RAND McNALLY

W9-BMZ-368

World
Atlas

Editors
Brett R. Gover
Anne Ford

Art Direction and Design
Rand McNally Art & Design

Cartography
Robert K. Argersinger
Gregory P. Babiak
Barbara Benstead-Strassheim
Kerry B. Chambers
Marzee L. Eckhoff
Susan K. Hudson
Nina Lusterman
John M. McAvoy
Robert L. Merrill
David R. Simmons
Raymond Tobiaski
Howard Veregin
Thomas F. Vitacco

Photo Credits

(l=left, r=right, c=center, t=top, b=bottom)

Jacket/cover

Cover images from left to right: © 2004 Diana Mayfield/Lonely Planet Images, Eddie Gerald/Lonely Planet Images, Andrew Drafffen/Lonely Planet Images, Feff Greenberg/Lonely Planet Images, David Tipling/Lonely Planet Images. Map: © 2005 Rand McNally

Contents

© North Wind Picture Archives, iv (figures 4, 6, and 7)

Tony Stone Images: © Nicholas Parfitt, x (background); © Christopher Arnesen, x (t r); © Johnny Johnson, x (b l); © Warren Jacobs, xi (background); © Nicholas DeVore, xi (t r), xv (background); © Stephen Studd, xi (b r); © Tony Stone Images, xii (background); © Kevin Schafer, xii (m); © Joel Bennett, xiii (background and t l); © Fred Felleman, xiii (b r); © Tony Stone Images, xiv (background); © Paul Harris, xiv (t r); © Keren Su, xiv (b l); © Sylvain Grandadam, xv (t l); © Anthony Cassidy, xv (b r); © Oliver Strewe, xvi (background); © Paul Chesley, xvi (t r); © Penny Tweedie, xvi (b l); © Stuart Westmorland, xvii (background); © Chad Ehlers, xvii (t l); © Fred Bavendam, xvii (b r); © Art Wolfe, xviii (background); © Joe Cornish, xviii (b l), xix (t l); © David Hiser, xviii (t r); © David Paterson, xix (background); © David Sutherland, xix (b r); © Richard During, xx (background); © John Running, xx (t r); © Tim Davis, xx (b l); © Darrell Gulin, xxi (background); © Robert Frerck, xxi (t l)

© 1997 PhotoDisc: iii (t), vi (figure 3), viii (background), ix (background and t l), xxi (b r), xxiv (Energy)

Copyright © Corel Corp.: xxii (background, t r, and b l), xxiii (background, t l, and b r), xxiv (Land, Population, and Growth)

Satellite photo, iv (figure 1), provided by Wally Jansen, WTJ Software Series

World Atlas

Copyright © 2005 by Rand McNally & Company

randmcnally.com

Published and printed in the United States of America

Rand McNally and Company.
  World atlas.
      p.   cm.
    Includes index.
    ISBN 0-528-96580-8 (hardback). - - ISBN 0-528-96581-6 (paperback)
      1. Atlases. I. Title.   II. Title: World atlas
  G1021 .R45   1997 <G&M>
  912- - DC21

97-11900
CIP
MAPS

Contents

INTRODUCTORY SECTION

Understanding Maps & Atlases . . . . iv - v
How to Use the Atlas . . . . vi-vii
The World & Its Seven Continents . viii - xxiv

MAPS

Index Map and Legend 1

World 2-5

World, Political 2-3
World, Physical 4-5

Europe 6-23

Europe, Political 6-7
Northern Europe 8-9
Scandinavia and the Baltic States 10-11
Northwest Europe 12-13
Mediterranean Lands 14-15
Southwest Europe 16-17
Southern Europe 18-19
Central and Eastern Europe 20-21
Eastern Europe 22-23

Asia 24-45

Asia, Political 24-25
Northern Eurasia 26-27
China, Mongolia, Korea, and Japan 28-29
Eastern China 30
Japan 31
Southeast Asia 32-33
Mainland Southeast Asia and the Philippines . . 34-35
Malaysia, Singapore, and Indonesia 36-37
Southwest Asia 38-39
India 40-41
The Middle East 42-43
Turkey and Transcaucasia 44-45

Africa 46-57

Africa, Political 46-47
Northern Africa 48-49

West Africa 50-51
Central and Southern Africa 52-53
Central Africa 54-55
Southern Africa and Madagascar 56-57

Australia and Oceania 58-63

Australia and Oceania, Political 58-59
Western Australia 60-61
Eastern Australia and New Zealand 62-63

Pacific and Indian Oceans 64-65
Atlantic Ocean 66

Antarctica 67

South America 68-74

South America, Political 68
Southern South America 69
Northern South America 70-71
Central South America 72-73
Northeast Brazil 74

North America 75-143

North America, Political 75
Mexico, Central America, and the Caribbean . . 76-77
Mexico 78-79
Central America and the Caribbean 80-81
Canada and Alaska 82-83
Canadian Province Maps 84-91
United States 92-93
U.S. State Maps 94-143

Arctic Region 144

INDEX

Index to the Reference Maps . . . . I•1-I•80

Understanding Maps & Atlases

figure 1

figure 2

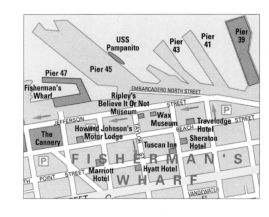

figure 3

What is a map?

A map is a representation, usually at a much-reduced size, of the location of things or places relative to one another. There are many different types of maps, including maps of the world, its regions or countries, cities, neighborhoods, and buildings. Figure 1 is an infrared satellite image of California's San Francisco Bay area; figure 2 shows the same area represented on a road map; and figure 3 provides street-level detail of one of the city's neighborhoods.

figure 4

A set of maps bound together is called an atlas. Abraham Ortelius' *Theatrum orbis terrarum*, published in 1570, is considered to be the first modern "atlas," although it was not referred to as such for almost 20 years. In 1589, Gerardus Mercator (figure 4) coined the term when he named his collection of maps after the mythological titan Atlas, who carried the Earth on his shoulders as punishment for warring against Zeus. Since then, the definition of "atlas" has been expanded, and atlases often include additional geographic information in diagrams, tables, and text.

History of Cartography

Around 500 B.C., on a tiny clay tablet the size of a hand, the Babylonians inscribed the Earth as a flat disk (figure 5) with Babylon at the center. Geographic knowledge was also highly developed among the Egyptians, who drew maps on papyrus and carved them into temple walls. Ancient Greek philosophers and scientists debated endlessly the nature of the Earth and its place in the universe; Ptolemy, the influential geographer and astronomer, made an early attempt to map the known world (figure 6). Roman maps most often depicted boundaries, physical features, and the infrastructure of the Roman Empire. Over the following centuries, territorial expansion directly increased geographic knowledge, which in turn greatly enhanced the cartography, or map-making, of the time.

figure 5

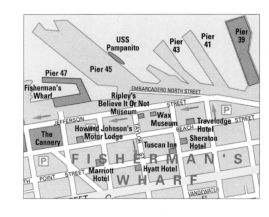

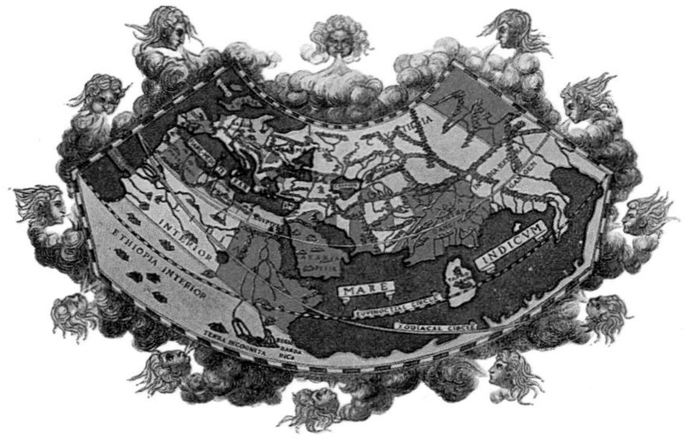

figure 6

As trade and navigation grew, maps were developed to guide merchants and explorers. The Cantino map of 1502 (figure 7) is an example of a *portolan* (sea) chart used by mariners traveling to the newly discovered Americas. Information gained from the past expeditions of John Cabot, Christopher Columbus, and Ferdinand Magellan led to great advances in the content and structure of world maps. As a result, many maps produced between 1600 and 1800, including the colored woodcut shown in figure 8, were works of art as well as geographical representations.

figure 8

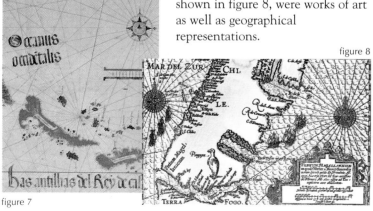

figure 7

Over the past three centuries, cartography throughout the world has become extremely precise, aided most recently by satellites which provide images of the Earth and, within the last 30 years, have led to the development of global positioning systems. Sophisticated computers now manage large amounts of geographic information used to produce maps for a variety of purposes, including business, science, government, and education.

Latitude and Longitude

The imaginary horizontal line that circles the Earth exactly halfway between the North and South poles is called the Equator, which represents 0° latitude and lies 90° from either pole. The other lines of latitude, or parallels, measure the distance from the Equator, either north or south (figure 9). The imaginary vertical line that measures 0° longitude runs through the Greenwich Observatory in the United Kingdom, and is called the Prime Meridian. The other lines of longitude, or meridians, measure distances east and west of the Prime Meridian (figure 10), up to a maximum of 180°. Lines of latitude and longitude cross each other, forming a pattern called a grid system (figure 11). Any point on Earth can be located by its precise latitude and longitude coordinates.

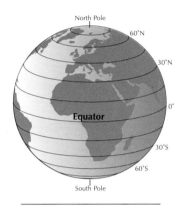

figure 9

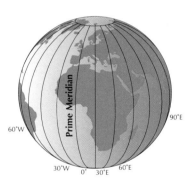

figure 10

figure 11

Map projections

Spherical representations of the Earth are called globes, while flat representations are called maps. Because globes are round and three-dimensional, they can show the continents and oceans undistorted and unbroken; therefore, they represent the Earth and its various features more correctly than do maps. Maps, however, generally feature larger scales and higher levels of detail.

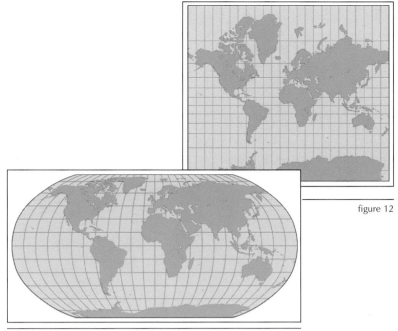

figure 12

figure 13

With the help of mathematics, cartographers are able to depict the curvature of the Earth on a two-dimensional surface. This process is called projecting a map, or creating a map projection. The size, shape, distance, area, and proportion of map features can be distorted, however, when the curves of a globe become the straight lines of a map. Distortion occurs because the Earth's spherical surface must be stretched and/or broken in places as it is flattened. Different map projections have specific properties that make them useful, and a cartographer must select the projection best-suited to the map's purpose.

The Mercator (figure 12) and the Robinson (figure 13) projections are commonly chosen for maps of the entire world. In this atlas, the Robinson is used along with four additional projections— the Lambert Azimuthal Equal Area, the Lambert Conformal Conic, the Sinusoidal, and the Azimuthal Equidistant.

Map scale

The scale of a map is the relationship between distances or areas shown on the map and the corresponding distances or areas on the Earth's surface. Large-scale maps generally show relatively small areas in greater detail than do small-scale maps, such as those of the world or the continents.

There are three different ways to express scale. Most often it is given as a ratio, such as 1:10,000,000, which means that the ratio of map distances to actual Earth distances is 1 to 10,000,000 (figure 14). Scale also can be expressed as a word phrase, such as, "One inch represents approximately 150 miles" (figure 15). Lastly, scale can be illustrated as a scale bar, labeled with miles on one side and kilometers on the other (figure 16). Any of these three scale expressions can be used to calculate distances on a map.

1:10 000 000

figure 14

One inch represents approximately 150 miles

figure 15

| 0 | 100 | 200 | 300 | 400 | | 600 | | 800 | | 1000 km |

| 0 | | 100 | | 200 | | | 400 | | | 600 miles |

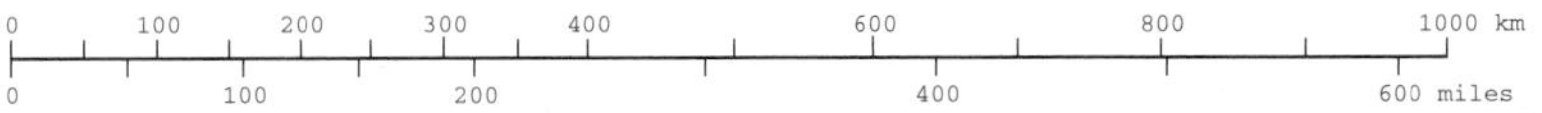

figure 16

How to Use the Atlas

figure 1

[1] Map title
[2] Page number
[3] Locator map
[4] Latitude
[5] Longitude
[6] Index reference letter
[7] Index reference number
[8] Scale bar

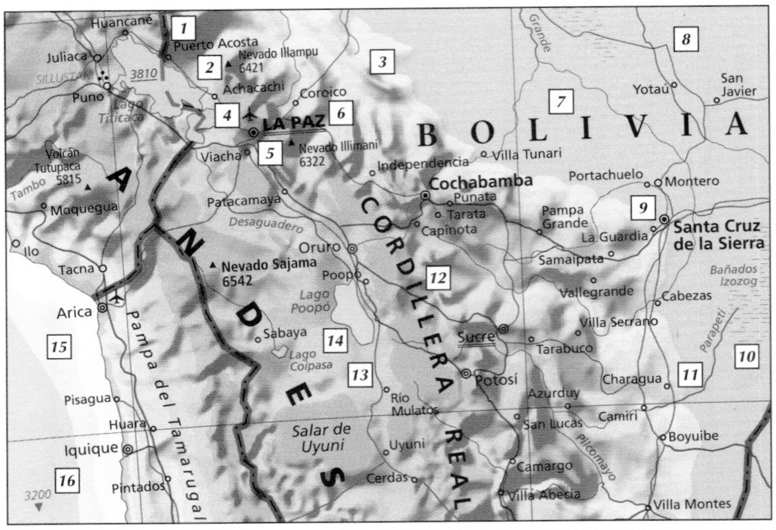

[9] Scale ratio
[10] Map projection
[11] Hypsometric/bathymetric scale bar
[12] Shaded relief
[13] Hypsometric tints
    (to show elevation)
[14] Bathymetric tints
    (to show water depths)

figure 2

[1] International boundary
[2] Mountain peak/elevation
[3] Hypsometric elevation tints
[4] International airport
[5] Urban area
[6] National capital
[7] Country name
[8] Road

[9] City/town
[10] Swamp
[11] River
[12] Mountain range
[13] Railroad
[14] Lake
[15] Bathymetric tints
[16] Depth of water (in meters)

What the *World Atlas* includes

At the core of the *World Atlas* is a collection of regional maps covering the entire world. The maps were designed to be as easy as possible to understand and use. Figure 1 is an example of a map spread contained in this atlas. The boxed numbers on this map, which correspond to items listed below it, highlight the features and information found on each map page—such as the map title, the locator map showing the area of the world depicted on the map, and the map scale.

Figure 2 is an enlarged section from the same map. As in figure 1, a few of the most common feature symbols have been highlighted. A more complete list of the map symbols used in this atlas can be found on page 1.

The atlas opens with a 17-page photographic essay devoted to the world and the continents (figure 3). Each of the seven continents is featured on two pages with photos and descriptive text. Fact blocks (figure 4) provide vital information about each continent's most notable characteristics and features.

Following the regional maps are individual maps of each of the United States, and the Canadian provinces (figure 5).

The last section of the *World Atlas* is an 80-page index with entries for approximately 45,000 places and geographic features that appear on the maps.

figure 4

Europe Facts

Land area: 3.8 million square miles
    (9.9 million sq km)
Continental rank (in area): 6th
Estimated population: 729.3 million
Population density: 192/square mile (74/sq km)
Highest point: Gora El'brus, Russia, 18,510 feet
    (5,642 m)
Lowest point: Caspian Sea, Europe-Asia,
    92 feet (28 m) below sea level
Longest river: Volga, 2,082 miles (3,351 km)
Largest island: Great Britain, 88,795 square miles
    (229,978 sq km)
Largest lake: Caspian Sea, Europe-Asia,
    144,400 square miles (374,000 sq km)
Number of countries and dependencies: 49
Largest country: Russia, Europe-Asia,
    6.6 million square miles (17.1 million sq km)
Smallest country (excl. dependencies):
    Vatican City, 0.2 square miles (0.4 sq km)
Most populous country: Russia, Europe-Asia,
    144.3 million
Largest city: Moscow, metro. area pop. 10.5 million

figure 3

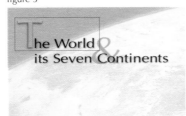

The World & its Seven Continents

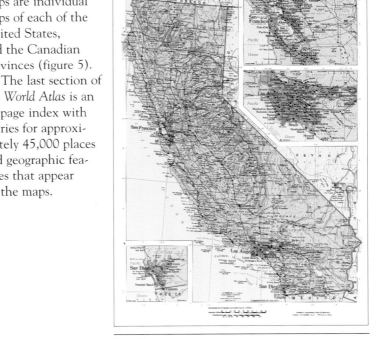

figure 5

Physical and Political Maps

The two main types of maps that appear in this atlas are physical maps and political maps. Physical maps, like the one shown in figure 6 (see next page), emphasize terrain, landforms, and elevation. Political maps, as in figure 7, emphasize countries and other political units over topography. The state and province maps found on pages 84-143 and pages 94-143 are both political and physical: they feature political coloration but also include shaded relief to depict landforms.

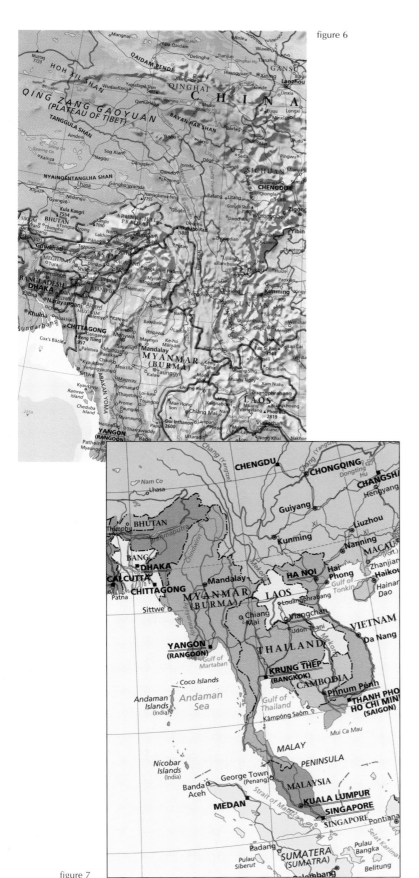

figure 6

figure 7

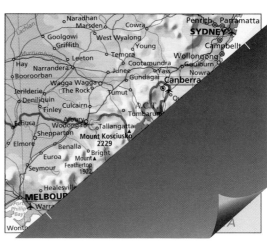

figure 8

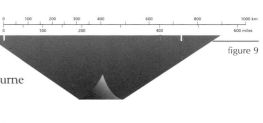

figure 9

between the 400-mile mark and the unlabeled 500-mile mark, indicating that the distance separating the two cities is approximately 450 miles (figure 9).

3) To confirm this measurement, make a third pencil mark (shown in red in figure 9) at the 400-mile mark. Slide the paper to the left so that the red mark lines up with 0. The white Sydney mark now falls very close to the 50-mile mark, which is unlabeled. Thus, Melbourne and Sydney are indeed approximately 450 (400 plus 50) miles apart.

Using the Index to Find Places

One of the most important purposes of an atlas is to help the reader locate places or features. In this atlas, each map is bordered by a letter and number grid. In the index, found in the back of the atlas on pages I•1 through I•80, every entry is assigned a map reference key, which consists of a letter and a number that correspond to a letter and a number on the grid. To locate places or features, follow the steps outlined in this example for Palembang, Indonesia:

P

Palanpur, India	.F5	40
Palaoa Point, C., Hi., U.S.	.C4	104
Palapye, Bots.	.F5	56
Palatine, Il., U.S.	.A5	106
Palatka, Fl., U.S.	.C5	102
Palau, ctry., Oc.	.B8	37
Palawan, i., Phil.	.B5	37
Palayankottai, India	.E8	41
Palembang, Indon.	.D2	36
Palencia, Spain.	.G6	17
Palermo, Italy	.D5	18
Palestine, Ar., U.S.	.C5	97
Palestine, Il., U.S.	.D6	106
Palestine, Tx., U.S.	.D5	136

figure 10

1) Look up Palembang in the index. The entry (figure 10) contains the following information: the feature name (Palembang), an abbreviation for the country (Indon.) in which Palembang is located, the map reference key (D2) that corresponds to Palembang's location on the map, and the page number (36) of the map on which Palembang can be found.

2) Turn to page 36. Look along either the left or right margin for the letter "D" —the letter code given for Palembang. The "D" denotes a narrow horizontal band, roughly 1½" wide, in which Palembang is located. Then, look along either the top or bottom margin for the number "2" —the numerical part of the code given for Palembang. The "2" denotes a narrow vertical band, also roughly 1½" wide, in which Palembang is located.

3) Using your finger, follow the "D" band and the "2" band to the area where they meet (figure 11). Palembang can be found within the darker shaded square where the bands overlap.

figure 11

Measuring Distances

Using a map scale bar, it is possible to calculate the distance between any two points on a map. To find the approximate distance between Melbourne and Sydney, Australia, for example, follow these steps:

1) Lay a piece of paper on the right-hand page of the "Eastern Australia and New Zealand" map found on pages 62-63, lining up its edge with the city dots for Melbourne and Sydney. Make a mark on the paper next to each dot (figure 8).

2) Place the paper along the scale bar found below the map, and position the first mark at 0. The second mark falls about halfway

The World & its Seven Continents

The world we humans inhabit—a world that sustains, inspires, and challenges us—is Planet Earth, a massive ball of rock spinning through the darkness of space.

On a human scale the Earth is immense, but on the incomprehensibly vast scale of the universe, it is no more significant than a grain of sand in a desert. Along with its companion planets, the Earth orbits a relatively small star we call the Sun, which is but one of 260 billion stars clustered in a great spiral-shaped galaxy known as the Milky Way, which is but one of billions of known galaxies.

Water dominates the surface of our planet; land covers only slightly more than a quarter of it. We arbitrarily call the largest pieces of land "continents": North America, South America, Africa, Antarctica, Australia, and Europe and Asia, which share a single landmass. All of the other pieces of land, from enormous Greenland to minuscule parcels of sand and rock breaking the ocean's surface, are considered islands.

Although life first appeared on the Earth perhaps 3.5 billion years ago, our own human species, Homo sapiens, has walked the planet for only 300,000 to 400,000 years—the blink of an eye in geologic time. Our distant ancestors led nomadic lives as hunters and gatherers, constantly on the move in search of prey and edible plants, fruits, and nuts. Over time they spread to every continent except Antarctica, even crossing wide seas to colonize Australia.

About 10,000 years ago, shortly after the end of the great Ice Age, a dramatic change swept through some areas of the world: humans began to cultivate crops—wheat and barley were probably the first—and to keep herds of domesticated animals, such as sheep, goats, and pigs. With the advent of agriculture came the first permanent settlements and ultimately the first civilizations.

Prior to these developments, the world's population had grown very slowly, and probably never exceeded ten million. But agriculture brought a much greater and more reliable supply of food, and the population began a climb that in modern times has reached explosive proportions. At the beginning of the first millennium A.D., perhaps 250 million people inhabited the planet. By 1850, this number had quadrupled to roughly 1.2 billion. Since then, it has more than quintupled: today the world holds a whopping 6.3 billion people.

Nevertheless, large parts of each continent remain unpopulated or only sparsely populated. Most such areas are hostile to human life: some are too hot and dry (deserts such as the Sahara and the Gobi); some are too cold or do not have adequate growing seasons (Antarctica and the northern regions of Asia, Europe, and North America); some are too densely vegetated (the rain forests of South America and central Africa); and some are too mountainous or poor in soil (western North America and western Asia). This leaves only a small part of the Earth's surface to support all of its people.

Until the last five or so centuries, the world's peoples and civilizations were largely isolated from one another, either by great distances or by natural barriers such as mountains, deserts, and seas. As a result, a myriad of languages and cultures arose, and inhabitants of one region or continent differed greatly from those of another. Recent advances in transportation and communication have reversed this situation, and now many local languages and traditions are slowly being replaced by an emerging global culture. Suddenly, our vast world is beginning to feel very small.

World
Facts

Land area: 57.9 million square miles (150.1 million sq km)
Estimated population: 6.3 billion
Population density: 109/square mile (42/sq km)
Highest point: Mt. Everest, China (Tibet)-Nepal, 29,028 feet (8,848 m)
Lowest point: Dead Sea, Israel-Jordan, 1,339 feet (408 m) below sea level
Longest river: Nile, Africa, 4,132 miles (6,650 km)
Largest island: Greenland, North America, 840,000 square miles (2.2 million sq km)
Largest lake: Caspian Sea, Asia-Europe, 144,400 square miles (374,000 sq km)
Number of countries and dependencies: 239
Largest country: Russia, Asia-Europe, 6.6 million square miles (17.1 million sq km)
Smallest country (excl. dependencies): Vatican City, Europe, 0.2 square miles (0.4 sq km)
Most populous country: China, Asia, 1.3 billion
Largest city: Tokyo, Japan, Asia, metro. area pop. 35.0 million

Africa

Africa is a land of vast spaces and infinite variety. Across its great length and breadth are found tropical rain forests, savannas teeming with wildlife, sun-scorched deserts, sprawling modern cities, and a kaleidoscope of peoples and cultures.

The Sahara, largest of the world's deserts, dominates the northern half of the continent. Reaching from the Atlantic Ocean to the Red Sea, the Sahara covers an area nearly as large as the entire continent of Europe. Few people inhabit this inhospitable landscape of shifting sand dunes, gravel-covered plains, and bare mountains, where rain seldom falls and hot, dust-laden winds blow relentlessly.

Southern Africa also contains large arid regions, most notably the Namib and Kalahari deserts. Along the equator, however, rain falls in abundance. Verdant rain forests blanket much of this region, alive with monkeys, gorillas, wild pigs, and countless species of birds and insects. Between the deserts and the rain forests lie the broad swaths of grassland known as savannas. Herds of zebras, wildebeests, giraffes, elephants, and many other animals graze on the savannas, always on the alert for lions, hyenas, and other predators. Poaching and destruction of habitat have decimated animal populations in many parts of Africa, but enormous concentrations still exist in places such as northern Botswana and the Serengeti Plain of Tanzania.

Africa's greatest rivers are the Congo, the Zambezi, the Niger, and of course the Nile, the longest river in the world. From its headwaters in Burundi, the Nile flows northward more

Left page: Acacia trees on the Serengeti Plain, Tanzania; Samburu girls, Kenya; African elephant.

Right page: Sahara near Arak, Algeria; brightly painted hut and its occupants, Lesotho; avenue of sphinxes, Luxor, Egypt.

than four thousand miles —through rugged mountains and highlands, the beautiful lake country of East Africa, and the wide marshy plain known as the Sudd—before spilling into the Mediterranean Sea.

Humans have farmed the fertile land of the Nile Delta from time immemorial, and it was here that the great civilization of the ancient Egyptians sprang up more than five thousand years ago. The marvelous archaeological legacies of this civilization include the Pyramids, the Sphinx, and the temples of Karnak and Luxor.

Among Africa's seven hundred million people there is tremendous ethnic and cultural diversity. More than eight hundred languages are spoken across the continent, and scores of distinct ethnic groups can be identified—groups such as the Tuareg and Berbers of Saharan Africa, the Masai and Kikuyu of the eastern savannas, the Fang and Bateke of the rain forests. Not surprisingly, few African countries are ethnically homogeneous.

Tremendous change has swept through Africa in the twentieth century. As recently as the 1940s, nearly the entire continent was controlled by colonial powers. In the wake of the Second World War, independence movements gathered strength, and by the end of the 1970s all of Africa's countries had shaken off their colonial shackles. For the first time in centuries, the continent was free to seek its own identity and destiny.

Africa Facts

Land area: 11.7 million square miles (30.3 million sq km)

Continental rank (in area): 2nd

Estimated population: 866.3 million

Population density: 74/square mile (29/sq km)

Highest point: Kilimanjaro, Tanzania, 19,340 feet (5,895 m)

Lowest point: Lac Assal, Djibouti, 509 feet (155 m) below sea level

Longest river: Nile, 4,132 miles (6,650 km)

Largest island: Madagascar, 227,000 square miles (588,000 sq km)

Largest lake: Lake Victoria, 26,600 square miles (68,900 sq km)

Number of countries and dependencies: 61

Largest country: Sudan, 967,500 square miles (2.5 million sq km)

Smallest country (excl. dependenci es): Seychelles, 176 square miles (455 sq km)

Most populous country: Nigeria, 135.6 million

Largest city: Cairo, metro. area pop. 10.8 million

Antarctica

The frozen continent of Antarctica lies at the very bottom of the world, buried beneath a great sheet of ice and encircled by frigid seas crowded with towering icebergs.

By far the coldest of the seven continents, Antarctica holds the record for the lowest temperature ever recorded on Earth: −128.6° F (−89.2° C) at Vostok Station on July 21, 1983. Even during the summer months, mean temperatures in the interior remain well below freezing. Coastal regions enjoy somewhat warmer temperatures but are whipped continuously by fierce winds blowing down from the high interior plateau.

Because of the extreme cold, most of the snow that falls over Antarctica's interior does not melt; instead, it accumulates and gradually compacts. Over the course of millions of years, this process has formed the ice sheet that now covers nearly the entire continent. Almost inconceivably massive, the sheet has an average thickness as great as the depth of the Grand Canyon; its maximum thickness is three times greater. It holds some ninety percent of all the ice on Earth, and seventy percent of the fresh water.

As the ice sheet slowly spreads outward under its own crushing weight, its edges spill into the surrounding seas, forming immense shelves that in some places extend hundreds of miles from the shore. The largest of these, the Ross Ice Shelf, covers an area as large as the entire country of France. Enormous pieces continuously break off, or "calve," from the margins of the shelves and drift northward as icebergs.

If all of Antarctica's ice were to melt, the consequences would be disastrous. Ocean levels would rise dramatically, flooding coastal regions around the world. Florida, for example, would disappear under water, as would southeast Asia's Malay Peninsula and the Low Countries of Europe. More than half of the world's people would be forced to relocate.

Antarctica's coasts, islands, and seas are as full of life as its interior is barren. Clamorous penguin rookeries, some containing tens of thousands of individuals, dot the coastline. Petrels, albatrosses, and cormorants sail the coastal skies, searching the sea for fish and crustaceans. Seven species of seal, including leopard seals, elephant seals, and crabeaters, swim the nutrient-rich Antarctic waters along with squid, octopuses, killer whales, blue whales, and more than a dozen other whale species.

To whom does Antarctica belong? This question has provoked a great deal of controversy in the twentieth century, as numerous countries have explored the continent, made territorial claims, or established research stations. The possibility of rich mineral deposits adds urgency to the question.

In 1959, twelve countries drafted and signed the Antarctic Treaty, which declares Antarctica a natural reserve to be used only for peaceful purposes, especially scientific investigation. So far, the treaty has met with great success, and today Antarctica enjoys a spirit of international cooperation unknown elsewhere in the world.

Left page: Sled and dog team; Emperor penguins.
Right page: Iceberg and ice floes; research ship anchored along sea ice; killer whale.

Antarctica Facts

Land area: 5.4 million square miles (14 million sq km)
Continental rank (in area): 5th
Estimated population: No permanent population
Highest point: Vinson Massif, 16,066 feet (4,897 m)
Lowest point: Bentley Subglacial Trench
Longest river: Antarctica has no true rivers
Largest island: Berkner Island, 20,005 square miles (51,829 sq km)
Number of countries with territorial claims: 7
Number of countries with research stations: 26

Asia

Three out of five people on Earth live in Asia, by far the world's largest and most heavily populated continent. With its myriad of landscapes, peoples, and historical treasures, and its swelling population, Asia represents a microcosm of the entire world.

Mountain systems—some ancient, some young and still rising—are the continent's signature landform. The Himalayas, which run through Pakistan, China, India, Nepal, and Bhutan, form the loftiest range in the world. Reaching more than five miles into the heavens, Mount Everest is the world's highest mountain, but nearby Kanchenjunga, Dhawalāgiri, Annapurna, and the peak known simply as K2 are hardly less formidable.

Seemingly endless expanses of semiarid grassland, or steppes, blanket much of the vast continental interior. Just north of the Himalayas lies the remote Tibetan Plateau, nicknamed the "Rooftop of the World": its average elevation is nearly half the height of Mount Everest.

The northern third of the continent is occupied by the region known as Siberia. Its name evokes images of a bitterly cold wasteland of snow and tundra, but visitors also discover vast, pristine forests, grassy plains, and extensive marshlands.

A long belt of desert stretches from the Arabian peninsula to eastern China. Most of this arid region is virtually uninhabited, and life is harsh for the few residents. The parched landscape of the Gobi, Asia's largest desert, contains little more than tough scrub vegetation and brackish lakes.

In the far west, the Arabian peninsula is a sea of sand dunes, punctuated by an occasional oasis where tall palm trees provide the desert's only shade.

In sharp contrast to these barren landscapes, the tropical lands and islands of Southeast Asia are awash in greenery. Crops and rain forests thrive in this wet region, where seasonal monsoon rains saturate the land for months at a time.

For centuries, rivers have been a lifeline for the people of the continent. Nestled between the Tigris and Euphrates rivers is the fertile land of Mesopotamia, which supported an advanced society that flourished as early as 4000 B.C. Ruins found in the lush Indus River valley of Pakistan tell of an advanced culture dating back to around 3000 B.C. And, almost 4,000 years ago, the ancient Chinese civilization developed along the banks of the Huang (Yellow) River.

Irrigation networks are vital to Asia because rocky terrain and minimal precipitation make much of the continent ill-suited for agriculture, and all arable land must be farmed intensively. The fertile valleys and coasts of eastern and southern Asia already strain to meet the demands of Asia's soaring population.

Recent economic and technological development has allowed Japan, Singapore, Indonesia, and Korea to rise to international prominence. It is likely that this trend will continue for these and other Asian countries into the 21st century, which many observers are already referring to as "the Asian Century." It will be a time for the countries of the continent to flex their collective muscle. Since Asia represents such a large percentage of the Earth's population, what happens there might dictate what the future brings to the rest of the world.

Left page: Mount Fuji and tea fields, Japan; Kazak man with hunting eagle, Mongolia; giant panda.

Right page: Mount Everest; Dome of the Rock, Omar Mosque, Jerusalem, Israel; schoolboys in Nāgaur, India.

Asia Facts

Land area: 17.3 million square miles (44.9 million sq km)

Continental rank (in area): 1st

Estimated population: 3.8 billion

Population density: 222/square mile (86/sq km)

Highest point: Mt. Everest, China (Tibet)-Nepal, 29,028 feet (8,848 m)

Lowest point: Dead Sea, Israel-Jordan, 1,339 feet (408 m) below sea level

Longest river: Yangtze (Chang), 3,915 miles (6,300 km)

Largest island: New Guinea, Asia-Oceania, 309,000 square miles (800,000 sq km)

Largest lake: Caspian Sea, Asia-Europe, 144,400 square miles (374,000 sq km)

Number of countries and dependencies: 49

Largest country: Russia, Asia-Europe, 6.6 million square miles (17.1 million sq km)

Smallest country (excl. dependencies): Maldives, 115 square miles (298 sq km)

Most populous country: China, 1.3 billion

Largest city: Tokyo, metro. area pop. 35.0 million

Australia & Oceania

The continent of Australia, along with its island neighbor New Zealand, is often classified as part of Oceania, a larger region that includes more than 25,000 islands, volcanic peaks, and coral atolls scattered across the southern Pacific Ocean.

The first European explorers to Australia came ashore near present-day Sydney and were so awed by the profusion of unfamiliar vegetation that they named the area Botany Bay. Today, eucalyptus and acacia trees, fuschias, and spear lilies thrive alongside exotic animal species such as kangaroos, wallabies, koala bears, kookaburras, and platypuses in Australia's warm climate.

Low, semiarid plateaus cover much of western Australia, taking in the Great Sandy Desert, the Gibson Desert, and the Great Victoria Desert. Here, scrubby grasses and spiky bushes break up stretches of pebble-covered land. This barren, largely uninhabited region is the Outback, whose harsh beauty and remoteness have come to epitomize "The Land Down Under" for many non-Australians.

Australia's indigenous people, called the Aborigines, arrived and settled the Outback and other parts of the continent perhaps 35,000 years prior to the Europeans. The complex Aboriginal society is based on kinship and the belief that humans, the environment, and time are intimately associated. Aborigines hold sacred numerous sites across Australia, including Uluru, or Ayers Rock, the world's largest monolith.

Left page: Dirt road through Australia's Outback; Aboriginal man, northern Australia; koala bear, Australia.

Right page: Rock Islands, Palau; Mount Cook (Aoraki), New Zealand's highest peak; school of sweetips.

Among Australia's most valuable natural resources are its vast grasslands, dotted with woolly herds of grazing sheep and fenced in by the paddocks of great ranches, or stations. Australia is a major world producer and exporter of wool, veal, and mutton. Sheep herding and grazing also dominate the economy of New Zealand, where sheep outnumber humans fourteen to one.

In this century, New Zealand has aggressively developed its own resources and now ranks among the world's most economically advanced countries. Cascading rivers provide water power for burgeoning industrial development, and rich reserves of minerals, natural gas, and timber drive a strong economy. With this wealth of resources, New Zealand has become a world leader in trade, much of which passes through the superb natural harbor of Wellington, the capital city.

New Zealand has two main islands, both of which are mountainous and ruggedly beautiful. On South Island, icy glaciers cut through the Southern Alps, and dazzling fjords such as Milford Sound indent the southwestern coast. The smaller North Island, home to three-quarters of the country's population, is dominated by a central volcanic plateau over which tower three impressive peaks: Ruapehu, Ngauruhoe, and Tongariro.

Papua New Guinea, on the eastern half of the island of New Guinea, is an uneven mixture of lush rain forests, swamplands, and steep volcanic mountains. Along with many of the smaller islands of Oceania, it lies on the southwestern section of the Ring of Fire—a band of active volcanoes that encircles the Pacific Ocean.

Every year, thousands of winter-weary tourists escape to Oceania's tropical island paradises, such as Tahiti, Fiji, and Guam. Here, they revel in the endless stretches of sandy beaches, secluded coves, and absolute isolation, half a world away from their homes.

Australia & Oceania Facts

Land area: 3.3 million square miles (8.5 million sq km)

Continental rank (in area): 7th

Estimated population: 32.2 million

Population density: 9.7/square mile (3.8/sq km)

Highest point: Mt. Wilhelm, Papua New Guinea, 14,793 feet (4,509 m)

Lowest point: Lake Eyre, South Australia, 50 feet (15 m) below sea level

Longest river: Murray-Darling, 2,169 miles (3,491 km)

Largest island: New Guinea, Oceania-Asia, 309,000 square miles (800,000 sq km)

Largest lake: Lake Eyre, 3,700 square miles (9,600 sq km)

Number of countries and dependencies: 29

Largest country: Australia, 3 million square miles (7.7 million sq km)

Smallest country (excl. dependencies): Nauru, 8.1 square miles (21 sq km)

Most populous country: Australia, 19.8 million

Largest city: Sydney, metro. area pop. 4.3 million

Europe

Human settlements and civilizations have flourished in Europe for more than four thousand years, benefiting from the generally mild climate and the abundance of arable land, navigable rivers, and natural resources. The continent today ranks with East Asia and South Asia as one of the three greatest population centers in the world.

The northern half of Europe bears dramatic evidence of past ice ages. During the Pleistocene epoch, immense sheets and rivers of ice plowed across the region, rounding the mountains of Scandinavia and Scotland, scouring river valleys to create Norway's deep fjords, and depositing a thick layer of sand, gravel, and boulder-filled clay across the landscape. This glacial deposition played a major part in the formation of the Great European Plain, which stretches in an arc from western France to the Urals. The western part of the plain is Europe's most intensively farmed region as well as its most densely populated, home to such great cities as Paris, Amsterdam, Berlin, Stockholm, Warsaw, and Moscow.

Uplands and mountain systems dominate the southern half of the continent. The Pyrenees, Alps, and Carpathians together form a nearly unbroken band of mountains stretching from the Atlantic to central Romania. Until the advent of modern transportation, this formidable natural barrier impeded overland travel between the Mediterranean region and the rest of Europe, especially when winter snows fell on the mountain passes. As a result, a distinct Mediterranean culture evolved, and it remains strong today.

Thanks to a warm ocean current called the North Atlantic Drift, northwestern Europe enjoys a climate far milder than those of lands at similar latitudes in North America and Asia. The current warms and moistens offshore air masses, which then flow across the British Isles, the Low Countries, France, Denmark, Germany, and surrounding lands. As this maritime air moves into eastern Europe, its effects become weaker and weaker, and climates become increasingly extreme. Mountain systems block the air masses from the Mediterranean region, which has a hotter, drier climate.

Europe has been home to many great civilizations, including those of the Minoans, Mycenaeans, Greeks, and Romans. With the collapse of the Roman Empire, Europe plunged into a period of relative decline and darkness, but emerged roughly one thousand years later into the light of the Renaissance, a glorious rebirth that pervaded nearly every field of human endeavor but especially art and science.

The Renaissance also marked the beginning of an era of exploration and expansion. Great powers such as England, Spain, Portugal, and France explored, conquered, and colonized lands all over the world—Africa, the Americas, Australia, India, and other parts of Asia. As gold, silver, and other riches poured into Europe, emigrants poured out, spreading European ideas, languages, and cultures to nearly every part of the globe. The Industrial and Agricultural revolutions further increased the continent's wealth and dominance. Through the first part of the 20th century, Europe held sway over the world as no continent had ever done before or is likely to do in the future.

Left page: Ibexes on mountainside above lake, Interlaken, Switzerland; farmer picking grapes, Italy; Big Ben, London.

Right page: Highlands of Scotland; Cibeles Fountain, Madrid; St. Basil's Cathedral, Moscow.

Europe Facts

Land area: 3.8 million square miles (9.9 million sq km)

Continental rank (in area): 6th

Estimated population: 729.3 million

Population density: 192/square mile (74/sq km)

Highest point: Gora El'brus, Russia, 18,510 feet (5,642 m)

Lowest point: Caspian Sea, Europe-Asia, 92 feet (28 m) below sea level

Longest river: Volga, 2,082 miles (3,351 km)

Largest island: Great Britain, 88,795 square miles (229,978 sq km)

Largest lake: Caspian Sea, Europe-Asia, 144,400 square miles (374,000 sq km)

Number of countries and dependencies: 49

Largest country: Russia, Europe-Asia, 6.6 million square miles (17.1 million sq km)

Smallest country (excl. dependencies): Vatican City, 0.2 square miles (0.4 sq km)

Most populous country: Russia, Europe-Asia, 144.3 million

Largest city: Moscow, metro. area pop. 10.5 million

North America

Almost 30,000 years ago, the first North Americans arrived on the continent after crossing the Bering land bridge from Asia. Before them lay a rich land of dense forests, virgin streams and lakes, and prairies where great herds of bison roamed.

These same treasures beckoned the first European settlers to North America in the early 16th century. For nearly 500 years, emigrants from all corners of the globe have been pouring onto the continent in search of a better life. Many have realized their dreams, and along the way North America has become the world's wealthiest and most influential continent.

Among its richest resources are vast tracts of arable land. The farmland of the Great Plains is so productive that this region has been called "the Breadbasket of the World." The United States and Canada are world leaders in food production, harvesting so much wheat, corn, barley, soybeans, oats, sugar, and fruit each year that thousands of surplus tons can be exported.

Sweeping mountain systems frame the plains in the east and west. Eastern North America is traversed by the ancient, well-weathered Appalachian Mountains, which stretch from Newfoundland south through Georgia. The soaring Rockies extend from western Canada into New Mexico, showcasing some of

Left page: Jasper National Park, Canadian Rockies, Alberta; Tarahumara man, Mexico; red-eyed tree frog, Central America.

Right page: farmhouse and fields near Moscow, Idaho; El Tajin, a Mayan temple in Veracruz, Mexico; spikes of wheat.

the continent's most dramatic landscapes. Mexico's greatest mountain ranges, the Sierra Madres, collide to form a spiny, volcanic backbone that continues into Central America.

Fed by hundreds of tributaries, the Mississippi-Missouri river system—North America's longest—cuts a path through the center of the continent. The mighty river both embraces and disregards those who settle along its banks, providing fertile farmland and access to a vital transport corridor, but also periodically flooding adjacent farms and towns.

Canada, the United States, and Mexico comprise almost 90% of North America. The United States and Canada have diversified, service-oriented economies, and increasingly urban populations. Mexico, although poorer than its northern neighbors, has in recent decades become a key manufacturing center and a popular tourist destination.

Brilliant tropical vegetation and exotic wildlife abound in the seven countries of Central America, which occupy a slender isthmus connecting Mexico and South America. Unlike the rest of North America, Central America has a population that is both dispersed and predominantly rural.

Many people in Mexico and Central America are of mixed Spanish and Indian ancestry, a rich heritage defined by a proud culture. This blending is less evident in remote areas, where Indian villages have remained virtually unchanged for centuries. In the cities, however, a strong Indian influence intermingles with architectural remnants of the colonial era and dramatic evidence of modern development.

To the east lie the balmy islands of the Caribbean Sea, including Cuba, Hispaniola, the West Indies, Jamaica, and Puerto Rico. Each boasts a colorful culture that reflects the diverse mix of peoples—Europeans, Africans, and Indians—who found themselves thrown together during the colonial past.

North America Facts

Land area: 9.5 million square miles (24.7 million sq km)

Continental rank (in area): 3rd

Estimated population: 505.8 million

Population density: 53/square mile (20/sq km)

Highest point: Mt. McKinley, Alaska, U.S., 20,320 feet (6,194 m)

Lowest point: Death Valley, California, U.S., 282 feet (86 m) below sea level

Longest river: Mississippi-Missouri, 3,710 miles (5,971 km)

Largest island: Greenland, 840,000 square miles (2.2 million sq km)

Largest lake: Lake Superior, Canada-U.S., 31,700 square miles (82,100 sq km)

Number of countries and dependencies: 36

Largest country: Canada, 3.9 million square miles (10 million sq km)

Smallest country (excl. dependencies): St. Kitts and Nevis, 101 square miles (261 sq km)

Most populous country: United States, 291.7 million

Largest city: Mexico City, metro. area pop. 18.7 million

South America

South America is a land of untamed beauty and tremendous diversity—in its landscapes, plant and animal life, and people.

Large parts of the continent remain as wild and pristine as they were when the first humans arrived more than eleven millennia ago. Human movement and settlement have been hindered by the rugged Andes mountains and the nearly impenetrable Amazonian rain forest.

The Andes, which curve along the continent's western edge from Venezuela in the north to Tierra del Fuego in the south, form the longest mountain system in the world. The loftiest Andean peaks reach greater heights than any others in the Western Hemisphere.

High in the Andes, clear, cold streams wander among moss-covered boulders, merge with one another, and eventually tumble out of the mountains as the Marañon and Ucayali rivers. These are the principal tributaries of the world's mightiest river, the Amazon. Crossing nearly the entire breadth of the continent, the Amazon carries one-fifth of all of the world's flowing water.

The rain forest that covers much of the Amazon's vast drainage basin holds an astonishing abundance and variety of life. Still largely unexplored, the rain forest is a torrid, watery realm of slow-moving rivers and sloughs, of colorful birds, insects, and flowers, and of trees growing so densely that little sunlight

Left page: Incan ruins, Machupicchu, Peru; Quechua woman and child, Peru; great blue heron, Galapagos Islands.

Right page: Iguassu Falls, Argentina-Brazil; colonial buildings, Bahia, Brazil; bird of paradise flower, Amazonia.

reaches the forest floor. Most of Amazonia's animals and insects live high up in the forest canopy and rarely descend to the ground.

Archaeologists believe that the first humans to reach South America were groups of hunters and gatherers migrating southward from North America some 11,000 to 14,000 years ago. Thousands of years later, the descendants of these first arrivals built several great civilizations on the continent, including the magnificent Inca Empire, which reached its maximum extent during the period AD 1100—1350. The city of Cusco, in present-day Peru, served as the Incas' capital, and today tourists are drawn to the many splendid ruins in and around the city.

The arrival of Europeans in the early 1500s, and their subsequent conquest and colonization of the continent, were disastrous to the indigenous peoples: it is estimated that three-quarters of the population died as a result of European diseases, warfare, and forced labor.

Although the colonial period came to an end in the 1800s, its architectural legacy endures in cathedrals, plazas, houses, and government buildings found in cities throughout the continent.

Nine out of ten South Americans live within 150 miles of the coast; much of the interior is only sparsely settled. For this reason, South America is sometimes spoken of as "the hollow continent." In recent decades, millions of people have abandoned their small farms and villages in search of a better life in the city.

This trend has greatly swollen the populations of many of the largest cities, including São Paulo, Rio de Janeiro, Buenos Aires, and Caracas. As a new millennium begins, the crowding and frenzy of such cities stand in sharp contrast to remote interior villages, where the people live just as they have for centuries and time seems to stand still.

South America Facts

Land area: 6.9 million square miles (17.8 million sq km)
Continental rank (in area): 4th
Estimated population: 366.6 million
Population density: 53/square mile (21/sq km)
Highest point: Cerro Aconcagua, Argentina, 22,831 feet (6,959 m)
Lowest point: Laguna del Carbón, Argentina, 344 feet (105 m) below sea level
Longest river: Amazon, 4,000 miles (6,400 km)
Largest island: Tierra del Fuego, 18,600 square miles (48,200 sq km)
Largest lake: Lake Titicaca, Bolivia-Peru, 3,200 square miles (8,300 sq km)
Number of countries and dependencies: 15
Largest country: Brazil, 3.3 million square miles (8.5 million sq km)
Smallest country (excl. dependencies): Suriname, 63,037 square miles (163,265 sq km)
Most populous country: Brazil, 183.1 million
Largest city: São Paulo, metro. area pop. 17.9 million

Land

The Earth has a total surface area of 197 million square miles (510.2 million sq km). Water, including oceans, seas, lakes, and rivers, covers nearly three-quarters of this area; land only one-quarter.

The largest landmass is Eurasia, shared by the continents of Europe and Asia. Eurasia represents 36.5% of the Earth's total land area (but only 10.7% of the total surface area). The largest continent is Asia, which accounts for 30% of the total land area. Africa ranks second, with 20% of the total land area.

The smallest continent by far is Australia, which holds only 5.1% of the world's land. When it is grouped with New Zealand and the other islands of Oceania, the figure rises only slightly, to 5.7%.

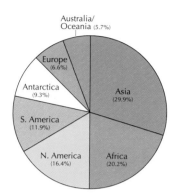

Australia/Oceania (5.7%)
Europe (6.6%)
Antarctica (9.3%)
S. America (11.9%)
N. America (16.4%)
Africa (20.2%)
Asia (29.9%)

Percentage of world land area

Energy

A large percentage of the world's energy is used for manufacturing. This fact helps explain the great variances among the continents in the consumption of energy. Highly developed North America, with only 8% of the world's population, consumes over 30% of the world's energy, and more than four times as much as Africa and South America combined.

For two continents, energy consumption exceeds production: North America produces roughly four-fifths of the energy it consumes, and Europe only three-fifths. In contrast, Africa consumes less than half of the energy it produces.

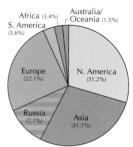

Africa (3.4%)
S. America (3.6%)
Australia/Oceania (1.5%)
Europe (22.1%)
N. America (31.2%)
Russia (7.1%)
Asia (31.1%)

Percentage of world energy consumption

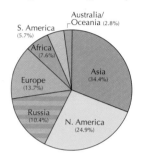

S. America (5.7%)
Africa (7.6%)
Australia/Oceania (2.8%)
Europe (13.7%)
Asia (34.4%)
Russia (10.4%)
N. America (24.9%)

Percentage of world energy production

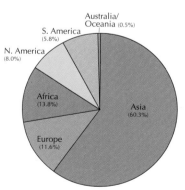

Population

Asia is the world's most populous continent, and has been for at least two millennia. Its current population of 3.8 billion represents an astonishing 60% of the world's people, more than four times as much as any other continent. It is home to the world's two most populous countries: China, with nearly 1.3 billion people, and India, with approximately 1.1 billion. Four other Asian countries rank among the ten most populous in the world: Indonesia (4th), Pakistan (6th), Bangladesh (8th), and Japan (10th).

Europe contains roughly 730 million people; Africa, about 870 million. Europe, however, has only one-third the land area of Africa, so its population density is three times greater. Antarctica has no permanent population and therefore does not appear on the graph.

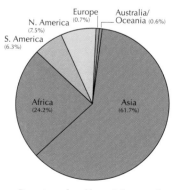

Australia/Oceania (0.5%)
S. America (5.8%)
N. America (8.0%)
Africa (13.8%)
Europe (11.6%)
Asia (60.3%)

Percentage of world population

population Growth

The world's population is growing at a rapid pace: at present, the annual rate of natural increase (births minus deaths) is 1.2%. Today, the world holds 6.3 billion people; some experts predict that by the year 2050 this number will have increased to 8.9 billion.

The largest part of the growth is taking place in Asia, which already is home to three-fifths of the world's people. Of every hundred people added to the Earth's population each year, 62 are Asian. Africa is also gaining a larger share of the world total: the continent's current population represents 14% of the world total, but its growth accounts for more than 24% of the annual world increase.

Europe, on the other hand, is seeing its share of the world population erode. Although Europe is the third most populous continent, its annual growth represents less than 1% of the world total.

Europe (0.7%)
Australia/Oceania (0.6%)
N. America (7.5%)
S. America (6.3%)
Africa (24.2%)
Asia (61.7%)

Percentage of world population growth

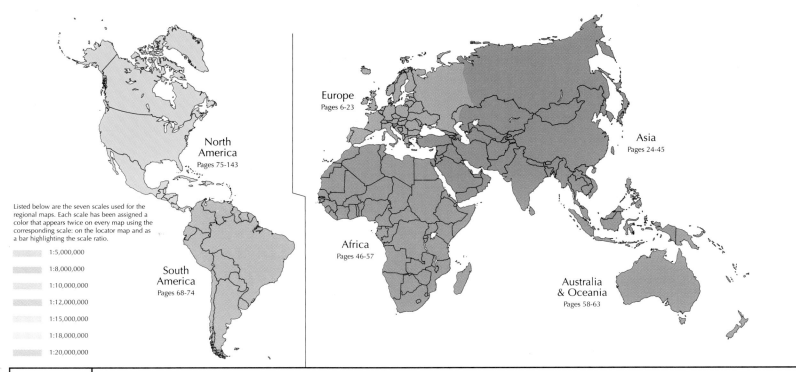

North America
Pages 75-143

South America
Pages 68-74

Europe
Pages 6-23

Asia
Pages 24-45

Africa
Pages 46-57

Australia & Oceania
Pages 58-63

Listed below are the seven scales used for the regional maps. Each scale has been assigned a color that appears twice on every map using the corresponding scale: on the locator map and as a bar highlighting the scale ratio.

1:5,000,000
1:8,000,000
1:10,000,000
1:12,000,000
1:15,000,000
1:18,000,000
1:20,000,000

Legend

World and Regional Maps

Hydrographic Features

	Perennial river
	Seasonal river
 Aswan High Dam	Dam
 Salto Ángel	Falls
	Lake, reservoir
	Seasonal lake
	Salt lake
	Seasonal salt lake
	Dry lake
395	Lake surface elevation
	Swamp, marsh
	Reef
	Glacier/ice sheet

Topographic Features

Elevations and depths are given in meters.

764 ▼ Depth of water
2278 ▲ Elevation above sea level
1700 ▼ Elevation below sea level
)(Mountain pass
Huo Shan 1774 Mountain peak/elevation

The highest elevation on each continent is underlined.
The highest elevation in each country is shown in boldface.

Transportation Features

	Major road
	Other road
	Trail
	Major railway
	Other railway
	Navigable canal
	Tunnel
	Ferry
✈	International airport
✈	Other airport

Political Features

International Boundaries (First-order political unit)

	International
	Disputed (de facto)
	Disputed (de jure)
	Indefinite/undefined
	Demarcation line

Internal Boundaries

	State/province

NORMANDIE
(Denmark)   Cultural/historic region
             Administering country

Cities and Towns

The size of symbol and type indicates the relative importance of the locality.

■ **LONDON**
▣ **CHICAGO**
◉ **Milwaukee**
◎ Tacna
⊙ Iquitos
o Old Crow
∘ Mettawa
 Urban area

Capitals

MEXICO CITY
Bratislava   Country, dependency

RIO DE JANEIRO
Perth   State, province

MANCHESTER
Chester   County

Cultural Features

⬚ or ■	National park
■	Point of interest
⌇	Wall
∴	Ruins

State and Province Maps

Pages 84-91 and Pages 94-143

⊙	Capital
∘	County seat
▲	Military installation
△	Point of interest
+	Mountain peak
	International boundary
	State/province boundary
	County boundary
	Road
	Railroad
✖	Urban area

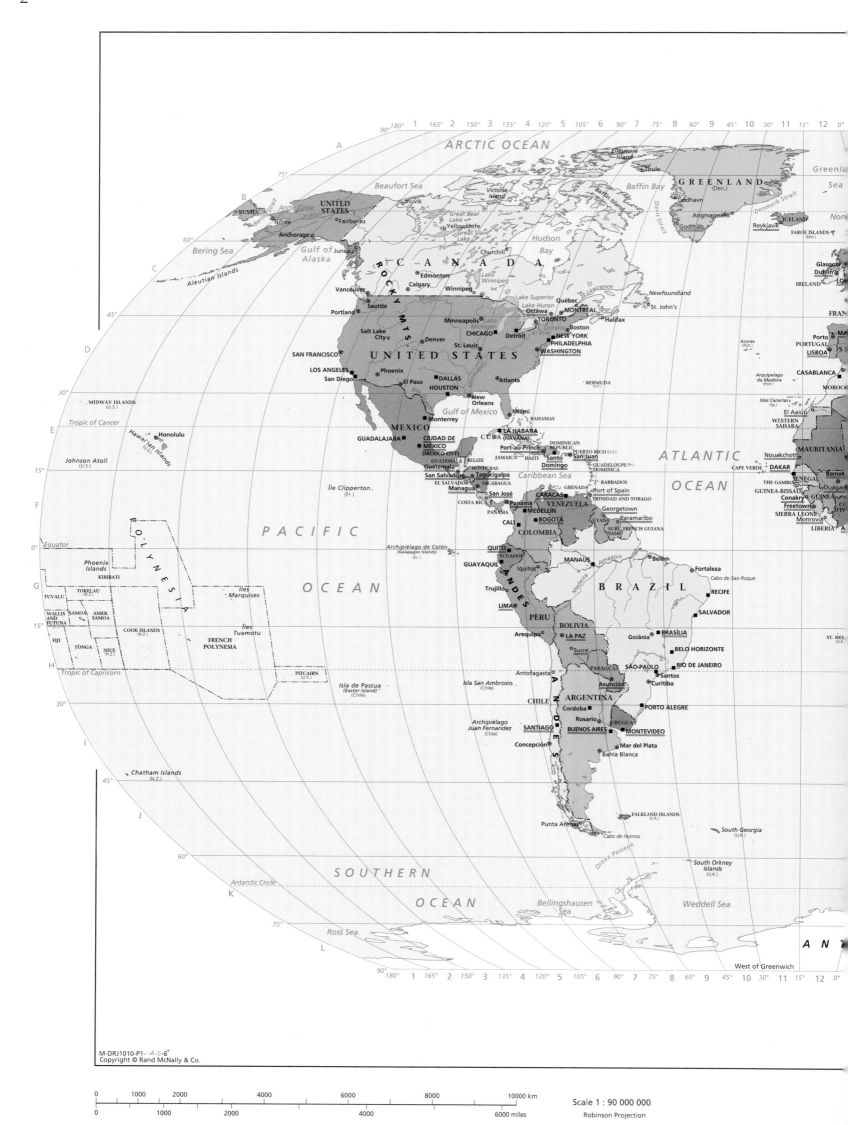

ARCTIC OCEAN

GREENLAND (Den.)

Ellesmere Island

Thule

Godhavn

Angmagssalik

Godthåb

Greenland Sea

Baffin Bay

Davis Strait

Denmark Strait

Reykjavík   ICELAND

FAROE ISLANDS (Den.)

Beaufort Sea

Victoria Island

Baffin Island

Inuvik

RUSSIA

Bering Strait

Nome

Arctic Circle

UNITED STATES

Yukon

Fairbanks

Anchorage

Gulf of Juneau
Alaska

Bering Sea

Aleutian Islands

Great Bear Lake

Yellowknife

Great Slave Lake

C A N A D A

ROCKY MTS.

Churchill

Hudson Bay

Edmonton

Calgary

Vancouver

Seattle

Portland

Lake Winnipeg

Winnipeg

Lake Superior

Lake Huron

Lake Michigan

Minneapolis

St. Lawrence

Québec

Ottawa

MONTREAL

TORONTO

Lake Ontario

Lake Erie

Newfoundland

St. John's

Halifax

Boston

NEW YORK

PHILADELPHIA

WASHINGTON

Detroit

CHICAGO

St. Louis

Denver

Salt Lake City

SAN FRANCISCO

UNITED STATES

Missouri

Mississippi

Atlanta

BERMUDA (U.K.)

LOS ANGELES

San Diego

Phoenix

El Paso

DALLAS

HOUSTON

Rio Grande

New Orleans

Monterrey

Gulf of Mexico

Miami

BAHAMAS

Acores (Port.)

Glasgow

Dublin

IRELAND

FRAN

Porto

PORTUGAL

LISBOA

CASABLANCA

MOROC

Arquipélago da Madeira (Port.)

Islas Canarias (Sp.)

El Aaiún

WESTERN SAHARA

ATLANTIC

OCEAN

MAURITANIA

Nouakchott

CAPE VERDE   DAKAR

THE GAMBIA

GUINEA-BISSAU   GUINEA

SENEGAL

Bamak

Ouaga

Conakry

Freetown

SIERRA LEONE

Monrovia

LIBERIA

CÔTE D'IV

Tropic of Cancer

MIDWAY ISLANDS (U.S.)

Honolulu

Hawaiian Islands (U.S.)

Johnson Atoll (U.S.)

MEXICO

GUADALAJARA

CIUDAD DE MÉXICO (MEXICO CITY)

GUATEMALA   BELIZE

Guatemala

HONDURAS

San Salvador

EL SALVADOR

Managua

NICARAGUA

Tegucigalpa

CUBA   LA HABANA (HAVANA)

Port-au-Prince

HAITI   Santo Domingo

JAMAICA

DOMINICAN REPUBLIC

PUERTO RICO (U.S.)

San Juan

GUADELOUPE (Fr.)

DOMINICA

BARBADOS

Caribbean Sea

San José

COSTA RICA

Panama

PANAMA

CARACAS

VENEZUELA

MEDELLÍN

CALI

BOGOTÁ

COLOMBIA

GRENADA

Port of Spain

TRINIDAD AND TOBAGO

Georgetown

GUYANA

Paramaribo

SUR.

FRENCH GUIANA

NAME

Île Clipperton (Fr.)

PACIFIC

OCEAN

Archipiélago de Colón (Galapagos Islands) (Ec.)

QUITO

ECUADOR

GUAYAQUIL

Iquitos

Equator

POLYNESIA

Phoenix Islands

KIRIBATI

TOKELAU (N.Z.)

TUVALU

WALLIS AND FUTUNA

SAMOA   AMER. SAMOA

COOK ISLANDS (N.Z.)

FIJI

TONGA

NIUE (N.Z.)

Îles Marquises

Îles Tuamotu

FRENCH POLYNESIA

PITCAIRN (U.K.)

Tropic of Capricorn

Isla de Pascua (Easter Island) (Chile)

MANAUS

Amazon

Madeira

Belem

Cabo de São Roque

Fortaleza

RECIFE

B R A Z I L

Trujillo

LIMA

PERU

ANDES

Arequipa

BOLIVIA

LA PAZ

Sucre

Goiânia

BRASÍLIA

SALVADOR

BELO HORIZONTE

RIO DE JANEIRO

SÃO PAULO   Santos

Curitiba

ST. HEL (U.K.)

Antofagasta

Isla San Ambrosio (Chile)

PARAGUAY

Asunción

ANDES

ARGENTINA

CHILE

Cordoba

Rosario

Archipiélago Juan Fernandez (Chile)

SANTIAGO

BUENOS AIRES

Concepción

PORTO ALEGRE

URUGUAY

MONTEVIDEO

Mar del Plata

Bahía Blanca

Chatham Islands (N.Z.)

Punta Arenas

Cabo de Hornos

FALKLAND ISLANDS (U.K.)

Drake Passage

South Georgia (U.K.)

SOUTHERN

OCEAN

Antarctic Circle

Bellingshausen Sea

South Orkney Islands (U.K.)

Weddell Sea

Ross Sea

A N

West of Greenwich

| 0 | 1000 | 2000 | 4000 | 6000 | 8000 | 10000 km |

| 0 | 1000 | 2000 | 4000 | 6000 miles |

Scale 1 : 90 000 000

Robinson Projection

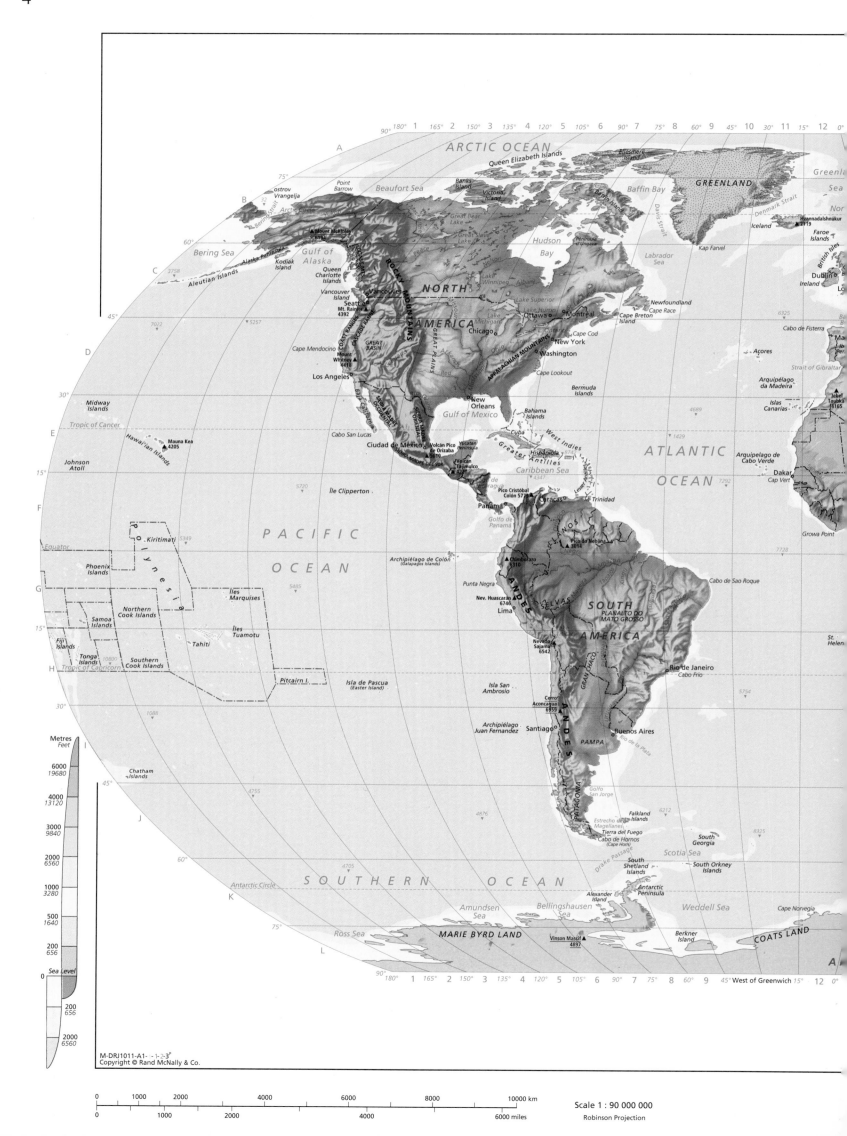

4

ARCTIC OCEAN

Queen Elizabeth Islands
Ellesmere Island
GREENLAND
Greenla

ostrov Vrangelja
Point Barrow
Beaufort Sea
Banks Island
Victoria Island
Baffin Bay
Baffin Island
Davis Strait
Denmark Strait
Sea
Nor

Bering Strait
Arctic Circle
Yukon
Great Bear Lake
Hvannadalshnúkur 2119
Iceland
Faroe Islands

Bering Sea
Mount McKinley 6194
Great Slave Lake
Peace
British Isles

Alaska Peninsula
Gulf of Alaska
NORTH
Nelson
Hudson Bay
Península d'Ungava
Kap Farvel
Dublin Ireland
Lo

3758
Kodiak Island
Queen Charlotte Islands
ROCKY MOUNTAINS
Lake Winnipeg
Albany
AMERICA
Labrador Sea

Aleutian Islands
7022
5257
Vancouver Island
Vancouver
Seattle
Mt. Rainier 4392
Lake Superior
Lake Huron
Ottawa
Montreal
Newfoundland
Cape Breton Island
Cape Race
6325

Cape Mendocino
CASCADE RANGE
COAST RANGES
GREAT BASIN
GREAT PLAINS
Chicago
Lake Michigan
L. Ontario
Cape Cod
Cabo de Fisterra

Mount Whitney 4418
APPALACHIAN MOUNTAINS
New York
Washington
Açores
Mai ib Peri

Los Angeles
Red
SIERRA MADRE OCCIDENTAL
Cape Lookout
Bermuda Islands
Strait of Gibraltar

Tropic of Cancer
Baja California
New Orleans
Gulf of Mexico
Bahama Islands
Arquipélago da Madeira
Jebel Toubkal 4165

Midway Islands
Cabo San Lucas
Ciudad de México
Volcán Pico de Orizaba 5610
Yucatán Peninsula
Cuba
West Indies
Greater Antilles
Hispaniola
4347
874
ATLANTIC
Islas Canarias

Hawai'ian Islands
Mauna Kea 4205
SIERRA MADRE DEL SUR
Volcán Tajumulco 4220
Caribbean Sea
1429
Arquipélago de Cabo Verde
OCEAN
Dakar
Cap Vert

Johnson Atoll
5720
Île Clipperton
LLANOS
Pico Cristóbal Colón 5775
Caracas
Trinidad
Lesser Antilles
7292
Growa Point

PACIFIC
Panamá
Golfo de Panamá
Pico da Neblina 3014

Equator
Kiritimati
5349
Archipiélago de Colón (Galápagos Islands)
Chimborazo 6310
SOUTH
7728

Phoenix Islands
OCEAN
Punta Negra
ANDES
SELVAS
AMERICA

Polynesia
5485
Nev. Huascarán 6746
Lima
PLANALTO DO MATO GROSSO
Cabo de São Roque

Íles Marquises
Northern Cook Islands
Tropic of Capricorn
Samoa Islands
Tahiti
Íles Tuamotu
Nevado Sajama 6542
GRAN CHACO
Rio de Janeiro
St. Helena

Fiji Islands
Tonga Islands
10800
Southern Cook Islands
Cabo Frio
5754

Pitcairn I.
Isla de Pascua (Easter Island)
Isla San Ambrosio
Cerro Aconcagua 6959
ANDES

Archipiélago Juan Fernández
Santiago
Buenos Aires
Rio de la Plata
1088
PAMPA

Metres Feet

6000 19680
Chatham Islands
4755
PATAGONIA
Golfo San Jorge
6212

4000 13120
4876
Estrecho de Magellanes
Tierra del Fuego
Falkland Islands
8325

3000 9840
Cabo de Hornos (Cape Horn)
South Georgia

2000 6560
Drake Passage
Scotia Sea

1000 3280
4705
South Shetland Islands
South Orkney Islands

500 1640
Antarctic Circle
SOUTHERN
OCEAN
Alexander Island
Antarctic Peninsula
Cape Norvegia

200 656
Amundsen Sea
Bellingshausen Sea
Weddell Sea

0 Sea Level
Ross Sea
MARIE BYRD LAND
Vinson Massif 4897
Berkner Island
COATS LAND

200 656

2000 6560

90° 180° 1 165° 2 150° 3 135° 4 120° 5 105° 6 90° 7 75° 8 60° 9 45° West of Greenwich 15° 12 0°

M-DRJ1011-A1- -1-2-3°
Copyright © Rand McNally & Co.

0   1000   2000   4000   6000   8000   10000 km

0   1000   2000   4000   6000 miles

Scale 1 : 90 000 000

Robinson Projection

ARCTIC OCEAN

Zemlja Franca-Iosefa
Severnaja
Zemlja
Novosibirskie
ostrova

Barents Sea
Novaja
Zemlja
Karskoe more
more Laptevyh
Vostočno-Sibirskoe
more

bergen
Nordkapp
Kol'skij
poluostrov
69
ZAPADNO-
SIBIRSKAJA
RAVNINA
Ekaterinberg
gora
Kamen
1701 ▲
SIBIR
(SIBERIA)
gora
Pobeda
3147 ▲

Ladožskoe
ozero
Moskva
ASIA
Kolyma
Kamčatka

ERLIN)
ROPE
CARPATHIAN MTS.
gora El'brus
5642 ▲
CAUCASUS
Ishim
Irtyš
Ob'
Nizhnjaja Tunguska
Angara
Irkutsk
ALTAI
Mt. Kujten
4374
Peak
Pobedy
7439
TIEN SHAN
ARDÍN
Sea of
Okhotsk
ostrov Sahalin
mys Lopatka
Bering Sea
4097
ostrov
Kamčatka

Roma
Black Sea
Istanbul
Aral
Syr Darja
Balhaš
Ulaanbaatar
GOBI
Kuril'skie
ostrova
60°

APPENNINO
Balkan
Peninsula
Sicilia
Kriti
Cyprus
Tehrān
KUHHA-YE ZAGROS
DASHT-E
KAVIR
Qolleh-ye
Damāvand
5604
HINDU KUSH
KUNLUN SHAN
Qing Zàng
Gaoyuan
Gongga Shan
7555
Beijing
Sea of
Japan
Hokkaidō
Honshū
Fuji-san
3776 ▲ Tōkyō
45°

Mediterranean Sea
El-Qāhira
Delhi
HIMALAYAS
Mount
Everest
8848
Shanghai
Yellow
Sea
East
China
Sea
Shikoku
Kyūshū
9695
Nansei-shotō
292
30°

GH
AR
A
TIBESTI
Em. Koussi
3415
NUBIAN
DESERT
ARABIAN
PENINSULA
AR-RUB' AL-KHALI
Mumbai
WESTERN GHATS
DECCAN
EASTERN GHATS
2359
Taiwan
Yu Shan
3997
Hainan Dao
PACIFIC
OCEAN
Tropic of Cancer
Mariana
Islands
E

AFRICA
N
Lake
Chad
Ras Dashen
Terara
4620
Arabian
Sea
Suquṭrā
Gees Gwardafuy
Bay of
Bengal
Krung Thep
Andaman
Islands
Andaman
Sea
INDOCHINA
South China
Sea
Luzon
Manila
Philippine
Islands
6057
Philippine
Sea
Mindanao
Palau
Islands
6674
Marshall
Islands
Micronesia
15°

Gulf of Aden
Ādīs Abeba
Cape Comorin
Pidurutalagala
2524
Maldive
Islands
Sri Lanka
5423
Nicobar
Islands
Malay
Peninsula
Gulf of
Thailand
Palawan
Gunong
Kinabalu
4101
Celebes
Sea
BORNEO
Halmahera
Palau
Islands
Caroline Islands
Equator

Margherita
Peak
5109
Kirinyaga
5199
Kilimanjaro
5895
Zanzibar
Seychelles
5340
Sumatera
Greater Sunda Islands
Jakarta
Jawa
Sulawesi
MALUKU
Laut
Banda
Seram
NEW
GUINEA
Mount Wilhelm
4509
New-
Britain
5040
Solomon
Islands
Melanesia

CONGO
BASIN
RIFT
Les
Amirantes
Tanjona
Bobaomby
Maromokotro
2875
MADAGASCAR
Réunion
Mauritius
5090
1706
INDIAN
OCEAN
Laut
Jawa
7125
Timor
Arafura Sea
Cape York
New
Hebrides
Fiji
Islands
5°

Cape Fria
NAMIB DESERT
KALAHARI
DESERT
Thabana-
Ntlenyana
3482
ORANGE
Mozambique Channel
Tanjona
Vohimena
6400
6658
North West Cape
Kimberley
Plateau
Great
Sandy
Desert
Cape York
Peninsula
Gulf of
Carpentaria
AUSTRALIA
Coral Sea
Nouvelle-
Calédonie
Tropic of Capricorn
5203
H

Cape Town
Cape of
Good Hope
Île Amsterdam
Mount
Meharry
1253
Mount
Woodroffe
1435
GREAT
VICTORIA
DESERT
Darling
GREAT DIVIDING RANGE
Sydney
North Cape
497
North Island
Mount Ruapehu
2797
30°

5536
Cape Leeuwin
Great
Australian
Bight
Melbourne
Mount
Kosciusko
2229
Tasman
Sea
I

Prince
Edward
Islands
3079
Archipel
Crozet
Îles
Kerguélen
2690
Mount Ossa
1617
Tasmania
South East Cape
South West Cape
Macquarie
Island
South Island
Mount Cook
3754
45°

Heard
Island
6089
4425
J
60°

SOUTHERN OCEAN
Cape Poinsett
Antarctic Circle

5124
ENDERBY LAND
WILKES LAND
VICTORIA LAND
Cape
Adare
K
75°

N MAUD LAND
TICA
of Greenwich
Ross
Sea
L

30° 15 45° 16 60° 17 75° 18 90° 19 105° 20 120° 21 135° 22 150° 23 165° 24 180° 90°
45° 16 60° 17 75° 18 90° 19 105° 20 120° 21 135° 22 150° 23 165° 24 180° 90°

Scale 1 : 15 000 000

Equidistant Conic Projection

NORWEGIAN SEA

ATLANTIC

OCEAN

ICELAND

Reykjavik

Ísafjördur
Horn
Siglufjördur
Borgarnes
Akureyri
Saudárkrókur
Húsavík
Rifstangi
Fontur
Breidafjördur
Húnaflói
Langjökull
Arctic Circle
Vestmannaeyjar
Selfoss
Hvannadalshnúkur 2119
Hekla 1510
Seydisfjördur
Neskaupstadur
Hofsjökull
Vatnajökull
Hernaey
Surtsey 1094
Keflavik
Thingvellir
Reykjanes
Faxaflói

NORWAY

LOFOTEN
VESTERÅLEN
HINNOYA
SENJA
KVALØY
RINGVAS
Narvik
Kebnekaise 211
Svolvær
Bodø
Fauske
Shotinden 1594
Mo i Rana
Okskorten 1915
Tårnaby
Arvid

SWEDEN

Vega
Mosjøen
Namsos
Steinkjer
Levanger
Smøla
Hitra
Frøya
Trondheim
Storlien
Helagsfjället 798
Röros
Dombås
Vikna
Vilhelmina
Gäddede
Lycksele
Åsele
Storuman
Ostersund
Kristiansund
Ålesund
Molde
Måløy
DOVREFJELL
Floro
Galdhøpiggen 2469
JOTUNHEIMEN
Lillehammer
Kramfors
Härnösand
Ånge
Sårna
Ljusdal
Hudiksvall
Siljan
Bergen
Voss
Fagernes
Hamar
Mora
Falun
Gävle
Haugesund
Rjukan
Drammen
Hønefoss
OSLO
Borlänge
Ludvika
Uppsala
Stavanger
Skien
Tønsberg
Moss
Fredrikstad
Larvik
Karlstad
Västerås
Eskilstuna
Örebro
Nora
STOCK
Eigersund
Afendal
Oslofjorden
690
Arvika
Säffle
Vänern
Mariestad
Skövde
Motala
Nyköping
Södert
Kristiansand
Lindesnes
Skagerrak
Uddevalla
Göteborg (Gothenburg)
Linköping
Norrköping
Vättern
Grenen
Hirtshals
Jönköping
Visby
Värnamo
Oskarshamn
Läsø
Frederikshavn
Ålborg
Varberg
Halmstad
Växjö
OLAND
Borgholm

DENMARK

Holstebro
Ringkøbing
Randers
Århus
JYLLAND
Kattegat
Helsingborg
Kristianstad
Karlskrona
Kalmar
BAL
Esbjerg
Kolding
KØBENHAVN (COPENHAGEN)
Odense
FYN
SJÆLLAND
Malmö
Trelleborg
BORNHOLM
Rønne
Sønderborg
Flensburg
NORTH FRISIAN ISLANDS
Svendborg
Nyköbing
LOLLAND
FALSTER
The Sound

UNITED KINGDOM
GREAT BRITAIN

SCOTLAND

ISLE OF LEWIS
Stornoway
HEBRIDES
St. Kilda
Cape Wrath
Kirkwall
ORKNEY ISLANDS
Duncansby Head
Thurso
Wick
Pentland Firth
Rona
Island of Skye
Inverness
Moray Firth
Kinnaird Head
Peterhead
Ben Nevis 1343
GRAMPIAN MOUNTAINS
Aberdeen
Island of Mull
Oban
Perth
Dundee
Greenock
GLASGOW
Kintyre
EDINBURGH
Firth of Forth
Kirkcaldy
The Minch
SHETLAND ISLANDS
MAINLAND
Lerwick

NORTH SEA

IRELAND

Clifden
Sligo
NORTHERN IRELAND
Londonderry
843
Galway
Galway Bay
Donegal Bay
Dundalk
Belfast
Stranraer
Carlisle
NEWCASTLE UPON TYNE
Sunderland
Malin Head
Islay
North Channel
ISLE OF MAN (U.K.)
Douglas
DUBLIN (BAILE ATHA CLIATH)
Dun Laoghaire
Middlesbrough
Scarborough
Kilkee
Limerick
Kilkenny
Blackpool
Bradford
York
Kingston upon Hull
Carrauntoohil 1038
Snowdon 1085
LIVERPOOL
Chester
LEEDS
MANCHESTER
Sheffield
Cork
Waterford
IRISH SEA
Stoke-on-Trent
Derby
Nottingham
Mizen Head
St. George's Channel
WALES
Wolverhampton
BIRMINGHAM
Leicester
ENGLAND
King's Lynn
Norwich
CELTIC SEA
Swansea
Gloucester
Newport
Coventry
Cambridge
Cardiff
Bristol
Oxford
Bristol Channel
Reading
LONDON
Ipswich
Land's End
Penzance
Lizard Point
Southampton
Bournemouth
ISLE OF WIGHT
Portsmouth
Brighton
Dover
Strait of Dover
ISLES OF SCILLY
Plymouth

Torshavn
FAROE ISLANDS (Den.)

Rockall (U.K.)

2300

Vega
3970

FRANCE

NETHERLANDS

Groningen
Wilhelmshaven
Bremerhaven
AMSTERDAM
Zwolle
Oldenburg
Bremen
's-Gravenhage (The Hague)
ROTTERDAM
Utrecht
Osnabrück
Hannover
Arnhem
ANTWERPEN
Eindhoven
ESSEN
Münster
BRUXELLES (BRUSSELS)
DÜSSELDORF
Dortmund
LILLE
BELGIUM
Charleroi
Liège
KÖLN (COLOGNE)
Bonn
Calais
Cambrai
Amiens
Laon
ARDENNES
LUXEMBOURG
Koblenz
Wiesbaden
Beauvais
Charleville
Rouen
Le Havre
Dieppe
Caen
CHANNEL ISLANDS (U.K.)
GUERNSEY
JERSEY
Cherbourg
Cap de la Hague
NORMANDIE
Saint-Malo
BRETAGNE
Brest
Pointe de Saint-Mathieu
Île d'Ouessant
Quimper
Lorient
Vannes
Saint-Nazaire
Belle-Île
Nantes
Île de Noirmoutier
Île d'Yeu
La Rochelle
Île de Ré
Île d'Oléron
Rennes
Laval
Le Mans
Angers
Saumur
Tours
Orléans
Chartres
Versailles
PARIS
Melun
Troyes
CHAMPAGNE
Reims
Marne
Metz
Nancy
Chaumont
Auxerre
BOURGOGNE
Dijon
Nevers
Bourges
Châteauroux
Poitiers
Loire
Montluçon
Mâcon
Le Creusot
Vichy
Limoges
Angoulême

GERMANY

Neumünster
Kiel
Lübeck
Schwerin
Rostock
Stralsund
Greifswald
RÜGEN
Neustrelitz
Schwedt
POMERANIA
Gdynia
Słupsk
Koszalin
Gdańsk
Świnoujście
Szczecin
Chojnice
Tczew
HAMBURG
Bielefeld
Braunschweig
BERLIN
Potsdam
Gorzów Wielkopolski
Piła
Bydgoszcz
Salzgitter
Magdeburg
Frankfurt
Poznań
Włocławek
Göttingen
Kassel
Halle
Leipzig
Cottbus
Zielona Góra
Lubin
POLAND
Erfurt
Dresden
Wuppertal
Chemnitz
Zwickau
ERZGEBIRGE
Wrocław
Opole
Częstochowa
Kalisz
Frankfurt am Main
Würzburg
Erlangen
PRAHA (PRAGUE)
BOHEMIA
Hradec Králové
Walbrzych
Ostrava
Rybnik
FRANKFURT AM MAIN
Darmstadt
Mannheim
Saarbrücken
Karlsruhe
STUTTGART
Nürnberg
Regensburg
Plzeň
BOHEMIAN FOREST
České Budějovice
Třebíč
Brno
CZECH REPUBLIC
MORAVA
Olomouc
Strasbourg
Freiburg
Ulm
BAYER
Ingolstadt
Passau
Linz
Trenčín
Piešť'any
Mulhouse
Basel
Augsburg
MÜNCHEN (MUNICH)
SCHWARZWALD
Bern
Zürich
Luzern
LIECHTENSTEIN
Kempten
Zugspitze
Innsbruck 2374
Salzburg
Steyr
WIEN (VIENNA)
Sankt Pölten
Győr
SWITZERLAND
AUSTRIA
Leoben
Bratislava
BUDAPEST
SL

Metres / Feet
4000 / 13120
3000 / 9840
2000 / 6560
1000 / 3280
500 / 1640
200 / 656
0 / Sea Level
200 / 656
2000 / 6560

West of Greenwich | 0° | East of Greenwich

0   100   200   300   400   600   800   1000 km
0   100   200   400   600 miles

Scale 1 : 10 000 000
Lambert Conformal Conic Projection

BARENTS SEA

OSTROV KOLGUEV

ZAPADNO-SIBIRSKAJA RAVNINA

URAL'SKIE GORY (URAL MOUNTAINS)

Nordkapp
NORDKINNHALVØYA
Berlevåg
VARANGERHALVØYA
Vardø
Varangerfjorden
Kirkenes

Hammerfest
Lakselv
Karasjok

Murmansk
Severomorsk

Harlovka

mys Kanin Nos
Kanin Nos
mys Svjatoj Nos
Šojna
Češskaja guba

Indiga
Nar'jan-Mar

Nižnjaja Peša

TIMANSKIJ KRJAŽ

KOMI

PERM'

FINLAND

Muonio
Inari
Sodankylä
Martti

Poljarnyj
Pečenga

Montegorsk
Olenegorsk
Apatity
Kovdor
Kandalakša

Umba
Kuzomen'

KOL'SKIJ POLUOSTROV

BELOE MORE

KARELIJA

Rovaniemi
Kemijärvi
Salla
Kuusamo

Zelenoborskij
Lesozavodskij
Louhi

SOLOVECKIE OSTROVA

Kem'
Belomorsk

Arhangel'sk
Severodvinsk
Novodvinsk
Onega
Samoded

Karpogory
Njuhča
Pinega

Mezen'
Safonovo
Kojda

Lešukonskoe

Ust'-Cil'ma

Pečora

Usinsk
Kožim
Verhnjaja Inta

Abez'
Hosedahard

Arctic Circle

Ust'-Lyža

Ust'-Usa
Uhta
Sosnogorsk

Vuktyl'
Sosnovka

Vol'Vož
Pečorsk
Troicko-Pečorsk
Anjudin
Jaksa

Ust'-Kulom

Jakša

Nyrov
Krasnovišersk
Berezniki
Solikamsk

Kuusamo

Oulu
Suomussalmi
Kajaani

Reboly
Valtimo

Juškozero
Segeža

Virandozero
Malošujka

Njandoma

Šenkursk

Velsk

Konoša

Njuksenica

Njandoma

Kuusamo

Tornio
Haparanda
Luleå
Hailuoto

Iisalmi
Kuopio

Kalevala

Medvežegorsk

Vytegra
Annenskij Most

Totma

Kotlas

Koslan
Vizinga
Sindor
Železnodorožnyj
Ust'-Kulom

Syktyvkar
Njuvčim

Timšer

Gajny

Kočevo
Kudymkar
Černoz

Dobrjanka

PERM'

Seinäjoki

Jyväskylä
Varkaus
Savonlinna

Petrozavodsk
Suojärvi
Sortavala
Pitkjaranta

Kondopoga
Onežskoe ozero

Kargopol'

Vožega

RUSSIA

Korjažma
Velikij Ustjug

Nikol'sk

Luza
Pinjug
Podosinovec

Omutninsk

SEVERNYE UVALY

Kočevo

Glazov
Balezino
Kez

UDMURTIJA
Votkinsk

Tampere
Lahti
Hämeenlinna

Mikkeli
Lappeenranta
Kouvola

HELSINKI
Espoo
Hanko

Kotka

SANKT-PETERBURG (SAINT PETERSBURG)

SALPAUSSELKÄ

Ladožskoe ozero
(Lake Ladoga)

Lodejnoe Pole
Podporože

ozero Beloe

Sokol
Vologda

Grjazovec

Galič
Manturovo

Šarja

Vetluga
Šahunja

Jaransk

Kotel'nič

Nolinsk
Svečka

Kirov
Novovjatsk

Kil'mez'

Iževsk

Vjatskie Poljany

Sarapul
Naberežnye Čelny
Nižnekamsk

Tallinn
Rakvere
Kohtla-Järve
Narva

Lomonosov
Kronštadt
Kolpino
Sestroreck
Gatčina
Kiriši

Tihvin

Babaevo
Čerepovec

Buj

Danilov

Kostroma

Kineško
Jurjevec
Semenov

Vetlužskij

EŠKAR-OLA
MARIJ EL

Volžsk
KAZAN'

TATARIJA
Al'met'evsk
Čistopol'

Gulf of Finland

Malaja Višera
Borovči

Rybinskoe vodohranilišče

Rybinsk
Danilov
Rostov

Jaroslavl'

Nerehta
Ivanovo

Gorodec
Bor

Gor'kovskoe vodohranilišče

NIŽNIJ NOVGOROD (GOR'KIJ)
Dzeržinsk

Čeboksary
ČUVAŠIJA
Šumerlja
Kanaš

Kujbyševskoe vodohranilišče

Haapsalu
ESTONIA
Pärnu
Viljandi
Tartu

Kingisepp

Gdov
Lake Peipus
Lake Pskov

Novgorod
Pljussa

Ljuban'

ozero Il'men'
Staraja Russa

Valdaj
Bologoe

Vyšnij Voloček

Uglič
Pereslavl'-Zalesskij

Kovrov

Pavlovo

Arzamas

Lukojanov

Sergač
Alatyr'

Uljanovsk

SAMARA (KUJBYŠEV)
Novokujbyševsk

Dimitrovgrad

Toljatti
Syzran'

MAA

LATVIA

Valga
Võru

Pskov
Ostrov

Dno

VALDAJSKAJA

Ostaškov

Toržok

VOZVYŠENNOST'

Tver'
Kimry

Klin

Sergiev Posad

Vladimir

Murom

Kasimov
Melenki
Kulebaki

MORDOVIJA
Saransk
Ruzaevka

Nikol'sk

Balakovo

Saratovskoe vodohranilišče

Pugačev

Riga
Jūrmala
Jelgava

Rēzekne

Velikie Luki

Nelidovo

Ržev

Noginsk

MOSKVA (MOSCOW)
Ljubercy
Podol'sk

Kolomna

Rjazan'

Sasovo

Kadom

Temnikov

Kovylkino

Penza

Kuzneck

Syzran'

NOVOKUJBYŠEV

PRIVOLŽSKAJA

Šiauliai
Telšiai

Daugavpils
Polack

Nevel'

Gagarin

Vjaz'ma

Obninsk
Serpuhov
Stupino

Kaluga
Aleksin

Tula

Skopin

Rjažsk
Moršansk

Kamenka

Serdobsk

Petrovsk

Atkarsk
VOZVYŠENNOST'

 Vol'sk

Balakovo

 Eršov

Dergači

LITHUANIA
Kaunas
Vilnius

Panevežys
Kēdainiai

Vicebsk
Orša

Smolensk
Počinok

Roslavl'
Kirov
Ljudinovo

Novomoskovsk

Bogorodick

Mičurinsk

Tambov

Kirsanov

Rtiščevo

Marks

SARATOV
Engel's

Novouzensk

Kaztalovka

Sovetsk
Černjahovsk

Vilnius

Maladzečna
Barysau

Mahilëu

M스tislavl'

Djat'kovo

Brjansk

Orel

SREDNERUSSKAJA VOZVYŠENNOST'

Livny

Elec
Efremov

Lipeck

Mordovo
Uvarovo

Žerdevka

Povorino

Elan'

Balašov

Volgogradskoe vodohranilišče

Kamyšin

Džanybek

ŁOMŽA

Białystok

Hrodna
Lida

Baranaviči
Sluck
Babrujsk

Svetlahorsk

MINSK

Homel'
Novozybkov

Unečka

Trubčevsk
Železnogorsk

Kursk

L'gov

Kastornoe

Staryj Oskol

Ostrogožsk

Liski

Kalač

Boguchar

Serafimovič

Kotel'nikovo

KAZAKHSTAN

VOLGOGRAD

Novaja Kazanka

WARSZAWA (WARSAW)
Siedlce
Lublin

Brest
Pinsk

PRIPET MARSHES

Mazyr

Rečyca

Čornobyl'
Kyivs'ke vodoskhovyshche

Nizhyn
Chernihiv

Romny
Pryluky

Sumy

Okhtyrka

Belgorod
Šebekino
Valujki

Rossoš'
Alekseevka

Vešenskaja

Millerovo

Morozovsk

Kalač-na-Donu
Dubovka

DONSKAJA GRJADA

Volžskij

Caspian Depression (Prikaspijskaja nizmennost')

Astrahan'

ŁÓDŹ

Lublin
Kovel'
Sarny

Luts'k
Rivne

Zhytomyr

KYÏV (KIEV)

Bila Tserkva

Poltava

KHARKIV

Izjum

Kup'jans'k

Lysychans'k
L7уhans'k

Šahty

Volgodonsk

Cimljanskoe vodohranilišče

KALMYKIJA

Kaspijskij

CASPIAN SEA

L'viv
Ternopil'
Khmel'nyts'kyi

Vinnytsia

Uman'
Pervomajs'k

Kirovohrad

DNIPROPETROVS'K

Zaporizhzhia

Kryvyi Rih
Nikopol'

Cherkasy
Smila

Kremenchuts'ke vodoskhovyshche
Kremenchuk

Dniprodzerzhyns'k

UKRAINE

Slov'ians'k
Kramators'k
Horlivka
Makiïvka

Stakhanov

Novošahtinsk
Novočerkassk

ROSTOV-NA-DONU

Azov
Taganrog

Mariupol'

Sea of Azov

Ejsk

Dinskoe
Krasnodar

Tihoreck
Kropotkin

Stavropol'

Budënnovsk

DAGESTAN

CARPATHIAN MOUNTAINS

Uzhhorod
Košice

hora Hoverla 2061

Ivano-Frankivs'k
Kam'ianets'-Podil's'kyi

Chernivtsi

PODIL'S'KA VYSOCHYNA

Kotovs'k

Voznesens'k

Mykolaïv

Melitopol'
Berdjans'k

Nova Kakhovka
Kakhovs'ke vodoskhovyshche

MOLDOVA
Bălți
Chișinău

ROMANIA

Nyíregyháza
Satu Mare
Suceava

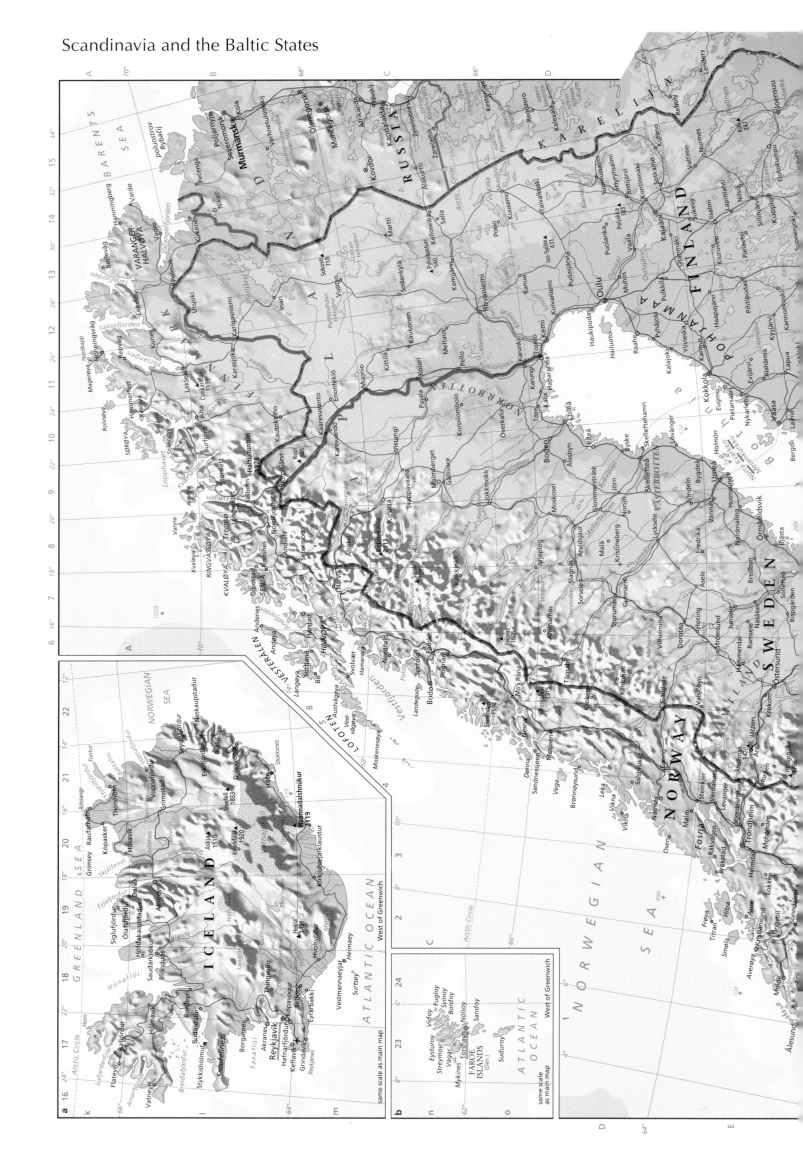

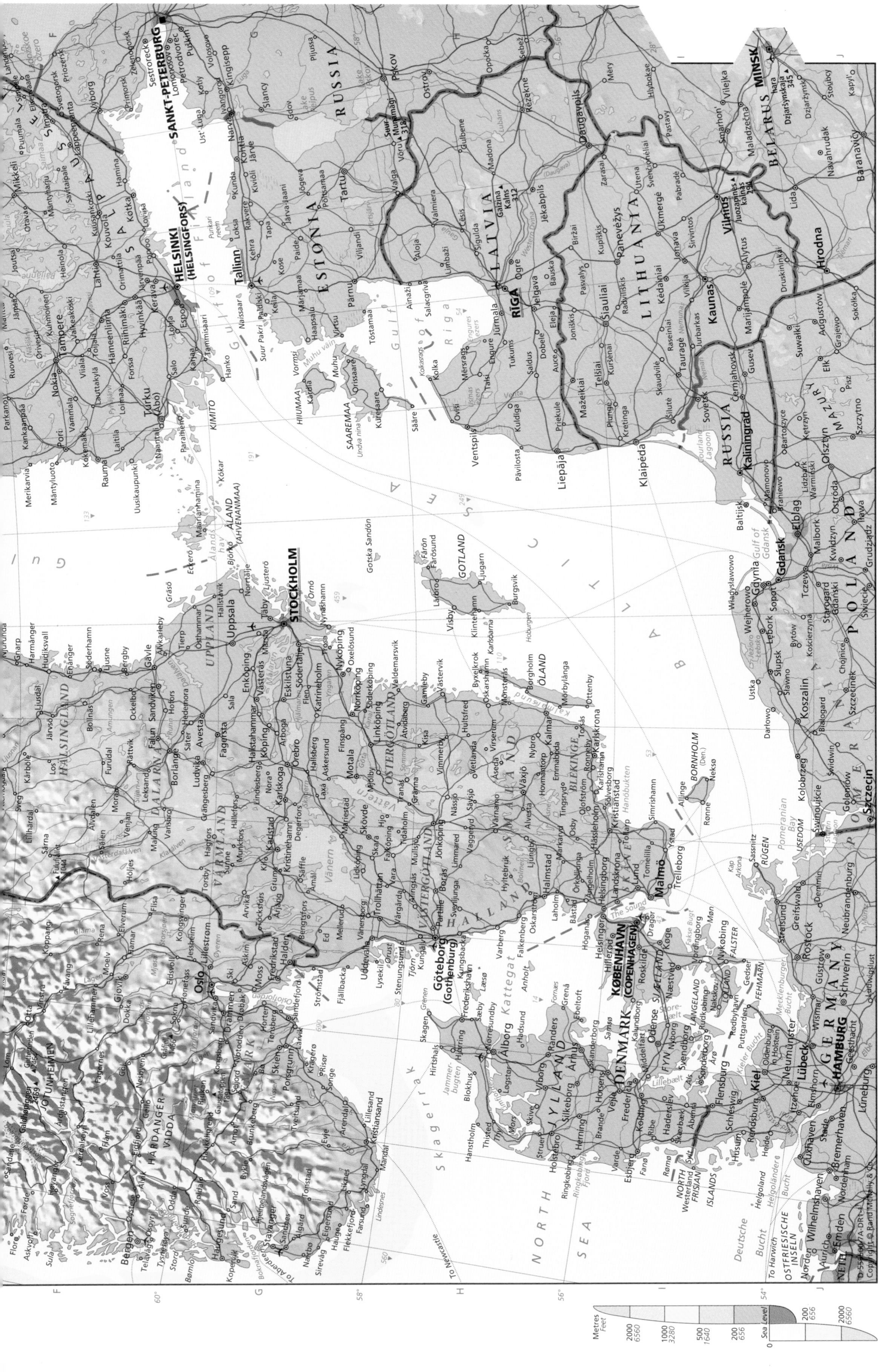

East of Greenwich

Scale 1 : 5 000 000

Lambert Conformal Conic Projection

Metres	Feet
2000	6560
1000	3280
500	1640
200	656
Sea level	
200	656
2000	6560

500 km
300 miles

12

SHETLAND ISLANDS (U.K.)
Unst
Fetlar
Yell
St. Magnus Bay
Whalsay
MAINLAND
Lerwick
Foula
Bressay

ATLANTIC OCEAN

Westray
Rousay
Sanday
Stronsay
MAINLAND
Kirkwall
ORKNEY ISLANDS
Hoy
South Ronaldsay
Pentland Firth
Thurso
Duncansby Head
John o' Groats

NORTH SEA

West of Greenwich

Fair Isle

Flannan Islands
Butt of Lewis
Cape Wrath
MAINLAND
To Bressay
Stronsay
Hoy
Kirkwall
ORKNEY ISLANDS
South Ronaldsay
Pentland Firth
Duncansby Head
John o' Groats
146
To Lerwick

OUTER HEBRIDES
ISLE OF LEWIS
Stornoway
St. Kilda
The Minch
Durness
Thurso
Wick
Helmsdale
Brora
Dornoch
Portsoy
Kinnaird Head
Fraserburgh
Peterhead

North Uist
Benbecula
South Uist
Lochboisdale
The Little Minch
INNER HEBRIDES
ISLAND OF SKYE
Portree
Kyle of Lochalsh
NORTH WEST HIGHLANDS
Ullapool
Lochinver
Ben More Assynt 998
Dingwall
Inverness
Nairn
Elgin
Loch Ness
Loch Ness
Ben Macdui 1309
GRAMPIAN MOUNTAINS
Aberdeen

Sea of the Hebrides
Rum
Eigg
Coll
Tiree
Tobermory
ISLAND OF MULL
Oban
Fort William
Ben Nevis 1343
Cairn Gorm 1182
Perth
Montrose
Stonehaven
Arbroath
Dundee

Barra
Firth of Lorn
Colonsay
JURA
ISLAY
Port Ellen
Kintyre
ISLAND OF ARRAN
Campbeltown
Inveraray
Loch Lomond
Greenock
GLASGOW
Kilmarnock
Ayr
Motherwell
EDINBURGH
Dunfermline
Kirkcaldy
Glenrothes
St. Andrews
Fife Ness
Firth of Forth
GREAT

Malin Head
GIANT'S CAUSEWAY
Rathlin Island
SOUTHERN UPLANDS
Girvan
843
Moffat
Galashiels
Berwick-upon-Tweed
Alnwick

Rocky Point
Aran Island
Errigal Mountain 752
Buncrana
Coleraine
Larne
Stranraer
Dumfries
HADRIAN'S WALL
Gatehouse of Fleet
Solway Firth
Carlisle
UNITED

Donegal
NORTHERN IRELAND
Omagh
Ballymena
Bangor
Belfast
Downpatrick
Newry
Whitehaven
Penrith
Lake District
Scafell Pikes 978
Kendal
NEWCASTLE UPON TYNE
Sunderland
Hartlepool
Durham
Darlington
Middlesbrough
Scarborough
KINGDOM

Donegal Bay
Sligo
Strabane
Lough Neagh
Portadown
Dundalk
Carrick on Shannon
Ballieborough
Drogheda
Dundalk Bay
Douglas
ISLE OF MAN (U.K.)
Barrow-in-Furness
Morecambe Bay
Lancaster
Blackpool
Preston
Ripon
York
Bridlington

Ballina
Castlebar
Clew Bay
Mweelrea 817
Clifden
CONNAUGHT
Roscommon
Longford
Athlone
Lough Ree
Lough Corrib
Galway
ARAN ISLANDS
Galway Bay
Ennistimon
CLIFFS OF MOHER
IRELAND
LEINSTER
Kildare
Port Laoise
Grand Canal
DUBLIN (BAILE ÁTHA CLIATH)
Dun Laoghaire
Holyhead
ANGLESEY
Bangor
Caernarfon
LIVERPOOL
Chester
Bolton
Preston
Blackburn
MANCHESTER
Huddersfield
LEEDS
Bradford
BRITAIN
Kingston upon Hull
Grimsby
Lincoln
Skegness
The Wash
Cromer
ENGLAND

Loop Head
Mouth of the Shannon
Kilkee
Tralee
Newcastle West
MUNSTER
Limerick
Mallow
Clonmel
Kilkenny
Carlow
Wicklow
WICKLOW MOUNTAINS 924
Arklow
Braich y Pwll
Pwllheli
Snowdon 1085
CAMBRIAN MOUNTAINS
Wrexham
Stoke-on-Trent
Stafford
Telford
Shrewsbury
Derby
Nottingham
Mansfield
Sheffield
Boston
King's Lynn
Peterborough
Norwich
Great Yarmouth
Lowestoft

Dingle Bay
Cahersiveen
Carrantuohill 1038
Killarney
Kenmare
Bantry
Bantry Bay
Mizen Head
Skull
Cork
Kinsale
Old Head of Kinsale
Blackwater
Dungarvan
Youghal
Waterford
Wexford
Enniscorthy
Rosslare
Carnsore Point
St. George's Channel
Fishguard
Cardigan
New Quay
Aberystwyth
Cardigan Bay
110
WALES
Llandovery
Builth Wells
Hereford
Worcester
Cheltenham
Gloucester
Dudley
Wolverhampton
Walsall
BIRMINGHAM
Coventry
Northampton
Banbury
Bedford
Milton Keynes
Ely
Cambridge
Bury Saint Edmunds
Ipswich
Leicester
Harwich

St. David's Head
Milford Haven
Pembroke
Carmarthen
Swansea
Merthyr Tydfil
Port Talbot
Newport
Cardiff
Bristol
Bath
Weston-super-Mare
Bridgwater
Taunton
Gloucester
Swindon
Reading
Oxford
Luton
LONDON
Slough
Colchester
Clacton-on-Sea
Chelmsford
Southend-on-Sea

128
CELTIC SEA
Lundy
Barnstaple
Bude
Newquay
Redruth
Penzance
ISLES OF SCILLY
Land's End
Lizard Point
Start Point
Bristol Channel
STONEHENGE
Basingstoke
Guildford
Reigate
Crawley
Winchester
Southampton
Bournemouth
Poole
Weymouth
Bill of Portland
ISLE OF WIGHT
Portsmouth
Worthing
Brighton
Eastbourne
Hastings
Canterbury
Dover
Folkestone
Ramsgate
Oostende

Exeter
Dorchester
Lyme Bay
Torquay
Plymouth
Saint Austell
Falmouth
CORNWALL

120
ATLANTIC OCEAN

English Channel
Alderney
Cap de la Hague
Cherbourg
Pointe de Barfleur
GUERNSEY (U.K.)
St. Peter Port
CHANNEL ISLANDS
Sark
Baie de la Seine
Dieppe
Fécam
Bolbec
Yvetot
Neufchâtel-en-Bray
Amiens
PICARDIE

JERSEY (U.K.)
St. Helier
Carteret
Coutances
Granville
Sillon de Talbert
Saint-Pol-de-Léon
Lannion
Morlaix
Guingamp
Saint-Malo
Golfe de Saint-Malo
LE MONT-ST-MICHEL
Saint-Lô
Bayeux
Caen
Le Havre
Lisieux
Rouen
Évreux
Saint-Denis
Versailles
PARIS
Creil
Beauvais
Compiègne
ÎLE-DE-FRANCE
Meaux

Île d'Ouessant
Pointe de Saint-Mathieu
Landerneau
Brest
Douarnenez
Pointe du Raz
Quimper
Concarneau
Quimperlé
Iroise
Châteaulin
Saint-Brieuc
Loudéac
Dinan
Fougères
BRETAGNE
Rennes
Vitré
Mayenne
Laval
Argentan
Alençon
Sablé-sur-Sarthe
Le Mans
Nogent-le-Rotrou
Dreux
Chartres
Châteaudun
Rambouillet
Étampes
Sens
Montargis

Pointe de Penmarc'h
Lorient
Hennebont
Vannes
Muzillac
Redon
Châteaubriant
Ancenis
Blain
Mauron
Segré
Angers
La Flèche
Vendôme
Blois
Orléans
Romorantin-Lanthenay
Vierzon
Bourges
Auxerre

Île de Groix
Quiberon
Belle-Île
Le Palais
La Baule-Escoublac
Saint-Nazaire
Nantes
Rezé
Cholet
Thouars
Bressuire
Châtellerault
Châteauroux
Issoudun
TOURAINE
Tours
Saumur
ANJOU
FRANCE

Noirmoutier
Île de Noirmoutier
Île d'Yeu
Saint-Jean-de-Monts
Machecoul
150
To Santander, Barakaldo

North Channel

IRISH SEA

NORTH SEA

Metres / Feet
3000 / 9840
2000 / 6560
1000 / 3280
500 / 1640
200 / 656
0 / Sea Level
200 / 656
2000 / 6560

Copyright © Rand McNally & Co.

0 50 100 150 200 300 400 500 km
0 50 100 200 300 miles

Scale 1 : 5 000 000
Lambert Conformal Conic Projection

West of Greenwich   East of Greenwich

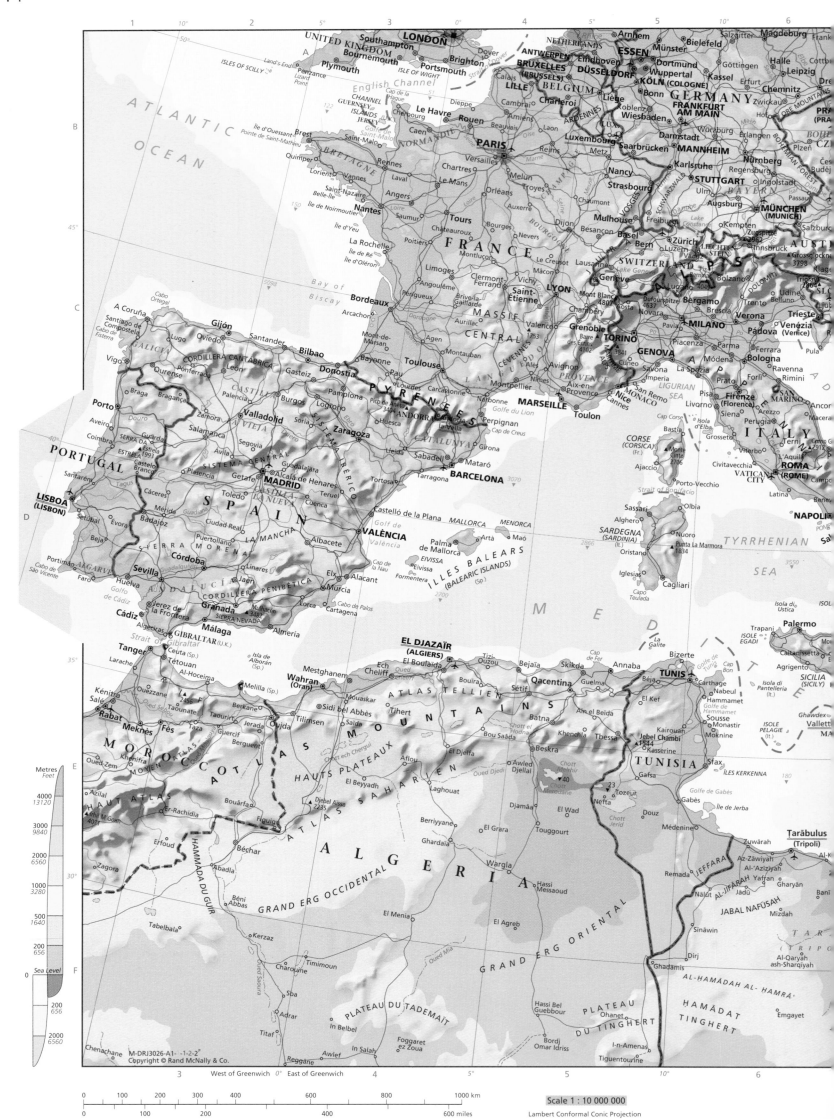

ATLANTIC OCEAN

UNITED KINGDOM

LONDON

Southampton
Bournemouth
Brighton
Portsmouth
Plymouth
Penzance
Land's End
ISLES OF SCILLY
Lizard Point

Dover
Calais
Cap de la Hague
Cherbourg
Le Havre
Rouen
Dieppe
Amiens
Beauvais
Caen
CHANNEL ISLANDS (U.K.)
GUERNSEY
JERSEY
Golfe de Saint-Malo
Saint-Malo
Rennes
Laval
Le Mans
Chartres
Versailles
PARIS
Melun
Orléans
Troyes
Auxerre

ANTWERPEN (BRUSSELS)
BRUXELLES
LILLE
BELGIUM
Charleroi
Liège
ARDENNES
Luxembourg
Reims
Metz
Nancy
Strasbourg

NETHERLANDS
Eindhoven
ESSEN
DÜSSELDORF
KÖLN (COLOGNE)
Bonn
Koblenz
Wiesbaden
FRANKFURT AM MAIN
Darmstadt
MANNHEIM
Saarbrücken
Karlsruhe

Arnhem
Münster
Dortmund
Wuppertal
GERMANY
Würzburg
Nürnberg
Regensburg

Bielefeld
Göttingen
Kassel
Erfurt

Salzgitter
Magdeburg
Halle
Leipzig
Chemnitz

ORE MOUNTAINS

Cottbus

PRA (PRA)
BOHEMIAN FOREST
Plzeň
CZ
BOHE

Erlangen
Ingolstadt
MÜNCHEN (MUNICH)
Passau
AUST
Salzburg

FRANCE

Brest
Pointe de Saint-Mathieu
Île d'Ouessant
Quimper
BRETAGNE
Lorient
Saint-Nazaire
Belle-Île
Île de Noirmoutier
Nantes
Île d'Yeu
La Rochelle
Île de Ré
Île d'Oléron
NORMANDIE
Vannes
Angers
Saumur
Tours
Poitiers
Châteauroux
Bordeaux
Arcachon
Périgueux
Angoulême
Brive-la-Gaillarde
Agen
Montauban
Toulouse

Bay of Biscay

Laon
Oise
Marne
Seine
Loire
Loire
Bourges
Nevers
Limoges
Clermont-Ferrand
Vichy
MASSIF CENTRAL
Aurillac
Aveyron

CHAMP
Chaumont
Dijon
BOURGOGNE
Mâcon
Saint-Étienne
LYON
Grenoble
Chambéry

VOSGES
Mulhouse
Basel
Bern
Genève
Lausanne
SWITZERLAND
Zürich
Luzern
LIECHTEN STEIN
Innsbruck
ALPS
Mont Blanc 4807
Dufourspitze 4637
San Remo
DOLOMITI
Grossglockner 3798
Triglav 2864

Lake Constance
Freiburg
Augsburg
Kempten
Zugspitze 2962
Bolzano

Valence
Avignon
Nîmes
Montpellier
Narbonne
Perpignan
Carcassonne
PROVENCE
Aix-en-Provence
MARSEILLE
Toulon
Cannes
Nice
MONACO
Golfe du Lion

Aosta
Novara
Pavia
MILANO
TORINO
Cuneo
GENOVA
Savona
La Spezia
LIGURIAN SEA
Bergamo
Brescia
Verona
PÀDOVA
VENÈZIA (Venice)
Trieste
SL
Udine
Belluno
Trento
Piacenza
Parma
Mòdena
Bologna
Ravenna
Rimini
Forli
Prato
FIRENZE (Florence)
Pisa
Livorno
Siena
Arezzo
Perùgia
ITALY
SAN MARINO
Pula

PORTUGAL

A Coruña
Cabo Ortegal
Santiago de Compostela
Cabo de Fisterra
Vigo
GALICIA
Lugo
Ourense
Braga
Bragança
Porto
Aveiro
Coimbra
SERRA DA ESTRELA 1993
Guarda
Castelo Branco
LISBOA (LISBON)
Santarém
Setúbal
Évora
Beja
Portimão
ALGARVE
Faro
Cabo de São Vicente

Gijón
Oviedo
Santander
Bilbao
CORDILLERA CANTÁBRICA
León
Palencia
Burgos
CASTI
Ponferrada
Zamora
Valladolid
Salamanca
Ávila
Segovia
SISTEMA CENTRAL
Plasencia
Cáceres
Guadalupe
Mérida
Badajoz
SIERRA MORENA
Ciudad Real
Puertollano
Córdoba
SPAIN
Guadiana
Sevilla
Huelva
Jaén
Linares
ANDALUCÍA
Granada
Mulhacén 3481
SIERRA NEVADA
Jerez de la Frontera
Málaga
Cádiz
Golfo de Cádiz
Algeciras
GIBRALTAR (U.K.)

Donostia
Gasteiz
Pamplona
Logroño
Soria
Zaragoza
Huesca
PYRÉNÉES
Pic d'Aneto 3404
ANDORRA la Vella
Lleida
CATALUNYA
Girona
Sabadell
Mataró
BARCELONA
Tarragona
Tortosa
Teruel
Cuenca
Guadalajara
Alcalá de Henares
MADRID
Getafe
Toledo
Aranjuez
Albacete
LA MANCHA
Cabo de Palos
Cartagena
Almería
Lorca
Murcia
Elx
Alacant
CORDILLERA PENIBÉTICA
Castelló de la Plana
VALÈNCIA
València
Gandía

Pau
Bayonne
Lourdes
Foix

EBRO
SISTEMA IBÉRICO

Golf de València
MALLORCA
MENORCA
Palma de Mallorca
Artà
Maó
Cap de la Nau
EIVISSA
Formentera
ILLES BALEARS (BALEARIC ISLANDS) (Sp.)

Cap de Creus

CORSE (CORSICA) (Fr.)
Bastia
Monte Cinto 2706
Ajaccio
Porto-Vecchio
Strait of Bonifacio
Cap Corse
Isola d'Elba

Grosseto
Civitavecchia
ROMA (ROME)
VATICAN CITY
L'Aquila
Viterbo
Latina
NAPOLI

MEDITERRANEAN

TYRRHENIAN SEA

SARDEGNA (SARDINIA) (It.)
Alghero
Nuoro
Oristano
Iglesias
Cagliari
Capo Teulada
Punta La Marmora 1834

Sassari
Olbia

Isola di Ustica
Trapani
ISOLE EGADI
Palermo
SICILIA (SICILY)
Caltanissetta
Agrigento
Isola di Pantelleria (It.)
Ghawdex (Gozo)
Valletta
MA
ISOLE PELAGIE (It.)

EL DJAZAÏR (ALGIERS)
El Boulaida
Ech Cheliff
Mestghanem
Wahran (Oran)
Tizi-Ouzou
Bejaïa
Skikda
Qacentina
Sétif
Batna
Bouïra
TUNIS
Bizerte
Carthage
Nabeul
Annaba
Cap de Fer
Guelma
Aïn el Beïda
El Kef
Kairouan
Sousse
Monastir
Mokmine
Sfax
ÎLES KERKENNA
Gafsa
TUNISIA
Gabès
Île de Jerba
Golfe de Gabès
La Galite
Cap Bon
Golfe de Hammamet
Hammamet
Sousse
Khenchla
Tbessa
Kasserine
Jebel Chambi 1544

ATLAS TELLIEN
ATLAS MOUNTAINS
Mouaskar
Sidi bel Abbès
Tihert
Saïda
Tilimsen
Berkane
Taourirt
Guercif
Oujda
Jerada
HAUTS PLATEAUX
El Djelfa
Aflou
Laghouat
ATLAS SAHARIEN
Djelfa
Bou Saâda
Beskra
Chott el Hodna
Chott Melrhir
Awled Djellal
Oued Djedi
Biskra
El Beyyadh
Tozeur
Nefta
Chott Jerid
Douz
Médenine
Remada
JEFFARA

Tanger
Ceuta (Sp.)
Tétouan
Al-Hoceima
Larache
Melilla (Sp.)
Isla de Alborán (Sp.)
Strait of Gibraltar
Kénitra
Salé
Rabat
Meknès
Fès
Taza
MOROCCO
MOYEN ATLAS
HAUT ATLAS
Khenifra
Azilal
Er-Rachidia
Irhil M'Goun 4071
Errachidia
Erfoud
Oued-Zem
Béni Mellal
Béchar
Bouârfa
Figuig
HAMMADA DU GUIR
Zagora
Abadla
Taurirt

MA
Taounate
Berguem
Oued
1456
Djebel Aïssa 2235

ATLAS SAHARIEN
ALGERIA
GRAND ERG OCCIDENTAL
Abadla
Béni Abbas
El Menia
El Agreb
El Grara
Ghardaïa
Berriyyane
Wargla
Hassi Messaoud
Touggourt
El Wad
GRAND ERG ORIENTAL
Ghadamis
Dirj
Sinawin
Nālūt
AL-JIFĀRAH
Az-Zāwiyah
Al-'Azīziyah
Gharyān
Yafran
Banī
Mizdah
JABAL NAFŪSAH
Tarābulus (Tripoli)
Zuwārah
Al-Qaryah ash-Sharqiyah

Tabelbala
Kerzaz
Charouine
Timimoun
Oued Siaoura
Sba
Adrar
Titaf
In Belbel
El Menia
AL-HAMĀDAH AL-HAMRĀ'
Hassi Bel Guebbour
Ohanet
HAMĀDAT TINGHERT
PLATEAU DU TINGHERT
Emgayet

PLATEAU DU TADEMAÏT
Chenachane
In Salah
Foggaret ez Zoua
Reggâne
Aoulef
Bordj Omar Idriss
I-n-Amenas
Tiguentourine

MOROCCO

Metres / Feet
4000 / 13120
3000 / 9840
2000 / 6560
1000 / 3280
500 / 1640
200 / 656
0 / Sea Level
200 / 656
2000 / 6560

West of Greenwich   0°   East of Greenwich

0 100 200 300 400 600 800 1000 km
0 100 200 400 600 miles

Scale 1 : 10 000 000

Lambert Conformal Conic Projection

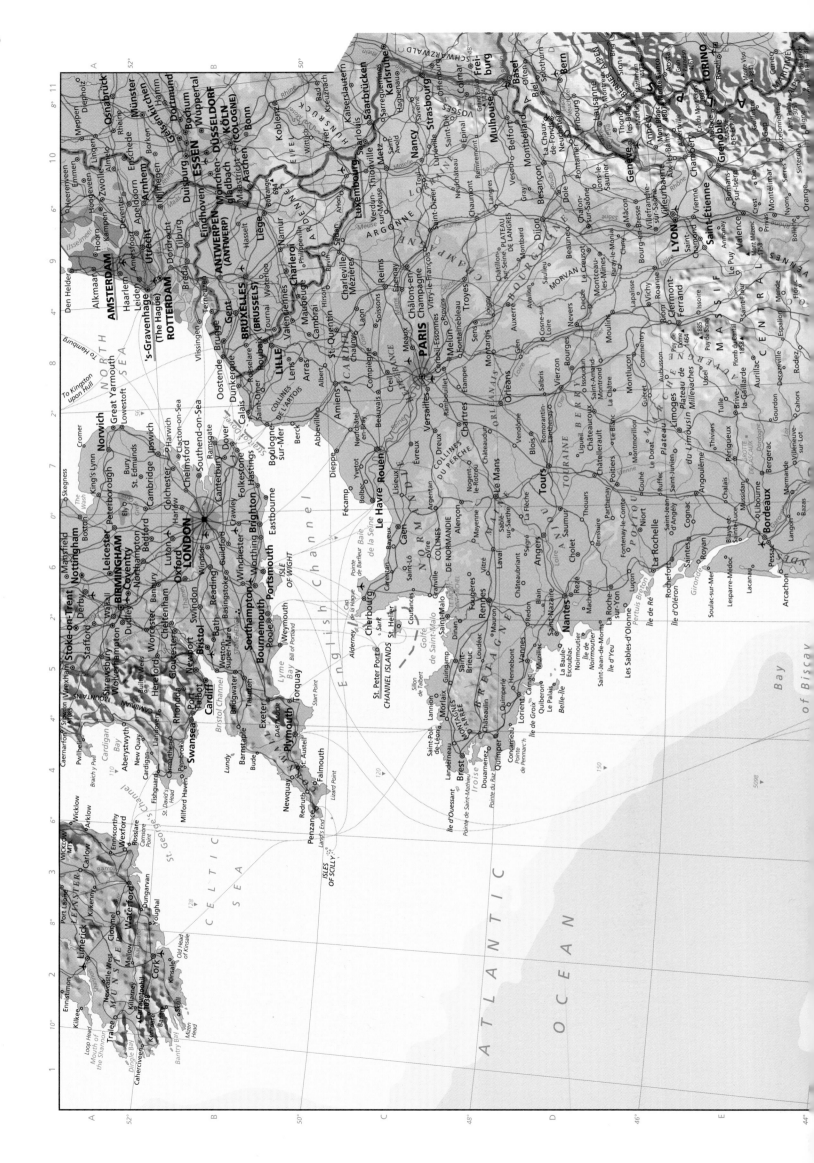

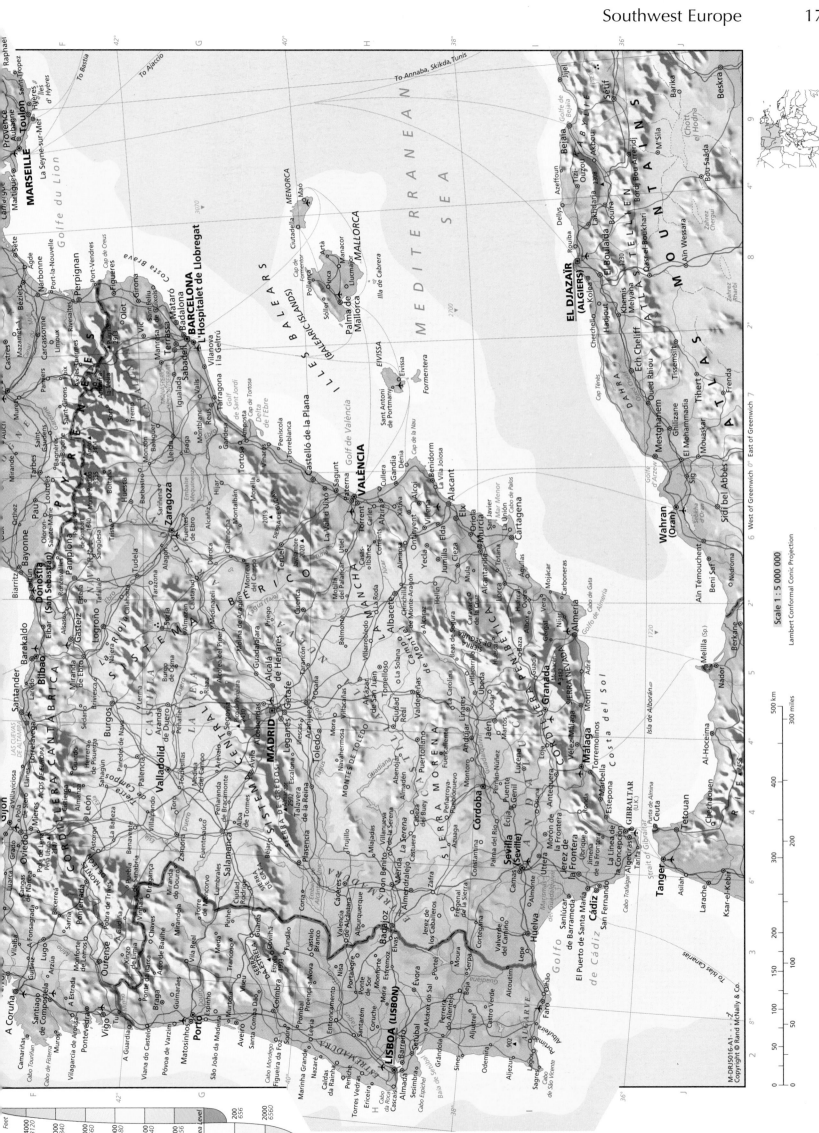

M-DR5016-A1-.-.-2°

Scale 1 : 5 000 000

Lambert Conformal Conic Projection

18

Metres / Feet
4000 / 13120
3000 / 9840
2000 / 6560
1000 / 3280
500 / 1640
200 / 656
0 / Sea Level
200 / 656
2000 / 6560

0   50 100 150 200   300   400   500 km
0   50   100   200   300 miles

Scale 1 : 5 000 000
Lambert Conformal Conic Projection

M-DRJSB17-A1-/-1-2.2"
Copyright © Rand McNally & Co.

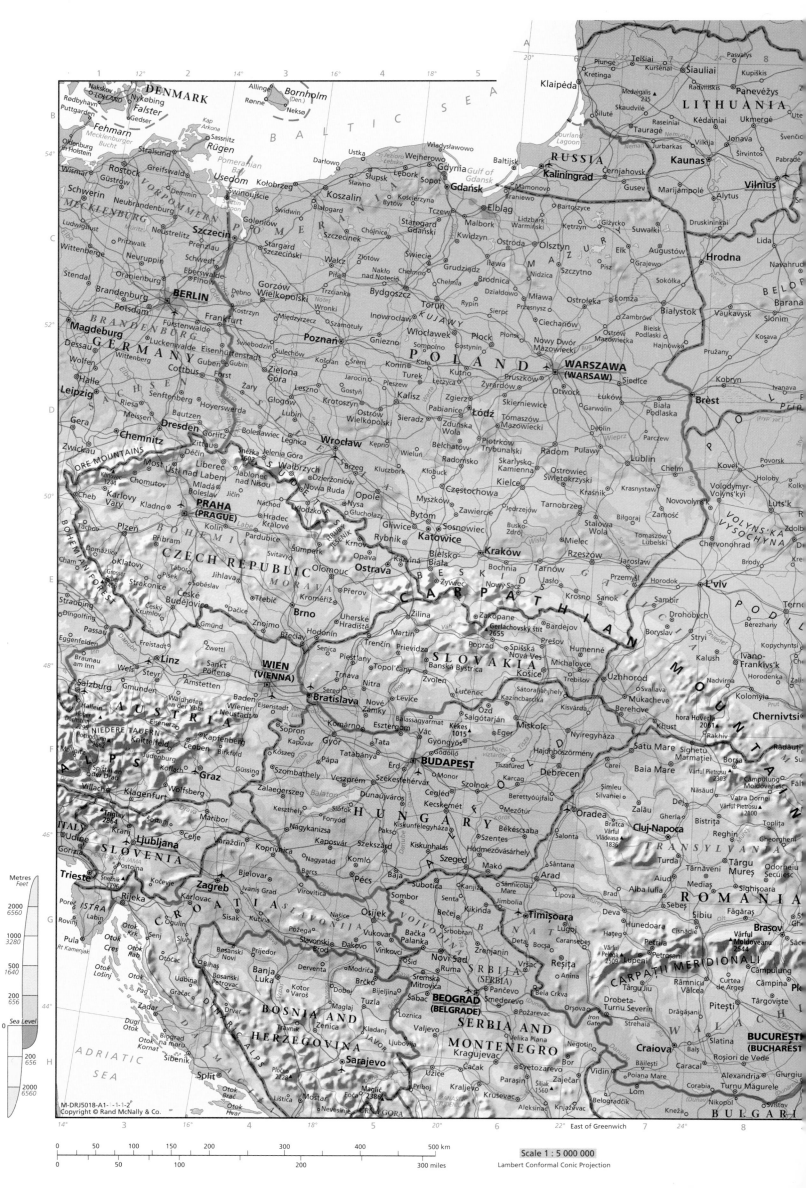

M-DRJ5018-A1-·-1-1-2"
Copyright © Rand McNally & Co.

Metres
Feet

2000
6560

1000
3280

500
1640

200
656

0
Sea Level

200
656

2000
6560

Scale 1 : 5 000 000
Lambert Conformal Conic Projection

East of Greenwich

0   50   100 150 200   300   400   500 km
0   50   100   200   300 miles

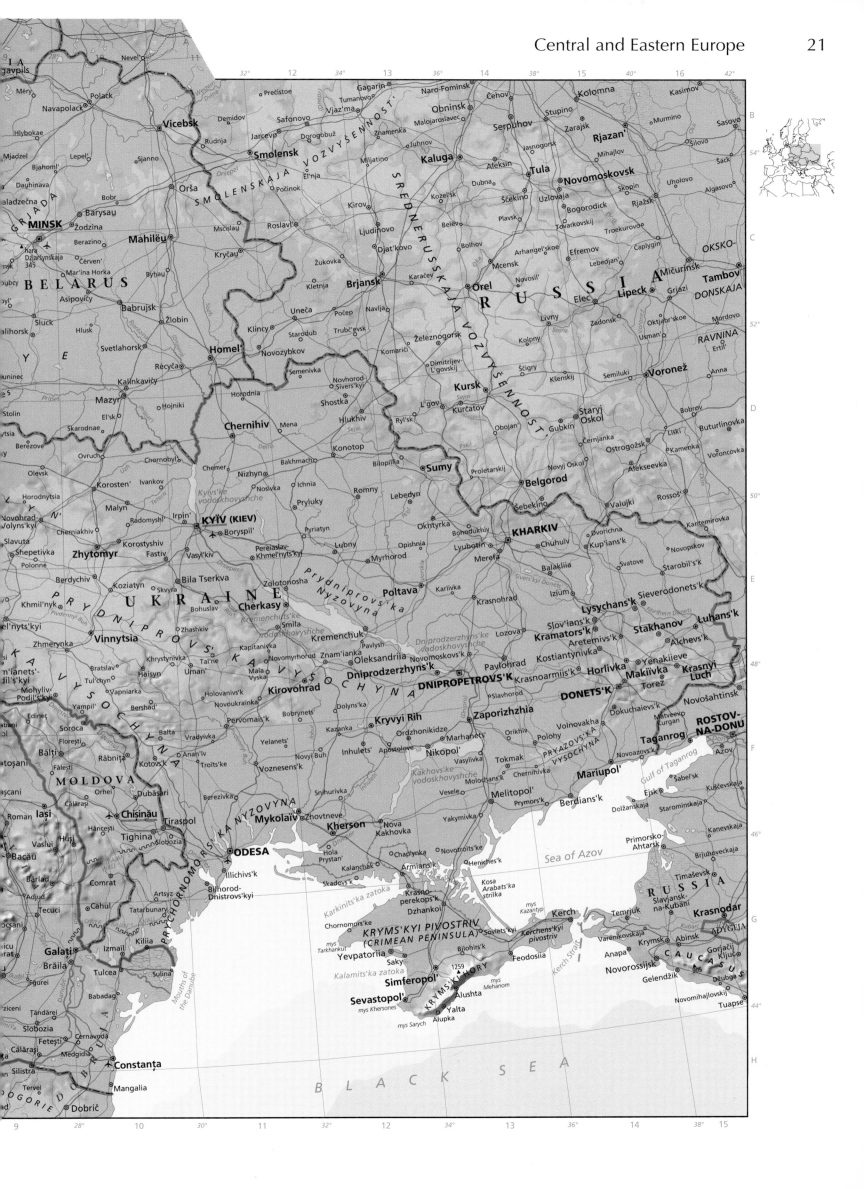

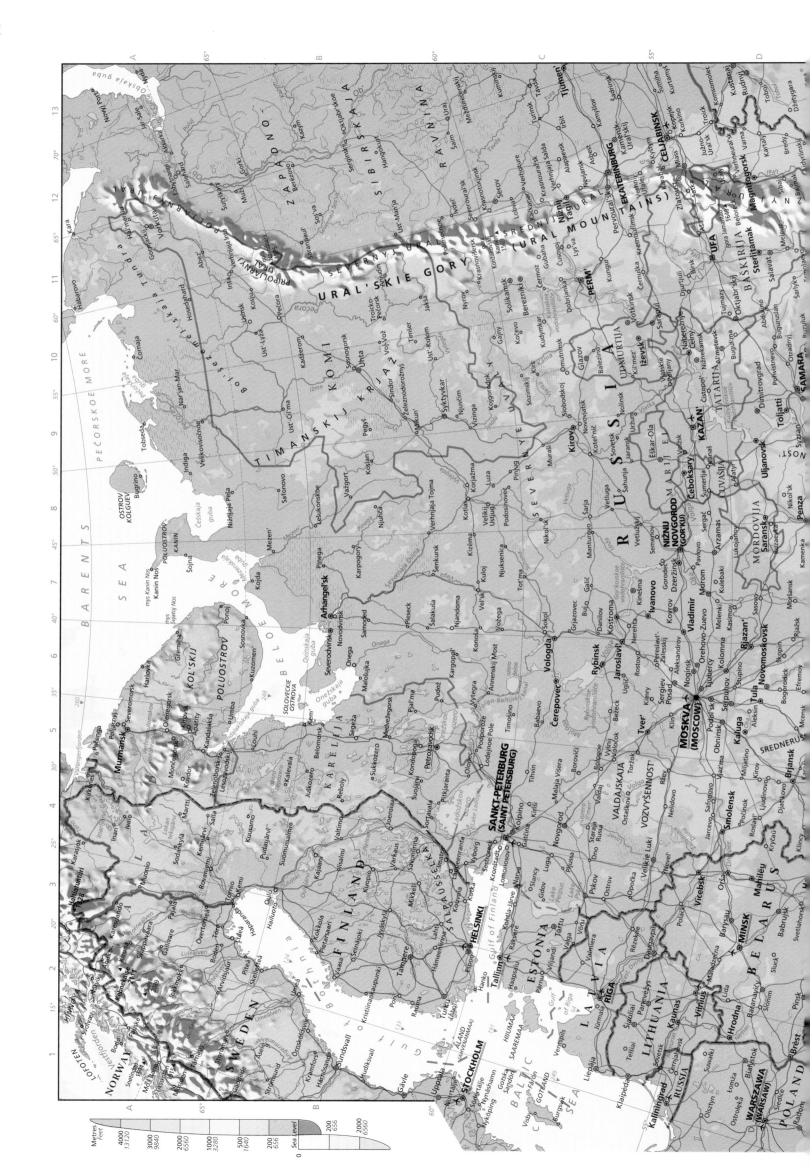

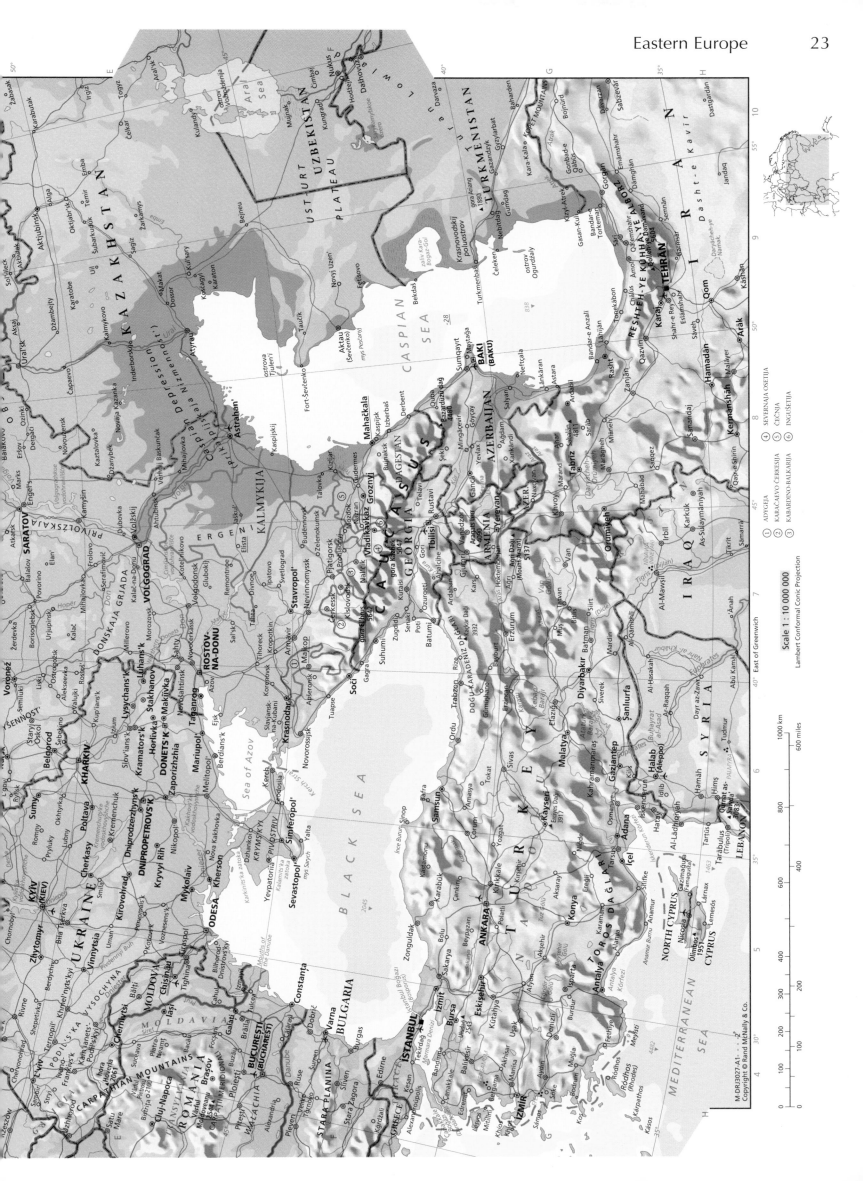

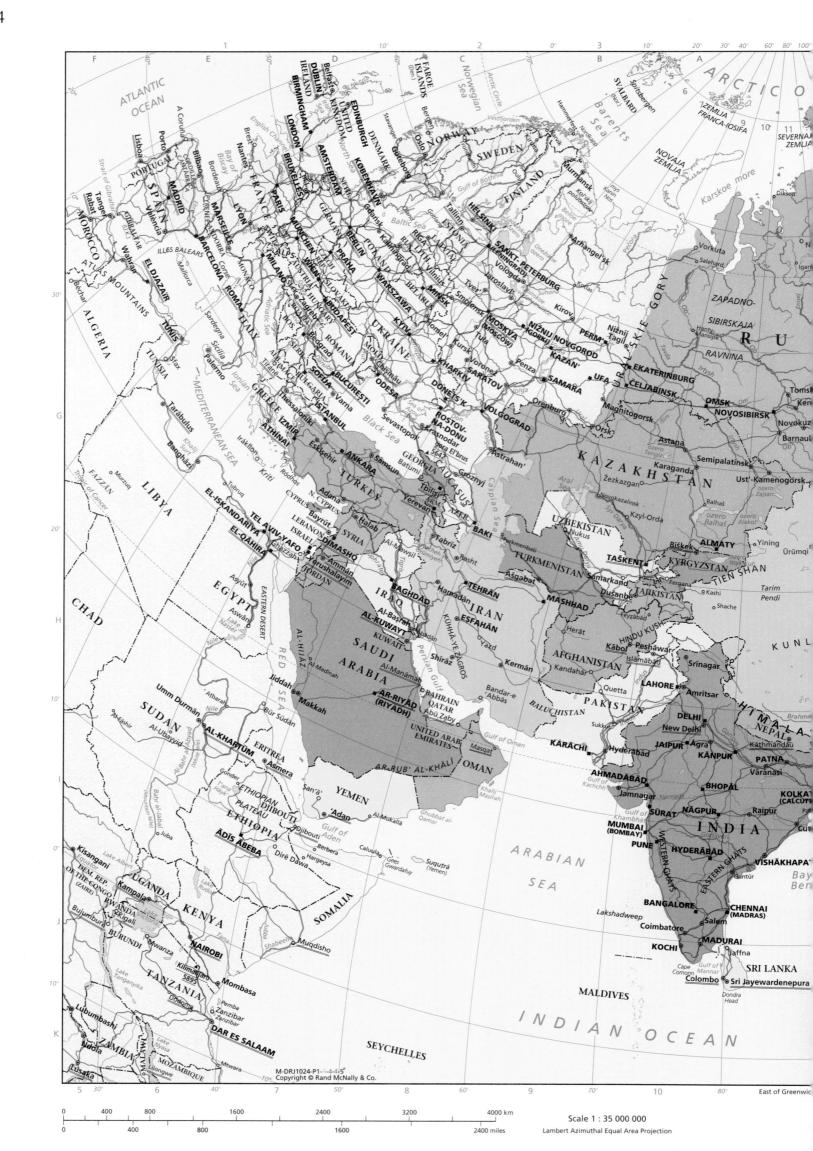

M-DRJ1024-P1-4-4-5°
Copyright © Rand McNally & Co.

0	400	800	1600	2400	3200	4000 km

0	400	800	1600	2400 miles

Scale 1 : 35 000 000
Lambert Azimuthal Equal Area Projection

East of Greenwich

Scale 1 : 20 000 000

Lambert Conformal Conic Projection

| 0 | 200 | 400 | 600 | 800 | | 1200 | | 1600 km |

| 0 | | 200 | | 400 | | 800 miles |

M.7099317 A.PR1 -4°
Copyright © Rand McNally & Co.

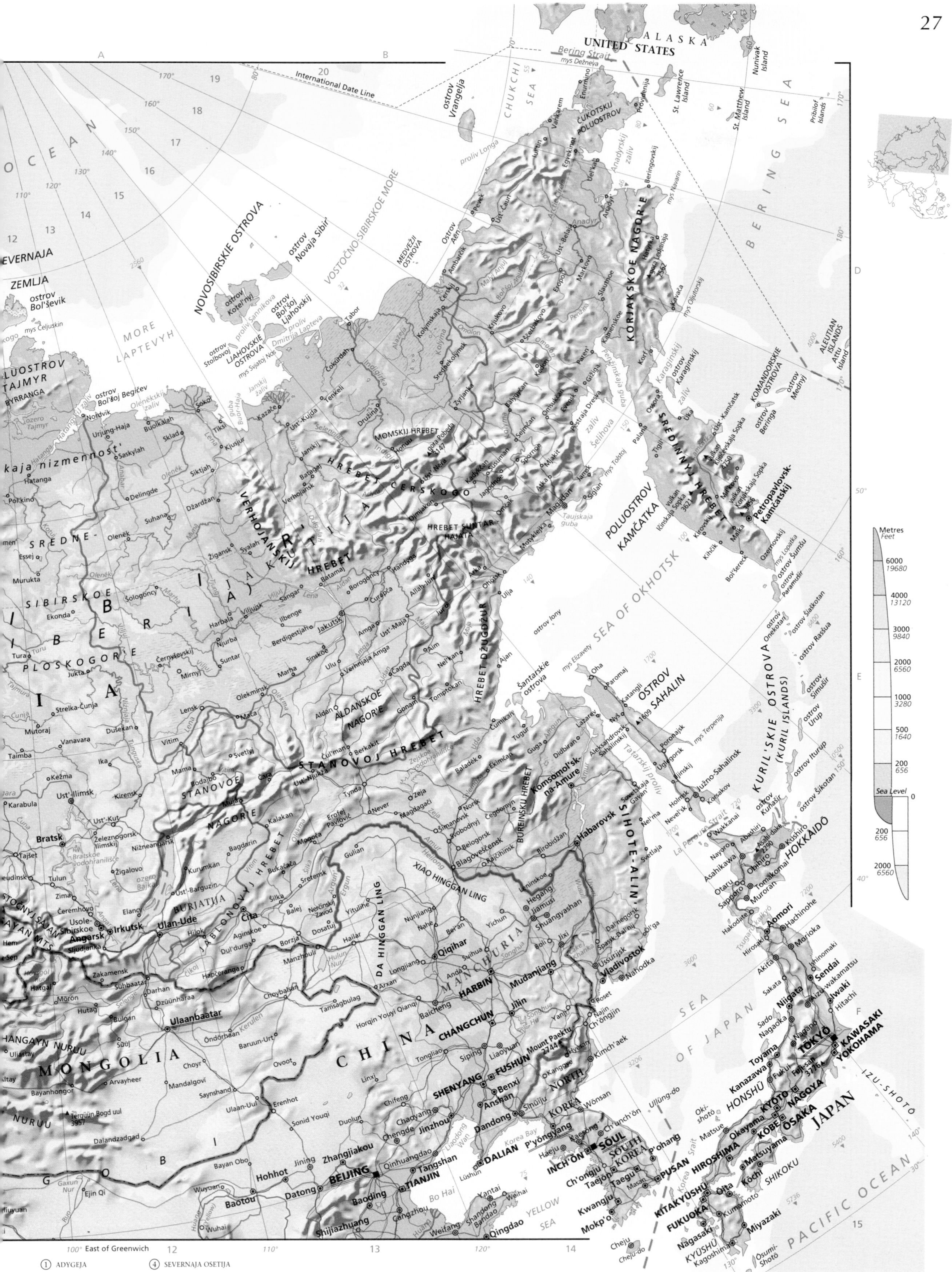

ALASKA

UNITED STATES

Bering Strait
mys Dežneva

CHUKCHI SEA

Nunivak Island

St. Lawrence Island

St. Matthew Island

Pribilof Islands

BERING SEA

ČUKOTSKIJ POLUOSTROV

proliv Longa

ostrov Vrangelja

OCEAN

NOVOSIBIRSKIE OSTROVA

ostrov Novaja Sibir'

ostrov Kotel'nyj

ostrov Bol'šoj Ljahovskij

LJAHOVSKIE OSTROVA

MEDVEŽ'I OSTROVA

MORE LAPTEVYH

kaja nizmennost'

SEVERNAJA ZEMLJA

ostrov Bol'ševik

PLUOSTROV TAJMYR

BYRRANGA

ozero Tajmyr

VOSTOČNO-SIBIRSKOE MORE

KORJAKSKOE NAGOR'E

SREDINNYJ HREBET

POLUOSTROV KAMČATKA

Petropavlovsk-Kamčatskij

KOMANDORSKIE OSTROVA

ostrov Bering

ostrov Mednyj

ALEUTIAN ISLANDS

Attu Island

SREDNE-SIBIRSKOE PLOSKOGOR'E

SIBERIA

VERHOJANSKIJ HREBET

HREBET ČERSKOGO

MOMSKIJ HREBET

HREBET SUNTAR-HAJATA

HREBET DŽUGDŽUR

ALDANSKOE NAGOR'E

SEA OF OKHOTSK

ostrov Iony

Šantarskie ostrova

OSTROV SAHALIN

Južno-Sahalinsk

Tatarskij proliv

La Pérouse Strait

KURIL'SKIE OSTROVA (KURIL ISLANDS)

ostrov Kunašir

ostrov Šikotan

ostrov Iturup

ostrov Urup

ostrov Simušir

ostrov Rasšua

ostrov Paramušir

ostrov Šiaškotan

Jakutsk

Lensk

Olekminsk

Mirnyj

Bratsk

Ust'-Ilimsk

Ust'-Kut

Irkutsk

Ulan-Ude

BURJATIJA

ozero Bajkal

Čita

STANOVOE NAGOR'E

STANOVOJ HREBET

JABLONOVYJ HREBET

BUREINSKIJ HREBET

Komsomol'sk-na-Amure

Habarovsk

SIHOTE-ALIN'

Birobidžan

Blagoveščensk

Vladivostok

Ussurijsk

Nahodka

VOSTOČNYJ SAJAN

SAJAN MTS

Angarsk

Zima

Tulun

MONGOLIA

Ulaanbaatar

Hovd

Altay

Bayanhongor

Hangayn Nuruu

Tergüün Bogd uul 3957

Darhan

Sühbaatar

Choybalsan

Baruun-Urt

Sainshand

Dalandzadgad

GOBI

DA HINGGAN LING

XIAO HINGGAN LING

MANCHURIA

CHINA

Qiqihar

HARBIN

CHANGCHUN

Jilin

Mudanjiang

SHENYANG

FUSHUN

Benxi

Anshan

DALIAN

NORTH KOREA

Mount Paektu 2744

P'yŏngyang

Wŏnsan

Hamhŭng

Ch'ŏngjin

SOUTH KOREA

SOUL

INCH'ŎN

Taejŏn

Taegu

PUSAN

Kwangju

Mokp'o

Cheju-do

BEIJING

TIANJIN

Hohhot

Baotou

Datong

Zhangjiakou

Tangshan

Qinhuangdao

Shijiazhuang

Baoding

Qingdao

Weifang

Yantai

Jinan

Bo Hai

YELLOW SEA

JAPAN

HOKKAIDŌ

Sapporo

Asahikawa

Otaru

Hakodate

Aomori

Akita

Sendai

Niigata

Toyama

Kanazawa

HONSHŪ

TOKYO

KAWASAKI

YOKOHAMA

NAGOYA

KYOTO

OSAKA

KOBE

HIROSHIMA

Matsuyama

KITAKYŪSHŪ

FUKUOKA

Nagasaki

Kumamoto

Miyazaki

Kagoshima

KYŪSHŪ

SHIKOKU

Kōchi

IZU-SHOTŌ

Ōsumi-Shotō

SEA OF JAPAN

PACIFIC OCEAN

International Date Line

East of Greenwich

Metres / Feet

6000 / 19680
4000 / 13120
3000 / 9840
2000 / 6560
1000 / 3280
500 / 1640
200 / 656
Sea Level 0
200 / 656
2000 / 6560

① ADYGEJA
② KARAČAEVO - ČERKESIJA
③ KABARDINO-BALKARIJA
④ SEVERNAJA OSETIJA
⑤ ČEČNJA
⑥ INGUŠETIJA

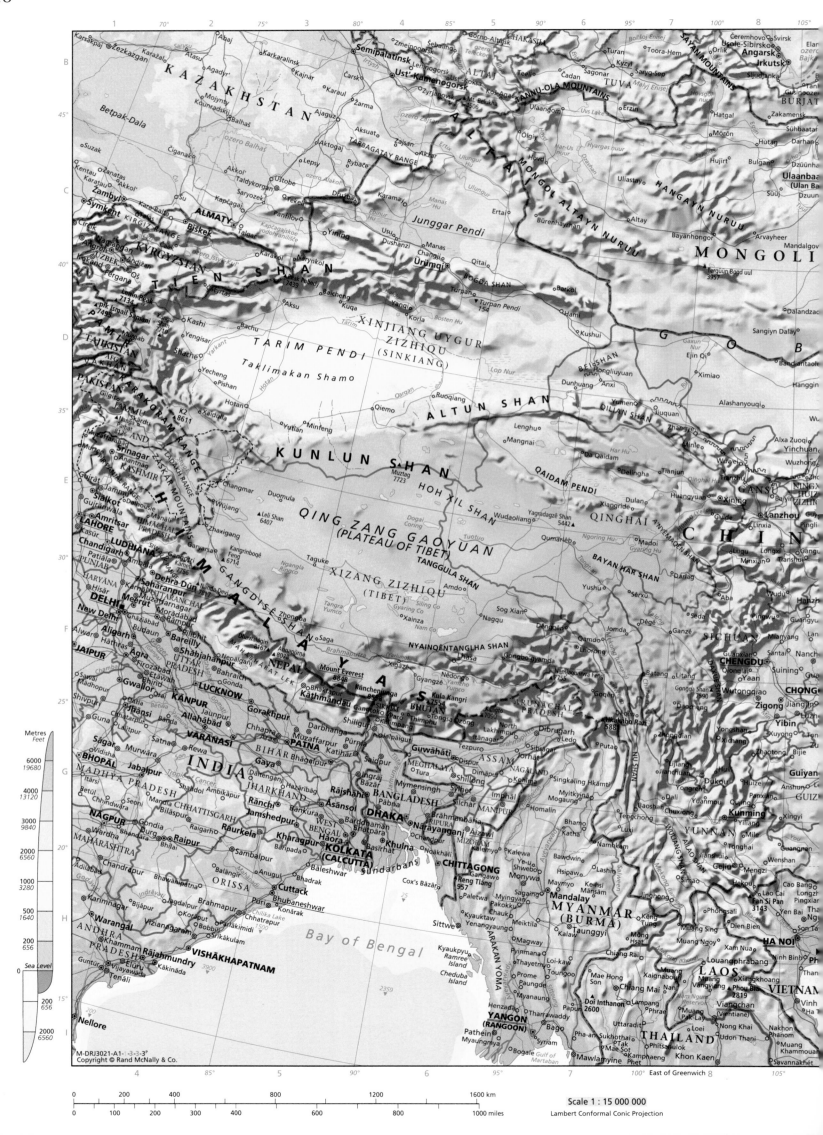

Metres / Feet

6000 / 19680
4000 / 13120
3000 / 9840
2000 / 6560
1000 / 3280
500 / 1640
200 / 656
Sea Level
0
200 / 656
2000 / 6560

M-DRJ3021-A1-|-3-3-3°
Copyright © Rand McNally & Co.

| 0 | 200 | 400 | 600 | 800 | 1200 | 1600 km |

| 0 | 100 | 200 | 300 | 400 | 600 | 800 | 1000 miles |

Scale 1 : 15 000 000

Lambert Conformal Conic Projection

East of Greenwich

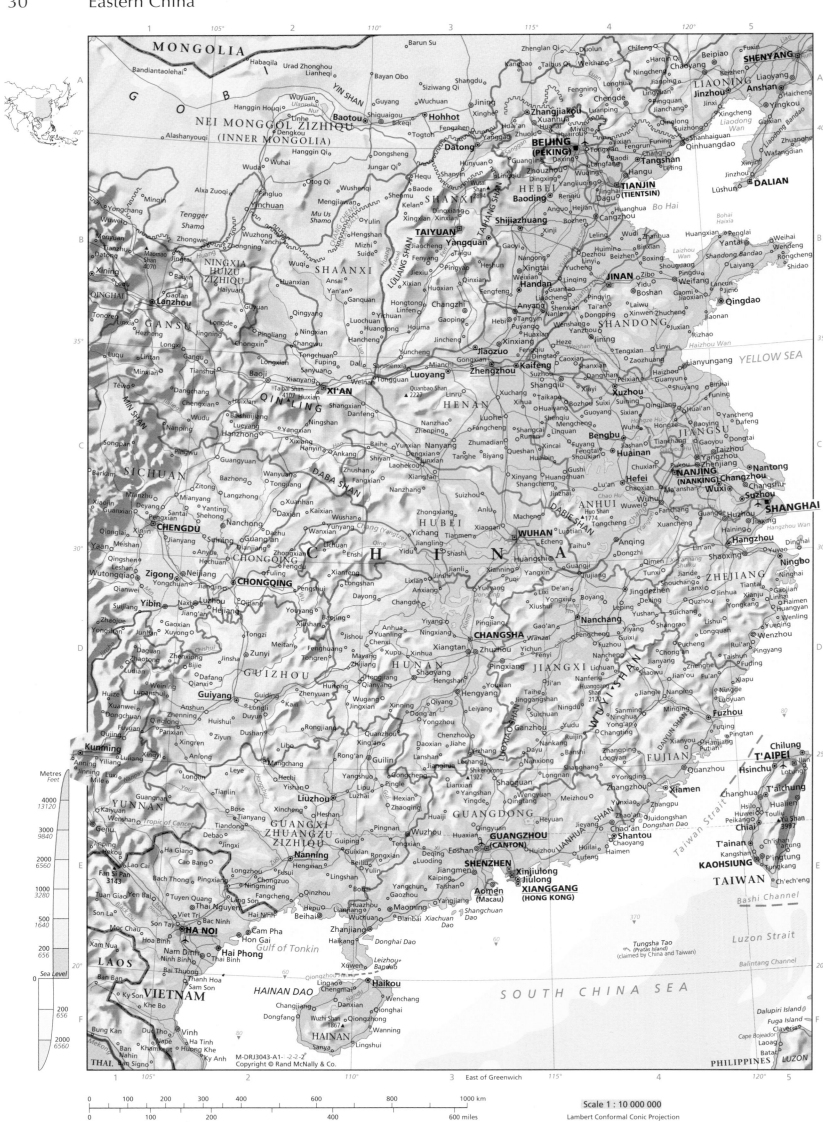

SEA OF OKHOTSK

Formerly part of Japan, Malaja Kuril'skaja, Šikotan, Kunašir, and Iturup, occupied by Russia since 1945, are claimed by Japan pending a final peace treaty.

SEA OF JAPAN

(EAST SEA)

JAPAN

HONSHŪ

PACIFIC OCEAN

EAST CHINA SEA

NANSEI-SHOTŌ (RYUKYU ISLANDS)

SHIKOKU

KYŪSHŪ

OSUMI-SHOTŌ (RYUKYU ISLANDS)

AMAMI-SHOTŌ

a same scale as main map

EAST CHINA SEA (DONG HAI)

NANSEI-SHOTŌ (RYUKYU ISLANDS)

JAPAN

PACIFIC OCEAN

OKINAWA-SHOTŌ

East of Greenwich

W-561500-7A-DR1-2
Copyright © Rand McNally & Co.

Metres	Feet
3000	9840
2000	6560
1000	3280
500	1640
200	656
Sea Level	0
200	656
2000	6560

Scale 1 : 8 000 000
Lambert Conformal Conic Projection

0   100   200   300   400   600   800 km
0   50   100   150   200   300   500 miles

32

Bay of Bengal

INDIAN OCEAN

Andaman Sea

Gulf of Thailand

BHUTAN

INDIA

BANGLADESH

MYANMAR (BURMA)

THAILAND

LAOS

VIETNAM

CAMBODIA

MALAYSIA

INDONESIA

SICHUAN

GUIZHOU

YUNNAN

CHINA

ANDAMAN ISLANDS

NICOBAR ISLANDS

ANDAMAN AND NICOBAR ISLANDS (India)

SUMATERA (SUMATRA)

Mouths of the Ganges

Tropic of Cancer

KOLKATA (CALCUTTA)

DHAKA

CHITTAGONG

Kunming

Guiyang

Mandalay

YANGON (RANGOON)

KRUNG THEP (BANGKOK)

Phnum Penh (Phnom Penh)

HA NOI

THANH PHO HO CHI MINH (SAIGON)

George Town (Penang)

Metres / Feet
6000 / 19680
4000 / 13120
3000 / 9840
2000 / 6560
1000 / 3280
500 / 1640
200 / 656
0 / Sea Level
200 / 656
2000 / 6560

M-DRJ3045-A1-1-3-3-3
Copyright © Rand McNally & Co.

Scale 1 : 10 000 000
Lambert Conformal Conic Projection
East of Greenwich

0   100   200   300   400   600   800   1000 km
0   100   200   300   400   500   600 miles

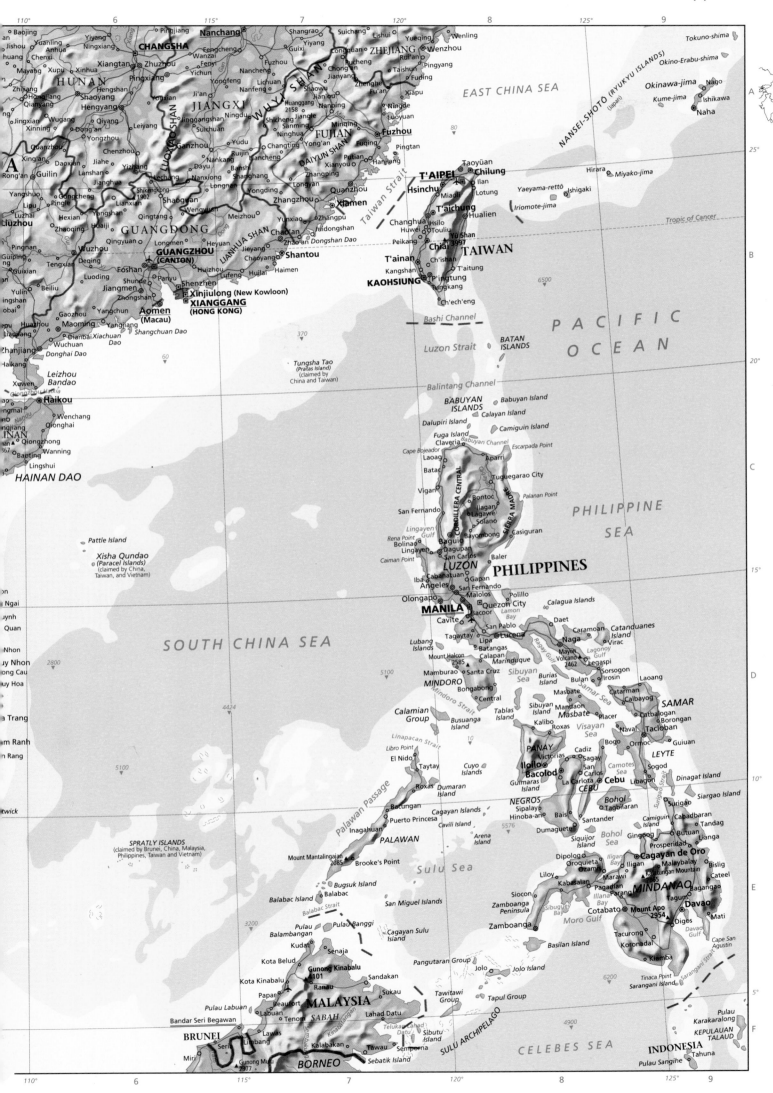

Mainland Southeast Asia and the Philippines

Baojing
Jishou
huang
Mayang Yuanling Ningxiang
Xupu Chenxi
Zhijiang Hongjiang
Qianyang
HUNAN
Jingxian
Anjiang
Rong'an Daoxian
Guilin
Yangshuo
Lipu Yangshan
Liuzhou Pingle
Hexian
Luzhai
Pingnan
Guiping
ng
Guixian
Yulin
ingshan
obai
pu Huazhou
Lianjiang Maoming
Zhanjiang Dianbai Xiachuan Dao
Wuchuan
Xuwen
Haikang
nmai Qiongzhong
nangan
357 Baoting
ngjiang Wanning
Lingshui
HAINAN DAO
Haikou
Wenchang
Qionghai
INAN
Qiongzhong
NANCHANG
Yiyang
Yichun Nancheng
Yongfeng Lichuan
Ji'an Nanfeng
Jinggangshan Guangchang
JIANGXI
Shicheng Jiangle
Ningdu
Yudu Ninghua
Ganzhou Changting Yong'an
Nankang Ruijin Liancheng
Shanghang
Longnan Yongding Longyan
Wuzhou
Qingyuan Yangchun
Heyuan
GUANGZHOU (CANTON)
Foshan
Shunde Panyu
Jiangmen Shenzhen
Zhongshan **Xinjiulong (New Kowloon)**
XIANGGANG (HONG KONG)
Aomen (Macau)
Shangchuan Dao
Donghai Dao
Leizhou Bandao

Pingjiang
Xiangtan
Xinhua

CHANGSHA
Zhuzhou
Wanzai
Fengcheng
Xingan
Lianhua
Hengyang
Shaoyang
Yongzhou
Lanshan
Jianghua

Shangrao Suichang Lishui
Shangrao **ZHEJIANG** Wenling
Guixi Wenzhou
Chong'an Taishun Pingyang
Shaowu Zhenghe Fuding
Huangganshan Ningde
2158 Minqing
Sanming Fuzhou
Shaxian
FUJIAN
Yong'an Fuqing Pingtan
Yunxiao Zhangpu
Zhao'an Dongshan Dao
Shantou
Chaoyang
Haimen
Lufeng Huilai

Changsha Zhuzhou
Hengshan
Hengyang Qiyang

EAST CHINA SEA

T'AIPEI Chilung
Hsinchu Ilan
Miaoli Lotung
T'aichung Hualien
Changhua Hsilo Touliu
Huwei Peikang **Chiai** 3997
Yu Shan
T'ainan
Kangshan Ch'ishan
KAOHSIUNG P'ingtung
Tungkang
Ch'ech'eng
TAIWAN

Taiwan Strait
Bashi Channel

PACIFIC OCEAN

Tokuno-shima
Okino-Erabu-shima
NANSEI-SHOTŌ (RYUKYU ISLANDS) (Japan)
Okinawa-jima Nago
Kume-jima Ishikawa
Naha
Hirara Miyako-jima
Yaeyama-rettō Ishigaki
Iriomote-jima
Tropic of Cancer

6500

370
60
Tungsha Tao
(Pratas Island)
(claimed by
China and Taiwan)

Luzon Strait BATAN ISLANDS
Balintang Channel
BABUYAN ISLANDS
Babuyan Island
Dalupiri Island Calayan Island
Fuga Island Camiguin Island
Claveria *Babuyan Channel*
Cape Bojeador Aparri
Laoag Escarpada Point
Batac Tuguegarao City
Vigan Bontoc
Ilagan Palanan Point
San Fernando Lagawe
Solano
Lingayen Bayombong Casiguran
Gulf Baguio
Rena Point Dagupan
Bolinao San Carlos Baler
Lingayen
Caiman Point **LUZON** **PHILIPPINES**
Iba Cabanatuan Gapan
Angeles San Fernando
Olongapo Malolos Polillo
MANILA Quezon City Calagua Islands
Bacoor Daet
Cavite San Pablo *Lamon Bay* Caramoan Catanduanes Island
Tagaytay Lipa Lucena Naga Virac
Batangas *Ragay Gulf*
Lubang Calapan Mayon *Lagonoy Gulf* Legaspi
Islands Mount Halcon Volcano Sorsogon
2585 Marinduque 2462 Irosin Laoang
Mamburao Santa Cruz Bulan Catarman
MINDORO Bongabong *Sibuyan Sea* Burias Island *Samar Sea*
Central Masbate Calbayog
Tablas Sibuyan Island Catbalogan
Mindoro Strait Island Mandaon **SAMAR**
Calamian Busuanga Kalibo **MASBATE** Naval Borongan
Group Island Roxas *Visayan Sea* Bogo Tacloban
Linapacan Strait Placer Ormoc Guiuan
Libro Point 10 **PANAY** Cadiz Sagay **LEYTE**
El Nido Victorias San *Camotes Sea*
Taytay Iloilo Carlos Libagon Sogod
Roxas Dumaran **Bacolod** La Carlota **Cebu** Dinagat Island
Island Guimaras Is. **NEGROS** Bohol *Surigao Strait*
Batungan Cagayan Islands Sipalay **CEBU** Siargao Island
Puerto Princesa Cavili Island Hinoba-an Tagbilaran Surigao
Inagahuan Arena Dumaguete Santander Camiguin Caraga
Island Siquijor **Bohol** Island Cabadbaran
PALAWAN Island *Bohol Sea* Gingoog Tandag
Mount Mantalingajan Dipolog Iligan Butuan Lianga
2085 Oroquieta Bay Malaybalay Prosperidad
Brooke's Point Ozamiz Iligan Bislig
Bugsuk Island Liloy Katanglad Mountain Cateel
Balabac Island Balabac Sioconc Marawi **MINDANAO** Bagangao
San Miguel Islands Kabasalan Pagadian Balingasag
Balabac Strait Zamboanga Illana Kidapawan Davao
3200 Peninsula Parang Bay Tagum **Davao**
Pulau Banggi Zamboanga Cotabato Mount Apo Mati
Balambangan 2954 Digos
Kudat Sibuguey *Davao Gulf*
Senaja Bay Tacurong Cape San
Kota Belud Pangutaran Group Koronadal Agustin
Kota Kinabalu Sandakan Jolo Kiamba
Gunong Kinabalu Ranau Jolo Island Tinaca Point
4101 Sukau Sarangani Island *Sarangani Strait*
Papar Tawitawi Tapul Group 6200
MALAYSIA Group Pulau
Beaufort Lahad Datu Karakaralong
Tenom Sandakan
SABAH Lahad Datu **KEPULAUAN TALAUD**
Bandar Seri Begawan Labuan Tawau
Lawas Semporna 4900
BRUNEI Seria Kalabakan **CELEBES SEA** **INDONESIA**
Miri Sebatik Island Pulau Sangihe
Gunong Mulu **SULU ARCHIPELAGO** Tahuna
2977
BORNEO

SOUTH CHINA SEA

Pattle Island
Xisha Qundao (Paracel Islands) (claimed by China, Taiwan, and Vietnam)

SPRATLY ISLANDS (claimed by Brunei, China, Malaysia, Philippines, Taiwan and Vietnam)

Sulu Sea
Palawan Passage

2800
5100
4424
5100
5576
3200
4900

PHILIPPINE SEA

Cordillera Central
Sierra Madre

Liuzhou
Luzhai

110° 6 115° 7 120° 8 125° 9

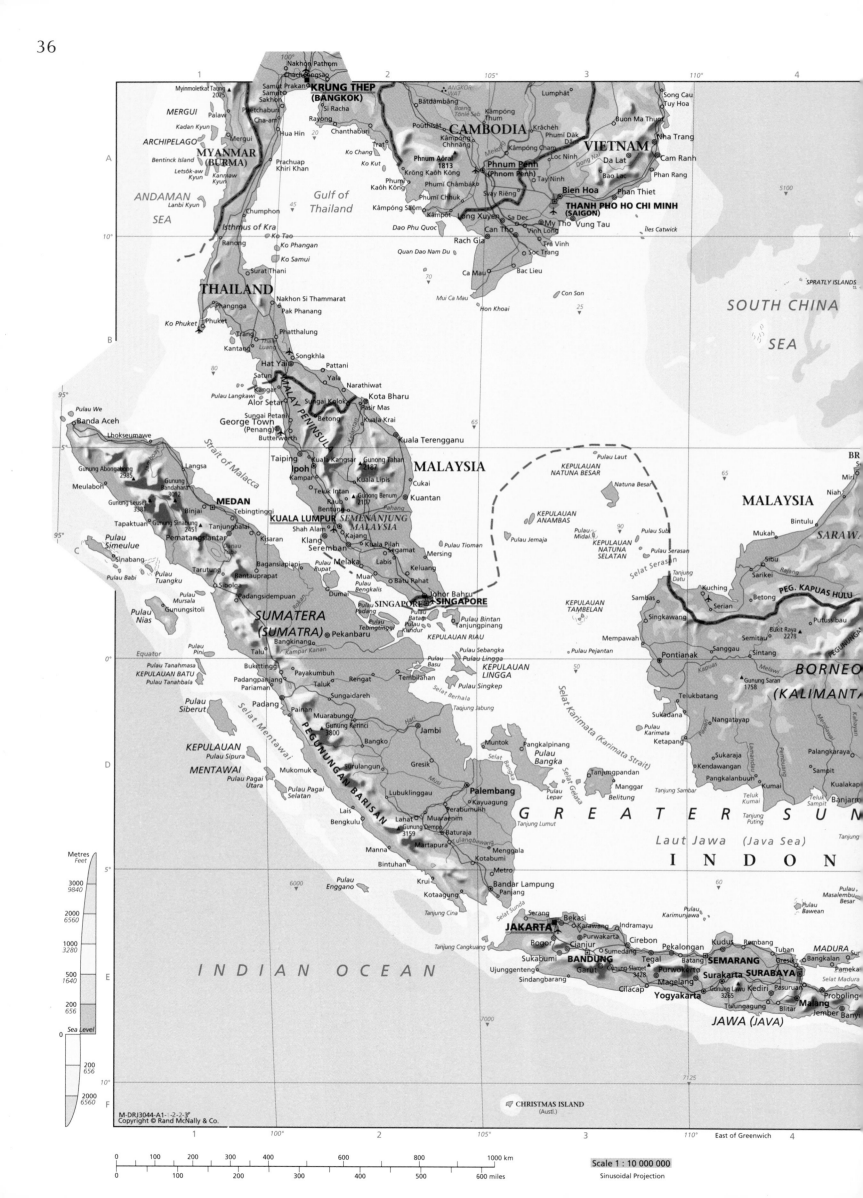

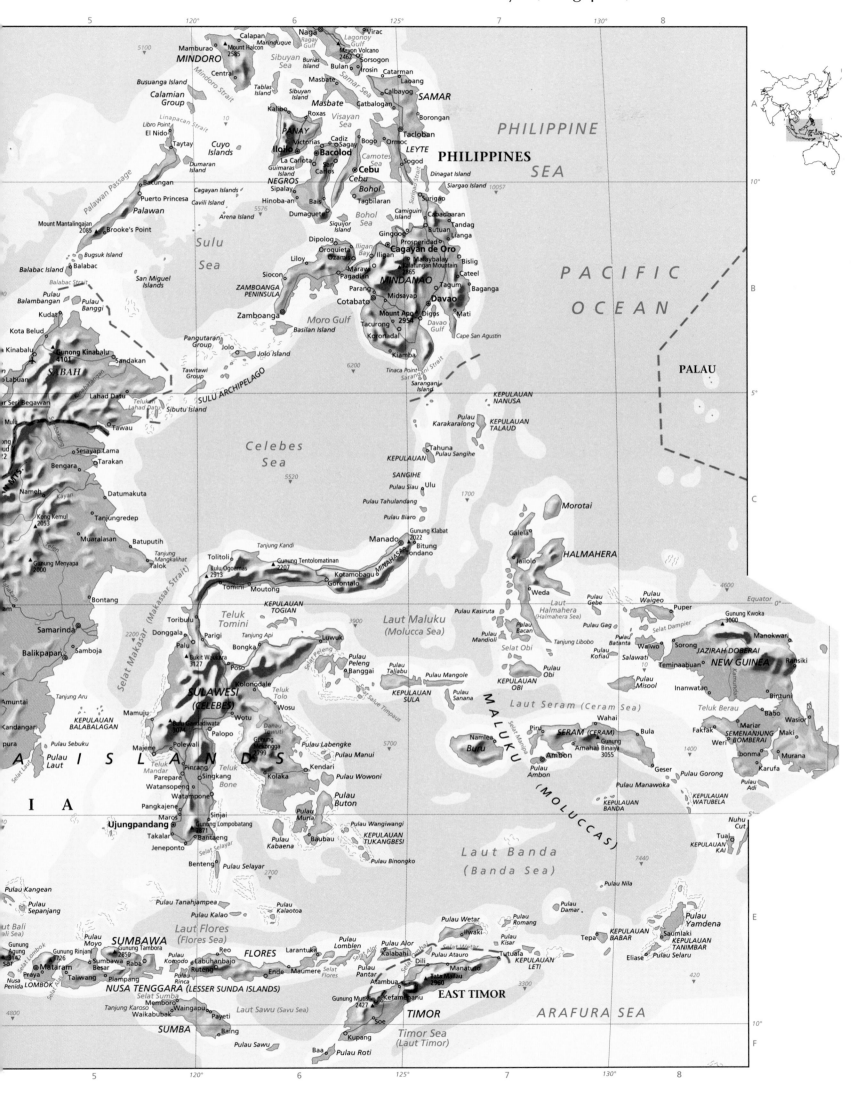

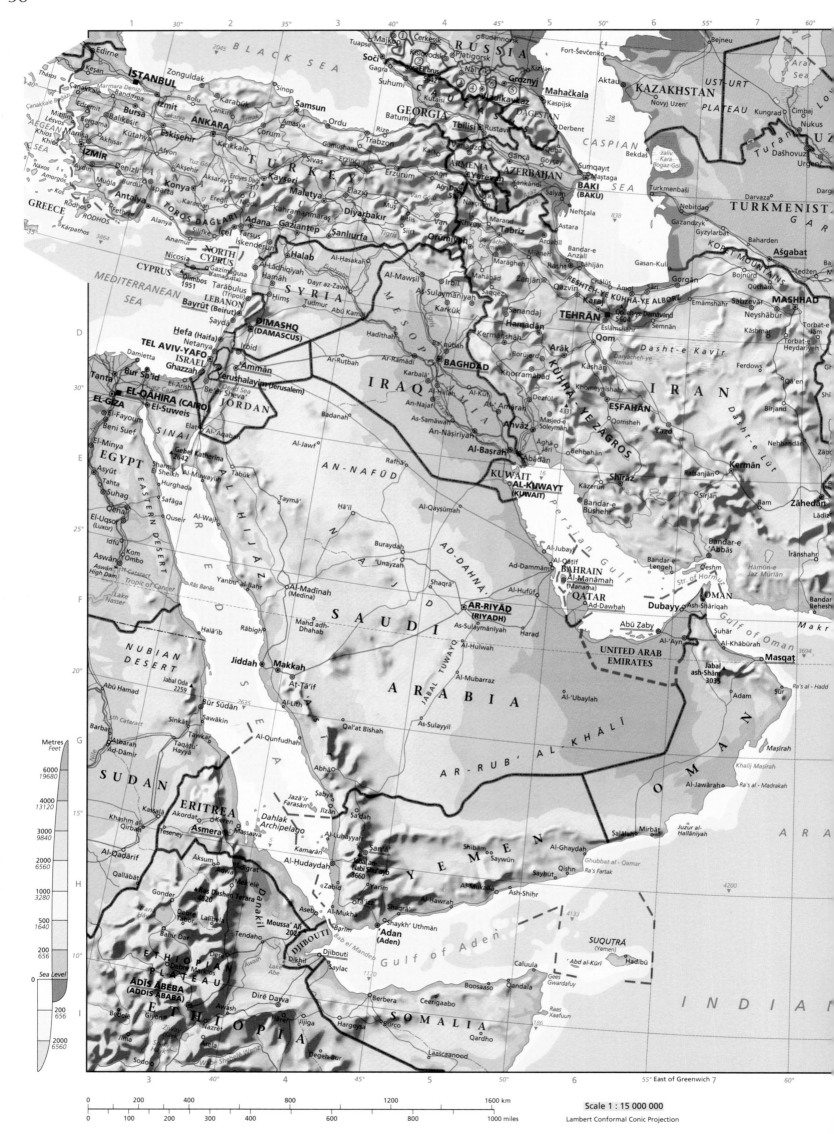

Metres Feet
6000 19680
4000 13120
3000 9840
2000 6560
1000 3280
500 1640
200 656
0 Sea Level
200 656
2000 6560

Scale 1 : 15 000 000
Lambert Conformal Conic Projection

55° East of Greenwich 7

0 200 400 800 1200 1600 km

0 100 200 300 400 600 800 1000 miles

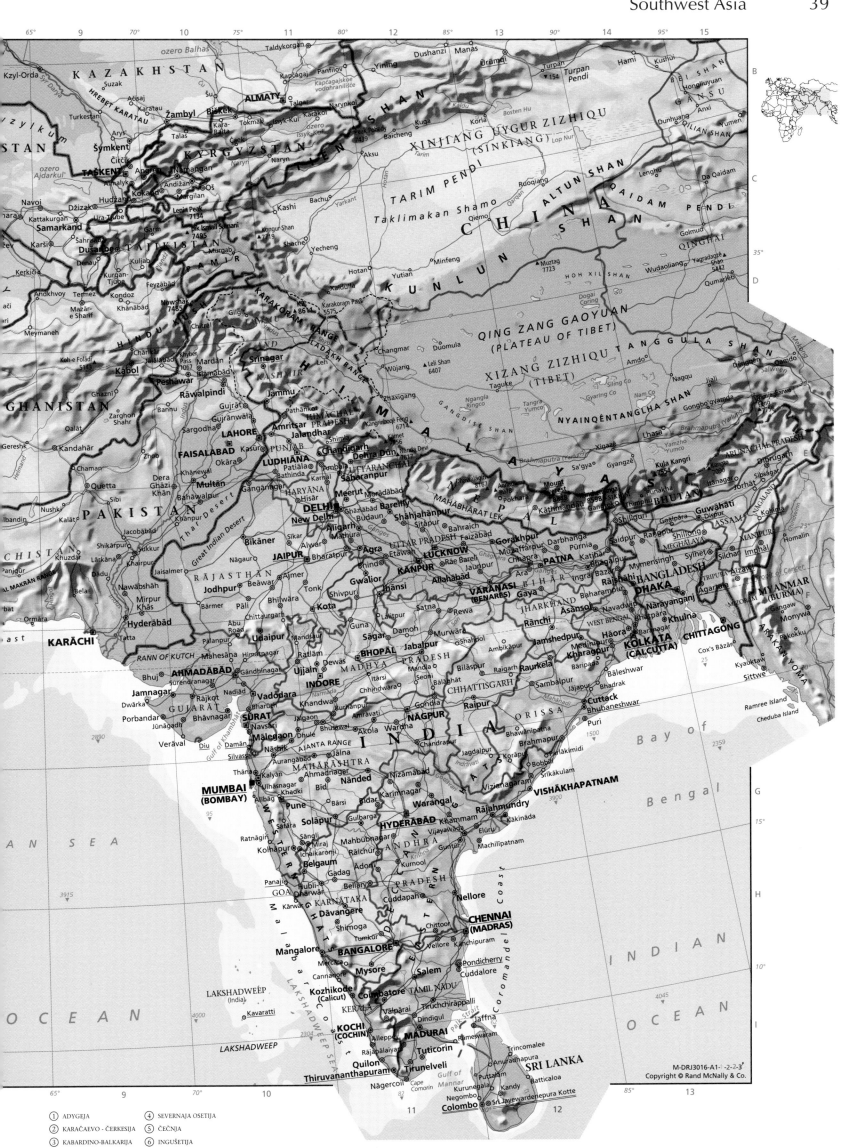

1 ADYGEJA
2 KARAČAEVO - ČERKESIJA
3 KABARDINO-BALKARIJA
4 SEVERNAJA OSETIJA
5 ČEČNJA
6 INGUŠETIJA

M-DRJ3016-A1- -2-2-3
Copyright © Rand McNally & Co.

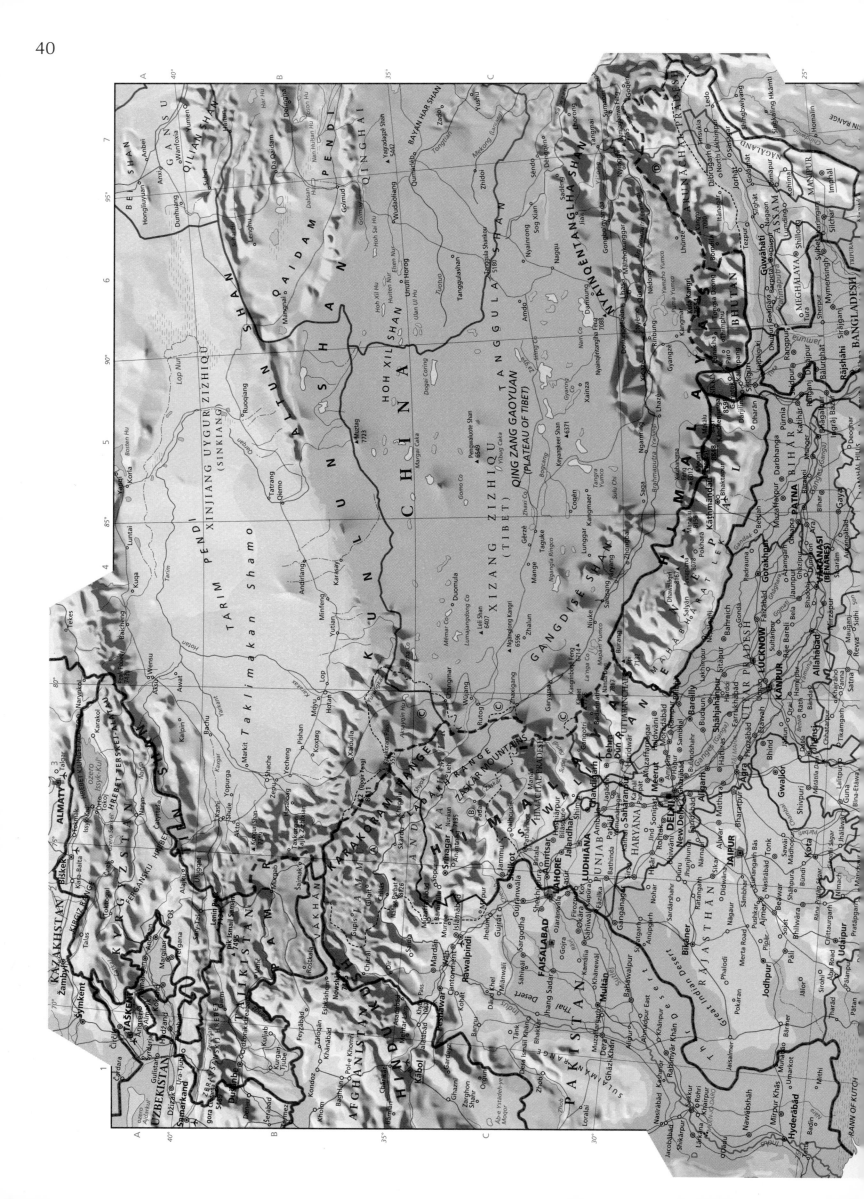

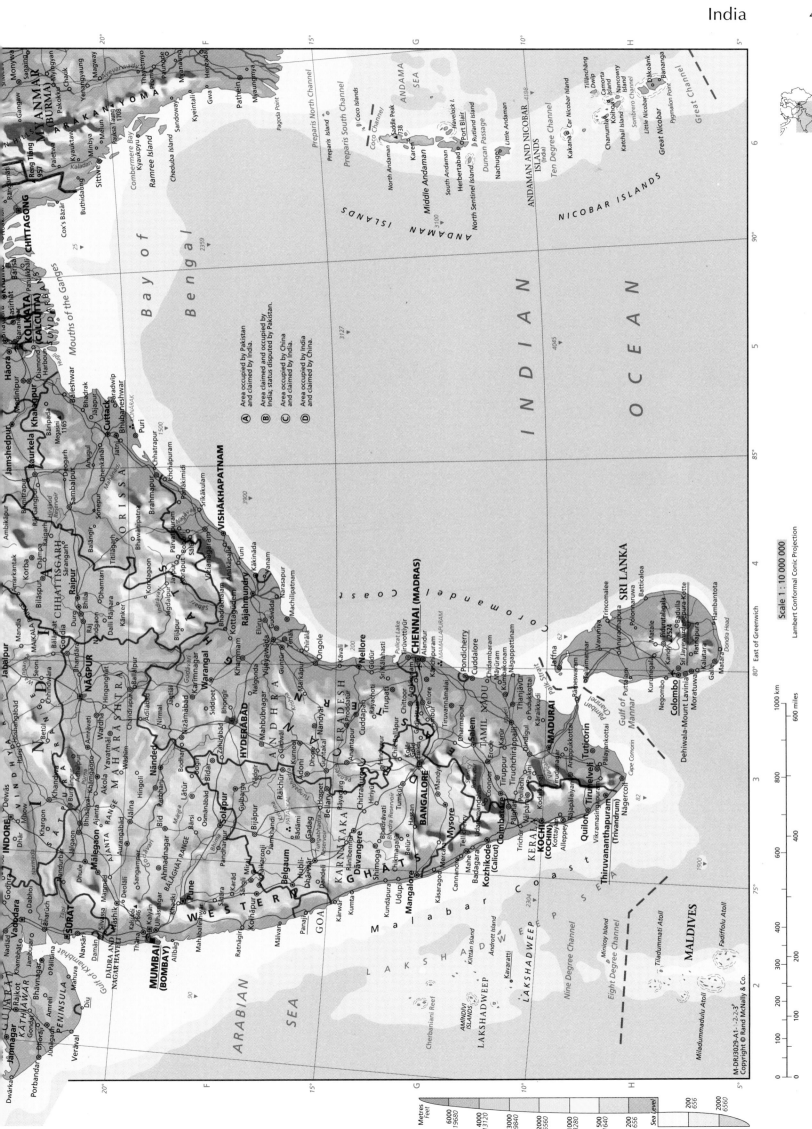

BLACK SEA

CASPIAN SEA

MEDITERRANEAN SEA

ROMANIA
Constanța

UKRAINE
Sea of Azov
Yevpatoriya
Kalamits'ka zatoka
Sevastopol'
Simferopol'
Feodosia
Yalta
mys Sarych
Kerch Strait
Novorossijsk
Krasnodar

RUSSIA
Tihoreck
Takta
Remontnoe
Elista
KALMYKIJA
Astrahan'
Atyrau
Tuapse
Apšeronsk
Majkop
Labinsk
Armavir
Nevinnomyssk
Stavropol'
Budënnovsk
Divnoe
Kropotkin
Ipatovo
Svetlograd
ostrov Tjulen'i
Kaspijskij
Fort-Ševčenko
Taučik

Soči
gora El'brus
Čerkessk
Pjatigorsk
Kislovodsk
Nal'čik
Mozdok
Groznyj
Gddermes
Kizljar
Aktau (Ševčenko)
mys Pesčanyj

Gagra
Suhumi
Zugdidi
Vladikavkaz
Nazran'
CAUCASUS
Mahačkala
Bujnaksk
Kaspijsk
Izberbaš
Bekdaš

 Zonguldak
İzmit
Sakarya
Bolu
Bafra
Sinop
İnce Burun
Trabzon
Rize
Batumi
Poti
Senaki
Kutaisi
Ardahan
Kars
Ozurgeti
Ahalcihe
Telavi
Tbilisi
Rustavi
GEORGIA
Derbent
Quba
Şeki
DAGESTAN
Bazardüzü dağ 4480
Sumqayıt
Maştaga
BAKI (BAKU)
Turkmenbaşı
Čeleke

Karabük
Kastamonu
Çankırı
Merzifon
Amasya
Ordu
Gümüşhane
Bayburt
Kaçkar Dağı 3932
Ağstafa
Vanadzor
Gjumri
Mingäçevir
Ganca
Göyçay
Neftçala
ostrov Ogurdžaly

ANKARA
Eskişehir
Polatlı
Çorum
Yozgat
Sivas
Erzincan
Erzurum
Karasu
Keban Baraji
ARMENIA
Aragats Leṙ 4090
Yerevan
AZERBAIJAN
Xankändi
AZER.
Naxçıvan
Salyan
Lənkəran
Astara

Afyon
Akşehir
Kırşehir
Nevşehir
Kayseri
Ercives Dağı 3917
Malatya
Elâzığ
Diyarbakır
Muş
Bitlis
Tatvan
Van
Hoktemberyan
Ağrı
Ağrı Dağı (Mount Ararat) 5137
Khvoy
Marand
Ahar
Sabalān 4811
Ardabil
Rasht
Lāhijān
Tonekābon

ANATOLIA
Konya
Aksaray
Niğde
Kahramanmaraş
Gaziantep
Şanlıurfa
Mardin
Batman
Siirt
Orūmiyeh
Marāgheh
Miāneh
Tabrīz
Sarāb
Bandar-e Anzalī
RESHTEH-YE KŪHHĀ-YE A

TOROS DAĞLARI
Karaman
Ereğli
Adana
Osmaniye
Kilis
Halab (Aleppo)
Al-Hasakah
Al-Qāmishlī
MESOPOTAMIA
Mahābād
Zanjān
Qazvīn
Čālūs
Āmol
Karaj
TEHRĀN

Alanya
Silifke
Anamur
Anamur Burnu
İçel
İskenderun
İskenderun Körfezi
Al-Lādhiqiyah
Idlib
Ar-Raqqah
Al-Mawşil
Irbil
Karkūk
As-Sulaymānīyah
Sanandaj
Saqqez
Shahr-e Rey
Qom
Daryācheh-ye Namak

NORTH CYPRUS
Nicosia
Ólimbos 1951
Gazimağusa (Famagusta)
Tartūs
Hamāh
Hims
Dayr az-Zawr
Tudmur
Abū Kamāl
Rāwah
Tikrīt
Sāmarrā
Qaşr-e Shirin
Kermānshāh (Bākhtarān)
Hamadān
Malāyer
Borūjerd
Arāk
Kāshān

CYPRUS
Lemesós
Lárnax
LEBANON
Tarābulus (Tripoli)
Bayrūt (Beirut)
An-Nabk
Dūmā
Ba'qūbah
Mandali
Ilām
Khorramābād
Do Rūd
Aligūdarz
Golpāyegān
Bād

Qurnat as- Sawdā' 3083
Zahlah
DIMASHQ (DAMASCUS)
BAGHDĀD
Dezfūl
Oshtoran Kūh 4331
Najafābād
Khomeynishahr
 EŞFAHĀN
Qomsheh

Şaydā
Mount Hermon 2814
Hefa (Haifa)
Nazerat
Țeverya
As-Suwaydā'
Ar-Rutbah
Ar-Ramādī
Karbalā'
An-Nu'māniyah
Al-Kūt
Masjed-e Soleymān
Shūshtar
Haft Gel
Shahr-e Kord

TEL AVIV-YAFO
Netanya
ISRAEL
Nābulus
Irbid
Dar'ā
JORDAN
Al-Hillah
An-Najaf
Al-Kūfah
Ad-Dīwānīyah
Al-'Amārah
Qal'at Sālih
Ahvāz
Rāmhormoz
Aghā Jārī
Behbahān

Ghazzah
Yerushalayim (Jerusalem)
Be'ér Sheva'
Az-Zarqā'
AMMĀN
SYRIAN DESERT
IRAQ
Ar-Rumaythah
As-Samāwah
An-Nāşirīyah
Eqlīd
Do Gonbadān
Gachsārān

EL-MANSŪRA
Tanta
Zagazig
EL-QAHIRA (CAIRO)
EL-GĪZA
El-Suweis (Suez)
Ma'ān
Badanah
Ad-Duwayd
Rafhā'
Al-Başrah
Khorramshahr
Ābādān
Bandar-e Khomeyni
Marv Dasht
SHIRĀZ

Baltim
Damietta
Būr Sa'īd (Port Said)
Ismailia
Qanā el-Suweis (Suez Canal)
El-'Arish
Elat
Jabal Ramm 1754
'Aqaba
Al-Jawf
AL-HARRAH
AL-HAJARAH
KUWAIT
Al-KUWAYT (KUWAIT)
Al-Jahrah
Mīnā' al-Ahmadī
Bandar-e Deylam
Kāzerūn

Beni Suef
SINAI
Abū Zenima
Gebel Katherîna 2637
Sharm El-Sheikh
Rās Mohammed
Al-Bi'r
Tabūk
Jabal al-Lawz 2549
AL-HUFRAH
AN-NAFŪD
Bandar-e Būshehr
Fīruzābād

EGYPT
Jamsah
Gebel Shâyib el-Banat 2187
Hurghada
Ash-Sharmah
Al-Muwayliḥ
Taymā'
Ḥā'il
Al-Qaysūmah
Al-Jubayl
Al-Qatīf
Ad-Dammām
Az-Zahrān
BAHRAIN
Al-Muharraq
Al-Manāmah (Manama)
Kangān

Safāga
Quseir
Al-Wajh
Umm Lajj
Al-'Ulā
Al-Ghazālah
Fayd
Buraydah
Ash-Shumlul
'Unayzah
Al-Majma'ah
AD-DAHNĀ'
'Ayn Dār
Buqayq
Al-Mubarraz
QATAR
Dukhān
Ad-Dawhah (Doha)
Qurayn Abā al-Bawl 105
Musay' id

Gebel Hamâtah 1977
Ra's Banās
Yanbu' al-Bahr
Al-Madīnah (Medina)
Abū Rubayq
Afif
SAUDI ARABIA
Shaqrā'
Nafi
Af-Hufūf
Yabrīn

AL-HIJAZ
RED SEA
Ra's Abū Madd
Rābigh
Mahd adh-Dhahab
AR-RIYĀD (RIYADH)
Al-Quway' iyah
As-Sulaymānīyah
Harad
Al-Hulwah

Administrative boundary
Halā'ib
Ra's al-Hadāribah
Al-Qadīmah
Al-Muwayh
Zalim
Yabrīn

SUDAN
Jabal Asoteriba 2217
Jiddah
Tropic of Cancer
Layla
UNI

East of Greenwich

| 0 | 100 | 200 | 300 | 400 | 600 | 800 | 1000 km |

| 0 | 100 | 200 | 400 | 600 miles |

Scale 1 : 10 000 000
Lambert Conformal Conic Projection

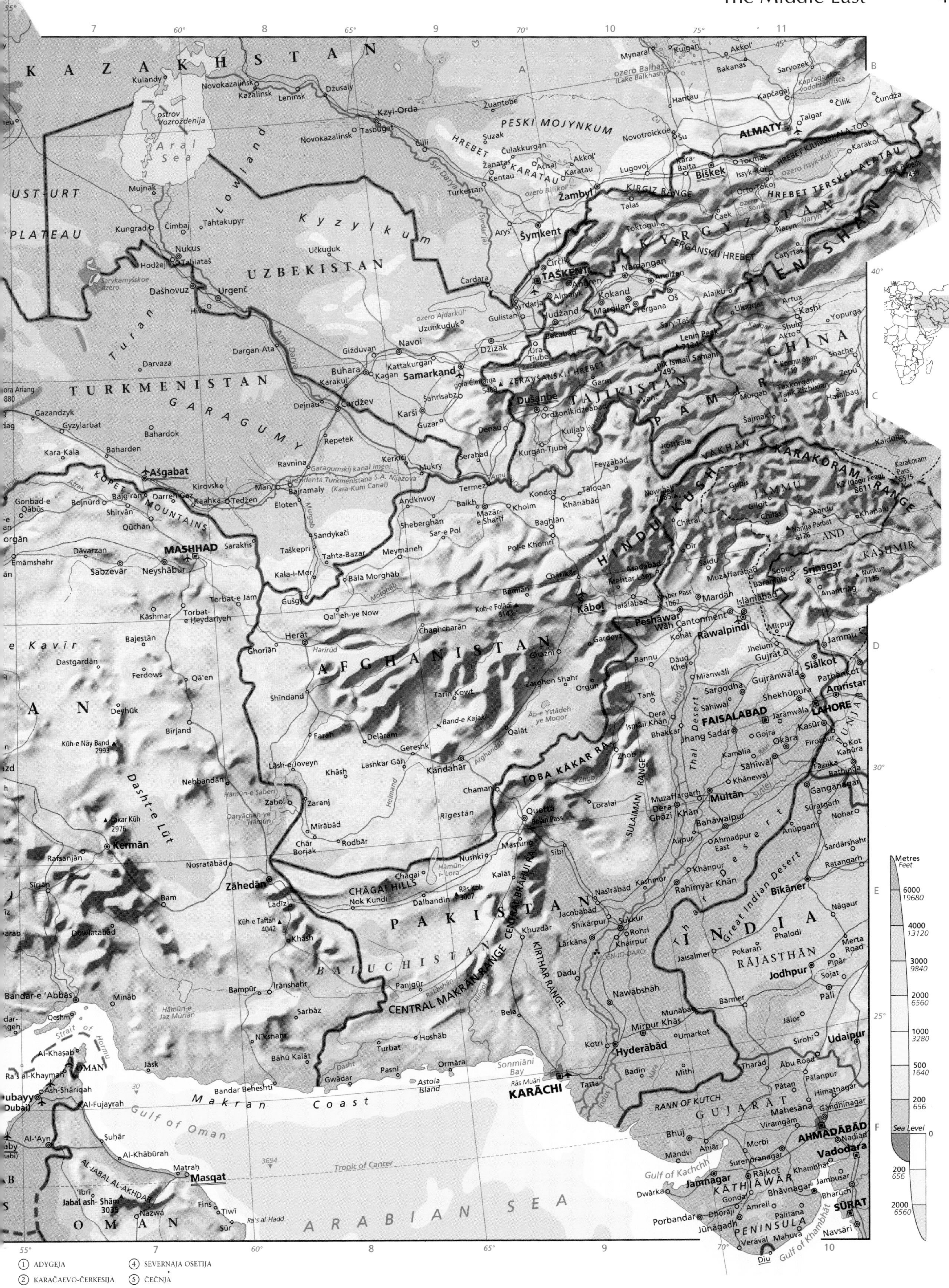

KAZAKHSTAN

Aral Sea

UST-URT PLATEAU

UZBEKISTAN

PESKI MOJYNKUM

KARATAU

ALMATY

BIŠKEK

KIRGIZ RANGE

KYRGYZSTAN

TIEN SHAN

TAŠKENT

Samarkand

TURKMENISTAN

GARAGUMY

Turan Lowland

Kyzylkum

ZERAVŠANSKIJ HREBET

Dušanbe

TAJIKISTAN

PAMIR

CHINA

KARAKORAM RANGE

HINDU KUSH

Ašgabat

KOPET MOUNTAINS

MASHHAD

JAMMU AND KASHMIR

Srinagar

Islāmābād

Rāwalpindi

Peshāwar

Kābol

AFGHANISTAN

Herāt

Kandahār

Quetta

TOBA KĀKAR RA.

SULAIMAN RANGE

KIRTHAR RANGE

PAKISTAN

LAHORE

Amritsar

Siālkot

FAISALABAD

Multan

Bahāwalpur

INDIA

RĀJASTHĀN

Jodhpur

Bīkāner

Great Indian Desert

Thar Desert

Dasht-e Lūt

Kermān

Zāhedān

CHĀGAI HILLS

BALUCHISTAN

CENTRAL MAKRAN RANGE

CENTRAL BRĀHUI RA.

Hyderābād

KARACHI

Makran Coast

Gulf of Oman

Masqat

OMAN

AL JABAL AL-AKHDAR

Dubai

Strait of Hormuz

Bandar-e 'Abbās

ARABIAN SEA

Tropic of Cancer

GUJARĀT

RANN OF KUTCH

AHMADĀBĀD

Vadodara

SŪRAT

KĀTHIĀWĀR PENINSULA

Jamnagar

Rājkot

Gulf of Khambhāt

Udaipur

Metres / Feet	
6000	19680
4000	13120
3000	9840
2000	6560
1000	3280
500	1640
200	656
Sea Level	0
200	656
2000	6560

① ADYGEJA
② KARAČAEVO-ČERKESIJA
③ KABARDINO-BALKARIJA
④ SEVERNAJA OSETIJA
⑤ ČEČNJA
⑥ INGUŠETIJA

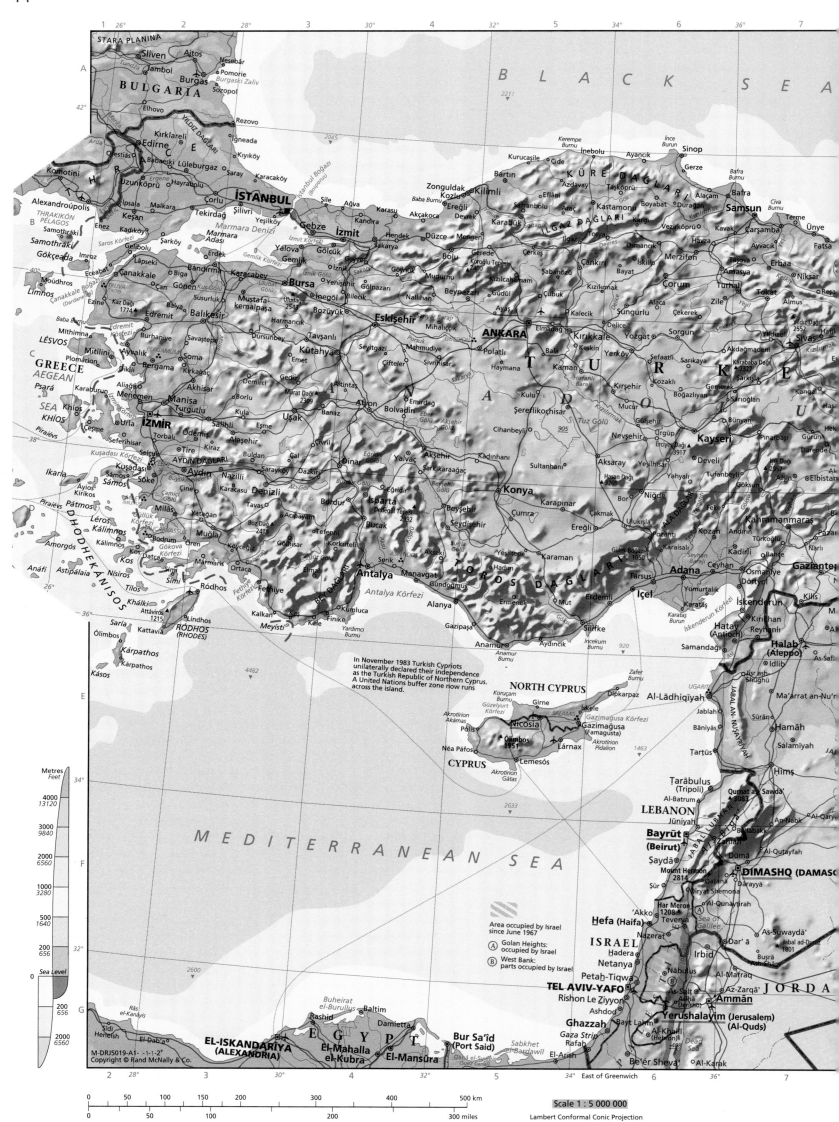

44

1 26° 2 28° 3 30° 4 32° 5 34° 6 36° 7

BLACK SEA

STARA PLANINA
Sliven
Aitos
Nesebăr
Pomorie
Jambol
Burgas
Burgaski Zaliv
Sozopol

A

BULGARIA

42°
Elhovo
Rezovo

Komotini
Edirne
Kırklareli
Iğneada
Kıyıköy

2045

Kerempe Burnu
İnce Burun
Kurucaşile
Cide
İnebolu
Ayancık
Sinop
Gerze
Bafra Burnu

THRAKIKÓN
PÉLAGOS
Alexandroúpolis
Ipsala
Uzunköprü
Keşan
Enez
Kadıköy
Malkara
Saray
Karacaköy
Çorlu
Tekirdağ
Şile
Ağva
Zonguldak
Kozlu
Ereğli
Devrek
Akçakoca
Azdavay
Taşköprü
Kastamonu
Boyabat
Durağan
Samsun
Çarşamba
Ünye
Fatsa

B
Samothráki
Gökçeada
İmroz
Gelibolu
Şarköy
Erdek
Bandırma
İSTANBUL
Gebze
İzmit
Yalova
Gölcük
Hendek
Düzce
Mengen
Bolu
Gerede
Çerkeş
Ilgaz
Tosya
Osmancık
Merzifon
Havza
Vezirköprü
Kavak
Amasya
Ayvacık
Terme

CYPRUS

In November 1983 Turkish Cypriots
unilaterally declared their independence
as the Turkish Republic of Northern Cyprus.
A United Nations buffer zone now runs
across the island.

NORTH CYPRUS

MEDITERRANEAN SEA

CYPRUS

Metres / Feet

4000 / 13120
3000 / 9840
2000 / 6560
1000 / 3280
500 / 1640
200 / 656
0 / Sea Level
200 / 656
2000 / 6560

M-DRJ5019-A1- -1-1-2°
Copyright © Rand McNally & Co.

2 28° 3 30° 4 32° 5 34° East of Greenwich 6 36° 7

0 50 100 150 200 300 400 500 km
0 50 100 200 300 miles

Scale 1 : 5 000 000

Lambert Conformal Conic Projection

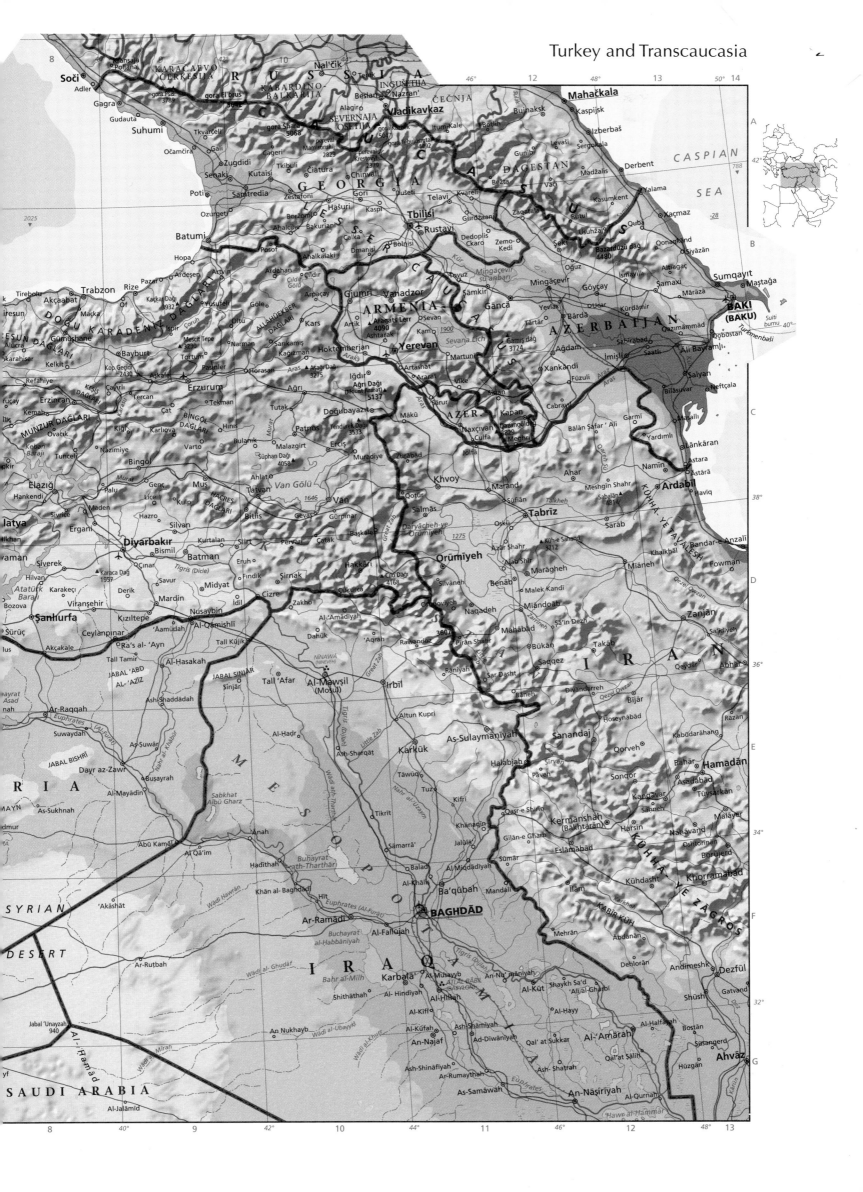

ATLANTIC OCEAN
CANADA
BAFFIN ISLAND
GREENLAND (Denmark)
ICELAND
NORWAY
SWEDEN
FINLAND
UNITED KINGDOM
IRELAND
FRANCE
SPAIN
PORTUGAL
ITALY
GERMANY
POLAND
UKRAINE
ROMANIA
BULGARIA
GREECE
TURKEY
SYRIA
IRAQ
IRAN
AFGHANISTAN
PAKISTAN
KAZAKHSTAN
UZBEKISTAN
TURKMENISTAN
RUSSIA
MOROCCO
ALGERIA
TUNISIA
LIBYA
EGYPT
WESTERN SAHARA
MAURITANIA
MALI
SAUDI ARABIA
OMAN
NORWEGIAN SEA
NORTH SEA
BARENTS SEA
GREENLAND SEA
BLACK SEA
CASPIAN SEA
MEDITERRANEAN SEA
RED SEA
URAL'SKIE GORY
LONDON
PARIS
MADRID
LISBOA
ROMA
BERLIN
WARSZAWA
MOSKVA
SANKT-PETERBURG
STOCKHOLM
HELSINKI
KØBENHAVN
DUBLIN
ATHÍNAI
İSTANBUL
ANKARA
EL-QÂHIRA
TEHRÂN
BAGHDAD
AR-RIYĀD
Kābol
TAŠKENT
ALMATY

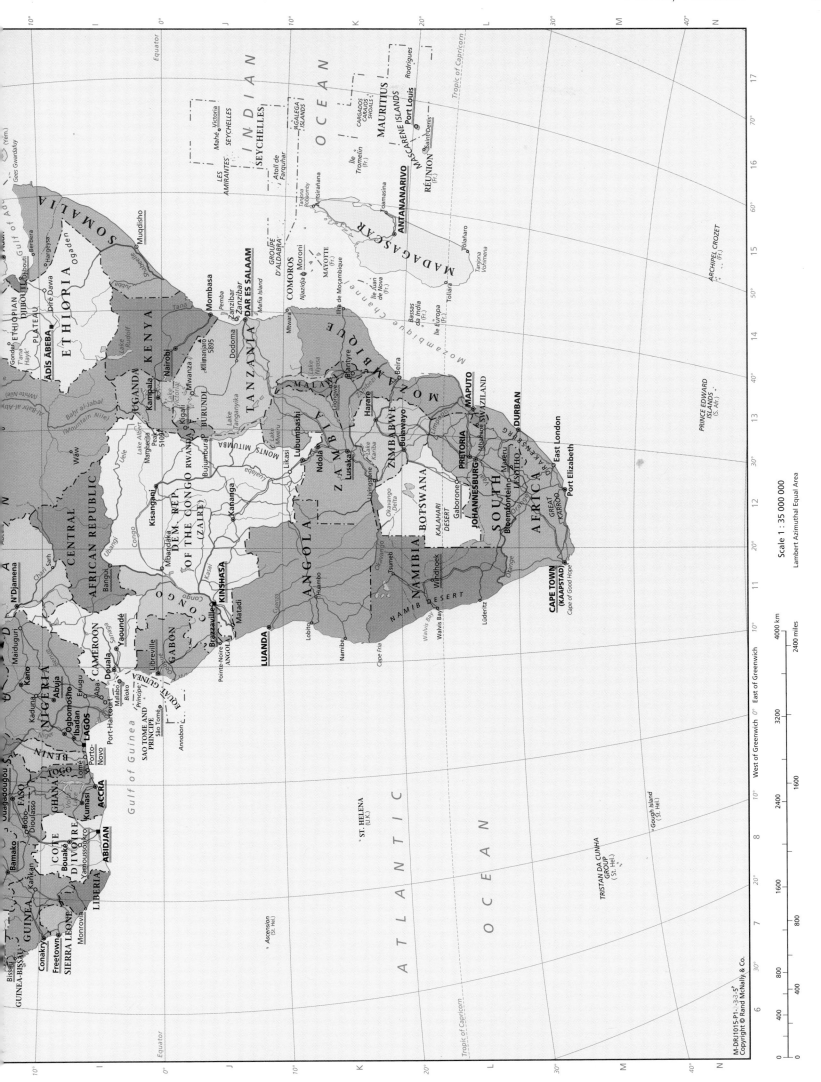

Scale 1 : 35 000 000

Lambert Azimuthal Equal Area

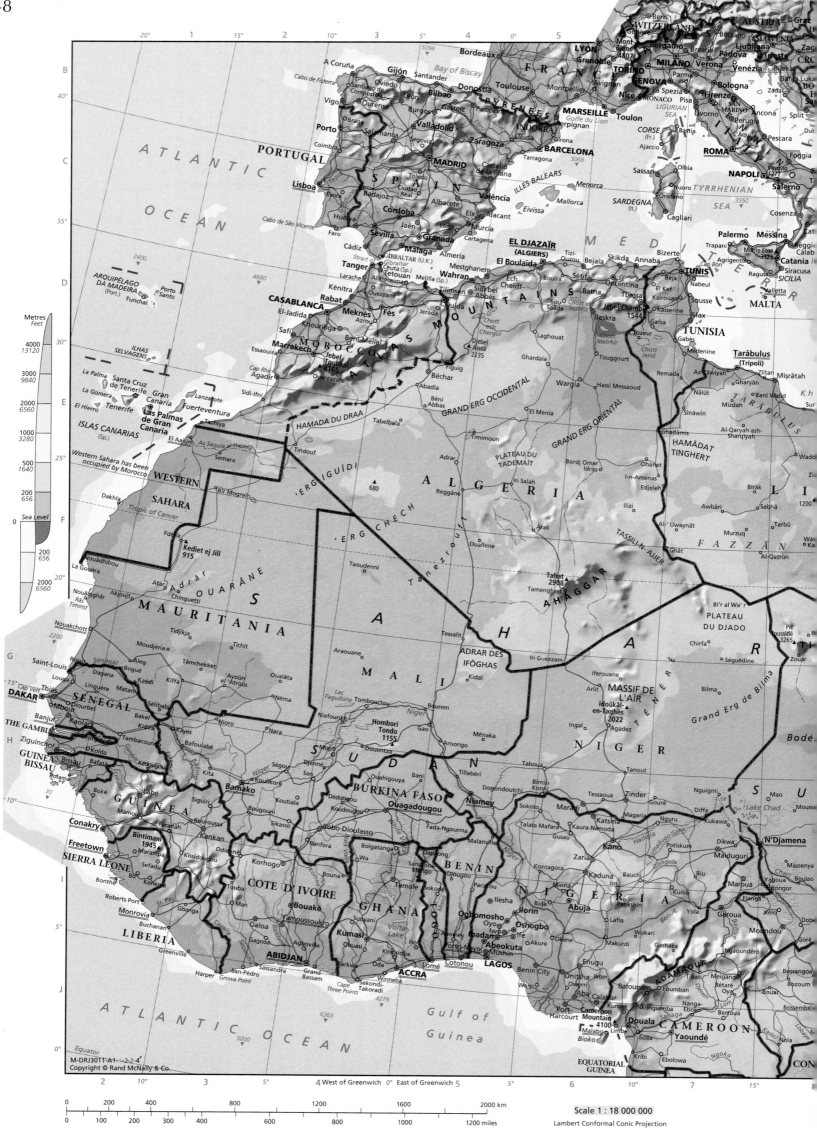

Scale 1 : 18 000 000

Lambert Conformal Conic Projection

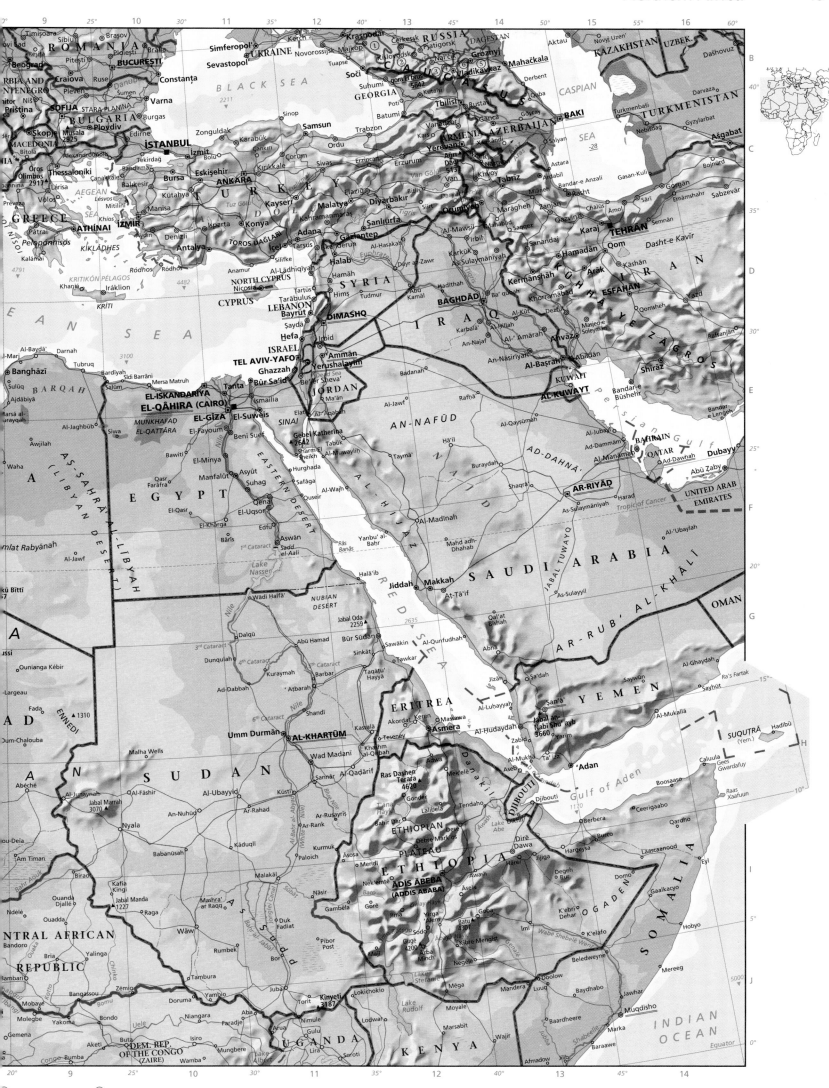

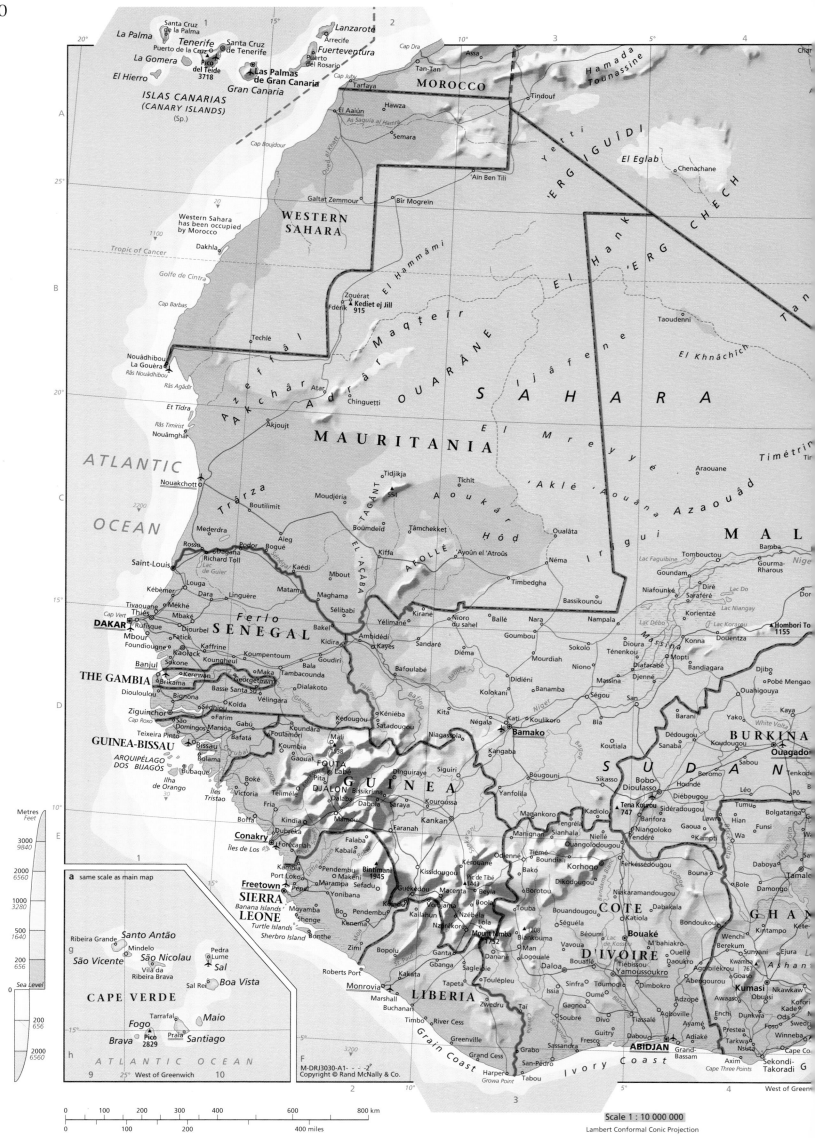

ATLANTIC

OCEAN

Santa Cruz
de la Palma
La Palma
Tenerife
Santa Cruz
de Tenerife
Puerto de la Cruz
La Gomera   Pico
del Teide
3718
El Hierro
Las Palmas
de Gran Canaria
Gran Canaria
ISLAS CANARIAS
(CANARY ISLANDS)
(Sp.)

Lanzarote
Arrecife
Fuerteventura
Puerto
del Rosario

Cap Dra

MOROCCO

Assa
Tan-Tan

Hamada
Tounassine

'ERG IGUÎDI

El Eglab
Chenachane

Tarfaya
El Aaiún
As Saguia al Hamra
Hawza
Semara

Tindouf

Cap Juby

WESTERN
SAHARA

Western Sahara
has been occupied
by Morocco

Galtat Zemmour

'Aïn Ben Tili

Bîr Mogreïn

Yetti

El Hank

'ERG CHECH

Tropic of Cancer

Dakhla

Golfe de Cintra

Cap Barbas

Cap Boujdour

El Hammâmi

Maqteir

Taoudenni

El Khnâchîch

Zouérat
Kediet ej Jill
915
Fdérik

OUARÂNE

SAHARA

Techlé

Akchâr

Adrâr

Atar
Chinguetti

Ijâfene

Araouane

Timétrin

Nouâdhibou
La Gouèra
Râs Nouâdhibou

Et Tidra
Râs Agâdir

Râs Timirist
Nouâmghâr

Akjoujt

Azef fâl

MAURITANIA

El Mreyyé
'Aklé 'Aouâna Azaouâd

ATLANTIC

Nouakchott

OCEAN

Tidjikja

Tichît

Aoukâr

Ouâlâta

MALI

Mederdra
Trarza
Boutilimit

Moudjéria

554
TAGANT

Hôd

Iri gui

Rosso
Dagana
Bogué
Podor
Aleg

Boûmdeïd
Tâmchekket

'Ayoûn el 'Atroûs

Néma

Nampala

Tombouctou
Bamba
Niger
Gourma-
Rharous

Saint-Louis
Richard Toll
Lac
de Guier
Kaédi
Kiffa
El 'ACÂBA
AFOLLÉ

Timbedgha
Bassikounou
Goundam

Niafounké
Diré
Lac Do
Saraféré
Lac Niangay

Kébèmer
Louga
Dara
Linguère
Matam
Mbout
Maghama
Sélibabi

Yélimané
Kirané
Nioro
du sahel
Ballé
Nara

Goumbou
Sokolo
Niono

Ténenkou
Diafarabé
Mopti
Massina
Konna
Douentza
Korientzé
Lac Korarou
Hombori To
1155

15°
Tivaouane
Thiès
Mékhé
Diourbel
Mbaké
DAKAR
Cap Vert
Rufisque

Ferlo

SENEGAL

Bakel
Kidira
Ambidédi
Kayes
Sandaré
Dièma
Mourdiah
Diéma

Diafarabé
Ségou
San
Djenné
Bandiagara
Djibo
Pobé Mengao

Mbour
Fatick
Kaffrine
Koumpentoum
Maka
Goudiri
Bafoulabé
Didiéni
Kolokani
Banamba

Foundiougne
Kaolack
Sokone
Koungheul
Bala
Tambacounda
Négala
Kati Koulikoro
Bla

Banjul
Kerewan
Georgetown
Dialakoto
Kédougou

Bamako
Kangaba
Koutiala

THE GAMBIA
Brikama
Basse Santa Su

Satadougou
Niagassola
Siguiri
Bougouni
Sikasso
Bobo-
Dioulasso
Dédougou
Koudougou

Diouloulou
Bignona
Sédhiou
Vélingara

Kita
Négala
Kolondiéba

Sanaba
Beromo
Houndé

BURKINA

Ziguinchor
Cap Roxo
São
Farim
Kolda
Kénieba
Kéniéba

Yanfolila
Tena Kourou
747
Diébougou
Léo
Pô

Teixeira Pinto
Mansôa
Koundâra
Foulamóri
Mali
1538
FOUTA

Mankono
Kadiolo
Banfora
Gaoua
Tumu
Bolgatanga

GUINEA-BISSAU
Bissau
Bolama
Koumbia
Gaoual
Labé
Dinguiraye
Kouroussa

Tengréla
Sianhala
Niellé
Niangoloko
Lawra
Hian
Funsi
Wa

ARQUIPÉLAGO
DOS BIJAGÓS
Bubaque
Boké
Pita
DJALON
Bissikrima
Siguiri

Odienné
Tiémé
Korhogo
Ferkéssédougou
Kampti
Daboya

Ilha
de Orango
Íles
Tristao
Victoria
Télimélé
Dalaba
Dabola
Saraya

Boundiali
Niakaramandougou
Bouna
Bole
Damongo

GUINEA

Fria
Boffa
Kindia
Mamou
Kankan

Manignan
Ouangolodougou
Dikodougou

Bondoukou
Tamale

Conakry
Dubréka
Íles de Los
Falaba
Kabala

Kérouane
Bako
Séguéla
Dabakala

Dimbokro

SIERRA
LEONE
Kambia
Port Loko
Pendembu
Makéni
Bintimani
1945
Kissidougou
Beyla
Borotou
Bouandougou
Bouaflé

Wenchi
Berekum

GHAN

Sunyani
Ejura

Ashan

Freetown
Marampa
Sefadu
Guékédou
Macenta
Nzébéla
Touba

COTE
Bouaké
M'bahiakro

Kumasi
Nkawkaw

Banana Islands
Turtle Islands
Moyamba
Shenge
Yonibana
Bo
Pendembu
Kenema

Koidu
Voinjama
Kailahun
Lola
Mount Nimba
1752
Biankouma
Man
Logoualé

D'IVOIRE
Bangolo
Vavoua
Béoumi
Lac
de Kossou

Yamoussoukro
Abengourou

Agboville
Obuasi

Sherbro Island
Bonthe
Zimi
Bopolu
Ganta
Danané
Daloa

Issia
Gagnoa
Divo
Tiassalé

Roberts Port
Nzérékoré
Tapeta
Toulépleu
Sinfra
Toumodi
Dimbokro
Adzopé

Adiaké
Ayamé
Aboisso

Monrovia
Marshall
Buchanan

Zwedru
Taï
Soubré
Gnagnoa
Dabou
ABIDJAN
Grand-
Bassam

LIBERIA

Timbo
River Cess
Greenville

Issia
Guitry
Fresco

Aximu
Tarkwa
Prestea
Enchi
Dunkwa

Grain Coast

Grabo
Sassandra
San-Pédro

Ivory Coast

a same scale as main map

Ribeira Grande
Santo Antão
Mindelo
São Vicente
São Nicolau
Pedra
Lume
Sal

Vila da
Ribeira Brava

Sal Rei
Boa Vista

CAPE VERDE

Tarrafal
Fogo
Maio
Pico
2829
Brava
Praia
Santiago

ATLANTIC OCEAN

25° West of Greenwich

M-DRJ3030-A1-   -2°
Copyright © Rand McNally & Co.

West of Green

Scale 1 : 10 000 000
Lambert Conformal Conic Projection

0   100   200   300   400   600   800 km

0   100   200   400 miles

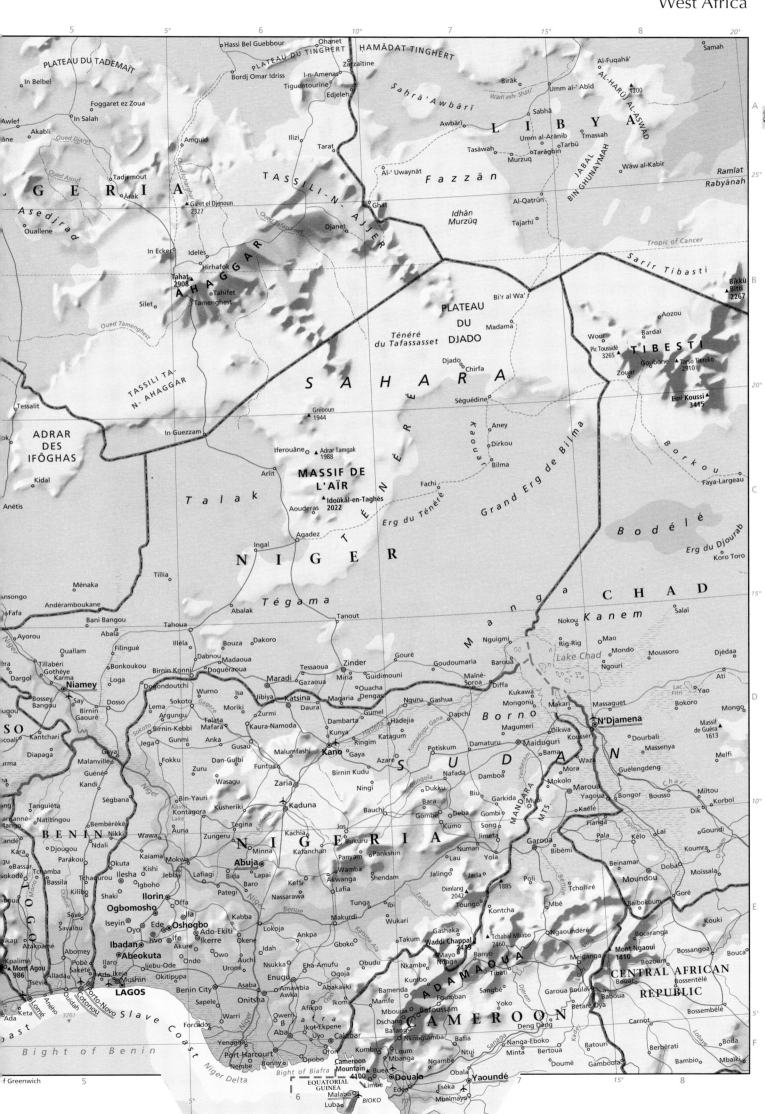

PLATEAU DU TADEMAÏT

In Belbel
Alwef
Akabli
âne
In Salah
Foggaret ez Zoua
Ouallene
Tessalit
Anétis
Kidal

GERIA

Asedirad

ADRAR
DES
IFÔGHAS

ok

SO
coalí
rma

BENIN

BURKINA

Hassi Bel Guebbour   Ohanet
Bordj Omar Idriss   I-n-Amenas
PLATEAU DU TINGHERT
Tiguentourine   Zarzaïtine
Edjeleh   HAMĀDAT TINGHERT
Amguid   Ilizi   Tarat
Garet el Djenoun
2327
In Ecker   Idelès   Djanet
Hirhafok
Tahat   AHAGGAR
2908   Tahifet
Silet   Tamenghest
Oued Tamenghest
TASSILI TA-
N- AHAGGAR
In Guezzam
Gréboun
1944
Iferouâne   Adrar Tamgak
1988
Arlit
MASSIF DE
L'AÏR
Talak   Idoûkâl-en-Taghès
2022
Aouderas
Agadez
Ingal   NIGER
Tillia
Ménaka   Abalak   Tanout
Andéramboukane   Tégama
ansongo
Fafa   Bani Bangou   Tahoua
Ayorou   Abala
Ouallam   Filingué   Illèla   Bouza   Dakoro
Tillabéri   Gothèye   Bonkoukou   Dabnou   Madaoua
Dargol   Karma   Birnin Konni   Doguéraoua
Niamey   Loga   Dogondoutchi
Bossey   Say   Birnin   Tessaoua   Zinder   Gouré
Bangou   Gaouré   Wurno   Isa   Jibiya   Katsina   Daura   Dengas
SO   Dosso   Sokoto   Moriki   Magaria
coalí   Lema   Argungu   Zurmi   Dambarta
Kantchari   Birnin-Kebbi   Kaura-Namoda   Kunya   Katagum
Diapaga   Jega   Gunmi   Anka   Gusau   Malumfashi   Ringim
Malanville   Fokku   Dan-Gulbi   Funtua   Azare
Guéné   Zuru   Wasagu   Birnin Kudu
Kandi   Zaria   Ningi
BENIN   Tanguiéta   Bin-Yauri   Kontagora   Kusheriki   Bauchi
amné   Natitingou   Wawa   Tegina   Jos
Kara   Nikki   Kaiama   Zungeru   Bukuru
Djougou   Ndali   Kishi   Mokwa   Minna
Bassar   Parakou   Okuta   Kafanchan   Panyam
okodé   Tchaourou   Jebba   Bida   NIGERIA
Bassila   Shaki   Lafiagi   Lapai   Keffi   Akwanga
Ilorin   Offa   Patigi   Nassarawa   Lafia
TOGO   Ogbomosho   Ila   Kabba   Tunga   Ibi
Iseyin   Oyo   Ede   Oshogbo   Lokoja   Makurdi   Wukari
Mont Agou   Ibadan   Iwo   Ife   Ado-Ekiti   Okene   Ankpa   Gboko
986   Abeokuta   Akure   Owo   Auchi   Idah
Abomey   Iseyin   Ikerre   Uromi
Kpalime   Allada   Ijebu-Ode   Nsukka   Eha-Amufu   Obudu
LAGOS   Okitipupa   Asaba   Enugu   Ogoja
Porto-Novo   Slave Coast   Benin City   Onitsha   Amawbia   Abakaliki
Cotonou   Awka   Ikom
Keta   Lomé   Warri   Owerri   Afikpo
Ouidah   Sapele   Onitsha   Mamfe

LIBYA

Samah
Birāk
Al-Fuqahā'
Umm al-' Abīd   1200
Sabhā   AL-HARŪJ AL-ASWAD
Umm al-Arānib   Tmassah
Tasāwah   Tarbū
Murzūq   Tarāghin
Al-' Uwaynāt   Wāw al-Kabīr
Ramlat
Al-Qatrūn   Rabyānah
Tajarhī
Tropic of Cancer
Sarīr Tibasti
Bikkū
Bī'r al Wa'r   Bitti
2267
PLATEAU
DU   Madama   Aozou
DJADO   Wour   Bardaï
Ténéré   Pic Toussidé   TIBESTI
du Tafassasset   Djado   Chirfa   3265   Goubone   Tarso Tieroko
Zouar   2910
SAHARA   Séguédine   Emi Koussi
3415
Aney
Kaoua   Dirkou   Borkou
Erg du Ténéré   Bilma   Faya-Largeau
Fachi   Bodélé
Grand Erg de Bilma   Erg du Djourab
Koro Toro
Manga   CHAD
Nokou   Kanem   Salal
Nguigmi   Rig-Rig   Mao
Goudoumaria   Baroua   Mondo   Moussoro   Djédaa
Maïné-   Lake Chad   Ngouri   Ati
Soroa   Diffa   Kukawa   Lac
Dapchi   Gashua   Mongonu   Makari   Fitri   Yao
Nguru   Massaguet   Bokoro   Mongo
Potiskum   Damaturu   Borno   Dikwa   N'Djamena
Magumeri   Kousséri   Dourbali   Massenya   Melfi
Nafada   Damboa   Maiduguri   Bama
Dukku   Biu   Mora   Waza   Guélengdeng
Bara   Deba   Garkida   Mubi   Mokolo   Maroua
Gombe   Gombi   Song   Mandara   Bongor   Bousso   Miltou   Korbol
Kumo   MTS   Garoua   Panda   Kélo   Lai   Goundi
Lau   Numan   Jimeta   Bibémi   Pala   Koumra
Jalingo   Yola   Jada   Poli   Beinamar   Doba   Moïssala
Dimlang   Toungo   Kontcha   Mbé   Moundou   Goré
2042   1885   Tchollire   Baïbokoum   Bossangoa
Gashaka   Takum   Mayo   Tchabal Mbabo   Ngaoundéré   Meiganga   Mont Ngaoui   Bocaranga
Waddi Chappal   Banyo   2460   1410   CENTRAL AFRICAN
2418   Mayo   Tibati   Sangbé   Foumban   Yoko   Bouar   Bossentélé   REPUBLIC
ADAMAOUA   Bamenda   Garoua Boulaï   Baboua   Bétaré Oya   Bossembélé
Nkambe   Kumbo   Bafoussam   Bouca
CAMEROON   Bafia   Deng Deng   Carnot
Dschang   Nkongsamba   Nanga-Eboko   Bertoua   Berbérati
Cameroon   Kumba   Loum   Ngambé   Minta   Doumé   Bambio
Mountain   Mbanga   Ntui   Batouri   Gamboula   Mbaïki
4100   Buea   Douala   Eséka   Yaoundé   Doumé   Boda
EQUATORIAL   Limbe   Obala   Edéa
GUINEA
Malabo   Mbalmayo
Lubao   BIOKO

Bight of Benin

Bight of Biafra

Niger Delta

5   5°   5°   10°   7   15°   8   20°

f Greenwich   5   7   8

ATLANTIC

OCEAN

Tropic of Capricorn

Metres Feet	
4000 13120	
3000 9840	
2000 6560	
1000 3280	
500 1640	
200 656	
0 Sea Level	
200 656	
2000 6560	

0   200   400   800   1200   1600   2000 km
0 100 200 300 400 500 600 700 800   1200 miles

Scale 1 : 18 000 000

Lambert Conformal Conic Projection

A

Kibre Mengist
Imi

ETHIOPIA

Negele

K'elafo

5°

Gaalkacyo

Mandera   *Doolow*   *Luuq*
Mado Gashi   *Baydhabo*   *Beledweyne*   *Hobyo*
nya

SOMALIA

Mereeg

B

Tana

Wajir   *Baardheere*   *Jawhar*
Garissa   *Jilib*   ○ Muqdisho
Marka

Baraawe

Equator   0°

Voi   *Buur Gaabo*
du   *Garsen*
Galana   *Lamu*

C

Malindi   5340 ▽

SEYCHELLES

INDIAN

Mombasa   Praslin
○   Victoria   ○ Mahé

Chake Chake   LES
Pemba ○   Poivre   AMIRANTES
Zanzibar ○   Atoll   Île
Zanzibar   Plate

OCEAN   5°

DAR ES SALAAM   ○ Alphonse   ○ Coëtivy

Mafia Island
Kilindoni

D

Kilwa Kivinje   SEYCHELLES
le   4406   6402
Lindi   GROUPE   ▽   ▽
D'ALDABRA   Île au Cerf

Palma   ATOLL DE   Atoll de
Masasi   COSMOLEDO   Farquhar
wea   Mocímboa   AGALEGA
da Praia   ÎLES GLORIEUSES   ISLANDS
Pemba   Njazidja   COMOROS   (Fr.)
Namapa   Moroni   Tanjona   E
Lhrio   Mwali   Nzwani   Bobaomby
Mutsamudu   Antsiranana
Nacala-a-Velha   5300   Dzaoudzi
Ilha de   MAYOTTE   Ambilobe   10°
Moçambique   (Fr.)
Mogincual   Ambanja   Maromokotro
ARCHIPEL DES COMORES   ▲ 2876   Sambava
Angoche   Analalava   Bealanana
Moma   Antalaha
Antsohihy   F
Mahajanga   Antsohihy   Maroantsetra
Île Juan   Mampikony   Mananara Avaratra   15°
de Nova   Soalala   Île Tromelin
(Fr.)   Besalampy   Nosy   (Fr.)
Maevatanana   Sainte Marie
Morafenobe   Ambatondrazaka   CARGADOS
Maintirano   Tsaratanana   CARAJOS
Tsiroanomandidy   MADAGASCAR   SHOALS
Miandrivazo   ANTANANARIVO   MAURITIUS
Ambatolampy   Toamasina
Morondava   Antsirabe   Vatomandry
Mahanoro   MASCARENE ISLANDS   Rodrigues
Ambositra
Mandabe   Port Louis
ssas da India   Manja   Fianarantsoa   Mananjary   Saint-Denis   Mauritius   20°
(Fr.)   Morombe   Ambalavao   Saint-Pierre
Île Europa   Ankazoabo   Ihosy   RÉUNION   4200
(Fr.)   Manakara   (Fr.)   ▽
Betroka   Farafangana
Toliara
G
Bekily
Ampanihy   Tropic of Capricorn
Tsiombe   Tolañaro
Tanjona   Ambovombe
Vohimena

4300 ▽   25°

H

30°

I

35°

Scale 1 : 10 000 000

Sinusoidal Projection

D-589500-7A-DR1-1°
Copyright © Rand McNally & Co.

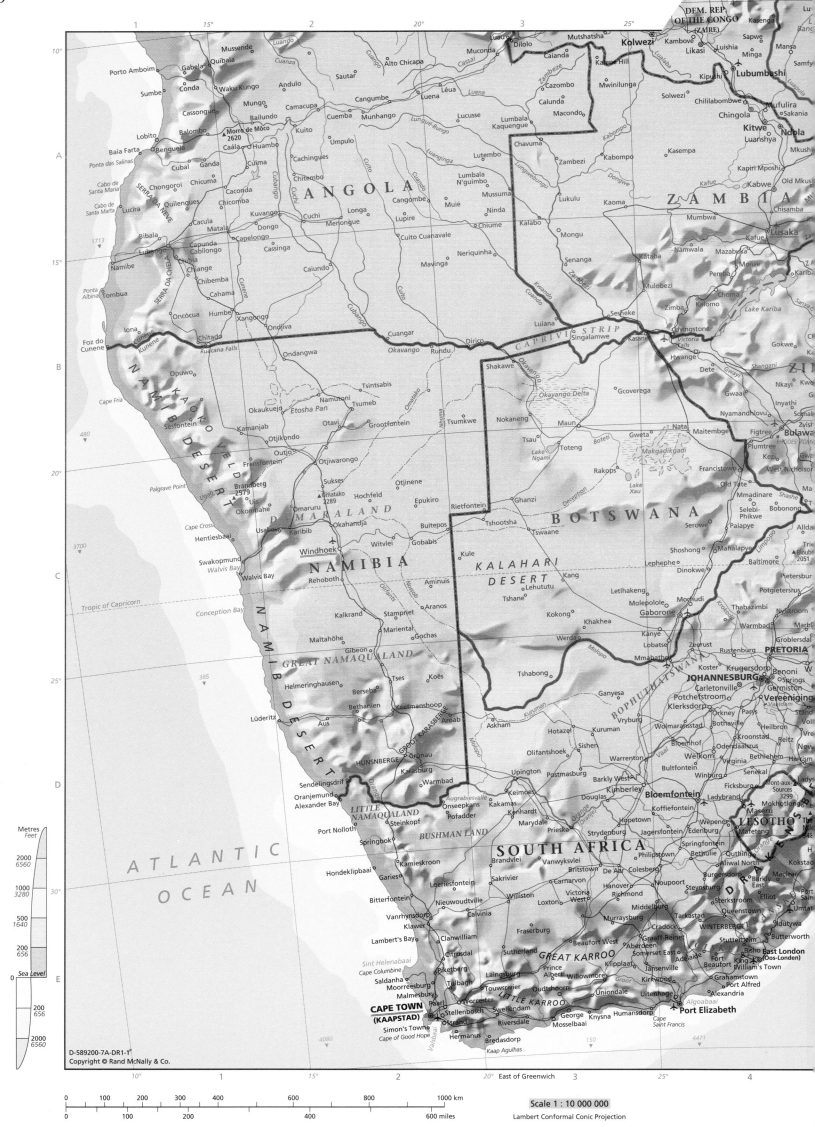

ATLANTIC OCEAN

ANGOLA

ZAMBIA

DEM. REP. OF THE CONGO (ZAIRE)

NAMIBIA

BOTSWANA

KALAHARI DESERT

SOUTH AFRICA

LESOTHO

NAMIB DESERT

KAOKO VELD

DAMARALAND

GREAT NAMAQUALAND

BUSHMAN LAND

GREAT KARROO

LITTLE KARROO

CAPRIVI STRIP

Tropic of Capricorn

10°

15°

20°

25°

Metres
Feet

2000
6560

1000
3280

500
1640

200
656

0
Sea Level

200
656

2000
6560

D-589200-7A-DR1-1°
Copyright © Rand McNally & Co.

East of Greenwich

Scale 1 : 10 000 000

Lambert Conformal Conic Projection

0   100   200   300   400   600   800   1000 km

0   100   200   400   600 miles

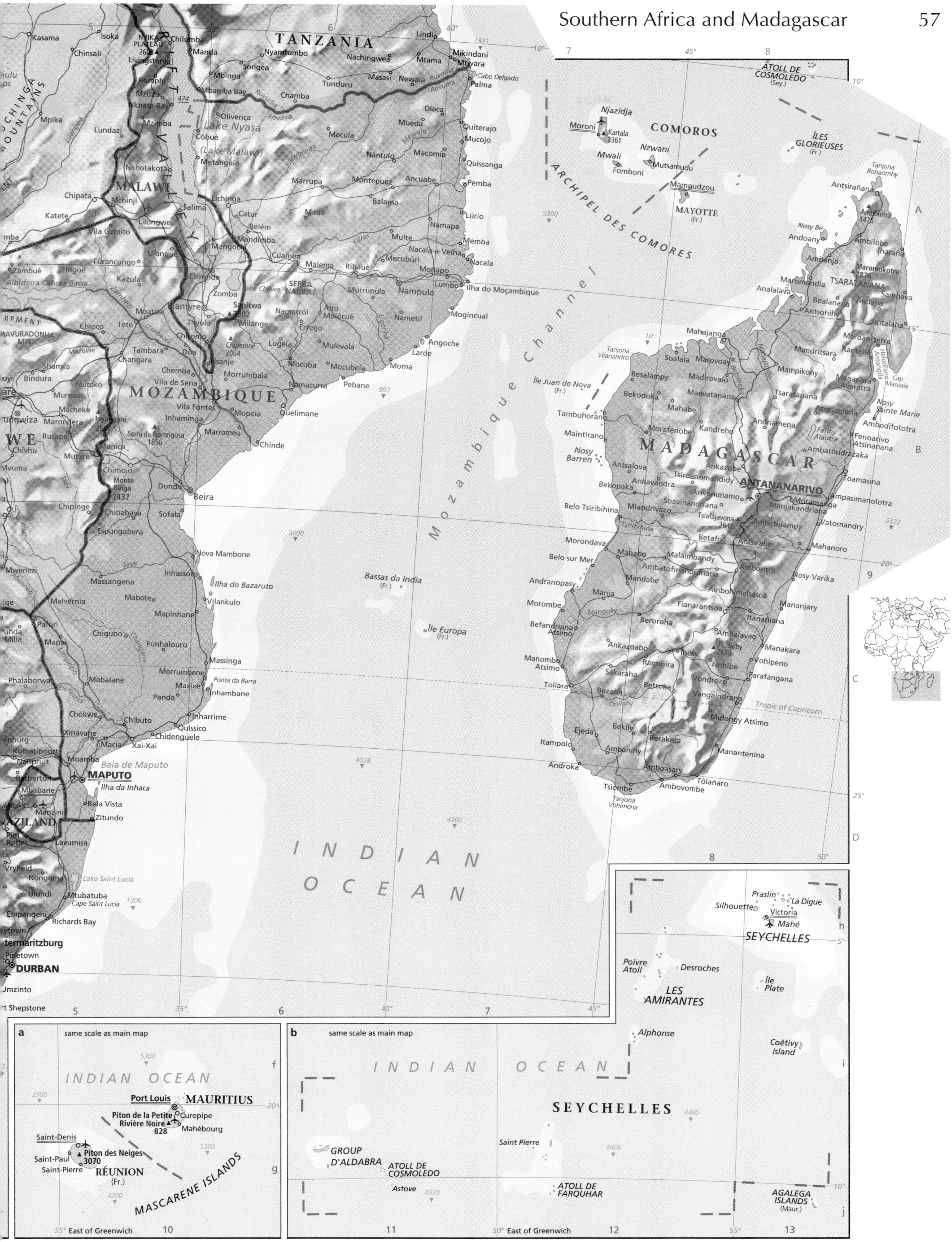

Kasama
Isoka
Chilumba
Manda
TANZANIA
Nyantumbo
Nachingwea
Lindi
ATOLL DE COSMOLEDO (Sey.)
Chinsali
NYIKA PLATEAU 2604
Livingstonia
Songea
Mbinga
Masasi
Newala
Mikindani
Mtwara
Mpika
Rumphi
Mzuzu
Mbamba Bay
Tunduru
Cabo Delgado
Palma

Lundazi
Nkhata Bay
Mzimba
474
Chamba
Diaca
Quiterajo
Mucojo
Njazidja
Moroni
Kartala 2361
COMOROS
ÍLES GLORIEUSES (Fr.)

Mpika
Olivença
Ruvuma
Mecula
Mueda
Nzwani
Mwali
Mutsamudu
Tanjona Bobaomby

Chipata
Katete
Nkhotakota
Lilongwe
MALAWI
Mchinji
Lichinga
Catur
Maúa
Montepuez
Balama
Nantulo
Macomia
Quissanga
Pemba
Mamoudzou
Fomboni
MAYOTTE (Fr.)
Antsiranana
Antohihi 1475
A

Vila Gamito
Furancungo
Ulóngue
Salima
Zomba
Namarrói
Errego
Ribáuè
Monapo
Nacala-a-Velha
Nacala
Nosy Be
Andoany
Ambilobe
Iharana
Maromokotro 2876

Zâmbuè
Kazula
Liwonde
Lake Chilwa
SERRA NAMULI
Alto Molócuè
Murrupula
Nampula
Lumbo
Ilha do Moçambique
Maromandia
Ambanja
Analalava
TSARATANANA
Sambava

Albufeira Cahora Bassa
Tete
Moatize
Blantyre
Sapitwa 3002
Thyolo
Milange
Lugela
Mocuba
Nametil
Mogincual
Andapa
Antsohihy
Bealanana

RPMENT
Chióco
Tambara
Dóa
Chiperone 2054
Mulevala
Mocubela
Moma
5300
Mahajanga
Soalala
Mandritsara
Maroantsetra
Helodrano Antongila
Cap Masoala

MAVURADONHA MTS.
Mazowe
Changara
Chemba
Vila de Sena
Morrumbala
Namacurra
Pebane
993
Tanjona Vilanandro
Besalampy
Madirovalo
Marovoay
Tsaratanana
Mampikony
Mananara Avaratra

Shamva
Bindura
Mutoko
Inyangani
Serra da Gorongosa 1856
Marromeu
Chinde
 Île Juan de Nova (Fr.)
Bekodoka
Mahabe
Kandreho
Andriamena
Andilamena
Nosy Sainte Marie

WE
Chivhu
Rusape
Mutare
Manica
Monte Binga 2437
Donde
Beira
Maintirano
Morafenobe
Nosy Barren
Antsalova
Ankazobe
Arivonimamo
Morarano
MADAGASCAR
ANTANANARIVO
Ampasimanolotra
Toamasina

Mvuma
Chimoio
Chibabava
Sofala
Morondava
Bekopaka
Ankavandra
Tsiroanomandidy
Soavinandriana
Tsiafajavona 2642
Ambatolampy
Antsirabe
5322

Chipinge
Espungabera
Nova Mambone
3000
Belo Tsiribihina
Miandrivazo
Betafo
Vatomandry

Mwenezi
Massangena
Inhassoro
Ilha do Bazaruto
Belo sur Mer
Mahabo
Malaimbandy
Ambatofinandrahana
Ambositra
Mahanoro

Mapai
Mabote
Vilankulo
Ile Europa (Fr.)
Mandabe
Manja
Ambohimahasoa

Milia
Chigubo
Funhalouro
Mapinhane
Andranopasy
Morombe
Befandriana Atsimo
Beroroha
Fianarantsoa
Ifanadiana
Mananjary

Phalaborwa
Mabalane
Massinga
Manombo Atsimo
Ankazoabo
Ihosy
Ambalavao
Pic Boby 2658
Ivohibe
Vohipeno
Nosy-Varika

Chókwè
Panda
Morrumbene
Maxixe
Inhambane
Ponta da Barra
Sakaraha
Bezaha
Toliara
Ranohira
Betroka
Vondrozo
Farafangana

Xinavane
Chibuto
Inharrime
Quissico
Chidenguele
4038
Onilahy
Tropic of Capricorn

enburg
Komatipoort
Nelspruit
Moamba
Macia
Xai-Xai
MAPUTO
Baie de Maputo
Ejeda
Bekily
Beraketa
Vangaindrano
Midongy Atsimo

Barberton
Mbabane
Bela Vista
Ilha da Inhaca
Itampolo
Ampanihy
Amboasary
Manantenina

SWAZILAND
Manzini
Zitundo
Androka
Androka
Ambovombe
Tôlañaro

Piet Retief
Lavumisa
Tsiombe
Tanjona Vohimena

Vryheid
Nongoma
Ulundi
Lake Saint Lucia
1306
4300

Empangeni
Mtubatuba
Cape Saint Lucia
INDIAN OCEAN

termaritzburg
Pinetown
Richards Bay

DURBAN

Jmzinto

t Shepstone

INDIAN OCEAN
Praslin
La Digue
Silhouette
Victoria
Mahé
SEYCHELLES

Poivre Atoll
Desroches
Île Plate

LES AMIRANTES
Alphonse
Coëtivy Island

ARCHIPEL DES COMORES
Mozambique Channel

a | same scale as main map

INDIAN OCEAN
5300
2300
Port Louis
MAURITIUS
Piton de la Petite Rivière Noire 828
Curepipe
Mahébourg
Saint-Denis
Piton des Neiges 3070
Saint-Paul
Saint-Pierre
RÉUNION (Fr.)
MASCARENE ISLANDS
4200
55° East of Greenwich   10

b | same scale as main map

INDIAN OCEAN
SEYCHELLES
4495
Saint Pierre
GROUP D'ALDABRA
ATOLL DE COSMOLEDO
Astove
4030
4406
ATOLL DE FARQUHAR
AGALEGA ISLANDS (Maur.)
11   50° East of Greenwich   12   55°   13

| 0 | 400 | 800 | 1600 | 2400 | 3200 | 4000 km |

| 0 | 400 | 800 | 1600 | 2400 miles |

Scale 1 : 35 000 000

Lambert Azimuthal Equal Area Projection

170°   11   180°   12   170°   13   160°   14   150°   15   140°   16   130°   17

A

30°

International Date Line

MIDWAY
ISLANDS
(U.S.)

B

Tropic of Cancer

HAWAI'IAN ISLANDS

Kaua'i   O'ahu
Honolulu   Moloka'i
Maui   UNITED STATES

AKE ISLAND
(U.S.)

Mauna Kea 4205   Hilo
Kalae   HAWAI'I

20°

MARSHALL
ISLANDS

Bikar

PACIFIC   OCEAN

C

elap

Maloelap

10°

ilinglaplap

Majuro

Butaritari

Tarawa   KIRIBATI

Kiritimati
(Christmas Island)

D

Abemama

URU

Banaba

KIRIBATI

Jarvis
Island
(U.S.)

LINE ISLANDS

Equator

0°

PHOENIX ISLANDS

Rawaki

POLYNESIA

Malden

NESIA

Nui

Starbuck

MON ISLANDS

TUVALU   Funafuti

TOKELAU
(N.Z.)

Penrhyn

E

Santa Cruz Islands

Niulakita

Banks

NEW
HEBRIDES

WALLIS AND FUTUNA
(Fr.)
Îles Wallis

SAMOA

AMERICAN
SAMOA
SAMOA ISLANDS

Nassau Island

Vostok

NORTHERN COOK
ISLANDS

Caroline

ÎLES
MARQUISES

iritu
anto

FIJI

Île Futuna

Savai'i   Apia
Upolu   Tutuila

Flint

alakula   Ambrym

Vanua Levu

Pago Pago

Suwarrow

FRENCH POLYNESIA

Éfaté
Port Vila

Viti
Levu   Suva

COOK ISLANDS
(N.Z.)

10°

LLE-
ONIE

Erromango

Koro
Sea

Vava'u

NIUE
(N.Z.)

Palmerston

Maupihaa

Îles du Désappointement

Lifou
Îles Loyauté

TONGA

Aitutaki   Manuae

ÎLES TUAMOTU

Anaa

Raraka

néa

Tongatapu   Nuku' alofa
'Eua

SOUTHERN
COOK
ISLANDS   Takutea

Tahiti   Papeete

Maruta

'Ata

Atiu

ARCHIPEL DE LA SOCIÉTÉ
(SOCIETY ISLANDS)

F

Rarotonga

Îles Maria

20°

Tubuai

NORFOLK ISLAND
(Austl.)

Îles Gambier

Kermadec
Islands
(N.Z.)

Tropic of Capricorn

Henderson Island

PITCAIRN
(U.K.)

G

North Cape

International Date Line

NEW
Auckland
NORTH ISLAND

Bay of
Plenty   East Cape

New Plymouth
Cape Egmont

Mount Ruapehu 2797
Hawke Bay
Napier

PACIFIC

ALAND   Wellington

TH ISLAND
Mount Cook   Christchurch
3754   Canterbury
Bight

Cook Strait

Chatham
Islands
(N.Z.)

30°

Dunedin
Invercargill

OCEAN

Island

West Cape

H

Auckland Islands
(N.Z.)

Campbell Island
(N.Z.)

50°

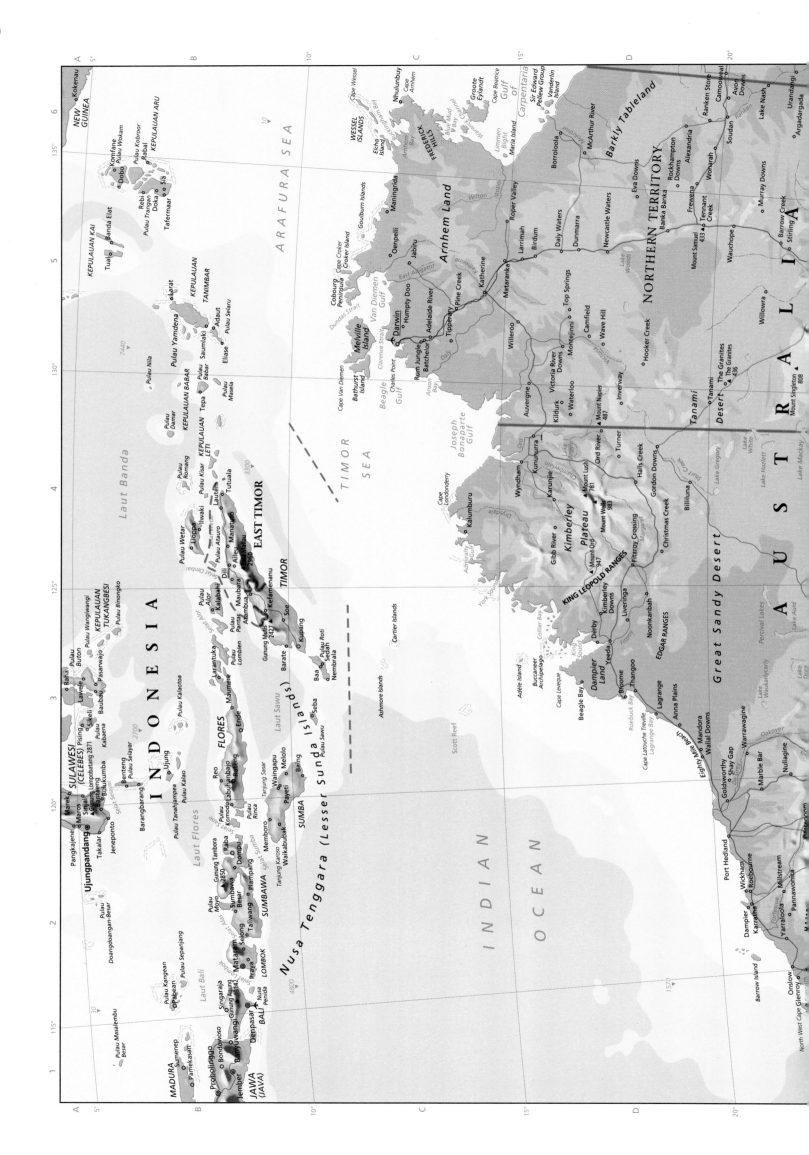

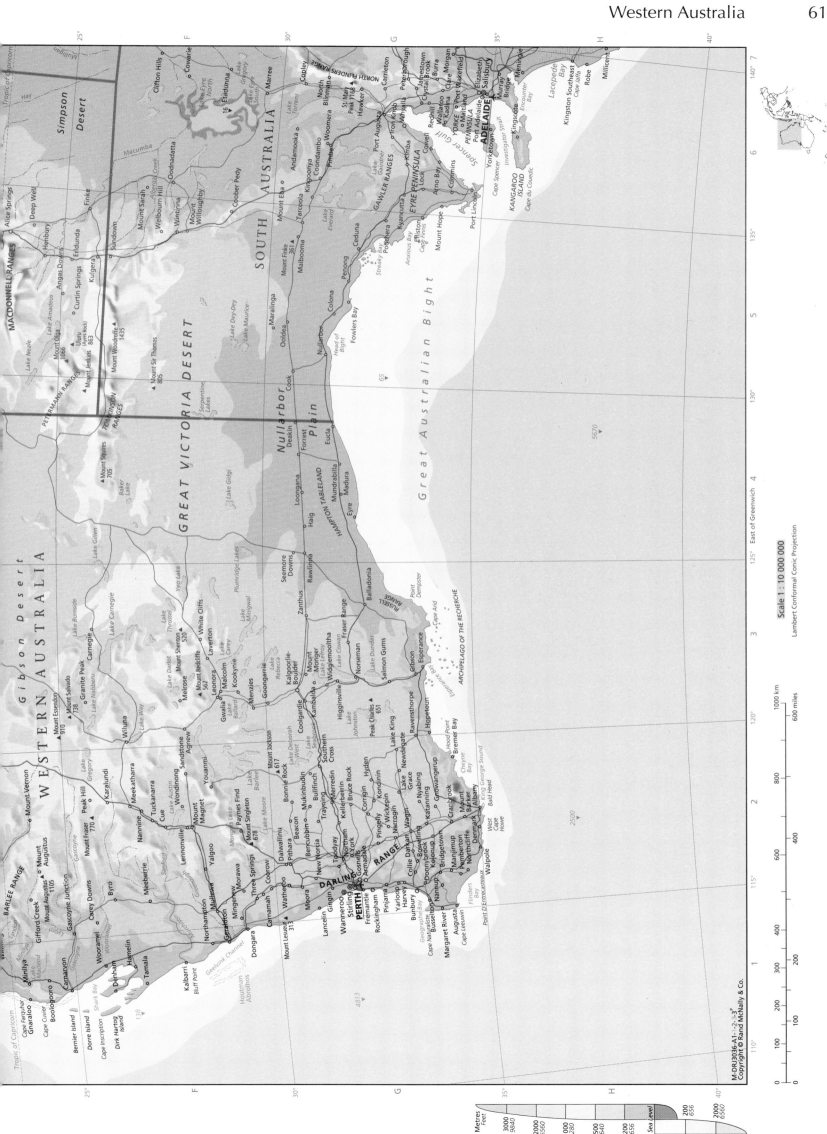

Scale 1 : 10 000 000

Lambert Conformal Conic Projection

M-DRJ3036-A1-·2·3·3°
Copyright © Rand McNally & Co.

Metres Feet
3000 9840
2000 6560
1000 3280
500 1640
200 656
0 Sea level
200 656
2000 6560

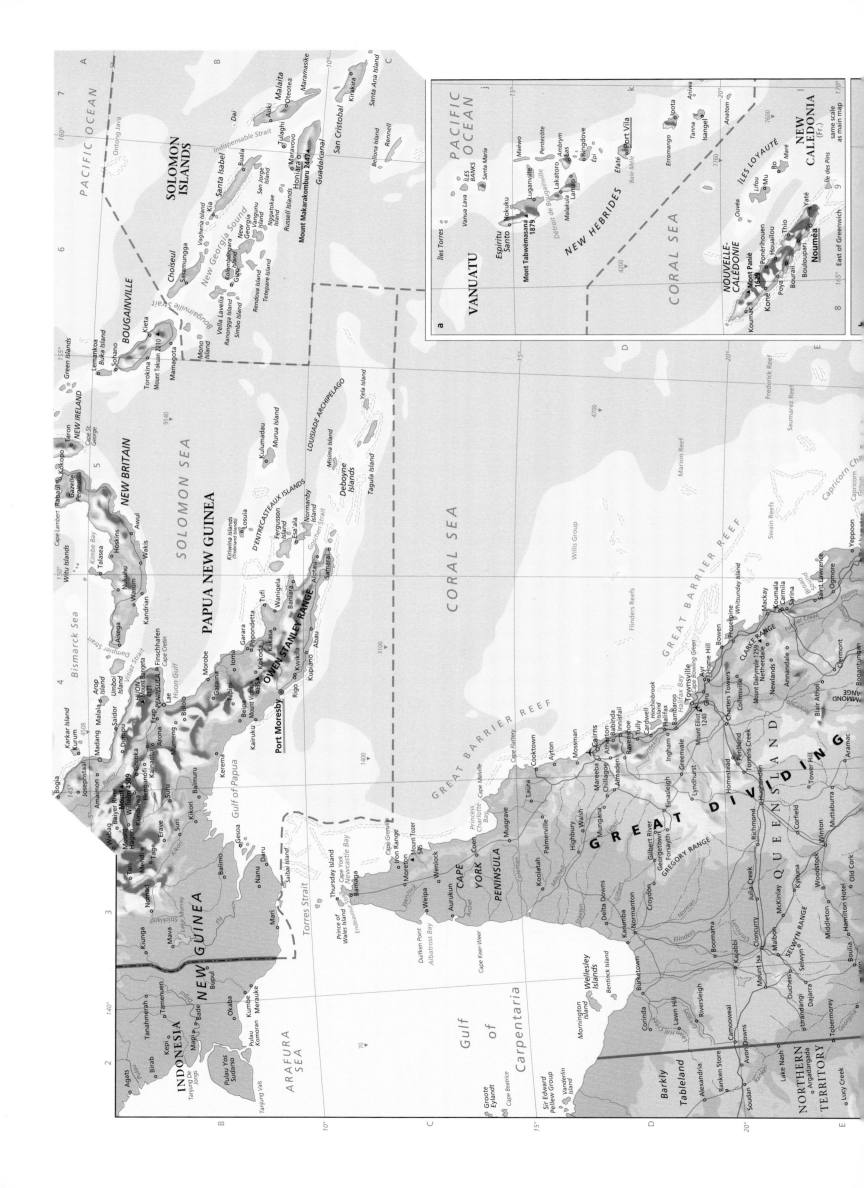

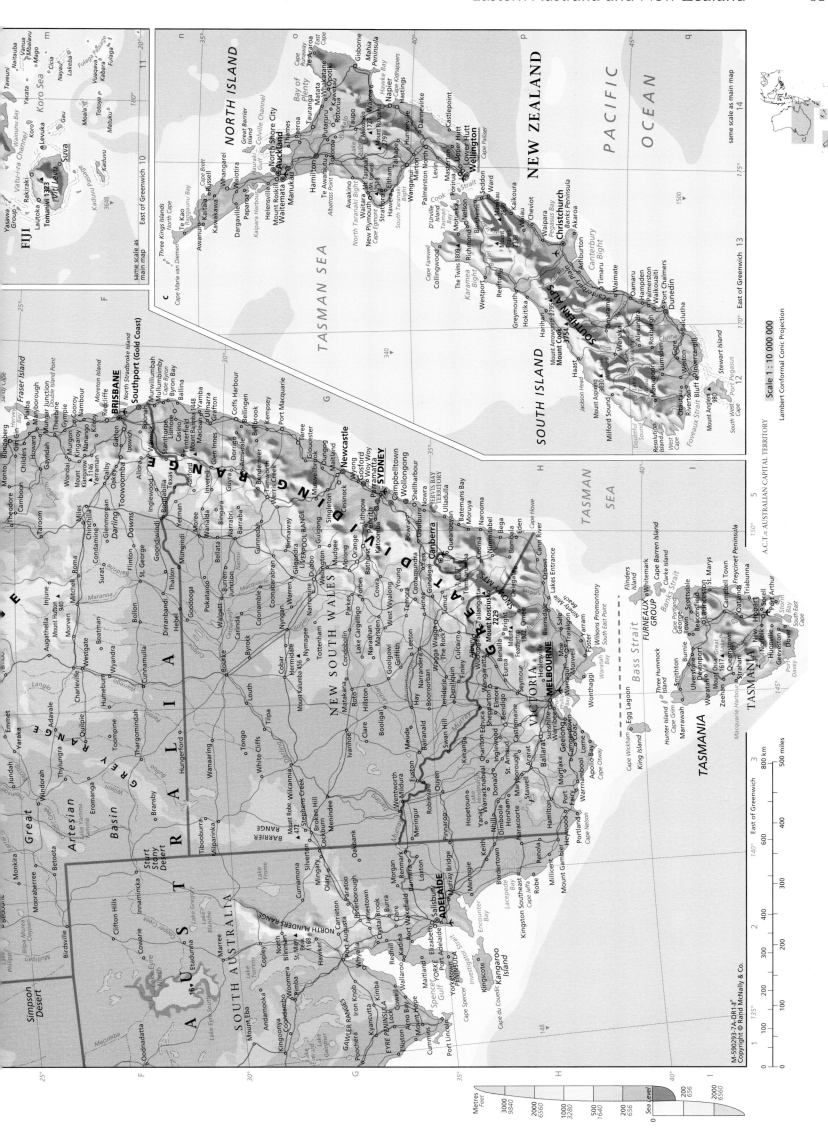

FIJI

NORTH ISLAND

NEW ZEALAND

PACIFIC OCEAN

TASMAN SEA

SOUTH ISLAND

SOUTHERN ALPS

Scale 1 : 10 000 000

Lambert Conformal Conic Projection

A.C.T. = AUSTRALIAN CAPITAL TERRITORY

AUSTRALIA

QUEENSLAND

NEW SOUTH WALES

SOUTH AUSTRALIA

VICTORIA

TASMANIA

BRISBANE
SYDNEY
Canberra
MELBOURNE
ADELAIDE

GREAT DIVIDING RANGE

Great Artesian Basin

Simpson Desert

Sturt Stony Desert

Bass Strait

Koro Sea

TASMAN SEA

Metres
Feet
3000 9840
2000 6560
1000 3280
500 1640
200 656
Sea Level
200 656
2000 6560

800 km
500 miles

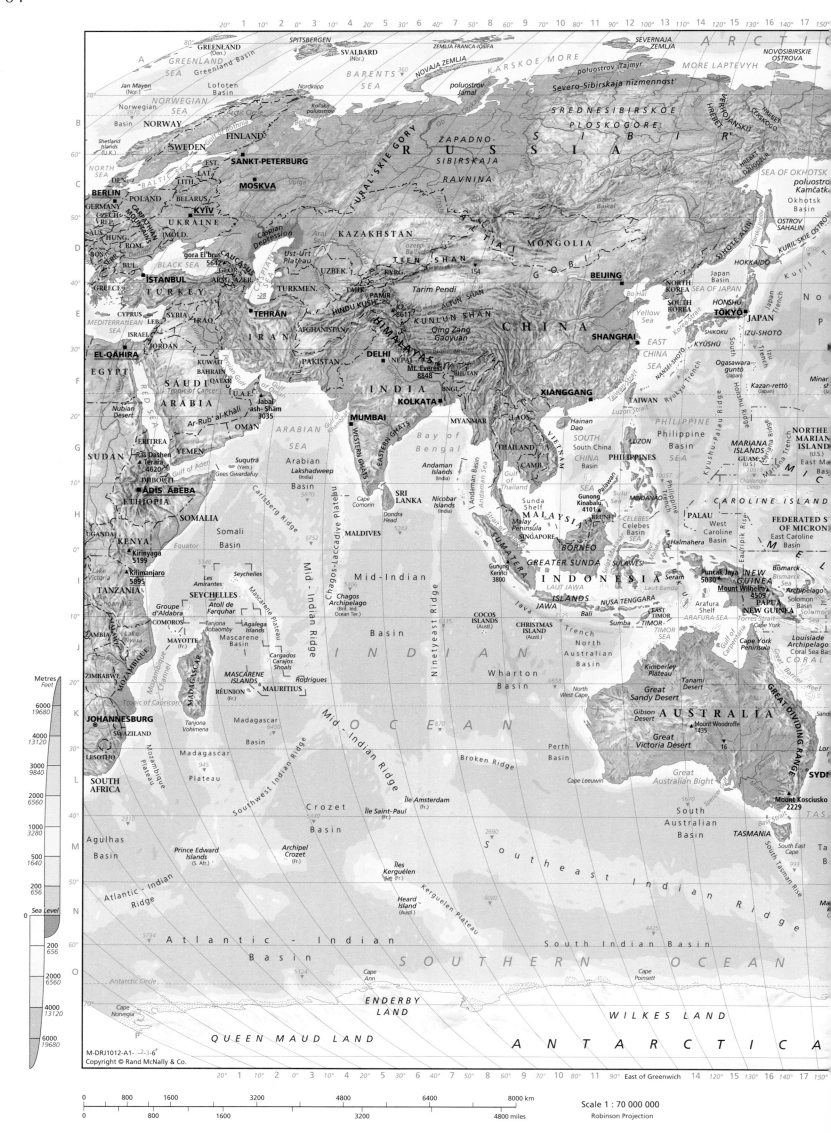

Metres
Feet

6000
19680

4000
13120

3000
9840

2000
6560

1000
3280

500
1640

200
656

0 Sea Level

200
656

2000
6560

4000
13120

6000
19680

M-DRJ1012-A1- -2-3-6°
Copyright © Rand McNally & Co.

0   800   1600   3200   4800   6400   8000 km
0   800   1600   3200   4800 miles

Scale 1 : 70 000 000
Robinson Projection

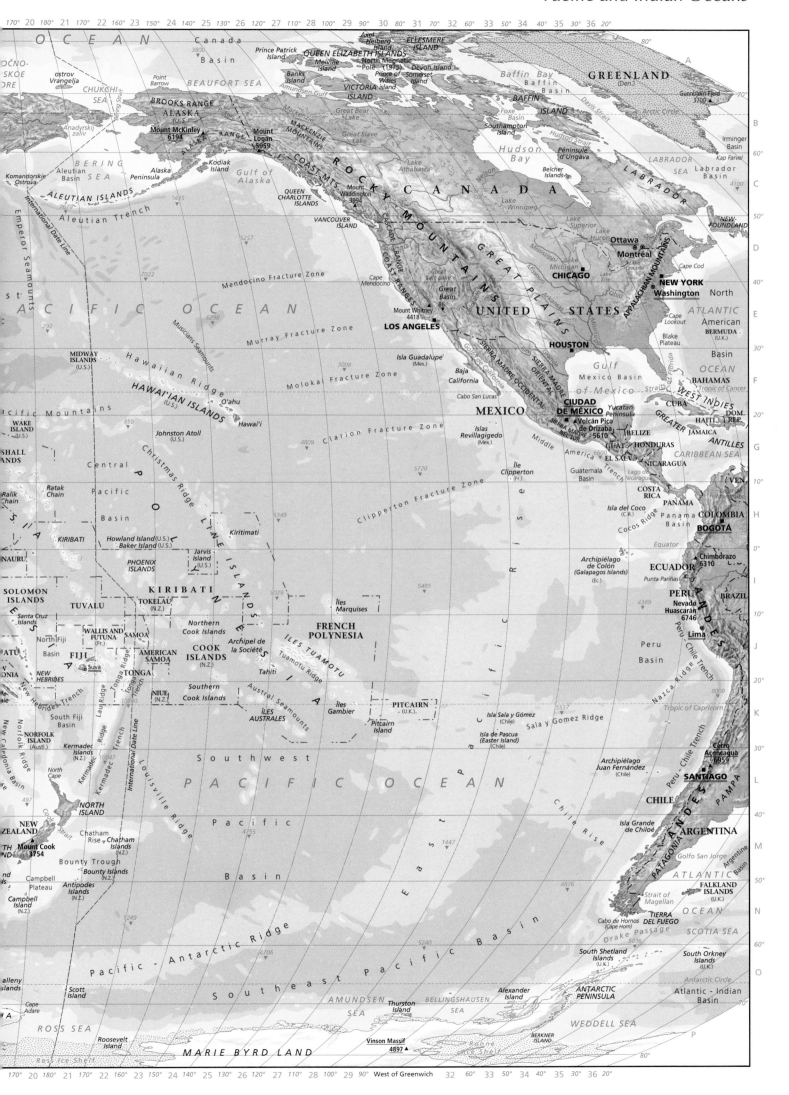

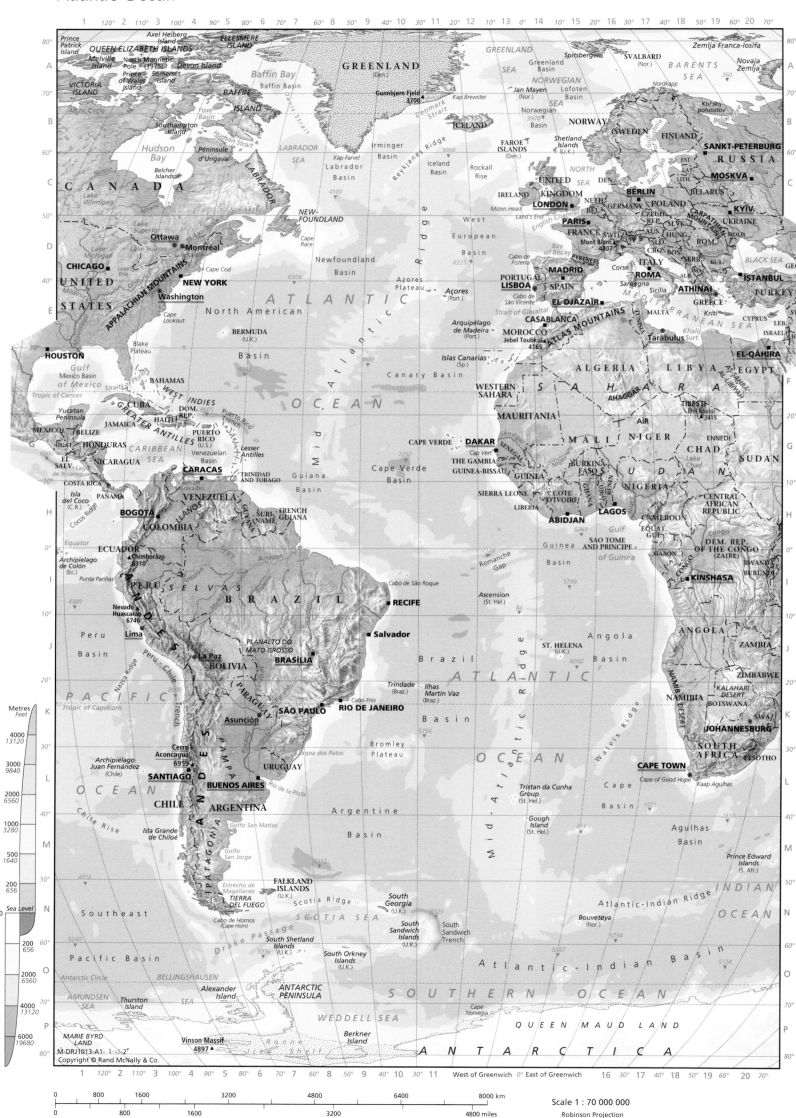

Scale 1 : 70 000 000

Robinson Projection

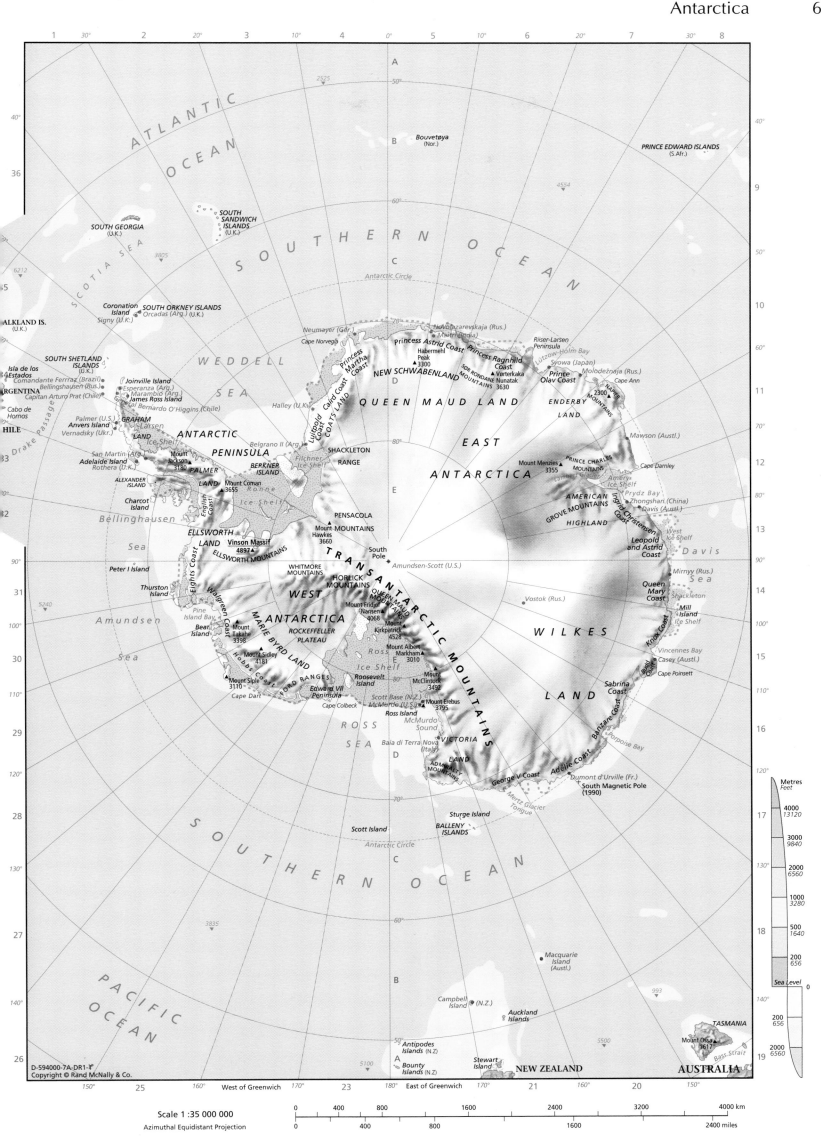

Scale 1:35 000 000

Azimuthal Equidistant Projection

| 0 | 400 | 800 | 1600 | 2400 | 3200 | 4000 km |

| 0 | 400 | 800 | 1600 | 2400 | 2400 miles |

UNITED STATES
Cape Canaveral
GULF OF
MEXICO   Tampa
                         MIAMI
                              Nassau
Straits of Florida
Tropic of Cancer   Tropic of Cancer
                                   BAHAMAS
          LA HABANA   TURKS AND CAICOS
                                     ISLANDS
Mérida   CUBA   Santiago de   (U.K.)
                        Cuba   DOMINICAN   PUERTO
MEXICO   CAYMAN   HAITI REPUBLIC RICO   ANGUILLA (U.K.)
              ISLANDS JAMAICA Port-au-Prince (U.S.)   ANTIGUA AND BARBUDA
BELIZE   (U.K.)   SANTO   SAN JUAN   GUADELOUPE
Belmopan   Kingston   DOMINGO   (Fr.)
HONDURAS   MONTSERRAT (U.K.) DOMINICA
Tegucigalpa   CARIBBEAN SEA   MARTINIQUE (Fr.)
EL SALVADOR   ARUBA   NETHERLANDS ST. LUCIA
NICARAGUA   Lago de   (Neth.) ANTILLES ST. VINCENT AND BARBADOS
Managua   Nicaragua Pico Cristóbal Colón THE GRENADINES GRENADA
                     Barranquilla 5775   TOBAGO
SAN JOSÉ   Colón Cartagena MARACAIBO CARACAS TRINIDAD AND TOBAGO
COSTA RICA   Panamá   Barquisimeto   TRINIDAD
Volcán Barú PANAMÁ   Cúcuta Ciudad Bolívar Ciudad Guayana
3475   Bucaramanga San Cristóbal VENEZUELA Georgetown
         MEDELLÍN   Puerto Ayacucho GUYANA Paramaribo
Manizales BOGOTÁ   Mount Roraima SURINAME Cayenne
Buenaventura   2875   FRENCH
         CALI COLOMBIA   Boa Vista   GUIANA
                    Mitú   Amapá
Esmeraldas   Pico da Neblina   Macapá Ilha de
QUITO   3014   Marajó BELÉM
ECUADOR   Amazon Óbidos Amazon   São Luís
GUAYAQUIL Cuenca   Fonte Boa Santarém   FORTALEZA
         Iquitos   MANAUS   Parnaíba
Chiclayo   Leticia   Teresina   Natal
Cajamarca Pucallpa   Rio   Negro Marabá   Campina Grande
Trujillo   Branco   Porto Velho Carolina   Caruaru João Pessoa
Nevado Huascarán PERU Cobija BRAZIL Paulistana Juazeiro RECIFE
6746   Riberalta Porto Nacional Represa de Maceió
Cerro de Pasco   Sobradinho Aracaju
Huancayo Puerto   Trinidad Mato Barra Itabuna SALVADOR
LIMA   Maldonado   PLANALTO DO Grosso Cuiabá
Ica Cusco   MATO GROSSO   Montes Claros BRASÍLIA
         Puno Lake Titicaca   Corumbá GOIÂNIA
Arequipa LA PAZ BOLIVIA Santa Cruz   BELO HORIZONTE
Mollendo Cochabamba de la Sierra   Ribeirão Vitória
Arica Nevado Sajama Sucre   Preto Campos
6542   Potosí   PARAGUAY   SÃO PAULO RIO DE JANEIRO
Iquique   GRAN CHACO Concepción   SANTOS
PACIFIC   Asunción CURITIBA
OCEAN Antofagasta   Villarrica Iguaçu Florianópolis
Tropic of Capricorn Salta Santiago Posadas   Tropic of Capricorn
         San Miguel del Estero Corrientes Santa Maria PORTO ALEGRE
         de Tucumán   Paraná Rivera Pelotas
         Nevado Ojos CÓRDOBA Santa Fe Salto Rio Grande
         del Salado San Juan   Paysandú
Coquimbo 6893 Mendoza ROSARIO URUGUAY
CHILE   Cerro Aconcagua BUENOS AIRES MONTEVIDEO
Valparaíso 6959   La Plata
SANTIAGO   ARGENTINA Mar del Plata
Concepción   Bahía Blanca
Valdivia Neuquén Negro Golfo San Matías
Osorno
Puerto Montt   Viedma
Archipiélago PATAGONIA Rawson
de los Chonos   Comodoro Rivadavia ATLANTIC
              Golfo San Jorge   OCEAN
         Wellington FALKLAND ISLANDS
         Río Gallegos West (U.K.) East
Punta Arenas Estrecho de Falkland Stanley Falkland
TIERRA DEL Magallanes
FUEGO   SOUTH GEORGIA
Ushuaia   (U.K.)
Cabo de Hornos
(Cape Horn)
Drake Passage

ATLANTIC

OCEAN

Archipiélago de Colón
(Galápagos Islands)
(Ec.)
Isla   Equator   Equator
Isabela

Archipiélago
Juan Fernández
(Chile)

ANDES
PERU
ANDES

0   400   800   1600   2400   3200   4000 km
0   400   800   1600   2400 miles
West of Greenwich
Scale 1 : 35 000 000
Lambert Azimuthal Equal Area Projection

Scale 1 : 15 000 000

Lambert Conformal Conic Projection

Metres	Feet
4000	13120
3000	9840
2000	6560
1000	3280
500	1640
200	656
Sea Level	0
200	656
2000	6560

Scale 1 : 15 000 000

Sinusoidal Projection

ATLANTIC

OCEAN

GRENADA
t George's
Scarborough
Tobago
Port of Spain
an Fernando
Trinidad
TRINIDAD AND TOBAGO

Morawhanna
Charity
Spring Garden
Georgetown
Parika
Bartica
Rockstone
Linden
New Amsterdam
Corriverton
Nieuw
Nickerie
Kwakoegron
Paramaribo
Nieuw Amsterdam
Saint-Laurent
du Maroni Île du Diable
Kourou
Cayenne
Régina
Cabo Orange
Saint-Georges
Oiapoque

Mount Roraima
2875
GUYANA
Lethem
SURINAME
Juliana Top
1230
FRENCH
GUIANA
Saül
Cunani
Calçoene
Amapá
Ilha de Maracá
AMAPÁ

Vista
Caracaraí
AIMA
Escaquibo
Brokopondo Stuwmeer
TUMUC-HUMAC MTS.
ACARAÍ MTS.
Serra do
Navio
Ilha Janaucu
Ilha Caviana de Fora
Ilha Mexiana
Macapá
Equator

MANAUS
capuru
ri
Careiro
Itacoatiara
Oriximiná
Faro
Parintins
Óbidos
Alenquer
Monte Alegre
Porto
de Moz
Portel
Breves
Cametá
Ilha
Grande
do Gurupa
ILHA DE
MARAJÓ
BELÉM
Bragança
Carutapera
Cururupu
Camiranga
Abaetetuba
São Luís
Pinheiro
Rosário
Parnaíba
Acaraú
Maués
Santarém
Altamira
Tucuruí
Viana
Monção
Itapecuru-Mirim
Brejo
Bacabal
Camocim
Sobral
Maranguape
FORTALEZA
Baturité
Aracati
CEARÁ

Borba
Novo Aripuanã
Manicoré
S
Prainha Nova
Itaituba
PARÁ
Marabá
São João do
Araguaia
Carajás
Imperatriz
Araguatins
Grajaú
SERRA DOS CARAJÁS
Codó
Pedreiras
Caxias
MARANHÃO
Barra do Corda
Colinas
Mirador
Teresina
Amarante
Campo
Maior
Ipu
Crateús
Senador
Pompeu
Quixadá
Areia Branca
Macau
Mossoró
RIO GRANDE
DO NORTE
Ceará-Mirim
Natal
Currais Novos
Cabo de São Roque

SERRA DO CACHIMBO
BRAZIL
Gradaús
Conceição do Araguaia
Araguacema
Pedro Afonso
Tocantinópolis
Carolina
Loreto
Balsas
Benedito Leite
Floriano
Oeiras
Picos
Juazeiro
do Norte
Sousa
Caicó
Rio Tinto
João Pessoa
Campina Grande
Olinda
PIAUÍ
PARAÍBA
Patos
Sertânia

SERRA DOS APIACÁS
SERRA FORMOSA
Xingu
Alto Parnaíba
Santa Filomena
São Raimundo
Nonato
Gilbués
Remanso
Juazeiro
Paulistana
Paulo Afonso
Jeremoabo
PERNAMBUCO
Serra
Talhada
Garanhuns
Caruaru
RECIFE
Barreiros

Vilhena
Roosevelt
Aripuanã
raná
Utiariti
Diamantino
MATO GROSSO
PLANALTO DO
MATO GROSSO
Tocantínia
Pium
Palmas
Porto Nacional
Cristalândia
Ilha do
Bananal
TOCANTINS
Gurupi
Dianópolis
Natividade
Paraná
Arraias
Parnaguá
Xique-Xique
Barra
Represa de
Sobradinho
Morro do Chapéu
Senhor do Bonfim
Tucano
Jacobina
Serrinha
Inhambupe
Alagoinhas
ALAGOAS
Arapiraca
Propriá
SERGIPE
Maceió
Itabaiana
Estância
Aracaju

Diamantino
Rosário Oeste
Cuiabá
Cáceres
Porto Esperidião
San Ignacio
de Velasco
Poxoréu
São Miguel
do Araguaia
Porangatu
Posse
Barreiras
Bom Jesus
da Lapa
Paramirim
Guanambi
Caetité
BAHIA
Santo Antônio
de Jesus
Mucujê
Jequié
Valença
SALVADOR
Santo Amaro
Candeias
Feira de Santana

Laguna Concepción
San José de Chiquitos
Roboré
Puerto Suárez
Corumbá
Pantanal de
São Lourenço
Rio Negro
MATO GROSSO
DO SUL
Taquari Novo
GOIÁS
Aruanã
DISTRITO
FEDERAL
BRASÍLIA
Formosa
Januária
São Francisco
Pedra Azul
Vitória da
Conquista
Monte Azul
Itabuna
Ibicaraí
Itapetinga
Ilhéus
Canavieiras
Belmonte

Porto
Esperança
Aquidauana
Campo Grande
Porto Murtinho
Bela Vista
ARAGUAY
iscal
irribia
Pedro Juan
Caballero
Ponta Porã
Amambaí
Umuarama
Apucarana
Concepción
Dourados
Presidente
Prudente
Marília
Bauru
Maringá
Londrina
Sorocaba
Araçatuba
São José
do Rio Preto
Barretos
Franca
Guaxupé
Poços
de Caldas
Ribeirão
Preto
Rio Claro
CAMPINAS
São José dos
Campos
SÃO PAULO
PARANÁ
SÃO PAULO

Santa Fé do Sul
Três Lagoas
Jataí
Coxim
Aragarças
Goiás
Iporá
GOIÂNIA
Rio Verde
Pires do Rio
Morrinhos
Catalão
Rondonópolis
Alto Araguaia
Anápolis
Luziânia
Montes Claros
Pirapora
Araguari
Ituiutaba
Uberlândia
Uberaba
Araxá
Ibiá
MINAS GERAIS
Corinto
Diamantina
Governador
Valadares
Araçuaí
Almenara
Nanuque
Prado
Alcobaça
Caravelas
Porto Seguro
São Mateus
ESPÍRITO
SANTO
Colatina
Aracruz
SERRA DO ESPINHAÇO

Represa de
Três Marias
Sete Lagoas
BELO
HORIZONTE
Itaúna
Divinópolis
Formiga
Passos
Represa de
Furnas
Conselheiro
Lafaiete
Ponte Nova
Caratinga
Itaguaí
Vitória
Vila Velha
Cachoeiro de Itapemirim
Campos
Cabo de São Tomé

Paranaíba
Represa de
Água Vermelha
Presidente
Prudente
Ourinhos
Maringá
Araguari
Rio Claro
Volta Redonda
Juiz de
Fora
Itaperuna
RIO DE JANEIRO
Nova Iguaçu
Niterói
RIO DE JANEIRO
Tropic of Capricorn

4600
4200
4600
110
5450
4000
5450
4000
4500
3600
4500
4900

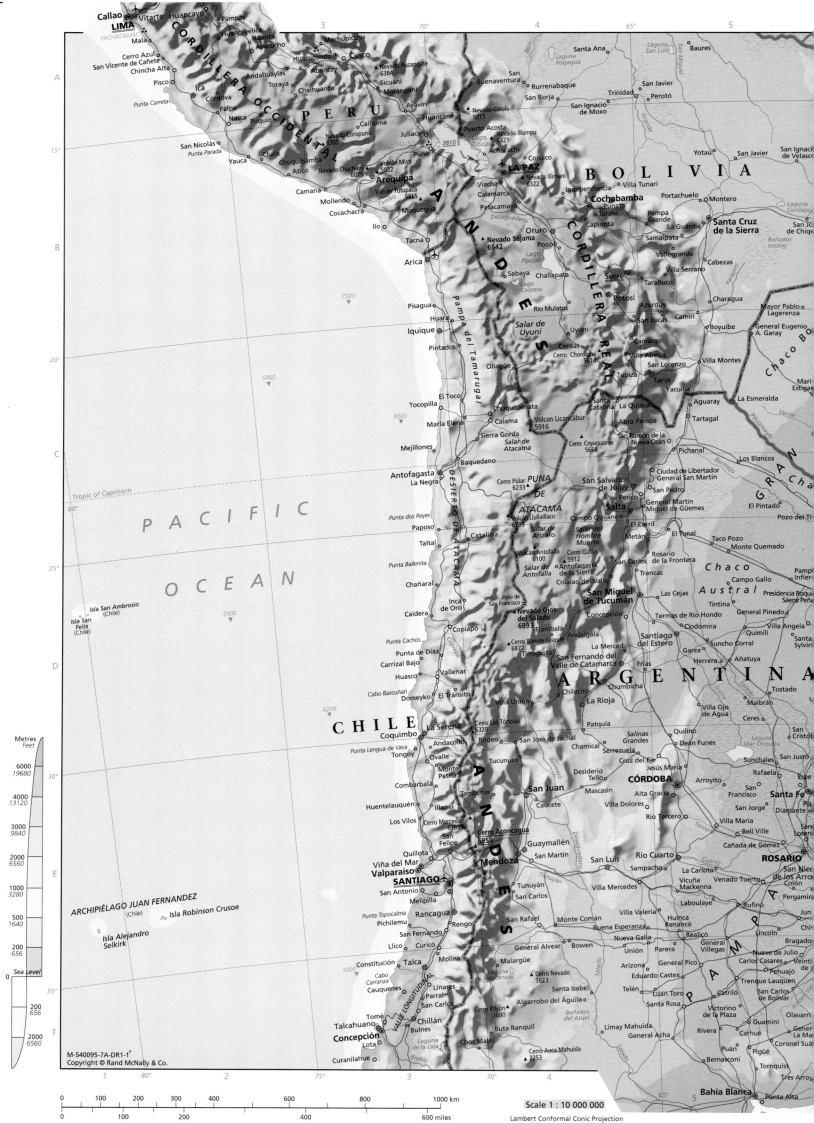

PACIFIC OCEAN

PERU

BOLIVIA

CHILE

ARGENTINA

CORDILLERA OCCIDENTAL

CORDILLERA REAL

A N D E S

P A M P A

Pampa del Tamarugal

Desierto de Atacama

PUNA DE ATACAMA

GRAN CHACO

Chaco Austral

Callao
LIMA
Vitarte
Huancayo
Pampas
PACHACAMAC
Mala
San Vicente de Cañete
Chincha Alta
Cerro Azul
Pisco
Ica
Córdova
Palpa
Nasca
Punta Carreta
San Nicolás
Punta Parada
Yauca
Chala
Chuquibamba
Atico
Camaná
Mollendo
Cocachacra
Ilo
Huancavelica
Huanta
Ayacucho
Andahuaylas
Toraya
Chalhuanca
Abancay
Huarocondo
Machupicchu
Cusco
Nevado Auzangate 6384
Sicuani
Marangani
Ayaviri
Cailloma
Juliaca
Nevado Coropuna 6305
Volcán Misti 5822
Puno
Arequipa
Volcán Tutupaca 5815
Tambo
Moquegua
Tacna
Arica
Nevado Chachani 6075

San Buenaventura
Rurrenabaque
Santa Ana
Laguna Rogagua
Boni
San Borja
Trinidad
San Ignacio de Moxo
San Javier
Perotó
Laguna San Luis
Baures
Santa Ana
San Javier de Velasco
Yotaú
Grande
San Miguel

Nevado Cololo 5915
Puerto Acosta
Achacachi
Huancané
Coroico
Nevado Illampu 6421
Nevado Illimani 6322
LA PAZ
Lago Titicaca
3810
SILLUSTANI
Viacha
Calamarca
Patacamaya
Desaguadero
Independencia
Villa Tunari
Cochabamba
Punata
Tarata
Pampa Grande
Capinota
La Guardia
Samaipata
Santa Cruz de la Sierra
Portachuelo
Montero
San José de Chiquitos
Laguna Concepción

Oruro
Poopó
Lago Poopó
Nevado Sajama 6542
Sabaya
Challapata
Lago Coipasa
Salar de Uyuni
Río Mulatos
Potosí
Sucre
Tarabuco
Vallegrande
Villa Serrano
Cabezas
Charagua
Bañados Izozog
Paraguay

Pisagua
Huara
Iquique
Pintados
El Toco
Tocopilla
María Elena
Calama
Chuquicamata
Ollagüe
Uyuni
Cerdas
Cerro Chorolque 5614
San Lucas
Azurduy
Camargo
Villa Abecia
Tupiza
Tarija
San Lorenzo
Yacuiba
Villa Montes
Camiri
Boyuibe
Mayor Pablo Lagerenza
General Eugenio A. Garay
La Esmeralda
Mariscal Estigarribia
Chaco Boreal
Pilcomayo
Verde

Mejillones
Sierra Gorda
Salar de Atacama
Baquedano
Antofagasta
La Negra
Tropic of Capricorn
Cerro Púlar 6233
Volcán Licancábur 5916
Santa Catalina
La Quiaca
Abra Pampa
San Ramón de la Nueva Orán
Pichanal
Cerro Coyaguaime 5668
San Salvador de Jujuy
Perico
San Pedro
Ciudad de Libertador General San Martín
Los Blancos
Bermejo
Gran Chaco
El Pintado
Pozo del Tigre

Punta dos Reyes
Paposo
Catalina
Taltal
Punta Ballenita
Chañaral
Punta Cachos
Caldera
Punta de Díaz
Carrizal Bajo
Huasco
Cabo Bascuñán
Domeyko
El Tránsito
Vallenar
Volcán Llullaillaco 6739
Salar de Arizaro
Salar del Hombre Muerto
Volcán Antofalla 6100
Salar de Antofalla
Cerro Galán 5912
Antofagasta de la Sierra
Colalao del Valle
El Carril
Salta
General Martín Miguel de Güemes
Metán
El Tunal
Rosario de la Frontera
San Carlos
Trancas
Campo Quijano
Las Cejas
Taco Pozo
Monte Quemado
Chaco
Campo Gallo
Presidencia Roque Sáenz Peña
Tintina
Clodomira
General Pinedo
Villa Ángela
Santa Sylvina

Inca de Oro
Copiapó
La Merced
Paso de San Francisco
Nevado Ojos del Salado 6893
Flambalá
Tinogasta
Cerro Bonete Grande 6872
Andalgalá
San Fernando del Valle de Catamarca
Frías
Herrera
Añatuya
San Miguel de Tucumán
Concepción
Termas de Río Hondo
Santiago del Estero
Suncho Corral
Garza
Quimilí

Cerro Las Tórtolas 6320
Villa Unión
Chilecito
Chumbicha
La Rioja
Patquía
Tostado
Villa Ojo de Agua
Ceres
Malbrán

La Serena
Coquimbo
Punta Lengua de Vaca
Tongoy
Andacollo
Rodeo
San José de Jáchal
Chamical
Salinas Grandes
Quilino
Deán Funes
Cruz del Eje
Jesús María
Sunchales
San Cristóbal
San Justo
Laguna Mar Chiquita

Ovalle
Monte Patria
Combarbalá
Tucunuco
San Juan
Caucete
Serrezuela
Desiderio Tello
Mascasín
CÓRDOBA
Arroyito
San Francisco
Santa Fe
Rafaela
Esperanza

Huentelauquén
Illapel
Cerro Mercedario 6769
Los Vilos
Tamberías
San Felipe
Cerro Aconcagua 6959
Guaymallén
San Martín
Villa Dolores
Alta Gracia
Río Tercero
Villa María
Bell Ville
Cañada de Gómez
San Jorge
Diamante

Quillota
Viña del Mar
Valparaíso
SANTIAGO
San Antonio
Mendoza
San Luis
Sampacho
Río Cuarto
La Carlota
Vicuña Mackenna
Venado Tuerto
ROSARIO
San Nicolás de los Arroyos
Colón
Pergamino

ARCHIPIÉLAGO JUAN FERNANDEZ (Chile)
Isla Robinson Crusoe
Isla Alejandro Selkirk

Isla San Ambrosio (Chile)
Isla San Félix (Chile)

Melipilla
Rancagua
Punta Topocalma
Pichilemu
San Fernando
Rengo
Llico
Curicó
Talca
Molina
Constitución
Cabo Carranza
Cauquenes
Linares
Parral
San Carlos
Tunuyán
San Carlos
San Rafael
Malargüe
Cerro Nevado 3823
Laguna Llancanelo
Monte Comán
Buena Esperanza
Nueva Galia
Unión
Parera
General Alvear
Bowen
Santa Isabel
Telén
Arizona
Eduardo Castex
General Pico
Carlos Casares
Pehuajó
Nueve de Julio
Villa Valeria
Huinca Renancó
Realicó
Lincoln
General Villegas
Bragado
Trenque Lauquen
Veinticinco de Mayo
Victorino de la Plaza
Guaminí
Olavarría
Coronel Suárez
Pigüé
Bernasconi
Tornquist
Bahía Blanca
Punta Alta
Tres Arroyos

Tomé
Talcahuano
Concepción
Lota
Chillán
Bulnes
Buta Ranquil
Chos Malal
Cerro Payún 3680
Laguna del Atuel
Limay Mahuida
General Acha
Rivera
Luan Toro
Santa Rosa
Catriló
San Carlos de Bolívar
Curanilahue
Biobío
Laguna de la Laja
Cerro Auca Mahuida 2253
Cerro Peteroa
Salado
VALLE LONGITUDINAL

Metres / Feet
6000 / 19680
4000 / 13120
3000 / 9840
2000 / 6560
1000 / 3280
500 / 1640
200 / 656
0 / Sea Level
200 / 656
2000 / 6560

0 100 200 300 400 600 800 1000 km
0 100 200 400 600 miles

Scale 1 : 10 000 000
Lambert Conformal Conic Projection

MATO GROSSO

Parecis
Arenápolis
Diamantino
Alto Paraguai
Rosário Oeste

Esperidião
Cuiabá
Várzea Grande
Cáceres
Poconé

DA DOS PARECIS

an Matias

Puerto
Suárez
Corumbá
Pantanal do
Rio Negro
Porto
Esperança

PLANALTO
DO
MATO
GROSSO

SERRA DO RONCADOR

Poxoréu
Jaciara
Rondonópolis
General Carneiro
Barra do Garças
Guiratinga

Pantanal de
São Lourenço

Alto Garças

Aruanã
Itapaci
Ceres

Porangatu
Bandeirantes

São Domingos

SERRA DOURADA

Nova Roma
Posse

São Francisco
da Lapa

Correntina

BAHIA

Paratinga

Bom Jesus

Paramirim

Cocos
Guanambi
Manga
Monte Azul

Caetité
Brumado
Caculé
Urandi

MATO GROSSO
DO SUL

Campo Grande
Aquidauana
Terenos
Sidrolândia
Jardim
Maracaju

Bela Vista
Porto Murtinho

Puerto
Bahía Negra
Fuerte Olimpo
Puerto Guaraní

Puerto Sastre
Puerto Fonciere
Pedro Juan Caballero
Ponta Porã

ARAGUAY

Concepción
Puerto Ybapobo
San Pedro de
Ycuamandiyú

Rosario

Asunción
Ypacaraí
Villarrica
Ciudad
del Este

Foz do Iguaçu

Coronel Oviedo
Puerto Esperanza

Quiindy
Yegros

San Juan
Bautista
San Ignacio
Pilar
Humaitá

Corrientes
Empedrado
Bella Vista
San Roque

Mercedes

BRAZIL

Goiás
Jaraguá
DISTRITO
FEDERAL

GOIÁS
Anápolis
Luziânia
BRASÍLIA

GOIÂNIA
Trindade
Anicuns
Pontalina
Morrinhos
Rio Verde

Cristalina

Formosa

Unaí

Paracatu

Pires
do Rio
Ipameri

João Pinheiro

MINAS GERAIS

Patos
de Minas
Patrocínio
Araxá
Ibiá
Uberlândia
Itumbiara
Araguari
Catalão
Diamantina
Corinto
Curvelo

Montes Claros
Bocaiúva

Pirapora

São Francisco
São Romão
Januária
Janaúba

Monte Azul

Itaobim
Pedra Azul

Teófilo Otoni

Araçuaí
Capelinha

SERRA DO ESPINHAÇO

Salinas
Coronel Murta

Carlos
Chagas

PORTO ALEGRE

URUGUAY

MONTEVIDEO

BUENOS AIRES

ATLANTIC

OCEAN

Tropic of Capricorn

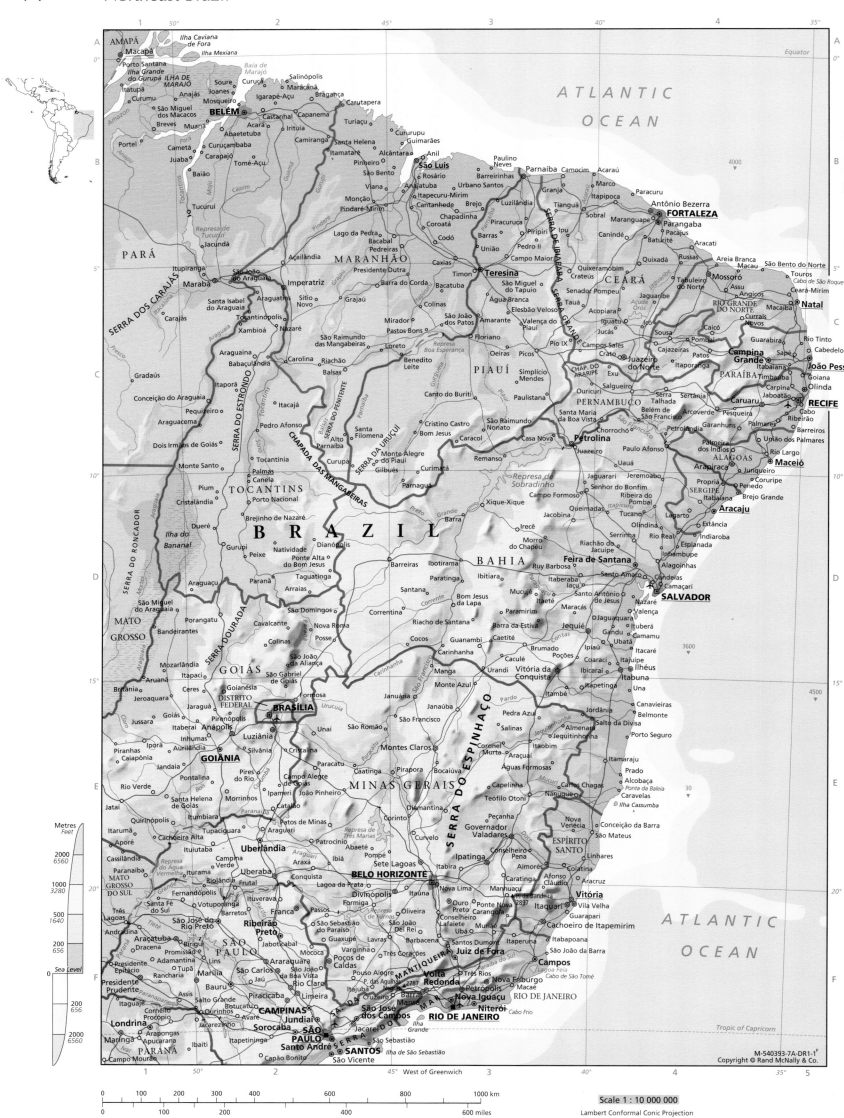

Scale 1 : 10 000 000

Lambert Conformal Conic Projection

M-540393-7A-DR1-1ª
Copyright © Rand McNally & Co.

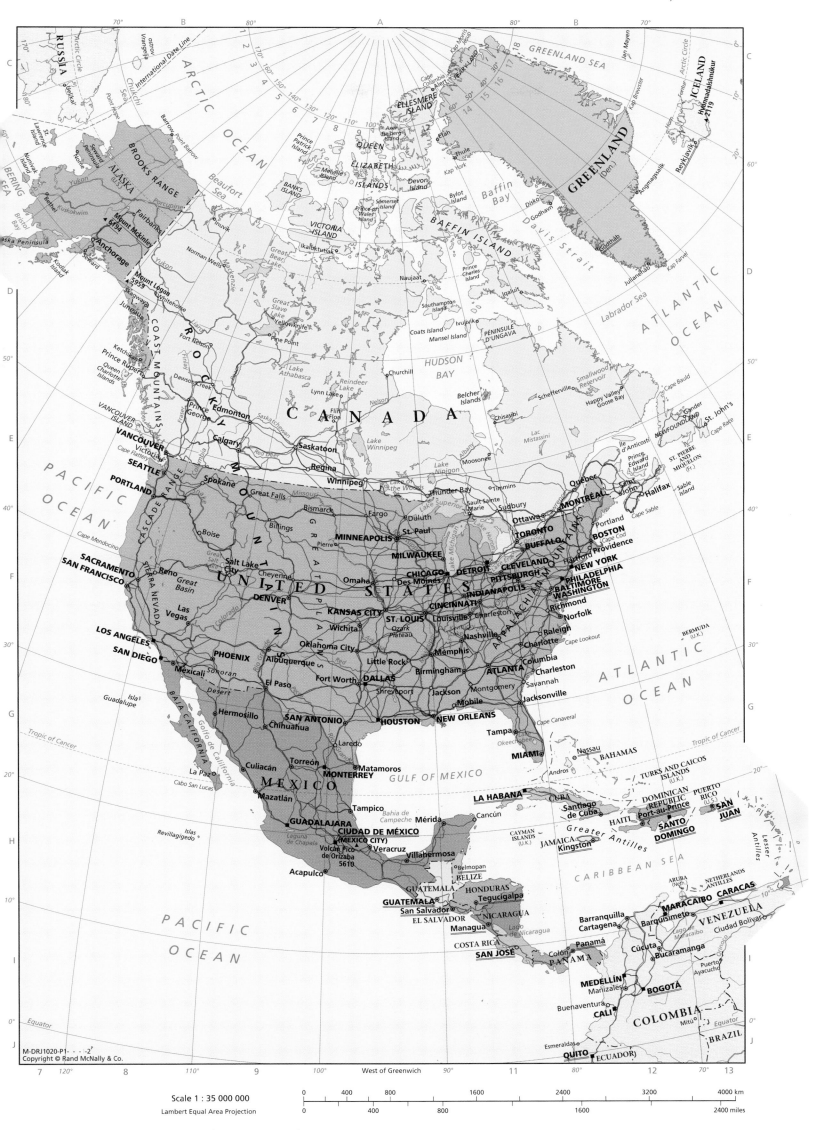

Scale 1 : 35 000 000

Lambert Equal Area Projection

0	400	800	1600	2400	3200	4000 km

0	400	800	1600	2400 miles

PACIFIC OCEAN

Gulf of Mex

UNITED STATES

MEXICO

GUATEMALA

EL SALVADOR

Metres
Feet

4000
13120

3000
9840

2000
6560

1000
3280

500
1640

200
656

0
Sea Level

200
656

2000
6560

M-530000-7A-DR1-1
Copyright © Rand McNally & Co.

| 0 | 200 | 400 | | 800 | | 1200 | | 1600 km |

| 0 | 100 | 200 | 300 | 400 | 600 | | 800 | 1000 miles |

Scale 1 : 15 000 000
Lambert Conformal Conic Projection

West of Greenwich

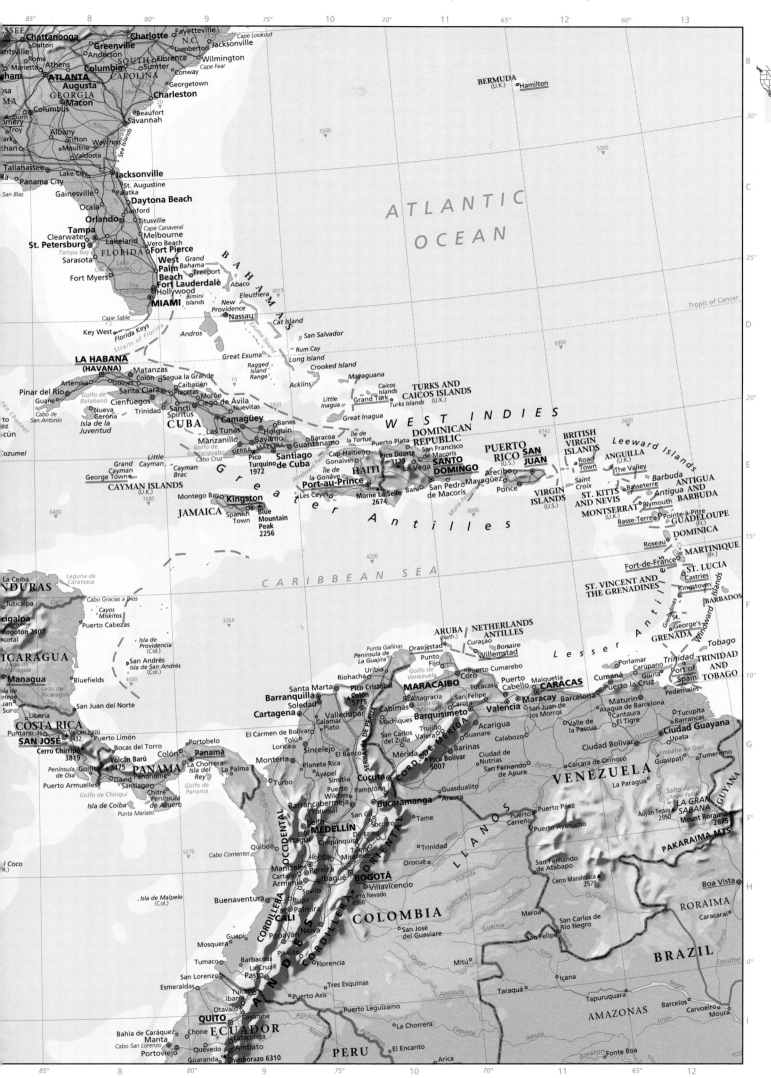

ATLANTIC
OCEAN

BERMUDA
(U.K.)   Hamilton

Tropic of Cancer

BAHAMAS

Chattanooga
Charlotte
Greenville
Anderson
Columbia
SOUTH
CAROLINA
Florence
Sumter
Wilmington
Cape Fear
N.C.
Fayetteville
Jacksonville
Cape Lookout
Rome
Athens
Marietta
ATLANTA
Augusta
GEORGIA
Macon
Columbus
Beaufort
Savannah
Charleston
Georgetown
Auburn
Albany
Tifton
Moultrie
Waycross
Valdosta
Tallahassee
Lake City
Jacksonville
Panama City
St. Augustine
Palatka
San Blas
Gainesville
Ocala
Daytona Beach
Sanford
Titusville
Orlando
Melbourne
Cape Canaveral
Tampa
Clearwater
Lakeland
Vero Beach
Fort Pierce
St. Petersburg
FLORIDA
West
Palm
Beach
Sarasota
Tampa Bay
Grand
Bahama
Freeport
Fort Myers
Fort Lauderdale
Hollywood
Cape Sable
MIAMI
Bimini
Islands
New
Providence
Nassau
Abaco
Eleuthera
Cat Island
Key West
Florida Keys
Andros
San Salvador
Straits of Florida
Exuma Sound
Great Exuma
Rum Cay
Long Island
Crooked Island
Ragged
Island
Range
Acklins
Mayaguana
LA HABANA
(HAVANA)
Matanzas
Colón
Sagua la Grande
Caibarién
Little
Inagua
Caicos
Islands
Grand Turk
TURKS AND
CAICOS ISLANDS
(U.K.)
Turks Islands
Pinar del Río
Artemisa
Güines
Santa Clara
Placetas
Morón
Ciego de Ávila
Nuevitas
Great Inagua
WEST INDIES
Guane
Golfo de
Batabanó
Nueva
Gerona
Trinidad
Sancti
Spíritus
Camagüey
Banes
Cabo de
San Antonio
Isla de la
Juventud
CUBA
Las Tunas
Holguín
Manzanillo
Bayamo
Baracoa
Île de
la Tortue
Puerto Plata
DOMINICAN
REPUBLIC
Golfo de
Guacanayabo
SIERRA
MAESTRA
Guantánamo
Cap-Haïtien
Gonaïves
San Francisco
de Macorís
BRITISH
VIRGIN
ISLANDS
(U.K.)
ANGUILLA
(U.K.)
Pico
Turquino
1972
Santiago
de Cuba
Pico Duarte
3175
La Vega
PUERTO
RICO
SAN
JUAN
Road
Town
The Valley
Leeward Islands
Grand
Cayman
Cayman
Brac
HAITI
SANTO
DOMINGO
Arecibo
Mayagüez
Barbuda
CAYMAN ISLANDS
(U.K.)
George Town
Port-au-Prince
Île de
la Gonâve
Bani
San Pedro
de Macorís
Ponce
Saint
Croix
ST. KITTS
AND NEVIS
Basseterre
ANTIGUA
Antigua AND
BARBUDA
Montego Bay
Les Cayes
Morne La Selle
2674
VIRGIN
ISLANDS
(U.S.)
Mona Passage
MONTSERRAT
(U.K.)
Plymouth
Basse-Terre
GUADELOUPE
(Fr.)
Pointe-à-Pitre
JAMAICA
Kingston
Spanish
Town
Blue
Mountain
Peak
2256
Greater
Antilles
Roseau
DOMINICA
MARTINIQUE
(Fr.)
La Ceiba
Laguna de
Caratasca
CARIBBEAN SEA
Fort-de-France
ST. LUCIA
Castries
NDURAS
Juticalpa
Coco
Cabo Gracias a Dios
Cayos
Miskitos
Puerto Cabezas
ST. VINCENT AND
THE GRENADINES
Kingstown
BARBADOS
Windward Islands
cigalpa
Mogotón 2107
ocal
Isla de
Providencia
(Col.)
3264
NETHERLANDS
ANTILLES
ARUBA
(Neth.)
Oranjestad
Curaçao
Bonaire
Willemstad
George's
GRENADA
Lesser Antilles
Grenadines
St.
Tobago
ICARAGUA
San Andrés
Isla de San Andrés
(Col.)
Bluefields
Punta Gallinas
Península de
La Guajira
Punto
Fijo
Golfo de
Venezuela
Puerto Cumarebo
Coro
Tucacas
Puerto
Cabello
Maiquetía
Porlamar
Cumaná
Carúpano
Güiria
Trinidad
Port of
Spain
TRINIDAD
AND
TOBAGO
Managua
la de
tepe
Lago de
Nicaragua
San Juan del Norte
Uribia
Ríohacha
Santa Marta
Barranquilla
Soledad
Pico Cristóbal
Colón
5775
Altagracia
MARACAIBO
Lago de
Maracaibo
Cabimas
San Felipe
Carora
Valencia
Maracay
Barcelona
San Juan de
los Morros
Barquisimeto
Valera
Acarigua
CARACAS
Puerto la Cruz
Maturín
Aragua de Barcelona
El Tigre
Pedernales
Tucupita
Barrancas
Costa Rica
Liberia
Puntarenas
Puerto Limón
Volcán Irazú
3432
Cartagena
El Carmen de Bolívar
Tolú
Valledupar
Plato
Machiques
San Carlos
del Zulia
Trujillo
Mérida
Barinas
Guanare
Calabozo
Ciudad de
Nutrias
San Fernando
de Apure
Valle de
la Pascua
Ciudad Bolívar
Ciudad Guayana
Upata
Guasipati
Tumeremo
SAN JOSÉ
Cerro Chirripó
3819
Bocas del Torro
Colón
PANAMÁ
Sincelejo
El Banco
Pico Bolívar
5007
Apure
Caicara del Orinoco
Embalse de Guri
Volcán Barú
3475
Panamónome
Pla Chorrera
Isla del
Rey
Montería
Planeta Rica
Ayapel
Simití
Puerto
Wilches
Pamplona
Cúcuta
Arauca
Guasdualito
Arauca
VENEZUELA
La Paragua
GUYANA
Península
de Osa
David
Santiago
Chitré
Península
de Azuero
La Palma
Turbo
Ayacay
Barrancabermeja
Bucaramanga
Tame
San Fernando
de Atabapo
Salto Ángel
(Angel Falls)
Auyán Tepuy
2950
LA GRAN
SABANA
Mount Roraima
2875
Puerto Armuelles
Golfo de Chiriquí
Isla de Coiba
Punta Mariato
Golfito
Quibdó
Betelu
MEDELLÍN
Itagüí
Yarumal
San Gil
Socorro
Puerto
Carreño
Puerto
Páez
Puerto Ayacucho
PAKARAIMA MTS.
I Coco
R.)
Cabo Corrientes
5276
Manizales
Pereira
Cartago
Armenia
Honda
Miraflores
Chiquinquirá
Duitama
Tunja
Orocué
Meta
Vichada
Cerro Marahuaca
2579
Boa Vista
Buenaventura
CALI
Palmira
Buga
Sevilla
Ibagué
BOGOTÁ
Villavicencio
Trinidad
San Fernando de
Atabapo
Caracaraí
RORAIMA
Mosquera
Guapi
Popayán
Neiva
Cerro Nevado
4560
San José
del Guaviare
Guaviare
Maroa
COLOMBIA
Isla de Malpelo
(Col.)
Barbacoas
La Cruz
Pitalito
Florencia
Tumaco
Pasto
Guainía
Mitú
Iça
Negro
San Carlos de
Río Negro
BRAZIL
San Lorenzo
Tulcán
Ibarra
Otavalo
Esmeraldas
Cayambe
Puerto Asís
Tres Esquinas
Puerto Leguizamo
Taraquá
Tapuruquara
Barcelos
Carveiro
Moura
Equator
QUITO
Bahía de Caráquez
Chone
Latacunga
ECUADOR
Ambato
Quevedo
PERU
Portoviejo
Guaranda
Chimborazo 6310
El Encanto
Arica
Fonte Boa
Cabo San Lorenzo
Manta
AMAZONAS

PACIFIC OCEAN

ISLAS
REVILLAGIGEDO
(Mex.)
Isla San Benedicto
Isla Roca Partida
Isla Socorro
Isla Clarión

BAJA
CALIFORNIA
SUR

BAJA CALIFORNIA

CALIFORNIA
ARIZONA
NEW MEXICO
SONORA
CHIHUAHUA
SINALOA
DURANGO
NAYARIT
JALISCO
COLIMA
ZACATECAS
COAH
U

SAN DIEGO
Tijuana
Mexicali
El Paso
Ciudad Juárez
Hermosillo
Chihuahua
Tucson
Culiacán
Durango
Mazatlán
Torreón
Gómez Palacio
La Paz
Aguascalientes
Zapopan GUADAL
Tlaque
Puerto Vallarta
Manzanillo
COLIMA

Metres
Feet
4000 / 13120
3000 / 9840
2000 / 6560
1000 / 3280
500 / 1640
200 / 656
0 / Sea Level
200 / 656
2000 / 6560

Scale 1 : 8 000 000
Lambert Conformal Conic Projection

W-532000-7A-DR1-2
Copyright © Rand McNally & Co.

West of Greenwich

0   100   200   300   400   600   800 km
0   50   100   150   200   300   400   500 miles

Gulf of Mexico

Bahía de Campeche

Caribbean Sea

Mexican State Abbreviations
AGS = AGUASCALIENTES
TLAX = TLAXCALA
D.F. = DISTRITO FEDERAL

GULF OF MEXICO

PACIFIC OCEAN

MEXICO

YUCATAN PENINSULA

CAMPECHE

QUINTANA ROO

BELIZE

GUATEMALA

HONDURAS

EL SALVADOR

NICARAGUA

COSTA RICA

PANAMA

CUBA

LA HABANA (HAVANA)

JAMAICA

Kingston

CAYMAN ISLANDS (U.K.)

George Town

Metres Feet

4000 13120
3000 9840
2000 6560
1000 3280
500 1640
200 656
Sea Level
200 656
2000 6560

W-530093-7A-DR1-2
Copyright © Rand McNally & Co.

0 100 200 300 400 600 800 km
0 50 100 150 200 300 400 500 miles

Scale 1 : 8 000 000

Lambert Conformal Conic Projection

West of Greenwich

ATLANTIC OCEAN

Tropic of Cancer
6900

BAHAMAS
Samana Cay
Crooked Island
Mayaguana
Acklins
North Caicos
Middle Caicos
East Caicos
Caicos Islands
Grand Turk
Turks Islands
Little Inagua
Matthew Town
Great Inagua
TURKS AND CAICOS ISLANDS (U.K.)

Cap à Foux
Île de la Tortue
HISPANIOLA
Manzanillo Bay
Cabo Isabela
Limbé
Cap-Haïtien
Puerto Plata
Cabo Francés Viejo
Gonaïves
Mao
Santiago de los Caballeros
San Francisco de Macorís
Cabo Samaná
HAITI
Pico Duarte 3175
Moca
La Vega
Sánchez
Saint-Marc
San Juan de la Maguana
Alto Bandera 2630
Higüey
Cabo Engaño
Golfe de la Gonâve
Port-au-Prince
Pétion-Ville
Azua
San Cristóbal
La Romana
Jérémie
Morne La Selle 2674
Bani
Pedro de Macorís
Isla Saona
Isla de Mona
PUERTO RICO (U.S.)
SAN JUAN
Arecibo
Bayamón
Caguas
Ponce
Mayagüez
Cerro de Punta 1338

BRITISH VIRGIN ISLANDS
Anegada
Charlotte Amalie
Road Town
Virgin Gorda
ANGUILLA (U.K.)
The Valley
St. Thomas
St. John
VIRGIN ISLANDS (U.S.)
St. Croix
Virgin Islands
Saint Martin (Fr.-Neth.)
St. Christopher (St. Kitts)
Barbuda
Saba (Neth.)
ST. KITTS AND NEVIS
Nevis
Basseterre
ANTIGUA AND BARBUDA
St. John's
Antigua
MONTSERRAT (U.K.)
Plymouth
Guadeloupe Passage
Grande-Terre
Basse-Terre
GUADELOUPE (Fr.)
Soufrière 1467
Pointe-à-Pitre
Marie Galante
Morne Diablotins 1447
DOMINICA
Roseau
Martinique Passage
Montagne Pelée 1397
Fort-de-France
MARTINIQUE (Fr.)
St. Lucia Channel
Mount Gimie 950
Castries
ST. LUCIA
Soufrière
St. Vincent Passage
ST. VINCENT AND THE GRENADINES
Soufrière 1234
St. Vincent
Kingstown
Mount Hillaby 340
Bridgetown
BARBADOS
Grenadines

LESSER ANTILLES
LEEWARD ISLANDS
WINDWARD ISLANDS
Anegada Passage

C A R I B B E A N   S E A

ARUBA (Neth.)
Oranjestad
NETHERLANDS ANTILLES
Curaçao
Bonaire
Kralendijk
Willemstad
Isla La Orchila
Isla Blanquilla
St. George's
GRENADA
Tobago
Scarborough
LESSER ANTILLES
Punta Gallinas
Puerto Bolívar
Cabo de La Vela
Punta Espada
Península de La Guajira
Uribia
Riohacha
Maicao
Golfo de Venezuela
Coro
Punta Fijo
Puerto Cumarebo
Islas de Aves
Islas Los Roques
Isla de Margarita
La Asunción
Porlamar
Isla La Tortuga
Pen. de Paria
Punta Piedras
Port of Spain
TRINIDAD AND TOBAGO
Santa Marta
Barranquilla
Uribia
Península de Paraguaná
Carúpano
Güiria
Arima
Trinidad
San Fernando
Río Claro
Point Fortin
Pico Cristóbal Colón 5775
MARACAIBO
La Concepción
Santa Rita
Ciudad Ojeda
Altagracia
Dabajuro
Churuguara
Tucacas
Maiquetía
CARACAS
Cumaná
Barcelona
Pozuelos
Puerto la Cruz
Boca de la Serpiente
Valledupar
Agustín Codazzi
Machiques
Cabimas
San Felipe
Puerto Cabello
La Victoria
Guarenas
Maracay
Chivacoa
Cúa
Ocumare del Tuy
Caripito
Maturín
Pedernales
Cerro Mu 2610
Ciénaga de Zapatosa
Paillas
Cerro Turimiquire 2596
Valencia
Cerro 1990
Barquisimeto
Valera
San Carlos
Tinaquillo
Tinaco
El Sombrero
Chaguaramas
Aragua de Barcelona
Anaco
Cantaura
Guanipa
Tucupita
DELTA DEL ORINOCO
Isla Tobejuba
Boca Grande
Corocoro Island
Gamarra
Aguachica
Simití
Ocaña
San Juan de Colón
Mene Grande
San Carlos del Zulia
Trujillo
Guanare
Calabozo
Valle de la Pascua
El Tigre
San José de Guanipa
Barrancas
Morawhanna
Encontrados
Mérida
Barinas
Ciudad Guayana
Upata
Pico Bolívar 5070
VENEZUELA
Ciudad Bolívar
Cúcuta
San Cristóbal
Ciudad de Nutrias
San Fernando de Apure
Caicara de Orinoco
Cabruta
Embalse de Guri
Guasipati
Matthews Ridge
Pamplona
Bucaramanga
Floridablanca
Guasdualito
Arauca
Elorza
Santa Rosa
La Urbana
Cerro Mato 1863
Cerro Bolívar 802
Ciudad Piar
El Callao
Tumeremo
Puerto Wilches
Riohacha
Arauca
Puerto Páez
La Paragua
El Dorado
GUYANA
COLOMBIA
San Gil
Socorro
Málaga
Tame
Casanare
Puerto Rondón
Meta
Puerto Carreño
Nueva Antioquia
Canaima
Salto Ángel Angel Fall
Piedecuesta
Barbosa
Duitama
Sogamoso
Yopal
Trinidad
Cerro Yaví 2441
Auyán Tepuy 2950
La Gran Sabana
Mount Roraima 2875
Villavicencio
Puerto López
Orocué
Puerto Nariño
Puerto Ayacucho
Arabelo
Iru Tepuy 2620
BOGOTÁ
Cerro Nevado 4560
San Martín
Granada
San Fernando de Atabapo
RORAIMA
Cerro Uquía 2500
BRAZIL
PAKARAIMA MOUNTAINS

ATLANTIC OCEAN
8742
7600
6900
6000
4200

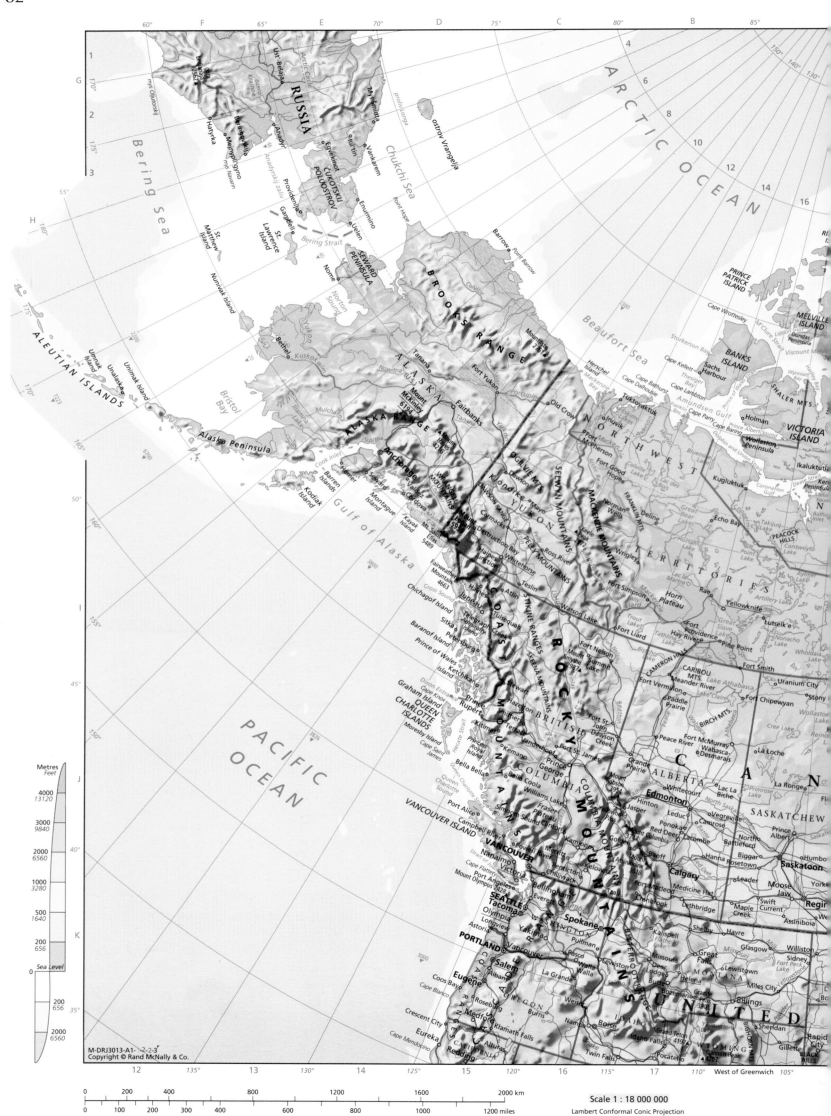

ARCTIC OCEAN

RUSSIA

Bering Sea

ALEUTIAN ISLANDS

BROOKS RANGE

ALASKA (U.S.)

Mount McKinley 6194

ALASKA RANGE

Gulf of Alaska

PACIFIC OCEAN

Beaufort Sea

PRINCE PATRICK ISLAND

BANKS ISLAND

VICTORIA ISLAND

MELVILLE ISLAND

NORTHWEST TERRITORIES

YUKON

MACKENZIE MOUNTAINS

OGILVIE MTS

SELWYN MOUNTAINS

ROCKY MOUNTAINS

BRITISH COLUMBIA

ALBERTA

SASKATCHEWAN

CANADA

COAST MOUNTAINS

QUEEN CHARLOTTE ISLANDS

VANCOUVER ISLAND

VANCOUVER

SEATTLE
Tacoma

PORTLAND

Salem

Eugene

Spokane

WASHINGTON

OREGON

IDAHO

MONTANA

WYOMING

UNITED STATES

Edmonton

Calgary

Saskatoon

Metres
Feet
4000 13120
3000 9840
2000 6560
1000 3280
500 1640
200 656
0 Sea Level
200 656
2000 6560

M-DRJ3013-A1- -2-2-3
Copyright © Rand McNally & Co.

0 200 400   800   1200   1600   2000 km
0 100 200 300 400   600   800   1000   1200 miles

Scale 1 : 18 000 000
Lambert Conformal Conic Projection

West of Greenwich

GREENLAND (Den.)

ICELAND
FAROE ISLANDS (Den.)
Tórshavn
Reykjavík
Akureyri
Ísafjörður
Vestmannaeyjar

Greenland Sea
Denmark Strait
Arctic Circle

ELLESMERE ISLAND
Barbeau Peak 2616
Cape Columbia
Alert
Peary Land
Lincoln Sea

AXEL HEIBERG ISLAND

DEVON ISLAND
Coburg Island
Cape Parker
Philpots Island
Cape Sherard

Thule (Qaanaaq)
Kap York
Etah

SOMERSET ISLAND
Cornwallis Island
Barrow Strait
Lancaster Sound
Jones Sound
Lady Ann Strait

BOOTHIA PENINSULA
BRODEUR PENINSULA
Borden Peninsula
Tununirusiq
Mittimatalik
Bylot Island

Baffin Bay
Davis Strait

BAFFIN ISLAND

Upernavik
Umanak
Qutdligssat
Disko
Godhavn
Egedesminde
Sukkertoppen
Godthåb (Nuuk)
Holsteinsborg
Strømfjord

Frederikshåb
Julianehåb
Kap Farvel

Labrador Sea

MELVILLE PENINSULA
Prince Charles Island
Air Force Island
Foxe Basin

Igloolik
Hall Peninsula
Iqaluit
Frobisher Bay
Resolution Island

FOXE PENINSULA
META INCOGNITA PENINSULA
Cumberland Peninsula
Pangnirtung
Cumberland Sound

Naujaat
Kinngait
Kimmirut
Cape Dorchester
Vansittart Island
Foxe Channel

NUNAVUT

SOUTHAMPTON ISLAND
Salliq
Coats Island
Mansel Island

Killiniq Island
Mount Caubvick 1652
Hebron
Nain
South Aulatsivik Island
Hopedale

PÉNINSULE D'UNGAVA
Kangirsuk
Ungava Bay
Kuujjuaq
Mont d'Iberville

NEWFOUNDLAND AND LABRADOR

Hudson Bay
All islands within Hudson Bay, James Bay, and Ungava Bay lie within Nunavut.

Arviat
Churchill
Cape Churchill

King George Islands
Belcher Islands

Povungnituk
Inukjuak
Hopewell Islands
Whapmagoostui

Happy Valley-Goose Bay
Cartwright
Battle Harbour
Belle Isle
St. Anthony
Grey Islands
Fogo Island
Gander
Bonavista
St. John's
Carbonear
Cape Race

Smallwood Reservoir
Schefferville
Labrador City
Churchill Falls

LONG RANGE MOUNTAINS
NEWFOUNDLAND
Corner Brook
Stephenville
Channel-Port aux Basques
SAINT PIERRE AND MIQUELON (Fr.)

MANITOBA
Norway House
Lake Winnipeg
Grand Rapids
Berens River

York Factory
Fort Severn
Winisk
Gillam
Wabowden

ONTARIO
QUÉBEC
MONTS OTISH

Sept-Îles
Gaspé
ÎLE D'ANTICOSTI
Gulf of St. Lawrence
Baie-Comeau
Matane
Rimouski

Chisasibi
Waskaganish
Eastmain
Attawapiskat
Fort Albany
Moosonee
James Bay
Akimiski Island
Charlton Island

Chibougamau
LAURENTIDES
Québec
Trois-Rivières
Shawinigan
Jonquière
Chicoutimi
Alma
NEW BRUNSWICK
Fredericton
Edmundston
Bathurst
Moncton
Saint John
NOVA SCOTIA
Halifax
Dartmouth
Liverpool
Yarmouth
Digby
PRINCE EDWARD ISLAND
Charlottetown
Sydney
New Glasgow
Glace Bay
CAPE BRETON ISLAND
Sable Island

Winnipeg
Selkirk
Gimli
Kenora
Dryden
Sioux Lookout
Red Lake
Pickle Lake
Armstrong
Geraldton
Hearst
Kapuskasing
Cochrane
Timmins
Val-d'Or
Rouyn-Noranda
La Sarre
Maniwaki
Ottawa
Hull
North Bay
Sudbury
Sault Sainte Marie
Elliot Lake
Wawa
Chapleau
New Liskeard
Pembroke
Peterborough
Belleville
Kingston
TORONTO
Hamilton
Kitchener
London
Windsor
Sarnia

Lake Superior
Lake Huron
Lake Michigan
Lake Erie
Lake Ontario

Thunder Bay
Atikokan
Fort Frances
International Falls
Duluth
Superior
Ironwood
Marquette
Escanaba
Green Bay
Appleton
Sheboygan
Milwaukee
Madison
La Crosse
MINNEAPOLIS
St. Paul
Eau Claire
Wausau
Marinette
MICHIGAN
WISCONSIN
MINNESOTA
Rochester
Fargo
Aberdeen
SOUTH DAKOTA
Sioux Falls
Bemidji
Brainerd
Moorhead
Grand Forks
Devils Lake

CHICAGO
Gary
Rockford
Flint
DETROIT
Grand Rapids
Lansing
Toledo
Buffalo
Rochester
Syracuse
Albany
Binghamton
Scranton
NEW YORK
NEWARK
NEW JERSEY
PHILADELPHIA
Trenton
New Haven
Hartford
MASSACHUSETTS
BOSTON
Providence
Cape Cod
Portland
Portsmouth
Concord
Augusta
Bangor
MAINE
Burlington
Montpelier
Sherbrooke
MONTRÉAL
Ottawa

Gulf of Maine

ATLANTIC OCEAN

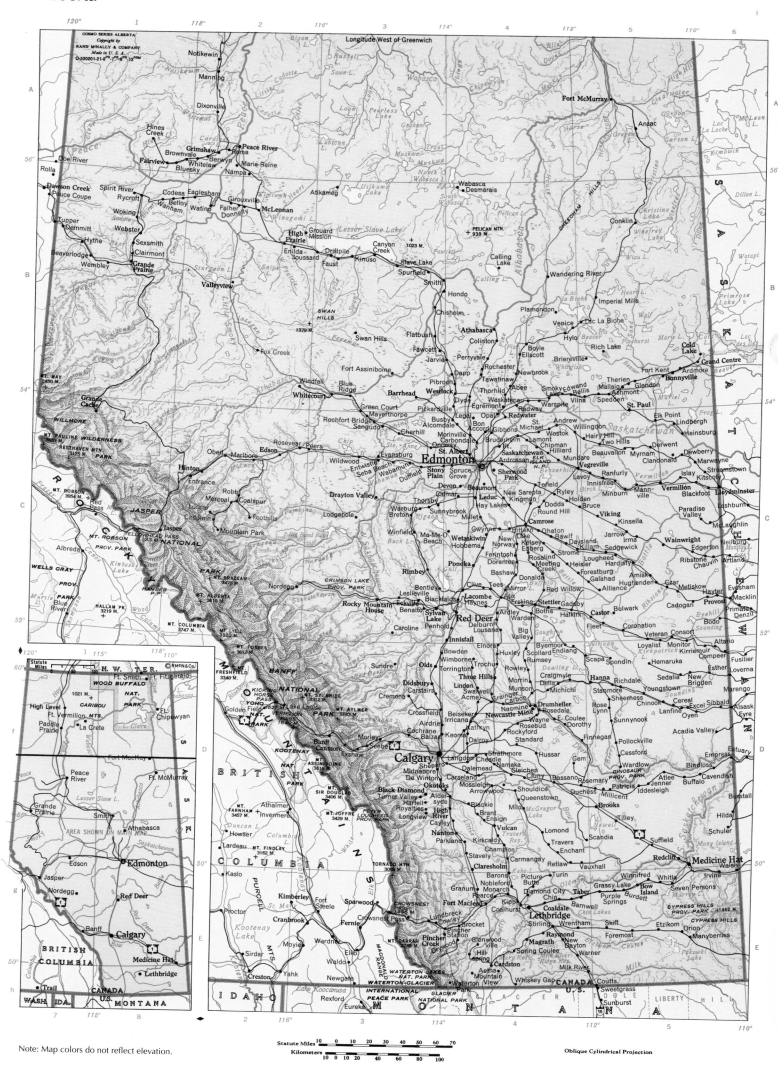

Longitude West of Greenwich

Note: Map colors do not reflect elevation.

Statute Miles 10   0   10   20   30   40   50   60   70
Kilometers 10 0 10 20 40   60   80   100

Oblique Cylindrical Projection

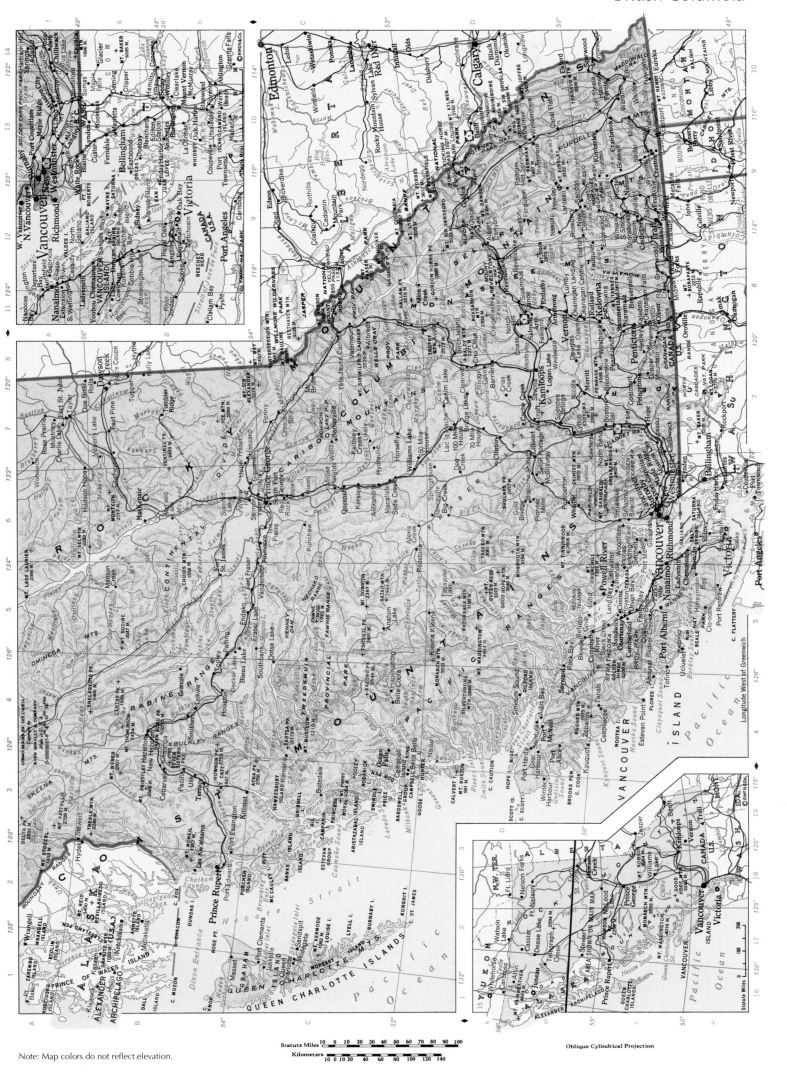

Note: Map colors do not reflect elevation.

Statute Miles 10 0 10 20 30 40 50 60 70 80 90 100
Kilometers 10 0 10 20 40 60 80 100 120 140

Oblique Cylindrical Projection

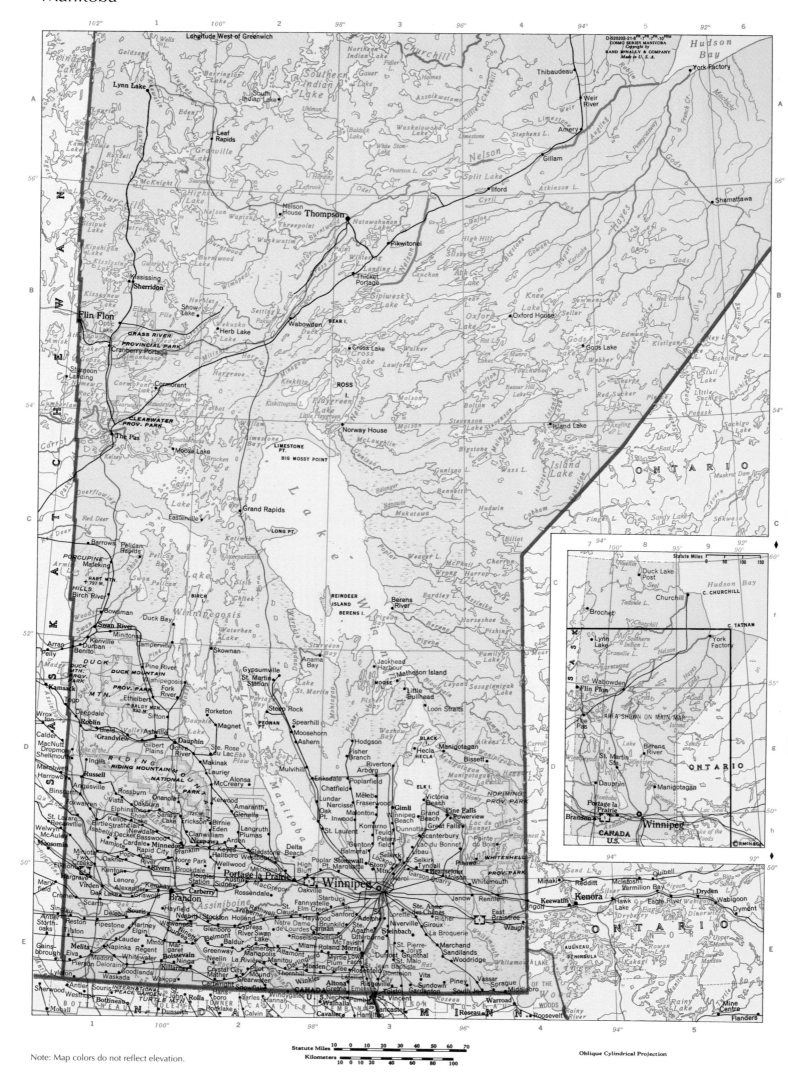

Note: Map colors do not reflect elevation.

Statute Miles 10   0 10 20 30 40 50 60 70
Kilometers 10 0 10 20   40   60   80   100

Oblique Cylindrical Projection

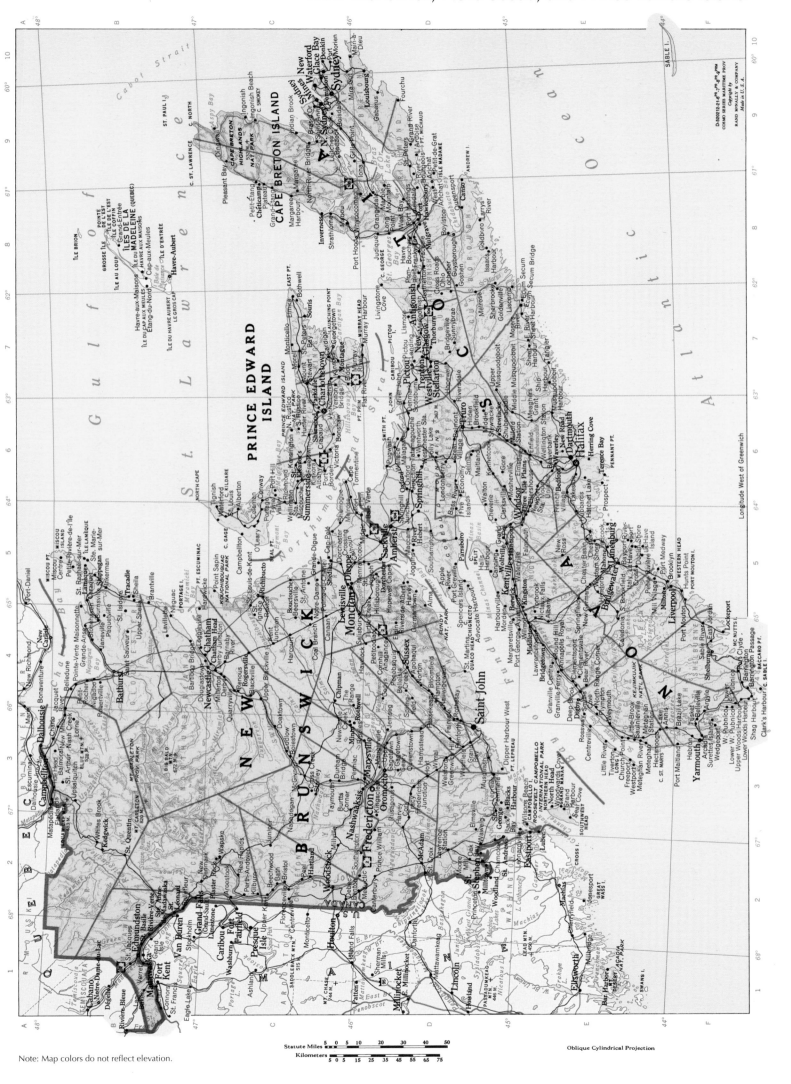

Note: Map colors do not reflect elevation.

Statute Miles 5 0 5 10   20   30   40   50
Kilometers 5 0 5 15 25 35 45 55 65 75

Oblique Cylindrical Projection

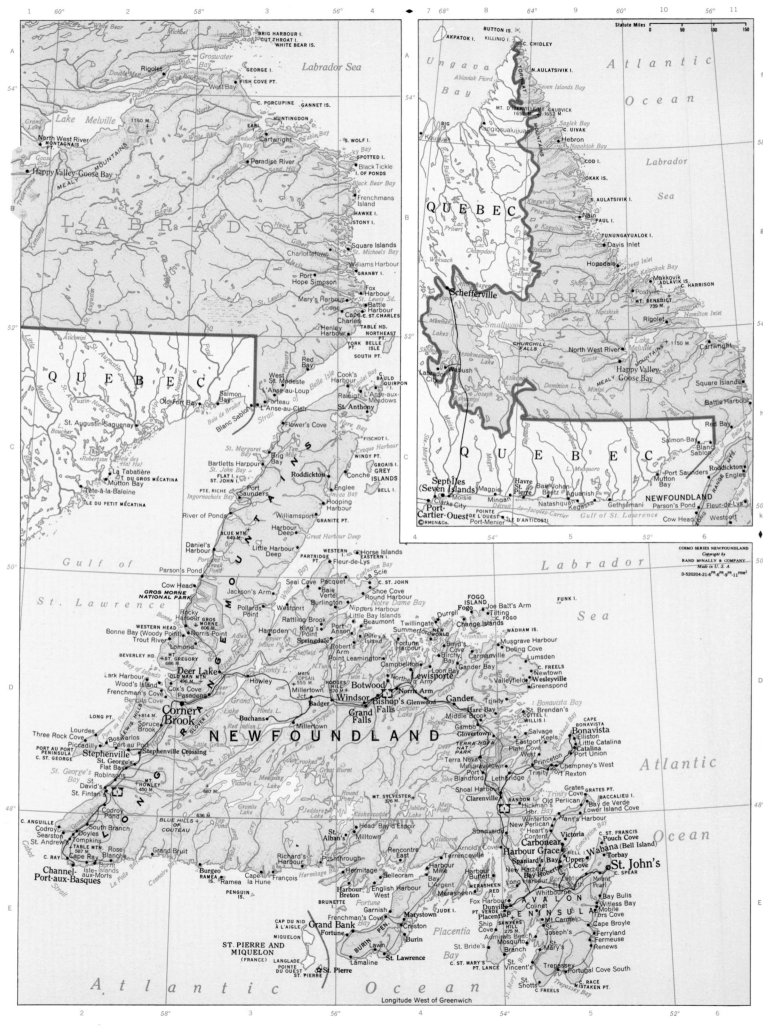

Note: Map colors do not reflect elevation.

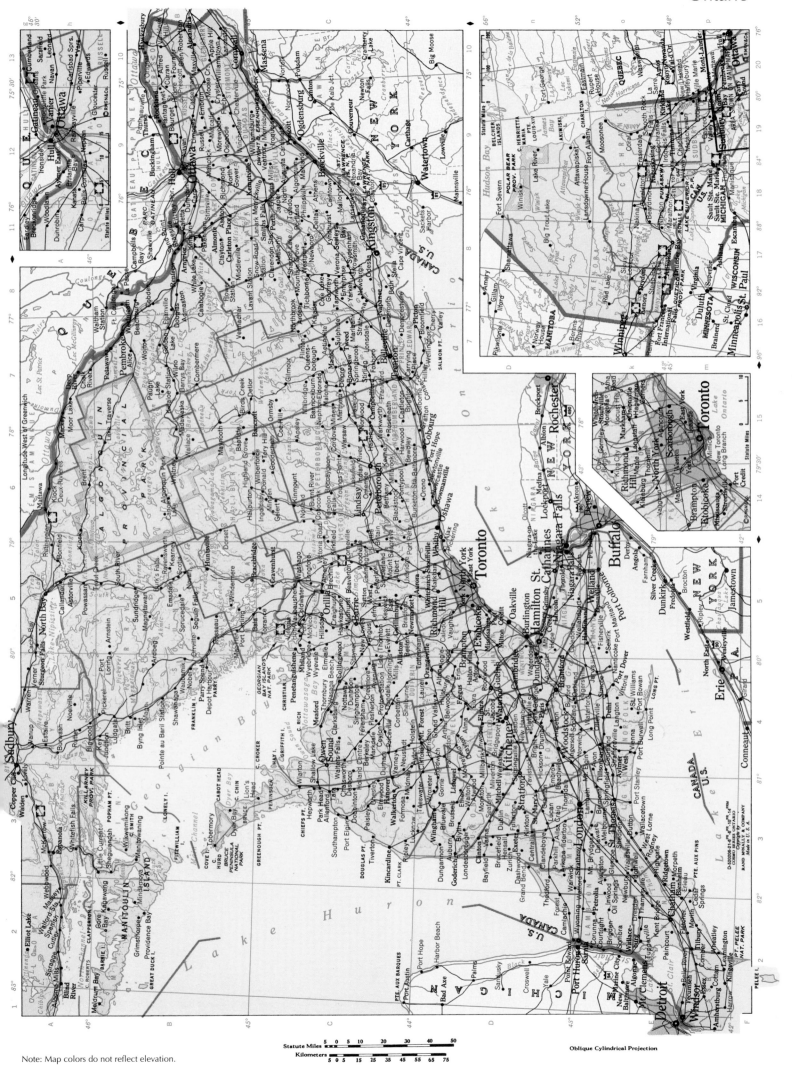

Note: Map colors do not reflect elevation.

Statute Miles 5 0 5 10 20 30 40 50
Kilometers 5 0 5 15 25 35 45 55 65 75

Oblique Cylindrical Projection

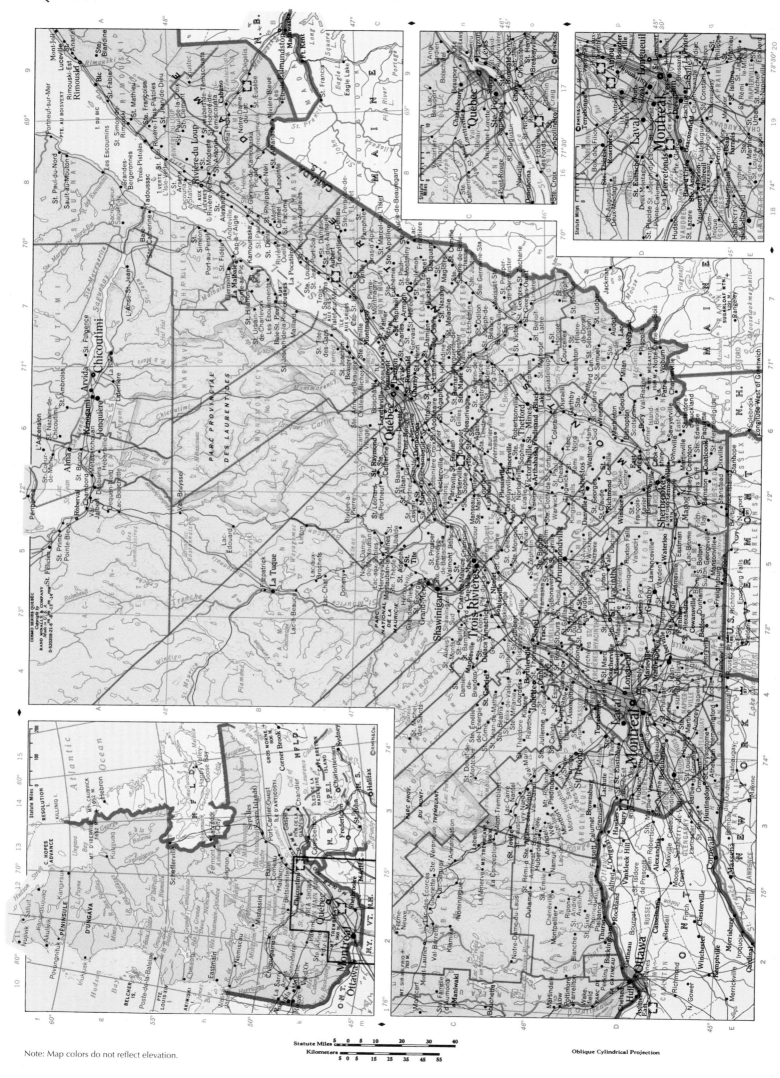

Note: Map colors do not reflect elevation.

Statute Miles 5 0 5 10   20   30   40
Kilometers 5 0 5 15 25 35 45 55

Oblique Cylindrical Projection

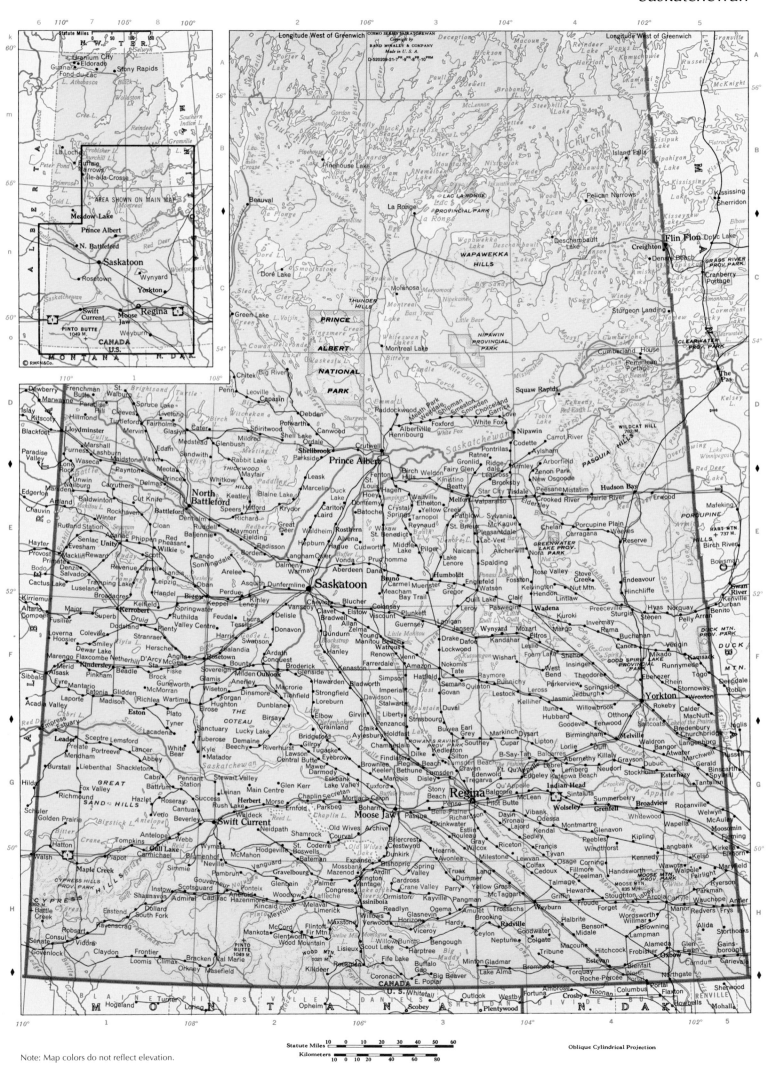

Note: Map colors do not reflect elevation.

Statute Miles
Kilometers

Oblique Cylindrical Projection

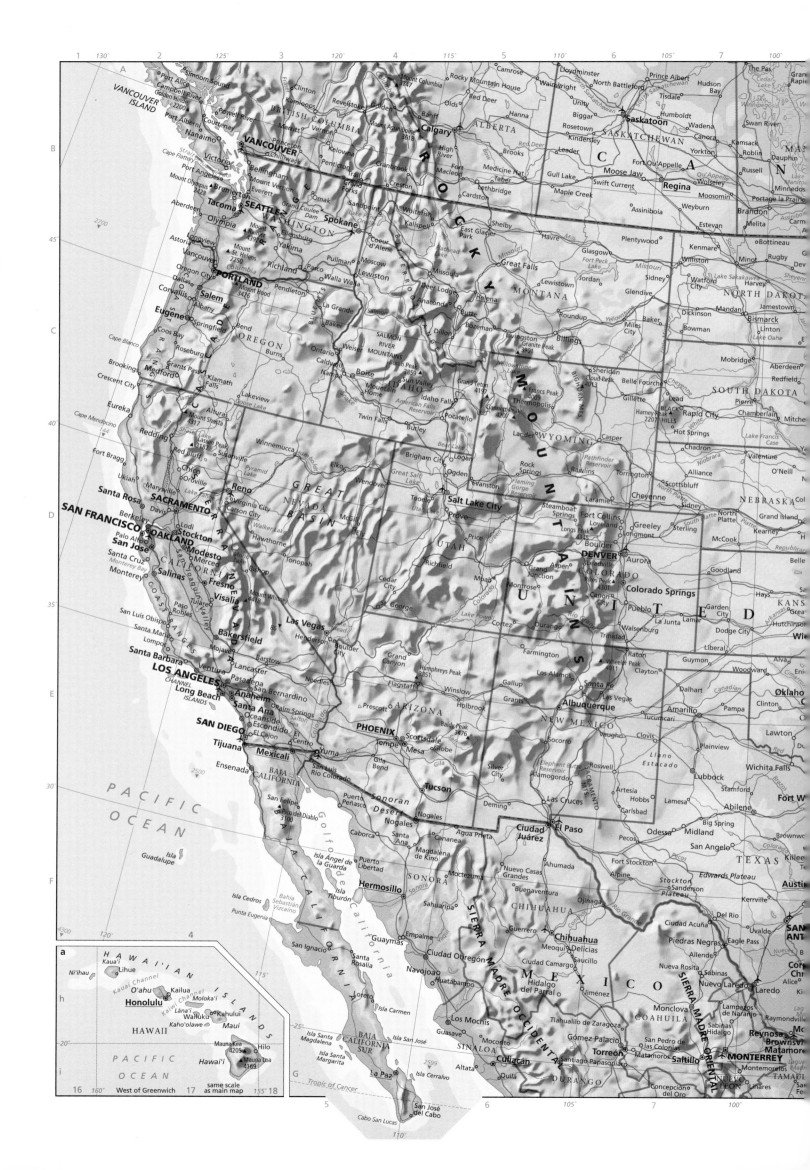

ONTARIO
QUÉBEC
MINNESOTA
WISCONSIN
MICHIGAN
IOWA
ILLINOIS
INDIANA
OHIO
MISSOURI
KENTUCKY
WEST VIRGINIA
VIRGINIA
TENNESSEE
NORTH CAROLINA
SOUTH CAROLINA
ARKANSAS
MISSISSIPPI
ALABAMA
GEORGIA
LOUISIANA
FLORIDA
PENNSYLVANIA
NEW YORK
MARYLAND
DELAWARE
NEW JERSEY
MAINE
VERMONT
N.H.
CONN.
R.I.
NEW BRUNSWICK

UNITED STATES

MINNEAPOLIS St. Paul
MILWAUKEE
CHICAGO
DETROIT
CLEVELAND
PITTSBURGH
NEW YORK
NEWARK
PHILADELPHIA
BALTIMORE
WASHINGTON
INDIANAPOLIS
CINCINNATI
ST. LOUIS
KANSAS CITY
MEMPHIS
NASHVILLE
ATLANTA
BIRMINGHAM
NEW ORLEANS
JACKSONVILLE
MIAMI
BOSTON
MONTRÉAL
TORONTO
OTTAWA
QUÉBEC

ATLANTIC OCEAN

Gulf of Mexico

Gulf of Maine

BAHAMAS

CUBA

Lake Superior
Lake Huron
Lake Michigan
Lake Erie
Lake Ontario

James Bay

Tropic of Cancer

Straits of Florida

Mississippi Delta

Chesapeake Bay
Delaware Bay

Cape Cod
Cape Hatteras
Cape Canaveral
Cape Sable
Key West

Metres
Feet
4000
13120
3000
9840
2000
6560
1000
3280
500
1640
200
656
Sea Level 0
200
656
2000
6560

Scale 1 : 12 000 000
Lambert Conformal Conic Projection

West of Greenwich

0   200   400   800   1200 km
0   100   200   400   600   800 miles

M-DRJ3023-A1-3
Copyright © Rand McNally & Co.

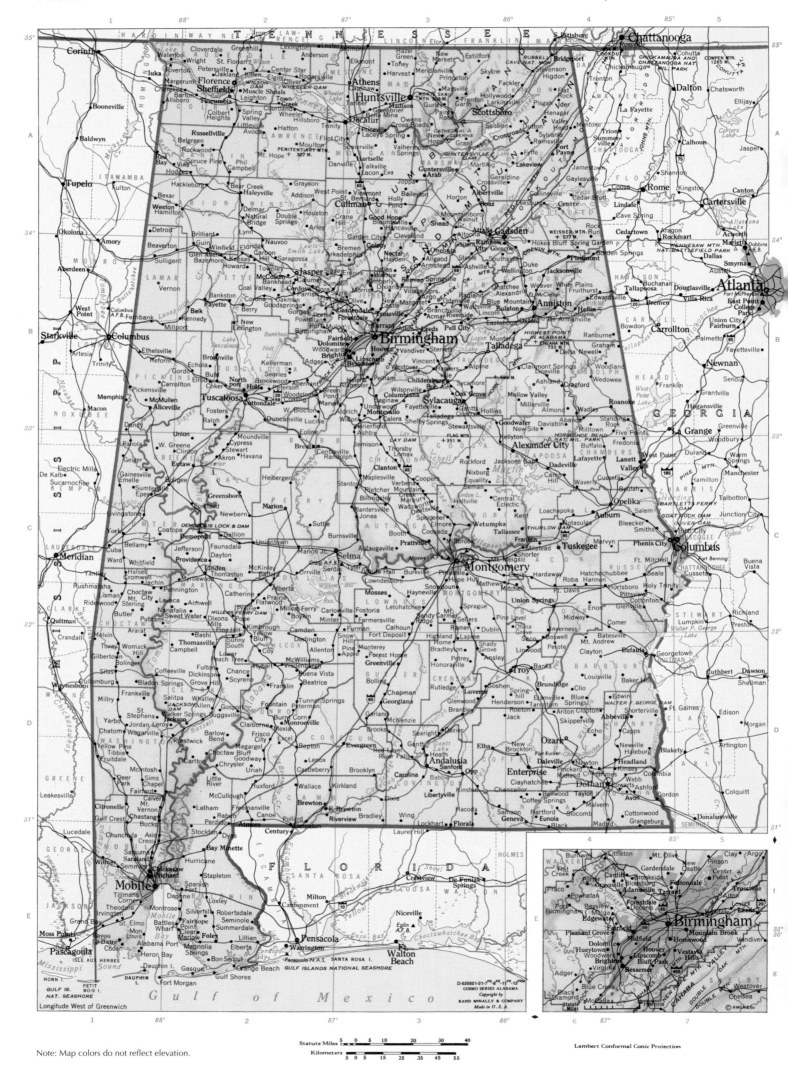

Note: Map colors do not reflect elevation.

Statute Miles 5 0 5 10 20 30 40
Kilometers 5 0 5 15 25 35 45 55

Lambert Conformal Conic Projection

D-520501-21-7⁷⁸-8⁸²-11⁷⁹-13⁹⁶
COSMO SERIES ALABAMA
Copyright by
RAND M⁰NALLY & COMPANY
Made in U. S. A.

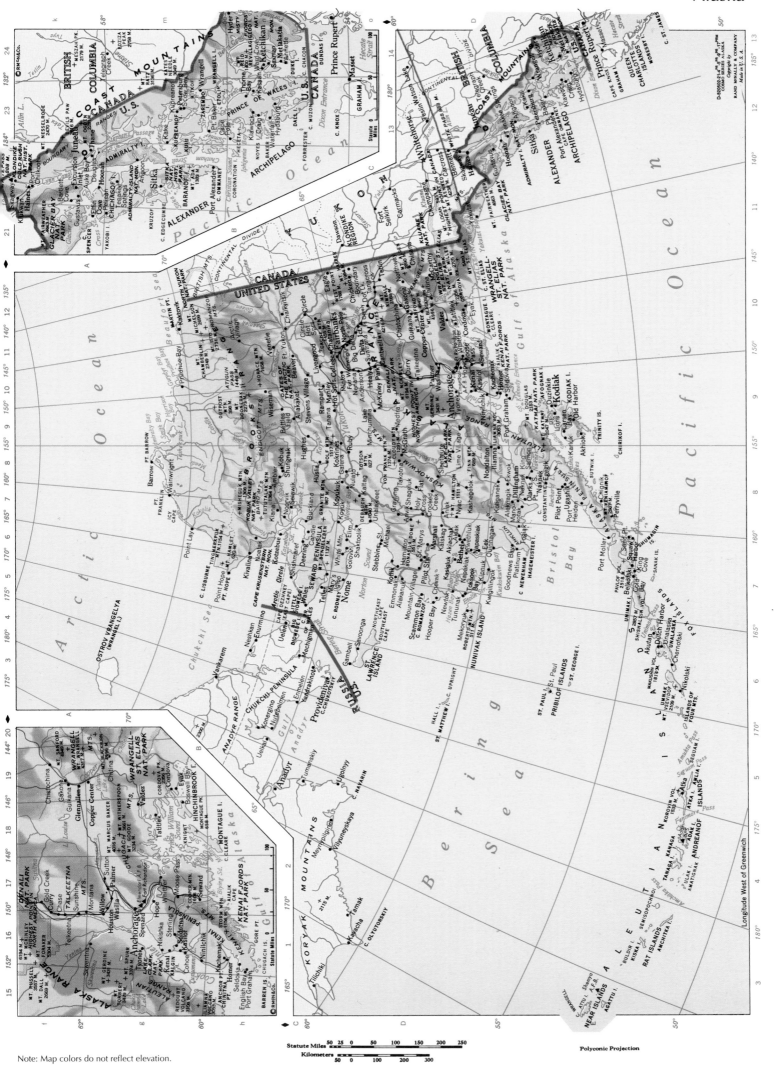

Note: Map colors do not reflect elevation.

Statute Miles 50 25 0   50   100   150   200   250
Kilometers 50 0   100   200   300

Polyconic Projection

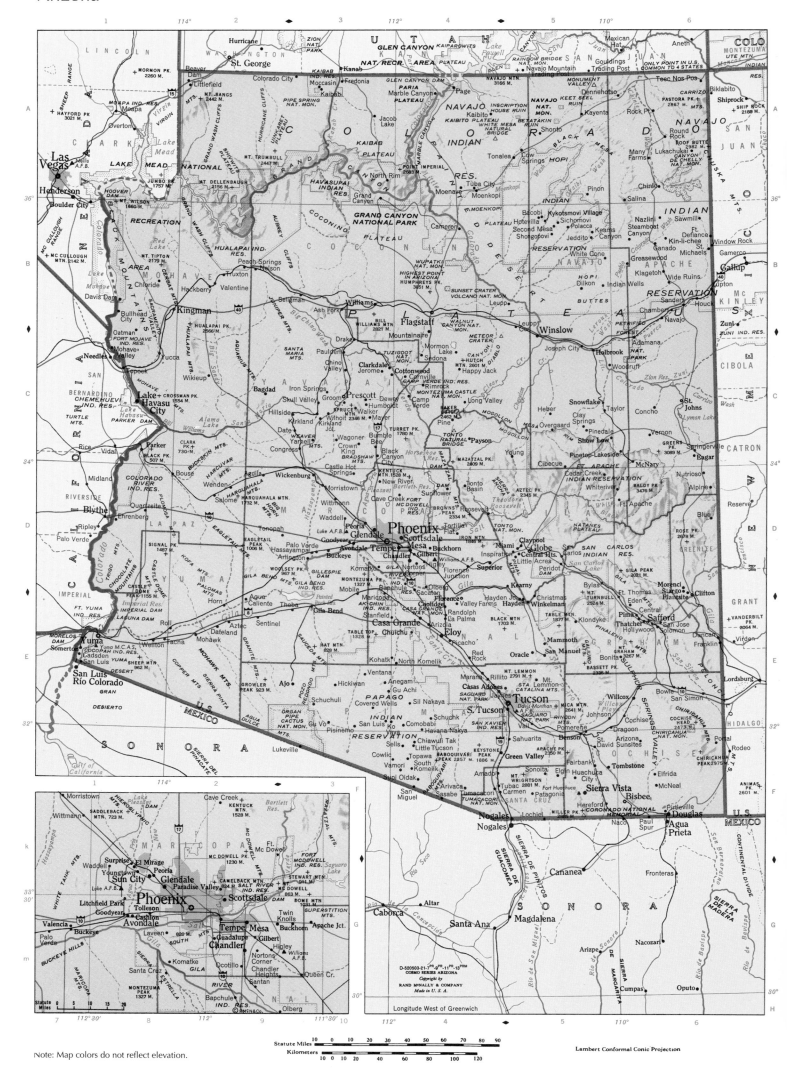

Note: Map colors do not reflect elevation.

Statute Miles
Kilometers

Lambert Conformal Conic Projection

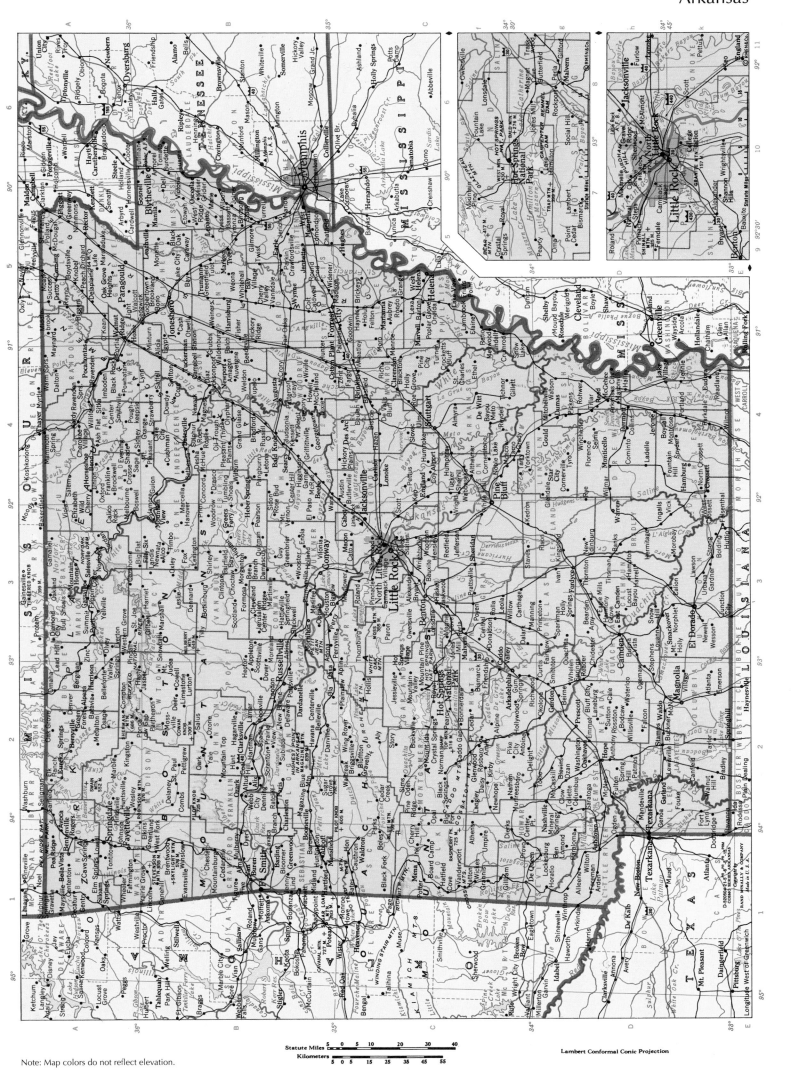

Note: Map colors do not reflect elevation.

Statute Miles   5 0 5 10   20   30   40
Kilometers   5 0 5 15   25   35   45   55

Lambert Conformal Conic Projection

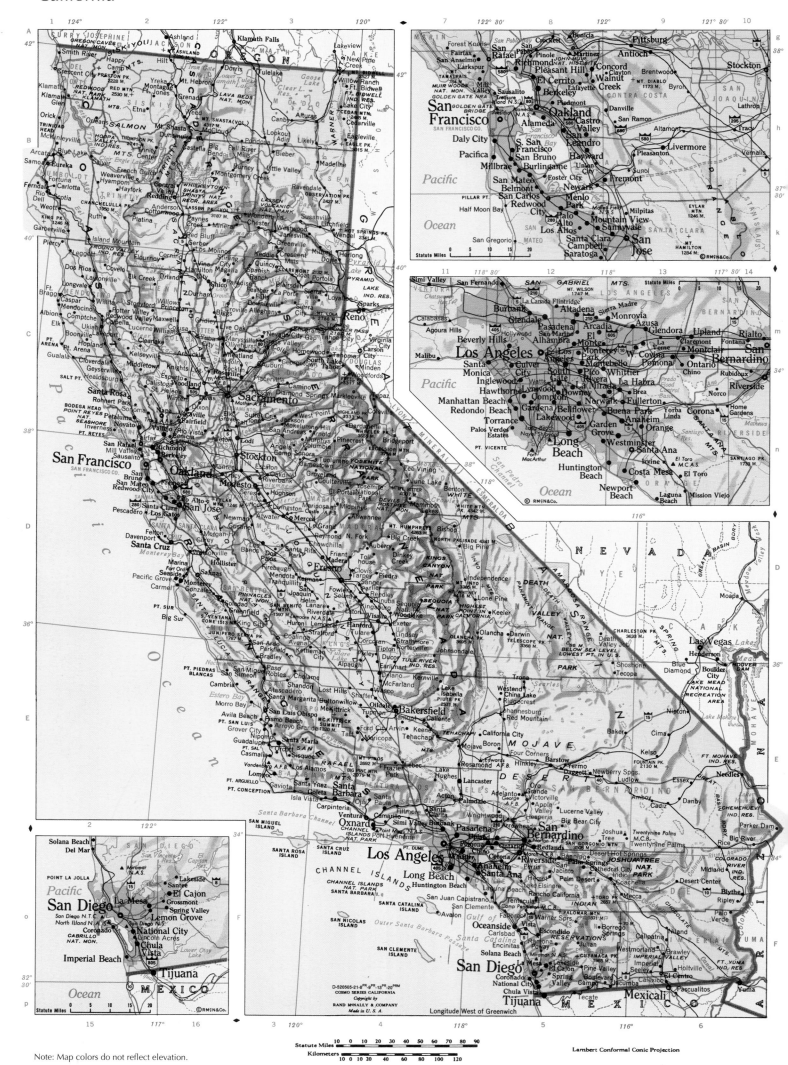

Note: Map colors do not reflect elevation.

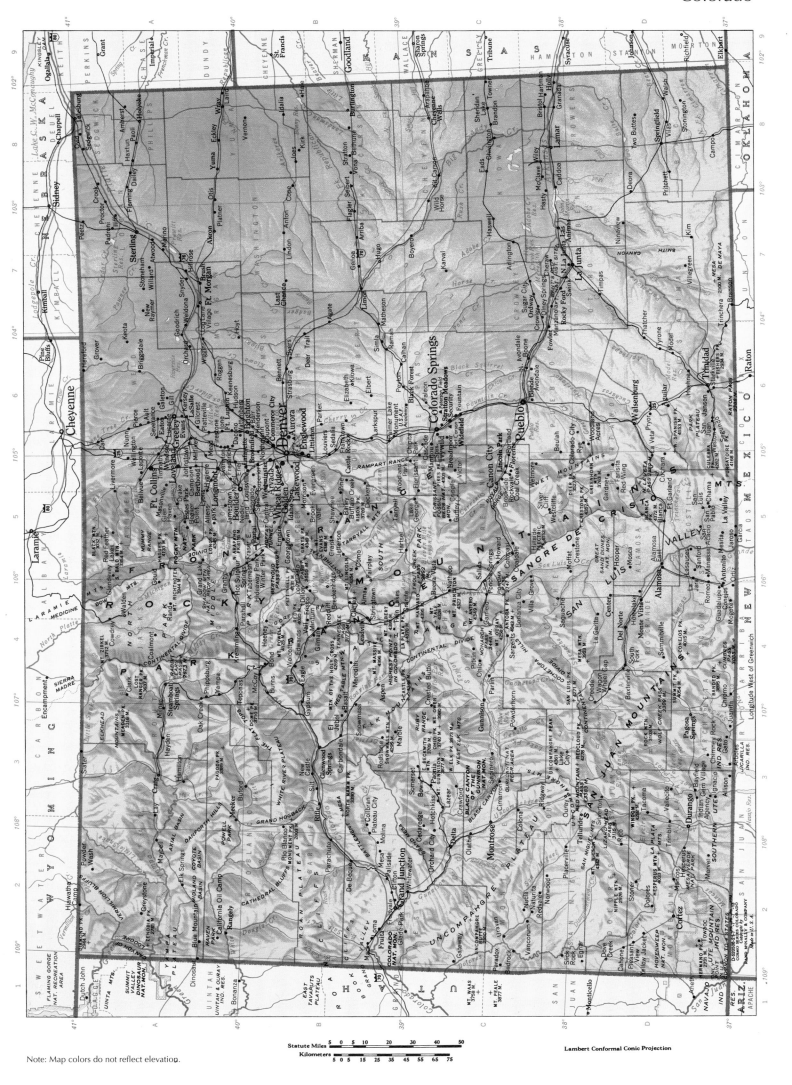

Note: Map colors do not reflect elevation.

Statute Miles 5 0 5 10   20   30   40   50
Kilometers 5 0 5 15 25 35 45 55 65 75

Lambert Conformal Conic Projection

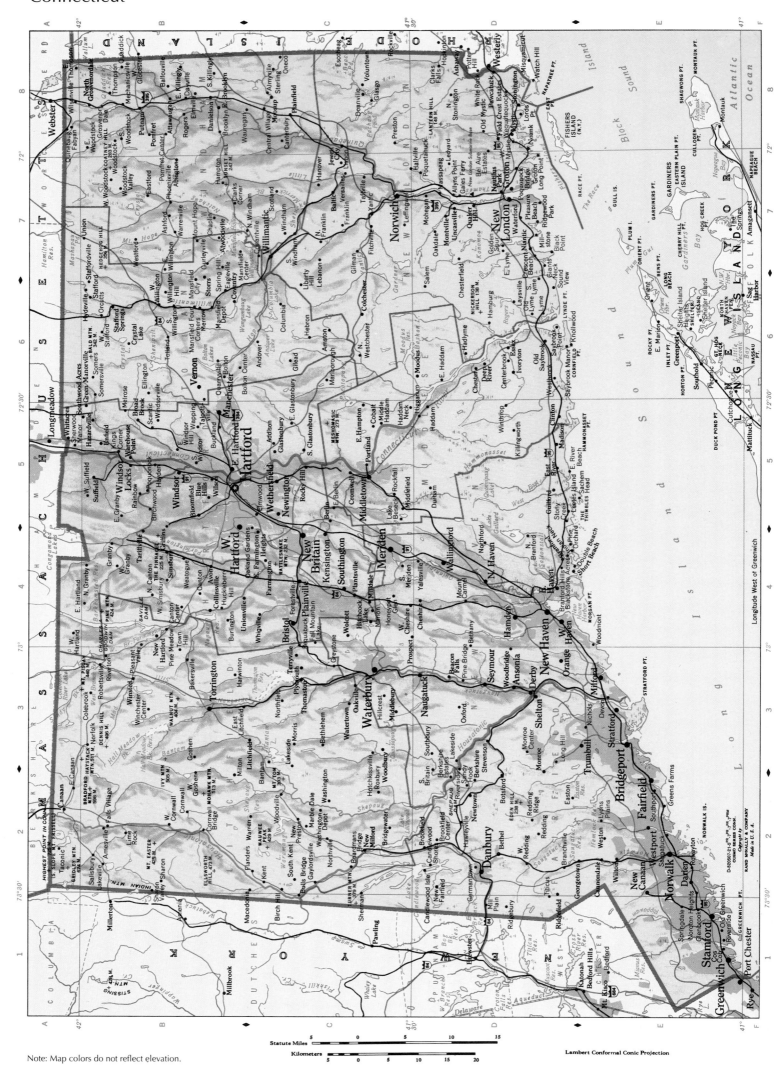

Note: Map colors do not reflect elevation.

Statute Miles

Kilometers

Lambert Conformal Conic Projection

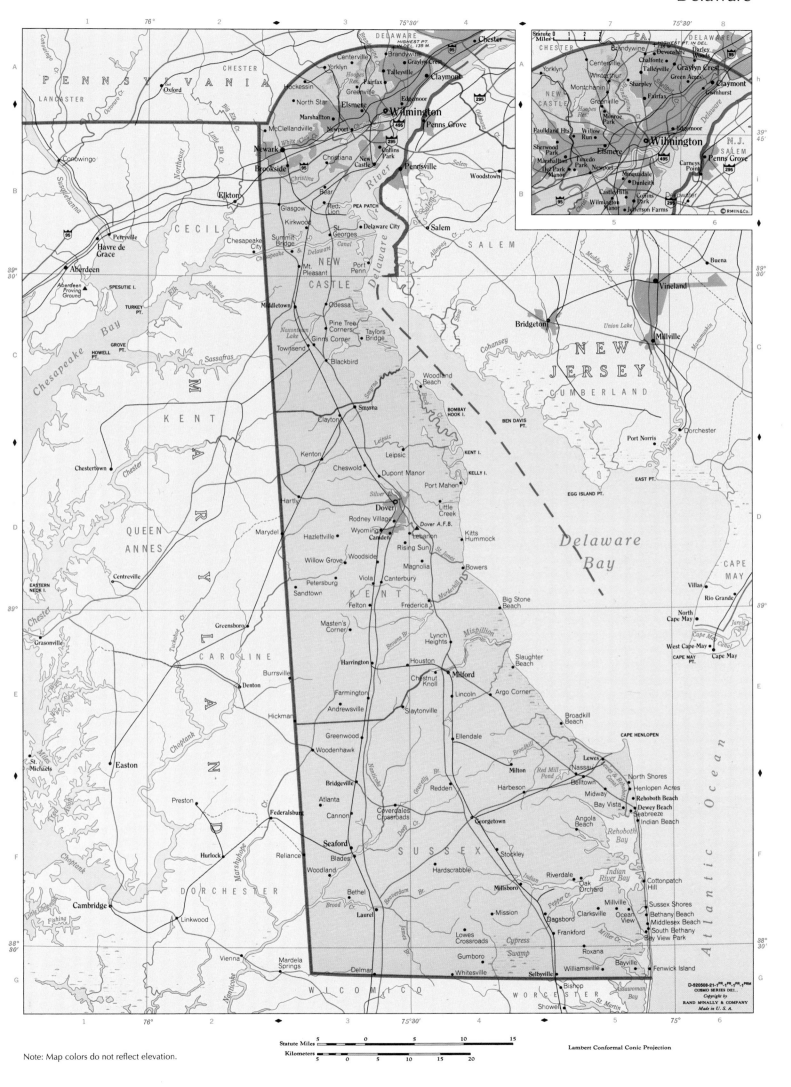

Note: Map colors do not reflect elevation.

Statute Miles
Kilometers

Lambert Conformal Conic Projection

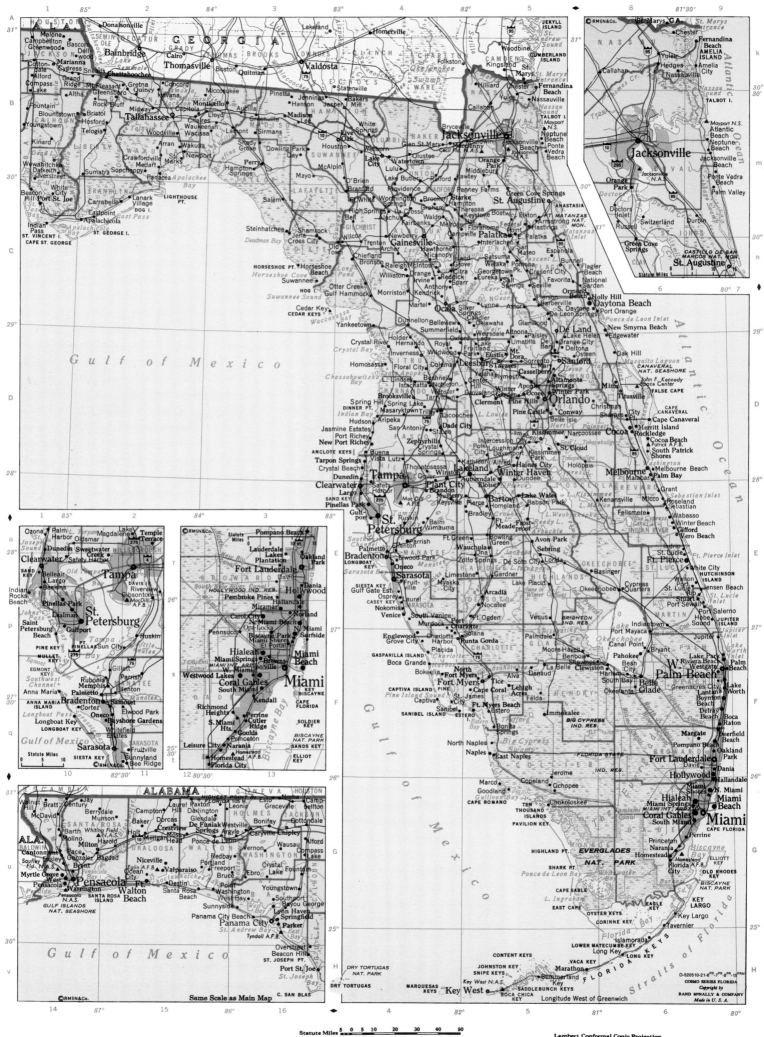

Note: Map colors do not reflect elevation.

Statute Miles 5 0 5 10   20   30   40   50
Kilometers 5 0 5 15 25 35 45 55 65

Lambert Conformal Conic Projection

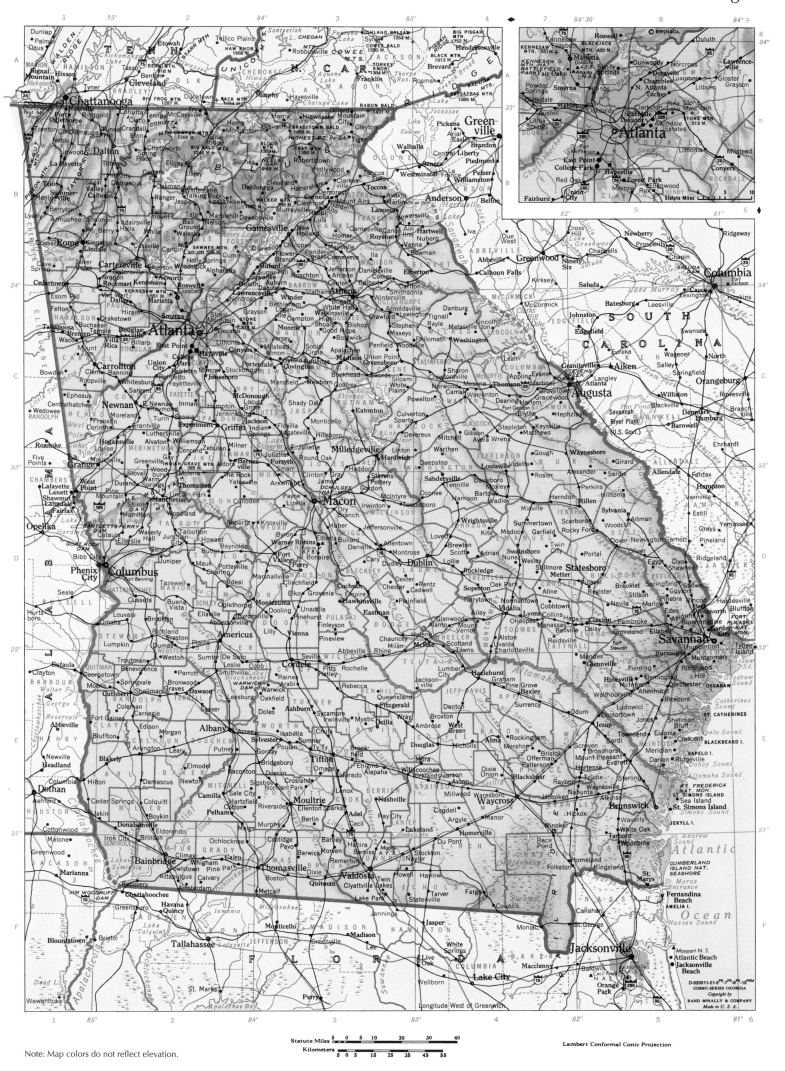

Note: Map colors do not reflect elevation.

Statute Miles 5 0 5 10   20   30   40
Kilometers 5 0 5 15 25 35 45 55

Lambert Conformal Conic Projection

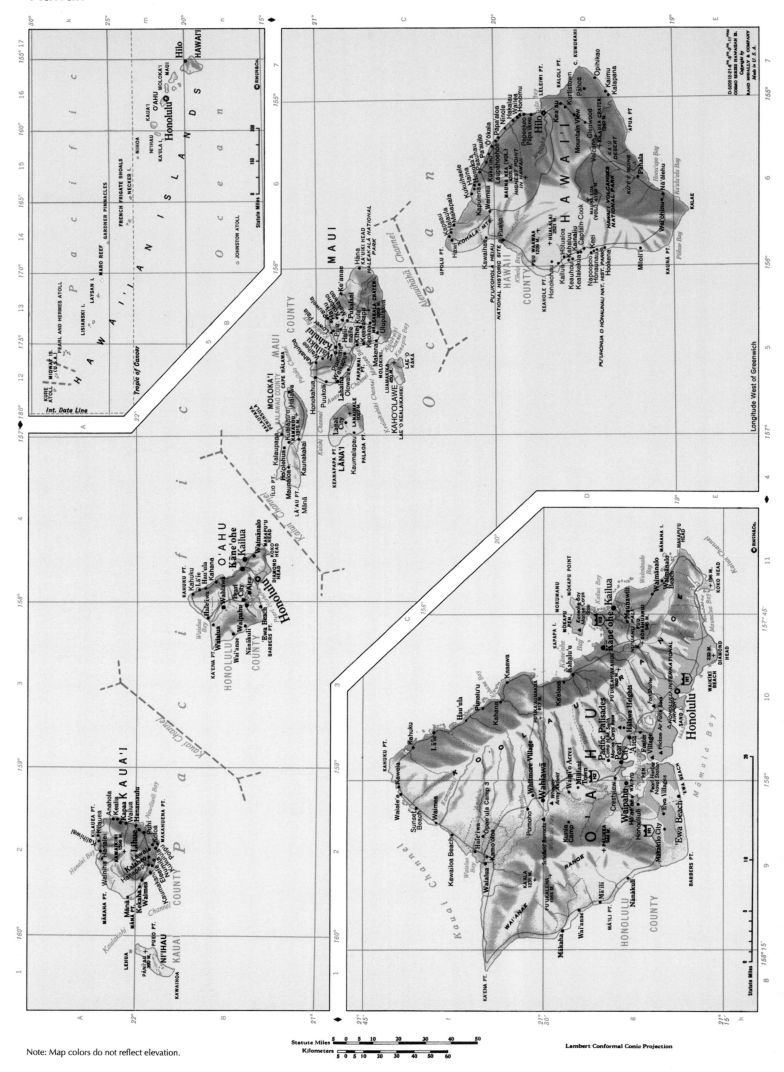

Note: Map colors do not reflect elevation.

Statute Miles
Kilometers

Lambert Conformal Conic Projection

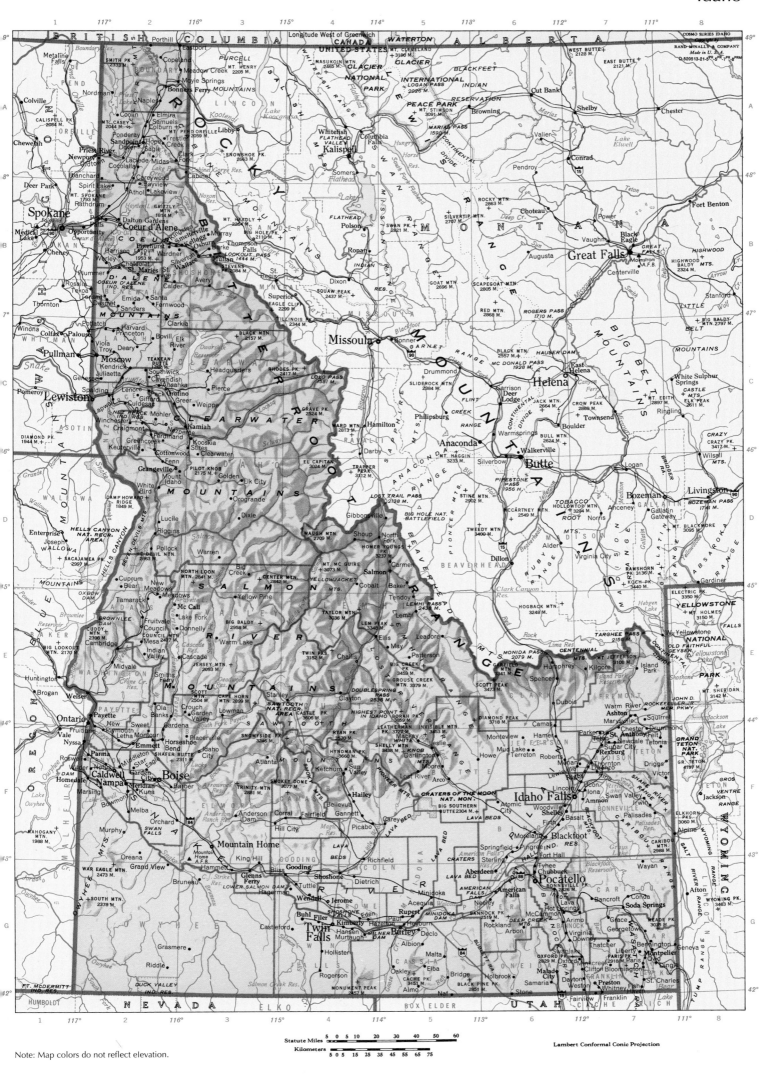

Note: Map colors do not reflect elevation.

Statute Miles   5 0 5 10   20   30   40   50   60
Kilometers   5 0 5 15   25   35   45   55   65   75

Lambert Conformal Conic Projection

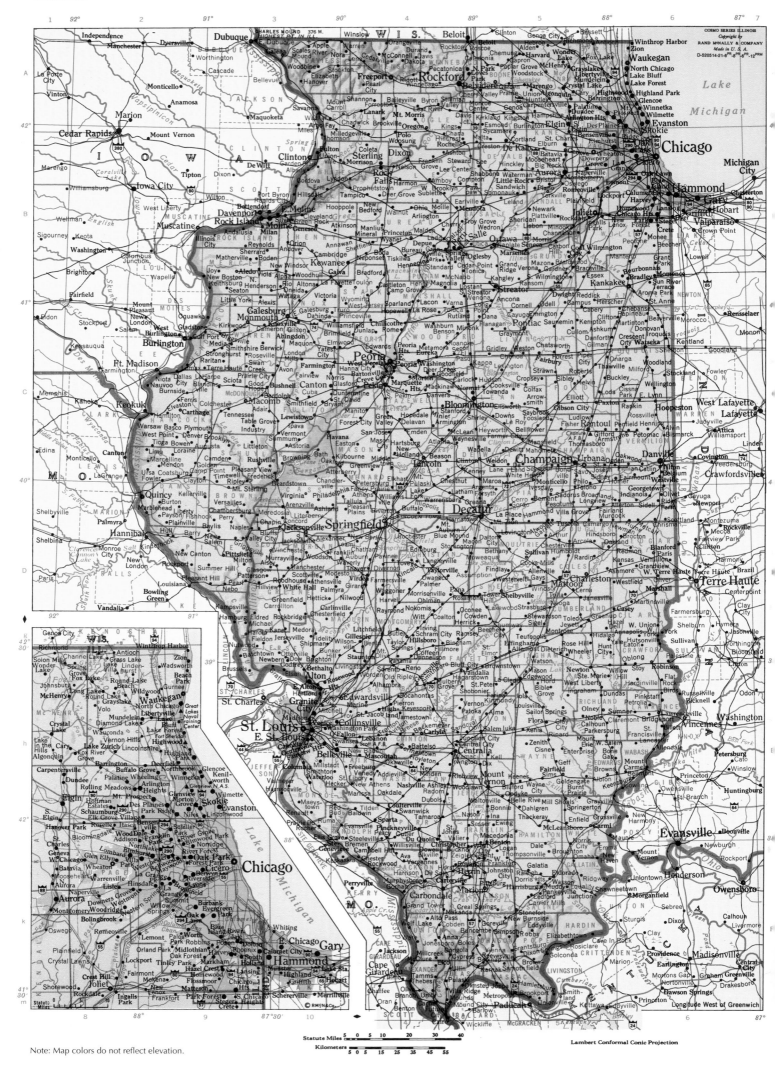

Note: Map colors do not reflect elevation.

Statute Miles
Kilometers

Lambert Conformal Conic Projection

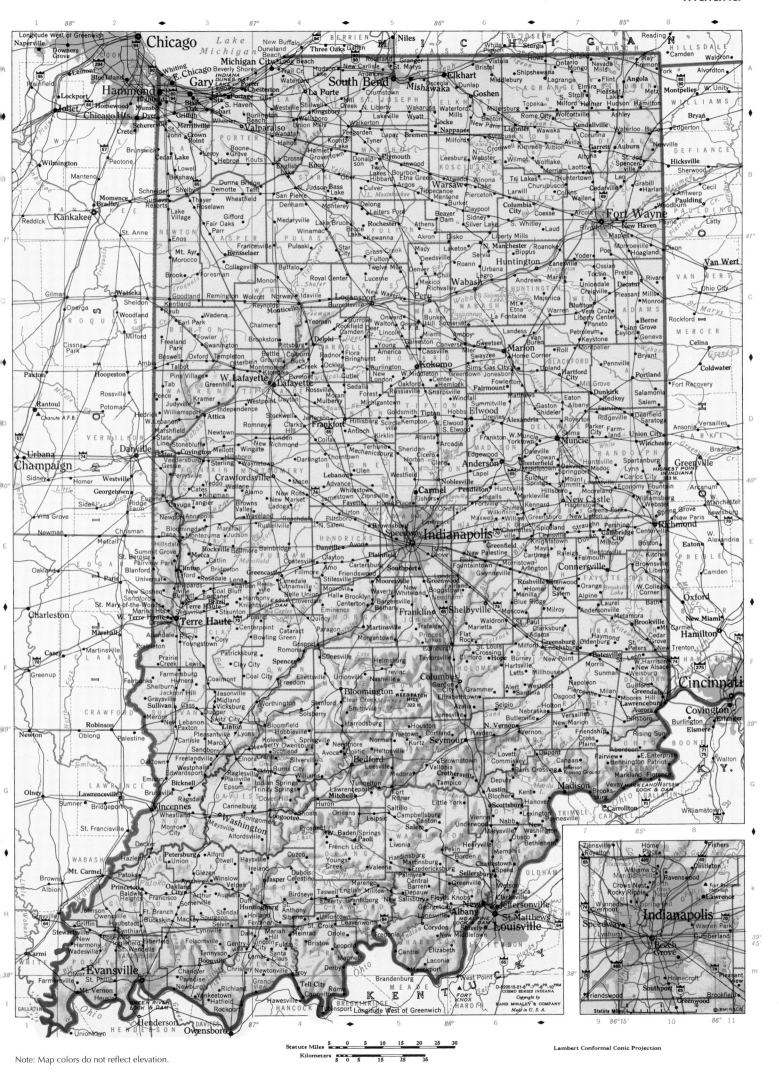

Note: Map colors do not reflect elevation.

Statute Miles
5 0 5   10   15   20   25   30
Kilometers
5 0 5   15   25   35

Lambert Conformal Conic Projection

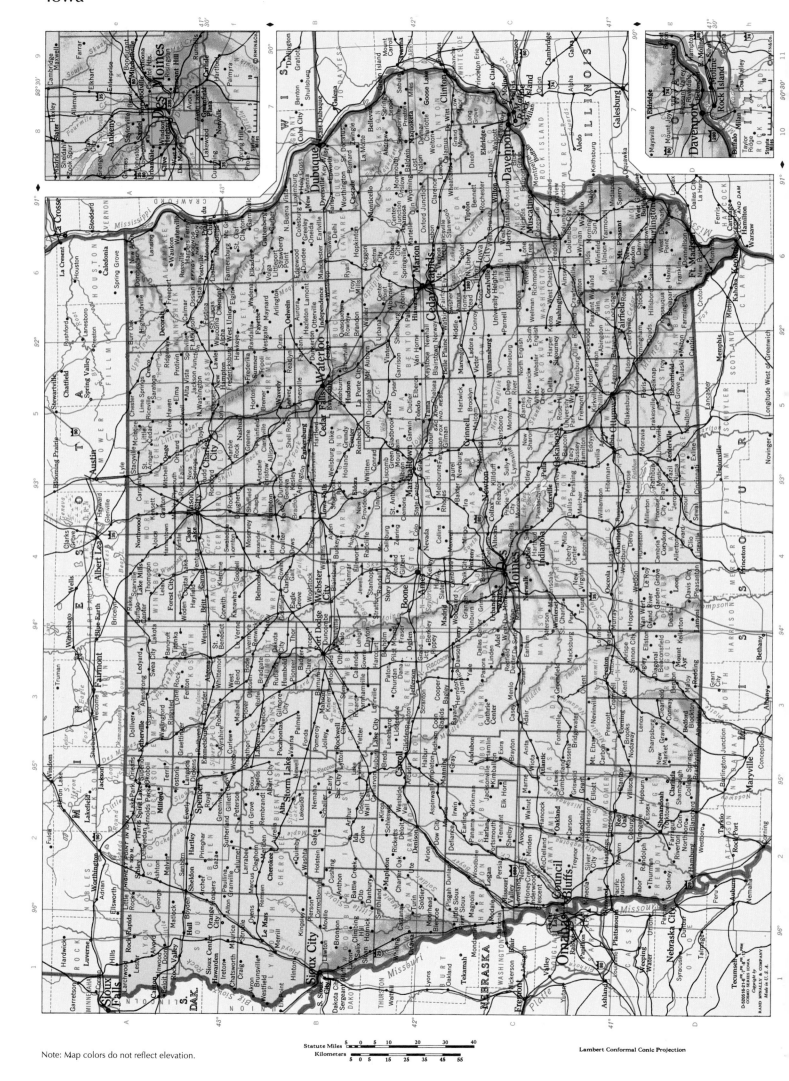

Note: Map colors do not reflect elevation.

Statute Miles 5 0 10   20   30   40
Kilometers 5 0 15 25 35 45 55

Lambert Conformal Conic Projection

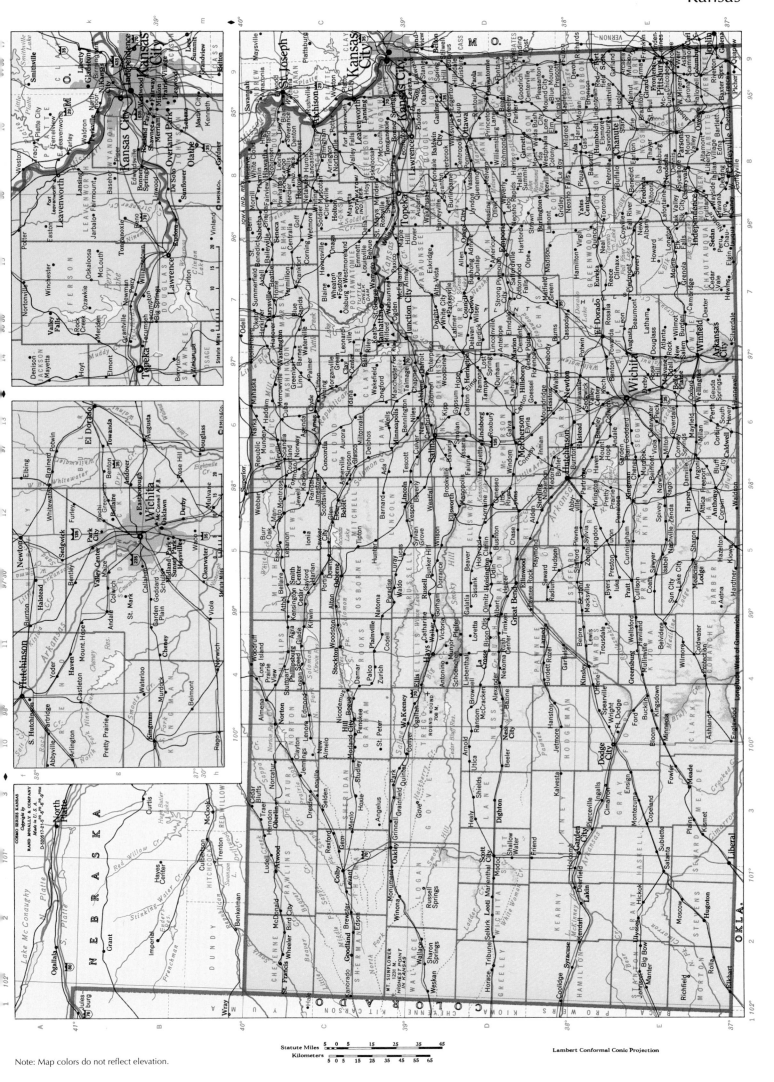

Note: Map colors do not reflect elevation.

Statute Miles 5 0 5 15 25 35 45

Kilometers 5 0 5 15 25 35 45 55 65

Lambert Conformal Conic Projection

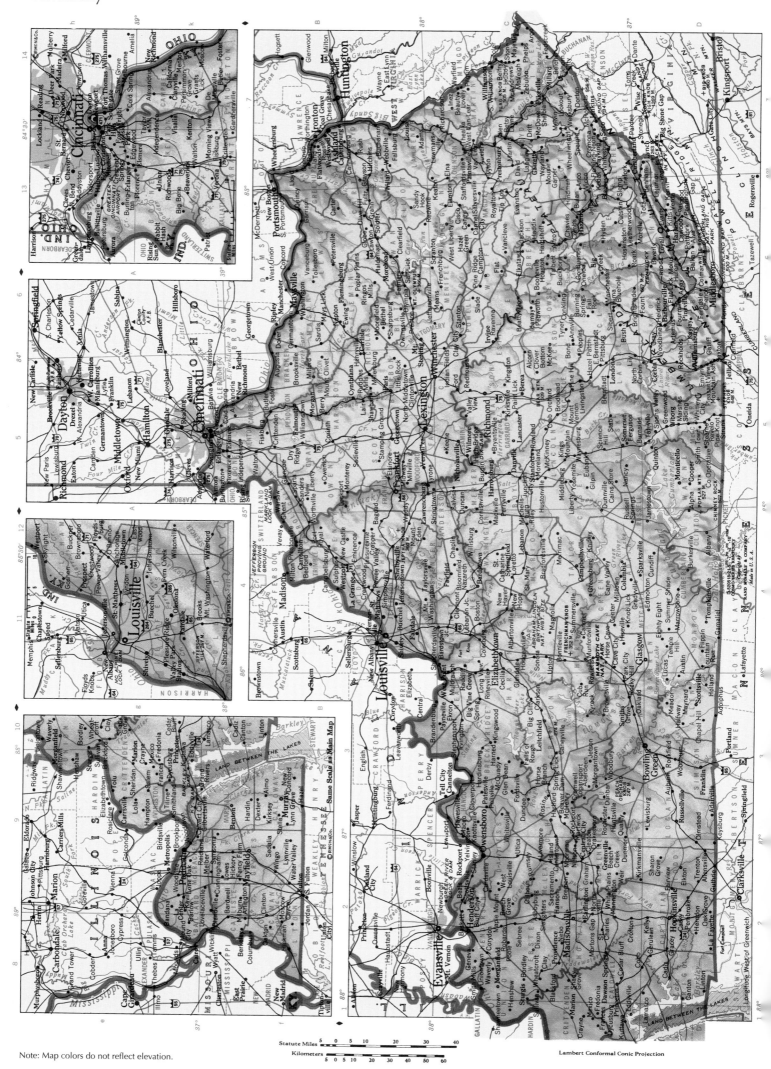

Note: Map colors do not reflect elevation.

Statute Miles 5 0 5 10   20   30   40

Kilometers 5 0 5 10 20 30 40 50 60

Lambert Conformal Conic Projection

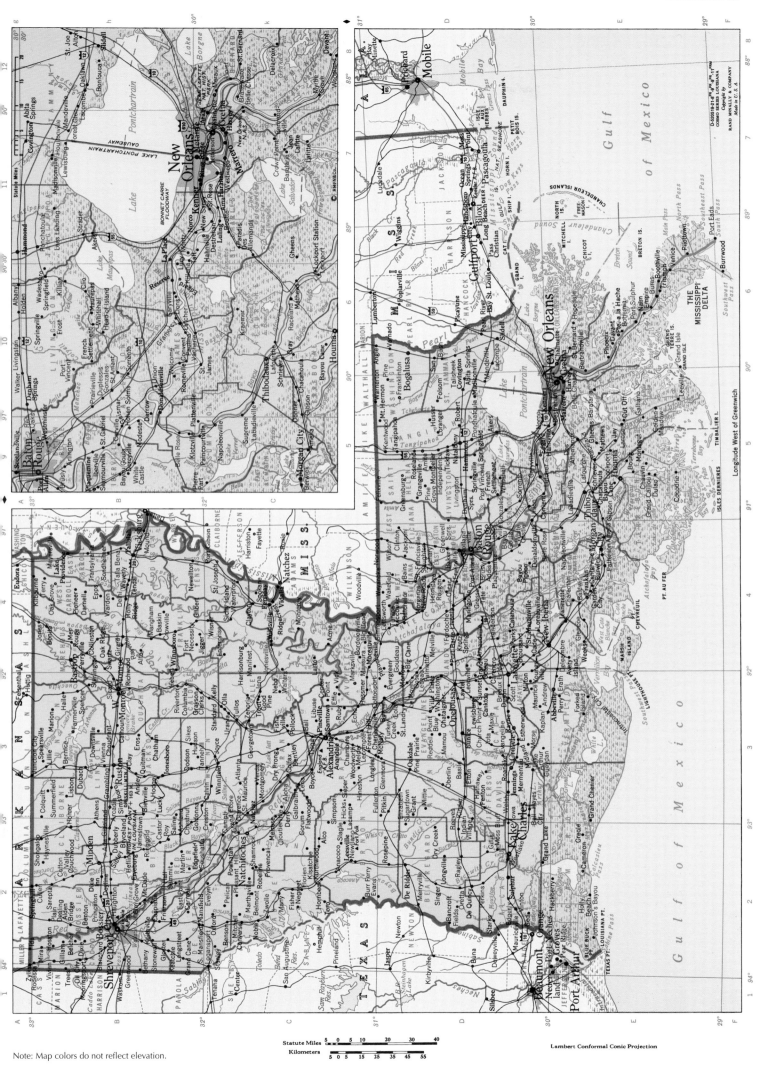

Note: Map colors do not reflect elevation.

Statute Miles 5 0 5 10 20 30 40
Kilometers 5 0 5 15 25 35 45 55

Lambert Conformal Conic Projection

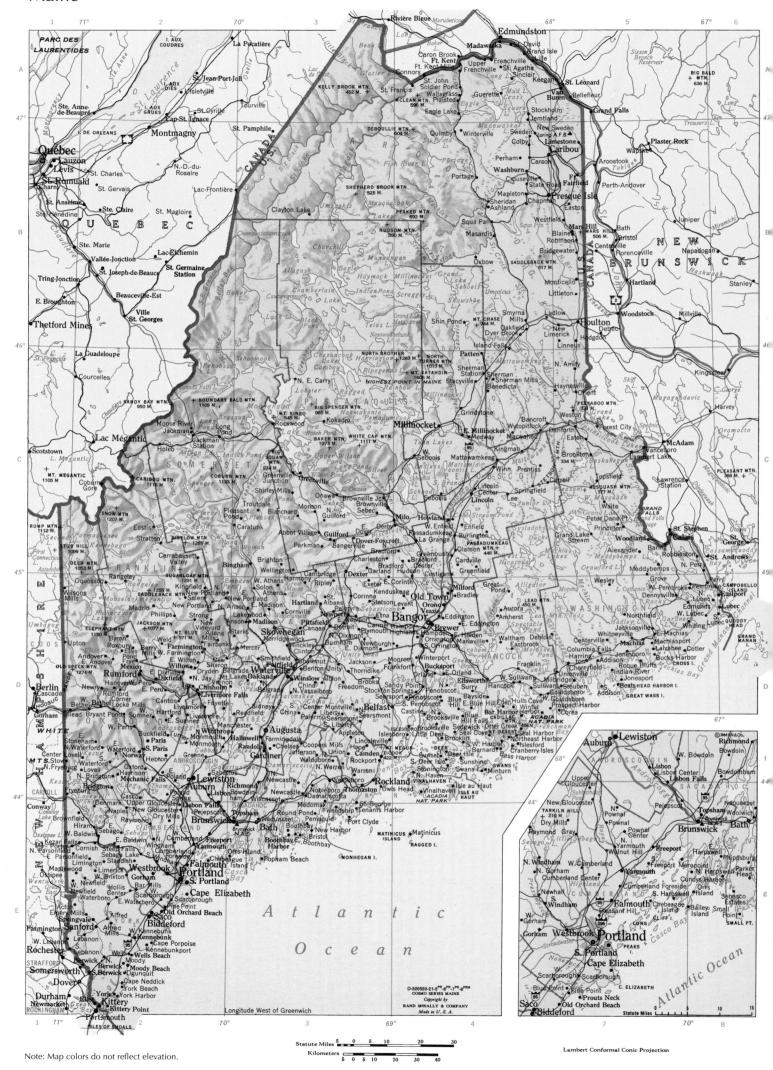

Note: Map colors do not reflect elevation.

Lambert Conformal Conic Projection

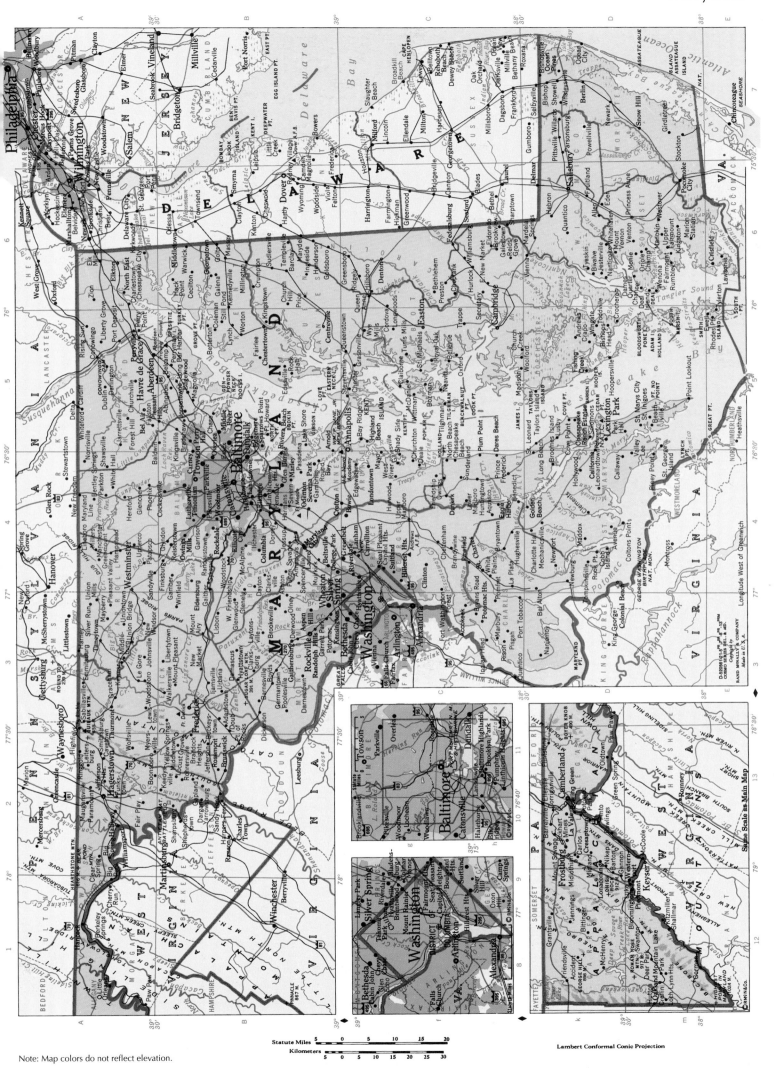

Note: Map colors do not reflect elevation.

Statute Miles 5   0   5   10   15   20
Kilometers 5 0 5 10 15 20 25 30

Lambert Conformal Conic Projection

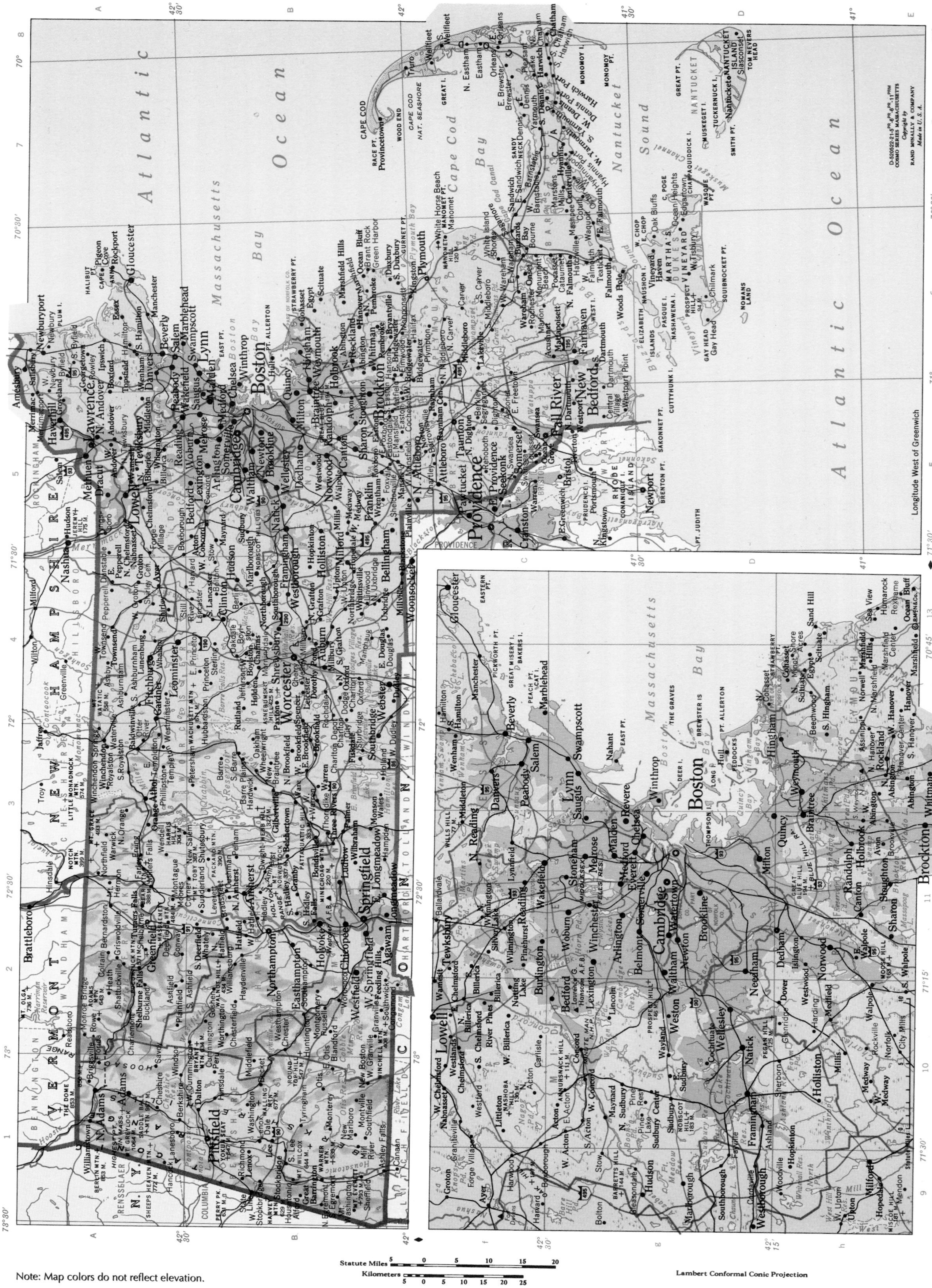

Atlantic Ocean

Massachusetts Bay

Cape Cod

Cape Cod Bay

Nantucket Sound

NANTUCKET ISLAND

MARTHA'S VINEYARD

NEW HAMPSHIRE

VERMONT

N. Y.

CONNECTICUT

RHODE ISLAND

Boston

Worcester

Springfield

Providence

Pittsfield

Brockton

New Bedford

Fall River

Longitude West of Greenwich

Note: Map colors do not reflect elevation.

Statute Miles

Kilometers

Lambert Conformal Conic Projection

D-520022-21-175 JFK JFK 11 PRM RAND M©NALLY & COMPANY Copyright © Made in U.S.A.

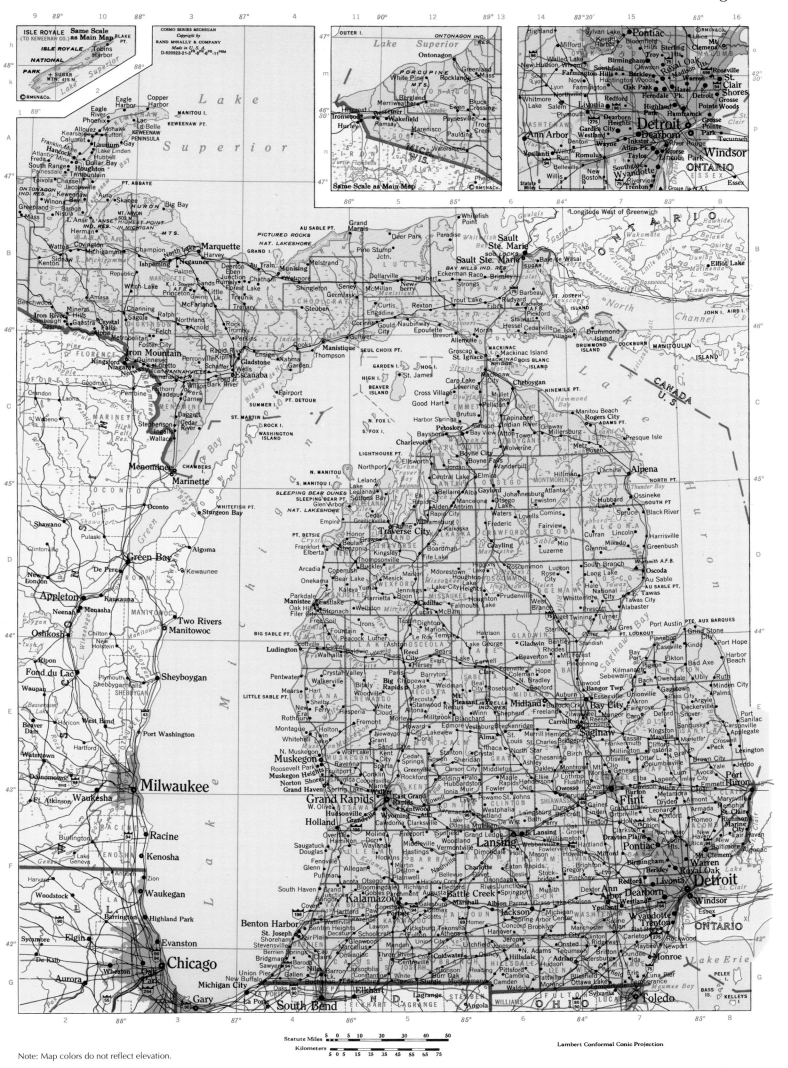

Note: Map colors do not reflect elevation.

Statute Miles
5 0 5 10   20   30   40   50
Kilometers
5 0 5 15 25 35 45 55 65 75

Lambert Conformal Conic Projection

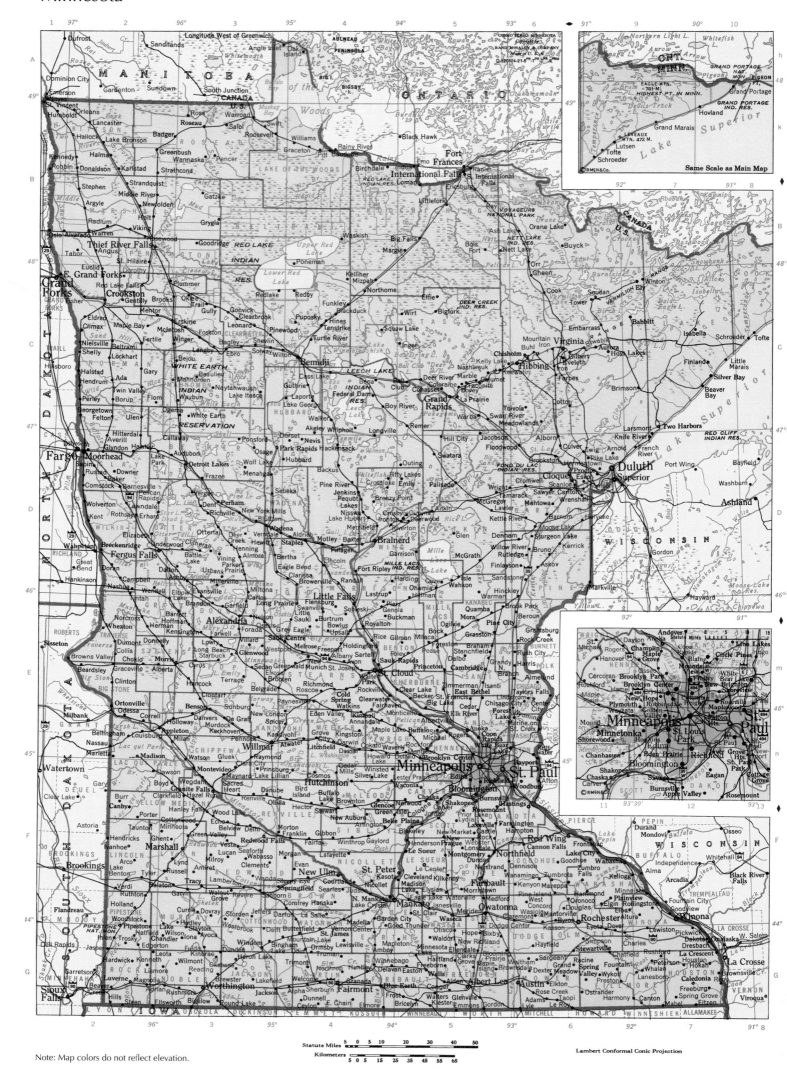

Note: Map colors do not reflect elevation.

Statute Miles 5 0 5 10 20 30 40 50
Kilometers 5 0 5 15 25 35 45 55 65

Lambert Conformal Conic Projection

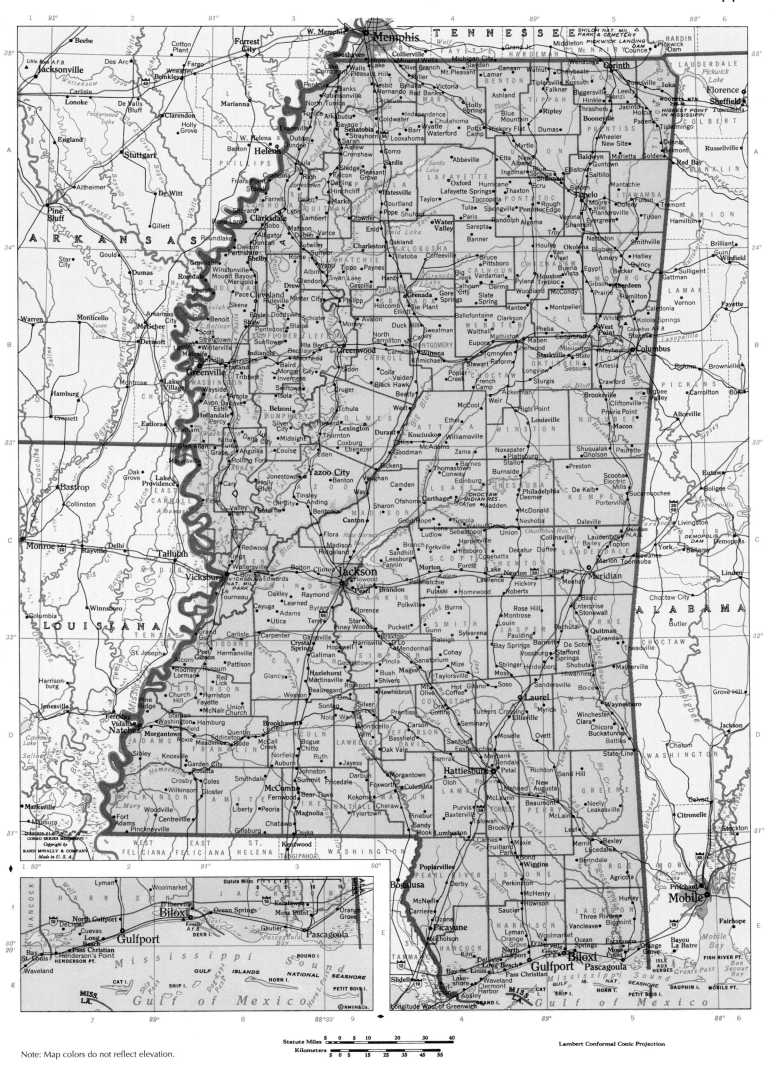

Note: Map colors do not reflect elevation.

Statute Miles
Kilometers

Lambert Conformal Conic Projection

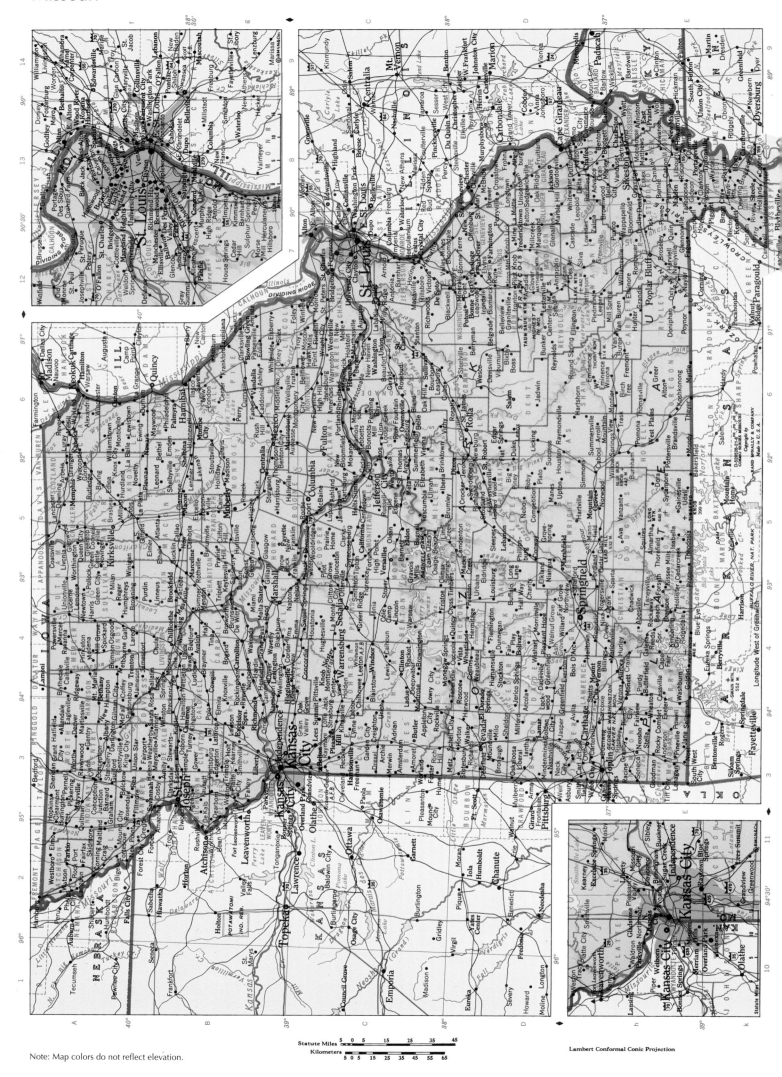

Note: Map colors do not reflect elevation.

Statute Miles   5 0 5   15   25   35   45
Kilometers   5 0 5 15 25 35 45 55 65

Lambert Conformal Conic Projection

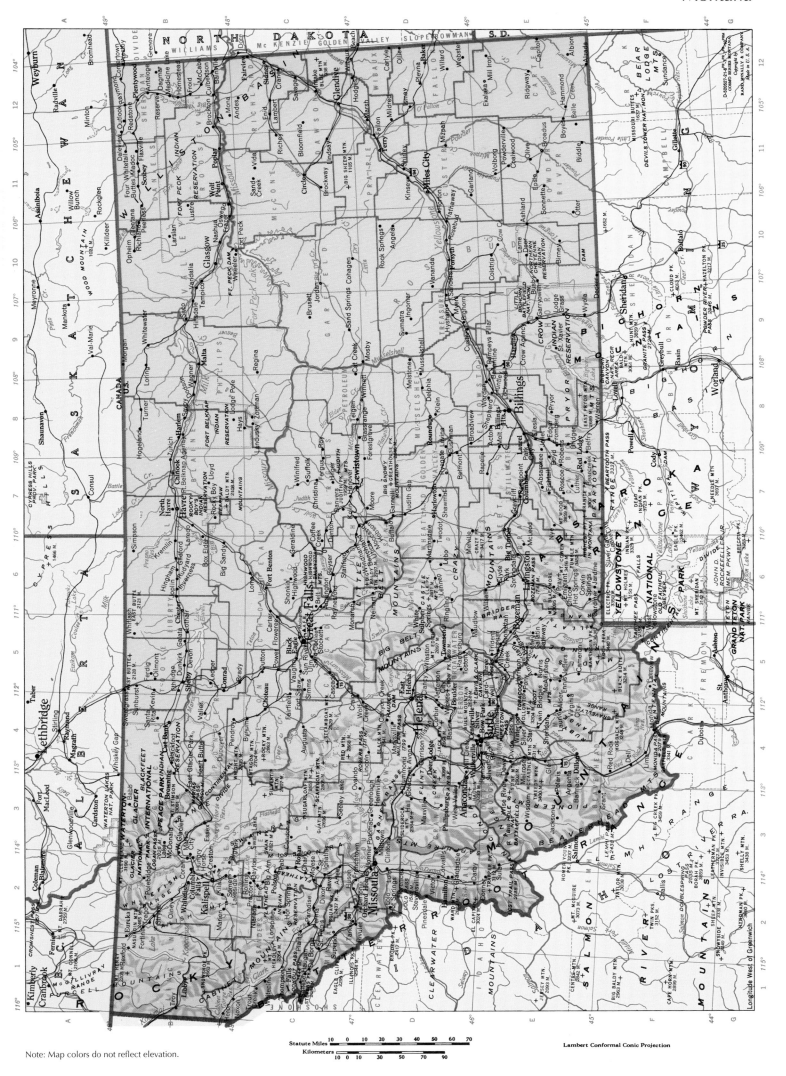

Note: Map colors do not reflect elevation.

Statute Miles   10 0 10 20 30 40 50 60 70
Kilometers   10 0 10   30   50   70   90

Lambert Conformal Conic Projection

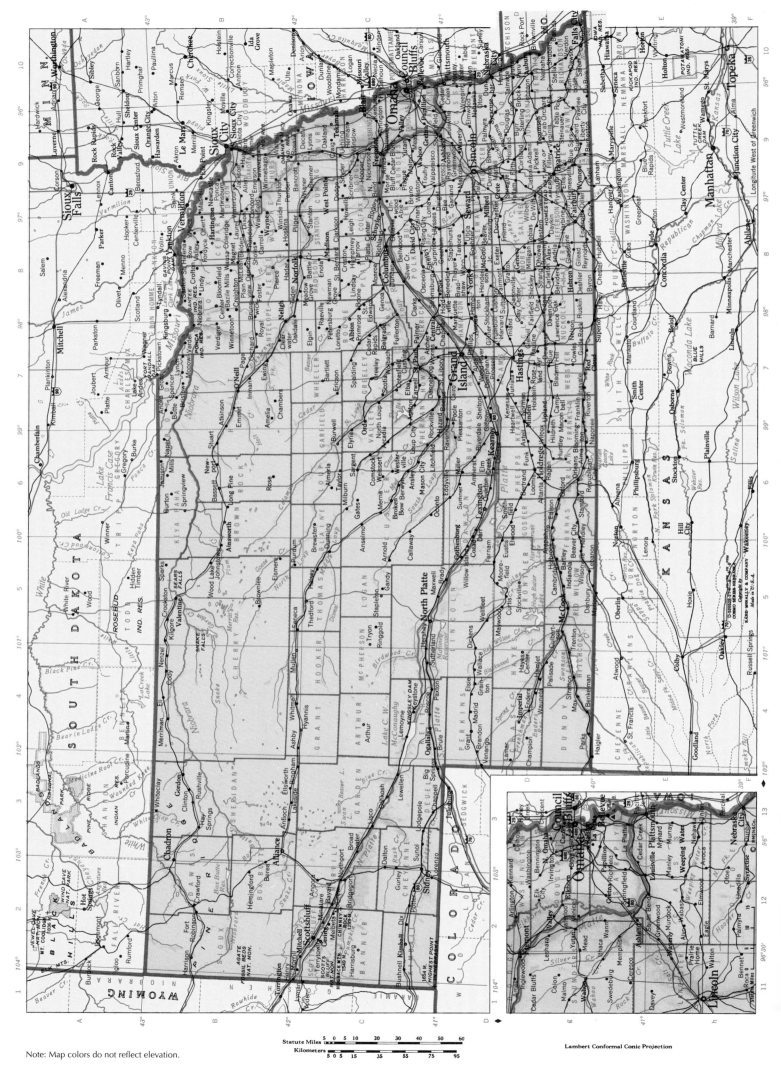

Note: Map colors do not reflect elevation.

Statute Miles   5 0 5 10   20   30   40   50   60
Kilometers   5 0 5 15   35   55   75   95

Lambert Conformal Conic Projection

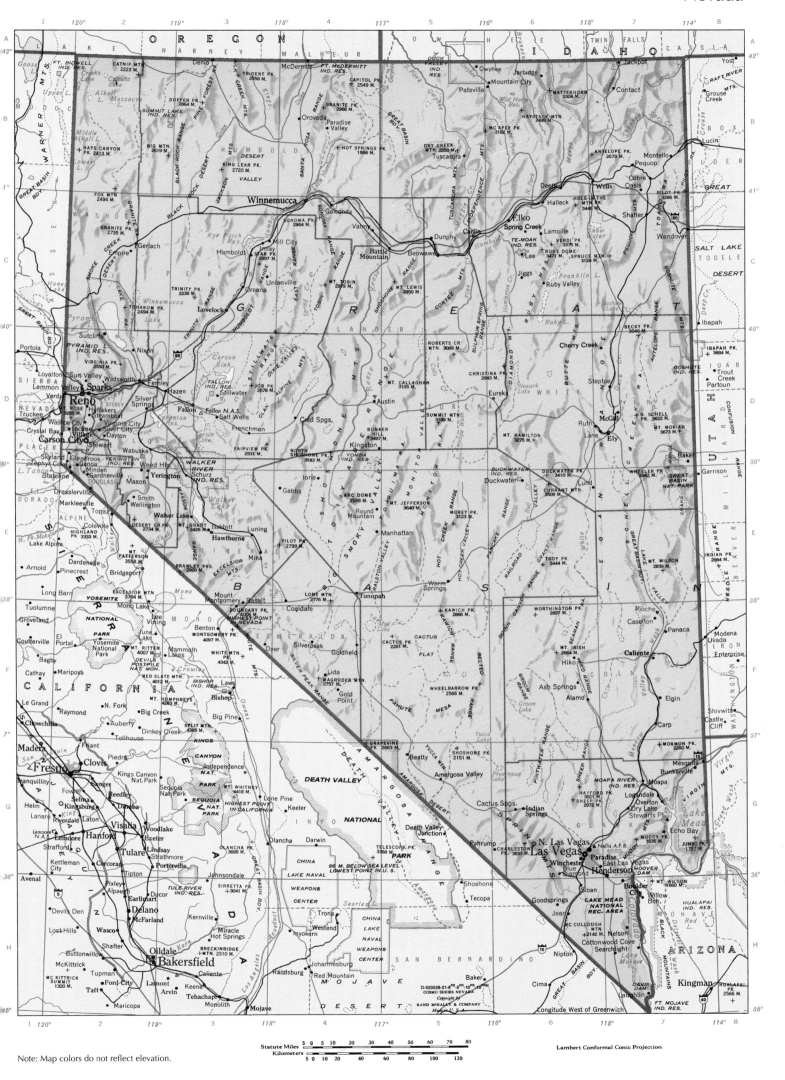

Note: Map colors do not reflect elevation.

Statute Miles   5 0 5 10   20   30   40   50   60   70   80

Kilometers   5 0 10 20   40   60   80   100   120

Lambert Conformal Conic Projection

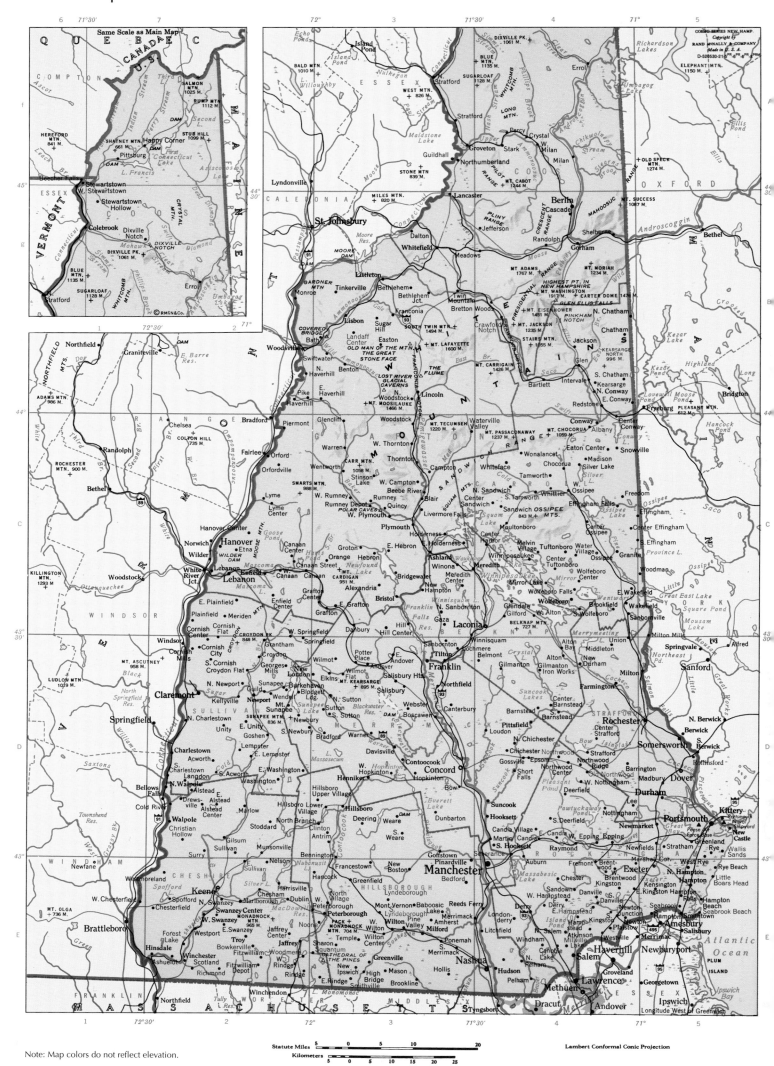

Note: Map colors do not reflect elevation.

Statute Miles 5 0 5 10 20
Kilometers 5 0 5 10 15 20 25

Lambert Conformal Conic Projection

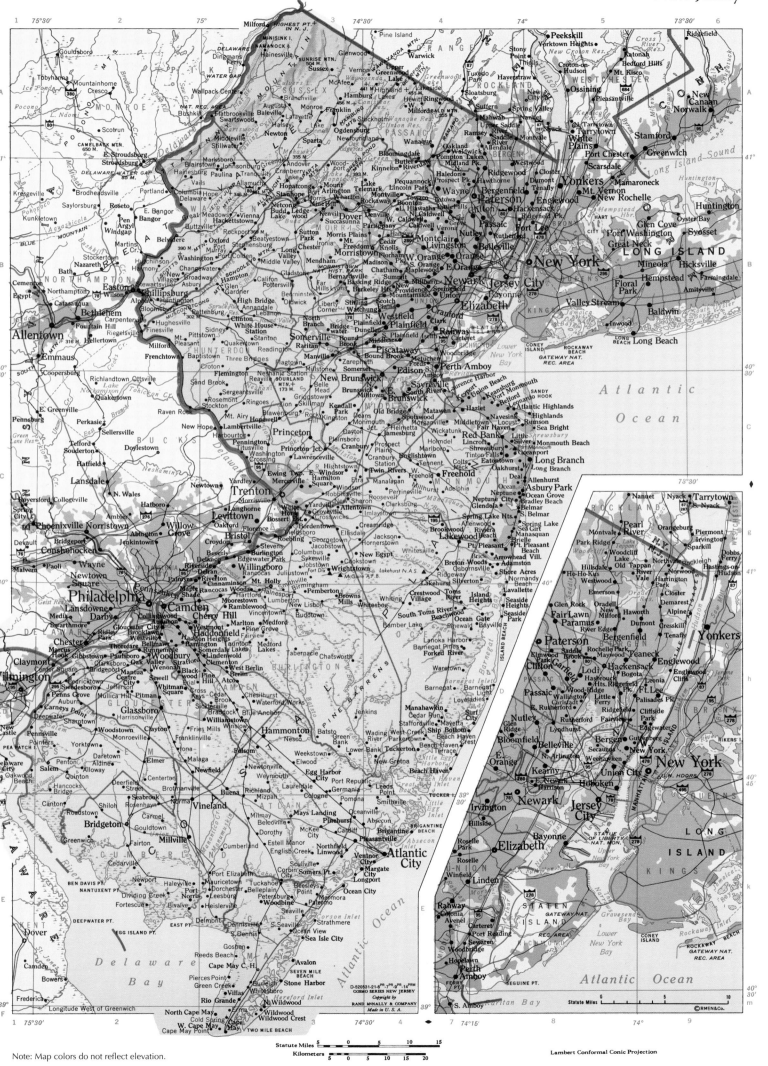

Note: Map colors do not reflect elevation.

Statute Miles 5 0 5 10 15
Kilometers 5 0 5 10 15 20

Lambert Conformal Conic Projection

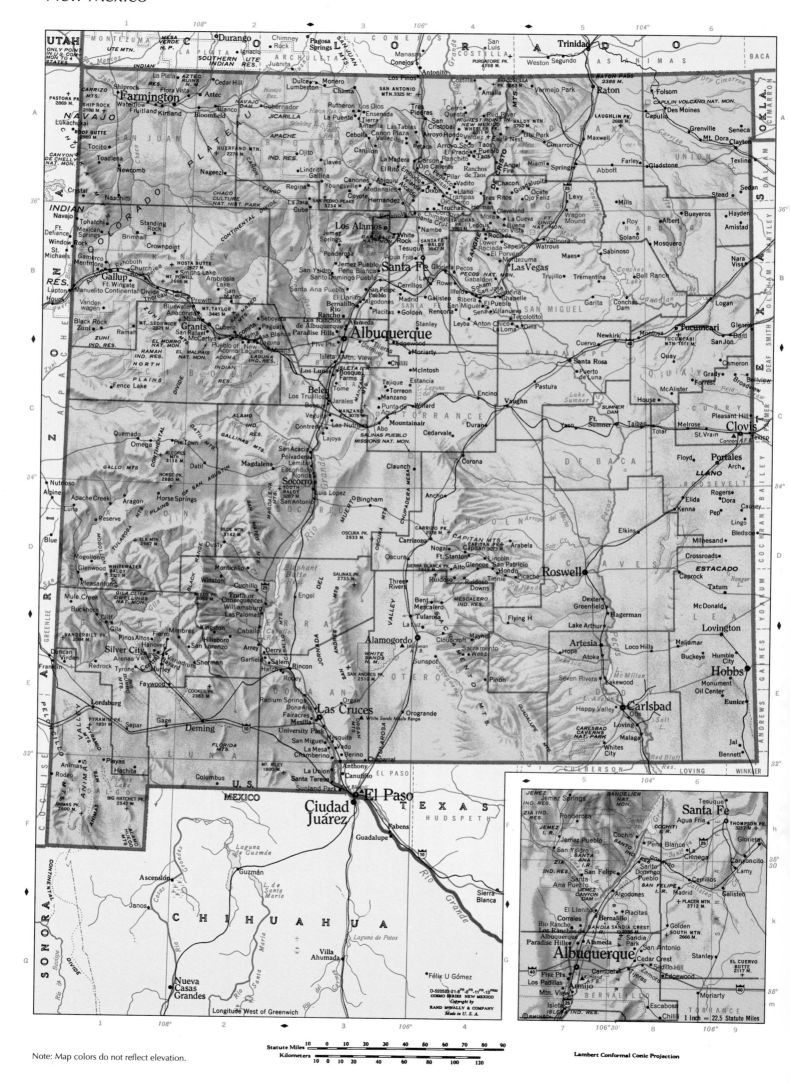

Note: Map colors do not reflect elevation.

Statute Miles
Kilometers

Lambert Conformal Conic Projection

1 Inch = 22.5 Statute Miles

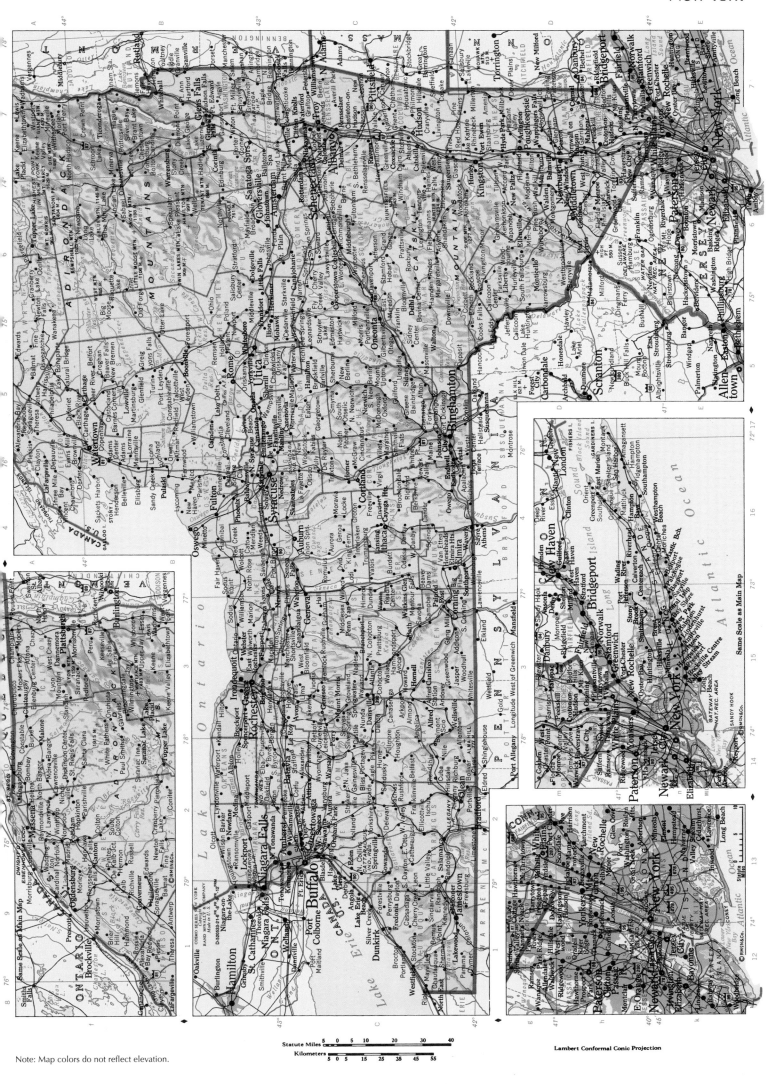

Note: Map colors do not reflect elevation.

Statute Miles 5 0 5 10 20 30 40

Kilometers 5 0 5 15 25 35 45 55

Lambert Conformal Conic Projection

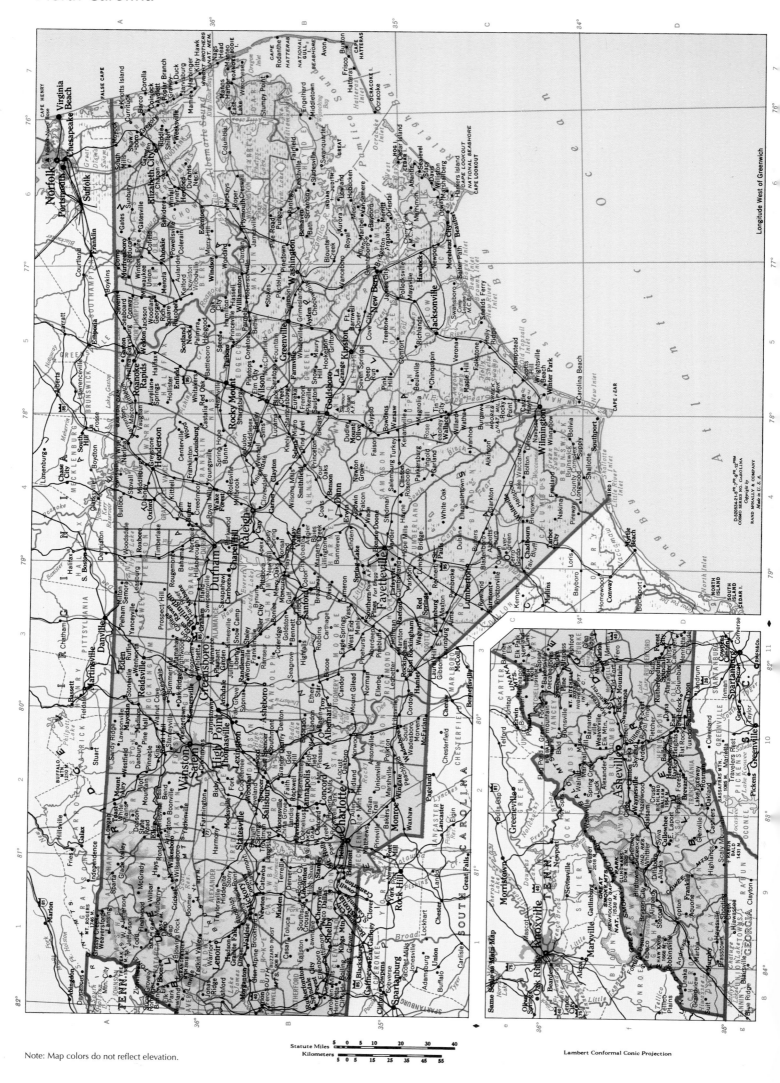

Note: Map colors do not reflect elevation.

Statute Miles 5 0 5 10 20 30 40
Kilometers 5 0 5 15 25 35 45 55

Lambert Conformal Conic Projection

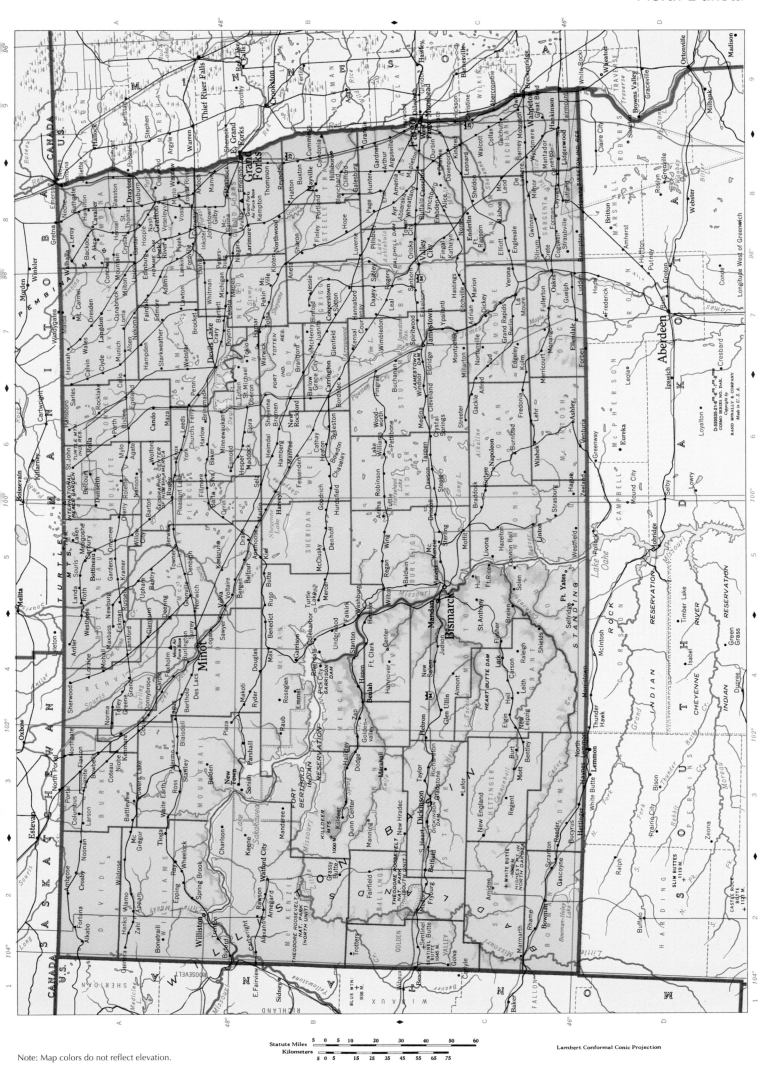

Note: Map colors do not reflect elevation.

Statute Miles
5 0 5 10   20   30   40   50   60
Kilometers
5 0 5 15 25 35 45 55 65 75

Lambert Conformal Conic Projection

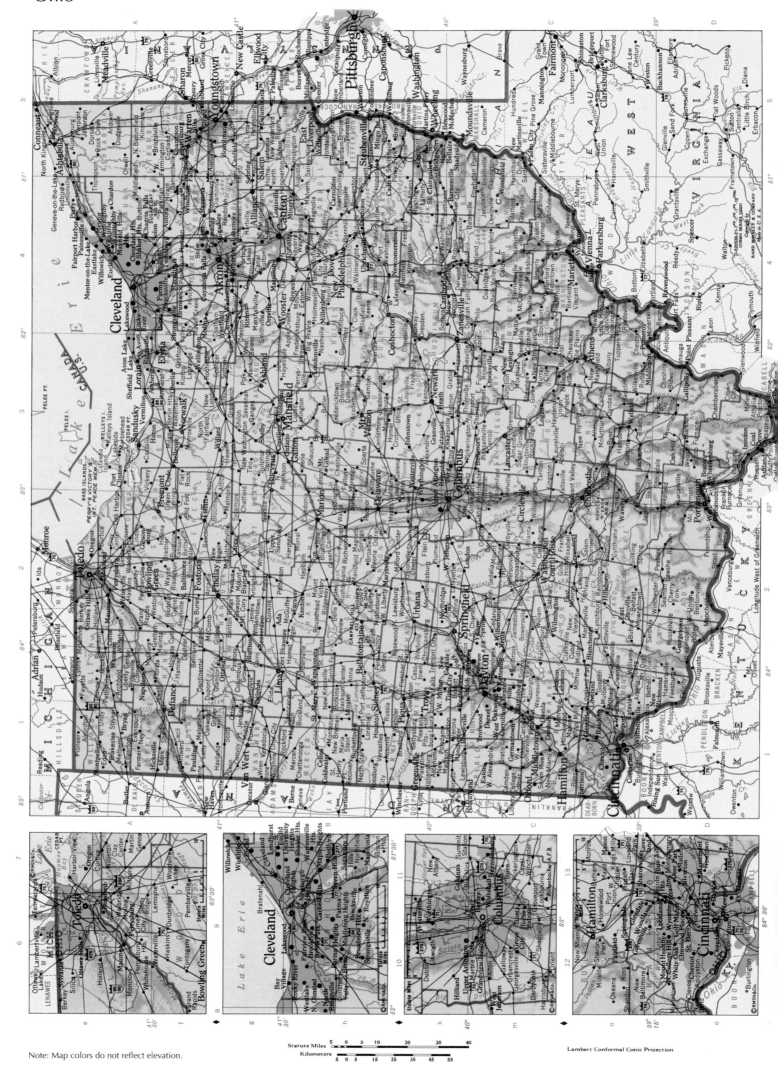

Note: Map colors do not reflect elevation.

Statute Miles   5   0   5   10   20   30   40

Kilometers   5   0   5   15   25   35   45   55

Lambert Conformal Conic Projection

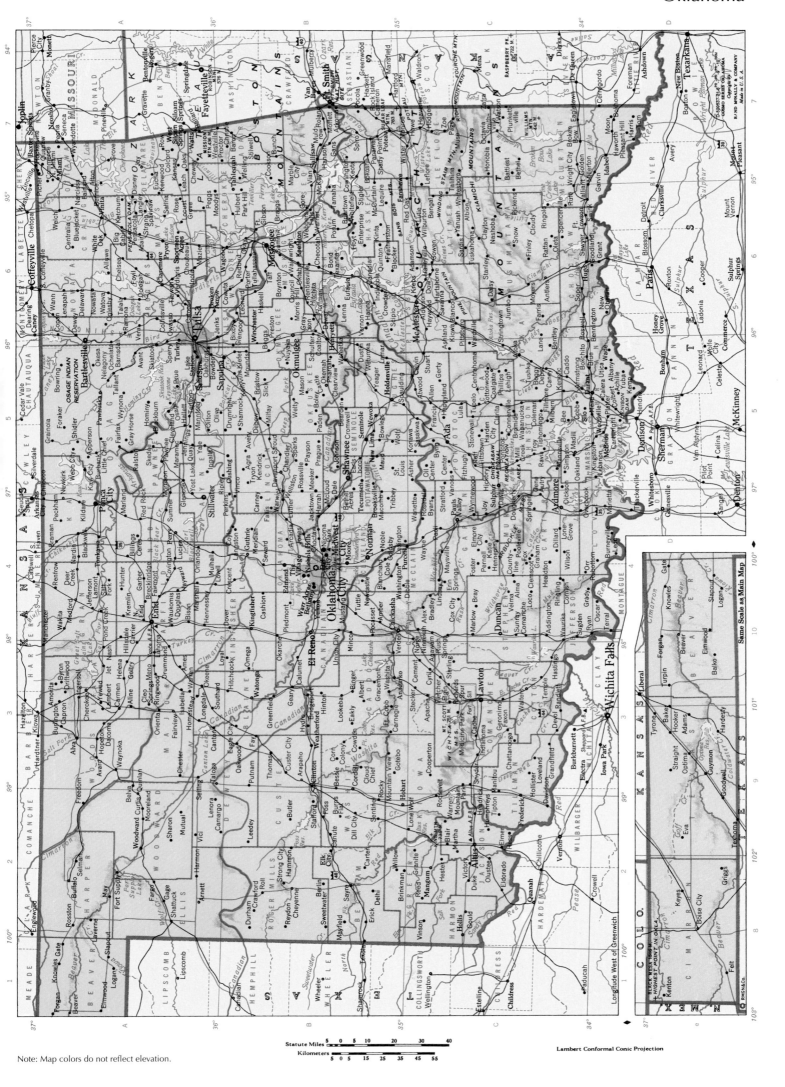

Statute Miles 5 0 5 10   20   30   40
Kilometers 5 0 5 15 25 35 45 55

Lambert Conformal Conic Projection

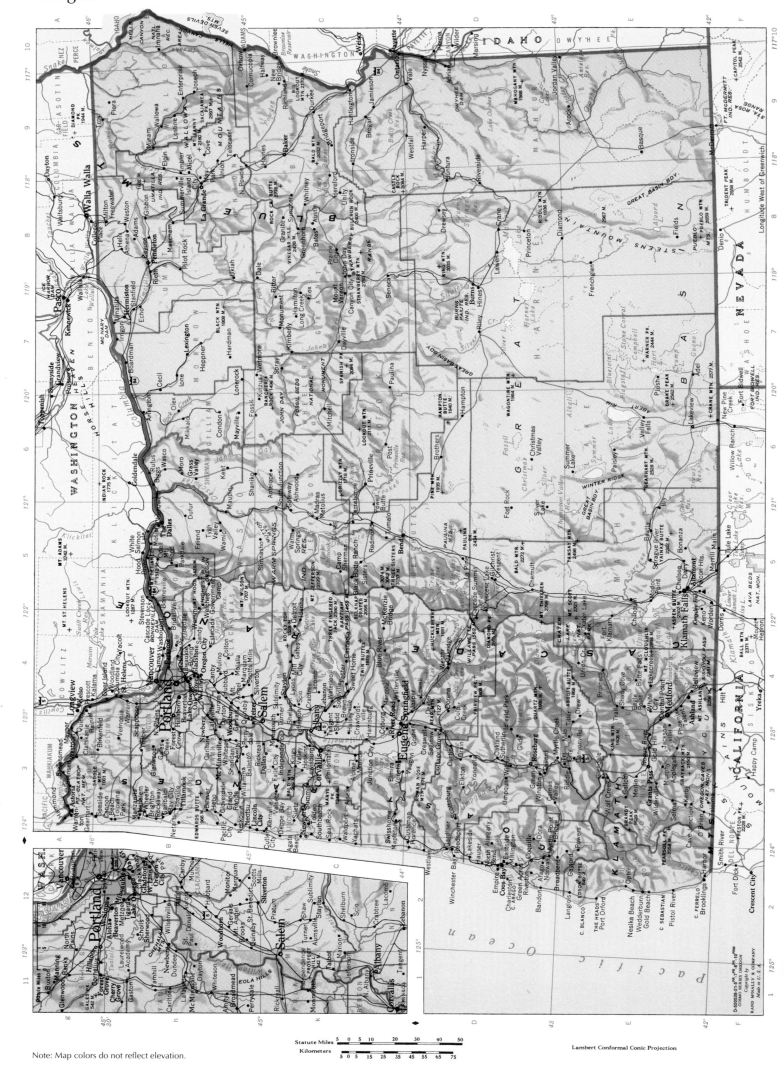

Note: Map colors do not reflect elevation.

Statute Miles 5 0 5 10   20   30   40   50

Kilometers 5 0 5 15 25 35 45 55 65 75

Lambert Conformal Conic Projection

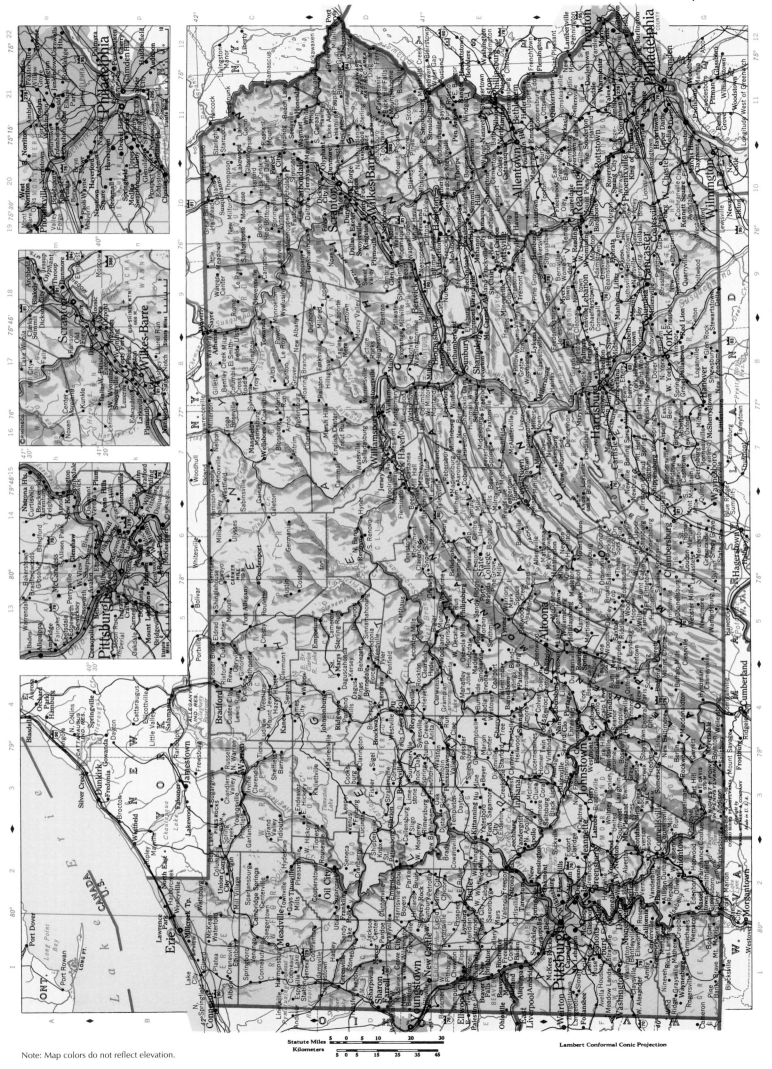

Note: Map colors do not reflect elevation.

Statute Miles
Kilometers

Lambert Conformal Conic Projection

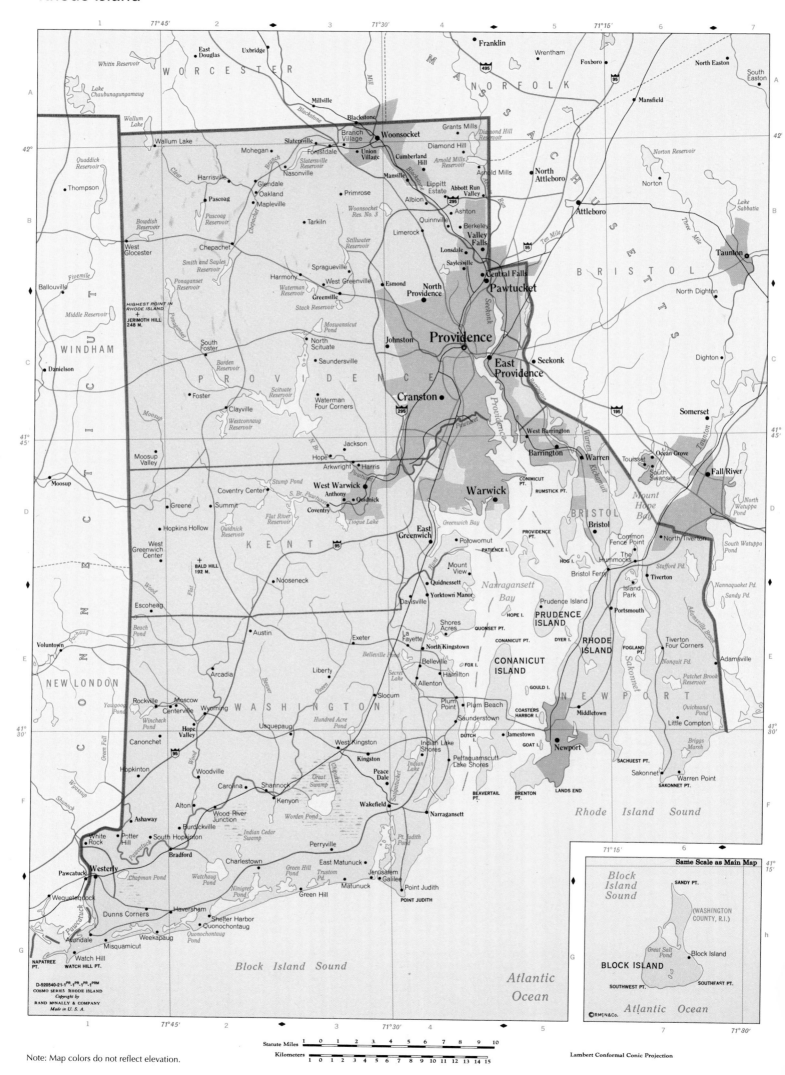

Note: Map colors do not reflect elevation.

Statute Miles 1 0 1 2 3 4 5 6 7 8 9 10

Kilometers 1 0 1 2 3 4 5 6 7 8 9 10 11 12 13 14 15

Lambert Conformal Conic Projection

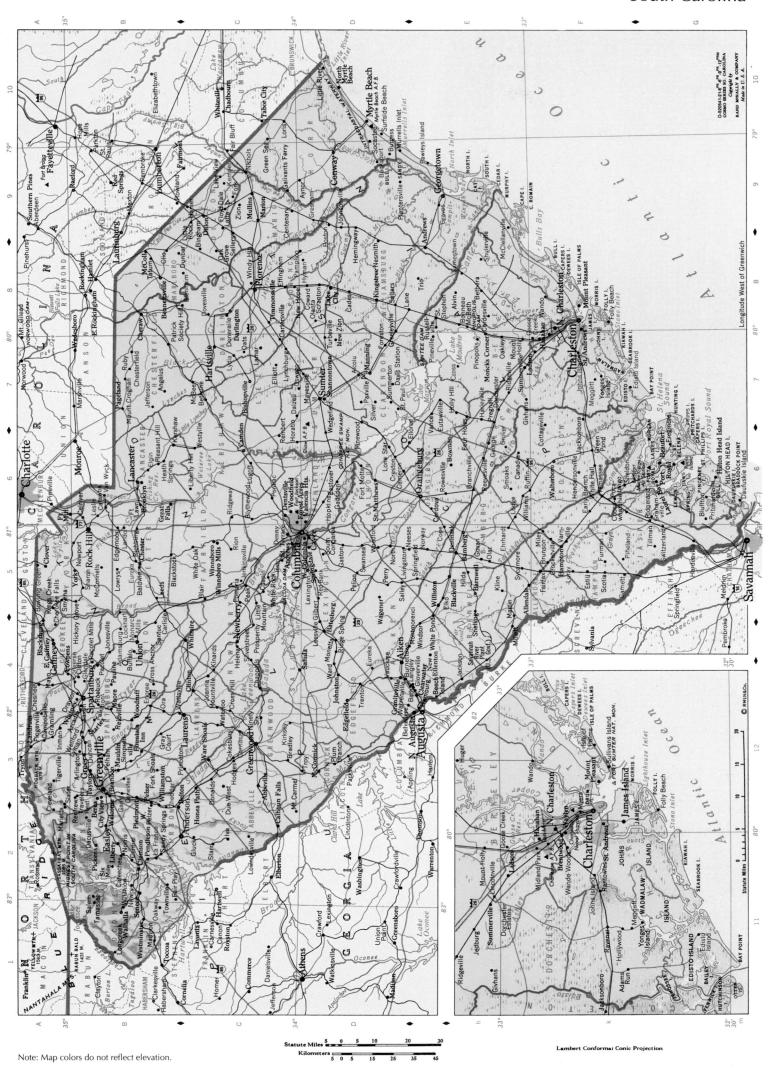

Note: Map colors do not reflect elevation.

Statute Miles 5 0 5 10   20   30

Kilometers 5 0   15   25   35   45

Lambert Conformal Conic Projection

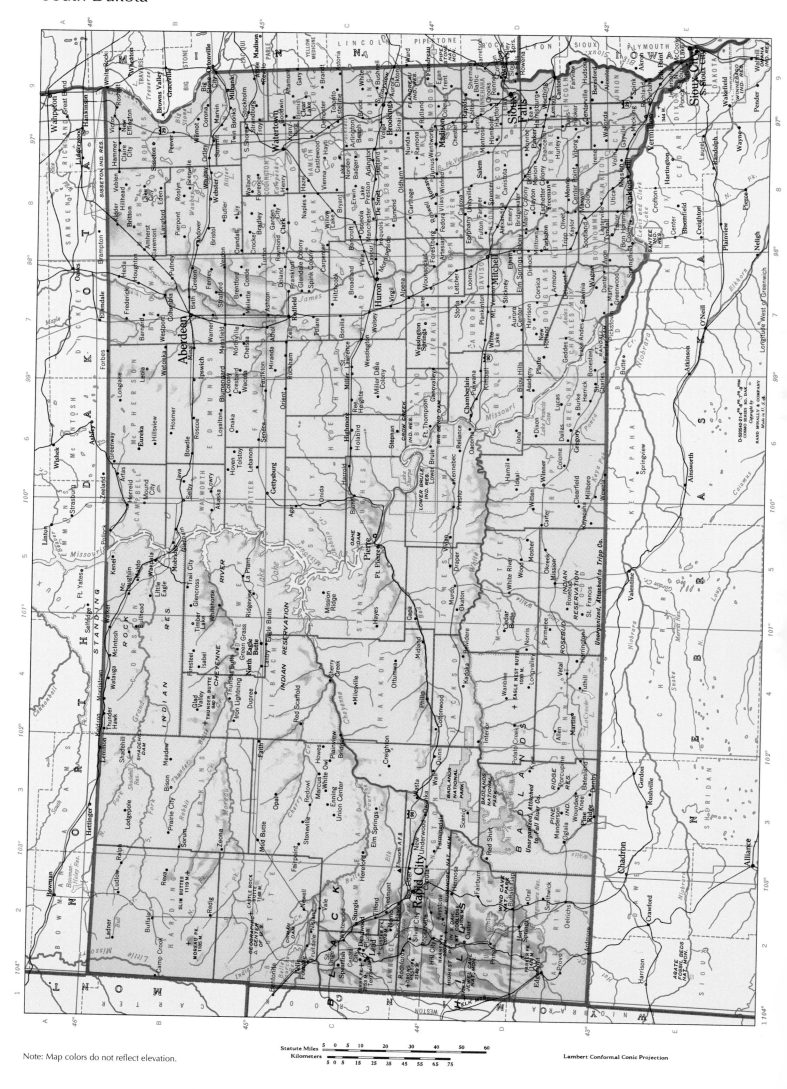

Note: Map colors do not reflect elevation.

Statute Miles
Kilometers

Lambert Conformal Conic Projection

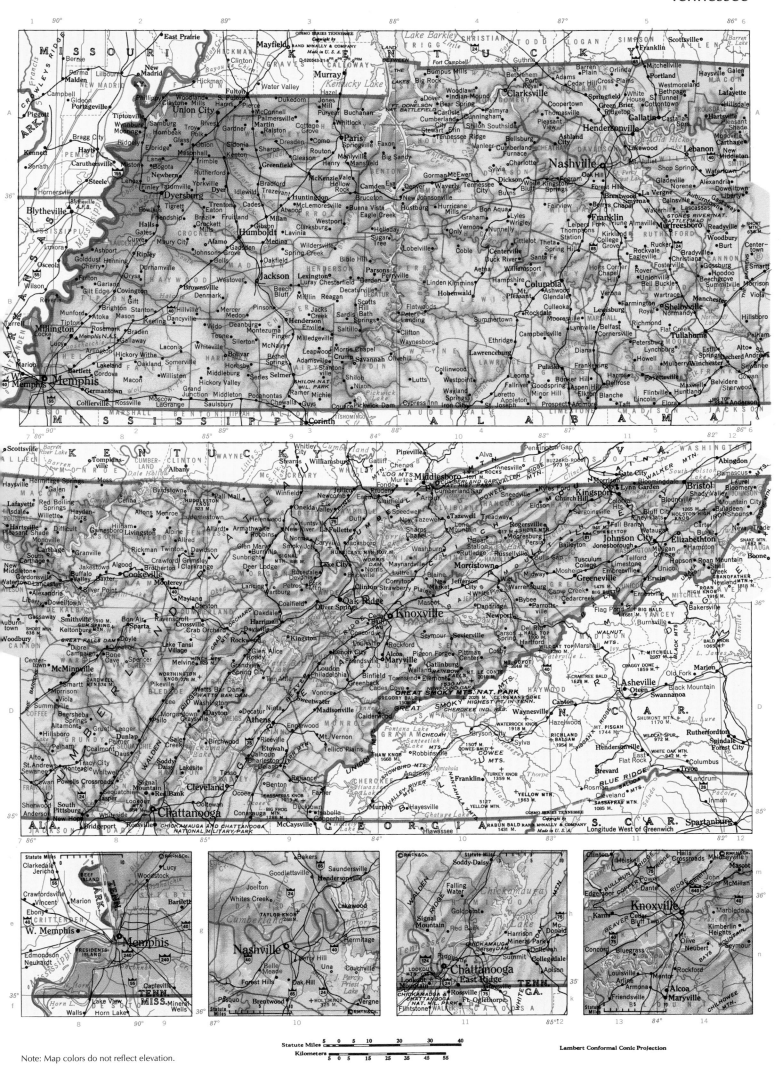

Note: Map colors do not reflect elevation.

Statute Miles
Kilometers

Lambert Conformal Conic Projection

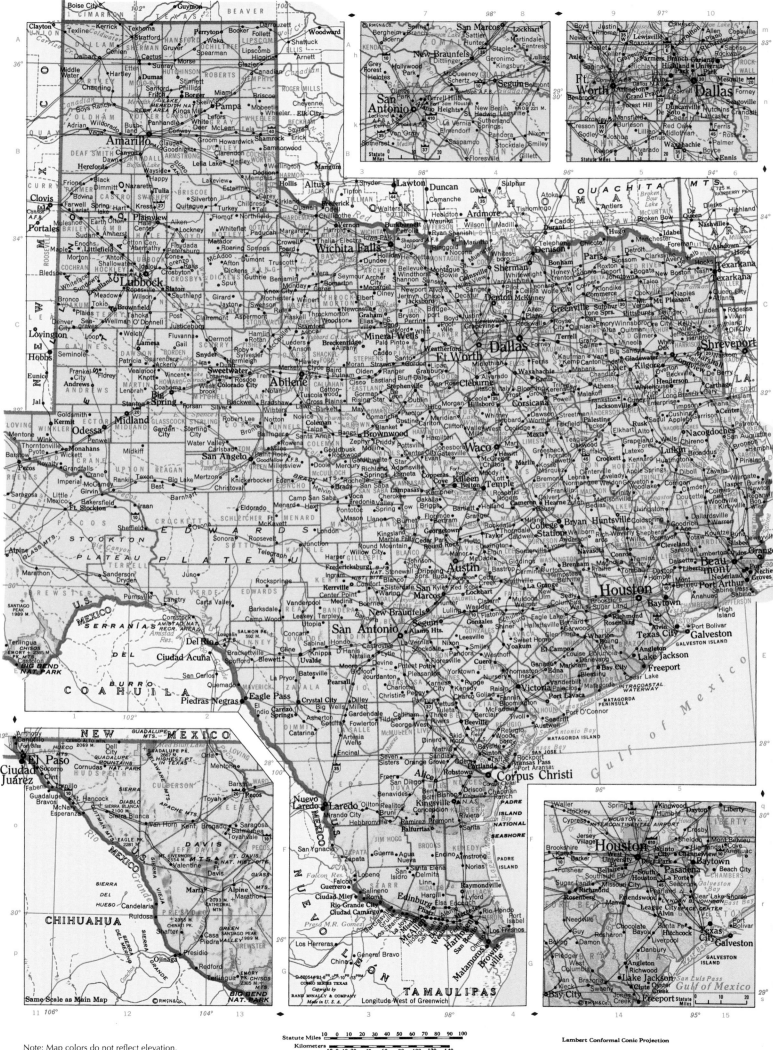

Note: Map colors do not reflect elevation.

Statute Miles
10 0 10 20 30 40 50 60 70 80 90 100
Kilometers
10 0 10 20 40 60 80 100 120 140

Lambert Conformal Conic Projection

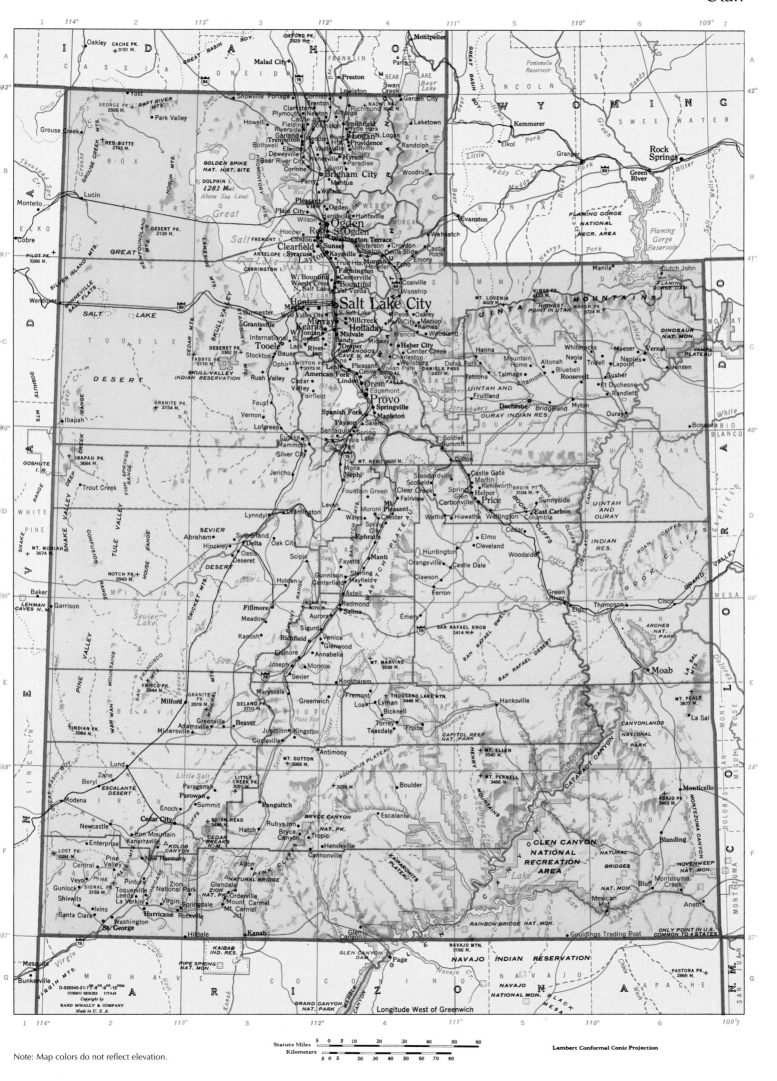

Statute Miles
Kilometers

Lambert Conformal Conic Projection

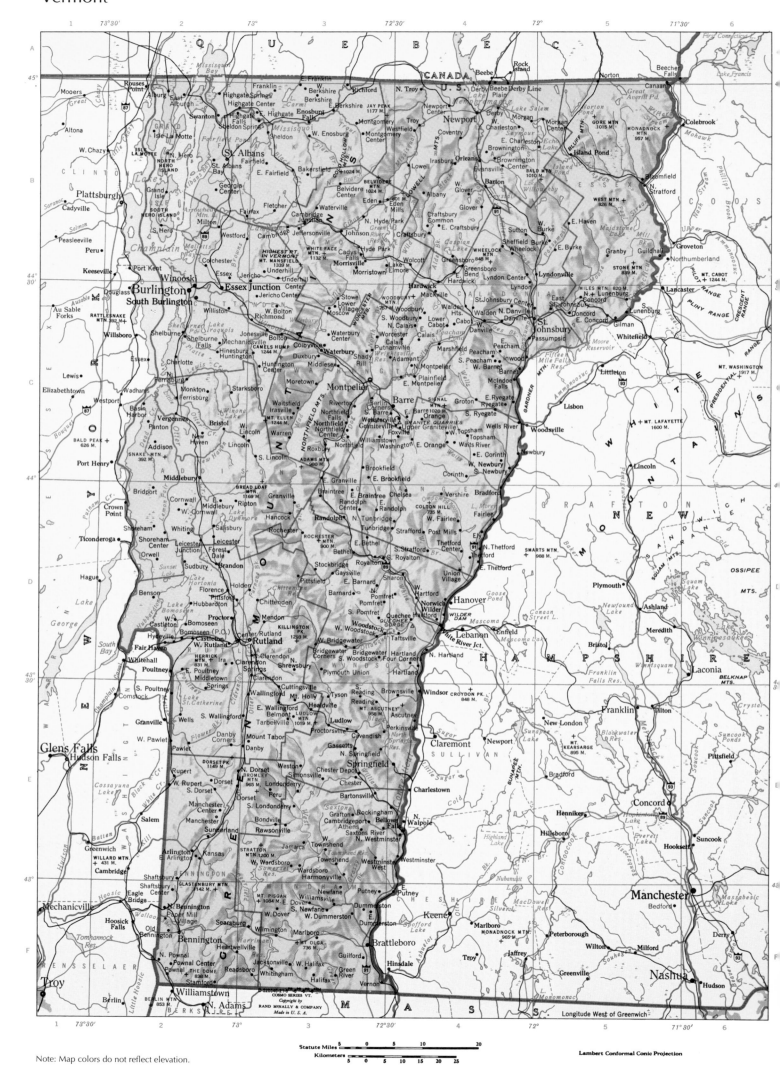

Note: Map colors do not reflect elevation.

Statute Miles 5 0 5 10 20
Kilometers 5 0 5 10 15 20 25

Lambert Conformal Conic Projection

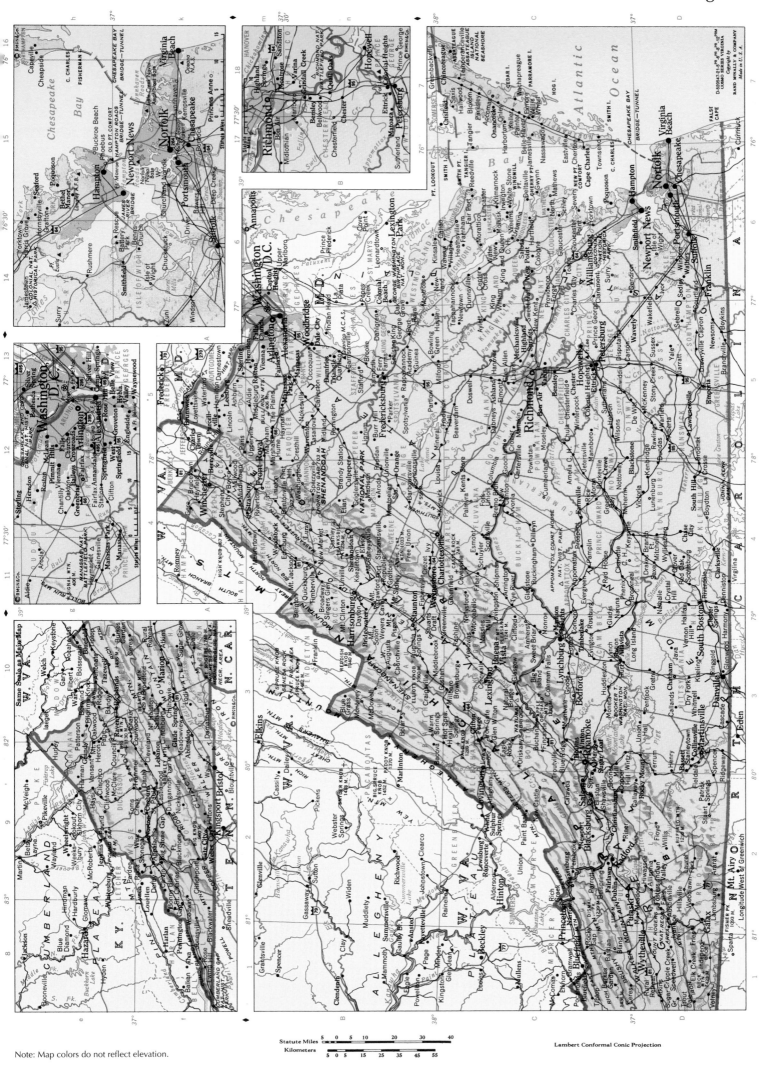

Note: Map colors do not reflect elevation.

Statute Miles   5 0 5   10   20   30   40
Kilometers   5 0 5   15   25   35   45   55

Lambert Conformal Conic Projection

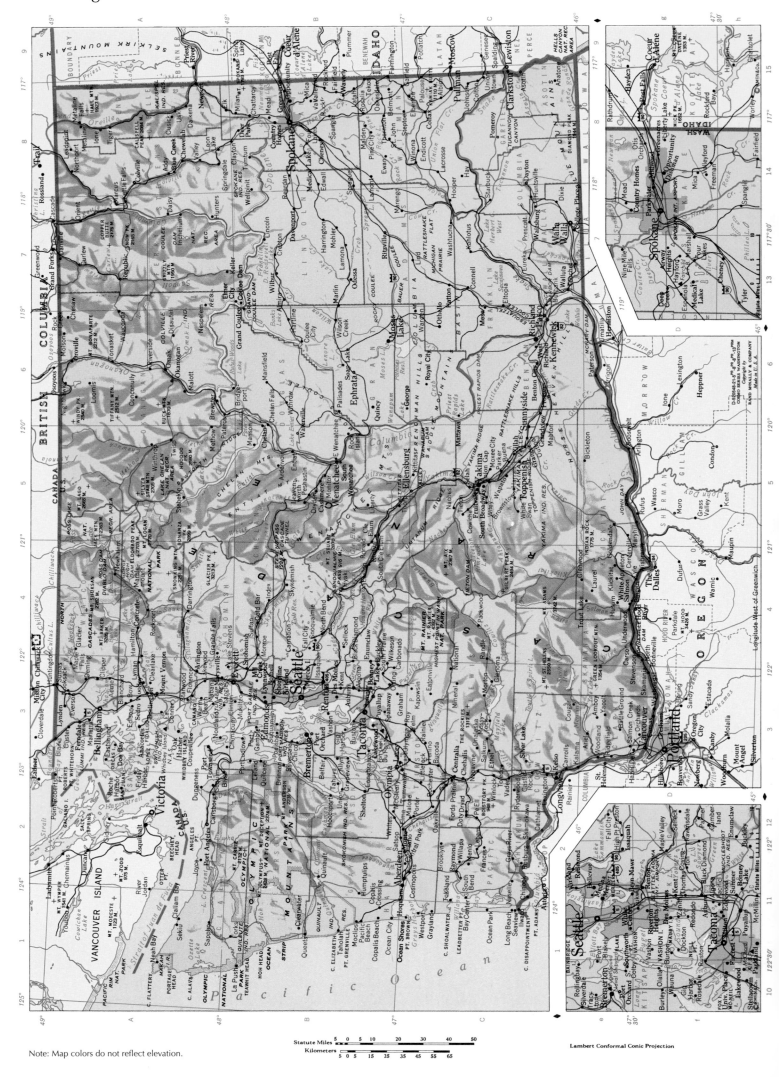

Note: Map colors do not reflect elevation.

Statute Miles 5 0 5 10   20   30   40   50
Kilometers 5 0 5 15 25 35 45 55 65

Lambert Conformal Conic Projection

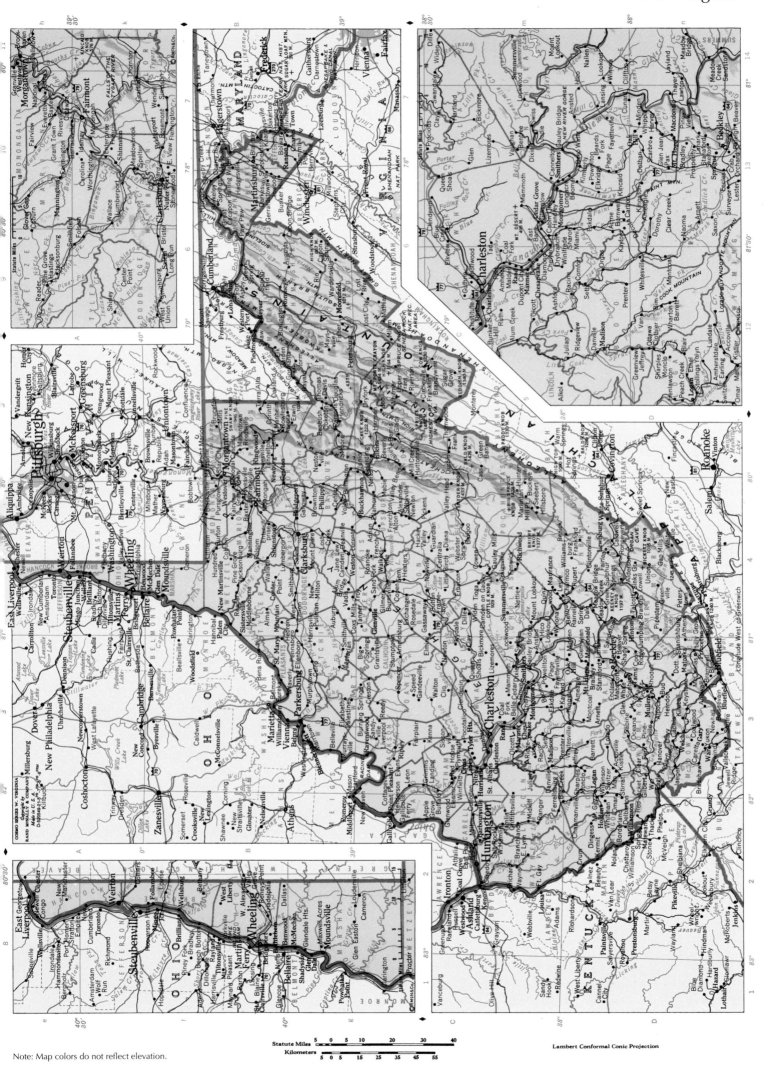

Note: Map colors do not reflect elevation.

Statute Miles 5 0 5 10 20 30 40
Kilometers 5 0 5 15 25 35 45 55

Lambert Conformal Conic Projection

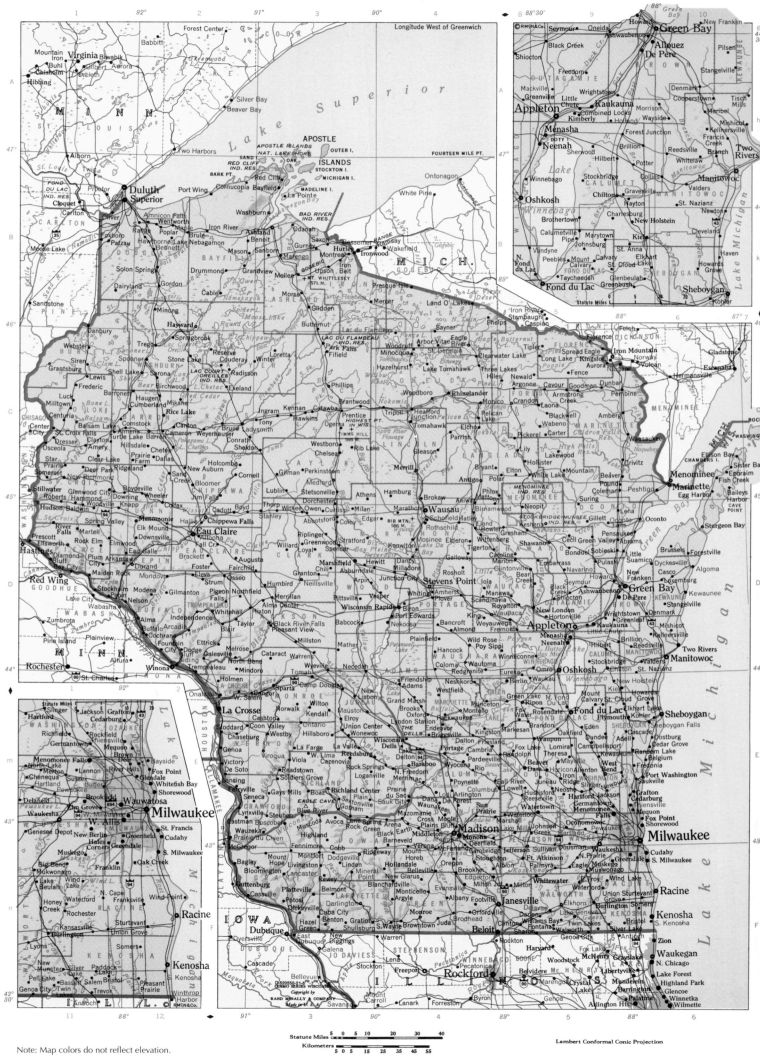

Note: Map colors do not reflect elevation.

Statute Miles
Kilometers

Lambert Conformal Conic Projection

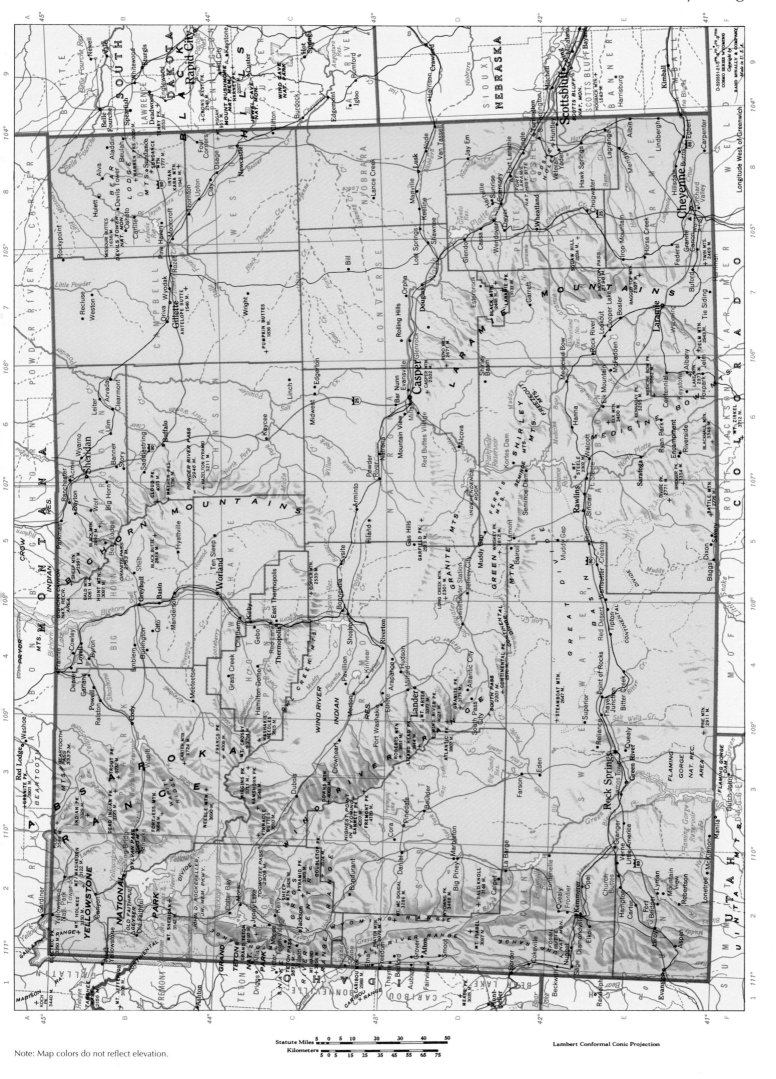

Note: Map colors do not reflect elevation.

Statute Miles
5 0 5 10   20   30   40   50
Kilometers
5 0 5 15   25   35   45   55   65   75

Lambert Conformal Conic Projection

Scale 1 : 35 000 000
Azimuthal Equidistant Projection

Index to World Reference Maps

Introduction to the Index

This index includes in a single alphabetical list approximately 45,000 names of features that appear on the reference maps. Each name is followed by the name of the country or continent in which it is located, a map reference key, and a page reference.

Names The names of cities appear in the index in regular type. The names of all other features appear in *italics*, followed by descriptive terms (hill, mtn., state) to indicate their nature.

Abbreviations of names on the maps have been standardized as much as possible. Names that are abbreviated on the maps are generally spelled out in full in the index.

Country names and names of features that extend beyond the boundaries of one country are followed by the name of the continent in which each is located. Country designations follow the names of all other places in the index. The locations of places in the United States, Canada, and the United Kingdom are further defined by abbreviations that indicate the state, province, or political division in which each is located.

All abbreviations used in the index are defined in the List of Abbreviations below.

Alphabetization Names are alphabetized in the order of the letters of the English alphabet. Spanish *ll* and *ch*, for example, are not treated as distinct letters. Furthermore, diacritical marks are disregarded in alphabetization—German or Scandinavian *ä* or *ö* are treated as *a* or *o*.

The names of physical features may appear inverted, since they are always alphabetized under the proper, not the generic, part of the name, thus: "Gibraltar, Strait of". Otherwise every entry, whether consisting of one word or more, is alphabetized as a single continuous entity. "Lakeland", for example, appears after La Crosse" and before "La Salle". Names beginning with articles (Le Havre, Den Helder, Al-Manāmah) are not inverted. Names beginning "St.", "Ste." and "Sainte" are alphabetized as though spelled "Saint".

In the case of identical names, towns are listed first, then political divisions, then physical features. Entries that are completely identical are listed alphabetically by country name.

Map Reference Keys and Page References The map reference keys and page references are found in the last two columns of each entry.

Each map reference key consists of a letter and number. The letters appear along the sides of the maps. Lowercase letters indicate reference to inset maps. Numbers appear across the tops and bottoms of the maps.

Map reference keys for point features, such as cities and mountain peaks, indicate the locations of the symbols. For other features, such as countries, mountain ranges, or rivers, locations are given for the names.

The page number generally refers to the main map for the country in which the feature is located. Page references to two-page maps always refer to the left-hand page.

Ab., Can.	Alberta, Can.
Afg.	Afghanistan
Afr.	Africa
Ak., U.S.	Alaska, U.S.
Al., U.S.	Alabama, U.S.
Alb.	Albania
Alg.	Algeria
Am. Sam.	American Samoa
And.	Andorra
anch.	anchorage
Ang.	Angola
Anguilla	Anguilla
Ant.	Antarctica
Antig.	Antigua and Barbuda
Ar., U.S.	Arkansas, U.S.
Arg.	Argentina
Arm.	Armenia
Aruba	Aruba
Asia	Asia
Aus.	Austria
Austl.	Australia
Az., U.S.	Arizona, U.S.
Azer.	Azerbaijan
b.	bay, gulf, inlet, lagoon
Bah.	Bahamas
Bahr.	Bahrain
Barb.	Barbados
B.C., Can.	British Columbia, Can.
Bdi.	Burundi
Bel.	Belgium
Belize	Belize
Bela.	Belarus
Benin	Benin
Ber.	Bermuda
Bhu.	Bhutan
B.I.O.T.	British Indian Ocean Territory
Bngl.	Bangladesh
Bol.	Bolivia
Bos.	Bosnia and Herzegovina
Bots.	Botswana
Braz.	Brazil
Br. Vir. Is.	British Virgin Islands
Bru.	Brunei
Bul.	Bulgaria
Burkina	Burkina Faso
c.	cape, point
Ca., U.S.	California, U.S.
Camb.	Cambodia
Cam.	Cameroon
Can.	Canada
C.A.R.	Central African Republic
Cay. Is.	Cayman Islands
Chad	Chad
Chile	Chile
China	China
Christ. I.	Christmas Island
C. Iv.	Cote d'Ivoire
clf.	cliff, escarpment
Co., U.S.	Colorado, U.S.
co.	county, parish
Cocos Is.	Cocos (Keeling) Islands
Col.	Colombia
Com.	Comoros
Congo	Congo
cont.	continent
Cook Is.	Cook Islands
C.R.	Costa Rica
crat.	crater
Cro.	Croatia
cst.	coast
Ct., U.S.	Connecticut, U.S.
ctry.	independent country
Cuba	Cuba
C.V.	Cape Verde
Cyp.	Cyprus
Czech Rep.	Czech Republic
D.C., U.S.	District of Columbia, U.S.
De., U.S.	Delaware, U.S.
Den.	Denmark
dep.	dependency, colony
depr.	depression
dept.	department, district
des.	desert
Dji.	Djibouti
Dom.	Dominica
Dom. Rep.	Dominican Republic
D.R.C.	Democratic Republic of the Congo
Ec.	Ecuador
Egypt	Egypt
El Sal.	El Salvador
Eng., U.K.	England, U.K.
Eq. Gui.	Equatorial Guinea
Erit.	Eritrea
Est.	Estonia
est.	estuary
Eth.	Ethiopia
E. Timor	East Timor
Eur.	Europe
Falk. Is.	Falkland Islands
Far. Is.	Faroe Islands
Fiji	Fiji
Fin.	Finland
Fl., U.S.	Florida, U.S.
for.	forest, moor
Fr.	France
Fr. Gu.	French Guiana
Fr. Poly.	French Polynesia
Ga., U.S.	Georgia, U.S.
Gabon	Gabon
Gam.	Gambia
Gaza Str.	Gaza Strip
Geor.	Georgia
Ger.	Germany
Ghana	Ghana
Gib.	Gibraltar
Golan Hts.	Golan Heights
Grc.	Greece
Gren.	Grenada
Grnld.	Greenland
Guad.	Guadeloupe
Guam	Guam
Guat.	Guatemala
Guernsey	Guernsey
Gui.	Guinea
Gui.-B.	Guinea-Bissau
Guy.	Guyana
Haiti	Haiti
Hi., U.S.	Hawaii, U.S.
hist.	historic site, ruins
hist. reg.	historic region
Hond.	Honduras
Hung.	Hungary
i.	island
Ia., U.S.	Iowa, U.S.
Ice.	Iceland
ice	ice feature, glacier
Id., U.S.	Idaho, U.S.
Il., U.S.	Illinois, U.S.
In., U.S.	Indiana, U.S.
India	India
Indon.	Indonesia
I. of Man	Isle of Man
Iran	Iran
Iraq	Iraq
Ire.	Ireland
Isr.	Israel
is.	islands
Italy	Italy
Jam.	Jamaica
Japan	Japan
Jersey	Jersey
Jer.	Jericho Area
Jord.	Jordan
Kaz.	Kazakhstan
Kenya	Kenya
Kir.	Kiribati
Ks., U.S.	Kansas, U.S.
Kuw.	Kuwait
Ky., U.S.	Kentucky, U.S.
Kyrg.	Kyrgyzstan
l.	lake, pond
La., U.S.	Louisiana, U.S.
Laos	Laos
Lat.	Latvia
Leb.	Lebanon
Leso.	Lesotho
Lib.	Liberia
Libya	Libya
Liech.	Liechtenstein
Lith.	Lithuania
Lux.	Luxembourg
Ma., U.S.	Massachusetts, U.S.
Mac.	Macedonia
Macau	Macau
Madag.	Madagascar
Malay.	Malaysia
Mald.	Maldives
Mali	Mali
Malta	Malta
Marsh. Is.	Marshall Islands
Mart.	Martinique
Maur.	Mauritania
May.	Mayotte
Mb., Can.	Manitoba, Can.
Md., U.S.	Maryland, U.S.
Me., U.S.	Maine, U.S.
Mex.	Mexico
Mi., U.S.	Michigan, U.S.
Micron.	Micronesia, Federated States of
Mid. Is.	Midway Islands
mil.	military installation
Mn., U.S.	Minnesota, U.S.
Mo., U.S.	Missouri, U.S.
Mol.	Moldova
Mon.	Monaco
Mong.	Mongolia
Monts.	Montserrat
Mor.	Morocco
Moz.	Mozambique
Mrts.	Mauritius
Ms., U.S.	Mississippi, U.S.
Mt., U.S.	Montana, U.S.
mth.	river mouth or channel
mtn.	mountain
mts.	mountains
Mwi.	Malawi
Myan.	Myanmar
N.A.	North America
Nauru	Nauru
N.B., Can.	New Brunswick, Can.
N.C., U.S.	North Carolina, U.S.
N. Cal.	New Caledonia
N. Cyp.	Cyprus, North
N.D., U.S.	North Dakota, U.S.
Ne., U.S.	Nebraska, U.S.
Nepal	Nepal
Neth.	Netherlands
Neth. Ant.	Netherlands Antilles
N.H., U.S.	New Hampshire, U.S.
Nic.	Nicaragua
Nig.	Nigeria
Niger	Niger
N. Ire., U.K.	Northern Ireland, U.K.
Niue	Niue
N.J., U.S.	New Jersey, U.S.
N. Kor.	Korea, North
N.L., Can.	Newfoundland and Labrador, Can.
N.M., U.S.	New Mexico, U.S.
N. Mar. Is.	Northern Mariana Islands
Nmb.	Namibia
Nor.	Norway
Norf. I.	Norfolk Island
N.S., Can.	Nova Scotia, Can.
N.T., Can.	Northwest Territories, Can.
Nu., Can.	Nunavut, Can.
Nv., U.S.	Nevada, U.S.
N.Y., U.S.	New York, U.S.
N.Z.	New Zealand
Oc.	Oceania
Oh., U.S.	Ohio, U.S.
Ok., U.S.	Oklahoma, U.S.
Oman	Oman
On., Can.	Ontario, Can.
Or., U.S.	Oregon, U.S.
Pa., U.S.	Pennsylvania, U.S.
Pak.	Pakistan
Palau	Palau
Pan.	Panama
Pap. N. Gui.	Papua New Guinea
Para.	Paraguay
P.E., Can.	Prince Edward Island, Can.
pen.	peninsula
Peru	Peru
Phil.	Philippines
Pit.	Pitcairn
pl.	plain, flat
plat.	plateau, highland
Pol.	Poland
Port.	Portugal
P.R.	Puerto Rico
prov.	province, region
Qatar	Qatar
Qc., Can.	Quebec, Can.
Reu.	Reunion
reg.	physical region
res.	reservoir
rf.	reef, shoal
R.I., U.S.	Rhode Island, U.S.
Rom.	Romania
Russia	Russia
Rw.	Rwanda
S.A.	South America
S. Afr.	South Africa
Samoa	Samoa
Sau. Ar.	Saudi Arabia
S.C., U.S.	South Carolina, U.S.
sci.	scientific station
Scot., U.K.	Scotland, U.K.
S.D., U.S.	South Dakota, U.S.
Sen.	Senegal
Serb.	Serbia and Montenegro
Sey.	Seychelles
S. Geor.	South Georgia and the South Sandwich Islands
Sing.	Singapore
Sk., Can.	Saskatchewan, Can.
S. Kor.	Korea, South
S.L.	Sierra Leone
Slvk.	Slovakia
Slvn.	Slovenia
S. Mar.	San Marino
Sol. Is.	Solomon Islands
Som.	Somalia
Spain	Spain
Sp. N. Afr.	Spanish North Africa
Sri L.	Sri Lanka
state	state, republic, canton
St. Hel.	St. Helena
St. K./N.	St. Kitts and Nevis
St. Luc.	St. Lucia
stm.	stream (river, creek)
St. P./M.	St. Pierre and Miquelon
strt.	strait
S. Tom./P.	Sao Tome and Principe
St. Vin.	St. Vincent and the Grenadines
Sudan	Sudan
Sur.	Suriname
Swaz.	Swaziland
sw.	swamp, marsh
Swe.	Sweden
Switz.	Switzerland
Syria	Syria
Tai.	Taiwan
Taj.	Tajikistan
Tan.	Tanzania
T./C. Is.	Turks and Caicos Islands
ter.	territory
Thai.	Thailand
Tn., U.S.	Tennessee, U.S.
Togo	Togo
Tok.	Tokelau
Tonga	Tonga
Trin.	Trinidad and Tobago
Tun.	Tunisia
Tur.	Turkey
Turk.	Turkmenistan
Tuvalu	Tuvalu
Tx., U.S.	Texas, U.S.
U.A.E.	United Arab Emirates
Ug.	Uganda
U.K.	United Kingdom
Ukr.	Ukraine
Ur.	Uruguay
U.S.	United States
Ut., U.S.	Utah, U.S.
Uzb.	Uzbekistan
Va., U.S.	Virginia, U.S.
val.	valley, watercourse
Vanuatu	Vanuatu
Vat.	Vatican City
Ven.	Venezuela
Viet.	Vietnam
V.I.U.S.	Virgin Islands (U.S.)
vol.	volcano
Vt., U.S.	Vermont, U.S.
Wa., U.S.	Washington, U.S.
Wake I.	Wake Island
Wales, U.K.	Wales, U.K.
Wal./F.	Wallis and Futuna
W.B.	West Bank
Wi., U.S.	Wisconsin, U.S.
W. Sah.	Western Sahara
wtfl.	waterfall
W.V., U.S.	West Virginia, U.S.
Wy., U.S.	Wyoming, U.S.
Yemen	Yemen
Yk., Can.	Yukon Territory, Can.
Zam.	Zambia
Zimb.	Zimbabwe

Name — Map Ref. — Page

A

Aachen, Ger. **E10** 12
Aali, Sadd el-, Egypt **F11** 48
Äänekoski, Fin. **E11** 10
Aba, China **E8** 28
Aba, Nig. **E6** 50
Abaco, i., Bah. **C9** 76
Ābādān, Iran **D5** 42
Ābādeh, Iran **D6** 42
Abadla, Alg. **D4** 48
Abaeté, Braz. **E2** 74
Abaetetuba, Braz. **B2** 74
Abag Qi, China **C10** 28
Abaj, Kaz. **B2** 28
Abajo Peak, mtn., Ut., U.S. **F6** 137
Abakaliki, Nig. **E6** 50
Abakan, Russia **D11** 26
Abala, Niger **D5** 50
Abancay, Peru **F5** 70
Abashiri, Japan **B4** 31
Abau, Pap. N. Gui. **I12** 32
Ābay see Blue Nile, stm., Afr. **H11** 48
Ābaya Hāyk', l., Eth. **B7** 54
Abaza, Russia **D11** 26
Abbaye, Point, c., Mi., U.S. **B2** 115
Abbeville, Fr. **B7** 16
Abbeville, Al., U.S. **D4** 94
Abbeville, Ga., U.S. **E3** 103
Abbeville, La., U.S. **E3** 111
Abbeville, S.C., U.S. **C3** 133
Abbeville, co., S.C., U.S. **C2** 133
Abbotsford, Wi., U.S. **D3** 142
Abbott Butte, mtn., Or., U.S. **E4** 130
Abbott Run, stm., U.S. **B4** 132
Abbott Run Valley, R.I., U.S. **B4** 132
Ābdānān, Iran **F12** 44
Abdulino, Russia **D9** 22
Abe, Lake, l., Afr. **H13** 48
Abéché, Chad **H9** 48
Abengourou, C. Iv. **E4** 50
Åbenrå, Den. **I3** 10
Abeokuta, Nig. **E5** 50
Aberdeen, Scot., U.K. **B5** 12
Aberdeen, Id., U.S. **G6** 105
Aberdeen, Md., U.S. **A5** 113
Aberdeen, Ms., U.S. **B5** 117
Aberdeen, N.C., U.S. **B3** 126
Aberdeen, Oh., U.S. **D2** 128
Aberdeen, S.D., U.S. **B7** 134
Aberdeen, Wa., U.S. **C2** 140
Aberdeen Lake, l., N.T., Can. **E20** 82
Abernathy, Tx., U.S. **C2** 136
Abert, Lake, l., Or., U.S. **E6** 130
Abert Rim, clf., Or., U.S. **E6** 130
Aberystwyth, Wales, U.K. **D4** 12
Abez', Russia **A11** 22
Abhā, Sau. Ar. **G4** 38
Abhar, Iran **D13** 44
Abidjan, C. Iv. **E4** 50
Abilene, Ks., U.S. **D6** 109
Abilene, Tx., U.S. **C3** 136
Abingdon, Il., U.S. **C3** 106
Abingdon, Md., U.S. **B5** 113
Abingdon, Va., U.S. **f10** 139
Abington, Ma., U.S. **B6** 114
Abington [Township], Pa., U.S. **o21** 131
Abinsk, Russia **G15** 20
Abisko, Swe. **B8** 10
Abita Springs, La., U.S. **D5** 111
Abitibi, stm., On., Can. **H23** 82
Åbo see Turku, Fin. **F10** 10
Abomey, Benin **E5** 50
Abongabong, Gunung, mtn., Indon. **C1** 36
Abong Mbang, Cam. **C2** 54
Abou-Deïa, Chad **H8** 48
Abraham Lake, res., Ab., Can. **C2** 84
Abraham Lincoln Birthplace National Historic Site, hist., Ky., U.S. **C4** 110
Abra Pampa, Arg. **C4** 72
Absaroka Range, mts., U.S. **F7** 143
Absarokee, Mt., U.S. **E7** 119
Absecon, N.J., U.S. **E4** 123
Absecon Inlet, b., N.J., U.S. **E4** 123
Abu Dhabi see Abū Ẓaby, U.A.E. **F6** 42
Abū Ḥamad, Sudan **G11** 48
Abuja, Nig. **E6** 50
Abū Kamāl, Syria **E9** 44
Abū Madd, Ra's, c., Sau. Ar. **F3** 42
Abū Maṭāriq, Sudan **A5** 54
Abunã, Braz. **E6** 70
Ābu Road, India **E2** 40
Abū Ẓaby (Abu Dhabi), U.A.E. **F6** 42
Abu Zenīma, Egypt **F10** 14
Abyad, Al-Baḥr al- (White Nile), stm., Sudan **H11** 48
Abyei, Sudan **B5** 54
Academia, Oh., U.S. **B3** 128
Acadia, co., La., U.S. **D3** 111
Acadia National Park, Me., U.S. **D4** 112
Açailândia, Braz. **B2** 74
Acámbaro, Mex. **C4** 78
Acaponeta, Mex. **C3** 78
Acapulco, Mex. **D5** 78
Acarai Mountains, mts., S.A. **C8** 70
Acaraú, Braz. **B3** 74
Acarigua, Ven. **B6** 70
Acayucan, Mex. **D5** 78
Accomack, co., Va., U.S. **C7** 139
Accoville, W.V., U.S. **D3** 141
Accra, Ghana **E4** 50
Achacachi, Bol. **B4** 72
Achalpur, India **E3** 40
Acheng, China **B13** 28
Acı Göl, l., Tur. **D3** 44
Ačinsk, Russia **D11** 26
Acireale, Italy **F5** 18
Ačisaj, Kaz. **B9** 42
Ackerman, Ms., U.S. **B4** 117
Ackley, Ia., U.S. **B4** 108
Acklins, i., Bah. **D10** 76
Acoma Indian Reservation, N.M., U.S. **C2** 124
Aconcagua, Cerro, mtn., Arg. **E4** 72
Acopiara, Braz. **C4** 74
Açores, is., Port. **F7** 46
A Coruña, Spain **F2** 16
Acre, state, Braz. **E5** 70
Acton, Ma., U.S. **B5** 114
Acton Vale, Qc., Can. **D5** 90
Acushnet, Ma., U.S. **C6** 114
Acworth, Ga., U.S. **B2** 103
Ada, Ghana **E5** 50
Ada, co., Id., U.S. **F2** 105
Ada, Mn., U.S. **C2** 116
Ada, Oh., U.S. **B2** 128
Ada, Ok., U.S. **C5** 129
Ada, Mount, mtn., Ak., U.S. **m22** 95
Adair, Ia., U.S. **C3** 108
Adair, co., Ia., U.S. **C3** 108
Adair, co., Ky., U.S. **C4** 110
Adair, co., Mo., U.S. **A5** 118
Adair, Ok., U.S. **A6** 129
Adair, co., Ok., U.S. **B7** 129
Adairsville, Ga., U.S. **B2** 103
Adairville, Ky., U.S. **D3** 110
Adak Island, i., Ak., U.S. **E4** 95
Adak Naval Station, mil., Ak., U.S. **E4** 95
Adam, Oman **F7** 38
Adamantina, Braz. **F1** 74
Adamaoua, mts., Afr. **B2** 54
Adamaoua, state, Cam. **E7** 50
Adamawa see Adamaoua, mts., Afr. **B2** 54
Adam Island, i., Md., U.S. **D5** 113
Adams, co., Co., U.S. **B6** 99
Adams, co., Ia., U.S. **C3** 108
Adams, co., Id., U.S. **E2** 105
Adams, co., Il., U.S. **D2** 106
Adams, co., In., U.S. **C8** 107
Adams, Ma., U.S. **A1** 114
Adams, Mn., U.S. **G6** 116
Adams, co., Ms., U.S. **D2** 117
Adams, co., N.D., U.S. **C3** 127
Adams, co., Ne., U.S. **D7** 120
Adams, N.Y., U.S. **B4** 125
Adams, co., Oh., U.S. **D2** 128
Adams, co., Pa., U.S. **G7** 131
Adams, co., Wa., U.S. **B7** 140
Adams, Wi., U.S. **E4** 142
Adams, co., Wi., U.S. **D4** 142
Adams, Mount, mtn., N.H., U.S. **B4** 122
Adams, Mount, mtn., Wa., U.S. **C4** 140
Adams Point, c., Mi., U.S. **C7** 115
Adams Run, S.C., U.S. **k11** 133
Adamstown, Pa., U.S. **F9** 131
Adamsville, Al., U.S. **f7** 94
Adamsville, R.I., U.S. **E6** 132
Adamsville, Tn., U.S. **B3** 135
Adamsville Brook, stm., R.I., U.S. **E6** 132
'Adan (Aden), Yemen **H5** 38
Adana, Tur. **D6** 44
Adare, Cape, c., Ant. **D22** 67
Adda, stm., Italy **B2** 18
Ad-Dabbah, Sudan **G11** 48
Ad-Dahnā', des., Sau. Ar. **E5** 38
Ad-Dāmir, Sudan **G2** 38
Ad-Dammām, Sau. Ar. **E5** 38
Ad-Dawḥah (Doha), Qatar **E6** 42
Ad-Ḍiffah (Libyan Plateau), plat., Afr. **E9** 14
Addis, La., U.S. **D4** 111
Addis Ababa see Ādīs Ābeba, Eth. **B7** 54
Addison, Al., U.S. **A2** 94
Addison, Ct., U.S. **C5** 100
Addison, Il., U.S. **k8** 106
Addison, N.Y., U.S. **C3** 125
Addison, co., Vt., U.S. **C2** 138
Ad-Dīwānīyah, Iraq **D5** 42
Addyston, Oh., U.S. **o12** 128
Adel, Ga., U.S. **E3** 103
Adel, Ia., U.S. **C3** 108
Adelaide, Austl. **G2** 62
Adelaide, S. Afr. **E4** 56
Adelaide Island, i., Ant. **C33** 67
Adelaide River, Austl. **C5** 60
Adelanto, Ca., U.S. **E5** 98
Adèle Island, i., Austl. **D3** 60
Adelie Coast, Ant. **C19** 67
Aden see 'Adan, Yemen **H5** 38
Aden, Gulf of, b. **H5** 38
Adi, Pulau, i., Indon. **D8** 36
Adiaké, C. Iv. **E4** 50
Adige, stm., Italy **B3** 18
Ādīgrat, Eth. **H3** 38
Ādilābād, India **F3** 40
Adimi, Russia **B15** 28
Adirondack Mountains, mts., N.Y., U.S. **A6** 125
Ādīs Ābeba (Addis Ababa), Eth. **B7** 54
Adıyaman, Tur. **D8** 44
Adjuntas, Presa de las see Vicente Guerrero, Presa, res., Mex. **C5** 78
Adler, Russia **A8** 44
Admiralty Bay, b., Ak., U.S. **A9** 95
Admiralty Gulf, b., Austl. **C4** 60
Admiralty Inlet, b., N.T., Can. **D22** 82
Admiralty Island, i., Ak., U.S. **m22** 95
Admiralty Islands, is., Pap. N. Gui. **G12** 32
Admiralty Mountains, mts., Ant. **D21** 67
Ado, Nig. **E5** 50
Adobe Creek Reservoir, res., Co., U.S. **C7** 99
Ado-Ekiti, Nig. **E6** 50
Ādoni, India **F3** 40
Adour, stm., Fr. **F6** 16
Adra, Spain **I5** 16
Adrar, Alg. **E4** 48
Adrâr, reg., Maur. **B2** 50
Adrian, Ga., U.S. **D4** 103
Adrian, Mi., U.S. **G6** 115
Adrian, Mn., U.S. **G3** 116
Adrian, Mo., U.S. **C3** 118
Adrianople see Edirne, Tur. **B2** 44
Adriatic Sea, s., Eur. **C5** 18
Adusa, D.R.C. **C5** 54
Advance, Mo., U.S. **D8** 118
Ādwa, Eth. **H12** 48
Adygeja, state, Russia **E5** 26
Adzopé, C. Iv. **E4** 50
Aegean Sea, s. **E10** 18
Aën, ostrov, i., Russia **C18** 26
A Estrada, Spain **F2** 16
Afadjoto, mtn., Ghana **E5** 50
Afars and Issas see Djibouti, ctry., Afr. **H13** 48
Afghanistan, ctry., Asia **D8** 42
Afgooye, Som. **C9** 54
Afikpo, Nig. **E6** 50
Aflou, Alg. **E4** 14
Afmadow, Som. **J13** 48
Afognak Island, i., Ak., U.S. **D9** 95
Africa, cont. **E14** 4
Afşin, Tur. **C7** 44
Afton, Ia., U.S. **C3** 108
Afton, Mn., U.S. **F6** 116
Afton, Ok., U.S. **A7** 129
Afton, Wy., U.S. **D2** 143
Afyon, Tur. **C4** 44
Agadez, Niger **C6** 50
Agadir, Mor. **D2** 48
Agadyr', Kaz. **E9** 26
Agalak, Sudan **A6** 54
Agalega Islands, is., Mrts. **E11** 52
Agana see Hagåtña, Guam **D11** 32
Agartala, India **E6** 40
Agate Fossil Beds National Monument, Ne., U.S. **B2** 120
Agattu Island, i., Ak., U.S. **E2** 95
Agawam, Ma., U.S. **B2** 114
Agboville, C. Iv. **E4** 50
Ağdam, Azer. **C12** 44
Agde, Fr. **F8** 16
Agen, Fr. **E7** 16
Agency, Ia., U.S. **D5** 108
Agency, Mo., U.S. **B3** 118
Āghā Jārī, Iran **D5** 42
Aginskoe, Russia **D13** 26
Agnew, Austl. **F3** 60
Agnibilékrou, C. Iv. **E4** 50
Agou, Mont, mtn., Togo **E5** 50
Agoura Hills, Ca., U.S. **m11** 98
Āgra, India **D3** 40
Ağrı, Tur. **C10** 44
Ağrı Dağı, mtn., Tur. **C11** 44
Agrigento, Italy **F4** 18
Agrihan, i., N. Mar. Is. **C12** 32
Agrínion, Grc. **E8** 18
Agrópoli, Italy **D5** 18
Água Branca, Braz. **C3** 74
Aguachica, Col. **D5** 80
Aguadas, Col. **D4** 80
Aguadulce, Pan. **D3** 80
Agua Fria, stm., Az., U.S. **D3** 96
Agua Fria, N.M., U.S. **B3** 124
Aguán, stm., Hond. **B2** 80
Agua Prieta, Mex. **A3** 78
A Guardia, Spain **G2** 16
Aguarico, stm., S.A. **D4** 70
Aguascalientes, state, Mex. **C4** 78
Aguascalientes, Mex. **C4** 78
Águas Formosas, Braz. **E3** 74
Água Vermelha, Represa de, res., Braz. **G9** 70
Aguelhok, Mali **C5** 50
Aguila, Az., U.S. **D2** 96
Águilas, Spain **I6** 16
Agulhas, Kaap, c., S. Afr. **E3** 56
Agulhas Basin **M15** 66
Agustín Codazzi, Col. **C5** 80
Ahaggar, mts., Alg. **F6** 48
Ahaggar, Tassili ta-n-, plat., Alg. **B5** 50
Ahalcihe, Geor. **B10** 44
Ahalkalaki, Geor. **B10** 44
Ahar, Iran **C5** 42
Ahklun Mountains, mts., Ak., U.S. **D7** 95
Ahlat, Tur. **C10** 44
Ahmadābād, India **E2** 40
Ahmadnagar, India **F2** 40
Ahmadpur East, Pak. **E10** 42
Ahmar Mountains, mts., Eth. **B8** 54
Ahoskie, N.C., U.S. **A6** 126
Ahtanum Creek, stm., Wa., U.S. **C5** 140
Ahtubinsk, Russia **E6** 26
Ahuacatlán, Mex. **C4** 78
Ahumada, Mex. **A3** 78
Ahvāz, Iran **D5** 42
Ahvenanmaa see Åland, is., Fin. **G9** 10
Aialik, Cape, c., Ak., U.S. **D10** 95
Aiea, Hi., U.S. **B4** 104
Aiken, S.C., U.S. **D4** 133
Aiken, co., S.C., U.S. **D4** 133
Ailao Shan, mts., China **G8** 28
Aileron, Austl. **E5** 60
Ailinglaplap, atoll, Marsh. Is. **D10** 58
Ailsa Craig, On., Can. **D3** 89
Aim, Russia **D15** 26
Aimorés, Braz. **E3** 74
Aïn el Beïda, Alg. **D5** 14
Ainslie Lake, l., N.S., Can. **C8** 87
Ainsworth, Ne., U.S. **B6** 120
Aïn Témouchent, Alg. **J6** 16
Aïn Wessara, Alg. **J8** 16
Aïr, Massif de l', mts., Niger **C6** 50
Airdrie, Ab., Can. **D3** 84
Aïssa, Djebel, mtn., Alg. **D4** 48
Aitape, Pap. N. Gui. **G11** 32
Aitkin, Mn., U.S. **D5** 116
Aitkin, co., Mn., U.S. **D5** 116
Aitutaki, at., Cook Is. **F14** 58
Aiud, Rom. **F7** 20
Aix, Mount, mtn., Wa., U.S. **C4** 140
Aix-en-Provence, Fr. **F9** 16
Aix-les-Bains, Fr. **E9** 16
Aíyina, i., Grc. **F9** 18
Aíyion, Grc. **E9** 18
Āīzawl, India **E6** 40
Aizu-wakamatsu, Japan **D16** 28
'Ajab Shīr, Iran **D11** 44
Ajaccio, Fr. **D2** 18
Ajaguz, Kaz. **E9** 26
Ajan, Russia **D15** 26
Ajanta, India **E3** 40
Ajanta Range, mts., India **E3** 40
Ajax, On., Can. **D6** 89
Ajdābiyā, Libya **D9** 48
Ajdarkul', ozero, l., Uzb. **B9** 42
Ajdyrlinskij, Russia **D10** 22
Ajjer, Tassili-n-, plat., Alg. **E6** 48
Ajmer, India **D2** 40
Ajo, Az., U.S. **E3** 96
Āk'ak'ī Besek'a, Eth. **B7** 54
'Akāshāt, Iraq **F8** 44
Akbou, Alg. **I9** 16
Akbulak, Russia **D10** 22
Akçaabat, Tur. **B8** 44
Akçadağ, Tur. **C7** 44
Akçakale, Tur. **D8** 44
Akçakoca, Tur. **B4** 44
Akchâr, reg., Maur. **C1** 50
Ak-Chin Indian Reservation, Az., U.S. **E3** 96
Akdağmadeni, Tur. **C6** 44
Aketi, D.R.C. **C4** 54
Akhḍar, Al-Jabal al-, mts., Oman **F7** 42
Akhisar, Tur. **C2** 44
Akiachak, Ak., U.S. **C7** 95
Akita, Japan **D16** 28
Akjoujt, Maur. **C2** 50
Akkajaure, l., Swe. **C7** 10
Akkol', Kaz. **E9** 26
Akkol', Kaz. **B10** 42
'Aklé (Aoûana), reg., Afr. **C3** 50
Akmola see Astana, Kaz. **D9** 26
Akok, Gabon **C1** 54
Akola, India **E3** 40
Akonolinga, Cam. **C2** 54
Akordat, Erit. **G12** 48
Akranes, Ice. **l17** 10a
Akron, Co., U.S. **A7** 99
Akron, Ia., U.S. **B1** 108
Akron, In., U.S. **B5** 107
Akron, N.Y., U.S. **B2** 125
Akron, Oh., U.S. **A4** 128
Akron, Pa., U.S. **F9** 131
Aksaj, Kaz. **D9** 22
Aksaray, Tur. **C6** 44
Aksarka, Russia **A12** 22
Akşehir, Tur. **C4** 44
Akşehir Gölü, l., Tur. **C4** 44
Akseki, Tur. **D4** 44
Aksu, China **C4** 28
Aksuat, Kaz. **E10** 26
Āksum, Eth. **H3** 38
Aktau, Kaz. **E7** 26
Aktjubinsk, Kaz. **D7** 26
Akto, China **B3** 40
Aktogaj, Kaz. **E9** 26
Akune, Japan **D1** 31
Akure, Nig. **E6** 50
Akureyri, Ice. **l19** 10a
Akwanga, Nig. **E6** 50
Akžar, Kaz. **B4** 28
Alabama, stm., Al., U.S. **D2** 94
Alabama, state, U.S. **C3** 94
Alabaster, Al., U.S. **B3** 94
Alaca, Tur. **B6** 44
Alaçam, Tur. **B6** 44
Alacant, Spain **H6** 16
Alachua, Fl., U.S. **C4** 102
Alachua, co., Fl., U.S. **C4** 102
Aladža manastir, rel., Blg. **C12** 18
Alagir, Russia **A11** 44
Alagoas, state, Braz. **C4** 74
Alagoinhas, Braz. **D4** 74
Alagón, Spain **G6** 16
Alahärmä, Fin. **E10** 10
Alajuela, C.R. **C3** 80
Alakanuk, Ak., U.S. **C7** 95
Alakol', ozero, l., Kaz. **E10** 26
Alalakeiki Channel, strt., Hi., U.S. **C5** 104
Al-'Amādīyah, Iraq **D10** 44
Alamagan, i., N. Mar. Is. **C12** 32
Alamance, co., N.C., U.S. **B3** 126
Al-'Amārah, Iraq **D5** 42
Alameda, Ca., U.S. **h8** 98
Alameda, co., Ca., U.S. **D3** 98
Alameda, N.M., U.S. **B3** 124
Alameda Naval Air Station, mil., Ca., U.S. **h8** 98
Alamito Creek, stm., Tx., U.S. **p12** 136
Alamo, Ga., U.S. **D4** 103
Alamo, Nv., U.S. **F6** 121
Alamo, Tn., U.S. **B2** 135
Alamo, Tx., U.S. **F3** 136
Alamogordo, N.M., U.S. **E4** 124
Alamo Heights, Tx., U.S. **E3** 136
Alamo Hueco Mountains, mts., N.M., U.S. **F1** 124
Alamo Indian Reservation, N.M., U.S. **C2** 124
Alamo Lake, res., Az., U.S. **C2** 96
Alamosa, Co., U.S. **D5** 99
Alamosa, stm., Co., U.S. **D4** 99
Alamosa, co., Co., U.S. **D5** 99
Alamosa Creek, stm., N.M., U.S. **D2** 124
Alamosa East, Co., U.S. **D5** 99
Åland, is., Fin. **G9** 10
Ålands hav, s., Eur. **F8** 10
Alandur, India **G4** 40
Alanya, Tur. **D4** 44
Alapaevsk, Russia **C11** 22
Alapaha, Ga., U.S. **E3** 103
Alapaha, stm., U.S. **E3** 103
Al-'Aqabah, Jord. **E3** 42
Alas, Selat, strt., Indon. **E5** 36
Alaşehir, Tur. **C3** 44
Alashanyouqi, China **C8** 28
Alaska, state, U.S. **C9** 95
Alaska, Gulf of, b., Ak., U.S. **D10** 95
Alaska Peninsula, pen., Ak., U.S. **D8** 95
Alaska Range, mts., Ak., U.S. **C9** 95
Alatna, stm., Ak., U.S. **B9** 95
Alatyr', Russia **D8** 22
Alava, Cape, c., Wa., U.S. **A1** 140
Alavus, Fin. **E10** 10
Al-'Ayn, U.A.E. **F7** 42
Al-'Azīzīyah, Libya **E6** 14
Alba, Italy **B2** 18
Al-Bāb, Syria **D7** 44
Albacete, Spain **H6** 16
Alba Iulia, Rom. **F7** 20
Albania, ctry., Eur. **D7** 18
Albano Laziale, Italy **D4** 18
Albany, Austl. **G2** 60
Albany, stm., On., Can. **o18** 89
Albany, Ga., U.S. **E2** 103
Albany, Il., U.S. **B3** 106
Albany, In., U.S. **D7** 107
Albany, Ky., U.S. **D4** 110
Albany, La., U.S. **g10** 111
Albany, Mn., U.S. **E4** 116
Albany, Mo., U.S. **A3** 118
Albany, N.Y., U.S. **C7** 125
Albany, co., N.Y., U.S. **C6** 125
Albany, Or., U.S. **C3** 130
Albany, Tx., U.S. **C3** 136
Albany, Wi., U.S. **F4** 142
Albany, co., Wy., U.S. **E7** 143
Al-Baṣrah, Iraq **D5** 42
Al-Batrā' (Petra), sci., Jord. **D3** 42
Al-Batrūn, Leb. **E6** 44
Al-Bayḍā', Libya **D9** 48
Albemarle, N.C., U.S. **B2** 126
Albemarle, co., Va., U.S. **C4** 139
Albemarle Island see Isabela, Isla, i., Ec. **D1** 70
Albemarle Lake, l., Ms., U.S. **C2** 117
Albemarle Sound, strt., N.C., U.S. **A6** 126
Albert, Fr. **B8** 16
Albert, Lake, l., Afr. **C6** 54
Alberta, prov., Can. **C4** 84
Alberta, Mount, mtn., Ab., Can. **C2** 84
Albert City, Ia., U.S. **B3** 108
Albert Lea, Mn., U.S. **G5** 116
Albert Markham, Mount, mtn., Ant. **E22** 67
Albert Nile, stm., Ug. **C6** 54
Alberton, P.E., Can. **C5** 87
Albertson, N.Y., U.S. **k13** 125
Albertville see Kalemie, D.R.C. **E5** 54
Albertville, Fr. **E10** 16
Albertville, Al., U.S. **A3** 94
Albertville, Mn., U.S. **E5** 116
Albi, Fr. **F8** 16
Albia, Ia., U.S. **C5** 108
Albion, Il., U.S. **E5** 106
Albion, In., U.S. **B7** 107
Albion, Mi., U.S. **F6** 115
Albion, Ne., U.S. **C7** 120
Albion, N.Y., U.S. **B2** 125
Albion, Pa., U.S. **C1** 131

Name — Map Ref. — Page

Albion, R.I., U.S. **B4** 132
Albion, Wa., U.S. **C8** 140
Al-Biqā', val., Leb. **F6** 44
Alborán, Isla de, i., Spain **J5** 16
Ålborg, Den. **H3** 10
Alborz, Reshteh-ye Kūhhā-ye, mts., Iran **C6** 42
Albox, Spain **I5** 16
Ālbū Gharz, Sabkhat, pl., Asia **E9** 44
Albuquerque, N.M., U.S. **B3** 124
Alburquerque, Spain **H3** 16
Alburtis, Pa., U.S. **F10** 131
Albury, Austl. **H4** 62
Alcalá de Henares, Spain **G5** 16
Alcalde, N.M., U.S. **A3** 124
Alcamo, Italy **F4** 18
Alcañiz, Spain **G6** 16
Alcántara Uno, Embalse de, res., Spain **H3** 16
Alcantarilla, Spain **I6** 16
Alcázar de San Juan, Spain **H5** 16
Alcazarquivir see Er-Rachidia, Mor. **E3** 14
Alcester, S.D., U.S. **D9** 134
Alchevs'k, Ukr. **E15** 20
Alcoa, Tn., U.S. **D10** 135
Alcobaça, Braz. **G12** 70
Alcobendas, Spain **G5** 16
Alcoi, Spain **H6** 16
Alcolu, S.C., U.S. **D7** 133
Alcona, co., Mi., U.S. **D7** 115
Alcorn, co., Ms., U.S. **A5** 117
Aldabra, Groupe d', i., Sey. **i11** 57b
Aldama, Mex. **B3** 78
Aldan, Russia **D14** 26
Aldan, stm., Russia **C15** 26
Aldan Plateau see Aldanskoe nagor'e, plat., Russia **D14** 26
Aldanskoe nagor'e, plat., Russia **D14** 26
Alden, Ia., U.S. **B4** 108
Alden, Mn., U.S. **G5** 116
Alden, N.Y., U.S. **C2** 125
Alder Brook, stm., Vt., U.S. **B4** 138
Alderney, i., Guern. **F5** 12
Alderson, W.V., U.S. **D4** 141
Aldrich, Al., U.S. **B3** 94
Aledo, Il., U.S. **B3** 106
Aleg, Maur. **C2** 50
Alegres Mountain, mtn., N.M., U.S. **C2** 124
Alegrete, Braz. **D6** 72
Alejandro Selkirk, Isla, i., Chile **E1** 72
Alejsk, Russia **D10** 26
Aleksandrov, Russia **C6** 22
Aleksandrovsk-Sahalinskij, Russia **D16** 26
Alekseevka, Russia **D15** 20
Aleksin, Russia **B14** 20
Aleksinac, Serb. **C8** 18
Alençon, Fr. **C7** 16
Alenquer, Braz. **D9** 70
Alenuihaha Channel, strt., Hi., U.S. **C5** 104
Aleppo see Ḥalab, Syria **D7** 44
Alert Bay, B.C., Can. **D4** 85
Alès, Fr. **E9** 16
Alessándria, Italy **B2** 18
Ålesund, Nor. **E2** 10
Aleutian Basin **B4** 144
Aleutian Islands, is., Ak., U.S. **E3** 95
Aleutian Range, mts., Ak., U.S. **D9** 95
Aleutian Trench **B4** 144
Aleutka, Russia **B18** 28
Alex, Ok., U.S. **C4** 129
Alexander, co., Il., U.S. **F4** 106
Alexander, co., N.C., U.S. **B1** 126
Alexander, Lake, l., Mn., U.S. **D4** 116
Alexander Archipelago, is., Ak., U.S. **D12** 95
Alexander Bay, S. Afr. **D2** 56
Alexander City, Al., U.S. **C4** 94
Alexander Island, i., Ant. **C33** 67
Alexandra, N.Z. **q12** 63c
Alexandretta see İskenderun, Tur. **D7** 44
Alexandria, On., Can. **B10** 89
Alexandria see El-Iskandarîya, Egypt **E9** 48
Alexandria, Rom. **H8** 20
Alexandria, S. Afr. **E4** 56
Alexandria, In., U.S. **D6** 107
Alexandria, Ky., U.S. **B5** 110
Alexandria, La., U.S. **C3** 111
Alexandria, Mn., U.S. **E3** 116
Alexandria, Tn., U.S. **A5** 135
Alexandria, Va., U.S. **B5** 139
Alexandroúpolis, Grc. **D10** 18
Alexis, Il., U.S. **B3** 106
Alfalfa, co., Ok., U.S. **A3** 129
Al-Fallūjah, Iraq **F10** 44
Al-Fāshir, Sudan **H10** 48
Alföld, pl., Hung. **F6** 20
Alfred, On., Can. **B10** 89
Alfred, N.Y., U.S. **C3** 125
Al-Fujayrah, U.A.E. **E7** 42
Al-Furāt see Euphrates, stm., Asia **D4** 42
Alga, Kaz. **E10** 22
Algarrobo del Águila, Arg. **F4** 72
Algarve, hist. reg., Port. **I2** 16
Algeciras, Spain **I4** 16
Alger, co., Mi., U.S. **B4** 115
Alger, Oh., U.S. **B2** 128
Algeria, ctry., Afr. **E5** 48
Al-Ghayḍah, Yemen **G6** 38
Al-Ghazālah, Sau. Ar. **E4** 42
Alghero, Italy **D2** 18
Algiers see El Djazaïr, Alg. **C5** 48
Algoabaai, b., S. Afr. **E4** 56
Algoma, Wi., U.S. **D6** 142
Algona, Ia., U.S. **A3** 108
Algona, Wa., U.S. **B3** 140
Algonac, Mi., U.S. **F8** 115
Algonquin, Il., U.S. **A5** 106
Algonquin Provincial Park, On., Can. **B6** 89
Algood, Tn., U.S. **C8** 135
Al-Ḥajarah, reg., Asia **E5** 42
Al-Ḥalfāyah, Iraq **G12** 44
Al-Ḥamād, pl., Sau. Ar. **G8** 44
Alhambra, Ca., U.S. **m12** 98
Al-Ḥarrah, lav., Sau. Ar. **D3** 42
Al-Harūj al-Aswad, Libya **A8** 50
Al-Ḥasakah, Syria **D9** 44
Al-Ḥawrah, Yemen **H5** 38
Al-Ḥayy, Iraq **F12** 44
Al-Ḥijāz, reg., Sau. Ar. **E3** 38
Al-Ḥillah, Iraq **D4** 42
Al-Hoceima, Mor. **C4** 48
Al-Ḥudaydah, Yemen **H4** 38
Al-Ḥufrah, reg., Sau. Ar. **E3** 42
Al-Hufūf, Sau. Ar. **E5** 38
Al-Ḥulwah, Sau. Ar. **F5** 38
Aliağo, Tur. **C2** 44
'Alī al-Gharbī, Iraq **F12** 44
Alībāg, India **F2** 40
Āli Bayramlı, Azer. **C13** 44
Alicante see Alacant, Spain **H6** 16
Alice, Tx., U.S. **F3** 136
Alice Lake, l., Mn., U.S. **C7** 116
Alice Springs, Austl. **E5** 60
Aliceville, Al., U.S. **B1** 94
Alīgarh, India **D3** 40
Alīgūdarz, Iran **D5** 42
Alingsås, Swe. **H5** 10
Alīpur, Pak. **E10** 42
Aliquippa, Pa., U.S. **E1** 131
Aliwal North, S. Afr. **E4** 56
Alix, Ab., Can. **C4** 84
Al-Jaghbūb, Libya **E9** 48
Al-Jahrah, Kuw. **E5** 42
Al-Jalāmīd, Sau. Ar. **G9** 44
Al-Jawārah, Oman **G7** 38
Al-Jawf, Libya **F9** 48
Al-Jawf, Sau. Ar. **E3** 38
Al-Jubayl, Sau. Ar. **E5** 38
Al-Junaynah, Sudan **H9** 48
Aljustrel, Port. **I2** 16
Alkali Lake, l., Nv., U.S. **B2** 121
Alkali Lake, l., Or., U.S. **E6** 130
Alkaline Lake, l., N.D., U.S. **C6** 127
Al-Karak, Jord. **G6** 44
Al-Khābūrah, Oman **F7** 38
Al-Khalīl (Hebron), W.B. **G6** 44
Al-Kharṭūm, Sudan **G11** 48
Al-Khaṣab, Oman **E7** 42
Al-Khums, Libya **E6** 14
Al-Kifl, Iraq **F11** 44
Alkmaar, Neth. **D9** 12
Al-Kūfah, Iraq **D4** 42
Al-Kūt, Iraq **D5** 42
Al-Kuwayt (Kuwait), Kuw. **E5** 42
Al-Lādhiqīyah, Syria **E6** 44
Allagash, stm., Me., U.S. **B3** 112
Allagash Lake, l., Me., U.S. **B3** 112
Allahābād, India **D4** 40
Allah-Jun', Russia **C15** 26
Allamakee, co., Ia., U.S. **A6** 108
Allan, Sk., Can. **F2** 91
Allanmyo, Mya. **C3** 34
Allardt, Tn., U.S. **C9** 135
Allatoona Lake, res., Ga., U.S. **B2** 103
Alldays, S. Afr. **C4** 56
Allegan, Mi., U.S. **F5** 115
Allegan, co., Mi., U.S. **F5** 115
Allegany, co., Md., U.S. **k13** 113
Allegany, N.Y., U.S. **C2** 125
Allegany, co., N.Y., U.S. **C2** 125
Allegany Indian Reservation, N.Y., U.S. **C2** 125
Alleghany, co., N.C., U.S. **A1** 126
Alleghany, co., Va., U.S. **C2** 139
Allegheny, co., Pa., U.S. **E2** 131
Allegheny, stm., U.S. **E2** 131
Allegheny Reservoir, res., U.S. **B4** 131
Allemands, Lac Des, l., La., U.S. **E5** 111
Allen, co., In., U.S. **B7** 107
Allen, co., Ks., U.S. **E8** 109
Allen, co., Ky., U.S. **D3** 110
Allen, co., La., U.S. **D3** 111
Allen, co., Oh., U.S. **B1** 128
Allen, Ok., U.S. **C5** 129
Allen, Mount, mtn., Ak., U.S. **C11** 95
Allendale, N.J., U.S. **A4** 123
Allendale, S.C., U.S. **E5** 133
Allendale, co., S.C., U.S. **F5** 133
Allende, Mex. **B4** 78
Allen Park, Mi., U.S. **p15** 115
Allenton, R.I., U.S. **E4** 132
Allenton, Wi., U.S. **E5** 142
Allentown, Pa., U.S. **E11** 131
Alleppey, India **H3** 40
Allerton, Point, c., Ma., U.S. **B6** 114
Alliance, Ne., U.S. **B3** 120
Alliance, Oh., U.S. **B4** 128
Allier, stm., Fr. **D8** 16
Alligator, stm., N.C., U.S. **B6** 126
Alligator Lake, l., Me., U.S. **D4** 112
Allison, Ia., U.S. **B5** 108
Allison, Pa., U.S. **G2** 131
Allison Park, Pa., U.S. **h14** 131
Alliston [Beeton Tecumseth and Tottenham], On., Can. **C5** 89
Al-Līth, Sau. Ar. **F4** 38
Allouez, Wi., U.S. **h9** 142
Alloway Creek, stm., N.J., U.S. **D2** 123
Al-Luḥayyah, Yemen **G4** 38
Allumette Lake, l., Can. **B7** 89
Allyn, Wa., U.S. **B3** 140
Alma, Qc., Can. **A6** 90
Alma, Ar., U.S. **B1** 97
Alma, Ga., U.S. **E4** 103
Alma, Ks., U.S. **C7** 109
Alma, Mi., U.S. **E6** 115
Alma, Ne., U.S. **D6** 120
Alma, Wi., U.S. **D2** 142
Alma-Ata see Almaty, Kaz. **E9** 26
Almada, Port. **H2** 16
Almadén, Spain **H4** 16
Al-Madīnah (Medina), Sau. Ar. **F3** 38
Al-Mafraq, Jord. **F7** 44
Almalyk, Uzb. **E8** 26
Al-Manāmah (Manama), Bahr. **E6** 42
Almanor, Lake, l., Ca., U.S. **B3** 98
Almansa, Spain **H6** 16
Al-Marj, Libya **D9** 48
Almaty, Kaz. **E9** 26
Al-Mawṣil, Iraq **C4** 42
Al-Mayādīn, Syria **E9** 44
Almelo, Neth. **D10** 12
Almenara, Braz. **E3** 74
Almendralejo, Spain **H3** 16
Almería, Spain **I5** 16
Almería, Golfo de, b., Spain **I5** 16
Al'metevsk, Russia **D7** 26
Al-Mijlad, Sudan **A5** 54
Al-Miqdādīyah, Iraq **F11** 44
Almirante, Pan. **D3** 80
Almont, Mi., U.S. **F7** 115
Almonte, On., Can. **B8** 89
Almonte, Spain **I3** 16
Al-Mubarraz, Sau. Ar. **E5** 42
Al-Mubarraz, Sau. Ar. **F5** 38
Al-Muḥarraq, Bahr. **E6** 42
Al-Mukallā, Yemen **H5** 38
Al-Mukhā, Yemen **H4** 38
Al-Muwayliḥ, Sau. Ar. **E3** 38
Alnön, i., Swe. **E7** 10
Alnwick, Eng., U.K. **C6** 12
Aloha, Or., U.S. **h12** 130
Alor, Pulau, i., Indon. **E6** 36
Alor Setar, Malay. **B2** 36
Alpena, Mi., U.S. **C7** 115
Alpena, co., Mi., U.S. **D7** 115
Alpha Cordillera **E33** 144
Alpharetta, Ga., U.S. **B2** 103
Alphonse, i., Sey. **i12** 57b
Alpine, Az., U.S. **D6** 96
Alpine, co., Ca., U.S. **C4** 98
Alpine, Tx., U.S. **D1** 136
Alpine, Ut., U.S. **C4** 137
Alps, mts., Eur. **B5** 14
Al-Qaḍārif, Sudan **H12** 48
Al-Qā'im, Iraq **E9** 44
Al-Qāmishlī, Syria **D9** 44
Al-Qaryah ash-Sharqīyah, Libya **D7** 48
Al-Qaryatayn, Syria **E7** 44
Al-Qaṭīf, Sau. Ar. **E6** 38
Al-Qaṭrūn, Libya **F7** 48
Al-Qayṣūmah, Sau. Ar. **E5** 38
Al-Quds see Jerusalem, Isr. **G6** 44
Al-Qunayṭirah, Syria **F6** 44
Al-Qunfudhah, Sau. Ar. **G4** 38
Al-Qurnah, Iraq **G12** 44
Al-Quṭayfah, Syria **F7** 44
Als, i., Den. **I3** 10
Alsace, hist. reg., Fr. **C10** 16
Alsasua, Spain **F5** 16
Alta, Nor. **B10** 10
Alta, Ia., U.S. **B2** 108
Altadena, Ca., U.S. **m12** 98
Alta Gracia, Arg. **E5** 72
Altagracia, Ven. **C5** 80
Altai, mts., Asia **B5** 28
Altai, mts., Asia **B5** 28
Altaj, state, Russia **A5** 28
Altamaha, stm., Ga., U.S. **E4** 103
Altamira, Braz. **D9** 70
Altamont, Il., U.S. **D5** 106
Altamont, Ks., U.S. **E8** 109
Altamont, Or., U.S. **E5** 130
Altamont, Tn., U.S. **D8** 135
Altamonte Springs, Fl., U.S. **D5** 102
Altamura, Italy **D6** 18
Altata, Mex. **C3** 78
Altavista, Va., U.S. **C3** 139
Altay, Mong. **B7** 28
Altay Mountains see Altai, mts., Asia **B5** 28
Altay Mountains see Altai, mts., Asia **B5** 28
Altevatnet, l., Nor. **B8** 10
Altheimer, Ar., U.S. **C4** 97
Alto, Ga., U.S. **B3** 103
Alto, N.M., U.S. **D4** 124
Alto Araguaia, Braz. **G9** 70
Alto Garças, Braz. **B7** 72
Alton, Ia., U.S. **B2** 108
Alton, Il., U.S. **E3** 106
Alton, Mo., U.S. **E6** 118
Alton, N.H., U.S. **D4** 122
Altona, Mb., Can. **E3** 86
Alton Bay, N.H., U.S. **D4** 122
Altoona, Al., U.S. **A3** 94
Altoona, Fl., U.S. **D5** 102
Altoona, Ia., U.S. **C4** 108
Altoona, Pa., U.S. **E5** 131
Altoona, Wi., U.S. **D2** 142
Alto Paraguai, Braz. **A6** 72
Alto Parnaíba, Braz. **E10** 70
Alto Río Senguer, Arg. **G2** 69
Altun Shan, mts., China **D5** 28
Alturas, Ca., U.S. **B3** 98
Altus, Ok., U.S. **C2** 129
Altus Air Force Base, mil., Ok., U.S. **C2** 129
Altus Reservoir, res., Ok., U.S. **C2** 129
Al-'Ubaylah, Sau. Ar. **F6** 38
Al-Ubayyiḍ, Sudan **H10** 48
Alucra, Tur. **B8** 44
Alum Bank, Pa., U.S. **F4** 131
Alum Creek, stm., Oh., U.S. **k11** 128
Alupka, Ukr. **G13** 20
Al-'Uqaylah, Libya **E7** 14
Alushta, Ukr. **G13** 20
Al-'Uwaynāt, Libya **E7** 48
Alva, Fl., U.S. **F5** 102
Alva, Ok., U.S. **A3** 129
Alvarado, Mex. **D5** 78
Alvarado, Tx., U.S. **C4** 136
Álvaro Obregón, Presa, res., Mex. **B3** 78
Älvdalen, Swe. **F6** 10
Alvin, Tx., U.S. **E5** 136
Alvinston, On., Can. **E3** 89
Älvkarleby, Swe. **F7** 10
Alvord Lake, l., Or., U.S. **E8** 130
Al-Wajh, Sau. Ar. **E3** 38
Alwar, India **D3** 40
Alxa Zuoqi, China **D9** 28
Alzira, Spain **H6** 16
Ama, La., U.S. **k11** 111
Amacuro, stm., S.A. **D7** 80
Amadeus, Lake, l., Austl. **E5** 60
Amador, co., Ca., U.S. **C3** 98
Amagansett, N.Y., U.S. **n16** 125
Amahai, Indon. **D7** 36
Amakusa-nada, s., Japan **D1** 31
Amakusa Sea see Amakusa-nada, s., Japan **D1** 31
Åmål, Swe. **G5** 10
Amalfi, Col. **D4** 80
Amalfi, Italy **D5** 18
Amaliás, Grc. **F8** 18
Amambaí, Braz. **H8** 70
Amami-Ō-shima, i., Japan **E1** 31
Amami-shotō, is., Japan **g6** 31a
Amana, Ia., U.S. **C6** 108
Amapá, Braz. **C9** 70
Amapá, state, Braz. **C9** 70
Amarante, Braz. **E11** 70
Amarapura, Mya. **B3** 34
Amargosa, stm., U.S. **D5** 98
Amargosa Desert, des., U.S. **G5** 121
Amargosa Range, mts., U.S. **G5** 121
Amargosa Valley, Nv., U.S. **G5** 121
Amarillo, Tx., U.S. **B2** 136
Amarkantak, India **E4** 40
Amasya, Tur. **B6** 44
Amatignak Island, i., Ak., U.S. **E4** 95
Amawbia Awka, Nig. **E6** 50
Amazon (Solimões) (Amazonas), stm., S.A. **D9** 70
Amazonas see Amazon, stm., S.A. **D9** 70
Ambāla, India **C3** 40
Ambalavao, Madag. **C8** 56
Ambanja, Madag. **A8** 56
Ambarčik, Russia **C18** 26
Ambato, Ec. **D4** 70
Ambatofinandrahana, Madag. **C8** 56
Ambatolampy, Madag. **B8** 56
Ambatondrazaka, Madag. **B8** 56
Amberg, Ger. **F12** 12
Ambikāpur, India **E4** 40
Ambilobe, Madag. **A8** 56
Ambler, Pa., U.S. **F11** 131
Amboasary, Madag. **C8** 56
Ambodifototra, Madag. **B8** 56
Ambon, Indon. **D7** 36
Ambon, Pulau, i., Indon. **D7** 36
Ambositra, Madag. **C8** 56
Ambovombe, Madag. **D8** 56
Amboy, Il., U.S. **B4** 106
Ambridge, Pa., U.S. **E1** 131
Ambriz, Ang. **E2** 54
Ambrym, i., Vanuatu **k9** 62a
Ambunti, Pap. N. Gui. **G11** 32
Āmbūr, India **G3** 40
Amchitka Island, i., Ak., U.S. **E3** 95
Amchitka Pass, strt., Ak., U.S. **E4** 95
Amderma, Russia **C8** 26
Amdo, China **E6** 28
Ameca, Mex. **C4** 78
Amelia, La., U.S. **E4** 111
Amelia, Oh., U.S. **C1** 128
Amelia, co., Va., U.S. **C4** 139
Amelia Court House, Va., U.S. **C5** 139
Amelia Island, i., Fl., U.S. **k9** 102
American, stm., Ca., U.S. **C3** 98
American Falls, Id., U.S. **G6** 105
American Falls Dam, Id., U.S. **G6** 105
American Falls Reservoir, res., Id., U.S. **F5** 105
American Fork, Ut., U.S. **C4** 137
American Highland, plat., Ant. **D12** 67
American Samoa, dep., Oc. **F12** 58
Americus, Ga., U.S. **D2** 103
Americus, Ks., U.S. **D7** 109
Amersfoort, Neth. **D9** 12
Amery, Wi., U.S. **C1** 142
Amery Ice Shelf, ice, Ant. **C12** 67
Ames, Ia., U.S. **B4** 108
Amesbury, Ma., U.S. **A6** 114
Amfilokhía, Grc. **E8** 18
Amga, Russia **C15** 26
Amga, stm., Russia **C14** 26
Amgun', stm., Russia **D15** 26
Amherst, Ma., U.S. **B2** 114
Amherst, N.H., U.S. **E3** 122
Amherst, N.Y., U.S. **C2** 125
Amherst, Oh., U.S. **A3** 128
Amherst, Va., U.S. **C3** 139
Amherst, co., Va., U.S. **C3** 139
Amherst, Wi., U.S. **D4** 142
Amherstburg, On., Can. **E1** 89
Amherstdale, W.V., U.S. **n12** 141
Amiens, Fr. **C8** 16
Aminuis, Nmb. **C2** 56
Amirantes, Les, is., Sey. **i12** 57b
Amisk Lake, l., Sk., Can. **C4** 91
Amistad, Presa de la (Amistad Reservoir), res., N.A. **B4** 78
Amistad National Recreation Area, Tx., U.S. **E2** 136
Amistad Reservoir (Amistad, Presa de la), res., N.A. **B4** 78
Amite, La., U.S. **D5** 111
Amite, stm., La., U.S. **D5** 111
Amite, co., Ms., U.S. **D3** 117
Amity, Or., U.S. **B3** 130
Amityville, N.Y., U.S. **E7** 125
Amlia Island, i., Ak., U.S. **E5** 95
'Ammān, Jord. **D3** 42
Ammon, Id., U.S. **F7** 105
Ammonoosuc, stm., N.H., U.S. **B3** 122
Āmol, Iran **C6** 42
Amorgós, i., Grc. **F10** 18
Amory, Ms., U.S. **B5** 117
Amos, Qc., Can. **k11** 90
Åmot, Nor. **G2** 10
Amoy see Xiamen, China **G11** 28
Ampanihy, Madag. **C7** 56
Ampasimanolotra, Madag. **B8** 56
Amposta, Spain **G7** 16
Amrāvati, India **E3** 40
Amreli, India **E2** 40
Amritsar, India **C2** 40
Amroha, India **D3** 40
Amsterdam, Neth. **D9** 12
Amsterdam, N.Y., U.S. **C6** 125
Amstetten, Aus. **F14** 12
Am Timan, Chad **A4** 54
Amu Darya, stm., Asia **B8** 42
Amukta Pass, strt., Ak., U.S. **E5** 95
Amundsen Gulf, b., N.T., Can. **D15** 82
Amundsen Sea, s., Ant. **C30** 67
Amuntai, Indon. **D5** 36
Amur (Heilong), stm., Asia **D16** 26
Amvrakikós Kólpos, b., Grc. **E8** 18
Anaa, at., Fr. Poly. **F15** 58
Anaco, Ven. **D7** 80
Anacoco, La., U.S. **C2** 111
Anaconda, Mt., U.S. **D4** 119
Anaconda Range, mts., Mt., U.S. **E3** 119
Anacortes, Wa., U.S. **A3** 140
Anacostia, stm., U.S. **C4** 113
Anacostia, Northwest Branch, stm., Md., U.S. **B3** 113
Anadarko, Ok., U.S. **B3** 129
Anadolu, hist. reg., Tur. **C6** 44
Anadyr', Russia **C19** 26
Anadyr', stm., Russia **C19** 26
Anadyr, Gulf of see Anadyrskij zaliv, b., Russia **C20** 26
Anadyrskij zaliv, b., Russia **C20** 26
'Ānah, Iraq **E9** 44
Anaheim, Ca., U.S. **F5** 98
Anahola, Hi., U.S. **A2** 104
Anahuac, Tx., U.S. **E5** 136
Anakāpalle, India **F4** 40
Analalava, Madag. **A8** 56
Ana María, Golfo de, b., Cuba **A4** 80
Anambas, Kepulauan, is., Indon. **C3** 36
Anamosa, Ia., U.S. **B6** 108
Anamur, Tur. **D5** 44
Anan, Japan **D2** 31
Anan'ïv, Ukr. **F11** 20
Anantapur, India **G3** 40
Anantnāg, India **C3** 40
Anapa, Russia **G14** 20
Anápolis, Braz. **E2** 74
Anastasia Island, i., Fl., U.S. **C5** 102

Name — Map Ref. — Page

Anatahan, i., N. Mar. Is. C12 32
Anatolia see Anadolu, hist. reg., Tur. C6 44
Anatom, i., Vanuatu I9 62a
Añatuya, Arg. D5 72
Anbei, China A7 40
Ancaster, On., Can. D4 89
Ancha, Sierra, mts., Az., U.S. D4 96
Anchorage, Ak., U.S. C10 95
Anchorage, Ky., U.S. g11 110
Anchor Point, Ak., U.S. D9 95
Anchor Point, c., Ak., U.S. h15 95
Ancienne-Lorette, Qc., Can. C6 90
Anclote Keys, is., Fl., U.S. D4 102
Ancona, Italy C4 18
Ancud, Chile F2 69
Anda, China B13 28
Andacollo, Chile E3 72
Andalgalá, Arg. D4 72
Åndalsnes, Nor. E2 10
Andalucía, hist. reg., Spain I4 16
Andalusia, Al., U.S. D3 94
Andalusia, Il., U.S. B3 106
Andaman and Nicobar Islands, mun., India G6 40
Andaman Basin H12 64
Andaman Islands, is., India G6 40
Andaman Sea, Asia E3 34
Andamooka, Austl. G2 62
Andapa, Madag. A8 56
Andéramboukane, Mali C5 50
Anderson, stm., N.T., Can. E14 82
Anderson, Ak., U.S. C10 95
Anderson, Ca., U.S. B2 98
Anderson, In., U.S. D6 107
Anderson, stm., In., U.S. H4 107
Anderson, co., Ks., U.S. D8 109
Anderson, co., Ky., U.S. C4 110
Anderson, Mo., U.S. E3 118
Anderson, S.C., U.S. B2 133
Anderson, co., S.C., U.S. B2 133
Anderson, co., Tn., U.S. C9 135
Anderson, co., Tx., U.S. D5 136
Anderson, Mount, mtn., Wa., U.S. B2 140
Anderson Ranch Reservoir, res., Id., U.S. F3 105
Andes, mts., S.A. B4 72
Andes, Lake, l., S.D., U.S. D7 134
Andfjorden, strt., Nor. B7 10
Andhra Pradesh, state, India F3 40
Andimeshk, Iran F13 44
Andirlang, China B4 40
Andižan, Uzb. E9 26
Andkhvoy, Afg. C9 42
Andoany, Madag. A8 56
Andong, S. Kor. D13 28
Andorra, ctry., Eur. F7 16
Andorra-la-Vella, And. F7 16
Andover, Ks., U.S. g12 109
Andover, Ma., U.S. A5 114
Andover, Mn., U.S. m12 116
Andover, Oh., U.S. A5 128
Andover Lake, res., Ct., U.S. C6 100
Andøya, i., Nor. B6 10
Andradina, Braz. F1 74
Andreanof Islands, is., Ak., U.S. E4 95
Andrew, co., Mo., U.S. B3 118
Andrew Island, i., N.S., Can. D9 87
Andrews, In., U.S. C6 107
Andrews, N.C., U.S. f9 126
Andrews, S.C., U.S. E8 133
Andrews, Tx., U.S. C1 136
Andrews, co., Tx., U.S. C1 136
Andrews Air Force Base, mil., Md., U.S. C4 113
Andria, Italy D6 18
Andriamena, Madag. B8 56
Androka, Madag. D7 56
Andropov see Rybinsk, Russia D5 26
Andros, i., Bah. D9 76
Ándros, i., Grc. F10 18
Androscoggin, co., Me., U.S. D2 112
Androscoggin, stm., Me., U.S. D2 112
Androscoggin Lake, l., Me., U.S. D2 112
Āndrott Island, i., India G2 40
Andudu, D.R.C. C5 54
Andújar, Spain H4 16
Andulo, Ang. F3 54
Anegada, i., Br. Vir. Is. B7 80
Anegada Passage, strt., N.A. B7 80
Anécho, Togo E5 50
Aneto, mtn., Spain F7 16
Aney, Niger C7 50
Ang'angxi, China B12 28
Angara, stm., Russia D11 26
Angarsk, Russia D12 26
Ånge, Swe. E6 10
Ángel, Salto (Angel Falls), wtfl., Ven. B7 70
Ángel de la Guarda, Isla, i., Mex. B2 78
Angeles, Phil. C8 34
Angeles Point, c., Wa., U.S. A2 140
Angel Falls see Ángel, Salto, wtfl., Ven. B7 70
Ängelholm, Swe. H5 10
Angelina, co., Tx., U.S. D5 136
Angels Camp, Ca., U.S. C3 98
Ångermanälven, stm., Swe. E7 10
Angers, Fr. D6 16
Angier, N.C., U.S. B4 126
Angkor Wat, hist., Camb. D4 34
Anglesey, i., Wales, U.K. D4 12
Angleton, Tx., U.S. E5 136
Angmagssalik, Grnld. E32 82
Ango, D.R.C. C5 54
Angoche, Moz. B6 56
Angol, Chile E2 69
Angola, ctry., Afr. F3 54
Angola, In., U.S. A8 107
Angola, N.Y., U.S. C1 125
Angola Basin J14 66
Angola Swamp, sw., N.C., U.S. C5 126
Angoon, Ak., U.S. D13 95
Angora see Ankara, Tur. C5 44
Angoram, Pap. N. Gui. G11 32
Angostura see Ciudad Bolívar, Ven. B7 70
Angostura, Presa de la, res., Mex. D6 78
Angostura Reservoir, res., S.D., U.S. D2 134
Angoulême, Fr. E7 16
Angren, Uzb. E9 26
Angu, D.R.C. C4 54
Anguilla, dep., N.A. E12 76
Anguilla, Ms., U.S. C3 117
Anguille, Cape, c., N.L., Can. E2 88
Anguo, China B4 30
Anholt, i., Den. H4 10
Anhua, China D3 30
Anhui, prov., China E11 28
Aniak, Ak., U.S. C8 95
Anil, Braz. B3 74
Animas, stm., U.S. D3 99
Animas Mountains, mts., N.M., U.S. F1 124
Animas Peak, mtn., N.M., U.S. F2 124
Animas Valley, val., N.M., U.S. F1 124
Anina, Rom. G6 20
Anita, Ia., U.S. C3 108
Aniva, zaliv, b., Russia B16 28
Aniwa, i., Vanuatu I9 62a
Anjār, India E2 40
Anjou, Qc., Can. p19 90
Anjou, hist. reg., Fr. D6 16
Anjouan see Nzwani, i., Com. A7 56
Anjudin, Russia B10 22
Ankang, China E9 28
Ankara, Tur. C5 44
Ankavandra, Madag. B8 56
Ankazoabo, Madag. C7 56
Ankazobe, Madag. B8 56
Ankeny, Ia., U.S. C4 108
Anking see Anqing, China E11 28
Ankoro, D.R.C. E5 54
Anlong, China D2 30
Anlu, China E10 28
Ann, Cape, c., Ma., U.S. A6 114
Anna, Russia D16 20
Anna, Il., U.S. F4 106
Anna, Oh., U.S. B1 128
Anna, Lake, res., Va., U.S. B5 139
Annaba, Alg. C6 48
An-Nabk, Syria E7 44
An-Nafūd, des., Sau. Ar. E4 38
An-Najaf, state, Iraq G11 44
An-Najaf, Iraq D4 42
Anna Maria, Fl., U.S. p10 102
Anna Maria Island, i., Fl., U.S. q10 102
Annandale, Mn., U.S. E4 116
Annandale, Va., U.S. g12 139
Anna Plains, Austl. D3 60
Annapolis, stm., N.S., Can. E4 87
Annapolis, Md., U.S. C5 113
Annapolis Junction, Md., U.S. B4 113
Annapolis Royal, N.S., Can. E4 87
Annapūrṇa, mtn., Nepal D4 40
Ann Arbor, Mi., U.S. F7 115
An-Nāṣirīyah, Iraq D5 42
Annawan, Il., U.S. B4 106
Anne Arundel, co., Md., U.S. B4 113
Annecy, Fr. E10 16
Annenkov Island, i., S. Geor. H9 69
Annette, Ak., U.S. n24 95
An Nhon, Viet. D5 34
Anning, China E1 30
Anniston, Al., U.S. B4 94
Annobón, i., Eq. Gui. C1 52
An-Nuhūd, Sudan H10 48
An Nukhayb, Iraq F10 44
An-Nu'mānīyah, Iraq D5 42
Annville, Pa., U.S. F8 131
Anoka, Mn., U.S. E5 116
Anoka, co., Mn., U.S. E5 116
Anori, Braz. D7 70
Anqing, China E11 28
Ansai, China B2 30
Ansbach, Ger. F12 12
Anshan, China C12 28
Anshun, China F9 28
Anson, Me., U.S. D3 112
Anson, co., N.C., U.S. B2 126
Anson, Tx., U.S. C3 136
Ansongo, Mali C5 50
Ansonia, Ct., U.S. D3 100
Ansonia, Oh., U.S. B1 128
Ansted, W.V., U.S. C3 141
Antalaha, Madag. A9 56
Antalya, Tur. D4 44
Antalya, Gulf of see Antalya Körfezi, b., Tur. D4 44
Antalya Körfezi, b., Tur. D4 44
Antananarivo, Madag. B8 56
Antarctica, cont. L13 4
Antarctic Peninsula, pen., Ant. D35 67
Antelope, co., Ne., U.S. B7 120
Antelope Creek, stm., Wy., U.S. C7 143
Antelope Island, i., Ut., U.S. B3 137
Antelope Peak, mtn., Nv., U.S. B7 121
Antelope Range, mts., Nv., U.S. D7 121
Antelope Reservoir, res., Or., U.S. E9 130
Antelope Wash, val., Nv., U.S. D5 121
Antequera, Spain I4 16
Antero, Mount, mtn., Co., U.S. C4 99
Antero Reservoir, res., Co., U.S. C5 99
Anthon, Ia., U.S. B2 108
Anthony, Fl., U.S. C4 102
Anthony, Ks., U.S. E5 109
Anthony, N.M., U.S. F3 124
Anthony, R.I., U.S. D3 132
Anthony, Tx., U.S. o11 136
Anthony Creek, stm., W.V., U.S. D4 141
Antibes, Fr. F10 16
Anticosti, Île d', i., Qc., Can. k14 90
Antietam National Battlefield, hist., Md., U.S. B2 113
Antigo, Wi., U.S. C4 142
Antigua, i., Antig. B7 80
Antigua and Barbuda, ctry., N.A. E12 76
Antioch see Hatay, Tur. D7 44
Antioch, Ca., U.S. h9 98
Antioch, Il., U.S. A5 106
Antioquia, Col. D4 80
Antipodes Islands, is., N.Z. N20 64
Antlers, Ok., U.S. C6 129
Antofagasta, Chile B2 69
Antofalla, Salar de, pl., Arg. D4 72
Anton, Tx., U.S. C1 136
Antongila, Helodrano, b., Madag. B8 56
Antônio Bezerra, Braz. B4 74
Antonito, Co., U.S. D5 99
Antora Peak, mtn., Co., U.S. C4 99
Antrim, co., Mi., U.S. C5 115
Antrim, N.H., U.S. D3 122
Antsalova, Madag. B7 56
Antsirabe, Madag. B8 56
Antsiraňana, Madag. A8 56
Antsohihy, Madag. A8 56
Antwerp see Antwerpen, Bel. E9 12
Antwerp, Oh., U.S. A1 128
Antwerpen (Antwerp), Bel. E9 12
Anugul, India E5 40
Anūpgarh, India D2 40
Anuradhapura, Sri L. H4 40
Anxi, China C7 28
Anxiang, China D3 30
Anyang, China D10 28
A'nyêmaqên Shan, mts., China D7 28
Anyue, China C2 30
Anžero-Sudžensk, Russia D10 26
Anzio, Italy D4 18
Aoga-shima, i., Japan E15 28
Aoji-ri, N. Kor. B2 31
Aomen (Macau), China B6 34
Aomori, Japan C16 28
Aoral, Mount see Aôral, Phnum, mtn., Camb. D4 34
Aôral, Phnum, mtn., Camb. D4 34
Aosta, Italy B1 18
'Aouâna ('Aklé), reg., Afr. C3 50
Aouderas, Niger C6 50
Aouk, Bahr, stm., Afr. I9 48
Aoukâr, reg., Maur. C3 50
Aozou, Chad B8 50
Apache, co., Az., U.S. B6 96
Apache, Ok., U.S. C3 129
Apache Junction, Az., U.S. m9 96
Apache Peak, mtn., Az., U.S. F5 96
Apalachee Bay, b., Fl., U.S. B2 102
Apalachicola, Fl., U.S. C2 102
Apalachicola, stm., Fl., U.S. B1 102
Apalachicola Bay, b., Fl., U.S. C2 102
Apaporis, stm., S.A. C5 70
Aparri, Phil. C8 34
Apartadó, Col. D4 80
Apatity, Russia C5 26
Apatzingán de la Constitución, Mex. D4 78
Apeldoorn, Neth. D9 12
Apennines see Appennino, mts., Italy C4 18
Apex, N.C., U.S. B4 126
Apia, Samoa F12 58
Apiacás, Serra dos, plat., Braz. E8 70
Apishapa, stm., Co., U.S. D6 99
Aplington, Ia., U.S. B5 108
Apo, Mount, mtn., Phil. E9 34
Apollo, Pa., U.S. E2 131
Apopka, Fl., U.S. D5 102
Apopka, Lake, l., Fl., U.S. D5 102
Apostle Islands, is., Wi., U.S. A3 142
Apostle Islands National Lakeshore, Wi., U.S. A3 142
Apóstoles, Arg. D6 72
Apostolove, Ukr. F12 20
Appalachia, Va., U.S. f9 139
Appalachian Mountains, mts., N.A. D11 92
Appanoose, co., Ia., U.S. D5 108
Appennino, mts., Italy C4 18
Appennino Ligure, mts., Italy B2 18
Apple, stm., Wi., U.S. C1 142
Apple Creek, Oh., U.S. B4 128
Applegate, stm., Or., U.S. E3 130
Applegate, Or., U.S. E3 130
Appleton, Mn., U.S. E2 116
Appleton, Wi., U.S. D5 142
Appleton City, Mo., U.S. C3 118
Apple Valley, Ca., U.S. E5 98
Apple Valley, Mn., U.S. n12 116
Appling, co., Ga., U.S. E4 103
Appomattox, Va., U.S. C4 139
Appomattox, co., Va., U.S. C4 139
Appomattox, stm., Va., U.S. C4 139
Appomattox Court House National Historical Park, Va., U.S. C4 139
Apšeronsk, Russia B3 42
Apua Point, c., Hi., U.S. D6 104
Apucarana, Braz. F1 74
Apure, stm., Ven. B6 70
Apurímac, stm., Peru 70
Apurímac, stm., Peru F5 70
Aqaba, Gulf of, b. E2 42
'Aqrah, Iraq D10 44
Aquarius Mountains, mts., Az., U.S. C2 96
Aquidauana, Braz. H8 70
Ara, India D4 40
Arab, Al., U.S. A3 94
'Arab, Baḥr al-, stm., Sudan A4 54
Arabi, La., U.S. k11 111
Arabian Basin G9 64
Arabian Desert see Eastern Desert, des., Egypt E11 48
Arabian Gulf see Persian Gulf, b., Asia E6 42
Arabian Sea G8 38
Aracaju, Braz. D4 74
Aracati, Braz. B4 74
Araçatuba, Braz. F1 74
Aracruz, Braz. E3 74
Araçuaí, Braz. E3 74
Arad, Rom. F6 20
Arafura Sea E7 58
Arafura Shelf I16 64
Aragac, gora see Aragats Lerr, mtn., Arm. B11 44
Aragarças, Braz. G9 70
Aragats Lerr, mtn., Arm. B11 44
Arago, Cape, c., Or., U.S. D2 130
Aragón, hist. reg., Spain G6 16
Aragon, Ga., U.S. B1 103
Araguacema, Braz. E10 70
Aragua de Barcelona, Ven. B7 70
Araguaia, stm., Braz. E10 70
Araguaína, Braz. C2 74
Araguari, Braz. E2 74
Araguatins, Braz. C2 74
Ârak, Alg. E5 48
Arāk, Iran D5 42
Arakan Yoma, mts., Mya. B2 34
Arakkonam, India G3 40
Araks (Aras) (Araz), stm., Asia B10 44
Aral see Aral'sk, Kaz. E8 26
Aral Sea, Asia B7 42
Aral'sk, Kaz. E8 26
Aranda de Duero, Spain G5 16
Aranjuez, Spain G5 16
Aranos, Nmb. C2 56
Aransas, co., Tx., U.S. E4 136
Aransas Bay, b., Tx., U.S. E4 136
Aransas Pass, Tx., U.S. F4 136
Aranyaprathet, Thai. D4 34
Araouane, Mali C4 50
Arapaho, Ok., U.S. B3 129
Arapahoe, co., Co., U.S. B6 99
Arapahoe, Ne., U.S. D6 120
Arapiraca, Braz. C4 74
Arapkir, Tur. C8 44
Arapongas, Braz. F1 74
Araranguá, Braz. D8 72
Araraquara, Braz. F2 74
Ararat, Arm. C11 44
Ararat, Austl. H3 62
Ararat, Mount see Ağrı Dağı, mtn., Tur. C11 44
Aras (Araks) (Araz), stm., Asia C12 44
Arauca, Col. D5 80
Arauquita, Col. D5 80
Araxá, Braz. E2 74
Araz (Araks) (Aras), stm., Asia C12 44
Ārba Minch', Eth. B7 54
Arboga, Swe. G6 10
Arborg, Mb., Can. D3 86
Arbroath, Scot., U.K. B5 12
Arbuckle, Lake, l., Fl., U.S. E5 102
Arbuckle Mountains, mts., Ok., U.S. C4 129
Arbuckles, Lake of the, res., Ok., U.S. C5 129
Arcachon, Fr. E6 16
Arcade, Ga., U.S. B3 103
Arcade, N.Y., U.S. C2 125
Arcadia, Ca., U.S. m12 98
Arcadia, Fl., U.S. E5 102
Arcadia, In., U.S. D5 107
Arcadia, La., U.S. B3 111
Arcadia, Mo., U.S. D7 118
Arcadia, S.C., U.S. B4 133
Arcadia, Wi., U.S. D2 142
Arcanum, Oh., U.S. C1 128
Arcata, Ca., U.S. B1 98
Arc Dome, mtn., Nv., U.S. E4 121
Archangel see Arhangel'sk, Russia C6 26
Archbald, Pa., U.S. m18 131
Archbold, Oh., U.S. A1 128
Archdale, N.C., U.S. B3 126
Archer, Fl., U.S. C4 102
Archer, co., Tx., U.S. C3 136
Archer City, Tx., U.S. C3 136
Arches National Park, Ut., U.S. E6 137
Archie, Mo., U.S. C3 118
Archuleta, co., Co., U.S. D3 99
Arco, Id., U.S. F5 105
Arcola, Il., U.S. D5 106
Arcoverde, Braz. C4 74
Arctic Ocean E36 144
Ardabīl, Iran C5 42
Ardahan, Tur. B10 44
Ardakān, Iran D6 42
Årdalstangen, Nor. F2 10
Ardennes, reg., Eur. B9 16
Ardeşen, Tur. B9 44
Ardmore, Al., U.S. A3 94
Ardmore, In., U.S. A5 107
Ardmore, Ok., U.S. C4 129
Ardmore, Tn., U.S. B5 135
Ardsley, N.Y., U.S. g13 125
Arecibo, P.R. B6 80
Areia Branca, Braz. B4 74
Arena, Point, c., Ca., U.S. C2 98
Arena, Punta, c., Mex. C3 78
Arenac, co., Mi., U.S. D7 115
Arenápolis, Braz. A6 72
Arenas, Cayo, i., Mex. C6 78
Arendal, Nor. G3 10
Arequipa, Peru G5 70
Arévalo, Spain G4 16
Arezzo, Italy C3 18
Argenta, Il., U.S. D5 106
Argentan, Fr. C6 16
Argentina, ctry., S.A. E3 69
Argentino, Lago, l., Arg. H2 69
Argentnie Basin L9 66
Argeș, stm., Rom. G8 20
Arghandāb, stm., Afg. D9 42
Argolikós Kólpos, b., Grc. F9 18
Argonne, reg., Fr. C9 16
Árgos, Grc. F9 18
Argos, In., U.S. B5 107
Argostólion, Grc. E8 18
Argun' (Ergun), stm., Asia A12 28
Argungu, Nig. D5 50
Argyle, Mn., U.S. B2 116
Argyle, Wi., U.S. F4 142
Arhangel'sk, Russia C6 26
Arhangel'skoe, Russia C14 20
Arhéa Epídavros, hist., Grc. F9 18
Århus, Den. H4 10
Arica, Chile A2 69
Arica, Col. D5 70
Arichat, N.S., Can. D8 87
Arid, Cape, c., Austl. G3 60
Arīḥā (Jericho), Gaza G6 44
Arikaree, stm., U.S. B8 99
Arima, Trin. C7 80
Arinos, stm., Braz. F8 70
Ariquemes, Braz. E7 70
Aristazabal Island, i., B.C., Can. C3 85
Ariton, Al., U.S. D4 94
Arivonimamo, Madag. B8 56
Arizaro, Salar de, pl., Arg. D4 72
Arizona, Arg. F4 72
Arizona, state, U.S. C4 96
Arizona Sunsites, Az., U.S. F6 96
Arjay, Ky., U.S. D6 110
Arjeplog, Swe. C7 10
Arjona, Col. C4 80
Arka, Russia C16 26
Arkabutla Lake, res., Ms., U.S. A4 117
Arkadelphia, Ar., U.S. C2 97
Arkalyk, Kaz. D8 26
Arkansas, co., Ar., U.S. C4 97
Arkansas, stm., U.S. D9 92
Arkansas, state, U.S. C3 97
Arkansas City, Ks., U.S. E6 109
Arkoma, Ok., U.S. B7 129

Name | Map Ref. | Page

Arktičeskogo Instituta, ostrova, is., Russia **B10** 26
Arles, Fr. **F9** 16
Arlington, Ga., U.S. **E2** 103
Arlington, Ma., U.S. **B5** 114
Arlington, Mn., U.S. **F4** 116
Arlington, N.C., U.S. **A2** 126
Arlington, Ne., U.S. **C9** 120
Arlington, N.Y., U.S. **D7** 125
Arlington, Oh., U.S. **B2** 128
Arlington, S.C., U.S. **B3** 133
Arlington, S.D., U.S. **C8** 134
Arlington, Tn., U.S. **B2** 135
Arlington, Tx., U.S. **n9** 136
Arlington, Va., U.S. **B5** 139
Arlington, co., Va., U.S. **g12** 139
Arlington, Vt., U.S. **E2** 138
Arlington, Wa., U.S. **A3** 140
Arlington, Lake, res., Tx., U.S. **n9** 136
Arlington Heights, Il., U.S. **A5** 106
Arlit, Niger **C6** 50
Arlon, Bel. **F9** 12
Arma, Ks., U.S. **E9** 109
Armada, Mi., U.S. **F8** 115
Armadale, Austl. **G2** 60
Armagh, Qc., Can. **C7** 90
Armagnac, hist. reg., Fr. **F7** 16
Armavir, Russia **B4** 42
Armenia, ctry., Asia **B11** 44
Armenia, Col. **C4** 70
Armians'k, Ukr. **F12** 20
Armidale, Austl. **G5** 62
Armijo, N.M., U.S. **k7** 124
Armour, S.D., U.S. **D7** 134
Armstrong, B.C., Can. **D8** 85
Armstrong, Ia., U.S. **A3** 108
Armstrong, co., Pa., U.S. **E2** 131
Armstrong, co., Tx., U.S. **B2** 136
Armstrong Creek, stm., W.V., U.S. **m13** 141
Arnaudville, La., U.S. **D4** 111
Arnett, W.V., U.S. **D3** 141
Arnhem, Neth. **E10** 12
Arnhem, Cape, c., Austl. **C6** 60
Arnhem Bay, b., Austl. **C6** 60
Arnhem Land, reg., Austl. **C5** 60
Arno, stm., Italy **C3** 18
Arnold, Mn., U.S. **D6** 116
Arnold, Mo., U.S. **C7** 118
Arnold, Ne., U.S. **C5** 120
Arnold, Pa., U.S. **h14** 131
Arnold Mills, R.I., U.S. **B4** 132
Arnold Mills Reservoir, res., R.I., U.S. **B4** 132
Arnold's Cove, N.L., Can. **E4** 88
Arnolds Park, Ia., U.S. **A2** 108
Arnøya, Nor. **A9** 10
Arnprior, On., Can. **B8** 89
Aroab, Nmb. **D2** 56
Aroostook, co., Me., U.S. **B4** 112
Ar-Rahad, Sudan **H11** 48
Arraias, Braz. **F10** 70
Ar-Ramādī, Iraq **D4** 42
Arran, Island of, i., Scot., U.K. **C4** 12
Ar-Rank, Sudan **H11** 48
Ar-Raqqah, Syria **E8** 44
Arras, Fr. **B8** 16
Arrecife, Spain **A2** 50
Arriaga, Mex. **D6** 78
Ar-Riyāḍ (Riyadh), Sau. Ar. **F5** 38
Arroio Grande, Braz. **E7** 72
Arrowhead Mountain Lake, res., Vt., U.S. **B2** 138
Arrowrock Reservoir, res., Id., U.S. **F3** 105
Arrowwood Lake, res., N.D., U.S. **B7** 127
Arroyito, Arg. **E5** 72
Arroyo Grande, Ca., U.S. **E3** 98
Ar-Rub' al-Khālī, des., Asia **G6** 38
Ar-Rumaythah, Iraq **D4** 42
Ar-Ruṣayriṣ, Sudan **H11** 48
Ar-Ruṭbah, Iraq **D4** 42
Arsenev, Russia **C14** 28
Árta, Grc. **E8** 18
Artà, Spain **H8** 16
Artašat (Artashat), Arm. **C11** 44
Artashat (Artašat), Arm. **C11** 44
Art'em, Russia **C14** 28
Artemisa, Cuba **A3** 80
Artemivs'k, Ukr. **E14** 20
Artëmovsk, Russia **D11** 26
Artemus, Ky., U.S. **D6** 110
Arter, Mount, mtn., Wy., U.S. **D4** 143
Artesia, N.M., U.S. **E5** 124
Arthabaska, Qc., Can. **C6** 90
Arthur, On., Can. **D4** 89
Arthur, Il., U.S. **D5** 106
Arthur, co., Ne., U.S. **C4** 120
Arthur, Lake, l., La., U.S. **D3** 111
Arthur, Lake, res., Pa., U.S. **E1** 131
Arthur Kill, stm., N.J., U.S. **k8** 123
Artigas, Ur. **E6** 72
Artik, Arm. **B10** 44
Artsyz, Ukr. **F10** 20
Artvin, Tur. **B9** 44
Aru, Kepulauan, is., Indon. **H10** 32
Aru, Tanjung, c., Indon. **D5** 36
Arua, Ug. **C6** 54
Aruanã, Braz. **G9** 70
Aruba, dep., N.A. **C6** 80
Arunāchal Pradesh, state, India **D6** 40
Aruppukkottai, India **H3** 40
Arusha, Tan. **D7** 54
Aruwimi, stm., D.R.C. **C4** 54
Arvada, Co., U.S. **B5** 99
Arvayheer, Mong. **B8** 28
Arvidsjaur, Swe. **D8** 10
Arvika, Swe. **G5** 10
Arvin, Ca., U.S. **E4** 98
Arvon, Mount, mtn., Mi., U.S. **B2** 115
Arvonia, Va., U.S. **C4** 139
Arxan, China **B11** 28
Arys', Kaz. **E8** 26
Arzamas, Russia **C7** 22
Arzew, Golfe d', b., Alg. **J6** 16
Aša, Russia **D10** 22
Asaba, Nig. **E6** 50
Asad, Buḥayrat al-, res., Syria **D8** 44
Asad, Lake see Asad, Buḥayrat al-, res., Syria **D8** 44
Asadābād, Afg. **C10** 42
Asadābād, Iran **E13** 44
Asahi-dake, vol., Japan **B4** 31
Asahikawa, Japan **C16** 28
Āsānsol, India **E5** 40
Asbest, Russia **C11** 22
Asbestos, Qc., Can. **D6** 90
Asbury Park, N.J., U.S. **C4** 123
Ascensión, Mex. **A3** 78
Ascension, i., St. Hel. **J8** 46
Ascension, co., La., U.S. **D5** 111
Ascoli Piceno, Italy **C4** 18
Aseb, Erit. **H13** 48
Åseda, Swe. **H6** 10
Asela, Eth. **B7** 54
Åsele, Swe. **D7** 10
Aşgabat, Turk. **F7** 26
Ashanti, state, Ghana **E4** 50
Ashaway, R.I., U.S. **F1** 132
Ashburn, Ga., U.S. **E3** 103
Ashburton, stm., Austl. **E2** 60
Ashburton, N.Z. **p13** 63c
Ashcroft, B.C., Can. **D7** 85
Ashdod, Isr. **G6** 44
Ashdown, Ar., U.S. **D1** 97
Ashe, co., N.C., U.S. **A1** 126
Asheboro, N.C., U.S. **B3** 126
Ashepoo, stm., S.C., U.S. **F6** 133
Ashern, Mb., Can. **D2** 86
Asherton, Tx., U.S. **E3** 136
Asheville, N.C., U.S. **f10** 126
Ash Flat, Ar., U.S. **A4** 97
Ashford, Al., U.S. **D4** 94
Ashford, W.V., U.S. **m12** 141
Ash Grove, Mo., U.S. **D4** 118
Ashikaga, Japan **C3** 31
Ashkhabad see Aşgabat, Turk. **F7** 26
Ashland, Al., U.S. **B4** 94
Ashland, Il., U.S. **D3** 106
Ashland, Ks., U.S. **E4** 109
Ashland, Ky., U.S. **B7** 110
Ashland, Ma., U.S. **g10** 114
Ashland, Me., U.S. **B4** 112
Ashland, Mo., U.S. **C5** 118
Ashland, Ne., U.S. **C9** 120
Ashland, N.H., U.S. **C3** 122
Ashland, Oh., U.S. **B3** 128
Ashland, co., Oh., U.S. **B3** 128
Ashland, Or., U.S. **E4** 130
Ashland, Pa., U.S. **E9** 131
Ashland, Va., U.S. **C5** 139
Ashland, Wi., U.S. **B3** 142
Ashland, co., Wi., U.S. **B3** 142
Ashland, Mount, mtn., Or., U.S. **E4** 130
Ashland City, Tn., U.S. **A4** 135
Ashland Reservoir, res., Ma., U.S. **h10** 114
Ashley, co., Ar., U.S. **D4** 97
Ashley, In., U.S. **A7** 107
Ashley, N.D., U.S. **C6** 127
Ashley, Oh., U.S. **B3** 128
Ashley, Pa., U.S. **n17** 131
Ashley, stm., S.C., U.S. **F7** 133
Ashley Creek, stm., Ut., U.S. **C6** 137
Ashmore, Il., U.S. **D5** 106
Ashmore Islands, is., Austl. **C3** 60
Ashokan Reservoir, res., N.Y., U.S. **D6** 125
Ash-Shaddādah, Syria **D9** 44
Ash-Shāmīyah, Iraq **F11** 44
Ash-Shāriqah, U.A.E. **E7** 42
Ash-Sharqāṭ, Iraq **E10** 44
Ash-Shaṭrah, Iraq **G12** 44
Ash-Shiḥr, Yemen **H5** 38
Ash-Shināfīyah, Iraq **G11** 44
Ashtabula, Oh., U.S. **A5** 128
Ashtabula, co., Oh., U.S. **A5** 128
Ashtabula, Lake, res., N.D., U.S. **B8** 127
Ashtarak, Arm. **B11** 44
Ashton, Id., U.S. **E7** 105
Ashton, Il., U.S. **B4** 106
Ashton, Md., U.S. **B3** 113
Ashton, R.I., U.S. **B4** 132
Ashuanipi Lake, l., N.L., Can. **h8** 88
Ashuelot, stm., N.H., U.S. **E2** 122
Ashville, Al., U.S. **B3** 94
Ashville, Oh., U.S. **C3** 128
Ashwaubenon, Wi., U.S. **D5** 142
Asi, stm., Asia **D7** 44
Asia, cont. **C19** 4
Asilah, Mor. **J3** 16
Asinara, Golfo dell', b., Italy **D2** 18
Asinara, Isola, i., Italy **D2** 18
Asino, Russia **D10** 26
Asipovičy, Bela. **C10** 20
'Asīr, reg., Sau. Ar. **G4** 38
Aşkale, Tur. **C9** 44
Askersund, Swe. **G6** 10
Askham, S. Afr. **D3** 56
Asmara see Asmera, Erit. **G12** 48
Asmera, Erit. **G12** 48
Āsosa, Eth. **A6** 54
Asotin, Wa., U.S. **C8** 140
Asotin, co., Wa., U.S. **C8** 140
Asotin Creek, stm., Wa., U.S. **C8** 140
Aspen, Co., U.S. **B4** 99
Aspen Butte, mtn., Or., U.S. **E4** 130
Aspendos, hist., Tur. **D4** 44
Aspermont, Tx., U.S. **C2** 136
Aspinwall, Pa., U.S. **k14** 131
Aspy Bay, b., N.S., Can. **C9** 87
Assa, Mor. **A3** 50
Assabet, stm., Ma., U.S. **g9** 114
As-Safīrah, Syria **D7** 44
As-Salṭ, Jord. **F6** 44
Assam, state, India **D6** 40
As-Samāwah, Iraq **D5** 42
Assateague Island, i., U.S. **D7** 113
Assateague Island National Seashore, U.S. **D7** 113
Assawoman Bay, b., Md., U.S. **D7** 113
Assiniboine, stm., Can. **E2** 86
Assiniboine, Mount, mtn., Can. **D3** 84
Assis, Braz. **F1** 74
Assu, Braz. **C4** 74
As-Sudd, reg., Sudan **I11** 48
As-Sulaymānīyah, Iraq **C5** 42
As-Sulaymānīyah, Sau. Ar. **F5** 38
As-Sulayyil, Sau. Ar. **F5** 38
As-Sumayḥ, Sudan **B5** 54
Assumption, Il., U.S. **D4** 106
Assumption, co., La., U.S. **E4** 111
As-Suwaydā', Syria **F7** 44
Astana, Kaz. **D9** 26
Astara, Azer. **C13** 44
Āstārā, Iran **C13** 44
Asti, Italy **B2** 18
Astipálaia, i., Grc. **F11** 18
Astorga, Spain **F3** 16
Astoria, Il., U.S. **C3** 106
Astoria, Or., U.S. **A3** 130
Astove, i., Sey. **j11** 57b
Astrahan', Russia **E6** 26
Asunción, Para. **D6** 72
Asuncion Island, i., N. Mar. Is. **C12** 32
Aswân, Egypt **F11** 48
Aswan High Dam see Aali, Sadd el-, Egypt **F11** 48
Asyût, Egypt **E11** 48
'Ata, i., Tonga **G12** 58
Atacama, Desierto de, des., Chile **C2** 69
Atacama, Puna de, plat., S.A. **C4** 72
Atacama, Salar de, pl., Chile **B3** 69
Atakpamé, Togo **E5** 50
Atambua, Indon. **E6** 36
Aṭar, Maur. **B2** 50
Atascadero, Ca., U.S. **E3** 98
Atascosa, co., Tx., U.S. **E3** 136
Atasu, Kaz. **E9** 26
Atatürk Barajı, res., Tur. **D8** 44
Atauro, Pulau, i., E. Timor **E7** 36
'Aṭbarah, Sudan **G11** 48
Atbasar, Kaz. **D8** 26
Atchafalaya, stm., La., U.S. **D4** 111
Atchafalaya Bay, b., La., U.S. **E4** 111
Atchison, Ks., U.S. **C8** 109
Atchison, co., Ks., U.S. **C8** 109
Atchison, co., Mo., U.S. **A2** 118
Athabasca, Ab., Can. **B4** 84
Athabasca, stm., Ab., Can. **G17** 82
Athabasca, Lake, l., Can. **G17** 82
Athena, Or., U.S. **B8** 130
Athens, On., Can. **C9** 89
Athens see Athínai, Grc. **E9** 18
Athens, Al., U.S. **A3** 94
Athens, Ga., U.S. **C3** 103
Athens, Il., U.S. **D4** 106
Athens, Mi., U.S. **F5** 115
Athens, N.Y., U.S. **C7** 125
Athens, Oh., U.S. **C3** 128
Athens, co., Oh., U.S. **C3** 128
Athens, Pa., U.S. **C8** 131
Athens, Tn., U.S. **D9** 135
Athens, Tx., U.S. **C5** 136
Athens, Wi., U.S. **C3** 142
Athens, W.V., U.S. **D3** 141
Atherton, Austl. **D4** 62
Athi, stm., Kenya **D7** 54
Athínai (Athens), Grc. **E9** 18
Athol, Ma., U.S. **A3** 114
Áthos, mtn., Grc. **D10** 18
Ati, Chad **D8** 50
Atiak, Ug. **C6** 54
Atik Lake, l., Mb., Can. **B4** 86
Atikonak Lake, l., N.L., Can. **h8** 88
Atiu, i., Cook Is. **G14** 58
Atka, Russia **C17** 26
Atka Island, i., Ak., U.S. **E5** 95
Atkarsk, Russia **D8** 22
Atkins, Ar., U.S. **B3** 97
Atkins, Va., U.S. **D1** 139
Atkinson, co., Ga., U.S. **E4** 103
Atkinson, Il., U.S. **B3** 106
Atkinson, Ne., U.S. **B7** 120
Atkinson, N.H., U.S. **E4** 122
Atlanta, Ga., U.S. **C2** 103
Atlanta, Il., U.S. **C4** 106
Atlanta, In., U.S. **D5** 107
Atlanta, Mi., U.S. **C6** 115
Atlanta, Tx., U.S. **C5** 136
Atlantic, Ia., U.S. **C2** 108
Atlantic, N.C., U.S. **C6** 126
Atlantic, co., N.J., U.S. **E3** 123
Atlantic Beach, Fl., U.S. **m9** 102
Atlantic City, N.J., U.S. **E4** 123
Atlantic Highlands, N.J., U.S. **C4** 123
Atlantic-Indian Basin **O12** 66
Atlantic-Indian Ridge **N14** 66
Atlantic Ocean **E9** 66
Atlantic Peak, mtn., Wy., U.S. **D3** 143
Atlas Mountains, mts., Afr. **D4** 48
Atlas Saharien, mts., Alg. **E3** 14
Atlas Tellien, mts., Alg. **D4** 14
Atlin Lake, l., Can. **G13** 82
Atmore, Al., U.S. **D2** 94
Atna Peak, mtn., B.C., Can. **C3** 85
Atoka, Ok., U.S. **C5** 129
Atoka, co., Ok., U.S. **C5** 129
Atoka, Tn., U.S. **B2** 135
Atoka Reservoir, res., Ok., U.S. **C5** 129
Atrak (Atrek), stm., Asia **C7** 42
Atrato, stm., Col. **B4** 70
Atrek (Atrak), stm., Asia **C6** 42
Aṭ-Ṭā'if, Sau. Ar. **F4** 38
Attala, co., Ms., U.S. **B4** 117
Attalla, Al., U.S. **A3** 94
Attapu, Laos **D5** 34
Attawapiskat, stm., On., Can. **n18** 89
Attica, In., U.S. **D3** 107
Attica, Ks., U.S. **E5** 109
Attica, N.Y., U.S. **C2** 125
Attica, Oh., U.S. **A3** 128
Attleboro, Ma., U.S. **C5** 114
Attu Island, i., Ak., U.S. **E2** 95
Atuel, Bañados del, sw., Arg. **F4** 72
Åtvidaberg, Swe. **G7** 10
Atwater, Ca., U.S. **D3** 98
Atwater, Mn., U.S. **E4** 116
Atwood, On., Can. **D3** 89
Atwood, Il., U.S. **D5** 106
Atwood, Ks., U.S. **C2** 109
Atwood, Tn., U.S. **B3** 135
Atwood Lake, res., Oh., U.S. **B4** 128
Atyrau, Kaz. **E7** 26
Auau Channel, strt., Hi., U.S. **C5** 104
Aubagne, Fr. **F9** 16
Auberry, Ca., U.S. **D4** 98
Auburn, Al., U.S. **C4** 94
Auburn, Ca., U.S. **C3** 98
Auburn, Ga., U.S. **B3** 103
Auburn, Il., U.S. **D4** 106
Auburn, In., U.S. **B7** 107
Auburn, Ks., U.S. **D8** 109
Auburn, Ky., U.S. **D3** 110
Auburn, Ma., U.S. **B4** 114
Auburn, Me., U.S. **D2** 112
Auburn, Mi., U.S. **E6** 115
Auburn, Ne., U.S. **D10** 120
Auburn, N.Y., U.S. **C4** 125
Auburn, Wa., U.S. **B3** 140
Auburndale, Fl., U.S. **D5** 102
Auburn Heights, Mi., U.S. **F7** 115
Aubusson, Fr. **E8** 16
Auch, Fr. **F7** 16
Auchi, Nig. **E6** 50
Aucilla, stm., Fl., U.S. **B3** 102
Auckland, N.Z. **o13** 63c
Auckland Islands, is., N.Z. **J10** 58
Audrain, co., Mo., U.S. **B6** 118
Audubon, Ia., U.S. **C3** 108
Audubon, co., Ia., U.S. **C2** 108
Audubon, N.J., U.S. **D2** 123
Augathella, Austl. **F4** 62
Auglaize, stm., Oh., U.S. **A1** 128
Auglaize, co., Oh., U.S. **B1** 128
Augrabiesvalle, wtfl., S. Afr. **D3** 56
Au Gres, Mi., U.S. **D7** 115
Augsburg, Ger. **F12** 12
Augusta, Austl. **G1** 60
Augusta, Italy **F5** 18
Augusta, Ar., U.S. **B4** 97
Augusta, Ga., U.S. **C5** 103
Augusta, Ks., U.S. **E7** 109
Augusta, Ky., U.S. **B6** 110
Augusta, Me., U.S. **D3** 112
Augusta, Mi., U.S. **F5** 115
Augusta, co., Va., U.S. **B3** 139
Augusta, Wi., U.S. **D2** 142
Augustów, Pol. **C7** 20
Augustus, Mount, mtn., Austl. **E2** 60
Aulander, N.C., U.S. **A5** 126
Aulneau Peninsula, pen., On., Can. **E4** 86
Ault, Co., U.S. **A6** 99
Aumsville, Or., U.S. **k12** 130
Aurangābād, India **E4** 40
Aurangābād, India **F3** 40
Aure, Nor. **E3** 10
Aurelia, Ia., U.S. **B2** 108
Aurich, Ger. **D10** 12
Aurillac, Fr. **E8** 16
Aurora, On., Can. **C5** 89
Aurora, Co., U.S. **B6** 99
Aurora, Il., U.S. **B5** 106
Aurora, In., U.S. **F8** 107
Aurora, Mn., U.S. **C6** 116
Aurora, Mo., U.S. **E4** 118
Aurora, Ne., U.S. **D7** 120
Aurora, Oh., U.S. **A4** 128
Aurora, S.D., U.S. **C9** 134
Aurora, co., S.D., U.S. **D7** 134
Aurora, Ut., U.S. **E4** 137
Aus, Nmb. **D2** 56
Au Sable, Mi., U.S. **D7** 115
Au Sable, stm., Mi., U.S. **D6** 115
Ausable, stm., N.Y., U.S. **f11** 125
Au Sable Forks, N.Y., U.S. **f11** 125
Au Sable Point, c., Mi., U.S. **D7** 115
Au Sable Point, c., Mi., U.S. **B4** 115
Austell, Ga., U.S. **h7** 103
Austin, In., U.S. **G6** 107
Austin, Mn., U.S. **G6** 116
Austin, Nv., U.S. **D4** 121
Austin, Tx., U.S. **D4** 136
Austin, co., Tx., U.S. **E4** 136
Austintown, Oh., U.S. **A5** 128
Austinville, Va., U.S. **D2** 139
Australia, i., Austl. **H21** 4
Australia, ctry., Oc. **G7** 58
Australian Capital Territory, state, Austl. **H4** 62
Austral Seamounts **K23** 64
Austria, ctry., Eur. **G14** 12
Autauga, co., Al., U.S. **C3** 94
Autaugaville, Al., U.S. **C3** 94
Autlán de Navarro, Mex. **D4** 78
Auvergne, hist. reg., Fr. **E8** 16
Auxerre, Fr. **D8** 16
Auxier, Ky., U.S. **C7** 110
Auxvasse, Mo., U.S. **B6** 118
Auyán Tepuy, mtn., Ven. **B7** 70
Auzangate, Nevado, mtn., Peru **F5** 70
Ava, Mo., U.S. **E5** 118
Avallon, Fr. **D8** 16
Avalon, Ca., U.S. **F4** 98
Avalon, Pa., U.S. **h13** 131
Avalon, Lake, res., N.M., U.S. **E5** 124
Avalon Peninsula, pen., N.L., Can. **E5** 88
Avaré, Braz. **F2** 74
Aveiro, Port. **G2** 16
Avella, Pa., U.S. **F1** 131
Avellaneda, Arg. **E6** 72
Avellino, Italy **D5** 18
Avenal, Ca., U.S. **E3** 98
Avery, co., N.C., U.S. **e11** 126
Aves, Islas de, is., Ven. **C6** 80
Avesta, Swe. **F7** 10
Avezzano, Italy **C4** 18
Avignon, Fr. **F9** 16
Ávila, Spain **G4** 16
Avilés, Spain **F4** 16
Avilla, In., U.S. **B7** 107
Avis, Pa., U.S. **D7** 131
Aviston, Il., U.S. **E4** 106
Avoca, Ia., U.S. **C2** 108
Avoca, Pa., U.S. **m18** 131
Avola, Italy **F5** 18
Avon, Ct., U.S. **B4** 100
Avon, Il., U.S. **C3** 106
Avon, Ma., U.S. **B5** 114
Avon, Mn., U.S. **E4** 116
Avon, N.Y., U.S. **C3** 125
Avon, Oh., U.S. **A3** 128
Avondale, Az., U.S. **D3** 96
Avondale, Co., U.S. **C6** 99
Avondale, Pa., U.S. **G10** 131
Avondale Estates, Ga., U.S. **h8** 103
Avon Lake, Ia., U.S. **e8** 108
Avon Lake, Oh., U.S. **A3** 128
Avonmore, Pa., U.S. **E3** 131
Avon Park, Fl., U.S. **E5** 102
Avoyelles, co., La., U.S. **C3** 111
Awaaso, Ghana **E4** 50
Āwarē, Eth. **B8** 54
Āwasa, Eth. **B7** 54
Āwash, Eth. **B8** 54
Āwash, stm., Eth. **H13** 48
Awbārī, Libya **E7** 48
Awbārī, Ṣaḥrā', reg., Libya **A7** 50
Awjilah, Libya **E9** 48
Awled Djellal, Alg. **E5** 14
Awlef, Alg. **F4** 14
Axim, Ghana **F4** 50
Axiós (Vardar), stm., Eur. **D9** 18
Axis, Al., U.S. **E1** 94
Axtell, Ne., U.S. **D6** 120
Ayacucho, Arg. **F6** 72
Ayacucho, Peru **F5** 70
Ayamé, C. Iv. **E4** 50
Ayancık, Tur. **B6** 44
Ayapel, Col. **D4** 80
Ayaviri, Peru **F5** 70
Ayden, N.C., U.S. **B5** 126
Aydın, Tur. **D2** 44
Ayer, Ma., U.S. **A4** 114
Ayers Cliff, Qc., Can. **D5** 90
Ayeyarwady, stm., Mya. **C3** 34

Name	Map Ref.	Page

Áyios Nikólaos, Grc.	G10	18
Ayíou Órous, Kólpos, b., Grc.	D10	18
Aylesford, N.S., Can.	D5	87
Aylmer, Mount, mtn., Ab., Can.	D3	84
Aylmer East, Qc., Can.	D2	90
Aylmer West, On., Can.	E4	89
'Ayn Dār, Sau. Ar.	E5	42
Ayorou, Niger	D5	50
Ayoûn el 'Atroûs, Maur.	C3	50
Ayr, Austl.	D4	62
Ayr, Scot., U.K.	C4	12
Ayvalik, Tur.	C2	44
Āzamgarh, India	D4	40
Azaouâd, reg., Mali	C4	50
Azare, Nig.	D7	50
Āžar Shahr, Iran	D11	44
Azdavay, Tur.	B5	44
Azeffâl, dunes, Afr.	B2	50
Azerbaijan, ctry., Asia	B12	44
Azilal, Mor.	E2	14
Aziscohos Lake, l., Me., U.S.	C1	112
Azle, Tx., U.S.	n9	136
Azogues, Ec.	D4	70
Azores see Açores, is., Port.	F7	46
Azores Plateau	D10	66
Azov, Russia	F15	20
Azov, Sea of, Eur.	F14	20
Azraq, Al-Baḥr al- see Blue Nile, stm., Afr.	H11	48
Azrou, Mor.	D3	48
Aztec, N.M., U.S.	A2	124
Aztec Peak, mtn., Az., U.S.	D5	96
Aztec Ruins National Monument, N.M., U.S.	A1	124
Azua, Dom. Rep.	B5	80
Azuaga, Spain	H4	16
Azuero, Península de, pen., Pan.	D3	80
Azul, Arg.	F6	72
Azurduy, Bol.	B5	72
Azusa, Ca., U.S.	m13	98
Az-Zahrān, Sau. Ar.	E5	42
Az-Zarqā', Jord.	D3	42
Az-Zāwiyah, Libya	D7	48

B

Baa, Indon.	F6	36
Baardheere, Som.	J13	48
Babadag, Rom.	G10	20
Babaeski, Tur.	B2	44
Babaevo, Russia	C6	22
Babanūsah, Sudan	H10	48
Babar, Kepulauan, is., Indon.	E7	36
Babb Creek, stm., Pa., U.S.	C7	131
Babbitt, Mn., U.S.	C7	116
Babbitt, Nv., U.S.	E3	121
Bab el Mandeb see Mandeb, Bab el, strt.	H4	38
Babelthuap, i., Palau	E9	32
Bābil, Aṭlāl (Babylon), hist., Iraq	F11	44
Babine, stm., B.C., Can.	B4	85
Babine Lake, l., B.C., Can.	B5	85
Babine Range, mts., B.C., Can.	B4	85
Babo, Indon.	D8	36
Baboquivari Mountains, mts., Az., U.S.	F4	96
Baboquivari Peak, mtn., Az., U.S.	F4	96
Babrujsk, Bela.	C10	20
Babuškin, Russia	A9	28
Babuyan Channel, strt., Phil.	C8	34
Babuyan Island, i., Phil.	C8	34
Babuyan Islands, is., Phil.	C8	34
Babylon see Bābil, Aṭlāl, hist., Iraq	F11	44
Babylon, N.Y., U.S.	n15	125
Baca, co., Co., U.S.	D8	99
Bacabal, Braz.	B3	74
Bacan, Pulau, i., Indon.	D7	36
Bacău, Rom.	F9	20
Bachu, China	D3	28
Back, stm., S.C., U.S.	h12	133
Bačka Palanka, Serb.	B7	18
Backbone Mountain, mtn., U.S.	m12	113
Bac Lieu, Viet.	E5	34
Bac Ninh, Viet.	B5	34
Bacolod, Phil.	D8	34
Bacon, co., Ga., U.S.	E4	103
Baconton, Ga., U.S.	E2	103
Bacoor, Phil.	D8	34
Bād, Iran	D6	42
Bad, stm., S.D., U.S.	C5	134
Bad, stm., Wi., U.S.	B3	142
Badagara, India	G3	40
Badajoz, Spain	H3	16
Badalona, Spain	G16	8
Bādāmi, India	F3	40
Badanah, Sau. Ar.	D4	42
Bad Axe, Mi., U.S.	E8	115
Baddeck, N.S., Can.	C9	87
Baden, Aus.	G14	12
Baden, On., Can.	D4	89
Baden, Pa., U.S.	E1	131
Baden-Baden, Ger.	F11	12
Badger, N.L., Can.	D3	88
Bad Hersfeld, Ger.	E11	12
Badīn, Pak.	F9	42

Badin, N.C., U.S.	B2	126
Badin Lake, res., N.C., U.S.	B2	126
Bad Kreuznach, Ger.	F10	12
Badlands, S.D., U.S.	D3	134
Badlands, reg., U.S.	C2	127
Badlands National Park, S.D., U.S.	D3	134
Bad Reichenhall, Ger.	G13	12
Bad River Indian Reservation, Wi., U.S.	B3	142
Bad Tölz, Ger.	G12	12
Badulla, Sri L.	H4	40
Badwater Creek, stm., Wy., U.S.	C5	143
Bafang, Cam.	B2	54
Bafatá, Gui.-B.	D2	50
Baffin Basin	C29	144
Baffin Bay, b., N.A.	D26	82
Baffin Bay, b., Tx., U.S.	E4	136
Baffin Bugt see Baffin Bay, b., N.A.	D26	82
Baffin Island, i., Can.	D24	82
Bafia, Cam.	C2	54
Bafing, stm., Afr.	D2	50
Bafoulabé, Mali	D2	50
Bafoussam, Cam.	B2	54
Bafra, Tur.	B6	44
Bafwasende, D.R.C.	C5	54
Bagaces, C.R.	C2	80
Bagamoyo, Tan.	E7	54
Baganga, Phil.	E9	34
Bagansiapiapi, Indon.	C2	36
Bagdad see Baghdād, Iraq	D4	42
Bagdad, Az., U.S.	C2	96
Bagdad, Fl., U.S.	u14	102
Bagdarin, Russia	D13	26
Bagé, Braz.	E7	72
Baggs, Wy., U.S.	E5	143
Baghdād, Iraq	D4	42
Bagheria, Italy	E4	18
Baghlān, Afg.	C9	42
Bagley, Mn., U.S.	C3	116
Bagnères-de-Bigorre, Fr.	F7	16
Bago, Mya.	C3	34
Baguio, Phil.	C8	34
Bahamas, ctry., N.A.	C9	76
Bahār, Iran	E13	44
Baharampur, India	E5	40
Baharden, Turk.	C7	42
Bahardok, Turk.	C7	42
Bahāwalpur, Pak.	E10	42
Bahçe, Tur.	D7	44
Bahia, state, Braz.	D3	74
Bahía, Islas de la, is., Hond.	B2	80
Bahía Blanca, Arg.	F5	72
Bahir Dar, Eth.	H12	48
Bahraich, India	D4	40
Bahrain, ctry., Asia	E6	42
Bahta, Russia	C10	26
Bāhū Kalāt, Iran	E8	42
Baía Farta, Ang.	F2	54
Baia Mare, Rom.	F7	20
Baicheng, China	C4	28
Baicheng, China	B12	28
Baidoa see Baydhabo, Som.	J13	48
Baie-Comeau, Qc., Can.	k13	90
Baie-d'Urfé, Qc., Can.	q19	90
Baie-Saint-Paul, Qc., Can.	B7	90
Baie Verte, N.L., Can.	D3	88
Baihe, China	C3	30
Baikal, Lake see Bajkal, ozero, l., Russia	D12	26
Baile Átha Cliath see Dublin, Ire.	D3	12
Băileşti, Rom.	G7	20
Bailey, co., Tx., U.S.	B1	136
Bailey Island, Me., U.S.	g8	112
Bailey Island, i., S.C., U.S.	k11	133
Baileys Crossroads, Va., U.S.	g12	139
Bailundo, Ang.	F3	54
Bainbridge, Ga., U.S.	F2	103
Bainbridge, In., U.S.	E4	107
Bainbridge, Oh., U.S.	C2	128
Bainbridge Island, i., Wa., U.S.	e10	140
Baing, Indon.	F6	36
Baird, Tx., U.S.	C3	136
Bairdford, Pa., U.S.	h14	131
Baird Inlet, b., Ak., U.S.	C7	95
Baird Mountains, mts., Ak., U.S.	B7	95
Bairin Zuoqi, China	C11	28
Bairnsdale, Austl.	H4	62
Bais, Phil.	E8	34
Baishuijiang, China	C2	30
Baitou Shan see Paektu, Mount, mtn., Asia	C13	28
Baiyin, China	D8	28
Baja, Hung.	F5	20
Baja California, pen., Mex.	B2	78
Baja California, state, Mex.	A1	78
Baja California Norte see Baja California, state, Mex.	A1	78
Baja California Sur, state, Mex.	B2	78
Bajestān, Iran	D7	42
Bajkal, ozero, l., Russia	D12	26
Bajkit, Russia	C11	26
Bajkonur, Kaz.	E8	26
Bajmak, Russia	D10	22
Bajo Boquete, Pan.	D3	80
Bajramaly, Turk.	C8	42
Bakala, C.A.R.	B4	54
Bakanas, Kaz.	B11	42

Bakel, Sen.	D2	50
Baker, co., Fl., U.S.	B4	102
Baker, co., Ga., U.S.	E2	103
Baker, La., U.S.	D4	111
Baker, Mt., U.S.	D12	119
Baker, stm., N.H., U.S.	C3	122
Baker, co., Or., U.S.	C9	130
Baker, Or., U.S.	C9	130
Baker, Mount, mtn., Wa., U.S.	A4	140
Baker Air Force Base, mil., Ar., U.S.	B6	97
Baker Butte, mtn., Az., U.S.	C4	96
Baker Island, i., Oc.	H21	64
Baker Island, i., Ak., U.S.	n22	95
Baker Lake, l., Austl.	F4	60
Baker Lake, l., Me., U.S.	B3	112
Baker Lake, res., Wa., U.S.	A4	140
Bakersfield, Ca., U.S.	E4	98
Bakers Island, i., Ma., U.S.	f12	114
Bakerstown, Pa., U.S.	h14	131
Bakhmach, Ukr.	D12	20
Bakı (Baku), Azer.	B13	44
Bako, Eth.	B7	54
Bakouma, C.A.R.	B4	54
Baku see Bakı, Azer.	B13	44
Bala, Sen.	D2	50
Balabac Island, i., Phil.	E7	34
Balabac Strait, strt., Asia	E7	34
Ba'labakk, Leb.	F7	44
Baladēk, Russia	D15	26
Balāghāt, India	E4	40
Balaguer, Spain	G7	16
Balakliia, Ukr.	E14	20
Balakovo, Russia	D6	26
Balama, Moz.	A6	56
Balambangan, Pulau, i., Malay.	B5	36
Bālā Morghāb, Afg.	C8	42
Balāngīr, India	E4	40
Balašov, Russia	D6	26
Balassagyarmat, Hung.	F5	20
Balaton, l., Hung.	F4	20
Balaton, Mn., U.S.	F3	116
Balbina, Represa, res., Braz.	D8	70
Balcad, Som.	C9	54
Balcarce, Arg.	F6	72
Balcarres, Sk., Can.	G4	91
Balclutha, N.Z.	p12	63c
Balcones Escarpment, clf., Tx., U.S.	E3	136
Bald Eagle Lake, l., Mn., U.S.	m12	116
Bald Eagle Lake, l., Mn., U.S.	C7	116
Baldhill Dam, N.D., U.S.	B7	127
Bald Knob, Ar., U.S.	B4	97
Bald Knoll, mtn., Wy., U.S.	D2	143
Bald Mountain, mtn., Or., U.S.	D5	130
Bald Mountain, mtn., Or., U.S.	C9	130
Bald Mountain, mtn., Wy., U.S.	B5	143
Bald Mountains, mts., N.C., U.S.	f10	126
Baldwin, co., Al., U.S.	E2	94
Baldwin, Fl., U.S.	B5	102
Baldwin, Ga., U.S.	B3	103
Baldwin, co., Ga., U.S.	C3	103
Baldwin, La., U.S.	E4	111
Baldwin, Mi., U.S.	E5	115
Baldwin, Pa., U.S.	k14	131
Baldwin, S.C., U.S.	B5	133
Baldwin, Wi., U.S.	D1	142
Baldwin City, Ks., U.S.	D8	109
Baldwinsville, N.Y., U.S.	B4	125
Baldwinville, Ma., U.S.	A3	114
Baldwyn, Ms., U.S.	A5	117
Baldy Mountain, mtn., B.C., Can.	D7	85
Baldy Mountain, mtn., Mb., Can.	D1	86
Baldy Mountain, mtn., Mt., U.S.	B7	119
Baldy Mountain, mtn., N.M., U.S.	A4	124
Baldy Peak, mtn., Az., U.S.	D6	96
Balearic Islands see Balears, Illes, is., Spain	H7	16
Balears, Illes (Balearic Islands), is., Spain	H7	16
Baleia, Ponta da, c., Braz.	E4	74
Baleine, Rivière à la, stm., Qc., Can.	g13	90
Balej, Russia	D13	26
Baler, Phil.	C8	34
Bāleshwar, India	E5	40
Balezino, Russia	C9	22
Balfate, Hond.	B2	80
Balfour, N.C., U.S.	f10	126
Balfour, Hond.	B2	80
Balhaš, China	D8	28
Balhaš, ozero, l., Kaz.	E9	26
Bali, i., Indon.	E5	36
Bali, Laut (Bali Sea), Indon.	E5	36
Balıkesir, Tur.	C2	44
Balikpapan, Indon.	D5	36
Balimo, Pap. N. Gui.	H11	32
Balintang Channel, strt., Phil.	C8	34
Bali Sea see Bali, Laut, Indon.	E5	36
Balkan Mountains see Stara Planina, mts., Eur.	C9	18
Balkaria see Kabardino-Balkarija, state, Russia	E6	26
Balkh, Afg.	C9	42

Balkhash, Lake see Balhaš, ozero, l., Kaz.	E9	26
Ball, Il., U.S.	C3	111
Balladonia, Austl.	G3	60
Ballālpur, India	F3	40
Ballarat, Austl.	H3	62
Ballard, co., Ky., U.S.	e8	110
Ball Club Lake, l., Mn., U.S.	C5	116
Balleny Islands, is., Ant.	C21	67
Ball Ground, Ga., U.S.	B2	103
Ballina, Austl.	F5	62
Ballina, Ire.	C2	12
Ballinger, Tx., U.S.	D3	136
Ball Mountain Lake, res., Vt., U.S.	E3	138
Ballston Spa, N.Y., U.S.	B7	125
Ballwin, Mo., U.S.	f12	118
Bally, Pa., U.S.	F10	131
Ballymena, N. Ire., U.K.	C3	12
Balmoral, N.B., Can.	B3	87
Balmoral Castle, hist., Scot., U.K.	B5	12
Balmville, N.Y., U.S.	D6	125
Balombo, Ang.	F2	54
Balqash Köli see Balhaš, ozero, l., Kaz.	E9	26
Balş, Rom.	G8	20
Balsam Lake, Wi., U.S.	C1	142
Balsam Lake, l., Wi., U.S.	C1	142
Balsas, Braz.	E10	70
Balsas, stm., Mex.	D4	78
Balta, Ukr.	F10	20
Baltasar Brum, Ur.	E6	72
Bălţi, Mol.	F9	20
Baltic, Ct., U.S.	C7	100
Baltic, S.D., U.S.	D9	134
Baltic Sea, Eur.	I7	10
Baltijsk, Russia	B5	20
Baltim, Egypt	E10	14
Baltimore, Md., U.S.	B4	113
Baltimore, co., Md., U.S.	B4	113
Baltimore, Oh., U.S.	C3	128
Baltimore Highlands, Md., U.S.	h11	113
Baluchistan, hist. reg., Asia	E8	42
Bālurghāt, India	D6	40
Balygyčan, Russia	C17	26
Bam, Iran	E7	42
Bama, Nig.	D7	50
Bamako, Mali	D3	50
Bamba, Mali	C4	50
Bambari, C.A.R.	B4	54
Bamberg, Ger.	F12	12
Bamberg, S.C., U.S.	E5	133
Bamberg, co., S.C., U.S.	E5	133
Bambesi, Eth.	B6	54
Bamenda, Cam.	B2	54
Bāmīān, Afg.	D9	42
Bamingui, C.A.R.	B4	54
Bampūr, Iran	E8	42
Banaba, i., Kir.	E10	58
Banalia, D.R.C.	C5	54
Banamba, Mali	D3	50
Banana River, b., Fl., U.S.	D6	102
Bananal, Ilha do, i., Braz.	D1	74
Banas, stm., India	D4	40
Banās, Rás, c., Egypt	F12	48
Banat, hist. reg., Eur.	G6	20
Banbury, Eng., U.K.	D6	12
Bancroft, On., Can.	B7	89
Bancroft, Ia., U.S.	A3	108
Bancroft see Chililabombwe, Zam.	A4	56
Bānda, India	D4	40
Banda, Kepulauan, is., Indon.	D7	36
Banda, Laut (Banda Sea), Indon.	E7	36
Banda Aceh, Indon.	B1	36
Bandama, stm., C. Iv.	E4	50
Bandar Beheshti, Iran	E8	42
Bandar-e 'Abbās, Iran	E7	42
Bandar-e Anzalī, Iran	C5	42
Bandar-e Būshehr, Iran	E6	42
Bandar-e Deylam, Iran	E6	42
Bandar-e Khomeynī, Iran	D5	42
Bandar-e Lengeh, Iran	E6	42
Bandar-e Torkeman, Iran	C6	42
Bandar Lampung, Indon.	E3	36
Bandar Seri Begawan, Bru.	C4	36
Banda Sea see Banda, Laut, Indon.	E7	36
Banded Peak, mtn., Co., U.S.	D4	99
Bandeira, Pico da, mtn., Braz.	F3	74
Bandeirantes, Braz.	B7	72
Bandelier National Monument, N.M., U.S.	B3	124
Bandera, co., Tx., U.S.	E3	136
Bandiagara, Mali	D4	50
Bandiantaolehai, China	C8	28
Bandırma, Tur.	B2	44
Bandon, Or., U.S.	D2	130
Ban Don, Ao, b., Thai.	E3	34
Bandundu, D.R.C.	D3	54
Bandung, Indon.	E3	36
Bāneh, Iran	E11	44
Banes, Cuba	A4	80
Banff National Park, Ab., Can.	D2	84
Banfora, Burkina	D4	50
Bangalore, India	G3	40
Bangassou, C.A.R.	C4	54

Banggai, Indon.	D6	36
Banggai, Kepulauan, is., Indon.	G7	32
Banggi, Pulau, i., Malay.	B5	36
Banghāzī, Libya	D9	48
Bangka, Pulau, i., Indon.	D3	36
Bangka, Selat, strt., Indon.	D3	36
Bangkalan, Indon.	E4	36
Bangkinang, Indon.	C2	36
Bangko, Indon.	D2	36
Bangkok see Krung Thep, Thai.	D4	34
Bangladesh, ctry., Asia	B2	34
Bang Mun Nak, Thai.	C4	34
Ban Gnômmarat Kèo, Laos	C5	34
Bangor, N. Ire., U.K.	C4	12
Bangor, Wales, U.K.	D4	12
Bangor, Me., U.S.	D4	112
Bangor, Mi., U.S.	F4	115
Bangor, Pa., U.S.	E11	131
Bangor, Wi., U.S.	E3	142
Bangor Township, Mi., U.S.	E7	115
Bangs, Tx., U.S.	D3	136
Bangs, Mount, mtn., Az., U.S.	A2	96
Bangui, C.A.R.	C3	54
Bangweulu, Lake, l., Zam.	A4	56
Ban Houayxay, Laos	B4	34
Bani, Burkina	D4	50
Baní, Dom. Rep.	B5	80
Baniara, Pap. N. Gui.	B4	62
Banister, stm., Va., U.S.	D4	139
Banī Walid, Libya	D7	48
Bāniyās, Syria	E6	44
Banja Luka, Bos.	B6	18
Banjarmasin, Indon.	D4	36
Banjul, Gam.	D1	50
Banka Banka, Austl.	D5	60
Bankhead Lake, res., Al., U.S.	B2	94
Banks, co., Ga., U.S.	B3	103
Banks, Îles, is., Vanuatu	j9	62a
Banks Island, i., B.C., Can.	C2	85
Banks Lake, res., Wa., U.S.	B6	140
Banks Strait, strt., Austl.	I4	62
Bānkura, India	E5	40
Ban Nalè, Laos	C4	34
Banner, co., Ne., U.S.	C2	120
Banner Elk, N.C., U.S.	A1	126
Banning, Ca., U.S.	F5	98
Bannock, co., Id., U.S.	G6	105
Bannock Peak, mtn., Id., U.S.	F6	105
Bannock Range, mts., Id., U.S.	G6	105
Bannu, Pak.	D10	42
Ban Pong, Thai.	D3	34
Ban Signo, Laos	C5	34
Banská Bystrica, Slvk.	E5	20
Bānswāra, India	E2	40
Bantaeng, Indon.	E6	36
Bantam, stm., Ct., U.S.	B3	100
Bantam Lake, l., Ct., U.S.	C3	100
Banyo, Cam.	B2	54
Banyuwangi, Indon.	E4	36
Banzare Coast, Ant.	C17	67
Baode, China	D10	28
Baodi, China	B4	30
Baoding, China	D11	28
Bao Ha, Viet.	B4	34
Baoji, China	E9	28
Baojing, China	D2	30
Bao Lac, Viet.	D5	34
Baoqing, China	A2	31
Baoshan, China	F7	28
Baoting, China	H9	28
Baotou, China	C9	28
Baoying, China	E11	28
Ba'qūbah, Iraq	D4	42
Baquedano, Chile	B2	69
Bara, Nig.	D7	50
Baraawe, Som.	J13	48
Baraboo, stm., Wi., U.S.	E3	142
Baraboo, Wi., U.S.	E4	142
Baracoa, Cuba	A5	80
Baraga, Mi., U.S.	B2	115
Baraga, co., Mi., U.S.	B2	115
Barahona, Dom. Rep.	B5	80
Barakaldo, Spain	F5	16
Baram, stm., Malay.	C4	36
Bārāmūla, India	C2	40
Baranagar, India	E5	40
Baranavičy, Bela.	C9	20
Barani, Burkina	D4	50
Baranof Island, i., Ak., U.S.	m22	95
Barataria, La., U.S.	E5	111
Barataria Bay, b., La., U.S.	E6	111
Barauni, India	D5	40
Barbacena, Braz.	F3	74
Barbacoas, Col.	D4	70
Barbados, ctry., N.A.	F12	76
Barbar, Sudan	G11	48
Barbas, Cap, c., W. Sah.	B1	50
Barbastro, Spain	F7	16
Barber, co., Ks., U.S.	E5	109
Barbers Point, c., Hi., U.S.	B3	104
Barbers Point Naval Air Station, mil., Hi., U.S.	g9	104
Barberton, S. Afr.	D5	56
Barberton, Oh., U.S.	A4	128
Barbour, co., Al., U.S.	D4	94
Barbour, co., W.V., U.S.	B4	141
Barboursville, W.V., U.S.	C2	141
Barbourville, Ky., U.S.	D6	110

Name | Map Ref. | Page

Barbuda, i., Antig. B7 80
Barcaldine, Austl. E4 62
Barcelona, Spain G8 16
Barcelona, Ven. B6 70
Barcelos, Braz. D7 70
Barcroft, Lake, res., Va., U.S. g12 139
Bärdä, Azer. B12 44
Bardaï, Chad B8 50
Bardawīl, Sabkhet el-, b., Egypt G5 44
Bardejov, Slvk. E6 20
Barden Reservoir, res., R.I., U.S. C2 132
Bardīyah, Libya D10 48
Bardstown, Ky., U.S. C4 110
Bardwell, Ky., U.S. f9 110
Bardwell Lake, res., Tx., U.S. C4 136
Bareilly, India D3 40
Barents Sea, Eur. B6 26
Barents Trough D20 144
Bargersville, In., U.S. E5 107
Bar Harbor, Me., U.S. D4 112
Bari, Italy D6 18
Barika, Alg. J9 16
Barillas, Guat. B1 80
Barīm, i., Yemen H4 38
Barinas, Ven. B6 70
Bāripada, India E5 40
Bârîs, Egypt F11 48
Barisāl, Bngl. E6 40
Barisan, Pegunungan, mts., Indon. D2 36
Barkam, China C1 30
Barker Heights, N.C., U.S. f10 126
Barkhamsted Reservoir, res., Ct., U.S. B3 100
Barkley, Lake, res., U.S. f10 110
Barkley Sound, strt., B.C., Can. E5 85
Barkly East, S. Afr. E4 56
Barkly Tableland, plat., Austl. D6 60
Barkol, China C6 28
Bark Point, c., Wi., U.S. B2 142
Barksdale Air Force Base, mil., La., U.S. B2 111
Bârlad, Rom. F9 20
Barlee, Lake, l., Austl. F2 60
Barletta, Italy D6 18
Barling, Ar., U.S. B1 97
Barlow, Ky., U.S. e8 110
Bārmer, India D2 40
Barmera, Austl. G3 62
Barnaul, Russia D10 26
Barnegat Bay, b., N.J., U.S. D4 123
Barnegat Inlet, b., N.J., U.S. D4 123
Barnes, co., N.D., U.S. B7 127
Barnesboro, Pa., U.S. E4 131
Barnes Sound, strt., Fl., U.S. G6 102
Barnesville, Ga., U.S. C2 103
Barnesville, Mn., U.S. D2 116
Barnesville, Oh., U.S. C4 128
Barnhart, Mo., U.S. C7 118
Barnsdall, Ok., U.S. A5 129
Barnstable, Ma., U.S. C7 114
Barnstable, co., Ma., U.S. C7 114
Barnstaple, Eng., U.K. E4 12
Barnwell, S.C., U.S. E5 133
Barnwell, co., S.C., U.S. E5 133
Baro, Nig. E6 50
Barpeta, India D6 40
Barqah (Cyrenaica), hist. reg., Libya E8 14
Barques, Pointe aux, c., Mi., U.S. D8 115
Barquisimeto, Ven. A6 70
Barra, Braz. D3 74
Barra, i., Scot., U.K. B3 12
Barra, Ponta da, c., Moz. C6 56
Barrackville, W.V., U.S. B4 141
Barra do Corda, Braz. C2 74
Barra do Cuanza, Ang. E2 54
Barra do Dande, Ang. E2 54
Barra do Garças, Braz. B7 72
Barra Mansa, Braz. F3 74
Barranca, Peru F4 70
Barrancabermeja, Col. B5 70
Barrancas, Ven. D7 80
Barranquilla, Col. A5 70
Barras, Braz. B3 74
Barre, Vt., U.S. C4 138
Barre, Lake, l., La., U.S. E5 111
Barre Falls Reservoir, res., Ma., U.S. B4 114
Barreiras, Braz. D3 74
Barreiro, Port. H2 16
Barreiros, Braz. C4 74
Barren, stm., Ky., U.S. C3 110
Barren, co., Ky., U.S. D4 110
Barren, Nosy, is., Madag. B7 56
Barren Island, i., Md., U.S. D5 113
Barren Islands, is., Ak., U.S. h15 95
Barren River Lake, res., Ky., U.S. D3 110
Barretos, Braz. F2 74
Barrett, W.V., U.S. D3 141
Barrhead, Ab., Can. B3 84
Barrie, On., Can. C5 89
Barrie Island, i., On., Can. B2 89
Barrière, B.C., Can. D7 85
Barrier Range, mts., Austl. G3 62
Barrington, Il., U.S. A5 106
Barrington, N.J., U.S. D2 123
Barrington, R.I., U.S. D5 132
Barrington, stm., R.I., U.S. C5 132
Barron, Wi., U.S. C2 142
Barron, co., Wi., U.S. C2 142
Barron Lake, Mi., U.S. G4 115
Barrow, Ak., U.S. A8 95
Barrow, co., Ga., U.S. B3 103
Barrow, Point, c., Ak., U.S. A8 95
Barrow Creek, Austl. E5 60
Barrow-in-Furness, Eng., U.K. C5 12
Barrow Island, i., Austl. E2 60
Barry, Il., U.S. D2 106
Barry, co., Mi., U.S. F5 115
Barry, co., Mo., U.S. E4 118
Barrys Bay, On., Can. B7 89
Bārsi, India F3 40
Barstow, Ca., U.S. E5 98
Bartholomew, co., In., U.S. F6 107
Bartholomew, Bayou, stm., U.S. D4 97
Bartica, Guy. B8 70
Bartın, Tur. B5 44
Bartlesville, Ok., U.S. A6 129
Bartlett, N.H., U.S. B4 122
Bartlett, Tn., U.S. B2 135
Bartlett, Tx., U.S. D4 136
Bartlett Reservoir, res., Az., U.S. D4 96
Bartletts Ferry Dam, U.S. C4 94
Barton, co., Ks., U.S. D5 109
Barton, co., Mo., U.S. D3 118
Barton, Oh., U.S. B5 128
Barton, Vt., U.S. B4 138
Barton, stm., Vt., U.S. B4 138
Bartonville, Il., U.S. C4 106
Bartoszyce, Pol. B6 20
Bartow, Fl., U.S. E5 102
Bartow, co., Ga., U.S. B2 103
Barú, Volcán, vol., Pan. D3 80
Barun Su, China A3 30
Baruun-Urt, Mong. B10 28
Barysau, Bela. B10 20
Basalt, Co., U.S. B3 99
Basankusu, D.R.C. C3 54
Bascuñán, Cabo, c., Chile D3 72
Basehor, Ks., U.S. k16 109
Basel, Switz. G10 12
Bashan Lake, l., Ct., U.S. D6 100
Bashaw, Ab., Can. C4 84
Bashi Channel, strt., Asia B8 34
Basilan Island, i., Phil. E8 34
Basile, La., U.S. D3 111
Basin, Wy., U.S. B4 143
Basingstoke, Eng., U.K. E6 12
Basīrhāt, India E5 40
Baskahegan Lake, l., Me., U.S. C5 112
Başkale, Tur. C10 44
Basking Ridge, N.J., U.S. B3 123
Baškirija, state, Russia D7 26
Basoko, D.R.C. C4 54
Basra see Al-Başrah, Iraq D5 42
Bassano, Ab., Can. D4 84
Bassar, Togo E5 50
Bassein see Pathein, Mya. C2 34
Basse Santa Su, Gam. D2 50
Basse-Terre, Guad. B7 80
Basse-Terre, i., Guad. B7 80
Basseterre, St. K./N. B7 80
Bassett, Ne., U.S. B6 120
Bassett, Va., U.S. D3 139
Bassett Peak, mtn., Az., U.S. E5 96
Bassikounou, Maur. C3 50
Bass Islands, is., Oh., U.S. A3 128
Bass Lake, In., U.S. B4 107
Bass Strait, strt., Austl. H4 62
Basswood Lake, l., Mn., U.S. B7 116
Båstad, Swe. H5 10
Bastia, Fr. C2 18
Bastrop, La., U.S. B4 111
Bastrop, Tx., U.S. D4 136
Bastrop, co., Tx., U.S. D4 136
Basu, Pulau, i., Indon. D2 36
Basutoland see Lesotho, ctry., Afr. D4 56
Bata, Eq. Gui. C1 54
Batabanó, Golfo de, b., Cuba A3 80
Batac, Phil. C8 34
Batagaj, Russia C15 26
Batala, India C3 40
Batamaj, Russia C14 26
Batang, China E7 28
Batang, Indon. E3 36
Batangafo, C.A.R. B3 54
Batangas, Phil. D8 34
Batan Islands, is., Phil. B8 34
Batanta, Pulau, i., Indon. D8 36
Batavia see Jakarta, Indon. E3 36
Batavia, Il., U.S. B5 106
Batavia, N.Y., U.S. C2 125
Batavia, Oh., U.S. C1 128
Batchelor, Austl. C5 60
Batchelor Bay, b., N.C., U.S. B6 126
Bătdâmbâng, Camb. D4 34
Batemans Bay, Austl. H5 62
Bates, co., Mo., U.S. C3 118
Batesburg, S.C., U.S. D4 133
Batesville, Ar., U.S. B4 97
Batesville, In., U.S. F7 107
Batesville, Ms., U.S. A4 117
Bath, N.B., Can. C2 87
Bath, On., Can. C8 89
Bath, Eng., U.K. E5 12
Bath, co., Ky., U.S. B6 110
Bath, Me., U.S. E3 112
Bath, N.Y., U.S. C3 125
Bath, Pa., U.S. E11 131
Bath, S.C., U.S. D4 133
Bath, co., Va., U.S. B3 139
Bathinda, India C3 40
Bathurst, Austl. G4 62
Bathurst, N.B., Can. B4 87
Bathurst see Banjul, Gam. D1 50
Bathurst Island, i., Austl. C5 60
Batiscan, stm., Qc., Can. B5 90
Batman, Tur. D9 44
Batna, Alg. C6 48
Baton Rouge, La., U.S. D4 111
Batouri, Cam. C2 54
Batsto, stm., N.J., U.S. D3 123
Batten Kill, stm., U.S. E2 138
Batticaloa, Sri L. H4 40
Battle, stm., Can. H17 82
Battle Creek, Ia., U.S. B2 108
Battle Creek, Mi., U.S. F5 115
Battle Creek, Ne., U.S. C8 120
Battle Ground, In., U.S. C4 107
Battle Ground, Wa., U.S. D3 140
Battle Lake, Mn., U.S. D3 116
Battle Mountain, Nv., U.S. C5 121
Battle Mountain, mtn., Wy., U.S. E5 143
Batu, mtn., Eth. B7 54
Batu, Kepulauan, is., Indon. D1 36
Batumi, Geor. B9 44
Batu Pahat, Malay. C2 36
Baturaja, Indon. D2 36
Baturité, Braz. B4 74
Baubau, Indon. E6 36
Bauchi, Nig. D6 50
Baudette, Mn., U.S. B4 116
Bauld, Cape, c., N.L., Can. C4 88
Baures, Bol. A5 72
Bauru, Braz. F2 74
Bauska, Lat. H11 10
Bautzen, Ger. E14 12
Bavispe, stm., Mex. A3 78
Bawdwin, Mya. B3 34
Bawean, Pulau, i., Indon. E4 36
Bawiti, Egypt E10 48
Baxley, Ga., U.S. E4 103
Baxter, co., Ar., U.S. A3 97
Baxter, Ia., U.S. C4 108
Baxter, Mn., U.S. D4 116
Baxter, Tn., U.S. C8 135
Baxter Springs, Ks., U.S. E9 109
Bay, Ar., U.S. B5 97
Bay, co., Fl., U.S. u16 102
Bay, co., Mi., U.S. E6 115
Bayamo, Cuba A4 80
Bayamón, P.R. B6 80
Bayan Har Shan, mts., China E7 28
Bayanhongor, Mong. B8 28
Bayano, Lago, res., Pan. D4 80
Bayan Obo, China C10 28
Bayard, Ne., U.S. C2 120
Bayard, N.M., U.S. E1 124
Bayboro, N.C., U.S. B6 126
Bay Bulls, N.L., Can. E5 88
Bayburt, Tur. B9 44
Bay City, Mi., U.S. E7 115
Bay City, Or., U.S. B3 130
Bay City, Tx., U.S. E5 136
Bay de Verde, N.L., Can. D5 88
Baydhabo, Som. J13 48
Bayeux, Fr. C6 16
Bayfield, On., Can. D3 89
Bayfield, Co., U.S. D3 99
Bayfield, Wi., U.S. B3 142
Bayfield, co., Wi., U.S. B2 142
Baylor, co., Tx., U.S. C3 136
Bay Mills Indian Reservation, Mi., U.S. B6 115
Bay Minette, Al., U.S. E2 94
Bayombong, Phil. C8 34
Bayonne, Fr. F6 16
Bayonne, N.J., U.S. B4 123
Bayou Bodcau Reservoir, res., La., U.S. B2 111
Bayou D'Arbonne Lake, res., La., U.S. B3 111
Bayou George, Fl., U.S. u16 102
Bayou Goula, La., U.S. D4 111
Bayou La Batre, Al., U.S. E1 94
Bayovar, Peru E3 70
Bay Point, c., S.C., U.S. G7 133
Bayport, Mn., U.S. E6 116
Bayport, N.Y., U.S. n15 125
Bayreuth, Ger. F12 12
Bay Ridge, Md., U.S. C5 113
Bay Roberts, N.L., Can. E5 88
Bayrūt (Beirut), Leb. F6 44
Bays, Lake of, l., On., Can. B5 89
Bay Saint Louis, Ms., U.S. E4 117
Bay Shore, N.Y., U.S. E7 125
Bayshore Gardens, Fl., U.S. q10 102
Bayside, Wi., U.S. m12 142
Bay Springs, Ms., U.S. D4 117
Bayt Laḩm, W.B. G6 44
Baytown, Tx., U.S. E5 136
Bayview, Al., U.S. f7 94
Bay Village, Oh., U.S. h9 128
Baza, Spain I5 16
Bazardjuzju, gora see Bazardüzü dağ, mtn., Azer. B12 44
Bazardüzü dağ, mtn., Azer. B12 44
Bazaruto, Ilha do, i., Moz. C6 56
Bazhong, China C2 30
Be, Nosy, i., Madag. A8 56
Beach, Il., U.S. h9 106
Beach, N.D., U.S. C1 127
Beachburg, On., Can. B8 89
Beach City, Oh., U.S. B4 128
Beach Haven Inlet, b., N.J., U.S. D4 123
Beach Pond, res., U.S. C8 100
Beachville, On., Can. D4 89
Beachwood, N.J., U.S. D4 123
Beacon, Austl. G2 60
Beacon, N.Y., U.S. D7 125
Beacon Falls, Ct., U.S. D3 100
Beaconsfield, Qc., Can. q19 90
Beadle, co., S.D., U.S. C7 134
Beagle Gulf, b., Austl. C4 60
Bealanana, Madag. A8 56
Beale, Cape, c., B.C., Can. E5 85
Beale Air Force Base, mil., Ca., U.S. C3 98
Bear, De., U.S. B3 101
Bear, stm., U.S. B3 137
Bear Creek, Al., U.S. A2 94
Bear Creek, stm., Or., U.S. E4 130
Bear Creek, stm., Wy., U.S. E8 143
Bear Creek, stm., U.S. E2 109
Bearden, Ar., U.S. D3 97
Beardstown, Il., U.S. C3 106
Bear Inlet, b., N.C., U.S. C5 126
Bear Island see Bjørnøya, i., Nor. B3 26
Bear Lake, co., Id., U.S. G7 105
Bear Lake, l., Wi., U.S. C2 142
Bear Lake, l., U.S. A4 137
Bear Lake, l., U.S. C5 92
Bear Lodge Mountains, mts., Wy., U.S. B8 143
Bear Mountain, mtn., Or., U.S. D4 130
Bearpaw Mountains, mts., Mt., U.S. B7 119
Bear River, N.S., Can. E4 87
Bear River City, Ut., U.S. B3 137
Beartooth Pass, Wy., U.S. B3 143
Beartooth Range, mts., U.S. E7 119
Bear Town, Ms., U.S. D3 117
Beās, stm., India C3 40
Beata, Isla, i., Dom. Rep. B5 80
Beatrice, Ne., U.S. D9 120
Beatrice, Cape, c., Austl. C2 62
Beatty, Nv., U.S. G5 121
Beattyville, Ky., U.S. C6 110
Beaufort, N.C., U.S. C6 126
Beaufort, co., N.C., U.S. B5 126
Beaufort, S.C., U.S. G6 133
Beaufort, co., S.C., U.S. G6 133
Beaufort Marine Corps Air Station, mil., S.C., U.S. F6 133
Beaufort Sea, N.A. D12 82
Beaufort West, S. Afr. E3 56
Beauharnois, Qc., Can. D4 90
Beau Lake, l., Me., U.S. A3 112
Beaumont, Ab., Can. C4 84
Beaumont, Ms., U.S. D5 117
Beaumont, Tx., U.S. D5 136
Beaune, Fr. D9 16
Beauport, Qc., Can. n17 90
Beaupré, Qc., Can. B7 90
Beauregard, co., La., U.S. D2 111
Beausejour, Mb., Can. D3 86
Beauvais, Fr. C8 16
Beauval, Sk., Can. B2 91
Beaver, stm., Can. B2 91
Beaver, stm., N.Y., U.S. B6 125
Beaver, co., Ok., U.S. e10 129
Beaver, Ok., U.S. A1 129
Beaver, Pa., U.S. E1 131
Beaver, co., Pa., U.S. E1 131
Beaver, stm., R.I., U.S. E2 132
Beaver, Ut., U.S. E3 137
Beaver, co., Ut., U.S. E2 137
Beaver, stm., Ut., U.S. E2 137
Beaver, W.V., U.S. D3 141
Beaver, stm., U.S. A2 129
Beaverbank, N.S., Can. E6 87
Beaver Brook, stm., U.S. E4 122
Beaver City, Ne., U.S. D6 120
Beaver Creek, stm., N.D., U.S. C1 127
Beaver Creek, stm., N.D., U.S. C5 127
Beavercreek, Oh., U.S. C1 128
Beaver Creek, stm., Ok., U.S. C3 129
Beaver Creek, stm., Tn., U.S. m13 135
Beaver Creek, stm., Wy., U.S. D4 143
Beaver Creek, stm., U.S. C8 143
Beaver Creek, stm., U.S. E4 120
Beaverdale, Pa., U.S. F4 131
Beaver Dam, Ky., U.S. C3 110
Beaver Dam, Wi., U.S. E5 142
Beaverdam Branch, stm., De., U.S. F3 101
Beaverdam Lake, res., Wi., U.S. E5 142
Beaver Falls, Pa., U.S. E1 131
Beaverhead, stm., Mt., U.S. E4 119
Beaverhead, co., Mt., U.S. E3 119
Beaverhead Mountains, mts., U.S. D5 105
Beaverhill Lake, l., Ab., Can. C4 84
Beaver Island, i., Mi., U.S. C5 115
Beaver Lake, res., Ar., U.S. A2 97
Beaverlodge, Ab., Can. B1 84
Beaver Meadows, Pa., U.S. E10 131
Beaver Run Reservoir, res., Pa., U.S. F2 131
Beavertail Point, c., R.I., U.S. F4 132
Beaverton, Mi., U.S. E6 115
Beaverton, Or., U.S. B4 130
Beāwar, India D2 40
Bebedouro, Braz. C8 72
Bécancour, Qc., Can. C5 90
Bečej, Serb. B8 18
Béchar, Alg. D4 48
Becharof Lake, l., Ak., U.S. D8 95
Bechuanaland see Botswana, ctry., Afr. C3 56
Beckemeyer, Il., U.S. E4 106
Becker, Mn., U.S. E5 116
Becker, co., Mn., U.S. D3 116
Beckham, co., Ok., U.S. B2 129
Beckley, W.V., U.S. D3 141
Becky Peak, mtn., Nv., U.S. D7 121
Bedelē, Eth. B7 54
Bedford, Qc., Can. D5 90
Bedford, Eng., U.K. D6 12
Bedford, Ia., U.S. D3 108
Bedford, In., U.S. G5 107
Bedford, Ky., U.S. B4 110
Bedford, Ma., U.S. B5 114
Bedford, N.H., U.S. E3 122
Bedford, Oh., U.S. A4 128
Bedford, Pa., U.S. F4 131
Bedford, co., Pa., U.S. G4 131
Bedford, co., Tn., U.S. B5 135
Bedford, Va., U.S. C3 139
Bedford, co., Va., U.S. C3 139
Bedford Hills, N.Y., U.S. D7 125
Bee, co., Tx., U.S. E4 136
Beebe, Qc., Can. D5 90
Beebe, Ar., U.S. B4 97
Beecher, Il., U.S. B6 106
Beech Fork, stm., Ky., U.S. C4 110
Beech Grove, In., U.S. E5 107
Beech Island, S.C., U.S. E4 133
Beemer, Ne., U.S. C9 120
Bee Ridge, Fl., U.S. q11 102
Beersheba see Be'ér Sheva', Isr. D2 42
Be'ér Sheva', Isr. D2 42
Beeton (part of Alliston Beeton Tecumseth and Tottenham), On., Can. C5 89
Beeville, Tx., U.S. E4 136
Befale, D.R.C. C4 54
Befandriana Atsimo, Madag. C7 56
Bega, Austl. H4 62
Beggs, Ok., U.S. B5 129
Behbahān, Iran D6 42
Behm Canal, strt., Ak., U.S. n24 95
Bei'an, China B13 28
Beigi, Eth. B6 54
Beihai, China G9 28
Beijing, China D11 28
Beiliu, China E3 30
Beipiao, China C12 28
Beira, Moz. B5 56
Beirut see Bayrūt, Leb. F6 44
Bei Shan, mts., China C7 28
Beitbridge, Zimb. C5 56
Beizhen, China B4 30
Beizhen, China A5 30
Beja, Port. I3 16
Béja, Tun. C6 48
Bejaïa, Alg. C6 48
Bejaïa, Golfe de, b., Alg. I9 16
Béjar, Spain G4 16
Bejneu, Kaz. E7 26
Bekaa Valley see Al-Biqā', val., Leb. F6 44
Bekabad, Uzb. B9 42
Bekasi, Indon. E3 36
Bekdaš, Turk. B6 42
Békéscsaba, Hung. F6 20
Bekily, Madag. C8 56
Bekodoka, Madag. B8 56
Bela, India D4 40
Bela, Pak. E9 42
Bela Crkva, Serb. B8 18
Bel Air, Md., U.S. A5 113
Bel Alton, Md., U.S. D4 113
Belarus, ctry., Eur. C9 20
Belau see Palau, ctry., Oc. F10 32
Bela Vista, Braz. H8 70
Bela Vista, Moz. D5 56
Belcamp, Md., U.S. B5 113
Bełchatów, Pol. D5 20
Belchertown, Ma., U.S. B3 114
Belcourt, N.D., U.S. A6 127
Belden, Ms., U.S. A5 117
Belding, Mi., U.S. E5 115
Beledweyne, Som. J13 48
Belém, Braz. B2 74
Belém, Moz. A6 56
Belém de São Francisco, Braz. C4 74
Belen, N.M., U.S. C3 124
Belëv, Russia C14 20
Belfair, Wa., U.S. B3 140

Name	Map Ref.	Page
Belfast, S. Afr.	D5	56
Belfast, N. Ire., U.K.	C4	12
Belfast, Me., U.S.	D3	112
Belfield, N.D., U.S.	C2	127
Belford, N.J., U.S.	C4	123
Belfort, Fr.	D10	16
Belfry, Ky., U.S.	C7	110
Belgaum, India	F2	40
Belgium, ctry., Eur.	B9	16
Belgium, Wi., U.S.	E6	142
Belgium, ctry., Eur.	B9	16
Belgium, Wi., U.S.	E6	142
Belgorod, Russia	D5	26
Belgrade, Mn., U.S.	E3	116
Belgrade, Mt., U.S.	E5	119
Belgrade see Beograd, Serb.	B8	18
Belhaven, N.C., U.S.	B6	126
Beliliou, i., Palau	E9	32
Belington, W.V., U.S.	B5	141
Belitung, i., Indon.	D3	36
Belize, ctry., N.A.	B2	80
Belize City, Belize	B2	80
Belknap, co., N.H., U.S.	C3	122
Belknap Crater, crat., Or., U.S.	C5	130
Bell, co., Ky., U.S.	D6	110
Bell, co., Tx., U.S.	D4	136
Bella Coola, stm., B.C., Can.	C4	85
Bellaire, Ks., U.S.	g12	109
Bellaire, Mi., U.S.	D5	115
Bellaire, Oh., U.S.	C5	128
Bellaire, Tx., U.S.	r14	136
Bellamy, Al., U.S.	C1	94
Bellary, India	F3	40
Bella Vista, Arg.	D6	72
Bellavista, Peru	E4	70
Bella Vista, Ar., U.S.	A1	97
Bellbrook, Oh., U.S.	C1	128
Belle, stm., La., U.S.	k9	111
Belle, Mo., U.S.	C6	118
Belle, W.V., U.S.	C3	141
Belleair, Fl., U.S.	p10	102
Belle Bay, b., N.L., Can.	E4	88
Belle Chasse, La., U.S.	E5	111
Bellefontaine, Oh., U.S.	B2	128
Bellefonte, Pa., U.S.	E6	131
Belle Fourche, S.D., U.S.	C2	134
Belle Fourche, stm., U.S.	C3	134
Belle Fourche Reservoir, res., S.D., U.S.	C2	134
Belle Glade, Fl., U.S.	F6	102
Belle-Île, i., Fr.	D5	16
Belle Isle, i., N.L., Can.	C4	88
Belle Isle, Fl., U.S.	D5	102
Belle Isle, Strait of, strt., N.L., Can.	C3	88
Belle Meade, Tn., U.S.	g10	135
Belle Plaine, Ia., U.S.	C5	108
Belle Plaine, Ks., U.S.	E6	109
Belle Plaine, Mn., U.S.	F5	116
Belle River, On., Can.	E2	89
Belle Rose, La., U.S.	D4	111
Belle Vernon, Pa., U.S.	F2	131
Belleview, Fl., U.S.	C4	102
Belle View, Va., U.S.	g12	139
Belleville, On., Can.	C7	89
Belleville, Il., U.S.	E4	106
Belleville, Ks., U.S.	C6	109
Belleville, Mi., U.S.	p15	115
Belleville, N.J., U.S.	B4	123
Belleville, Pa., U.S.	E6	131
Belleville, Wi., U.S.	F4	142
Belleville Pond, l., R.I., U.S.	E4	132
Bellevue, Ia., U.S.	B7	108
Bellevue, Id., U.S.	F4	105
Bellevue, Ky., U.S.	h13	110
Bellevue, Mi., U.S.	F5	115
Bellevue, Ne., U.S.	C10	120
Bellevue, Oh., U.S.	A3	128
Bellevue, Pa., U.S.	F1	131
Bellevue, Wa., U.S.	e11	140
Bellflower, Ca., U.S.	n12	98
Bellingham, Ma., U.S.	B5	114
Bellingham, Wa., U.S.	A3	140
Bellingshausen Sea, Ant.	C32	67
Bellinzona, Switz.	A2	18
Bell Island, i., N.L., Can.	C4	88
Bellmawr, N.J., U.S.	D2	123
Bello, Col.	B4	70
Bellows Falls, Vt., U.S.	E4	138
Bellport, N.Y., U.S.	n16	125
Bells, Tn., U.S.	B2	135
Bells Creek, stm., W.V., U.S.	m13	141
Belluno, Italy	A4	18
Bell Ville, Arg.	E5	72
Bellville, Oh., U.S.	B3	128
Bellville, Tx., U.S.	E4	136
Bellwood, Il., U.S.	k9	106
Bellwood, Pa., U.S.	E5	131
Bellwood, Va., U.S.	n18	139
Belmar, N.J., U.S.	C4	123
Belmond, Ia., U.S.	B4	108
Belmont, On., Can.	E3	89
Belmont, Ca., U.S.	h8	98
Belmont, Ma., U.S.	g11	114
Belmont, Ms., U.S.	A5	117
Belmont, N.C., U.S.	B1	126
Belmont, N.H., U.S.	D4	122
Belmont, co., Oh., U.S.	C4	128
Belmont, Wi., U.S.	F3	142
Belmont, W.V., U.S.	B3	141
Belmonte, Braz.	G12	70
Belmopan, Belize	B2	80
Bel-Nor, Mo., U.S.	f13	118
Beloe, ozero, l., Russia	C5	26
Beloeil, Qc., Can.	D4	90
Beloe more, Russia	C5	26
Belogorsk, Russia	D14	26
Belo Horizonte, Braz.	E3	74
Beloit, Ks., U.S.	C5	109
Beloit, Oh., U.S.	B5	128
Beloit, Wi., U.S.	F4	142
Belomorsk, Russia	C5	26
Beloreck, Russia	D10	22
Belorussia see Belarus, ctry., Eur.	C9	20
Belo Tsiribihina, Madag.	B7	56
Belpre, Oh., U.S.	C4	128
Belt, Mt., U.S.	C6	119
Belted Range, mts., Nv., U.S.	F5	121
Belton, Mo., U.S.	C3	118
Belton, S.C., U.S.	B3	133
Belton, Tx., U.S.	D4	136
Belton Lake, res., Tx., U.S.	D4	136
Beltrami, co., Mn., U.S.	B3	116
Beltsville, Md., U.S.	B4	113
Beluha, gora, mtn., Asia	B5	28
Belūr, India	G3	40
Belvedere, S.C., U.S.	D4	133
Belvidere, Il., U.S.	A5	106
Belvidere, N.J., U.S.	B2	123
Belyj, ostrov, i., Russia	B8	26
Belyj Jar, Russia	D10	26
Belzoni, Ms., U.S.	B3	117
Bembèrèkè, Benin	D5	50
Bement, Il., U.S.	D5	106
Bemidji, Mn., U.S.	C4	116
Bemidji, Lake, l., Mn., U.S.	C4	116
Benāb, Iran	D11	44
Bena-Dibele, D.R.C.	D4	54
Benalla, Austl.	H4	62
Benares see Vārānasi, India	D4	40
Benavente, Spain	F4	16
Benavides, Tx., U.S.	F3	136
Benbecula, i., Scot., U.K.	B3	12
Benbrook Lake, res., Tx., U.S.	n9	136
Bencubbin, Austl.	G2	60
Bend, Or., U.S.	C5	130
Ben Davis Point, c., N.J., U.S.	E2	123
Bendeleben, Mount, mtn., Ak., U.S.	B7	95
Bendigo, Austl.	H3	62
Benedict, Md., U.S.	C4	113
Benedito Leite, Braz.	E11	70
Benevento, Italy	D5	18
Benewah, co., Id., U.S.	B2	105
Bengal, Bay of, b., Asia	F5	40
Bengbu, China	E11	28
Benghazi see Banghāzī, Libya	D9	48
Bengkalis, Pulau, i., Indon.	C2	36
Bengkulu, Indon.	D2	36
Bengtsfors, Swe.	G5	10
Benguela, Ang.	F2	54
Bengweulu Swamps, sw., Zam.	A5	56
Benham, Ky., U.S.	D7	110
Ben Hill, co., Ga., U.S.	E3	103
Beni, stm., Bol.	F6	70
Beni, D.R.C.	C5	54
Béni Abbas, Alg.	D4	48
Benicia, Ca., U.S.	C2	98
Benidorm, Spain	H6	16
Beni-Mellal, Mor.	D3	48
Benin, ctry., Afr.	D5	50
Benin, Bight of, b., Afr.	E5	50
Benin City, Nig.	E6	50
Beni Saf, Alg.	J6	16
Beni Suef, Egypt	E11	48
Benito Juárez, Arg.	F6	72
Benjamin Constant, Braz.	D5	70
Benkelman, Ne., U.S.	D4	120
Benld, Il., U.S.	D4	106
Bennett, Co., U.S.	B6	99
Bennett, co., S.D., U.S.	D4	134
Bennettsville, S.C., U.S.	B8	133
Bennington, Ne., U.S.	g12	120
Bennington, N.H., U.S.	D3	122
Bennington, Vt., U.S.	F2	138
Bennington, co., Vt., U.S.	E2	138
Benoit, Ms., U.S.	B2	117
Benoni, S. Afr.	D4	56
Bénoué see Benue, stm., Afr.	E6	50
Bensenville, Il., U.S.	B6	106
Bensheim, Ger.	F11	12
Bensley, Va., U.S.	C5	139
Benson, Az., U.S.	F5	96
Benson, Mn., U.S.	E3	116
Benson, N.C., U.S.	B4	126
Benson, co., N.D., U.S.	A6	127
Bent, co., Co., U.S.	D7	99
Benteng, Indon.	E6	36
Bentinck Island, i., Austl.	D2	62
Bentinck Island, i., Mya.	D3	34
Bentley, Ab., Can.	C3	84
Bentleyville, Pa., U.S.	F1	131
Benton, Ar., U.S.	C3	97
Benton, co., Ar., U.S.	A1	97
Benton, co., Ia., U.S.	B5	108
Benton, Il., U.S.	E5	106
Benton, co., In., U.S.	C3	107
Benton, Ks., U.S.	E6	109
Benton, Ky., U.S.	f9	110
Benton, La., U.S.	B2	111
Benton, co., Mn., U.S.	E4	116
Benton, co., Mo., U.S.	C4	118
Benton, co., Ms., U.S.	A4	117
Benton, co., Or., U.S.	C3	130
Benton, Pa., U.S.	D9	131
Benton, Tn., U.S.	B7	135
Benton, co., Tn., U.S.	A3	135
Benton, co., Wa., U.S.	C6	140
Benton, Wi., U.S.	F3	142
Benton City, Wa., U.S.	C6	140
Benton Harbor, Mi., U.S.	F4	115
Benton Heights, Mi., U.S.	F4	115
Bentonville, Ar., U.S.	A1	97
Ben Tre, Viet.	D5	34
Bent's Old Fort National Historic Site, hist., Co., U.S.	C7	99
Bentung, Malay.	C2	36
Benue, stm., Afr.	E6	50
Benwood, W.V., U.S.	f8	141
Benxi, China	C12	28
Benzie, co., Mi., U.S.	D4	115
Beograd (Belgrade), Serb.	B8	18
Béoumi, C. Iv.	E3	50
Beowawe, Nv., U.S.	C5	121
Beppu, Japan	D2	31
Beraketa, Madag.	C8	56
Berat, Alb.	D7	18
Berau, Teluk, b., Indon.	D8	36
Berazino, Bela.	C10	20
Berbera, Som.	H14	48
Berbérati, C.A.R.	C3	54
Berck, Fr.	B7	16
Berdians'k, Ukr.	F14	20
Berdigestjah, Russia	C14	26
Berdychiv, Ukr.	E10	20
Berea, Ky., U.S.	C5	110
Berea, Oh., U.S.	A4	128
Berea, S.C., U.S.	B3	133
Berehove, Ukr.	E7	20
Berekum, Ghana	E4	50
Berens, stm., Can.	C3	86
Beresford, S.D., U.S.	D9	134
Berettyóújfalu, Hung.	F6	20
Berezhany, Ukr.	E8	20
Berezivka, Ukr.	F11	20
Berezniki, Russia	D7	26
Berëzovo, Russia	C8	26
Berg, Swe.	F7	10
Bergama, Tur.	C2	44
Bergamo, Italy	B2	18
Bergen, Ger.	D12	12
Bergen, Nor.	F1	10
Bergen, co., N.J., U.S.	A4	123
Bergenfield, N.J., U.S.	B4	123
Bergerac, Fr.	E7	16
Bergland, Mi., U.S.	m12	115
Berguent, Mor.	E3	14
Berhala, Selat, strt., Indon.	D2	36
Beringa, ostrov, i., Russia	D18	26
Beringov proliv see Bering Strait, strt.	F6	82
Beringovskij, Russia	C19	26
Bering Sea	G3	82
Bering Strait, strt.	F6	82
Berkakit, Russia	D14	26
Berkane, Mor.	E3	14
Berkeley, co., S.C., U.S.	D2	98
Berkeley, Ca., U.S.	D2	98
Berkeley, Mo., U.S.	f13	118
Berkeley, R.I., U.S.	B4	132
Berkeley, co., S.C., U.S.	E8	133
Berkeley, co., W.V., U.S.	B6	141
Berkeley Heights, N.J., U.S.	B4	123
Berkeley Springs, W.V., U.S.	B6	141
Berkley, Mi., U.S.	F7	115
Berks, co., Pa., U.S.	F9	131
Berkshire, co., Ma., U.S.	B1	114
Berkshire Hills, Ma., U.S.	B1	114
Berlevåg, Nor.	A13	10
Berlin, Ger.	D13	12
Berlin, Ct., U.S.	C5	100
Berlin, Md., U.S.	D7	113
Berlin, N.H., U.S.	B4	122
Berlin, N.J., U.S.	D3	123
Berlin, Pa., U.S.	G4	131
Berlin, Wi., U.S.	E5	142
Berlin Lake, res., Oh., U.S.	A4	128
Bermejo, stm., S.A.	C5	72
Bermuda, dep., N.A.	B12	76
Bern, Switz.	A1	18
Bernalillo, N.M., U.S.	B3	124
Bernalillo, co., N.M., U.S.	C3	124
Bernardsville, N.J., U.S.	B3	123
Bernasconi, Arg.	F5	72
Berne see Bern, Switz.	A1	18
Berne, In., U.S.	C8	107
Berner Alpen, mts., Switz.	A1	18
Bernese Alps see Berner Alpen, mts., Switz.	A1	18
Bernice, La., U.S.	B3	111
Bernie, Mo., U.S.	E8	118
Bernier Island, i., Austl.	E1	60
Bernina, Piz, mtn., Eur.	A2	18
Beroroha, Madag.	C8	56
Berrien, co., Ga., U.S.	E3	103
Berrien, co., Mi., U.S.	F4	115
Berrien Springs, Mi., U.S.	G4	115
Berry, hist. reg., Fr.	D7	16
Berry, Al., U.S.	B2	94
Berryessa, Lake, res., Ca., U.S.	C2	98
Berry Hill, Tn., U.S.	g10	135
Berryville, Ar., U.S.	A2	97
Berryville, Va., U.S.	A5	139
Berseba, Nmb.	D2	56
Bershad', Ukr.	E10	20
Berthierville, Qc., Can.	C4	90
Berthoud, Co., U.S.	A5	99
Berthoud Pass, Co., U.S.	B5	99
Bertie, co., N.C., U.S.	A5	126
Bertoua, Cam.	C2	54
Bertrand, Mo., U.S.	E8	118
Bertrand, Ne., U.S.	D6	120
Berwick, Ia., U.S.	e8	108
Berwick, La., U.S.	E4	111
Berwick, Me., U.S.	E2	112
Berwick, Pa., U.S.	D9	131
Berwick-upon-Tweed, Eng., U.K.	C6	12
Berwyn, Ab., Can.	A2	84
Berwyn, Il., U.S.	k9	106
Berwyn, Pa., U.S.	o20	131
Besalampy, Madag.	B7	56
Besançon, Fr.	D9	16
Beskids, mts., Eur.	E5	20
Beskra, Alg.	D6	48
Beslan, Russia	A11	44
Besni, Tur.	D7	44
Bessemer, Al., U.S.	B3	94
Bessemer, Mi., U.S.	n11	115
Bessemer, Pa., U.S.	E1	131
Bessemer City, N.C., U.S.	B1	126
Bétaré Oya, Cam.	B2	54
Betatakin Ruin, hist., Az., U.S.	A5	96
Bethalto, Il., U.S.	E3	106
Bethanien, Nmb.	D2	56
Bethany, Ct., U.S.	D4	100
Bethany, Il., U.S.	D5	106
Bethany, Mo., U.S.	A3	118
Bethany, Ok., U.S.	B4	129
Bethany, W.V., U.S.	A4	141
Bethany Beach, De., U.S.	F5	101
Bethel, Ak., U.S.	C7	95
Bethel, Ct., U.S.	D2	100
Bethel, Me., U.S.	D2	112
Bethel, N.C., U.S.	B5	126
Bethel, Oh., U.S.	D1	128
Bethel, Vt., U.S.	D3	138
Bethel Park, Pa., U.S.	k14	131
Bethel Springs, Tn., U.S.	B3	135
Bethesda, Md., U.S.	C3	113
Bethesda, Oh., U.S.	B4	128
Bethlehem, S. Afr.	D4	56
Bethlehem, Ct., U.S.	C3	100
Bethlehem, N.H., U.S.	B3	122
Bethlehem, Pa., U.S.	E11	131
Bethlehem see Bayt Laḥm, W.B.	G6	44
Bethulie, S. Afr.	E4	56
Betong, Malay.	C4	36
Betong, Thai.	E4	34
Betoota, Austl.	F3	62
Betpak-Dala, des., Kaz.	E8	26
Betroka, Madag.	C8	56
Betsiboka, stm., Madag.	B8	56
Betsie, Point, c., Mi., U.S.	D4	115
Betsy Layne, Ky., U.S.	C7	110
Bettendorf, Ia., U.S.	C7	108
Bettiah, India	D4	40
Betūl, India	E3	40
Betwa, stm., India	D3	40
Betzdorf, Ger.	E10	12
Beulah, Co., U.S.	C6	99
Beulah, N.D., U.S.	B4	127
Beulah, Lake, l., Ms., U.S.	B3	117
Beulaville, N.C., U.S.	C5	126
Beuthen see Bytom, Pol.	D5	20
B. Everett Jordan Lake, res., N.C., U.S.	B3	126
Beverley Head, c., N.L., Can.	D2	88
Beverly, Ma., U.S.	A6	114
Beverly, N.J., U.S.	C3	123
Beverly, Oh., U.S.	C4	128
Beverly, W.V., U.S.	C5	141
Beverly Hills, Ca., U.S.	m12	98
Beverly Shores, In., U.S.	A4	107
Bexar, co., Tx., U.S.	E3	136
Bexley, Oh., U.S.	m11	128
Beyla, Gui.	E3	50
Beypazarı, Tur.	B4	44
Beyşehir, Tur.	D4	44
Beyşehir Gölü, l., Tur.	D4	44
Bežeck, Russia	C6	22
Béziers, Fr.	F8	16
Bhadohi, India	D4	40
Bhadrāchalam, India	F4	40
Bhadrak, India	E5	40
Bhadra Reservoir, res., India	G3	40
Bhadrāvati, India	G3	40
Bhāgalpur, India	D5	40
Bhāgīrathi see Ganges, stm., India	D5	40
Bhakkar, Pak.	D10	42
Bhaktapur, Nepal	D5	40
Bhamo, Mya.	B3	34
Bhandāra, India	E3	40
Bharatpur, India	D3	40
Bharūch, India	E2	40
Bhātpāra, India	E5	40
Bhāvnagar, India	E2	40
Bhawānipatna, India	F4	40
Bhilai, India	E4	40
Bhīlwāra, India	D2	40
Bhīma, stm., India	F3	40
Bhind, India	D3	40
Bhiwāni, India	D3	40
Bhongīr, India	F3	40
Bhopāl, India	E3	40
Bhubaneshwar, India	E5	40
Bhuj, India	E1	40
Bhusāwal, India	E3	40
Bhutan, ctry., Asia	D6	40
Bia, Mount see Bia, Phou, mtn., Laos	C4	34
Bia, Phou, mtn., Laos	C4	34
Biafra, Bight of, b., Afr.	C1	54
Biak, i., Indon.	G10	32
Biała Podlaska, Pol.	D7	20
Białogard, Pol.	B4	20
Białystok, Pol.	C7	20
Bianco, Monte (Blanc, Mont), mtn., Eur.	B1	18
Biankouma, C. Iv.	E3	50
Biaora, India	E3	40
Biaro, Pulau, i., Indon.	C7	36
Biarritz, Fr.	F6	16
Bibala, Ang.	A1	56
Bibb, co., Al., U.S.	C2	94
Bibb, co., Ga., U.S.	D3	103
Bibémi, Cam.	B2	54
Biberach an der Riss, Ger.	F11	12
Bic, Qc., Can.	A9	90
Bic, Île du, i., Qc., Can.	A9	90
Biche, Lac la, l., Ab., Can.	B4	84
Bicknell, In., U.S.	G3	107
Bīd, India	F3	40
Bida, Nig.	E6	50
Bīdar, India	F3	40
Biddeford, Me., U.S.	E2	112
Bidwell, Mount, mtn., Ca., U.S.	B3	98
Biel, Switz.	A1	18
Bielefeld, Ger.	E11	12
Biella, Italy	B2	18
Bielsko-Biała, Pol.	E5	20
Bielsk Podlaski, Pol.	C7	20
Bien Hoa, Viet.	D5	34
Bienville, co., La., U.S.	B2	111
Bienville, Lac, l., Qc., Can.	g12	90
Big, stm., Mo., U.S.	c7	118
Biga, Tur.	B2	44
Big Bald, mtn., Ga., U.S.	B2	103
Big Bald Mountain, mtn., N.B., Can.	B3	87
Big Baldy, mtn., Id., U.S.	E3	105
Big Baldy Mountain, mtn., Mt., U.S.	D6	119
Big Bay De Noc, b., Mi., U.S.	C4	115
Big Bear City, Ca., U.S.	E5	98
Big Belt Mountains, mts., Mt., U.S.	D5	119
Big Bend, Wi., U.S.	n11	142
Big Bend Dam, S.D., U.S.	C6	134
Big Bend National Park, Tx., U.S.	E1	136
Big Birch Lake, l., Mn., U.S.	E4	116
Big Black, stm., Me., U.S.	B3	112
Big Black, stm., Ms., U.S.	C3	117
Big Blue, stm., In., U.S.	E6	107
Big Burro Mountains, mts., N.M., U.S.	E1	124
Big Cabin Creek, stm., Ok., U.S.	A6	129
Big Coal, stm., W.V., U.S.	C3	141
Big Costilla Peak, mtn., N.M., U.S.	A4	124
Big Creek, stm., Tn., U.S.	e8	135
Big Creek Lake, res., Al., U.S.	E1	94
Big Creek Peak, mtn., Id., U.S.	E5	105
Big Cypress Indian Reservation, Fl., U.S.	F5	102
Big Cypress Swamp, sw., Fl., U.S.	F5	102
Big Darby Creek, stm., Oh., U.S.	C2	128
Big Delta, Ak., U.S.	C10	95
Big Duke Dam, N.C., U.S.	B2	126
Big Eau Pleine, stm., Wi., U.S.	D3	142
Big Eau Pleine Reservoir, res., Wi., U.S.	D4	142
Big Escambia Creek, stm., U.S.	D2	94
Big Flats, N.Y., U.S.	C4	125
Big Fork, stm., Mn., U.S.	B5	116
Bigfork, Mt., U.S.	B2	119
Biggs, Ca., U.S.	C3	98
Big Hatchet Peak, mtn., N.M., U.S.	F1	124
Big Hole, stm., Mt., U.S.	E4	119
Big Hole National Battlefield, hist., Mt., U.S.	E3	119
Big Horn, co., Mt., U.S.	E9	119
Big Horn, co., Wy., U.S.	B4	143
Bighorn Canyon National Recreation Area, U.S.	F8	119
Bighorn Lake, res., U.S.	E8	119
Big Horn Mountains, mts., Az., U.S.	D2	96
Bighorn Mountains, mts., U.S.	B5	143
Bighorn Mountains, mts., U.S.	C6	92
Bight, Head of, b., Austl.	G5	60
Big Kandiyohi Lake, l., Mn., U.S.	F4	116
Big Lake, l., Me., U.S.	C5	112
Big Lake, Mn., U.S.	E5	116
Big Lake, Tx., U.S.	D2	136
Biglerville, Pa., U.S.	G7	131
Big Lookout Mountain, mtn., Or., U.S.	C9	130

Name | Map Ref. | Page

Big Lost, stm., Id., U.S. F5 105
Big Mossy Point, c., Mb., Can. C2 86
Big Mountain, mtn., Nv., U.S. B2 121
Big Muddy, stm., Il., U.S. F4 106
Big Nemaha, stm., Ne., U.S. D10 120
Bignona, Sen. D1 50
Big Otter, stm., Va., U.S. C3 139
Big Pine Lake, l., Mn., U.S. D3 116
Big Pine Mountain, mtn., Ca., U.S. E4 98
Big Piney, stm., Mo., U.S. D5 118
Big Piney, Wy., U.S. D2 143
Bigpoint, Ms., U.S. E5 117
Big Rapids, Mi., U.S. E5 115
Big Rib, stm., Wi., U.S. C3 142
Big River, Sk., Can. D2 91
Big Sable Point, c., Mi., U.S. D4 115
Big Sandy, stm., Az., U.S. C2 96
Big Sandy, Mt., U.S. B6 119
Big Sandy, stm., Tn., U.S. B3 135
Big Sandy, Tx., U.S. C5 136
Big Sandy, stm., Wy., U.S. D3 143
Big Sandy, stm., U.S. C2 141
Big Sandy Creek, stm., W.V., U.S. C3 141
Big Sandy Lake, l., Mn., U.S. D5 116
Big Sandy Reservoir, res., Wy., U.S. D3 143
Big Sheep Mountain, mtn., Mt., U.S. C11 119
Big Sioux, stm., U.S. E9 134
Big Smoky Valley, val., Nv., U.S. E4 121
Big Snowy Mountains, mts., Mt., U.S. D7 119
Big Southern Butte, mtn., Id., U.S. F5 105
Big South Fork, stm., Ky., U.S. k13 110
Big Spring, Tx., U.S. C2 136
Big Stone, co., Mn., U.S. E2 116
Big Stone City, S.D., U.S. B9 134
Big Stone Gap, Va., U.S. f9 139
Big Stone Lake, l., U.S. E2 116
Big Sunflower, stm., Ms., U.S. B3 117
Big Thompson, stm., Co., U.S. A5 99
Big Timber, Mt., U.S. E7 119
Big Trout Lake, l., On., Can. n17 89
Big Walnut Creek, stm., Oh., U.S. m11 128
Big Wood, stm., Id., U.S. F4 105
Bihać, Bos. B5 18
Bihār, India D5 40
Bihār, state, India D5 40
Biharamulo, Tan. D6 54
Bijagós, Arquipélago dos, is., Gui.-B. D1 50
Bijāpur, India F3 40
Bījār, Iran E12 44
Bijeljina, Bos. B7 18
Bijie, China F9 28
Bijsk, Russia D10 26
Bīkāner, India D2 40
Bikar, atoll, Marsh. Is. C10 58
Bikeqi, China C10 28
Bikin, Russia B14 28
Bikini, atoll, Marsh. Is. C10 58
Bikkū Bīttī, mtn., Libya F8 48
Bikoro, D.R.C. D3 54
Bilāspur, India E4 40
Bilāspur, India C3 40
Biläsuvar, Azer. C13 44
Bila Tserkva, Ukr. E11 20
Bilauktaung Range, mts., Asia D3 34
Bilbao, Spain F5 16
Bilecik, Tur. B4 44
Biłgoraj, Pol. D7 20
Bilhorod-Dnistrovs'kyi, Ukr. F11 20
Bili, D.R.C. C5 54
Bilk Creek Mountains, mts., Nv., U.S. B3 121
Billerica, Ma., U.S. A5 114
Billings, Mo., U.S. D4 118
Billings, Mt., U.S. E8 119
Billings, co., N.D., U.S. B2 127
Billings Heights, Mt., U.S. E8 119
Bill Williams, stm., Az., U.S. C1 96
Bill Williams Mountain, mtn., Az., U.S. B3 96
Bilma, Niger C7 50
Bilohirs'k, Ukr. G13 20
Bilopillia, Ukr. D13 20
Biloxi, Ms., U.S. E5 117
Biloxi, stm., Ms., U.S. E4 117
Biloxi Bay, b., Ms., U.S. f8 117
Biltmore Forest, N.C., U.S. f10 126
Bimbo, C.A.R. C3 54
Bimini Islands, is., Bah. C9 76
Bina-Etāwa, India E3 40
Bindura, Zimb. B5 56
Binga, D.R.C. C4 54
Binga, Monte, mtn., Afr. B5 56
Bingamon Creek, stm., W.V., U.S. k10 141
Bingara, Austl. F5 62
Bingen, Wa., U.S. D4 140
Binger, Ok., U.S. B3 129
Bingham, co., Id., U.S. F6 105
Bingham, Me., U.S. C3 112
Binghamton, N.Y., U.S. C5 125
Bingöl, Tur. C9 44
Binhai, China E12 28
Binh Son, Viet. C5 34
Binjai, Indon. C1 36
Binongko, Pulau, i., Indon. E6 36
Bintan, Pulau, i., Indon. C2 36
Bintimani, mtn., S.L. E2 50
Bintuhan, Indon. D2 36
Bintulu, Malay. C4 36
Bintuni, Indon. D8 36
Binxian, China B4 30
Binyang, China B5 34
Bin-Yauri, Nig. D5 50
Binzert see Bizerte, Tun. C6 48
Biobío, stm., Chile F3 72
Bioko, i., Eq. Gui. C1 54
Birāk, Libya E7 48
Bi'r al Wa'r, Libya F7 48
Birao, C.A.R. A4 54
Birch, stm., W.V., U.S. C4 141
Birch Island, i., Mb., Can. C2 86
Birch Lake, l., Mn., U.S. C7 116
Birch River, Mb., Can. C1 86
Birch Run, Mi., U.S. E7 115
Birchy Bay, N.L., Can. D4 88
Bird Creek, stm., Ok., U.S. A6 129
Bird Island, Mn., U.S. F4 116
Bird Island, i., N.C., U.S. D4 126
Birdsboro, Pa., U.S. F10 131
Birdum, Austl. D5 60
Birecik, Tur. D8 44
Birigui, Braz. F1 74
Bīrjand, Iran D7 42
Birmingham, Eng., U.K. D6 12
Birmingham, Al., U.S. B3 94
Birmingham, Mi., U.S. F7 115
Birmitrapur, India E4 40
Bîr Mogreïn, Maur. A2 50
Birnin-Kebbi, Nig. D5 50
Birnin Konni, Niger D6 50
Birnin Kudu, Nig. D6 50
Birobidžan, Russia E15 26
Biron, Wi., U.S. D4 142
Birsk, Russia C10 22
Birtle, Mb., Can. D1 86
Biržai, Lith. H11 10
Bisbee, Az., U.S. F6 96
Biscay, Bay of (Gascogne, Golfe de), b., Eur. E5 16
Biscayne, Key, i., Fl., U.S. s13 102
Biscayne Bay, b., Fl., U.S. G6 102
Biscayne National Monument, Fl., U.S. G6 102
Biscayne Park, Fl., U.S. s13 102
Biscoe, N.C., U.S. B3 126
Bishkek see Biškek, Kyrg. E9 26
Bishop, Ca., U.S. D4 98
Bishop, Tx., U.S. F4 136
Bishop's Falls, N.L., Can. D4 88
Bishopville, S.C., U.S. C7 133
Biškek, Kyrg. E9 26
Bislig, Phil. E9 34
Bismarck, Il., U.S. C6 106
Bismarck, Mo., U.S. D7 118
Bismarck, N.D., U.S. C5 127
Bismarck Archipelago, is., Pap. N. Gui. G12 32
Bismarck Range, mts., Pap. N. Gui. H11 32
Bismarck Sea, Pap. N. Gui. G12 32
Bismil, Tur. D9 44
Bison Peak, mtn., Co., U.S. B5 99
Bissau, Gui.-B. D1 50
Bissikrima, Gui. D2 50
Bistineau, Lake, res., La., U.S. B2 111
Bistrița, Rom. F8 20
Bitam, Gabon C2 54
Bitlis, Tur. C10 44
Bitola, Mac. D8 18
Bitou, Burkina D4 50
Bitter Creek, stm., Wy., U.S. E4 143
Bitterfontein, S. Afr. E2 56
Bitter Lake, l., S.D., U.S. B8 134
Bitterroot, stm., Mt., U.S. D2 119
Bitterroot Range, mts., U.S. B3 105
Bitterroot Range, mts., U.S. B4 92
Bitung, Indon. C7 36
Biu, Nig. D7 50
Biwabik, Mn., U.S. C6 116
Biwa-ko, l., Japan C3 31
Bixby, Ok., U.S. B6 129
Biyang, China C3 30
Bizerte, Tun. C6 48
Bjala, Blg. C10 18
Bjarèzina, stm., Bela. C10 20
Bjelovar, Cro. B6 18
Bjørnøya, i., Nor. B3 26
Bla, Mali D3 50
Black, stm., Asia B4 34
Black, stm., Ar., U.S. B4 97
Black, stm., Az., U.S. D5 96
Black, stm., La., U.S. C4 111
Black, stm., Mi., U.S. E8 115
Black, stm., N.C., U.S. C4 126
Black, stm., N.Y., U.S. B4 125
Black, stm., S.C., U.S. D8 133
Black, stm., Vt., U.S. E3 138
Black, stm., Wi., U.S. D3 142
Blackall, Austl. E4 62
Black Bear Creek, stm., Ok., U.S. A4 129
Blackbeard Island, i., Ga., U.S. E5 103
Blackburn, Mount, mtn., Ak., U.S. C11 95
Black Butte, mtn., Mt., U.S. F5 119
Black Butte Lake, res., Ca., U.S. C2 98
Black Canyon, Co., U.S. C3 99
Black Canyon City, Az., U.S. C3 96
Black Canyon of the Gunnison National Monument, Co., U.S. C3 99
Black Creek, B.C., Can. E5 85
Black Creek, stm., S.C., U.S. B7 133
Black Creek, Wi., U.S. D5 142
Black Creek, stm., U.S. B1 124
Black Diamond, Ab., Can. D3 84
Black Diamond, Wa., U.S. B4 140
Blackduck, Mn., U.S. C4 116
Black Eagle, Mt., U.S. C5 119
Black Earth, Wi., U.S. E4 142
Blackfalds, Ab., Can. C4 84
Blackfeet Indian Reservation, Mt., U.S. B4 119
Blackfoot, Id., U.S. F6 105
Blackfoot, stm., Mt., U.S. C3 119
Blackfoot Mountains, mts., Id., U.S. F7 105
Blackfoot Reservoir, res., Id., U.S. G7 105
Blackford, co., In., U.S. D7 107
Black Forest see Schwarzwald, mts., Ger. F11 12
Black Forest, Co., U.S. C6 99
Blackhall Mountain, mtn., Wy., U.S. E6 143
Black Hawk, co., Ia., U.S. B5 108
Black Hawk, S.D., U.S. C2 134
Black Hills, mts., U.S. C2 134
Blackjack Mountain, mtn., Ga., U.S. h8 103
Black Lake, Qc., Can. C6 90
Black Lake, l., Mi., U.S. C6 115
Black Lake, l., N.Y., U.S. f9 125
Black Lick, Pa., U.S. F3 131
Black Mesa, mtn., Ok., U.S. e8 129
Black Mingo Creek, stm., S.C., U.S. D9 133
Blackmore, Mount, mtn., Mt., U.S. E6 119
Black Mountain, mtn., Az., U.S. E4 96
Black Mountain, mtn., Co., U.S. A5 99
Black Mountain, mtn., Id., U.S. C3 105
Black Mountain, mtn., Mt., U.S. D4 119
Black Mountain, N.C., U.S. f10 126
Black Mountain, mtn., Or., U.S. B7 130
Black Mountain, mtn., Wy., U.S. B5 143
Black Mountain, mtn., Wy., U.S. D7 143
Black Mountain, mtn., U.S. D7 110
Black Mountains, mts., Az., U.S. B1 96
Black Peak, mtn., Az., U.S. C1 96
Black Pine Peak, mtn., Id., U.S. G5 105
Blackpool, Eng., U.K. D5 12
Black Range, mts., N.M., U.S. D2 124
Black River Falls, Wi., U.S. D3 142
Black Rock, rock, S. Geor. H8 69
Black Rock, Ar., U.S. A4 97
Black Rock, N.M., U.S. B1 124
Black Rock Desert, des., Nv., U.S. B3 121
Black Rock Range, mts., Nv., U.S. B3 121
Blacksburg, S.C., U.S. A4 133
Blacksburg, Va., U.S. C2 139
Black Sea E5 22
Blacks Fork, stm., U.S. E3 143
Blacks Harbour, N.B., Can. D3 87
Blackshear, Ga., U.S. E4 103
Blackstone, Ma., U.S. B4 114
Blackstone, stm., R.I., U.S. B4 132
Blackstone, Va., U.S. C5 139
Black Thunder Creek, stm., Wy., U.S. C8 143
Blackville, N.B., Can. C4 87
Blackville, S.C., U.S. E5 133
Black Volta, stm., Afr. D4 50
Blackwalnut Point, c., Md., U.S. C5 113
Black Warrior, stm., Al., U.S. C2 94
Blackwater, stm., Ire. D2 12
Blackwater, stm., Fl., U.S. u15 102
Blackwater, stm., Md., U.S. D5 113
Blackwater, stm., N.H., U.S. D3 122
Blackwater, stm., Va., U.S. D6 139
Blackwater Reservoir, res., N.H., U.S. D3 122
Blackwell, Ok., U.S. A4 129
Blackwood, N.J., U.S. D2 123
Bladen, co., N.C., U.S. C4 126
Bladenboro, N.C., U.S. C4 126
Bladensburg, Md., U.S. f9 113
Blades, De., U.S. F3 101
Blagoevgrad, Blg. D9 18
Blagoveščensk, Russia D14 26
Blaine, co., Id., U.S. F4 105
Blaine, Me., U.S. B5 112
Blaine, Mn., U.S. m12 116
Blaine, co., Mt., U.S. B7 119
Blaine, co., Ne., U.S. C6 120
Blaine, co., Ok., U.S. B3 129
Blaine, Tn., U.S. C10 135
Blaine, Wa., U.S. A3 140
Blaine Lake, Sk., Can. E2 91
Blair, Ne., U.S. C9 120
Blair, Ok., U.S. C2 129
Blair, co., Pa., U.S. E5 131
Blair, Wi., U.S. D2 142
Blair, W.V., U.S. n12 141
Blairstown, Ia., U.S. C5 108
Blairsville, Pa., U.S. F3 131
Blake Island, i., Wa., U.S. e11 140
Blakely, Ga., U.S. E2 103
Blakely, Pa., U.S. m18 131
Blake Plateau E6 66
Blake Point, c., Mi., U.S. h10 115
Blanc, Cap see Nouâdhibou, Râs, c., Afr. B1 50
Blanc, Mont (Bianco, Monte), mtn., Eur. B1 18
Blanca Peak, mtn., Co., U.S. D5 99
Blanchard, La., U.S. B2 111
Blanchard, stm., Oh., U.S. A1 128
Blanchard, Ok., U.S. B4 129
Blanchardville, Wi., U.S. F4 142
Blanchester, Oh., U.S. C2 128
Blanco, Tx., U.S. D3 136
Blanco, co., Tx., U.S. D3 136
Blanco, Cape, c., Or., U.S. E2 130
Bland, Mo., U.S. C6 118
Bland, co., Va., U.S. C1 139
Blanding, Ut., U.S. F6 137
Blandinsville, Il., U.S. C3 106
Blanquilla, Isla, i., Ven. C7 80
Blantyre, Mwi. B5 56
Blasdell, N.Y., U.S. C2 125
Blawnox, Pa., U.S. k14 131
Bleckley, co., Ga., U.S. D3 103
Bledsoe, co., Tn., U.S. D8 135
Blekinge, hist. reg., Swe. H6 10
Blende, Co., U.S. C6 99
Blenheim, On., Can. E3 89
Blenheim, N.Z. p13 63c
Blennerhassett, W.V., U.S. B3 141
Blind, stm., La., U.S. h10 111
Blind River, On., Can. A2 89
Blissfield, Mi., U.S. G7 115
Blitar, Indon. E4 36
Block Island, i., R.I., U.S. h7 132
Block Island, R.I., U.S. h7 132
Block Island Sound, strt., U.S. G2 132
Bloemfontein, S. Afr. D4 56
Bloemhof, S. Afr. D4 56
Blois, Fr. D7 16
Blommestein Meer see Brokopondo Stuwmeer, res., Sur. C8 70
Blönduós, Ice. l18 10a
Blood Mountain, mtn., Ga., U.S. B3 103
Bloodsworth Island, i., Md., U.S. D5 113
Bloodvein, stm., Can. D3 86
Bloomer, Wi., U.S. C2 142
Bloomfield, On., Can. D7 89
Bloomfield, Ct., U.S. B5 100
Bloomfield, Ia., U.S. D5 108
Bloomfield, In., U.S. F4 107
Bloomfield, Ky., U.S. C4 110
Bloomfield, Mo., U.S. E8 118
Bloomfield, Ne., U.S. B8 120
Bloomfield, N.J., U.S. h8 123
Bloomfield, N.M., U.S. A2 124
Bloomfield Hills, Mi., U.S. o15 115
Bloomingdale, Ga., U.S. D5 103
Bloomingdale, Il., U.S. k8 106
Bloomingdale, N.J., U.S. A4 123
Bloomingdale, Tn., U.S. C11 135
Blooming Prairie, Mn., U.S. G5 116
Bloomington, Il., U.S. C4 106
Bloomington, In., U.S. F4 107
Bloomington, Mn., U.S. F5 116
Bloomington, Tx., U.S. E4 136
Bloomington, Wi., U.S. F3 142
Bloomington, Lake, res., Il., U.S. C5 106
Bloomsburg, Pa., U.S. E9 131
Bloomville, Oh., U.S. A2 128
Blossburg, Pa., U.S. C7 131
Blossom, Tx., U.S. C5 136
Blount, co., Al., U.S. B3 94
Blount, co., Tn., U.S. D10 135
Blountstown, Fl., U.S. B1 102
Blountsville, Al., U.S. A3 94
Blountville, Tn., U.S. C11 135
Blowing Rock, N.C., U.S. A1 126
Blue, stm., Co., U.S. B4 99
Blue, stm., In., U.S. H5 107
Blue, stm., Mo., U.S. k10 118
Blue, stm., Ok., U.S. C5 129
Blue Ash, Oh., U.S. o13 128
Blue Buck Point, c., La., U.S. E2 111
Blue Creek, W.V., U.S. m13 141
Blue Creek, stm., W.V., U.S. m13 141
Blue Cypress Lake, l., Fl., U.S. E6 102
Blue Diamond, Nv., U.S. G6 121
Blue Earth, Mn., U.S. G4 116
Blue Earth, co., Mn., U.S. G4 116
Blue Earth, stm., Mn., U.S. G4 116
Bluefield, Va., U.S. C1 139
Bluefield, W.V., U.S. D3 141
Bluefields, Nic. C3 80
Blue Grass, Ia., U.S. C7 108
Blue Hill, Me., U.S. D4 112
Blue Hill, Ne., U.S. D7 120
Blue Hill Range, Ma., U.S. h11 114
Blue Hills, Ct., U.S. B5 100
Blue Island, Il., U.S. B6 106
Bluejoint Lake, l., Or., U.S. E7 130
Blue Lake, Ca., U.S. B2 98
Blue Mesa Reservoir, res., Co., U.S. C3 99
Blue Mound, Il., U.S. D4 106
Blue Mountain, Ms., U.S. A4 117
Blue Mountain, mtn., Mt., U.S. C12 119
Blue Mountain, mtn., N.M., U.S. D2 124
Blue Mountain, mtn., Pa., U.S. F6 131
Blue Mountain Lake, res., Ar., U.S. B2 97
Blue Mountain Peak, mtn., Jam. B4 80
Blue Mountains, mts., U.S. B4 92
Blue Nile, stm., Afr. H11 48
Blue Point, Me., U.S. g7 112
Blue Rapids, Ks., U.S. C7 109
Blue Ridge, Va., U.S. C3 139
Blue Ridge, mtn., U.S. C11 92
Blue Ridge, mts., U.S. D11 92
Blue Ridge Summit, Pa., U.S. G7 131
Blue Springs, Mo., U.S. h11 118
Bluestone, stm., W.V., U.S. D3 141
Bluestone Lake, res., U.S. D4 141
Bluewell, W.V., U.S. D3 141
Bluff, N.Z. q12 63c
Bluff City, Tn., U.S. C11 135
Bluff Creek, stm., Ok., U.S. A4 129
Bluff Lake, res., Ms., U.S. B5 117
Bluff Park, Al., U.S. g7 94
Bluffs, Il., U.S. D3 106
Bluffton, In., U.S. C7 107
Bluffton, Oh., U.S. B2 128
Bluffton, S.C., U.S. G6 133
Blumenau, Braz. D8 72
Bly, Or., U.S. E5 130
Blying Sound, strt., Ak., U.S. h17 95
Blyth, On., Can. D3 89
Blythe, Ca., U.S. F6 98
Blytheville, Ar., U.S. B6 97
Bo, S.L. E2 50
Boaco, Nic. C2 80
Boa Esperança, Represa, res., Braz. E11 70
Boalsburg, Pa., U.S. E6 131
Boardman, Oh., U.S. A5 128
Boardman, Or., U.S. B7 130
Boa Vista, Braz. C7 70
Boa Vista, i., C.V. g10 50a
Boaz, Al., U.S. A3 94
Bobai, China E2 30
Bobaomby, Tanjona, c., Madag. A8 56
Bobbili, India F4 40
Bobcaygeon, On., Can. C6 89
Bobo-Dioulasso, Burkina D4 50
Bobonong, Bots. C4 56
Bobrov, Russia D16 20
Bobrynets', Ukr. E12 20
Bobtown, Pa., U.S. G2 131
Boby, mtn., Madag. C8 56
Boca Chica Key, i., Fl., U.S. H5 102
Boca Ciega Bay, b., Fl., U.S. p10 102
Boca do Acre, Braz. E6 70
Boca Grande, Fl., U.S. F4 102
Bocaiúva, Braz. E3 74
Bocaranga, C.A.R. B3 54
Boca Raton, Fl., U.S. F6 102
Bocas del Toro, Pan. D3 80
Bochnia, Pol. E6 20
Bochum, Ger. E10 12
Boconó, Ven. D5 80
Bocșa, Rom. G6 20
Bodajbo, Russia D13 26
Bodega Head, c., Ca., U.S. C2 98
Bodélé, reg., Chad C8 50
Boden, Swe. D9 10
Bodhan, India F3 40
Bodie Island, i., N.C., U.S. B7 126
Bodkin Point, c., Md., U.S. B5 113
Bodø, Nor. C6 10
Bodrum, Tur. D2 44
Boende, D.R.C. D4 54
Boerne, Tx., U.S. E3 136
Boeuf, stm., La., U.S. C4 111
Boeuf, Lake, l., La., U.S. k10 111
Boffa, Gui. D2 50
Bogale, Mya. C3 34
Bogalusa, La., U.S. D6 111
Bogangolo, C.A.R. B3 54
Bogart, Ga., U.S. C3 103
Bogata, Tx., U.S. C5 136
Boğazlıyan, Tur. C6 44
Bogda Shan, mts., China C5 28
Boger City, N.C., U.S. B1 126
Bogo, Phil. D8 34
Bogor, Indon. E3 36

Name	Map Ref.	Page
Bogorodick, Russia	**C15**	20
Bogotá, Col.	**C5**	70
Bogota, N.J., U.S.	**h8**	123
Bogué, Maur.	**C2**	50
Bogue Chitto, Ms., U.S.	**D3**	117
Bogue Chitto, stm., U.S.	**D5**	111
Bogue Inlet, b., N.C., U.S.	**C5**	126
Bogue Phalia, stm., Ms., U.S.	**B3**	117
Bo Hai, b., China	**D11**	28
Bohai Haixia, strt., China	**D12**	28
Bohemia, hist. reg., Czech Rep.	**E3**	20
Bohodukhiv, Ukr.	**D13**	20
Bohol, i., Phil.	**E8**	34
Bohol Sea, Phil.	**E8**	34
Bohuslav, Ukr.	**E11**	20
Boiling Springs, N.C., U.S.	**B1**	126
Boiling Springs, Pa., U.S.	**F7**	131
Bois Blanc Island, i., Mi., U.S.	**C6**	115
Bois Brule, stm., Wi., U.S.	**B2**	142
Boischâtel, Qc., Can.	**C6**	90
Bois-des-Filion, Qc., Can.	**p19**	90
Bois de Sioux, stm., Mn., U.S.	**E2**	116
Boise, Id., U.S.	**F2**	105
Boise, co., Id., U.S.	**F3**	105
Boise City, Ok., U.S.	**e8**	129
Boissevain, Mb., Can.	**E1**	86
Boissevain, Va., U.S.	**e10**	139
Boistfort Peak, mtn., Wa., U.S.	**C2**	140
Bojeador, Cape, c., Phil.	**C8**	34
Bojnūrd, Iran	**C7**	42
Boké, Gui.	**D2**	50
Boknafjorden, strt., Nor.	**G1**	10
Boko, Congo	**D2**	54
Bokoro, Chad	**D8**	50
Bokungu, D.R.C.	**D4**	54
Bolama, Gui.-B.	**D1**	50
Bolbec, Fr.	**C7**	16
Bole, Ghana	**E4**	50
Bolesławiec, Pol.	**D3**	20
Boley, Ok., U.S.	**B5**	129
Bolgatanga, Ghana	**D4**	50
Bolhov, Russia	**C14**	20
Boli, China	**B14**	28
Bolingbrook, Il., U.S.	**k8**	106
Bolivar, Mo., U.S.	**D4**	118
Bolivar, co., Ms., U.S.	**B3**	117
Bolivar, Oh., U.S.	**B4**	128
Bolivar, Tn., U.S.	**B3**	135
Bolivar, W.V., U.S.	**B7**	141
Bolívar, Cerro, mtn., Ven.	**B6**	70
Bolivar, Lake, l., Ms., U.S.	**B3**	117
Bolívar, Pico, mtn., Ven.	**B5**	70
Bolivia, ctry., S.A.	**G7**	70
Bollinger, co., Mo., U.S.	**D7**	118
Bollnäs, Swe.	**F7**	10
Bolnisi, Geor.	**B11**	44
Bolobo, D.R.C.	**D3**	54
Bologna, Italy	**B3**	18
Bologoe, Russia	**C5**	22
Bolomba, D.R.C.	**C3**	54
Bol'šaja Murta, Russia	**D11**	26
Bolsena, Lago di, l., Italy	**C3**	18
Bol'šereck, Russia	**D17**	26
Bol'ševik, ostrov, i., Russia	**B12**	26
Bol'šezemel'skaja Tundra, reg., Russia	**A9**	22
Bol'šoj Begičev, ostrov, i., Russia	**B13**	26
Bol'šoj Enisej, stm., Russia	**A7**	28
Bol'šoj Kamen', Russia	**B2**	31
Bol'šoj Ljahovskij, ostrov, i., Russia	**B16**	26
Bolton, Eng., U.K.	**D5**	12
Bolton, Ms., U.S.	**C3**	117
Bolton Lakes, l., Ct., U.S.	**B6**	100
Bolton Landing, N.Y., U.S.	**B7**	125
Bolu, Tur.	**B4**	44
Bolvadin, Tur.	**C4**	44
Bolzano, Italy	**A3**	18
Boma, D.R.C.	**E2**	54
Bombay see Mumbai, India	**F2**	40
Bombay Hook Island, i., De., U.S.	**C4**	101
Bomberai, Semenanjung, pen., Indon.	**D8**	36
Bom Despacho, Braz.	**B8**	72
Bomdila, India	**D6**	40
Bom Jesus da Lapa, Braz.	**D3**	74
Bomongo, D.R.C.	**C3**	54
Bomoseen, Lake, l., Vt., U.S.	**D2**	138
Bomu, stm., Afr.	**C4**	54
Bon, Cap, c., Tun.	**C7**	48
Bon Accord, Ab., Can.	**C4**	84
Bon Air, Va., U.S.	**C5**	139
Bonaire, i., Neth. Ant.	**C6**	80
Bonaire, Ga., U.S.	**D3**	103
Bonanza Peak, mtn., Wa., U.S.	**A5**	140
Bonaparte, Mount, mtn., Wa., U.S.	**A6**	140
Bonasila Dome, mtn., Ak., U.S.	**C7**	95
Bonaventure, Qc., Can.	**A4**	87
Bonavista, N.L., Can.	**D5**	88
Bonavista, Cape, c., N.L., Can.	**D5**	88
Bonavista Bay, b., N.L., Can.	**D5**	88
Bond, co., Il., U.S.	**E4**	106
Bondo, D.R.C.	**D4**	54
Bondo, D.R.C.	**C4**	54
Bondoukou, C. Iv.	**E4**	50
Bondsville, Ma., U.S.	**B3**	114
Bonduel, Wi., U.S.	**D5**	142
Bondurant, Ia., U.S.	**C4**	108
Bône see Annaba, Alg.	**C6**	48
Bone, Gulf of see Bone, Teluk, b., Indon.	**D6**	36
Bone, Teluk, b., Indon.	**D6**	36
Bone Lake, l., Wi., U.S.	**C1**	142
Bongandanga, D.R.C.	**C4**	54
Bongka, Indon.	**D6**	36
Bongo, Massif des, mts., C.A.R.	**B4**	54
Bongor, Chad	**D8**	50
Bonham, Tx., U.S.	**C4**	136
Bon Homme, co., S.D., U.S.	**D8**	134
Bonifacio, Strait of, strt., Eur.	**D2**	18
Bonifay, Fl., U.S.	**u16**	102
Bonin Islands see Ogasawara-guntō, is., Japan	**F16**	64
Bonita Springs, Fl., U.S.	**F5**	102
Bonkoukou, Niger	**D5**	50
Bonn, Ger.	**E10**	12
Bonneauville, Pa., U.S.	**G7**	131
Bonne Bay, b., N.L., Can.	**D3**	88
Bonner, co., Id., U.S.	**A2**	105
Bonners Ferry, Id., U.S.	**A2**	105
Bonner Springs, Ks., U.S.	**C9**	109
Bonnet Carre Floodway, La., U.S.	**h11**	111
Bonne Terre, Mo., U.S.	**D7**	118
Bonneville, co., Id., U.S.	**F7**	105
Bonneville Dam, U.S.	**B4**	130
Bonneville Peak, mtn., Id., U.S.	**F6**	105
Bonneville Salt Flats, pl., Ut., U.S.	**C2**	137
Bonney Lake, Wa., U.S.	**B3**	140
Bonnie Doone, N.C., U.S.	**B4**	126
Bonnie Rock, Austl.	**G2**	60
Bonny, Nig.	**F6**	50
Bonny Reservoir, res., Co., U.S.	**B8**	99
Bonnyville, Ab., Can.	**B5**	84
Bono, Ar., U.S.	**B5**	97
Bon Secour, Al., U.S.	**E2**	94
Bonthe, S.L.	**E2**	50
Bontoc, Phil.	**C8**	34
Booker, Tx., U.S.	**A2**	136
Booker T. Washington National Monument, Va., U.S.	**C3**	139
Boola, Gui.	**E3**	50
Boolaloo, Austl.	**E2**	60
Boomer, W.V., U.S.	**C3**	141
Boone, co., Ar., U.S.	**A2**	97
Boone, Ia., U.S.	**B4**	108
Boone, co., Ia., U.S.	**B3**	108
Boone, stm., Ia., U.S.	**B4**	108
Boone, co., Il., U.S.	**A5**	106
Boone, co., In., U.S.	**D4**	107
Boone, co., Ky., U.S.	**B5**	110
Boone, co., Mo., U.S.	**B5**	118
Boone, N.C., U.S.	**A1**	126
Boone, co., Ne., U.S.	**C7**	120
Boone, co., W.V., U.S.	**C3**	141
Boone Lake, res., Tn., U.S.	**C11**	135
Booneville, Ar., U.S.	**B2**	97
Booneville, Ms., U.S.	**A5**	117
Boonsboro, Md., U.S.	**A2**	113
Boonton, N.J., U.S.	**B4**	123
Boonville, In., U.S.	**H3**	107
Boonville, Mo., U.S.	**C5**	118
Boonville, N.C., U.S.	**A2**	126
Boonville, N.Y., U.S.	**B5**	125
Boosaaso, Som.	**H14**	48
Boothbay Harbor, Me., U.S.	**E3**	112
Boothia, Gulf of, b., N.T., Can.	**D21**	82
Booths Creek, stm., W.V., U.S.	**h11**	141
Boothville, La., U.S.	**E6**	111
Booué, Gabon	**D2**	54
Bophuthatswana, hist. reg., S. Afr.	**D4**	56
Bopolu, Lib.	**E2**	50
Bor, Sudan	**I11**	48
Bor, Tur.	**D6**	44
Bor, Serb.	**B9**	18
Borah Peak, mtn., Id., U.S.	**E5**	105
Borås, Swe.	**H5**	10
Borba, Braz.	**D8**	70
Bordeaux, Fr.	**E6**	16
Borden, co., Tx., U.S.	**C2**	136
Bordentown, N.J., U.S.	**C3**	123
Bordj Bou Arreridj, Alg.	**J9**	16
Bordj Omar Idriss, Alg.	**E6**	48
Borðoy, i., Far. Is.	**n23**	10b
Borgarnes, Ice.	**l17**	10a
Borger, Tx., U.S.	**B2**	136
Borgholm, Swe.	**H7**	10
Borgne, Lake, b., La., U.S.	**D6**	111
Borisoglebsk, Russia	**D7**	22
Borken, Ger.	**E10**	12
Borkou, reg., Chad	**C8**	50
Borlänge, Swe.	**F6**	10
Borneo (Kalimantan), i., Asia	**D4**	36
Bornholm, i., Den.	**I6**	10
Borno, state, Nig.	**D7**	50
Borogoncy, Russia	**C15**	26
Boromo, Burkina	**D4**	50
Boron, Ca., U.S.	**E5**	98
Borongan, Phil.	**D9**	34
Boroviči, Russia	**D5**	26
Borrego Springs, Ca., U.S.	**F5**	98
Borroloola, Austl.	**D6**	60
Borşa, Rom.	**F8**	20
Borūjerd, Iran	**D5**	42
Boryslav, Ukr.	**E7**	20
Boryspil', Ukr.	**D11**	20
Borzja, Russia	**D13**	26
Boržomi, Geor.	**B10**	44
Bosanski Novi, Bos.	**B6**	18
Boscobel, Wi., U.S.	**E3**	142
Bose, China	**G9**	28
Boshan, China	**D11**	28
Bosna, stm., Bos.	**B6**	18
Bosnia and Herzegovina, ctry., Eur.	**B6**	18
Bosnik, Indon.	**G10**	32
Bosobolo, D.R.C.	**C3**	54
Bosporus see İstanbul Boğazı, strt., Tur.	**B3**	44
Bosque, co., Tx., U.S.	**D4**	136
Bossangoa, C.A.R.	**B3**	54
Bossembélé, C.A.R.	**B3**	54
Bossentélé, C.A.R.	**B3**	54
Bossier, co., La., U.S.	**B2**	111
Bossier City, La., U.S.	**B2**	111
Bostān, Iran	**G13**	44
Bosten Hu, l., China	**C5**	28
Boston, Eng., U.K.	**D6**	12
Boston, Ga., U.S.	**F3**	103
Boston, Ma., U.S.	**B5**	114
Boston Bay, b., Ma., U.S.	**B6**	114
Boston Mountains, mts., Ar., U.S.	**B2**	97
Boswell, In., U.S.	**C3**	107
Boswell, Ok., U.S.	**C6**	129
Boswell, Pa., U.S.	**F3**	131
Botetourt, co., Va., U.S.	**C3**	139
Bothell, Wa., U.S.	**B3**	140
Bothnia, Gulf of, b., Eur.	**F8**	10
Bothwell, On., Can.	**E3**	89
Botkins, Oh., U.S.	**B1**	128
Botlih, Russia	**A12**	44
Botoşani, Rom.	**F9**	20
Bo Trach, Viet.	**C5**	34
Botswana, ctry., Afr.	**C3**	56
Bottineau, N.D., U.S.	**A5**	127
Bottineau, co., N.D., U.S.	**A4**	127
Botucatu, Braz.	**F2**	74
Botwood, N.L., Can.	**D4**	88
Bouaflé, C. Iv.	**E3**	50
Bouaké, C. Iv.	**E3**	50
Bouar, C.A.R.	**B3**	54
Bouarfa, Mor.	**E3**	14
Bouca, C.A.R.	**B3**	54
Boucherville, Qc., Can.	**D4**	90
Bouctouche, N.B., Can.	**C5**	87
Boudreaux, Lake, l., La., U.S.	**E5**	111
Bougainville, i., Pap. N. Gui.	**B6**	62
Bougainville, Détroit de, strt., Vanuatu	**k9**	62a
Bougie see Bejaïa, Alg.	**C6**	48
Bougouni, Mali	**D3**	50
Bouïra, Alg.	**C5**	48
Boujdour, Cap, c., W. Sah.	**A2**	50
Boulder, Co., U.S.	**A5**	99
Boulder, co., Co., U.S.	**A5**	99
Boulder, Mt., U.S.	**D4**	119
Boulder City, Nv., U.S.	**H7**	121
Boulevard Heights, Md., U.S.	**f9**	113
Boulia, Austl.	**E2**	62
Boulogne-sur-Mer, Fr.	**B7**	16
Boulsa, Burkina	**D4**	50
Bouna, C. Iv.	**E4**	50
Boundary, co., Id., U.S.	**A2**	105
Boundary Bay, b., Wa., U.S.	**A3**	140
Boundary Peak, mtn., Nv., U.S.	**F3**	121
Bound Brook, N.J., U.S.	**B3**	123
Boundiali, C. Iv.	**E3**	50
Bountiful, Ut., U.S.	**C4**	137
Bounty Islands, is., N.Z.	**M21**	64
Bounty Trough	**M20**	64
Bourail, N. Cal.	**I9**	62a
Bourbeuse, stm., Mo., U.S.	**C6**	118
Bourbon, In., U.S.	**B5**	107
Bourbon, co., Ks., U.S.	**E9**	109
Bourbon, co., Ky., U.S.	**B5**	110
Bourbon, Mo., U.S.	**C6**	118
Bourbonnais, Il., U.S.	**B6**	106
Bourem, Mali	**C4**	50
Bourg, La., U.S.	**E5**	111
Bourg-en-Bresse, Fr.	**D9**	16
Bourges, Fr.	**D8**	16
Bourgogne, hist. reg., Fr.	**D9**	16
Bourke, Austl.	**G4**	62
Bournemouth, Eng., U.K.	**E5**	12
Bou Saâda, Alg.	**C5**	48
Bouse, Az., U.S.	**D2**	96
Bousso, Chad	**D8**	50
Boutilimit, Maur.	**C2**	50
Boutte, La., U.S.	**k11**	111
Bouvetøya, i., Ant.	**B5**	67
Bouza, Niger	**D6**	50
Bovey, Mn., U.S.	**C5**	116
Bovina, Tx., U.S.	**B1**	136
Bow, stm., Ab., Can.	**D4**	84
Bow, N.H., U.S.	**D3**	122
Bowden, Ab., Can.	**D4**	84
Bowdish Reservoir, res., R.I., U.S.	**B1**	132
Bowdon, Ga., U.S.	**C1**	103
Bowen, Arg.	**F4**	72
Bowen, Austl.	**D4**	62
Bowie, Az., U.S.	**E6**	96
Bowie, Md., U.S.	**C4**	113
Bowie, Tx., U.S.	**C4**	136
Bowie, co., Tx., U.S.	**C5**	136
Bow Island, Ab., Can.	**E5**	84
Bow Lake, l., N.H., U.S.	**D4**	122
Bowling Green, Fl., U.S.	**E5**	102
Bowling Green, Ky., U.S.	**D3**	110
Bowling Green, Mo., U.S.	**B6**	118
Bowling Green, Oh., U.S.	**A2**	128
Bowling Green, S.C., U.S.	**A5**	133
Bowling Green, Va., U.S.	**B5**	139
Bowling Green, Cape, c., Austl.	**D4**	62
Bowman, Ga., U.S.	**B3**	103
Bowman, N.D., U.S.	**C2**	127
Bowman, co., N.D., U.S.	**C2**	127
Bowman, S.C., U.S.	**E6**	133
Bowman Creek, stm., Pa., U.S.	**m16**	131
Bowman-Haley Lake, res., N.D., U.S.	**C2**	127
Bowral, Austl.	**G5**	62
Bowron, stm., B.C., Can.	**C7**	85
Bowstring Lake, l., Mn., U.S.	**C5**	116
Box Butte, co., Ne., U.S.	**B2**	120
Box Butte Reservoir, res., Ne., U.S.	**B2**	120
Box Elder, S.D., U.S.	**C2**	134
Box Elder, co., Ut., U.S.	**B2**	137
Boxford, Ma., U.S.	**A6**	114
Boxing, China	**B4**	30
Boyabat, Tur.	**B6**	44
Boyang, China	**D4**	30
Boyce, La., U.S.	**C3**	111
Boyceville, Wi., U.S.	**C1**	142
Boyd, co., Ky., U.S.	**B7**	110
Boyd, co., Ne., U.S.	**B7**	120
Boyd, Tx., U.S.	**C4**	136
Boyden, Ia., U.S.	**A2**	108
Boyd Lake, l., Me., U.S.	**C4**	112
Boyer, stm., Ia., U.S.	**C2**	108
Boyertown, Pa., U.S.	**F10**	131
Boykins, Va., U.S.	**D5**	139
Boyle, Ab., Can.	**B4**	84
Boyle, co., Ky., U.S.	**C5**	110
Boyle, Ms., U.S.	**B3**	117
Boyne City, Mi., U.S.	**C6**	115
Boynton Beach, Fl., U.S.	**F6**	102
Boyoma Falls see Stanley Falls, wtfl., D.R.C.	**C5**	54
Boysen Reservoir, res., Wy., U.S.	**C4**	143
Boys Town, Ne., U.S.	**g12**	120
Bozeman, Mt., U.S.	**E5**	119
Bozeman Pass, Mt., U.S.	**E6**	119
Bozhen, China	**D11**	28
Bozhou, China	**C4**	30
Bozoum, C.A.R.	**B3**	54
Bozova, Tur.	**D8**	44
Bozüyük, Tur.	**C3**	44
Bra, Italy	**B1**	18
Bracebridge, On., Can.	**B5**	89
Bräcke, Swe.	**E6**	10
Bracken, co., Ky., U.S.	**B5**	110
Brackenridge, Pa., U.S.	**h15**	131
Brackettville, Tx., U.S.	**E2**	136
Brad, Rom.	**F7**	20
Braddock, Pa., U.S.	**k14**	131
Braddock Heights, Md., U.S.	**B2**	113
Braddock Point, c., S.C., U.S.	**G6**	133
Bradenton, Fl., U.S.	**E4**	102
Bradenville, Pa., U.S.	**F3**	131
Bradford, Eng., U.K.	**D5**	12
Bradford, Ar., U.S.	**B4**	97
Bradford, co., Fl., U.S.	**C4**	102
Bradford, Oh., U.S.	**B1**	128
Bradford, co., Pa., U.S.	**C8**	131
Bradford, Pa., U.S.	**C4**	131
Bradford, R.I., U.S.	**F2**	132
Bradford, Tn., U.S.	**A3**	135
Bradford, Vt., U.S.	**D4**	138
Bradford [West Gwillimbury], On., Can.	**C5**	89
Bradfordwoods, Pa., U.S.	**h13**	131
Bradley, co., Ar., U.S.	**D3**	97
Bradley, Il., U.S.	**B6**	106
Bradley, Me., U.S.	**D4**	112
Bradley, co., Tn., U.S.	**D9**	135
Bradley, W.V., U.S.	**D3**	141
Bradley Beach, N.J., U.S.	**C4**	123
Bradner, Oh., U.S.	**A2**	128
Bradshaw, Md., U.S.	**B5**	113
Bradshaw Mountains, mts., Az., U.S.	**C3**	96
Brady, Tx., U.S.	**D3**	136
Braga, Port.	**G2**	16
Bragado, Arg.	**F5**	72
Bragança, Braz.	**B2**	74
Bragança, Port.	**G3**	16
Braham, Mn., U.S.	**E5**	116
Brāhmanbāria, Bngl.	**E6**	40
Brahmapur, India	**F4**	40
Brahmaputra (Yarlung), stm., Asia	**D6**	40
Braidwood, Il., U.S.	**B5**	106
Brăila, Rom.	**G9**	20
Brainerd, Mn., U.S.	**D4**	116
Braintree, Ma., U.S.	**B5**	114
Brampton, On., Can.	**D5**	89
Bramwell, W.V., U.S.	**D3**	141
Branch, co., Mi., U.S.	**G5**	115
Branch, stm., R.I., U.S.	**B3**	132
Branch, stm., Wi., U.S.	**h10**	142
Branch Lake, l., Me., U.S.	**D4**	112
Branch Village, R.I., U.S.	**B3**	132
Branchville, S.C., U.S.	**E6**	133
Branco, stm., Braz.	**C7**	70
Brandberg, mtn., Nmb.	**C1**	56
Brandenburg, Ger.	**D13**	12
Brandenburg, Ky., U.S.	**C3**	110
Brandon, Mb., Can.	**E2**	86
Brandon, Fl., U.S.	**E4**	102
Brandon, Ms., U.S.	**C4**	117
Brandon, S.C., U.S.	**B3**	133
Brandon, S.D., U.S.	**D9**	134
Brandon, Vt., U.S.	**D2**	138
Brandon, Wi., U.S.	**E5**	142
Brandvlei, S. Afr.	**E3**	56
Brandy Peak, mtn., Or., U.S.	**E3**	130
Brandywine, Md., U.S.	**C4**	113
Brandywine Creek, stm., U.S.	**A3**	101
Branford, Ct., U.S.	**D4**	100
Branford Hills, Ct., U.S.	**D4**	100
Branson, Mo., U.S.	**E4**	118
Brantford, On., Can.	**D4**	89
Brantley, Al., U.S.	**D3**	94
Brantley, co., Ga., U.S.	**E4**	103
Brant Rock, Ma., U.S.	**B6**	114
Brantville, N.B., Can.	**B5**	87
Bras d'Or Lake, l., N.S., Can.	**D9**	87
Brasil, ctry., S.A.	**D2**	74
Brasiléia, Braz.	**F6**	70
Brasília, Braz.	**E2**	74
Braşov, Rom.	**G8**	20
Brasstown Bald, mtn., Ga., U.S.	**B3**	103
Brassua Lake, res., Me., U.S.	**C3**	112
Bratenahl, Oh., U.S.	**g9**	128
Bratislava, Slvk.	**E4**	20
Bratsk, Russia	**D12**	26
Bratskoe vodohranilišče, res., Russia	**D12**	26
Bratsk Reservoir see Bratskoe vodohranilišče, res., Russia	**D12**	26
Brattleboro, Vt., U.S.	**F3**	138
Braunau am Inn, Aus.	**F13**	12
Braunschweig, Ger.	**D12**	12
Brava, i., C.V.	**h10**	50a
Bravo (Rio Grande), stm., N.A.	**B5**	78
Brawley, Ca., U.S.	**F6**	98
Brawley Peaks, mts., Nv., U.S.	**E3**	121
Braxton, co., W.V., U.S.	**C4**	141
Bray, Ok., U.S.	**C4**	129
Braymer, Mo., U.S.	**B4**	118
Brazeau, stm., Ab., Can.	**C2**	84
Brazil, ctry., S.A.	**D5**	68
Brazil, In., U.S.	**E3**	107
Brazil Basin	**J11**	66
Brazoria, co., Tx., U.S.	**E5**	136
Brazoria, Tx., U.S.	**r14**	136
Brazos, stm., Tx., U.S.	**D4**	136
Brazos, co., Tx., U.S.	**D4**	136
Brazzaville, Congo	**D3**	54
Brčko, Bos.	**B7**	18
Brea, Ca., U.S.	**n13**	98
Breakenridge, Mount, mtn., B.C., Can.	**E7**	85
Breathitt, co., Ky., U.S.	**C6**	110
Breaux Bridge, La., U.S.	**D4**	111
Breckenridge, Co., U.S.	**B4**	99
Breckenridge, Mi., U.S.	**E6**	115
Breckenridge, Mn., U.S.	**D2**	116
Breckenridge, Tx., U.S.	**C3**	136
Breckinridge, co., Ky., U.S.	**C3**	110
Brecksville, Oh., U.S.	**A4**	128
Břeclav, Czech Rep.	**E4**	20
Breda, Neth.	**E9**	12
Bredasdorp, S. Afr.	**E3**	56
Bredy, Russia	**D11**	22
Breese, Il., U.S.	**E4**	106
Breiðafjörður, b., Ice.	**l17**	10a
Brejo, Braz.	**D11**	70
Bremen, Ger.	**D11**	12
Bremen, Ga., U.S.	**C1**	103
Bremen, In., U.S.	**B5**	107
Bremen, Oh., U.S.	**C3**	128
Bremer, co., Ia., U.S.	**B5**	108
Bremer Bay, Austl.	**G2**	60
Bremerhaven, Ger.	**D11**	12
Bremerton, Wa., U.S.	**B3**	140
Bremond, Tx., U.S.	**D4**	136
Brenham, Tx., U.S.	**D4**	136
Brenner Pass, Eur.	**A3**	18
Brent, Al., U.S.	**C2**	94
Brent, Fl., U.S.	**u14**	102
Brenton Point, c., R.I., U.S.	**F5**	132
Brentwood, Ca., U.S.	**h9**	98
Brentwood, Md., U.S.	**f9**	113
Brentwood, Mo., U.S.	**f13**	118
Brentwood, N.Y., U.S.	**E7**	125
Brentwood, Pa., U.S.	**k14**	131
Brentwood, S.C., U.S.	**k11**	133
Brentwood, Tn., U.S.	**A5**	135
Brescia, Italy	**B3**	18
Breslau see Wrocław, Pol.	**D4**	20
Bressuire, Fr.	**D6**	16
Brèst, Bela.	**C7**	20
Brest, Fr.	**C4**	16
Bretagne, hist. reg., Fr.	**C5**	16
Breton, Pertuis, strt., Fr.	**D6**	16
Breton Islands, is., La., U.S.	**E6**	111

Name | Map Ref. | Page

Breton Sound, strt., La., U.S. E6 111
Breueh, Pulau, i., Indon. E1 32
Brevard, co., Fl., U.S. E6 102
Brevard, N.C., U.S. f10 126
Breves, Braz. B1 74
Brevoort Lake, l., Mi., U.S. B6 115
Brewer, Me., U.S. D4 112
Brewster, Ma., U.S. C7 114
Brewster, N.Y., U.S. D7 125
Brewster, Oh., U.S. B4 128
Brewster, co., Tx., U.S. E1 136
Brewster, Wa., U.S. A6 140
Brewster, Kap, c., Grnld. D35 82
Brewster Islands, is., Ma., U.S. g12 114
Brewton, Al., U.S. D2 94
Brezhnev see Naberežnye Čelny, Russia D7 26
Bria, C.A.R. B4 54
Brian Boru Peak, mtn., B.C., Can. B4 85
Brian Head, mtn., Ut., U.S. F3 137
Briceville, Tn., U.S. C9 135
Brick [Township], N.J., U.S. C4 123
Bridal Veil Falls, wtfl., Ut., U.S. C4 137
Bridgehampton, N.Y., U.S. n16 125
Bridgeport, Al., U.S. A4 94
Bridgeport, Ct., U.S. E3 100
Bridgeport, Il., U.S. E6 106
Bridgeport, Mi., U.S. E7 115
Bridgeport, Ne., U.S. C2 120
Bridgeport, Oh., U.S. B5 128
Bridgeport, Pa., U.S. o20 131
Bridgeport, Tx., U.S. C4 136
Bridgeport, Wa., U.S. B6 140
Bridgeport, W.V., U.S. B4 141
Bridger, Mt., U.S. E8 119
Bridger Peak, mtn., Wy., U.S. E5 143
Bridger Range, mts., Mt., U.S. E6 119
Bridgeton, Mo., U.S. C7 118
Bridgeton, N.J., U.S. E2 123
Bridgetown, Austl. G2 60
Bridgetown, Barb. C7 80
Bridgetown, N.S., Can. E4 87
Bridgeville, De., U.S. F3 101
Bridgeville, Pa., U.S. k13 131
Bridgewater, Ma., U.S. C6 114
Bridgewater, N.J., U.S. B3 123
Bridgewater, Va., U.S. B4 139
Bridgman, Mi., U.S. G4 115
Bridgton, Me., U.S. D2 112
Bridgwater, Eng., U.K. E5 12
Bridlington, Eng., U.K. C6 12
Brielle, N.J., U.S. C4 123
Brigantine, N.J., U.S. E4 123
Brigantine Beach, N.J., U.S. E4 123
Brigden, On., Can. E2 89
Briggs Marsh, sw., R.I., U.S. F6 132
Brigham City, Ut., U.S. B3 137
Bright, Austl. H4 62
Brighton, On., Can. C7 89
Brighton, Eng., U.K. E6 12
Brighton, Al., U.S. B3 94
Brighton, Co., U.S. B6 99
Brighton, Ia., U.S. C6 108
Brighton, Il., U.S. D3 106
Brighton, Mi., U.S. F7 115
Brighton, N.Y., U.S. B3 125
Brighton, Tn., U.S. B2 135
Brighton Indian Reservation, Fl., U.S. E5 102
Brikama, Gam. D1 50
Brilliant, Al., U.S. A2 94
Brilliant, Oh., U.S. B5 128
Brillion, Wi., U.S. D5 142
Brimfield, Il., U.S. C4 106
Brindisi, Italy D6 18
Brinkley, Ar., U.S. C4 97
Brinnon, Wa., U.S. B3 140
Brisbane, Austl. F5 62
Briscoe, co., Tx., U.S. B2 136
Bristol, N.B., Can. C2 87
Bristol, Eng., U.K. E5 12
Bristol, Ct., U.S. C4 100
Bristol, In., U.S. A6 107
Bristol, co., Ma., U.S. C5 114
Bristol, N.H., U.S. C3 122
Bristol, R.I., U.S. D5 132
Bristol, co., R.I., U.S. D5 132
Bristol, Tn., U.S. C11 135
Bristol, Va., U.S. f9 139
Bristol, Vt., U.S. C2 138
Bristol Bay, b., Ak., U.S. D7 95
Bristol Channel, strt., U.K. E5 12
Bristol [Township], Pa., U.S. F12 131
Bristow, Ok., U.S. B5 129
British Columbia, prov., Can. C6 85
British Guiana see Guyana, ctry., S.A. B8 70
British Honduras see Belize, ctry., N.A. B2 80
British Indian Ocean Teritory, dep., Afr. I10 64
British Isles, is., Eur. I10 4
British Virgin Islands, dep., N.A. E12 76
Britstown, S. Afr. E3 56
Britt, Ia., U.S. A4 108
Brittany see Bretagne, hist. reg., Fr. C5 16
Britton, S.D., U.S. B8 134
Brive-la-Gaillarde, Fr. E7 16
Brjansk, Russia D5 26
Brjuhoveckaja, Russia G15 20
Brno, Czech Rep. E4 20
Broad, stm., S.C., U.S. C5 133
Broad Brook, Ct., U.S. B5 100
Broadkill, stm., De., U.S. E4 101
Broadkill Beach, De., U.S. E5 101
Broad Run, stm., Va., U.S. g11 139
Broad Sound, b., Austl. E4 62
Broadus, Mt., U.S. E11 119
Broadview Heights, Oh., U.S. h9 128
Broadwater, co., Mt., U.S. D5 119
Broadway, N.C., U.S. B3 126
Broadway, Va., U.S. B4 139
Brockman, Mount, mtn., Austl. E2 60
Brockport, N.Y., U.S. B3 125
Brockton, Ma., U.S. B5 114
Brockton Reservoir, res., Ma., U.S. h11 114
Brockville, On., Can. C9 89
Brockway, Pa., U.S. D4 131
Brodhead, Ky., U.S. C5 110
Brodhead, Wi., U.S. F4 142
Brodheadsville, Pa., U.S. E11 131
Brodnica, Pol. C5 20
Brody, Ukr. D8 20
Broken Arrow, Ok., U.S. A6 129
Broken Bow, Ne., U.S. C6 120
Broken Bow, Ok., U.S. C7 129
Broken Bow Lake, res., Ok., U.S. C7 129
Broken Hill, Austl. G3 62
Broken Hill see Kabwe, Zam. A4 56
Broken Ridge L12 64
Brokopondo, Sur. C8 70
Brokopondo Stuwmeer, res., Sur. C8 70
Brome, Lac, l., Qc., Can. D5 90
Bromley Plateau K10 66
Bromptonville, Qc., Can. D6 90
Bronson, Mi., U.S. G5 115
Bronx, co., N.Y., U.S. E7 125
Bronxville, N.Y., U.S. h13 125
Brook, In., U.S. C3 107
Brooke, co., W.V., U.S. A4 141
Brookfield, N.S., Can. D6 87
Brookfield, Ct., U.S. D2 100
Brookfield, Il., U.S. k9 106
Brookfield, Mo., U.S. B4 118
Brookfield, Wi., U.S. m11 142
Brookfield Center, Ct., U.S. D2 100
Brookhaven, Ms., U.S. D3 117
Brookhaven, W.V., U.S. h11 141
Brookings, Or., U.S. E2 130
Brookings, S.D., U.S. C9 134
Brookings, co., S.D., U.S. C9 134
Brookland, Ar., U.S. B5 97
Brooklandville, Md., U.S. g10 113
Brooklet, Ga., U.S. D5 103
Brookline, Ma., U.S. B5 114
Brooklyn, N.S., Can. E5 87
Brooklyn, Ct., U.S. B8 100
Brooklyn, Ia., U.S. C5 108
Brooklyn, In., U.S. E5 107
Brooklyn, Mi., U.S. F6 115
Brooklyn, Ms., U.S. D4 117
Brooklyn, Oh., U.S. h9 128
Brooklyn, S.C., U.S. B6 133
Brooklyn, Wi., U.S. F4 142
Brooklyn Center, Mn., U.S. E5 116
Brooklyn Park, Md., U.S. h11 113
Brooklyn Park, Mn., U.S. m12 116
Brookneal, Va., U.S. C4 139
Brook Park, Oh., U.S. h9 128
Brookport, Il., U.S. F5 106
Brooks, Ab., Can. D5 84
Brooks, co., Ga., U.S. F3 103
Brooks, Ky., U.S. g11 110
Brooks, co., Tx., U.S. F3 136
Brooks Air Force Base, mil., Tx., U.S. k7 136
Brookshire, Tx., U.S. E5 136
Brookside, Al., U.S. f7 94
Brookside, De., U.S. B3 101
Brooks Range, mts., Ak., U.S. B9 95
Brookston, In., U.S. C4 107
Brooksville, Fl., U.S. D4 102
Brooksville, Ky., U.S. B5 110
Brooksville, Ms., U.S. B5 117
Brookville, In., U.S. F8 107
Brookville, Oh., U.S. C1 128
Brookville, Pa., U.S. D3 131
Brookville Lake, res., In., U.S. E7 107
Brookwood, Al., U.S. B2 94
Brookwood, N.J., U.S. C4 123
Broomall, Pa., U.S. p20 131
Broome, Austl. D3 60
Broome, co., N.Y., U.S. C5 125
Broomfield, Co., U.S. B5 99
Brossard, Qc., Can. q20 90
Broussard, La., U.S. D4 111
Broward, co., Fl., U.S. F6 102
Browerville, Mn., U.S. D4 116
Brown, co., Il., U.S. D3 106
Brown, co., In., U.S. F5 107
Brown, co., Ks., U.S. C8 109
Brown, co., Mn., U.S. F4 116
Brown, co., Ne., U.S. B6 120
Brown, co., Oh., U.S. D2 128
Brown, co., S.D., U.S. B7 134
Brown, co., Tx., U.S. D3 136
Brown, co., Wi., U.S. D6 142
Brown, Point, c., Wa., U.S. C1 140
Brown City, Mi., U.S. E8 115
Brown Deer, Wi., U.S. m12 142
Brownfield, Tx., U.S. C1 136
Browning, Mt., U.S. B3 119
Brownlee Dam, U.S. E2 105
Brownlee Reservoir, res., U.S. C10 130
Browns, stm., Vt., U.S. B2 138
Browns Branch, stm., De., U.S. E3 101
Brownsburg, Qc., Can. D3 90
Brownsburg, In., U.S. E5 107
Brownsdale, Mn., U.S. G6 116
Browns Inlet, b., N.C., U.S. C5 126
Browns Mills, N.J., U.S. D3 123
Browns Peak, mtn., Az., U.S. D4 96
Brownstown, In., U.S. G5 107
Browns Valley, Mn., U.S. E2 116
Brownsville, Fl., U.S. s13 102
Brownsville, Ky., U.S. C3 110
Brownsville, Or., U.S. C4 130
Brownsville, Pa., U.S. F2 131
Brownsville, Tn., U.S. B2 135
Brownsville, Tx., U.S. G4 136
Brownton, Mn., U.S. F4 116
Brownville Junction, Me., U.S. C3 112
Brownwood, Tx., U.S. D3 136
Brownwood, Lake, res., Tx., U.S. D3 136
Broxton, Ga., U.S. E4 103
Bruce, Ms., U.S. B4 117
Bruce, Wi., U.S. C2 142
Bruce, Mount, mtn., Austl. E2 60
Bruce National Park, On., Can. B3 89
Bruce Peninsula, pen., On., Can. B3 89
Bruce Rock, Austl. G2 60
Bruceton, Tn., U.S. A3 135
Bruderheim, Ab., Can. C4 84
Brugge, Bel. E8 12
Bruin Point, mtn., Ut., U.S. D5 137
Brule, co., S.D., U.S. D6 134
Brule, stm., U.S. C5 142
Brule Lake, l., Mn., U.S. k9 116
Brumado, Braz. D3 74
Brundidge, Al., U.S. D4 94
Bruneau, stm., U.S. G3 105
Brunei, ctry., Asia F6 34
Brunei see Bandar Seri Begawan, Bru. C4 36
Bruno, Sk., Can. E3 91
Brunswick see Braunschweig, Ger. D12 12
Brunswick, Ga., U.S. E5 103
Brunswick, Md., U.S. B2 113
Brunswick, Me., U.S. E3 112
Brunswick, Mo., U.S. B4 118
Brunswick, co., N.C., U.S. C4 126
Brunswick, Oh., U.S. A4 128
Brunswick, co., Va., U.S. D5 139
Brunswick, Península, pen., Chile H2 69
Brunswick Naval Air Station, mil., Me., U.S. E3 112
Brush, Co., U.S. A7 99
Brushy Mountains, mts., N.C., U.S. B1 126
Brusly, La., U.S. D4 111
Brusque, Braz. D8 72
Brussels see Bruxelles, Bel. E9 12
Brussels, On., Can. D3 89
Bruxelles (Brussels), Bel. E9 12
Bryan, co., Ga., U.S. D5 103
Bryan, Oh., U.S. A1 128
Bryan, co., Ok., U.S. D5 129
Bryan, Tx., U.S. D4 136
Bryans Road, Md., U.S. C3 113
Bryant, Ar., U.S. C3 97
Bryantville, Ma., U.S. B6 114
Bryce Canyon National Park, Ut., U.S. F3 137
Bryn Mawr, Wa., U.S. e11 140
Bryson City, N.C., U.S. f9 126
Brzeg, Pol. D4 20
Bua Yai, Thai. C4 34
Bu'ayrat al-Hasun, Libya E7 14
Bubaque, Gui.-B. D1 50
Bucak, Tur. D4 44
Bucaramanga, Col. B5 70
Buccaneer Archipelago, is., Austl. D3 60
Buchanan, Lib. E2 50
Buchanan, Ga., U.S. C1 103
Buchanan, co., Ia., U.S. B6 108
Buchanan, Mi., U.S. G4 115
Buchanan, co., Mo., U.S. B3 118
Buchanan, co., Va., U.S. e9 139
Buchanan, Va., U.S. C3 139
Buchans, N.L., Can. D3 88
Bucharest see București, Rom. G9 20
Buckatunna, Ms., U.S. D5 117
Buckeye, Az., U.S. D3 96
Buckeye Lake, Oh., U.S. C3 128
Buckhannon, W.V., U.S. C4 141
Buck Hill Falls, Pa., U.S. D11 131
Buckhorn Lake, res., Ky., U.S. C6 110
Buckingham, Qc., Can. D2 90
Buckingham, co., Va., U.S. C4 139
Buckley, Wa., U.S. B3 140
Bucklin, Ks., U.S. E4 109
Bucklin, Mo., U.S. B5 118
Buck Mountain, mtn., Wa., U.S. A6 140
Buckner, Mo., U.S. h11 118
Bucks, co., Pa., U.S. F11 131
Buckskin Mountains, mts., Az., U.S. C2 96
Bucksport, Me., U.S. D4 112
Bucksport, S.C., U.S. D9 133
Buco Zau, Ang. D2 54
București (Bucharest), Rom. G9 20
Bucyrus, Oh., U.S. B3 128
Buda, Tx., U.S. D4 136
Budapest, Hung. F5 20
Budaun, India D3 40
Budd Lake, l., N.J., U.S. B3 123
Bude, Ms., U.S. D3 117
Budënnovsk, Russia B4 42
Búðir, Ice. I21 10a
Budjala, D.R.C. C3 54
Buea, Cam. C1 54
Buechel, Ky., U.S. B4 110
Buena, N.J., U.S. D3 123
Buena, Wa., U.S. C5 140
Buena Esperanza, Arg. E4 72
Buena Park, Ca., U.S. n12 98
Buenaventura, Col. C4 70
Buenaventura, Mex. B3 78
Buena Vista, Co., U.S. C4 99
Buena Vista, Fl., U.S. D4 102
Buena Vista, Ga., U.S. D2 103
Buena Vista, co., Ia., U.S. B2 108
Buena Vista, Va., U.S. C3 139
Buenos Aires, Arg. E6 72
Buffalo, stm., Ar., U.S. B3 97
Buffalo, Ia., U.S. C7 108
Buffalo, Mn., U.S. E5 116
Buffalo, stm., Mn., U.S. D2 116
Buffalo, Mo., U.S. D4 118
Buffalo, co., Ne., U.S. D6 120
Buffalo, N.Y., U.S. C2 125
Buffalo, Ok., U.S. A2 129
Buffalo, S.C., U.S. B4 133
Buffalo, co., S.D., U.S. C6 134
Buffalo, stm., Tn., U.S. B4 135
Buffalo, Tx., U.S. D5 136
Buffalo, Wi., U.S. D2 142
Buffalo, co., Wi., U.S. D2 142
Buffalo, stm., Wi., U.S. D2 142
Buffalo, W.V., U.S. C3 141
Buffalo, Wy., U.S. B6 143
Buffalo Bill Reservoir, res., Wy., U.S. B3 143
Buffalo Center, Ia., U.S. A4 108
Buffalo Creek, stm., W.V., U.S. n12 141
Buffalo Creek, stm., W.V., U.S. h10 141
Buffalo Creek, stm., U.S. f8 141
Buffalo Grove, Il., U.S. h9 106
Buffalo Lake, l., Ab., Can. C4 84
Buffalo Lake, Mn., U.S. F4 116
Buffalo Lake, res., Tx., U.S. B1 136
Buffalo Lake, res., Wi., U.S. E4 142
Buffumville Lake, res., Ma., U.S. B4 114
Buford, Ga., U.S. B2 103
Bug, stm., Eur. C6 20
Buga, Col. C4 70
Bugsuk Island, i., Phil. E7 34
Bugt, China B12 28
Bugul'ma, Russia D9 22
Buguruslan, Russia D9 22
Buhara, Uzb. F8 26
Buhl, Id., U.S. G4 105
Buhl, Mn., U.S. C6 116
Buhler, Ks., U.S. D6 109
Buies Creek, N.C., U.S. B4 126
Buitepos, Nmb. C2 56
Buj, Russia C7 22
Bujnaksk, Russia A12 44
Bujumbura, Bdi. D5 54
Bukačača, Russia D13 26
Bukama, D.R.C. E5 54
Būkān, Iran D12 44
Bukavu, D.R.C. D5 54
Bukeya, D.R.C. F5 54
Bukittinggi, Indon. D2 36
Bukoba, Tan. D6 54
Bula, Indon. D8 36
Bulan, Phil. D8 34
Bulan, Ky., U.S. C6 110
Bulancak, Tur. B8 44
Bulandshahr, India D3 40
Bulanık, Tur. C10 44
Bulawayo, Zimb. C4 56
Buldan, Tur. C3 44
Bulgan, Mong. B8 28
Bulgaria, ctry., Eur. C10 18
Bulkley, stm., B.C., Can. B4 85
Bullaxaar, Som. A8 54
Bull Creek, stm., S.D., U.S. B2 134
Bullfinch, Austl. G2 60
Bullfrog Creek, stm., Ut., U.S. F5 137
Bullhead City, Az., U.S. B1 96
Bull Island, i., S.C., U.S. G6 133
Bull Island, i., S.C., U.S. D9 133
Bull Island, i., S.C., U.S. F8 133
Bullitt, co., Ky., U.S. C4 110
Bull Mountain, mtn., Mt., U.S. D4 119
Bulloch, co., Ga., U.S. D5 103
Bullock, co., Al., U.S. C4 94
Bullock Creek, Mi., U.S. E6 115
Bull Run, stm., Va., U.S. g11 139
Bullrun Rock, mtn., Or., U.S. C8 130
Bulls Bay, b., S.C., U.S. F8 133
Bulls Gap, Tn., U.S. C10 135
Bull Shoals, Ar., U.S. A3 97
Bull Shoals Lake, res., U.S. A3 97
Bull Shoals Lake, res., U.S. D9 92
Bully Creek Reservoir, res., Or., U.S. C9 130
Bultfontein, S. Afr. D4 56
Bumba, D.R.C. C4 54
Bumping, stm., Wa., U.S. C4 140
Buna, Tx., U.S. D6 136
Bunbury, Austl. G2 60
Buncombe, co., N.C., U.S. f10 126
Bundaberg, Austl. E5 62
Būndi, India D3 40
Bungoma, Kenya C6 54
Bungo-suidō, strt., Japan E14 28
Bunia, D.R.C. C6 54
Bunker Hill, Il., U.S. D4 106
Bunker Hill, In., U.S. C5 107
Bunker Hill, mtn., Nv., U.S. D4 121
Bunker Hill, W.V., U.S. B6 141
Bunker Hill, W.V., U.S. m12 141
Bunkerville, Nv., U.S. G7 121
Bunkie, La., U.S. D3 111
Bunnell, Fl., U.S. C5 102
Buntok, Indon. D4 36
Bünyan, Tur. C6 44
Buolkalah, Russia B13 26
Buon Ma Thuot, Viet. D5 34
Buor-Haja, guba, b., Russia B15 26
Buqayq, Sau. Ar. E5 42
Bura, Kenya D7 54
Burang, China C5 40
Buras, La., U.S. E6 111
Buraydah, Sau. Ar. E4 38
Burbank, Ca., U.S. E4 98
Burbank, Il., U.S. k9 106
Burbank, Wa., U.S. C7 140
Burco, Som. I14 48
Burdickville, R.I., U.S. F2 132
Burdur, Tur. D4 44
Burdur Gölü, l., Tur. D4 44
Bureau, co., Il., U.S. B4 106
Bureinskij hrebet, mts., Russia D15 26
Bürenhayrhan, Mong. B6 28
Burfjord, Nor. B10 10
Burgas, Blg. C11 18
Burgaski Zaliv, b., Blg. C11 18
Burgaw, N.C., U.S. C5 126
Burgeo, N.L., Can. E3 88
Burgersdorp, S. Afr. E4 56
Burgettstown, Pa., U.S. F1 131
Burgin, Ky., U.S. C5 110
Burgo de Osma, Spain G5 16
Burgos, Spain F5 16
Burgundy see Bourgogne, hist. reg., Fr. D9 16
Burhaniye, Tur. C2 44
Burhānpur, India E3 40
Burias Island, i., Phil. D8 34
Burin, N.L., Can. E4 88
Burin Peninsula, pen., N.L., Can. E4 88
Buri Ram, Thai. C4 34
Burjatija, state, Russia D13 26
Burkburnett, Tx., U.S. B3 136
Burke, co., Ga., U.S. C4 103
Burke, co., N.C., U.S. B1 126
Burke, co., N.D., U.S. A3 127
Burke, S.D., U.S. D6 134
Burke Channel, strt., B.C., Can. C4 85
Burkesville, Ky., U.S. D4 110
Burketown, Austl. D2 62
Burkina Faso, ctry., Afr. D4 50
Burk's Falls, On., Can. B5 89
Burleigh, co., N.D., U.S. C5 127
Burleson, Tx., U.S. n9 136
Burleson, co., Tx., U.S. D4 136
Burley, Id., U.S. G5 105
Burlingame, Ca., U.S. h8 98
Burlingame, Ks., U.S. D8 109
Burlington, On., Can. D5 89
Burlington, Co., U.S. B8 99
Burlington, Ia., U.S. D6 108
Burlington, Ks., U.S. D8 109
Burlington, Ky., U.S. A5 110
Burlington, Ma., U.S. f11 114
Burlington, N.C., U.S. A3 126
Burlington, N.D., U.S. A4 127
Burlington, N.J., U.S. C3 123
Burlington, co., N.J., U.S. D3 123
Burlington, Vt., U.S. C2 138
Burlington, Wa., U.S. A3 140
Burlington, Wi., U.S. F5 142
Burlington Beach, In., U.S. B3 107
Burlington Junction, Mo., U.S. A2 118
Burlit, Russia A2 31
Burma see Myanmar, ctry., Asia B3 34

Name	Map Ref.	Page
Burnaby, B.C., Can.	E6	85
Burnet, Tx., U.S.	D3	136
Burnet, co., Tx., U.S.	D3	136
Burnett, co., Wi., U.S.	C1	142
Burney, Ca., U.S.	B3	98
Burnham, Pa., U.S.	E6	131
Burnie, Austl.	I4	62
Burns, Or., U.S.	D7	130
Burns, Tn., U.S.	A4	135
Burns, Wy., U.S.	E8	143
Burns Flat, Ok., U.S.	B2	129
Burnside, Ky., U.S.	D5	110
Burns Lake, B.C., Can.	B5	85
Burns Paiute Indian Reservation, Or., U.S.	D7	130
Burnsville, Mn., U.S.	F5	116
Burnsville, Ms., U.S.	A5	117
Burnsville, N.C., U.S.	f10	126
Burnsville Lake, res., W.V., U.S.	C4	141
Burnt Islands, N.L., Can.	E2	88
Burnt Mills, Lake, l., Va., U.S.	k14	139
Burntside Lake, l., Mn., U.S.	C6	116
Burntwood, stm., Mb., Can.	B2	86
Burra, Austl.	G2	62
Burrel, Alb.	D8	18
Burr Oak, Mi., U.S.	G5	115
Burr Oak Reservoir, res., Oh., U.S.	C3	128
Burrton, Ks., U.S.	D6	109
Bursa, Tur.	B3	44
Bûr Sa'îd, Egypt	D11	48
Bûr Sûdân, Sudan	G12	48
Burt, co., Ne., U.S.	C9	120
Burt Lake, l., Mi., U.S.	C6	115
Burton, Mi., U.S.	F7	115
Burton, Oh., U.S.	A4	128
Burtts Corner, N.B., Can.	C3	87
Buru, i., Indon.	D7	36
Burullus, Buheirat el-, l., Egypt	G4	44
Burundi, ctry., Afr.	D5	54
Burwell, Ne., U.S.	C6	120
Bury Saint Edmunds, Eng., U.K.	D7	12
Busanga, D.R.C.	D4	54
Bushman Land, hist. reg., S. Afr.	D2	56
Bushnell, Fl., U.S.	D4	102
Bushnell, Il., U.S.	C3	106
Bush River, b., Md., U.S.	B5	113
Busia, Ug.	C6	54
Businga, D.R.C.	C4	54
Busira, stm., D.R.C.	D3	54
Busko-Zdrój, Pol.	D6	20
Buşrá ash-Shām, Syria	F7	44
Busselton, Austl.	G2	60
Busuanga Island, i., Phil.	D8	34
Busu-Djanoa, D.R.C.	C4	54
Buta, D.R.C.	C4	54
Butare, Rw.	D5	54
Butaritari, atoll, Kir.	D11	58
Bute Inlet, b., B.C., Can.	D5	85
Butembo, D.R.C.	C5	54
Butere, Kenya	C6	54
Buthidaung, Mya.	B2	34
Butiaba, Ug.	C6	54
Butler, Al., U.S.	C1	94
Butler, co., Al., U.S.	D3	94
Butler, Ga., U.S.	D2	103
Butler, co., Ia., U.S.	B5	108
Butler, In., U.S.	B8	107
Butler, co., Ks., U.S.	E7	109
Butler, Ky., U.S.	B5	110
Butler, co., Ky., U.S.	C3	110
Butler, Mo., U.S.	C3	118
Butler, co., Mo., U.S.	E7	118
Butler, co., Ne., U.S.	C8	120
Butler, N.J., U.S.	B4	123
Butler, Oh., U.S.	B3	128
Butler, co., Oh., U.S.	C1	128
Butler, Pa., U.S.	E2	131
Butler, co., Pa., U.S.	E2	131
Butler, Wi., U.S.	m11	142
Butner, N.C., U.S.	A4	126
Buton, Pulau, i., Indon.	D6	36
Butrint, hist., Alb.	E8	18
Buttahatchee, stm., U.S.	B5	117
Butte, co., Ca., U.S.	C3	98
Butte, co., Id., U.S.	F5	105
Butte, Mt., U.S.	E4	119
Butte, co., S.D., U.S.	C2	134
Butte des Morts, Lake, l., Wi., U.S.	D5	142
Butte Mountains, mts., Nv., U.S.	D6	121
Butternut Lake, l., Wi., U.S.	C5	142
Butterworth, Malay.	B2	36
Buttonwillow, Ca., U.S.	E4	98
Butts, co., Ga., U.S.	C3	103
Butuan, Phil.	E9	34
Buturlinovka, Russia	D16	20
Buulobarde, Som.	C9	54
Buur Gaabo, Som.	D8	54
Buxton, N.C., U.S.	B7	126
Büyük Ağrı Dağı see Ağrı Dağı, mtn., Tur.	C11	44
Büyükmenderes, stm., Tur.	D2	44
Buzuluk, Russia	D9	22
Buzzards Bay, Ma., U.S.	C6	114
Buzzards Bay, b., Ma., U.S.	C6	114
Bwendi, D.R.C.	C5	54
Bydgoszcz, Pol.	C5	20
Byelorussia see Belarus, ctry., Eur.	C9	20
Byers, Co., U.S.	B6	99
Byesville, Oh., U.S.	C4	128
Byhalia, Ms., U.S.	A4	117
Byhaŭ, Bela.	C11	20
Bylas, Az., U.S.	D5	96
Byng, Ok., U.S.	C5	129
Byrdstown, Tn., U.S.	C8	135
Byro, Austl.	F2	60
Byron, Ga., U.S.	D3	103
Byron, Il., U.S.	A4	106
Byron, Mn., U.S.	F6	116
Byron, Wy., U.S.	B4	143
Byron, Cape, c., Austl.	F5	62
Byron Bay, Austl.	F5	62
Byrranga, gory, mts., Russia	B12	26
Bytom, Pol.	D5	20
Bytów, Pol.	B4	20
Byzantium see İstanbul, Tur.	B3	44

C

Name	Map Ref.	Page
Caála, Ang.	F3	54
Caatinga, Braz.	B8	72
Cabadbaran, Phil.	E9	34
Cabaiguán, Cuba	A4	80
Caballo Mountains, mts., N.M., U.S.	E2	124
Caballo Reservoir, res., N.M., U.S.	E2	124
Cabanatuan, Phil.	C8	34
Cabano, Qc., Can.	B9	90
Cabarrus, co., N.C., U.S.	B2	126
Cabbage Swamp, sw., Fl., U.S.	m9	102
Cabedelo, Braz.	C5	74
Cabell, co., W.V., U.S.	C2	141
Cabeza del Buey, Spain	H4	16
Cabimas, Ven.	A5	70
Cabin Creek, W.V., U.S.	m13	141
Cabin Creek, stm., W.V., U.S.	m13	141
Cabinda, Ang.	E2	54
Cabinet Gorge Reservoir, res., U.S.	B1	119
Cabinet Mountains, mts., Mt., U.S.	B1	119
Cabin John, Md., U.S.	C3	113
Cabo, Braz.	C4	74
Cabo Blanco, Arg.	G3	69
Cabonga, Réservoir, res., Qc., Can.	I24	82
Cabool, Mo., U.S.	D5	118
Caborca, Mex.	C2	78
Cabot, Ar., U.S.	C3	97
Cabot, Mount, mtn., N.H., U.S.	A4	122
Cabot Head, c., On., Can.	B3	89
Cabrayıl, Azer.	C12	44
Cabri, Sk., Can.	G1	91
Cabrillo National Monument, Ca., U.S.	o15	98
Caçador, Braz.	D7	72
Čačak, Serb.	C8	18
Caçapava do Sul, Braz.	E7	72
Cacapon, stm., W.V., U.S.	B6	141
Cáceres, Braz.	G8	70
Cáceres, Spain	H3	16
Cache, stm., Ar., U.S.	C4	97
Cache, stm., Il., U.S.	F4	106
Cache, Ok., U.S.	C3	129
Cache, co., Ut., U.S.	B4	137
Cache Bay, On., Can.	A5	89
Cache Creek, B.C., Can.	D7	85
Cache la Poudre, stm., Co., U.S.	A5	99
Cache Mountain, mtn., Ak., U.S.	B10	95
Cache Peak, mtn., Id., U.S.	G5	105
Cachimbo, Serra do, mts., Braz.	E8	70
Cachingues, Ang.	F3	54
Cachoeira do Sul, Braz.	E7	72
Cachoeiro de Itapemirim, Braz.	F3	74
Cacolo, Ang.	F3	54
Caconda, Ang.	A2	56
Cactus Flat, pl., Nv., U.S.	F5	121
Cactus Peak, mtn., Nv., U.S.	F5	121
Cacuaco, Ang.	E2	54
Caculé, Braz.	A9	72
Čadan, Russia	D11	26
Caddo, stm., Ar., U.S.	C2	97
Caddo, co., La., U.S.	B2	111
Caddo, Ok., U.S.	C5	129
Caddo, co., Ok., U.S.	B3	129
Caddo Creek, stm., Ok., U.S.	C4	129
Caddo Lake, res., U.S.	B2	111
Cadillac, Mi., U.S.	D5	115
Cadillac Mountain, mtn., Me., U.S.	D4	112
Cadiz, Phil.	D8	34
Cádiz, Spain	I3	16
Cadiz, Ky., U.S.	D2	110
Cadiz, Oh., U.S.	B4	128
Cádiz, Golfo de, b., Eur.	I3	16
Cadiz, Gulf of see Cádiz, Golfo de, b., Eur.	I3	16
Cadott, Wi., U.S.	D2	142
Čaek, Kyrg.	A2	40
Caen, Fr.	C6	16
Caernarfon, Wales, U.K.	D4	12
Caesar Creek Lake, res., Oh., U.S.	C2	128
Caetité, Braz.	D3	74
Cagayan de Oro, Phil.	E8	34
Cagayan Islands, is., Phil.	E8	34
Cagayan Sulu Island, i., Phil.	E7	34
Čagda, Russia	D15	26
Cagles Mill Lake, res., In., U.S.	F4	107
Cagliari, Italy	E2	18
Cagliari, Golfo di, b., Italy	E2	18
Caguas, P.R.	B6	80
Cahaba, stm., Al., U.S.	C2	94
Cahama, Ang.	B1	56
Cahokia, Il., U.S.	E3	106
Cahora Bassa, Albufeira, res., Moz.	B5	56
Cahors, Fr.	E7	16
Cahul, Mol.	G10	20
Caiapó, Serra do, mts., Braz.	B7	72
Caibarién, Cuba	A4	80
Caicara de Orinoco, Ven.	D6	80
Caicó, Braz.	C4	74
Caicos Islands, is., T./C. Is.	A5	80
Caicos Passage, strt., N.A.	A5	80
Cailloma, Peru	B3	72
Caillou Bay, b., La., U.S.	E5	111
Caillou Lake, l., La., U.S.	E5	111
Caimanera, Cuba	B4	80
Cairnbrook, Pa., U.S.	F4	131
Cairns, Austl.	D4	62
Cairo see El-Qâhira, Egypt	D11	48
Cairo, Ga., U.S.	F2	103
Cairo, Il., U.S.	F4	106
Cairo, Ne., U.S.	D7	120
Caiundo, Ang.	B2	56
Cajamarca, Peru	E4	70
Cajazeiras, Braz.	C4	74
Calabar, Nig.	F6	50
Calabozo, Ven.	B6	70
Calagua Islands, is., Phil.	D8	34
Calahorra, Spain	F6	16
Calais, Fr.	B7	16
Calais, Me., U.S.	C5	112
Calama, Chile	B3	69
Calamian Group, is., Phil.	D7	34
Calamus, stm., Ne., U.S.	B6	120
Calapan, Phil.	D8	34
Călăraşi, Mol.	F10	20
Călăraşi, Rom.	G9	20
Calatayud, Spain	G6	16
Calaveras, co., Ca., U.S.	C3	98
Calayan Island, i., Phil.	C8	34
Calbayog, Phil.	D8	34
Calcasieu, stm., La., U.S.	D2	111
Calcasieu, co., La., U.S.	D2	111
Calcasieu Lake, l., La., U.S.	E2	111
Calcasieu Pass, strt., La., U.S.	E2	111
Calçoene, Braz.	C9	70
Calcutta see Kolkata, India	E5	40
Calcutta, Oh., U.S.	B5	128
Calcutta Lake, l., Nv., U.S.	B2	121
Caldas da Rainha, Port.	H2	16
Caldera, Chile	C2	69
Calderwood, Tn., U.S.	D10	135
Caldron Falls Reservoir, res., Wi., U.S.	C5	142
Caldwell, Id., U.S.	F2	105
Caldwell, Ks., U.S.	E6	109
Caldwell, co., Ky., U.S.	C2	110
Caldwell, co., La., U.S.	B3	111
Caldwell, co., Mo., U.S.	B3	118
Caldwell, co., N.C., U.S.	B1	126
Caldwell, N.J., U.S.	B4	123
Caldwell, Oh., U.S.	C4	128
Caldwell, Tx., U.S.	D4	136
Caldwell, co., Tx., U.S.	E4	136
Caledon, On., Can.	D5	89
Caledonia, Mi., U.S.	F5	115
Caledonia, Mn., U.S.	G7	116
Caledonia, Ms., U.S.	B5	117
Caledonia, N.Y., U.S.	C3	125
Caledonia, co., Vt., U.S.	C4	138
Calera, Al., U.S.	B3	94
Calera, Ok., U.S.	D5	129
Calexico, Ca., U.S.	F6	98
Calgary, Ab., Can.	D3	84
Calhoun, co., Al., U.S.	B4	94
Calhoun, co., Ar., U.S.	D3	97
Calhoun, co., Fl., U.S.	B1	102
Calhoun, Ga., U.S.	B2	103
Calhoun, co., Ga., U.S.	E2	103
Calhoun, co., Ia., U.S.	B3	108
Calhoun, co., Il., U.S.	D3	106
Calhoun, Ky., U.S.	C2	110
Calhoun, co., Mi., U.S.	F5	115
Calhoun, co., Ms., U.S.	B4	117
Calhoun, co., S.C., U.S.	D6	133
Calhoun, co., Tx., U.S.	E4	136
Calhoun, co., W.V., U.S.	C3	141
Calhoun City, Ms., U.S.	B4	117
Calhoun Falls, S.C., U.S.	C2	133
Cali, Col.	C4	70
Calico Rock, Ar., U.S.	A3	97
Calicut see Kozhikode, India	G3	40
Caliente, Nv., U.S.	F7	121
California, Mo., U.S.	C5	118
California, Pa., U.S.	F2	131
California, state, U.S.	D4	98
California, Golfo de, b., Mex.	B2	78
California, Gulf of see California, Golfo de, b., Mex.	B2	78
California Aqueduct, aq., Ca., U.S.	E4	98
Calipatria, Ca., U.S.	F6	98
Calispell Peak, mtn., Wa., U.S.	A8	140
Calistoga, Ca., U.S.	C2	98
Callaghan, Mount, mtn., Nv., U.S.	D5	121
Callahan, co., Tx., U.S.	C3	136
Callao, Peru	F4	70
Callaway, co., Mo., U.S.	C6	118
Calling Lake, l., Ab., Can.	B4	84
Calloway, co., Ky., U.S.	f9	110
Calmar, Ab., Can.	C4	84
Calmar, Ia., U.S.	A6	108
Caloosahatchee, stm., Fl., U.S.	F5	102
Caltanissetta, Italy	F4	18
Calulo, Ang.	E2	54
Calumet, Qc., Can.	D3	90
Calumet, Mi., U.S.	A2	115
Calumet, co., Wi., U.S.	D5	142
Calumet, Lake, l., Il., U.S.	k9	106
Calumet City, Il., U.S.	B6	106
Calunda, Ang.	F4	54
Caluula, Som.	H15	48
Calvert, co., Md., U.S.	C4	113
Calvert, Tx., U.S.	D4	136
Calvert City, Ky., U.S.	e9	110
Calverton Park, Mo., U.S.	f13	118
Calvillo, Mex.	C4	78
Calvinia, S. Afr.	E2	56
Camabatela, Ang.	E3	54
Camaçari, Braz.	D4	74
Camacupa, Ang.	F3	54
Camagüey, Cuba	A4	80
Camaná, Peru	G5	70
Camanche, Ia., U.S.	C7	108
Camano Island, i., Wa., U.S.	A3	140
Camaquã, Braz.	E7	72
Camará, Braz.	D7	70
Camargo, Bol.	C4	72
Camargue, reg., Fr.	F9	16
Camarones, Arg.	F3	69
Camas, Spain	I3	16
Camas, co., Id., U.S.	F4	105
Camas, Wa., U.S.	D3	140
Ca Mau, Viet.	E5	34
Ca Mau, Mui, c., Viet.	E4	34
Cambodia, ctry., Asia	D4	34
Cambrai, Fr.	B8	16
Cambria, Ca., U.S.	E3	98
Cambria, co., Pa., U.S.	E4	131
Cambria, Wi., U.S.	E4	142
Cambridge, On., Can.	D4	89
Cambridge, Eng., U.K.	D7	12
Cambridge, Ia., U.S.	C4	108
Cambridge, Il., U.S.	B3	106
Cambridge, Ma., U.S.	B5	114
Cambridge, Md., U.S.	C5	113
Cambridge, Mn., U.S.	E5	116
Cambridge, Ne., U.S.	D5	120
Cambridge, N.Y., U.S.	B7	125
Cambridge, Oh., U.S.	B4	128
Cambridge, Wi., U.S.	F4	142
Cambridge City, In., U.S.	E7	107
Cambridge Reservoir, res., Ma., U.S.	g10	114
Cambridge Springs, Pa., U.S.	C1	131
Cambulo, Ang.	E4	54
Cambundi-Catembo, Ang.	F3	54
Camden, Al., U.S.	D2	94
Camden, Ar., U.S.	D3	97
Camden, De., U.S.	D3	101
Camden, co., Ga., U.S.	F5	103
Camden, In., U.S.	C4	107
Camden, Me., U.S.	D3	112
Camden, co., Mo., U.S.	C5	118
Camden, co., N.C., U.S.	A6	126
Camden, N.J., U.S.	D2	123
Camden, co., N.J., U.S.	D3	123
Camden, N.Y., U.S.	B5	125
Camden, Oh., U.S.	C1	128
Camden, S.C., U.S.	C6	133
Camden, Tn., U.S.	A3	135
Camdenton, Mo., U.S.	D5	118
Camelback Mountain, mtn., Az., U.S.	k9	96
Cameron, Az., U.S.	B4	96
Cameron, La., U.S.	E2	111
Cameron, co., La., U.S.	E2	111
Cameron, Mo., U.S.	B3	118
Cameron, co., Pa., U.S.	D5	131
Cameron, Tx., U.S.	D4	136
Cameron, co., Tx., U.S.	F4	136
Cameron, Wi., U.S.	C2	142
Cameron, W.V., U.S.	B4	141
Cameron Hills, Can.	G16	82
Cameroon, ctry., Afr.	J7	48
Cameroon Mountain, vol., Cam.	C1	54
Cametá, Braz.	B2	74
Çamiçi Gölü, l., Tur.	D2	44
Camiguin Island, i., Phil.	C8	34
Camiguin Island, i., Phil.	E8	34
Camilla, Ga., U.S.	E2	103
Camino, Ca., U.S.	C3	98
Camiranga, Braz.	D10	70
Camiri, Bol.	C5	72
Camissombo, Ang.	E4	54
Cammack Village, Ar., U.S.	C3	97
Camocim, Braz.	B3	74
Camooweal, Austl.	D2	62
Camorta Island, i., India	H6	40
Camotes Sea, Phil.	D8	34
Camp, co., Tx., U.S.	C5	136
Campana, Arg.	E6	72
Campbell, Ca., U.S.	k8	98
Campbell, Fl., U.S.	D5	102
Campbell, co., Ky., U.S.	B5	110
Campbell, Mo., U.S.	E7	118
Campbell, Oh., U.S.	A5	128
Campbell, co., S.D., U.S.	B5	134
Campbell, co., Tn., U.S.	C9	135
Campbell, co., Va., U.S.	C3	139
Campbell, co., Wy., U.S.	B7	143
Campbellford, On., Can.	C7	89
Campbell Hill, Oh., U.S.	B2	128
Campbell Island, i., N.Z.	J10	58
Campbell Lake, l., Or., U.S.	E7	130
Campbell Plateau	M20	64
Campbellsburg, In., U.S.	G5	107
Campbellsburg, Ky., U.S.	B4	110
Campbells Creek, stm., W.V., U.S.	m13	141
Campbellsport, Wi., U.S.	E5	142
Campbellsville, Ky., U.S.	C4	110
Campbellton, N.B., Can.	A3	87
Campbellton, N.L., Can.	D4	88
Campbelltown, Austl.	G5	62
Campbeltown, Scot., U.K.	C4	12
Campeche, state, Mex.	D6	78
Campeche, Mex.	D6	78
Campeche, Bahía de, b., Mex.	D6	78
Campeche, Gulf of see Campeche, Bahía de, b., Mex.	D6	78
Camperdown, Austl.	H3	62
Camperville, Mb., Can.	D1	86
Cam Pha, Viet.	B5	34
Camp Hill, Al., U.S.	C4	94
Camp Hill, Pa., U.S.	F8	131
Camp H. M. Smith Marine Corps Base, mil., Hi., U.S.	g10	104
Camp Howard Ridge, mtn., Id., U.S.	D2	105
Câmpina, Rom.	G8	20
Campina Grande, Braz.	C4	74
Campinas, Braz.	F2	74
Campina Verde, Braz.	E2	74
Camp Lejeune Marine Corps Base, mil., N.C., U.S.	C5	126
Campo, Cam.	C1	54
Campobasso, Italy	D5	18
Campobello Island, i., N.B., Can.	E3	87
Campo de la Cruz, Col.	C5	80
Campo Formoso, Braz.	D3	74
Campo Gallo, Arg.	D5	72
Campo Grande, Braz.	H9	70
Campo Maior, Braz.	B3	74
Campo Mourão, Braz.	F1	74
Campos, Braz.	F3	74
Campos Sales, Braz.	C3	74
Camp Pendleton Marine Corps Base, mil., Ca., U.S.	F5	98
Camp Point, Il., U.S.	C2	106
Camp Springs, Md., U.S.	f9	113
Campti, La., U.S.	C2	111
Campton, N.H., U.S.	C3	122
Câmpulung, Rom.	G8	20
Câmpulung Moldovenesc, Rom.	F8	20
Camp Verde, Az., U.S.	C4	96
Camp Verde Indian Reservation, Az., U.S.	C4	96
Cam Ranh, Viet.	D5	34
Camrose, Ab., Can.	C4	84
Çan, Tur.	B2	44
Canaan, stm., N.B., Can.	C4	87
Canaan, Ct., U.S.	A2	100
Canaan, N.H., U.S.	C2	122
Canada, ctry., N.A.	G17	82
Canada Basin	D1	144
Canada Bay, b., N.L., Can.	C3	88
Cañada de Gómez, Arg.	E5	72
Canada Falls Lake, res., Me., U.S.	C2	112
Canadensis, Pa., U.S.	D11	131
Canadian, co., Ok., U.S.	B3	129
Canadian, Tx., U.S.	B2	136
Canadian, stm., U.S.	D7	92
Canaima, Ven.	D7	80
Canajoharie, N.Y., U.S.	C6	125
Çanakkale, Tur.	B2	44
Çanakkale Boğazı (Dardanelles), strt., Tur.	C1	44
Canal Flats, B.C., Can.	D10	85
Canal Fulton, Oh., U.S.	B4	128
Canal Winchester, Oh., U.S.	C3	128
Canandaigua, N.Y., U.S.	C3	125
Canandaigua Lake, l., N.Y., U.S.	C3	125
Cananea, Mex.	A2	78
Canarias, Islas (Canary Islands), is., Spain	A1	50
Canary Basin	F10	66
Canary Islands see Canarias, Islas, is., Spain	A1	50
Cañasgordas, Col.	D4	80
Canastota, N.Y., U.S.	B5	125
Canaveral, Cape, c., Fl., U.S.	D6	102
Canaveral National Seashore, Fl., U.S.	D6	102

Name — Map Ref. — Page

Canaveral National Seashore, Fl., U.S. D6 102
Canavieiras, Braz. E4 74
Canberra, Austl. H4 62
Canby, Mn., U.S. F2 116
Canby, Or., U.S. B4 130
Cancún, Mex. C7 78
Candeias, Braz. D4 74
Candia see Iráklion, Grc. G10 18
Candiac, Qc., Can. q19 90
Candle Lake, l., Sk., Can. D3 91
Candler, co., Ga., U.S. D4 103
Candlewood, Lake, l., Ct., U.S. D1 100
Candlewood Isle, Ct., U.S. D2 100
Candlewood Shores, Ct., U.S. D2 100
Cando, N.D., U.S. A6 127
Candor, N.C., U.S. B3 126
Cane, stm., La., U.S. C2 111
Canelones, Ur. E6 72
Caney, Ks., U.S. E8 109
Caney, stm., Ok., U.S. A5 129
Caney Creek, stm., Tx., U.S. r14 136
Caney Fork, stm., Tn., U.S. C8 135
Canfield, Oh., U.S. A5 128
Cangas de Narcea, Spain F3 16
Cangkuang, Tanjung, c., Indon. E3 36
Cangombe, Ang. A2 56
Canguçu, Braz. E7 72
Cangumbe, Ang. F3 54
Cangyuan, China B3 34
Cangzhou, China D11 28
Caniapiscau, stm., Qc., Can. g13 90
Canicattì, Italy F4 18
Canindé, Braz. B4 74
Canistear Reservoir, res., N.J., U.S. A4 123
Canisteo, stm., N.Y., U.S. C3 125
Canisteo, N.Y., U.S. C3 125
Canistota, S.D., U.S. D8 134
Çankırı, Tur. B5 44
Canmore, Ab., Can. D3 84
Cannanore, India G3 40
Cannelton, In., U.S. I4 107
Cannes, Fr. F10 16
Canning, N.S., Can. D5 87
Cannon, stm., Mn., U.S. F5 116
Cannon, co., Tn., U.S. B5 135
Cannon Air Force Base, mil., N.M., U.S. C6 124
Cannonball, stm., N.D., U.S. C5 127
Cannon Beach, Or., U.S. B3 130
Cannondale, Ct., U.S. E2 100
Cannon Falls, Mn., U.S. F6 116
Cannonsburg, Ky., U.S. B7 110
Cannonsville Reservoir, res., N.Y., U.S. C5 125
Canoas, Braz. D7 72
Canoinhas, Braz. D7 72
Canon, Ga., U.S. B3 103
Canon City, Co., U.S. C5 99
Canonsburg, Pa., U.S. F1 131
Cantabrian Mountains see Cantábrica, Cordillera, mts., Spain F4 16
Cantábrica, Cordillera, mts., Spain F4 16
Cantaura, Ven. B7 70
Canterbury, Eng., U.K. E7 12
Canterbury, De., U.S. D3 101
Canterbury Bight, b., N.Z. p13 63c
Can Tho, Viet. E5 34
Canton see Guangzhou, China E3 30
Canton, Ct., U.S. B4 100
Canton, Ga., U.S. B2 103
Canton, Il., U.S. C3 106
Canton, Ks., U.S. D6 109
Canton, Ma., U.S. B5 114
Canton, Mo., U.S. A6 118
Canton, Ms., U.S. C3 117
Canton, N.C., U.S. f10 126
Canton, N.Y., U.S. f9 125
Canton, Oh., U.S. B4 128
Canton, Ok., U.S. A3 129
Canton, Pa., U.S. C8 131
Canton, S.D., U.S. D9 134
Canton, Tx., U.S. C5 136
Canton Lake, res., Ok., U.S. A3 129
Cantonment, Fl., U.S. u14 102
Canutama, Braz. E7 70
Canutillo, Tx., U.S. o11 136
Čany, ozero, l., Russia D9 26
Canyon, co., Id., U.S. F2 105
Canyon, Tx., U.S. B2 136
Canyon City, Or., U.S. C8 130
Canyon de Chelly National Monument, Az., U.S. A6 96
Canyon Ferry Lake, res., Mt., U.S. D5 119
Canyon Lake, Tx., U.S. E3 136
Canyon Lake, res., Tx., U.S. E3 136
Canyonlands National Park, Ut., U.S. E6 137
Canyonville, Or., U.S. E3 130
Cao Bang, Viet. B5 34
Caoxian, China C4 30
Capac, Mi., U.S. F8 115
Čapaevo, Kaz. D9 22
Cap-à-l'Aigle, Qc., Can. B7 90
Capanema, Braz. B2 74
Capão Bonito, Braz. F2 74
Cap-aux-Meules, Qc., Can. B8 87
Cap-de-la-Madeleine, Qc., Can. C5 90
Cape Barren Island, i., Austl. I4 62
Cape Basin L14 66
Cape Breton Highlands National Park, N.S., Can. C9 87
Cape Breton Island, i., N.S., Can. C9 87
Cape Broyle, N.L., Can. E5 88
Cape Canaveral, Fl., U.S. D6 102
Cape Charles, Va., U.S. C6 139
Cape Coast, Ghana E4 50
Cape Cod Bay, b., Ma., U.S. C7 114
Cape Cod Canal, Ma., U.S. C6 114
Cape Cod National Seashore, Ma., U.S. C7 114
Cape Coral, Fl., U.S. F5 102
Cape Elizabeth, Me., U.S. E2 112
Cape Fear, stm., N.C., U.S. C4 126
Cape Girardeau, Mo., U.S. D8 118
Cape Girardeau, co., Mo., U.S. D8 118
Cape Hatteras National Seashore, N.C., U.S. B7 126
Cape Horn Mountain, mtn., Id., U.S. E3 105
Cape Island, i., S.C., U.S. E9 133
Capelinha, Braz. E3 74
Capelongo, Ang. A2 56
Cape Lookout National Seashore, N.C., U.S. C6 126
Cape May, N.J., U.S. F3 123
Cape May, co., N.J., U.S. E3 123
Cape May Court House, N.J., U.S. E3 123
Capers Inlet, b., S.C., U.S. k12 133
Capers Island, i., S.C., U.S. G6 133
Capers Island, i., S.C., U.S. F8 133
Cape Sable Island, i., N.S., Can. F4 87
Cape Town (Kaapstad), S. Afr. E2 56
Cape Verde, ctry., Afr. 50a
Cape Verde, ctry., Afr. 50a
Cape Verde G10 66
Cape York Peninsula, pen., Austl. C3 62
Cap-Haïtien, Haiti B5 80
Capinota, Bol. B4 72
Capitan, N.M., U.S. D4 124
Capitan Mountains, mts., N.M., U.S. D4 124
Capitan Peak, mtn., N.M., U.S. D4 124
Capitol Heights, Ia., U.S. e8 108
Capitol Heights, Md., U.S. C4 113
Capitol Peak, mtn., Nv., U.S. B4 121
Capitol Reef National Park, Ut., U.S. E4 137
Čaplygin, Russia C15 20
Cap-Pelé, N.B., Can. C5 87
Capreol, On., Can. p19 89
Capri, Isola di, i., Italy D5 18
Capricorn Channel, strt., Austl. E5 62
Capricorn Group, is., Austl. E5 62
Caprivi Strip, hist. reg., Nmb. B3 56
Cap-Rouge, Qc., Can. n17 90
Cap-Saint-Ignace, Qc., Can. B7 90
Captain Cook, Hi., U.S. D6 104
Captiva, Fl., U.S. F4 102
Captiva Island, i., Fl., U.S. F4 102
Capulin Volcano National Monument, N.M., U.S. A6 124
Capunda Cabilongo, Ang. F2 54
Caquetá (Japurá), stm., S.A. D5 70
Čara, Russia D13 26
Caracal, Rom. G8 20
Caracaraí, Braz. C7 70
Caracas, Ven. A6 70
Carajás, Braz. E9 70
Carajás, Serra dos, Braz. E9 70
Carangola, Braz. F3 74
Caransebeș, Rom. G7 20
Caraquet, N.B., Can. B5 87
Caratasca, Laguna de, b., Hond. B3 80
Caratinga, Braz. E3 74
Carauari, Braz. D6 70
Caravaca de la Cruz, Spain H6 16
Caravelas, Braz. G12 70
Caraway, Ar., U.S. B5 97
Carazinho, Braz. D7 72
Carberry, Mb., Can. E2 86
Carbon, co., Mt., U.S. E7 119
Carbon, co., Pa., U.S. E10 131
Carbon, co., Ut., U.S. D5 137
Carbon, co., Wy., U.S. E5 143
Carbondale, Co., U.S. B3 99
Carbondale, Il., U.S. F4 106
Carbondale, Ks., U.S. D8 109
Carbondale, Pa., U.S. C10 131
Carbonear, N.L., Can. E5 88
Carbon Hill, Al., U.S. B2 94
Carbonia, Italy E2 18
Carcassonne, Fr. F8 16
Čardara, Kaz. B9 42
Cárdenas, Cuba A3 80
Cárdenas, Mex. H14 78
Cardiff, Wales, U.K. E5 12
Cardigan, Wales, U.K. D4 12
Cardigan Bay, b., P.E., Can. C7 87
Cardigan Bay, b., Wales, U.K. D4 12
Cardinal, On., Can. C9 89
Cardington, Oh., U.S. B3 128
Cardston, Ab., Can. E4 84
Cardwell, Mo., U.S. E7 118
Čardžev, Turk. F8 26
Carei, Rom. F7 20
Careiro, Braz. D8 70
Carelia see Karelia, hist. reg., Eur. C12 6
Carencro, La., U.S. D3 111
Carentan, Fr. C6 16
Caretta, W.V., U.S. D3 141
Carey, Id., U.S. F5 105
Carey, Oh., U.S. B2 128
Carey Downs, Austl. F2 60
Cargados Carajos Shoals, is., Mrts. F11 52
Caribbean Sea C4 80
Cariboo Mountains, mts., B.C., Can. C7 85
Caribou, co., Id., U.S. G7 105
Caribou, Me., U.S. B5 112
Caribou Island, i., N.S., Can. D7 87
Caribou Lake, l., Me., U.S. C3 112
Caribou Mountain, mtn., Id., U.S. F7 105
Caribou Mountains, mts., Ab., Can. f7 84
Caribou Range, mts., Id., U.S. F7 105
Caripito, Ven. C7 80
Carl Blackwell, Lake, res., Ok., U.S. A4 129
Carlet, Spain H6 16
Carleton, Mi., U.S. F7 115
Carleton, Mount, mtn., N.B., Can. B3 87
Carleton Place, On., Can. B8 89
Carletonville, S. Afr. D4 56
Carlin, Nv., U.S. C5 121
Carlinville, Il., U.S. D4 106
Carlisle, Eng., U.K. C5 12
Carlisle, Ar., U.S. C4 97
Carlisle, Ia., U.S. C4 108
Carlisle, In., U.S. G3 107
Carlisle, Ky., U.S. B5 110
Carlisle, co., Ky., U.S. f8 110
Carlisle, Oh., U.S. C1 128
Carlisle, Pa., U.S. F7 131
Carl Junction, Mo., U.S. D3 118
Carlos Casares, Arg. F5 72
Carlos Chagas, Braz. E3 74
Carlow, Ire. D3 12
Carlsbad see Karlovy Vary, Czech Rep. D2 20
Carlsbad, Ca., U.S. F5 98
Carlsbad, N.M., U.S. E5 124
Carlsbad Caverns National Park, N.M., U.S. E5 124
Carlsberg Ridge H8 64
Carlstadt, N.J., U.S. h8 123
Carlton, Mn., U.S. D6 116
Carlton, co., Mn., U.S. D6 116
Carlton, Or., U.S. B3 130
Carlyle, Il., U.S. E4 106
Carlyle Lake, res., Il., U.S. E4 106
Carman, Mb., Can. E2 86
Carmanville, N.L., Can. D4 88
Carmarthen, Wales, U.K. E4 12
Carmel, Ca., U.S. D3 98
Carmel, In., U.S. E5 107
Carmel, N.Y., U.S. D7 125
Carmelo, Ur. E6 72
Carmen, Isla, i., Mex. B2 78
Carmen, Isla del, i., Mex. H15 78
Carmen de Patagones, Arg. F4 69
Carmi, Il., U.S. E5 106
Carmi, Lake, l., Vt., U.S. B3 138
Carnamah, Austl. F2 60
Carnarvon, Austl. E1 60
Carnarvon, S. Afr. E3 56
Carnation, Wa., U.S. B4 140
Carnegie, Ok., U.S. B3 129
Carnegie, Pa., U.S. F1 131
Carnegie, Lake, l., Austl. F3 60
Carneys Point, N.J., U.S. D2 123
Carnic Alps, mts., Eur. A4 18
Car Nicobar Island, i., India H6 40
Carnot, C.A.R. C3 54
Caro, Mi., U.S. E7 115
Carol City, Fl., U.S. s13 102
Caroleen, N.C., U.S. B1 126
Carolina, Braz. C2 74
Carolina, R.I., U.S. F2 132
Carolina, W.V., U.S. k10 141
Carolina Beach, N.C., U.S. C5 126
Caroline, atoll, Kir. E15 58
Caroline, co., Md., U.S. C6 113
Caroline, co., Va., U.S. C5 139
Caroline Islands, is., Oc. D8 58
Caroní, stm., Ven. C7 70
Carora, Ven. C5 80
Carpathian Mountains, mts., Eur. E6 20
Carpații Meridionali, mts., Rom. G7 20
Carpentaria, Gulf of, b., Austl. F7 58
Carpenter Dam, Ar., U.S. g7 97
Carpentersville, Il., U.S. A5 106
Carpentras, Fr. E9 16
Carpina, Braz. C4 74
Carpinteria, Ca., U.S. E4 98
Carrabelle, Fl., U.S. C2 102
Carranza, Cabo, c., Chile F3 72
Carrara, Italy B3 18
Carrauntoohil, mtn., Ire. D2 12
Carrboro, N.C., U.S. B3 126
Carreta, Punta, c., Peru F4 70
Carrick on Shannon, Ire. C3 12
Carrie, Mount, mtn., Wa., U.S. B2 140
Carriere, Ms., U.S. E4 117
Carrier Mills, Il., U.S. F5 106
Carrington, N.D., U.S. B6 127
Carrington Island, i., Ut., U.S. C3 137
Carrizal Bajo, Chile C2 69
Carrizo Creek, stm., U.S. A1 136
Carrizo Mountain, mtn., N.M., U.S. D4 124
Carrizo Mountains, mts., U.S. A6 96
Carrizozo, N.M., U.S. D4 124
Carroll, co., Ar., U.S. A2 97
Carroll, co., Ga., U.S. C1 103
Carroll, Ia., U.S. B3 108
Carroll, co., Ia., U.S. B3 108
Carroll, co., Il., U.S. A4 106
Carroll, co., In., U.S. C4 107
Carroll, co., Ky., U.S. B4 110
Carroll, co., Md., U.S. A3 113
Carroll, co., Mo., U.S. B4 118
Carroll, co., Ms., U.S. B4 117
Carroll, co., N.H., U.S. C4 122
Carroll, co., Oh., U.S. B4 128
Carroll, co., Tn., U.S. B3 135
Carroll, co., Va., U.S. D2 139
Carrollton, Al., U.S. B1 94
Carrollton, Ga., U.S. C1 103
Carrollton, Il., U.S. D3 106
Carrollton, Ky., U.S. B4 110
Carrollton, Mi., U.S. E7 115
Carrollton, Mo., U.S. B4 118
Carrollton, Oh., U.S. B4 128
Carrolltown, Pa., U.S. E4 131
Carrot, stm., Can. D4 91
Carry Falls Reservoir, res., N.Y., U.S. f10 125
Çarşamba, Tur. B7 44
Čarsk, Kaz. B4 28
Carson, Ia., U.S. C2 108
Carson, stm., Nv., U.S. D2 121
Carson, co., Tx., U.S. B2 136
Carson, Wa., U.S. D4 140
Carson City, Mi., U.S. E6 115
Carson City, Nv., U.S. D2 121
Carson Lake, l., Nv., U.S. D3 121
Carson Sink, l., Nv., U.S. D3 121
Carson Spring, Tn., U.S. D10 135
Carstairs, Ab., Can. D3 84
Cartagena, Col. A4 70
Cartagena, Spain I6 16
Cartago, C.R. D3 80
Carter, co., Ky., U.S. B6 110
Carter, co., Mo., U.S. E7 118
Carter, co., Mt., U.S. E12 119
Carter, co., Ok., U.S. C4 129
Carter, co., Tn., U.S. C11 135
Carteret, co., N.C., U.S. C6 126
Carteret, N.J., U.S. B4 123
Carter Lake, Ia., U.S. C2 108
Carter Mountain, mtn., Wy., U.S. B3 143
Carters Lake, res., Ga., U.S. B2 103
Cartersville, Ga., U.S. B2 103
Carterville, Il., U.S. F4 106
Carterville, Mo., U.S. D3 118
Carthage, hist., Tun. F3 18
Carthage, Tun. F3 18
Carthage, Il., U.S. C2 106
Carthage, In., U.S. E6 107
Carthage, Mo., U.S. D3 118
Carthage, Ms., U.S. C4 117
Carthage, N.C., U.S. B3 126
Carthage, N.Y., U.S. B5 125
Carthage, Tn., U.S. C8 135
Carthage, Tx., U.S. C5 136
Cartier Islands, is., Austl. C3 60
Cartwright, N.L., Can. B3 88
Cartwright, Ok., U.S. D5 129
Caruaru, Braz. C4 74
Carúpano, Ven. A7 70
Carutapera, Braz. D10 70
Caruthersville, Mo., U.S. E8 118
Carver, Ma., U.S. C6 114
Carver, Mn., U.S. F5 116
Carver, co., Mn., U.S. F5 116
Carville, La., U.S. h9 111
Carvoeiro, Braz. D7 70
Cary, Il., U.S. A5 106
Cary, N.C., U.S. B4 126
Caryville, Tn., U.S. C9 135
Casablanca, Mor. D3 48
Casa Grande, Az., U.S. E4 96
Casa Grande National Monument, Az., U.S. E4 96
Casale Monferrato, Italy B2 18
Casa Nova, Braz. C3 74
Casas Adobes, Az., U.S. E5 96
Cascade, Co., U.S. C6 99
Cascade, Ia., U.S. B6 108
Cascade, Id., U.S. E2 105
Cascade, Mt., U.S. C5 119
Cascade, co., Mt., U.S. C5 119
Cascade Locks, Or., U.S. B5 130
Cascade Range, mts., N.A. C3 92
Cascade Reservoir, res., Id., U.S. E3 105
Cascade Tunnel, Wa., U.S. B4 140
Cascais, Port. H2 16
Cascavel, Braz. D7 72
Casco Bay, b., Me., U.S. E3 112
Caserta, Italy D5 18
Caseville, Mi., U.S. E7 115
Casey, Il., U.S. D6 106
Casey, co., Ky., U.S. C5 110
Casey, Mount, mtn., Id., U.S. A2 105
Casey Key, i., Fl., U.S. E4 102
Cashion, Az., U.S. m8 96
Cashmere, Wa., U.S. B5 140
Cashton, Wi., U.S. E3 142
Casino, Austl. F5 62
Casper, Wy., U.S. D6 143
Casper Mountain, mtn., Wy., U.S. D6 143
Caspian, Mi., U.S. B2 115
Caspian Depression (Prikaspijskaja nizmennost'), pl. E8 22
Caspian Lake, l., Vt., U.S. B4 138
Caspian Sea F9 22
Cass, co., Ia., U.S. C3 108
Cass, co., Il., U.S. D3 106
Cass, co., In., U.S. C5 107
Cass, stm., Mi., U.S. E7 115
Cass, co., Mi., U.S. G4 115
Cass, co., Mn., U.S. D4 116
Cass, co., Mo., U.S. C3 118
Cass, co., N.D., U.S. C8 127
Cass, co., Ne., U.S. D9 120
Cass, co., Tx., U.S. C5 136
Cassai (Kasai), stm., Afr. F4 54
Cass City, Mi., U.S. E7 115
Casselberry, Fl., U.S. D5 102
Casselman, On., Can. B9 89
Casselman, stm., U.S. k12 113
Casselton, N.D., U.S. C8 127
Cassia, co., Id., U.S. G5 105
Cassiar, B.C., Can. m17 85
Cassilândia, Braz. E1 74
Cassinga, Ang. B2 56
Cassino, Italy D4 18
Cass Lake, Mn., U.S. C4 116
Cass Lake, l., Mn., U.S. C4 116
Cassongue, Ang. F2 54
Cassopolis, Mi., U.S. G4 115
Cassumba, Ilha, i., Braz. E4 74
Cassville, Ga., U.S. B2 103
Cassville, Mo., U.S. E4 118
Cassville, Wi., U.S. F3 142
Castalia, Oh., U.S. A3 128
Castanea, Pa., U.S. D7 131
Castanhal, Braz. B2 74
Castellammare, Golfo di, b., Italy E4 18
Castelló de la Plana, Spain H6 16
Castelo Branco, Port. H3 16
Castelsarrasin, Fr. F7 16
Castelvetrano, Italy F4 18
Castilla, Peru E3 70
Castilla la Nueva, hist. reg., Spain H4 16
Castilla la Vieja, hist. reg., Spain G5 16
Castillo de San Marcos National Monument, Fl., U.S. n9 102
Castine, Me., U.S. D4 112
Castlebar, Ire. D2 12
Castleberry, Al., U.S. D2 94
Castle Dale, Ut., U.S. D4 137
Castle Dome Mountains, mts., Az., U.S. D1 96
Castle Dome Peak, mtn., Az., U.S. D1 96
Castlegar, B.C., Can. E9 85
Castle Hayne, N.C., U.S. C5 126
Castle Hills, De., U.S. i7 101
Castlemaine, Austl. H3 62
Castle Mountains, mts., Mt., U.S. D6 119
Castle Peak, mtn., Co., U.S. B4 99
Castle Peak, mtn., Id., U.S. E4 105
Castle Point, Mo., U.S. f13 118
Castle Rock, Co., U.S. B6 99
Castle Rock, mtn., Or., U.S. C8 130
Castle Rock, Wa., U.S. C3 140
Castle Rock Lake, res., Wi., U.S. E4 142
Castleton, Vt., U.S. D2 138
Castlewood, Va., U.S. f9 139
Castor, Ab., Can. C5 84
Castor, stm., Mo., U.S. D7 118
Castres, Fr. F8 16
Castries, St. Luc. C7 80
Castro, Braz. C7 72
Castro, Chile F2 69
Castro, co., Tx., U.S. B1 136
Castro Valley, Ca., U.S. h8 98
Castrovillari, Italy E6 18
Castroville, Tx., U.S. E3 136
Castuera, Spain H4 16
Caswell, co., N.C., U.S. A3 126
Cataguazes, Braz. C9 72
Catahoula, co., La., U.S. C4 111
Catahoula Lake, l., La., U.S. C3 111
Catalão, Braz. E2 74
Catalina, N.L., Can. D5 88
Catalina, Chile C3 69

Name | Map Ref. | Page

Catalunya, hist. reg., Spain **F7** 16
Catanduanes Island, i., Phil. **D8** 34
Catania, Italy **F5** 18
Catanzaro, Italy **E6** 18
Cataouatche, Lake, l., La., U.S. **k11** 111
Catarino Rodríguez, Mex. **C4** 78
Catarman, Phil. **D8** 34
Catasauqua, Pa., U.S. **E11** 131
Cataumet, Ma., U.S. **C6** 114
Catawba, co., N.C., U.S. **B1** 126
Catawba, stm., S.C., U.S. **B6** 133
Catawba, South Fork, stm., N.C., U.S. **B1** 126
Catawissa, Pa., U.S. **E9** 131
Catbalogan, Phil. **D8** 34
Catete, Ang. **E2** 54
Cathance, Lake, l., Me., U.S. **D5** 112
Cathedral City, Ca., U.S. **F5** 98
Cathedral of the Pines, rel., N.H., U.S. **E3** 122
Catherine, Lake, res., Ar., U.S. **C3** 97
Cat Island, i., Bah. **D9** 76
Cat Island, i., Ma., U.S. **f12** 114
Cat Island, i., Ms., U.S. **E4** 117
Cat Island, i., S.C., U.S. **E9** 133
Catlettsburg, Ky., U.S. **B7** 110
Catlin, Il., U.S. **C6** 106
Catnip Mountain, mtn., Nv., U.S. **B2** 121
Catoche, Cabo, c., Mex. **C7** 78
Catonsville, Md., U.S. **B4** 113
Catoosa, co., Ga., U.S. **B1** 103
Catoosa, Ok., U.S. **A6** 129
Catriló, Arg. **F5** 72
Catron, co., N.M., U.S. **D1** 124
Catskill, N.Y., U.S. **C7** 125
Catskill Mountains, mts., N.Y., U.S. **C6** 125
Catt, Mount, mtn., B.C., Can. **B3** 85
Cattaraugus, co., N.Y., U.S. **C2** 125
Cattaraugus Creek, stm., N.Y., U.S. **C2** 125
Cattaraugus Indian Reservation, N.Y., U.S. **C2** 125
Čatyrtaš, Kyrg. **A3** 40
Caubvick, Mount (Mont d'Iberville), mtn., Can. **f9** 88
Cauca, stm., Col. **B5** 70
Caucasia, Col. **D4** 80
Caucasus, mts. **A10** 44
Caucete, Arg. **E4** 72
Caucomgomoc Lake, l., Me., U.S. **B3** 112
Caungula, Ang. **E3** 54
Cauquenes, Chile **E2** 69
Caura, stm., Ven. **B7** 70
Cavalier, N.D., U.S. **A8** 127
Cavalier, co., N.D., U.S. **A7** 127
Cave City, Ar., U.S. **B4** 97
Cave City, Ky., U.S. **C4** 110
Cave Creek, Az., U.S. **D4** 96
Cave Junction, Or., U.S. **E3** 130
Cave Point, c., Wi., U.S. **D6** 142
Cave Run Lake, res., Ky., U.S. **B6** 110
Cave Spring, Ga., U.S. **B1** 103
Cave Spring, Va., U.S. **C2** 139
Cavetown, Md., U.S. **A2** 113
Caviana de Fora, Ilha, i., Braz. **A2** 74
Cavite, Phil. **D8** 34
Cawood, Ky., U.S. **D6** 110
Cawston, B.C., Can. **E8** 85
Caxias, Braz. **B3** 74
Caxias do Sul, Braz. **D7** 72
Caxito, Ang. **E2** 54
Cayambe, vol., Ec. **C4** 70
Cayce, S.C., U.S. **D5** 133
Cayenne, Fr. Gu. **C9** 70
Cayman Brac, i., Cay. Is. **B4** 80
Cayman Islands, dep., N.A. **E8** 76
Cayuga, In., U.S. **E3** 107
Cayuga, co., N.Y., U.S. **C4** 125
Cayuga Heights, N.Y., U.S. **C4** 125
Cayuga Lake, l., N.Y., U.S. **C4** 125
Cazenovia, N.Y., U.S. **C5** 125
Cazombo, Ang. **F4** 54
Ceará, state, Braz. **C4** 74
Ceará-Mirim, Braz. **C4** 74
Ceballos, Mex. **B4** 78
Čeboksary, Russia **D6** 26
Cebu, i., Phil. **D8** 34
Cebu, Phil. **D8** 34
Cecil, co., Md., U.S. **A6** 113
Cecil Field Naval Air Station, mil., Fl., U.S. **B5** 102
Cecilia, Ky., U.S. **C4** 110
Cecina, Italy **C3** 18
Čečnja, state, Russia **E6** 26
Cedar, co., Ia., U.S. **C6** 108
Cedar, co., Mo., U.S. **D4** 118
Cedar, stm., Ne., U.S. **B7** 120
Cedar, co., Ne., U.S. **B8** 120
Cedar, stm., Wa., U.S. **B4** 140
Cedar, stm., U.S. **C6** 108
Cedar Bluff, Al., U.S. **A4** 94
Cedar Bluff Reservoir, res., Ks., U.S. **D4** 109
Cedar Bluff Two, Tn., U.S. **D9** 135
Cedar Breaks National Monument, Ut., U.S. **F3** 137
Cedarburg, Wi., U.S. **E6** 142
Cedar City, Ut., U.S. **F2** 137
Cedar Creek, stm., N.D., U.S. **C3** 127
Cedar Creek, stm., N.J., U.S. **D4** 123
Cedar Creek, stm., Oh., U.S. **e7** 128
Cedar Creek Lake, res., Tx., U.S. **C4** 136
Cedar Crest, N.M., U.S. **k8** 124
Cedaredge, Co., U.S. **C3** 99
Cedar Falls, Ia., U.S. **B5** 108
Cedar Grove, N.J., U.S. **B4** 123
Cedar Grove, Wi., U.S. **E6** 142
Cedar Grove, W.V., U.S. **C3** 141
Cedar Hill, Mo., U.S. **g12** 118
Cedar Hill, Tx., U.S. **n10** 136
Cedarhurst, N.Y., U.S. **k13** 125
Cedar Island, i., N.C., U.S. **C6** 126
Cedar Island, i., S.C., U.S. **E9** 133
Cedar Island, i., Va., U.S. **C7** 139
Cedar Key, Fl., U.S. **C3** 102
Cedar Keys, is., Fl., U.S. **C3** 102
Cedar Lake, res., Mb., Can. **C1** 86
Cedar Lake, res., Il., U.S. **F4** 106
Cedar Lake, In., U.S. **B3** 107
Cedar Mountain, mtn., Ca., U.S. **B3** 98
Cedar Point, c., Md., U.S. **D5** 113
Cedar Point, c., Oh., U.S. **e7** 128
Cedar Point, c., Oh., U.S. **A3** 128
Cedar Rapids, Ia., U.S. **C6** 108
Cedar Springs, Mi., U.S. **E5** 115
Cedartown, Ga., U.S. **B1** 103
Cedar Vale, Ks., U.S. **E7** 109
Cedarville, Oh., U.S. **C2** 128
Cedros, Isla, i., Mex. **B1** 78
Ceduna, Austl. **G5** 60
Ceerigaabo, Som. **H14** 48
Cefalonia see Kefallinía, i., Grc. **E8** 18
Cefalù, Italy **F5** 18
Čegdomyn, Russia **D15** 26
Cegléd, Hung. **F5** 20
Čehov, Russia **A4** 31
Čehov, Russia **B14** 20
Çekerek, stm., Tur. **C6** 44
Çekerek, Tur. **B6** 44
Celaya, Mex. **C4** 78
Celebes see Sulawesi, i., Indon. **D6** 36
Celebes Basin **H15** 64
Celebes Sea, Asia **C6** 36
Çeleken, Turk. **C6** 42
Celina, Oh., U.S. **B1** 128
Celina, Tn., U.S. **C8** 135
Celina, Tx., U.S. **C4** 136
Čeljabinsk, Russia **D8** 26
Celje, Slvn. **A5** 18
Čeljuskin, mys, c., Russia **B12** 26
Čelkar, Kaz. **E7** 26
Celle, Ger. **D11** 12
Celtic Sea, Eur. **B3** 16
Cement, Ok., U.S. **C3** 129
Cementon, Pa., U.S. **E10** 131
Cenderawasih, Teluk, b., Indon. **G10** 32
Cenderawasih Bay see Cenderawasih, Teluk, b., Indon. **G10** 32
Centennial Mountains, mts., Id., U.S. **E7** 105
Center, Co., U.S. **D4** 99
Center, N.D., U.S. **B4** 127
Center, Tx., U.S. **D5** 136
Centerbrook, Ct., U.S. **D6** 100
Centerburg, Oh., U.S. **B3** 128
Centereach, N.Y., U.S. **n15** 125
Centerfield, Ut., U.S. **D4** 137
Center Hill Lake, res., Tn., U.S. **C8** 135
Center Moriches, N.Y., U.S. **n16** 125
Center Mountain, mtn., Id., U.S. **D3** 105
Center Point, Al., U.S. **f7** 94
Center Point, Ia., U.S. **B6** 108
Centerville, Ia., U.S. **D5** 108
Centerville, In., U.S. **E8** 107
Centerville, La., U.S. **E4** 111
Centerville, Ma., U.S. **C7** 114
Centerville, Oh., U.S. **C1** 128
Centerville, Pa., U.S. **F2** 131
Centerville, S.D., U.S. **D9** 134
Centerville, Tn., U.S. **B4** 135
Centerville, Ut., U.S. **C4** 137
Central, Phil. **D8** 34
Central, N.M., U.S. **E1** 124
Central, S.C., U.S. **B2** 133
Central, Cordillera, mts., Col. **E4** 80
Central, Cordillera, mts., Peru **E4** 70
Central, Massif, mts., Fr. **E8** 16
Central, Sistema, mts., Spain **G4** 16
Central African Republic, ctry., Afr. **B3** 54
Central City, Co., U.S. **B5** 99
Central City, Ia., U.S. **B6** 108
Central City, Il., U.S. **E4** 106
Central City, Ky., U.S. **C2** 110
Central City, Ne., U.S. **C7** 120
Central City, Pa., U.S. **F4** 131
Central Falls, R.I., U.S. **B4** 132
Central Heights, Az., U.S. **D5** 96
Centralia, Il., U.S. **E4** 106
Centralia, Mo., U.S. **B5** 118
Centralia, Wa., U.S. **C3** 140
Central Islip, N.Y., U.S. **n15** 125
Central Lake, Mi., U.S. **C5** 115
Central Makrān Range, mts., Pak. **E8** 42
Central Pacific Basin **G21** 64
Central Park, Wa., U.S. **C2** 140
Central Point, Or., U.S. **E4** 130
Central Siberian Uplands see Srednesibirskoe ploskogor'e, plat., Russia **C12** 26
Central Square, N.Y., U.S. **B4** 125
Central Valley, Ca., U.S. **B2** 98
Central Valley, N.Y., U.S. **D6** 125
Central Village, Ct., U.S. **C8** 100
Centre, Al., U.S. **A4** 94
Centre, co., Pa., U.S. **E6** 131
Centre Hall, Pa., U.S. **E6** 131
Centreville, Al., U.S. **C2** 94
Centreville, Il., U.S. **E3** 106
Centreville, Md., U.S. **B5** 113
Centreville, Mi., U.S. **G5** 115
Centreville, Ms., U.S. **D2** 117
Centuria, Wi., U.S. **C1** 142
Century, Fl., U.S. **u14** 102
Ceos see Kéa, i., Grc. **F10** 18
Ceram see Seram, i., Indon. **D7** 36
Ceram Sea see Seram, Laut, Indon. **D7** 36
Cerbat Mountains, mts., Az., U.S. **B1** 96
Cerdas, Bol. **C4** 72
Ceredo, W.V., U.S. **C2** 141
Čeremhovo, Russia **D12** 26
Čerepovec, Russia **D5** 26
Ceres, Arg. **D5** 72
Ceres, Braz. **E2** 74
Ceres, Ca., U.S. **D3** 98
Ceresco, Ne., U.S. **C9** 120
Cerignola, Italy **D5** 18
Čerkessk, Russia **E6** 26
Čerlak, Russia **D9** 26
Čermoz, Russia **C10** 22
Cernavodă, Rom. **G10** 20
Černjahovsk, Russia **B6** 20
Černjanka, Russia **D14** 20
Černobyl', Ukr. **D11** 20
Černuška, Russia **C10** 22
Černyševskij, Russia **C13** 26
Cerralvo, Isla, i., Mex. **C3** 78
Cerritos, Mex. **C4** 78
Cerro Azul, Peru **A2** 72
Cerro de Pasco, Peru **F4** 70
Cerro Gordo, co., Ia., U.S. **A4** 108
Cerro Gordo, Il., U.S. **D5** 106
Čerskij, Russia **C18** 26
Čerskogo, hrebet, mts., Russia **C15** 26
Červen', Bela. **C10** 20
Cervino see Matterhorn, mtn., Eur. **A1** 18
Cesena, Italy **B4** 18
Cēsis, Lat. **H11** 10
České Budějovice, Czech Rep. **E3** 20
Çeşme, Tur. **C2** 44
Češskaja guba, b., Russia **A8** 22
Cessnock, Austl. **G5** 62
Cetinje, Serb. **C7** 18
Ceuta, Sp. N. Afr. **J4** 16
Cévennes, reg., Fr. **E8** 16
Ceyhan, stm., Tur. **D6** 44
Ceyhan, Tur. **D6** 44
Ceylanpınar, Tur. **D9** 44
Ceylon see Sri Lanka, ctry., Asia **H4** 40
Cha-am, Thai. **D3** 34
Chachani, Nevado, vol., Peru **G5** 70
Chachapoyas, Peru **E4** 70
Chachoengsao, Thai. **D4** 34
Chaco, stm., N.M., U.S. **A1** 124
Chaco Austral, reg., Arg. **D5** 72
Chaco Boreal, reg., Para. **C5** 72
Chaco Central, reg., Arg. **C5** 72
Chaco Culture National Historic Park, N.M., U.S. **A2** 124
Chacon, Cape, c., Ak., U.S. **n24** 95
Chad, ctry., Chad **G8** 48
Chad, Lake, l., Afr. **D7** 50
Chadbourn, N.C., U.S. **C4** 126
Chadds Ford, Pa., U.S. **G10** 131
Chadron, Ne., U.S. **B3** 120
Chadwicks, N.Y., U.S. **B5** 125
Chaffee, co., Co., U.S. **C4** 99
Chaffee, Mo., U.S. **D8** 118
Chaffin, Ma., U.S. **B4** 114
Chaghcharān, Afg. **D9** 42
Chagos Archipelago, is., B.I.O.T. **I10** 64
Chagos-Laccadive Plateau **I10** 64
Chagrin Falls, Oh., U.S. **A4** 128
Chaguaramas, Ven. **D6** 80
Chai Nat, Thai. **C4** 34
Chaiyaphum, Thai. **C4** 34
Chajarí, Arg. **E6** 72
Chakachamna Lake, l., Ak., U.S. **g15** 95
Chakari, Zimb. **B4** 56
Chakasija, state, Russia **A5** 28
Chala, Peru **B3** 72
Chalatenango, El Sal. **C2** 80
Chalbi Desert, des., Kenya **C7** 54
Chalcidice see Khalkidhikí, hist. reg., Grc. **D9** 18
Chalcis see Khalkís, Grc. **E9** 18
Chaleur Bay, b., Can. **B4** 87
Chalfonte, De., U.S. **h7** 101
Chalk River, On., Can. **A7** 89
Challapata, Bol. **B4** 72
Challenger Deep **G17** 64
Challis, Id., U.S. **E4** 105
Chalmette, La., U.S. **E6** 111
Châlons-en-Champagne, Fr. **C9** 16
Chalon-sur-Saône, Fr. **D9** 16
Chālūs, Iran **C6** 42
Chama, N.M., U.S. **A3** 124
Chama, Rio, stm., N.M., U.S. **A3** 124
Chaman, Pak. **D9** 42
Chambal, stm., India **D3** 40
Chamberlain, S.D., U.S. **D6** 134
Chamberlain Lake, l., Me., U.S. **B3** 112
Chamberlin, Mount, mtn., Ak., U.S. **B10** 95
Chambers, co., Al., U.S. **C4** 94
Chambers, co., Tx., U.S. **E5** 136
Chambersburg, Pa., U.S. **G6** 131
Chambers Island, i., Wi., U.S. **C6** 142
Chambéry, Fr. **E9** 16
Chambi, Jebel, mtn., Tun. **C6** 48
Chamblee, Ga., U.S. **h8** 103
Chambly, Qc., Can. **D4** 90
Chamical, Arg. **E4** 72
Chamisal, N.M., U.S. **A4** 124
Chāmpa, India **E4** 40
Champagne, hist. reg., Fr. **C9** 16
Champaign, Il., U.S. **C5** 106
Champaign, co., Il., U.S. **C5** 106
Champaign, co., Oh., U.S. **B2** 128
Champasak, Laos **D5** 34
Champion, Oh., U.S. **A5** 128
Champlain, Lake, l., N.A. **C13** 92
Champlin, Mn., U.S. **m12** 116
Champotón, Mex. **D6** 78
Chañaral, Chile **C2** 69
Chance, Md., U.S. **D6** 113
Chanchelulla Peak, mtn., Ca., U.S. **B2** 98
Chandalar, stm., Ak., U.S. **B10** 95
Chandeleur Islands, is., La., U.S. **E7** 111
Chandeleur Sound, strt., La., U.S. **E6** 111
Chandīgarh, India **C3** 40
Chandler, Qc., Can. **k14** 90
Chandler, Az., U.S. **D4** 96
Chandler, In., U.S. **H3** 107
Chandler, Ok., U.S. **B5** 129
Chandler, Tx., U.S. **C5** 136
Chandler Heights, Az., U.S. **m9** 96
Chāndpur, Bngl. **E6** 40
Chandrapur, India **F3** 40
Chang (Yangtze), stm., China **E9** 28
Chang, Ko, i., Thai. **D4** 34
Changane, stm., Moz. **C5** 56
Changara, Moz. **B5** 56
Chang Cheng (Great Wall), China **B2** 30
Changchun, China **C13** 28
Changde, China **F10** 28
Changhua, Tai. **E5** 30
Changji, China **C5** 28
Changjiang, China **H9** 28
Changli, China **B4** 30
Changmar, China **E3** 28
Changning, China **B3** 34
Changsha, China **F10** 28
Changshu, China **C5** 30
Changting, China **F11** 28
Changwu, China **B2** 30
Changzhi, China **D10** 28
Changzhou, China **E12** 28
Chanhassen, Mn., U.S. **n11** 116
Channahon, Il., U.S. **B5** 106
Channel Islands, is., Eur. **C5** 16
Channel Islands National Park, Ca., U.S. **F4** 98
Channel Lake, Il., U.S. **H8** 106
Channel-Port-aux-Basques, N.L., Can. **E2** 88
Channelview, Tx., U.S. **r14** 136
Chanthaburi, Thai. **D4** 34
Chantilly, Va., U.S. **g12** 139
Chanute, Ks., U.S. **E8** 109
Chao'an, China **G11** 28
Chao Hu, l., China **E11** 28
Chaoxian, China **C4** 30
Chaoyang, China **E4** 30
Chaoyang, China **C12** 28
Chapadinha, Braz. **B3** 74
Chapala, Laguna de, l., Mex. **C4** 78
Chaparral, Col. **E4** 80
Chapecó, Braz. **D7** 72
Chapel Hill, N.C., U.S. **B3** 126
Chapel Hill, Tn., U.S. **B5** 135
Chaplin, stm., Ky., U.S. **C4** 110
Chaplin Lake, l., Sk., Can. **G2** 91
Chaplynka, Ukr. **F12** 20
Chapman, Ks., U.S. **D6** 109
Chapman Pond, l., R.I., U.S. **F1** 132
Chapmanville, W.V., U.S. **D2** 141
Chappaquiddick Island, i., Ma., U.S. **D7** 114
Chappell, Ne., U.S. **C3** 120
Charagua, Bol. **B5** 72
Chār Borjak, Afg. **D8** 42
Charcas, Mex. **C4** 78
Chardon, Oh., U.S. **A4** 128
Charenton, La., U.S. **E4** 111
Chari, stm., Afr. **H8** 48
Chārīkār, Afg. **C9** 42
Chariton, Ia., U.S. **C4** 108
Chariton, co., Mo., U.S. **B4** 118
Chariton, stm., U.S. **A5** 118
Charity, Guy. **B8** 70
Charleroi, Bel. **E9** 12
Charleroi, Pa., U.S. **F2** 131
Charles, stm., Ma., U.S. **B5** 114
Charles, co., Md., U.S. **C3** 113
Charles, Cape, c., Va., U.S. **C6** 139
Charles A. Goodwin Dam, Ct., U.S. **B3** 100
Charlesbourg, Qc., Can. **n17** 90
Charles City, Ia., U.S. **A5** 108
Charles City, co., Va., U.S. **C5** 139
Charles Mill Lake, res., Oh., U.S. **B3** 128
Charles Mix, co., S.D., U.S. **D7** 134
Charles Mound, Il., U.S. **A3** 106
Charleston, Ar., U.S. **B1** 97
Charleston, Il., U.S. **D5** 106
Charleston, Mo., U.S. **E8** 118
Charleston, Ms., U.S. **A3** 117
Charleston, Or., U.S. **D2** 130
Charleston, co., S.C., U.S. **F8** 133
Charleston, S.C., U.S. **F8** 133
Charleston, Tn., U.S. **D9** 135
Charleston, W.V., U.S. **C3** 141
Charleston Air Force Base, mil., S.C., U.S. **k11** 133
Charleston Naval Shipyard, mil., S.C., U.S. **k12** 133
Charleston Peak, mtn., Nv., U.S. **G6** 121
Charlestown, In., U.S. **H6** 107
Charlestown, N.H., U.S. **D2** 122
Charlestown, R.I., U.S. **F2** 132
Charles Town, W.V., U.S. **B7** 141
Charleville, Austl. **F4** 62
Charleville-Mézières, Fr. **C9** 16
Charlevoix, Mi., U.S. **C5** 115
Charlevoix, co., Mi., U.S. **C5** 115
Charlevoix, Lake, l., Mi., U.S. **C5** 115
Charlo, N.B., Can. **B3** 87
Charlotte, co., Fl., U.S. **F5** 102
Charlotte, Mi., U.S. **F6** 115
Charlotte, N.C., U.S. **B2** 126
Charlotte, Tn., U.S. **A4** 135
Charlotte, Tx., U.S. **E3** 136
Charlotte, co., Va., U.S. **C4** 139
Charlotte Amalie, V.I.U.S. **B6** 80
Charlotte Hall, Md., U.S. **D4** 113
Charlotte Harbor, Fl., U.S. **F4** 102
Charlotte Harbor, b., Fl., U.S. **F4** 102
Charlottesville, Va., U.S. **B4** 139
Charlottetown, P.E., Can. **C6** 87
Charlton, co., Ga., U.S. **F4** 103
Charmco, W.V., U.S. **C4** 141
Charny, Qc., Can. **C6** 90
Charters Towers, Austl. **E4** 62
Chartres, Fr. **C7** 16
Chascomús, Arg. **F6** 72
Chase, B.C., Can. **D8** 85
Chase, co., Ks., U.S. **D7** 109
Chase, Md., U.S. **B5** 113
Chase, co., Ne., U.S. **D4** 120
Chase City, Va., U.S. **D4** 139
Chaska, Mn., U.S. **F5** 116
Chassahowitzka Bay, b., Fl., U.S. **D4** 102
Chassell, Mi., U.S. **B2** 115
Châteaubriant, Fr. **D6** 16
Châteaudun, Fr. **C7** 16
Châteauguay, Qc., Can. **D4** 90
Château-Richer, Qc., Can. **C6** 90
Châteauroux, Fr. **D7** 16
Châtellerault, Fr. **D7** 16
Chatfield, Mn., U.S. **G6** 116
Chatham, N.B., Can. **B4** 87
Chatham, On., Can. **E2** 89
Chatham, co., Ga., U.S. **E5** 103
Chatham, Il., U.S. **D4** 106
Chatham, La., U.S. **B3** 111
Chatham, Ma., U.S. **C8** 114
Chatham, co., N.C., U.S. **B3** 126
Chatham, N.J., U.S. **B4** 123
Chatham, N.Y., U.S. **C7** 125
Chatham, Va., U.S. **D3** 139
Chatham Islands, is., N.Z. **I12** 58
Chatham Rise **M21** 64
Chatham Strait, strt., Ak., U.S. **m22** 95
Châtillon-sur-Seine, Fr. **D9** 16
Chatom, Al., U.S. **D1** 94
Chatsworth, Ga., U.S. **B2** 103
Chatsworth, Il., U.S. **C5** 106
Chatsworth Reservoir, res., Ca., U.S. **m11** 98
Chattahoochee, Fl., U.S. **B2** 102
Chattahoochee, co., Ga., U.S. **D2** 103
Chattahoochee, stm., U.S. **E1** 103
Chattanooga, Tn., U.S. **D8** 135

Name — Map Ref. — Page

Chattaroy, W.V., U.S. **D2** 141
Chattooga, co., Ga., U.S. **B1** 103
Chattooga, stm., U.S. **B1** 133
Chatuge Lake, res., U.S. **g9** 126
Chaudière, stm., Qc., Can. **C7** 90
Chauk, Mya. **B2** 34
Chaumont, Fr. **C9** 16
Chauncey, Oh., U.S. **C3** 128
Chauny, Fr. **C8** 16
Chautauqua, co., Ks., U.S. **E7** 109
Chautauqua, co., N.Y., U.S. **C1** 125
Chautauqua Lake, l., N.Y., U.S. **C1** 125
Chauvin, La., U.S. **E5** 111
Chaves, Port. **G3** 16
Chaves, co., N.M., U.S. **D5** 124
Cheaha Mountain, mtn., Al., U.S. **B4** 94
Cheat, Shavers Fork, stm., W.V., U.S. **B5** 141
Cheatham, co., Tn., U.S. **A4** 135
Cheb, Czech Rep. **D2** 20
Chebanse, Il., U.S. **C6** 106
Cheboygan, Mi., U.S. **C6** 115
Cheboygan, co., Mi., U.S. **C6** 115
Chech, 'Erg, des., Afr. **B4** 50
Chechaouen, Mor. **J4** 16
Chechnya see Čečnja, state, Russia **E6** 26
Checotah, Ok., U.S. **B6** 129
Chedabucto Bay, b., N.S., Can. **D8** 87
Cheduba Island, i., Mya. **C2** 34
Cheektowaga, N.Y., U.S. **C2** 125
Cheeseman Lake, res., Co., U.S. **B5** 99
Chehalem Mountains, mts., Or., U.S. **h12** 130
Chehalis, Wa., U.S. **C3** 140
Chehalis, stm., Wa., U.S. **C2** 140
Cheju, S. Kor. **E13** 28
Cheju-do, i., S. Kor. **E13** 28
Chekhov see Čehov, Russia **A4** 31
Chekhov see Čehov, Russia **B14** 20
Chelan, Wa., U.S. **B5** 140
Chelan, co., Wa., U.S. **B4** 140
Chelan, Lake, l., Wa., U.S. **A5** 140
Chelan Mountains, mts., Wa., U.S. **A5** 140
Chelif, Oued, stm., Alg. **D4** 14
Chełm, Pol. **D7** 20
Chełmno, Pol. **C5** 20
Chelmsford, Eng., U.K. **E7** 12
Chelmsford, Ma., U.S. **A5** 114
Chelsea, Qc., Can. **D2** 90
Chelsea, Al., U.S. **g7** 94
Chelsea, Ma., U.S. **B5** 114
Chelsea, Mi., U.S. **F6** 115
Chelsea, Ok., U.S. **A6** 129
Cheltenham, Eng., U.K. **E5** 12
Cheltenham, Md., U.S. **C4** 113
Chelyabinsk see Čeljabinsk, Russia **D8** 26
Chelyan, W.V., U.S. **C3** 141
Chemba, Moz. **B5** 56
Chemehuevi Indian Reservation, Ca., U.S. **E6** 98
Chemnitz, Ger. **E13** 12
Chemquasabamticook Lake (Ross Lake), l., Me., U.S. **B3** 112
Chemung, co., N.Y., U.S. **C4** 125
Chemung, stm., Pa., U.S. **C8** 131
Chemung Lake, l., On., Can. **C6** 89
Chenāb, stm., Asia **C2** 40
Chenango, stm., N.Y., U.S. **C5** 125
Chenango, co., N.Y., U.S. **C5** 125
Chenango Bridge, N.Y., U.S. **C5** 125
Chenes, River Aux, b., La., U.S. **k12** 111
Chénéville, Qc., Can. **D2** 90
Cheney, Ks., U.S. **E6** 109
Cheney, Wa., U.S. **B8** 140
Cheney Reservoir, res., Ks., U.S. **E6** 109
Cheneyville, La., U.S. **C3** 111
Chengde, China **C11** 28
Chengdu, China **E8** 28
Chengmai, China **F2** 30
Chengshan Jiao, c., China **D12** 28
Chengxian, China **C2** 30
Chennai (Madras), India **G4** 40
Chenoa, Il., U.S. **C5** 106
Chenoweth, Or., U.S. **B5** 130
Chenxi, China **D3** 30
Chenzhou, China **F10** 28
Chepachet, R.I., U.S. **B2** 132
Chepachet, stm., R.I., U.S. **B2** 132
Chequamegon Bay, b., Wi., U.S. **B3** 142
Cher, stm., Fr. **D7** 16
Cheraw, S.C., U.S. **B8** 133
Cherbaniani Reef, rf., India **G2** 40
Cherbourg, Fr. **C6** 16
Cherchell, Alg. **I8** 16
Chergui, Chott ech, l., Alg. **D5** 48
Cherkasy, Ukr. **E11** 20
Cherkessia see Karačaevo-Čerkesija, state, Russia **E6** 26
Cherniakhiv, Ukr. **D10** 20
Chernihiv, Ukr. **D11** 20
Chernivtsi, Ukr. **E8** 20
Chernobyl see Černobyl', Ukr. **D11** 20
Cherokee, Al., U.S. **A2** 94
Cherokee, co., Al., U.S. **A4** 94
Cherokee, co., Ga., U.S. **B2** 103
Cherokee, Ia., U.S. **B2** 108
Cherokee, co., Ia., U.S. **B2** 108
Cherokee, co., Ks., U.S. **E9** 109
Cherokee, Ks., U.S. **E9** 109
Cherokee, co., N.C., U.S. **f8** 126
Cherokee, Ok., U.S. **A3** 129
Cherokee, co., Ok., U.S. **B6** 129
Cherokee, co., S.C., U.S. **A4** 133
Cherokee, co., Tx., U.S. **D5** 136
Cherokee Indian Reservation, N.C., U.S. **f9** 126
Cherokee Lake, res., Tn., U.S. **C10** 135
Cherokees, Lake O' The, res., Ok., U.S. **A7** 129
Cherokee Village, Ar., U.S. **A4** 97
Cherry, co., Ne., U.S. **B4** 120
Cherry Creek, stm., S.D., U.S. **C3** 134
Cherry Hill, N.J., U.S. **D2** 123
Cherry Point, c., Va., U.S. **C6** 139
Cherry Point Marine Corps Air Station, mil., N.C., U.S. **C6** 126
Cherryvale, Ks., U.S. **E8** 109
Cherry Valley, Ar., U.S. **B5** 97
Cherry Valley, Il., U.S. **A5** 106
Cherryville, N.C., U.S. **B1** 126
Cherskiy Mountains see Čerskogo, hrebet, mts., Russia **C15** 26
Chervonohrad, Ukr. **D8** 20
Chesaning, Mi., U.S. **E6** 115
Chesapeake, Oh., U.S. **D3** 128
Chesapeake, Va., U.S. **D6** 139
Chesapeake, W.V., U.S. **C3** 141
Chesapeake and Delaware Canal, U.S. **B3** 101
Chesapeake Bay, b., U.S. **D12** 92
Chesapeake Bay Bridge-Tunnel, Va., U.S. **D7** 139
Chesapeake Beach, Md., U.S. **C4** 113
Chesapeake City, Md., U.S. **A6** 113
Chesdin, Lake, res., Va., U.S. **C5** 139
Chesha Bay see Češskaja guba, b., Russia **A8** 22
Cheshire, Ct., U.S. **D4** 100
Cheshire, co., N.H., U.S. **E2** 122
Cheshire Reservoir, res., Ma., U.S. **A1** 114
Chesley, On., Can. **C3** 89
Chesnee, S.C., U.S. **A4** 133
Chester, Eng., U.K. **D5** 12
Chester, Ca., U.S. **B3** 98
Chester, Ct., U.S. **D6** 100
Chester, Ga., U.S. **D3** 103
Chester, Il., U.S. **F4** 106
Chester, Md., U.S. **C5** 113
Chester, stm., Md., U.S. **B5** 113
Chester, Mt., U.S. **B6** 119
Chester, N.H., U.S. **E4** 122
Chester, N.Y., U.S. **D6** 125
Chester, Pa., U.S. **G11** 131
Chester, co., Pa., U.S. **G10** 131
Chester, S.C., U.S. **B5** 133
Chester, co., S.C., U.S. **B5** 133
Chester, co., Tn., U.S. **B3** 135
Chester, Va., U.S. **C5** 139
Chester, Vt., U.S. **E3** 138
Chester, W.V., U.S. **A4** 141
Chester Basin, N.S., Can. **E5** 87
Chester Depot, Vt., U.S. **E3** 138
Chesterfield, In., U.S. **D6** 107
Chesterfield, S.C., U.S. **B7** 133
Chesterfield, co., S.C., U.S. **B7** 133
Chesterfield, co., Va., U.S. **C5** 139
Chesterton, In., U.S. **A3** 107
Chestertown, Md., U.S. **B5** 113
Chesterville, On., Can. **B9** 89
Chesuncook Lake, l., Me., U.S. **C3** 112
Cheswick, Pa., U.S. **h14** 131
Cheswold, De., U.S. **D3** 101
Cheta see Heta, stm., Russia **B11** 26
Chetac, Lake, l., Wi., U.S. **C2** 142
Chetco, stm., Or., U.S. **E2** 130
Chetek, Wi., U.S. **C2** 142
Chetek, Lake, l., Wi., U.S. **C2** 142
Chetopa, Ks., U.S. **E8** 109
Chetumal, Mex. **D7** 78
Chetumal, Bahía, b., N.A. **B2** 80
Chetwynd, B.C., Can. **B7** 85
Chevak, Ak., U.S. **C6** 95
Cheviot, Oh., U.S. **C1** 128
Chevreuil, Point, c., La., U.S. **E4** 111
Chevy Chase, Md., U.S. **C3** 113
Chewack, stm., Wa., U.S. **A5** 140
Chewelah, Wa., U.S. **A8** 140
Cheyenne, co., Co., U.S. **C8** 99
Cheyenne, co., Ks., U.S. **C2** 109
Cheyenne, co., Ne., U.S. **C2** 120
Cheyenne, Ok., U.S. **B2** 129
Cheyenne, Wy., U.S. **E8** 143
Cheyenne, stm., U.S. **C7** 92
Cheyenne, stm., U.S. **C4** 134
Cheyenne, Dry Fork, stm., Wy., U.S. **C7** 143
Cheyenne River Indian Reservation, S.D., U.S. **B4** 134
Cheyenne Wells, Co., U.S. **C8** 99
Chhapra, India **D4** 40
Chhatarpur, India **E3** 40
Chhatrapur, India **F5** 40
Chhattisgarh, state, India **E4** 40
Chhindwāra, India **E3** 40
Chi, stm., Thai. **C4** 34
Chiai, Tai. **E5** 30
Chiange, Ang. **B1** 56
Chiang Kham, Thai. **C4** 34
Chiang Khan, Thai. **C4** 34
Chiang Mai, Thai. **C3** 34
Chiang Rai, Thai. **C3** 34
Chiapas, state, Mex. **D6** 78
Chiba, Japan **C4** 31
Chiblow Lake, l., On., Can. **A1** 89
Chibougamau, Qc., Can. **k12** 90
Chibuto, Moz. **C5** 56
Chicago, Il., U.S. **B6** 106
Chicago Heights, Il., U.S. **B6** 106
Chicago Sanitary and Ship Canal, Il., U.S. **k8** 106
Chicamacomico, stm., Md., U.S. **D6** 113
Chicapa, stm., Afr. **E4** 54
Chichagof Island, i., Ak., U.S. **m22** 95
Chichén Itzá, hist., Mex. **C7** 78
Chickahominy, stm., Va., U.S. **C5** 139
Chickamauga, Ga., U.S. **B1** 103
Chickamauga and Chattanooga National Military Park, U.S. **k11** 135
Chickamauga Dam, Tn., U.S. **h11** 135
Chickamauga Lake, res., Tn., U.S. **D8** 135
Chickasaw, Al., U.S. **E1** 94
Chickasaw, co., Ia., U.S. **A5** 108
Chickasaw, co., Ms., U.S. **B5** 117
Chickasawhay, stm., Ms., U.S. **D5** 117
Chickasaw National Recreation Area, Ok., U.S. **C5** 129
Chickasha, Ok., U.S. **B4** 129
Chickasha, Lake, res., Ok., U.S. **B3** 129
Chickwolnepy Stream, stm., N.H., U.S. **A4** 122
Chiclayo, Peru **E4** 70
Chico, stm., Arg. **F3** 69
Chico, Ca., U.S. **C3** 98
Chicomba, Ang. **A1** 56
Chicopee, Ga., U.S. **B3** 103
Chicopee, Ma., U.S. **B2** 114
Chicora, Pa., U.S. **E2** 131
Chicot, Lake, l., Ar., U.S. **D4** 97
Chicot Island, i., La., U.S. **E6** 111
Chicoutimi, Qc., Can. **A6** 90
Chicoutimi, stm., Qc., Can. **A6** 90
Chidambaram, India **G3** 40
Chiefland, Fl., U.S. **C4** 102
Chieti, Italy **C5** 18
Chifeng, China **C11** 28
Chignecto, Cape, c., N.S., Can. **D5** 87
Chignecto Bay, b., Can. **D5** 87
Chigubo, Moz. **C5** 56
Chihli, Gulf of see Bo Hai, b., China **D11** 28
Chihuahua, Mex. **B3** 78
Chihuahua, state, Mex. **B3** 78
Chihuahuan Desert, des., N.A. **A3** 78
Chikaskia, stm., U.S. **A4** 129
Chik Ballāpur, India **G3** 40
Chikmagalūr, India **G3** 40
Chilās, Pak. **C10** 42
Childersburg, Al., U.S. **B3** 94
Childress, Tx., U.S. **B2** 136
Childress, co., Tx., U.S. **B2** 136
Chile, ctry., S.A. **D2** 69
Chilecito, Arg. **D4** 72
Chile Rise **L29** 64
Chilhowie, Va., U.S. **f10** 139
Chililabombwe, Zam. **A4** 56
Chilko, stm., B.C., Can. **D6** 85
Chilko Lake, l., B.C., Can. **D5** 85
Chillán, Chile **E2** 69
Chillicothe, Il., U.S. **C4** 106
Chillicothe, Mo., U.S. **B4** 118
Chillicothe, Oh., U.S. **C3** 128
Chilliwack, B.C., Can. **E7** 85
Chillum, Md., U.S. **f9** 113
Chiloé, Isla Grande de, i., Chile **F2** 69
Chiloquin, Or., U.S. **E5** 130
Chilpancingo de los Bravo, Mex. **D5** 78
Chilton, co., Al., U.S. **C3** 94
Chilton, Wi., U.S. **D5** 142
Chiluage, Ang. **E4** 54
Chilung, Tai. **D5** 30
Chimacum, Wa., U.S. **A3** 140
Chimayo, N.M., U.S. **A4** 124
Chimborazo, vol., Ec. **D4** 70
Chimbote, Peru **E4** 70
Chimney Rock, mtn., Ne., U.S. **C2** 120
Chimoio, Moz. **B5** 56
China, ctry., Asia **D8** 28
China Grove, N.C., U.S. **B2** 126
China Lake, l., Me., U.S. **D3** 112
Chinandega, Nic. **C2** 80
Chincha Alta, Peru **F4** 70
Chinchilla, Austl. **F5** 62
Chincoteague, Va., U.S. **C7** 139
Chincoteague Bay, b., U.S. **D7** 113
Chinde, Moz. **B6** 56
Chindwinn, stm., Mya. **A3** 34
Chingola, Zam. **A4** 56
Chinguețți, Maur. **B2** 50
Chin Hills, Mya. **B2** 34
Chinhoyi, Zimb. **B5** 56
Chinitna Point, c., Ak., U.S. **h15** 95
Chinju, S. Kor. **D13** 28
Chinle, Az., U.S. **A6** 96
Chino, Ca., U.S. **F5** 98
Chinook, Mt., U.S. **B7** 119
Chinook, Wa., U.S. **C2** 140
Chinook, Lake, res., Or., U.S. **C5** 130
Chino Valley, Az., U.S. **C3** 96
Chinsali, Zam. **A5** 56
Chinvali, Geor. **A10** 44
Chioco, Moz. **B5** 56
Chioggia, Italy **B4** 18
Chios see Khíos, Grc. **E11** 18
Chipata, Zam. **A5** 56
Chipita Park, Co., U.S. **C6** 99
Chipley, Fl., U.S. **u16** 102
Chipman, N.B., Can. **C4** 87
Chipola, stm., Fl., U.S. **B1** 102
Chippewa, co., Mi., U.S. **B6** 115
Chippewa, co., Mn., U.S. **E3** 116
Chippewa, stm., Mn., U.S. **E3** 116
Chippewa, stm., Wi., U.S. **D2** 142
Chippewa, co., Wi., U.S. **C2** 142
Chippewa, Lake, l., Wi., U.S. **C2** 142
Chippewa Falls, Wi., U.S. **D2** 142
Chipuxet, stm., R.I., U.S. **F3** 132
Chiquimula, Guat. **C2** 80
Chiquinquirá, Col. **B5** 70
Chirāla, India **F4** 40
Chirfa, Niger **B7** 50
Chiricahua Mountains, mts., Az., U.S. **E6** 96
Chiricahua National Monument, Az., U.S. **F6** 96
Chiricahua Peak, mtn., Az., U.S. **F6** 96
Chirikof Island, i., Ak., U.S. **D8** 95
Chiriquí, Golfo de, b., Pan. **D3** 80
Chiriquí, Laguna de, b., Pan. **D3** 80
Chiromo, Mwi. **B6** 56
Chirripó, Cerro, mtn., C.R. **D3** 80
Chisago, co., Mn., U.S. **E6** 116
Chisago City, Mn., U.S. **E6** 116
Ch'ishan, Tai. **E5** 30
Chisholm, Me., U.S. **D2** 112
Chisholm, Mn., U.S. **C6** 116
Chishui, stm., China **D2** 30
Chişinău, Mol. **F10** 20
Chisos Mountains, mts., Tx., U.S. **E1** 136
Chita see Čita, Russia **D13** 26
Chitado, Ang. **B1** 56
Chitato, Ang. **E4** 54
Chitembo, Ang. **F3** 54
Chitina, stm., Ak., U.S. **g19** 95
Chitose, Japan **B4** 31
Chitradurga, India **G3** 40
Chitrāl, Pak. **C10** 42
Chitré, Pan. **D3** 80
Chittagong, Bngl. **E6** 40
Chittaurgarh, India **E2** 40
Chittenango, N.Y., U.S. **B5** 125
Chittenden, co., Vt., U.S. **C2** 138
Chittenden Reservoir, res., Vt., U.S. **D3** 138
Chittoor, India **G3** 40
Chitungwiza, Zimb. **B5** 56
Chiumbe (Tshumbe), stm., Afr. **E4** 54
Chiume, Ang. **B3** 56
Chivacoa, Ven. **C6** 80
Chivilcoy, Arg. **E5** 72
Chŏâm Khsant, Camb. **D4** 34
Chocolate Mountains, mts., U.S. **F6** 98
Chocope, Peru **E4** 70
Choctaw, co., Al., U.S. **C1** 94
Choctaw, co., Ms., U.S. **B4** 117
Choctaw, Ok., U.S. **B4** 129
Choctaw, co., Ok., U.S. **C6** 129
Choctawhatchee Bay, b., Fl., U.S. **u15** 102
Choctaw Indian Reservation, Ms., U.S. **C4** 117
Choele Choel, Arg. **E3** 69
Chojnice, Pol. **C4** 20
Chókwe, Moz. **C5** 56
Cholet, Fr. **D6** 16
Choluteca, Hond. **C2** 80
Choluteca, stm., Hond. **C2** 80
Choma, Zam. **B4** 56
Chomutov, Czech Rep. **D2** 20
Chon Buri, Thai. **D4** 34
Chone, Ec. **D3** 70
Chong'an, China **D4** 30
Ch'ŏngjin, N. Kor. **C13** 28
Ch'ŏngju, S. Kor. **D13** 28
Chongqing, China **F9** 28
Chongqing, prov., China **E9** 28
Chongxin, China **B2** 30
Chongzuo, China **G9** 28
Chŏnju, S. Kor. **D13** 28
Chonos, Archipiélago de los, is., Chile **G2** 69
Choptank, stm., Md., U.S. **C6** 113
Chornomors'ke, Ukr. **G12** 20
Chortkiv, Ukr. **E8** 20
Chōshi, Japan **C4** 31
Chos Malal, Arg. **F3** 72
Choteau, Mt., U.S. **C4** 119
Chouteau, co., Mt., U.S. **C6** 119
Chouteau, Ok., U.S. **A6** 129
Chowan, stm., N.C., U.S. **A6** 126
Chowan, co., N.C., U.S. **A6** 126
Chowchilla, Ca., U.S. **D3** 98
Choybalsan, Mong. **B10** 28
Choyr, Mong. **B9** 28
Chrisman, Il., U.S. **D6** 106
Christchurch, N.Z. **p13** 63c
Christian, co., Il., U.S. **D4** 106
Christian, co., Ky., U.S. **D2** 110
Christian, co., Mo., U.S. **E4** 118
Christiana, De., U.S. **B3** 101
Christiana, Pa., U.S. **G9** 131
Christiansburg, Va., U.S. **C2** 139
Christian Sound, strt., Ak., U.S. **n22** 95
Christina, stm., Ab., Can. **A5** 84
Christina, stm., De., U.S. **B3** 101
Christina, Lake, l., Mn., U.S. **D3** 116
Christina Peak, mtn., Nv., U.S. **D6** 121
Christmas, Fl., U.S. **D5** 102
Christmas Island, i., Christ. I. **F4** 58
Christmas Island see Kiritimati, atoll, Kir. **D14** 58
Christmas Island, dep., Oc. **I4** 32
Christmas Lake, l., Or., U.S. **D6** 130
Christmas Ridge **G22** 64
Christopher, Il., U.S. **F4** 106
Chubbuck, Id., U.S. **G6** 105
Chubut, stm., Arg. **F3** 69
Chugach Islands, is., Ak., U.S. **h16** 95
Chugach Mountains, mts., Ak., U.S. **g18** 95
Chugwater, Wy., U.S. **E8** 143
Chugwater Creek, stm., Wy., U.S. **E8** 143
Chuhuïv, Ukr. **E14** 20
Chukchi Sea **E5** 82
Chukotsk Peninsula see Čukotskij poluostrov, pen., Russia **C20** 26
Chula Vista, Ca., U.S. **F5** 98
Chulucanas, Peru **E3** 70
Chumbicha, Arg. **D4** 72
Chumphon, Thai. **D3** 34
Chum Saeng, Thai. **C4** 34
Chunchula, Al., U.S. **E1** 94
Chungking see Chongqing, China **F9** 28
Chuntuquí, Guat. **B1** 80
Chupadera Mesa, mtn., N.M., U.S. **D3** 124
Chuquibamba, Peru **B3** 72
Chuquicamata, Chile **B3** 69
Chur, Switz. **A2** 18
Church Hill, Tn., U.S. **C11** 135
Churchill, Mb., Can. **f9** 86
Churchill, stm., N.L., Can. **h9** 88
Churchill, stm., Can. **G21** 82
Churchill, co., Nv., U.S. **D3** 121
Churchill, Cape, c., Mb., Can. **f9** 86
Churchill, Mount, mtn., B.C., Can. **E6** 85
Churchill Falls, wtfl., N.L., Can. **h8** 88
Churchill Lake, l., Sk., Can. **m7** 91
Churchill Lake, l., Me., U.S. **B3** 112
Church Point, La., U.S. **D3** 111
Church Rock, N.M., U.S. **B1** 124
Churchton, Md., U.S. **C4** 113
Churchville, N.Y., U.S. **B3** 125
Chūru, India **D2** 40
Churubusco, In., U.S. **B7** 107
Chuska Mountains, mts., Az., U.S. **A6** 96
Chuuk Islands, is., Micron. **D9** 58
Chuvashia see Čuvašija, state, Russia **D6** 26
Chuxian, China **C4** 30
Chuxiong, China **F8** 28
Cianjur, Indon. **E3** 36
Cianorte, Braz. **C7** 72
Čiatura, Geor. **A10** 44
Cibecue, Az., U.S. **C5** 96
Cibola, co., N.M., U.S. **C1** 124
Cibolo Creek, stm., Tx., U.S. **h7** 136
Cicero, Il., U.S. **B6** 106
Cicero, In., U.S. **D5** 107
Cide, Tur. **B5** 44
Ciechanów, Pol. **C6** 20
Ciego de Ávila, Cuba **A4** 80
Cienfuegos, Cuba **A3** 80
Cieza, Spain **H6** 16
Çifteler, Tur. **C4** 44
Čiganak, Kaz. **E9** 26
Cihanbeyli, Tur. **C5** 44
Čiili, Kaz. **B9** 42
Čikoj, stm., Asia **D12** 26
Cilacap, Indon. **E3** 36
Çıldır Gölü, l., Tur. **B10** 44

Name — Map Ref. — Page

Čilik, Kaz. B11 42
Cimarron, Ks., U.S. E3 109
Cimarron, N.M., U.S. A5 124
Cimarron, co., Ok., U.S. e8 129
Cimarron, stm., U.S. D8 92
Čimbaj, Uzb. B7 42
Cimljanskoe vodohranilišče, res., Russia E7 22
Cina, Tanjung, c., Indon. E2 36
Çınar, Tur. D9 44
Cincinnati, Oh., U.S. C1 128
Çine, Tur. D3 44
Cinnaminson, N.J., U.S. D3 123
Cintalapa, Mex. D6 78
Cinto, Monte, mtn., Fr. C2 18
Cintra, Golfe de, b., W. Sah. B1 50
Cipolletti, Arg. E3 69
Čirčik, Uzb. E8 26
Circle, Ak., U.S. B11 95
Circle, Mt., U.S. C11 119
Circle Pines, Mn., U.S. m12 116
Circleville, Oh., U.S. C3 128
Cirebon, Indon. E3 36
Cirò Marina, Italy E6 18
Cisco, Tx., U.S. C3 136
Ciskei, hist. reg., S. Afr. E4 56
Cisnădie, Rom. G8 20
Cispus, stm., Wa., U.S. C4 140
Cissna Park, Il., U.S. C6 106
Čistopol', Russia C9 22
Čita, Russia D13 26
Citlaltépetl, Volcán see Pico de Orizaba, Volcán, vol., Mex. D5 78
Citra, Fl., U.S. C4 102
Citronelle, Al., U.S. D1 94
Citrus, co., Fl., U.S. D4 102
City of Refuge National Historical Park, Hi., U.S. D5 104
City View, S.C., U.S. B3 133
Ciudad Acuña, Mex. B4 78
Ciudad Anáhuac, Mex. B4 78
Ciudad Bolívar, Ven. B7 70
Ciudad Camargo, Mex. B5 78
Ciudad Camargo, Mex. B3 78
Ciudad Constitución, Mex. C2 78
Ciudad del Carmen, Mex. D6 78
Ciudad del Este, Para. D7 72
Ciudad de Libertador General San Martín, Arg. C5 72
Ciudad de México (Mexico City), Mex. D5 78
Ciudad de Nutrias, Ven. D6 80
Ciudad Guayana, Ven. B7 70
Ciudad Juárez, Mex. A3 78
Ciudad Madero, Mex. C5 78
Ciudad Mante, Mex. C5 78
Ciudad Miguel Alemán, Mex. B5 78
Ciudad Netzahualcóyotl, Mex. D5 78
Ciudad Obregón, Mex. B3 78
Ciudad Ojeda, Ven. C5 80
Ciudad Real, Spain H5 16
Ciudad Rodrigo, Spain G3 16
Ciudad Valles, Mex. C5 78
Ciudad Victoria, Mex. C5 78
Ciutadella, Spain G8 16
Civitanova Marche, Italy C4 18
Civitavecchia, Italy C3 18
Çivril, Tur. C3 44
Cizre, Tur. D10 44
C.J. Strike Reservoir, res., Id., U.S. G3 105
Clackamas, Or., U.S. h12 130
Clackamas, co., Or., U.S. B4 130
Clacton-on-Sea, Eng., U.K. E7 12
Claflin, Ks., U.S. D5 109
Claiborne, co., La., U.S. B2 111
Claiborne, co., Ms., U.S. D3 117
Claiborne, co., Tn., U.S. C10 135
Claiborne, Lake, res., La., U.S. B3 111
Clair, N.B., Can. B1 87
Claire, Lake, l., Ab., Can. f8 84
Clair Engle Lake, res., Ca., U.S. B2 98
Clairton, Pa., U.S. F2 131
Clallam, co., Wa., U.S. B1 140
Clallam Bay, Wa., U.S. A1 140
Clam Lake, l., Wi., U.S. C1 142
Clan Alpine Mountains, mts., Nv., U.S. D4 121
Clanton, Al., U.S. C3 94
Clanwilliam, S. Afr. E2 56
Clara City, Mn., U.S. F3 116
Clara Peak, mtn., Az., U.S. C2 96
Clare, Mi., U.S. E6 115
Clare, co., Mi., U.S. E6 115
Claremont, Ca., U.S. m13 98
Claremont, mtn., Ca., U.S. C3 98
Claremont, N.C., U.S. B1 126
Claremont, N.H., U.S. D2 122
Claremore, Ok., U.S. A6 129
Clarence, Ia., U.S. C6 108
Clarence, Mo., U.S. B5 118
Clarence Strait, strt., Austl. C5 60
Clarence Strait, strt., Ak., U.S. n23 95
Clarendon, Ar., U.S. C4 97
Clarendon, co., S.C., U.S. D7 133
Clarendon, Tx., U.S. B2 136
Clarendon, stm., Vt., U.S. E2 138
Clarendon Hills, Il., U.S. k9 106
Clarenville, N.L., Can. D4 88
Claresholm, Ab., Can. D4 84
Claridge, Pa., U.S. F2 131
Clarinda, Ia., U.S. D2 108
Clarion, Ia., U.S. B4 108
Clarion, Pa., U.S. D3 131
Clarion, stm., Pa., U.S. D3 131
Clarion, co., Pa., U.S. D3 131
Clarión, Isla, i., Mex. D2 78
Clarion Fracture Zone G25 64
Clarissa, Mn., U.S. D4 116
Clark, co., Ar., U.S. C2 97
Clark, co., Id., U.S. E6 105
Clark, co., Il., U.S. D6 106
Clark, co., In., U.S. H6 107
Clark, co., Ks., U.S. E4 109
Clark, co., Ky., U.S. C5 110
Clark, co., Mo., U.S. A6 118
Clark, N.J., U.S. B4 123
Clark, co., Nv., U.S. G6 121
Clark, co., Oh., U.S. C2 128
Clark, S.D., U.S. C8 134
Clark, co., S.D., U.S. C8 134
Clark, co., Wa., U.S. D3 140
Clark, co., Wi., U.S. D3 142
Clark, Lake, l., Ak., U.S. C9 95
Clark, Point, c., On., Can. C3 89
Clarkdale, Az., U.S. C3 96
Clarkdale, Ga., U.S. h7 103
Clarke, co., Al., U.S. D2 94
Clarke, co., Ga., U.S. C3 103
Clarke, co., Ia., U.S. D4 108
Clarke, co., Ms., U.S. C5 117
Clarke, co., Va., U.S. A4 139
Clarke Island, i., Austl. I4 62
Clarkesville, Ga., U.S. B3 103
Clarkfield, Mn., U.S. F3 116
Clark Fork, stm., U.S. C1 119
Clarks, stm., Ky., U.S. f9 110
Clarks, La., U.S. B3 111
Clarksburg, Md., U.S. B3 113
Clarksburg, W.V., U.S. B4 141
Clarksdale, Ms., U.S. A3 117
Clarks Grove, Mn., U.S. G5 116
Clark's Harbour, N.S., Can. F4 87
Clarks Hill, In., U.S. D4 107
Clarks Hill Lake, res., U.S. E11 92
Clarkson, Ky., U.S. C3 110
Clarkson, Ne., U.S. C8 120
Clarks Summit, Pa., U.S. m18 131
Clarkston, Ga., U.S. h8 103
Clarkston, Mi., U.S. F7 115
Clarkston, Ut., U.S. B3 137
Clarkston, Wa., U.S. C8 140
Clarksville, Ar., U.S. B2 97
Clarksville, De., U.S. F5 101
Clarksville, Ia., U.S. B5 108
Clarksville, In., U.S. H6 107
Clarksville, Tn., U.S. A4 135
Clarksville, Tx., U.S. C5 136
Clarksville, Va., U.S. D4 139
Clarkton, Mo., U.S. E8 118
Clarkton, N.C., U.S. C4 126
Clatskanie, Or., U.S. A3 130
Clatsop, co., Or., U.S. A3 130
Claude, Tx., U.S. B2 136
Clawson, Mi., U.S. o15 115
Claxton, Ga., U.S. D5 103
Clay, co., Al., U.S. B4 94
Clay, co., Ar., U.S. A5 97
Clay, co., Fl., U.S. B5 102
Clay, co., Ga., U.S. E2 103
Clay, co., Ia., U.S. A2 108
Clay, co., Il., U.S. E5 106
Clay, co., In., U.S. F3 107
Clay, co., Ks., U.S. C6 109
Clay, co., Ky., U.S. C6 110
Clay, Ky., U.S. C2 110
Clay, co., Mn., U.S. D2 116
Clay, co., Mo., U.S. B3 118
Clay, co., Ms., U.S. B5 117
Clay, co., N.C., U.S. f9 126
Clay, co., Ne., U.S. D7 120
Clay, co., S.D., U.S. E8 134
Clay, co., Tn., U.S. C8 135
Clay, co., Tx., U.S. C3 136
Clay, co., W.V., U.S. C3 141
Clay Center, Ks., U.S. C6 109
Clay Center, Ne., U.S. D7 120
Clay City, Il., U.S. E5 106
Clay City, In., U.S. F3 107
Clay City, Ky., U.S. C6 110
Clay Creek, stm., S.D., U.S. D8 134
Claymont, De., U.S. A4 101
Clayoquot Sound, strt., B.C., Can. E4 85
Claypool, Az., U.S. D5 96
Claysburg, Pa., U.S. F5 131
Claysville, Pa., U.S. F1 131
Clayton, Al., U.S. D4 94
Clayton, De., U.S. C3 101
Clayton, Ga., U.S. B3 103
Clayton, co., Ga., U.S. C2 103
Clayton, co., Ia., U.S. B6 108
Clayton, In., U.S. E4 107
Clayton, La., U.S. C4 111
Clayton, Mo., U.S. f13 118
Clayton, N.C., U.S. B4 126
Clayton, N.J., U.S. D2 123
Clayton, N.M., U.S. A6 124
Clayton, N.Y., U.S. A4 125
Clayton, Ok., U.S. C6 129
Claytor Lake, res., Va., U.S. C2 139
Clear, stm., R.I., U.S. B2 132
Clear Boggy Creek, stm., Ok., U.S. C5 129
Clear Creek, co., Co., U.S. B5 99
Clear Creek, stm., Tn., U.S. C9 135
Clear Creek, stm., Wy., U.S. B6 143
Cleare, Cape, c., Ak., U.S. D10 95
Clearfield, Ky., U.S. B6 110
Clearfield, Pa., U.S. D5 131
Clearfield, co., Pa., U.S. D5 131
Clearfield, Ut., U.S. B3 137
Clear Fork, stm., W.V., U.S. D3 141
Clear Fork, stm., W.V., U.S. n13 141
Clearlake, Ca., U.S. C2 98
Clear Lake, res., Ca., U.S. C2 98
Clear Lake, Ia., U.S. A4 108
Clear Lake, l., Ia., U.S. A4 108
Clear Lake, S.D., U.S. C9 134
Clear Lake, l., Ut., U.S. D3 137
Clearlake, Wa., U.S. A3 140
Clear Lake, Wi., U.S. C1 142
Clear Lake Reservoir, res., Ca., U.S. B3 98
Clear Lake Shores, Tx., U.S. r15 136
Clear Stream, stm., N.H., U.S. g7 122
Clearwater, B.C., Can. D7 85
Clearwater, stm., Can. A5 84
Clearwater, Fl., U.S. E4 102
Clearwater, stm., Id., U.S. C2 105
Clearwater, co., Id., U.S. C3 105
Clearwater, Ks., U.S. E6 109
Clearwater, stm., Mn., U.S. C3 116
Clearwater, co., Mn., U.S. C3 116
Clearwater, S.C., U.S. E4 133
Clearwater Lake, res., Mo., U.S. D7 118
Clearwater Mountains, mts., Id., U.S. C2 105
Cleburne, co., Al., U.S. B4 94
Cleburne, co., Ar., U.S. B3 97
Cleburne, Tx., U.S. C4 136
Cle Elum, Wa., U.S. B5 140
Cle Elum, stm., Wa., U.S. B4 140
Cle Elum Lake, res., Wa., U.S. B4 140
Clementon, N.J., U.S. D3 123
Clemmons, N.C., U.S. A2 126
Clemson, S.C., U.S. B2 133
Clendenin, W.V., U.S. C3 141
Clendening Lake, res., Oh., U.S. B4 128
Cleona, Pa., U.S. F9 131
Clermont, Austl. E4 62
Clermont, Qc., Can. B7 90
Clermont, Fl., U.S. D5 102
Clermont, co., Oh., U.S. C1 128
Clermont-Ferrand, Fr. E8 16
Cleveland, Al., U.S. A3 94
Cleveland, co., Ar., U.S. D3 97
Cleveland, Ga., U.S. B3 103
Cleveland, Mn., U.S. F5 116
Cleveland, Ms., U.S. B3 117
Cleveland, N.C., U.S. B2 126
Cleveland, co., N.C., U.S. B1 126
Cleveland, Oh., U.S. A4 128
Cleveland, Ok., U.S. A5 129
Cleveland, co., Ok., U.S. B4 129
Cleveland, Tn., U.S. D9 135
Cleveland, Tx., U.S. D5 136
Cleveland, Wi., U.S. k10 142
Cleveland, Mount, mtn., Mt., U.S. B3 119
Cleveland Heights, Oh., U.S. A4 128
Cleves, Oh., U.S. o12 128
Clew Bay, b., Ire. D2 12
Clewiston, Fl., U.S. F6 102
Cliff Island, i., Me., U.S. g7 112
Clifford, On., Can. D4 89
Cliffside, N.C., U.S. B1 126
Cliffside Park, N.J., U.S. h9 123
Clifton, Az., U.S. D6 96
Clifton, Co., U.S. B2 99
Clifton, Il., U.S. C6 106
Clifton, N.J., U.S. B4 123
Clifton, S.C., U.S. B4 133
Clifton, Tn., U.S. B4 135
Clifton, Tx., U.S. D4 136
Clifton Forge, Va., U.S. C3 139
Clifton Knolls, N.Y., U.S. C7 125
Clifton Springs, N.Y., U.S. C3 125
Clinch, co., Ga., U.S. F4 103
Clinch, stm., U.S. D9 135
Clinchco, Va., U.S. e9 139
Clinch Mountain, mtn., U.S. C10 135
Clingmans Dome, mtn., U.S. D10 135
Clinton, B.C., Can. D7 85
Clinton, On., Can. D3 89
Clinton, Ar., U.S. B3 97
Clinton, Ct., U.S. D5 100
Clinton, Ia., U.S. C7 108
Clinton, co., Ia., U.S. C7 108
Clinton, Il., U.S. C5 106
Clinton, co., Il., U.S. E4 106
Clinton, In., U.S. E3 107
Clinton, co., In., U.S. D4 107
Clinton, Ky., U.S. f9 110
Clinton, co., Ky., U.S. D4 110
Clinton, La., U.S. D4 111
Clinton, Ma., U.S. B4 114
Clinton, Md., U.S. C4 113
Clinton, Me., U.S. D3 112
Clinton, Mi., U.S. F7 115
Clinton, co., Mi., U.S. F6 115
Clinton, Mo., U.S. C4 118
Clinton, co., Mo., U.S. B3 118
Clinton, Ms., U.S. C3 117
Clinton, N.C., U.S. C4 126
Clinton, N.Y., U.S. B5 125
Clinton, co., N.Y., U.S. f11 125
Clinton, co., Oh., U.S. C2 128
Clinton, Ok., U.S. B3 129
Clinton, co., Pa., U.S. D6 131
Clinton, S.C., U.S. C4 133
Clinton, Tn., U.S. C9 135
Clinton, Ut., U.S. B3 137
Clinton, Wa., U.S. B3 140
Clinton, Wi., U.S. F5 142
Clinton, Lake, res., Il., U.S. C5 106
Clinton Lake, res., Ks., U.S. m15 109
Clinton Reservoir, res., N.J., U.S. A4 123
Clintonville, Wi., U.S. D5 142
Clintwood, Va., U.S. e9 139
Clio, Al., U.S. D4 94
Clio, Mi., U.S. E7 115
Clio, S.C., U.S. B8 133
Clipperton, Île, atoll, Oc. G28 64
Clipperton Fracture Zone H25 64
Clive, Ia., U.S. e8 108
Clodomira, Arg. D5 72
Cloncurry, Austl. E3 62
Clonmel, Ire. D3 12
Cloquet, Mn., U.S. D6 116
Cloquet, stm., Mn., U.S. C6 116
Clorinda, Arg. D6 72
Closter, N.J., U.S. B5 123
Clothier, W.V., U.S. n12 141
Cloud, co., Ks., U.S. C6 109
Cloudcroft, N.M., U.S. E4 124
Cloud Peak, mtn., Wy., U.S. B5 143
Clover, S.C., U.S. A5 133
Cloverdale, Al., U.S. A2 94
Cloverdale, Ca., U.S. C2 98
Cloverdale, In., U.S. E4 107
Cloverport, Ky., U.S. C3 110
Clovis, Ca., U.S. D4 98
Clovis, N.M., U.S. C6 124
Cluj-Napoca, Rom. F7 20
Clute, Tx., U.S. r14 136
Clyde, Ks., U.S. C6 109
Clyde, N.C., U.S. f10 126
Clyde, N.Y., U.S. B4 125
Clyde, Oh., U.S. A3 128
Clyde, Tx., U.S. C3 136
Clyde, Firth of, b., Scot., U.K. C4 12
Clymer, Pa., U.S. E3 131
Cnossus see Knossós, hist., Grc. G10 18
Coachella, Ca., U.S. F5 98
Coachella Canal, Ca., U.S. F6 98
Coahoma, co., Ms., U.S. A3 117
Coahoma, Tx., U.S. C2 136
Coahuila, state, Mex. B4 78
Coal, co., Ok., U.S. C5 129
Coal, stm., W.V., U.S. C3 141
Coal Branch, N.B., Can. C4 87
Coal City, Il., U.S. B5 106
Coal Creek, stm., Ok., U.S. B6 129
Coaldale, Ab., Can. E4 84
Coal Fork, W.V., U.S. C3 141
Coal Fork, stm., W.V., U.S. m13 141
Coalgate, Ok., U.S. C5 129
Coal Grove, Oh., U.S. D3 128
Coal Hill, Ar., U.S. B2 97
Coalhurst, Ab., Can. E4 84
Coalinga, Ca., U.S. D3 98
Coalmont, Tn., U.S. D8 135
Coalville, Ut., U.S. C4 137
Coalwood, W.V., U.S. D3 141
Coaraci, Braz. D4 74
Coari, Braz. D7 70
Coasters Harbor Island, i., R.I., U.S. E5 132
Coast Mountains, mts., N.A. G13 82
Coast Ranges, mts., U.S. C3 92
Coatesville, Pa., U.S. G10 131
Coaticook, Qc., Can. D6 90
Coats, N.C., U.S. B4 126
Coats Land, reg., Ant. D2 67
Coatzacoalcos, Mex. D6 78
Cobalt, On., Can. p19 89
Cobán, Guat. B1 80
Cobar, Austl. G4 62
Cobb, co., Ga., U.S. C2 103
Cobb, stm., Mn., U.S. G5 116
Cobble Mountain Reservoir, res., Ma., U.S. B2 114
Cobbosseecontee Lake, l., Me., U.S. D3 112
Cobden, On., Can. B8 89
Cobden, Il., U.S. F4 106
Cobequid Mountains, mts., N.S., Can. D5 87
Cobham, stm., Can. C4 86
Cobija, Bol. F6 70
Cobleskill, N.Y., U.S. C6 125
Cobourg, On., Can. D6 89
Cobourg Peninsula, pen., Austl. C5 60
Cóbuè, Moz. A5 56
Cobun Creek, stm., W.V., U.S. h11 141
Coburg, Ger. E12 12
Coburg, Or., U.S. C3 130
Cocachacra, Peru B3 72
Cochabamba, Bol. B4 72
Cocheco, stm., N.H., U.S. D5 122
Cochin see Kochi, India H3 40
Cochise, co., Az., U.S. F5 96
Cochise Head, mtn., Az., U.S. E6 96
Cochiti Indian Reservation, N.M., U.S. h8 124
Cochiti Reservoir, res., N.M., U.S. B3 124
Cochituate, Ma., U.S. g10 114
Cochituate, Lake, l., Ma., U.S. g10 114
Cochran, Ga., U.S. D3 103
Cochran, co., Tx., U.S. C1 136
Cochrane, Ab., Can. D3 84
Cochrane, On., Can. o19 89
Cochranton, Pa., U.S. C1 131
Cocke, co., Tn., U.S. D10 135
Cockeysville, Md., U.S. B4 113
Cockrell Hill, Tx., U.S. n10 136
Coco, stm., N.A. F8 76
Coco, Cayo, i., Cuba A4 80
Coco, Isla del, i., C.R. D2 80
Cocoa, Fl., U.S. D6 102
Cocoa Beach, Fl., U.S. D6 102
Coco Channel, strt., Asia D2 34
Coco Islands, is., Mya. D2 34
Coconino, co., Az., U.S. B3 96
Cocopah Indian Reservation, Az., U.S. E1 96
Cocos Islands, dep., Oc. F3 58
Cocos Ridge H5 66
Cod, Cape, c., Ma., U.S. C7 114
Codajás, Braz. D7 70
Coden, Al., U.S. E1 94
Codington, co., S.D., U.S. C8 134
Codó, Braz. B3 74
Cody, Wy., U.S. B3 143
Coeburn, Va., U.S. f9 139
Coen, Austl. C3 62
Coeroeni (Corentyne), stm., S.A. C8 70
Coëtivy, i., Sey. i13 57b
Coeur d'Alene, Id., U.S. B2 105
Coeur d'Alene, stm., Id., U.S. B2 105
Coeur d'Alene Indian Reservation, Id., U.S. B2 105
Coeur d'Alene Lake, res., Id., U.S. B2 105
Coeur d'Alene Mountains, mts., Id., U.S. B2 105
Coffee, co., Al., U.S. D3 94
Coffee, co., Ga., U.S. E4 103
Coffee, co., Tn., U.S. B5 135
Coffeeville, Ms., U.S. B4 117
Coffey, co., Ks., U.S. D8 109
Coffeyville, Ks., U.S. E8 109
Coffs Harbour, Austl. G5 62
Coggon, Ia., U.S. B6 108
Cognac, Fr. E6 16
Cohansey, stm., N.J., U.S. E2 123
Cohasset, Ma., U.S. B6 114
Cohasset, Mn., U.S. C5 116
Cohocton, stm., N.Y., U.S. C3 125
Cohoes, N.Y., U.S. C7 125
Cohoon, Lake, res., Va., U.S. k14 139
Cohutta Mountain, mtn., Ga., U.S. B2 103
Coiba, Isla de, i., Pan. D3 80
Coihaique, Chile G2 69
Coimbatore, India G3 40
Coimbra, Port. G2 16
Coipasa, Lago, l., Bol. B4 72
Cojutepeque, El Sal. C2 80
Cokato, Mn., U.S. E4 116
Coke, co., Tx., U.S. D2 136
Cokeville, Wy., U.S. D2 143
Čokurdah, Russia B16 26
Colac, Austl. H3 62
Colatina, Braz. E3 74
Colbeck, Cape, c., Ant. D25 67
Colbert, co., Al., U.S. A2 94
Colbert, Ok., U.S. D5 129
Colborne, On., Can. C7 89
Colby, Ks., U.S. C2 109
Colby, Wi., U.S. D3 142
Colchester, Eng., U.K. E7 12
Colchester, Ct., U.S. C6 100
Colchester, Il., U.S. C3 106
Colcord, Ok., U.S. A7 129
Cold, stm., N.H., U.S. C4 122
Cold, stm., N.H., U.S. D2 122
Cold Bay, Ak., U.S. E7 95
Cold Lake, Ab., Can. B5 84
Cold Spring, Ky., U.S. A5 110
Cold Spring, Mn., U.S. E4 116
Coldwater, On., Can. C5 89
Coldwater, Ks., U.S. E4 109
Coldwater, Mi., U.S. G5 115
Coldwater, stm., Ms., U.S. A3 117
Coldwater, Ms., U.S. A4 117
Coldwater, Oh., U.S. B1 128
Coldwater Creek, stm., U.S. e9 129
Cole, co., Mo., U.S. C5 118
Colebrook, N.H., U.S. g7 122
Colebrook River Lake, res., Ct., U.S. A3 100
Cole Camp, Mo., U.S. C4 118
Coleen, stm., Ak., U.S. B11 95
Coleman, Mi., U.S. E6 115
Coleman, Tx., U.S. D3 136
Coleman, co., Tx., U.S. D3 136
Coleman, Wi., U.S. C5 142
Coleraine, N. Ire., U.K. C3 12

Name — Map Ref. — Page

Coleraine, Mn., U.S. **C5** 116
Coles, co., Il., U.S. **D5** 106
Colesberg, S. Afr. **E4** 56
Colfax, Ca., U.S. **C3** 98
Colfax, Ia., U.S. **C4** 108
Colfax, Il., U.S. **C5** 106
Colfax, In., U.S. **D4** 107
Colfax, La., U.S. **C3** 111
Colfax, co., Ne., U.S. **C8** 120
Colfax, co., N.M., U.S. **A5** 124
Colfax, Wa., U.S. **C8** 140
Colfax, Wi., U.S. **D2** 142
Colhué Huapi, Lago, l., Arg. **G3** 69
Colima, Mex. **D4** 78
Colima, state, Mex. **D4** 78
Colinas, Braz. **C3** 74
Coll, i., Scot., U.K. **B3** 12
College, Ak., U.S. **B10** 95
Collegedale, Tn., U.S. **h11** 135
College Park, Ga., U.S. **C2** 103
College Park, Md., U.S. **C4** 113
College Place, Wa., U.S. **C7** 140
College Station, Ar., U.S. **C3** 97
College Station, Tx., U.S. **D4** 136
Collegeville, In., U.S. **C3** 107
Collegeville, Pa., U.S. **F11** 131
Colleton, co., S.C., U.S. **F6** 133
Collie, Austl. **G2** 60
Collier, co., Fl., U.S. **F5** 102
Colliers, W.V., U.S. **f8** 141
Collierville, Tn., U.S. **B2** 135
Collin, co., Tx., U.S. **C4** 136
Collingdale, Pa., U.S. **p20** 131
Collingswood, N.J., U.S. **D2** 123
Collingsworth, co., Tx., U.S. **B2** 136
Collingwood, On., Can. **C4** 89
Collins, Ms., U.S. **D4** 117
Collins Park, De., U.S. **B3** 101
Collinsville, Al., U.S. **A4** 94
Collinsville, Ct., U.S. **B4** 100
Collinsville, Il., U.S. **E4** 106
Collinsville, Ms., U.S. **C5** 117
Collinsville, Ok., U.S. **A6** 129
Collinwood, Tn., U.S. **B4** 135
Collipulli, Chile **E2** 69
Colmar, Fr. **C10** 16
Colmar Manor, Md., U.S. **f9** 113
Colo, Ia., U.S. **B4** 108
Cologne see Köln, Ger. **E10** 12
Coloma, Mi., U.S. **F4** 115
Colombia, ctry., S.A. **C5** 70
Colombo, Braz. **D8** 72
Colombo, Sri L. **H3** 40
Colón, Arg. **E5** 72
Colón, Cuba **A3** 80
Colón, Pan. **D3** 80
Colon, Mi., U.S. **G5** 115
Colón, Archipiélago de (Galapagos Islands), is., Ec. **C2** 70
Colonial Beach, Va., U.S. **B6** 139
Colonial Heights, Tn., U.S. **C11** 135
Colonial Heights, Va., U.S. **C5** 139
Colonial National Historical Park, Va., U.S. **C6** 139
Colonie, N.Y., U.S. **C7** 125
Colorado, stm., Arg. **E4** 69
Colorado, stm., N.A. **E5** 92
Colorado, stm., Tx., U.S. **D3** 136
Colorado, co., Tx., U.S. **E4** 136
Colorado, state, U.S. **B5** 99
Colorado City, Az., U.S. **A3** 96
Colorado City, Co., U.S. **D6** 99
Colorado City, Tx., U.S. **C2** 136
Colorado City, Lake, res., Tx., U.S. **C2** 136
Colorado National Monument, Co., U.S. **B2** 99
Colorado River Aqueduct, aq., Ca., U.S. **F6** 98
Colorado River Indian Reservation, U.S. **D1** 96
Colorado Springs, Co., U.S. **C6** 99
Colquitt, Ga., U.S. **E2** 103
Colquitt, co., Ga., U.S. **E3** 103
Colstrip, Mt., U.S. **E10** 119
Colton, S.D., U.S. **D9** 134
Coltons Point, Md., U.S. **D4** 113
Columbia, stm., N.A. **B3** 92
Columbia, Al., U.S. **D4** 94
Columbia, co., Ar., U.S. **D2** 97
Columbia, co., Fl., U.S. **B4** 102
Columbia, co., Ga., U.S. **C4** 103
Columbia, Il., U.S. **E3** 106
Columbia, Ky., U.S. **C4** 110
Columbia, Md., U.S. **B4** 113
Columbia, Mo., U.S. **C5** 118
Columbia, Ms., U.S. **D4** 117
Columbia, N.C., U.S. **B6** 126
Columbia, co., N.Y., U.S. **C7** 125
Columbia, co., Or., U.S. **B3** 130
Columbia, Pa., U.S. **F9** 131
Columbia, co., Pa., U.S. **D9** 131
Columbia, S.C., U.S. **C5** 133
Columbia, Tn., U.S. **B4** 135
Columbia, co., Wa., U.S. **C7** 140
Columbia, co., Wi., U.S. **E4** 142
Columbia, Mount, mtn., Can. **C2** 84
Columbia City, In., U.S. **B7** 107
Columbia City, Or., U.S. **B4** 130
Columbia Falls, Mt., U.S. **B2** 119
Columbia Heights, Mn., U.S. **m12** 116
Columbia Lake, res., Ct., U.S. **C6** 100
Columbia Mountains, mts., B.C., Can. **C7** 85
Columbia Mountains, mts., N.A. **H15** 82
Columbiana, Al., U.S. **B3** 94
Columbiana, Oh., U.S. **B5** 128
Columbiana, co., Oh., U.S. **B5** 128
Columbiaville, Mi., U.S. **E7** 115
Columbus, Ga., U.S. **D2** 103
Columbus, In., U.S. **F6** 107
Columbus, Ks., U.S. **E9** 109
Columbus, Ms., U.S. **B5** 117
Columbus, Mt., U.S. **E7** 119
Columbus, N.C., U.S. **f10** 126
Columbus, co., N.C., U.S. **C4** 126
Columbus, Ne., U.S. **C8** 120
Columbus, N.M., U.S. **F2** 124
Columbus, Oh., U.S. **C2** 128
Columbus, Tx., U.S. **E4** 136
Columbus, Wi., U.S. **E4** 142
Columbus Air Force Base, mil., Ms., U.S. **B5** 117
Columbus Grove, Oh., U.S. **B1** 128
Columbus Junction, Ia., U.S. **C6** 108
Columbus Lake, res., Ms., U.S. **B5** 117
Colusa, Ca., U.S. **C2** 98
Colusa, co., Ca., U.S. **C2** 98
Colver, Pa., U.S. **E4** 131
Colville, stm., Ak., U.S. **B9** 95
Colville, Wa., U.S. **A8** 140
Colville, stm., Wa., U.S. **A8** 140
Colville Indian Reservation, Wa., U.S. **A6** 140
Colvos Passage, strt., Wa., U.S. **f10** 140
Colwich, Ks., U.S. **E6** 109
Colwood, B.C., Can. **h12** 85
Comacchio, Italy **B4** 18
Comacchio, Valli di, l., Italy **B4** 18
Comal, co., Tx., U.S. **E3** 136
Comalcalco, Mex. **D6** 78
Coman, Mount, mtn., Ant. **D34** 67
Comanche, co., Ks., U.S. **E4** 109
Comanche, Ok., U.S. **C4** 129
Comanche, co., Ok., U.S. **C3** 129
Comanche, co., Tx., U.S. **D3** 136
Comanche, Tx., U.S. **D3** 136
Comandante Fontana, Arg. **D6** 72
Comayagua, Hond. **C2** 80
Combahee, stm., S.C., U.S. **F6** 133
Combarbalá, Chile **D2** 69
Comber, On., Can. **E2** 89
Combermere Bay, b., Mya. **C2** 34
Combined Locks, Wi., U.S. **h9** 142
Combs, Ky., U.S. **C6** 110
Comer, Ga., U.S. **B3** 103
Comfort, Tx., U.S. **E3** 136
Comilla, Bngl. **E6** 40
Comitán, Mex. **D6** 78
Comite, stm., La., U.S. **D4** 111
Commerce, Ga., U.S. **B3** 103
Commerce, Ok., U.S. **A7** 129
Commerce, Tx., U.S. **C5** 136
Commerce City, Co., U.S. **B6** 99
Committee Bay, b., N.T., Can. **E22** 82
Common Fence Point, R.I., U.S. **D6** 132
Communism Peak see Ismail Samani, pik, mtn., Taj. **F9** 26
Como, Italy **B2** 18
Como, Ms., U.S. **A4** 117
Como, Lago di, l., Italy **B2** 18
Comodoro Rivadavia, Arg. **G3** 69
Comores, Archipel des, is., Afr. **A7** 56
Comorin, Cape, c., India **H3** 40
Comoros, ctry., Afr. **A7** 56
Comox, B.C., Can. **E5** 85
Compiègne, Fr. **C8** 16
Compostela, Mex. **C4** 78
Compton, Qc., Can. **D6** 90
Compton, Ca., U.S. **n12** 98
Comrat, Mol. **F10** 20
Comstock, Mi., U.S. **F5** 115
Conakry, Gui. **E2** 50
Conanicut Island, i., R.I., U.S. **E5** 132
Conanicut Point, c., R.I., U.S. **E5** 132
Concarneau, Fr. **D5** 16
Conceição da Barra, Braz. **E4** 74
Conceição do Araguaia, Braz. **C2** 74
Concepción, Arg. **D4** 72
Concepción, Chile **E2** 69
Concepción, Para. **C6** 72
Concepción del Oro, Mex. **C4** 78
Concepción del Uruguay, Arg. **E6** 72
Conception, Point, c., Ca., U.S. **E3** 98
Conception Bay, b., N.L., Can. **E5** 88
Conception Bay South, N.L., Can. **E5** 88
Conchas Lake, res., N.M., U.S. **B5** 124
Concho, stm., Tx., U.S. **D2** 136
Concho, co., Tx., U.S. **D3** 136
Conchos, stm., Mex. **B3** 78
Concord, Ca., U.S. **h8** 98
Concord, Ma., U.S. **B5** 114
Concord, stm., Ma., U.S. **A5** 114
Concord, Mi., U.S. **F6** 115
Concord, Mo., U.S. **g13** 118
Concord, N.C., U.S. **B2** 126
Concord, N.H., U.S. **D3** 122
Concordia, Arg. **E6** 72
Concórdia, Braz. **D7** 72
Concordia, co., La., U.S. **C4** 111
Concordia, Ks., U.S. **C6** 109
Concordia, Mo., U.S. **C4** 118
Concrete, Wa., U.S. **A4** 140
Conda, Ang. **F2** 54
Condobolin, Austl. **G4** 62
Condon, Or., U.S. **B6** 130
Condoto, Col. **D4** 80
Conecuh, co., Al., U.S. **D2** 94
Conecuh, stm., U.S. **D3** 94
Conejos, stm., Co., U.S. **D4** 99
Conejos, co., Co., U.S. **D4** 99
Conejos Peak, mtn., Co., U.S. **D4** 99
Conemaugh, Pa., U.S. **F4** 131
Conemaugh River Lake, res., Pa., U.S. **F3** 131
Congamond Lakes, l., U.S. **A4** 100
Congaree, stm., S.C., U.S. **D6** 133
Congaree Swamp National Monument, S.C., U.S. **D6** 133
Congo, ctry., Afr. **D3** 54
Congo (Zaire), stm., Afr. **D2** 54
Congo, Democratic Republic of the, ctry., Afr. **D4** 54
Congress, Az., U.S. **C3** 96
Conimicut Point, c., R.I., U.S. **D5** 132
Conklin, N.Y., U.S. **C5** 125
Connaught, hist. reg., Ire. **D2** 12
Conneaut, Oh., U.S. **A5** 128
Conneaut Creek, stm., Oh., U.S. **A5** 128
Conneaut Lake, l., Pa., U.S. **C1** 131
Connecticut, stm., U.S. **C5** 100
Connecticut, state, U.S. **C5** 100
Connell, Wa., U.S. **C7** 140
Connellsville, Pa., U.S. **F2** 131
Connersville, In., U.S. **E7** 107
Conover, N.C., U.S. **B1** 126
Conowingo, Md., U.S. **A5** 113
Conrad, Ia., U.S. **B5** 108
Conrad, Mt., U.S. **B5** 119
Conroe, Tx., U.S. **D5** 136
Conselheiro Lafaiete, Braz. **F3** 74
Conselheiro Pena, Braz. **E3** 74
Conshohocken, Pa., U.S. **F11** 131
Consolación del Sur, Cuba **A3** 80
Con Son, is., Viet. **E5** 34
Consort, Ab., Can. **C5** 84
Constance see Konstanz, Ger. **G11** 12
Constance, Lake, l., Eur. **A2** 18
Constanța, Rom. **G10** 20
Constantina, Spain **I4** 16
Constantine see Qacentina, Alg. **C6** 48
Constantine, Mi., U.S. **G5** 115
Constantine, Cape, c., Ak., U.S. **D8** 95
Constantinople see İstanbul, Tur. **B3** 44
Constitución, Chile **E2** 69
Contas, stm., Braz. **D3** 74
Content Keys, is., Fl., U.S. **H5** 102
Continental, Oh., U.S. **A1** 128
Continental Peak, mtn., Wy., U.S. **D4** 143
Continental Reservoir, res., Co., U.S. **D3** 99
Contoocook, N.H., U.S. **D3** 122
Contoocook, stm., N.H., U.S. **D3** 122
Contra Costa, co., Ca., U.S. **D3** 98
Contrecoeur, Qc., Can. **D4** 90
Converse, In., U.S. **C6** 107
Converse, S.C., U.S. **B4** 133
Converse, co., Wy., U.S. **C7** 143
Convoy, Oh., U.S. **B1** 128
Conway, Ar., U.S. **B3** 97
Conway, co., Ar., U.S. **B3** 97
Conway, Fl., U.S. **D5** 102
Conway, Mo., U.S. **D5** 118
Conway, N.C., U.S. **A5** 126
Conway, N.H., U.S. **C4** 122
Conway, Pa., U.S. **E1** 131
Conway, S.C., U.S. **D9** 133
Conway, Lake, res., Ar., U.S. **B3** 97
Conway Lake, l., N.H., U.S. **C4** 122
Conway Springs, Ks., U.S. **E6** 109
Conyers, Ga., U.S. **C2** 103
Coober Pedy, Austl. **F5** 60
Cook, co., Ga., U.S. **E3** 103
Cook, co., Il., U.S. **B6** 106
Cook, Mn., U.S. **C6** 116
Cook, co., Mn., U.S. **k9** 116
Cook, Cape, c., B.C., Can. **D4** 85
Cook, Mount, mtn., N.Z. **p12** 63c
Cooke, co., Tx., U.S. **C4** 136
Cookes Peak, mtn., N.M., U.S. **E2** 124
Cookeville, Tn., U.S. **C8** 135
Cook Inlet, b., Ak., U.S. **D9** 95
Cook Islands, dep., Oc. **F13** 58
Cook Point, c., Md., U.S. **C5** 113
Cookshire, Qc., Can. **D6** 90
Cookson, Ok., U.S. **B7** 129
Cook Strait, strt., N.Z. **p13** 63c
Cooktown, Austl. **D4** 62
Cooleemee, N.C., U.S. **B2** 126
Coolgardie, Austl. **G3** 60
Coolidge, Az., U.S. **E4** 96
Coolidge, Ga., U.S. **E3** 103
Cooma, Austl. **H4** 62
Coonabarabran, Austl. **G4** 62
Coonamble, Austl. **G4** 62
Coonoor, India **G3** 40
Coon Rapids, Ia., U.S. **C3** 108
Coon Rapids, Mn., U.S. **E5** 116
Coon Valley, Wi., U.S. **E2** 142
Cooper, co., Mo., U.S. **C5** 118
Cooper, stm., S.C., U.S. **F8** 133
Cooper, Tx., U.S. **C5** 136
Cooper Creek, stm., Austl. **F2** 62
Cooper Mountain, mtn., Ak., U.S. **g17** 95
Coopersburg, Pa., U.S. **F11** 131
Cooperstown, N.D., U.S. **B7** 127
Cooperstown, N.Y., U.S. **C6** 125
Coopersville, Mi., U.S. **E5** 115
Coorow, Austl. **F2** 60
Coos, co., N.H., U.S. **A4** 122
Coos, co., Or., U.S. **D2** 130
Coos, stm., Or., U.S. **D2** 130
Coosa, co., Al., U.S. **C3** 94
Coosa, stm., U.S. **C3** 94
Coosada, Al., U.S. **C3** 94
Coosawhatchie, stm., S.C., U.S. **F5** 133
Coos Bay, Or., U.S. **D2** 130
Cootamundra, Austl. **G4** 62
Copalis Beach, Wa., U.S. **B1** 140
Copan, Ok., U.S. **A6** 129
Copan Reservoir, res., Ok., U.S. **A6** 129
Copenhagen see København, Den. **I5** 10
Copiah, co., Ms., U.S. **D3** 117
Copiapó, Chile **C2** 69
Coplay, Pa., U.S. **E10** 131
Copper, stm., Ak., U.S. **C11** 95
Copperas Cove, Tx., U.S. **D4** 136
Copper Butte, mtn., Wa., U.S. **A7** 140
Copper Mountain, mtn., Wy., U.S. **C5** 143
Copper Mountains, mts., Az., U.S. **E2** 96
Coquille, Or., U.S. **D2** 130
Coquimbo, Chile **C2** 69
Corabia, Rom. **H8** 20
Coral Gables, Fl., U.S. **G6** 102
Coral Sea, Oc. **F9** 58
Coral Sea Basin **J18** 64
Coralville, Ia., U.S. **C6** 108
Coralville Lake, res., Ia., U.S. **C5** 108
Coraopolis, Pa., U.S. **E1** 131
Corbeil-Essonnes, Fr. **C8** 16
Corbin, Ky., U.S. **D5** 110
Corcoran, Ca., U.S. **D4** 98
Corcoran, Mn., U.S. **m11** 116
Corcovado, Golfo, b., Chile **F2** 69
Corcovado, Volcán, vol., Chile **F2** 69
Cordele, Ga., U.S. **E3** 103
Cordell, Ok., U.S. **B3** 129
Cordell Hull Lake, res., Tn., U.S. **C8** 135
Córdoba, Arg. **E5** 72
Córdoba, Mex. **D5** 78
Córdoba, Spain **I4** 16
Córdova, Peru **A2** 72
Cordova see Córdoba, Spain **I4** 16
Cordova, Ak., U.S. **C10** 95
Cordova, Al., U.S. **B2** 94
Cordova, N.C., U.S. **C3** 126
Cordova, N.M., U.S. **A4** 124
Cordova Peak, mtn., Ak., U.S. **C10** 95
Corentyne (Coeroeni), stm., S.A. **C8** 70
Corfu see Kérkira, i., Grc. **E7** 18
Corfu see Kérkira, Grc. **E7** 18
Coria, Spain **H3** 16
Corinna, Me., U.S. **D3** 112
Corinne, Ut., U.S. **B3** 137
Corinne Key, i., Fl., U.S. **G6** 102
Corinth see Kórinthos, Grc. **F9** 18
Corinth, Ms., U.S. **A5** 117
Corinth, N.Y., U.S. **B7** 125
Corinth, Gulf of see Korinthiakós Kólpos, b., Grc. **E9** 18
Corinto, Braz. **E3** 74
Corisco, Isla de, i., Eq. Gui. **C1** 54
Cork, Ire. **E2** 12
Çorlu, Tur. **B2** 44
Cormorant Lake, l., Mb., Can. **B1** 86
Cornelia, Ga., U.S. **B3** 103
Cornélio Procópio, Braz. **F1** 74
Cornelius, N.C., U.S. **B2** 126
Cornelius, Or., U.S. **g11** 130
Cornell, Wi., U.S. **C2** 142
Corner Brook, N.L., Can. **D3** 88
Cornersville, Tn., U.S. **B5** 135
Cornfield Point, c., Ct., U.S. **D6** 100
Cornie Bayou, stm., U.S. **D3** 97
Corning, Ar., U.S. **A5** 97
Corning, Ca., U.S. **C2** 98
Corning, Ia., U.S. **D3** 108
Corning, N.Y., U.S. **C3** 125
Cornish, Me., U.S. **E2** 112
Corno Grande, mtn., Italy **C4** 18
Cornville, Az., U.S. **C4** 96
Cornwall, On., Can. **B10** 89
Cornwall, hist. reg., Eng., U.K. **E4** 12
Cornwall, Pa., U.S. **F9** 131
Cornwall on Hudson, N.Y., U.S. **D6** 125
Coro, Ven. **A6** 70
Coroatá, Braz. **B3** 74
Corocoro Island, i., S.A. **D7** 80
Čoroh, stm., Asia **B9** 44
Coroico, Bol. **B4** 72
Coromandel Coast, India **G4** 40
Corona, Ca., U.S. **F5** 98
Coronado, Ca., U.S. **F5** 98
Coronado, Bahía de, b., C.R. **D3** 80
Coronado National Memorial, Az., U.S. **F5** 96
Coronation, Ab., Can. **C5** 84
Coronation Gulf, b., N.T., Can. **E17** 82
Coronation Island, i., Ant. **B36** 67
Coronation Island, i., Ak., U.S. **n22** 95
Coronel Murta, Braz. **B9** 72
Coronel Oviedo, Para. **D6** 72
Coronel Suárez, Arg. **F5** 72
Coronel Vivida, Braz. **D7** 72
Coropuna, Nevado, vol., Peru **G5** 70
Corozal, Belize **B2** 80
Corozal, Col. **D4** 80
Corpus Christi, Tx., U.S. **F4** 136
Corpus Christi Naval Air Station, mil., Tx., U.S. **F4** 136
Correctionville, Ia., U.S. **B2** 108
Correntina, Braz. **A9** 72
Corrib, Lough, l., Ire. **D2** 12
Corrientes, Arg. **D6** 72
Corrientes, Cabo, c., Col. **B4** 70
Corrientes, Cabo, c., Mex. **C3** 78
Corrigan, Tx., U.S. **D5** 136
Corriganville, Md., U.S. **k13** 113
Corrigin, Austl. **G2** 60
Corriverton, Guy. **B8** 70
Corry, Pa., U.S. **C2** 131
Corse (Corsica), i., Fr. **C2** 18
Corse, Cap, c., Fr. **C2** 18
Corsica see Corse, i., Fr. **C2** 18
Corsica, S.D., U.S. **D7** 134
Corsicana, Tx., U.S. **C4** 136
Corson, co., S.D., U.S. **B4** 134
Corson Inlet, b., N.J., U.S. **E3** 123
Cort Adelaer, Kap, c., Grnld. **F31** 82
Corte, Fr. **C2** 18
Cortés, Mar de see California, Golfo de, b., Mex. **B2** 78
Cortez, Co., U.S. **D2** 99
Cortez, Fl., U.S. **q10** 102
Cortez, Sea of see California, Golfo de, b., Mex. **B2** 78
Cortez Mountains, mts., Nv., U.S. **C5** 121
Cortland, Il., U.S. **B5** 106
Cortland, N.Y., U.S. **C4** 125
Cortland, co., N.Y., U.S. **C4** 125
Cortland, Oh., U.S. **A5** 128
Çorum, Tur. **B6** 44
Corumbá, Braz. **G8** 70
Corunna see A Coruña, Spain **F2** 16
Corunna, Mi., U.S. **F6** 115
Coruripe, Braz. **D4** 74
Corvallis, Or., U.S. **C3** 130
Corydon, Ia., U.S. **D4** 108
Corydon, In., U.S. **H5** 107
Corydon, Ky., U.S. **C2** 110
Coryell, co., Tx., U.S. **D4** 136
Cos see Kos, i., Grc. **F11** 18
Cosenza, Italy **E6** 18
Coshocton, Oh., U.S. **B4** 128
Coshocton, co., Oh., U.S. **B4** 128
Cosmoledo, Atoll de, i., Sey. **i11** 57b
Cosmopolis, Wa., U.S. **C2** 140
Cosmos, Mn., U.S. **F4** 116
Cosne-sur-Loire, Fr. **D8** 16
Cossatot, stm., Ar., U.S. **C1** 97
Costa Mesa, Ca., U.S. **n13** 98
Costa Rica, Mex. **C3** 78
Costa Rica, ctry., N.A. **F8** 76
Costilla, co., Co., U.S. **D5** 99
Coswig, Ger. **E13** 12
Cotabato, Phil. **E8** 34
Coteau-Landing, Qc., Can. **D3** 90
Cote d'Ivoire, ctry., C. Iv. **E3** 50
Cotonou, Benin **E5** 50
Cotopaxi, vol., Ec. **D4** 70
Cottage Grove, Mn., U.S. **n13** 116
Cottage Grove, Or., U.S. **D3** 130
Cottage Grove Reservoir, res., Or., U.S. **D3** 130
Cottam, On., Can. **E2** 89
Cottbus, Ger. **E14** 12

Name — Map Ref. — Page

Cotter, Ar., U.S. A3 97
Cottle, co., Tx., U.S. B2 136
Cottleville, Mo., U.S. f12 118
Cotton, co., Ok., U.S. C3 129
Cottondale, Al., U.S. B2 94
Cotton Plant, Ar., U.S. B4 97
Cottonport, La., U.S. C3 111
Cotton Valley, La., U.S. B2 111
Cottonwood, Al., U.S. D4 94
Cottonwood, Az., U.S. C3 96
Cottonwood, Ca., U.S. B2 98
Cottonwood, Id., U.S. C2 105
Cottonwood, stm., Ks., U.S. D7 109
Cottonwood, Mn., U.S. F3 116
Cottonwood, co., Mn., U.S. F3 116
Cottonwood, stm., Mn., U.S. F3 116
Cottonwood Creek, stm., Wy., U.S. C4 143
Cottonwood Falls, Ks., U.S. D7 109
Cotuit, Ma., U.S. C7 114
Cotulla, Tx., U.S. E3 136
Coudersport, Pa., U.S. C5 131
Cougar Reservoir, res., Or., U.S. C4 130
Coulee Creek, stm., Wa., U.S. g13 140
Coulee Dam, Wa., U.S. B7 140
Coulee Dam National Recreation Area, Wa., U.S. A7 140
Coulterville, Il., U.S. E4 106
Counce, Tn., U.S. B3 135
Council, Id., U.S. E2 105
Council Bluffs, Ia., U.S. C2 108
Council Grove, Ks., U.S. D7 109
Council Grove Lake, res., Ks., U.S. D7 109
Council Mountain, mtn., Id., U.S. E2 105
Country Homes, Wa., U.S. B8 140
Coupeville, Wa., U.S. A3 140
Courland Lagoon, b., Eur. B6 20
Courtenay, B.C., Can. E5 85
Courte Oreilles, Lac, l., Wi., U.S. C2 142
Courtland, On., Can. E4 89
Courtland, Al., U.S. A2 94
Courtland, Va., U.S. D5 139
Coushatta, La., U.S. B2 111
Cove Creek, stm., Ut., U.S. E3 137
Covedale, Oh., U.S. o12 128
Coventry, Eng., U.K. D6 12
Coventry, Ct., U.S. B6 100
Coventry, R.I., U.S. D3 132
Cove Point, c., Md., U.S. D5 113
Covilhã, Port. G3 16
Covina, Ca., U.S. m13 98
Covington, co., Al., U.S. D3 94
Covington, Ga., U.S. C3 103
Covington, In., U.S. D3 107
Covington, Ky., U.S. A5 110
Covington, La., U.S. D5 111
Covington, co., Ms., U.S. D4 117
Covington, Oh., U.S. B1 128
Covington, Tn., U.S. B2 135
Covington, Va., U.S. C3 139
Cowan, Tn., U.S. B5 135
Cowansville, Qc., Can. D5 90
Cowarts, Al., U.S. D4 94
Cow Creek, stm., Wa., U.S. C7 140
Cowee Mountains, mts., N.C., U.S. f9 126
Cowell, Austl. G2 62
Cowen, Mount, mtn., Mt., U.S. E6 119
Coweta, co., Ga., U.S. C2 103
Coweta, Ok., U.S. B6 129
Cow Head, N.L., Can. D3 88
Cowichan Bay, B.C., Can. g12 85
Cow Lakes, l., Or., U.S. D9 130
Cowley, co., Ks., U.S. E7 109
Cowley, Wy., U.S. B4 143
Cowlington, Ok., U.S. B7 129
Cowlitz, co., Wa., U.S. C2 140
Cowlitz, stm., Wa., U.S. C3 140
Cowpasture, stm., Va., U.S. B3 139
Cowpen Mountain, mtn., Ga., U.S. B2 103
Cowpens, S.C., U.S. A4 133
Cowra, Austl. G4 62
Coxim, Braz. G9 70
Coxsackie, N.Y., U.S. C7 125
Cox's Bāzār, Bngl. E6 40
Cox's Cove, N.L., Can. D2 88
Coyuca de Catalán, Mex. D4 78
Cozad, Ne., U.S. D6 120
Cozumel, Mex. C7 78
Cozumel, Isla, i., Mex. C7 78
Crab Creek, stm., Wa., U.S. C6 140
Crab Creek, stm., Wa., U.S. B7 140
Crab Orchard, Ky., U.S. C5 110
Crab Orchard, Tn., U.S. D9 135
Crab Orchard, W.V., U.S. n13 141
Crab Orchard Lake, res., Il., U.S. F4 106
Crabtree, Pa., U.S. F3 131
Crabtree Mills, Qc., Can. D4 90
Cracow see Kraków, Pol. D5 20
Cradock, S. Afr. E4 56
Crafton, Pa., U.S. k13 131
Craig, Ak., U.S. D13 95
Craig, Co., U.S. A3 99
Craig, co., Ok., U.S. A6 129
Craig, co., Va., U.S. C2 139
Craig Air Force Base, mil., Al., U.S. C3 94
Craig Creek, stm., Va., U.S. C2 139
Craighead, co., Ar., U.S. B5 97
Craigsville, Va., U.S. B3 139
Craigsville, W.V., U.S. C4 141
Craiova, Rom. G7 20
Cramerton, N.C., U.S. B1 126
Cranberry Lake, l., N.Y., U.S. A6 125
Cranberry Portage, Mb., Can. B1 86
Cranbrook, Austl. G2 60
Cranbrook, B.C., Can. E10 85
Crandall, Tx., U.S. n10 136
Crandon, Wi., U.S. C5 142
Crane, Mo., U.S. E4 118
Crane, co., Tx., U.S. D1 136
Crane, Tx., U.S. D1 136
Crane Creek, stm., Oh., U.S. e7 128
Crane Creek Reservoir, res., Id., U.S. E2 105
Crane Lake, l., Il., U.S. C3 106
Crane Lake, l., Mn., U.S. B6 116
Crane Mountain, mtn., Or., U.S. E6 130
Crane Prairie Reservoir, res., Or., U.S. D5 130
Cranford, N.J., U.S. B4 123
Cranston, R.I., U.S. C4 132
Crater Lake, l., Or., U.S. E4 130
Crater Lake National Park, Or., U.S. E4 130
Craters of the Moon National Monument, Id., U.S. F5 105
Crateús, Braz. C3 74
Crato, Braz. C4 74
Craven, co., N.C., U.S. B5 126
Crawford, co., Ar., U.S. B1 97
Crawford, Ga., U.S. C3 103
Crawford, co., Ga., U.S. D3 103
Crawford, co., Ia., U.S. B2 108
Crawford, co., Il., U.S. D6 106
Crawford, co., In., U.S. H4 107
Crawford, co., Ks., U.S. E9 109
Crawford, co., Mi., U.S. D6 115
Crawford, co., Mo., U.S. D6 118
Crawford, Ms., U.S. B5 117
Crawford, Ne., U.S. B2 120
Crawford, co., Oh., U.S. B3 128
Crawford, co., Pa., U.S. C1 131
Crawford, co., Wi., U.S. E3 142
Crawford Lake, l., Me., U.S. C5 112
Crawford Notch State Park, N.H., U.S. B4 122
Crawfordsville, Ar., U.S. B5 97
Crawfordsville, In., U.S. D4 107
Crawfordville, Fl., U.S. B2 102
Crawley, Eng., U.K. E6 12
Crazy Mountains, mts., Mt., U.S. D6 119
Crazy Peak, mtn., Mt., U.S. D6 119
Crazy Woman Creek, stm., Wy., U.S. B6 143
Creal Springs, Il., U.S. F5 106
Creedmoor, N.C., U.S. A4 126
Creek, co., Ok., U.S. B5 129
Cree Lake, l., Sk., Can. m7 91
Creemore, On., Can. C4 89
Creighton, Ne., U.S. B8 120
Creighton, Pa., U.S. h14 131
Creil, Fr. C8 16
Crema, Italy B2 18
Cremona, Italy B3 18
Crenshaw, co., Al., U.S. D3 94
Crenshaw, Ms., U.S. A3 117
Creola, Al., U.S. E1 94
Cres, Otok, i., Cro. B5 18
Cresaptown, Md., U.S. k13 113
Crescent, Ok., U.S. B4 129
Crescent, Or., U.S. D5 130
Crescent, Lake, l., Wa., U.S. A2 140
Crescent City, Ca., U.S. B1 98
Crescent City, Fl., U.S. C5 102
Crescent Lake, l., Fl., U.S. C5 102
Crescent Lake, l., Or., U.S. D5 130
Crescent Springs, Ky., U.S. h13 110
Cresco, Ia., U.S. A5 108
Cresskill, N.J., U.S. h9 123
Cresson, Pa., U.S. F4 131
Cressona, Pa., U.S. E9 131
Crested Butte, Co., U.S. C4 99
Crest Hill, Il., U.S. k8 106
Crestline, Oh., U.S. B3 128
Creston, B.C., Can. E9 85
Creston, Ia., U.S. C3 108
Creston, Oh., U.S. B4 128
Crestone Peak, mtn., Co., U.S. D5 99
Crestview, Fl., U.S. u15 102
Crestview, Hi., U.S. g10 104
Crestwood, Ky., U.S. B4 110
Crestwood Village, N.J., U.S. D4 123
Creswell, Or., U.S. D3 130
Crete see Kríti, i., Grc. G10 18
Crete, Il., U.S. B6 106
Crete, Ne., U.S. D9 120
Crete, Sea of see Kritikón Pélagos, Grc. G10 18
Creve Coeur, Il., U.S. C4 106
Crewe, Va., U.S. C4 139
Criciúma, Braz. D8 72
Cricket, N.C., U.S. A1 126
Cridersville, Oh., U.S. B1 128
Crimean Mountains see Kryms'ki hory, mts., Ukr. G13 20
Crimean Peninsula see Kryms'kyi pivostriv, pen., Ukr. G12 20
Crisfield, Md., U.S. E6 113
Crisp, co., Ga., U.S. E3 103
Cristalândia, Braz. F10 70
Cristalina, Braz. E2 74
Cristóbal Colón, Pico, mtn., Col. A5 70
Crittenden, co., Ar., U.S. B5 97
Crittenden, Ky., U.S. B5 110
Crittenden, co., Ky., U.S. e9 110
Crivitz, Wi., U.S. C6 142
Crna Gora (Montenegro), state, Serb. C7 18
Croatia, ctry., Eur. B5 18
Crocker, Mo., U.S. D5 118
Crockett, Ca., U.S. g8 98
Crockett, co., Tn., U.S. B2 135
Crockett, Tx., U.S. D5 136
Crockett, co., Tx., U.S. D2 136
Crofton, Ky., U.S. C2 110
Crofton, Md., U.S. B4 113
Crofton, Ne., U.S. B8 120
Croix, Lac la, l., Mn., U.S. B6 116
Croker, Cape, c., Austl. C5 60
Croker, Cape, c., On., Can. C4 89
Croker Island, i., Austl. C5 60
Cromona, Ky., U.S. C7 110
Cromwell, Ct., U.S. C5 100
Crook, co., Or., U.S. C6 130
Crook, co., Wy., U.S. B8 143
Crooked, stm., Or., U.S. C6 130
Crooked Creek, stm., Pa., U.S. C7 131
Crooked Creek, stm., U.S. E3 109
Crooked Creek Lake, res., Pa., U.S. E3 131
Crooked Island, i., Bah. D10 76
Crooked Island Passage, strt., Bah. A5 80
Crooked Lake, l., Fl., U.S. E5 102
Crooked Lake, l., Mn., U.S. B7 116
Crooks, S.D., U.S. D9 134
Crooks Lake, l., Nv., U.S. B2 121
Crookston, Mn., U.S. C2 116
Crooksville, Oh., U.S. C3 128
Crosby, Mn., U.S. D5 116
Crosby, N.D., U.S. A2 127
Crosby, Tx., U.S. r14 136
Crosby, co., Tx., U.S. C2 136
Crosby, Mount, mtn., Wy., U.S. C3 143
Crosbyton, Tx., U.S. C2 136
Cross, co., Ar., U.S. B5 97
Cross Bay, b., Mb., Can. C2 86
Cross City, Fl., U.S. C3 102
Cross Creek, stm., W.V., U.S. f8 141
Crossett, Ar., U.S. D4 97
Crossfield, Ab., Can. D3 84
Cross Island, i., Me., U.S. D5 112
Cross Lake, Mb., Can. B3 86
Cross Lake, res., La., U.S. B2 111
Cross Lake, l., Me., U.S. A4 112
Crosslake, Mn., U.S. D4 116
Cross Lanes, W.V., U.S. C3 141
Crossman Peak, mtn., Az., U.S. C1 96
Cross Plains, Tn., U.S. A5 135
Cross Plains, Tx., U.S. C3 136
Cross Plains, Wi., U.S. E4 142
Cross Sound, strt., Ak., U.S. k21 95
Crossville, Al., U.S. A4 94
Crossville, Il., U.S. E5 106
Crossville, Tn., U.S. D8 135
Croswell, Mi., U.S. E8 115
Crothersville, In., U.S. G6 107
Crotone, Italy E6 18
Croton-on-Hudson, N.Y., U.S. D7 125
Crouse, N.C., U.S. B1 126
Crow, stm., Mn., U.S. F4 116
Crow Agency, Mt., U.S. E9 119
Crow Creek, stm., U.S. A6 99
Crow Creek Indian Reservation, S.D., U.S. C6 134
Crowder, Ms., U.S. A3 117
Crowell, Tx., U.S. C3 136
Crow Indian Reservation, Mt., U.S. E9 119
Crowley, co., Co., U.S. C7 99
Crowley, La., U.S. D3 111
Crowley, Tx., U.S. n9 136
Crowley, Lake, res., Ca., U.S. D4 98
Crowleys Ridge, mtn., U.S. B5 97
Crown Point, In., U.S. B3 107
Crown Point, La., U.S. k11 111
Crownpoint, N.M., U.S. B1 124
Crow Peak, mtn., Mt., U.S. D5 119
Crowsnest Pass, Ab., Can. E3 84
Crowsnest Pass, Can. E3 84
Crow Wing, stm., Mn., U.S. D4 116
Crow Wing, co., Mn., U.S. D4 116
Crozet, Va., U.S. B4 139
Crozet, Archipel, is., Afr. N15 46
Crozet Basin L9 64
Cruces, Cuba A3 80
Crump Lake, l., Or., U.S. E7 130
Cruz, Cabo, c., Cuba B4 80
Cruz Alta, Braz. D7 72
Cruz del Eje, Arg. E5 72
Cruzeiro, Braz. F2 74
Cruzeiro do Sul, Braz. E5 70
Crystal, stm., Co., U.S. B3 99
Crystal, Mn., U.S. m12 116
Crystal Bay, b., Fl., U.S. D4 102
Crystal Bay, Nv., U.S. D1 121
Crystal Beach, Fl., U.S. D4 102
Crystal City, Mb., Can. E2 86
Crystal City, Mo., U.S. C7 118
Crystal City, Tx., U.S. E3 136
Crystal Falls, Mi., U.S. B2 115
Crystal Lake, Ct., U.S. B6 100
Crystal Lake, l., Ct., U.S. B6 100
Crystal Lake, Fl., U.S. u16 102
Crystal Lake, Il., U.S. A5 106
Crystal Lake, l., Mi., U.S. D4 115
Crystal Lake, l., N.H., U.S. D4 122
Crystal Lake, l., Vt., U.S. B4 138
Crystal Lawns, Il., U.S. k8 106
Crystal Pond, res., Ct., U.S. B7 100
Crystal River, Fl., U.S. D4 102
Crystal Springs, Ms., U.S. D3 117
Ču, stm., Asia B10 42
Cúa, Ven. C6 80
Cuamba, Moz. A6 56
Cuando (Kwando), stm., Afr. B3 56
Cuangar, Ang. B2 56
Cuango (Kwango), stm., Afr. E3 54
Cuango, Ang. E3 54
Cuango, Ang. E3 54
Cuanza, stm., Ang. E3 52
Cuauhtémoc, Mex. C7 78
Cuba, ctry., N.A. D9 76
Cuba, Il., U.S. C3 106
Cuba, Mo., U.S. C6 118
Cuba, N.M., U.S. A3 124
Cuba, N.Y., U.S. C2 125
Cuba City, Wi., U.S. F3 142
Cubal, Ang. F2 54
Cubango (Okavango), stm., Afr. B2 56
Cubero, N.M., U.S. B2 124
Çubuk, Tur. B5 44
Cucharas, stm., Co., U.S. D6 99
Cúcuta, Col. B5 70
Cudahy, Wi., U.S. F6 142
Cuddalore, India G3 40
Cuddapah, India G3 40
Cuddy Mountain, mtn., Id., U.S. E2 105
Cue, Austl. F2 60
Cuenca, Ec. D4 70
Cuenca, Spain G5 16
Cuencamé de Ceniceros, Mex. C4 78
Cuernavaca, Mex. D5 78
Cuero, Tx., U.S. E4 136
Cuiabá, Braz. G8 70
Cuilo (Kwilu), stm., Afr. E3 54
Cuima, Ang. A2 56
Cuíto, stm., Ang. B2 56
Cuito Cuanavale, Ang. B2 56
Cuitzeo, Lago de, l., Mex. D4 78
Cuivre, West Fork, stm., Mo., U.S. B6 118
Cukai, Malay. C2 36
Čukotskij poluostrov, pen., Russia C20 26
Çulakkurgan, Kaz. B9 42
Culberson, co., Tx., U.S. o12 136
Culbertson, Mt., U.S. B12 119
Culbertson, Ne., U.S. D5 120
Culebra Peak, mtn., Co., U.S. D5 99
Culfa, Azer. C11 44
Culiacán, Mex. C3 78
Cullen, La., U.S. B2 111
Cullera, Spain H6 16
Cullman, co., Al., U.S. A3 94
Cullman, Al., U.S. A3 94
Culloden, W.V., U.S. C2 141
Cullowhee, N.C., U.S. f9 126
Čul'man, Russia D14 26
Culpeper, Va., U.S. B4 139
Culpeper, co., Va., U.S. B5 139
Culver, In., U.S. B5 107
Culver City, Ca., U.S. m12 98
Culvers Lake, l., N.J., U.S. A3 123
Čulym, Russia D10 26
Čulym, stm., Russia D10 26
Cumaná, Ven. A7 70
Cumberland, B.C., Can. E5 85
Cumberland, co., Il., U.S. D5 106
Cumberland, Ky., U.S. D7 110
Cumberland, co., Ky., U.S. D4 110
Cumberland, Md., U.S. k13 113
Cumberland, co., Me., U.S. E2 112
Cumberland, co., N.C., U.S. C4 126
Cumberland, co., N.J., U.S. E2 123
Cumberland, co., Pa., U.S. F7 131
Cumberland, co., Tn., U.S. D8 135
Cumberland, co., Va., U.S. C4 139
Cumberland, Wi., U.S. C2 142
Cumberland, stm., U.S. D4 110
Cumberland, Lake, res., Ky., U.S. D5 110
Cumberland Center, Me., U.S. g7 112
Cumberland Foreside, Me., U.S. E2 112
Cumberland Gap, U.S. D6 110
Cumberland Gap National Historical Park, U.S. D6 110
Cumberland Hill, R.I., U.S. B4 132
Cumberland Island National Seashore, Ga., U.S. F5 103
Cumberland Lake, l., Sk., Can. C4 91
Cumbres Pass, Co., U.S. D4 99
Čumikan, Russia D15 26
Cuming, co., Ne., U.S. C9 120
Cumming, Ga., U.S. B2 103
Çumra, Tur. D5 44
Čunani, Braz. C9 70
Čundža, Kaz. B11 42
Cunene (Kunene), stm., Afr. B1 56
Cuneo, Italy B1 18
Čunja, stm., Russia C11 26
Cunnamulla, Austl. F4 62
Cunningham, Ky., U.S. f9 110
Cupar, Sk., Can. G3 91
Curaçao, i., Neth. Ant. C6 80
Curanilahue, Chile E2 69
Čurapča, Russia C15 26
Curecanti National Recreation Area, Co., U.S. C3 99
Curepipe, Mrts. g10 57a
Curicó, Chile D2 69
Curitiba, Braz. D8 72
Curitibanos, Braz. D7 72
Curlew Creek, stm., Wa., U.S. A7 140
Curlew Lake, l., Wa., U.S. A7 140
Currais Novos, Braz. C4 74
Currant Mountain, mtn., Nv., U.S. E6 121
Current, stm., U.S. A5 97
Currituck, co., N.C., U.S. A6 126
Curry, co., N.M., U.S. C6 124
Curry, co., Or., U.S. E2 130
Curtea de Argeş, Rom. G8 20
Curtin Springs, Austl. F5 60
Curtis, Ne., U.S. D5 120
Curtis Island, i., Austl. E5 62
Curtisville, Pa., U.S. E2 131
Cururupu, Braz. B3 74
Curuzú Cuatiá, Arg. D6 72
Curvelo, Braz. E3 74
Curwensville, Pa., U.S. E4 131
Curwensville Lake, res., Pa., U.S. E4 131
Curwood, Mount, mtn., Mi., U.S. B2 115
Cusco, Peru F5 70
Cushing, Ok., U.S. B5 129
Cushman, Lake, res., Wa., U.S. B2 140
Čusovoj, Russia C10 22
Cusseta, Ga., U.S. D2 103
Custer, co., Co., U.S. C5 99
Custer, co., Id., U.S. E4 105
Custer, co., Mt., U.S. D11 119
Custer, co., Ne., U.S. C6 120
Custer, co., Ok., U.S. B2 129
Custer, S.D., U.S. D2 134
Custer, co., S.D., U.S. D2 134
Custer Battlefield National Monument, Mt., U.S. E9 119
Cut, Nuhu, i., Indon. E8 36
Cut Bank, Mt., U.S. B4 119
Cut Bank Creek, stm., N.D., U.S. A4 127
Cutchogue, N.Y., U.S. m16 125
Cuthbert, Ga., U.S. E2 103
Cutler Ridge, Fl., U.S. s13 102
Cut Off, La., U.S. E5 111
Cuttack, India E5 40
Cuttyhunk Island, i., Ma., U.S. D6 114
Čuvašija, state, Russia D6 26
Cuvier, Cape, c., Austl. E1 60
Cuxhaven, Ger. D11 12
Cuyahoga, stm., Oh., U.S. A4 128
Cuyahoga, co., Oh., U.S. A4 128
Cuyahoga Falls, Oh., U.S. A4 128
Cuyama, stm., Ca., U.S. E4 98
Cuyamaca Peak, mtn., Ca., U.S. F5 98
Cuyo Islands, is., Phil. D8 34
Cuyuni, stm., S.A. D7 80
C.W. McConaughy, Lake, res., Ne., U.S. C4 120
Cyclades see Kikládhes, is., Grc. F10 18
Cynthiana, In., U.S. H2 107
Cynthiana, Ky., U.S. B5 110
Cypress Creek, stm., Tx., U.S. r14 136
Cypress Hills Provincial Park, Sk., Can. H1 91
Cypress Lake, l., Fl., U.S. D5 102
Cypress Quarters, Fl., U.S. E6 102
Cypress Swamp, sw., U.S. F4 101
Cyprus, ctry., Asia E5 44
Cyprus, North see North Cyprus, ctry., Asia E5 44
Cyrenaica see Barqah, hist. reg., Libya E8 14
Cyril, Ok., U.S. C3 129
Cythera see Kíthira, i., Grc. F9 18
Cythnos see Kíthnos, i., Grc. F10 18
Czech Republic, ctry., Eur. E3 20
Częstochowa, Pol. D5 20

D

Dabajuro, Ven. C5 80
Dabeiba, Col. D4 80
Dabhoi, India E2 40
Dabie Shan, mts., China E11 28
Dabola, Gui. D2 50
Dabou, C. Iv. E4 50
Daboya, Ghana E4 50
Dacca see Dhaka, Bngl. E6 40
Dac Glei, Viet. C5 34
Dachau, Ger. F12 12

Name	Map Ref.	Page
Dacono, Co., U.S.	**A6**	99
Dacula, Ga., U.S.	**C3**	103
Dade, co., Fl., U.S.	**G6**	102
Dade, co., Ga., U.S.	**B1**	103
Dade, co., Mo., U.S.	**D4**	118
Dade City, Fl., U.S.	**D4**	102
Dadeville, Al., U.S.	**C4**	94
Dādra and Nagar Haveli, ter., India	**E2**	40
Dādu, Pak.	**E9**	42
Daet, Phil.	**D8**	34
Dafang, China	**D2**	30
Dafeng, China	**C5**	30
Daga Medo, Eth.	**B8**	54
Dagana, Sen.	**C1**	50
Dagestan, state, Russia	**E6**	26
Dagestan see Altaj, state, Russia	**A5**	28
Daggett, co., Ut., U.S.	**C6**	137
Dagsboro, De., U.S.	**F5**	101
Dagu, China	**B4**	30
Daguan, China	**D1**	30
Dagupan, Phil.	**C8**	34
Da Hinggan Ling, mts., China	**B12**	28
Dahlak Archipelago, is., Erit.	**G4**	38
Dahlonega, Ga., U.S.	**B3**	103
Dāhod, India	**E2**	40
Dahomey see Benin, ctry., Afr.	**D5**	50
Dahra, Libya	**E8**	48
Dahūk, Iraq	**D10**	44
Dailing, China	**A1**	31
Daingerfield, Tx., U.S.	**C5**	136
Dairen see Dalian, China	**D12**	28
Dakar, Sen.	**D1**	50
Dakhla, W. Sah.	**B1**	50
Dākoānk, India	**H6**	40
Dakoro, Niger	**D6**	50
Dakota, co., Mn., U.S.	**F5**	116
Dakota, co., Ne., U.S.	**B9**	120
Dakota City, Ia., U.S.	**B3**	108
Dakota City, Ne., U.S.	**B9**	120
Ðakovica, Serb.	**C8**	18
Ðakovo, Cro.	**B7**	18
Dalaba, Gui.	**D2**	50
Dalälven, stm., Swe.	**F7**	10
Dalandzadgad, Mong.	**C8**	28
Dalarna, hist. reg., Swe.	**F6**	10
Da Lat, Viet.	**D5**	34
Dālbandin, Pak.	**E8**	42
Dalby, Austl.	**F5**	62
Dale, co., Al., U.S.	**D4**	94
Dale, In., U.S.	**H4**	107
Dale City, Va., U.S.	**B5**	139
Dale Hollow Lake, res., U.S.	**C8**	135
Daleville, Al., U.S.	**D4**	94
Daleville, In., U.S.	**D6**	107
Dalhart, Tx., U.S.	**A1**	136
Dalhousie, N.B., Can.	**A3**	87
Dalhousie, India	**C3**	40
Dali, China	**F8**	28
Dali, China	**C2**	30
Dalian, China	**D12**	28
Dall, Mount, mtn., Ak., U.S.	**f15**	95
Dallam, co., Tx., U.S.	**A1**	136
Dallas, co., Al., U.S.	**C2**	94
Dallas, co., Ar., U.S.	**D3**	97
Dallas, Ga., U.S.	**C2**	103
Dallas (part of Melcher), Ia., U.S.	**C4**	108
Dallas, co., Ia., U.S.	**C3**	108
Dallas, co., Mo., U.S.	**D4**	118
Dallas, N.C., U.S.	**B1**	126
Dallas, Or., U.S.	**C3**	130
Dallas, Pa., U.S.	**D10**	131
Dallas, Tx., U.S.	**C4**	136
Dallas, co., Tx., U.S.	**C4**	136
Dallas Center, Ia., U.S.	**C4**	108
Dallas City, Il., U.S.	**C2**	106
Dallas Naval Air Station, mil., Tx., U.S.	**n9**	136
Dallastown, Pa., U.S.	**G8**	131
Dalli Rājhara, India	**E4**	40
Dall Island, i., Ak., U.S.	**n23**	95
Dalmacija, hist. reg., Eur.	**C6**	18
Dalmatia see Dalmacija, hist. reg., Eur.	**C6**	18
Dal'negorsk, Russia	**E15**	26
Dal'nerečensk, Russia	**B14**	28
Daloa, C. Iv.	**E3**	50
Dalqū, Sudan	**F11**	48
Dāltenganj, India	**E4**	40
Dalton, Ga., U.S.	**B2**	103
Dalton, Ma., U.S.	**B1**	114
Dalton, Oh., U.S.	**B4**	128
Dalton, Pa., U.S.	**C10**	131
Dalton Gardens, Id., U.S.	**B2**	105
Dalupiri Island, i., Phil.	**C8**	34
Dalvík, Ice.	**l19**	10a
Dalwallinu, Austl.	**G2**	60
Daly, stm., Austl.	**C5**	60
Daly City, Ca., U.S.	**h8**	98
Daly Waters, Austl.	**D5**	60
Damān, India	**E2**	40
Damanhûr, Egypt	**E10**	14
Damar, Pulau, i., Indon.	**E7**	36
Damaraland, hist. reg., Nmb.	**C2**	56
Damariscotta, Me., U.S.	**D3**	112
Damariscotta Lake, l., Me., U.S.	**D3**	112
Damascus see Dimashq, Syria	**F7**	44
Damascus, Md., U.S.	**B3**	113
Damascus, Va., U.S.	**f10**	139
Damaturu, Nig.	**D7**	50
Damāvand, Qolleh-ye, vol., Iran	**C6**	42
Damba, Ang.	**E3**	54
Dambarta, Nig.	**D6**	50
Dāmghān, Iran	**C6**	42
Damietta, Egypt	**E10**	14
Damoh, India	**E3**	40
Damongo, Ghana	**E4**	50
Dampier, Austl.	**E2**	60
Dampier, Selat, strt., Indon.	**D8**	36
Dan, stm., U.S.	**D3**	139
Dana, In., U.S.	**E3**	107
Danakil, reg., Afr.	**H13**	48
Danané, C. Iv.	**E3**	50
Da Nang, Viet.	**C5**	34
Danbury, Ct., U.S.	**D2**	100
Danbury, Tx., U.S.	**r14**	136
Dandeli, India	**F2**	40
Dandong, China	**C12**	28
Dandridge, Tn., U.S.	**C10**	135
Dane, co., Wi., U.S.	**E4**	142
Danfeng, China	**C3**	30
Dangchang, China	**C1**	30
Dangriga, Belize	**B2**	80
Dangshan, China	**C4**	30
Dania, Fl., U.S.	**F6**	102
Daniels, co., Mt., U.S.	**B11**	119
Danielson, Ct., U.S.	**B8**	100
Daniels Pass, Ut., U.S.	**C4**	137
Danilov, Russia	**C7**	22
Danlí, Hond.	**C2**	80
Dannemora, N.Y., U.S.	**f11**	125
Dannevirke, N.Z.	**p14**	63c
Dansville, N.Y., U.S.	**C3**	125
Dante, Va., U.S.	**f9**	139
Danube, stm., Eur.	**C9**	14
Danube, Mouths of the, mth., Eur.	**G10**	20
Danvers, Il., U.S.	**C4**	106
Danvers, Ma., U.S.	**A6**	114
Danville, Qc., Can.	**D5**	90
Danville, Ar., U.S.	**B2**	97
Danville, Ca., U.S.	**h9**	98
Danville, Ia., U.S.	**D6**	108
Danville, Il., U.S.	**C6**	106
Danville, In., U.S.	**E4**	107
Danville, Ky., U.S.	**C5**	110
Danville, Oh., U.S.	**B3**	128
Danville, Pa., U.S.	**E8**	131
Danville, Va., U.S.	**D3**	139
Danxian, China	**F2**	30
Danzig see Gdańsk, Pol.	**B5**	20
Daocheng, China	**F8**	28
Daoukro, C. Iv.	**E4**	50
Daoxian, China	**D3**	30
Dapaong, Togo	**D5**	50
Dapchi, Nig.	**D7**	50
Daphne, Al., U.S.	**E2**	94
Da Qaidam, China	**D7**	28
Dar'ā, Syria	**F7**	44
Dārāb, Iran	**E6**	42
Darabani, Rom.	**E9**	20
Dārayyā, Syria	**F7**	44
Darbhanga, India	**D5**	40
Darby, Mt., U.S.	**D2**	119
Darby, Pa., U.S.	**G11**	131
Dardanelle, Ar., U.S.	**B2**	97
Dardanelle Lake, res., Ar., U.S.	**B2**	97
Dardanelles see Çanakkale Boğazı, strt., Tur.	**C1**	44
Dare, co., N.C., U.S.	**B7**	126
Darende, Tur.	**C7**	44
Dar es Salaam, Tan.	**E7**	54
Dargan-Ata, Turk.	**B8**	42
Dargaville, N.Z.	**o13**	63c
Darhan, Mong.	**B9**	28
Darien, Ct., U.S.	**E2**	100
Darien, Ga., U.S.	**E5**	103
Darien, Wi., U.S.	**F5**	142
Dārjiling, India	**D5**	40
Darke, co., Oh., U.S.	**B1**	128
Darlag, China	**E7**	28
Darley Woods, De., U.S.	**h8**	101
Darling, stm., Austl.	**G3**	62
Darling, Lake, res., N.D., U.S.	**A4**	127
Darling Range, mts., Austl.	**G2**	60
Darlington, Eng., U.K.	**C6**	12
Darlington, In., U.S.	**D4**	107
Darlington, Md., U.S.	**A5**	113
Darlington, S.C., U.S.	**C8**	133
Darlington, co., S.C., U.S.	**C8**	133
Darlington, Wi., U.S.	**F3**	142
Darłowo, Pol.	**B4**	20
Darmstadt, Ger.	**F11**	12
Darnah, Libya	**D9**	48
Darnley, Cape, c., Ant.	**C12**	67
Darrah, Mount, mtn., Can.	**E3**	84
Darreh Gaz, Iran	**C7**	42
Darrington, Wa., U.S.	**A4**	140
Dart, Cape, c., Ant.	**D27**	67
Daru, Pap. N. Gui.	**H11**	32
Darvaza, Turk.	**E7**	26
Darwin, Austl.	**C5**	60
Dašhovuz, Turk.	**E7**	26
Dassel, Mn., U.S.	**E4**	116
Dastgardān, Iran	**D7**	42
Date, Japan	**B4**	31
Datia, India	**D3**	40
Datil Mountains, mts., N.M., U.S.	**C2**	124
Datong, China	**B1**	30
Datong, China	**C10**	28
Datu, Tanjung, c., Asia	**C3**	36
Daufuskie Island, i., S.C., U.S.	**G6**	133
Daung Kyun, i., Mya.	**D3**	34
Dauphin, Mb., Can.	**D1**	86
Dauphin, stm., Mb., Can.	**D2**	86
Dauphin, co., Pa., U.S.	**F8**	131
Dauphin Island, Al., U.S.	**E1**	94
Dauphin Island, i., Al., U.S.	**E1**	94
Dauphin Lake, l., Mb., Can.	**D2**	86
Dāvangere, India	**G3**	40
Davao, Phil.	**E9**	34
Davao Gulf, b., Phil.	**E9**	34
Dāvarzan, Iran	**C7**	42
Daveluyville, Qc., Can.	**C5**	90
Davenport, Fl., U.S.	**D5**	102
Davenport, Ia., U.S.	**C7**	108
Davenport, Ok., U.S.	**B5**	129
Davenport, Wa., U.S.	**B7**	140
David, Pan.	**D3**	80
David City, Ne., U.S.	**C8**	120
Davidson, N.C., U.S.	**B2**	126
Davidson, co., N.C., U.S.	**B2**	126
Davidson, co., Tn., U.S.	**A5**	135
Davidsville, Pa., U.S.	**F4**	131
Davie, Fl., U.S.	**F6**	102
Davie, co., N.C., U.S.	**B2**	126
Daviess, co., In., U.S.	**G3**	107
Daviess, co., Ky., U.S.	**C2**	110
Daviess, co., Mo., U.S.	**B3**	118
Davis, Ca., U.S.	**C3**	98
Davis, co., Ia., U.S.	**D5**	108
Davis, Ok., U.S.	**C4**	129
Davis, co., Ut., U.S.	**C3**	137
Davis, W.V., U.S.	**B5**	141
Davis, Mount, mtn., Pa., U.S.	**G3**	131
Davis Creek, stm., W.V., U.S.	**m12**	141
Davis Dam, U.S.	**H7**	121
Davis Islands, is., Fl., U.S.	**p11**	102
Davis Lake, l., Or., U.S.	**E5**	130
Davis-Monthan Air Force Base, mil., Az., U.S.	**E5**	96
Davison, Mi., U.S.	**E7**	115
Davison, co., S.D., U.S.	**D7**	134
Davis Sea, Ant.	**C13**	67
Davisstrædet see Davis Strait, strt., N.A.	**E28**	82
Davis Strait, strt., N.A.	**E28**	82
Davisville, R.I., U.S.	**E4**	132
Dawa, stm., Afr.	**C7**	54
Dawei, Mya.	**D3**	34
Dawes, co., Ne., U.S.	**B2**	120
Dawna Range, mts., Mya.	**C3**	34
Daws Island, i., S.C., U.S.	**G6**	133
Dawson, Ga., U.S.	**E2**	103
Dawson, co., Ga., U.S.	**B2**	103
Dawson, Mn., U.S.	**F2**	116
Dawson, co., Mt., U.S.	**C11**	119
Dawson, co., Ne., U.S.	**D6**	120
Dawson, co., Tx., U.S.	**C1**	136
Dawson, Isla, i., Chile	**H2**	69
Dawson, Mount, mtn., B.C., Can.	**D9**	85
Dawson Creek, B.C., Can.	**B7**	85
Dawson Springs, Ky., U.S.	**C2**	110
Dax, Fr.	**F6**	16
Daxian, China	**E9**	28
Daxing, China	**B4**	30
Daxue Shan, mts., China	**E8**	28
Day, co., S.D., U.S.	**B8**	134
Dayao, China	**A4**	34
Dayong, China	**D3**	30
Dayr az-Zawr, Syria	**E9**	44
Daysland, Ab., Can.	**C4**	84
Dayton, Ia., U.S.	**B3**	108
Dayton, In., U.S.	**D4**	107
Dayton, Ky., U.S.	**h14**	110
Dayton, Md., U.S.	**B4**	113
Dayton, Mn., U.S.	**m12**	116
Dayton, Nv., U.S.	**D2**	121
Dayton, Oh., U.S.	**C1**	128
Dayton, Or., U.S.	**B3**	130
Dayton, Tn., U.S.	**D8**	135
Dayton, Tx., U.S.	**D5**	136
Dayton, Va., U.S.	**B4**	139
Dayton, Wa., U.S.	**C8**	140
Dayton, Wy., U.S.	**B5**	143
Daytona Beach, Fl., U.S.	**C5**	102
Dayu, China	**F10**	28
Da Yunhe (Grand Canal), China	**D11**	28
Dayville, Ct., U.S.	**B8**	100
Dazhu, China	**C2**	30
De Aar, S. Afr.	**E3**	56
Dead, North Branch, stm., Me., U.S.	**C2**	112
Dead, South Branch, stm., Me., U.S.	**C2**	112
Dead Creek, stm., Vt., U.S.	**C2**	138
Dead Diamond, stm., N.H., U.S.	**g7**	122
Dead Indian Peak, mtn., Wy., U.S.	**B3**	143
Dead Lake, l., Mn., U.S.	**D3**	116
Dead Lakes, l., Fl., U.S.	**B1**	102
Deadman Bay, b., Fl., U.S.	**C3**	102
Deadman Creek, stm., Wa., U.S.	**g14**	140
Dead Sea, l., Asia	**G6**	44
Deadwood, S.D., U.S.	**C2**	134
Deadwood Reservoir, res., Id., U.S.	**E3**	105
Deaf Smith, co., Tx., U.S.	**B1**	136
Deakin, Austl.	**G4**	60
Deale, Md., U.S.	**C4**	113
Deal Island, Md., U.S.	**D6**	113
Deal Island, i., Md., U.S.	**D6**	113
Dean, stm., B.C., Can.	**C4**	85
De'an, China	**D4**	30
Dean Channel, strt., B.C., Can.	**C4**	85
Deán Funes, Arg.	**E5**	72
Dearborn, co., In., U.S.	**F7**	107
Dearborn, Mi., U.S.	**F7**	115
Dearborn Heights, Mi., U.S.	**p15**	115
Death Valley, val., Ca., U.S.	**D5**	98
Death Valley National Park, U.S.	**D5**	98
Deba, Nig.	**D7**	50
De Baca, co., N.M., U.S.	**C5**	124
Debao, China	**E2**	30
De Bary, Fl., U.S.	**D5**	102
Debauch Mountain, mtn., Ak., U.S.	**C8**	95
Dęblin, Pol.	**D6**	20
Debre Birhan, Eth.	**B7**	54
Debrecen, Hung.	**F6**	20
Debre Mark'os, Eth.	**A7**	54
Debre Tabor, Eth.	**H3**	38
Debre Zeyit, Eth.	**B7**	54
De Cade, Lake, l., La., U.S.	**E5**	111
Decatur, Al., U.S.	**A3**	94
Decatur, Ar., U.S.	**A1**	97
Decatur, Ga., U.S.	**C2**	103
Decatur, co., Ga., U.S.	**F2**	103
Decatur, co., Ia., U.S.	**D4**	108
Decatur, Il., U.S.	**D5**	106
Decatur, In., U.S.	**C8**	107
Decatur, co., In., U.S.	**F6**	107
Decatur, co., Ks., U.S.	**C3**	109
Decatur, Mi., U.S.	**F5**	115
Decatur, Ms., U.S.	**C4**	117
Decatur, Ne., U.S.	**B9**	120
Decatur, Tn., U.S.	**D9**	135
Decatur, co., Tn., U.S.	**B3**	135
Decatur, Tx., U.S.	**C4**	136
Decatur, Lake, res., Il., U.S.	**D5**	106
Decaturville, Tn., U.S.	**B3**	135
Decazeville, Fr.	**E8**	16
Deccan, plat., India	**G3**	40
Deception, Mount, mtn., Wa., U.S.	**B2**	140
Decherd, Tn., U.S.	**B5**	135
Děčín, Czech Rep.	**D3**	20
Decize, Fr.	**D8**	16
Deckerville, Mi., U.S.	**E8**	115
Decorah, Ia., U.S.	**A6**	108
Dedham, Ma., U.S.	**B5**	114
Dedoplis Ckaro, Geor.	**B12**	44
Dédougou, Burkina	**D4**	50
Deep, stm., N.C., U.S.	**B3**	126
Deep Creek, stm., Ut., U.S.	**C2**	137
Deep Creek, stm., Ut., U.S.	**F3**	137
Deep Creek, stm., Ut., U.S.	**B3**	137
Deep Creek, stm., Wa., U.S.	**g13**	140
Deep Creek Lake, res., Md., U.S.	**K12**	113
Deep Creek Mountains, mts., Id., U.S.	**G6**	105
Deep Fork, stm., Ok., U.S.	**B5**	129
Deep Inlet, b., N.L., Can.	**g10**	88
Deep Red Creek, stm., Ok., U.S.	**C3**	129
Deep River, On., Can.	**A7**	89
Deep River, Ct., U.S.	**D6**	100
Deer Creek, stm., Oh., U.S.	**C2**	128
Deer Creek Indian Reservation, Mn., U.S.	**C5**	116
Deerfield, Il., U.S.	**h9**	106
Deerfield, Ks., U.S.	**E2**	109
Deerfield, Ma., U.S.	**A2**	114
Deerfield, Mi., U.S.	**G7**	115
Deerfield, Wi., U.S.	**E4**	142
Deerfield, stm., U.S.	**A2**	114
Deerfield Beach, Fl., U.S.	**F6**	102
Deer Island, pen., Ma., U.S.	**g12**	114
Deer Island, i., Ms., U.S.	**f8**	117
Deer Isle, i., Me., U.S.	**D4**	112
Deer Lake, l., N.L., Can.	**D3**	88
Deer Lake, N.L., Can.	**D3**	88
Deer Lake, l., Mn., U.S.	**C5**	116
Deer Lodge, Mt., U.S.	**D4**	119
Deer Lodge, co., Mt., U.S.	**E3**	119
Deer Park, N.Y., U.S.	**n15**	125
Deer Park, Oh., U.S.	**o13**	128
Deer Park, Wa., U.S.	**B8**	140
Deer Peak, mtn., Co., U.S.	**C5**	99
Deer River, Mn., U.S.	**C5**	116
Defiance, Oh., U.S.	**A1**	128
Defiance, co., Oh., U.S.	**A1**	128
Defiance, Mount, mtn., Or., U.S.	**B5**	130
De Forest, Wi., U.S.	**E4**	142
De Funiak Springs, Fl., U.S.	**u15**	102
Dêgê, China	**E7**	28
Degeh Bur, Eth.	**B8**	54
Dégelis, Qc., Can.	**B9**	90
Degerfors, Swe.	**G6**	10
De Graff, Oh., U.S.	**B2**	128
De Gray Lake, res., Ar., U.S.	**C2**	97
Dehiwala-Mount Lavinia, Sri L.	**H3**	40
Dehlorān, Iran	**F12**	44
Dehra Dūn, India	**C3**	40
Dehui, China	**C13**	28
Dej, Rom.	**F7**	20
Dejnau, Turk.	**C8**	42
De Kalb, co., Al., U.S.	**A4**	94
De Kalb, co., Ga., U.S.	**C2**	103
De Kalb, Il., U.S.	**B5**	106
De Kalb, co., Il., U.S.	**B5**	106
De Kalb, co., In., U.S.	**B7**	107
De Kalb, co., Mo., U.S.	**B3**	118
De Kalb, Ms., U.S.	**C5**	117
De Kalb, co., Tn., U.S.	**D8**	135
De Kalb, Tx., U.S.	**C5**	136
Dekese, D.R.C.	**D4**	54
Delafield, Wi., U.S.	**m11**	142
Delanco, N.J., U.S.	**C3**	123
De Land, Fl., U.S.	**C5**	102
Delano, Ca., U.S.	**E4**	98
Delano, Mn., U.S.	**E5**	116
Delano Peak, mtn., Ut., U.S.	**E3**	137
Delārām, Afg.	**D8**	42
Delaronde Lake, l., Sk., Can.	**C2**	91
Delavan, Il., U.S.	**C4**	106
Delavan, Wi., U.S.	**F5**	142
Delaware, co., Ia., U.S.	**B6**	108
Delaware, co., In., U.S.	**D7**	107
Delaware, stm., Ks., U.S.	**C8**	109
Delaware, co., N.Y., U.S.	**C5**	125
Delaware, Oh., U.S.	**B2**	128
Delaware, co., Oh., U.S.	**B2**	128
Delaware, co., Ok., U.S.	**A7**	129
Delaware, co., Pa., U.S.	**G11**	131
Delaware, stm., U.S.	**G11**	131
Delaware, state, U.S.	**D3**	101
Delaware, East Branch, stm., N.Y., U.S.	**C5**	125
Delaware Bay, b., U.S.	**D13**	92
Delaware City, De., U.S.	**B3**	101
Delaware Lake, res., Oh., U.S.	**B3**	128
Delaware Water Gap, N.J., U.S.	**B2**	123
Delaware Water Gap National Recreation Area, U.S.	**B2**	123
Delbarton, W.V., U.S.	**D2**	141
Delcambre, La., U.S.	**E4**	111
Del City, Ok., U.S.	**B4**	129
De Leon, Tx., U.S.	**C3**	136
De Leon Springs, Fl., U.S.	**C5**	102
Delfzijl, Neth.	**D10**	12
Delgado, Cabo, c., Moz.	**A7**	56
Delhi, India	**D3**	40
Delhi, La., U.S.	**B4**	111
Delhi, N.Y., U.S.	**C6**	125
Delice, stm., Tur.	**B6**	44
Delicias, Mex.	**B3**	78
Delingde, Russia	**B13**	26
Delingha, China	**D7**	28
De Lisle, Ms., U.S.	**E4**	117
Dellenbaugh, Mount, mtn., Az., U.S.	**A2**	96
Dell Rapids, S.D., U.S.	**D9**	134
Dellys, Alg.	**I8**	16
Del Mar, Ca., U.S.	**o15**	98
Delmar, De., U.S.	**G3**	101
Delmar, Md., U.S.	**D6**	113
Delmar, N.Y., U.S.	**C7**	125
Delmenhorst, Ger.	**D11**	12
Del Norte, co., Ca., U.S.	**B2**	98
Del Norte, Co., U.S.	**D4**	99
Deloraine, Mb., Can.	**E1**	86
Delos see Dhílos, hist., Grc.	**F10**	18
Del Park Manor, De., U.S.	**i7**	101
Delphi see Dhelfoí, hist., Grc.	**E9**	18
Delphi, In., U.S.	**C4**	107
Delphos, Oh., U.S.	**B1**	128
Delran, N.J., U.S.	**C3**	123
Delray Beach, Fl., U.S.	**F6**	102
Del Rio, Tx., U.S.	**E2**	136
Delson, Qc., Can.	**q19**	90
Delta, Co., U.S.	**C2**	99
Delta, co., Co., U.S.	**C3**	99
Delta, co., Mi., U.S.	**C3**	115
Delta, reg., Ms., U.S.	**B3**	117
Delta, Oh., U.S.	**A2**	128
Delta, co., Tx., U.S.	**C5**	136
Delta, Ut., U.S.	**D3**	137
Delta Junction, Ak., U.S.	**C10**	95
Delta Peak, mtn., B.C., Can.	**A3**	85
Delta Reservoir, res., N.Y., U.S.	**B5**	125
Deltaville, Va., U.S.	**C6**	139
Deltona, Fl., U.S.	**D5**	102
Del Verme Falls, wtfl., Eth.	**B8**	54
Demarest, N.J., U.S.	**h9**	123
Demba, D.R.C.	**E4**	54
Dembia, C.A.R.	**B4**	54
Dembī Dolo, Eth.	**B6**	54
Demidov, Russia	**B11**	20
Deming, N.M., U.S.	**E2**	124
Demirci, Tur.	**C3**	44
Demjanskoe, Russia	**D8**	26
Demmin, Ger.	**D13**	12
Democratic Republic of the Congo see Congo, Democratic Republic of the, ctry., Afr.	**D4**	52
Demopolis, Al., U.S.	**C2**	94
Demorest, Ga., U.S.	**B3**	103
Demotte, In., U.S.	**B3**	107
Dempo, Gunung, vol., Indon.	**D2**	36
Demta, Indon.	**G11**	32

Name — Map Ref. — Page

Denakil see Danakil, reg., Afr. H13 48
Denali National Park, Ak., U.S. C9 95
Denan, Eth. B8 54
Denare Beach, Sk., Can. C4 91
Denau, Uzb. F8 26
Dengas, Niger D6 50
Dengkou, China A2 30
Dêngqên, China E7 28
Dengxian, China C3 30
Denham, Austl. F1 60
Denham, Mount, mtn., Jam. B4 80
Denham Springs, La., U.S. D5 111
Den Helder, Neth. D9 12
Dénia, Spain H7 16
Deniliquin, Austl. H4 62
Denison, Ia., U.S. B2 108
Denison, Tx., U.S. C4 136
Denison Dam, U.S. D5 129
Denizli, Tur. D3 44
Denmark, Austl. G2 60
Denmark, ctry., Eur. I4 10
Denmark, S.C., U.S. E5 133
Denmark, Wi., U.S. D6 142
Denmark Strait, strt. E34 82
Dennehotso, Az., U.S. A6 96
Dennis, Ma., U.S. C7 114
Dennison, Oh., U.S. B4 128
Dennis Port, Ma., U.S. C7 114
Denny Terrace, S.C., U.S. C5 133
Denpasar, Indon. E5 36
Dent, co., Mo., U.S. D6 118
Denton, Md., U.S. C6 113
Denton, N.C., U.S. B2 126
Denton, Tx., U.S. C4 136
Denton, co., Tx., U.S. C4 136
D'Entrecasteaux, Point, c., Austl. G2 60
D'Entrecasteaux Islands, is., Pap. N. Gui. H13 32
Dentsville, S.C., U.S. C6 133
Denver, Co., U.S. B6 99
Denver, co., Co., U.S. B6 99
Denver, Ia., U.S. B5 108
Denver, Pa., U.S. F9 131
Denver City, Tx., U.S. C1 136
Denville, N.J., U.S. B4 123
Deoghar, India E5 40
Deolāli, India F2 40
De Pere, Wi., U.S. D5 142
Depew, N.Y., U.S. C2 125
Depoe Bay, Or., U.S. C2 130
Deposit, N.Y., U.S. C5 125
Depue, Il., U.S. B4 106
Dêqên, China F7 28
Deqing, China E3 30
De Queen, Ar., U.S. C1 97
De Queen Reservoir, res., Ar., U.S. C1 97
De Quincy, La., U.S. D2 111
Dera Ghāzi Khān, Pak. E10 42
Dera Ismāīl Khān, Pak. D10 42
Derbent, Russia E6 26
Derby, Austl. D3 60
Derby, Eng., U.K. D6 12
Derby, Ct., U.S. D3 100
Derby, Ks., U.S. E6 109
Derby, Vt., U.S. B4 138
Derby Line, Vt., U.S. A4 138
Derg, Lough, l., Ire. D2 12
Dergači, Russia D8 22
De Ridder, La., U.S. D2 111
Derik, Tur. D9 44
Derma, Ms., U.S. B4 117
Dermott, Ar., U.S. D4 97
Dernieres, Isles, is., La., U.S. E5 111
Derry see Londonderry, N. Ire., U.K. C3 12
Derry, N.H., U.S. E4 122
Derry, Pa., U.S. F3 131
Derventa, Bos. B6 18
Derwood, Md., U.S. B3 113
Des Allemands, La., U.S. E5 111
Désappointement, Îles du, is., Fr. Poly. F15 58
Des Arc, Ar., U.S. C4 97
Desbiens, Qc., Can. A6 90
Descanso, Mex. A1 78
Deschaillons [-sur-Saint-Laurent], Qc., Can. C5 90
Deschambault, Qc., Can. C6 90
Deschambault Lake, l., Sk., Can. C4 91
Deschutes, stm., Or., U.S. B6 130
Deschutes, co., Or., U.S. D5 130
Desē, Eth. H12 48
Deseado, stm., Arg. G3 69
Desengaño, Punta, c., Arg. G3 69
Deseret Peak, mtn., Ut., U.S. C3 137
Deseronto, On., Can. C7 89
Desert Creek Peak, mtn., Nv., U.S. E2 121
Desert Hot Springs, Ca., U.S. F5 98
Desert Peak, mtn., Ut., U.S. B2 137
Desert Valley, val., Nv., U.S. B3 121
Desha, Ar., U.S. B4 97
Desha, co., Ar., U.S. D4 97
Deshler, Ne., U.S. D8 120
Deshler, Oh., U.S. A2 128
Des Lacs, stm., N.D., U.S. A4 127
Desloge, Mo., U.S. D7 118
De Smet, S.D., U.S. C8 134
Des Moines, Ia., U.S. C4 108
Des Moines, co., Ia., U.S. D6 108
Des Moines, Wa., U.S. B3 140
Des Moines, stm., U.S. D5 108
Desna, stm., Eur. D11 20
De Soto, co., Fl., U.S. E5 102
De Soto, Ia., U.S. C3 108
De Soto, Il., U.S. F4 106
De Soto, Ks., U.S. D9 109
De Soto, co., La., U.S. B2 111
De Soto, Mo., U.S. C7 118
De Soto, co., Ms., U.S. A3 117
Despard, W.V., U.S. k10 141
Des Peres, Mo., U.S. f13 118
Des Plaines, Il., U.S. A6 106
Des Plaines, stm., U.S. k8 106
Desroches, i., Sey. i12 57b
Dessau, Ger. E13 12
Destin, Fl., U.S. u15 102
Destrehan, La., U.S. E5 111
Detour, Point, c., Mi., U.S. C4 115
Detroit, Mi., U.S. F7 115
Detroit Lake, res., Or., U.S. C4 130
Detroit Lakes, Mn., U.S. D3 116
Dettifoss, wtfl., Ice. l20 10a
Deuel, co., Ne., U.S. C3 120
Deuel, co., S.D., U.S. C9 134
Deutsche Bucht, b., Ger. C10 12
Deux-Montagnes, Qc., Can. p19 90
Deux Montagnes, Lac des, l., Qc., Can. q19 90
Deva, Rom. G7 20
De Valls Bluff, Ar., U.S. C4 97
Develi, Tur. C6 44
Deventer, Neth. D10 12
DeView, Bayou, stm., Ar., U.S. B4 97
Devils Island see Diable, Île du, i., Fr. Gu. B9 70
Devils Lake, N.D., U.S. A7 127
Devils Lake, l., N.D., U.S. A6 127
Devils Paw, mtn., Ak., U.S. k23 95
Devils Postpile National Monument, Ca., U.S. D4 98
Devils Tower National Monument, Wy., U.S. B8 143
Devil Track Lake, l., Mn., U.S. k9 116
Devine, Tx., U.S. E3 136
DeVola, Oh., U.S. C4 128
Devon, Ab., Can. C4 84
Devonport, Austl. I4 62
Devonshire, De., U.S. h7 101
Devrek, Tur. B4 44
Dewar, Ok., U.S. B6 129
Dewās, India E3 40
Dewees Inlet, b., S.C., U.S. k12 133
Dewees Island, i., S.C., U.S. F8 133
Dewey, Az., U.S. C3 96
Dewey, Ok., U.S. A6 129
Dewey, co., Ok., U.S. B2 129
Dewey, co., S.D., U.S. B4 134
Dewey Beach, De., U.S. F5 101
Dewey Lake, res., Ky., U.S. C7 110
Deweyville, Tx., U.S. D6 136
De Witt, Ar., U.S. C4 97
De Witt, Ia., U.S. C7 108
De Witt, co., Il., U.S. C4 106
De Witt, Mi., U.S. F6 115
De Witt, N.Y., U.S. B4 125
De Witt, co., Tx., U.S. E4 136
Dexing, China D4 30
Dexter, Ia., U.S. C3 108
Dexter, Me., U.S. C3 112
Dexter, Mi., U.S. F7 115
Dexter, Mo., U.S. E8 118
Dexter, N.M., U.S. D5 124
Dexter, Lake, l., Fl., U.S. C5 102
Dezfūl, Iran D5 42
Dezhou, China D11 28
Dežneva, mys, c., Russia C21 26
Dhahran see Az-Zahrān, Sau. Ar. E5 42
Dhaka, Bngl. E6 40
Dhamtari, India E4 40
Dhanbād, India E5 40
Dhār, India E3 40
Dharān, Nepal D5 40
Dharmapuri, India G3 40
Dhawalāgiri, mtn., Nepal D4 40
Dhelfoí, hist., Grc. E9 18
Dhenkānāl, India E5 40
Dhílos, hist., Grc. F10 18
Dhodhekánisos, is., Grc. F11 18
Dhone, India F3 40
Dhoomadheere, Som. C8 54
Dhorāji, India E2 40
Dhuburi, India D5 40
Dhule, India E2 40
Diable, Île du, i., Fr. Gu. B9 70
Diablo, Canyon, Az., U.S. C4 96
Diablo, Mount, mtn., Ca., U.S. h9 98
Diablo, Pico del, mtn., Mex. A1 78
Diablo Dam, Wa., U.S. A4 140
Diablo Lake, res., Wa., U.S. A4 140
Diablo Range, mts., Ca., U.S. D3 98
Diablotins, Morne, vol., Dom. B7 80
Diaca, Moz. A6 56
Dialakoto, Sen. D2 50
Diamante, Arg. E5 72
Diamantina, stm., Austl. E3 62
Diamantina, Braz. E3 74
Diamantino, Braz. F8 70
Diamond Harbour, India E5 40
Diamond Head, crat., Hi., U.S. B4 104
Diamond Hill, R.I., U.S. B4 132
Diamond Hill Reservoir, res., R.I., U.S. A4 132
Diamond Lake, Il., U.S. h9 106
Diamond Lake, l., Or., U.S. D4 130
Diamond Mountains, mts., Nv., U.S. D6 121
Diamond Peak, mtn., Co., U.S. A2 99
Diamond Peak, mtn., Id., U.S. E5 105
Diamond Peak, mtn., Or., U.S. D4 130
Diamond Peak, mtn., Wa., U.S. C8 140
Diamondville, Wy., U.S. E2 143
Dianbai, China E3 30
Dianjiang, China C2 30
Dianópolis, Braz. F10 70
Diapaga, Burkina D5 50
Diaz, Ar., U.S. B4 97
Dibaya, D.R.C. E4 54
D'Iberville, Ms., U.S. E5 117
Diboll, Tx., U.S. D5 136
Dibrugarh, India D6 40
Dickens, co., Tx., U.S. C2 136
Dickenson, co., Va., U.S. e9 139
Dickerson, Md., U.S. B3 113
Dickey, co., N.D., U.S. C7 127
Dickeyville, Wi., U.S. F3 142
Dickinson, co., Ia., U.S. A2 108
Dickinson, co., Ks., U.S. D6 109
Dickinson, co., Mi., U.S. B3 115
Dickinson, N.D., U.S. C3 127
Dickinson Dam, N.D., U.S. C3 127
Dickson, Ok., U.S. C5 129
Dickson, Tn., U.S. A4 135
Dickson, co., Tn., U.S. A4 135
Dickson City, Pa., U.S. D10 131
Dicle see Tigris, stm., Asia D5 42
Didao, China A2 31
Didbiran, Russia D15 26
Didsbury, Ab., Can. D3 84
Dīdwāna, India D2 40
Diefenbaker, Lake, res., Sk., Can. F2 91
Diego de Almagro, Isla, i., Chile H1 69
Diégo-Suarez see Antsiranana, Madag. A8 56
Diéma, Mali D3 50
Dien Bien, Viet. B4 34
Diepholz, Ger. D11 12
Dieppe, N.B., Can. C5 87
Dieppe, Fr. C7 16
Dierks, Ar., U.S. C1 97
Di'er Songhua see Songhua, stm., China B14 28
Dif, Kenya C8 54
Diffa, Niger D7 50
Dighton, Ks., U.S. D3 109
Digne, Fr. E10 16
Digos, Phil. E9 34
Digul, stm., Indon. H10 32
Diinsor, Som. C8 54
Dijlah see Tigris, stm., Asia D5 42
Dijon, Fr. D9 16
Dike, Ia., U.S. B5 108
Dikhil, Dji. H13 48
Dikili, Tur. C2 44
Dikson, Russia B10 26
Dikwa, Nig. D7 50
Dīla, Eth. B7 54
Dili, E. Timor E7 36
Dillard, Or., U.S. D3 130
Dill City, Ok., U.S. B2 129
Dilley, Tx., U.S. E3 136
Dillingham, Ak., U.S. D8 95
Dillon, Mt., U.S. E4 119
Dillon, co., S.C., U.S. C9 133
Dillon, S.C., U.S. C9 133
Dillon Lake, res., Oh., U.S. B3 128
Dillon Reservoir, res., Co., U.S. B4 99
Dillonvale, Oh., U.S. B5 128
Dillsboro, In., U.S. F7 107
Dillsburg, Pa., U.S. F7 131
Dilolo, D.R.C. F4 54
Dilworth, Mn., U.S. D2 116
Dimāpur, India D6 40
Dimashq (Damascus), Syria F7 44
Dimbokro, C. Iv. E4 50
Dimitrovgrad, Blg. C10 18
Dimitrovgrad, Russia D6 26
Dimlang, mtn., Nig. E7 50
Dimmit, co., Tx., U.S. E3 136
Dimmitt, Tx., U.S. B1 136
Dimondale, Mi., U.S. F6 115
Dinagat Island, i., Phil. D9 34
Dinājpur, Bngl. D5 40
Dinan, Fr. C5 16
Dinar, Tur. C4 44
Dinaric Alps, mts., Eur. G4 20
Dindigul, India G3 40
Dinghai, China E12 28
Dingle Bay, b., Ire. D1 12
Dingmans Ferry, Pa., U.S. D12 131
Dingolfing, Ger. F13 12
Dingtao, China B4 30
Dinguiraye, Gui. D2 50
Dingxiang, China B3 30
Dingxing, China B4 30
Dinner Point, c., Fl., U.S. D4 102
Dinokwe, Bots. C4 56
Dinosaur National Monument, U.S. C6 137
Dinuba, Ca., U.S. D4 98
Dinwiddie, co., Va., U.S. C5 139
Dioura, Mali D3 50
Diourbel, Sen. D1 50
Dipolog, Phil. E8 34
Dīr, Pak. C10 42
Diré, Mali C4 50
Dirē Dawa, Eth. B8 54
Dirico, Ang. B3 56
Dirj, Libya E6 14
Dirk Hartog Island, i., Austl. F1 60
Dirkou, Niger C7 50
Dirty Devil, stm., Ut., U.S. E5 137
Disappointment, Cape, c., S. Geor. H9 69
Disappointment, Cape, c., Wa., U.S. C1 140
Disappointment, Lake, l., Austl. E3 60
Dishman, Wa., U.S. g14 140
Disko, i., Grnld. E28 82
Dismal, stm., Ne., U.S. C5 120
Dispur, India D6 40
Disraëli, Qc., Can. D6 90
District of Columbia, state, U.S. f8 113
Distrito Federal, state, Braz. E2 74
Distrito Federal, state, Mex. D5 78
Diu, India E2 40
Dīvāndarreh, Iran E12 44
Divernon, Il., U.S. D4 106
Divide, co., N.D., U.S. A2 127
Divide Peak, mtn., Wy., U.S. E5 143
Divinópolis, Braz. F3 74
Divisor, Serra do, plat., S.A. E5 70
Divnoe, Russia A4 42
Divo, C. Iv. E3 50
Divriği, Tur. C8 44
Dix, stm., Ky., U.S. C5 110
Dixfield, Me., U.S. D2 112
Dixie, co., Fl., U.S. C3 102
Dixie Valley, val., Nv., U.S. D4 121
Dixon, Ca., U.S. C3 98
Dixon, Il., U.S. B4 106
Dixon, Mo., U.S. D5 118
Dixon, co., Ne., U.S. B9 120
Dixon, N.M., U.S. A4 124
Dixon Entrance, strt., N.A. H13 82
Dixonville, Pa., U.S. E3 131
Diyarbakır, Tur. D9 44
Djado, Plateau du, plat., Niger B7 50
Djamâa, Alg. E5 14
Djambala, Congo D2 54
Djanet, Alg. B6 50
Djat'kovo, Russia C13 20
Djemila, hist., Alg. I9 16
Djenné, Mali D4 50
Djibo, Burkina D4 50
Djibouti, ctry., Afr. H13 48
Djibouti, Dji. H13 48
Djoku-Punda, D.R.C. E4 54
Djougou, Benin E5 50
Djoum, Cam. C2 54
Djugu, D.R.C. C6 54
Djurtjuli, Russia C9 22
Dmitrija Lapteva, proliv, strt., Russia B16 26
Dmitrijev-L'govskij, Russia C13 20
Dnepropetrovsk see Dnipropetrovs'k, Ukr. E13 20
Dnestr see Dniester, stm., Eur. F11 20
Dnieper (Dnepr) (Dnipro), stm., Eur. F12 20
Dniester (Nistru) (Dnister), stm., Eur. F11 20
Dniprodzerzhyns'k, Ukr. E13 20
Dniprodzerzhyns'ke vodoskhovyshche, res., Ukr. E13 20
Dnipropetrovs'k, Ukr. E13 20
Dnister see Dniester, stm., Eur. F11 20
Dno, Russia C5 22
Dôa, Moz. B5 56
Doaktown, N.B., Can. C3 87
Doba, Chad E8 50
Dobbs Ferry, N.Y., U.S. g13 125
Dobele, Lat. H10 10
Doberai, Jazirah, pen., Indon. D8 36
Dobo, Indon. H9 32
Doboj, Bos. B7 18
Dobrič, Blg. C11 18
Dobrjanka, Russia C10 22
Dobruja, hist. reg., Eur. H9 20
Dobson, N.C., U.S. A2 126
Doce, stm., Braz. E3 74
Docena, Al., U.S. f7 94
Doctors Lake, l., Fl., U.S. m8 102
Doddridge, co., W.V., U.S. B4 141
Dodecanese see Dhodhekánisos, is., Grc. F11 18
Dodge, co., Ga., U.S. D3 103
Dodge, co., Mn., U.S. G6 116
Dodge, Ne., U.S. C9 120
Dodge, co., Ne., U.S. C9 120
Dodge, co., Wi., U.S. E5 142
Dodge Center, Mn., U.S. F6 116
Dodge City, Ks., U.S. E3 109
Dodgeville, Wi., U.S. F3 142
Dodoma, Tan. E7 54
Doerun, Ga., U.S. E3 103
Doe Run, Mo., U.S. D7 118
Dog, stm., Vt., U.S. C3 138
Dogai Coring, l., China E5 28
Dog Island, i., Fl., U.S. C2 102
Dog Keys Pass, strt., Ms., U.S. g8 117
Dog Lake, l., Mb., Can. D2 86
Do Gonbadān, Iran D6 42
Dogondoutchi, Niger D5 50
Doğubayazıt, Tur. C11 44
Doğu Karadeniz Dağları, mts., Tur. B8 44
Doha see Ad-Dawḥah, Qatar E6 42
Dokka, Nor. F4 10
Dokuchaievs'k, Ukr. F14 20
Dolbeau, Qc., Can. k12 90
Dole, Fr. D9 16
Dolgeville, N.Y., U.S. B6 125
Dolinsk, Russia B16 28
Dollar Bay, Mi., U.S. A2 115
Dolomite, Al., U.S. B3 94
Dolomites see Dolomiti, mts., Italy A3 18
Dolomiti, mts., Italy A3 18
Dolores, Arg. E6 72
Dolores, Ur. F6 72
Dolores, Co., U.S. D2 99
Dolores, co., Co., U.S. D2 99
Dolores, stm., U.S. E7 137
Dolphin Island, i., Ut., U.S. B3 137
Dolton, Il., U.S. k9 106
Dolyns'ka, Ukr. E12 20
Dombås, Nor. E3 10
Dome Mountain, mtn., Az., U.S. k9 96
Dome Peak, mtn., Co., U.S. B3 99
Domeyko, Chile C2 69
Dominica, ctry., N.A. E12 76
Dominican Republic, ctry., N.A. H12 75
Dominique, Canal de la see Martinique Passage, strt., N.A. B7 80
Domo, Eth. I14 48
Dom Pedrito, Braz. E7 72
Don, stm., Russia E6 26
Dona Ana, N.M., U.S. E3 124
Dona Ana, co., N.M., U.S. E2 124
Donaldsonville, La., U.S. D4 111
Donalsonville, Ga., U.S. E2 103
Donau see Danube, stm., Eur. C9 14
Donauwörth, Ger. F12 12
Don Benito, Spain H4 16
Dondo, Ang. E2 54
Dondo, Moz. B5 56
Dondra Head, c., Sri L. H4 40
Donegal, Ire. C2 12
Donegal Bay, b., Ire. C2 12
Doneraile, S.C., U.S. C8 133
Donets'k, Ukr. F14 20
Dong, stm., China B7 34
Dong'an, China D3 30
Dongara, Austl. F1 60
Dongchuan, China D1 30
Dongfang, China H9 28
Donggala, Indon. D5 36
Donghai Dao, i., China G10 28
Dong Hoi, Viet. C5 34
Dongjingcheng, China B1 31
Dongo, Ang. A2 56
Dongping, China B4 30
Dongsheng, China B3 30
Dongtai, China C5 30
Dongting Hu, l., China F10 28
Dongzhi, China C4 30
Doniphan, co., Ks., U.S. C8 109
Doniphan, Mo., U.S. E7 118
Doniphan, Ne., U.S. D7 120
Donkey Creek, stm., Wy., U.S. B7 143
Donkin, N.S., Can. C10 87
Donley, co., Tx., U.S. B2 136
Dønna, Nor. C5 10
Donna, Tx., U.S. F3 136
Donnacona, Qc., Can. C6 90
Donnellson, Ia., U.S. D6 108
Donner Pass, Ca., U.S. C3 98
Donnybrook, Austl. G2 60
Donora, Pa., U.S. F2 131
Donostia (San Sebastián), Spain F6 16
Donskaja grjada, Eur. E7 22
Don Upland see Donskaja grjada, Eur. E7 22
Doolow, Som. J13 48
Dooly, co., Ga., U.S. D3 103
Doonerak, Mount, mtn., Ak., U.S. B9 95
Door, co., Wi., U.S. D6 142
Dora, Al., U.S. B2 94
Doraville, Ga., U.S. h8 103
Dorcheat, Bayou, stm., U.S. B2 111
Dorchester, N.B., Can. D5 87
Dorchester, Eng., U.K. E5 12
Dorchester, co., Md., U.S. D5 113
Dorchester, Ne., U.S. D8 120
Dorchester, co., S.C., U.S. E7 133
Dordogne, stm., Fr. E7 16

Name **Map Ref.** **Page**

Dordrecht, Neth. **E9** 12
Doré Lake, l., Sk., Can. **C2** 91
Dorena Lake, res., Or., U.S. **D3** 130
Dori, Burkina **D4** 50
Dorion-Vaudreuil, Qc., Can. **q18** 90
Dormont, Pa., U.S. **k13** 131
Dornbirn, Aus. **G11** 12
Dorogobuž, Russia **B12** 20
Dorohoi, Rom. **F9** 20
Dorothy Pond, Ma., U.S. **B4** 114
Dorr, Mi., U.S. **F5** 115
Dorre Island, i., Austl. **F1** 60
Dorset, Vt., U.S. **E2** 138
Dorsey, Md., U.S. **B4** 113
Dortmund, Ger. **E10** 12
Dorton, Ky., U.S. **C7** 110
Dörtyol, Tur. **D7** 44
Do Rūd, Iran **D5** 42
Doruma, D.R.C. **C5** 54
Dorval, Qc., Can. **q19** 90
Dosatuj, Russia **D13** 26
Dos Bahías, Cabo, c., Arg. **G3** 69
Dosso, Niger **D5** 50
Dossor, Kaz. **E9** 22
Dothan, Al., U.S. **D4** 94
Douala, Cam. **C1** 54
Douarnenez, Fr. **C4** 16
Double Beach, Ct., U.S. **D4** 100
Double Island Point, c., Austl. **F5** 62
Doublespring Pass, Id., U.S. **E5** 105
Double Springs, Al., U.S. **A2** 94
Doubletop Peak, mtn., Wy., U.S. **C2** 143
Doubs, stm., Eur. **D9** 16
Douentza, Mali **C4** 50
Dougherty, co., Ga., U.S. **E2** 103
Douglas, I. of Man **C4** 12
Douglas, S. Afr. **D3** 56
Douglas, Az., U.S. **F6** 96
Douglas, co., Co., U.S. **B6** 99
Douglas, Ga., U.S. **E4** 103
Douglas, co., Ga., U.S. **C2** 103
Douglas, co., Il., U.S. **D5** 106
Douglas, co., Ks., U.S. **D8** 109
Douglas, Mi., U.S. **F4** 115
Douglas, co., Mn., U.S. **E3** 116
Douglas, co., Mo., U.S. **E5** 118
Douglas, co., Ne., U.S. **C9** 120
Douglas, co., Nv., U.S. **E2** 121
Douglas, co., Or., U.S. **D3** 130
Douglas, co., S.D., U.S. **D7** 134
Douglas, co., Wa., U.S. **B6** 140
Douglas, co., Wi., U.S. **B2** 142
Douglas, Wy., U.S. **D7** 143
Douglas, Mount, mtn., Ak., U.S. **D9** 95
Douglas Channel, strt., B.C., Can. **C3** 85
Douglas Lake, l., Mi., U.S. **C6** 115
Douglas Lake, res., Tn., U.S. **D10** 135
Douglass, Ks., U.S. **E7** 109
Douglastown, N.B., Can. **B4** 87
Douglasville, Ga., U.S. **C2** 103
Dourados, Braz. **H9** 70
Dourbali, Chad **D8** 50
Douro (Duero), stm., Eur. **G2** 16
Dousman, Wi., U.S. **E5** 142
Dove Creek, Co., U.S. **D2** 99
Dover, Eng., U.K. **E7** 12
Dover, Ar., U.S. **B2** 97
Dover, De., U.S. **D3** 101
Dover, Fl., U.S. **D4** 102
Dover, Ma., U.S. **h10** 114
Dover, N.H., U.S. **D5** 122
Dover, N.J., U.S. **B3** 123
Dover, Oh., U.S. **B4** 128
Dover, Pa., U.S. **F8** 131
Dover, Tn., U.S. **A4** 135
Dover, Strait of, strt., Eur. **B7** 16
Dover Air Force Base, mil., De., U.S. **D4** 101
Dover-Foxcroft, Me., U.S. **C3** 112
Dover Plains, N.Y., U.S. **D7** 125
Dowagiac, Mi., U.S. **G4** 115
Dowlatābād, Iran **E7** 42
Downers Grove, Il., U.S. **B5** 106
Downey, Ca., U.S. **n12** 98
Downey, Id., U.S. **G6** 105
Downingtown, Pa., U.S. **F10** 131
Downpatrick, N. Ire., U.K. **C4** 12
Downs, Ks., U.S. **C5** 109
Downs Mountain, mtn., Wy., U.S. **C3** 143
Downton, Mount, mtn., B.C., Can. **C5** 85
Dows, Ia., U.S. **B4** 108
Doylestown, Oh., U.S. **B4** 128
Doylestown, Pa., U.S. **F11** 131
Doyline, La., U.S. **B2** 111
Draa, Hamada du, des., Alg. **E3** 48
Dracena, Braz. **F1** 74
Dracut, Ma., U.S. **A5** 114
Drăgășani, Rom. **G8** 20
Dragør, Den. **I5** 10
Drain, Or., U.S. **D3** 130
Drakensberg, mts., Afr. **D4** 56
Drake Passage, strt. **B33** 67
Drake Peak, mtn., Or., U.S. **E6** 130
Dráma, Grc. **D10** 18
Drammen, Nor. **G4** 10
Draper, Ut., U.S. **C4** 137
Drau (Dráva), stm., Eur. **F2** 20
Dráva (Drau), stm., Eur. **G4** 20
Drayton, On., Can. **D4** 89
Drayton, N.D., U.S. **A8** 127
Drayton, S.C., U.S. **B4** 133
Drayton Plains, Mi., U.S. **F7** 115
Drayton Valley, Ab., Can. **C3** 84
Dresden, On., Can. **E2** 89
Dresden, Ger. **E13** 12
Dresden, Oh., U.S. **B3** 128
Dresden, Tn., U.S. **A3** 135
Dresslerville, Nv., U.S. **E2** 121
Dreux, Fr. **C7** 16
Drew, co., Ar., U.S. **D4** 97
Drew, Ms., U.S. **B3** 117
Drews Reservoir, res., Or., U.S. **E6** 130
Drexel, Mo., U.S. **C3** 118
Drexel, N.C., U.S. **B1** 126
Drexel, Oh., U.S. **C1** 128
Drift, Ky., U.S. **C7** 110
Driggs, Id., U.S. **F7** 105
Drinit, Gjiri i, b., Alb. **D7** 18
Driskill Mountain, La., U.S. **B3** 111
Drobeta-Turnu Severin, Rom. **G7** 20
Drogheda, Ire. **D3** 12
Drohobych, Ukr. **E7** 20
Drumheller, Ab., Can. **D4** 84
Drum Island, i., S.C., U.S. **k12** 133
Drummond, Lake, l., Va., U.S. **D6** 139
Drummond Island, i., Mi., U.S. **C7** 115
Drummondville, Qc., Can. **D5** 90
Drumright, Ok., U.S. **B5** 129
Druskininkai, Lith. **I11** 10
Družba, Kaz. **B4** 28
Družina, Russia **C16** 26
Drybranch, W.V., U.S. **m13** 141
Dry Cimarron, stm., U.S. **A6** 124
Dry Creek Mountain, mtn., Nv., U.S. **B5** 121
Dryden, On., Can. **o16** 89
Dryden, N.Y., U.S. **C4** 125
Dry Fork, stm., Mo., U.S. **D6** 118
Dry Fork, stm., W.V., U.S. **D3** 141
Dry Fork, stm., W.V., U.S. **B5** 141
Dry Ridge, Ky., U.S. **B5** 110
Dry Tortugas, is., Fl., U.S. **H5** 102
Dschang, Cam. **B1** 54
Duarte, Pico, mtn., Dom. Rep. **B5** 80
Dubach, La., U.S. **B3** 111
Dubai see Dubayy, U.A.E. **E7** 42
Dubăsari, Mol. **F10** 20
Du Bay, Lake, res., Wi., U.S. **D4** 142
Dubayy (Dubai), U.A.E. **E7** 42
Dubbo, Austl. **G4** 62
Dublin (Baile Átha Cliath), Ire. **D3** 12
Dublin, Ga., U.S. **D4** 103
Dublin, In., U.S. **E7** 107
Dublin, N.H., U.S. **E2** 122
Dublin, Oh., U.S. **k10** 128
Dublin, Pa., U.S. **F11** 131
Dublin, Tx., U.S. **C3** 136
Dublin, Va., U.S. **C2** 139
Dubno, Ukr. **D8** 20
Dubois, In., U.S. **H4** 107
Dubois, co., In., U.S. **H4** 107
Du Bois, Pa., U.S. **D4** 131
Dubois, Wy., U.S. **C3** 143
Duboistown, Pa., U.S. **D7** 131
Dubovka, Russia **E7** 22
Dubréka, Gui. **E2** 50
Dubrovnik, Cro. **C7** 18
Dubrovytsia, Ukr. **D9** 20
Dubuque, Ia., U.S. **B7** 108
Dubuque, co., Ia., U.S. **B7** 108
Duchesne, Ut., U.S. **C5** 137
Duchesne, stm., Ut., U.S. **C5** 137
Duchesne, co., Ut., U.S. **C5** 137
Duck, stm., Tn., U.S. **B4** 135
Duck Bay, Mb., Can. **C1** 86
Duck Creek, stm., Oh., U.S. **C4** 128
Duck Creek, stm., Wi., U.S. **h9** 142
Duck Lake, Sk., Can. **E2** 91
Duck Lake, l., Me., U.S. **C4** 112
Duck Mountain Provincial Park, Sk., Can. **F5** 91
Duck Valley Indian Reservation, U.S. **B5** 121
Duckwater Indian Reservation, Nv., U.S. **E6** 121
Duckwater Peak, mtn., Nv., U.S. **E6** 121
Du Couedic, Cape, c., Austl. **H2** 62
Dudinka, Russia **C10** 26
Dudley, Eng., U.K. **D5** 12
Dudley, Ma., U.S. **B4** 114
Duenweg, Mo., U.S. **D3** 118
Duero (Douro), stm., Eur. **G4** 16
Due West, S.C., U.S. **C3** 133
Duffer Peak, mtn., Nv., U.S. **B3** 121
Dufourspitze, mtn., Eur. **B1** 18
Dugdemona, stm., La., U.S. **B3** 111
Dugger, In., U.S. **F3** 107
Dugi Otok, i., Cro. **C5** 18
Duifken Point, c., Austl. **C3** 62
Duisburg, Ger. **E10** 12
Duitama, Col. **B5** 70
Duke Island, i., Ak., U.S. **n24** 95
Dukes, co., Ma., U.S. **D6** 114
Duk Fadiat, Sudan **I11** 48
Dukhān, Qatar **E6** 42
Dukku, Nig. **D7** 50
Dukou, China **F8** 28
Dulan, China **D7** 28
Dulce, stm., Arg. **E5** 72
Dulce, N.M., U.S. **A2** 124
Dul'durga, Russia **D13** 26
Duluth, Ga., U.S. **B2** 103
Duluth, Mn., U.S. **D6** 116
Dūmā, Syria **F7** 44
Dumaguete, Phil. **E8** 34
Dumai, Indon. **C2** 36
Dumaran Island, i., Phil. **D7** 34
Dumas, Ar., U.S. **D4** 97
Dumas, Tx., U.S. **B2** 136
Dumfries, Scot., U.K. **C5** 12
Dumfries, Va., U.S. **B5** 139
Dumont, Ia., U.S. **B5** 108
Dumont, N.J., U.S. **B5** 123
Dumraon, India **D4** 40
Duna see Danube, stm., Eur. **C9** 14
Dunai see Danube, stm., Eur. **C9** 14
Dunaïvtsi, Ukr. **E9** 20
Dunaj see Danube, stm., Eur. **C9** 14
Dunărea see Danube, stm., Eur. **C9** 14
Dunaújváros, Hung. **F5** 20
Dunav see Danube, stm., Eur. **C9** 14
Dunay see Danube, stm., Eur. **C9** 14
Dunbar, Pa., U.S. **G2** 131
Dunbar, W.V., U.S. **C3** 141
Duncan, B.C., Can. **E6** 85
Duncan, Az., U.S. **E6** 96
Duncan, Ok., U.S. **C4** 129
Duncan, S.C., U.S. **B3** 133
Duncan Falls, Oh., U.S. **C4** 128
Duncan Lake, res., B.C., Can. **D9** 85
Duncannon, Pa., U.S. **F7** 131
Duncan Passage, strt., India **G6** 40
Duncansville, Pa., U.S. **F5** 131
Duncanville, Tx., U.S. **n10** 136
Dundalk, On., Can. **C4** 89
Dundalk, Ire. **C3** 12
Dundalk, Md., U.S. **B4** 113
Dundalk Bay, b., Ire. **D3** 12
Dundas, On., Can. **D5** 89
Dundee, S. Afr. **D5** 56
Dundee, Scot., U.K. **B5** 12
Dundee, Fl., U.S. **D5** 102
Dundee, Il., U.S. **A5** 106
Dundee, Mi., U.S. **G7** 115
Dundee, N.Y., U.S. **C4** 125
Dundee, Or., U.S. **h11** 130
Dundy, co., Ne., U.S. **D4** 120
Dunedin, N.Z. **q13** 63c
Dunedin, Fl., U.S. **D4** 102
Dunellen, N.J., U.S. **B4** 123
Dunfermline, Scot., U.K. **B5** 12
Dūngarpur, India **E2** 40
Dungarvan, Ire. **D3** 12
Dungeness, stm., Wa., U.S. **A2** 140
Dungu, D.R.C. **C5** 54
Dunham, Qc., Can. **D5** 90
Dunhuang, China **C6** 28
Dunkard Creek, stm., U.S. **B4** 141
Dunkerque, Fr. **B8** 16
Dunkerton, Ia., U.S. **B5** 108
Dunkirk see Dunkerque, Fr. **B8** 16
Dunkirk, In., U.S. **D7** 107
Dunkirk, N.Y., U.S. **C1** 125
Dunkirk, Oh., U.S. **B2** 128
Dunklin, co., Mo., U.S. **E7** 118
Dunkwa, Ghana **E4** 50
Dún Laoghaire, Ire. **D3** 12
Dunlap, Ia., U.S. **C2** 108
Dunlap, Il., U.S. **C4** 106
Dunlap, In., U.S. **A6** 107
Dunlap, Tn., U.S. **D8** 135
Dunleary see Dún Laoghaire, Ire. **D3** 12
Dunleith, De., U.S. **i7** 101
Dunloup Creek, stm., W.V., U.S. **n13** 141
Dunmore, Pa., U.S. **D10** 131
Dunmore, Lake, l., Vt., U.S. **D2** 138
Dunn, N.C., U.S. **B4** 126
Dunn, co., N.D., U.S. **B3** 127
Dunn, co., Wi., U.S. **D2** 142
Dunnellon, Fl., U.S. **C4** 102
Dunnville, On., Can. **E5** 89
Dunqulah, Sudan **G11** 48
Dunseith, N.D., U.S. **A5** 127
Dunsmuir, Ca., U.S. **B2** 98
Dunville, N.L., Can. **E5** 88
Dunwoody, Ga., U.S. **h8** 103
Duolun, China **C11** 28
Duomula, China **E4** 28
Du Page, stm., Il., U.S. **k8** 106
Du Page, co., Il., U.S. **B5** 106
Duplin, co., N.C., U.S. **C5** 126
Dupnica, Blg. **C9** 18
Dupont, Co., U.S. **B6** 99
Dupont, Pa., U.S. **n18** 131
Dupont City, W.V., U.S. **m12** 141
Dupont Manor, De., U.S. **D3** 101
Dupont Manor, De., U.S. **B1** 101
Duque de York, Isla, i., Chile **H1** 69
Duquesne, Pa., U.S. **F2** 131
Du Quoin, Il., U.S. **E4** 106
Durand, Il., U.S. **A4** 106
Durand, Mi., U.S. **F6** 115
Durand, Wi., U.S. **D2** 142
Durango, Mex. **E8** 78
Durango, state, Mex. **E8** 78
Durango, Co., U.S. **D3** 99
Durant, Ia., U.S. **C7** 108
Durant, Ms., U.S. **B4** 117
Durant, Ok., U.S. **D5** 129
Durazno, Ur. **E6** 72
Durban, S. Afr. **D5** 56
Durg, India **E4** 40
Durgāpur, India **E5** 40
Durham, On., Can. **C4** 89
Durham, Eng., U.K. **C6** 12
Durham, Ca., U.S. **C3** 98
Durham, Ct., U.S. **D5** 100
Durham, co., N.C., U.S. **A4** 126
Durham, N.C., U.S. **B4** 126
Durham, N.H., U.S. **D5** 122
Durmitor, mtn., Serb. **C7** 18
Durrell, N.L., Can. **D4** 88
Durrës, Alb. **D7** 18
Dursunbey, Tur. **C3** 44
D'Urville Island, i., N.Z. **p13** 63c
Duryea, Pa., U.S. **D10** 131
Dušanbe, Taj. **F8** 26
Dušekan, Russia **C12** 26
Dushan, China **F9** 28
Dushanbe see Dušanbe, Taj. **F8** 26
Dushanzi, China **C4** 28
Duson, La., U.S. **D3** 111
Düsseldorf, Ger. **E10** 12
Dutchess, co., N.Y., U.S. **D7** 125
Dutch Island, i., R.I., U.S. **F4** 132
Dutton, On., Can. **E3** 89
Dutton, Mount, mtn., Ut., U.S. **E3** 137
Duval, co., Fl., U.S. **B5** 102
Duval, co., Tx., U.S. **F3** 136
Duxbury, Ma., U.S. **B6** 114
Duyun, China **F9** 28
Düzce, Tur. **B4** 44
Dvina Bay see Dvinskaja guba, b., Russia **A6** 22
Dvinskaja guba, b., Russia **A6** 22
Dwārka, India **E1** 40
Dwight, Il., U.S. **B5** 106
Dwight D. Eisenhower Lock, N.Y., U.S. **f9** 125
Dworshak Reservoir, res., Id., U.S. **C3** 105
Dyer, In., U.S. **A2** 107
Dyer, Tn., U.S. **A3** 135
Dyer, co., Tn., U.S. **A2** 135
Dyer Island, i., R.I., U.S. **E5** 132
Dyersburg, Tn., U.S. **A2** 135
Dyersville, Ia., U.S. **B6** 108
Dyess Air Force Base, mil., Tx., U.S. **C3** 136
Dysart, Ia., U.S. **B5** 108
Džalinda, Russia **A12** 28
Džambejty, Kaz. **D9** 22
Džanybek, Kaz. **E8** 22
Džardžan, Russia **C14** 26
Dzaudzhikau see Vladikavkaz, Russia **E6** 26
Dzerzhinsk see Dzjaržynsk, Bela. **C9** 20
Dzerzhinsk see Dzeržinsk, Russia **C7** 22
Dzeržinsk, Russia **C7** 22
Džetygara, Kaz. **D8** 26
Dzhambul see Žambyl, Kaz. **E9** 26
Dzhankoi, Ukr. **G13** 20
Dzierżoniów, Pol. **D4** 20
Džizak, Uzb. **E8** 26
Dzjaržynsk, Bela. **C9** 20
Džubga, Russia **G15** 20
Džugdžur, hrebet, mts., Russia **D15** 26
Dzungarian Basin see Junggar Pendi, bas., China **B5** 28
Džusaly, Kaz. **A8** 42
Dzüünharaa, Mong. **B9** 28
Dzuunmod, Mong. **B9** 28

E

Eads, Co., U.S. **C8** 99
Eagan, Mn., U.S. **n12** 116
Eagar, Az., U.S. **C6** 96
Eagle, stm., N.L., Can. **B2** 88
Eagle, Co., U.S. **B4** 99
Eagle, co., Co., U.S. **B4** 99
Eagle, Id., U.S. **F2** 105
Eagle, Ne., U.S. **h12** 120
Eagle, Wi., U.S. **F5** 142
Eagle Creek Reservoir, res., In., U.S. **E5** 107
Eagle Grove, Ia., U.S. **B4** 108
Eagle Key, i., Fl., U.S. **G6** 102
Eagle Lake, l., Ca., U.S. **B3** 98
Eagle Lake, Me., U.S. **A4** 112
Eagle Lake, l., Me., U.S. **B3** 112
Eagle Lake, l., Me., U.S. **A4** 112
Eagle Lake, Mn., U.S. **F5** 116
Eagle Lake, l., Ms., U.S. **C3** 117
Eagle Lake, Tx., U.S. **E4** 136
Eagle Lake, l., Wi., U.S. **C4** 142
Eagle Mountain, mtn., Mn., U.S. **k9** 116
Eagle Mountain Lake, res., Tx., U.S. **m9** 136
Eagle Nest Lake, l., N.M., U.S. **A4** 124
Eagle Pass, Tx., U.S. **E2** 136
Eagle Peak, mtn., Ca., U.S. **B3** 98
Eagle Point, Or., U.S. **E4** 130
Eagle River, Wi., U.S. **C4** 142
Eagletail Mountains, mts., Az., U.S. **D2** 96
Eagletail Peak, mtn., Az., U.S. **D2** 96
Eagletown, Ok., U.S. **C7** 129
Earle, Ar., U.S. **B5** 97
Earlham, Ia., U.S. **C3** 108
Earlimart, Ca., U.S. **E4** 98
Earlington, Ky., U.S. **C2** 110
Earlville, Ia., U.S. **B6** 108
Earlville, Il., U.S. **B5** 106
Early, co., Ga., U.S. **E2** 103
Early, Ia., U.S. **B2** 108
Earth, Tx., U.S. **B1** 136
Easley, S.C., U.S. **B2** 133
East, stm., Ct., U.S. **D5** 100
East, stm., N.Y., U.S. **k13** 125
East, stm., Wi., U.S. **h9** 142
East Alton, Il., U.S. **E3** 106
East Angus, Qc., Can. **D6** 90
East Arlington, Vt., U.S. **E2** 138
East Aurora, N.Y., U.S. **C2** 125
East Bangor, Pa., U.S. **E11** 131
East Bank, W.V., U.S. **m13** 141
East Barre, Vt., U.S. **C4** 138
East Baton Rouge, co., La., U.S. **D4** 111
East Bay, b., Fl., U.S. **u16** 102
East Bay, b., Tx., U.S. **R15** 136
East Beckwith Mountain, mtn., Co., U.S. **C3** 99
East Berlin, Ct., U.S. **C5** 100
East Berlin, Pa., U.S. **G8** 131
East Bernard, Tx., U.S. **E4** 136
East Bernstadt, Ky., U.S. **C5** 110
East Bethel, Mn., U.S. **E5** 116
East Billerica, Ma., U.S. **f11** 114
Eastborough, Ks., U.S. **g12** 109
Eastbourne, Eng., U.K. **E7** 12
East Brady, Pa., U.S. **E2** 131
East Branch Clarion River Lake, res., Pa., U.S. **C4** 131
East Brewton, Al., U.S. **D2** 94
East Bridgewater, Ma., U.S. **B6** 114
East Brimfield Lake, res., Ma., U.S. **B3** 114
East Brooklyn, Ct., U.S. **B8** 100
East Broughton, Qc., Can. **C6** 90
East Brunswick, N.J., U.S. **C4** 123
East Butte, mtn., Mt., U.S. **B5** 119
East Cache Creek, stm., Ok., U.S. **C3** 129
East Caicos, i., T./C. Is. **A5** 80
East Cape, c., N.Z. **o14** 63c
East Cape, c., Fl., U.S. **G5** 102
East Carbon, Ut., U.S. **D5** 137
East Caroline Basin **H17** 64
East Carroll, co., La., U.S. **B4** 111
East Chicago, In., U.S. **A3** 107
East China Sea, Asia **F12** 28
East Chop, c., Ma., U.S. **D6** 114
East Cleveland, Oh., U.S. **g9** 128
East Cote Blanche Bay, b., La., U.S. **E4** 111
East Dennis, Ma., U.S. **C7** 114
East Derry, N.H., U.S. **E4** 122
East Detroit, Mi., U.S. **p16** 115
East Douglas, Ma., U.S. **B4** 114
East Dubuque, Il., U.S. **A3** 106
Eastend, Sk., Can. **H1** 91
Easter Island see Pascua, Isla de, i., Chile **K28** 64
Eastern Bay, b., Md., U.S. **C5** 113
Eastern Desert, des., Egypt **E11** 48
Eastern Ghāts, mts., India **G3** 40
Eastern Neck Island, i., Md., U.S. **B5** 113
Eastern Point, c., Ma., U.S. **f13** 114
Eastern Sayans see Vostočnyj Sajan, mts., Russia **D11** 26
Easterville, Mb., Can. **C2** 86
East Falkland, i., Falk. Is. **H5** 69
East Falmouth, Ma., U.S. **C6** 114
East Feliciana, co., La., U.S. **D4** 111
East Flat Rock, N.C., U.S. **f10** 126
East Fork, stm., Wy., U.S. **D3** 143
East Fork Lake, res., Oh., U.S. **C1** 128
East Frisian Islands see Ostfriesische Inseln, is., Ger. **D10** 12
East Gaffney, S.C., U.S. **A4** 133
East Galesburg, Il., U.S. **C3** 106
East Granby, Ct., U.S. **B5** 100
East Grand Forks, Mn., U.S. **C2** 116
East Grand Rapids, Mi., U.S. **F5** 115
East Greenville, Pa., U.S. **F10** 131
East Greenwich, R.I., U.S. **D4** 132
East Gwillimbury, On., Can. **C5** 89
East Hampstead, N.H., U.S. **E4** 122
East Hampton, Ct., U.S. **C5** 100
Easthampton, Ma., U.S. **B2** 114
East Hartford, Ct., U.S. **B5** 100
East Hartland, Ct., U.S. **B4** 100

Name	Map Ref.	Page
East Jordan, Mi., U.S.	C5	115
Eastlake, Oh., U.S.	A4	128
East Lake Tohopekaliga, l., Fl., U.S.	D5	102
Eastland, Tx., U.S.	C3	136
Eastland, co., Tx., U.S.	C3	136
East Lansing, Mi., U.S.	F6	115
East Las Vegas, Nv., U.S.	G6	121
East Liverpool, Oh., U.S.	B5	128
East London (Oos-Londen), S. Afr.	E4	56
East Longmeadow, Ma., U.S.	B2	114
East Los Angeles, Ca., U.S.	m12	98
East Lyme, Ct., U.S.	D7	100
East Lynn Lake, res., W.V., U.S.	C2	141
Eastmain-Opinaca, Réservoir, res., Qc., Can.	h11	90
Eastman, Qc., Can.	D5	90
Eastman, Ga., U.S.	D3	103
East Mariana Basin	G18	64
East Matunuck, R.I., U.S.	F3	132
East Middlebury, Vt., U.S.	D2	138
East Millinocket, Me., U.S.	C4	112
East Moline, Il., U.S.	B3	106
East Montpelier, Vt., U.S.	C4	138
East Naples, Fl., U.S.	F5	102
East Newnan, Ga., U.S.	C2	103
East Nishnabotna, stm., Ia., U.S.	C2	108
East Norriton, Pa., U.S.	o20	131
East Olympia, Wa., U.S.	C3	140
Easton, Md., U.S.	C5	113
Easton, Pa., U.S.	E11	131
Easton Reservoir, res., Ct., U.S.	E2	100
East Orange, N.J., U.S.	B4	123
East Orleans, Ma., U.S.	C8	114
Eastover, S.C., U.S.	D6	133
East Pacific Rise	M27	64
East Pakistan see Bangladesh, ctry., Asia	B2	34
East Palatka, Fl., U.S.	C5	102
East Palestine, Oh., U.S.	B5	128
East Pass, strt., Fl., U.S.	C2	102
East Pea Ridge, W.V., U.S.	C2	141
East Peoria, Il., U.S.	C4	106
East Pepperell, Ma., U.S.	A4	114
East Petersburg, Pa., U.S.	F9	131
East Pittsburgh, Pa., U.S.	k14	131
East Point, c., P.E., Can.	C8	87
Eastpoint, Fl., U.S.	C2	102
East Point, Ga., U.S.	C2	103
East Point, c., Ma., U.S.	B6	114
East Point, c., N.J., U.S.	E2	123
Eastport, N.L., Can.	D5	88
Eastport, Me., U.S.	D6	112
East Prairie, Mo., U.S.	E8	118
East Providence, R.I., U.S.	C4	132
East Pryor Mountain, mtn., Mt., U.S.	E8	119
East Quogue, N.Y., U.S.	n16	125
East Range, mts., Nv., U.S.	C4	121
East Ridge, Tn., U.S.	h11	135
East River, Ct., U.S.	D5	100
East Rochester, N.Y., U.S.	B3	125
East Rockingham, N.C., U.S.	C3	126
East Rutherford, N.J., U.S.	h8	123
East Saint Louis, Il., U.S.	E3	106
East Sea see Japan, Sea of, Asia	C14	28
East Selkirk, Mb., Can.	D3	86
East Siberian Sea see Vostočno-Sibirskoe more, Russia	B17	26
Eastsound, Wa., U.S.	A3	140
East Spencer, N.C., U.S.	B2	126
East Stroudsburg, Pa., U.S.	D11	131
East Tawas, Mi., U.S.	D7	115
East Timor, ctry., Asia	E7	36
East Troy, Wi., U.S.	F5	142
East Vestal, N.Y., U.S.	C4	125
East View, W.V., U.S.	k10	141
East Walker, stm., U.S.	E2	121
East Walpole, Ma., U.S.	h11	114
East Wareham, Ma., U.S.	C6	114
East Washington, Pa., U.S.	F1	131
East Wenatchee, Wa., U.S.	B5	140
East Windsor, N.J., U.S.	C3	123
East York, On., Can.	D5	89
Eaton, Co., U.S.	A6	99
Eaton, In., U.S.	D7	107
Eaton, co., Mi., U.S.	F6	115
Eaton, Oh., U.S.	C1	128
Eaton Rapids, Mi., U.S.	F6	115
Eatonton, Ga., U.S.	C3	103
Eatontown, N.J., U.S.	C4	123
Eatonville, Wa., U.S.	C3	140
Eau Claire, Wi., U.S.	D2	142
Eau Claire, co., Wi., U.S.	D2	142
Eau Claire, stm., Wi., U.S.	D2	142
Eau Claire, Lac à l', l., Qc., Can.	g11	90
Eauripik Rise	H17	64
Ebano, Mex.	C5	78
Ebebiyín, Eq. Gui.	C2	54
Ebensburg, Pa., U.S.	F4	131
Eber Gölü, l., Tur.	C4	44
Eberswalde-Finow, Ger.	D13	12
Ebetsu, Japan	B4	31
Ebinur Hu, l., China	B4	28
Ebolowa, Cam.	C2	54
Ebre see Ebro, stm., Spain	G7	16
Ebre, Delta de l', Spain	G7	16
Ebro, stm., Spain	G7	16
Eccles, W.V., U.S.	n13	141
Ech Cheliff, Alg.	C5	48
Echeng, China	C3	30
Echo Bay, Nv., U.S.	G7	121
Echo Lake, l., Me., U.S.	D3	112
Echo Lake, l., Vt., U.S.	B5	138
Echols, co., Ga., U.S.	F4	103
Echuca, Austl.	H3	62
Écija, Spain	I4	16
Eckerö, i., Fin.	F8	10
Eckhart Mines, Md., U.S.	k13	113
Eckville, Ab., Can.	C3	84
Eclectic, Al., U.S.	C3	94
Econfina, stm., Fl., U.S.	B3	102
Écorces, Rivière aux, stm., Qc., Can.	A6	90
Ecorse, Mi., U.S.	p15	115
Ecru, Ms., U.S.	A4	117
Ector, co., Tx., U.S.	D1	136
Ecuador, ctry., S.A.	D4	70
Edcouch, Tx., U.S.	F4	136
Eddy, co., N.D., U.S.	B7	127
Eddy, co., N.M., U.S.	E5	124
Eddystone, Pa., U.S.	p20	131
Eddyville, Ia., U.S.	C5	108
Eddyville, Ky., U.S.	e9	110
Ede, Nig.	E5	50
Edéa, Cam.	C2	54
Eden, Ga., U.S.	D5	103
Eden, Md., U.S.	D6	113
Eden, N.C., U.S.	A3	126
Eden, N.Y., U.S.	C2	125
Eden, Tx., U.S.	D3	136
Edenburg, S. Afr.	D4	56
Eden Prairie, Mn., U.S.	n12	116
Edenton, N.C., U.S.	A6	126
Eden Valley, Mn., U.S.	E4	116
Edfu, Egypt	F11	48
Edgar, co., Il., U.S.	D6	106
Edgar, Ne., U.S.	D8	120
Edgar, Wi., U.S.	D4	142
Edgard, La., U.S.	D5	111
Edgartown, Ma., U.S.	D6	114
Edgecombe, co., N.C., U.S.	B5	126
Edgecumbe, Cape, c., Ak., U.S.	m21	95
Edgefield, S.C., U.S.	D4	133
Edgefield, co., S.C., U.S.	D4	133
Edgeley, N.D., U.S.	C7	127
Edgemere, Md., U.S.	B5	113
Edgemont, S.D., U.S.	D2	134
Edgemoor, De., U.S.	A3	101
Edgeøya, i., Nor.	B4	26
Edgerton, Ks., U.S.	D8	109
Edgerton, Mn., U.S.	G2	116
Edgerton, Oh., U.S.	A1	128
Edgerton, Wi., U.S.	F4	142
Edgerton, Wy., U.S.	C6	143
Edgewater, Al., U.S.	f7	94
Edgewater, Fl., U.S.	D6	102
Edgewater, Md., U.S.	C4	113
Edgewater, N.J., U.S.	h9	123
Edgewater Park, N.J., U.S.	C3	123
Edgewood, Ia., U.S.	B6	108
Edgewood, In., U.S.	D6	107
Edgewood, Ky., U.S.	h13	110
Edgewood, Md., U.S.	B5	113
Edgewood, N.M., U.S.	B3	124
Edgewood, Oh., U.S.	A5	128
Edgewood, Pa., U.S.	k14	131
Edgewood, Wa., U.S.	f11	140
Edgeworth, Pa., U.S.	h13	131
Édhessa, Grc.	D9	18
Edina, Mn., U.S.	F5	116
Edina, Mo., U.S.	A5	118
Edinboro, Pa., U.S.	C1	131
Edinburg, Il., U.S.	D4	106
Edinburg, Tx., U.S.	F3	136
Edinburg, Va., U.S.	B4	139
Edinburgh, Scot., U.K.	C5	12
Edinburgh, In., U.S.	F6	107
Edineț, Mol.	E9	20
Edirne, Tur.	B2	44
Edison, Ga., U.S.	E2	103
Edison, N.J., U.S.	B4	123
Edisto, stm., S.C., U.S.	E6	133
Edisto Island, i., S.C., U.S.	F7	133
Edith, Mount, mtn., Mt., U.S.	D5	119
Edjeleh, Alg.	E6	48
Edmond, Ok., U.S.	B4	129
Edmonds, Wa., U.S.	B3	140
Edmonson, co., Ky., U.S.	C3	110
Edmonton, Ab., Can.	C4	84
Edmonton, Ky., U.S.	D4	110
Edmore, Mi., U.S.	E5	115
Edmunds, co., S.D., U.S.	B6	134
Edmundston, N.B., Can.	B1	87
Edna, Tx., U.S.	E4	136
Edon, Oh., U.S.	A1	128
Édouard, Lac, l., Qc., Can.	B5	90
Edremit, Tur.	C2	44
Edremit Körfezi, b., Tur.	C2	44
Edson, Ab., Can.	C2	84
Edson Butte, mtn., Or., U.S.	E2	130
Eduardo Castex, Arg.	F5	72
Edward, Lake, l., Afr.	D5	54
Edwards, co., Il., U.S.	E5	106
Edwards, co., Ks., U.S.	E4	109
Edwards, Ms., U.S.	C3	117
Edwards, co., Tx., U.S.	E2	136
Edwards Air Force Base, mil., Ca., U.S.	E5	98
Edwardsburg, Mi., U.S.	G4	115
Edwards Butte, mtn., Or., U.S.	B3	130
Edwardsville, Il., U.S.	E4	106
Edwardsville, Ks., U.S.	k16	109
Edwardsville, Pa., U.S.	n17	131
Edward VII Peninsula, pen., Ant.	D25	67
Eel, stm., Ca., U.S.	B2	98
Eel, stm., In., U.S.	F3	107
Eel, stm., In., U.S.	C6	107
Éfaté, i., Vanuatu	k9	62a
Efes (Ephesus), hist., Tur.	D2	44
Effigy Mounds National Monument, Ia., U.S.	A6	108
Effingham, co., Ga., U.S.	D5	103
Effingham, Il., U.S.	D5	106
Effingham, co., Il., U.S.	D5	106
Efland, N.C., U.S.	A3	126
Efremov, Russia	C15	20
Egadi, Isole, is., Italy	E4	18
Egan Range, mts., Nv., U.S.	E7	121
Eganville, On., Can.	B7	89
Egedesminde, Grnld.	E29	82
Eger, Hung.	F6	20
Eggenfelden, Ger.	F13	12
Egg Harbor City, N.J., U.S.	D3	123
Egg Island Point, c., N.J., U.S.	E2	123
Egijn, stm., Mong.	A8	28
Eglin Air Force Base, mil., Fl., U.S.	u15	102
Egmont, Cape, c., N.Z.	o13	63c
Egmont, Mount see Taranaki, Mount, vol., N.Z.	o13	63c
Egmont Bay, b., P.E., Can.	C5	87
Egmont Channel, strt., Fl., U.S.	p10	102
Egmont Key, i., Fl., U.S.	p10	102
Eğridir, Tur.	D4	44
Eğridir Gölü, l., Tur.	C4	44
Egvekinot, Russia	C20	26
Egypt, ctry., Afr.	E10	48
Egypt, Lake of, res., Il., U.S.	F5	106
Eha-Amufu, Nig.	E6	50
Ehrenberg, Az., U.S.	D1	96
Eibar, Spain	F5	16
Eielson Air Force Base, mil., Ak., U.S.	C10	95
Eigersund, Nor.	G2	10
Eight Degree Channel, strt., Asia	H2	40
Eights Coast, Ant.	D31	67
Eighty Mile Beach, Austl.	D3	60
Eindhoven, Neth.	E9	12
Eirunepé, Braz.	E6	70
Eisenach, Ger.	E12	12
Eisenerz, Aus.	G14	12
Eisenhower, Mount, mtn., N.H., U.S.	B4	122
Eisenhüttenstadt, Ger.	D14	12
Eisenstadt, Aus.	G15	12
Eivissa, Spain	H7	16
Eivissa (Ibiza), i., Spain	H7	16
Ejin Qi, China	C8	28
Ejsk, Russia	F15	20
Ejura, Ghana	E4	50
Ekaterinburg, Russia	D8	26
Ekibastuz, Kaz.	D9	26
Ekimčan, Russia	D15	26
Ekonda, Russia	C12	26
Ela, Mya.	C3	34
El Aaiún, W. Sah.	A2	50
Elaine, Ar., U.S.	C5	97
El-Alamein, Egypt	E9	14
Elan', Russia	D7	22
Elancy, Russia	D12	26
El-Arish, Egypt	E10	14
Elat, Isr.	E2	42
Elat, Gulf of see Aqaba, Gulf of, b.	E2	42
Elath see Elat, Isr.	E2	42
Elazığ, Tur.	C8	44
Elba, Al., U.S.	D3	94
Elba, Isola d', i., Italy	C3	18
El Banco, Col.	D5	80
Elbasan, Alb.	D7	18
Elbe see Labe, stm., Eur.	E14	12
Elberfeld, In., U.S.	H3	107
Elbert, co., Co., U.S.	B6	99
Elbert, co., Ga., U.S.	B4	103
Elbert, Mount, mtn., Co., U.S.	B4	99
Elberta, Ga., U.S.	D3	103
Elberton, Ga., U.S.	B4	103
El Beyyadh, Alg.	E4	14
Elbistan, Tur.	C7	44
Elbląg, Pol.	B5	20
El Boulaïda, Alg.	C5	48
Elbow, stm., Ab., Can.	D3	84
Elbow Lake, Mn., U.S.	E3	116
El'brus, gora, mtn., Russia	E6	26
Elbrus, Mount see El'brus, gora, mtn., Russia	E6	26
Elburn, Il., U.S.	B5	106
Elburz Mountains see Alborz, Reshteh-ye Kūhhā-ye, mts., Iran	C6	42
El Cajon, Ca., U.S.	F5	98
El Calafate, Arg.	H2	69
El Callao, Ven.	D7	80
El Campo, Tx., U.S.	E4	136
El Capitan, mtn., Mt., U.S.	D2	119
El Capitan Reservoir, res., Ca., U.S.	o16	98
El Carmen de Bolívar, Col.	B4	70
El Centro, Ca., U.S.	F6	98
El Cerrito, Ca., U.S.	h8	98
Elcho Island, i., Austl.	C6	60
El Cuervo Butte, mtn., N.M., U.S.	k9	124
Elda, Spain	H6	16
El-Dab'a, Egypt	G3	44
El Djazaïr (Algiers), Alg.	C5	48
El Djelfa, Alg.	E4	14
Eldon, Ia., U.S.	D5	108
Eldon, Mo., U.S.	C5	118
Eldora, Ia., U.S.	B4	108
Eldorado, Arg.	D7	72
El Dorado, Ar., U.S.	D3	97
El Dorado, co., Ca., U.S.	C3	98
Eldorado, Il., U.S.	F5	106
El Dorado, Ks., U.S.	E7	109
Eldorado, Tx., U.S.	D2	136
El Dorado, Ven.	D7	80
Eldorado Peak, mtn., Wa., U.S.	A4	140
Eldorado Springs, Co., U.S.	B5	99
El Dorado Springs, Mo., U.S.	D3	118
Eldoret, Kenya	C7	54
Eldridge, Ia., U.S.	C7	108
Eleanor, W.V., U.S.	C3	141
Elec, Russia	D5	26
Electra, Tx., U.S.	C3	136
Electra Lake, res., Co., U.S.	D3	99
Electric Peak, mtn., Co., U.S.	C5	99
Electric Peak, mtn., Mt., U.S.	E6	119
Elefantes (Olifants), stm., Afr.	C5	56
El Encanto, Col.	D5	70
Elephant Butte Reservoir, res., N.M., U.S.	D2	124
Eleuthera, i., Bah.	C9	76
Eleven Mile Canyon Reservoir, res., Co., U.S.	C5	99
Eleven Point, stm., U.S.	A4	97
El-Fayoum, Egypt	E11	48
Elgin, Scot., U.K.	B5	12
Elgin, Ia., U.S.	B6	108
Elgin, Il., U.S.	A5	106
Elgin, Mn., U.S.	F6	116
Elgin, N.D., U.S.	C4	127
Elgin, Ne., U.S.	C7	120
Elgin, Ok., U.S.	C3	129
Elgin, Or., U.S.	B9	130
Elgin, S.C., U.S.	B6	133
Elgin, Tx., U.S.	D4	136
El-Gîza, Egypt	E11	48
Elgon, Mount, mtn., Afr.	C6	54
El Grara, Alg.	E4	14
El Ḥammâmi, reg., Maur.	B2	50
El Ḥank, clf., Afr.	B3	50
El Hierro, i., Spain	A1	50
Elhovo, Blg.	C11	18
Eliase, Indon.	E8	36
Elida, Oh., U.S.	B1	128
El-Iskandarîya, Egypt	D10	48
Elista, Russia	E6	26
Elizabeth, Austl.	G2	62
Elizabeth, Co., U.S.	B6	99
Elizabeth, N.J., U.S.	B4	123
Elizabeth, W.V., U.S.	B3	141
Elizabeth, Cape, c., Wa., U.S.	B1	140
Elizabeth City, N.C., U.S.	A6	126
Elizabeth Islands, is., Ma., U.S.	D6	114
Elizabethton, Tn., U.S.	C11	135
Elizabethtown, Ky., U.S.	C4	110
Elizabethtown, N.C., U.S.	C4	126
Elizabethtown, Pa., U.S.	F8	131
Elizabethville, Pa., U.S.	E8	131
Elizavety, mys, c., Russia	D16	26
El-Jadida, Mor.	D3	48
El Jebel, Co., U.S.	B3	99
Ełk, Pol.	C7	20
Elk, stm., Co., U.S.	A4	99
Elk, stm., Ks., U.S.	E7	109
Elk, co., Ks., U.S.	E7	109
Elk, co., Pa., U.S.	D4	131
Elk, stm., Wi., U.S.	C3	142
Elk, stm., W.V., U.S.	C3	141
Elk, stm., U.S.	A2	94
Elkader, Ia., U.S.	B6	108
Elk City, Id., U.S.	D3	105
Elk City, Ok., U.S.	B2	129
Elk City Lake, res., Ks., U.S.	E7	109
Elk Creek, stm., Ok., U.S.	B2	129
Elk Creek, stm., S.D., U.S.	C3	134
El Kef, Tun.	C6	48
Ēl Kerē, Eth.	B8	54
Elkford, B.C., Can.	D10	85
Elk Grove, Ca., U.S.	C3	98
Elk Grove Village, Il., U.S.	h9	106
El-Khârga, Egypt	E11	48
Elkhart, In., U.S.	A6	107
Elkhart, stm., In., U.S.	B6	107
Elkhart, co., In., U.S.	A6	107
Elkhart, Ks., U.S.	E2	109
Elkhart, Tx., U.S.	D5	136
Elkhart Lake, Wi., U.S.	E5	142
Elkhead Mountains, mts., Co., U.S.	A3	99
Elkhorn, Mb., Can.	E1	86
Elk Horn, Ia., U.S.	C2	108
Elkhorn, stm., Ne., U.S.	B7	120
Elkhorn, Ne., U.S.	g12	120
Elkhorn, Wi., U.S.	F5	142
Elkhorn City, Ky., U.S.	C7	110
Elkhorn Peaks, mts., Id., U.S.	F7	105
Elkin, N.C., U.S.	A2	126
Elkins, Ar., U.S.	A1	97
Elkins, W.V., U.S.	C5	141
Elkland, Pa., U.S.	C7	131
Elk Mills, Md., U.S.	A6	113
Elk Mound, Wi., U.S.	D2	142
Elk Mountain, mtn., N.M., U.S.	D1	124
Elk Mountain, Wy., U.S.	E6	143
Elk Mountain, mtn., Wy., U.S.	E6	143
Elk Mountains, mts., Co., U.S.	B3	99
Elk Mountains, mts., U.S.	D1	134
Elko, Nv., U.S.	C6	121
Elko, co., Nv., U.S.	B6	121
Elk Peak, mtn., Mt., U.S.	D6	119
Elk Point, Ab., Can.	C5	84
Elk Point, S.D., U.S.	E9	134
Elk Rapids, Mi., U.S.	D5	115
Elkridge, Md., U.S.	B4	113
Elk River, Mn., U.S.	E5	116
Elkton, Ky., U.S.	D2	110
Elkton, Md., U.S.	A6	113
Elkton, Mi., U.S.	E7	115
Elkton, S.D., U.S.	C9	134
Elkton, Va., U.S.	B4	139
Elkview, W.V., U.S.	m13	141
Elkville, Il., U.S.	F4	106
Ellaville, Ga., U.S.	D2	103
Ellen, Mount, mtn., Ut., U.S.	E5	137
Ellendale, De., U.S.	E4	101
Ellendale, N.D., U.S.	C7	127
Ellensburg, Wa., U.S.	C5	140
Ellenton, Fl., U.S.	E4	102
Ellenville, N.Y., U.S.	D6	125
Ellerbe, N.C., U.S.	B3	126
Ellerslie, Md., U.S.	k13	113
Ellesmere Island, i., Can.	B24	82
Ellettsville, In., U.S.	F4	107
Ellice Islands see Tuvalu, ctry., Oc.	E11	58
Ellicott City, Md., U.S.	B4	113
Ellijay, Ga., U.S.	B2	103
Ellington, Ct., U.S.	B6	100
Ellington, Mo., U.S.	D7	118
Ellinwood, Ks., U.S.	D5	109
Elliot, S. Afr.	E4	56
Elliot Lake, On., Can.	A2	89
Elliott, co., Ky., U.S.	B6	110
Elliott, Ms., U.S.	B4	117
Elliott Bay, b., Wa., U.S.	e11	140
Elliott Key, i., Fl., U.S.	G6	102
Ellis, Ks., U.S.	D4	109
Ellis, co., Ks., U.S.	D4	109
Ellis, stm., N.H., U.S.	B4	122
Ellis, co., Ok., U.S.	A2	129
Ellis, co., Tx., U.S.	C4	136
Elliston, Va., U.S.	C2	139
Ellisville, Mo., U.S.	f12	118
Ellisville, Ms., U.S.	D4	117
Ellore see Elūru, India	F4	40
Elloree, S.C., U.S.	D6	133
Ellport, Pa., U.S.	E1	131
Ellsworth, Ks., U.S.	D5	109
Ellsworth, co., Ks., U.S.	D5	109
Ellsworth, Me., U.S.	D4	112
Ellsworth, Pa., U.S.	F1	131
Ellsworth, Wi., U.S.	D1	142
Ellsworth Air Force Base, mil., S.D., U.S.	C2	134
Ellsworth Land, reg., Ant.	D32	67
Ellsworth Mountains, mts., Ant.	D32	67
Ellwood City, Pa., U.S.	E1	131
Elm, stm., N.D., U.S.	B8	127
Elma, Ia., U.S.	A5	108
Elma, Wa., U.S.	C2	140
Elmadağ, Tur.	C5	44
El-Mahalla el-Kubra, Egypt	G4	44
Elmalı, Tur.	D3	44
El-Mansûra, Egypt	E10	14
Elm City, N.C., U.S.	B5	126
Elm Creek, Ne., U.S.	D6	120
Elmendorf Air Force Base, mil., Ak., U.S.	C10	95
El Menia, Alg.	D5	48
Elm Grove, Wi., U.S.	m11	142
Elmhurst, Il., U.S.	B6	106
Elmhurst, Pa., U.S.	D10	131
El-Minya, Egypt	E11	48
Elmira, N.Y., U.S.	C4	125
El Mirage, Az., U.S.	k8	96
Elmira Heights, N.Y., U.S.	C4	125
El Mohammadia, Alg.	J7	16
Elmont, N.Y., U.S.	k13	125
Elmora, Pa., U.S.	E4	131
Elmore, co., Al., U.S.	C3	94
Elmore, co., Id., U.S.	F3	105
Elmore, Mn., U.S.	G4	116
Elmore, Oh., U.S.	A2	128
El Morro National Monument, N.M., U.S.	B1	124
El Mreyyé, reg., Maur.	C3	50
Elmsdale, N.S., Can.	E6	87
Elmshorn, Ger.	D11	12
Elm Springs, Ar., U.S.	A1	97
Elmvale, On., Can.	C5	89
Elmwood, Il., U.S.	C3	106
Elmwood, Wi., U.S.	D1	142
Elmwood Park, Il., U.S.	k9	106

Name Map Ref. Page

Elmwood Park, N.J., U.S. h8 123
Elmwood Place, Oh., U.S. o13 128
Elnora, In., U.S. G3 107
Eloise, Fl., U.S. E5 102
Elon College, N.C., U.S. A3 126
Elora, On., Can. D4 89
Elorza, Ven. D6 80
Eloten, Turk. C8 42
Eloy, Az., U.S. E4 96
El Paso, co., Co., U.S. C6 99
El Paso, Il., U.S. C4 106
El Paso, Tx., U.S. o11 136
El Paso, co., Tx., U.S. o11 136
El Pital, Cerro, mtn., N.A. C2 80
El Portal, Fl., U.S. s13 102
El Prado, N.M., U.S. A4 124
El Progreso, Hond. B2 80
El Puerto de Santa María, Spain I3 16
El-Qâhira (Cairo), Egypt D10 48
El-Qasr, Egypt E10 48
El Reno, Ok., U.S. B4 129
Elrose, Sk., Can. F1 91
Elroy, Wi., U.S. E3 142
Elsa, Tx., U.S. F3 136
Elsah, Il., U.S. E3 106
El Salto, Mex. C3 78
El Salvador, ctry., N.A. C2 80
El Sauzal, Mex. A1 78
Elsberry, Mo., U.S. B7 118
Elsie, Mi., U.S. E6 115
Elsinore, Ut., U.S. E3 137
El'sk, Bela. D10 20
Elsmere, De., U.S. B3 101
Elsmere, Ky., U.S. B5 110
El Sueco, Mex. B3 78
El-Suweis, Egypt E11 48
Eltham, N.Z. o13 63c
El Tigre, Ven. B7 70
El Toco, Chile C4 72
Elton, La., U.S. D3 111
El Toro Marine Corps Air Station, mil., Ca., U.S. n13 98
El Turbio, Arg. H2 69
El-Uqsor, Egypt E11 48
Elūru, India F4 40
El Vado Reservoir, res., N.M., U.S. A3 124
Elvas, Port. H3 16
Elvins, Mo., U.S. D7 118
El Wad, Alg. E5 14
El Wak, Kenya C8 54
Elwell, Lake, res., Mt., U.S. B5 119
Elwha, stm., Wa., U.S. A2 140
Elwood, In., U.S. D6 107
Elwood, Ks., U.S. C9 109
Elwood, Ne., U.S. D6 120
Elx, Spain H6 16
Ely, Eng., U.K. D7 12
Ely, Mn., U.S. C7 116
Ely, Nv., U.S. D7 121
Elyria, Oh., U.S. A3 128
Elysburg, Pa., U.S. E8 131
Emāmshahr, Iran C7 42
Emanuel, co., Ga., U.S. D4 103
Emba, stm., Kaz. E7 26
Emba, Kaz. E10 22
Embarrass, stm., Il., U.S. E6 106
Embarrass, stm., Wi., U.S. D5 142
Embro, On., Can. D4 89
Embu, Kenya D7 54
Emden, Ger. D10 12
Emerald, Austl. E4 62
Emerson, Mb., Can. E3 86
Emerson, Ga., U.S. B2 103
Emerson, Ne., U.S. B9 120
Emerson, N.J., U.S. h8 123
Emery, co., Ut., U.S. E5 137
Emet, Tur. C3 44
Emiliano Zapata, Mex. D6 78
Emily, Mn., U.S. D5 116
Emily, Lake, l., Mn., U.S. E3 116
Eminence, Ky., U.S. B4 110
Emirdağ, Tur. C4 44
Emmaus, Pa., U.S. E11 131
Emmen, Neth. D10 12
Emmet, co., Ia., U.S. A3 108
Emmet, co., Mi., U.S. C6 115
Emmetsburg, Ia., U.S. A3 108
Emmett, Id., U.S. F2 105
Emmitsburg, Md., U.S. A3 113
Emmonak, Ak., U.S. C7 95
Emmons, co., N.D., U.S. C5 127
Emory Peak, mtn., Tx., U.S. E1 136
Empalme, Mex. B2 78
Empangeni, S. Afr. D5 56
Empedrado, Arg. D6 72
Emperor Seamounts D19 64
Empire, La., U.S. E6 111
Empire, Nv., U.S. C2 121
Empoli, Italy C3 18
Emporia, Ks., U.S. D7 109
Emporia, Va., U.S. D5 139
Emporium, Pa., U.S. D5 131
Empty Quarter see Ar-Rub' al-Khālī, des., Asia G6 38
Emsworth, Pa., U.S. h13 131
Encampment, Wy., U.S. E6 143
Encarnación, Para. D6 72
Enchilayas, Mex. A2 78
Encinitas, Ca., U.S. F5 98
Encontrados, Ven. D5 80
Encounter Bay, b., Austl. H2 62
Ende, Indon. E6 36
Enderby, B.C., Can. D8 85
Enderby Land, reg., Ant. D9 67
Enderlin, N.D., U.S. C8 127
Enders Reservoir, res., Ne., U.S. D4 120
Endicott, N.Y., U.S. C4 125
Endicott Mountains, mts., Ak., U.S. B9 95
Endless Lake, l., Me., U.S. C4 112
Endwell, N.Y., U.S. C4 125
Enewetak, atoll, Marsh. Is. C10 58
Enfield (Thompsonville), Ct., U.S. B5 100
Enfield, N.C., U.S. A5 126
Enfield, N.H., U.S. C2 122
Engel's, Russia D6 26
Enggano, Pulau, i., Indon. E2 36
England, state, U.K. D6 12
England, Ar., U.S. C4 97
Englee, N.L., Can. C3 88
Engleside, Va., U.S. g12 139
Englewood, Co., U.S. B6 99
Englewood, Fl., U.S. F4 102
Englewood, N.J., U.S. B5 123
Englewood, Oh., U.S. C1 128
Englewood, Tn., U.S. D9 135
Englewood Cliffs, N.J., U.S. h9 123
English, In., U.S. H5 107
English Bāzār see Ingrāj Bāzār, India E5 40
English Channel, strt., Eur. C5 16
English Coast, Ant. D33 67
Enid, Ok., U.S. A4 129
Enid Lake, res., Ms., U.S. A4 117
Enigma, Ga., U.S. E3 103
Enisej (Yenisey), stm., Russia C10 26
eNjesuthi, mtn., Afr. D4 56
Enka, N.C., U.S. f10 126
Enköping, Swe. G7 10
Enna, Italy F5 18
Ennedi, plat., Chad G9 48
Ennis, Mt., U.S. E5 119
Ennis, Tx., U.S. C4 136
Enoch, Ut., U.S. F2 137
Enola, Pa., U.S. F8 131
Enontekiö, Fin. B10 10
Enoree, stm., S.C., U.S. B3 133
Enoree, S.C., U.S. B4 133
Enosburg Falls, Vt., U.S. B3 138
Enriquillo, Lago, l., Dom. Rep. B5 80
Enschede, Neth. D10 12
Ensenada, Mex. A1 78
Enshi, China E9 28
Enshu Bay see Enshū-nada, Japan D3 31
Enshū-nada, Japan D3 31
Ensley, Fl., U.S. u14 102
Entebbe, Ug. C6 54
Enterprise, Al., U.S. D4 94
Enterprise, Ks., U.S. D6 109
Enterprise, Or., U.S. B9 130
Enterprise, Ut., U.S. F2 137
Enterprise, W.V., U.S. B4 141
Entiat, stm., Wa., U.S. B5 140
Entiat, Lake, l., Wa., U.S. B5 140
Entiat Mountains, mts., Wa., U.S. B5 140
Entroncamento, Port. H2 16
Enugu, Nig. E6 50
Enumclaw, Wa., U.S. B4 140
Enurmino, Russia C20 26
Enyamba, D.R.C. D5 54
Eola Hills, Or., U.S. h11 130
Epena, Congo C3 54
Epernay, Fr. C8 16
Ephesus see Efes, hist., Tur. D2 44
Ephraim, Ut., U.S. D4 137
Ephrata, Pa., U.S. F9 131
Ephrata, Wa., U.S. B6 140
Epi, i., Vanuatu I9 62a
Épinal, Fr. C10 16
Epirus see Ípeiros, hist. reg., Grc. E8 18
Epping, N.H., U.S. D4 122
Epukiro, Nmb. C2 56
Epworth, Ia., U.S. B7 108
Eqlid, Iran D6 42
Equatorial Guinea, ctry., Afr. C1 54
Erath, La., U.S. E3 111
Erath, co., Tx., U.S. C3 136
Erbaa, Tur. B7 44
Erciş, Tur. C10 44
Erciyes Dağı, vol., Tur. C6 44
Érd, Hung. F5 20
Erdek, Tur. B2 44
Erdemli, Tur. D6 44
Erdene see Ulaan-Uul, Mong. C10 28
Erebus, Mount, mtn., Ant. D21 67
Erechim, Braz. D7 72
Ereğli, Tur. B4 44
Ereğli, Tur. D5 44
Erenhot, China C10 28
Erfoud, Mor. E3 14
Erfurt, Ger. E12 12
Ergani, Tur. C8 44
Ergel, Mong. C9 28
Ergene, stm., Tur. B2 44
Ergeni, Russia E6 26
Ergun see Argun', stm., Asia D14 26
Erick, Ok., U.S. B2 129
Erickson, Mb., Can. D2 86
Erie, Co., U.S. A5 99
Erie, Il., U.S. B3 106
Erie, Ks., U.S. E8 109
Erie, Mi., U.S. G7 115
Erie, co., N.Y., U.S. C2 125
Erie, co., Oh., U.S. A3 128
Erie, Pa., U.S. B1 131
Erie, co., Pa., U.S. C1 131
Erie, Lake, l., N.A. C11 92
Erie Canal, N.Y., U.S. B5 125
Erimo-misaki, c., Japan C16 28
Erin, On., Can. D4 89
Erin, Tn., U.S. A4 135
Eritrea, ctry., Afr. G12 48
Erlangen, Ger. F12 12
Erlanger, Ky., U.S. A5 110
Erling, Lake, res., Ar., U.S. D2 97
Ermelo, S. Afr. D4 56
Ermenek, Tur. D5 44
Ermolaevo, Russia D10 22
Ermoúpolis, Grc. F10 18
Erne, Lower Lough, l., N. Ire., U.K. C3 12
Erne, Upper Lough, l., Eur. C3 12
Erode, India G3 40
Erofej Pavlovič, Russia D14 26
Eropol, Russia C18 26
Er-Rachidia, Mor. E3 14
Errego, Moz. B6 56
Erromango, i., Vanuatu I9 62a
Eršov, Russia D8 22
Ertai, China B6 28
Ertil', Russia D16 20
Ertis see Irtysh, stm., Asia D8 26
Ertix see Irtysh, stm., Asia D8 26
Erwin, N.C., U.S. B4 126
Erwin, Tn., U.S. C11 135
Eryuan, China A3 34
Erzgebirge, mts., Eur. E9 8
Erzin, Russia D11 26
Erzincan, Tur. C8 44
Erzurum, Tur. C9 44
Esa'ala, Pap. N. Gui. H13 32
Esbjerg, Den. I3 10
Escalante, Ut., U.S. F4 137
Escalante, stm., Ut., U.S. F4 137
Escalon, Ca., U.S. D3 98
Escambia, co., Al., U.S. D2 94
Escambia, stm., Fl., U.S. u14 102
Escambia, co., Fl., U.S. u14 102
Escanaba, Mi., U.S. C3 115
Escanaba, stm., Mi., U.S. B3 115
Escárcega, Mex. D6 78
Escarpada Point, c., Phil. C8 34
Escatawpa, Ms., U.S. E5 117
Escatawpa, stm., U.S. D5 117
Escondido, stm., Nic. C3 80
Escondido, Ca., U.S. F5 98
Escoumins, Rivière des, stm., Qc., Can. A8 90
Escuinapa de Hidalgo, Mex. C3 78
Escuintla, Guat. C1 80
Escuminac, Point, c., N.B., Can. B5 87
Eséka, Cam. C2 54
Eşfahān, Iran D6 42
Esil', Kaz. D8 26
Èskar-Ola, Russia D6 26
Eskilstuna, Swe. G7 10
Eskimo Lakes, l., N.T., Can. E13 82
Eskişehir, Tur. C4 44
Esla, stm., Spain G4 16
Eslāmābād, Iran E12 44
Eslāmshahr, Iran C6 42
Eşme, Tur. C3 44
Esmeralda, co., Nv., U.S. F4 121
Esmeraldas, Ec. C4 70
Esmond, R.I., U.S. B4 132
Espanola, On., Can. A3 89
Espanola, N.M., U.S. B3 124
Esparto, Ca., U.S. C2 98
Esperança, Braz. D6 70
Esperance, Austl. G3 60
Esperance Bay, b., Austl. G3 60
Esperanza, Arg. E5 72
Esperanza, Mex. B3 78
Espinhaço, Serra do, mts., Braz. E3 74
Espinho, Port. G2 16
Espírito Santo, state, Braz. E3 74
Espiritu Santo, i., Vanuatu j9 62a
Espíritu Santo, Isla del, i., Mex. C2 78
Esplanada, Braz. D4 74
Espoo, Fin. F11 10
Espungabera, Moz. C5 56
Espy, Pa., U.S. D9 131
Esquel, Arg. F2 69
Esquimalt, B.C., Can. E6 85
Esquina, Arg. D6 72
Essaouira, Mor. D3 48
Essej, Russia C12 26
Essen, Ger. E10 12
Essendon, Mount, mtn., Austl. E3 60
Essequibo, stm., Guy. C8 70
Essex, On., Can. E2 89
Essex, Ct., U.S. D6 100
Essex, Ia., U.S. D2 108
Essex, Ma., U.S. A6 114
Essex, co., Ma., U.S. A5 114
Essex, Md., U.S. B5 113
Essex, co., N.J., U.S. B4 123
Essex, co., N.Y., U.S. B7 125
Essex, co., Va., U.S. C6 139
Essex, Vt., U.S. B2 138
Essex, co., Vt., U.S. B5 138
Essex Junction, Vt., U.S. C2 138
Essexville, Mi., U.S. E7 115
Esslingen am Neckar, Ger. F11 12
Estacada, Or., U.S. B4 130
Estacado, Llano, pl., U.S. C1 136
Estacado, Llano, pl., U.S. E7 92
Estados, Isla de los, i., Arg. H4 69
Eşţahbān, Iran E6 42
Estância, Braz. D4 74
Estancia, N.M., U.S. C3 124
Estcourt, S. Afr. D4 56
Estelí, Nic. C2 80
Estella, Spain F5 16
Estelline, S.D., U.S. C9 134
Estepona, Spain I4 16
Estero Bay, b., Ca., U.S. E3 98
Estero Bay, b., Fl., U.S. F5 102
Estero Island, i., Fl., U.S. F5 102
Estes Park, Co., U.S. A5 99
Estherville, Ia., U.S. A3 108
Estherwood, La., U.S. D3 111
Estill, co., Ky., U.S. C6 110
Estill, S.C., U.S. F5 133
Estill Springs, Tn., U.S. B5 135
Estonia, ctry., Eur. G11 10
Estremadura, hist. reg., Port. H2 16
Esztergom, Hung. F5 20
Etah, Grnld. C25 82
Étampes, Fr. C8 16
Étang-du-Nord, Qc., Can. B8 87
Etāwah, India D3 40
Ethel, W.V., U.S. n12 141
Ethel Creek, Austl. E3 60
Ethiopia, ctry., Afr. I12 48
Etna, Pa., U.S. k14 131
Etna, Monte, vol., Italy F5 18
Etobicoke, On., Can. D5 89
Etolin Island, i., Ak., U.S. m23 95
Etolin Strait, strt., Ak., U.S. C6 95
Etosha Pan, pl., Nmb. B2 56
Etowah, co., Al., U.S. A3 94
Etowah, stm., Ga., U.S. B2 103
Etowah, Tn., U.S. D9 135
Et Tîdra, i., Maur. C1 50
Ettrick, Va., U.S. C5 139
Eua, i., Tonga G12 58
Euboea see Évvoia, i., Grc. E9 18
Euboea, Gulf of see Vórios Evvoïkós Kólpos, b., Grc. E9 18
Eucla, Austl. G4 60
Euclid, Oh., U.S. A4 128
Eudora, Ar., U.S. D4 97
Eudora, Ks., U.S. D8 109
Eufaula, Al., U.S. D4 94
Eufaula, Ok., U.S. B6 129
Eufaula Lake, res., Ok., U.S. B6 129
Eugene, Or., U.S. C3 130
Eugenia, Punta, c., Mex. B1 78
Eugmo, i., Fin. E10 10
Eunice, La., U.S. D3 111
Eunice, N.M., U.S. E6 124
Euphrates (Al-Furāt), stm., Asia D4 42
Eupora, Ms., U.S. B4 117
Eureka, Ca., U.S. B1 98
Eureka, Il., U.S. C4 106
Eureka, Ks., U.S. E7 109
Eureka, Mo., U.S. f12 118
Eureka, Mt., U.S. B1 119
Eureka, co., Nv., U.S. D5 121
Eureka, Nv., U.S. D6 121
Eureka, S.C., U.S. B5 133
Eureka, S.D., U.S. B6 134
Eureka Springs, Ar., U.S. A2 97
Euroa, Austl. H4 62
Europe, cont. C13 4
Eustis, Fl., U.S. D5 102
Eutaw, Al., U.S. C2 94
Eutsuk Lake, l., B.C., Can. C4 85
Evangeline, co., La., U.S. D3 111
Evans, Co., U.S. A6 99
Evans, Ga., U.S. C4 103
Evans, co., Ga., U.S. D5 103
Evans, W.V., U.S. C3 141
Evans, Mount, mtn., Co., U.S. B5 99
Evansburg, Ab., Can. C3 84
Evans City, Pa., U.S. E1 131
Evansdale, Ia., U.S. B5 108
Evanston, Il., U.S. A6 106
Evanston, Wy., U.S. E2 143
Evansville, Il., U.S. E4 106
Evansville, In., U.S. I2 107
Evansville, Wi., U.S. F4 142
Evansville, Wy., U.S. D6 143
Eva Perón see La Plata, Arg. F6 72
Evart, Mi., U.S. E5 115
Evarts, Ky., U.S. D6 110
Eveleth, Mn., U.S. C6 116
Evensk, Russia C17 26
Everest, Mount, mtn., Asia D5 40
Everett, Ma., U.S. g11 114
Everett, Pa., U.S. F5 131
Everett, Wa., U.S. B3 140
Everett Lake, res., N.H., U.S. D3 122
Everglades National Park, Fl., U.S. G5 102
Evergreen, Al., U.S. D3 94
Evergreen, Co., U.S. B5 99
Evergreen Park, Il., U.S. k9 106
Everly, Ia., U.S. A2 108
Everson, Wa., U.S. A3 140
Evje, Nor. G2 10
Évora, Port. H3 16
Évreux, Fr. C7 16
Évros (Marica) (Meriç), stm., Eur. D11 18
E.V. Spence Reservoir, res., Tx., U.S. D2 136
Évvoia, i., Grc. E9 18
'Ewa Beach, Hi., U.S. B3 104
'Ewa Beach, cst., Hi., U.S. g9 104
'Ewa Villages, Hi., U.S. B3 104
Ewing Township, N.J., U.S. C3 123
Ewo, Congo D2 54
Excelsior Mountain, mtn., Ca., U.S. C4 98
Excelsior Mountains, mts., Nv., U.S. E3 121
Excelsior Springs, Mo., U.S. B3 118
Exeter, On., Can. D3 89
Exeter, Eng., U.K. E5 12
Exeter, Ca., U.S. D4 98
Exeter, Ne., U.S. D8 120
Exeter, N.H., U.S. E5 122
Exeter, stm., N.H., U.S. E5 122
Exeter, Pa., U.S. D10 131
Exira, Ia., U.S. C3 108
Exmore, Va., U.S. C7 139
Exmouth, Austl. E1 60
Exmouth Gulf, b., Austl. E1 60
Experiment, Ga., U.S. C2 103
Exploits, stm., N.L., Can. D3 88
Exploits, Bay of, b., N.L., Can. D4 88
Export, Pa., U.S. F2 131
Extremadura, hist. reg., Spain H3 16
Exuma Cays, is., Bah. A4 80
Exuma Sound, strt., Bah. D9 76
Eyasi, Lake, l., Tan. D7 54
Eyl, Som. I14 48
Eylar Mountain, mtn., Ca., U.S. D3 98
Eyota, Mn., U.S. G6 116
Eyre, Austl. G4 60
Eyre North, Lake, l., Austl. F2 62
Eyre Peninsula, pen., Austl. G2 62
Ezequiel Ramos Mexía, Embalse, res., Arg. E3 69
Ezine, Tur. C2 44

F

Fabens, Tx., U.S. o11 136
Fabius, stm., Mo., U.S. A6 118
Fabriano, Italy C4 18
Fachi, Niger C7 50
Factoryville, Pa., U.S. C10 131
Fada, Chad G9 48
Fada-Ngourma, Burkina D5 50
Faenza, Italy B3 18
Faeroe Islands see Faroe Islands, is., Far. Is. B12 4
Făgăraş, Rom. G8 20
Fagernes, Nor. F3 10
Fagersta, Swe. G6 10
Fairacres, N.M., U.S. E3 124
Fairbank, Ia., U.S. B5 108
Fairbanks, Ak., U.S. C10 95
Fair Bluff, N.C., U.S. C3 126
Fairborn, Oh., U.S. C1 128
Fairburn, Ga., U.S. C2 103
Fairbury, Il., U.S. C5 106
Fairbury, Ne., U.S. D8 120
Fairchance, Pa., U.S. G2 131
Fairchild Air Force Base, mil., Wa., U.S. g13 140
Fairdale, Ky., U.S. B4 110
Fairfax, Ca., U.S. C2 98
Fairfax, De., U.S. A3 101
Fairfax, Ia., U.S. C6 108
Fairfax, Mn., U.S. F4 116
Fairfax, Mo., U.S. A2 118
Fairfax, Ok., U.S. A5 129
Fairfax, S.C., U.S. F5 133
Fairfax, Va., U.S. B5 139
Fairfax, co., Va., U.S. B5 139
Fairfield, Al., U.S. B3 94
Fairfield, Ca., U.S. C2 98
Fairfield, Ct., U.S. E2 100
Fairfield, co., Ct., U.S. D2 100
Fairfield, Ia., U.S. C6 108
Fairfield, Il., U.S. E5 106
Fairfield, Me., U.S. D3 112
Fairfield, Mt., U.S. C5 119
Fairfield, Oh., U.S. n12 128
Fairfield, co., Oh., U.S. C3 128
Fairfield, co., S.C., U.S. C5 133
Fairfield, Tx., U.S. D4 136
Fairfield Bay, Ar., U.S. B3 97
Fairfield Pond, l., Vt., U.S. B3 138
Fair Grove, Mo., U.S. D4 118
Fair Grove, N.C., U.S. B2 126
Fairhaven, Ma., U.S. C6 114
Fair Haven, Mi., U.S. F8 115
Fair Haven, N.J., U.S. C4 123
Fair Haven, Vt., U.S. D2 138
Fairhope, Al., U.S. E2 94
Fair Isle, i., Scot., U.K. i19 12a
Fairland, In., U.S. E6 107
Fairland, Ok., U.S. A7 129
Fair Lawn, N.J., U.S. h8 123
Fairlawn, Va., U.S. C2 139
Fairlea, W.V., U.S. D4 141
Fairmont, Il., U.S. C6 106
Fairmont, Mn., U.S. G4 116
Fairmont, N.C., U.S. C3 126

Name — Map Ref. — Page

Fairmont, Mn., U.S. G4 116
Fairmont, N.C., U.S. C3 126
Fairmont, Ne., U.S. D8 120
Fairmont, W.V., U.S. B4 141
Fairmount, Ga., U.S. B2 103
Fairmount, In., U.S. D6 107
Fairmount Heights, Md., U.S. f9 113
Fair Oaks, Ga., U.S. h7 103
Fairoaks, Pa., U.S. h13 131
Fair Plain, Mi., U.S. F4 115
Fairport, N.Y., U.S. B3 125
Fairport Harbor, Oh., U.S. A4 128
Fairvale, N.B., Can. D4 87
Fairview, Ab., Can. A1 84
Fairview, Mt., U.S. C12 119
Fairview, N.J., U.S. h8 123
Fairview, Ok., U.S. A3 129
Fairview, Pa., U.S. B1 131
Fairview, Tn., U.S. B4 135
Fairview, Ut., U.S. D4 137
Fairview Heights, Il., U.S. E3 106
Fairview Park, In., U.S. E3 107
Fairview Park, Oh., U.S. g9 128
Fairview Peak, mtn., Nv., U.S. D3 121
Fairview Peak, mtn., Or., U.S. D4 130
Fairway, Ks., U.S. k16 109
Fairweather Mountain, mtn., N.A. G12 82
Fais, i., Micron. E11 32
Faisalabad, Pak. D10 42
Faison, N.C., U.S. B4 126
Faizābād, India D4 40
Fakfak, Indon. D8 36
Fakse Bugt, b., Den. I5 10
Faku, China C12 28
Falaba, S.L. E2 50
Falam, Mya. B2 34
Falconer, N.Y., U.S. C1 125
Falcon Heights, Mn., U.S. n12 116
Falcon Heights, Or., U.S. E5 130
Fălești, Mol. F9 20
Falfurrias, Tx., U.S. F3 136
Falher, Ab., Can. B2 84
Falkenberg, Swe. H5 10
Falkland Islands, is., Falk. Is. H4 69
Falkland Sound, strt., Falk. Is. H4 69
Falköping, Swe. G5 10
Falkville, Al., U.S. A3 94
Fall, stm., Ks., U.S. E7 109
Fall Branch, Tn., U.S. C11 135
Fallbrook, Ca., U.S. F5 98
Fall City, Wa., U.S. B4 140
Fall Creek, Wi., U.S. D2 142
Falling Creek, stm., Va., U.S. n17 139
Falling Rock Creek, stm., W.V., U.S. m13 141
Fall Mountain Lake, Ct., U.S. C4 100
Fallon, co., Mt., U.S. D12 119
Fallon, Nv., U.S. D3 121
Fallon Indian Reservation, Nv., U.S. D3 121
Fallon Naval Air Station, mil., Nv., U.S. D3 121
Fall River, Ma., U.S. C5 114
Fall River, co., S.D., U.S. D2 134
Fall River, Wi., U.S. E4 142
Fall River Lake, res., Ks., U.S. E7 109
Falls, co., Tx., U.S. D4 136
Falls Church, Va., U.S. g12 139
Falls City, Ne., U.S. D10 120
Falls City, Or., U.S. C3 130
Falls Creek, Pa., U.S. D4 131
Fallston, Md., U.S. A5 113
Falmouth, N.S., Can. E5 87
Falmouth, Eng., U.K. E4 12
Falmouth, Ky., U.S. B5 110
Falmouth, Ma., U.S. C6 114
Falmouth, Me., U.S. E2 112
Falmouth, Va., U.S. B5 139
False Bay see Valsbaai, b., S. Afr. E2 56
False Cape, c., Fl., U.S. D6 102
False Cape, c., Va., U.S. D7 139
Falster, i., Den. I5 10
Fălticeni, Rom. F9 20
Falun, Swe. F6 10
Fanchang, China C4 30
Fancy Farm, Ky., U.S. f9 110
Fangak, Sudan B6 54
Fangcheng, China C3 30
Fangcheng, China E2 30
Fangxian, China C3 30
Fangzheng, China A1 31
Fannin, co., Ga., U.S. B2 103
Fannin, co., Tx., U.S. C4 136
Fanny, Mount, mtn., Or., U.S. B9 130
Fano, Italy C4 18
Fan Si Pan, mtn., Viet. B4 34
Faradje, D.R.C. C5 54
Faradofay see Tôlanaro, Madag. D8 56
Farafangana, Madag. C8 56
Farāh, Afg. D8 42
Farallon de Medinilla, i., N. Mar. Is. C12 32
Farallon de Pajaros, i., N. Mar. Is. B12 32
Faranah, Gui. D2 50
Farasān, Jazā'ir, is., Sau. Ar. G4 38
Farewell, Cape, c., N.Z. p13 63c
Fargo, Ga., U.S. F4 103
Fargo, N.D., U.S. C9 127
Faribault, Mn., U.S. F5 116
Faribault, co., Mn., U.S. G4 116
Farīdābād, India D3 40
Farley, Ia., U.S. B6 108
Farmer City, Il., U.S. C5 106
Farmers Branch, Tx., U.S. n10 136
Farmersburg, In., U.S. F3 107
Farmerville, La., U.S. B3 111
Farmingdale, Me., U.S. D3 112
Farmington, Ar., U.S. A1 97
Farmington, Ct., U.S. C4 100
Farmington, stm., Ct., U.S. B4 100
Farmington, Ia., U.S. D6 108
Farmington, Il., U.S. C3 106
Farmington, Me., U.S. D2 112
Farmington, Mi., U.S. p15 115
Farmington, Mn., U.S. F5 116
Farmington, Mo., U.S. D7 118
Farmington, N.H., U.S. D4 122
Farmington, N.M., U.S. A1 124
Farmington, Ut., U.S. C4 137
Farmington Hills, Mi., U.S. o15 115
Farmland, In., U.S. D7 107
Farmville, N.C., U.S. B5 126
Farmville, Va., U.S. C4 139
Farnham, Qc., Can. D5 90
Faro, Braz. D8 70
Faro, Port. I3 16
Faroe Islands, dep., Eur. o23 10b
Faroe Islands, is., Far. Is. B12 4
Fårön, i., Swe. H8 10
Fårösund, Swe. H8 10
Farquhar, Atoll de, is., Sey. j12 57b
Farrell, Pa., U.S. D1 131
Farrukhābād, India D3 40
Fartak, Ra's, c., Yemen G6 38
Farvel, Kap, c., Grnld. G31 82
Farwell, Mi., U.S. E6 115
Farwell, Tx., U.S. B1 136
Fasā, Iran E6 42
Fastiv, Ukr. D10 20
Fatick, Sen. D1 50
Fatsa, Tur. B7 44
Faulk, co., S.D., U.S. B6 134
Faulkland Heights, De., U.S. i7 101
Faulkner, co., Ar., U.S. B3 97
Faulkton, S.D., U.S. B6 134
Fauquier, co., Va., U.S. B5 139
Fauske, Nor. C6 10
Fawnie Nose, mtn., B.C., Can. C5 85
Faxaflói, b., Ice. l17 10a
Faya-Largeau, Chad C8 50
Fayd, Sau. Ar. E4 42
Fayette, Al., U.S. B2 94
Fayette, co., Al., U.S. B3 94
Fayette, co., Ga., U.S. C2 103
Fayette, Ia., U.S. B6 108
Fayette, co., Ia., U.S. B6 108
Fayette, co., Il., U.S. D5 106
Fayette, co., In., U.S. E7 107
Fayette, co., Ky., U.S. B5 110
Fayette, Mo., U.S. B5 118
Fayette, Ms., U.S. D2 117
Fayette, Oh., U.S. A1 128
Fayette, co., Oh., U.S. C2 128
Fayette, co., Pa., U.S. G2 131
Fayette, co., Tn., U.S. B2 135
Fayette, co., Tx., U.S. E4 136
Fayette, co., W.V., U.S. C3 141
Fayetteville, Ar., U.S. A1 97
Fayetteville, Ga., U.S. C2 103
Fayetteville, N.C., U.S. B4 126
Fayetteville, Pa., U.S. G6 131
Fayetteville, Tn., U.S. B5 135
Fayetteville, W.V., U.S. C3 141
Fāzilka, India C2 40
Fazzān, hist. reg., Libya A7 50
Fdérik, Maur. B2 50
Fear, Cape, c., N.C., U.S. D5 126
Feather, stm., Ca., U.S. C3 98
Fécamp, Fr. C7 16
Federal, Arg. E6 72
Federalsburg, Md., U.S. C6 113
Federated States of Micronesia see Micronesia, Federated States of, ctry., Oc. D8 58
Feeding Hills, Ma., U.S. B2 114
Fehmarn, i., Ger. C12 12
Feijó, Braz. E5 70
Feira de Santana, Braz. D4 74
Felipe Carrillo Puerto, Mex. D7 78
Fellsmere, Fl., U.S. E6 102
Felton, Ca., U.S. D2 98
Felton, De., U.S. D3 101
Femunden, l., Nor. E4 10
Fence, stm., Mi., U.S. B2 115
Fence Lake, l., Wi., U.S. C4 142
Fenelon Falls, On., Can. C6 89
Fengcheng, China F11 28
Fengdu, China F9 28
Fengfeng, China B3 30
Fenghuang, China D2 30
Fengning, China A4 30
Fengqing, China B3 34
Fengqiu, China B3 30
Fengrun, China B4 30
Fengtai, China C4 30
Fengzhen, China A3 30
Fenimore Pass, strt., Ak., U.S. E4 95
Fennimore, Wi., U.S. F3 142
Fennville, Mi., U.S. F4 115
Fenoarivo Atsinanana, Madag. B8 56
Fenton, Mi., U.S. F7 115
Fentress, co., Tn., U.S. C9 135
Fenwick Island, i., S.C., U.S. k11 133
Fenyang, China D10 28
Fenyi, China D3 30
Feodosiia, Ukr. G13 20
Fer, Point au, c., La., U.S. E4 111
Ferdinand, In., U.S. H4 107
Ferdows, Iran D7 42
Fergana, Uzb. E9 26
Fergana Mountains see Ferganskij hrebet, mts., Kyrg. A2 40
Ferganskij hrebet, mts., Kyrg. A2 40
Fergus, On., Can. D4 89
Fergus, co., Mt., U.S. C7 119
Fergus Falls, Mn., U.S. D2 116
Ferguson, Ky., U.S. C5 110
Ferguson, Mo., U.S. C7 118
Ferkéssédougou, C. Iv. E3 50
Ferlo, reg., Sen. C2 50
Ferme-Neuve, Qc., Can. C2 90
Fermo, Italy C4 18
Fermont, Qc., Can. h13 90
Fernandina Beach, Fl., U.S. B5 102
Fernandópolis, Braz. F1 74
Fernando Póo see Bioko, i., Eq. Gui. C1 54
Fernán-Núñez, Spain I4 16
Fern Creek, Ky., U.S. g11 110
Ferndale, Ca., U.S. B1 98
Ferndale, Md., U.S. B4 113
Ferndale, Mi., U.S. P15 115
Ferndale, Pa., U.S. F4 131
Ferndale, Wa., U.S. A3 140
Fernie, B.C., Can. E10 85
Fernley, Nv., U.S. D2 121
Fern Ridge Lake, res., Or., U.S. C3 130
Fernwood, Id., U.S. B2 105
Fernwood, Ms., U.S. D3 117
Feroe Islands see Faroe Islands, dep., Far. Is. C5 8
Ferrara, Italy B3 18
Ferrelo, Cape, c., Or., U.S. E2 130
Ferriday, La., U.S. C4 111
Ferris, Tx., U.S. C4 136
Ferris Mountains, mts., Wy., U.S. D5 143
Ferro see El Hierro, i., Spain A1 50
Ferrol, Spain F2 16
Ferron, Ut., U.S. D4 137
Ferrum, Va., U.S. D2 139
Ferry, co., Wa., U.S. A7 140
Ferry Farms, Va., U.S. B5 139
Ferryland, N.L., Can. E5 88
Ferry Point, c., N.J., U.S. k7 123
Fertile, Mn., U.S. C2 116
Fès, Mor. D4 48
Feshi, D.R.C. E3 54
Fessenden, N.D., U.S. B6 127
Festus, Mo., U.S. C7 118
Fetești, Rom. G9 20
Fethiye, Tur. D3 44
Fetisovo, Kaz. B6 42
Feuilles, Rivière aux, stm., Qc., Can. g12 90
Feyzābād, Afg. C10 42
Fianarantsoa, Madag. C8 56
Fianga, Chad E8 50
Fichē, Eth. B7 54
Ficksburg, S. Afr. D4 56
Fidalgo Island, i., Wa., U.S. A3 140
Fieldale, Va., U.S. D3 139
Fields, Lake, l., Fl., U.S. B3 102
Fields, Lake, l., La., U.S. k10 111
Fier, Alb. D7 18
Fifteenmile Creek, stm., Wy., U.S. B4 143
Fifteen Mile Falls Reservoir, res., U.S. C5 138
Fifth Cataract, wtfl., Sudan G11 48
Figtree, Zimb. C4 56
Figueira da Foz, Port. G2 16
Figueres, Spain F8 16
Figuig, Mor. D4 48
Fiji, ctry., Oc. m10 63b
Filchner Ice Shelf, ice, Ant. D1 67
Filer, Id., U.S. G4 105
Filingué, Niger D5 50
Filippoi, hist., Grc. D10 18
Fillmore, Ca., U.S. E4 98
Fillmore, co., Mn., U.S. G6 116
Fillmore, co., Ne., U.S. D8 120
Fillmore, Ut., U.S. E3 137
Fimi, stm., D.R.C. D3 54
Findlay, Il., U.S. D5 106
Findlay, Oh., U.S. A2 128
Fíngoè, Moz. B5 56
Finike, Tur. D4 44
Finke, Austl. F5 60
Finland, ctry., Eur. E12 10
Finland, Gulf of, b., Eur. G10 10
Finley, Austl. H4 62
Finley, Tn., U.S. A2 135
Finney, co., Ks., U.S. D3 109
Finnmark, state, Nor. B11 10
Finn Mountain, mtn., Ak., U.S. C8 95
Fins, Oman F7 42
Finspång, Swe. G6 10
Fircrest, Wa., U.S. f10 140
Firebaugh, Ca., U.S. D3 98
Firenze (Florence), Italy C3 18
Firestone, Co., U.S. A6 99
Fīrozābād, India D3 40
Firozpur, India C2 40
First Cataract, wtfl., Egypt F11 48
First Connecticut Lake, l., N.H., U.S. f7 122
Fīrūzābād, Iran E6 42
Fish, stm., Al., U.S. E2 94
Fish, stm., Me., U.S. A4 112
Fish Creek, stm., W.V., U.S. g8 141
Fisher, Il., U.S. C5 106
Fisher, co., Tx., U.S. C2 136
Fisher Bay, b., Mb., Can. D3 86
Fishermans Island, i., Va., U.S. h15 139
Fishers, In., U.S. E5 107
Fishers Island, i., N.Y., U.S. m16 125
Fishers Peak, mtn., Co., U.S. D6 99
Fishersville, Va., U.S. B4 139
Fishing Bay, b., Md., U.S. D5 113
Fishing Creek, Md., U.S. D5 113
Fishing Creek, stm., N.C., U.S. A5 126
Fishing Creek, stm., S.C., U.S. B5 133
Fishing Creek, stm., W.V., U.S. B4 141
Fishing Creek Reservoir, res., S.C., U.S. B6 133
Fishkill, N.Y., U.S. D7 125
Fish Lake, l., Ut., U.S. E4 137
Fish River Lake, l., Me., U.S. B4 112
Fishtrap Lake, res., Ky., U.S. C7 110
Fiskdale, Ma., U.S. B3 114
Fisterra, Cabo de, c., Spain F2 16
Fitchburg, Ma., U.S. A4 114
Fitri, Lac, l., Chad D8 50
Fitzgerald, Ga., U.S. E3 103
Fitz Roy, Arg. G3 69
Fitzroy, stm., Austl. D3 60
Fitzroy Crossing, Austl. D4 60
Fitzwilliam, N.H., U.S. E2 122
Fitzwilliam Island, i., On., Can. B3 89
Fiume see Rijeka, Cro. B5 18
Five Island Lake, l., Ia., U.S. A3 108
Fivemile Creek, stm., Wy., U.S. C4 143
Five Points, N.M., U.S. B3 124
Fizi, D.R.C. D5 54
Flagler, co., Fl., U.S. C5 102
Flagler Beach, Fl., U.S. C5 102
Flagstaff, Az., U.S. B4 96
Flagstaff Lake, l., Or., U.S. E7 130
Flambeau, stm., Wi., U.S. C3 142
Flaming Gorge Dam, Ut., U.S. C6 137
Flaming Gorge National Recreation Area, U.S. E3 143
Flaming Gorge Reservoir, res., U.S. E3 143
Flaming Gorge Reservoir, res., U.S. C6 92
Flanagan, Il., U.S. C5 106
Flandreau, S.D., U.S. C9 134
Flandreau Indian Reservation, S.D., U.S. C9 134
Flat, stm., Mi., U.S. E5 115
Flat, stm., N.C., U.S. A4 126
Flat, stm., R.I., U.S. E2 132
Flat Brook, stm., N.J., U.S. A3 123
Flathead, co., Mt., U.S. B2 119
Flathead, South Fork, stm., Mt., U.S. C3 119
Flathead Indian Reservation, Mt., U.S. C2 119
Flathead Lake, l., Mt., U.S. C2 119
Flathead Valley, val., Mt., U.S. C2 119
Flat Lake, l., La., U.S. k9 111
Flat Lick, Ky., U.S. D6 110
Flatonia, Tx., U.S. E4 136
Flat River, Mo., U.S. D7 118
Flat River Reservoir, res., R.I., U.S. D3 132
Flatrock, stm., In., U.S. F6 107
Flat Rock, Mi., U.S. F7 115
Flat Rock, N.C., U.S. f10 126
Flattery, Cape, c., Austl. C4 62
Flattery, Cape, c., Wa., U.S. A1 140
Flatwoods, Ky., U.S. B7 110
Fleetwood, Pa., U.S. F10 131
Fleming, co., Ky., U.S. B6 110
Fleming-Neon, Ky., U.S. C7 110
Flemingsburg, Ky., U.S. B6 110
Flemington, N.J., U.S. B3 123
Flemington, Pa., U.S. D7 131
Flen, Swe. G7 10
Flensburg, Ger. C11 12
Fletcher, N.C., U.S. f10 126
Fletcher, Ok., U.S. C3 129
Flinders, stm., Austl. D3 62
Flinders Bay, b., Austl. G2 60
Flinders Island, i., Austl. H4 62
Flinders Reefs, rf., Austl. D4 62
Flin Flon, Mb., Can. B1 86
Flint, i., Kir. F14 58
Flint, stm., Ga., U.S. E2 103
Flint, Mi., U.S. E7 115
Flint City, Al., U.S. A3 94
Flint Creek Range, mts., Mt., U.S. D3 119
Flint Run, stm., W.V., U.S. k9 141
Flippin, Ar., U.S. A3 97
Flisa, Nor. F5 10
Flomaton, Al., U.S. D2 94
Flora, Il., U.S. E5 106
Flora, In., U.S. C4 107
Flora, Ms., U.S. C3 117
Florala, Al., U.S. D3 94
Floral City, Fl., U.S. D4 102
Florence see Firenze, Italy C3 18
Florence, Al., U.S. A2 94
Florence, Az., U.S. D4 96
Florence, Co., U.S. C5 99
Florence, Ks., U.S. D7 109
Florence, Ky., U.S. A5 110
Florence, Ms., U.S. C3 117
Florence, N.J., U.S. C3 123
Florence, Or., U.S. D2 130
Florence, co., S.C., U.S. C8 133
Florence, S.C., U.S. C8 133
Florence, co., Wi., U.S. C5 142
Florenceville, N.B., Can. C2 87
Florencia, Col. C4 70
Flores, i., Indon. E6 36
Flores, Laut (Flores Sea), Indon. E6 36
Flores Sea see Flores, Laut, Indon. E6 36
Florești, Mol. F10 20
Floresville, Tx., U.S. E3 136
Florham Park, N.J., U.S. B4 123
Floriano, Braz. C3 74
Florianópolis, Braz. D8 72
Florida, Cuba A4 80
Florida, Ur. E6 72
Florida, N.Y., U.S. D6 125
Florida, state, U.S. E5 102
Florida, Cape, c., Fl., U.S. G6 102
Florida, Straits of, strt., N.A. G11 92
Florida Bay, b., Fl., U.S. H6 102
Floridablanca, Col. D5 80
Florida City, Fl., U.S. G6 102
Florida Keys, is., Fl., U.S. H6 102
Florida Mountains, mts., N.M., U.S. E2 124
Florida State Indian Reservation, Fl., U.S. F5 102
Florien, La., U.S. C2 111
Flórina, Grc. D8 18
Florissant, Mo., U.S. f13 118
Florissant Fossil Beds National Monument, Co., U.S. C5 99
Florø, Nor. F1 10
Flossmoor, Il., U.S. k9 106
Flovilla, Ga., U.S. C3 103
Flower Brook, stm., Vt., U.S. E2 138
Flowery Branch, Ga., U.S. B3 103
Flowood, Ms., U.S. C3 117
Floyd, co., Ga., U.S. B1 103
Floyd, stm., Ia., U.S. B1 108
Floyd, co., Ia., U.S. A5 108
Floyd, co., In., U.S. H6 107
Floyd, co., Ky., U.S. C7 110
Floyd, co., Tx., U.S. B2 136
Floyd, co., Va., U.S. D2 139
Floydada, Tx., U.S. C2 136
Floyds Fork, stm., Ky., U.S. B4 110
Floyds Knobs, In., U.S. H6 107
Flushing see Vlissingen, Neth. E8 12
Flushing, Mi., U.S. E7 115
Flushing, Oh., U.S. B4 128
Fluvanna, co., Va., U.S. C4 139
Foard, co., Tx., U.S. B3 136
Foča, Bos. C7 18
Focșani, Rom. G9 20
Foggia, Italy D5 18
Fogland Point, c., R.I., U.S. E6 132
Fogo, N.L., Can. D4 88
Fogo, i., C.V. g10 50a
Fogo, Cape, c., N.L., Can. D5 88
Fogo Island, i., N.L., Can. D4 88
Foix, Fr. F7 16
Fokku, Nig. D5 50
Folādī, Koh-e, mtn., Afg. D9 42
Folda, b., Nor. C6 10
Foley, Al., U.S. E2 94
Foley, Mn., U.S. E5 116
Foligno, Italy C4 18
Folkestone, Eng., U.K. E7 12
Folkston, Ga., U.S. F4 103
Follansbee, W.V., U.S. A4 141
Folly Beach, S.C., U.S. F8 133
Folly Island, i., S.C., U.S. F8 133
Folsom, Ca., U.S. C3 98
Fomboni, Com. A7 56
Fonda, Ia., U.S. B3 108
Fond du Lac, Wi., U.S. E5 142
Fond du Lac, co., Wi., U.S. E5 142
Fond du Lac Indian Reservation, Mn., U.S. D6 116
Fonseca, Golfo de, b., N.A. C2 80
Fontainebleau, Fr. C8 16
Fontana, Ca., U.S. m14 98
Fontana, Wi., U.S. F5 142
Fontana Lake, res., N.C., U.S. f9 126
Fontanelle, Ia., U.S. C3 108
Fonte Boa, Braz. D6 70
Fontenay-le-Comte, Fr. D6 16
Fontenelle Reservoir, res., Wy., U.S. D2 143
Fontur, c., Ice. k21 10a
Foochow see Fuzhou, China F11 28
Footville, Wi., U.S. F4 142
Foraker, Mount, mtn., Ak., U.S. f16 95

Name | Map Ref. | Page

Forbes, Austl. G4 62
Forbes, Mount, mtn., Ab., Can. D2 84
Forcados, Nig. E6 50
Forchheim, Ger. F12 12
Ford, co., Il., U.S. C5 106
Ford, co., Ks., U.S. E4 109
Ford, stm., Mi., U.S. C3 115
Ford City, Ca., U.S. E4 98
Ford City, Pa., U.S. E2 131
Fordoche, La., U.S. D4 111
Fords Prairie, Wa., U.S. C2 140
Fordyce, Ar., U.S. D3 97
Forécariah, Gui. E2 50
Forel, Mont, mtn., Grnld. E32 82
Foreman, Ar., U.S. D1 97
Forest, On., Can. D2 89
Forest, Ms., U.S. C4 117
Forest, stm., N.D., U.S. A8 127
Forest, Oh., U.S. B2 128
Forest, co., Pa., U.S. C3 131
Forest, co., Wi., U.S. C5 142
Forest Acres, S.C., U.S. C6 133
Forestburg, Ab., Can. C4 84
Forest City, Ia., U.S. A4 108
Forest City, N.C., U.S. B1 126
Forest City, Pa., U.S. C11 131
Forestdale, R.I., U.S. B3 132
Forest Dale, Vt., U.S. D2 138
Forest Glen, La., U.S. h12 111
Forest Grove, Or., U.S. B3 130
Forest Hill, Md., U.S. A5 113
Forest Hills, Pa., U.S. k14 131
Forest Knolls, Ca., U.S. g7 98
Forest Lake, Mn., U.S. E6 116
Forest Park, Ga., U.S. h8 103
Forest Park, Il., U.S. k9 106
Forillon, Parc National de, Qc., Can. k14 90
Fork Creek, stm., W.V., U.S. m12 141
Forked Deer, stm., Tn., U.S. B2 135
Forkland, Al., U.S. C2 94
Forks, Wa., U.S. B1 140
Forlì, Italy B4 18
Formentera, i., Spain H7 16
Formia, Italy D4 18
Formiga, Braz. F2 74
Formosa, Arg. D6 72
Formosa see Taiwan, ctry., Asia B8 34
Formosa, Braz. E2 74
Formosa, Serra, plat., Braz. F9 70
Formosa Strait see Taiwan Strait, strt., Asia E4 30
Forney, Tx., U.S. C4 136
Forrest, Austl. G4 60
Forrest, Il., U.S. C5 106
Forrest, co., Ms., U.S. D4 117
Forrest City, Ar., U.S. B5 97
Forrester Island, i., Ak., U.S. n23 95
Forreston, Il., U.S. A4 106
Forsayth, Austl. D3 62
Forst, Ger. E14 12
Forsyth, Ga., U.S. C3 103
Forsyth, co., Ga., U.S. B2 103
Forsyth, Il., U.S. D5 106
Forsyth, Mo., U.S. E4 118
Forsyth, Mt., U.S. D10 119
Forsyth, co., N.C., U.S. A2 126
Fortaleza, Braz. B4 74
Fort Apache Indian Reservation, Az., U.S. D5 96
Fort-Archambault see Sarh, Chad B3 54
Fort Ashby, W.V., U.S. B6 141
Fort Atkinson, Wi., U.S. F5 142
Fort Beaufort, S. Afr. E4 56
Fort Belknap Indian Reservation, Mt., U.S. B8 119
Fort Belvoir, mil., Va., U.S. g12 139
Fort Bend, co., Tx., U.S. E5 136
Fort Benjamin Harrison, mil., In., U.S. k10 107
Fort Benning, mil., Ga., U.S. D2 103
Fort Benton, Mt., U.S. C6 119
Fort Berthold Indian Reservation, N.D., U.S. B3 127
Fort Bidwell Indian Reservation, Ca., U.S. B3 98
Fort Bliss, mil., Tx., U.S. o11 136
Fort Bragg, Ca., U.S. C2 98
Fort Bragg, mil., N.C., U.S. B3 126
Fort Branch, In., U.S. H2 107
Fort Calhoun, Ne., U.S. C9 120
Fort Campbell, mil., U.S. A4 135
Fort Carson, mil., Co., U.S. C6 99
Fort Chipewyan, Ab., Can. f8 84
Fort Clatsop National Memorial, hist., Or., U.S. A3 130
Fort Cobb, Ok., U.S. B3 129
Fort Cobb Reservoir, res., Ok., U.S. B3 129
Fort Collins, Co., U.S. A5 99
Fort Coulonge, Qc., Can. B8 89
Fort-Dauphin see Tôlañaro, Madag. D8 56
Fort Davis, Tx., U.S. o13 136
Fort Davis National Historic Site, hist., Tx., U.S. o13 136
Fort Defiance, Az., U.S. B6 96
Fort-de-France, Mart. C7 80
Fort Deposit, Al., U.S. D3 94
Fort Detrick, mil., Md., U.S. B3 113
Fort Dix, mil., N.J., U.S. C3 123
Fort Dodge, Ia., U.S. B3 108
Fort Donelson National Battlefield, Tn., U.S. A4 135
Fort Edward, N.Y., U.S. B7 125
Fort Erie, On., Can. E6 89
Fort Eustis, mil., Va., U.S. h14 139
Fort Fairfield, Me., U.S. B5 112
Fort Frances, On., Can. o16 89
Fort Gaines, Ga., U.S. E1 103
Fort Gay, W.V., U.S. C2 141
Fort Gibson, Ok., U.S. B6 129
Fort Gibson Lake, res., Ok., U.S. A6 129
Fort Gordon, mil., Ga., U.S. C4 103
Fort Greely, mil., Ak., U.S. C10 95
Forth, Firth of, b., Scot., U.K. B5 12
Fort Hall, Id., U.S. F6 105
Fort Hall Indian Reservation, Id., U.S. F6 105
Fort Hood, mil., Tx., U.S. D4 136
Fort Howard, Md., U.S. B5 113
Fort Huachuca, mil., Az., U.S. F5 96
Fort Jackson, mil., S.C., U.S. C6 133
Fort Jefferson National Monument, Fl., U.S. H4 102
Fort Kent, Me., U.S. A4 112
Fort Knox, mil., Ky., U.S. B4 110
Fort-Lamy see N'Djamena, Chad D8 50
Fort Laramie, Wy., U.S. D8 143
Fort Laramie National Historic Site, hist., Wy., U.S. D8 143
Fort Lauderdale, Fl., U.S. F6 102
Fort Lawn, S.C., U.S. B6 133
Fort Leavenworth, mil., Ks., U.S. C9 109
Fort Lee, N.J., U.S. B5 123
Fort Lee, mil., Va., U.S. C5 139
Fort Leonard Wood, mil., Mo., U.S. D5 118
Fort Lewis, mil., Wa., U.S. B3 140
Fort Loramie, Oh., U.S. B1 128
Fort Loudon, Pa., U.S. G6 131
Fort Loudoun Lake, res., Tn., U.S. D9 135
Fort Lupton, Co., U.S. A6 99
Fort MacArthur, mil., Ca., U.S. n12 98
Fort Macleod, Ab., Can. E4 84
Fort Madison, Ia., U.S. D6 108
Fort Matanzas National Monument, Fl., U.S. C5 102
Fort McClellan, mil., Al., U.S. B4 94
Fort McDermitt Indian Reservation, U.S. B4 121
Fort McDowell Indian Reservation, Az., U.S. D4 96
Fort McHenry National Monument and Historic Shrine, Md., U.S. g11 113
Fort McMurray, Ab., Can. A5 84
Fort Meade, Fl., U.S. E5 102
Fort Meade, mil., Md., U.S. B4 113
Fort Meadow Reservoir, res., Ma., U.S. g9 114
Fort Mill, S.C., U.S. A6 133
Fort Mitchell, Al., U.S. C4 94
Fort Mitchell, Ky., U.S. h13 110
Fort Mojave Indian Reservation, U.S. C1 96
Fort Monmouth, mil., N.J., U.S. C4 123
Fort Monroe, mil., Va., U.S. h15 139
Fort Morgan, Co., U.S. A7 99
Fort Myer, mil., Va., U.S. g12 139
Fort Myers, Fl., U.S. F5 102
Fort Myers Beach, Fl., U.S. F5 102
Fort Nelson, B.C., Can. m18 85
Fort Oglethorpe, Ga., U.S. B1 103
Fort Payne, Al., U.S. A4 94
Fort Peck Indian Reservation, Mt., U.S. B11 119
Fort Peck Lake, res., Mt., U.S. C9 119
Fort Pierce, Fl., U.S. E6 102
Fort Pierce Inlet, b., Fl., U.S. E6 102
Fort Pierre, S.D., U.S. C5 134
Fort Plain, N.Y., U.S. C6 125
Fort Polk, mil., La., U.S. C2 111
Fort Portal, Ug. C6 54
Fort Randall Dam, S.D., U.S. D7 134
Fort Recovery, Oh., U.S. B1 128
Fortress Mountain, mtn., Wy., U.S. B3 143
Fort Richardson, mil., Ak., U.S. C10 95
Fort Riley, mil., Ks., U.S. C7 109
Fort Ritchie, mil., Md., U.S. A3 113
Fort Rucker, mil., Al., U.S. D4 94
Fort Saint James, B.C., Can. B5 85
Fort Saint John, B.C., Can. A7 85
Fort Sam Houston, mil., Tx., U.S. k7 136
Fort Saskatchewan, Ab., Can. C4 84
Fort Scott, Ks., U.S. E9 109
Fort-Ševčenko, Kaz. E7 26
Fort Shafter, mil., Hi., U.S. g10 104
Fort Shawnee, Oh., U.S. B1 128
Fort Sill, mil., Ok., U.S. C3 129
Fort Smith, Ar., U.S. B1 97
Fort Stewart, mil., Ga., U.S. D5 103
Fort Stockton, Tx., U.S. D1 136
Fort Sumner, N.M., U.S. C5 124
Fort Sumter National Monument, S.C., U.S. k12 133
Fort Supply Lake, res., Ok., U.S. A2 129
Fort Thomas, Ky., U.S. h14 110
Fort Totten, N.D., U.S. B7 127
Fort Totten Indian Reservation, N.D., U.S. B7 127
Fortuna, Ca., U.S. B1 98
Fortune, N.L., Can. E4 88
Fortune Bay, b., N.L., Can. E4 88
Fort Union National Monument, N.M., U.S. B5 124
Fort Valley, Ga., U.S. D3 103
Fort Vermilion, Ab., Can. f7 84
Fortville, In., U.S. E6 107
Fort Wainwright, mil., Ak., U.S. C10 95
Fort Walton Beach, Fl., U.S. u15 102
Fort Washington Forest, Md., U.S. C4 113
Fort Wayne, In., U.S. B7 107
Fort William, Scot., U.K. B4 12
Fort Wingate, N.M., U.S. B1 124
Fort Worth, Tx., U.S. C4 136
Fort Wright, Ky., U.S. h13 110
Forty Fort, Pa., U.S. D10 131
Fort Yukon, Ak., U.S. B10 95
Fort Yuma Indian Reservation, Ca., U.S. F6 98
Foshan, China G10 28
Foso, Ghana E4 50
Fossano, Italy B1 18
Fossil Butte National Monument, Wy., U.S. E2 143
Fossil Lake, l., Or., U.S. D6 130
Foss Reservoir, res., Ok., U.S. B2 129
Fosston, Mn., U.S. C3 116
Foster, co., N.D., U.S. B6 127
Foster, Or., U.S. C4 130
Foster Village, Hi., U.S. g10 104
Fostoria, Oh., U.S. A2 128
Fougamou, Gabon D2 54
Fougères, Fr. C6 16
Fouke, Ar., U.S. D2 97
Foulamôri, Gui. D2 50
Foumban, Cam. B2 54
Foundiougne, Sen. D1 50
Fountain, Co., U.S. C6 99
Fountain, co., In., U.S. D3 107
Fountain City, In., U.S. E8 107
Fountain City, Wi., U.S. D2 142
Fountain Hill, Pa., U.S. E11 131
Fountain Inn, S.C., U.S. B3 133
Fountain Peak, mtn., Ca., U.S. E6 98
Fourche LaFave, stm., Ar., U.S. C2 97
Fourche Maline, stm., Ok., U.S. C6 129
Four Mountains, Islands of, is., Ak., U.S. E6 95
Four Oaks, N.C., U.S. B4 126
Fourth Cataract, wtfl., Sudan G11 48
Fouta Djalon, reg., Gui. D2 50
Foveaux Strait, strt., N.Z. q12 63c
Fowler, Ca., U.S. D4 98
Fowler, Co., U.S. C6 99
Fowler, In., U.S. C3 107
Fowler, Mi., U.S. E6 115
Fowlerville, Mi., U.S. F6 115
Fowman, Iran D13 44
Fox, stm., Mb., Can. B4 86
Fox, stm., Mi., U.S. B4 115
Fox, stm., Wi., U.S. D5 142
Fox, stm., U.S. B5 106
Fox, stm., U.S. A6 118
Foxboro, On., Can. C7 89
Foxboro, Ma., U.S. B5 114
Fox Creek, Ab., Can. B2 84
Foxe Basin, b., N.T., Can. E24 82
Fox Island, i., R.I., U.S. E4 132
Fox Island, i., Wa., U.S. f10 140
Fox Islands, is., Ak., U.S. E6 95
Fox Lake, Il., U.S. A5 106
Fox Lake, l., Il., U.S. h8 106
Fox Lake, Wi., U.S. E5 142
Fox Mountain, mtn., Nv., U.S. B2 121
Fox Point, Wi., U.S. E6 142
Fox River Grove, Il., U.S. h8 106
Foxworth, Ms., U.S. D4 117
Foz do Cunene, Ang. B1 56
Foz do Iguaçu, Braz. D7 72
Frackville, Pa., U.S. E9 131
Fraga, Spain G7 16
Fram Basin E22 144
Framingham, Ma., U.S. B5 114
Franca, Braz. F2 74
Franca-Iosifa, Zemlja, is., Russia B7 26
France, ctry., Eur. D8 16
Francesville, In., U.S. C4 107
Franceville, Gabon D2 54
Francis, Lake, l., N.H., U.S. f7 122
Francis Case, Lake, res., S.D., U.S. D6 134
Francistown, Bots. C4 56
Franconia, N.H., U.S. B3 122
Franconia Notch, N.H., U.S. B3 122
Francs Peak, mtn., Wy., U.S. C3 143
Franken, hist. reg., Ger. E11 12
Frankenmuth, Mi., U.S. E7 115
Frankford, On., Can. C7 89
Frankford, De., U.S. F5 101
Frankfort, Il., U.S. m9 106
Frankfort, In., U.S. D4 107
Frankfort, Ks., U.S. C7 109
Frankfort, Ky., U.S. B5 110
Frankfort, Mi., U.S. D4 115
Frankfort, N.Y., U.S. B5 125
Frankfort, Oh., U.S. C2 128
Frankfurt, Ger. D14 12
Frankfurt am Main, Ger. E11 12
Franklin, co., Al., U.S. A2 94
Franklin, co., Ar., U.S. B2 97
Franklin, co., Fl., U.S. C2 102
Franklin, Ga., U.S. C1 103
Franklin, co., Ga., U.S. B3 103
Franklin, co., Ia., U.S. B4 108
Franklin, co., Id., U.S. G7 105
Franklin, co., Il., U.S. E4 106
Franklin, In., U.S. F5 107
Franklin, co., In., U.S. F7 107
Franklin, co., Ks., U.S. D8 109
Franklin, Ky., U.S. D3 110
Franklin, co., Ky., U.S. B5 110
Franklin, La., U.S. E4 111
Franklin, co., La., U.S. B4 111
Franklin, Ma., U.S. B5 114
Franklin, co., Ma., U.S. A2 114
Franklin, co., Me., U.S. C2 112
Franklin, co., Mo., U.S. C6 118
Franklin, co., Ms., U.S. D3 117
Franklin, N.C., U.S. f9 126
Franklin, co., N.C., U.S. A4 126
Franklin, Ne., U.S. D7 120
Franklin, co., Ne., U.S. D7 120
Franklin, N.H., U.S. D3 122
Franklin, N.J., U.S. A3 123
Franklin, co., N.Y., U.S. f10 125
Franklin, Oh., U.S. C1 128
Franklin, co., Oh., U.S. B2 128
Franklin, Pa., U.S. D2 131
Franklin, co., Pa., U.S. G6 131
Franklin, Tn., U.S. B5 135
Franklin, co., Tn., U.S. B5 135
Franklin, Tx., U.S. D4 136
Franklin, co., Tx., U.S. C5 136
Franklin, Va., U.S. D6 139
Franklin, co., Va., U.S. D3 139
Franklin, co., Vt., U.S. B2 138
Franklin, co., Wa., U.S. C6 140
Franklin, Wi., U.S. n11 142
Franklin, W.V., U.S. C5 141
Franklin, Point, c., Ak., U.S. A8 95
Franklin D. Roosevelt Lake, res., Wa., U.S. B7 140
Franklin Falls Reservoir, res., N.H., U.S. C3 122
Franklin Grove, Il., U.S. B4 106
Franklin Lake, l., Nv., U.S. C6 121
Franklin Park, Il., U.S. k9 106
Franklinton, La., U.S. D5 111
Franklinton, N.C., U.S. A4 126
Franklinville, N.Y., U.S. C2 125
Frankston, Tx., U.S. C5 136
Frankton, In., U.S. D6 107
Fransfontein, Nmb. C2 56
Franz Josef Land see Franca-Iosifa, Zemlja, is., Russia B7 26
Fraser, stm., B.C., Can. E7 85
Fraser, stm., N.L., Can. g9 88
Fraser, Mount, mtn., Can. C8 85
Fraserburg, S. Afr. E3 56
Fraserburgh, Scot., U.K. B5 12
Fraser Island, i., Austl. F5 62
Fraser Lake, B.C., Can. B5 85
Fraser Plateau, plat., B.C., Can. D6 85
Frazee, Mn., U.S. D3 116
Frazeysburg, Oh., U.S. B3 128
Frazier Park, Ca., U.S. E4 98
Frederic, Wi., U.S. C1 142
Frederica, De., U.S. D4 101
Fredericia, Den. I3 10
Frederick, Co., U.S. A6 99
Frederick, Md., U.S. B3 113
Frederick, co., Md., U.S. B3 113
Frederick, Ok., U.S. C2 129
Frederick, co., Va., U.S. A4 139
Fredericksburg, Ia., U.S. B5 108
Fredericksburg, Tx., U.S. D3 136
Fredericksburg, Va., U.S. B5 139
Frederick Sound, strt., Ak., U.S. m23 95
Fredericktown, Mo., U.S. D7 118
Fredericktown, Oh., U.S. B3 128
Fredericktown, Pa., U.S. F1 131
Fredericton, N.B., Can. D3 87
Fredericton Junction, N.B., Can. D3 87
Frederikshåb, Grnld. F29 82
Frederikshavn, Den. H4 10
Fredonia, Az., U.S. A3 96
Fredonia, Ks., U.S. E8 109
Fredonia, N.Y., U.S. C1 125
Fredonia, Wi., U.S. E6 142
Fredrikstad, Nor. G4 10
Freeborn, co., Mn., U.S. G5 116
Freeburg, Il., U.S. E4 106
Freedom, Pa., U.S. E1 131
Freedom, Wy., U.S. D2 143
Freehold, N.J., U.S. C4 123
Freeland, Mi., U.S. E6 115
Freeland, Pa., U.S. D10 131
Freelandville, In., U.S. G3 107
Freel Peak, mtn., Ca., U.S. C4 98
Freels, Cape, c., N.L., Can. D5 88
Freels, Cape, c., N.L., Can. E5 88
Freeman, S.D., U.S. D8 134
Freeman, Lake, l., In., U.S. C4 107
Freemansburg, Pa., U.S. E11 131
Freemason Island, i., La., U.S. E7 111
Freeport, Bah. C9 76
Freeport, Il., U.S. A4 106
Freeport, Me., U.S. E2 112
Freeport, N.Y., U.S. n15 125
Freeport, Pa., U.S. E2 131
Freeport, Tx., U.S. E5 136
Freer, Tx., U.S. F3 136
Freestone, co., Tx., U.S. D4 136
Freetown, S.L. E2 50
Freetown, In., U.S. G5 107
Freezeout Mountains, mts., Wy., U.S. D6 143
Fregenal de la Sierra, Spain H3 16
Freiburg, Ger. G10 12
Freising, Ger. F12 12
Freistadt, Aus. F14 12
Fréjus, Fr. F10 16
Fremantle, Austl. G2 60
Fremont, Ca., U.S. D2 98
Fremont, co., Co., U.S. C5 99
Fremont, Ia., U.S. C5 108
Fremont, co., Ia., U.S. D2 108
Fremont, co., Id., U.S. E7 105
Fremont, In., U.S. A8 107
Fremont, Mi., U.S. E5 115
Fremont, N.C., U.S. B5 126
Fremont, Ne., U.S. C9 120
Fremont, Oh., U.S. A2 128
Fremont, stm., Ut., U.S. E4 137
Fremont, co., Wy., U.S. C4 143
Fremont Island, i., Ut., U.S. B3 137
Fremont Lake, l., Wy., U.S. D3 143
Fremont Peak, mtn., Wy., U.S. C3 143
French Broad, stm., U.S. D10 135
Frenchburg, Ky., U.S. C6 110
French Creek, stm., Pa., U.S. C2 131
French Frigate Shoals, rf., Hi., U.S. m14 104
French Guiana, dep., S.A. C9 70
French Lick, In., U.S. G4 107
Frenchman Bay, b., Me., U.S. D4 112
Frenchman Creek, stm., U.S. D4 120
Frenchman Hills, Wa., U.S. C6 140
Frenchman Lake, l., Nv., U.S. G6 121
French Polynesia, dep., Oc. F15 58
French Settlement, La., U.S. D5 111
French Somaliland see Djibouti, ctry., Afr. H13 48
Frenda, Alg. J7 16
Freshfield, Mount, mtn., Can. D2 84
Fresnillo, Mex. F9 78
Fresno, Ca., U.S. D4 98
Fresno, co., Ca., U.S. D4 98
Fresno Reservoir, res., Mt., U.S. B6 119
Frewsburg, N.Y., U.S. C1 125
Freycinet Peninsula, pen., Austl. I4 62
Fria, Gui. D2 50
Fria, Cape, c., Nmb. B1 56
Friars Point, Ms., U.S. A3 117
Frías, Arg. D4 72
Fribourg, Switz. A1 18
Friday Harbor, Wa., U.S. A2 140
Fridley, Mn., U.S. m12 116
Fridtjof Nansen, Mount, mtn., Ant. E25 67
Friedrichshafen, Ger. G11 12
Friend, Ne., U.S. D8 120
Friendsville, Tn., U.S. D9 135
Fries, Va., U.S. D2 139
Frio, co., Tx., U.S. E3 136
Frio, stm., Tx., U.S. E3 136
Frio, Cabo, c., Braz. F3 74
Friona, Tx., U.S. B1 136
Fripps Island, i., S.C., U.S. G7 133
Frisco, Co., U.S. B4 99
Frisco City, Al., U.S. D2 94
Frisco Peak, mtn., Ut., U.S. E2 137
Frisian Islands, is., Eur. D9 12
Frissell, Mount, mtn., U.S. A2 100
Fritch, Tx., U.S. B2 136
Friza, proliv, strt., Russia B17 28
Frobisher Bay, b., N.T., Can. F26 82
Frobisher Lake, l., Sk., Can. m7 91
Frolovo, Russia E7 22
Frome, Lake, l., Austl. G3 62
Frontenac, Ks., U.S. E9 109
Frontera, Mex. B4 78
Frontera, Mex. D6 78
Frontier, co., Ne., U.S. D5 120
Front Range, mts., Co., U.S. A5 99
Front Royal, Va., U.S. B4 139
Frosinone, Italy D4 18
Frostburg, Md., U.S. k13 113

Name / Map Ref. / Page

Frostproof, Fl., U.S. E5 102
Frøya, i., Nor. E3 10
Fruita, Co., U.S. B2 99
Fruit Heights, Ut., U.S. B4 137
Fruitland, Id., U.S. F2 105
Fruitland, Md., U.S. D6 113
Fruitland, N.M., U.S. A1 124
Fruitland Park, Fl., U.S. D5 102
Fruitport, Mi., U.S. E4 115
Fruitvale, B.C., Can. E9 85
Fruitvale, Co., U.S. B2 99
Fruitvale, Wa., U.S. C5 140
Fruitville, Fl., U.S. E4 102
Frunze see Biškek, Kyrg. E9 26
Frutal, Braz. E2 74
Fryeburg, Me., U.S. D2 112
Fu'an, China D4 30
Fuding, China D5 30
Fuerte, stm., Mex. B3 78
Fuerte Olimpo, Para. C6 72
Fuerteventura, i., Spain A2 50
Fuga Island, i., Phil. C8 34
Fuji, Japan C3 31
Fuji, Mount see Fuji-san, vol., Japan D15 28
Fujian, prov., China F11 28
Fujin, China B14 28
Fuji-san, vol., Japan D15 28
Fujiyama see Fuji-san, vol., Japan D15 28
Fukui, Japan D15 28
Fukuoka, Japan E14 28
Fukushima, Japan C4 31
Fukuyama, Japan D2 31
Fulaga Passage, i., Fiji m11 63b
Fulda, Ger. E11 12
Fulda, Mn., U.S. G3 116
Fuling, China D2 30
Fullerton, Ca., U.S. n13 98
Fullerton, Ne., U.S. C8 120
Fulton, co., Ar., U.S. A4 97
Fulton, co., Ga., U.S. C2 103
Fulton, co., Il., U.S. C3 106
Fulton, Il., U.S. B3 106
Fulton, co., In., U.S. B5 107
Fulton, Ky., U.S. f9 110
Fulton, co., Ky., U.S. f8 110
Fulton, Md., U.S. B4 113
Fulton, Mo., U.S. C6 118
Fulton, Ms., U.S. A5 117
Fulton, N.Y., U.S. B4 125
Fulton, co., N.Y., U.S. B6 125
Fulton, co., Oh., U.S. A1 128
Fulton, co., Pa., U.S. G5 131
Fultondale, Al., U.S. f7 94
Funafuti, i., Tuvalu E11 58
Funchal, Port. D1 48
Fundy, Bay of, b., Can. D4 87
Fundy National Park, N.B., Can. D4 87
Funhalouro, Moz. C5 56
Funing, China C4 30
Funing, China B4 30
Funkstown, Md., U.S. A2 113
Funsi, Ghana D4 50
Funtua, Nig. D6 50
Fuping, China C2 30
Fuqing, China D4 30
Fuquay-Varina, N.C., U.S. B4 126
Furnace Brook, stm., Vt., U.S. D3 138
Furnas, co., Ne., U.S. D6 120
Furnas, Represa de, res., Braz. F2 74
Furneaux Group, is., Austl. I4 62
Fürstenwalde, Ger. D14 12
Furudal, Swe. F6 10
Fushun, China C12 28
Fusui, China G9 28
Futuna, Île, i., Wal./F. F12 58
Fuxin, China A5 30
Fuyang, China E11 28
Fuyu, China B12 28
Fuyuan, China D1 30
Fuzhou, China F11 28
Fuzhou, China F11 28
Füzuli, Azer. C12 44
Fyffe, Al., U.S. A4 94
Fyn, i., Den. I4 10

G

Gaalkacyo, Som. I14 48
Gabbs, Nv., U.S. E4 121
Gabela, Ang. F2 54
Gaberones see Gaborone, Bots. C4 56
Gabès, Tun. D7 48
Gabon, ctry., Afr. D2 54
Gaborone, Bots. C4 56
Gabriola, B.C., Can. f12 85
Gabrovo, Blg. C10 18
Gabú, Gui.-B. D2 50
Gachsārān, Iran D6 42
Gadag, India F3 40
Gäddede, Swe. D6 10
Gadsden, Al., U.S. A3 94
Gadsden, co., Fl., U.S. B2 102
Gadwāl, India F3 40
Gaeta, Italy D4 18
Gaeta, Golfo di, b., Italy D4 18
Gaffney, S.C., U.S. A4 133
Gafsa, Tun. D6 48
Gag, Pulau, i., Indon. D7 36
Gagarin, Russia B13 20
Gage, co., Ne., U.S. D9 120
Gagetown, N.B., Can. D3 87
Gagnoa, C. Iv. E3 50
Gagra, Geor. A9 44
Gahanna, Oh., U.S. k11 128
Gaillard, Lake, l., Ct., U.S. D5 100
Gaines, co., Tx., U.S. C1 136
Gainesboro, Tn., U.S. C8 135
Gaines Creek, stm., Ok., U.S. C6 129
Gainesville, Fl., U.S. C4 102
Gainesville, Ga., U.S. B3 103
Gainesville, Mo., U.S. E5 118
Gainesville, Tx., U.S. C4 136
Gainesville, Va., U.S. g11 139
Gairdner, Lake, l., Austl. G2 62
Gaithersburg, Md., U.S. B3 113
Gaixian, China C12 28
Gaizina Kalns, Lat. H11 10
Gajny, Russia B9 22
Galán, Cerro, mtn., Arg. D4 72
Galapagos Islands see Colón, Archipiélago de, is., Ec. C2 70
Galashiels, Scot., U.K. C5 12
Galați, Rom. G9 20
Galatia, Il., U.S. F5 106
Galax, Va., U.S. D2 139
Galdhøpiggen, mtn., Nor. F3 10
Galela, Indon. C7 36
Galena, Ak., U.S. C8 95
Galena, Il., U.S. A3 106
Galena, Ks., U.S. E9 109
Galesburg, Il., U.S. C3 106
Galesburg, Mi., U.S. F5 115
Gales Ferry, Ct., U.S. D7 100
Galesville, Md., U.S. C4 113
Galesville, Wi., U.S. D2 142
Galeton, Pa., U.S. C6 131
Gali, Geor. A9 44
Galič, Russia C7 22
Galicia, hist. reg., Eur. E7 20
Galilee, Sea of, l., Isr. F6 44
Galion, Oh., U.S. B3 128
Galisteo Creek, stm., N.M., U.S. k8 124
Galiuro Mountains, mts., Az., U.S. E5 96
Gallant, Al., U.S. B3 94
Gallatin, co., Il., U.S. F5 106
Gallatin, co., Ky., U.S. B5 110
Gallatin, Mo., U.S. B4 118
Gallatin, co., Mt., U.S. E5 119
Gallatin, stm., Mt., U.S. E5 119
Gallatin, Tn., U.S. A5 135
Gallatin Range, mts., Mt., U.S. E5 119
Gallaway, Tn., U.S. B2 135
Galle, Sri L. H4 40
Gallia, co., Oh., U.S. D3 128
Galliano, La., U.S. E5 111
Gallinas, Punta, c., Col. A5 70
Gallinas Mountains, mts., N.M., U.S. C2 124
Gallipoli, Italy D6 18
Gallipoli see Gelibolu, Tur. B2 44
Gallipolis, Oh., U.S. D3 128
Gallitzin, Pa., U.S. F4 131
Gällivare, Swe. C9 10
Gallo Mountains, mts., N.M., U.S. C1 124
Galloo Island, i., N.Y., U.S. B4 125
Gallup, N.M., U.S. B1 124
Galt, Ca., U.S. C3 98
Galtat Zemmour, W. Sah. A2 50
Galva, Il., U.S. B3 106
Galva, Ks., U.S. D6 109
Galveston, In., U.S. C5 107
Galveston, Tx., U.S. E5 136
Galveston, co., Tx., U.S. E5 136
Galveston Bay, b., Tx., U.S. E5 136
Galveston Island, i., Tx., U.S. E5 136
Galway, Ire. D2 12
Galway Bay, b., Ire. D2 12
Gamarra, Col. B5 70
Gambēla, Eth. B6 54
Gambell, Ak., U.S. C5 95
Gambia, stm., Afr. D2 50
Gambia, The, ctry., Afr. D1 50
Gambier, Oh., U.S. B3 128
Gambier, Îles, is., Fr. Poly. G16 58
Gambo, N.L., Can. D4 88
Gamboma, Congo D3 54
Gamboula, C.A.R. C3 54
Gambrills, Md., U.S. B4 113
Gan, stm., China D4 30
Ganado, Az., U.S. B6 96
Ganado, Tx., U.S. E4 136
Gananoque, On., Can. C8 89
Găncă, Azer. B12 44
Gand see Gent, Bel. E8 12
Ganda, Ang. F2 54
Gandajika, D.R.C. E4 54
Gandak, stm., Asia D4 40
Gander, N.L., Can. D4 88
Gander, stm., N.L., Can. D4 88
Gander Lake, l., N.L., Can. D4 88
Gandesa, Spain G7 16
Gāndhinagar, India E2 40
Gandhi Reservoir see Gāndhi Sāgar, res., India E3 40
Gāndhi Sāgar, res., India E3 40
Gandia, Spain H6 16
Gandu, Braz. D4 74
Ganga see Ganges, stm., Asia D5 40
Gangānagar, India D2 40
Gangaw, Mya. B2 34
Gangdisê Shan, mts., China E4 28
Ganges (Ganga), stm., Asia D5 40
Ganges, B.C., Can. g12 85
Ganges, Mouths of the, mth., Asia B1 34
Gang Mills, N.Y., U.S. C3 125
Gangotri, India C3 40
Gangtok, India D5 40
Gangu, China E9 28
Gannett Peak, mtn., Wy., U.S. C3 143
Ganquan, China B2 30
Gansu, prov., China D8 28
Gantt, S.C., U.S. B3 133
Gantt Lake, res., Al., U.S. D3 94
Ganzê, China E8 28
Ganzhou, China F10 28
Gao, Mali C4 50
Gao'an, China D4 30
Gaolan, China B1 30
Gaomi, China B4 30
Gaoping, China B3 30
Gaoua, Burkina D4 50
Gaoual, Gui. D2 50
Gaoxian, China D1 30
Gaoyi, China B3 30
Gaoyou, China C4 30
Gaoyou Hu, l., China C4 30
Gaozhou, China E3 30
Gap, Fr. E10 16
Gap, Pa., U.S. G9 131
Gapan, Phil. C8 34
Garagumskij kanal imeni Prezidenta Turkmenistana S.A. Nijazova (Kara-Kum Canal), Turk. C8 42
Garagumy, des., Turk. F7 26
Garanhuns, Braz. C4 74
Garber, Ok., U.S. A4 129
Garberville, Ca., U.S. B2 98
Garda, Lago di, l., Italy B3 18
Garden, co., Ne., U.S. C3 120
Gardena, Ca., U.S. n12 98
Garden City, Ga., U.S. D5 103
Garden City, Id., U.S. F2 105
Garden City, Ks., U.S. E3 109
Garden City, Mi., U.S. p15 115
Garden City, Mo., U.S. C3 118
Gardendale, Al., U.S. B3 94
Garden Grove, Ca., U.S. n13 98
Garden Island, i., Mi., U.S. C5 115
Garden Plain, Ks., U.S. E6 109
Gardeyz, Afg. D9 42
Gardiner, Me., U.S. D3 112
Gardiner, Mt., U.S. E6 119
Gardiner, Or., U.S. D2 130
Gardiners Island, i., N.Y., U.S. m16 125
Gardner, Il., U.S. B5 106
Gardner, Ks., U.S. D9 109
Gardner, Ma., U.S. A4 114
Gardner Canal, strt., B.C., Can. C3 85
Gardner Lake, l., Ct., U.S. C6 100
Gardner Lake, l., Me., U.S. D5 112
Gardner Pinnacles, Hi., U.S. k14 104
Gardnerville, Nv., U.S. E2 121
Garfield, co., Co., U.S. B2 99
Garfield, co., Mt., U.S. C9 119
Garfield, co., Ne., U.S. C6 120
Garfield, N.J., U.S. h8 123
Garfield, co., Ok., U.S. A4 129
Garfield, co., Ut., U.S. F4 137
Garfield, co., Wa., U.S. C8 140
Garfield Heights, Oh., U.S. h9 128
Garfield Mountain, mtn., Mt., U.S. F4 119
Garfield Peak, mtn., Wy., U.S. D5 143
Garibaldi, Or., U.S. B3 130
Garibaldi, Mount, mtn., B.C., Can. E6 85
Garies, S. Afr. E2 56
Garissa, Kenya D7 54
Garland, co., Ar., U.S. C2 97
Garland, N.C., U.S. C4 126
Garland, Tx., U.S. n10 136
Garland, Ut., U.S. B3 137
Garm, Taj. C10 42
Garmī, Iran C13 44
Garmisch-Partenkirchen, Ger. G12 12
Garmsār, Iran C6 42
Garnavillo, Ia., U.S. B6 108
Garner, Ia., U.S. A4 108
Garner, N.C., U.S. B4 126
Garnet Range, mts., Mt., U.S. D3 119
Garnett, Ks., U.S. D8 109
Garnish, N.L., Can. E4 88
Garonne, stm., Eur. E6 16
Garoua, Cam. B2 54
Garoua Boulaï, Cam. B2 54
Garrard, co., Ky., U.S. C5 110
Garretson, S.D., U.S. D9 134
Garrett, In., U.S. B7 107
Garrett, co., Md., U.S. k12 113
Garrett Park, Md., U.S. B3 113
Garrettsville, Oh., U.S. A4 128
Garrison, Ky., U.S. B6 110
Garrison, Md., U.S. B4 113
Garrison, N.D., U.S. B4 127
Garrison Dam, N.D., U.S. B4 127
Garsen, Kenya D8 54
Garut, Indon. E3 36
Garvin, co., Ok., U.S. C4 129
Garwolin, Pol. D6 20
Gary, In., U.S. A3 107
Gary, W.V., U.S. D3 141
Garyarsa, China E4 28
Garysburg, N.C., U.S. A5 126
Garyville, La., U.S. D5 111
Garza, co., Tx., U.S. C2 136
Garza-Little Elm Reservoir, res., Tx., U.S. C4 136
Gasan-Kuli, Turk. C6 42
Gas City, In., U.S. D6 107
Gascogne, hist. reg., Fr. F7 16
Gasconade, stm., Mo., U.S. C6 118
Gasconade, co., Mo., U.S. C6 118
Gascony see Gascogne, hist. reg., Fr. F7 16
Gascoyne, stm., Austl. E1 60
Gascoyne Junction, Austl. F2 60
Gashaka, Nig. E7 50
Gashua, Nig. D7 50
Gasparilla Island, i., Fl., U.S. F4 102
Gaspé, Qc., Can. k14 90
Gaspésie, Péninsule de la, pen., Qc., Can. k13 90
Gassaway, W.V., U.S. C4 141
Gassville, Ar., U.S. A3 97
Gasteiz, Spain F5 16
Gaston, In., U.S. D7 107
Gaston, N.C., U.S. A5 126
Gaston, co., N.C., U.S. B1 126
Gaston, S.C., U.S. D5 133
Gaston, Lake, res., U.S. A5 126
Gaston Dam, N.C., U.S. A5 126
Gastonia, N.C., U.S. B1 126
Gastre, Arg. F3 69
Gatčina, Russia C5 22
Gate City, Va., U.S. f9 139
Gates, co., N.C., U.S. A6 126
Gates, Tn., U.S. B2 135
Gates of the Arctic National Park, Ak., U.S. B9 95
Gatesville, Tx., U.S. D4 136
Gatineau, Qc., Can. D2 90
Gatineau, stm., Qc., Can. D2 90
Gatineau, Parc de la, Qc., Can. D2 90
Gatlinburg, Tn., U.S. D10 135
Gatton, Austl. F5 62
Gauley, stm., W.V., U.S. C3 141
Gauley Bridge, W.V., U.S. C3 141
Gaustatoppen, mtn., Nor. G3 10
Gautier, Ms., U.S. f8 117
Gávdhos, i., Grc. G10 18
Gavins Point Dam, U.S. B8 120
Gävle, Swe. F7 10
Gawler Ranges, mts., Austl. G2 62
Gaya, India E5 40
Gaya, Nig. D6 50
Gaya, Niger D5 50
Gay Head, c., Ma., U.S. D6 114
Gaylord, Mi., U.S. C6 115
Gaylord, Mn., U.S. F4 116
Gayndah, Austl. F5 62
Gaza see Ghazzah, Gaza G6 44
Gazandžyk, Turk. C7 42
Gazaoua, Niger D6 50
Gaza Strip, Asia G6 44
Gaziantep, Tur. D7 44
Gazimağusa (Famagusta), N. Cyp. E5 44
Gazimağusa Körfezi, b., N. Cyp. E6 44
Gazipaşa, Tur. D5 44
Gbanga, Lib. E3 50
Gboko, Nig. E6 50
Gdańsk, Pol. B5 20
Gdov, Russia G12 10
Gdynia, Pol. B5 20
Gearhart, Or., U.S. A3 130
Gearhart Mountain, mtn., Or., U.S. E6 130
Geary, N.B., Can. D3 87
Geary, co., Ks., U.S. D7 109
Geary, Ok., U.S. B3 129
Geauga, co., Oh., U.S. A4 128
Gebe, Pulau, i., Indon. D7 36
Gebze, Tur. B3 44
Gediz, Tur. C3 44
Geelong, Austl. H3 62
Geesthacht, Ger. D12 12
Geilo, Nor. F3 10
Geistown, Pa., U.S. F4 131
Geist Reservoir, res., In., U.S. E6 107
Geita, Tan. D6 54
Gejiu, China G8 28
Gela, Italy F5 18
Gelasa, Selat, strt., Indon. D3 36
Gelendžik, Russia G15 20
Gelibolu, Tur. B2 44
Gelsenkirchen, Ger. E10 12
Gem, co., Id., U.S. E2 105
Gemena, D.R.C. C3 54
Gemlik, Tur. B3 44
Gemlik Körfezi, b., Tur. B3 44
Genalē (Jubba), stm., Afr. B8 54
Genç, Tur. C9 44
General Acha, Arg. F5 72
General Alvear, Arg. F4 72
General Carneiro, Braz. B7 72
General Carrera, Lago, l., S.A. G2 69
General Conesa, Arg. F4 69
General Eugenio A. Garay, Para. C5 72
General Juan José Ríos, Mex. B3 78
General Juan Madariaga, Arg. F6 72
General La Madrid, Arg. F5 72
General Pico, Arg. F5 72
General Pinedo, Arg. D5 72
General Roca, Arg. E3 69
General Villegas, Arg. F5 72
Genesee, Id., U.S. C2 105
Genesee, co., Mi., U.S. E7 115
Genesee, Mi., U.S. E7 115
Genesee, co., N.Y., U.S. B2 125
Genesee, stm., N.Y., U.S. C2 125
Geneseo, Il., U.S. B3 106
Geneseo, N.Y., U.S. C3 125
Geneva see Genève, Switz. A1 18
Geneva, Al., U.S. D4 94
Geneva, co., Al., U.S. D4 94
Geneva, Il., U.S. B5 106
Geneva, In., U.S. C8 107
Geneva, Ne., U.S. D8 120
Geneva, N.Y., U.S. C4 125
Geneva, Oh., U.S. A5 128
Geneva, Lake, l., Eur. A1 18
Geneva, Lake, l., Wi., U.S. F5 142
Geneva-on-the-Lake, Oh., U.S. A5 128
Genève (Geneva), Switz. A1 18
Gengma, China B3 34
Genoa see Genova, Italy B2 18
Genoa, Il., U.S. A5 106
Genoa, Ne., U.S. C8 120
Genoa, Nv., U.S. D2 121
Genoa, Oh., U.S. A2 128
Genoa, Gulf of see Genova, Golfo di, b., Italy B2 18
Genoa City, Wi., U.S. F5 142
Genola, Ut., U.S. D4 137
Genova, Italy B2 18
Genova, Golfo di, b., Italy B2 18
Gent, Bel. E8 12
Gentry, Ar., U.S. A1 97
Gentry, co., Mo., U.S. A3 118
Geographe Bay, b., Austl. G2 60
George, stm., Qc., Can. g13 90
George, S. Afr. E3 56
George, Ia., U.S. A2 108
George, co., Ms., U.S. E5 117
George, Cape, c., N.S., Can. D8 87
George, Lake, l., Fl., U.S. C5 102
George, Lake, l., N.Y., U.S. B7 125
George B. Stevenson Reservoir, res., Pa., U.S. D6 131
George Peak, mtn., Ut., U.S. B2 137
George Town, Austl. I4 62
Georgetown, Austl. D3 62
Georgetown, P.E., Can. C7 87
George Town, Cay. Is. B3 80
Georgetown, Gam. D2 50
Georgetown, Guy. B8 70
George Town (Penang), Malay. B2 36
Georgetown, Ca., U.S. C3 98
Georgetown, Co., U.S. B5 99
Georgetown, Ct., U.S. D2 100
Georgetown, De., U.S. F4 101
Georgetown, Ga., U.S. E1 103
Georgetown, Il., U.S. D6 106
Georgetown, In., U.S. H6 107
Georgetown, Ky., U.S. B5 110
Georgetown, Ma., U.S. A6 114
Georgetown, Oh., U.S. D2 128
Georgetown, S.C., U.S. E9 133
Georgetown, co., S.C., U.S. E9 133
Georgetown, Tx., U.S. D4 136
George V Coast, Ant. C20 67
George Washington Birthplace National Monument, Va., U.S. B6 139
George Washington Carver National Monument, Mo., U.S. E3 118
George West, Tx., U.S. E3 136
Georgia, ctry., Asia A10 44
Georgia, state, U.S. D3 103
Georgiana, Al., U.S. D3 94
Georgian Bay, b., On., Can. B3 89
Georgina, stm., Austl. E2 62
Gera, Ger. E13 12
Gerald, Mo., U.S. C6 118
Geraldine, Al., U.S. A4 94
Geraldton, Austl. F1 60
Geraldton, On., Can. o18 89
Gerber Reservoir, res., Or., U.S. E5 130
Gerdine, Mount, mtn., Ak., U.S. C9 95
Gerede, Tur. B5 44
Gereshk, Afg. D8 42
Gering, Ne., U.S. C2 120
Gerlach, Nv., U.S. C2 121
Gerlachovský štít, mtn., Slvk. E6 20
Germantown, Il., U.S. E4 106
Germantown, Md., U.S. B3 113

Name	Map Ref.	Page
Germantown, Oh., U.S.	C1	128
Germantown, Tn., U.S.	B2	135
Germantown, Wi., U.S.	E5	142
Germany, ctry., Eur.	E12	12
Germiston, S. Afr.	D4	56
Gerona see Girona, Spain	G8	16
Geronimo, Ok., U.S.	C3	129
Gervais, Or., U.S.	B4	130
Gêrzê, China	C4	40
Geser, Indon.	D8	36
Getafe, Spain	G5	16
Gettysburg, Pa., U.S.	G7	131
Gettysburg, S.D., U.S.	C6	134
Geyve, Tur.	B4	44
Ghadāmis, Libya	E6	48
Ghāghara, stm., Asia	D4	40
Ghana, ctry., Afr.	E4	50
Ghanzi, Bots.	C3	56
Ghardaïa, Alg.	D5	48
Gharyān, Libya	D7	48
Ghāt, Libya	F7	48
Ghawdex, i., Malta	F5	18
Ghazāl, Baḥr al-, stm., Sudan	B5	54
Ghāziābād, India	D3	40
Ghāzīpur, India	D4	40
Ghaznī, Afg.	D9	42
Ghazzah, Gaza	G6	44
Gheen, Mn., U.S.	C6	116
Gheorgheni, Rom.	F8	20
Gherla, Rom.	F7	20
Ghilizane, Alg.	J7	16
Ghoriān, Afg.	D8	42
Gianitsá, Grc.	D9	18
Giant's Causeway, N. Ire., U.K.	C3	12
Giants Neck, Ct., U.S.	D7	100
Gibara, Cuba	A4	80
Gibbon, Mn., U.S.	F4	116
Gibbon, Ne., U.S.	D7	120
Gibbons, Ab., Can.	C4	84
Gibb River, Austl.	D4	60
Gibbstown, N.J., U.S.	D2	123
Gibeon, Nmb.	D2	56
Gibraltar, dep., Eur.	I4	16
Gibraltar, Strait of, strt.	J4	16
Gibsland, La., U.S.	B2	111
Gibson, Ga., U.S.	C4	103
Gibson, co., In., U.S.	H2	107
Gibson, co., Tn., U.S.	A3	135
Gibsonburg, Oh., U.S.	A2	128
Gibson City, Il., U.S.	C5	106
Gibson Desert, des., Austl.	E3	60
Gibsonia, Pa., U.S.	h14	131
Gibson Island, i., Md., U.S.	B5	113
Gibsons, B.C., Can.	E6	85
Gibsonton, Fl., U.S.	p11	102
Gibsonville, N.C., U.S.	A3	126
Giddings, Tx., U.S.	D4	136
Gideon, Mo., U.S.	E8	118
Gien, Fr.	D8	16
Giessen, Ger.	E11	12
Gifford, Fl., U.S.	E6	102
Gifford, Il., U.S.	C5	106
Gifford Creek, Austl.	E2	60
Gifu, Japan	D15	28
Gig Harbor, Wa., U.S.	B3	140
Giglio, Isola del, i., Italy	C3	18
Gihon, stm., Vt., U.S.	B3	138
Gijón, Spain	F4	16
Gila, co., Az., U.S.	D5	96
Gila, stm., U.S.	E5	92
Gila Bend, Az., U.S.	E3	96
Gila Bend Indian Reservation, Az., U.S.	D3	96
Gila Bend Mountains, mts., Az., U.S.	D2	96
Gila Cliff Dwellings National Monument, N.M., U.S.	D1	124
Gila Mountains, mts., Az., U.S.	D6	96
Gila Peak, mtn., Az., U.S.	D6	96
Gila River Indian Reservation, Az., U.S.	D4	96
Gilbert, Az., U.S.	D4	96
Gilbert, Ia., U.S.	B4	108
Gilbert, La., U.S.	B4	111
Gilbert, Mn., U.S.	C6	116
Gilbert Islands see Kiribati, is., Kir.	D11	58
Gilbert Peak, mtn., Wa., U.S.	C4	140
Gilbert Plains, Mb., Can.	D1	86
Gilbertsville, Ky., U.S.	f9	110
Gilbertsville, Pa., U.S.	F10	131
Gilbertville, Ia., U.S.	B5	108
Gilbués, Braz.	E10	70
Gilchrist, co., Fl., U.S.	C4	102
Gilchrist, Or., U.S.	D5	130
Gilcrest, Co., U.S.	A6	99
Giles, co., Tn., U.S.	B4	135
Giles, co., Va., U.S.	C2	139
Gilford Island, i., B.C., Can.	D4	85
Gilgandra, Austl.	G4	62
Gilgil, Kenya	D7	54
Gilgit, Pak.	C10	42
Gillam, Mb., Can.	A4	86
Gillespie, Il., U.S.	D4	106
Gillespie, co., Tx., U.S.	D3	136
Gillespie Dam, Az., U.S.	D3	96
Gillett, Ar., U.S.	C4	97
Gillett, Wi., U.S.	D5	142
Gillette, Wy., U.S.	B7	143
Gilliam, co., Or., U.S.	B6	130
Gilman, Il., U.S.	C5	106
Gilman, Vt., U.S.	C5	138
Gilmanton, N.H., U.S.	D4	122
Gilmer, co., Ga., U.S.	B2	103
Gilmer, Tx., U.S.	C5	136
Gilmer, co., W.V., U.S.	C4	141
Gilpin, co., Co., U.S.	B5	99
Gilroy, Ca., U.S.	D3	98
Gīmbī, Eth.	B7	54
Gimie, Mount, vol., St. Luc.	C7	80
Gimli, Mb., Can.	D3	86
Gingoog, Phil.	E9	34
Gīnīr, Eth.	B8	54
Giralia, Austl.	E1	60
Girard, Il., U.S.	D4	106
Girard, Ks., U.S.	E9	109
Girard, Oh., U.S.	A5	128
Girard, Pa., U.S.	B1	131
Girardot, Col.	E5	80
Girardville, Pa., U.S.	E9	131
Giresun, Tur.	B8	44
Girona, Spain	G8	16
Gironde, est., Fr.	E6	16
Girvan, Scot., U.K.	C4	12
Gisborne, N.Z.	o14	63c
Gitarama, Rw.	D5	54
Gitega, Bdi.	D5	54
Giurgiu, Rom.	H8	20
Giyon, Eth.	B7	54
Giza see El-Gîza, Egypt	E11	48
Giza, Pyramids of, Egypt	F10	14
Giždruvan, Uzb.	B8	42
Gižiga, Russia	C18	26
Giżycko, Pol.	B6	20
Gjirokastër, Alb.	D8	18
Gjøvik, Nor.	F4	10
Gjumri, Arm.	B10	44
Glacier, co., Mt., U.S.	B3	119
Glacier Bay, b., Ak., U.S.	k21	95
Glacier Bay National Park, Ak., U.S.	D12	95
Glacier National Park, B.C., Can.	D9	85
Glacier National Park, Mt., U.S.	B2	119
Glacier Peak, mtn., Wa., U.S.	A4	140
Gladbrook, Ia., U.S.	B5	108
Glade Creek, stm., Wa., U.S.	C6	140
Glade Creek, stm., W.V., U.S.	n14	141
Glade Creek, stm., W.V., U.S.	n13	141
Glades, co., Fl., U.S.	F5	102
Glade Spring, Va., U.S.	f10	139
Gladewater, Tx., U.S.	C5	136
Gladstone, Austl.	E5	62
Gladstone, Mb., Can.	D2	86
Gladstone, Mi., U.S.	C4	115
Gladstone, Mo., U.S.	h10	118
Gladstone, Or., U.S.	B4	130
Gladwin, Mi., U.S.	E6	115
Gladwin, co., Mi., U.S.	D6	115
Glåma, stm., Nor.	F4	10
Glascock, co., Ga., U.S.	C4	103
Glasford, Il., U.S.	C4	106
Glasgow, Scot., U.K.	C4	12
Glasgow, Ky., U.S.	C4	110
Glasgow, Mo., U.S.	B5	118
Glasgow, Mt., U.S.	B10	119
Glasgow, Va., U.S.	C3	139
Glasgow, W.V., U.S.	m13	141
Glassboro, N.J., U.S.	D2	123
Glasscock, co., Tx., U.S.	D2	136
Glassport, Pa., U.S.	F2	131
Glastonbury, Ct., U.S.	C5	100
Glazier Lake, l., Me., U.S.	A3	112
Glazov, Russia	D7	26
Gleason, Tn., U.S.	A3	135
Glen Allan, Ms., U.S.	B2	117
Glen Allen, Va., U.S.	C5	139
Glenboro, Mb., Can.	E2	86
Glenbrook, Nv., U.S.	D2	121
Glen Burnie, Md., U.S.	B4	113
Glen Canyon Dam, Az., U.S.	A4	96
Glen Canyon National Recreation Area, U.S.	F5	137
Glencoe, On., Can.	E3	89
Glencoe, Al., U.S.	B4	94
Glencoe, Il., U.S.	A6	106
Glencoe, Mn., U.S.	F4	116
Glen Cove, N.Y., U.S.	h13	125
Glendale, Az., U.S.	D3	96
Glendale, Ca., U.S.	m12	98
Glendale, Ms., U.S.	D4	117
Glendale, Oh., U.S.	C1	128
Glendale, Or., U.S.	E3	130
Glendale, R.I., U.S.	B2	132
Glendale, S.C., U.S.	B4	133
Glendale, Wi., U.S.	m12	142
Glen Dale, W.V., U.S.	B4	141
Glendale Heights, W.V., U.S.	g8	141
Glendive, Mt., U.S.	C12	119
Glendo, Wy., U.S.	D7	143
Glendora, Ca., U.S.	m13	98
Glendo Reservoir, res., Wy., U.S.	D8	143
Glenelg, Md., U.S.	B4	113
Glen Ellis Falls, wtfl., N.H., U.S.	B4	122
Glen Ellyn, Il., U.S.	k8	106
Glenham, N.Y., U.S.	D7	125
Glen Innes, Austl.	F5	62
Glen Jean, W.V., U.S.	D3	141
Glen Lake, l., Mi., U.S.	D5	115
Glen Lyon, Pa., U.S.	D9	131
Glenmora, La., U.S.	D3	111
Glenn, co., Ca., U.S.	C2	98
Glennallen, Ak., U.S.	f19	95
Glenns Ferry, Id., U.S.	G3	105
Glennville, Ga., U.S.	E5	103
Glenolden, Pa., U.S.	p20	131
Glenpool, Ok., U.S.	B5	129
Glen Raven, N.C., U.S.	A3	126
Glen Ridge, N.J., U.S.	h8	123
Glen Rock, N.J., U.S.	h8	123
Glen Rock, Pa., U.S.	G8	131
Glenrock, Wy., U.S.	D7	143
Glen Rose, Tx., U.S.	C4	136
Glenrothes, Scot., U.K.	B5	12
Glenroy, Austl.	E1	60
Glens Falls, N.Y., U.S.	B7	125
Glen Ullin, N.D., U.S.	C4	127
Glenview, Il., U.S.	h9	106
Glenville, Mn., U.S.	G5	116
Glenville, W.V., U.S.	C4	141
Glenwood, N.L., Can.	D4	88
Glenwood, Ar., U.S.	C2	97
Glenwood, Ga., U.S.	D4	103
Glenwood, Ia., U.S.	C2	108
Glenwood, Mn., U.S.	E3	116
Glenwood, Va., U.S.	D3	139
Glenwood City, Wi., U.S.	C1	142
Glenwood Springs, Co., U.S.	B3	99
Glidden, Ia., U.S.	B3	108
Glide, Or., U.S.	D3	130
Glittertinden, mtn., Nor.	F3	10
Gliwice, Pol.	D5	20
Globe, Az., U.S.	D5	96
Głogów, Pol.	D4	20
Gloster, Ms., U.S.	D2	117
Gloucester, On., Can.	h12	89
Gloucester, Eng., U.K.	E5	12
Gloucester, Ma., U.S.	A6	114
Gloucester, co., N.J., U.S.	D2	123
Gloucester, Va., U.S.	C6	139
Gloucester, co., Va., U.S.	C6	139
Gloucester City, N.J., U.S.	D2	123
Gloucester Point, Va., U.S.	C6	139
Glouster, Oh., U.S.	C3	128
Glover Island, i., N.L., Can.	D3	88
Gloversville, N.Y., U.S.	B6	125
Glovertown, N.L., Can.	D4	88
Gloverville, S.C., U.S.	E4	133
Glubokij, Russia	E7	22
Głuchołazy, Pol.	D4	20
Gluck, S.C., U.S.	C2	133
Glyndon, Md., U.S.	B4	113
Glyndon, Mn., U.S.	D2	116
Glynn, co., Ga., U.S.	E5	103
Gmünd, Aus.	F14	12
Gmunden, Aus.	G13	12
Gnadenhutten, Oh., U.S.	B4	128
Gnarp, Swe.	E7	10
Gniezno, Pol.	C4	20
Gnowangerup, Austl.	G2	60
Goa, state, India	F2	40
Goālpāra, India	D6	40
Goat Island, i., R.I., U.S.	F5	132
Goat Mountain, mtn., Mt., U.S.	C3	119
Goat Rock Dam, U.S.	C4	94
Goba, Eth.	B7	54
Gobabis, Nmb.	C2	56
Gobernador Gregores, Arg.	G2	69
Gobi, des., Asia	C7	28
Gobles, Mi., U.S.	F5	115
Gobō, Japan	D3	31
Goðafoss, wtfl., Ice.	l20	10a
Godāvari, stm., India	F3	40
Goddard, Ks., U.S.	E6	109
Goderich, On., Can.	D3	89
Godfrey, Il., U.S.	E3	106
Godhavn, Grnld.	E29	82
Godhra, India	E2	40
Gödöllő, Hung.	F5	20
Gods, stm., Mb., Can.	A5	86
Gods Lake, l., Mb., Can.	B4	86
Godthåb (Nuuk), Grnld.	F29	82
Goff Creek, stm., Ok., U.S.	e9	129
Goffstown, N.H., U.S.	D3	122
Gogebic, co., Mi., U.S.	n12	115
Gogebic, Lake, l., Mi., U.S.	m12	115
Goiana, Braz.	C5	74
Goianésia, Braz.	E2	74
Goiânia, Braz.	E2	74
Goiás, state, Braz.	F10	70
Goiás, Braz.	E1	74
Gojra, Pak.	D10	42
Gök, stm., Tur.	B6	44
Gökçeada, i., Tur.	B1	44
Gökova Körfezi, b., Tur.	D2	44
Göksun, Tur.	C7	44
Gokwe, Zimb.	B4	56
Golāghāt, India	D6	40
Golconda, Il., U.S.	F5	106
Golconda, Nv., U.S.	C4	121
Gölcük, Tur.	B3	44
Gold Bar, Wa., U.S.	B4	140
Gold Beach, Or., U.S.	E2	130
Gold Coast see Southport, Austl.	F5	62
Golden, B.C., Can.	D9	85
Golden, Co., U.S.	B5	99
Golden City, Mo., U.S.	D3	118
Goldendale, Wa., U.S.	D5	140
Golden Gate Bridge, Ca., U.S.	h7	98
Golden Gate National Recreation Area, Ca., U.S.	h7	98
Golden Hinde, mtn., B.C., Can.	E5	85
Golden Meadow, La., U.S.	E5	111
Golden Spike National Historic Site, hist., Ut., U.S.	B3	137
Golden Valley, Mn., U.S.	n12	116
Golden Valley, co., Mt., U.S.	D7	119
Golden Valley, co., N.D., U.S.	B2	127
Goldfield, Ia., U.S.	B4	108
Goldfield, Nv., U.S.	F4	121
Gold Hill, Or., U.S.	E3	130
Goldsboro, N.C., U.S.	B5	126
Goldsby, Ok., U.S.	B4	129
Goldsworthy, Austl.	E2	60
Goldthwaite, Tx., U.S.	D3	136
Goleniów, Pol.	C3	20
Goleta, Ca., U.S.	E4	98
Golfito, C.R.	D3	80
Golf Manor, Oh., U.S.	o13	128
Gölhisar, Tur.	D3	44
Goliad, Tx., U.S.	E4	136
Goliad, co., Tx., U.S.	E4	136
Gölköy, Tur.	B7	44
Golmud, China	B6	40
Golpāyegān, Iran	D6	42
Goma, D.R.C.	D5	54
Gomati, stm., India	D4	40
Gombe, Nig.	D7	50
Gombi, Nig.	D7	50
Gomel see Homel', Bela.	C11	20
Gómez Palacio, Mex.	B4	78
Gonaïves, Haiti	B5	80
Gonam, Russia	D15	26
Gonâve, Golfe de la, b., Haiti	B5	80
Gonâve, Île de la, i., Haiti	B5	80
Gonbad-e Qābūs, Iran	C7	42
Gonda, India	D4	40
Gondal, India	E2	40
Gonder, Eth.	H12	48
Gondia, India	E4	40
Gönen, Tur.	B2	44
Gongbo'gyamda, China	E6	28
Gongcheng, China	E3	30
Gongga Shan, mtn., China	F8	28
Gongxian, China	C3	30
Gongzhuling, China	C12	28
Gonzales, Ca., U.S.	D3	98
Gonzales, La., U.S.	D5	111
Gonzales, co., Tx., U.S.	E4	136
Gonzales, Tx., U.S.	E4	136
González, Mex.	C5	78
Gonzalez, Fl., U.S.	u14	102
Goochland, co., Va., U.S.	C5	139
Goode, Mount, mtn., Ak., U.S.	g18	95
Goodfellow Air Force Base, mil., Tx., U.S.	D2	136
Good Hope, Cape of, c., S. Afr.	E2	56
Good Hope Mountain, mtn., B.C., Can.	D5	85
Goodhue, co., Mn., U.S.	F6	116
Gooding, Id., U.S.	G4	105
Gooding, co., Id., U.S.	F4	105
Goodland, In., U.S.	C3	107
Goodland, Ks., U.S.	C2	109
Goodlettsville, Tn., U.S.	g10	135
Goodman, Mo., U.S.	E3	118
Goodman, Ms., U.S.	C4	117
Good Pine, La., U.S.	C3	111
Goodsprings, Nv., U.S.	H6	121
Goodview, Mn., U.S.	F7	116
Goodwater, Al., U.S.	B3	94
Goodwell, Ok., U.S.	e9	129
Goodyear, Az., U.S.	D3	96
Goondiwindi, Austl.	F5	62
Goose, stm., N.D., U.S.	B8	127
Goose Bay, b., N.L., Can.	B1	88
Gooseberry Creek, stm., Wy., U.S.	B4	143
Goose Creek, S.C., U.S.	F7	133
Goose Creek, stm., Va., U.S.	C3	139
Goose Creek, stm., U.S.	G5	105
Goose Creek Reservoir, res., S.C., U.S.	k11	133
Goose Lake, l., U.S.	B3	98
Goose Lake, l., U.S.	C3	92
Goose Pond, l., N.H., U.S.	C2	122
Goqên, China	F7	28
Gorakhpur, India	D4	40
Gorda, Punta, c., Cuba	A3	80
Gordion, hist., Tur.	C4	44
Gordo, Al., U.S.	B2	94
Gordon, Ga., U.S.	D3	103
Gordon, co., Ga., U.S.	B2	103
Gordon, Ne., U.S.	B3	120
Gordon Downs, Austl.	D4	60
Gordonsville, Tn., U.S.	C8	135
Gordonsville, Va., U.S.	B4	139
Goré, Chad	E8	50
Gorē, Eth.	B7	54
Gore, N.Z.	q12	63c
Gore, Ok., U.S.	B6	129
Gore Bay, On., Can.	B2	89
Gore Point, c., Ak., U.S.	h16	95
Gore Range, mts., Co., U.S.	B4	99
Goreville, Il., U.S.	F5	106
Gorgān, Iran	C6	42
Gorge High Dam, Wa., U.S.	A4	140
Gorham, Me., U.S.	E2	112
Gorham, N.H., U.S.	B4	122
Gori, Geor.	A11	44
Gorizia, Italy	B4	18
Gorjačij Ključ, Russia	G15	20
Gor'kij see Nižnij Novgorod, Russia	D6	26
Gorkiy Reservoir see Gor'kovskoe vodohranilišče, res., Russia	C7	22
Gor'kovskoe vodohranilišče, res., Russia	C7	22
Görlitz, Ger.	E14	12
Gorlovka see Horlivka, Ukr.	E15	20
Gorman, Tx., U.S.	C3	136
Gorna Orjahovica, Blg.	C10	18
Gornjackij, Russia	A11	22
Gorno-Altajsk, Russia	D10	26
Gornozavodsk, Russia	B16	28
Gorodec, Russia	C7	22
Goroka, Pap. N. Gui.	H12	32
Gorong, Pulau, i., Indon.	D8	36
Gorontalo, Indon.	C6	36
Gorzów Wielkopolski, Pol.	C3	20
Gosford, Austl.	G5	62
Goshen, In., U.S.	A6	107
Goshen, N.Y., U.S.	D6	125
Goshen, Oh., U.S.	C1	128
Goshen, co., Wy., U.S.	D8	143
Goshute Indian Reservation, U.S.	D7	121
Goshute Lake, l., Nv., U.S.	C7	121
Goshute Mountains, mts., Nv., U.S.	C7	121
Goslar, Ger.	E12	12
Gosnells, Austl.	G2	60
Gosper, co., Ne., U.S.	D6	120
Gosport, In., U.S.	F4	107
Gossinga, Sudan	B5	54
Gostivar, Mac.	D8	18
Gostyń, Pol.	D4	20
Gostynin, Pol.	C5	20
Göteborg (Gothenburg), Swe.	H4	10
Gothenburg see Göteborg, Swe.	H4	10
Gothenburg, Ne., U.S.	D5	120
Gotland, i., Swe.	H8	10
Gotō-rettō, is., Japan	E13	28
Gotska Sandön, i., Swe.	G8	10
Göttingen, Ger.	E11	12
Goubone, Chad	B8	50
Goudoumaria, Niger	D7	50
Gough Island, i., St. Hel.	N9	46
Gouin, Réservoir, res., Qc., Can.	I25	82
Goulburn, Austl.	G4	62
Goulburn Islands, is., Austl.	C5	60
Gould, Ar., U.S.	D4	97
Goulding, Fl., U.S.	u14	102
Gould Island, i., R.I., U.S.	E5	132
Goulds, Fl., U.S.	s13	102
Goundam, Mali	C4	50
Goundi, Chad	E8	50
Gouré, Niger	D7	50
Gouverneur, N.Y., U.S.	f9	125
Gove, co., Ks., U.S.	D3	109
Governador Valadares, Braz.	E3	74
Govind Ballabh Pant Reservoir see Govind Ballabh Pant Sāgar, res., India	E4	40
Govind Ballabh Pant Sāgar, res., India	E4	40
Gowanda, N.Y., U.S.	C2	125
Gower, Mo., U.S.	B3	118
Gowrie, Ia., U.S.	B3	108
Goya, Arg.	D6	72
Göyçay, Azer.	B12	44
Gozo see Ghawdex, i., Malta	F5	18
Graaff-Reinet, S. Afr.	E3	56
Grabill, In., U.S.	B8	107
Grabo, C. Iv.	F3	50
Grace, Id., U.S.	G7	105
Graceville, Fl., U.S.	u16	102
Graceville, Mn., U.S.	E2	116
Gracewood, Ga., U.S.	C4	103
Gracias a Dios, Cabo, c., N.A.	F8	76
Gradaús, Braz.	E9	70
Grady, co., Ga., U.S.	F2	103
Grady, co., Ok., U.S.	C4	129
Graettinger, Ia., U.S.	A3	108
Grafton, Austl.	F5	62
Grafton, Il., U.S.	E3	106
Grafton, Ma., U.S.	B4	114
Grafton, N.D., U.S.	A8	127
Grafton, co., N.H., U.S.	C3	122
Grafton, Oh., U.S.	A3	128
Grafton, Va., U.S.	h15	139
Grafton, Wi., U.S.	E6	142
Grafton, W.V., U.S.	B4	141
Graham, co., Az., U.S.	E5	96
Graham, co., Ks., U.S.	C4	109
Graham, N.C., U.S.	A3	126
Graham, co., N.C., U.S.	f9	126
Graham, Tx., U.S.	C3	136
Graham, Lake, res., Tx., U.S.	C3	136
Graham, Mount, mtn., Az., U.S.	E6	96
Graham Island, i., B.C., Can.	C1	85

Name | Map Ref. | Page

Graham Lake, l., Me., U.S. D4 112
Graham Land, reg., Ant. C34 67
Grahamstown, S. Afr. E4 56
Grahn, Ky., U.S. B6 110
Grainger, co., Tn., U.S. C10 135
Grain Valley, Mo., U.S. B3 118
Grajaú, Braz. C2 74
Grajewo, Pol. C7 20
Grambling, La., U.S. B3 111
Gramercy, La., U.S. h10 111
Granada, Col. E5 80
Granada, Nic. C2 80
Granada, Spain I5 16
Granbury, Tx., U.S. C4 136
Granby, Qc., Can. D5 90
Granby, Co., U.S. A5 99
Granby, Ct., U.S. B4 100
Granby, Mo., U.S. E3 118
Granby, Lake, res., Co., U.S. A5 99
Gran Canaria, i., Spain A1 50
Gran Chaco, reg., S.A. C5 72
Grand, stm., On., Can. D4 89
Grand, co., Co., U.S. A4 99
Grand, stm., Mi., U.S. E5 115
Grand, stm., Mo., U.S. A3 118
Grand, stm., Oh., U.S. A4 128
Grand, stm., S.D., U.S. B4 134
Grand, co., Ut., U.S. E6 137
Grand Bahama, i., Bah. C9 76
Grand Bank, N.L., Can. E4 88
Grand-Bassam, C. Iv. E4 50
Grand Bay, N.B., Can. D3 87
Grand Bay, Al., U.S. E1 94
Grand Bend, On., Can. D3 89
Grand Blanc, Mi., U.S. F7 115
Grand Caillou, La., U.S. E5 111
Grand Canal see Da Yunhe, China D11 28
Grand Canyon, Az., U.S. A3 96
Grand Canyon, Az., U.S. A3 96
Grand Canyon National Park, Az., U.S. B3 96
Grand Cayman, i., Cay. Is. B3 80
Grand Centre, Ab., Can. B5 84
Grand Cess, Lib. F3 50
Grand Coteau, La., U.S. D3 111
Grand Coulee, Wa., U.S. B6 140
Grand Coulee Dam, Wa., U.S. B6 140
Grande, stm., Bol. G7 70
Grande, stm., Braz. F1 74
Grande, stm., Ven. D7 80
Grande, Bahía, b., Arg. H3 69
Grande, Boca, mth., Ven. D7 80
Grande, Ilha, i., Braz. F3 74
Grande, Rio see Rio Grande, stm., N.A. B5 78
Grande-Anse, N.B., Can. B4 87
Grande Cache, Ab., Can. C1 84
Grande Comore see Njazidja, i., Com. A7 56
Grande de Matagalpa, stm., Nic. C3 80
Grande de Santiago, stm., Mex. C4 78
Grande do Gurupá, Ilha, i., Braz. B1 74
Grand-Entrée, Qc., Can. B8 87
Grande Prairie, Ab., Can. B1 84
Grand Erg de Bilma, des., Niger C7 50
Grand Erg Occidental, des., Alg. D5 48
Grand Erg Oriental, des., Alg. D6 48
Grande rivière de la Baleine, stm., Qc., Can. g11 90
Grande Ronde, stm., U.S. C8 140
Grandes, Salinas, pl., Arg. E4 72
Grandes-Bergeronnes, Qc., Can. A8 90
Grande-Terre, i., Guad. B7 80
Grand Falls (Grand-Sault), N.B., Can. B2 87
Grand Falls, wtfl., Me., U.S. C5 112
Grand Falls [-Windsor], N.L., Can. D4 88
Grandfather Mountain, mtn., N.C., U.S. A1 126
Grandfield, Ok., U.S. C3 129
Grand Forks, B.C., Can. E8 85
Grand Forks, N.D., U.S. B8 127
Grand Forks, co., N.D., U.S. B8 127
Grand Forks Air Force Base, mil., N.D., U.S. B8 127
Grand Harbour, N.B., Can. E3 87
Grand Haven, Mi., U.S. E4 115
Grand Island, i., La., U.S. D6 111
Grand Island, i., Mi., U.S. B4 115
Grand Island, Ne., U.S. D7 120
Grand Isle, La., U.S. E6 111
Grand Isle, i., La., U.S. E6 111
Grand Isle, co., Vt., U.S. B2 138
Grand Junction, Co., U.S. B2 99
Grand Junction, Ia., U.S. B3 108
Grand Lake, l., N.B., Can. D3 87
Grand Lake, l., N.L., Can. D3 88
Grand Lake, l., La., U.S. E6 111
Grand Lake, l., La., U.S. E3 111
Grand Lake, l., Mi., U.S. C7 115
Grand Lake, l., Oh., U.S. B1 128
Grand Lake Matagamon, l., Me., U.S. B4 112
Grand Lake Seboeis, l., Me., U.S. B4 112
Grand Ledge, Mi., U.S. F6 115
Grand Manan Island, i., N.B., Can. E3 87
Grand Marais, Mn., U.S. k9 116
Grand Meadow, Mn., U.S. G6 116
Grand-Mère, Qc., Can. C5 90
Grand Mound, Ia., U.S. C7 108
Grand Portage Indian Reservation, Mn., U.S. k10 116
Grand Portage National Monument, Mn., U.S. h10 116
Grand Prairie, Tx., U.S. n10 136
Grand Rapids, Mi., U.S. F5 115
Grand Rapids, Mn., U.S. C5 116
Grand Rapids, Oh., U.S. f6 128
Grand Saline, Tx., U.S. C5 136
Grand Terre Islands, is., La., U.S. E6 111
Grand Teton, mtn., Wy., U.S. C2 143
Grand Teton National Park, Wy., U.S. C2 143
Grand Tower, Il., U.S. F4 106
Grand Traverse, co., Mi., U.S. D5 115
Grand Traverse Bay, b., Mi., U.S. C5 115
Grand Turk, T./C. Is. A5 80
Grand Valley, On., Can. D4 89
Grandview, Mb., Can. D1 86
Grandview, In., U.S. I4 107
Grandview, Mo., U.S. C3 118
Grandview, Wa., U.S. C6 140
Grandview Heights, Oh., U.S. m10 128
Grandville, Mi., U.S. F5 115
Grandy, N.C., U.S. A7 126
Granger, Ia., U.S. C4 108
Granger, In., U.S. A5 107
Granger, Tx., U.S. D4 136
Granger, Wa., U.S. C5 140
Grängesberg, Swe. F6 10
Grangeville, Id., U.S. D2 105
Gran Guardia, Arg. D6 72
Granisle, B.C., Can. B4 85
Granite, co., Mt., U.S. D3 119
Granite, Ok., U.S. C2 129
Granite City, Il., U.S. E3 106
Granite Falls, Mn., U.S. F3 116
Granite Falls, N.C., U.S. B1 126
Granite Falls, Wa., U.S. A4 140
Granite Lake, res., N.L., Can. D3 88
Granite Mountain, mtn., Ak., U.S. B7 95
Granite Mountains, mts., Az., U.S. E2 96
Granite Mountains, mts., Wy., U.S. D5 143
Granite Pass, Wy., U.S. B5 143
Granite Peak, mtn., Mt., U.S. E7 119
Granite Peak, mtn., Nv., U.S. C2 121
Granite Peak, mtn., Nv., U.S. B4 121
Granite Peak, mtn., Ut., U.S. C2 137
Granite Peak, mtn., Ut., U.S. E3 137
Granite Peak, mtn., Wy., U.S. D4 143
Granite Quarry, N.C., U.S. B2 126
Granite Range, mts., Nv., U.S. C2 121
Graniteville, S.C., U.S. D4 133
Graniteville, Vt., U.S. C4 138
Granja, Braz. B3 74
Grant, Al., U.S. A3 94
Grant, co., Ar., U.S. C3 97
Grant, co., In., U.S. D6 107
Grant, co., Ks., U.S. E2 109
Grant, co., Ky., U.S. B5 110
Grant, co., La., U.S. C3 111
Grant, Mi., U.S. E5 115
Grant, co., Mn., U.S. E2 116
Grant, co., N.D., U.S. C4 127
Grant, Ne., U.S. D4 120
Grant, co., Ne., U.S. C4 120
Grant, co., N.M., U.S. E1 124
Grant, co., Ok., U.S. A4 129
Grant, co., Or., U.S. C7 130
Grant, co., S.D., U.S. B8 134
Grant, co., Wa., U.S. B6 140
Grant, co., Wi., U.S. F3 142
Grant, co., W.V., U.S. B5 141
Grant, Mount, mtn., Nv., U.S. E3 121
Grant City, Mo., U.S. A3 118
Grant Park, Il., U.S. B6 106
Grant Range, mts., Nv., U.S. E6 121
Grants, N.M., U.S. B2 124
Grantsburg, Wi., U.S. C1 142
Grants Pass, Or., U.S. E3 130
Grantsville, Ut., U.S. C3 137
Grantsville, W.V., U.S. C3 141
Grant Town, W.V., U.S. B4 141
Grantville, Ga., U.S. C2 103
Granville, Fr. C6 16
Granville, Il., U.S. B4 106
Granville, co., N.C., U.S. A4 126
Granville, N.Y., U.S. B7 125
Granville, Oh., U.S. B3 128
Granville, W.V., U.S. h11 141
Granville Lake, l., Mb., Can. A1 86
Grapeland, Tx., U.S. D5 136
Grapeview, Wa., U.S. B3 140
Grapevine, Tx., U.S. C4 136
Grapevine Lake, res., Tx., U.S. n9 136
Grapevine Peak, mtn., Nv., U.S. G4 121
Gräsö, i., Swe. F8 10
Grasonville, Md., U.S. C5 113
Grass, stm., Mb., Can. B2 86
Grass, stm., N.Y., U.S. f9 125
Grasse, Fr. F10 16
Grass Lake, l., Il., U.S. h8 106
Grass Lake, Il., U.S. h8 106
Grass Lake, Mi., U.S. F6 115
Grass Valley, Ca., U.S. C3 98
Grassy Brook, stm., Vt., U.S. E3 138
Grassy Lake, l., La., U.S. k9 111
Grates Point, c., N.L., Can. D5 88
Gratiot, co., Mi., U.S. E6 115
Gratis, Oh., U.S. C1 128
Grave Creek, stm., W.V., U.S. g8 141
Gravelly Branch, stm., De., U.S. F4 101
Gravelly Range, mts., Mt., U.S. E4 119
Gravenhage, 's- see 's-Gravenhage, Neth. D8 12
Gravenhurst, On., Can. C5 89
Grave Peak, mtn., Id., U.S. C4 105
Graves, co., Ky., U.S. f9 110
Gravette, Ar., U.S. A1 97
Gray, Fr. D9 16
Gray, Ga., U.S. C3 103
Gray, co., Ks., U.S. E3 109
Gray, Ky., U.S. D5 110
Gray, La., U.S. k10 111
Gray, Me., U.S. g7 112
Gray, co., Tx., U.S. B2 136
Grayback Mountain, mtn., Or., U.S. E3 130
Gray Court, S.C., U.S. B3 133
Grayland, Wa., U.S. C1 140
Grayling, Mi., U.S. D6 115
Graylyn Crest, De., U.S. A3 101
Grays Harbor, b., Wa., U.S. C1 140
Grays Harbor, co., Wa., U.S. B2 140
Grays Lake, sw., Id., U.S. F7 105
Grayslake, Il., U.S. A5 106
Grayson, Ky., U.S. B7 110
Grayson, co., Ky., U.S. C3 110
Grayson, co., Tx., U.S. C4 136
Grayson, co., Va., U.S. D1 139
Grayson Lake, res., Ky., U.S. B7 110
Grays Peak, mtn., Co., U.S. B5 99
Gray Summit, Mo., U.S. g12 118
Graysville, Al., U.S. f7 94
Graysville, Tn., U.S. D8 135
Grayville, Il., U.S. E5 106
Graz, Aus. G14 12
Great Alfold see Alföld, pl., Hung. F6 20
Great Artesian Basin, bas., Austl. F3 62
Great Australian Bight, b., Austl. G4 60
Great Averill Pond, l., Vt., U.S. B5 138
Great Barrier Island, i., N.Z. o14 63c
Great Barrier Reef, rf., Austl. D4 62
Great Barrington, Ma., U.S. B1 114
Great Basin, bas., U.S. C4 92
Great Basin National Park, Nv., U.S. E7 121
Great Bay, b., N.H., U.S. D5 122
Great Bay, b., N.J., U.S. D4 123
Great Bear Lake, l., N.T., Can. E15 82
Great Belt see Storebælt, strt., Den. I4 10
Great Bend, Ks., U.S. D5 109
Great Britain see United Kingdom, ctry., Eur. C6 12
Great Captain Island, i., Ct., U.S. F1 100
Great Channel, strt., Asia E2 34
Great Dismal Swamp, sw., U.S. D6 139
Great Divide Basin, bas., Wy., U.S. E4 143
Great Dividing Range, mts., Austl. H4 62
Great East Lake, l., U.S. C5 122
Great Egg Harbor, stm., N.J., U.S. D3 123
Greater Antilles, is., N.A. E9 76
Greater Khingan Range see Da Hinggan Ling, mts., China B12 28
Greater Sunda Islands, is., Asia D3 36
Great Exuma, i., Bah. D9 76
Great Falls, wtfl., Md., U.S. B3 113
Great Falls, Mt., U.S. C5 119
Great Falls, S.C., U.S. B6 133
Great Falls Dam, Tn., U.S. D6 135
Greathouse Peak, mtn., Mt., U.S. D7 119
Great Inagua, i., Bah. D10 76
Great Indian Desert (Thar Desert), des., Asia D2 40
Great Island, spit, Ma., U.S. C7 114
Great Island, i., N.C., U.S. B6 126
Great Karroo, plat., S. Afr. E3 56
Great Lakes Naval Training Center, mil., Il., U.S. h9 106
Great Miami, stm., U.S. C1 128
Great Misery Island, i., Ma., U.S. f12 114
Great Moose Lake, l., Me., U.S. D3 112
Great Namaqualand, hist. reg., Nmb. D2 56
Great Neck, N.Y., U.S. h13 125
Great Nicobar, i., India H6 40
Great Ouse, stm., Eng., U.K. D7 12
Great Pee Dee, stm., U.S. D9 133
Great Plains, pl., N.A. E9 75
Great Point, c., Ma., U.S. D7 114
Great Ruaha, stm., Tan. E7 54
Great Sacandaga Lake, l., N.Y., U.S. C6 125
Great Salt Lake, l., Ut., U.S. B3 137
Great Salt Lake Desert, des., Ut., U.S. C2 137
Great Salt Plains Lake, res., Ok., U.S. A3 129
Great Salt Pond, b., R.I., U.S. h7 132
Great Sand Dunes National Monument, Co., U.S. D5 99
Great Sandy Desert, des., Austl. E3 60
Great Slave Lake, l., N.T., Can. F17 82
Great Smoky Mountains, mts., U.S. B8 135
Great Smoky Mountains National Park, U.S. B8 135
Great Swamp, sw., R.I., U.S. F3 132
Great Victoria Desert, des., Austl. F4 60
Great Village, N.S., Can. D6 87
Great Wall see Chang Cheng, hist., China B2 30
Great Wass Island, i., Me., U.S. D5 112
Great Yarmouth, Eng., U.K. D7 12
Great Zab, stm., Asia D10 44
Gréboun, mtn., Niger C6 50
Greece, ctry., Eur. E8 18
Greece, N.Y., U.S. B3 125
Greeley, Co., U.S. A6 99
Greeley, co., Ks., U.S. D2 109
Greeley, co., Ne., U.S. C7 120
Greeley, Pa., U.S. D12 131
Green, stm., Il., U.S. B4 106
Green, stm., Ky., U.S. C2 110
Green, co., Ky., U.S. C4 110
Green, Or., U.S. D3 130
Green, stm., Wa., U.S. B3 140
Green, co., Wi., U.S. F4 142
Green, stm., U.S. A1 99
Green, stm., U.S. D6 92
Green Acres, De., U.S. h8 101
Greenacres, Wa., U.S. B8 140
Greenacres City, Fl., U.S. F6 102
Greenback, Tn., U.S. D9 135
Green Bay, Wi., U.S. D6 142
Green Bay, b., U.S. D3 115
Green Bay, b., U.S. B10 92
Greenbelt, Md., U.S. C4 113
Greenbriar, Va., U.S. g12 139
Greenbrier, Ar., U.S. B3 97
Green Brier, Tn., U.S. A5 135
Greenbrier, stm., W.V., U.S. D4 141
Greenbrier, co., W.V., U.S. D4 141
Greenbush, Mn., U.S. B2 116
Greencastle, In., U.S. E4 107
Greencastle, Pa., U.S. G6 131
Green City, Mo., U.S. A5 118
Green Cove Springs, Fl., U.S. C5 102
Greendale, In., U.S. F8 107
Greendale, Wi., U.S. F6 142
Greene, co., Al., U.S. C1 94
Greene, co., Ar., U.S. A5 97
Greene, co., Ga., U.S. C3 103
Greene, Ia., U.S. B5 108
Greene, co., Ia., U.S. B3 108
Greene, co., Il., U.S. D3 106
Greene, co., In., U.S. F4 107
Greene, co., Mo., U.S. D4 118
Greene, co., Ms., U.S. D5 117
Greene, co., N.C., U.S. B5 126
Greene, N.Y., U.S. C5 125
Greene, co., N.Y., U.S. C6 125
Greene, co., Oh., U.S. C2 128
Greene, co., Pa., U.S. G1 131
Greene, co., Tn., U.S. C11 135
Greene, co., Va., U.S. B4 139
Greeneville, Tn., U.S. C11 135
Green Fall, stm., U.S. F1 132
Greenfield, Ca., U.S. D3 98
Greenfield, Ia., U.S. C3 108
Greenfield, Il., U.S. D3 106
Greenfield, In., U.S. E6 107
Greenfield, Ma., U.S. A2 114
Greenfield, Mo., U.S. D4 118
Greenfield, N.H., U.S. E3 122
Greenfield, Oh., U.S. C2 128
Greenfield, Tn., U.S. A3 135
Greenfield, Wi., U.S. n12 142
Greenfield Plaza, Ia., U.S. e8 108
Green Forest, Ar., U.S. A2 97
Green Harbor, Ma., U.S. B6 114
Green Hill Pond, l., R.I., U.S. G3 132
Greenhills, Oh., U.S. n12 128
Green Lake, l., Me., U.S. D4 112
Green Lake, Wi., U.S. E5 142
Green Lake, l., Wi., U.S. E5 142
Green Lake, co., Wi., U.S. E4 142
Greenland, dep., N.A. D30 82
Greenland, Ar., U.S. B1 97
Greenland, N.H., U.S. D5 122
Greenland Basin D23 144
Greenland Sea B9 46
Greenlee, co., Az., U.S. D6 96
Green Lookout Mountain, mtn., Wa., U.S. D3 140
Green Mountain, mtn., Wy., U.S. D5 143
Green Mountain Reservoir, res., Co., U.S. B4 99
Green Mountains, mts., Vt., U.S. F2 138
Greenock, Scot., U.K. C4 12
Greenock, Pa., U.S. F2 131
Green Peter Lake, res., Or., U.S. C4 130
Green Pond, Al., U.S. B2 94
Green Pond, l., N.J., U.S. A4 123
Greenport, N.Y., U.S. m16 125
Green River, Ut., U.S. E5 137
Green River, Wy., U.S. E3 143
Green River Lake, res., Ky., U.S. C4 110
Green River Lock and Dam, U.S. I2 107
Green River Reservoir, res., Vt., U.S. B3 138
Green Rock, Il., U.S. B3 106
Greensboro, Al., U.S. C2 94
Greensboro, Ga., U.S. C3 103
Greensboro, Md., U.S. C6 113
Greensboro, N.C., U.S. A3 126
Greensburg, In., U.S. F7 107
Greensburg, Ks., U.S. E4 109
Greensburg, Ky., U.S. C4 110
Greensburg, Pa., U.S. F2 131
Greens Peak, mtn., Az., U.S. C6 96
Green Springs, Oh., U.S. A2 128
Greensville, co., Va., U.S. D5 139
Green Swamp, sw., N.C., U.S. C4 126
Greentown, In., U.S. D6 107
Greenup, Il., U.S. D5 106
Greenup, Ky., U.S. B7 110
Greenup, co., Ky., U.S. B7 110
Green Valley, Az., U.S. F5 96
Greenview, Il., U.S. C4 106
Greenville, Lib. E3 50
Greenville, Al., U.S. D3 94
Greenville, Ca., U.S. B3 98
Greenville, De., U.S. A3 101
Greenville, Ga., U.S. C2 103
Greenville, Il., U.S. E4 106
Greenville, Ky., U.S. C2 110
Greenville, Me., U.S. C3 112
Greenville, Mi., U.S. E5 115
Greenville, Ms., U.S. B2 117
Greenville, N.C., U.S. B5 126
Greenville, N.H., U.S. E3 122
Greenville, Oh., U.S. B1 128
Greenville, Pa., U.S. D1 131
Greenville, R.I., U.S. C3 132
Greenville, S.C., U.S. B3 133
Greenville, co., S.C., U.S. B3 133
Greenville, Tx., U.S. C4 136
Greenville Creek, stm., Oh., U.S. B1 128
Greenville Junction, Me., U.S. C3 112
Greenwich, Ct., U.S. E1 100
Greenwich, N.Y., U.S. B7 125
Greenwich, Oh., U.S. A3 128
Greenwich Bay, b., R.I., U.S. D4 132
Greenwich Point, c., Ct., U.S. E1 100
Greenwood, B.C., Can. E8 85
Greenwood, Ar., U.S. B1 97
Greenwood, De., U.S. E3 101
Greenwood, In., U.S. E5 107
Greenwood, co., Ks., U.S. E7 109
Greenwood, La., U.S. B2 111
Greenwood, Mo., U.S. k11 118
Greenwood, Ms., U.S. B3 117
Greenwood, Pa., U.S. E5 131
Greenwood, S.C., U.S. C3 133
Greenwood, co., S.C., U.S. C3 133
Greenwood, Wi., U.S. D3 142
Greenwood, Lake, res., In., U.S. G4 107
Greenwood, Lake, res., S.C., U.S. C4 133
Greenwood Lake, l., Mn., U.S. C7 116
Greenwood Lake, N.Y., U.S. D6 125
Greenwood Lake, l., U.S. A4 123
Greer, co., Ok., U.S. C2 129
Greer, S.C., U.S. B3 133
Greers Ferry Lake, res., Ar., U.S. B3 97
Greeson, Lake, res., Ar., U.S. C2 97
Gregg, co., Tx., U.S. C5 136
Gregory, S.D., U.S. D6 134
Gregory, co., S.D., U.S. D6 134
Gregory Range, mts., Austl. D3 62
Greifswald, Ger. C13 12
Greilickville, Mi., U.S. D5 115

Name — Map Ref. — Page

Gremiha, Russia **C5** 26
Grenada, ctry., N.A. **F12** 76
Grenada, Ms., U.S. **B4** 117
Grenada, co., Ms., U.S. **B4** 117
Grenada Lake, res., Ms., U.S. **B4** 117
Grenadines, is., N.A. **F12** 76
Grenen, c., Den. **H4** 10
Grenoble, Fr. **E9** 16
Grenville, Qc., Can. **D3** 90
Grenville, Cape, c., Austl. **C3** 62
Grenville, Point, c., Wa., U.S. **B1** 140
Gresham, Or., U.S. **B4** 130
Gresik, Indon. **D2** 36
Gresik, Indon. **E4** 36
Gretna, Mb., Can. **E3** 86
Gretna, Fl., U.S. **B2** 102
Gretna, La., U.S. **E5** 111
Gretna, Ne., U.S. **C9** 120
Gretna, Va., U.S. **D3** 139
Grevená, Grc. **D8** 18
Grey, stm., N.L., Can. **E3** 88
Greybull, Wy., U.S. **B4** 143
Greybull, stm., Wy., U.S. **B4** 143
Greylock, Mount, mtn., Ma., U.S. **A1** 114
Greymouth, N.Z. **p13** 63c
Grey Range, mts., Austl. **F3** 62
Greys, stm., Wy., U.S. **C2** 143
Greytown, S. Afr. **D5** 56
Gridley, Ca., U.S. **C3** 98
Gridley, Il., U.S. **C5** 106
Griffin, Ga., U.S. **C2** 103
Griffiss Air Force Base, mil., N.Y., U.S. **B5** 125
Griffith, Austl. **G4** 62
Griffith, In., U.S. **A3** 107
Grifton, N.C., U.S. **B5** 126
Griggs, co., N.D., U.S. **B7** 127
Griggsville, Il., U.S. **D3** 106
Grim, Cape, c., Austl. **I3** 62
Grimes, Ia., U.S. **C4** 108
Grimes, co., Tx., U.S. **D4** 136
Grimsby, On., Can. **D5** 89
Grimsby, Eng., U.K. **D7** 12
Grímsey, i., Ice. **k20** 10a
Grimshaw, Ab., Can. **A2** 84
Grimsley, Tn., U.S. **C9** 135
Grímsstaðir, Ice. **l20** 10a
Grindall Creek, Va., U.S. **n18** 139
Grinnell, Ia., U.S. **C5** 108
Griswold, Ia., U.S. **C2** 108
Grizzly Mountain, mtn., Id., U.S. **B2** 105
Grizzly Mountain, mtn., Or., U.S. **C6** 130
Grizzly Mountain, mtn., Wa., U.S. **A7** 140
Grjazi, Russia **C15** 20
Grjazovec, Russia **C7** 22
Grois Island, i., N.L., Can. **C4** 88
Groblersdal, S. Afr. **D4** 56
Grodno see Hrodnoo, Bela. **C7** 20
Groesbeck, Tx., U.S. **D4** 136
Groningen, Neth. **D10** 12
Groom Lake, l., Nv., U.S. **F6** 121
Groom Range, mts., Nv., U.S. **F6** 121
Groote Eylandt, i., Austl. **C6** 60
Grootfontein, Nmb. **B2** 56
Gros Morne National Park, N.L., Can. **D3** 88
Grosse Isle Naval Air Station, mil., Mi., U.S. **p15** 115
Grosse Pointe Park, Mi., U.S. **p16** 115
Grosse Pointe Woods, Mi., U.S. **p16** 115
Grosseto, Italy **C3** 18
Grossglockner, mtn., Aus. **G13** 12
Grossmont, Ca., U.S. **o16** 98
Gros Ventre, stm., Wy., U.S. **C2** 143
Gros Ventre Range, mts., Wy., U.S. **C2** 143
Groswater Bay, b., N.L., Can. **H28** 82
Groton, Ct., U.S. **D7** 100
Groton, N.Y., U.S. **C4** 125
Groton, S.D., U.S. **B7** 134
Groton Long Point, Ct., U.S. **D7** 100
Grottoes, Va., U.S. **B4** 139
Grouse Creek, stm., Ut., U.S. **B2** 137
Grouse Creek Mountain, mtn., Id., U.S. **E5** 105
Grove, Ok., U.S. **A7** 129
Grove City, Fl., U.S. **F4** 102
Grove City, Oh., U.S. **C2** 128
Grove City, Pa., U.S. **D1** 131
Grove Hill, Al., U.S. **D2** 94
Groveland, Fl., U.S. **D5** 102
Groveland, Ma., U.S. **A5** 114
Grove Mountains, mts., Ant. **D12** 67
Grove Point, c., Md., U.S. **B5** 113
Groveport, Oh., U.S. **C3** 128
Grover City, Ca., U.S. **E3** 98
Groves, Tx., U.S. **E6** 136
Groveton, N.H., U.S. **A3** 122
Groveton, Tx., U.S. **D5** 136
Groveton, Va., U.S. **g12** 139
Grovetown, Ga., U.S. **C4** 103
Groveville, N.J., U.S. **C3** 123
Growa Point, c., Lib. **F3** 50
Growler Peak, mtn., Az., U.S. **E2** 96
Groznyj, Russia **E6** 26
Grudziądz, Pol. **C5** 20
Gruetli-Laager, Tn., U.S. **D8** 135
Grulla, Tx., U.S. **F3** 136
Grünau, Nmb. **D2** 56
Grundy, co., Ia., U.S. **B5** 108
Grundy, co., Il., U.S. **B5** 106
Grundy, co., Mo., U.S. **A4** 118
Grundy, co., Tn., U.S. **D8** 135
Grundy, Va., U.S. **e9** 139
Grundy Center, Ia., U.S. **B5** 108
Grunthal, Mb., Can. **E3** 86
Gruver, Tx., U.S. **A2** 136
Guacanayabo, Golfo de, b., Cuba **A4** 80
Guadalajara, Mex. **C4** 78
Guadalajara, Spain **G5** 16
Guadalcanal, i., Sol. Is. **B7** 62
Guadalquivir, stm., Spain **I4** 16
Guadalquivir, Marismas del, sw., Spain **I3** 16
Guadalupe, Mex. **C4** 78
Guadalupe, Mex. **B4** 78
Guadalupe, Az., U.S. **m9** 96
Guadalupe, Ca., U.S. **E3** 98
Guadalupe, co., N.M., U.S. **C5** 124
Guadalupe, co., Tx., U.S. **E4** 136
Guadalupe, Isla, i., Mex. **B1** 78
Guadalupe Mountains, mts., U.S. **E5** 124
Guadalupe Mountains National Park, Tx., U.S. **o12** 136
Guadalupe Peak, mtn., Tx., U.S. **o12** 136
Guadeloupe, dep., N.A. **E12** 76
Guadeloupe Passage, strt., N.A. **B7** 80
Guadiana, stm., Eur. **I3** 16
Guadix, Spain **I5** 16
Guaíra, Braz. **C7** 72
Guajará-Mirim, Braz. **F6** 70
Guaje, Laguna del, l., Mex. **B4** 78
Gualeguay, Arg. **E6** 72
Gualeguaychú, Arg. **E6** 72
Guam, dep., Oc. **D12** 32
Guaminí, Arg. **F5** 72
Guamúchil, Mex. **B3** 78
Guanaja, Isla de, i., Hond. **B2** 80
Guanajuato, Mex. **C4** 78
Guanajuato, state, Mex. **C4** 78
Guanambi, Braz. **D3** 74
Guanare, Ven. **B6** 70
Guane, Cuba **A3** 80
Guang'an, China **E9** 28
Guangde, China **C4** 30
Guangdong, prov., China **G10** 28
Guangji, China **D4** 30
Guangling, China **B3** 30
Guangnan, China **G8** 28
Guangxi Zhuangzu Zizhiqu, prov., China **G9** 28
Guangyuan, China **E9** 28
Guangzhou (Canton), China **E3** 30
Guano Lake, l., Or., U.S. **E7** 130
Guantánamo, Cuba **A4** 80
Guantao, China **B4** 30
Guanxian, China **E8** 28
Guanyun, China **C4** 30
Guapí, Col. **C4** 70
Guápiles, C.R. **C3** 80
Guaporé, stm., S.A. **F7** 70
Guarabira, Braz. **C4** 74
Guarapari, Braz. **F3** 74
Guarapuava, Braz. **D7** 72
Guaratuba, Braz. **D8** 72
Guarda, Port. **G3** 16
Guardafui, Cape see Gwardafuy, Gees, c., Som. **H15** 48
Guardo, Spain **F4** 16
Guarenas, Ven. **C6** 80
Guárico, stm., Ven. **D6** 80
Guasave, Mex. **B3** 78
Guasdualito, Ven. **B5** 70
Guasipati, Ven. **B7** 70
Guatemala, Guat. **C1** 80
Guatemala, ctry., N.A. **D6** 78
Guatemala Basin **G29** 64
Guaviare, stm., Col. **C6** 70
Guaxupé, Braz. **F2** 74
Guayana see Guyana, ctry., S.A. **B8** 70
Guayana see Ciudad Guayana, Ven. **B7** 70
Guayape, stm., Hond. **C2** 80
Guayaquil, Ec. **D3** 70
Guayaquil, Golfo de, b., S.A. **D3** 70
Guaymallén, Arg. **E4** 72
Guaymas, Mex. **B2** 78
Gubaha, Russia **C10** 22
Gubbio, Italy **C4** 18
Guben, Ger. **E14** 12
Guben (Gubin), Pol. **D3** 20
Gubin (Guben), Pol. **D3** 20
Gubkin, Russia **D14** 20
Gudauta, Geor. **A9** 44
Gudermes, Russia **B5** 42
Gudivāda, India **F4** 40
Gudiyāttam, India **G3** 40
Güdür, India **G3** 40
Guékédou, Gui. **E2** 50
Guélengdeng, Chad **D8** 50
Guelma, Alg. **D5** 14
Guelph, On., Can. **D4** 89
Guercif, Mor. **E3** 14
Güere, stm., Ven. **D7** 80
Guéret, Fr. **D7** 16
Guernsey, dep., Eur. **F5** 12
Guernsey, co., Oh., U.S. **B4** 128
Guernsey, Wy., U.S. **D8** 143
Guerrero, Mex. **B3** 78
Guerrero, state, Mex. **D4** 78
Guerrero Negro, Mex. **B2** 78
Gueydan, La., U.S. **D3** 111
Guga, Russia **D15** 26
Gugē, mtn., Eth. **B7** 54
Guguan, i., N. Mar. Is. **C12** 32
Guiana Basin **G9** 66
Guide, China **D8** 28
Guiding, China **D2** 30
Guildford, Eng., U.K. **E6** 12
Guilford, Ct., U.S. **D5** 100
Guilford, Me., U.S. **C3** 112
Guilford, co., N.C., U.S. **A3** 126
Guilin, China **F10** 28
Guimarães, Port. **G2** 16
Guimaras Island, i., Phil. **D8** 34
Guin, Al., U.S. **B2** 94
Guinea, ctry., Afr. **D2** 50
Guinea, Gulf of, b., Afr. **I10** 46
Guinea Basin **H13** 66
Guinea-Bissau, ctry., Afr. **D1** 50
Güines, Cuba **A3** 80
Guingamp, Fr. **C5** 16
Guiping, China **E3** 30
Güira de Melena, Cuba **A3** 80
Guiratinga, Braz. **B7** 72
Güiria, Ven. **A7** 70
Guitry, C. Iv. **E3** 50
Guiuan, Phil. **D9** 34
Guixi, China **D4** 30
Guixian, China **G9** 28
Guiyang, China **F9** 28
Guizhou, prov., China **F9** 28
Gujarāt, state, India **E2** 40
Gujrānwāla, Pak. **D10** 42
Gujrāt, Pak. **D10** 42
Gulbarga, India **F3** 40
Gulbene, Lat. **H12** 10
Gulf, co., Fl., U.S. **C1** 102
Gulf, The see Persian Gulf, b., Asia **E6** 42
Gulf Gate Estates, Fl., U.S. **E4** 102
Gulf Islands National Seashore, U.S. **E5** 117
Gulf of Alaska Seamount Province **B1** 144
Gulfport, Fl., U.S. **E4** 102
Gulfport, Ms., U.S. **E4** 117
Gulf Shores, Al., U.S. **E2** 94
Gulgong, Austl. **G4** 62
Gulian, China **A12** 28
Gulistan, Uzb. **B9** 42
Gullfoss, wtfl., Ice. **l19** 10a
Gull Island, i., N.C., U.S. **B7** 126
Gullivan Bay, b., Fl., U.S. **G5** 102
Gull Lake, l., Ab., Can. **C4** 84
Gull Lake, l., Mn., U.S. **D4** 116
Güllük Körfezi, b., Tur. **D2** 44
Gulu, Ug. **C6** 54
Gumboro, De., U.S. **G4** 101
Gumdag, Turk. **C6** 42
Gumel, Nig. **D6** 50
Gümüşhane, Tur. **B8** 44
Guna, India **E3** 40
Gundagai, Austl. **H4** 62
Gundji, D.R.C. **C4** 54
Gungu, D.R.C. **E3** 54
Gunisao, stm., Mb., Can. **C3** 86
Gunmi, Nig. **D6** 50
Gunnbjørn Fjeld, mtn., Grnld. **E34** 82
Gunnedah, Austl. **G5** 62
Gunnison, Co., U.S. **C4** 99
Gunnison, co., Co., U.S. **C3** 99
Gunnison, stm., Co., U.S. **C2** 99
Gunnison, Ms., U.S. **B3** 117
Gunnison, Ut., U.S. **D4** 137
Gunnison, Mount, mtn., Co., U.S. **C3** 99
Gunpowder Neck, c., Md., U.S. **B5** 113
Gunpowder River, b., Md., U.S. **B5** 113
Guntakal, India **F3** 40
Gunter Air Force Base, mil., Al., U.S. **C3** 94
Guntersville, Al., U.S. **A3** 94
Guntersville Lake, res., Al., U.S. **A3** 94
Guntown, Ms., U.S. **A5** 117
Guntūr, India **F4** 40
Gunungsitoli, Indon. **C1** 36
Guoyang, China **C4** 30
Gupis, Pak. **C10** 42
Gurdon, Ar., U.S. **D2** 97
Gurdžaani, Geor. **B11** 44
Guri, Embalse de, res., Ven. **B7** 70
Gurley, Al., U.S. **A3** 94
Gurnee, Il., U.S. **h9** 106
Gurnet Point, c., Ma., U.S. **B6** 114
Gurskøya, i., Nor. **E1** 10
Gürün, Tur. **C7** 44
Gurupi, stm., Braz. **B2** 74
Gurupi, Braz. **D2** 74
Gusau, Nig. **D6** 50
Gusev, Russia **B7** 20
Gušgy, Turk. **F8** 26
Gushi, China **C4** 30
Gusinoozersk, Russia **A9** 28
Guspini, Italy **E2** 18
Gustav Holm, Kap, c., Grnld. **E33** 82
Gustine, Ca., U.S. **D3** 98
Güstrow, Ger. **D13** 12
Guthrie, co., Ia., U.S. **C3** 108
Guthrie, Ky., U.S. **D2** 110
Guthrie, Ok., U.S. **B4** 129
Guthrie, W.V., U.S. **m12** 141
Guthrie Center, Ia., U.S. **C3** 108
Guttenberg, Ia., U.S. **B6** 108
Guttenberg, N.J., U.S. **h8** 123
Guwāhāti, India **D6** 40
Guyana, ctry., S.A. **B8** 70
Guyandotte, stm., W.V., U.S. **C2** 141
Guyang, China **A3** 30
Guymon, Ok., U.S. **e9** 129
Guysborough, N.S., Can. **D8** 87
Guyton, Ga., U.S. **D5** 103
Guyuan, China **D9** 28
Guzar, Uzb. **C9** 42
Güzelyurt Körfezi, b., N. Cyp. **E5** 44
Guzmán, Mex. **D4** 78
Gwaai, Zimb. **B4** 56
Gwādar, Pak. **E8** 42
Gwalia, Austl. **F3** 60
Gwalior, India **D3** 40
Gwanda, Zimb. **C4** 56
Gwardafuy, Gees, c., Som. **H15** 48
Gwayi, stm., Zimb. **B4** 56
Gweru, Zimb. **B4** 56
Gweta, Bots. **C4** 56
Gwinhurst, De., U.S. **h8** 101
Gwinn, Mi., U.S. **B3** 115
Gwinner, N.D., U.S. **C8** 127
Gwinnett, co., Ga., U.S. **C2** 103
Gwydyr Bay, b., Ak., U.S. **A10** 95
Gwynns Falls, stm., Md., U.S. **g10** 113
Gyangzê, China **F5** 28
Gyaring Co, l., China **E5** 28
Gyaring Hu, l., China **E7** 28
Gyda, Russia **B9** 26
Gydanskij poluostrov, pen., Russia **B9** 26
Gyldenløves Fjord, b., Grnld. **F31** 82
Gympie, Austl. **F5** 62
Gyöngyös, Hung. **F5** 20
Győr, Hung. **F4** 20
Gypsum, Co., U.S. **B4** 99
Gyzylarbat, Turk. **F7** 26

H

Haakon, co., S.D., U.S. **C4** 134
Haapsalu, Est. **G10** 10
Haarlem, Neth. **D9** 12
Haast, N.Z. **p12** 63c
Habarovo, Russia **A11** 22
Habarovsk, Russia **E15** 26
Ḥabbānīyah, Buḥayrat al-, res., Iraq **F10** 44
Habersham, co., Ga., U.S. **B3** 103
Hachijō-jima, i., Japan **E15** 28
Hachinohe, Japan **C16** 28
Hachiōji, Japan **C3** 31
Hackberry, La., U.S. **E2** 111
Hackensack, N.J., U.S. **B4** 123
Hackensack, stm., N.J., U.S. **h8** 123
Hackettstown, N.J., U.S. **B3** 123
Hackleburg, Al., U.S. **A2** 94
Haddam, Ct., U.S. **D5** 100
Haddock, Ga., U.S. **C3** 103
Haddonfield, N.J., U.S. **D2** 123
Haddon Heights, N.J., U.S. **D2** 123
Hadejia, stm., Nig. **D6** 50
Hadejia, Nig. **D7** 50
Ḥadera, Isr. **F6** 44
Haderslev, Den. **I3** 10
Hadībū, Yemen **H6** 38
Ḥadīthah, Iraq **D4** 42
Hadjout, Alg. **I8** 16
Hadley Lake, l., Me., U.S. **D5** 112
Hadrian's Wall, Eng., U.K. **C5** 12
Haeju, N. Kor. **D13** 28
Hafik, Tur. **C7** 44
Hafnarfjörður, Ice. **l17** 10a
Haft Gel, Iran **D5** 42
Hagan, Ga., U.S. **D5** 103
Hagåtña (Agana), Guam **D11** 32
Hagemeister Island, i., Ak., U.S. **D7** 95
Hagerman, Id., U.S. **G4** 105
Hagerman, N.M., U.S. **D5** 124
Hagerstown, In., U.S. **E7** 107
Hagerstown, Md., U.S. **A2** 113
Hagfors, Swe. **F5** 10
Haggin, Mount, mtn., Mt., U.S. **D3** 119
Hagi, Japan **D2** 31
Ha Giang, Viet. **B5** 34
Hague, Sk., Can. **E2** 91
Haguenau, Fr. **C10** 16
Hagues Peak, mtn., Co., U.S. **A5** 99
Ha! Ha!, Baie des, b., Qc., Can. **C2** 88
Hahira, Ga., U.S. **F3** 103
Hahnville, La., U.S. **E5** 111
Haicheng, China **A5** 30
Hai Duong, Viet. **B5** 34
Haifa see Ḥefa, Isr. **D2** 42
Haig, Austl. **G4** 60
Haikang, China **E3** 30
Haikou, China **G10** 28
Haiku, Hi., U.S. **C5** 104
Ḥā'il, Sau. Ar. **E4** 38
Hailar, China **B11** 28
Hailey, Id., U.S. **F4** 105
Haileybury, On., Can. **p20** 89
Haileyville, Ok., U.S. **C6** 129
Hailin, China **B1** 31
Hailun, China **B13** 28
Haimen, China **E4** 30
Haimen, China **F12** 28
Hainan, prov., China **H9** 28
Hainan Dao, i., China **H9** 28
Hainan Island see Hainan Dao, i., China **H9** 28
Haines, Ak., U.S. **D12** 95
Haines City, Fl., U.S. **D5** 102
Haining, China **C5** 30
Hai Ninh, Viet. **B5** 34
Hai Phong, Viet. **B5** 34
Haisyn, Ukr. **E10** 20
Haiti, ctry., N.A. **H12** 75
Haitun, China **B7** 40
Haiyuan, China **B2** 30
Haizhou, China **E11** 28
Haizhou Wan, b., China **B4** 30
Hajdúböszörmény, Hung. **F6** 20
Hajnówka, Pol. **C7** 20
Hakkâri, Tur. **D10** 44
Hakodate, Japan **C16** 28
Ḥalab (Aleppo), Syria **D7** 44
Halachó, Mex. **C6** 78
Ḥalā'ib, Sudan **F12** 48
Halawa, Cape, c., Hi., U.S. **B5** 104
Halawa Heights, Hi., U.S. **g10** 104
Halberstadt, Ger. **E12** 12
Halden, Nor. **G4** 10
Haldimand, On., Can. **E5** 89
Haldwāni, India **D3** 40
Hale, co., Al., U.S. **C2** 94
Hale, co., Tx., U.S. **B2** 136
Haleakala Crater, crat., Hi., U.S. **C5** 104
Haleakala National Park, Hi., U.S. **C6** 104
Hale Center, Tx., U.S. **B2** 136
Haleiwa, Hi., U.S. **B3** 104
Hales Corners, Wi., U.S. **n11** 142
Halethorpe, Md., U.S. **B4** 113
Haleyville, Al., U.S. **A2** 94
Half Moon Bay, Ca., U.S. **k8** 98
Halfway, Md., U.S. **A2** 113
Haliburton, On., Can. **B6** 89
Halibut Point, c., Ma., U.S. **A6** 114
Halicarnassus, hist., Tur. **D2** 44
Halifax, N.S., Can. **E6** 87
Halifax, co., N.C., U.S. **A5** 126
Halifax, Va., U.S. **D4** 139
Halifax, co., Va., U.S. **D4** 139
Haliimaile, Hi., U.S. **C5** 104
Hall, co., Ga., U.S. **B3** 103
Hall, co., Ne., U.S. **D7** 120
Hall, co., Tx., U.S. **B2** 136
Halla, Mount see Halla-san, mtn., S. Kor. **E13** 28
Hallam Peak, mtn., B.C., Can. **C8** 85
Hallandale, Fl., U.S. **G6** 102
Ḥallānīyah, Juzur al-, is., Oman **G7** 38
Halla-san, mtn., S. Kor. **E13** 28
Halle, Ger. **E12** 12
Hällefors, Swe. **G6** 10
Hallein, Aus. **G13** 12
Hallettsville, Tx., U.S. **E4** 136
Hallie, Wi., U.S. **D2** 142
Hall Island, i., Ak., U.S. **C5** 95
Hall Meadow Brook Reservoir, res., Ct., U.S. **B3** 100
Hall Mountain, mtn., Wa., U.S. **A8** 140
Hallock, Mn., U.S. **B2** 116
Hallowell, Me., U.S. **D3** 112
Halls, Tn., U.S. **B2** 135
Hallsberg, Swe. **G6** 10
Halls Creek, Austl. **D4** 60
Halls Creek, stm., Ut., U.S. **F5** 137
Halls Crossroads, Tn., U.S. **m14** 135
Halls Stream, stm., N.H., U.S. **f7** 122
Hallstahammar, Swe. **G7** 10
Hallstead, Pa., U.S. **C10** 131
Hallsville, Mo., U.S. **B5** 118
Hallsville, Tx., U.S. **C5** 136
Halmahera, i., Indon. **C7** 36
Halmahera, Laut (Halmahera Sea), Indon. **D7** 36
Halmahera Sea see Halmahera, Laut, Indon. **D7** 36
Hal'mer-Ju, Russia **A11** 22
Halmstad, Swe. **H5** 10
Halsey, Or., U.S. **C3** 130
Hälsingland, hist. reg., Swe. **F7** 10
Halstad, Mn., U.S. **C2** 116
Halstead, Ks., U.S. **E6** 109
Haltiatunturi, mtn., Eur. **B9** 10
Halton Hills, On., Can. **D5** 89
Hamada, Japan **D2** 31
Hamadān, Iran **D5** 42
Ḥamāh, state, Syria **E7** 44
Ḥamāh, Syria **E7** 44

Name	Map Ref.	Page
Hamarøya, Nor.	B6	10
Hambantota, Sri L.	H4	40
Hamblen, co., Tn., U.S.	C10	135
Hamburg, Ger.	D12	12
Hamburg, Ar., U.S.	D4	97
Hamburg, Ia., U.S.	D2	108
Hamburg, N.Y., U.S.	C2	125
Hamburg, Pa., U.S.	E10	131
Hamden, Ct., U.S.	D4	100
Hamden, Oh., U.S.	C3	128
Hämeenlinna, Fin.	F11	10
Hamel, Mn., U.S.	m11	116
Hameln, Ger.	D11	12
Hamersley Range, mts., Austl.	E2	60
Hami, China	C6	28
Hamilton, Austl.	H3	62
Hamilton, Ber.	B12	76
Hamilton, On., Can.	D5	89
Hamilton, N.Z.	o14	63c
Hamilton, Al., U.S.	A2	94
Hamilton, co., Fl., U.S.	B3	102
Hamilton, co., Ia., U.S.	B4	108
Hamilton, Il., U.S.	C2	106
Hamilton, co., Il., U.S.	E5	106
Hamilton, In., U.S.	A8	107
Hamilton, co., In., U.S.	D5	107
Hamilton, co., Ks., U.S.	E2	109
Hamilton, Mi., U.S.	F4	115
Hamilton, Mo., U.S.	B3	118
Hamilton, Ms., U.S.	B5	117
Hamilton, Mt., U.S.	D2	119
Hamilton, co., Ne., U.S.	D7	120
Hamilton, N.Y., U.S.	C5	125
Hamilton, co., N.Y., U.S.	B6	125
Hamilton, Oh., U.S.	C1	128
Hamilton, co., Oh., U.S.	C1	128
Hamilton, co., Tn., U.S.	D8	135
Hamilton, co., Tx., U.S.	D3	136
Hamilton, Tx., U.S.	D3	136
Hamilton, Va., U.S.	A5	139
Hamilton, Lake, res., Ar., U.S.	C2	97
Hamilton, Mount, mtn., Ak., U.S.	C8	95
Hamilton, Mount, mtn., Ca., U.S.	k9	98
Hamilton, Mount, mtn., Nv., U.S.	D6	121
Hamilton Inlet, b., N.L., Can.	A2	88
Hamilton Reservoir, res., Ma., U.S.	B3	114
Hamilton Sound, strt., N.L., Can.	D4	88
Hamilton Square, N.J., U.S.	C3	123
Hamina, Fin.	F12	10
Hamiota, Mb., Can.	D1	86
Hamīrpur, India	D4	40
Hamlet, In., U.S.	B4	107
Hamlet, N.C., U.S.	C3	126
Hamlet, Mount, mtn., Ak., U.S.	B6	95
Hamlin, Pa., U.S.	D11	131
Hamlin, co., S.D., U.S.	C8	134
Hamlin, Tx., U.S.	C2	136
Hamlin, W.V., U.S.	C2	141
Hamlin Lake, l., Mi., U.S.	D4	115
Hamm, Ger.	E10	12
Hammamet, Tun.	F3	18
Hammamet, Golfe de, b., Tun.	F3	18
Hammam Lif, Tun.	F3	18
Ḩammār, Hawr al-, l., Iraq	G12	44
Hammerfest, Nor.	A10	10
Hammon, Ok., U.S.	B2	129
Hammonasset, stm., Ct., U.S.	D5	100
Hammonasset Point, c., Ct., U.S.	E5	100
Hammond, In., U.S.	A2	107
Hammond, La., U.S.	D5	111
Hammond, Wi., U.S.	D1	142
Hammond Bay, b., Mi., U.S.	C6	115
Hammonton, N.J., U.S.	D3	123
Hamningberg, Nor.	A14	10
Hampden, N.L., Can.	D3	88
Hampden, co., Ma., U.S.	B2	114
Hampden, Me., U.S.	D4	112
Hampden Highlands, Me., U.S.	D4	112
Hampshire, Il., U.S.	A5	106
Hampshire, co., Ma., U.S.	B2	114
Hampshire, co., W.V., U.S.	B6	141
Hampstead, Md., U.S.	A4	113
Hampstead, N.C., U.S.	C5	126
Hampton, N.B., Can.	D4	87
Hampton, Ar., U.S.	D3	97
Hampton, Ga., U.S.	C2	103
Hampton, Ia., U.S.	B4	108
Hampton, N.H., U.S.	E5	122
Hampton, S.C., U.S.	F5	133
Hampton, co., S.C., U.S.	F5	133
Hampton, Tn., U.S.	C11	135
Hampton, Va., U.S.	C6	139
Hampton Bays, N.Y., U.S.	n16	125
Hampton Beach, N.H., U.S.	E5	122
Hampton Butte, mtn., Or., U.S.	D6	130
Hampton Roads, anch., Va., U.S.	k15	139
Hampton Roads Bridge-Tunnel, Va., U.S.	k15	139
Ḩamrā', Al-Ḩamādah al-, des., Libya	F6	14
Hamra, As Saquia al, stm., W. Sah.	A2	50
Hams Fork, stm., Wy., U.S.	E2	143
Hamtramck, Mi., U.S.	p15	115
Hāmūn, Daryācheh-ye, l., Iran	D8	42
Han, stm., China	E9	28
Hāna, Hi., U.S.	C6	104
Hanahan, S.C., U.S.	F7	133
Hanalei Bay, b., Hi., U.S.	A2	104
Hanamaki, Japan	D16	28
Hanamaulu, Hi., U.S.	B2	104
Hanapēpē, Hi., U.S.	B2	104
Hâncești, Mol.	F10	20
Hanceville, Al., U.S.	A3	94
Hancheng, China	D10	28
Hancock, co., Ga., U.S.	C3	103
Hancock, co., Ia., U.S.	A4	108
Hancock, co., Il., U.S.	C2	106
Hancock, co., In., U.S.	E6	107
Hancock, co., Ky., U.S.	C3	110
Hancock, Md., U.S.	A1	113
Hancock, co., Me., U.S.	D4	112
Hancock, Mi., U.S.	A2	115
Hancock, Mn., U.S.	E3	116
Hancock, co., Ms., U.S.	E4	117
Hancock, co., Oh., U.S.	A2	128
Hancock, co., Tn., U.S.	C10	135
Hancock, co., W.V., U.S.	A4	141
Hand, co., S.D., U.S.	C6	134
Handan, China	D10	28
Handyga, Russia	C15	26
Hanford, Ca., U.S.	D4	98
Hangayn nuruu, mts., Mong.	B7	28
Hangchow see Hangzhou, China	E12	28
Hanggin Houqi, China	C9	28
Hanggin Qi, China	D9	28
Hangman Creek, stm., Wa., U.S.	B8	140
Hangokurt, Russia	B11	22
Hangu, China	B4	30
Hangzhou, China	E12	28
Hangzhou Wan, b., China	C5	30
Hanjiang, China	F11	28
Hankinson, N.D., U.S.	C9	127
Hanko, Fin.	G10	10
Hanna, Ab., Can.	D5	84
Hanna, Wy., U.S.	E6	143
Hanna City, Il., U.S.	C4	106
Hannahville Indian Reservation, Mi., U.S.	C3	115
Hannibal, Mo., U.S.	B6	118
Hannover, Ger.	D11	12
Hanöbukten, b., Swe.	I6	10
Ha Noi, Viet.	B5	34
Hanover, On., Can.	C3	89
Hanover see Hannover, Ger.	D11	12
Hanover, Il., U.S.	A3	106
Hanover, In., U.S.	G7	107
Hanover, Ks., U.S.	C7	109
Hanover, Ma., U.S.	B6	114
Hanover, Mn., U.S.	m11	116
Hanover, N.H., U.S.	C2	122
Hanover, Pa., U.S.	G8	131
Hanover, co., Va., U.S.	C5	139
Hanover Park, Il., U.S.	k8	106
Hansen, Id., U.S.	G4	105
Hansford, co., Tx., U.S.	A2	136
Hanson, Ma., U.S.	B6	114
Hanson, co., S.D., U.S.	D8	134
Hanstholm, Den.	H3	10
Hantsport, N.S., Can.	D5	87
Hanty-Mansijsk, Russia	C8	26
Hanyin, China	C2	30
Hanzhong, China	E9	28
Hāora, India	E5	40
Haparanda, Swe.	D11	10
Hapčeranga, Russia	E13	26
Hapeville, Ga., U.S.	C2	103
Happy Valley, N.M., U.S.	E5	124
Happy Valley-Goose Bay, N.L., Can.	B1	88
Hāpur, India	D3	40
Ḩaraḍ, Sau. Ar.	F5	38
Harahan, La., U.S.	k11	111
Haralson, co., Ga., U.S.	C1	103
Harare, Zimb.	B5	56
Harazé Mangueigne, Chad	B4	54
Harbala, Russia	C14	26
Harbeson, De., U.S.	F4	101
Harbin, China	B13	28
Harbor, Or., U.S.	E2	130
Harbor Beach, Mi., U.S.	E8	115
Harborcreek, Pa., U.S.	B2	131
Harbor Springs, Mi., U.S.	C6	115
Harbour Breton, N.L., Can.	E4	88
Harbour Grace, N.L., Can.	E5	88
Harcuvar Mountains, mts., Az., U.S.	D2	96
Hardangerfjorden, b., Nor.	F2	10
Hardee, co., Fl., U.S.	E5	102
Hardeeville, S.C., U.S.	G5	133
Hardeman, co., Tn., U.S.	B2	135
Hardeman, co., Tx., U.S.	B3	136
Hardin, co., Ia., U.S.	B4	108
Hardin, Il., U.S.	D3	106
Hardin, co., Il., U.S.	F5	106
Hardin, co., Ky., U.S.	C4	110
Hardin, Mt., U.S.	E9	119
Hardin, co., Oh., U.S.	B2	128
Hardin, co., Tn., U.S.	B3	135
Hardin, co., Tx., U.S.	D5	136
Harding, S. Afr.	E4	56
Harding, co., N.M., U.S.	B5	124
Harding, co., S.D., U.S.	B2	134
Harding, Lake, res., U.S.	C4	94
Hardinsburg, Ky., U.S.	C3	110
Hardisty, Ab., Can.	C5	84
Hardoi, India	D4	40
Hardwick, Ga., U.S.	C3	103
Hardwick, Vt., U.S.	B4	138
Hardwood Ridge, mtn., Pa., U.S.	D11	131
Hardy, co., W.V., U.S.	B6	141
Hardy Lake, res., In., U.S.	G6	107
Hare Bay, N.L., Can.	D4	88
Hare Bay, b., N.L., Can.	C4	88
Hārer, Eth.	B8	54
Harford, co., Md., U.S.	A5	113
Hargeysa, Som.	I13	48
Har Hu, l., China	D7	28
Hari, stm., Indon.	D2	36
Haridwār, India	D3	40
Harīrūd, stm., Asia	D8	42
Harkers Island, N.C., U.S.	C6	126
Harlan, Ia., U.S.	C2	108
Harlan, In., U.S.	B8	107
Harlan, Ky., U.S.	D6	110
Harlan, co., Ky., U.S.	D6	110
Harlan, co., Ne., U.S.	D6	120
Harlan County Lake, res., Ne., U.S.	E6	120
Harlem, Fl., U.S.	F6	102
Harlem, Ga., U.S.	C4	103
Harlem, Mt., U.S.	B8	119
Harleyville, S.C., U.S.	E7	133
Harlingen, Tx., U.S.	F4	136
Harlow, Eng., U.K.	E7	12
Harlowton, Mt., U.S.	D7	119
Harmånger, Swe.	F7	10
Harmanli, Blg.	D10	18
Harmon, co., Ok., U.S.	C2	129
Harmon Creek, stm., W.V., U.S.	f8	141
Harmony, In., U.S.	E3	107
Harmony, Mn., U.S.	G6	116
Harmony, Pa., U.S.	E1	131
Harmony, R.I., U.S.	B3	132
Harnett, co., N.C., U.S.	B4	126
Harney, co., Or., U.S.	D7	130
Harney, Lake, l., Fl., U.S.	D5	102
Harney Lake, l., Or., U.S.	D7	130
Harney Peak, mtn., S.D., U.S.	D2	134
Härnösand, Swe.	E7	10
Haro Strait, strt., Wa., U.S.	A2	140
Harper, Lib.	F3	50
Harper, Ks., U.S.	E5	109
Harper, co., Ks., U.S.	E5	109
Harper, co., Ok., U.S.	A2	129
Harper, Mount, mtn., Ak., U.S.	C11	95
Harpers Ferry, W.V., U.S.	B7	141
Harpers Ferry National Historical Park, W.V., U.S.	B7	141
Harpersville, Al., U.S.	B3	94
Harpeth, stm., Tn., U.S.	A5	135
Harqin Qi, China	A4	30
Harquahala Mountain, mtn., Az., U.S.	D2	96
Harquahala Mountains, mts., Az., U.S.	D2	96
Harrah, Ok., U.S.	B4	129
Harricana, stm., Can.	H24	82
Harriman, Tn., U.S.	D9	135
Harriman Reservoir, res., Vt., U.S.	F3	138
Harrington, De., U.S.	E3	101
Harrington Park, N.J., U.S.	h9	123
Harris, co., Ga., U.S.	D2	103
Harris, Mn., U.S.	E6	116
Harris, R.I., U.S.	D3	132
Harris, co., Tx., U.S.	E5	136
Harris, Lake, l., Fl., U.S.	D5	102
Harrisburg, Ar., U.S.	B5	97
Harrisburg, Il., U.S.	F5	106
Harrisburg, Or., U.S.	C3	130
Harrisburg, Pa., U.S.	F8	131
Harrisburg, S.D., U.S.	D9	134
Harrismith, S. Afr.	D4	56
Harrison, Ar., U.S.	A2	97
Harrison, co., Ia., U.S.	C2	108
Harrison, co., In., U.S.	H5	107
Harrison, co., Ky., U.S.	B5	110
Harrison, Mi., U.S.	D6	115
Harrison, co., Mo., U.S.	A3	118
Harrison, co., Ms., U.S.	E4	117
Harrison, N.J., U.S.	k8	123
Harrison, N.Y., U.S.	h13	125
Harrison, co., Oh., U.S.	B4	128
Harrison, Oh., U.S.	C1	128
Harrison, Tn., U.S.	h11	135
Harrison, co., Tx., U.S.	C5	136
Harrison, co., W.V., U.S.	B4	141
Harrison, Cape, c., N.L., Can.	g10	88
Harrison Bay, b., Ak., U.S.	A9	95
Harrisonburg, Va., U.S.	B4	139
Harrison Hot Springs, B.C., Can.	f14	85
Harrison Lake, l., B.C., Can.	E7	85
Harrisonville, Mo., U.S.	C3	118
Harriston, On., Can.	D4	89
Harristown, Il., U.S.	D4	106
Harrisville, R.I., U.S.	B2	132
Harrisville, Ut., U.S.	B4	137
Harrisville, W.V., U.S.	B3	141
Harrodsburg, Ky., U.S.	C5	110
Harrow, On., Can.	E2	89
Harry S. Truman Reservoir, res., Mo., U.S.	C4	118
Harry Strunk Lake, res., Ne., U.S.	D5	120
Harsīn, Iran	E12	44
Harstad, Nor.	B7	10
Hart, co., Ga., U.S.	B4	103
Hart, co., Ky., U.S.	C4	110
Hart, Mi., U.S.	E4	115
Hart, Tx., U.S.	B1	136
Hart, Lake, l., Fl., U.S.	D5	102
Hartford, Al., U.S.	D4	94
Hartford, Ar., U.S.	B1	97
Hartford, Ct., U.S.	B5	100
Hartford, co., Ct., U.S.	B4	100
Hartford, Ia., U.S.	C4	108
Hartford, Il., U.S.	E3	106
Hartford, Ky., U.S.	C3	110
Hartford, Mi., U.S.	F4	115
Hartford, S.D., U.S.	D9	134
Hartford, Vt., U.S.	D4	138
Hartford, Wi., U.S.	E5	142
Hartford City, In., U.S.	D7	107
Hartington, Ne., U.S.	B8	120
Hart Lake, l., Or., U.S.	E7	130
Hartland, N.B., Can.	C2	87
Hartland, Me., U.S.	D3	112
Hartland, Wi., U.S.	E5	142
Hartlepool, Eng., U.K.	C6	12
Hartley, Ia., U.S.	A2	108
Hartley, co., Tx., U.S.	B1	136
Hartney, Mb., Can.	E1	86
Hartselle, Al., U.S.	A3	94
Hartshorne, Ok., U.S.	C6	129
Hartsville, S.C., U.S.	C7	133
Hartsville, Tn., U.S.	A5	135
Hartville, Oh., U.S.	B4	128
Hartwell, Ga., U.S.	B4	103
Hartwell Lake, res., U.S.	B1	133
Harvard, Il., U.S.	A5	106
Harvard, Ne., U.S.	D7	120
Harvard, Mount, mtn., Co., U.S.	C4	99
Harvey, Il., U.S.	B6	106
Harvey, co., Ks., U.S.	D6	109
Harvey, La., U.S.	E5	111
Harvey, Mi., U.S.	B3	115
Harvey, N.D., U.S.	B6	127
Harvey Lake, res., Pa., U.S.	m16	131
Harveys Creek, stm., Pa., U.S.	n16	131
Harwich, Eng., U.K.	E7	12
Harwich Port, Ma., U.S.	C7	114
Harwinton, Ct., U.S.	B3	100
Haryāna, state, India	D3	40
Hasalbag, China	B3	40
Hasbrouck Heights, N.J., U.S.	h8	123
Haskell, Ar., U.S.	C3	97
Haskell, co., Ks., U.S.	E3	109
Haskell, Ok., U.S.	B6	129
Haskell, co., Ok., U.S.	B6	129
Haskell, co., Tx., U.S.	C3	136
Haskell, Tx., U.S.	C3	136
Haskovo, Blg.	D10	18
Hassan, India	G3	40
Hassayampa, stm., Az., U.S.	D3	96
Hasselt, Bel.	E9	12
Hassi Messaoud, Alg.	D6	48
Hässleholm, Swe.	H5	10
Hastings, On., Can.	C7	89
Hastings, N.Z.	o14	63c
Hastings, Eng., U.K.	E7	12
Hastings, Mi., U.S.	F5	115
Hastings, Mn., U.S.	F6	116
Hastings, Ne., U.S.	D7	120
Hastings, Pa., U.S.	E4	131
Hastings-on-Hudson, N.Y., U.S.	h13	125
Hašuri, Geor.	B10	44
Hatanga, stm., Russia	B12	26
Hatanga, Russia	B12	26
Hatangskij zaliv, b., Russia	B12	26
Hatay (Antioch), Tur.	D7	44
Hatch, N.M., U.S.	E2	124
Hatchet Lake, N.S., Can.	E6	87
Hatchie, stm., Tn., U.S.	B2	135
Hatchineha, Lake, l., Fl., U.S.	D5	102
Hat Creek, stm., S.D., U.S.	E2	134
Hatfield, In., U.S.	I3	107
Hatfield, Pa., U.S.	F11	131
Hatgal, Mong.	A8	28
Hāthras, India	D3	40
Ha Tinh, Viet.	C5	34
Hat Mountain, mtn., Az., U.S.	E3	96
Hatteras, N.C., U.S.	B7	126
Hatteras, Cape, c., N.C., U.S.	B7	126
Hatteras Inlet, b., N.C., U.S.	B7	126
Hattiesburg, Ms., U.S.	D4	117
Hatton, N.D., U.S.	B8	127
Hat Yai, Thai.	E4	34
Hatyrka, Russia	C19	26
Haubstadt, In., U.S.	H2	107
Haugesund, Nor.	G1	10
Haughton, La., U.S.	B2	111
Haukeligrend, Nor.	G2	10
Haukivesi, l., Fin.	E13	10
Hauraki Gulf, b., N.Z.	o13	63c
Hauser, Or., U.S.	D2	130
Haut, Isle au, i., Me., U.S.	D4	112
Haut Atlas, mts., Mor.	E2	14
Hau'ula, Hi., U.S.	B4	104
Havana see La Habana, Cuba	A3	80
Havana, Fl., U.S.	B2	102
Havana, Il., U.S.	C3	106
Havasu, Lake, res., U.S.	C1	96
Havasupai Indian Reservation, Az., U.S.	A3	96
Havelock, On., Can.	C7	89
Havelock, N.C., U.S.	C6	126
Havelock Island, i., India	G6	40
Haven, Ks., U.S.	E6	109
Haverford [Township], Pa., U.S.	o20	131
Haverhill, Ma., U.S.	A5	114
Haverstraw, N.Y., U.S.	D7	125
Haviland, Ks., U.S.	E4	109
Havre see Le Havre, Fr.	C7	16
Havre, Mt., U.S.	B7	119
Havre de Grace, Md., U.S.	A5	113
Havre North, Mt., U.S.	B7	119
Havza, Tur.	B6	44
Haw, stm., N.C., U.S.	B3	126
Hawai'i, i., Hi., U.S.	D6	104
Hawaii, state, U.S.	C5	104
Hawai'ian Islands, is., Hi., U.S.	m14	104
Hawaiian Ridge	F22	64
Hawaii County, co., Hi., U.S.	D6	104
Hawai'i Volcanoes National Park, Hi., U.S.	D6	104
Hawarden, Ia., U.S.	A1	108
Hawera, N.Z.	o13	63c
Hawesville, Ky., U.S.	C3	110
Hawi, Hi., U.S.	C6	104
Hawke Bay, b., N.Z.	o14	63c
Hawker, Austl.	G2	62
Hawkes, Mount, mtn., Ant.	E34	67
Hawkesbury, On., Can.	B10	89
Hawkesbury Island, i., B.C., Can.	C3	85
Hawkins, co., Tn., U.S.	C11	135
Hawkinsville, Ga., U.S.	D3	103
Hawley, Mn., U.S.	D2	116
Hawley, Pa., U.S.	D11	131
Haworth, N.J., U.S.	h9	123
Haw River, N.C., U.S.	A3	126
Hawthorne, Ca., U.S.	n12	98
Hawthorne, Fl., U.S.	C4	102
Hawthorne, N.J., U.S.	B4	123
Hawthorne, Nv., U.S.	E3	121
Hawthorne, N.Y., U.S.	g13	125
Hawza, W. Sah.	A2	50
Haxtun, Co., U.S.	A8	99
Hay, Austl.	G3	62
Hayden, Az., U.S.	E5	96
Hayden, Co., U.S.	A3	99
Hayden Lake, l., Id., U.S.	B2	105
Hayes, stm., Mb., Can.	B5	86
Hayes, La., U.S.	D3	111
Hayes, co., Ne., U.S.	D4	120
Hayes, Mount, mtn., Ak., U.S.	C10	95
Hayfield, Mn., U.S.	G6	116
Hayford Peak, mtn., Nv., U.S.	G6	121
Haymock Lake, l., Me., U.S.	B3	112
Haynesville, La., U.S.	B2	111
Hayneville, Al., U.S.	C3	94
Hayrabolu, Tur.	B2	44
Hays, Ks., U.S.	D4	109
Hays, N.C., U.S.	A1	126
Hays, co., Tx., U.S.	D3	136
Hays Canyon Peak, mtn., Nv., U.S.	B2	121
Hay Springs, Ne., U.S.	B3	120
Haystack Mountain, mtn., Nv., U.S.	B6	121
Haysville, Ks., U.S.	g12	109
Hayti, Mo., U.S.	E8	118
Hayti Heights, Mo., U.S.	E8	118
Hayward, Ca., U.S.	h8	98
Hayward, Wi., U.S.	B2	142
Haywood, co., N.C., U.S.	f9	126
Haywood, co., Tn., U.S.	B2	135
Hazard, Ky., U.S.	C6	110
Hazardville, Ct., U.S.	B5	100
Hazārībāg, India	E5	40
Hazel Crest, Il., U.S.	k9	106
Hazel Dell, Wa., U.S.	D3	140
Hazel Green, Al., U.S.	A3	94
Hazel Green, Wi., U.S.	F3	142
Hazel Park, Mi., U.S.	p15	115
Hazelton Pyramid, mtn., Wy., U.S.	B5	143
Hazelwood, N.C., U.S.	f10	126
Hazen, Ar., U.S.	C4	97
Hazen, N.D., U.S.	B4	127
Hazen Bay, b., Ak., U.S.	C6	95
Hazlehurst, Ga., U.S.	E4	103
Hazlehurst, Ms., U.S.	D3	117
Hazlet, N.J., U.S.	C4	123
Hazleton, Ia., U.S.	B6	108
Hazleton, Pa., U.S.	E10	131
Head Harbor Island, i., Me., U.S.	D5	112
Headland, Al., U.S.	D4	94
Headley, Mount, mtn., Mt., U.S.	C1	119
Healdsburg, Ca., U.S.	C2	98
Healdton, Ok., U.S.	C4	129
Healesville, Austl.	H4	62
Healy, Ak., U.S.	C10	95
Heard, co., Ga., U.S.	C1	103

Name — Map Ref. — Page

Hearne, Tx., U.S. D4 136
Hearst, On., Can. o19 89
Heart, stm., N.D., U.S. C3 127
Heart Butte Dam, N.D., U.S. C4 127
Heart Lake, l., Wy., U.S. B2 143
Heart's Content, N.L., Can. E5 88
Heath, Oh., U.S. B3 128
Heath Springs, S.C., U.S. B6 133
Heavener, Ok., U.S. C7 129
Hebbronville, Tx., U.S. F3 136
Hebei, prov., China D11 28
Heber, Az., U.S. C5 96
Heber City, Ut., U.S. C4 137
Heber Springs, Ar., U.S. B3 97
Hébertville, Qc., Can. A6 90
Hebgen Lake, res., Mt., U.S. F5 119
Hebi, China D10 28
Hebrides, is., Scot., U.K. D4 6
Hebrides, Sea of the, Scot., U.K. B3 12
Hebron, N.S., Can. F3 87
Hebron, Il., U.S. A5 106
Hebron, In., U.S. B3 107
Hebron, Ky., U.S. h13 110
Hebron, Md., U.S. D6 113
Hebron, N.D., U.S. C3 127
Hebron, Ne., U.S. D8 120
Hebron, Oh., U.S. C3 128
Hebron see Al-Khalīl, W.B. G6 44
Hecate Strait, strt., B.C., Can. C2 85
Hecelchakán, Mex. C6 78
Heceta Island, i., Ak., U.S. n23 95
Hechi, China G9 28
Hechuan, China D2 30
Hecla Island, i., Mb., Can. D3 86
Hector, Mn., U.S. F4 116
Hedemora, Swe. F6 10
He Devil, mtn., Id., U.S. D2 105
Hedrick, Ia., U.S. C5 108
Ḥefa (Haifa), Isr. D2 42
Hefei, China E11 28
Heflin, Al., U.S. B4 94
Hefner, Lake, res., Ok., U.S. B4 129
Hegang, China B14 28
Hegins, Pa., U.S. E9 131
Heide, Ger. C11 12
Heidelberg, Ger. F11 12
Heidelberg, Ms., U.S. D5 117
Heidrick, Ky., U.S. D6 110
Heilbron, S. Afr. D4 56
Heilbronn, Ger. F11 12
Heilong (Amur), stm., Asia D14 26
Heilongjiang see Amur, stm., Asia D16 26
Heilongjiang see Heilong, stm., Asia D16 26
Heilongjiang, prov., China B13 28
Heinävesi, Fin. E13 10
Hejaz see Al-Ḥijāz, reg., Sau. Ar. E3 38
Hejian, China B4 30
Hejiang, China D2 30
Hekimhan, Tur. C7 44
Hekla, vol., Ice. l19 10a
Hekou, China G8 28
Helagsfjället, mtn., Swe. E5 10
Helena, Al., U.S. B3 94
Helena, Ar., U.S. C5 97
Helena, Ga., U.S. D4 103
Helena, Mt., U.S. D4 119
Helena, Ok., U.S. A3 129
Helensville, N.Z. o13 63c
Helgoländer Bucht, b., Ger. C11 12
Heli, China A2 31
Hellam, Pa., U.S. G8 131
Hellertown, Pa., U.S. E11 131
Hellín, Spain H6 16
Hells Canyon, U.S. B10 130
Hells Canyon National Recreation Area, U.S. B10 130
Hell-Ville see Andoany, Madag. A8 56
Helmand, stm., Asia D8 42
Helmeringhausen, Nmb. D2 56
Helmstedt, Ger. D12 12
Helotes, Tx., U.S. h7 136
Helper, Ut., U.S. D5 137
Helsingborg, Swe. H5 10
Helsingfors see Helsinki, Fin. F11 10
Helsingør, Den. H5 10
Helsinki (Helsingfors), Fin. F11 10
Hematite, Mo., U.S. C7 118
Hemet, Ca., U.S. F5 98
Hemingford, Ne., U.S. B2 120
Hemingway, S.C., U.S. D9 133
Hemlock, Mi., U.S. E6 115
Hemlock Reservoir, res., Ct., U.S. E2 100
Hemmingford, Qc., Can. D4 90
Hemphill, Tx., U.S. D6 136
Hemphill, co., Tx., U.S. B2 136
Hempstead, co., Ar., U.S. D2 97
Hempstead, N.Y., U.S. n15 125
Hempstead, Tx., U.S. D4 136
Hemsön, i., Swe. E8 10
Henagar, Al., U.S. A4 94
Henan, prov., China E10 28
Hendek, Tur. B4 44
Henderson, co., Il., U.S. C3 106
Henderson, Ky., U.S. C2 110
Henderson, co., Ky., U.S. C2 110
Henderson, La., U.S. D4 111
Henderson, Mn., U.S. F5 116
Henderson, co., N.C., U.S. f10 126
Henderson, N.C., U.S. A4 126
Henderson, Ne., U.S. D8 120
Henderson, Nv., U.S. G7 121
Henderson, co., Tn., U.S. B3 135
Henderson, Tn., U.S. B3 135
Henderson, Tx., U.S. C5 136
Henderson, co., Tx., U.S. C5 136
Henderson Island, i., Pit. G17 58
Henderson's Point, Ms., U.S. g7 117
Hendersonville, N.C., U.S. f10 126
Hendersonville, Tn., U.S. A5 135
Hendricks, co., In., U.S. E4 107
Hendricks, Mn., U.S. F2 116
Hendry, co., Fl., U.S. F5 102
Hengshan, China D3 30
Hengshan, China D9 28
Hengxian, China E2 30
Hengyang, China F10 28
Heniches'k, Ukr. F13 20
Henlawson, W.V., U.S. n12 141
Henlopen, Cape, c., De., U.S. E5 101
Hennebont, Fr. D5 16
Hennepin, co., Mn., U.S. E5 116
Hennessey, Ok., U.S. A4 129
Henniker, N.H., U.S. D3 122
Henning, Mn., U.S. D3 116
Henning, Tn., U.S. B2 135
Henrico, co., Va., U.S. C5 139
Henrietta, N.C., U.S. B1 126
Henrietta, Tx., U.S. C3 136
Henrietta Maria, Cape, c., On., Can. n19 89
Henry, co., Al., U.S. D4 94
Henry, co., Ga., U.S. C2 103
Henry, co., Ia., U.S. C6 108
Henry, Il., U.S. B4 106
Henry, co., Il., U.S. B3 106
Henry, co., In., U.S. E7 107
Henry, co., Ky., U.S. B4 110
Henry, co., Mo., U.S. C4 118
Henry, co., Oh., U.S. A1 128
Henry, co., Tn., U.S. A3 135
Henry, co., Va., U.S. D3 139
Henry, Mount, mtn., Mt., U.S. B1 119
Henryetta, Ok., U.S. B6 129
Henrys Fork, stm., U.S. E2 143
Henryville, Qc., Can. D4 90
Henryville, In., U.S. G6 107
Hensall, On., Can. D3 89
Hentiesbaai, Nmb. C1 56
Henzada, Mya. C3 34
Hephzibah, Ga., U.S. C4 103
Heppner, Or., U.S. B7 130
Hepu, China G9 28
Hequ, China B3 30
Herāt, Afg. D8 42
Herbert G. West, Lake, res., Wa., U.S. C7 140
Herbes, Isle aux, i., Al., U.S. E1 94
Herculaneum, Mo., U.S. C7 118
Hereford, Eng., U.K. D5 12
Hereford, Md., U.S. A4 113
Hereford, Tx., U.S. B1 136
Hereford Inlet, b., N.J., U.S. E3 123
Herford, Ger. D11 12
Herington, Ks., U.S. D7 109
Herkimer, co., N.Y., U.S. B5 125
Herkimer, N.Y., U.S. B6 125
Hermann, Mo., U.S. C6 118
Hermano Peak, mtn., Co., U.S. D2 99
Hermantown, Mn., U.S. D6 116
Hermanus, S. Afr. E2 56
Herminie, Pa., U.S. F2 131
Hermiston, Or., U.S. B7 130
Hermitage, N.L., Can. E4 88
Hermitage, Ar., U.S. D3 97
Hermitage Bay, b., N.L., Can. E3 88
Hermit Islands, is., Pap. N. Gui. G12 32
Hermon, Mount, mtn., Asia F6 44
Hermosillo, Mex. B2 78
Hernando, Fl., U.S. D4 102
Hernando, co., Fl., U.S. D4 102
Hernando, Ms., U.S. A4 117
Herndon, Va., U.S. B5 139
Herning, Den. H3 10
Heron Lake, Mn., U.S. G3 116
Herrera, Arg. D5 72
Herrin, Il., U.S. F4 106
Herring Bay, b., Md., U.S. C4 113
Herring Cove, N.S., Can. E6 87
Herrington Lake, res., Ky., U.S. C5 110
Herscher, Il., U.S. B5 106
Hershey, Pa., U.S. F8 131
Hertford, N.C., U.S. A6 126
Hertford, co., N.C., U.S. A5 126
Hervey Bay, b., Austl. E5 62
Heshan, China E2 30
Heshun, China B3 30
Hesperia, Ca., U.S. E5 98
Hesperia, Mi., U.S. E4 115
Hesperus Mountain, mtn., Co., U.S. D2 99
Hesston, Ks., U.S. D6 109
Heta, stm., Russia B11 26
Hettinger, N.D., U.S. D3 127
Hettinger, co., N.D., U.S. C3 127
Hexian, China G10 28
Heyburn, Id., U.S. G5 105
Heyuan, China E3 30
Heywort h, Il., U.S. C5 106
Heze, China B4 30
Hialeah, Fl., U.S. G6 102
Hiawatha, Ia., U.S. B6 108
Hiawatha, Ks., U.S. C8 109
Hibbing, Mn., U.S. C6 116
Hickam Air Force Base, mil., Hi., U.S. g10 104
Hickman, Ky., U.S. f8 110
Hickman, co., Ky., U.S. f8 110
Hickman, Ne., U.S. D9 120
Hickman, co., Tn., U.S. B4 135
Hickory, co., Mo., U.S. D4 118
Hickory, N.C., U.S. B1 126
Hicksville, N.Y., U.S. E7 125
Hicksville, Oh., U.S. A1 128
Hico, Tx., U.S. D3 136
Hico, W.V., U.S. C3 141
Hidalgo, Mex. C5 78
Hidalgo, state, Mex. C5 78
Hidalgo, co., N.M., U.S. F1 124
Hidalgo, co., Tx., U.S. F3 136
Hidalgo, Tx., U.S. F3 136
Hidalgo del Parral, Mex. B3 78
Hiddenite, N.C., U.S. B1 126
Hieroglyphic Mountains, mts., Az., U.S. k8 96
Higbee, Mo., U.S. B5 118
Higganum, Ct., U.S. D5 100
Higgins Lake, l., Mi., U.S. D6 115
Higgins Millpond, res., Md., U.S. C6 113
Higginsville, Mo., U.S. B4 118
High Bridge, N.J., U.S. B3 123
High Falls Reservoir, res., Wi., U.S. C5 142
High Island, i., Mi., U.S. C5 115
Highland, Il., U.S. E4 106
Highland, In., U.S. A3 107
Highland, Ks., U.S. C8 109
Highland, Mi., U.S. o14 115
Highland, N.Y., U.S. D7 125
Highland, co., Oh., U.S. C2 128
Highland, co., Va., U.S. B3 139
Highland, Wi., U.S. E3 142
Highland Lake, l., Me., U.S. g7 112
Highland Lakes, N.J., U.S. A4 123
Highland Park, Il., U.S. A6 106
Highland Park, Mi., U.S. p15 115
Highland Park, Tx., U.S. n10 136
Highland Peak, mtn., Ca., U.S. C4 98
Highland Point, c., Fl., U.S. G5 102
Highlands, co., Fl., U.S. E5 102
Highlands, N.C., U.S. f9 126
Highlands, N.J., U.S. C5 123
Highlands, Tx., U.S. r14 136
Highland Springs, Va., U.S. C5 139
High Level, Ab., Can. F7 84
Highmore, S.D., U.S. C6 134
High Point, N.C., U.S. B2 126
High Prairie, Ab., Can. B2 84
High Ridge, Mo., U.S. g12 118
High River, Ab., Can. D4 84
Highrock Lake, l., Mb., Can. B1 86
High Rock Lake, res., N.C., U.S. B2 126
High Spire, Pa., U.S. F8 131
High Springs, Fl., U.S. C4 102
Hightstown, N.J., U.S. C3 123
Highwood, Il., U.S. A6 106
Highwood Baldy, mtn., Mt., U.S. C6 119
Highwood Mountains, mts., Mt., U.S. C6 119
Higuera de Abuya, Mex. C3 78
Higüey, Dom. Rep. B6 80
Hiiumaa, i., Est. G10 10
Hiko Range, mts., Nv., U.S. F6 121
Hilbert, Wi., U.S. D5 142
Hildale, Ut., U.S. F3 137
Hilden, N.S., Can. D6 87
Hildesheim, Ger. D11 12
Hill, co., Mt., U.S. B6 119
Hill, co., Tx., U.S. D4 136
Hillaby, Mount, mtn., Barb. C8 80
Hill City, Ks., U.S. C4 109
Hill City, S.D., U.S. D2 134
Hillcrest, Il., U.S. B4 106
Hillcrest Heights, Md., U.S. C4 113
Hillerød, Den. I5 10
Hilliard, Fl., U.S. B5 102
Hilliard, Oh., U.S. k10 128
Hill Lake, l., Ar., U.S. h10 97
Hills, Ia., U.S. C6 108
Hills, Mn., U.S. G2 116
Hillsboro, Il., U.S. D4 106
Hillsboro, Ks., U.S. D6 109
Hillsboro, Mo., U.S. C7 118
Hillsboro, N.D., U.S. B8 127
Hillsboro, N.H., U.S. D3 122
Hillsboro, Oh., U.S. C2 128
Hillsboro, Or., U.S. B4 130
Hillsboro, Tx., U.S. C4 136
Hillsboro, Wi., U.S. E3 142
Hillsboro Canal, Fl., U.S. F6 102
Hillsborough, N.B., Can. D5 87
Hillsborough, co., Fl., U.S. E4 102
Hillsborough, N.C., U.S. A3 126
Hillsborough, co., N.H., U.S. E3 122
Hillsborough Bay, b., P.E., Can. C6 87
Hillsburgh, On., Can. D4 89
Hills Creek Lake, res., Or., U.S. D4 130
Hillsdale, Mi., U.S. G6 115
Hillsdale, co., Mi., U.S. G6 115
Hillsdale, N.J., U.S. g8 123
Hillside, N.J., U.S. k8 123
Hillsville, Pa., U.S. D1 131
Hillsville, Va., U.S. D2 139
Hilo, Hi., U.S. D6 104
Hilo Bay, b., Hi., U.S. D6 104
Hilok, Russia D13 26
Hilton, N.Y., U.S. B3 125
Hilton Head Island, i., S.C., U.S. G6 133
Hilton Head Island, S.C., U.S. G6 133
Hilvan, Tur. D8 44
Himāchal Pradesh, state, India C3 40
Himalayas, mts., Asia C3 40
Himatnagar, India E2 40
Himeji, Japan D2 31
Ḥimṣ, Syria E7 44
Hinchinbrook Island, i., Austl. D4 62
Hinchinbrook Island, i., Ak., U.S. g18 95
Hinckley, Il., U.S. B5 106
Hinckley, Mn., U.S. D6 116
Hinckley, Ut., U.S. D3 137
Hinckley Reservoir, res., N.Y., U.S. B5 125
Hindman, Ky., U.S. C7 110
Hinds, co., Ms., U.S. C3 117
Hindu Kush, mts., Asia C1 40
Hindupur, India G3 40
Hines, Or., U.S. D7 130
Hinesville, Ga., U.S. E5 103
Hinganghāt, India E3 40
Hingham, Ma., U.S. B6 114
Hingham Bay, b., Ma., U.S. g12 114
Hingol, stm., Pak. E9 42
Hingoli, India F3 40
Hınıs, Tur. C9 44
Hinnøya, i., Nor. B6 10
Hinsdale, co., Co., U.S. D3 99
Hinsdale, Il., U.S. k9 106
Hinsdale, N.H., U.S. E2 122
Hinton, Ab., Can. C2 84
Hinton, Ia., U.S. B1 108
Hinton, Ok., U.S. B3 129
Hinton, W.V., U.S. D4 141
Hīrākud Reservoir, res., India E4 40
Hiram, Ga., U.S. C2 103
Hiram, Oh., U.S. A4 128
Hirara, Japan B9 34
Hirfanlı Barajı, res., Tur. C5 44
Hiriyūr, India G3 40
Hirosaki, Japan C16 28
Hiroshima, Japan E14 28
Hirson, Fr. C9 16
Hirtshals, Den. H3 10
Hisār, India D3 40
Hispaniola, i., N.A. A5 80
Hita, Japan D2 31
Hitachi, Japan D16 28
Hitchcock, co., Ne., U.S. D4 120
Hitchcock, Tx., U.S. r14 136
Hitchcock Lake, Ct., U.S. C4 100
Hitoyoshi, Japan D2 31
Hitra, i., Nor. E3 10
Hiva, Uzb. B8 42
Hiwassee, stm., Tn., U.S. D9 135
Hiwassee Lake, res., N.C., U.S. f8 126
Hjälmaren, l., Swe. G6 10
Hjelmelandsvågen, Nor. G2 10
Hjørring, Den. H3 10
Hkakabo Razi, mtn., Mya. A3 34
Hlukhiv, Ukr. D12 20
Hlusk, Bela. C10 20
Hlybokae, Bela. B9 20
Ho, Ghana E5 50
Hoa Binh, Viet. B5 34
Hoagland, In., U.S. C8 107
Hoback, stm., Wy., U.S. C2 143
Hobart, Austl. I4 62
Hobart, In., U.S. A3 107
Hobart, Ok., U.S. B2 129
Hobbs, N.M., U.S. E6 124
Hobbs Coast, Ant. D28 67
Hobe Sound, Fl., U.S. E6 102
Hoboken, N.J., U.S. k8 123
Hobyo, Som. I14 48
Ho Chi Minh City see Thanh Pho Ho Chi Minh, Viet. D5 34
Hockessin, De., U.S. A3 101
Hocking, co., Oh., U.S. C3 128
Hocking, stm., Oh., U.S. C3 128
Hockley, co., Tx., U.S. C1 136
Ḥōd, reg., Maur. C3 50
Hodeida see Al-Ḥudaydah, Yemen H4 38
Hodgeman, co., Ks., U.S. D4 109
Hodgenville, Ky., U.S. C4 110
Hodges Village Reservoir, res., Ma., U.S. B4 114
Hódmezővásárhely, Hung. F6 20
Hodna, Chott el, l., Alg. C5 48
Hodonín, Czech Rep. E4 20
Hodžejli, Uzb. B7 42
Hoeryŏng-ŭp, N. Kor. B1 31
Hof, Ger. E12 12
Höfðakaupstaður, Ice. l18 10a
Hoffman Estates, Il., U.S. h8 106
Hofors, Swe. F7 10
Hofsjökull, ice, Ice. l19 10a
Hōfu, Japan D2 31
Höganäs, Swe. H5 10
Hogansville, Ga., U.S. C2 103
Hogback Mountain, mtn., Mt., U.S. F4 119
Hoggar see Ahaggar, mts., Alg. F6 48
Hog Island, i., Fl., U.S. C3 102
Hog Island, i., Mi., U.S. C5 115
Hog Island, i., N.C., U.S. B6 126
Hog Island, i., R.I., U.S. D5 132
Hog Island, i., Va., U.S. C7 139
Hoh, stm., Wa., U.S. B1 140
Hohenwald, Tn., U.S. B4 135
Hoh Head, c., Wa., U.S. B1 140
Hohhot, China C10 28
Hohoe, Ghana E5 50
Ho-Ho-Kus, N.J., U.S. h8 123
Hoh Xil Shan, mts., China D5 28
Hoi An, Viet. C5 34
Hoima, Ug. C6 54
Hoisington, Ks., U.S. D5 109
Ḫojniki, Bela. D10 20
Hokah, Mn., U.S. G7 116
Hoke, co., N.C., U.S. B3 126
Hokes Bluff, Al., U.S. B4 94
Hokitika, N.Z. p13 63c
Hokkaidō, i., Japan C16 28
Hoktemberjan, Arm. B11 44
Hola Prystan', Ukr. F12 20
Holbrook, Az., U.S. C5 96
Holbrook, Ma., U.S. B5 114
Holcomb, Ks., U.S. E3 109
Holden, Ma., U.S. B4 114
Holden, Mo., U.S. C4 118
Holden, W.V., U.S. D2 141
Holdenville, Ok., U.S. B5 129
Holdrege, Ne., U.S. D6 120
Hole in the Mountain Peak, mtn., Nv., U.S. C6 121
Holgate, Oh., U.S. A1 128
Holguín, Cuba A4 80
Holladay, Ut., U.S. C4 137
Holland, In., U.S. H3 107
Holland, Mi., U.S. F4 115
Holland, Oh., U.S. A2 128
Holland, Tx., U.S. D4 136
Hollandale, Ms., U.S. B3 117
Hollandia see Jayapura, Indon. G11 32
Holland Island, i., Md., U.S. D5 113
Holland Point, c., Md., U.S. C4 113
Holland Straits, strt., Md., U.S. D5 113
Holley, N.Y., U.S. B2 125
Holliday, Tx., U.S. C3 136
Hollidaysburg, Pa., U.S. F5 131
Hollins, Va., U.S. C3 139
Hollis, Ok., U.S. C2 129
Hollister, Ca., U.S. D3 98
Hollister, Mo., U.S. E4 118
Holliston, Ma., U.S. B5 114
Holloman Air Force Base, mil., N.M., U.S. E3 124
Hollow Rock, Tn., U.S. A3 135
Hollowtop Mountain, mtn., Mt., U.S. E4 119
Holly, Co., U.S. C8 99
Holly, Mi., U.S. F7 115
Holly Grove, Ar., U.S. C4 97
Holly Hill, Fl., U.S. C5 102
Holly Hill, S.C., U.S. E7 133
Holly Pond, Al., U.S. A3 94
Holly Ridge, N.C., U.S. C5 126
Holly Shelter Swamp, sw., N.C., U.S. C5 126
Holly Springs, Ga., U.S. B2 103
Holly Springs, Ms., U.S. A4 117
Holly Springs, N.C., U.S. B4 126
Hollywood, Al., U.S. A4 94
Hollywood, Fl., U.S. F6 102
Hollywood, Md., U.S. D4 113
Hollywood, S.C., U.S. k11 133
Hollywood Indian Reservation, Fl., U.S. r3 102
Holmen, Wi., U.S. E2 142
Holmes, co., Fl., U.S. u16 102
Holmes, co., Ms., U.S. B3 117
Holmes, co., Oh., U.S. B4 128
Holmes, Mount, mtn., Wy., U.S. B2 143
Holmsk, Russia E16 26
Holoby, Ukr. D8 20
Holstebro, Den. H3 10
Holstein, Ia., U.S. B2 108
Holsteinsborg, Grnld. E29 82
Holston, stm., Tn., U.S. C11 135
Holston, Middle Fork, stm., Va., U.S. f10 139
Holston High Knob, mtn., Tn., U.S. C11 135
Holt, Al., U.S. B2 94
Holt, Mi., U.S. F6 115
Holt, co., Mo., U.S. A2 118
Holt, co., Ne., U.S. B7 120
Holt Lake, res., Al., U.S. B2 94
Holton, Ks., U.S. C8 109

Name — Map Ref. — Page

Holtville, Ca., U.S. F6 98
Holualoa, Hi., U.S. D6 104
Holy Cross, Mountain of the, mtn., Co., U.S. B4 99
Holyhead, Wales, U.K. D4 12
Holyoke, Co., U.S. A8 99
Holyoke, Ma., U.S. B2 114
Holyoke Range, Ma., U.S. B2 114
Homalin, Mya. B2 34
Hombori Tondo, mtn., Mali C4 50
Hombre Muerto, Salar del, pl., Arg. D4 72
Homecroft, In., U.S. m10 107
Homedale, Id., U.S. F2 105
Home Hill, Austl. D4 62
Homel', Bela. C11 20
Homeland, Ga., U.S. F4 103
Home Place, In., U.S. E5 107
Homer, Ak., U.S. D9 95
Homer, Ga., U.S. B3 103
Homer, Il., U.S. C6 106
Homer, La., U.S. B2 111
Homer, Mi., U.S. F6 115
Homer, N.Y., U.S. C4 125
Homer City, Pa., U.S. E3 131
Homerville, Ga., U.S. E4 103
Homer Youngs Peak, mtn., Mt., U.S. E3 119
Homestead, Fl., U.S. G6 102
Homestead, Pa., U.S. k14 131
Homestead National Monument of America, Ne., U.S. D9 120
Homewood, Al., U.S. g7 94
Homewood, Il., U.S. B6 106
Homewood, Oh., U.S. C1 128
Hominy, Ok., U.S. A5 129
Hominy Creek, stm., Ok., U.S. A5 129
Homme Dam, N.D., U.S. A8 127
Homochitto, stm., Ms., U.S. D2 117
Homosassa, Fl., U.S. D4 102
Homs see Al-Khums, Libya E6 14
Homs see Ḥimṣ, Syria E7 44
Honaker, Va., U.S. e10 139
Honan see Henan, prov., China E10 28
Honaunau, Hi., U.S. D6 104
Honda, Col. B5 70
Hondo, stm., N.A. B2 80
Hondo, Tx., U.S. E3 136
Hondo, Rio, stm., N.M., U.S. D4 124
Honduras, ctry., N.A. C2 80
Honduras, Gulf of, b., N.A. B2 80
Honea Path, S.C., U.S. C3 133
Hønefoss, Nor. F4 10
Honeoye Falls, N.Y., U.S. C3 125
Honesdale, Pa., U.S. C11 131
Honey Brook, Pa., U.S. F10 131
Honey Grove, Tx., U.S. C5 136
Honey Lake, l., Ca., U.S. B3 98
Honeypot Glen, Ct., U.S. C4 100
Honeyville, Ut., U.S. B3 137
Hong, Song see Red, stm., Asia B4 34
Hon Gai, Viet. B5 34
Honga River, b., Md., U.S. D5 113
Hongjiang, China F9 28
Hong Kong see Xianggang, China E3 30
Hongliuyuan, China C7 28
Hongshui, stm., China G9 28
Hongtong, China B3 30
Hongze, China C4 30
Hongze Hu, l., China E11 28
Honiara, Sol. Is. B6 62
Honjō, Japan C3 31
Honokaa, Hi., U.S. C6 104
Honolulu, co., Hi., U.S. B3 104
Honolulu, Hi., U.S. B4 104
Honolulu International Airport, Hi., U.S. g10 104
Honomu, Hi., U.S. D6 104
Honouliuli, Hi., U.S. g9 104
Honshū, i., Japan D16 28
Honuapo Bay, b., Hi., U.S. D6 104
Honuu, Russia C16 26
Hood, co., Tx., U.S. C4 136
Hood, Mount, mtn., Or., U.S. B5 130
Hood Canal, b., Wa., U.S. B2 140
Hoodoo Peak, mtn., Wa., U.S. A5 140
Hood Point, c., Austl. G2 60
Hood River, Or., U.S. B5 130
Hood River, co., Or., U.S. B5 130
Hoodsport, Wa., U.S. B2 140
Hoogeveen, Neth. D10 12
Hooker, co., Ne., U.S. C4 120
Hooker, Ok., U.S. e9 129
Hooker Creek, Austl. D5 60
Hooksett, N.H., U.S. D4 122
Hoonah, Ak., U.S. D12 95
Hoopa Valley Indian Reservation, Ca., U.S. B2 98
Hooper, Ne., U.S. C9 120
Hooper Bay, Ak., U.S. C6 95
Hooper Islands, is., Md., U.S. D5 113
Hooper Strait, strt., Md., U.S. D5 113
Hoopes Reservoir, res., De., U.S. A3 101
Hoopeston, Il., U.S. C6 106
Hoorn, Neth. D9 12
Hoosac Range, mts., U.S. A1 114
Hoosic, stm., U.S. C7 125
Hoosick Falls, N.Y., U.S. C7 125
Hoover Dam, U.S. G7 121
Hoover Reservoir, res., Oh., U.S. B3 128
Hooverson Heights, W.V., U.S. f8 141
Hopa, Tur. B9 44
Hopatcong, N.J., U.S. B3 123
Hopatcong, Lake, l., N.J., U.S. A3 123
Hope, B.C., Can. E7 85
Hope, Ar., U.S. D2 97
Hope, In., U.S. F6 107
Hope, R.I., U.S. D3 132
Hope, Point, c., Ak., U.S. B6 95
Hopedale, Il., U.S. C4 106
Hopedale, Ma., U.S. B4 114
Hope Island, i., R.I., U.S. E5 132
Hopelchén, Mex. D7 78
Hope Mills, N.C., U.S. C4 126
Hopër, stm., Russia D7 22
Hopes Advance, Cap, c., Qc., Can. f13 90
Hopetoun, Austl. G3 60
Hopetown, S. Afr. D3 56
Hope Valley, R.I., U.S. E2 132
Hopewell, Va., U.S. C5 139
Hopewell Junction, N.Y., U.S. D7 125
Hopi Indian Reservation, Az., U.S. A5 96
Hopkins, co., Ky., U.S. C2 110
Hopkins, Mn., U.S. n12 116
Hopkins, S.C., U.S. D6 133
Hopkins, co., Tx., U.S. C5 136
Hopkinsville, Ky., U.S. D2 110
Hopkinton, Ia., U.S. B6 108
Hopkinton, Ma., U.S. B4 114
Hopkinton, R.I., U.S. F1 132
Hopkinton Lake, res., N.H., U.S. D3 122
Hopwood, Pa., U.S. G2 131
Hoquiam, Wa., U.S. C2 140
Hor, Russia A2 31
Horace, N.D., U.S. C9 127
Horace Mountain, mtn., Ak., U.S. B10 95
Horasan, Tur. B10 44
Horatio, Ar., U.S. D1 97
Horicon, Wi., U.S. E5 142
Horine, Mo., U.S. C7 118
Horlick Mountains, mts., Ant. E29 67
Horlivka, Ukr. E15 20
Hormuz, Strait of, strt., Asia E7 42
Horn, c., Ice. k17 10a
Horn, Cape see Hornos, Cabo de, c., Chile I3 69
Hornavan, l., Swe. C7 10
Hornell, N.Y., U.S. C3 125
Hornersville, Mo., U.S. E7 118
Horn Island, i., Ms., U.S. E5 117
Horn Island Pass, strt., Ms., U.S. g8 117
Horn Lake, Ms., U.S. A3 117
Hornos, Cabo de (Cape Horn), c., Chile I3 69
Horodenka, Ukr. E8 20
Horodnia, Ukr. D11 20
Horodok, Ukr. E7 20
Horqin Youyi Qianqi, China B12 28
Horry, co., S.C., U.S. D10 133
Horse, stm., Ct., U.S. C6 100
Horse Cave, Ky., U.S. C4 110
Horse Creek, stm., U.S. E8 143
Horse Creek Reservoir, res., Co., U.S. C7 99
Horsehead Lake, l., N.D., U.S. B6 127
Horseheads, N.Y., U.S. C4 125
Horse Heaven Hills, Wa., U.S. C6 140
Horsens, Den. I3 10
Horse Peak, mtn., N.M., U.S. D1 124
Horseshoe Bend, Id., U.S. F2 105
Horseshoe Bend National Military Park, Al., U.S. C4 94
Horseshoe Cove, b., Fl., U.S. C3 102
Horseshoe Point, c., Fl., U.S. C3 102
Horseshoe Reservoir, res., Az., U.S. C4 96
Horsham, Austl. H3 62
Horten, Nor. G4 10
Horton, stm., N.T., Can. E15 82
Horton, Ks., U.S. C8 109
Hortonia, Lake, l., Vt., U.S. D2 138
Hortonville, Wi., U.S. D5 142
Horyn', stm., Eur. D9 20
Hosa'ina, Eth. B7 54
Hoschton, Ga., U.S. B3 103
Hosedahard, Russia A10 22
Hoshāb, Pak. E8 42
Hoshangābād, India E3 40
Hoshiārpur, India C3 40
Hospers, Ia., U.S. A2 108
Hospet, India F3 40
Hosta Butte, mtn., N.M., U.S. B1 124
Hotan, China D3 28
Hotan, stm., China A4 40
Hotazel, S. Afr. D3 56
Hotchkiss, Co., U.S. C3 99
Hot Creek Range, mts., Nv., U.S. E5 121
Hot Creek Valley, val., Nv., U.S. E5 121
Hot Spring, co., Ar., U.S. C2 97
Hot Springs, S.D., U.S. D2 134
Hot Springs, co., Wy., U.S. C4 143
Hot Springs National Park, Ar., U.S. C2 97
Hot Springs National Park, Ar., U.S. C2 97
Hot Springs Peak, mtn., Ca., U.S. B3 98
Hot Springs Peak, mtn., Nv., U.S. B4 121
Houaïlou, N. Cal. I9 62a
Houghton, Mi., U.S. A2 115
Houghton, co., Mi., U.S. B2 115
Houghton, N.Y., U.S. C2 125
Houghton Lake, Mi., U.S. D6 115
Houghton Lake, l., Mi., U.S. D6 115
Houghton Lake Heights, Mi., U.S. D6 115
Houlton, Me., U.S. B5 112
Houma, China D10 28
Houma, La., U.S. E5 111
Housatonic, stm., U.S. D3 100
House Springs, Mo., U.S. g12 118
Houston, co., Al., U.S. D4 94
Houston, De., U.S. E3 101
Houston, co., Ga., U.S. D3 103
Houston, stm., La., U.S. D2 111
Houston, co., Mn., U.S. G7 116
Houston, Mn., U.S. G7 116
Houston, Mo., U.S. D6 118
Houston, Ms., U.S. B4 117
Houston, Pa., U.S. F1 131
Houston, co., Tn., U.S. A4 135
Houston, Tx., U.S. E5 136
Houston, co., Tx., U.S. D5 136
Houston, Lake, res., Tx., U.S. r14 136
Houston Intercontinental Airport, Tx., U.S. r14 136
Houtman Abrolhos, is., Austl. F1 60
Houtzdale, Pa., U.S. E5 131
Hovd, Mong. B6 28
Hovd, stm., Mong. B6 28
Hovenweep National Monument, Ut., U.S. F6 137
Hoverla, hora, mtn., Ukr. E8 20
Hovmantorp, Swe. H6 10
Hövsgöl nuur, l., Mong. A8 28
Howard, co., Ar., U.S. C2 97
Howard, co., Ia., U.S. A5 108
Howard, co., In., U.S. C5 107
Howard, Ks., U.S. E7 109
Howard, co., Md., U.S. B4 113
Howard, co., Mo., U.S. B5 118
Howard, co., Ne., U.S. C7 120
Howard, S.D., U.S. C8 134
Howard, co., Tx., U.S. C2 136
Howard, Wi., U.S. D5 142
Howard City, Mi., U.S. E5 115
Howard Hanson Reservoir, res., Wa., U.S. B4 140
Howard Lake, Mn., U.S. E4 116
Howard Prairie Lake, res., Or., U.S. E4 130
Howards Grove-Millersville, Wi., U.S. E6 142
Howe, Cape, c., Austl. H5 62
Howell, Mi., U.S. F7 115
Howell, co., Mo., U.S. E6 118
Howells, Ne., U.S. C8 120
Howe Sound, strt., B.C., Can. E6 85
Howick, Qc., Can. D4 90
Howland, Me., U.S. C4 112
Howland Island, i., Oc. H21 64
Hoxie, Ar., U.S. A5 97
Hoxie, Ks., U.S. C3 109
Hoyerswerda, Ger. E14 12
Hoyt Lakes, Mn., U.S. C6 116
Hradec Králové, Czech Rep. D3 20
Hrodno, Bela. C7 20
Hron, stm., Slvk. E5 20
Hsilo, Tai. E5 30
Hsinchu, Tai. E5 30
Hsipaw, Mya. B3 34
Huacho, Peru F4 70
Huachuca City, Az., U.S. F5 96
Hua Hin, Thai. D3 34
Huai'an, China E11 28
Huai'an, China A3 30
Huaibin, China C4 30
Huaiji, China E3 30
Huailai, China A4 30
Huainan, China E11 28
Huairou, China A4 30
Huaiyang, China E11 28
Huajuapan de León, Mex. D5 78
Hualalai, vol., Hi., U.S. D6 104
Hualapai Indian Reservation, Az., U.S. B2 96
Hualapai Mountains, mts., Az., U.S. C2 96
Hualapai Peak, mtn., Az., U.S. B2 96
Hualien, Tai. E5 30
Huallaga, stm., Peru E4 70
Huambo, Ang. F3 54
Huanan, China A2 31
Huancavelica, Peru F4 70
Huancayo, Peru F4 70
Huang (Yellow), stm., China D11 28
Huangchuan, China E11 28
Huangho see Huang, stm., China D11 28
Huanghua, China B4 30
Huanglong, China B2 30
Huangshi, China E11 28
Huangxian, China B5 30
Huangyan, China D5 30
Huangyuan, China D8 28
Huanta, Peru A3 72
Huánuco, Peru E4 70
Huanxian, China B2 30
Huaral, Peru F4 70
Huarocondo, Peru A3 72
Huascarán, Nevado, mtn., Peru E4 70
Huasco, Chile C2 69
Huatabampo, Mex. B3 78
Huauchinango, Mex. C5 78
Huaxian, China B3 30
Huaxian, China E3 30
Huazhou, China E3 30
Hubbard, Ia., U.S. B4 108
Hubbard, co., Mn., U.S. C4 116
Hubbard, Oh., U.S. A5 128
Hubbard, Or., U.S. B4 130
Hubbard, Tx., U.S. D4 136
Hubbard Creek Lake, res., Tx., U.S. C3 136
Hubbard Lake, l., Mi., U.S. D7 115
Hubbardton, stm., Vt., U.S. D2 138
Hubbell, Mi., U.S. A2 115
Hubei, prov., China E10 28
Hubli-Dhārwār, India F3 40
Huckleberry Mountain, mtn., Or., U.S. D4 130
Huddersfield, Eng., U.K. D6 12
Hudiksvall, Swe. F7 10
Hudson, Qc., Can. D3 90
Hudson, Co., U.S. A6 99
Hudson, Fl., U.S. D4 102
Hudson, Ia., U.S. B5 108
Hudson, Il., U.S. C5 106
Hudson, Ma., U.S. B4 114
Hudson, Mi., U.S. G6 115
Hudson, N.C., U.S. B1 126
Hudson, N.H., U.S. E4 122
Hudson, co., N.J., U.S. B4 123
Hudson, N.Y., U.S. C7 125
Hudson, Oh., U.S. A4 128
Hudson, Wi., U.S. D1 142
Hudson, Wy., U.S. D4 143
Hudson, stm., U.S. E7 125
Hudson, Lake, res., Ok., U.S. A6 129
Hudson Bay, b., Can. G24 82
Hudson Falls, N.Y., U.S. B7 125
Hudson Hope, B.C., Can. A6 85
Hudson Lake, In., U.S. A4 107
Hudson Strait, strt., Can. F25 82
Hudsonville, Mi., U.S. F5 115
Hudspeth, co., Tx., U.S. o12 136
Hudžand, Taj. E8 26
Hue, Viet. C5 34
Huehuetenango, Guat. B1 80
Huelva, Spain I3 16
Huércal-Overa, Spain I6 16
Huerfano, stm., Co., U.S. D6 99
Huerfano, co., Co., U.S. D5 99
Huerfano Mountain, mtn., N.M., U.S. A2 124
Huesca, Spain F6 16
Huéscar, Spain I5 16
Huetamo de Núñez, Mex. D4 78
Hueytown, Al., U.S. g6 94
Huffakers, Nv., U.S. D2 121
Ḥufrat an-Naḥās, Sudan B4 54
Hugh Butler Lake, res., Ne., U.S. D5 120
Hughenden, Austl. E3 62
Hughes, Ar., U.S. C5 97
Hughes, co., Ok., U.S. B5 129
Hughes, co., S.D., U.S. C5 134
Hughes, North Fork, stm., W.V., U.S. B3 141
Hughes, South Fork, stm., W.V., U.S. B3 141
Hughesville, Md., U.S. C4 113
Hughesville, Pa., U.S. D8 131
Hugli, stm., India E5 40
Hugo, Co., U.S. B7 99
Hugo, Mn., U.S. m13 116
Hugo, Ok., U.S. C6 129
Hugo Lake, res., Ok., U.S. C6 129
Hugoton, Ks., U.S. E2 109
Hŭich'ŏn, N. Kor. C13 28
Huilai, China E4 30
Huili, China F8 28
Huimin, China B4 30
Huinca Renancó, Arg. E5 72
Huishui, China D2 30
Huitong, China D2 30
Huixian, China C2 30
Huixtla, Mex. D6 78
Huize, China F8 28
Huizhou, China E3 30
Hujirt, Mong. B8 28
Hulah Lake, res., Ok., U.S. A5 129
Hulett, Wy., U.S. B8 143
Hulin, China B14 28
Hull, Qc., Can. D2 90
Hull, Ia., U.S. A1 108
Hull, Ma., U.S. B6 114
Huma, China A13 28
Humaitá, Braz. E7 70
Humaitá, Para. D6 72
Humansdorp, S. Afr. E3 56
Humansville, Mo., U.S. D4 118
Humbe, Ang. B1 56
Humble, Tx., U.S. E5 136
Humboldt, Az., U.S. C3 96
Humboldt, co., Ca., U.S. B2 98
Humboldt, Ia., U.S. B3 108
Humboldt, co., Ia., U.S. B3 108
Humboldt, Ks., U.S. E8 109
Humboldt, Ne., U.S. D10 120
Humboldt, stm., Nv., U.S. C3 121
Humboldt, co., Nv., U.S. B3 121
Humboldt, Tn., U.S. B3 135
Humboldt Range, mts., Nv., U.S. C3 121
Humenné, Slvk. E6 20
Hummels Wharf, Pa., U.S. E8 131
Humphrey, Ar., U.S. C4 97
Humphrey, Ne., U.S. C8 120
Humphreys, co., Ms., U.S. B3 117
Humphreys, co., Tn., U.S. A4 135
Humphreys, Mount, mtn., Ca., U.S. D4 98
Humphreys Peak, mtn., Az., U.S. B4 96
Humpty Doo, Austl. C5 60
Hun, stm., China A5 30
Hūn, Libya F7 14
Húnaflói, b., Ice. k18 10a
Hunan, prov., China F10 28
Hunchun, China B2 31
Hundred Acre Pond, l., R.I., U.S. E3 132
Hunedoara, Rom. G7 20
Hungary, ctry., Eur. F5 20
Hŭngdŏki-dong, N. Kor. D13 28
Hungry Horse, Mt., U.S. B2 119
Hungry Horse Reservoir, res., Mt., U.S. B3 119
Hunjiang, China C13 28
Hunsberge, mts., Nmb. D2 56
Hunt, stm., R.I., U.S. D4 132
Hunt, co., Tx., U.S. C4 136
Hunterdon, co., N.J., U.S. B3 123
Hunter Island, i., Austl. I3 62
Hunter Island, i., B.C., Can. D3 85
Huntertown, In., U.S. B7 107
Huntingburg, In., U.S. H4 107
Huntingdon, Qc., Can. D3 90
Huntingdon, Pa., U.S. F6 131
Huntingdon, co., Pa., U.S. F5 131
Huntingdon, Tn., U.S. A3 135
Hunting Island, i., S.C., U.S. G7 133
Huntington, Ar., U.S. B1 97
Huntington, In., U.S. C7 107
Huntington, co., In., U.S. C6 107
Huntington, N.Y., U.S. E7 125
Huntington, Tx., U.S. D5 136
Huntington, Ut., U.S. D5 137
Huntington, W.V., U.S. C2 141
Huntington Beach, Ca., U.S. F4 98
Huntington Lake, res., In., U.S. C7 107
Huntington Woods, Mi., U.S. p15 115
Huntingtown, Md., U.S. C4 113
Huntland, Tn., U.S. B5 135
Huntley, Il., U.S. A5 106
Hunt Mountain, mtn., Wy., U.S. B5 143
Huntsville, On., Can. B5 89
Huntsville, Al., U.S. A3 94
Huntsville, Ar., U.S. A2 97
Huntsville, Mo., U.S. B5 118
Huntsville, Tn., U.S. C9 135
Huntsville, Tx., U.S. D5 136
Hunucmá, Mex. C7 78
Hunyuan, China D10 28
Huon Gulf, b., Pap. N. Gui. H12 32
Huoxian, China B3 30
Hurd, Cape, c., On., Can. B3 89
Hurghada, Egypt E11 48
Hurley, Ms., U.S. E5 117
Hurley, N.M., U.S. E1 124
Hurley, N.Y., U.S. D6 125
Hurley, Wi., U.S. B3 142
Hurlock, Md., U.S. C6 113
Huron, stm., Mi., U.S. p14 115
Huron, co., Mi., U.S. E7 115
Huron, Oh., U.S. A3 128
Huron, co., Oh., U.S. A3 128
Huron, S.D., U.S. C7 134
Huron, Lake, l., N.A. C11 92
Huron Mountains, Mi., U.S. B3 115
Hurricane, Ut., U.S. F2 137
Hurricane, W.V., U.S. C2 141
Hurst, Il., U.S. F4 106
Hurt, Va., U.S. C3 139
Hurtsboro, Al., U.S. C4 94
Húsavík, Ice. k20 10a
Huşi, Rom. F10 20
Hustisford, Wi., U.S. E5 142
Husum, Ger. C11 12
Hutag, Mong. B8 28
Hutchins, Tx., U.S. n10 136
Hutchinson, Ks., U.S. D6 109
Hutchinson, Mn., U.S. F4 116
Hutchinson, co., S.D., U.S. D8 134
Hutchinson, co., Tx., U.S. B2 136

Name	Map Ref.	Page
Hutchinson Island, i., Fl., U.S.	E6	102
Hutchinson Island, i., S.C., U.S.	k11	133
Hutch Mountain, mtn., Az., U.S.	C4	96
Huttig, Ar., U.S.	D3	97
Huwei, Tai.	E5	30
Huxian, China	C2	30
Huxley, Ia., U.S.	C4	108
Hūzgān, Iran	G13	44
Huzhou, China	E12	28
Hužir, Russia	A9	28
Hvannadalshnúkur, mtn., Ice.	m20	10a
Hwange, Zimb.	B4	56
Hwang Ho see Huang, stm., China	D11	28
Hyannis, Ma., U.S.	C7	114
Hyannis Port, Ma., U.S.	C7	114
Hyargas nuur, l., Mong.	B6	28
Hyattsville, Md., U.S.	C4	113
Hybla Valley, Va., U.S.	g12	139
Hyco, stm., Va., U.S.	D3	139
Hyco Lake, res., N.C., U.S.	A3	126
Hydaburg, Ak., U.S.	D13	95
Hyde, co., N.C., U.S.	B6	126
Hyde, Pa., U.S.	D5	131
Hyde, co., S.D., U.S.	C6	134
Hyden, Austl.	G2	60
Hyde Park, N.Y., U.S.	D7	125
Hyde Park, Ut., U.S.	B4	137
Hyder, Ak., U.S.	D13	95
Hyderābād, India	F3	40
Hyderābād, Pak.	E9	42
Hydeville, Vt., U.S.	D2	138
Hydra see Ídhra, i., Grc.	F9	18
Hydro, Ok., U.S.	B3	129
Hyères, Fr.	F10	16
Hyesan, N. Kor.	C13	28
Hymera, In., U.S.	F3	107
Hyndman, Pa., U.S.	G4	131
Hyndman Peak, mtn., Id., U.S.	F4	105
Hyrum, Ut., U.S.	B4	137
Hythe, Ab., Can.	B1	84
Hyvinkää, Fin.	F11	10

I

Name	Map Ref.	Page
Iaçu, Braz.	D3	74
Ialomiţa, stm., Rom.	G9	20
Iamonia, Lake, l., Fl., U.S.	B2	102
Iaşi, Rom.	F9	20
Iatt, Lake, res., La., U.S.	C3	111
Iba, Phil.	C7	34
Ibadan, Nig.	E5	50
Ibagué, Col.	C4	70
Ibaiti, Braz.	F1	74
Ibapah Peak, mtn., Ut., U.S.	D2	137
Ibarra, Ec.	C4	70
Ibembo, D.R.C.	C4	54
Iberia, co., La., U.S.	E4	111
Iberia, Mo., U.S.	C5	118
Iberian Mountains see Ibérico, Sistema, mts., Spain	G5	16
Ibérico, Sistema, mts., Spain	G5	16
Iberville, Qc., Can.	D4	90
Iberville, co., La., U.S.	D4	111
Iberville, Mont d' (Mount Caubvick), mtn., Can.	g14	90
Ibiá, Braz.	E2	74
Ibicaraí, Braz.	D4	74
Ibiza see Eivissa, i., Spain	H7	16
Ibonma, Indon.	D8	36
Ibotirama, Braz.	D3	74
'Ibrī, Oman	F7	42
Ica, Peru	F4	70
Içá (Putumayo), stm., S.A.	D6	70
Içana, Braz.	C6	70
Içana (Isana), stm., S.A.	C6	70
Ice Harbor Dam, Wa., U.S.	C7	140
İçel, Tur.	D6	44
Iceland, ctry., Eur.	l18	10a
Iceland Basin	B25	144
Ichaikaronji, India	F2	40
Ichchāpuram, India	F4	40
Ichnia, Ukr.	D12	20
Icicle Creek, stm., Wa., U.S.	B5	140
Ičinskaja Sopka, vulkan, vol., Russia	D17	26
Icó, Braz.	C4	74
Icy Cape, c., Ak., U.S.	A7	95
Icy Strait, strt., Ak., U.S.	k22	95
Ida, co., Ia., U.S.	B2	108
Ida, Mi., U.S.	G7	115
Ida, Lake, l., Mn., U.S.	D3	116
Idabel, Ok., U.S.	D7	129
Ida Grove, Ia., U.S.	B2	108
Idah, Nig.	E6	50
Idaho, co., Id., U.S.	D3	105
Idaho, state, U.S.	E3	105
Idaho Falls, Id., U.S.	F6	105
Idaho Springs, Co., U.S.	B5	99
Idalou, Tx., U.S.	C2	136
Idamay, W.V., U.S.	k10	141
Idaville, In., U.S.	C4	107
Ider, Al., U.S.	A4	94
Ídhi Óros, mtn., Grc.	G10	18
Ídhra, i., Grc.	F9	18
İdil, Tur.	D9	44
Idiofa, D.R.C.	D3	54
Idlib, state, Syria	E7	44
Idoûkâl-en-Taghès, mtn., Niger	C6	50
Idutywa, S. Afr.	E4	56
Ifakara, Tan.	E7	54
Ife, Nig.	E5	50
Iferouâne, Niger	C6	50
Ifôghas, Adrar des, mts., Afr.	C5	50
Iganga, Ug.	C6	54
Igarapé-Açu, Braz.	B2	74
Igarka, Russia	C10	26
Igboho, Nig.	E5	50
Iğdır, Tur.	C11	44
Iglesias, Italy	E2	18
Ignacio, Co., U.S.	D3	99
Iguaçu, stm., S.A.	D7	72
Iguala, Mex.	D5	78
Igualada, Spain	G7	16
Iguatu, Braz.	C4	74
Iguazú see Iguaçu, stm., S.A.	D7	72
Iguéla, Gabon	D1	54
Iguîdi, 'Erg, dunes, Afr.	A3	50
Iharaña, Madag.	A8	56
Iheya-shima, i., Japan	g6	31a
Ihosy, Madag.	C8	56
Iisalmi, Fin.	E12	10
Iizuka, Japan	D2	31
Ijâfene, des., Maur.	B3	50
Ijebu-Ode, Nig.	E5	50
IJsselmeer, l., Neth.	D9	12
Ijuí, Braz.	D7	72
Ika, Russia	D12	26
Ikaría, i., Grc.	F11	18
Ikeja, Nig.	E5	50
Ikela, D.R.C.	D4	54
Ikerre, Nig.	E6	50
Ikom, Nig.	E6	50
Ikot-Ekpene, Nig.	E6	50
Ila, Nig.	E5	50
Ilagan, Phil.	C8	34
Īlām, Iran	D5	42
Ilan, Tai.	E5	30
Ilaro, Nig.	E5	50
Iława, Pol.	C5	20
Ilbenge, Russia	C14	26
Île-à-la-Crosse, Lac, l., Sk., Can.	B2	91
Ilebo, D.R.C.	D4	54
Île-de-France, hist. reg., Fr.	C8	16
Île-Perrot, Qc., Can.	q19	90
Ilesha, Nig.	E5	50
Ilha de Moçambique, Moz.	B7	56
Ilhéus, Braz.	D4	74
Iliamna Lake, l., Ak., U.S.	D8	95
Iliamna Volcano, vol., Ak., U.S.	C9	95
Iligan, Phil.	E8	34
Iligan Bay, b., Phil.	E8	34
Ilion, N.Y., U.S.	B5	125
Ilio Point, c., Hi., U.S.	B4	104
Ilizi, Alg.	E6	48
Il'jinskij, Russia	E16	26
Illampu, Nevado, mtn., Bol.	G6	70
Illana Bay, b., Phil.	E8	34
Illapel, Chile	D2	69
Illéla, Niger	D6	50
Illichivs'k, Ukr.	F11	20
Illimani, Nevado, mtn., Bol.	B4	72
Illinois, stm., Il., U.S.	B5	106
Illinois, stm., Or., U.S.	E3	130
Illinois, stm., U.S.	A7	129
Illinois, state, U.S.	C4	106
Illinois Peak, mtn., Id., U.S.	B3	105
Illiopolis, Il., U.S.	D4	106
Illmo, Mo., U.S.	D8	118
Il'men', ozero, l., Russia	C5	22
Ilo, Peru	G5	70
Iloilo, Phil.	D8	34
Ilorin, Nig.	E5	50
Ilovlja, Russia	F15	8
Ilwaco, Wa., U.S.	C1	140
Ilwaki, Indon.	E7	36
Imabari, Japan	D2	31
Imandra, ozero, l., Russia	C15	10
Imatra, Fin.	F13	10
Imboden, Ar., U.S.	A4	97
Īmī, Eth.	B8	54
İmişli, Azer.	C13	44
Imlay, Nv., U.S.	C3	121
Imlay City, Mi., U.S.	E7	115
Immokalee, Fl., U.S.	F5	102
Imnaha, stm., Or., U.S.	B10	130
Imola, Italy	B3	18
Imperatriz, Braz.	C2	74
Imperia, Italy	C2	18
Imperial, co., Ca., U.S.	F6	98
Imperial, Ca., U.S.	F6	98
Imperial, Mo., U.S.	C7	118
Imperial, Ne., U.S.	D4	120
Imperial, Pa., U.S.	k13	131
Imperial Beach, Ca., U.S.	o15	98
Imperial Dam, U.S.	E1	96
Imperial Reservoir, res., U.S.	E1	96
Imperial Valley, val., Ca., U.S.	F6	98
Impfondo, Congo	C3	54
Imphāl, India	E6	40
I-n-Amenas, Alg.	E6	48
Inanwatan, Indon.	D8	36
Inari, Fin.	B12	10
Inarijärvi, l., Fin.	B12	10
In Belbel, Alg.	F4	14
Inca, Spain	H8	16
Inca de Oro, Chile	C3	69
İnce Burun, c., Tur.	A6	44
Inch'ŏn, S. Kor.	D13	28
Incline Village, Nv., U.S.	D2	121
Indé, Mex.	B3	78
Independence, co., Ar., U.S.	B4	97
Independence, Ia., U.S.	B6	108
Independence, Ks., U.S.	E8	109
Independence, Ky., U.S.	B5	110
Independence, La., U.S.	D5	111
Independence, Mo., U.S.	B3	118
Independence, stm., N.Y., U.S.	B5	125
Independence, Or., U.S.	C3	130
Independence, Va., U.S.	D1	139
Independence, Wi., U.S.	D2	142
Independence Mountains, mts., Nv., U.S.	C5	121
Independence National Historical Park, Pa., U.S.	p21	131
Independence Rock, mtn., Wy., U.S.	D5	143
Inderborskij, Kaz.	E7	26
India, ctry., Asia	E3	40
Indian, stm., On., Can.	B7	89
Indian, stm., De., U.S.	F4	101
Indian, stm., Mi., U.S.	B4	115
Indian, stm., N.Y., U.S.	A5	125
Indiana, Pa., U.S.	E3	131
Indiana, co., Pa., U.S.	E3	131
Indiana, state, U.S.	E5	107
Indiana Dunes National Lakeshore, In., U.S.	A3	107
Indianapolis, In., U.S.	E5	107
Indian Bay, b., Fl., U.S.	D4	102
Indian Cedar Swamp, sw., R.I., U.S.	F2	132
Indian Creek, stm., Oh., U.S.	C1	128
Indian Creek, stm., S.D., U.S.	B2	134
Indian Creek, stm., Tn., U.S.	B3	135
Indian Creek, stm., W.V., U.S.	D4	141
Indian Creek, stm., W.V., U.S.	k9	141
Indian Head, Md., U.S.	C3	113
Indian Island, i., N.C., U.S.	B6	126
Indian Lake, l., Mi., U.S.	C4	115
Indian Lake, l., N.Y., U.S.	B6	125
Indian Lake, l., Oh., U.S.	B2	128
Indian Lake, l., R.I., U.S.	F4	132
Indian Neck, Ct., U.S.	D4	100
Indian Ocean	J11	64
Indianola, Ia., U.S.	C4	108
Indianola, Ms., U.S.	B3	117
Indianola, Ne., U.S.	D5	120
Indian Peak, mtn., Ut., U.S.	E2	137
Indian Peak, mtn., Wy., U.S.	B3	143
Indian Prairie Canal, Fl., U.S.	E5	102
Indian River, b., Fl., U.S.	D6	102
Indian River, co., Fl., U.S.	E6	102
Indian River Bay, b., De., U.S.	F5	101
Indian Rock, mtn., Wa., U.S.	D5	140
Indian Rocks Beach, Fl., U.S.	p10	102
Indian Springs, Nv., U.S.	G6	121
Indian Stream, stm., N.H., U.S.	f7	122
Indiantown, Fl., U.S.	E6	102
Indian Trail, N.C., U.S.	B2	126
Indiga, Russia	A8	22
Indigirka, stm., Russia	C16	26
Indio, Ca., U.S.	F5	98
Indochina, reg., Asia	C4	34
Indonesia, ctry., Asia	D4	36
Indore, India	E3	40
Indramayu, Indon.	E3	36
Indrāvati, stm., India	F4	40
Indus, stm., Asia	D1	40
İnegöl, Tur.	B3	44
Infiernillo, Presa del, res., Mex.	D4	78
Ingal, Niger	C6	50
Ingalls, In., U.S.	E6	107
Ingalls Park, Il., U.S.	B5	106
Ingende, D.R.C.	D3	54
Ingersoll, On., Can.	D4	89
Ingham, Austl.	D4	62
Ingham, co., Mi., U.S.	F6	115
Ingleside, Tx., U.S.	F4	136
Inglewood, Ca., U.S.	n12	98
Ingolstadt, Ger.	F12	12
Ingraham, Lake, l., Fl., U.S.	G5	102
Ingrāj Bāzār, India	E5	40
Ingram, Pa., U.S.	k13	131
Ingrid Christensen Coast, Ant.	D12	67
In Guezzam, Alg.	G6	48
Ingušetija, state, Russia	E6	26
Ingushetia see Ingušetija, state, Russia	E6	26
Inhaca, Ilha da, i., Moz.	D5	56
Inhambane, Moz.	C6	56
Inhambupe, Braz.	F12	70
Inhaminga, Moz.	B6	56
Inharrime, Moz.	C6	56
Inhassoro, Moz.	C6	56
Inhulets', Ukr.	F12	20
Inhumas, Braz.	E2	74
Inírida, stm., Col.	C6	70
Inkerman, N.B., Can.	B5	87
Inkom, Id., U.S.	G6	105
Inkster, Mi., U.S.	p15	115
Inland Sea see Seto-naikai, Japan	E14	28
Inman, Ks., U.S.	D6	109
Inman, S.C., U.S.	A3	133
Inn, stm., Eur.	G12	12
Inner Channel, strt., Belize	B2	80
Inner Hebrides, is., Scot., U.K.	B3	12
Inner Mongolia see Nei Monggol Zizhiqu, prov., China	C10	28
Innisfail, Austl.	D4	62
Innisfail, Ab., Can.	C4	84
Innsbruck, Aus.	G12	12
Inola, Ok., U.S.	A6	129
Inongo, D.R.C.	D3	54
Inowrocław, Pol.	C5	20
In Salah, Alg.	E5	48
Inscription House Ruin, hist., Az., U.S.	A5	96
Institute, W.V., U.S.	m12	141
Inta, Russia	C8	26
Interlachen, Fl., U.S.	C5	102
International Falls, Mn., U.S.	B5	116
Inthanon, Doi, mtn., Thai.	C3	34
Intracoastal Waterway, U.S.	E4	111
Inukjuak, Qc., Can.	g11	90
Invercargill, N.Z.	q12	63c
Inverell, Austl.	F5	62
Inver Grove Heights, Mn., U.S.	n12	116
Invermere, B.C., Can.	D9	85
Inverness, Scot., U.K.	B4	12
Inverness, Ca., U.S.	C2	98
Inverness, Fl., U.S.	D4	102
Inverness, Ms., U.S.	B3	117
Inverway, Austl.	D4	60
Investigator Strait, strt., Austl.	H2	62
Invisible Mountain, mtn., Id., U.S.	F5	105
Inwood, Ia., U.S.	A1	108
Inwood, N.Y., U.S.	k13	125
Inwood, W.V., U.S.	B6	141
Inyangani, mtn., Zimb.	B5	56
Inyan Kara Creek, stm., Wy., U.S.	B8	143
Inyan Kara Mountain, mtn., Wy., U.S.	B8	143
Inyo, co., Ca., U.S.	D5	98
Inyo, Mount, mtn., Ca., U.S.	D5	98
Inyo Mountains, mts., Ca., U.S.	D4	98
Ioánnina, Grc.	E8	18
Iola, Ks., U.S.	E8	109
Iola, Wi., U.S.	D4	142
Iona, Id., U.S.	F7	105
Ione, Ca., U.S.	C3	98
Iongo, Ang.	E3	54
Ionia, Mi., U.S.	F5	115
Ionia, co., Mi., U.S.	F5	115
Ionian Islands see Iónioi Nísoi, is., Grc.	E7	18
Ionian Sea, Eur.	E7	18
Iónioi Nísoi (Ionian Islands), is., Grc.	E7	18
Iony, ostrov, i., Russia	D16	26
Íos, i., Grc.	F10	18
Iosco, co., Mi., U.S.	D7	115
Iota, La., U.S.	D3	111
Iowa, stm., Ia., U.S.	C6	108
Iowa, co., Ia., U.S.	C5	108
Iowa, La., U.S.	D2	111
Iowa, co., Wi., U.S.	E3	142
Iowa, state, U.S.	C4	108
Iowa, West Branch, stm., Ia., U.S.	B4	108
Iowa City, Ia., U.S.	C6	108
Iowa Falls, Ia., U.S.	B4	108
Iowa Indian Reservation, U.S.	C8	109
Iowa Lake, l., U.S.	A3	108
Iowa Park, Tx., U.S.	C3	136
Ipameri, Braz.	E2	74
Ipatinga, Braz.	E3	74
Ipatovo, Russia	A4	42
Ipeiros, hist. reg., Grc.	E8	18
Iphigenia Bay, b., Ak., U.S.	n22	95
Ipiales, Col.	C4	70
Ipiaú, Braz.	D4	74
Ipoh, Malay.	C2	36
Iporã, Braz.	E1	74
Ippy, C.A.R.	B4	54
Ipswich, Austl.	F5	62
Ipswich, Eng., U.K.	D7	12
Ipswich, stm., Ma., U.S.	A5	114
Ipswich, Ma., U.S.	A6	114
Ipswich, S.D., U.S.	B6	134
Ipu, Braz.	B3	74
Iquique, Chile	B2	69
Iquitos, Peru	D5	70
Iraan, Tx., U.S.	D2	136
Iráklion, Grc.	G10	18
Iran, ctry., Asia	D6	42
Iran Mountains, mts., Asia	C5	36
Īrānshahr, Iran	E8	42
Irapuato, Mex.	C4	78
Iraq, ctry., Asia	D4	42
Irati, Braz.	D7	72
Irazú, Volcán, vol., C.R.	C3	80
Irbid, Jord.	D3	42
Irbil, Iraq	C4	42
Irbit, Russia	C11	22
Irecê, Braz.	D3	74
Iredell, co., N.C., U.S.	B2	126
Ireland, ctry., Eur.	D2	12
Irgiz, Kaz.	E8	26
Irigui, reg., Afr.	C3	50
Iriklinskij, Russia	D10	22
Iringa, Tan.	E7	54
Iriomote-jima, i., Japan	B8	34
Irion, co., Tx., U.S.	D2	136
Iriri, stm., Braz.	D9	70
Irish, Mount, mtn., Nv., U.S.	F6	121
Irish Sea, Eur.	D4	12
Irkutsk, Russia	D12	26
Irminger Basin	C26	144
Irmo, S.C., U.S.	C5	133
Iroise, b., Fr.	C4	16
Iron, co., Mi., U.S.	B2	115
Iron, co., Mo., U.S.	D7	118
Iron, co., Ut., U.S.	F2	137
Iron, co., Wi., U.S.	B3	142
Irondale, Al., U.S.	f7	94
Irondequoit, N.Y., U.S.	B3	125
Iron Gate, Eur.	G7	20
Iron Gate Reservoir, res., Ca., U.S.	B2	98
Iron Knob, Austl.	G2	62
Iron Mountain, mtn., Az., U.S.	D4	96
Iron Mountain, Mi., U.S.	C2	115
Iron Mountains, mts., U.S.	D1	139
Iron Ridge, Wi., U.S.	E5	142
Iron River, Mi., U.S.	B2	115
Iron River, Wi., U.S.	B2	142
Ironton, Mo., U.S.	D7	118
Ironton, Oh., U.S.	D3	128
Ironwood, Mi., U.S.	n11	115
Iroquois, On., Can.	C9	89
Iroquois, co., Il., U.S.	C6	106
Iroquois, stm., U.S.	C6	106
Iroquois, Lake, l., Vt., U.S.	B2	138
Iroquois Falls, On., Can.	o19	89
Irosin, Phil.	D8	34
Irpin', Ukr.	D11	20
Irrawaddy see Ayeyarwady, stm., Mya.	C3	34
Irricana, Ab., Can.	D4	84
Irrigon, Or., U.S.	B7	130
Irtyš see Irtysh, stm., Asia	D8	26
Irtysh, stm., Asia	D8	26
Irtyshsk, Kaz.	D9	26
Irtysj see Irtysh, stm., Asia	D8	26
Irumu, D.R.C.	C5	54
Irún, Spain	F6	16
Iruña see Pamplona, Spain	F6	16
Irvine, Ca., U.S.	n13	98
Irvine, Ky., U.S.	C6	110
Irving, Tx., U.S.	n10	136
Irvington, Al., U.S.	E1	94
Irvington, Il., U.S.	E4	106
Irvington, Ky., U.S.	C3	110
Irvington, N.J., U.S.	k8	123
Irvington, N.Y., U.S.	g13	125
Irwin, co., Ga., U.S.	E3	103
Irwin, Pa., U.S.	F2	131
Irwinton, Ga., U.S.	D3	103
Isa, Nig.	D6	50
Isabel, Mount, mtn., Wy., U.S.	D2	143
Isabela, Isla, i., Ec.	D1	70
Isabella, co., Mi., U.S.	E6	115
Isabella Indian Reservation, Mi., U.S.	E6	115
Isabella Lake, l., Mn., U.S.	C7	116
Ísafjarðardjúp, b., Ice.	k17	10a
Ísafjörður, Ice.	k17	10a
Isana (Içana), stm., S.A.	C5	70
Isanga, D.R.C.	D4	54
Isangel, Vanuatu	k9	62a
Isanti, Mn., U.S.	E5	116
Isanti, co., Mn., U.S.	E5	116
Isar, stm., Eur.	F13	12
Ischia, Isola d', i., Italy	D4	18
Ise, Japan	D3	31
Isernia, Italy	D5	18
Iset', stm., Russia	D8	26
Iseyin, Nig.	E5	50
Isfahan see Eşfahān, Iran	D6	42
Ishigaki, Japan	B8	34
Ishikari, stm., Japan	B4	31
Ishikawa, Japan	A9	34
Ishinomaki, Japan	D16	28
Ishpeming, Mi., U.S.	B3	115
Išim, stm., Asia	D9	26
Išim, Russia	D8	26
Isinglass, stm., N.H., U.S.	D4	122
Isiolo, Kenya	C7	54
Isiro, D.R.C.	C5	54
Iskăr, stm., Blg.	C10	18
İskenderun, Tur.	D7	44
İskenderun Körfezi, b., Tur.	D6	44
İskilip, Tur.	B6	44
Islāmābād, Pak.	D10	42
Islamorada, Fl., U.S.	H6	102
Islamorada, Fl., U.S.	H6	102
Island, co., Wa., U.S.	A3	140
Island Beach, N.J., U.S.	D4	123
Island City, Or., U.S.	B8	130
Island Falls, Me., U.S.	B4	112
Island Lake, l., Mb., Can.	C4	86
Island Park, R.I., U.S.	E6	132
Island Park Reservoir, res., Id., U.S.	E7	105
Island Pond, l., N.H., U.S.	E4	122
Island Pond, Vt., U.S.	B5	138
Islands, Bay of, b., N.L., Can.	D2	88

Name — Map Ref. — Page

Isla Vista, Ca., U.S. E4 98
Islay, i., Scot., U.K. C3 12
Isle-aux-Morts, N.L., Can. E2 88
Isle of Man, dep., Eur. C4 12
Isle of Palms, S.C., U.S. k12 133
Isle of Wight, co., Va., U.S. D6 139
Isle of Wight Bay, b., Md., U.S. D7 113
Isle Royale National Park, Mi., U.S. h9 115
Islesboro Island, i., Me., U.S. D4 112
Isleta, N.M., U.S. C3 124
Isleta Indian Reservation, N.M., U.S. C3 124
Islington, Ma., U.S. h11 114
Ismailia, Egypt D11 48
Ismail Samani, pik (Kommunizma, pik), mtn., Taj. F9 26
İsmayıllı, Azer. B13 44
Isoka, Zam. A5 56
Isola, Ms., U.S. B3 117
Isparta, Tur. D4 44
İspir, Tur. B9 44
Israel, ctry., Asia D2 42
Israel, stm., N.H., U.S. B3 122
Issaquah, Wa., U.S. B3 140
Issaquena, co., Ms., U.S. C2 117
Issia, C. Iv. E3 50
Issoire, Fr. E8 16
Issoudun, Fr. D8 16
Issyk-Kul', Kyrg. E9 26
Issyk-Kul', ozero, l., Kyrg. E9 26
İstanbul, Tur. B3 44
İstanbul Boğazı (Bosporus), strt., Tur. B3 44
Isto, Mount, mtn., Ak., U.S. B11 95
Istokpoga, Lake, l., Fl., U.S. E5 102
Itabaiana, Braz. D4 74
Itabaiana, Braz. C4 74
Itaberaba, Braz. D3 74
Itaberaí, Braz. E2 74
Itabira, Braz. E3 74
Itabuna, Braz. D4 74
Itacoatiara, Braz. D8 70
Itagüí, Col. B4 70
Itaipu Reservoir, res., S.A. C7 72
Itaituba, Braz. D8 70
Itajaí, Braz. D8 72
Itajubá, Braz. F2 74
Itajuípe, Braz. D4 74
Italy, ctry., Eur. C4 18
Italy, Tx., U.S. C4 136
Itamaraju, Braz. E4 74
Itambé, Braz. E3 74
Itānagar, India D6 40
Itaobim, Braz. E3 74
Itapecuru-Mirim, Braz. B3 74
Itaperuna, Braz. F3 74
Itapetinga, Braz. E3 74
Itapetininga, Braz. F2 74
Itapipoca, Braz. B4 74
Itapiranga, Braz. D7 72
Itaporanga, Braz. C4 74
Itaquari, Braz. F3 74
Itaqui, Braz. D6 72
Itārsi, India E3 40
Itasca, Il., U.S. k8 106
Itasca, co., Mn., U.S. C5 116
Itasca, Tx., U.S. C4 136
Itasca, Lake, l., Mn., U.S. C3 116
Itaúna, Braz. F3 74
Itawamba, co., Ms., U.S. A5 117
Itenes see Guaporé, stm., S.A. F7 70
Iténez see Guaporé, stm., S.A. F7 70
Ithaca see Itháki, i., Grc. E8 18
Ithaca, Mi., U.S. E6 115
Ithaca, N.Y., U.S. C4 125
Itháki, i., Grc. E8 18
Itimbiri, stm., D.R.C. C4 54
Itoigawa, Japan C3 31
Itoko, D.R.C. D4 54
Itta Bena, Ms., U.S. B3 117
Ituango, Col. D4 80
Ituberá, Braz. D4 74
Ituiutaba, Braz. E2 74
Itumbiara, Braz. E2 74
Iturama, Braz. E1 74
Iturup, ostrov, i., Russia E16 26
Ituverava, Braz. F2 74
Itzehoe, Ger. D11 12
Iuka, Ms., U.S. A5 117
Iul'tin, Russia C20 26
Iva, S.C., U.S. C2 133
Ivanava, Bela. C8 20
Ivangorod, Russia G13 10
Ivanhoe, Mn., U.S. F2 116
Ivankov, Ukr. D10 20
Ivano-Frankivs'k, Ukr. E8 20
Ivanovo, Russia D6 26
Ivdel', Russia C8 26
Ivigtut, Grnld. F30 82
Ivins, Ut., U.S. F2 137
Ivohibe, Madag. C8 56
Ivory Coast see Cote d'Ivoire, ctry., Afr. E3 50
Ivoryton, Ct., U.S. D6 100
Ivrea, Italy B1 18
Iwaki, Japan D16 28
Iwo, Nig. E5 50
Ixmiquilpan, Mex. C5 78
Ixtapa, Mex. D4 78
Ixtepec, Mex. D5 78
Izabal, Lago de, l., Guat. B2 80
Izamal, Mex. C7 78
Izard, co., Ar., U.S. A4 97
Izberbaš, Russia A12 44
Iževsk, Russia D7 26
Iziaslav, Ukr. D9 20
Izium, Ukr. E14 20
Ižma, stm., Russia A9 22
Izmaïl, Ukr. G10 20
İzmir, Tur. C2 44
İzmir Körfezi, b., Tur. C2 44
İzmit, Tur. B3 44
İzmit Körfezi, b., Tur. B3 44
İznik, Tur. B3 44
İznik Gölü, l., Tur. B3 44
Izucar de Matamoros, Mex. D5 78
Izu-shotō, is., Japan E15 28
Izu Trench F17 64

J

Jabal, Baḥr al- (Mountain Nile), stm., Sudan I11 48
Jabalpur, India E3 40
Jabiru, Austl. C5 60
Jablah, Syria E6 44
Jablonec nad Nisou, Czech Rep. D3 20
Jablonovyj hrebet, mts., Russia D13 26
Jaboatão, Braz. C4 74
Jaboticabal, Braz. F2 74
Jacareí, Braz. F2 74
Jacarezinho, Braz. F2 74
Jaciara, Braz. B7 72
Jacinto City, Tx., U.S. r14 136
Jack, co., Tx., U.S. C3 136
Jackfish Lake, l., Sk., Can. D1 91
Jackman, Me., U.S. C2 112
Jackman Station, Me., U.S. C2 112
Jack Mountain, mtn., Mt., U.S. D4 119
Jack Mountain, mtn., Wa., U.S. A5 140
Jackpot, Nv., U.S. B7 121
Jacksboro, Tn., U.S. C9 135
Jacksboro, Tx., U.S. C3 136
Jacks Mountain, mtn., Pa., U.S. E6 131
Jackson, Al., U.S. D2 94
Jackson, co., Al., U.S. A3 94
Jackson, co., Ar., U.S. B4 97
Jackson, Ca., U.S. C3 98
Jackson, co., Co., U.S. A4 99
Jackson, co., Fl., U.S. B1 102
Jackson, Ga., U.S. C3 103
Jackson, co., Ga., U.S. B3 103
Jackson, co., Ia., U.S. B7 108
Jackson, co., Il., U.S. F4 106
Jackson, co., In., U.S. G5 107
Jackson, co., Ks., U.S. C8 109
Jackson, Ky., U.S. C6 110
Jackson, co., Ky., U.S. C5 110
Jackson, La., U.S. D4 111
Jackson, co., La., U.S. B3 111
Jackson, Mi., U.S. F6 115
Jackson, co., Mi., U.S. F6 115
Jackson, co., Mn., U.S. G3 116
Jackson, Mn., U.S. G4 116
Jackson, Mo., U.S. D8 118
Jackson, co., Mo., U.S. B3 118
Jackson, Ms., U.S. C3 117
Jackson, co., Ms., U.S. E5 117
Jackson, co., N.C., U.S. f9 126
Jackson, Oh., U.S. C3 128
Jackson, co., Oh., U.S. C3 128
Jackson, co., Ok., U.S. C2 129
Jackson, co., Or., U.S. E4 130
Jackson, S.C., U.S. E4 133
Jackson, co., S.D., U.S. D4 134
Jackson, Tn., U.S. B3 135
Jackson, co., Tn., U.S. C8 135
Jackson, co., Tx., U.S. E4 136
Jackson, stm., Va., U.S. C3 139
Jackson, Wi., U.S. E5 142
Jackson, co., Wi., U.S. D3 142
Jackson, co., W.V., U.S. C3 141
Jackson, Wy., U.S. C2 143
Jackson, Lake, l., Fl., U.S. B2 102
Jackson, Lake, l., Fl., U.S. E5 102
Jackson, Mount, mtn., Ant. D34 67
Jackson, Mount, mtn., N.H., U.S. B4 122
Jackson Center, Oh., U.S. B1 128
Jackson Lake, res., Wy., U.S. C2 143
Jackson Mountains, mts., Nv., U.S. B3 121
Jackson's Arm, N.L., Can. D3 88
Jacksons Gap, Al., U.S. C4 94
Jacksonville, Al., U.S. B4 94
Jacksonville, Ar., U.S. C3 97
Jacksonville, Fl., U.S. B5 102
Jacksonville, Il., U.S. D3 106
Jacksonville, N.C., U.S. C5 126
Jacksonville, Or., U.S. E4 130
Jacksonville, Tx., U.S. D5 136
Jacksonville Beach, Fl., U.S. B5 102
Jacksonville Naval Air Station, mil., Fl., U.S. B5 102
Jacks Peak, mtn., Ut., U.S. E3 137
Jacmel, Haiti B5 80
Jacobābād, Pak. E9 42
Jacobina, Braz. D3 74
Jacques-Cartier, stm., Qc., Can. B6 90
Jacques-Cartier, Détroit de, strt., Qc., Can. I27 82
Jacquet River, N.B., Can. B4 87
Jacundá, Braz. B2 74
Jada, Nig. E7 50
Jaén, Peru E4 70
Jaén, Spain I5 16
Jaffa, Cape, c., Austl. H2 62
Jaffna, Sri L. H4 40
Jaffrey, N.H., U.S. E2 122
Jagādhri, India C3 40
Jagdalpur, India F4 40
Jagersfontein, S. Afr. D4 56
Jagodnoe, Russia C16 26
Jagtiāl, India F3 40
Jaguaquara, Braz. D4 74
Jaguarão, Braz. E7 72
Jaguaribe, Braz. C4 74
Jahrom, Iran E6 42
Jailolo, Indon. C7 36
Jaipur, India D3 40
Jaisalmer, India D2 40
Jājapur, India E5 40
Jakarta, Indon. E3 36
Jakobshavn, Grnld. E29 82
Jakša, Russia B10 22
Jakutija, state, Russia C14 26
Jakutsk, Russia C14 26
Jal, N.M., U.S. E6 124
Jalālābād, Afg. D10 42
Jalandhar, India C3 40
Jalapa see Xalapa, Mex. D5 78
Jālaun, India D3 40
Jālgaon, India E3 40
Jalingo, Nig. E7 50
Jalisco, state, Mex. C4 78
Jālna, India F3 40
Jālor, India D2 40
Jalostotitlán, Mex. C4 78
Jalpāiguri, India D5 40
Jalūlā', Iraq E11 44
Jamaica, ctry., N.A. E9 76
Jamaica Bay, b., N.Y., U.S. k13 125
Jamaica Channel, strt., N.A. B4 80
Jamal, poluostrov, pen., Russia B8 26
Jamantau, gora, mtn., Russia D7 26
Jambi, Indon. D2 36
Jambol, Blg. C11 18
Jambusar, India E2 40
James, stm., Mo., U.S. E4 118
James, stm., Va., U.S. C5 139
James, stm., U.S. C8 92
James, Lake, l., In., U.S. A7 107
James, Lake, res., N.C., U.S. B1 126
James Bay, b., Can. H23 82
James Branch, stm., De., U.S. F3 101
Jamesburg, N.J., U.S. C4 123
James City, N.C., U.S. B5 126
James City, co., Va., U.S. C6 139
James Island, i., Md., U.S. C5 113
James Island, S.C., U.S. k12 133
James Island, i., S.C., U.S. F8 133
James River Bridge, Va., U.S. k15 139
Jamestown, Austl. G2 62
Jamestown, In., U.S. E4 107
Jamestown, Ky., U.S. D4 110
Jamestown, N.C., U.S. B3 126
Jamestown, N.D., U.S. C7 127
Jamestown, N.Y., U.S. C1 125
Jamestown, Oh., U.S. C2 128
Jamestown, R.I., U.S. F5 132
Jamestown, Tn., U.S. C9 135
James Town, Wy., U.S. E3 143
Jamestown Dam, N.D., U.S. C7 127
Jamestown Reservoir, res., N.D., U.S. C7 127
Jamkhandi, India F3 40
Jammerbugten, b., Den. H3 10
Jammu, India C2 40
Jammu and Kashmir, hist. reg., Asia C10 38
Jamnagar, India E2 40
Jämsä, Fin. F11 10
Jamshedpur, India E5 40
Jamsk, Russia D17 26
Jämtland, hist. reg., Swe. E6 10
Jamuna, stm., Bngl. D5 40
Jana, stm., Russia C15 26
Janaúba, Braz. E3 74
Janaucu, Ilha, i., Braz. C10 70
Janesville, Ca., U.S. C3 98
Janesville, Ia., U.S. B5 108
Janesville, Mn., U.S. F5 116
Janesville, Wi., U.S. F4 142
Jan Mayen, i., Nor. D23 144
Jan Mayen Ridge C24 144
Jansenville, S. Afr. E3 56
Janskij, Russia C15 26
Janskij zaliv, b., Russia B15 26
Januária, Braz. E3 74
Jaora, India E3 40
Japan, ctry., Asia D15 28
Japan, Sea of (East Sea), Asia C14 28
Japan Basin D16 64
Japan Trench E17 64
Japurá (Caquetá), stm., S.A. D6 70
Jaraguá, Braz. E2 74
Jaransk, Russia C8 22
Jarānwāla, Pak. D10 42
Jarcevo, Russia B12 20
Jardim, Braz. C6 72
Jardín América, Arg. D6 72
Jari, stm., Braz. C9 70
Jarocin, Pol. D4 20
Jaroslavl', Russia D6 26
Jarosław, Pol. D7 20
Jarrettsville, Md., U.S. A5 113
Jar-Sale, Russia A13 22
Järva-Jaani, Est. G11 10
Järvenpää, Fin. F11 10
Jarvis Island, i., Oc. E13 58
Jasikan, Ghana E5 50
Jāsk, Iran E7 42
Jaškul', Russia A5 42
Jasło, Pol. E6 20
Jasmine Estates, Fl., U.S. D4 102
Jasnogorsk, Russia B14 20
Jason Islands, is., Falk. Is. H4 69
Jasonville, In., U.S. F3 107
Jasper, Al., U.S. B2 94
Jasper, Fl., U.S. B4 102
Jasper, Ga., U.S. B2 103
Jasper, co., Ga., U.S. C3 103
Jasper, co., Ia., U.S. C4 108
Jasper, co., Il., U.S. D5 106
Jasper, In., U.S. H4 107
Jasper, co., In., U.S. B3 107
Jasper, Mo., U.S. D3 118
Jasper, co., Mo., U.S. D3 118
Jasper, co., Ms., U.S. C4 117
Jasper, co., S.C., U.S. G5 133
Jasper, Tn., U.S. D8 135
Jasper, co., Tx., U.S. D5 136
Jasper, Tx., U.S. D6 136
Jasper National Park, Ab., Can. C1 84
Jataí, Braz. E1 74
Jatni, India E5 40
Jaú, Braz. F2 74
Jaunpur, India D4 40
Java see Jawa, i., Indon. E3 36
Javari (Yavarí), stm., S.A. D5 70
Java Sea see Jawa, Laut, Indon. D3 36
Java Trench I13 64
Jawa (Java), i., Indon. E3 36
Jawa, Laut (Java Sea), Indon. D3 36
Jawhar, Som. J14 48
Jay, co., In., U.S. D7 107
Jay, Ok., U.S. A7 129
Jaya, Puncak, mtn., Indon. G10 32
Jayapura, Indon. G11 32
Jaypur, India F4 40
Jaz Mūrīān, Hāmūn-e, l., Iran E7 42
J. B. Thomas, Lake, res., Tx., U.S. C2 136
Jean, Nv., U.S. H6 121
Jeanerette, La., U.S. E4 111
Jean Lafitte National Historical Park, La., U.S. k12 111
Jeannette, Pa., U.S. F2 131
Jebba, Nig. E5 50
Jeddore Lake, res., N.L., Can. D3 88
Jędrzejów, Pol. D6 20
Jeff Davis, co., Ga., U.S. E4 103
Jeff Davis, co., Tx., U.S. o12 136
Jefferson, co., Al., U.S. B3 94
Jefferson, co., Ar., U.S. C3 97
Jefferson, co., Co., U.S. B5 99
Jefferson, co., Fl., U.S. B3 102
Jefferson, Ga., U.S. B3 103
Jefferson, co., Ga., U.S. C4 103
Jefferson, co., Ia., U.S. C5 108
Jefferson, Ia., U.S. B3 108
Jefferson, co., Id., U.S. F6 105
Jefferson, co., Il., U.S. E5 106
Jefferson, co., In., U.S. G6 107
Jefferson, co., Ks., U.S. C8 109
Jefferson, co., Ky., U.S. B4 110
Jefferson, La., U.S. k11 111
Jefferson, co., La., U.S. E5 111
Jefferson, co., Mo., U.S. C7 118
Jefferson, co., Ms., U.S. D2 117
Jefferson, co., Mt., U.S. D4 119
Jefferson, stm., Mt., U.S. E5 119
Jefferson, N.C., U.S. A1 126
Jefferson, co., Ne., U.S. D8 120
Jefferson, co., N.Y., U.S. A5 125
Jefferson, Oh., U.S. A5 128
Jefferson, co., Oh., U.S. B5 128
Jefferson, co., Ok., U.S. C4 129
Jefferson, Or., U.S. C3 130
Jefferson, co., Or., U.S. C5 130
Jefferson, co., Pa., U.S. D3 131
Jefferson, S.C., U.S. B7 133
Jefferson, co., Tn., U.S. C10 135
Jefferson, Tx., U.S. C5 136
Jefferson, co., Tx., U.S. E5 136
Jefferson, co., Wa., U.S. B1 140
Jefferson, Wi., U.S. E5 142
Jefferson, co., Wi., U.S. E5 142
Jefferson, co., W.V., U.S. B7 141
Jefferson, Mount, mtn., Id., U.S. E7 105
Jefferson, Mount, mtn., Nv., U.S. E5 121
Jefferson, Mount, mtn., Or., U.S. C5 130
Jefferson City, Mo., U.S. C5 118
Jefferson City, Tn., U.S. C10 135
Jefferson Davis, co., La., U.S. D3 111
Jefferson Davis, co., Ms., U.S. D4 117
Jefferson Farms, De., U.S. i7 101
Jefferson Proving Ground, mil., In., U.S. G7 107
Jeffersontown, Ky., U.S. B4 110
Jeffersonville, Ga., U.S. D3 103
Jeffersonville, In., U.S. H6 107
Jeffersonville, Ky., U.S. C6 110
Jeffersonville, Oh., U.S. C2 128
Jeffrey, W.V., U.S. D3 141
Jeffrey City, Wy., U.S. D5 143
Jeffries Creek, stm., S.C., U.S. C8 133
Jega, Nig. D5 50
Jehossee Island, i., S.C., U.S. k11 133
Jēkabpils, Lat. H11 10
Jekyll Island, i., Ga., U.S. E5 103
Jelenia Góra, Pol. D3 20
Jelgava, Lat. H10 10
Jellico, Tn., U.S. C9 135
Jelm Mountain, mtn., Wy., U.S. E7 143
Jemaja, Pulau, i., Indon. C3 36
Jember, Indon. E4 36
Jemez, stm., N.M., U.S. k7 124
Jemez Canyon Dam, N.M., U.S. k7 124
Jemez Indian Reservation, N.M., U.S. h7 124
Jemez Pueblo, N.M., U.S. B3 124
Jemison, Al., U.S. C3 94
Jena, Ger. E12 12
Jena, La., U.S. C3 111
Jeneponto, Indon. E5 36
Jenkins, co., Ga., U.S. D5 103
Jenkins, Ky., U.S. C7 110
Jenkintown, Pa., U.S. o21 131
Jenks, Ok., U.S. A6 129
Jennings, co., In., U.S. G6 107
Jennings, La., U.S. D3 111
Jennings, Mo., U.S. f13 118
Jensen Beach, Fl., U.S. E6 102
Jens Munks Ø, i., Grnld. F32 82
Jequié, Braz. D3 74
Jequitinhonha, Braz. E3 74
Jequitinhonha, stm., Braz. E3 74
Jerada, Mor. D4 48
Jerauld, co., S.D., U.S. C7 134
Jérémie, Haiti B5 80
Jeremoabo, Braz. D4 74
Jerez de García Salinas, Mex. C4 78
Jerez de la Frontera, Spain I3 16
Jerez de los Caballeros, Spain H3 16
Jericho see Arīḥā, Gaza G6 44
Jericho, Vt., U.S. B3 138
Jerid, Chott, l., Tun. D6 48
Jerimoth Hill, R.I., U.S. C1 132
Jermyn, Pa., U.S. C10 131
Jerome, Id., U.S. G4 105
Jerome, co., Id., U.S. G4 105
Jerome, Pa., U.S. F4 131
Jersey, dep., Eur. F5 12
Jersey, co., Il., U.S. D3 106
Jersey City, N.J., U.S. B4 123
Jersey Mountain, mtn., Id., U.S. E3 105
Jersey Shore, Pa., U.S. D7 131
Jerseyville, Il., U.S. D3 106
Jerusalem see Yerushalayim, Isr. G6 42
Jervis Inlet, b., B.C., Can. D6 85
Jesi, Italy C4 18
Jessamine, co., Ky., U.S. C5 110
Jesselton see Kota Kinabalu, Malay. B5 36
Jessore, Bngl. E5 40
Jessup, Md., U.S. B4 113
Jessup, Pa., U.S. m18 131
Jesup, Ga., U.S. E5 103
Jesup, Ia., U.S. B5 108
Jesup, Lake, l., Fl., U.S. D5 102
Jésus, Île, i., Qc., Can. p19 90
Jesús Carranza, Mex. I13 78
Jesús María, Arg. E5 72
Jetmore, Ks., U.S. D4 109
Jewel Cave National Monument, S.D., U.S. D2 134
Jewell, Ia., U.S. B4 108
Jewell, co., Ks., U.S. C5 109
Jewett City, Ct., U.S. C8 100
Jhālāwār, India E3 40
Jhang Sadar, Pak. D10 42
Jhānsi, India D3 40
Jharkhand, state, India E4 40
Jhelum, Pak. D10 42
Jhunjhunūn, India D3 40
Jiahe, China D3 30
Jiali, China C6 40
Jialing, stm., China E8 28
Jiamusi, China B14 28
Ji'an, China D3 30
Jianchang, China A4 30
Jianchuan, China F8 28
Jiande, China D4 30
Jiang'an, China D2 30
Jiangcheng, China B4 34
Jiangjin, China F9 28
Jiangle, China D4 30
Jiangling, China C3 30

Name | Map Ref. | Page

Jiangmen, China G10 28
Jiangsu, prov., China E11 28
Jiangxi, prov., China F11 28
Jianli, China D3 30
Jian'ou, China F11 28
Jianping, China A4 30
Jianshui, China G8 28
Jianyang, China D4 30
Jianyang, China C1 30
Jiaocheng, China B3 30
Jiaonan, China B4 30
Jiaoxian, China D12 28
Jiaozuo, China D10 28
Jiashan, China C4 30
Jibiya, Nig. D6 50
Jicarilla Apache Indian Reservation, N.M., U.S. A2 124
Jičín, Czech Rep. D3 20
Jiddah, Sau. Ar. F3 38
Jiexiu, China B3 30
Jieyang, China G11 28
Jihlava, Czech Rep. E3 20
Jijel, Alg. I9 16
Jijiga, Eth. B8 54
Jilib, Som. J13 48
Jilin, prov., China C13 28
Jilin, China C13 28
Jill, Kediet ej, mtn., Maur. B2 50
Jima, Eth. B7 54
Jimbolia, Rom. G6 20
Jiménez (Ciudad Jiménez), Mex. B4 78
Jimeta, Nig. E7 50
Jim Hogg, co., Tx., U.S. F3 136
Jim Lake, res., N.D., U.S. B7 127
Jimo, China B5 30
Jim Thorpe, Pa., U.S. E10 131
Jim Wells, co., Tx., U.S. F3 136
Jinan, China D11 28
Jincheng, China B3 30
Jind, India D3 40
Jingdezhen, China F11 28
Jinggangshan, China F10 28
Jinghai, China B4 30
Jinghong, China G8 28
Jingning, China B2 30
Jingxi, China E2 30
Jingxian, China D2 30
Jinhua, China F11 28
Jining, China D11 28
Jining, China C10 28
Jinja, Ug. C6 54
Jinning, China E1 30
Jinsha, China D2 30
Jinshi, China F10 28
Jinzhai, China C4 30
Jinzhou, China C12 28
Jinzhou, China D12 28
Ji-Paraná, Braz. F7 70
Jishou, China D2 30
Jisr ash-Shughūr, Syria E7 44
Jiu, stm., Rom. G7 20
Jiujiang, China F11 28
Jiulong (Kowloon), China E3 30
Jiuquan, China D7 28
Jiutai, China C13 28
Jixi, China B14 28
Jixian, China C11 28
Jīzān, Sau. Ar. G4 38
Joanna, S.C., U.S. C4 133
João Pessoa, Braz. C5 74
João Pinheiro, Braz. E2 74
Job Peak, mtn., Nv., U.S. D3 121
Jocassee, Lake, res., U.S. B1 133
Jódar, Spain I5 16
Jo Daviess, co., Il., U.S. A3 106
Jodhpur, India D2 40
Joe Batt's Arm [-Barr'd Islands-Shoal Bay], N.L., Can. D4 88
Joensuu, Fin. E13 10
Joes Brook, stm., Vt., U.S. C4 138
Joes Creek, stm., W.V., U.S. m12 141
Joetsu, Japan D15 28
Joffre, Mount, mtn., Can. D3 84
Johannesburg, S. Afr. D4 56
John, Cape, c., N.S., Can. D6 87
John Day, Or., U.S. C8 130
John Day, stm., Or., U.S. B6 130
John Day Dam, U.S. D5 140
John Day Fossil Beds National Monument, Or., U.S. C6 130
John F. Kennedy Space Center, hist., Fl., U.S. D6 102
John H. Kerr Dam, Va., U.S. D4 139
John H. Kerr Reservoir, res., U.S. D4 139
John Martin Reservoir, res., Co., U.S. C7 99
John Muir National Historical Site, hist., Ca., U.S. h8 98
John Redmond Reservoir, res., Ks., U.S. D8 109
John Sevier, Tn., U.S. m14 135
Johns Island, i., S.C., U.S. F7 133
Johnson, co., Ar., U.S. B2 97
Johnson, co., Ga., U.S. D4 103
Johnson, co., Ia., U.S. C6 108
Johnson, co., Il., U.S. F5 106
Johnson, co., In., U.S. F5 107
Johnson, Ks., U.S. E2 109
Johnson, co., Ks., U.S. D9 109
Johnson, co., Ky., U.S. C7 110
Johnson, co., Mo., U.S. C4 118
Johnson, co., Ne., U.S. D9 120
Johnson, co., Tn., U.S. C12 135
Johnson, co., Tx., U.S. C4 136
Johnson, Vt., U.S. B3 138
Johnson, co., Wy., U.S. B6 143
Johnsonburg, Pa., U.S. D4 131
Johnson City, N.Y., U.S. C5 125
Johnson City, Tn., U.S. C11 135
Johnson City, Tx., U.S. D3 136
Johnson Creek, Wi., U.S. E5 142
Johnsonville, S.C., U.S. D9 133
Johns Pass, strt., Fl., U.S. p10 102
Johnston, Ia., U.S. e8 108
Johnston, co., N.C., U.S. B4 126
Johnston, co., Ok., U.S. C5 129
Johnston, R.I., U.S. C4 132
Johnston, S.C., U.S. D4 133
Johnston Atoll, atoll, Oc. G22 64
Johnston City, Il., U.S. F5 106
Johnston Key, i., Fl., U.S. H5 102
Johnstown, Co., U.S. A6 99
Johnstown, N.Y., U.S. B6 125
Johnstown, Oh., U.S. B3 128
Johnstown, Pa., U.S. F4 131
John W. Flannagan Reservoir, res., Va., U.S. e9 139
Johor Bahru, Malay. C2 36
Joigny, Fr. C8 16
Joiner, Ar., U.S. B5 97
Joinville, Braz. D8 72
Jokkmokk, Swe. C8 10
Jolfā, Iran C11 44
Joliet, Il., U.S. B5 106
Joliette, Qc., Can. C4 90
Jolo, Phil. E8 34
Jolo Island, i., Phil. E8 34
Jomda, China E7 28
Jones, co., Ga., U.S. C3 103
Jones, co., Ia., U.S. B6 108
Jones, co., Ms., U.S. D4 117
Jones, co., N.C., U.S. B5 126
Jones, Ok., U.S. B4 129
Jones, co., S.D., U.S. D5 134
Jones, co., Tx., U.S. C3 136
Jonesboro, Ar., U.S. B5 97
Jonesboro, Ga., U.S. C2 103
Jonesboro, Il., U.S. F4 106
Jonesboro, In., U.S. D6 107
Jonesboro, La., U.S. B3 111
Jonesborough, Tn., U.S. C11 135
Jonesburg, Mo., U.S. C6 118
Jones Creek, Tx., U.S. s14 136
Jones Mill, Ar., U.S. C3 97
Jonesport, Me., U.S. D5 112
Jonestown, Ms., U.S. A3 117
Jonesville, La., U.S. C4 111
Jonesville, Mi., U.S. G6 115
Jonesville, N.C., U.S. A2 126
Jonesville, S.C., U.S. B4 133
Jonesville, Va., U.S. f8 139
Joniškis, Lith. H10 10
Jonquière, Qc., Can. A6 90
Jonuta, Mex. D6 78
Joplin, Mo., U.S. D3 118
Joppatowne, Md., U.S. B5 113
Jordan, ctry., Asia D3 42
Jordan, stm., Asia F6 44
Jordan, Mn., U.S. F5 116
Jordan, stm., Ut., U.S. C4 137
Jordan Creek, stm., U.S. E9 130
Jordan Lake, res., Al., U.S. C3 94
Jorhāt, India D6 40
Jornado del Muerto, des., N.M., U.S. D3 124
Joroinen, Fin. E12 10
Jos, Nig. E6 50
José de San Martín, Arg. F2 69
Joseph, Or., U.S. B9 130
Joseph, Lac, l., N.L., Can. h8 88
Joseph Bonaparte Gulf, b., Austl. C4 60
Joseph City, Az., U.S. C5 96
Josephine, co., Or., U.S. E3 130
Joshua, Tx., U.S. n9 136
Joshua Tree, Ca., U.S. E5 98
Joshua Tree National Monument, Ca., U.S. F6 98
Jostedalsbreen, ice, Nor. F2 10
Jourdanton, Tx., U.S. E3 136
Jovellanos, Cuba A3 80
J. Percy Priest Lake, res., Tn., U.S. A5 135
Juab, co., Ut., U.S. D2 137
Juan Aldama, Mex. C4 78
Juan de Fuca, Strait of, strt., N.A. B3 92
Juan Fernandez, Archipiélago, is., Chile E1 72
Juanjuí, Peru E4 70
Juazeiro, Braz. C3 74
Juazeiro do Norte, Braz. C4 74
Juba, Sudan J11 48
Jubba (Genalē), stm., Afr. C8 54
Juby, Cap, c., Mor. A2 50
Júcar, stm., Spain H6 16
Juchitán de Zaragoza, Mex. D5 78
Judenburg, Aus. G14 12
Judith, stm., Mt., U.S. C7 119
Judith, Point, c., R.I., U.S. G4 101
Judith Basin, co., Mt., U.S. C6 119
Judith Island, i., N.C., U.S. B6 126
Judith Mountains, mts., Mt., U.S. C7 119
Judith Peak, mtn., Mt., U.S. C7 119
Judsonia, Ar., U.S. B4 97
Juhnov, Russia B13 20
Juidongshan, China E4 30
Juiz de Fora, Braz. F3 74
Jukta, Russia C12 26
Julesburg, Co., U.S. A8 99
Juliaca, Peru G5 70
Julia Creek, Austl. E3 62
Julian, Ca., U.S. F5 98
Julian, W.V., U.S. C3 141
Julian Alps, mts., Eur. A4 18
Juliana Top, mtn., Sur. C8 70
Julianehåb, Grnld. F30 82
Jumba, Som. D8 54
Jumbo Peak, mtn., Nv., U.S. G7 121
Jumilla, Spain H6 16
Jump, stm., Wi., U.S. C3 142
Jūnāgadh, India E2 40
Junction, Tx., U.S. D3 136
Junction City, Ar., U.S. D3 97
Junction City, Ks., U.S. C7 109
Junction City, Ky., U.S. C5 110
Junction City, La., U.S. A3 111
Junction City, Or., U.S. C3 130
Jundiaí, Braz. F2 74
Juneau, Ak., U.S. D13 95
Juneau, Wi., U.S. E5 142
Juneau, co., Wi., U.S. E3 142
Junee, Austl. G4 62
June in Winter, Lake, l., Fl., U.S. E5 102
Jungar Qi, China D10 28
Junggar Pendi, bas., China B5 28
Juniata, Ne., U.S. D7 120
Juniata, co., Pa., U.S. F7 131
Juniata, stm., Pa., U.S. F7 131
Junín, Arg. E5 72
Junior Lake, l., Me., U.S. C4 112
Juniper Mountains, mts., Az., U.S. B2 96
Junipero Serra Peak, mtn., Ca., U.S. D3 98
Jūniyah, Leb. F6 44
Junlian, China D1 30
Junxian, China E10 28
Jupiter, Fl., U.S. F6 102
Jupiter Inlet, b., Fl., U.S. F6 102
Jupiter Island, i., Fl., U.S. E6 102
Jur, Russia D15 26
Jura, i., Scot., U.K. C4 12
Jurga, Russia D10 26
Jūrmala, Lat. H10 10
Juruá, stm., S.A. E6 70
Juruena, stm., Braz. F8 70
Jurumirim, Represa, res., Braz. C8 72
Juškozero, Russia B5 22
Jussara, Braz. B7 72
Justin, Tx., U.S. C4 136
Jutaí, stm., Braz. D6 70
Jutiapa, Guat. C1 80
Juticalpa, Hond. C2 80
Jutland see Jylland, reg., Den. I3 10
Juventud, Isla de la, i., Cuba A3 80
Juxian, China B4 30
Južno-Sahalinsk, Russia E16 26
Južno-Ural'sk, Russia D11 22
Jylland, reg., Den. I3 10
Jyväskylä, Fin. E11 10

K

K2 (Qogir Feng), mtn., Asia B3 40
Kaaawa, Hi., U.S. f10 104
Kaahka, Turk. C7 42
Kaala, mtn., Hi., U.S. f9 104
Kaalualu Bay, b., Hi., U.S. E6 104
Kaaumakua, Puu, mtn., Hi., U.S. f10 104
Kabaena, Pulau, i., Indon. E6 36
Kabala, S.L. E2 50
Kabale, Ug. D5 54
Kabalega Falls, wtfl., Ug. C6 54
Kabalo, D.R.C. E5 54
Kabambare, D.R.C. D5 54
Kabardino-Balkarija, state, Russia E6 26
Kabba, Nig. E6 50
Kabetogama Lake, l., Mn., U.S. B5 116
Kabinda, D.R.C. E4 54
Kabīr Kūh, mts., Iran F12 44
Kābol, Afg. D9 42
Kabompo, stm., Zam. A3 56
Kabongo, D.R.C. E5 54
Kabūdarāhang, Iran E13 44
Kābul see Kābol, Afg. D9 42
Kabwe, Zam. A4 56
Kabylie, reg., Alg. I9 16
Kachchh, Gulf of, b., India E1 40
Kachess Lake, res., Wa., U.S. B4 140
Kačkanar, Russia C10 22
Kadan Kyun, i., Mya. D3 34
Kade, Ghana E4 50
Kadınhanı, Tur. C5 44
Kadiolo, Mali D3 50
Kadirli, Tur. D7 44
Kadoka, S.D., U.S. D4 134
Kadoma, Zimb. B4 56
Kaduna, stm., Nig. D6 50
Kaduna, Nig. D6 50
Kāduqlī, Sudan H10 48
Kadykčan, Russia C16 26
Kadžerom, Russia B10 22
Kaédi, Maur. C2 50
Kaélé, Cam. A2 54
Kaena Point, c., Hi., U.S. B3 104
Kafanchan, Nig. E6 50
Kaffrine, Sen. D1 50
Kafia Kingi, Sudan I9 48
Kafue, Zam. B4 56
Kafue, stm., Zam. A4 56
Kaga, Japan C3 31
Kaga Bandoro, C.A.R. B3 54
Kagan, Uzb. C8 42
Kagera, stm., Afr. D6 54
Kağızman, Tur. B10 44
Kagoshima, Japan E14 28
Kagul see Cahul, Mol. G10 20
Kahaluu, Hi., U.S. g10 104
Kahaluu, Hi., U.S. D6 104
Kahama, Tan. D6 54
Kahana Bay, b., Hi., U.S. f10 104
Kahemba, D.R.C. E3 54
Kahoka, Mo., U.S. A6 118
Kahoolawe, i., Hi., U.S. C5 104
Kahramanmaraş, Tur. D7 44
Kahuku, Hi., U.S. B4 104
Kahuku Point, c., Hi., U.S. B4 104
Kahului, Hi., U.S. C5 104
Kahului Bay, b., Hi., U.S. C5 104
Kai, Kepulauan, is., Indon. E8 36
Kaibab Indian Reservation, Az., U.S. A3 96
Kaifeng, China E10 28
Kaikoura, N.Z. p13 63c
Kailahun, S.L. E2 50
Kailas see Kangrinboqê Feng, mtn., China E4 28
Kailas Range see Gangdisê Shan, mts., China E4 28
Kaili, China D2 30
Kailu, China C12 28
Kailua, Hi., U.S. B4 104
Kailua Bay, b., Hi., U.S. g11 104
Kailua Kona, Hi., U.S. D6 104
Kainji Lake, res., Nig. D5 50
Kaiping, China E3 30
Kairouan, Tun. C7 48
Kaiserslautern, Ger. F10 12
Kaitaia, N.Z. o13 63c
Kaithal, India D3 40
Kaiwi Channel, strt., Hi., U.S. B4 104
Kaiwi Channel, strt., Hi., U.S. h17 92a
Kaixian, China C2 30
Kaiyuan, China E1 30
Kaiyuan, China C12 28
Kajaani, Fin. D12 10
Kajakī, Band-e, res., Afg. D9 42
Kajang, Malay. C2 36
Kajiado, Kenya D7 54
Kajnar, Kaz. E9 26
Kaka, Sudan A6 54
Kakamas, S. Afr. D3 56
Kakamega, Kenya C6 54
Kaka Point, c., Hi., U.S. C5 104
Kakata, Lib. E2 50
Kake, Ak., U.S. D13 95
Kakhovka Reservoir see Kakhovs'ke vodoskhovyshche, res., Ukr. F13 20
Kakhovs'ke vodoskhovyshche, res., Ukr. F13 20
Kākināda, India F4 40
Kalaa Kebira, Tun. G3 18
Kalaallit Nunaat see Greenland, dep., N.A. D30 82
Kalabahi, Indon. E6 36
Kalabo, Zam. B3 56
Kalač, Russia D7 22
Kalač-na-Donu, Russia E7 22
Kaladan, stm., Asia B2 34
Ka Lae, c., Hi., U.S. E6 104
Kalahari Desert, des., Afr. C3 56
Kalaheo, Hi., U.S. B2 104
Kalajoki, Fin. D10 10
Kalakan, Russia D13 26
Kalama, Wa., U.S. C3 140
Kalámai, Grc. F8 18
Kalamazoo, Mi., U.S. F5 115
Kalamazoo, stm., Mi., U.S. F5 115
Kalamazoo, co., Mi., U.S. F5 115
Kalamits'ka zatoka, b., Ukr. G12 20
Kalanchak, Ukr. F12 20
Kalao, Pulau, i., Indon. E6 36
Kalaotoa, Pulau, i., Indon. E6 36
Kalasin, Thai. C4 34
Kalāt, Pak. E9 42
Kalaupapa Peninsula, pen., Hi., U.S. B5 104
Kalaw, Mya. B3 34
Kalawao, co., Hi., U.S. B5 104
Kalbarri, Austl. F1 60
Kale, Tur. D3 44
Kalecik, Tur. B5 44
Kaleden, B.C., Can. E8 85
Kalemie, D.R.C. E5 54
Kalemyo, Mya. B2 34
Kalena, Puu, mtn., Hi., U.S. g9 104
Kalene Hill, Zam. A3 56
Kalevala, Russia D14 10
Kalewa, Mya. B2 34
Kalgin Island, i., Ak., U.S. g16 95
Kalgoorlie-Boulder, Austl. G3 60
Kalibo, Phil. D8 34
Kalima, D.R.C. D5 54
Kalimantan see Borneo, i., Asia D4 36
Kálimnos, Grc. F11 18
Kálimnos, i., Grc. F11 18
Kālimpang, India D5 40
Kalinin see Tver', Russia D5 26
Kaliningrad, Russia D4 26
Kalinkavičy, Bela. C10 20
Kalispel Indian Reservation, Wa., U.S. A8 140
Kalispell, Mt., U.S. B2 119
Kalisz, Pol. D5 20
Kalixälven, stm., Swe. C9 10
Kalkaska, Mi., U.S. D5 115
Kalkaska, co., Mi., U.S. D5 115
Kallavesi, l., Fin. E12 10
Kalmar, Swe. H7 10
Kalmarsund, strt., Swe. H7 10
Kalmykija, state, Russia E6 26
Kalohi Channel, strt., Hi., U.S. C4 104
Kaloli Point, c., Hi., U.S. D7 104
Kalomo, Zam. B4 56
Kalona, Ia., U.S. C6 108
Kalone Peak, mtn., B.C., Can. C4 85
Kalpin, China A3 40
Kalsūbai, mtn., India F2 40
Kaluga, Russia D5 26
Kalundborg, Den. I4 10
Kalush, Ukr. E8 20
Kalutara, Sri L. H4 40
Kalyān, India F2 40
Kama, D.R.C. D5 54
Kama, stm., Russia D7 26
Kamaishi, Japan D16 28
Kamakou, mtn., Hi., U.S. B5 104
Kamālia, Pak. D10 42
Kaman, Tur. C5 44
Kamarān, i., Yemen G4 38
Kama Reservoir see Kamskoe vodohranilišče, res., Russia C10 22
Kamas, Ut., U.S. C4 137
Kambalda, Austl. G3 60
Kambove, D.R.C. F5 54
Kamčatka, poluostrov, pen., Russia D17 26
Kamchatka Peninsula see Kamčatka, poluostrov, pen., Russia D17 26
Kamen', gora, mtn., Russia C11 26
Kamenka, Russia D15 20
Kamenka, Russia D7 22
Kamen'-na-Obi, Russia D10 26
Kamenskoe, Russia C18 26
Kamensk-Ural'skij, Russia C11 22
Kāmet, mtn., Asia C3 40
Kamiah, Id., U.S. C2 105
Kamiak Butte, mtn., Wa., U.S. C8 140
Kam'ianets'-Podil's'kyi, Ukr. E9 20
Kamina, D.R.C. E5 54
Kamloops, B.C., Can. D7 85
Kamo, Arm. B11 44
Kampala, Ug. C6 54
Kampar, Malay. C2 36
Kampen, Neth. D9 12
Kampeska, Lake, l., S.D., U.S. C8 134
Kamphaeng Phet, Thai. C3 34
Kâmpóng Cham, Camb. D5 34
Kâmpóng Chhnăng, Camb. D4 34
Kâmpóng Saôm, Camb. D4 34
Kâmpóng Thum, Camb. D4 34
Kâmpôt, Camb. D4 34
Kampti, Burkina D4 50
Kampuchea see Cambodia, ctry., Asia D4 34
Kamskoe vodohranilišče, res., Russia C10 22
Kamuela (Waimea), Hi., U.S. C6 104
Kamyšin, Russia D6 26
Kamyšlov, Russia C11 22
Kanab, Ut., U.S. F3 137
Kanab Creek, stm., U.S. A3 96
Kanabec, co., Mn., U.S. E5 116
Kanaga Island, i., Ak., U.S. E4 95
Kanairiktok, stm., N.L., Can. g9 88
Kananga, D.R.C. E4 54
Kanapou Bay, b., Hi., U.S. C5 104
Kanaš, Russia C8 22
Kanata, On., Can. B9 89
Kanawha, Ia., U.S. B4 108
Kanawha, stm., W.V., U.S. C3 141
Kanawha, co., W.V., U.S. C3 141
Kanazawa, Japan D15 28
Kānchenjunga, mtn., Asia D5 40
Kānchipuram, India G3 40
Kandahār, Afg. D9 42
Kandalakša, Russia C15 10
Kandalaksha Bay see Kandalakšskaja guba, b., Russia A5 22
Kandalakšskaja guba, b., Russia A5 22
Kandale, D.R.C. E3 54
Kandangan, Indon. D5 36
Kandi, Benin D5 50
Kandıra, Tur. B4 44
Kandiyohi, co., Mn., U.S. E3 116
Kandy, Sri L. H4 40
Kane, co., Il., U.S. B5 106

Name — Map Ref. — Page

Kane, Pa., U.S. C4 131
Kane, co., Ut., U.S. F3 137
Kanem, state, Chad D8 50
Kāne'ohe, Hi., U.S. B4 104
Kāne'ohe Bay, b., Hi., U.S. g10 104
Kaneohe Bay Marine Corps Base, mil., Hi., U.S. g10 104
Kangaba, Mali D3 50
Kangal, Tur. C7 44
Kangân, Iran E6 42
Kangar, Malay. B2 36
Kangaroo Island, i., Austl. H2 62
Kangāvar, Iran E12 44
Kangbao, China A3 30
Kangean, Pulau, i., Indon. E5 36
Kanggye, N. Kor. C13 28
Kango, Gabon C2 54
Kangpu, China A3 34
Kangrinboqê Feng, mtn., China E4 28
Kangshan, Tai. E5 30
Kangto, mtn., Asia A2 34
Kaniama, D.R.C. E4 54
Kaniet Islands, is., Pap. N. Gui. G12 32
Kanin, poluostrov, pen., Russia C6 26
Kaningo, Kenya D7 54
Kanin Nos, Russia A7 22
Kanin Nos, mys, c., Russia C6 26
Kanjiža, Serb. A8 18
Kankakee, Il., U.S. B6 106
Kankakee, co., Il., U.S. B6 106
Kankakee, stm., U.S. B5 106
Kankan, Gui. D3 50
Kānker, India E4 40
Kanmaw Kyun, i., Mya. D3 34
Kannapolis, N.C., U.S. B2 126
Kannonkoski, Fin. E11 10
Kano, Nig. D6 50
Kanopolis, Ks., U.S. D5 109
Kanopolis Lake, res., Ks., U.S. D5 109
Kanoya, Japan D2 31
Kānpur, India D4 40
Kansas, Il., U.S. D6 106
Kansas, stm., Ks., U.S. C7 109
Kansas, state, U.S. D5 109
Kansas City, Ks., U.S. C9 109
Kansas City, Mo., U.S. B3 118
Kansk, Russia D11 26
Kantang, Thai. E3 34
Kantchari, Burkina D5 50
Kantemirovka, Russia E15 20
Kanye, Bots. D4 56
Kaohsiung, Tai. E5 30
Kaoko Veld, plat., Nmb. B1 56
Kaolack, Sen. D1 50
Kaoma, Zam. A3 56
Kaouar, reg., Niger C7 50
Kapaa, Hi., U.S. A2 104
Kapaau, Hi., U.S. C6 104
Kapan, Arm. C12 44
Kapanga, D.R.C. E4 54
Kapapa Island, i., Hi., U.S. g10 104
Kapčagaj, Kaz. B11 42
Kapčagajskoe vodohranilišče, res., Kaz. B11 42
Kapchagay Reservoir see Kapčagajskoe vodohranilišče, res., Kaz. B11 42
Kapfenberg, Aus. G14 12
Kapiri Mposhi, Zam. A4 56
Kaplan, La., U.S. D3 111
Kapoeta, Sudan C6 54
Kaposvár, Hung. F4 20
Kaptai Lake see Karnaphuli Reservoir, res., Bngl. E6 40
Kapuas, stm., Indon. D4 36
Kapuas, stm., Indon. D3 36
Kapuas Hulu, Pegunungan (Kapuas Hulu, Pergunungan), mts., Asia C4 36
Kapuas Hulu, Pergunungan (Kapuas Hulu, Pegunungan), mts., Asia C4 36
Kapuskasing, On., Can. o19 89
Kapuvár, Hung. F4 20
Kapyl', Bela. C9 20
Kara, Russia C8 26
Kara-Balta, Kyrg. A2 40
Karabaš, Russia C11 22
Kara-Bogaz-Gol, zaliv, b., Turk. E7 26
Kara-Bogaz-Gol Gulf see Kara-Bogaz-Gol, zaliv, b., Turk. E7 26
Karabük, Tur. B5 44
Karabula, Russia D11 26
Karaburun, Tur. C2 44
Karabutak, Kaz. E11 22
Karacabey, Tur. B3 44
Karačaevo-Čerkesija, state, Russia E6 26
Karačev, Russia C13 20
Karāchi, Pak. F9 42
Karād, India F2 40
Karaganda, Kaz. E9 26
Karaginskij, ostrov, i., Russia D18 26
Karaginskij zaliv, b., Russia D18 26
Kāraikkudi, India G3 40
Karaj, Iran C6 42
Karakaya Barajı, res., Tur. C8 44
Karakelong, Pulau, i., Indon. E8 32
Karakol, Kyrg. E9 26
Karakoram Pass, Asia B3 40
Karakoram Range, mts., Asia B3 40
Karakul', Uzb. C8 42
Kara-Kum Canal see Garagumskij kanal imeni Prezidenta Turkmenistana S.A. Nijazova, Turk. C8 42
Karaman, Tur. D5 44
Karamay, China B4 28
Karamea Bight, b., N.Z. p13 63c
Karapınar, Tur. D5 44
Karasay, China B4 40
Karasburg, Nmb. D2 56
Kara Sea see Karskoe more, Russia B8 26
Karasu, stm., Tur. C9 44
Karasu, Tur. B4 44
Karasuk, Russia D9 26
Karatau, Kaz. B10 42
Karatau, hrebet, mts., Kaz. E8 26
Karatobe, Kaz. E9 22
Karaton, Kaz. A6 42
Karatsu, Japan D1 31
Karaul, Kaz. B3 28
Karaul, Russia B10 26
Karawang, Indon. E3 36
Karažal, Kaz. B2 28
Karbalā', Iraq D4 42
Karbalā', state, Iraq F10 44
Kårböle, Swe. F6 10
Karcag, Hung. F6 20
Kardeljevo, Cro. C6 18
Kardhítsa, Grc. E8 18
Kărdžali, Blg. D10 18
Karelia, hist. reg., Eur. C12 6
Karelia see Karelija, state, Russia C5 26
Karelija, state, Russia C5 26
Karema, Tan. E6 54
Karesuando, Swe. B10 10
Kargopol', Russia C5 26
Kariba, Zimb. B4 56
Kariba, Lake, res., Afr. B4 56
Karibib, Nmb. C2 56
Karigasniemi, Fin. B11 10
Karimata, Selat (Karimata Strait), strt., Indon. D3 36
Karimata Strait see Karimata, Selat, strt., Indon. D3 36
Karīmganj, India E6 40
Karīmnagar, India F3 40
Karimunjawa, Pulau, i., Indon. E4 36
Karisimbi, Volcan, vol., Afr. D5 54
Karkaralinsk, Kaz. B3 28
Karkar Island, i., Pap. N. Gui. G12 32
Karkheh, stm., Iran G12 44
Karkinits'ka zatoka, b., Ukr. G12 20
Karkūk, Iraq C4 42
Karlivka, Ukr. E13 20
Karl-Marx-Stadt see Chemnitz, Ger. E13 12
Karlovac, Cro. B5 18
Karlovy Vary, Czech Rep. D2 20
Karlshamn, Swe. H6 10
Karlskoga, Swe. G6 10
Karlskrona, Swe. H6 10
Karlsruhe, Ger. F11 12
Karlstad, Swe. G5 10
Karlstad, Mn., U.S. B2 116
Karma, Niger D5 50
Karnāl, India D3 40
Karnaphuli Reservoir, res., Bngl. E6 40
Karnātaka, state, India G3 40
Karnes, co., Tx., U.S. E4 136
Karnes City, Tx., U.S. E4 136
Karns, Tn., U.S. n13 135
Kárpathos, i., Grc. G11 18
Karpogory, Russia B7 22
Karratha, Austl. E2 60
Kars, Tur. B10 44
Karsakpaj, Kaz. B1 28
Karši, Uzb. F8 26
Karskie Vorota, proliv, strt., Russia B7 26
Karskoe more, Russia B8 26
Kartaly, Russia D8 26
Karufa, Indon. D8 36
Kārūn, stm., Iran G13 44
Karūr, India G3 40
Karviná, Czech Rep. E5 20
Kārwār, India G2 40
Karymskoe, Russia A10 28
Kasai (Cassai), stm., Afr. D3 54
Kasaji, D.R.C. F4 54
Kasama, Zam. A5 56
Kasane, Bots. B4 56
Kasanga, Tan. E6 54
Kasangulu, D.R.C. D3 54
Kāsaragod, India G3 40
Kasempa, Zam. A4 56
Kasenga, D.R.C. F5 54
Kasenye, D.R.C. C6 54
Kasese, D.R.C. D5 54
Kasese, Ug. C6 54
Kāshān, Iran D6 42
Kashgar see Kashi, China D3 28
Kashi, China D3 28
Kāshmar, Iran C7 42
Kasimov, Russia B16 20
Kasiruta, Pulau, i., Indon. D7 36
Kaskaskia, stm., Il., U.S. D5 106
Kaslo, B.C., Can. E9 85
Kasongo, D.R.C. D5 54
Kasongo-Lunda, D.R.C. E3 54
Kásos, i., Grc. G11 18
Kasota, Mn., U.S. F5 116
Kaspi, Geor. B11 44
Kaspijsk, Russia A12 44
Kaspijskij, Russia E6 26
Kassalā, Sudan G12 48
Kassandra, Gulf of see Kassándras, Kólpos, b., Grc. D9 18
Kassándras, Kólpos, b., Grc. D9 18
Kassel, Ger. E11 12
Kasserine, Tun. C6 48
Kasson, Mn., U.S. F6 116
Kastamonu, Tur. B5 44
Kastoría, Grc. D8 18
Kasulu, Tan. D6 54
Kasūr, Pak. D10 42
Kataba, Zam. B4 56
Katahdin, Mount, mtn., Me., U.S. C4 112
Katako-Kombe, D.R.C. D4 54
Katanga, hist. reg., D.R.C. E4 54
Katangli, Russia D16 26
Katanning, Austl. G2 60
Katchall Island, i., India H6 40
Kateríni, Grc. D9 18
Kates Needle, mtn., Ak., U.S. m24 95
Katha, Mya. B3 34
Katherîna, Gebel, mtn., Egypt E11 48
Katherine, Austl. C5 60
Kāthiāwār Peninsula, pen., India E2 40
Kathleen, Fl., U.S. D4 102
Kāṭhmāṇḍāu, Nepal D5 40
Kati, Mali D3 50
Katihār, India D5 40
Katiola, C. Iv. E3 50
Katmai, Mount, mtn., Ak., U.S. D9 95
Katmai National Park, Ak., U.S. D9 95
Kātmāndu see Kāṭhmāṇḍāu, Nepal D5 40
Katompi, D.R.C. E5 54
Katoomba, Austl. G5 62
Katowice, Pol. D5 20
Katrineholm, Swe. G7 10
Katsina, Nig. D6 50
Kattakurgan, Uzb. C9 42
Kattegat, strt., Eur. B12 12
Katy, Tx., U.S. r14 136
Kaua'i, i., Hi., U.S. A2 104
Kauai Channel, strt., Hi., U.S. B3 104
Kauai County, co., Hi., U.S. B1 104
Ka'ū Desert, des., Hi., U.S. D6 104
Kaufbeuren, Ger. G12 12
Kaufman, Tx., U.S. C4 136
Kaufman, co., Tx., U.S. C4 136
Ka'uiki Head, c., Hi., U.S. C6 104
Kaujuitoq see Resolute, N.T., Can. D20 82
Kaukauna, Wi., U.S. D5 142
Ka'ula Island, i., Hi., U.S. m15 104
Kaulakahi Channel, strt., Hi., U.S. A2 104
Kaumakani, Hi., U.S. B2 104
Kaunakakai, Hi., U.S. B4 104
Kaunā Point, c., Hi., U.S. D6 104
Kaura-Namoda, Nig. D6 50
Kavača, Russia C19 26
Kavadarci, Mac. D8 18
Kavála, Grc. D10 18
Kavalerovo, Russia C15 28
Kāvali, India G4 40
Kavaratti, India G2 40
Kāveri, stm., India G3 40
Kavieng, Pap. N. Gui. G13 32
Kavīr, Dasht-e, des., Iran D6 42
Kawaihoa Point, c., Hi., U.S. B1 104
Kawaikini, mtn., Hi., U.S. A2 104
Kawambwa, Zam. E5 54
Kawasaki, Japan D15 28
Kawerau, N.Z. o14 63c
Kawich Peak, mtn., Nv., U.S. F5 121
Kawich Range, mts., Nv., U.S. F5 121
Kaw Lake, res., Ok., U.S. A5 129
Kaxgar, stm., China B3 40
Kay, co., Ok., U.S. A4 129
Kaya, Burkina D4 50
Kaycee, Wy., U.S. C6 143
Kayenta, Az., U.S. A5 96
Kayes, Mali D2 50
Kayseri, Tur. C6 44
Kaysville, Ut., U.S. B4 137
Kayuagung, Indon. D2 36
Kazače, Russia B15 26
Kazahskij melkosopočnik, Kaz. D9 26
Kazakh Hills see Kazahskij melkosopočnik, Kaz. D9 26
Kazakhstan, ctry., Asia E8 26
Kazalinsk, Kaz. A8 42
Kazan', Russia D6 26
Kazanka, Ukr. F12 20
Kazanlăk, Blg. C10 18
Kazan-rettō, is., Japan F17 64
Kazbek, gora, vol. A11 44
Kāzerūn, Iran E6 42
Kazincbarcika, Hung. E6 20
Kaztalovka, Kaz. E8 22
Kazym, Russia B12 22
Kéa, i., Grc. F10 18
Kea'au, Hi., U.S. D6 104
Keahole Point, c., Hi., U.S. D5 104
Kealaikahiki, Lae 'O, c., Hi., U.S. C5 104
Kealaikahiki Channel, strt., Hi., U.S. C5 104
Kealakekua, Hi., U.S. D6 104
Kealia, Hi., U.S. A2 104
Keams Canyon, Az., U.S. B5 96
Keanapapa Point, c., Hi., U.S. C4 104
Keansburg, N.J., U.S. C4 123
Kearney, Mo., U.S. B3 118
Kearney, Ne., U.S. D6 120
Kearney, co., Ne., U.S. D7 120
Kearns, Ut., U.S. C4 137
Kearny, Az., U.S. D5 96
Kearny, co., Ks., U.S. D2 109
Kearny, N.J., U.S. h8 123
Keban Barajı, res., Tur. C8 44
Keban Reservoir see Keban Barajı, res., Tur. C8 44
Kébèmer, Sen. C1 50
Kebnekaise, mtn., Swe. C8 10
K'ebrī Dehar, Eth. B8 54
Kecskemét, Hung. F5 20
Kedges Straits, strt., Md., U.S. D5 113
Kedgwick, N.B., Can. B2 87
Kediri, Indon. E4 36
Kedon, Russia C17 26
Kédougou, Sen. D2 50
Keego Harbor, Mi., U.S. o15 115
Keene, N.H., U.S. E2 122
Keene, Tx., U.S. n9 136
Keer-Weer, Cape, c., Austl. C3 62
Keeseville, N.Y., U.S. f11 125
Keesler Air Force Base, mil., Ms., U.S. E5 117
Keetmanshoop, Nmb. D2 56
Keet Seel Ruin, hist., Az., U.S. A5 96
Keewatin, On., Can. E4 86
Keewatin, Mn., U.S. C5 116
Kefallinía, i., Grc. E8 18
Kefamenanu, Indon. E6 36
Keffi, Nig. E6 50
Keflavík, Ice. m17 10a
Kegonsa, Lake, l., Wi., U.S. F4 142
Kehra, Est. G11 10
Ke-hsi Mānsām, Mya. B3 34
Keila, Est. G11 10
Keiser, Ar., U.S. B5 97
Keith, co., Ne., U.S. C4 120
Keizer, Or., U.S. C3 130
Kejimkujik National Park, N.S., Can. E4 87
Kekaha, Hi., U.S. B2 104
Kékes, mtn., Hung. F5 20
K'elafo, Eth. B8 54
Kelan, China B3 30
Kelantan, stm., Malay. B2 36
Kelibia, Tun. F3 18
Kelkit, stm., Tur. B7 44
Kelkit, Tur. B8 44
Keller, Tx., U.S. n9 136
Kellerberrin, Austl. G2 60
Kelleys Island, i., Oh., U.S. A3 128
Kellogg, Ia., U.S. C5 108
Kellogg, Id., U.S. B2 105
Kelloselkä, Fin. C13 10
Kelly Air Force Base, mil., Tx., U.S. k7 136
Kelly Island, i., De., U.S. D4 101
Kellyville, Ok., U.S. B5 129
Kélo, Chad E8 50
Kelowna, B.C., Can. E8 85
Kelso, Wa., U.S. C3 140
Keluang, Malay. C2 36
Kem', Russia C5 26
Kembé, C.A.R. C4 54
Kemerovo, Russia D10 26
Kemi, Fin. D11 10
Kemijärvi, Fin. C12 10
Kemijoki, stm., Fin. C11 10
Kemmerer, Wy., U.S. E2 143
Kemp, Tx., U.S. C4 136
Kemp, Lake, res., Tx., U.S. C3 136
Kemper, co., Ms., U.S. C5 117
Kempsey, Austl. G5 62
Kempten, Ger. G12 12
Kemptville, On., Can. B9 89
Kemul, Kong, mtn., Indon. C5 36
Kenai, Ak., U.S. C9 95
Kenai Fjords National Park, Ak., U.S. D10 95
Kenai Mountains, mts., Ak., U.S. h16 95
Kenai Peninsula, pen., Ak., U.S. h16 95
Kenansville, N.C., U.S. C5 126
Kenbridge, Va., U.S. D4 139
Kendal, Eng., U.K. C5 12
Kendall, Fl., U.S. s13 102
Kendall, co., Il., U.S. B5 106
Kendall, co., Tx., U.S. E3 136
Kendall Park, N.J., U.S. C3 123
Kendallville, In., U.S. B7 107
Kendari, Indon. D6 36
Kendawangan, Indon. D4 36
Kenedy, Tx., U.S. E4 136
Kenedy, co., Tx., U.S. F4 136
Kenema, S.L. E2 50
Kenesaw, Ne., U.S. D7 120
Kenge, D.R.C. D3 54
Kēng Tung, Mya. B3 34
Kenhardt, S. Afr. D3 56
Kenilworth, Il., U.S. h9 106
Kénitra, Mor. D3 48
Kenly, N.C., U.S. B4 126
Kenmare, N.D., U.S. A3 127
Kenmore, N.Y., U.S. C2 125
Kennaday Peak, mtn., Wy., U.S. E6 143
Kennebago Lake, l., Me., U.S. C2 112
Kennebec, co., Me., U.S. D3 112
Kennebec, stm., Me., U.S. D3 112
Kennebunk, Me., U.S. E2 112
Kennebunkport, Me., U.S. E2 112
Kennedy, Cape see Canaveral, Cape, c., Fl., U.S. F11 92
Kennedy Entrance, strt., Ak., U.S. D9 95
Kenner, La., U.S. E5 111
Kennesaw, Ga., U.S. B2 103
Kennesaw Mountain, mtn., Ga., U.S. C2 103
Kennett, Mo., U.S. E7 118
Kennett Square, Pa., U.S. G10 131
Kennewick, Wa., U.S. C6 140
Keno, Or., U.S. E5 130
Kénogami, Lac, l., Qc., Can. A6 90
Kenora, On., Can. o16 89
Kenosha, Wi., U.S. F6 142
Kenosha, co., Wi., U.S. F5 142
Kenova, W.V., U.S. C2 141
Kensett, Ar., U.S. B4 97
Kensico Reservoir, res., N.Y., U.S. g13 125
Kensington, P.E., Can. C6 87
Kensington, Ct., U.S. C4 100
Kensington, Md., U.S. B3 113
Kent, co., De., U.S. D3 101
Kent, co., Md., U.S. B5 113
Kent, co., Mi., U.S. E5 115
Kent, Oh., U.S. A4 128
Kent, co., R.I., U.S. D2 132
Kent, co., Tx., U.S. C2 136
Kent, Wa., U.S. B3 140
Kentau, Kaz. B9 42
Kent City, Mi., U.S. E5 115
Kent Island, i., De., U.S. D4 101
Kent Island, i., Md., U.S. C5 113
Kentland, In., U.S. C3 107
Kenton, De., U.S. D3 101
Kenton, co., Ky., U.S. B5 110
Kenton, Oh., U.S. B2 128
Kenton, Tn., U.S. A2 135
Kent Point, c., Md., U.S. C5 113
Kentucky, stm., Ky., U.S. B5 110
Kentucky, state, U.S. C4 110
Kentucky Lake, res., U.S. D10 92
Kentwood, La., U.S. D5 111
Kentwood, Mi., U.S. F5 115
Kenvil, N.J., U.S. B3 123
Kenvir, Ky., U.S. D6 110
Kenya, ctry., Afr. C7 54
Kenya, Mount see Kirinyaga, mtn., Kenya D7 54
Kenyon, Mn., U.S. F6 116
Kenyon, R.I., U.S. F2 132
Keokea, Hi., U.S. C5 104
Keokuk, Ia., U.S. D6 108
Keokuk, co., Ia., U.S. C5 108
Keokuk Lock and Dam, U.S. D6 108
Keosauqua, Ia., U.S. D6 108
Keota, Ia., U.S. C6 108
Keota, Ok., U.S. B7 129
Keowee, Lake, res., S.C., U.S. B2 133
Kępno, Pol. D4 20
Kerala, state, India G3 40
Kerang, Austl. H3 62
Kerava, Fin. F11 10
Kerch, Ukr. G14 20
Kerch Strait, strt., Eur. G14 20
Keremeos, B.C., Can. E8 85
Keren, Erit. G12 48
Kerens, Tx., U.S. C4 136
Kerguélen, Îles, is., Afr. M10 64
Kerguelen Plateau N10 64
Kerhonkson, N.Y., U.S. D6 125
Kericho, Kenya D7 54
Kerinci, Gunung, vol., Indon. D2 36
Kerkhoven, Mn., U.S. E3 116
Kerki, Turk. C9 42
Kerkiči, Turk. F8 26
Kérkira, Grc. E7 18
Kérkira (Corfu), i., Grc. E7 18
Kermadec Islands, is., N.Z. G12 58
Kermadec Ridge L20 64
Kermadec Trench L21 64
Kermān, Iran D7 42
Kermānshāh (Bākhtarān), Iran D5 42
Kermit, Tx., U.S. D1 136

Name — Map Ref. — Page

Kermode, Mount, mtn., B.C., Can. C2 85
Kern, stm., Ca., U.S. E4 98
Kern, co., Ca., U.S. E4 98
Kernersville, N.C., U.S. A2 126
Kernville, Ca., U.S. E4 98
Kérouané, Gui. E3 50
Kerr, co., Tx., U.S. D3 136
Kerr, Lake, l., Fl., U.S. C5 102
Kerrville, Tx., U.S. D3 136
Kersey, Co., U.S. A6 99
Kershaw, S.C., U.S. B6 133
Kershaw, co., S.C., U.S. C6 133
Kerulen, stm., Asia B10 28
Keşan, Tur. B2 44
Kesennuma, Japan D16 28
Keshena, Wi., U.S. D5 142
Keskin, Tur. C5 44
Kesten'ga, Russia D14 10
Keszthely, Hung. F4 20
Ket', stm., Russia D10 26
Keta, Ghana E5 50
Ketapang, Indon. D3 36
Ketchikan, Ak., U.S. D13 95
Ketchum, Id., U.S. F4 105
Kete-Krachi, Ghana E4 50
Kętrzyn, Pol. B6 20
Kettering, Oh., U.S. C1 128
Kettle, stm., Mn., U.S. D6 116
Kettle Creek, stm., Pa., U.S. D6 131
Kettle Creek Lake, res., Pa., U.S. D6 131
Kettle Falls, Wa., U.S. A7 140
Keuka Lake, l., N.Y., U.S. C3 125
Kewanee, Il., U.S. B4 106
Kewaskum, Wi., U.S. E5 142
Kewaunee, Wi., U.S. D6 142
Kewaunee, co., Wi., U.S. D6 142
Keweenaw, co., Mi., U.S. A2 115
Keweenaw Bay, b., Mi., U.S. B2 115
Keweenaw Peninsula, pen., Mi., U.S. A3 115
Keweenaw Point, c., Mi., U.S. A3 115
Keya Paha, co., Ne., U.S. B6 120
Keya Paha, stm., U.S. A5 120
Keyhole Reservoir, res., Wy., U.S. B8 143
Key Largo, Fl., U.S. G6 102
Keyport, N.J., U.S. C4 123
Keyser, W.V., U.S. B6 141
Keystone, W.V., U.S. D3 141
Keystone Heights, Fl., U.S. C4 102
Keystone Lake, res., Ok., U.S. A5 129
Keystone Peak, mtn., Az., U.S. F4 96
Keysville, Va., U.S. C4 139
Key West, Fl., U.S. H5 102
Key West Naval Air Station, mil., Fl., U.S. H5 102
Kezar Falls, Me., U.S. E2 112
Kezar Lake, l., Me., U.S. D2 112
Kezi, Zimb. C4 56
Kežma, Russia D12 26
Khābūr, Nahr al-, stm., Asia E9 44
Khadki, India F2 40
Khairpur, Pak. E9 42
Khajrāho, India E4 40
Khakhea, Bots. C3 56
Khalkhāl, Iran D13 44
Khalkidhikí, hist. reg., Grc. D9 18
Khalkís, Grc. E9 18
Khambhāt, India E2 40
Khambhāt, Gulf of, b., India E2 40
Khāmgaon, India E3 40
Khammam, India F4 40
Khānābād, Afg. C9 42
Khān al-Baghdādī, Iraq F10 44
Khānaqīn, Iraq E11 44
Khandwa, India E3 40
Khānewāl, Pak. D10 42
Khaniá, Grc. G9 18
Khaníon, Kólpos, b., Grc. G9 18
Khanka, Lake, l., Asia C14 28
Khānpur, Pak. E10 42
Kharagpur, India E5 40
Khargon, India E3 40
Kharkiv, Ukr. E14 20
Khartoum see Al-Kharṭūm, Sudan G11 48
Khāsh, Afg. D8 42
Khāsh, Iran E8 42
Khashm al-Qirbah, Sudan H12 48
Khemis Melyana, Alg. I8 16
Khenchla, Alg. D5 14
Khenifra, Mor. E2 14
Kherson, Ukr. F12 20
Khíos, Grc. E11 18
Khíos, i., Grc. E10 18
Khmel'nyts'kyi, Ukr. E9 20
Khmil'nyk, Ukr. E9 20
Kholm, Afg. C9 42
Khomeynīshahr, Iran D6 42
Khong see Mekong, stm., Asia C4 34
Khon Kaen, Thai. C4 34
Khorramābād, Iran D5 42
Khorramshahr, Iran D5 42
Khotyn, Ukr. E9 20
Khouribga, Mor. D3 48
Khrystynivka, Ukr. E10 20
Khulna, Bngl. E5 40
Khust, Ukr. E7 20
Khuzdār, Pak. E9 42
Khvoy, Iran C4 42
Khyber Pass, Asia C2 40
Kiama, D.R.C. E3 54
Kiamba, Phil. E8 34
Kiamichi, stm., Ok., U.S. C6 129
Kiamika, stm., Qc., Can. C2 90
Kiana, Ak., U.S. B7 95
Kiangarow, Mount, mtn., Austl. F5 62
Kiawah Island, i., S.C., U.S. F7 133
Kibangou, Congo D2 54
Kibombo, D.R.C. D5 54
Kibondo, Tan. D6 54
Kibre Mengist, Eth. B7 54
Kičevo, Mac. D8 18
Kickamuit, stm., R.I., U.S. D5 132
Kickapoo, stm., Wi., U.S. E3 142
Kickapoo, Lake, res., Tx., U.S. C3 136
Kickapoo Indian Reservation, Ks., U.S. C8 109
Kicking Horse Pass, Can. D2 84
Kidal, Mali C5 50
Kidatu, Tan. E7 54
Kidder, co., N.D., U.S. C6 127
Kidira, Sen. D2 50
Kiefer, Ok., U.S. B5 129
Kiel, Ger. C12 12
Kiel, Wi., U.S. E5 142
Kiel Bay see Kieler Bucht, b., Ger. C12 12
Kiel Canal see Nord-Ostsee-Kanal, Ger. C11 12
Kielce, Pol. D6 20
Kieler Bucht, b., Ger. C12 12
Kiester, Mn., U.S. G5 116
Kiev see Kyïv, Ukr. D11 20
Kiev Reservoir see Kyïvs'ke vodoskhovyshche, res., Ukr. D11 20
Kiffa, Maur. C2 50
Kigali, Rw. D6 54
Kigoma, Tan. D5 54
Kihčik, Russia D17 26
Kihei, Hi., U.S. C5 104
Kiholo Bay, b., Hi., U.S. D5 104
Kii Strait see Kii-suidō, strt., Japan E15 28
Kii-suidō, strt., Japan E15 28
Kikinda, Serb. B8 18
Kikládhes, is., Grc. F10 18
Kikori, Pap. N. Gui. H11 32
Kikwit, D.R.C. E3 54
Kil, Swe. G5 10
Kilauea, Hi., U.S. A2 104
Kilauea Crater, crat., Hi., U.S. D6 104
Kilauea Point, c., Hi., U.S. A2 104
Kilchu-ŭp, N. Kor. B1 31
Kildurk, Austl. D4 60
Kilgore, Tx., U.S. C5 136
Kilibo, Benin E5 50
Kiliia, Ukr. G10 20
Kilimanjaro, mtn., Tan. D7 54
Kilimli, Tur. B4 44
Kilindoni, Tan. E7 54
Kilis, Tur. D7 44
Kilkenny, Ire. D3 12
Kilkís, Grc. D9 18
Killaloe Station, On., Can. B7 89
Killam, Ab., Can. C5 84
Killarney, Mb., Can. E2 86
Killarney Provincial Park, On., Can. A3 89
Killdeer, N.D., U.S. B3 127
Killeen, Tx., U.S. D4 136
Killen, Al., U.S. A2 94
Killian, La., U.S. h10 111
Killik, stm., Ak., U.S. B9 95
Killiniq Island, i., Can. F27 82
Killona, La., U.S. h11 111
Kilmarnock, Scot., U.K. C4 12
Kilmarnock, Va., U.S. C6 139
Kilmichael, Ms., U.S. B4 117
Kiln, Ms., U.S. E4 117
Kilomines, D.R.C. C6 54
Kilosa, Tan. E7 54
Kilttān Island, i., India G2 40
Kilwa, D.R.C. E5 54
Kilwa Kivinje, Tan. E7 54
Kimba, Austl. G2 62
Kimball, Mn., U.S. E4 116
Kimball, Ne., U.S. C2 120
Kimball, co., Ne., U.S. C2 120
Kimball, S.D., U.S. D7 134
Kimball, Mount, mtn., Ak., U.S. C11 95
Kimberley, B.C., Can. E9 85
Kimberley, S. Afr. D3 56
Kimberley Plateau, plat., Austl. D4 60
Kimberlin Heights, Tn., U.S. n14 135
Kimberly, Al., U.S. B3 94
Kimberly, Id., U.S. G4 105
Kimberly, Wi., U.S. h9 142
Kimberly, W.V., U.S. m13 141
Kimble, co., Tx., U.S. D3 136
Kimch'aek, N. Kor. C13 28
Kimito, i., Fin. G10 10
Kimry, Russia C6 22
Kinabalu, Gunong, mtn., Malay. B5 36
Kinabatangan, stm., Malay. B5 36
Kinbasket Lake, res., B.C., Can. D8 85
Kincaid, Il., U.S. D4 106
Kincaid, W.V., U.S. m13 141
Kincaid, Lake, res., Il., U.S. D4 106
Kincardine, On., Can. C3 89
Kincheloe Air Force Base, mil., Mi., U.S. B6 115
Kinda, D.R.C. E5 54
Kinder, La., U.S. D3 111
Kindia, Gui. D2 50
Kindu, D.R.C. D5 54
Kinešma, Russia C7 22
King, N.C., U.S. A2 126
King, co., Tx., U.S. C2 136
King, co., Wa., U.S. B3 140
King, Wi., U.S. D4 142
King and Queen, co., Va., U.S. C6 139
Kingaroy, Austl. F5 62
King City, Ca., U.S. D3 98
King City, Mo., U.S. A3 118
King Cove, Ak., U.S. E7 95
Kingfield, Me., U.S. D2 112
Kingfisher, Ok., U.S. B4 129
Kingfisher, co., Ok., U.S. B3 129
King George, co., Va., U.S. B5 139
Kingisepp, Russia G13 10
King Island, i., Austl. H3 62
King Island, i., B.C., Can. C4 85
King Lear Peak, mtn., Nv., U.S. B3 121
King Leopold Ranges, mts., Austl. D3 60
Kingman, Az., U.S. B1 96
Kingman, Ks., U.S. E5 109
Kingman, co., Ks., U.S. E5 109
King Mountain, mtn., Or., U.S. E3 130
King Mountain, mtn., Or., U.S. D8 130
Kingombe, D.R.C. D5 54
King Peak, mtn., Ca., U.S. B1 98
Kings, stm., Ar., U.S. A2 97
Kings, stm., Ca., U.S. D4 98
Kings, co., Ca., U.S. D4 98
Kings, Ms., U.S. C3 117
Kings, stm., Nv., U.S. B3 121
Kings, co., N.Y., U.S. E7 125
King Salmon, Ak., U.S. D8 95
Kingsburg, Ca., U.S. D4 98
Kingsbury, co., S.D., U.S. C8 134
Kings Canyon National Park, Ca., U.S. D4 98
Kingsey-Falls, Qc., Can. D5 90
Kingsford, Mi., U.S. C2 115
Kingsland, Ga., U.S. F5 103
Kingsland, Tx., U.S. D3 136
Kingsley, Ia., U.S. B2 108
Kingsley, Mi., U.S. D5 115
King's Lynn, Eng., U.K. D7 12
Kings Mountain, N.C., U.S. B1 126
King Sound, strt., Austl. D3 60
Kings Peak, mtn., Ut., U.S. C5 137
King's Point, N.L., Can. D3 88
Kingsport, Tn., U.S. C11 135
Kingston, On., Can. C8 89
Kingston, Jam. B4 80
Kingston, Ga., U.S. B2 103
Kingston, Id., U.S. B2 105
Kingston, Ma., U.S. C6 114
Kingston, N.H., U.S. E4 122
Kingston, N.Y., U.S. D6 125
Kingston, Oh., U.S. C3 128
Kingston, Ok., U.S. D5 129
Kingston, Pa., U.S. D10 131
Kingston, R.I., U.S. F3 132
Kingston, Tn., U.S. D9 135
Kingston Springs, Tn., U.S. A4 135
Kingston upon Hull, Eng., U.K. D6 12
Kingstown see Dún Laoghaire, Ire. D3 12
Kingstown, St. Vin. C7 80
Kingstown, Md., U.S. B5 113
Kingstree, S.C., U.S. D8 133
Kingsville, On., Can. E2 89
Kingsville, Md., U.S. B5 113
Kingsville (North Kingsville), Oh., U.S. A5 128
Kingsville, Tx., U.S. F4 136
Kingsville Naval Air Station, mil., Tx., U.S. F4 136
King William, co., Va., U.S. C5 139
King William's Town, S. Afr. E4 56
Kingwood, W.V., U.S. B5 141
Kinistino, Sk., Can. E3 91
Kinkaid Lake, res., Il., U.S. F4 106
Kinkala, Congo D2 54
Kinloch, Mo., U.S. f13 118
Kinmundy, Il., U.S. E5 106
Kinnaird Head, c., Scot., U.K. B6 12
Kinnelon, N.J., U.S. B4 123
Kinney, co., Tx., U.S. E2 136
Kinsey, Al., U.S. D4 94
Kinshasa, D.R.C. D3 54
Kinsley, Ks., U.S. E4 109
Kinston, N.C., U.S. B5 126
Kintampo, Ghana E4 50
Kintyre, pen., Scot., U.K. C4 12
Kinyeti, mtn., Sudan J11 48
Kinzia, D.R.C. D3 54
Kiowa, co., Co., U.S. C8 99
Kiowa, co., Ks., U.S. E4 109
Kiowa, Ks., U.S. E5 109
Kiowa, Ok., U.S. C6 129
Kiowa, co., Ok., U.S. C2 129
Kiowa Creek, stm., Ok., U.S. A1 129
Kiparissiakós Kólpos, b., Grc. F8 18
Kipembawe, Tan. E6 54
Kipengere Range, mts., Tan. E6 54
Kipili, Tan. E6 54
Kipini, Kenya D8 54
Kipnuk, Ak., U.S. C7 95
Kipushi, D.R.C. F5 54
Kirbyville, Tx., U.S. D6 136
Kirensk, Russia D12 26
Kirgiz Range, mts., Asia A2 40
Kiri, D.R.C. D3 54
Kiribati, is., Kir. D11 58
Kiribati, ctry., Oc. E12 58
Kırıkhan, Tur. D7 44
Kırıkkale, Tur. C5 44
Kirinyaga (Kenya, Mount), mtn., Kenya D7 54
Kiriši, Russia C5 22
Kiritimati (Christmas Island), atoll, Kir. D14 58
Kırkağaç, Tur. C2 44
Kirkcaldy, Scot., U.K. B5 12
Kirkenes, Nor. B14 10
Kirkjubæjarklaustur, Ice. m19 10a
Kirkland, Il., U.S. A5 106
Kirkland, Wa., U.S. B3 140
Kirkland Lake, On., Can. o19 89
Kırklareli, Tur. B2 44
Kirklin, In., U.S. D5 107
Kirkpatrick, Mount, mtn., Ant. E22 67
Kirksville, Mo., U.S. A5 118
Kirkwall, Scot., U.K. A5 12
Kirkwood, S. Afr. E4 56
Kirkwood, De., U.S. B3 101
Kirkwood, Il., U.S. C3 106
Kirkwood, Mo., U.S. f13 118
Kirov, Russia B13 20
Kirov, Russia D6 26
Kirovabad see Gäncä, Azer. B12 44
Kirovakan see Vanadzor, Arm. B11 44
Kirovohrad, Ukr. E12 20
Kirovsk, Russia A5 22
Kirovsk, Turk. C8 42
Kirovskij, Russia D17 26
Kirovskij, Russia A2 31
Kirs, Russia C9 22
Kirsanov, Russia D7 22
Kırşehir, Tur. C6 44
Kīrthar Range, mts., Pak. E9 42
Kirtland, N.M., U.S. A1 124
Kirtland Air Force Base, mil., N.M., U.S. k7 124
Kiruna, Swe. C9 10
Kirwin Reservoir, res., Ks., U.S. C4 109
Kisangani, D.R.C. C5 54
Kisar, Pulau, i., Indon. E7 36
Kisaran, Indon. C1 36
Kishangarh Bās, India D2 40
Kishi, Nig. E5 50
Kishinev see Chişinău, Mol. F10 20
Kishiwada, Japan D3 31
Kishwaukee, stm., Il., U.S. A5 106
Kisii, Kenya D6 54
Kisiju, Tan. E7 54
Kiska Island, i., Ak., U.S. E3 95
Kiskunfélegyháza, Hung. F5 20
Kiskunhalas, Hung. F5 20
Kislovodsk, Russia B4 42
Kismaayo, Som. D8 54
Kissidougou, Gui. E2 50
Kissimmee, stm., Fl., U.S. E5 102
Kissimmee, Fl., U.S. D5 102
Kissimmee, Lake, l., Fl., U.S. E5 102
Kississing Lake, l., Mb., Can. B1 86
Kistler, W.V., U.S. D3 141
Kisumu, Kenya D6 54
Kisvárda, Hung. E7 20
Kita, Mali D3 50
Kitaibaraki, Japan C4 31
Kitakyūshū, Japan E14 28
Kitale, Kenya C7 54
Kitami, Japan B4 31
Kit Carson, co., Co., U.S. B8 99
Kitchener, On., Can. D4 89
Kíthira, i., Grc. F9 18
Kíthnos, i., Grc. F10 18
Kitimat, B.C., Can. B3 85
Kitsap, co., Wa., U.S. B3 140
Kitscoty, Ab., Can. C5 84
Kittanning, Pa., U.S. E2 131
Kittatinny Mountain, mtn., U.S. B2 123
Kittery, Me., U.S. E2 112
Kittery Point, Me., U.S. E2 112
Kittitas, co., Wa., U.S. B4 140
Kittitas, Wa., U.S. C5 140
Kitts, Ky., U.S. D6 110
Kittson, co., Mn., U.S. B2 116
Kitty Hawk, N.C., U.S. A7 126
Kitty Hawk Bay, b., N.C., U.S. A7 126
Kitui, Kenya D7 54
Kitwe, Zam. A4 56
Kiunga, Kenya D8 54
Kiviõli, Est. G12 10
Kivu, Lac, l., Afr. D5 54
Kizëma, Russia B7 22
Kızılcahamam, Tur. B5 44
Kızılırmak, stm., Tur. B6 44
Kızıltepe, Tur. D9 44
Kizljar, Russia B5 42
Kizyl-Atrek, Turk. C6 42
Kjusjur, Russia B14 26
Kjustendil, Blg. C9 18
Klabat, Gunung, vol., Indon. C7 36
Kladno, Czech Rep. D3 20
Klagenfurt, Aus. G14 12
Klaipėda, Lith. I9 10
Klamath, co., Or., U.S. E5 130
Klamath, stm., U.S. B2 98
Klamath Falls, Or., U.S. E5 130
Klamath Mountains, mts., U.S. E2 130
Klang, Malay. C2 36
Klatovy, Czech Rep. E2 20
Klawer, S. Afr. E2 56
Klawock, Ak., U.S. D13 95
Kleberg, co., Tx., U.S. F4 136
Klerksdorp, S. Afr. D4 56
Kletna, Russia C12 20
Klickitat, Wa., U.S. D4 140
Klickitat, co., Wa., U.S. D4 140
Klickitat, stm., Wa., U.S. C4 140
Klimpfjäll, Swe. D6 10
Klin, Russia C6 22
Klincy, Russia C12 20
Klipplaat, S. Afr. E3 56
Ključevskaja Sopka, vulkan, vol., Russia D18 26
Kłobuck, Pol. D5 20
Kłodzko, Pol. D4 20
Klondike, hist. reg., Yk., Can. F12 82
Klondike Gold Rush National Historical Park, Ak., U.S. k22 95
Kluczbork, Pol. D5 20
Klutina Lake, l., Ak., U.S. g19 95
Knapp Creek, stm., W.V., U.S. C5 141
Knee Lake, l., Mb., Can. B4 86
Kneža, Blg. C10 18
Knife, stm., N.D., U.S. B3 127
Knightdale, N.C., U.S. B4 126
Knight Inlet, b., B.C., Can. D5 85
Knight Island, i., Ak., U.S. g18 95
Knightstown, In., U.S. E6 107
Knightsville, In., U.S. E3 107
Knightville Reservoir, res., Ma., U.S. B2 114
Knittelfeld, Aus. G14 12
Knob Noster, Mo., U.S. C4 118
Knollwood, W.V., U.S. m12 141
Knossós, hist., Grc. G10 18
Knott, co., Ky., U.S. C6 110
Knox, co., Il., U.S. B3 106
Knox, In., U.S. B4 107
Knox, co., In., U.S. G3 107
Knox, co., Ky., U.S. D6 110
Knox, co., Me., U.S. D4 112
Knox, co., Mo., U.S. A5 118
Knox, co., Ne., U.S. B8 120
Knox, co., Oh., U.S. B3 128
Knox, Pa., U.S. D2 131
Knox, co., Tn., U.S. C10 135
Knox, co., Tx., U.S. C3 136
Knox, Cape, c., B.C., Can. B1 85
Knox City, Tx., U.S. C3 136
Knox Coast, Ant. C15 67
Knoxville, Ia., U.S. C4 108
Knoxville, Il., U.S. C3 106
Knoxville, Tn., U.S. D10 135
Knysna, S. Afr. E3 56
Kōbe, Japan E15 28
København (Copenhagen), Den. I5 10
Koblenz, Ger. E10 12
Kobroor, Pulau, i., Indon. H9 32
Kobryn, Bela. C8 20
Kobuk, stm., Ak., U.S. B8 95
Kobuk Valley National Park, Ak., U.S. B8 95
Kočani, Mac. D9 18
Kočevo, Russia C9 22
Kochi (Cochin), India H3 40
Kōchi, Japan E14 28
Koch Peak, mtn., Mt., U.S. E5 119
Kodaikānal, India G3 40
Kodiak, Ak., U.S. D9 95
Kodiak Island, i., Ak., U.S. D9 95
Kodok, Sudan B6 54
Koës, Nmb. D2 56
Kofa Mountains, mts., Az., U.S. D2 96
Köflach, Aus. G14 12
Koforidua, Ghana E4 50
Kōfu, Japan D15 28
Kohala Mountains, mts., Hi., U.S. C6 104
Kohāt, Pak. D10 42
Kohima, India D6 40
Kohler, Wi., U.S. E6 142
Kohtla-Järve, Est. G12 10
Koihoa, India H6 40
Koindu, S.L. E2 50
Kojgorodok, Russia B9 22
Kojonup, Austl. G2 60
Kokand, Uzb. E9 26
Kokanee Glacier Provincial Park, B.C., Can. E9 85
Kokčetav, Kaz. D8 26
Kokemäki, Fin. F10 10
Kokenau, Indon. G10 32
Kokkola, Fin. E10 10
Kokoda, Pap. N. Gui. H12 32
Koko Head, c., Hi., U.S. B4 104
Kokolik, stm., Ak., U.S. B7 95

Name — Map Ref. — Page

Kokomo, In., U.S. D5 107
Koko Nor see Qinghai Hu, l., China D8 28
Kokosing, stm., Oh., U.S. B3 128
Kokstad, S. Afr. E4 56
Kola, Russia B15 10
Kolaka, Indon. D6 36
Kola Peninsula see Kol'skij poluostrov, pen., Russia C5 26
Kolār Gold Fields, India G3 40
Kolbio, Kenya D8 54
Kolda, Sen. D2 50
Kolding, Den. I3 10
Kole, D.R.C. D4 54
Kolea, Alg. I8 16
Kolguev, ostrov, i., Russia C6 26
Kolhāpur, India F2 40
Kolka, Lat. H10 10
Kolkata (Calcutta), India E5 40
Kolmogorovo, Russia D11 26
Köln (Cologne), Ger. E10 12
Koło, Pol. C5 20
Koloa, Hi., U.S. B2 104
Kołobrzeg, Pol. B3 20
Kolokani, Mali D3 50
Kolomna, Russia D5 26
Kolonia see Palikir, Micron. D9 58
Kolonodale, Indon. D6 36
Kolpaševo, Russia D10 26
Kolpino, Russia C5 22
Kol'skij poluostrov, pen., Russia C5 26
Kolwezi, D.R.C. F5 54
Kolyma, stm., Russia C17 26
Kolymskaja, Russia C17 26
Komandorskie ostrova, is., Russia D18 26
Komandorski Islands see Komandorskie ostrova, is., Russia D18 26
Komárno, Slvk. F5 20
Komatipoort, S. Afr. D5 56
Kome Island, i., Ug. D6 54
Komi, state, Russia C7 26
Komló, Hung. F5 20
Kommunarsk see Alchevs'k, Ukr. E15 20
Kommunizma, pik see Ismail Samani, pik, mtn., Taj. F9 26
Komodo, Pulau, i., Indon. E5 36
Komoé, stm., Afr. E4 50
Komotiní, Grc. D10 18
Komsomolec, Kaz. D11 22
Komsomolec, ostrov, i., Russia A11 26
Komsomol'sk-na-Amure, Russia D15 26
Kōnāhuanui, mtn., Hi., U.S. g10 104
Konārak, hist., India F5 40
Konawa, Ok., U.S. C5 129
Kondagaon, India F4 40
Kondinin, Austl. G2 60
Kondoa, Tan. D7 54
Kondopoga, Russia C5 26
Kondoz, Afg. C9 42
Koné, N. Cal. I8 62a
Kong, stm., Asia C5 34
Kongolo, D.R.C. E5 54
Kongor, Sudan B6 54
Kongsvinger, Nor. F5 10
Kongur Shan, mtn., China D3 28
Königsberg see Kaliningrad, Russia D4 26
Konin, Pol. C5 20
Konna, Mali D4 50
Konomoc, Lake, res., Ct., U.S. D7 100
Konoša, Russia C6 26
Konotop, Ukr. D12 20
Konstanz, Ger. G11 12
Kontagora, Nig. D6 50
Kontcha, Cam. B2 54
Kon Tum, Viet. D5 34
Konya, Tur. D5 44
Konza, Kenya D7 54
Konžakovskij Kamen', gora, mtn., Russia C10 22
Koochiching, co., Mn., U.S. B4 116
Kookynie, Austl. F3 60
Ko'olau Range, mts., Hi., U.S. f10 104
Koontz Lake, In., U.S. B5 107
Kooskia, Id., U.S. C3 105
Kootenai, co., Id., U.S. B2 105
Kootenay Lake, l., B.C., Can. E9 85
Kootenay National Park, B.C., Can. D9 85
Kópasker, Ice. k20 10a
Kópavogur, Ice. l18 10a
Kopejsk, Russia C11 22
Kopet Mountains, mts., Asia C7 42
Köping, Swe. G6 10
Koppang, Nor. F4 10
Koppel, Pa., U.S. E1 131
Koprivnica, Cro. A6 18
Korab (Korabit, Maja e), mtn., Eur. D8 18
Korabit, Maja e (Korab), mtn., Eur. D8 18
Korāput, India F4 40
Korba, India E4 40
Korbol, Chad D8 50
Korçë, Alb. D8 18
Korea, North, ctry., Asia C13 28
Korea, South, ctry., Asia D10 28
Korea Bay, b., Asia D12 28
Korea Strait, strt., Asia E13 28
Korenovsk, Russia A3 42
Korf, Russia C18 26
Korfovskij, Russia A3 31
Korhogo, C. Iv. E3 50
Korinthiakós Kólpos, b., Grc. E9 18
Kórinthos, Grc. F9 18
Kōriyama, Japan C4 31
Korjakskaja Sopka, vulkan, vol., Russia D17 26
Korjakskoe nagor'e, mts., Russia C18 26
Korjažma, Russia B8 22
Korkino, Russia D11 22
Korkuteli, Tur. D4 44
Korla, China C5 28
Korliki, Russia C10 26
Kornat, Otok, i., Cro. C5 18
Korogwe, Tan. E7 54
Koronadal, Phil. E8 34
Koronis, Lake, l., Mn., U.S. E4 116
Koror, Palau E9 32
Koro Sea, Fiji F12 58
Korosten', Ukr. D10 20
Korostyshiv, Ukr. D10 20
Korovin Volcano, vol., Ak., U.S. E5 95
Korsakov, Russia E16 26
Korsnäs, Fin. E9 10
Kos, i., Grc. F11 18
Koš-Agač, Russia D10 26
Koščagyl, Kaz. A6 42
Kościan, Pol. C4 20
Kościerzyna, Pol. B4 20
Kosciusko, co., In., U.S. B6 107
Kosciusko, Ms., U.S. B4 117
Kosciusko, Mount, mtn., Austl. H4 62
Koshkonong, Lake, l., Wi., U.S. F5 142
Košice, Slvk. E6 20
Kosju, Russia A10 22
Koslan, Russia B8 22
Kosovska Mitrovica, Serb. C8 18
Kossou, Lac de, res., C. Iv. E3 50
Kossuth, co., Ia., U.S. A3 108
Kostiantynivka, Ukr. E14 20
Kostopil', Ukr. D9 20
Kostroma, Russia C7 22
Kostrzyn, Pol. C3 20
Koszalin, Pol. B4 20
Kőszeg, Hung. F4 20
Kota, India D3 40
Kotaagung, Indon. E2 36
Kotabaru, Indon. G6 32
Kotabaru see Jayapura, Indon. G11 32
Kota Belud, Malay. B5 36
Kota Bharu, Malay. B2 36
Kotabumi, Indon. D2 36
Kota Kinabalu, Malay. B5 36
Kotamobagu, Indon. C6 36
Kotel'nič, Russia C8 22
Kotel'nikovo, Russia E7 22
Kotel'nyj, ostrov, i., Russia B15 26
Kotido, Ug. C6 54
Kotka, Fin. F12 10
Kot Kapūra, India C2 40
Kotlas, Russia C6 26
Kotlik, Ak., U.S. C7 95
Kotovs'k, Ukr. F10 20
Kotri, Pak. E9 42
Kottagūdem, India F4 40
Kottayam, India H3 40
Kotte see Sri Jayewardenepura Kotte, Sri L. H4 40
Kotto, stm., C.A.R. B4 54
Kotuj, stm., Russia C12 26
Kotzebue, Ak., U.S. B7 95
Kotzebue Sound, strt., Ak., U.S. B7 95
Kouchibouguac National Park, N.B., Can. C5 87
Koudougou, Burkina D4 50
Kouki, C.A.R. B3 54
Koulamoutou, Gabon D2 54
Koulikoro, Mali D3 50
Koumac, N. Cal. I8 62a
Koumbia, Gui. D2 50
Koumra, Chad E8 50
Koundâra, Gui. D2 50
Kounradskij, Kaz. B2 28
Kountze, Tx., U.S. D5 136
Kourou, Fr. Gu. B9 70
Kouroussa, Gui. D3 50
Kousséri, Cam. D8 50
Koussi, Emi, mtn., Chad C8 50
Koutiala, Mali D3 50
Kouts, In., U.S. B3 107
Kouvola, Fin. F12 10
Kovdor, Russia C14 10
Kovdozero, ozero, res., Russia C15 10
Kovel', Ukr. D8 20
Kovrov, Russia C7 22
Kowloon see Jiulong, China E3 30
Koyukuk, stm., Ak., U.S. B8 95
Kozan, Tur. D6 44
Kozáni, Grc. D8 18
Kozel'sk, Russia B13 20
Kozhikode (Calicut), India G3 40
Koziatyn, Ukr. E10 20
Kozlu, Tur. B4 44
Kpalimé, Togo E5 50
Kra, Isthmus of, isth., Asia D3 34
Krâchéh, Camb. D5 34
Kragerø, Nor. G3 10
Kragujevac, Serb. B8 18
Kraków, Pol. D5 20
Kralendijk, Neth. Ant. C6 80
Kraljevo, Serb. C8 18
Kramators'k, Ukr. E14 20
Kramfors, Swe. E7 10
Kranj, Slvn. A5 18
Kraśnik, Pol. D7 20
Krasnoarmiis'k, Ukr. E14 20
Krasnodar, Russia E5 26
Krasnogorsk, Russia B16 28
Krasnohrad, Ukr. E13 20
Krasnojarsk, Russia D11 26
Krasnoperekops'k, Ukr. G12 20
Krasnosel'kup, Russia C10 26
Krasnoturjinsk, Russia C11 22
Krasnoufimsk, Russia C10 22
Krasnoural'sk, Russia D8 26
Krasnovišersk, Russia B10 22
Krasnovodsk see Turkmenbaši, Turk. E7 26
Krasnoyarsk see Krasnojarsk, Russia D11 26
Krasnoznamenskoje, Kaz. D8 26
Krasnyi Luch, Ukr. E15 20
Krasnystaw, Pol. D7 20
Krasyliv, Ukr. E9 20
Krebs, Ok., U.S. C6 129
Kremenchug Reservoir see Kremenchuts'ke vodoskhovyshche, res., Ukr. E12 20
Kremenchuk, Ukr. E12 20
Kremenchuts'ke vodoskhovyshche, res., Ukr. E12 20
Kremenets', Ukr. D8 20
Kremmling, Co., U.S. A4 99
Kretinga, Lith. I9 10
Kreuztal, Ger. E11 12
Kribi, Cam. C1 54
Krishna, stm., India F3 40
Krishnanagar, India E5 40
Kristiansand, Nor. G3 10
Kristianstad, Swe. I6 10
Kristiansund, Nor. E2 10
Kristiinankaupunki, Fin. E9 10
Kristineberg, Swe. D8 10
Kristinehamn, Swe. G6 10
Kríti (Crete), i., Grc. G10 18
Kritikón Pélagos, Grc. G10 18
Krjukovo, Russia C17 26
Krk, Otok, i., Cro. B5 18
Krnov, Czech Rep. D4 20
Kroměříž, Czech Rep. E4 20
Krŏng Kaôh Kŏng, Camb. D4 34
Kronštadt, Russia B4 22
Kroonstad, S. Afr. D4 56
Kropotkin, Russia A4 42
Krosno, Pol. E6 20
Krotoszyn, Pol. D4 20
Krotz Springs, La., U.S. D4 111
Krugersdorp, S. Afr. D4 56
Krui, Indon. E2 36
Krung Thep (Bangkok), Thai. D4 34
Kruševac, Serb. C8 18
Kruzof Island, i., Ak., U.S. m21 95
Kryčau, Bela. C11 20
Krymsk, Russia G14 20
Kryms'ki hory, mts., Ukr. G13 20
Kryms'kyi pivostriv (Crimean Peninsula), pen., Ukr. G12 20
Kryvyi Rih, Ukr. F12 20
Ksar-el-Kebir, Mor. J4 16
Ksenevka, Russia A11 28
Ksenskij, Russia D14 20
Kuala Kangsar, Malay. C2 36
Kualakapuas, Indon. D4 36
Kuala Krai, Malay. B2 36
Kuala Lipis, Malay. C2 36
Kuala Lumpur, Malay. C2 36
Kuala Pilah, Malay. C2 36
Kuala Terengganu, Malay. B2 36
Kuantan, Malay. C2 36
Kuban', stm., Russia E6 26
Kuching, Malay. C4 36
Kuçovë, Alb. D8 18
Kudat, Malay. B5 36
Kudus, Indon. E4 36
Kudymkar, Russia C9 22
Kū'ē'ē Ruins, hist., Hi., U.S. D6 104
Kufstein, Aus. G13 12
Kūhdasht, Iran F12 44
Kuito, Ang. F3 54
Kuiu Island, i., Ak., U.S. m23 95
Kujawy, reg., Pol. C5 20
Kujbyšev see Samara, Russia D7 26
Kujbyševe, Russia D9 26
Kujbyševskoe vodohranilišče, res., Russia D8 22
Kujgan, Kaz. A10 42
Kujū-san, vol., Japan D2 31
Kukawa, Nig. D7 50
Kula, Tur. C3 44
Kula, Hi., U.S. C5 104
Kula Kangri, mtn., Bhu. D6 40
Kuldīga, Lat. H9 10
Kule, Bots. C3 56
Kulebaki, Russia C7 22
Kuljab, Taj. F8 26
Kulmbach, Ger. E12 12
Kuloj, Russia B7 22
Kulpmont, Pa., U.S. E9 131
Kul'sary, Kaz. E7 26
Kulu, Tur. C5 44
Kulumadau, Pap. N. Gui. H13 32
Kumagaya, Japan C3 31
Kumai, Indon. D4 36
Kumai, Teluk, b., Indon. D4 36
Kumamoto, Japan E14 28
Kumanovo, Mac. C8 18
Kumasi, Ghana E4 50
Kumba, Cam. C1 54
Kumbakonam, India G3 40
Kume-jima, i., Japan A9 34
Kuminskij, Russia C12 22
Kumluca, Tur. D4 44
Kumo, Nig. E7 50
Kumta, India G2 40
Kumukahi, Cape, c., Hi., U.S. D7 104
Kuna, Id., U.S. F2 105
Kunašir, ostrov, i., Russia E16 26
Kunda, Est. G12 10
Kundāpura, India G2 40
Kundur, Pulau, i., Indon. C2 36
Kunene (Cunene), stm., Afr. B1 56
Kunghit Island, i., B.C., Can. C2 85
Kungrad, Uzb. B7 42
Kungur, Russia C10 22
Kunhing, Mya. B3 34
Kunlun Shan, mts., China D5 28
Kunming, China F8 28
Kununurra, Austl. D4 60
Kunya, Nig. D6 50
Kuopio, Fin. E12 10
Kupang, Indon. F6 36
Kup'ians'k, Ukr. E14 20
Kupreanof Island, i., Ak., U.S. m23 95
Kuqa, China C4 28
Kuqa, China C4 28
Kür, stm., Asia C13 44
Kurashiki, Japan D2 31
Kuraymah, Sudan G11 48
Kurčatov, Russia D13 20
Kürdämir, Azer. B13 44
Kurdistan, hist. reg., Asia D10 44
Kure, Japan D2 31
Kure Atoll, i., Hi., U.S. k12 104
Kurejka, stm., Russia C10 26
Kuresaare, Est. G10 10
Kurgan, Russia D8 26
Kurgan-Tjube, Taj. C9 42
Kuril Islands see Kuril'skie ostrova, is., Russia E16 26
Kuril'sk, Russia B17 28
Kuril'skie ostrova (Kuril Islands), is., Russia E16 26
Kuril Trench A7 144
Kurmuk, Sudan H11 48
Kurnool, India F3 40
Kursk, Russia D5 26
Kurtalan, Tur. D9 44
Kurtamyš, Russia D11 22
Kurtistown, Hi., U.S. D6 104
Kuruman, stm., S. Afr. D3 56
Kuruman, S. Afr. D3 56
Kurume, Japan D2 31
Kurumkan, Russia D13 26
Kurunegala, Sri L. H4 40
Kuşadası, Tur. D2 44
Kuşadası Körfezi, b., Tur. D2 44
Kuščevskaja, Russia F15 20
Kuş Gölü, l., Tur. B2 44
Kushiro, Japan C16 28
Kushui, China C6 28
Kuskokwim, stm., Ak., U.S. C8 95
Kuskokwim Bay, b., Ak., U.S. D7 95
Kuskokwim Mountains, mts., Ak., U.S. C8 95
Kustanaj, Kaz. D8 26
Kūstī, Sudan H11 48
Kut, Ko, i., Thai. D4 34
Kütahya, Tur. C3 44
Kutaisi, Geor. A10 44
Kutch see Kachchh, Gulf of, b., India E1 40
Kutch, Gulf of see Kachchh, Gulf of, b., India E1 40
Kutch, Rann of, reg., Asia E1 40
Kutina, Cro. B6 18
Kutno, Pol. C5 20
Kutu, D.R.C. D3 54
Kutztown, Pa., U.S. E10 131
Kuujjuaq, Qc., Can. g13 90
Kuusamo, Fin. D13 10
Kuusankoski, Fin. F12 10
Kuvango, Ang. A2 56
Kuwait, ctry., Asia E5 42
Kuwait see Al-Kuwayt, Kuw. E5 42
Kuybyshev see Samara, Russia D7 26
Kuybyshev see Kujbyšev, Russia D9 26
Kuybyshev Reservoir see Kujbyševskoe vodohranilišče, res., Russia D8 22
Kuytun, Mount, mtn., Asia E10 26
Kuz'movka, Russia C11 26
Kuzneck, Russia D6 26
Kuzomen', Russia A6 22
Kvænangen, b., Nor. A9 10
Kvaløya, i., Nor. B8 10
Kvareli, Geor. B11 44
Kwa, stm., D.R.C. D3 54
Kwakoegron, Sur. B8 70
Kwamouth, D.R.C. D3 54
Kwando (Cuando), stm., Afr. B3 56
Kwangju, S. Kor. D13 28
Kwango (Cuango), stm., Afr. D3 54
Kwangsi Chuang see Guangxi Zhuangzu Zizhiqu, state, China G9 28
Kwekwe, Zimb. B4 56
Kwenge, stm., Afr. E3 54
Kwethluk, Ak., U.S. C7 95
Kwidzyn, Pol. C5 20
Kwigillingok, Ak., U.S. D7 95
Kwilu (Cuilo), stm., Afr. D3 54
Kyaikto, Mya. C3 34
Kyaukkyi, Mya. C3 34
Kyaukme, Mya. B3 34
Kyaukpyu, Mya. C2 34
Kyaukse, Mya. B3 34
Kyauktaw, Mya. B2 34
Kyaunggon, Mya. C3 34
Kyïv (Kiev), Ukr. D11 20
Kyïvs'ke vodoskhovyshche, res., Ukr. D11 20
Kyle, Tx., U.S. E4 136
Kyoga, Lake, l., Ug. C6 54
Kyŏngju, S. Kor. C1 31
Kyŏngsŏng-ŭp, N. Kor. B1 31
Kyōto, Japan D15 28
Kyrgyzstan, ctry., Asia A2 40
Kyštovka, Russia D9 26
Kyštym, Russia C11 22
Kyuquot Sound, strt., B.C., Can. E4 85
Kyūshū, i., Japan E14 28
Kyushu-Palau Ridge G16 64
Kyyiv see Kyïv, Ukr. D11 20
Kyyjärvi, Fin. E11 10
Kyzyl, Russia D11 26
Kyzylkum, des., Asia B8 42
Kzyl-Orda, Kaz. E8 26
Kzyltu, Kaz. D9 26

L

Laascaanood, Som. I14 48
La Asunción, Ven. C7 80
Lā'au Point, c., Hi., U.S. B4 104
Laayoune see El Aaiún, W. Sah. A2 50
Labadieville, La., U.S. E5 111
La Bañeza, Spain F4 16
La Barca, Mex. C4 78
La Barge, Wy., U.S. D2 143
La Barge Creek, stm., Wy., U.S. D2 143
La Baule-Escoublac, Fr. D5 16
Labe, stm., Eur. E14 12
Labé, Gui. D2 50
La Belle, Fl., U.S. F5 102
La Belle, Mo., U.S. A6 118
Labette, co., Ks., U.S. E8 109
Labinsk, Russia B4 42
Labis, Malay. C2 36
Laboulaye, Arg. E5 72
Labrador, reg., N.L., Can. g9 88
Labrador Basin B28 144
Labrador City, N.L., Can. h8 88
Labrador Sea, N.A. F29 82
Lábrea, Braz. E7 70
Labuan, Malay. B5 36
Labuan, Pulau, i., Malay. B5 36
Labuha, Indon. G8 32
Labuhanbajo, Indon. E5 36
Labytnangi, Russia A12 22
Laç, Alb. D7 18
La Canada Flintridge, Ca., U.S. m12 98
La Carlota, Arg. E5 72
La Carlota, Phil. D8 34
La Carolina, Spain H5 16
Lac-Bouchette, Qc., Can. A5 90
Lac-Brome, Qc., Can. D5 90
Laccadive, Minicoy and Amīndivi Islands see Lakshadweep, ter., India G2 40
Laccadive Islands see Lakshadweep, is., India G2 40
Lac-Carré, Qc., Can. C3 90
Lac Courte Oreilles Indian Reservation, Wi., U.S. C2 142
Lac du Bonnet, Mb., Can. D3 86
Lac du Flambeau, Wi., U.S. B4 142
Lac du Flambeau Indian Reservation, Wi., U.S. C3 142
La Ceiba, Hond. B2 80
La Center, Ky., U.S. e9 110
Lac-Etchemin, Qc., Can. C7 90
Lacey, Wa., U.S. B3 140
La Chaux-de-Fonds, Switz. A1 18
Lachine, Qc., Can. D4 90
La Chorrera, Col. D5 70
La Chorrera, Pan. D3 80
Lachute, Qc., Can. D3 90
La Citadelle, hist., Haiti B5 80
Lackawanna, N.Y., U.S. C2 125

Name / Map Ref. / Page

Lackawanna, co., Pa., U.S. D10 131
Lackland Air Force Base, mil., Tx., U.S. k7 136
Lac La Biche, Ab., Can. B5 84
Lac la Hache, B.C., Can. D7 85
Laclede, co., Mo., U.S. D5 118
Lac-Mégantic, Qc., Can. D7 90
Lacolle, Qc., Can. D4 90
La Columna see Bolívar, Pico, mtn., Ven. B5 70
Lacombe, Ab., Can. C4 84
Lacombe, La., U.S. D6 111
Lacon, Il., U.S. B4 106
La Concepción, Pan. D3 80
La Concepción, Ven. C5 80
Laconia, N.H., U.S. C4 122
Laconia, Gulf of see Lakonikós Kólpos, b., Grc. F9 18
La Conner, Wa., U.S. A3 140
Lacoochee, Fl., U.S. D4 102
La Coruña see A Coruña, Spain F2 16
Lac qui Parle, stm., Mn., U.S. F2 116
Lac qui Parle, co., Mn., U.S. F2 116
La Creek Lake, l., S.D., U.S. D4 134
La Crescent, Mn., U.S. G7 116
La Crete, Ab., Can. f7 84
La Crosse, In., U.S. B4 107
La Crosse, Ks., U.S. D4 109
La Crosse, Wi., U.S. E2 142
La Crosse, co., Wi., U.S. E2 142
La Crosse, stm., Wi., U.S. E3 142
La Cygne, Ks., U.S. D9 109
Ladākh Range, mts., Asia C3 40
Ladd, Il., U.S. B4 106
Ladies Island, i., S.C., U.S. G6 133
La Digue, i., Sey. h13 57b
Lādīz, Iran E8 42
Ladoga, In., U.S. E4 107
Ladoga, Lake see Ladožskoe ozero, l., Russia C5 26
La Dorada, Col. D5 80
Ladožskoe ozero, l., Russia C5 26
Ladson, S.C., U.S. F7 133
Ladybrand, S. Afr. D4 56
Lady Lake, Fl., U.S. D5 102
Lady Laurier, Mount, mtn., B.C., Can. A6 85
Ladysmith, B.C., Can. E6 85
Ladysmith, S. Afr. D4 56
Ladysmith, Wi., U.S. C2 142
Lae, Pap. N. Gui. H12 32
La Encantada, Mex. B4 78
Læsø, i., Den. H4 10
La Esperanza, Hond. C2 80
La Estrada see A Estrada, Spain F2 16
La Farge, Wi., U.S. E3 142
Lafayette, Al., U.S. C4 94
Lafayette, co., Ar., U.S. D2 97
Lafayette, Co., U.S. B5 99
Lafayette, co., Fl., U.S. C3 102
Lafayette, Ga., U.S. B1 103
Lafayette, In., U.S. D4 107
Lafayette, La., U.S. D3 111
Lafayette, co., La., U.S. D3 111
Lafayette, co., Mo., U.S. B4 118
Lafayette, co., Ms., U.S. A4 117
Lafayette, N.C., U.S. B3 126
Lafayette, Or., U.S. B3 130
La Fayette, R.I., U.S. E4 132
Lafayette, Tn., U.S. A5 135
Lafayette, co., Wi., U.S. F3 142
Lafayette, Mount, mtn., N.H., U.S. B3 122
La Feria, Tx., U.S. F4 136
Lafia, Nig. E6 50
Lafiagi, Nig. E6 50
Lafitte, La., U.S. k11 111
La Flèche, Fr. D6 16
La Follette, Tn., U.S. C9 135
La Fontaine, In., U.S. C6 107
Lafourche, La., U.S. E5 111
Lafourche, co., La., U.S. E5 111
La France, S.C., U.S. B2 133
La Galite, i., Tun. F2 18
Lagarto, Braz. D4 74
Lagawe, Phil. C8 34
Lågen, stm., Nor. F3 10
Lages, Braz. D7 72
Laghouat, Alg. D5 48
Lago, Mount, mtn., Wa., U.S. A5 140
Lagoa da Prata, Braz. F2 74
Lago da Pedra, Braz. B2 74
La Gomera, i., Spain A1 50
Lagonoy Gulf, b., Phil. D8 34
Lagos, Nig. E5 50
Lagos, Port. I2 16
Lagos de Moreno, Mex. C4 78
La Gouèra, W. Sah. B1 50
La Grande, stm., Qc., Can. h11 90
La Grande, Or., U.S. B8 130
La Grande Deux, Réservoir, res., Qc., Can. h11 90
Lagrange, Austl. D3 60
La Grange, Ga., U.S. C1 103
La Grange, Il., U.S. B6 106
Lagrange, co., In., U.S. A7 107
Lagrange, In., U.S. A7 107
La Grange, Ky., U.S. B4 110
La Grange, Mo., U.S. A6 118
La Grange, N.C., U.S. B5 126
Lagrange, Oh., U.S. A3 128
La Grange, Tx., U.S. E4 136
La Grange Park, Il., U.S. k9 106
La Gran Sabana, pl., Ven. B7 70
La Guadeloupe (Saint-Evariste), Qc., Can. D7 90
La Guajira, Península de, pen., S.A. A5 70
La Guardia, Bol. B5 72
La Guardia see A Guardia, Spain G2 16
Laguna, Braz. D8 72
Laguna, N.M., U.S. B2 124
Laguna Beach, Ca., U.S. F5 98
Laguna Dam, U.S. E1 96
Laguna Indian Reservation, N.M., U.S. C2 124
La Habana (Havana), Cuba A3 80
La Habra, Ca., U.S. n13 98
Lahad Datu, Malay. C5 36
Lahad Datu, Telukan, b., Malay. C5 36
Lahaina, Hi., U.S. C5 104
La Harpe, Il., U.S. C3 106
La Harpe, Ks., U.S. E8 109
Lahat, Indon. D2 36
La Have, stm., N.S., Can. E5 87
Lahdenpohja, Russia F14 10
Lāhījān, Iran C6 42
Lahoma, Ok., U.S. A3 129
Lahontan Reservoir, res., Nv., U.S. D2 121
Lahore, Pak. D10 42
Lahti, Fin. F11 10
Laï, Chad E8 50
Lai Chau, Viet. B4 34
Laie, Hi., U.S. B4 104
Lai-hka, Mya. B3 34
Laingsburg, S. Afr. E3 56
Laingsburg, Mi., U.S. F6 115
Lainioälven, stm., Swe. B9 10
Lais, Indon. D2 36
Laisamis, Kenya C7 54
Laiwu, China B4 30
Laiwui, Indon. G8 32
Laiyang, China B5 30
Laizhou Wan, b., China D11 28
La Jara, Co., U.S. D5 99
La Jolla, Point, c., Ca., U.S. o15 98
La Junta, Co., U.S. D7 99
Lakatoro, Vanuatu k9 62a
Lake, co., Ca., U.S. C2 98
Lake, co., Co., U.S. B4 99
Lake, co., Fl., U.S. D5 102
Lake, co., Il., U.S. A6 106
Lake, co., In., U.S. B3 107
Lake, co., Mi., U.S. E5 115
Lake, co., Mn., U.S. C7 116
Lake, co., Mt., U.S. C2 119
Lake, co., Oh., U.S. A4 128
Lake, co., Or., U.S. E6 130
Lake, co., S.D., U.S. C8 134
Lake, co., Tn., U.S. A2 135
Lake Alfred, Fl., U.S. D5 102
Lake Andes, S.D., U.S. D7 134
Lake Ariel, Pa., U.S. D11 131
Lake Arrowhead, Ca., U.S. E5 98
Lake Arthur, La., U.S. D3 111
Lakeba, i., Fiji m11 63b
Lake Benton, Mn., U.S. F2 116
Lake Bluff, Il., U.S. A6 106
Lake Butler, Fl., U.S. B4 102
Lake Cargelligo, Austl. G4 62
Lake Charles, La., U.S. D2 111
Lake Chelan National Recreation Area, Wa., U.S. A5 140
Lake City, Ar., U.S. B5 97
Lake City, Fl., U.S. B4 102
Lake City, Ia., U.S. B3 108
Lake City, Mi., U.S. D5 115
Lake City, Mn., U.S. F6 116
Lake City, Pa., U.S. B1 131
Lake City, S.C., U.S. D8 133
Lake City, Tn., U.S. C9 135
Lake Clark National Park, Ak., U.S. C9 95
Lake Cowichan, B.C., Can. g11 85
Lake Creek, stm., Wa., U.S. B7 140
Lake Crystal, Mn., U.S. F4 116
Lake Delta, N.Y., U.S. B5 125
Lake Delton, Wi., U.S. E4 142
Lake District, reg., Eng., U.K. C5 12
Lake Elsinore, Ca., U.S. F5 98
Lake Erie Beach, N.Y., U.S. C1 125
Lakefield, On., Can. C6 89
Lakefield, Mn., U.S. G3 116
Lake Forest, Il., U.S. A6 106
Lake Fork, stm., Ut., U.S. C5 137
Lake Geneva, Wi., U.S. F5 142
Lake Hamilton, Ar., U.S. g7 97
Lake Havasu City, Az., U.S. C1 96
Lake Helen, Fl., U.S. D5 102
Lakehurst, N.J., U.S. C4 123
Lakehurst Naval Air Station, mil., N.J., U.S. C4 123
Lake in the Hills, Il., U.S. h8 106
Lake Jackson, Tx., U.S. r14 136
Lake Katrine, N.Y., U.S. D7 125
Lake King, Austl. G2 60
Lakeland, Fl., U.S. D5 102
Lakeland, Ga., U.S. E3 103
Lake Linden, Mi., U.S. A2 115
Lake Louise, Ab., Can. D2 84
Lake Magdalene, Fl., U.S. o11 102
Lake Mary, Fl., U.S. D5 102
Lake Mead National Recreation Area, U.S. H7 121
Lake Meredith National Recreation Area, Tx., U.S. B2 136
Lake Mills, Ia., U.S. A4 108
Lake Mills, Wi., U.S. E5 142
Lakemore, Oh., U.S. A4 128
Lake Mountain, mtn., Wy., U.S. E6 143
Lake Nebagamon, Wi., U.S. B2 142
Lake Odessa, Mi., U.S. F5 115
Lake of the Woods, co., Mn., U.S. B4 116
Lake Orion, Mi., U.S. F7 115
Lake Oswego, Or., U.S. B4 130
Lake Ozark, Mo., U.S. C5 118
Lake Park, Fl., U.S. F6 102
Lake Park, Ia., U.S. A2 108
Lake Park, Mn., U.S. D2 116
Lake Placid, Fl., U.S. E5 102
Lake Placid, N.Y., U.S. A7 125
Lake Pontchartrain Causeway, La., U.S. h11 111
Lakeport, Ca., U.S. C2 98
Lake Preston, S.D., U.S. C8 134
Lake Providence, La., U.S. B4 111
Lake Range, mts., Nv., U.S. C2 121
Lakes Entrance, Austl. H4 62
Lake Shore, Md., U.S. B5 113
Lakeshore, Ms., U.S. E4 117
Lakeside, Az., U.S. C6 96
Lakeside, Ca., U.S. F5 98
Lakeside, Ct., U.S. D3 100
Lakeside, Mt., U.S. B2 119
Lakeside, Oh., U.S. A3 128
Lakeside, Or., U.S. D2 130
Lakeside Park, Ky., U.S. h13 110
Lake Station, In., U.S. A3 107
Lake Station, Ok., U.S. A5 129
Lake Stevens, Wa., U.S. A3 140
Lake Superior Provincial Park, On., Can. p18 89
Lake Swamp, stm., S.C., U.S. D8 133
Lake Tansi Village, Tn., U.S. D8 135
Lake Valley, val., Nv., U.S. E7 121
Lake View, Ia., U.S. B2 108
Lakeview, Mi., U.S. E5 115
Lakeview, Oh., U.S. B2 128
Lakeview, Or., U.S. E6 130
Lake View, S.C., U.S. C9 133
Lake Villa, Il., U.S. h8 106
Lake Village, Ar., U.S. D4 97
Lake Village, In., U.S. B3 107
Lakeville, Ct., U.S. B2 100
Lakeville, In., U.S. A5 107
Lakeville, Ma., U.S. C6 114
Lakeville, Mn., U.S. F5 116
Lake Waccamaw, N.C., U.S. C4 126
Lake Wales, Fl., U.S. E5 102
Lakewood, Ca., U.S. n12 98
Lakewood, Co., U.S. B5 99
Lakewood, Ia., U.S. f8 108
Lakewood, Il., U.S. D5 106
Lakewood, N.J., U.S. C4 123
Lakewood, N.Y., U.S. C1 125
Lakewood, Oh., U.S. A4 128
Lakewood, Wa., U.S. B3 140
Lake Worth, Fl., U.S. F6 102
Lake Worth Inlet, b., Fl., U.S. F7 102
Lake Zurich, Il., U.S. h8 106
Lakhdaria, Alg. I8 16
Lakhimpur, India D4 40
Lakin, Ks., U.S. E2 109
Lakonikós Kólpos, b., Grc. F9 18
Lakota, N.D., U.S. A7 127
Laksefjorden, b., Nor. A12 10
Lakshadweep, ter., India G2 40
Lakshadweep, is., India G2 40
Lakshadweep Sea, Asia G2 40
Lalara, Gabon C2 54
Lalībela, Eth. H12 48
La Libertad, Guat. B1 80
La Línea de la Concepción, Spain I4 16
Lalitpur, India E3 40
La Loche see Churchill, stm., Sk., Can. G21 82
La Luz, N.M., U.S. E4 124
La Malbaie, Qc., Can. B7 90
La Mancha, reg., Spain H5 16
La Manche see English Channel, strt., Eur. C5 16
Lamap, Vanuatu k9 62a
Lamar, co., Al., U.S. B1 94
Lamar, Ar., U.S. B2 97
Lamar, Co., U.S. C8 99
Lamar, co., Ga., U.S. C2 103
Lamar, Mo., U.S. D3 118
Lamar, co., Ms., U.S. D4 117
Lamar, Pa., U.S. D7 131
Lamar, S.C., U.S. C7 133
Lamar, co., Tx., U.S. C5 136
Lamar, stm., Wy., U.S. B2 143
La Mauricie, Parc National de, Qc., Can. C5 90
Lamb, co., Tx., U.S. B1 136
Lambaréné, Gabon D2 54
Lambayeque, Peru E4 70
Lambert, Ms., U.S. A3 117
Lambert Glacier, ice, Ant. D11 67
Lamberton, Mn., U.S. F3 116
Lambert's Bay, S. Afr. E2 56
Lambertville, Mi., U.S. G7 115
Lambertville, N.J., U.S. C3 123
Lame Deer, Mt., U.S. E10 119
Lamèque, N.B., Can. B5 87
Lamèque, Île, i., N.B., Can. B5 87
La Mesa, Ca., U.S. F5 98
La Mesa, N.M., U.S. E3 124
Lamesa, Tx., U.S. C2 136
Lamía, Grc. E9 18
Lamoille, Nv., U.S. C6 121
Lamoille, stm., Vt., U.S. B3 138
Lamoille, co., Vt., U.S. B3 138
La Moine, stm., Il., U.S. C3 106
Lamon Bay, b., Phil. D8 34
Lamoni, Ia., U.S. D4 108
Lamont, Ab., Can. C4 84
Lamont, Ca., U.S. E4 98
La Monte, Mo., U.S. C4 118
La Motte, Isle, i., Vt., U.S. B2 138
La Moure, co., N.D., U.S. C7 127
La Moure, N.D., U.S. C7 127
Lampang, Thai. C3 34
Lampasas, Tx., U.S. D3 136
Lampasas, co., Tx., U.S. D3 136
Lampazos de Naranjo, Mex. B4 78
Lamphun, Thai. C3 34
Lampman, Sk., Can. H4 91
Lamprey, stm., N.H., U.S. D4 122
Lamu, Kenya D8 54
Lanai, i., Hi., U.S. C4 104
Lanai City, Hi., U.S. C5 104
Lanaihale, mtn., Hi., U.S. C5 104
Lanark, On., Can. C8 89
Lanark, Il., U.S. A4 106
Lanark, W.V., U.S. D3 141
Lanbi Kyun, i., Mya. D3 34
Lancang see Mekong, stm., Asia A3 34
Lancaster, On., Can. B10 89
Lancaster, Eng., U.K. C5 12
Lancaster, Ca., U.S. E4 98
Lancaster, Ky., U.S. C5 110
Lancaster, Mo., U.S. A5 118
Lancaster, co., Ne., U.S. D9 120
Lancaster, N.H., U.S. B3 122
Lancaster, N.Y., U.S. C2 125
Lancaster, Oh., U.S. C3 128
Lancaster, Pa., U.S. F9 131
Lancaster, co., Pa., U.S. G9 131
Lancaster, S.C., U.S. B6 133
Lancaster, co., S.C., U.S. B6 133
Lancaster, Tx., U.S. n10 136
Lancaster, co., Va., U.S. C6 139
Lancaster, Wi., U.S. F3 142
Lance Creek, stm., Wy., U.S. C8 143
Lanchow see Lanzhou, China D8 28
Lanciano, Italy C5 18
Lancun, China B5 30
Lāndana, Ang. E2 54
Land Between the Lakes, U.S. f9 110
Landeck, Aus. G12 12
Landegode, Nor. C6 10
Lander, co., Nv., U.S. C4 121
Lander, Wy., U.S. D4 143
Landerneau, Fr. C4 16
Landes, reg., Fr. E6 16
Landess, In., U.S. C6 107
Landis, N.C., U.S. B2 126
Lando, S.C., U.S. B5 133
Landrum, S.C., U.S. A3 133
Land's End, c., Eng., U.K. E4 12
Lands End, c., R.I., U.S. F5 132
Landshut, Ger. F13 12
Landskrona, Swe. I5 10
Lane, co., Ks., U.S. D3 109
Lane, co., Or., U.S. C4 130
La Negra, Chile C3 72
Lanesboro, Mn., U.S. G7 116
Lanett, Al., U.S. C4 94
Langdon, N.D., U.S. A7 127
Langeland, i., Den. I4 10
Langeloth, Pa., U.S. F1 131
Langfang, China B4 30
Langhorne, Pa., U.S. F12 131
Langjökull, ice, Ice. l20 10a
Langkawi, Pulau, i., Malay. B1 36
Langlade, co., Wi., U.S. C4 142
Langley, B.C., Can. f13 85
Langley, S.C., U.S. E4 133
Langley, Wa., U.S. A3 140
Langley Air Force Base, mil., Va., U.S. h15 139
Langley Park, Md., U.S. f9 113
Langøya, i., Nor. B6 10
Langres, Fr. D9 16
Langsa, Indon. C1 36
Lang Son, Viet. B5 34
Langston, Ok., U.S. B4 129
Languedoc, hist. reg., Fr. F8 16
L'Anguille, stm., Ar., U.S. B5 97
Langzhong, China E9 28
Lanham, Md., U.S. C4 113
Lanier, co., Ga., U.S. E3 103
Länkäran, Azer. C13 44
Lannion, Fr. C5 16
Lannon, Wi., U.S. m11 142
L'Annonciation, Qc., Can. C3 90
Lanping, China A3 34
Lansdale, Pa., U.S. F11 131
Lansdowne, Md., U.S. B4 113
L'Anse, Mi., U.S. B2 115
L'Anse-au-Loup, N.L., Can. C3 88
L'Anse Indian Reservation, Mi., U.S. B2 115
Lansford, Pa., U.S. E10 131
Lanshan, China D3 30
Lansing, Ia., U.S. A6 108
Lansing, Il., U.S. B6 106
Lansing, Ks., U.S. C9 109
Lansing, Mi., U.S. F6 115
Lantana, Fl., U.S. F6 102
Lanxi, China F11 28
Lanzarote, i., Spain A2 50
Lanzhou, China D8 28
Laoag, Phil. C8 34
Laoang, Phil. D9 34
Lao Cai, Viet. B4 34
Laoha, stm., China C12 28
Laohekou, China E10 28
Laon, Fr. C8 16
La Orchila, Isla, i., Ven. C6 80
La Oroya, Peru F4 70
Laos, ctry., Asia B3 32
La Palma, Pan. D4 80
La Palma, i., Spain A1 50
La Paragua, Ven. B7 70
La Paz, Arg. E6 72
La Paz, Bol. B4 72
La Paz, Mex. C2 78
La Paz, co., Az., U.S. D2 96
Lapeer, Mi., U.S. E7 115
Lapeer, co., Mi., U.S. E7 115
Lapel, In., U.S. D6 107
La Perouse Strait, strt., Asia B16 28
La Pine, Or., U.S. D5 130
Lapinlahti, Fin. E12 10
La Place, La., U.S. h11 111
Lapland (Lappland), hist. reg., Eur. B8 10
La Plata, Arg. F6 72
La Plata, co., Co., U.S. D3 99
La Plata, Md., U.S. C4 113
La Plata, Mo., U.S. A5 118
La Plata Mountains, mts., Co., U.S. D3 99
La Plata Peak, mtn., Co., U.S. B4 99
La Platte, stm., Vt., U.S. C2 138
La Pocatière, Qc., Can. B7 90
Laporte, Co., U.S. A5 99
La Porte, In., U.S. A4 107
La Porte, co., In., U.S. A4 107
La Porte, Tx., U.S. r14 136
La Porte City, Ia., U.S. B5 108
Lappeenranta, Fin. F13 10
Lappland (Lapland), hist. reg., Eur. B8 10
La Prairie, Qc., Can. D4 90
La Pryor, Tx., U.S. E3 136
Laptev Sea see Laptevyh, more, Russia B14 26
Laptevyh, more, Russia B14 26
La Push, Wa., U.S. B1 140
Lapwai, Id., U.S. C2 105
La Quiaca, Arg. C4 72
L'Áquila, Italy C4 18
Lār, Iran E6 42
Larache, Mor. C3 48
Laramie, co., Wy., U.S. E8 143
Laramie, Wy., U.S. E7 143
Laramie, stm., U.S. E7 143
Laramie Mountains, mts., Wy., U.S. D7 143
Laramie Peak, mtn., Wy., U.S. D7 143
Larantuka, Indon. E6 36
Lärbro, Swe. H8 10
Larchmont, N.Y., U.S. h13 125
Larchwood, Ia., U.S. A1 108
Laredo, Spain F5 16
Laredo, Tx., U.S. F3 136
Largo, Fl., U.S. E4 102
Largo, Cañon, val., N.M., U.S. A2 124
Largo, Key, i., Fl., U.S. G6 102
Larimer, co., Co., U.S. A5 99
Larimore, N.D., U.S. B8 127
La Rioja, Arg. D4 72
La Rioja, reg., Spain F5 16
Lárisa, Grc. E9 18
Lārkāna, Pak. E9 42
Lark Harbour, N.L., Can. D2 88
Larkspur, Ca., U.S. h7 98
Larksville, Pa., U.S. n17 131
Larnaca see Lárnax, Cyp. E5 44
Lárnax, Cyp. E5 44
Larne, N. Ire., U.K. C4 12
Larned, Ks., U.S. D4 109
La Rochelle, Fr. D6 16
La Roche-sur-Yon, Fr. D6 16
La Roda, Spain H5 16
La Romana, Dom. Rep. B6 80
Larose, La., U.S. E5 111
Larrimah, Austl. D5 60
Larsen Ice Shelf, ice, Ant. C34 67
Larue, co., Ky., U.S. C4 110
Larvik, Nor. G4 10
LaSalle, Qc., Can. q19 90
La Salle, Co., U.S. A6 99
La Salle, Il., U.S. B4 106
La Salle, co., Il., U.S. B4 106
La Salle, co., La., U.S. C3 111
La Salle, co., Tx., U.S. E3 136
Las Animas, Co., U.S. C7 99

Name — Map Ref. — Page

Las Animas, co., Co., U.S. . . D6 99
La Sarre, Qc., Can. k11 90
Las Casitas, mtn., Mex. C3 78
Las Choapas, Mex. D6 78
La Scie, N.L., Can. D4 88
Las Cruces, N.M., U.S. E3 124
La Selle, Morne, mtn., Haiti B5 80
La Serena, Chile C2 69
La Serena, reg., Spain H4 16
La Seyne-sur-Mer, Fr. F9 16
Las Flores, Arg. F6 72
Lāsh-e Joveyn, Afg. D8 42
Las Heras, Arg. G3 69
Lashio, Mya. B3 34
Lashkar Gāh, Afg. D8 42
Las Margaritas, Mex. D6 78
Las Minas, Cerro, mtn., Hond. C2 80
La Solana, Spain H5 16
Las Palmas de Gran Canaria, Spain A1 50
La Spezia, Italy B2 18
Las Piedras, Ur. E6 72
Las Plumas, Arg. F3 69
Las Rosas, Mex. D6 78
Lassen, co., Ca., U.S. B3 98
Lassen Peak, vol., Ca., U.S. B3 98
Lassen Volcanic National Park, Ca., U.S. B3 98
L'Assomption, Qc., Can. D4 90
Las Tablas, Pan. D3 80
Last Mountain Lake, l., Sk., Can. F3 91
Lastoursville, Gabon D2 54
Las Tunas, Cuba A4 80
Las Varas, Mex. B3 78
Las Varas, Mex. C3 78
Las Vegas, N.M., U.S. B4 124
Las Vegas, Nv., U.S. G6 121
Latah, co., Id., U.S. C2 105
Latakia see Al-Lādhiqīyah, Syria E6 44
Lathrop, Mo., U.S. B3 118
Latimer, co., Ok., U.S. C6 129
Latina, Italy D4 18
Laton, Ca., U.S. D4 98
La Tortuga, Isla, i., Ven. . . . C6 80
Latouche Treville, Cape, c., Austl. D3 60
Latour Peak, mtn., Id., U.S. . B2 105
Latrobe, Pa., U.S. F3 131
Latta, S.C., U.S. C9 133
La Tuque, Qc., Can. B5 90
Lātūr, India F3 40
Latvia, ctry., Eur. H11 10
Lauderdale, co., Al., U.S. . . . A2 94
Lauderdale, Ms., U.S. C5 117
Lauderdale, co., Ms., U.S. . . C5 117
Lauderdale, co., Tn., U.S. . . B2 135
Lauderdale Lakes, Fl., U.S. . . r13 102
Laughlin, Nv., U.S. H7 121
Laughlin Air Force Base, mil., Tx., U.S. E2 136
Laughlin Peak, mtn., N.M., U.S. A5 124
Laughlintown, Pa., U.S. . . . F3 131
Launceston, Austl. I4 62
Launching Point, c., P.E., Can. C7 87
La Unión, Chile F2 69
La Unión, El Sal. C2 80
La Unión, Spain I6 16
Laurel, De., U.S. F3 101
Laurel, Fl., U.S. E4 102
Laurel, stm., Ky., U.S. D5 110
Laurel, co., Ky., U.S. C5 110
Laurel, Md., U.S. B4 113
Laurel, Ms., U.S. D4 117
Laurel, Mt., U.S. E8 119
Laurel, Ne., U.S. B8 120
Laurel, Va., U.S. C5 139
Laurel Bay, S.C., U.S. G6 133
Laurel Creek, stm., W.V., U.S. m12 141
Laurel Creek, stm., W.V., U.S. n14 141
Laureldale, Pa., U.S. F10 131
Laurel Fork, stm., W.V., U.S. C5 141
Laurel Hill, N.C., U.S. C3 126
Laurel River Lake, res., Ky., U.S. D5 110
Laurence G. Hanscom Air Force Base, mil., Ma., U.S. g10 114
Laurence Harbor, N.J., U.S. . C4 123
Laurens, co., Ga., U.S. D4 103
Laurens, Ia., U.S. B3 108
Laurens, S.C., U.S. C3 133
Laurens, co., S.C., U.S. C4 133
Laurentides, Qc., Can. D4 90
Laurentides, Parc Provincial des, Qc., Can. B6 90
Lau Ridge K21 64
Laurier, Qc., Can. C6 90
Laurierville, Qc., Can. C6 90
Laurinburg, N.C., U.S. C3 126
Laurium, Mi., U.S. A2 115
Lausanne, Switz. A1 18
Laut, Pulau, i., Indon. D5 36
Laut, Pulau, i., Indon. C3 36
Laut, Selat, strt., Indon. D5 36
Lautaro, Chile E2 69
Lauzon (part of Lévis-Lauzon), Qc., Can. C6 90
Lava Beds National Monument, Ca., U.S. . . . B3 98
Lavaca, Ar., U.S. B1 97
Lavaca, co., Tx., U.S. E4 136
Laval, Qc., Can. D4 90
Laval, Fr. C6 16
La Vale, Md., U.S. k13 113
La Vall d'Uixó, Spain H6 16
Lavaltrie, Qc., Can. D4 90
Laveen, Az., U.S. m8 96
La Vega, Dom. Rep. B5 80
L'Avenir, Qc., Can. D5 90
La Vergne, Tn., U.S. A5 135
La Verkin, Ut., U.S. F2 137
La Verne, Ca., U.S. m13 98
Laverne, Ok., U.S. A2 129
Laverton, Austl. F3 60
La Veta, Co., U.S. D5 99
La Victoria, Ven. C6 80
La Vila Joiosa, Spain H6 16
La Vista, Ne., U.S. g12 120
Lavonia, Ga., U.S. B3 103
Lavon Lake, res., Tx., U.S. . . m10 136
Lavras, Braz. F2 74
Lavumisa, Swaz. D5 56
Lawai, Hi., U.S. B2 104
Lawn, N.L., Can. E4 88
Lawra, Ghana D4 50
Lawrence, co., Al., U.S. A2 94
Lawrence, co., Ar., U.S. A4 97
Lawrence, co., Il., U.S. E6 106
Lawrence, In., U.S. E5 107
Lawrence, co., In., U.S. G4 107
Lawrence, Ks., U.S. D8 109
Lawrence, co., Ky., U.S. B7 110
Lawrence, Ma., U.S. A5 114
Lawrence, Mi., U.S. F4 115
Lawrence, co., Mo., U.S. . . . D4 118
Lawrence, co., Ms., U.S. D3 117
Lawrence, N.Y., U.S. k13 125
Lawrence, co., Oh., U.S. . . . D3 128
Lawrence, co., Pa., U.S. E1 131
Lawrence, co., Tn., U.S. B4 135
Lawrenceburg, In., U.S. F8 107
Lawrenceburg, Ky., U.S. B5 110
Lawrenceburg, Tn., U.S. B4 135
Lawrence Park, Pa., U.S. . . . B1 131
Lawrenceville, Ga., U.S. C3 103
Lawrenceville, Il., U.S. E6 106
Lawrenceville, Va., U.S. D5 139
Lawson, Mo., U.S. B3 118
Lawsonia, Md., U.S. E6 113
Lawtell, La., U.S. D3 111
Lawton, Mi., U.S. F5 115
Lawton, Ok., U.S. C3 129
Lawz, Jabal al-, mtn., Sau. Ar. E3 42
Laxå, Swe. G6 10
Lay Lake, res., Al., U.S. B3 94
Laysan Island, i., Hi., U.S. . . k13 104
Layton, Ut., U.S. B4 137
Lazarev, Russia D16 26
Lázaro Cárdenas, Mex. D4 78
Lazo, Russia B2 31
Leachville, Ar., U.S. B5 97
Lead, S.D., U.S. C2 134
Leadbetter Point, c., Wa., U.S. C1 140
Leadville, Co., U.S. B4 99
Leadwood, Mo., U.S. D7 118
Leaf, stm., Ms., U.S. D5 117
Leaf Rapids, Mb., Can. A1 86
Leake, co., Ms., U.S. C4 117
Leakesville, Ms., U.S. D5 117
Lealman, Fl., U.S. p10 102
Leamington, On., Can. E2 89
Leary, Ga., U.S. E2 103
Leatherman Peak, mtn., Id., U.S. E5 105
Leavenworth, Ks., U.S. C9 109
Leavenworth, co., Ks., U.S. . . C8 109
Leavenworth, Wa., U.S. B5 140
Leavittsburg, Oh., U.S. A5 128
Leawood, Ks., U.S. D9 109
Lebanon, ctry., Asia E6 44
Lebanon, De., U.S. D4 101
Lebanon, Il., U.S. E4 106
Lebanon, In., U.S. D5 107
Lebanon, Ky., U.S. C4 110
Lebanon, Mo., U.S. D5 118
Lebanon, N.H., U.S. C2 122
Lebanon, Oh., U.S. C1 128
Lebanon, Or., U.S. C4 130
Lebanon, Pa., U.S. F9 131
Lebanon, co., Pa., U.S. F8 131
Lebanon, Tn., U.S. A5 135
Lebanon, Va., U.S. f9 139
Lebanon Junction, Ky., U.S. C4 110
Lebanon Mountains see Lubnān, Jabal, mts., Leb. . F6 44
Lebedjan', Russia C15 20
Lebedyn, Ukr. D13 20
Lebesby, Nor. A12 10
Lebjaže, Kaz. D9 26
Lebo, Ks., U.S. D8 109
Lębork, Pol. B4 20
Lebu, Chile E2 69
Lecce, Italy D7 18
Lecco, Italy B2 18
Le Center, Mn., U.S. F5 116
Lechang, China D3 30
Le Claire, Ia., U.S. C7 108
Lecompte, La., U.S. C3 111
Lecompton, Ks., U.S. C8 109
Le Creusot, Fr. D9 16
Łęczyca, Pol. C5 20
Ledjanaja, gora, mtn., Russia C19 26
Ledo, India D7 40
Ledu, China B1 30
Leduc, Ab., Can. C4 84
Lee, co., Al., U.S. C4 94
Lee, co., Ar., U.S. C5 97
Lee, co., Fl., U.S. F5 102
Lee, co., Ga., U.S. E2 103
Lee, co., Ia., U.S. D6 108
Lee, co., Il., U.S. B4 106
Lee, co., Ky., U.S. C6 110
Lee, Ma., U.S. B1 114
Lee, co., Ms., U.S. A5 117
Lee, co., N.C., U.S. B3 126
Lee, co., S.C., U.S. C7 133
Lee, co., Tx., U.S. D4 136
Lee, co., Va., U.S. f8 139
Lee, Lake, l., Ms., U.S. B3 117
Leechburg, Pa., U.S. E2 131
Leech Lake, l., Mn., U.S. . . . C4 116
Leech Lake Indian Reservation, Mn., U.S. . . C4 116
Lee Creek, stm., U.S. B1 97
Leeds, Eng., U.K. D6 12
Leeds, Al., U.S. B3 94
Leelanau, co., Mi., U.S. D5 115
Leelanau, Lake, l., Mi., U.S. . C5 115
Lee Park, Pa., U.S. n17 131
Leer, Ger. D10 12
Leesburg, Fl., U.S. D5 102
Leesburg, Ga., U.S. E2 103
Leesburg, Oh., U.S. C2 128
Leesburg, Va., U.S. A5 139
Lees Summit, Mo., U.S. C3 118
Leesville, La., U.S. C2 111
Leesville, S.C., U.S. D4 133
Leesville Lake, res., Va., U.S. C3 139
Leeton, Austl. G4 62
Leeton, Mo., U.S. C4 118
Leetonia, Oh., U.S. B5 128
Leetsdale, Pa., U.S. h13 131
Leeuwarden, Neth. D9 12
Leeuwin, Cape, c., Austl. . . . G1 60
Leeward Islands, is., N.A. . . . E12 76
Leflore, co., Ms., U.S. B3 117
Le Flore, co., Ok., U.S. C7 129
Lega Hida, Eth. B8 54
Legal, Ab., Can. C4 84
Leganés, Spain G5 16
Legaspi, Phil. D8 34
Leghorn see Livorno, Italy . . C3 18
Legnica, Pol. D4 20
Le Grand, Ca., U.S. D3 98
Le Grand, Ia., U.S. B5 108
Leh, India C3 40
Le Havre, Fr. C7 16
Lehi, Ut., U.S. C4 137
Lehigh, stm., Pa., U.S. E10 131
Lehigh, co., Pa., U.S. E10 131
Lehigh Acres, Fl., U.S. F5 102
Lehighton, Pa., U.S. E10 131
Lehua Island, i., Hi., U.S. . . . A1 104
Lehututu, Bots. C3 56
Leicester, Eng., U.K. D6 12
Leicester, Ma., U.S. B4 114
Leiden, Neth. D9 12
Leighton, Al., U.S. A2 94
Leinster, hist. reg., Ire. D3 12
Leipsic, stm., De., U.S. C3 101
Leipsic, De., U.S. D3 101
Leipsic, Oh., U.S. A2 128
Leipzig, Ger. E13 12
Leiria, Port. H2 16
Leisler, Mount, mtn., Austl. . . E4 60
Leisure City, Fl., U.S. s13 102
Leitchfield, Ky., U.S. C3 110
Leiyang, China D3 30
Leizhou Bandao, pen., China E3 30
Leka, Nor. D4 10
Leland, Il., U.S. B5 106
Leland, Ms., U.S. B3 117
Leleiwi Point, c., Hi., U.S. . . D7 104
Leleque, Arg. F2 69
Leling, China B4 30
Leli Shan, mtn., China E4 28
Le Mans, Fr. C7 16
Le Mars, Ia., U.S. B1 108
Lema Shilindi, Eth. C8 54
Lemesós, Cyp. E5 44
Lemhi, stm., Id., U.S. E5 105
Lemhi, co., Id., U.S. E4 105
Lemhi Pass, Id., U.S. E5 105
Lemhi Range, mts., Id., U.S. E5 105
Lemmon, S.D., U.S. B3 134
Lemmon, Mount, mtn., Az., U.S. E5 96
Lemmon Valley, Nv., U.S. . . . D2 121
Lemnos see Límnos, i., Grc. . E10 18
Lemon, Lake, l., In., U.S. . . . F5 107
Lemon Fair, stm., Vt., U.S. . . C2 138
Lemon Grove, Ca., U.S. o15 98
Lemon Island, i., S.C., U.S. . . G6 133
Lemont, Il., U.S. B5 106
Lemont, Pa., U.S. E6 131
Lemonweir, stm., Wi., U.S. . . D3 142
Lemoore, Ca., U.S. D4 98
Lemoore Naval Air Station, mil., Ca., U.S. D4 98
Lempa, stm., N.A. C2 80
Lem Peak, mtn., Id., U.S. . . . E5 105
Lena, stm., Russia B14 26
Lena, Il., U.S. A4 106
Lenawee, co., Mi., U.S. G6 115
Lenexa, Ks., U.S. D9 109
Lenghu, China D6 28
Leninakan see Gjumri, Arm. B10 44
Leningrad see Sankt-Peterburg, Russia D5 26
Leninogorsk, Kaz. A4 28
Lenin Peak, mtn., Asia B2 40
Leninsk, Kaz. E8 26
Leninsk-Kuzneckij, Russia . . . D10 26
Leninskoe, Russia E15 26
Lennonville, Austl. F2 60
Lennox, S.D., U.S. D9 134
Lennoxville, Qc., Can. D6 90
Lenoir, N.C., U.S. B1 126
Lenoir, co., N.C., U.S. B5 126
Lenoir City, Tn., U.S. D9 135
Lenore Lake, l., Sk., Can. . . . E3 91
Lenore Lake, l., Wa., U.S. . . . B6 140
Lenox, Ga., U.S. E3 103
Lenox, Ia., U.S. D3 108
Lenox, Ma., U.S. B1 114
Lens, Fr. B8 16
Lensk, Russia C13 26
Lentini, Italy F5 18
Léo, Burkina D4 50
Leo, In., U.S. B7 107
Leoben, Aus. G14 12
Leominster, Ma., U.S. A4 114
León, Mex. C4 78
León, Nic. C2 80
León, Spain F4 16
Leon, co., Fl., U.S. B2 102
Leon, Ia., U.S. D4 108
Leon, Ks., U.S. E7 109
Leon, co., Tx., U.S. D4 136
Leonard, Tx., U.S. C4 136
Leonardo, N.J., U.S. C4 123
Leonardtown, Md., U.S. D4 113
Leonia, N.J., U.S. h9 123
Leonora, Austl. F3 60
Leonville, La., U.S. D4 111
Leopold and Astrid Coast, Ant. C13 67
Léopoldville see Kinshasa, D.R.C. D3 54
Leoti, Ks., U.S. D2 109
Lepanto, Ar., U.S. B5 97
Lepar, Pulau, i., Indon. D3 36
Lepe, Spain I3 16
Lepel', Bela. B10 20
Leping, China D4 30
L'Épiphanie, Qc., Can. D4 90
Lepsy, Kaz. B3 28
Le Puy, Fr. E8 16
Le Roy, Il., U.S. C5 106
Le Roy, Mn., U.S. G6 116
Le Roy, N.Y., U.S. C3 125
Lerwick, Scot., U.K. h19 12a
Léry, Qc., Can. q19 90
Lery, Lake, l., La., U.S. k12 111
Lesbos see Lésvos, i., Grc. . . E10 18
Les Cayes, Haiti B5 80
Leskovac, Serb. C8 18
Leslie, co., Ky., U.S. C6 110
Leslie, Mi., U.S. F6 115
Leslie, S.C., U.S. B6 133
Lesosibirsk, Russia D11 26
Lesotho, ctry., Afr. D4 56
Lesozavodsk, Russia B14 28
Les Sables-d'Olonne, Fr. D6 16
Lesser Antilles, is. F12 76
Lesser Caucasus, mts., Asia . . B11 44
Lesser Khingan Range see Xiao Hinggan Ling, mts., China A1 31
Lesser Slave Lake, l., Ab., Can. B3 84
Lesser Sunda Islands see Tenggara, Nusa, is., Indon. E5 36
Lester Prairie, Mn., U.S. F4 116
Le Sueur, Mn., U.S. F5 116
Le Sueur, co., Mn., U.S. F5 116
Lešukonskoe, Russia B8 22
Lésvos, i., Grc. E10 18
Leszno, Pol. D4 20
Letcher, co., Ky., U.S. C7 110
Lethbridge, Ab., Can. E4 84
Lethbridge, N.L., Can. D5 88
Lethem, Guy. C8 70
Leti, Kepulauan, is., Indon. . . E7 36
Leticia, Col. D6 70
Leting, China B4 30
Letlhakeng, Bots. C3 56
Letsôk-aw Kyun, i., Mya. . . . D3 34
Levádhia, Grc. E9 18
Levanger, Nor. E4 10
Levelland, Tx., U.S. C1 136
Leveque, Cape, c., Austl. . . . D3 60
Levice, Slvk. E5 20
Levin, N.Z. p14 63c
Levisa Fork, stm., U.S. C7 110
Lévis [-Lauzon], Qc., Can. . . . C6 90
Levittown, N.Y., U.S. E7 125
Levittown, Pa., U.S. F12 131
Levkás, i., Grc. E8 18
Levy, co., Fl., U.S. C4 102
Levy Lake, l., Fl., U.S. C4 102
Lewes, De., U.S. E5 101
Lewes and Rehoboth Canal, De., U.S. F5 101
Lewis, co., Id., U.S. C2 105
Lewis, co., Ky., U.S. B6 110
Lewis, co., Mo., U.S. A6 118
Lewis, co., N.Y., U.S. B5 125
Lewis, co., Tn., U.S. B4 135
Lewis, stm., Wa., U.S. C4 140
Lewis, co., Wa., U.S. C3 140
Lewis, co., W.V., U.S. C4 141
Lewis, stm., Wy., U.S. B2 143
Lewis, Isle of, i., Scot., U.K. A3 12
Lewis, Mount, mtn., Nv., U.S. C5 121
Lewis and Clark, co., Mt., U.S. C4 119
Lewis and Clark Cavern, Mt., U.S. D5 119
Lewis and Clark Lake, res., U.S. E8 134
Lewisburg, Ky., U.S. D3 110
Lewisburg, Oh., U.S. C1 128
Lewisburg, Pa., U.S. E8 131
Lewisburg, Tn., U.S. B5 135
Lewisburg, W.V., U.S. D4 141
Lewis Creek, stm., Vt., U.S. . C2 138
Lewis Lake, l., Wy., U.S. . . . B2 143
Lewisport, Ky., U.S. C3 110
Lewisporte, N.L., Can. D4 88
Lewis Smith Lake, res., Al., U.S. B2 94
Lewiston, Id., U.S. C1 105
Lewiston, Me., U.S. D2 112
Lewiston, Mn., U.S. G7 116
Lewiston, N.Y., U.S. B1 125
Lewiston, Ut., U.S. B4 137
Lewiston Peak, mtn., Ut., U.S. C3 137
Lewiston Woodville, N.C., U.S. A5 126
Lewistown, Il., U.S. C3 106
Lewistown, Mt., U.S. C7 119
Lewistown, Pa., U.S. E6 131
Lewisville, Ar., U.S. D2 97
Lewisville, Tx., U.S. C4 136
Lewisville Lake, res., Tx., U.S. C4 136
Lexington, Al., U.S. A2 94
Lexington, Il., U.S. C5 106
Lexington, Ky., U.S. B5 110
Lexington, Ma., U.S. B5 114
Lexington, Mi., U.S. E8 115
Lexington, Mo., U.S. B4 118
Lexington, Ms., U.S. B3 117
Lexington, N.C., U.S. B2 126
Lexington, Ne., U.S. D6 120
Lexington, Oh., U.S. B3 128
Lexington, Ok., U.S. B4 129
Lexington, S.C., U.S. D5 133
Lexington, co., S.C., U.S. . . . D5 133
Lexington, Tn., U.S. B3 135
Lexington, Va., U.S. C3 139
Lexington Park, Md., U.S. . . . D5 113
Leye, China E2 30
Leyte, i., Phil. D9 34
Lezhë, Alb. D7 18
L'gov, Russia D13 20
Lhasa, China F6 28
Lhazê, China D5 40
Lhokseumawe, Indon. B1 36
Lhorong, China E7 28
L'Hospitalet de Llobregat, Spain G8 16
Lhünzê, China D6 40
Liancheng, China A7 34
Lianga, Phil. E9 34
Lianjiang, China E3 30
Lianxian, China G10 28
Lianyungang, China E11 28
Liao, stm., China C12 28
Liaocheng, China B4 30
Liaodong Bandao, pen., China D12 28
Liaodong Bay see Liaodong Wan, b., China C12 28
Liaodong Wan, b., China . . . C12 28
Liaoning, prov., China C12 28
Liaotung, Gulf of see Liaodong Wan, b., China C12 28
Liaotung Bay see Liaodong Wan, b., China C12 28
Liaoyang, China A5 30
Liaoyuan, China C13 28
Liard, stm., Can. F15 82
Libagon, Phil. D9 34
Libby, Mt., U.S. B1 119
Libenge, D.R.C. C3 54
Liberal, Ks., U.S. E3 109
Liberal, Mo., U.S. D3 118
Liberec, Czech Rep. D3 20
Liberia, ctry., Afr. E3 50
Liberia, C.R. C2 80
Liberty, co., Fl., U.S. B2 102
Liberty, co., Ga., U.S. E5 103
Liberty, In., U.S. E8 107
Liberty, Ky., U.S. C5 110
Liberty, Mo., U.S. B3 118
Liberty, Ms., U.S. D3 117
Liberty, co., Mt., U.S. B5 119
Liberty, N.C., U.S. B3 126
Liberty, N.Y., U.S. D6 125
Liberty, S.C., U.S. B2 133
Liberty, Tx., U.S. D5 136
Liberty, co., Tx., U.S. D5 136
Liberty Center, Oh., U.S. . . . A1 128
Liberty Lake, res., Md., U.S. . B4 113
Liberty Lake, Wa., U.S. g14 140
Libertyville, Il., U.S. A6 106
Lībīyah, Aṣ-Ṣaḥrā' al- (Libyan Desert), des., Afr. E9 48
Libo, China D2 30

Name — Map Ref. — Page

Libourne, Fr. E6 16
Libreville, Gabon C1 54
Libuse, La., U.S. C3 111
Libya, ctry., Afr. E8 48
Libyan Desert see Lībīyah, Aṣ-Ṣaḥrā' al-, des., Afr. E9 48
Licancábur, Cerro, vol., S.A. C4 72
Licata, Italy F4 18
Lice, Tur. C9 44
Lichinga, Moz. A6 56
Lichuan, China D4 30
Lichuan, China C2 30
Lick Creek, stm., Tn., U.S. C11 135
Licking, stm., Ky., U.S. B6 110
Licking, Mo., U.S. D6 118
Licking, co., Oh., U.S. B3 128
Lida, Bela. C8 20
Lida, Lake, l., Mn., U.S. D3 116
Liden, Swe. E7 10
Lidgerwood, N.D., U.S. C8 127
Lidköping, Swe. G5 10
Lido di Ostia, ngh., Italy D4 18
Lidzbark Warmiński, Pol. B6 20
Liebig, Mount, mtn., Austl. E5 60
Liechtenstein, ctry., Eur. A2 18
Liège, Bel. E9 12
Lienz, Aus. G13 12
Liepāja, Lat. H9 10
Lièvre, Rivière du, stm., Qc., Can. D2 90
Lifou, i., N. Cal. I9 62a
Lighthouse Inlet, b., S.C., U.S. k12 133
Lighthouse Point, c., Fl., U.S. C2 102
Lighthouse Point, c., La., U.S. E3 111
Lighthouse Point, c., Mi., U.S. C5 115
Lightning Creek, stm., Wy., U.S. C8 143
Ligonier, In., U.S. B6 107
Ligonier, Pa., U.S. F3 131
Ligurian Apennines see Appennino Ligure, mts., Italy B2 18
Ligurian Sea, Eur. C2 18
Lihue, Hi., U.S. B2 104
Lijiang, China F8 28
Likasi, D.R.C. F5 54
Likati, D.R.C. C4 54
Lilbourn, Mo., U.S. E8 118
Lilburn, Ga., U.S. h8 103
Lille, Fr. B8 16
Lillebælt, strt., Den. I3 10
Lillehammer, Nor. F4 10
Lillesand, Nor. G3 10
Lillestrøm, Nor. G4 10
Lillian, Al., U.S. E2 94
Lillington, N.C., U.S. B4 126
Lillinonah, Lake, l., Ct., U.S. C2 100
Lillooet, B.C., Can. D7 85
Lillooet, stm., B.C., Can. D6 85
Lilly, Pa., U.S. F4 131
Lilly Fork, stm., W.V., U.S. m13 141
Lilly Grove, W.V., U.S. D3 141
Lilongwe, Mwi. A5 56
Liloy, Phil. E8 34
Lily, Ky., U.S. C5 110
Lima, Peru F4 70
Lima, N.Y., U.S. C3 125
Lima, Oh., U.S. B1 128
Lima Reservoir, res., Mt., U.S. F4 119
Limay Mahuida, Arg. F4 72
Limbe, Cam. C1 54
Limbé, Haiti B5 80
Limeira, Braz. F2 74
Limerick, Ire. D2 12
Limestone, co., Al., U.S. A2 94
Limestone, Me., U.S. B5 112
Limestone, co., Tx., U.S. D4 136
Limestone Point, pen., Mb., Can. C2 86
Limfjorden, l., Den. H3 10
Limingen, l., Nor. D5 10
Limmen Bight, b., Austl. C6 60
Límnos, i., Grc. E10 18
Limoges, On., Can. B9 89
Limoges, Fr. E7 16
Limón, Hond. B2 80
Limon, Co., U.S. B7 99
Limoux, Fr. F8 16
Limpopo, stm., Afr. C5 56
Lin'an, China C4 30
Linapacan Strait, strt., Phil. D7 34
Linares, Chile E2 69
Linares, Mex. C5 78
Linares, Spain H5 16
Lincoln, Arg. E5 72
Lincoln, On., Can. D5 89
Lincoln, Eng., U.K. D6 12
Lincoln, Al., U.S. B3 94
Lincoln, Ar., U.S. B1 97
Lincoln, co., Ar., U.S. D4 97
Lincoln, Ca., U.S. C3 98
Lincoln, co., Co., U.S. C7 99
Lincoln, De., U.S. E4 101
Lincoln, co., Ga., U.S. C4 103
Lincoln, Id., U.S. F6 105
Lincoln, co., Id., U.S. G4 105
Lincoln, Il., U.S. C4 106
Lincoln, co., Ks., U.S. C5 109
Lincoln, Ks., U.S. C5 109
Lincoln, co., Ky., U.S. C5 110
Lincoln, co., La., U.S. B3 111
Lincoln, Ma., U.S. g10 114
Lincoln, Me., U.S. C4 112
Lincoln, co., Me., U.S. D3 112
Lincoln, co., Mn., U.S. F2 116
Lincoln, Mo., U.S. C4 118
Lincoln, co., Mo., U.S. B7 118
Lincoln, co., Ms., U.S. D3 117
Lincoln, co., Mt., U.S. B1 119
Lincoln, co., N.C., U.S. B1 126
Lincoln, Ne., U.S. D9 120
Lincoln, co., Ne., U.S. D5 120
Lincoln, N.H., U.S. B3 122
Lincoln, co., N.M., U.S. D4 124
Lincoln, co., Nv., U.S. F6 121
Lincoln, co., Ok., U.S. B5 129
Lincoln, co., Or., U.S. C3 130
Lincoln, co., S.D., U.S. D9 134
Lincoln, co., Tn., U.S. B5 135
Lincoln, co., Wa., U.S. B7 140
Lincoln, co., Wi., U.S. C4 142
Lincoln, co., W.V., U.S. C2 141
Lincoln, co., Wy., U.S. D2 143
Lincoln, Mount, mtn., Co., U.S. B4 99
Lincoln Acres, Ca., U.S. o15 98
Lincoln City, Or., U.S. C3 130
Lincoln Hav see Lincoln Sea, N.A. B28 82
Lincoln Heights, Oh., U.S. o13 128
Lincoln Park, Co., U.S. C5 99
Lincoln Park, Ga., U.S. D2 103
Lincoln Park, Mi., U.S. p15 115
Lincoln Park, N.J., U.S. B4 123
Lincoln Sea, N.A. B28 82
Lincolnshire, Il., U.S. h9 106
Lincoln Tomb State Memorial, hist., Il., U.S. D4 106
Lincolnton, Ga., U.S. C4 103
Lincolnton, N.C., U.S. B1 126
Lincolnville, S.C., U.S. h11 133
Lincolnwood, Il., U.S. h9 106
Lincroft, N.J., U.S. C4 123
Lindale, Ga., U.S. B1 103
Lindale, Tx., U.S. C5 136
Linden, Guy. B8 70
Linden, Al., U.S. C2 94
Linden, In., U.S. D4 107
Linden, Mi., U.S. F7 115
Linden, N.J., U.S. k8 123
Linden, Tn., U.S. B4 135
Linden, Tx., U.S. C5 136
Lindenhurst, Il., U.S. h8 106
Lindenhurst, N.Y., U.S. n15 125
Lindenwold, N.J., U.S. D3 123
Lindesberg, Swe. G6 10
Lindesnes, c., Nor. H2 10
Lindi, Tan. E7 54
Lindon, Ut., U.S. C4 137
Lindsay, On., Can. C6 89
Lindsay, Ca., U.S. D4 98
Lindsay, Ok., U.S. C4 129
Lindsborg, Ks., U.S. D6 109
Lindstrom, Mn., U.S. E6 116
Line Islands, is., Oc. E14 58
Linesville, Pa., U.S. C1 131
Lineville, Al., U.S. B4 94
Linfen, China D10 28
Lingao, China F2 30
Lingayen, Phil. C8 34
Lingayen Gulf, b., Phil. C8 34
Lingen, Ger. D10 12
Lingga, Kepulauan, is., Indon. D3 36
Lingga, Pulau, i., Indon. D2 36
Lingle, Wy., U.S. D8 143
Linglestown, Pa., U.S. F8 131
Lingqiu, China B3 30
Lingshan, China E2 30
Lingshui, China F3 30
Linguère, Sen. C1 50
Lingyuan, China A4 30
Linhai, China F12 28
Linhares, Braz. E3 74
Linhe, China C9 28
Linière, Qc., Can. C7 90
Linköping, Swe. G6 10
Linkou, China B14 28
Linn, co., Ia., U.S. B6 108
Linn, co., Ks., U.S. D9 109
Linn, Mo., U.S. C6 118
Linn, co., Mo., U.S. B4 118
Linn, co., Or., U.S. C4 130
Lino Lakes, Mn., U.S. m12 116
Linqing, China B4 30
Linquan, China C4 30
Linru, China E10 28
Lins, Braz. F2 74
Lintan, China C1 30
Linthicum Heights, Md., U.S. B4 113
Linton, In., U.S. F3 107
Linton, N.D., U.S. C5 127
Linwood, N.J., U.S. E3 123
Linxi, China C11 28
Linxia, China D8 28
Linyi, China D11 28
Linyi, China B4 30
Linz, Aus. F14 12
Lion, Golfe du, b., Fr. F9 16
Lion, Gulf of see Lion, Golfe du, b., Fr. F9 16
Lipa, Phil. D8 34
Lipeck, Russia D5 26
Lipova, Rom. F6 20
Lipscomb, Al., U.S. B3 94
Lipscomb, co., Tx., U.S. A2 136
Lipu, China E3 30
Lira, Ug. C6 54
Lisala, D.R.C. C4 54
Lisboa (Lisbon), Port. H2 16
Lisbon see Lisboa, Port. H2 16
Lisbon, Ia., U.S. C6 108
Lisbon, Md., U.S. B3 113
Lisbon, Me., U.S. D2 112
Lisbon, N.D., U.S. C8 127
Lisbon, N.H., U.S. B3 122
Lisbon, Oh., U.S. B5 128
Lisbon Center, Me., U.S. f7 112
Lisbon Falls, Me., U.S. E2 112
Lisburne, Cape, c., Ak., U.S. B6 95
Lishui, China F11 28
Lisianski Island, i., Hi., U.S. k13 104
Lisieux, Fr. C7 16
Liski, Russia D5 26
Lisle, Il., U.S. k8 106
L'Islet-sur-Mer, Qc., Can. B7 90
L'Isle-Verte, Qc., Can. A8 90
Lismore, Austl. F5 62
Listowel, On., Can. D4 89
Litang, China G9 28
Litang, China E8 28
Litchfield, Ct., U.S. C3 100
Litchfield, co., Ct., U.S. B2 100
Litchfield, Il., U.S. D4 106
Litchfield, Mi., U.S. F6 115
Litchfield, Mn., U.S. E4 116
Litchfield Park, Az., U.S. m8 96
Lithgow, Austl. G5 62
Lithia Springs, Ga., U.S. h7 103
Lithonia, Ga., U.S. C2 103
Lithuania, ctry., Eur. B7 20
Lititz, Pa., U.S. F9 131
Litovko, Russia B15 28
Little, stm., Ct., U.S. C7 100
Little, stm., Ky., U.S. D2 110
Little, stm., La., U.S. C3 111
Little, stm., N.C., U.S. B3 126
Little, stm., Ok., U.S. B5 129
Little, stm., S.C., U.S. C2 133
Little, stm., Tn., U.S. n14 135
Little, stm., Va., U.S. D2 139
Little, stm., Va., U.S. D7 129
Little, stm., Vt., U.S. C3 138
Little, stm., U.S. B5 97
Little Acres, Az., U.S. D5 96
Little Andaman, i., India G6 40
Little Arkansas, stm., Ks., U.S. D6 109
Little Belt see Lillebælt, strt., Den. I3 10
Little Belt Mountains, mts., Mt., U.S. D6 119
Little Bighorn, stm., U.S. E9 119
Little Black, stm., Me., U.S. A3 112
Little Blue, stm., In., U.S. H5 107
Little Blue, stm., U.S. C6 109
Little Bow, stm., Ab., Can. D4 84
Little Cacapon, stm., W.V., U.S. B6 141
Little Catalina, N.L., Can. D5 88
Little Cayman, i., Cay. Is. B3 80
Little Cedar, stm., Ia., U.S. A5 108
Little Churchill, stm., Mb., Can. A4 86
Little Chute, Wi., U.S. D5 142
Little Coal, stm., W.V., U.S. C3 141
Little Colorado, stm., Az., U.S. B4 96
Little Compton, R.I., U.S. E6 132
Little Creek, De., U.S. D4 101
Little Creek Naval Amphibious Base, mil., Va., U.S. k15 139
Little Creek Peak, mtn., Ut., U.S. F3 137
Little Current, On., Can. B3 89
Little Diomede Island, i., Ak., U.S. B6 95
Little Egg Harbor, b., N.J., U.S. D4 123
Little Egg Inlet, b., N.J., U.S. E4 123
Little Falls, Mn., U.S. E4 116
Little Falls, N.J., U.S. B4 123
Little Falls, N.Y., U.S. B6 125
Little Ferry, N.J., U.S. h8 123
Littlefield, Tx., U.S. C1 136
Little Fishing Creek, stm., W.V., U.S. h9 141
Littlefork, Mn., U.S. B5 116
Little Fork, stm., Mn., U.S. B5 116
Little Goose Creek, stm., Wy., U.S. B6 143
Little Gunpowder Falls, stm., Md., U.S. A4 113
Little Humboldt, stm., Nv., U.S. B4 121
Little Inagua, i., Bah. D10 76
Little Kanawha, stm., W.V., U.S. C4 141
Little Karroo, plat., S. Afr. E3 56
Little Lake, l., La., U.S. E5 111
Little Lake, Mi., U.S. B3 115
Little Lynches, stm., S.C., U.S. C7 133
Little Manatee, stm., Fl., U.S. p11 102
Little Mecatina, stm., Can. h9 88
Little Miami, stm., Oh., U.S. C1 128
Little Minch, The, strt., Scot., U.K. B3 12
Little Missouri, stm., Ar., U.S. D2 97
Little Missouri, stm., U.S. B7 92
Little Muddy, stm., Il., U.S. E4 106
Little Muddy, stm., N.D., U.S. A2 127
Little Namaqualand, hist. reg., S. Afr. D2 56
Little Nicobar, i., India H6 40
Little Osage, stm., U.S. E9 109
Little Otter Creek, stm., Vt., U.S. C2 138
Little Owyhee, stm., U.S. B5 121
Little Pee Dee, stm., S.C., U.S. C9 133
Little Powder, stm., U.S. F11 119
Little Red, stm., Ar., U.S. B4 97
Little River, co., Ar., U.S. D1 97
Little River Inlet, b., S.C., U.S. D10 133
Little Rock, Ar., U.S. C3 97
Little Rock, stm., U.S. A1 108
Little Rock Air Force Base, mil., Ar., U.S. C3 97
Little Sable Point, c., Mi., U.S. E4 115
Little Salt Lake, l., Ut., U.S. F3 137
Little Sandy, stm., Ky., U.S. B6 110
Little Sandy Creek, stm., Wy., U.S. D3 143
Little Sebago Lake, l., Me., U.S. g7 112
Little Silver, N.J., U.S. C4 123
Little Sioux, stm., U.S. B2 108
Little Sioux, West Fork, stm., Ia., U.S. B2 108
Little Smoky, stm., Ab., Can. B2 84
Little Snake, stm., U.S. A2 99
Little Spokane, stm., Wa., U.S. B8 140
Littlestown, Pa., U.S. G7 131
Little Tallapoosa, stm., U.S. B4 94
Little Tenmile Creek, stm., W.V., U.S. k10 141
Little Tennessee, stm., U.S. D9 135
Littleton, Co., U.S. B6 99
Littleton, Ma., U.S. f10 114
Littleton, Me., U.S. B5 112
Littleton, N.C., U.S. A5 126
Littleton, N.H., U.S. B3 122
Littleville, Al., U.S. A2 94
Little Wabash, stm., Il., U.S. E5 106
Little Walnut, stm., Ks., U.S. g13 109
Little White, stm., S.D., U.S. D5 134
Little Wolf, stm., Wi., U.S. D4 142
Little Wood, stm., Id., U.S. F4 105
Little Zab, stm., Asia E10 44
Liucheng, China G9 28
Liuzhou, China G9 28
Live Oak, Ca., U.S. C3 98
Live Oak, Fl., U.S. B4 102
Live Oak, co., Tx., U.S. E3 136
Livermore, Ca., U.S. h9 98
Livermore, Ky., U.S. C2 110
Livermore, Mount, mtn., Tx., U.S. o12 136
Livermore Falls, Me., U.S. D2 112
Liverpool, Eng., U.K. D5 12
Lívingston, Guat. B2 80
Livingston, Al., U.S. C1 94
Livingston, Ca., U.S. D3 98
Livingston, Il., U.S. E4 106
Livingston, co., Il., U.S. C5 106
Livingston, co., Ky., U.S. e9 110
Livingston, La., U.S. D5 111
Livingston, co., La., U.S. D5 111
Livingston, co., Mi., U.S. F7 115
Livingston, co., Mo., U.S. B4 118
Livingston, Mt., U.S. E6 119
Livingston, N.J., U.S. B4 123
Livingston, co., N.Y., U.S. C3 125
Livingston, Tn., U.S. C8 135
Livingston, Tx., U.S. D5 136
Livingston, Lake, res., Tx., U.S. D5 136
Livingstone, Zam. B4 56
Livingstone Falls, wtfl., Afr. E2 54
Livingstonia, Mwi. A5 56
Livny, Russia C14 20
Livonia, La., U.S. D4 111
Livonia, Mi., U.S. F7 115
Livorno, Italy C3 18
Liwale, Tan. E7 54
Liwonde, Mwi. B6 56
Lixi, China F10 28
Lixian, China D3 30
Lizard Head Pass, Co., U.S. D3 99
Lizard Head Peak, mtn., Wy., U.S. D3 143
Lizella, Ga., U.S. D3 103
Ljahovskie ostrova, is., Russia B15 26
Ljubercy, Russia C6 22
Ljubljana, Slvn. A5 18
Ljudinovo, Russia C13 20
Ljungby, Swe. H5 10
Ljusdal, Swe. F7 10
Ljusnan, stm., Swe. E6 10
Ljusterö, i., Swe. G8 10
Llancanelo, Laguna, l., Arg. F4 72
Llano, Tx., U.S. D3 136
Llano, stm., Tx., U.S. D3 136
Llano, co., Tx., U.S. D3 136
Llano Estacado see Estacado, Llano, pl., U.S. E7 92
Llanos, pl., S.A. B6 70
Lleida, Spain G7 16
Llera de Canales, Mex. C5 78
Lloyd, Ky., U.S. B7 110
Lloydminster, Ab., Can. C5 84
Lloyds, stm., N.L., Can. D3 88
Llucmajor, Spain H8 16
Llullaillaco, Volcán, vol., S.A. C4 72
Loami, Il., U.S. D4 106
Loange, stm., Afr. E3 54
Lobamba, Swaz. D5 56
Lobatse, Bots. D4 56
Lobelville, Tn., U.S. B4 135
Lobería, Arg. F6 72
Lobito, Ang. F2 54
Lobos, Cay, i., Bah. A4 80
Lobster Lake, l., Me., U.S. C3 112
Lobva, Russia C11 22
Locarno, Switz. A2 18
Loch Raven Reservoir, res., Md., U.S. B4 113
Lochsa, stm., Id., U.S. C3 105
Lockeport, N.S., Can. F4 87
Lockesburg, Ar., U.S. D1 97
Lockhart, Tx., U.S. E4 136
Lock Haven, Pa., U.S. D7 131
Lockland, Oh., U.S. o13 128
Lockney, Tx., U.S. B2 136
Lockport, Il., U.S. B5 106
Lockport, La., U.S. E5 111
Lockport, N.Y., U.S. B2 125
Lockwood, Mo., U.S. D4 118
Lockwood, Mt., U.S. E8 119
Loc Ninh, Viet. D5 34
Locust, N.C., U.S. B2 126
Locust Fork, stm., Al., U.S. B3 94
Locust Grove, Ga., U.S. C2 103
Locust Grove, Ok., U.S. A6 129
Lodejnoe Pole, Russia B5 22
Lodgepole Creek, stm., U.S. C3 120
Lodi, Italy B2 18
Lodi, Ca., U.S. C3 98
Lodi, N.J., U.S. h8 123
Lodi, Oh., U.S. A3 128
Lodi, Wi., U.S. E4 142
Lodja, D.R.C. D4 54
Lodore, Canyon of, Co., U.S. A2 99
Lodwar, Kenya C7 54
Łódź, Pol. D5 20
Loei, Thai. C4 34
Lofoten, is., Nor. B5 10
Lofoten Basin D21 144
Loga, Niger D5 50
Logan, co., Ar., U.S. B2 97
Logan, co., Co., U.S. A7 99
Logan, Ia., U.S. C2 108
Logan, co., Il., U.S. C4 106
Logan, Ks., U.S. C4 109
Logan, co., Ks., U.S. D2 109
Logan, co., Ky., U.S. D3 110
Logan, co., N.D., U.S. C6 127
Logan, co., Ne., U.S. C5 120
Logan, N.M., U.S. B6 124
Logan, Oh., U.S. C3 128
Logan, co., Oh., U.S. B2 128
Logan, co., Ok., U.S. B4 129
Logan, Ut., U.S. B4 137
Logan, W.V., U.S. D3 141
Logan, co., W.V., U.S. D3 141
Logan, Mount, mtn., Yk., Can. F11 82
Logan, Mount, mtn., Wa., U.S. A5 140
Logandale, Nv., U.S. G7 121
Logan Lake, B.C., Can. D7 85
Logan Martin Lake, res., Al., U.S. B3 94
Logan Pass, Mt., U.S. B2 119
Logansport, In., U.S. C5 107
Logansport, La., U.S. C2 111
Loganville, Ga., U.S. C3 103
Loganville, Pa., U.S. G8 131
Loggieville, N.B., Can. B4 87
Log Lane Village, Co., U.S. A7 99
Logone, stm., Afr. B3 54
Logroño, Spain F5 16
Løgstør, Den. H3 10
Loi-kaw, Mya. C3 34
Loimaa, Fin. F10 10
Loire, stm., Fr. D6 16
Loja, Ec. D4 70
Loja, Spain I4 16
Lokandu, D.R.C. D5 54
Lokan tekojärvi, res., Fin. C12 10
Lokichokio, Kenya C6 54
Lokoja, Nig. E6 50
Lokolama, D.R.C. D3 54
Lola, Gui. E3 50
Lola, Mount, mtn., Ca., U.S. C3 98
Loliondo, Tan. D7 54
Lolland, i., Den. I4 10
Lolo, Mt., U.S. D2 119
Lolo Pass, U.S. C4 105
Lom, Blg. C9 18
Lomami, stm., D.R.C. C4 54
Lomas de Zamora, Arg. E6 72

Name	Map Ref.	Page
Lombard, Il., U.S.	**k8**	106
Lomblen, Pulau, i., Indon.	**E6**	36
Lombok, i., Indon.	**E5**	36
Lombok, Selat, strt., Indon.	**E5**	36
Lomé, Togo	**E5**	50
Lomela, D.R.C.	**D4**	54
Lomié, Cam.	**C2**	54
Lomira, Wi., U.S.	**E5**	142
Lomonosov, Russia	**G13**	10
Lomonosov Ridge	**E8**	144
Lompoc, Ca., U.S.	**E3**	98
Lom Sak, Thai.	**C4**	34
Łomża, Pol.	**C7**	20
Lonaconing, Md., U.S.	**k13**	113
Loncoche, Chile	**E2**	69
London, On., Can.	**E3**	89
London, Eng., U.K.	**E6**	12
London, Ar., U.S.	**B2**	97
London, Ky., U.S.	**C5**	110
London, Oh., U.S.	**C2**	128
Londonderry, N. Ire., U.K.	**C3**	12
Londonderry, N.H., U.S.	**E4**	122
Londonderry, Cape, c., Austl.	**C4**	60
Londonderry, Isla, i., Chile	**I2**	69
Londontown, Md., U.S.	**C4**	113
Londrina, Braz.	**F1**	74
Lone Grove, Ok., U.S.	**C4**	129
Lone Mountain, mtn., Nv., U.S.	**E4**	121
Lone Pine, Ca., U.S.	**D4**	98
Lone Tree, Ia., U.S.	**C6**	108
Long, co., Ga., U.S.	**E5**	103
Longa, proliv, strt., Russia	**B19**	26
Long Bar Harbor, Md., U.S.	**B5**	113
Long Beach, Ca., U.S.	**F4**	98
Long Beach, In., U.S.	**A4**	107
Long Beach, Md., U.S.	**D5**	113
Long Beach, Ms., U.S.	**g7**	117
Long Beach, N.Y., U.S.	**E7**	125
Long Beach, Wa., U.S.	**C1**	140
Longboat Key, Fl., U.S.	**q10**	102
Longboat Key, i., Fl., U.S.	**E4**	102
Longboat Pass, strt., Fl., U.S.	**q10**	102
Long Branch, N.J., U.S.	**C5**	123
Longbranch, Wa., U.S.	**B3**	140
Long Creek Mountain, mtn., Wy., U.S.	**D5**	143
Longde, China	**B2**	30
Longford, Ire.	**D3**	12
Long Grove, Ia., U.S.	**C7**	108
Long Harbour [-Mount Arlington Heights], N.L., Can.	**E5**	88
Longhua, China	**A4**	30
Longiram, Indon.	**D5**	36
Long Island, i., Bah.	**D10**	76
Long Island, i., N.S., Can.	**E3**	87
Long Island, i., Ma., U.S.	**g12**	114
Long Island, i., Me., U.S.	**g7**	112
Long Island, i., N.Y., U.S.	**E7**	125
Long Island Sound, strt., U.S.	**E7**	125
Longjiang, China	**B12**	28
Long Key, i., Fl., U.S.	**H6**	102
Long Lake, Il., U.S.	**h8**	106
Long Lake, l., Me., U.S.	**A4**	112
Long Lake, l., Me., U.S.	**D2**	112
Long Lake, l., Mi., U.S.	**C7**	115
Long Lake, l., Mi., U.S.	**D5**	115
Long Lake, l., Mn., U.S.	**D4**	116
Long Lake, l., N.D., U.S.	**C6**	127
Long Lake, l., N.Y., U.S.	**B6**	125
Long Lake, l., Wa., U.S.	**f10**	140
Long Lake, l., Wi., U.S.	**C2**	142
Longli, China	**F9**	28
Longling, China	**B3**	34
Longmeadow, Ma., U.S.	**B2**	114
Longmen, China	**B6**	34
Longmont, Co., U.S.	**A5**	99
Longnan, China	**E3**	30
Long Point, c., Mb., Can.	**C2**	86
Long Point, pen., On., Can.	**E4**	89
Long Pond, res., Fl., U.S.	**C4**	102
Long Prairie, Mn., U.S.	**E4**	116
Longquan, China	**D4**	30
Long Range Mountains, mts., N.L., Can.	**D3**	88
Longreach, Austl.	**E3**	62
Longshan, China	**D2**	30
Longs Peak, mtn., Co., U.S.	**A5**	99
Long Strait see Longa, proliv, strt., Russia	**B19**	26
Longueuil, Qc., Can.	**D4**	90
Long View, N.C., U.S.	**B1**	126
Longview, Tx., U.S.	**C5**	136
Longview, Wa., U.S.	**C3**	140
Longxi, China	**E8**	28
Longxian, China	**C2**	30
Long Xuyen, Viet.	**D5**	34
Longyan, China	**D4**	30
Longzhou, China	**G9**	28
Lonoke, Ar., U.S.	**C4**	97
Lonoke, co., Ar., U.S.	**C4**	97
Lonsdale, Mn., U.S.	**F5**	116
Lonsdale, R.I., U.S.	**B4**	132
Lons-le-Saunier, Fr.	**D9**	16
Loogootee, In., U.S.	**G4**	107
Lookout, Ky., U.S.	**C7**	110
Lookout, Cape, c., N.C., U.S.	**C6**	126
Lookout, Point, c., Mi., U.S.	**d7**	115
Lookout Mountain, mtn., Or., U.S.	**C6**	130
Lookout Mountain, Tn., U.S.	**h11**	135
Lookout Mountain, mtn., U.S.	**D8**	135
Lookout Pass, U.S.	**B3**	105
Lookout Point Lake, res., Or., U.S.	**D4**	130
Loongana, Austl.	**G4**	60
Loon Lake, l., Me., U.S.	**B3**	112
Loon Lake, Wa., U.S.	**A8**	140
Loop Creek, stm., W.V., U.S.	**m13**	141
Loosahatchie, stm., Tn., U.S.	**B2**	135
Lop, China	**B4**	40
Lopatka, mys, c., Russia	**D17**	26
Lop Buri, Thai.	**D4**	34
Lopez, Cap, c., Gabon	**D1**	54
Lopez Island, i., Wa., U.S.	**A3**	140
Lop Nor (Lop Nur), l., China	**C6**	28
Lop Nur (Lop Nor), l., China	**C6**	28
Lopphavet, Nor.	**A9**	10
Lora, Hāmūn-i-, l., Asia	**E8**	42
Lorain, co., Oh., U.S.	**A3**	128
Lorain, Oh., U.S.	**A3**	128
Loramie, Lake, res., Oh., U.S.	**B1**	128
Lorca, Spain	**I6**	16
Lord Howe Rise	**K19**	64
Lordsburg, N.M., U.S.	**E1**	124
Loreauville, La., U.S.	**D4**	111
Lorenzo, Tx., U.S.	**C2**	136
Loreto, Braz.	**E10**	70
Loreto, Mex.	**B2**	78
Lorette, Mb., Can.	**E3**	86
Loretteville, Qc., Can.	**C6**	90
Loretto, Ky., U.S.	**C4**	110
Loretto, Pa., U.S.	**F4**	131
Loretto, Tn., U.S.	**B4**	135
Lorica, Col.	**B4**	70
Lorient, Fr.	**D5**	16
L'Orignal, On., Can.	**B10**	89
Loris, S.C., U.S.	**C10**	133
Lorn, Firth of, b., Scot., U.K.	**B4**	12
Lorne, Austl.	**H3**	62
Lorne, N.B., Can.	**B3**	87
Lorraine, hist. reg., Fr.	**C9**	16
Los, Îles de, is., Gui.	**E2**	50
Los Alamos, N.M., U.S.	**B3**	124
Los Alamos, co., N.M., U.S.	**B3**	124
Los Altos, Ca., U.S.	**k8**	98
Los Angeles, Ca., U.S.	**E4**	98
Los Angeles, co., Ca., U.S.	**E4**	98
Los Angeles Aqueduct, aq., Ca., U.S.	**E4**	98
Los Banos, Ca., U.S.	**D3**	98
Los Blancos, Arg.	**C5**	72
Los Fresnos, Tx., U.S.	**F4**	136
Los Gatos, Ca., U.S.	**D2**	98
Lošinj, Otok, i., Cro.	**B5**	18
Los Lunas, N.M., U.S.	**C3**	124
Los Mochis, Mex.	**B3**	78
Los Pinos, stm., Co., U.S.	**D3**	99
Los Ranchos de Albuquerque, N.M., U.S.	**B3**	124
Los Roques, Islas, is., Ven.	**C6**	80
Lost, stm., In., U.S.	**G4**	107
Lost, stm., Wa., U.S.	**A5**	140
Lost, stm., W.V., U.S.	**B6**	141
Lost Creek, stm., Wy., U.S.	**D4**	143
Lost Peak, mtn., Ut., U.S.	**F2**	137
Lost Ranger Peak, mtn., Co., U.S.	**A4**	99
Lost River Glacial Caverns, N.H., U.S.	**B3**	122
Lost River Range, mts., Id., U.S.	**E5**	105
Lost Trail Pass, U.S.	**D5**	105
Losuia, Pap. N. Gui.	**H13**	32
Los Vilos, Chile	**D2**	69
Lot, stm., Fr.	**E7**	16
Lota, Chile	**F3**	72
Lotawana, Lake, res., Mo., U.S.	**k11**	118
Lotbinière, Qc., Can.	**C6**	90
Loto, D.R.C.	**D4**	54
Lotung, Tai.	**E5**	30
Louang Namtha, Laos	**B4**	34
Louangphrabang, Laos	**C4**	34
Loubomo, Congo	**D2**	54
Loudon, Tn., U.S.	**D9**	135
Loudon, co., Tn., U.S.	**D9**	135
Loudonville, Oh., U.S.	**B3**	128
Loudoun, co., Va., U.S.	**A5**	139
Louga, Sen.	**C1**	50
Louhi, Russia	**A5**	22
Louisa, co., Ia., U.S.	**C6**	108
Louisa, Ky., U.S.	**B7**	110
Louisa, Va., U.S.	**B4**	139
Louisa, co., Va., U.S.	**C5**	139
Louisa, Lake, l., Fl., U.S.	**D5**	102
Louisbourg, N.S., Can.	**D10**	87
Louisburg, Ks., U.S.	**D9**	109
Louisburg, N.C., U.S.	**A4**	126
Louisdale, N.S., Can.	**D8**	87
Louise, Lake, l., Ak., U.S.	**f18**	95
Louise Island, i., B.C., Can.	**C2**	85
Louiseville, Qc., Can.	**C5**	90
Louisiana, Mo., U.S.	**B6**	118
Louisiana, state, U.S.	**C3**	111
Louisiana Point, c., La., U.S.	**E2**	111
Louis Trichardt, S. Afr.	**C4**	56
Louisville, Al., U.S.	**D4**	94
Louisville, Co., U.S.	**B5**	99
Louisville, Ga., U.S.	**C4**	103
Louisville, Il., U.S.	**E5**	106
Louisville, Ky., U.S.	**B4**	110
Louisville, Ms., U.S.	**B4**	117
Louisville, Ne., U.S.	**D9**	120
Louisville, Oh., U.S.	**B4**	128
Louisville Ridge	**L22**	64
Louis-XIV, Pointe, c., Qc., Can.	**h11**	90
Loum, Cam.	**C1**	54
Loup, stm., Ne., U.S.	**C8**	120
Loup, co., Ne., U.S.	**C6**	120
Loup City, Ne., U.S.	**C7**	120
Lourdes, N.L., Can.	**D2**	88
Lourdes, Fr.	**F6**	16
Lourenço Marques see Maputo, Moz.	**D5**	56
Louviers, Co., U.S.	**B6**	99
Love, co., Ok., U.S.	**D4**	129
Loveč, Blg.	**C10**	18
Loveland, Co., U.S.	**A5**	99
Loveland, Oh., U.S.	**n13**	128
Loveland Park, Oh., U.S.	**C1**	128
Loveland Pass, Co., U.S.	**B5**	99
Lovell, Wy., U.S.	**B4**	143
Lovelock, Nv., U.S.	**C3**	121
Lovely, Ky., U.S.	**C7**	110
Lovenia, Mount, mtn., Ut., U.S.	**C5**	137
Love Point, c., Md., U.S.	**B5**	113
Loves Park, Il., U.S.	**A4**	106
Lovettsville, Va., U.S.	**A5**	139
Loving, N.M., U.S.	**E5**	124
Loving, co., Tx., U.S.	**D1**	136
Lovington, Ia., U.S.	**e8**	108
Lovington, Il., U.S.	**D5**	106
Lovington, N.M., U.S.	**E6**	124
Lóvua, Ang.	**E4**	54
Lowden, Ia., U.S.	**C7**	108
Lowell, Ar., U.S.	**A1**	97
Lowell, In., U.S.	**B3**	107
Lowell, Ma., U.S.	**A5**	114
Lowell, Mi., U.S.	**F5**	115
Lowell, N.C., U.S.	**B1**	126
Lowell, Or., U.S.	**D4**	130
Lowell, Lake, res., Id., U.S.	**F2**	105
Lowellville, Oh., U.S.	**A5**	128
Lower Arrow Lake, res., B.C., Can.	**E8**	85
Lower Brule Indian Reservation, S.D., U.S.	**C6**	134
Lower California see Baja California, pen., Mex.	**B2**	78
Lower Hutt, N.Z.	**p14**	63c
Lower Klamath Lake, l., Ca., U.S.	**B3**	98
Lower Matecumbe Key, i., Fl., U.S.	**H6**	102
Lower New York Bay, b., N.J., U.S.	**B4**	123
Lower Otay Lake, res., Ca., U.S.	**o16**	98
Lower Paia, Hi., U.S.	**C5**	104
Lower Red Lake, l., Mn., U.S.	**C3**	116
Lower Rice Lake, l., Mn., U.S.	**C3**	116
Lower Salmon Dam, Id., U.S.	**G4**	105
Lower Trajan's Wall, hist., Eur.	**G10**	20
Lower West Pubnico, N.S., Can.	**F4**	87
Lowestoft, Eng., U.K.	**D7**	12
Lowndes, co., Al., U.S.	**C3**	94
Lowndes, co., Ga., U.S.	**F3**	103
Lowndes, co., Ms., U.S.	**B5**	117
Lowry City, Mo., U.S.	**C4**	118
Lowville, N.Y., U.S.	**B5**	125
Loxley, Al., U.S.	**E2**	94
Loxton, Austl.	**G3**	62
Loyal, Wi., U.S.	**D3**	142
Loyall, Ky., U.S.	**D6**	110
Loyalsock Creek, stm., Pa., U.S.	**D8**	131
Loyalty Islands see Loyauté, Îles, is., N. Cal.	**I9**	62a
Loyauté, Îles, is., N. Cal.	**I9**	62a
Loznica, Serb.	**B7**	18
Lozova, Ukr.	**E14**	20
Lualaba, stm., Afr.	**D5**	54
Lua Makika, crat., Hi., U.S.	**C5**	104
Lu'an, China	**C4**	30
Luan, stm., China	**C11**	28
Luanda, Ang.	**E2**	54
Luang, Thale, l., Thai.	**E4**	34
Luanginga, stm., Afr.	**A3**	56
Luangwa, stm., Afr.	**A5**	56
Luanping, China	**A4**	30
Luanshya, Zam.	**A4**	56
Luan Toro, Arg.	**F4**	72
Luapula, stm., Afr.	**A4**	56
Luau, Ang.	**F4**	54
Luba, Eq. Gui.	**C1**	54
Lubang Islands, is., Phil.	**D8**	34
Lubango, Ang.	**A1**	56
Lubbock, Tx., U.S.	**C2**	136
Lubbock, co., Tx., U.S.	**C2**	136
Lubec, Me., U.S.	**D6**	112
Lübeck, Ger.	**D12**	12
Lubefu, D.R.C.	**D4**	54
Lubin, Pol.	**D4**	20
Lublin, Pol.	**D7**	20
Lubnān, Jabal, mts., Leb.	**F6**	44
Lubny, Ukr.	**D12**	20
Lubudi, D.R.C.	**F5**	54
Lubuklinggau, Indon.	**D2**	36
Lubumbashi, D.R.C.	**F5**	54
Lubutu, D.R.C.	**D5**	54
Lucama, N.C., U.S.	**B4**	126
Lucan, On., Can.	**D3**	89
Lucapa, Ang.	**E4**	54
Lucas, co., Ia., U.S.	**C4**	108
Lucas, co., Oh., U.S.	**A2**	128
Lucasville, Oh., U.S.	**D3**	128
Lucca, Italy	**C3**	18
Luce, co., Mi., U.S.	**B5**	115
Lucedale, Ms., U.S.	**E5**	117
Lucena, Phil.	**D8**	34
Lucena, Spain	**I4**	16
Lučenec, Slvk.	**E5**	20
Lucera, Italy	**D5**	18
Lucerne see Luzern, Switz.	**A2**	18
Lucerne, Ca., U.S.	**C2**	98
Lucerne, Lake see Vierwaldstätter See, l., Switz.	**A2**	18
Lucernemines, Pa., U.S.	**E3**	131
Lucerne Valley, Ca., U.S.	**E5**	98
Luceville, Qc., Can.	**A9**	90
Lucira, Ang.	**A1**	56
Luck, Wi., U.S.	**C1**	142
Luckenwalde, Ger.	**E13**	12
Lucknow, On., Can.	**D3**	89
Lucknow, India	**D4**	40
Lucky Peak Lake, res., Id., U.S.	**F3**	105
Luçon, Fr.	**D6**	16
Lucusse, Ang.	**A3**	56
Lüda see Dalian, China	**D12**	28
Lüderitz, Nmb.	**D2**	56
Ludhiāna, India	**C3**	40
Ludington, Mi., U.S.	**E4**	115
Ludlow, Ky., U.S.	**h13**	110
Ludlow, Ma., U.S.	**B3**	114
Ludlow, Vt., U.S.	**E3**	138
Ludogorie, reg., Blg.	**C11**	18
Ludowici, Ga., U.S.	**E5**	103
Ludvika, Swe.	**F6**	10
Ludwigsburg, Ger.	**F11**	12
Ludwigslust, Ger.	**D12**	12
Luebo, D.R.C.	**E4**	54
Luena, Ang.	**F3**	54
Luena, D.R.C.	**E5**	54
Lueyang, China	**C2**	30
Lufeng, China	**E4**	30
Lufkin, Tx., U.S.	**D5**	136
Luga, Russia	**C4**	22
Lugano, Switz.	**A2**	18
Luganville, Vanuatu	**k9**	62a
Lugards Falls, wtfl., Kenya	**D7**	54
Lugela, Moz.	**B6**	56
Lugo, Italy	**B3**	18
Lugo, Spain	**F3**	16
Lugoff, S.C., U.S.	**C6**	133
Lugoj, Rom.	**G6**	20
Lugovoj, Kaz.	**B10**	42
Luhans'k, Ukr.	**E15**	20
Luishia, D.R.C.	**F5**	54
Luiza, D.R.C.	**E4**	54
Lukachukai, Az., U.S.	**A6**	96
Luke Air Force Base, mil., Az., U.S.	**D3**	96
Lukenie, stm., D.R.C.	**D3**	54
Lukojanov, Russia	**D7**	22
Lukolela, D.R.C.	**E4**	54
Lukolela, D.R.C.	**D3**	54
Lukula, D.R.C.	**E2**	54
Lukulu, Zam.	**A3**	56
Lula, Ga., U.S.	**B3**	103
Luleå, Swe.	**D10**	10
Luleälven, stm., Swe.	**C9**	10
Lüleburgaz, Tur.	**B2**	44
Luliang, China	**D1**	30
Lüliang Shan, mts., China	**D10**	28
Luling, La., U.S.	**k11**	111
Luling, Tx., U.S.	**E4**	136
Lulua, stm., D.R.C.	**E4**	54
Lumana, D.R.C.	**D5**	54
Lumbala N'guimbo, Ang.	**A3**	56
Lumber, stm., U.S.	**C9**	133
Lumber City, Ga., U.S.	**E4**	103
Lumberport, W.V., U.S.	**B4**	141
Lumberton, Ms., U.S.	**D4**	117
Lumberton, N.C., U.S.	**C3**	126
Lumbo, Moz.	**B7**	56
Lumby, B.C., Can.	**D8**	85
Lumding, India	**D6**	40
Lummi Indian Reservation, Wa., U.S.	**A3**	140
Lumpkin, Ga., U.S.	**D2**	103
Lumpkin, co., Ga., U.S.	**B2**	103
Lumsden, N.L., Can.	**D5**	88
Lumut, Tanjung, c., Indon.	**D3**	36
Luna, co., N.M., U.S.	**E2**	124
Luna Pier, Mi., U.S.	**G7**	115
Lund, Swe.	**I5**	10
Lund, Nv., U.S.	**E6**	121
Lundar, Mb., Can.	**D2**	86
Lundazi, Zam.	**A5**	56
Lüneburg, Ger.	**D12**	12
Lunenburg, Ma., U.S.	**A4**	114
Lunenburg, co., Va., U.S.	**D4**	139
Lunéville, Fr.	**C10**	16
Lungué-Bungo (Lungwebungu), stm., Afr.	**A2**	56
Lungwebungu (Lungué-Bungo), stm., Afr.	**A3**	56
Luninec, Bela.	**C9**	20
Luobei, China	**A2**	31
Luochuan, China	**B2**	30
Luoding, China	**E3**	30
Luohe, China	**E10**	28
Luotian, China	**C4**	30
Luoyang, China	**E10**	28
Luoyuan, China	**D4**	30
Luozi, D.R.C.	**E2**	54
Lupanshui, China	**D1**	30
Lupeni, Rom.	**G7**	20
Luputa, D.R.C.	**E4**	54
Luqu, China	**E8**	28
Luray, Va., U.S.	**B4**	139
Lure, Lake, res., N.C., U.S.	**f10**	126
Luremo, Ang.	**E3**	54
Lúrio, Moz.	**A7**	56
Lúrio, stm., Moz.	**A6**	56
Lusaka, Zam.	**B4**	56
Lusambo, D.R.C.	**D4**	54
Lusanga, D.R.C.	**D3**	54
Lusangi, D.R.C.	**D5**	54
Lusby, Md., U.S.	**D5**	113
Luseland, Sk., Can.	**E1**	91
Lushnjë, Alb.	**D7**	18
Lushoto, Tan.	**D7**	54
Lüshun, China	**D12**	28
Lusk, Wy., U.S.	**D8**	143
Lūt, dasht-e, des., Iran	**D7**	42
Lutcher, La., U.S.	**D5**	111
Luther, Ok., U.S.	**B4**	129
Lutherstadt Eisleben, Ger.	**E12**	12
Lutherstadt Wittenberg, Ger.	**E13**	12
Luthersville, Ga., U.S.	**C2**	103
Lutherville-Timonium, Md., U.S.	**B4**	113
Luton, Eng., U.K.	**E6**	12
Łutselk'e, N.T., Can.	**F17**	82
Luts'k, Ukr.	**D8**	20
Luttrell, Tn., U.S.	**C10**	135
Lutz, Fl., U.S.	**D4**	102
Lutzow-Holm Bay, b., Ant.	**C8**	67
Luuq, Som.	**J13**	48
Luverne, Al., U.S.	**D3**	94
Luverne, Mn., U.S.	**G2**	116
Luwingu, Zam.	**A4**	56
Luwuk, Indon.	**D6**	36
Luxapallila Creek, stm., U.S.	**B5**	117
Luxembourg, ctry., Eur.	**C10**	16
Luxembourg, Lux.	**F9**	12
Luxemburg, Wi., U.S.	**D6**	142
Luxi, China	**G7**	28
Luxomni, Ga., U.S.	**h8**	103
Luxor see El-Uqsor, Egypt	**E11**	48
Luxora, Ar., U.S.	**B6**	97
Luza, Russia	**B8**	22
Luzern, Switz.	**A2**	18
Luzerne, co., Pa., U.S.	**D9**	131
Luzerne, Pa., U.S.	**n17**	131
Luzhai, China	**E2**	30
Luzhou, China	**F9**	28
Luziânia, Braz.	**E2**	74
Luzilândia, Braz.	**B3**	74
Luzon, i., Phil.	**C8**	34
Luzon Strait, strt., Asia	**B8**	34
L'viv, Ukr.	**E8**	20
L'vov see L'viv, Ukr.	**E8**	20
Lyallpur see Faisalabad, Pak.	**D10**	42
Lycksele, Swe.	**D8**	10
Lycoming, co., Pa., U.S.	**D7**	131
Lycoming Creek, stm., Pa., U.S.	**D7**	131
Lydenburg, S. Afr.	**D5**	56
Lyell, Mount, mtn., Can.	**D2**	84
Lyford, Tx., U.S.	**F4**	136
Lykens, Pa., U.S.	**E8**	131
Lyle, Wa., U.S.	**D4**	140
Lyman, S.C., U.S.	**B3**	133
Lyman, co., S.D., U.S.	**D6**	134
Lyman, Wy., U.S.	**E2**	143
Lyman Lake, res., Az., U.S.	**C6**	96
Lyme Bay, b., Eng., U.K.	**E5**	12
Lynch, Ky., U.S.	**D7**	110
Lynchburg, Oh., U.S.	**C2**	128
Lynchburg, Tn., U.S.	**B5**	135
Lynchburg, Va., U.S.	**C3**	139
Lynches, stm., S.C., U.S.	**D8**	133
Lynden, Wa., U.S.	**A3**	140
Lynde Point, c., Ct., U.S.	**D6**	100
Lyndhurst, N.J., U.S.	**h8**	123
Lyndhurst, Oh., U.S.	**g9**	128
Lyndon, Ks., U.S.	**D8**	109
Lyndon, Ky., U.S.	**g11**	110
Lyndon B. Johnson National Historical Site, hist., Tx., U.S.	**D3**	136
Lyndon B. Johnson Space Center, hist., Tx., U.S.	**r14**	136
Lyndonville, Vt., U.S.	**B4**	138
Lyndora, Pa., U.S.	**E2**	131
Lyngen, b., Nor.	**B9**	10
Lynn, Al., U.S.	**A2**	94
Lynn, In., U.S.	**D8**	107
Lynn, Ma., U.S.	**B6**	114
Lynn, co., Tx., U.S.	**C2**	136
Lynn, Lake, res., W.V., U.S.	**B5**	141
Lynn Canal, b., Ak., U.S.	**k22**	95
Lynnfield, Ma., U.S.	**f11**	114
Lynn Garden, Tn., U.S.	**C11**	135
Lynn Haven, Fl., U.S.	**u16**	102
Lynnhaven Roads, b., Va., U.S.	**k15**	139
Lynnville, In., U.S.	**H3**	107
Lynnwood, Wa., U.S.	**B3**	140
Lynwood, Ca., U.S.	**n12**	98
Lyon, Fr.	**E9**	16
Lyon, co., Ia., U.S.	**A1**	108
Lyon, co., Ks., U.S.	**D7**	109
Lyon, co., Ky., U.S.	**C1**	110
Lyon, co., Mn., U.S.	**F3**	116

Name | Map Ref. | Page

Lyon, co., Nv., U.S. D2 121
Lyons, Co., U.S. A5 99
Lyons, Ga., U.S. D4 103
Lyons, Il., U.S. k9 106
Lyons, In., U.S. G3 107
Lyons, Ks., U.S. D5 109
Lyons, Mi., U.S. F6 115
Lyons, Ne., U.S. C9 120
Lyons, N.Y., U.S. B3 125
Lyons, Or., U.S. C4 130
Lysekil, Swe. G4 10
Lyster Station, Qc., Can. C6 90
Lys'va, Russia D7 26
Lysychans'k, Ukr. E15 20
Lytle, Tx., U.S. E3 136
Lyubotyn, Ukr. E13 20

M

Maalaea Bay, b., Hi., U.S. C5 104
Ma'ān, Jord. D3 42
Ma'anshan, China C4 30
Maarianhamina, Fin. F8 10
Ma'arrat an-Nu'mān, Syria E7 44
Maas (Meuse), stm., Eur. B9 16
Maastricht, Neth. E9 12
Mabank, Tx., U.S. C4 136
Mabel, Mn., U.S. G7 116
Maben, Ms., U.S. B4 117
Mableton, Ga., U.S. h7 103
Mabote, Moz. C5 56
Mabscott, W.V., U.S. D3 141
Mabton, Wa., U.S. C5 140
Mača, Russia D13 26
Macaé, Braz. F3 74
Macaíba, Braz. C4 74
Macapá, Braz. A1 74
Macará, Ec. D4 70
Macau, Braz. C4 74
Macau see Aomen, China B6 34
MacClenny, Fl., U.S. B4 102
MacDill Air Force Base, mil., Fl., U.S. E4 102
MacDonnell Ranges, mts., Austl. E5 60
MacDowell Reservoir, res., N.H., U.S. E2 122
Macedonia, ctry., Eur. D8 18
Macedonia, hist. reg., Eur. D9 18
Macedonia, Oh., U.S. A4 128
Maceió, Braz. C4 74
Macenta, Gui. E3 50
Macerata, Italy C4 18
Maces Bay, b., N.B., Can. D3 87
MacGregor, Mb., Can. E2 86
Machado, stm., Braz. E7 70
Machakos, Kenya D7 54
Machala, Ec. D4 70
Macheke, Zimb. B5 56
Macheng, China C3 30
Machias, Me., U.S. D5 112
Machias, stm., Me., U.S. D5 112
Machias, stm., Me., U.S. B4 112
Machias Bay, b., Me., U.S. D5 112
Machias Lakes, l., Me., U.S. C5 112
Machilīpatnam, India F4 40
Machiques, Ven. A5 70
Macho, Arroyo del, val., N.M., U.S. C4 124
Machupicchu, Peru F5 70
Machupicchu, hist., Peru A3 72
Mackay, Austl. E4 62
Mackay, Lake, l., Austl. E4 60
MacKenzie, B.C., Can. B6 85
Mackenzie, stm., N.T., Can. E13 82
Mackenzie Bay, b., Can. E12 82
Mackenzie Mountains, mts., Can. F14 82
Mackinac, co., Mi., U.S. B5 115
Mackinac, Straits of, strt., Mi., U.S. C6 115
Mackinac Bridge, Mi., U.S. C6 115
Mackinac Island, i., Mi., U.S. C6 115
Mackinaw, Il., U.S. C4 106
Mackinaw, stm., Il., U.S. C4 106
Mackinaw City, Mi., U.S. C6 115
Mackinnon Road, Kenya D7 54
Maclean, Austl. F5 62
Maclear, S. Afr. E4 56
Macleod, Lake, l., Austl. E1 60
Maclovio Herrera, Mex. B3 78
Macomb, Il., U.S. C3 106
Macomb, co., Mi., U.S. F8 115
Macomer, Italy D2 18
Mâcon, Fr. D9 16
Macon, co., Al., U.S. C4 94
Macon, Ga., U.S. D3 103
Macon, co., Ga., U.S. D2 103
Macon, Il., U.S. D5 106
Macon, co., Il., U.S. D4 106
Macon, Mo., U.S. B5 118
Macon, co., Mo., U.S. B5 118
Macon, Ms., U.S. B5 117
Macon, co., N.C., U.S. f9 126
Macon, co., Tn., U.S. A5 135
Macon, Bayou, stm., U.S. B4 111
Macoupin, co., Il., U.S. D4 106
Macquarie Island, i., Austl. J23 4
Macquarie Ridge N18 64
MacTier, On., Can. B5 89
Macungie, Pa., U.S. E10 131
Macuspana, Mex. D6 78
Mad, stm., Ca., U.S. B2 98
Mad, stm., Ct., U.S. B3 100
Mad, stm., N.H., U.S. C3 122
Mad, stm., Oh., U.S. C2 128
Mad, stm., Vt., U.S. C3 138
Madagascar, ctry., Afr. B8 56
Madagascar Basin K8 64
Madagascar Plateau L7 64
Madame, Isle, i., N.S., Can. D9 87
Madang, Pap. N. Gui. H12 32
Madaoua, Niger D6 50
Madawaska, stm., On., Can. B7 89
Madawaska, stm., Can. B9 90
Madawaska, Me., U.S. A4 112
Madawaska Lake, l., Me., U.S. A4 112
Madaya, Mya. B3 34
Madeira, stm., S.A. E7 70
Madeira, Oh., U.S. o13 128
Madeira, Arquipélago da, is., Port. D1 48
Madeira Islands see Madeira, Arquipélago da, is., Port. D1 48
Madeleine, Îles de la, is., Qc., Can. B8 87
Madelia, Mn., U.S. F4 116
Madeline Island, i., Wi., U.S. B3 142
Maden, Tur. C8 44
Madera, Mex. B3 78
Madera see Madeira, stm., S.A. E7 70
Madera, Ca., U.S. D3 98
Madera, co., Ca., U.S. D4 98
Madhya Pradesh, state, India E3 40
Madill, Ok., U.S. C5 129
Madimba, D.R.C. D3 54
Madingo-Kayes, Congo D2 54
Madingou, Congo D2 54
Madirovalo, Madag. B8 56
Madison, Al., U.S. A3 94
Madison, co., Al., U.S. A3 94
Madison, Ar., U.S. B5 97
Madison, co., Ar., U.S. B2 97
Madison, Ct., U.S. D5 100
Madison, Fl., U.S. B3 102
Madison, co., Fl., U.S. B3 102
Madison, Ga., U.S. C3 103
Madison, co., Ga., U.S. B3 103
Madison, co., Ia., U.S. C3 108
Madison, co., Id., U.S. F7 105
Madison, Il., U.S. E3 106
Madison, co., Il., U.S. E4 106
Madison, In., U.S. G7 107
Madison, co., In., U.S. D6 107
Madison, Ks., U.S. D7 109
Madison, co., Ky., U.S. C5 110
Madison, co., La., U.S. B4 111
Madison, Me., U.S. D3 112
Madison, Mn., U.S. E2 116
Madison, co., Mo., U.S. D7 118
Madison, Ms., U.S. C3 117
Madison, co., Ms., U.S. C4 117
Madison, co., Mt., U.S. E5 119
Madison, stm., Mt., U.S. E5 119
Madison, N.C., U.S. A3 126
Madison, co., N.C., U.S. f10 126
Madison, Ne., U.S. C8 120
Madison, co., Ne., U.S. C8 120
Madison, N.J., U.S. B4 123
Madison, co., N.Y., U.S. C5 125
Madison, Oh., U.S. A4 128
Madison, co., Oh., U.S. C2 128
Madison, S.D., U.S. D8 134
Madison, co., Tn., U.S. B3 135
Madison, co., Tx., U.S. D5 136
Madison, co., Va., U.S. B4 139
Madison, Wi., U.S. E4 142
Madison, W.V., U.S. C3 141
Madison Heights, Mi., U.S. o15 115
Madison Heights, Va., U.S. C3 139
Madison Lake, Mn., U.S. F5 116
Madison Range, mts., Mt., U.S. E5 119
Madisonville, Ky., U.S. C2 110
Madisonville, La., U.S. D5 111
Madisonville, Tn., U.S. D9 135
Madisonville, Tx., U.S. D5 136
Madoc, On., Can. C7 89
Mado Gashi, Kenya C7 54
Madoi, China E7 28
Madona, Lat. H12 10
Madrakah, Ra's al-, c., Oman G7 38
Madras see Chennai, India G4 40
Madras see Tamil Nādu, state, India G3 40
Madras, Or., U.S. C5 130
Madre, Laguna, l., Mex. B5 78
Madre, Laguna, b., Tx., U.S. F4 136
Madre, Sierra, mts., Phil. C8 34
Madre de Dios, stm., S.A. F6 70
Madre de Dios, Isla, i., Chile H1 69
Madre del Sur, Sierra, mts., Mex. D5 78
Madre Occidental, Sierra, mts., Mex. B3 78
Madre Oriental, Sierra, mts., Mex. C4 78
Madrid, Spain G5 16
Madrid, Ia., U.S. C4 108
Madura, i., Indon. E4 36
Madura, Selat, strt., Indon. E4 36
Madurai, India H3 40
Maebashi, Japan D15 28
Mae Hong Son, Thai. C3 34
Mae Sariang, Thai. C3 34
Maeser, Ut., U.S. C6 137
Mae Sot, Thai. C3 34
Maestra, Sierra, mts., Cuba B4 80
Maevatanana, Madag. B8 56
Maéwo, i., Vanuatu k9 62a
Mafeteng, Leso. D4 56
Mafia Island, i., Tan. E7 54
Magadan, Russia D17 26
Magadi, Kenya D7 54
Magallanes, Estrecho de (Magellan, Strait of), strt., S.A. H2 69
Magangué, Col. B5 70
Magaria, Niger D6 50
Magazine, Ar., U.S. B2 97
Magazine Mountain, mtn., Ar., U.S. B2 97
Magdagači, Russia D14 26
Magdalena, Bol. F7 70
Magdalena, stm., Col. D5 80
Magdalena, stm., Mex. A2 78
Magdalena, N.M., U.S. C2 124
Magdalena, Isla, i., Chile F2 69
Magdalena de Kino, Mex. A2 78
Magdalena Mountains, mts., N.M., U.S. D2 124
Magdeburg, Ger. D12 12
Magee, Ms., U.S. D4 117
Magelang, Indon. E4 36
Magellan, Strait of see Magallanes, Estrecho de, strt., S.A. H2 69
Maggie Creek, stm., Nv., U.S. C5 121
Maggiore, Lago, l., Eur. B2 18
Maghâgha, Egypt F10 14
Maghama, Maur. C2 50
Magic Reservoir, res., Id., U.S. F4 105
Maglie, Italy D7 18
Magna, Ut., U.S. C3 137
Magnetawan, stm., On., Can. B4 89
Magnitogorsk, Russia D7 26
Magnolia, Ar., U.S. D2 97
Magnolia, Ky., U.S. C4 110
Magnolia, Ms., U.S. D3 117
Magnolia, N.C., U.S. C4 126
Magnolia, Oh., U.S. B4 128
Magoffin, co., Ky., U.S. C6 110
Magog, Qc., Can. D5 90
Magothy River, b., Md., U.S. B4 113
Magrath, Ab., Can. E4 84
Magruder Mountain, mtn., Nv., U.S. F4 121
Magway, Mya. B2 34
Mahābād, Iran C5 42
Mahābaleshwar, India F2 40
Mahabe, Madag. B8 56
Mahābhārat Lek, mts., Nepal D4 40
Mahabo, Madag. C7 56
Mahačkala, Russia E6 26
Mahagi, D.R.C. C6 54
Mahajanga, Madag. B8 56
Mahakam, stm., Indon. C5 36
Mahalapye, Bots. C4 56
Mahānadi, stm., India E4 40
Mahanoro, Madag. B8 56
Mahanoy City, Pa., U.S. E9 131
Mahārāshtra, state, India E3 40
Maha Sarakham, Thai. C4 34
Mahaska, co., Ia., U.S. C5 108
Mahbūbnagar, India F3 40
Mahd adh-Dhahab, Sau. Ar. F4 38
Mahdia, Tun. G3 18
Mahe, India G3 40
Mahé, i., Sey. h13 57b
Mahébourg, Mrts. g10 57a
Mahenge, Tan. E7 54
Mahesāna, India E2 40
Mahi, stm., India E2 40
Mahilëu, Bela. C11 20
Mahnomen, Mn., U.S. C3 116
Mahnomen, co., Mn., U.S. C3 116
Mahogany Mountain, mtn., Or., U.S. D9 130
Mahomet, Il., U.S. C5 106
Mahón see Maó, Spain H9 16
Mahone Bay, N.S., Can. E5 87
Mahoning, co., Oh., U.S. B5 128
Mahoning, stm., U.S. A5 128
Mahopac, N.Y., U.S. D7 125
Mahuva, India E2 40
Mahwah, N.J., U.S. A4 123
Maicao, Col. C5 80
Maiden, N.C., U.S. B1 126
Maidstone Lake, l., Vt., U.S. B5 138
Maiduguri, Nig. D7 50
Maili, Hi., U.S. g9 104
Maili Point, c., Hi., U.S. g9 104
Main, stm., Ger. F11 12
Main Channel, strt., On., Can. B3 89
Mai-Ndombe, Lac, l., D.R.C. D3 54
Maine, hist. reg., Fr. C6 16
Maine, state, U.S. C3 112
Maine, Gulf of, b., N.A. C14 92
Mainland, i., Scot., U.K. h19 12a
Mainland, i., Scot., U.K. A5 12
Main Pass, strt., La., U.S. E6 111
Maintirano, Madag. B7 56
Mainz, Ger. E11 12
Maio, i., C.V. g10 50a
Maipú, Arg. F6 72
Maiquetía, Ven. A6 70
Maisonnette, N.B., Can. B4 87
Maitembge, Bots. C4 56
Maitland, Austl. G5 62
Maitland, On., Can. C9 89
Maíz, Islas del, is., Nic. C3 80
Maize, Ks., U.S. g12 109
Maizuru, Japan C3 31
Maja, stm., Russia C15 26
Majene, Indon. D5 36
Majī, Eth. B7 54
Majkop, Russia E6 26
Major, co., Ok., U.S. A3 129
Majorca see Mallorca, i., Spain H8 16
Majuro, atoll, Marsh. Is. D11 58
Maka, Sen. D2 50
Makabana, Congo D2 54
Makaha, Hi., U.S. g9 104
Makaha Point, c., Hi., U.S. A2 104
Makah Indian Reservation, Wa., U.S. A1 140
Makahuena Point, c., Hi., U.S. B2 104
Makakilo City, Hi., U.S. g9 104
Makapuu Head, c., Hi., U.S. B4 104
Makarakomburu, Mount, mtn., Sol. Is. B6 62
Makarov, Russia B16 28
Makarov Basin E34 144
Makasar see Ujungpandang, Indon. E5 36
Makasar, Selat (Makassar Strait), strt., Indon. D5 36
Makassar Strait see Makasar, Selat, strt., Indon. D5 36
Makat, Kaz. E7 26
Makawao, Hi., U.S. C5 104
Makaweli, Hi., U.S. B2 104
Makeni, S.L. E2 50
Makgadikgadi, pl., Bots. C4 56
Makiïvka, Ukr. E14 20
Makindu, Kenya D7 54
Makkah, Sau. Ar. F3 38
Makó, Hung. F6 20
Makokou, Gabon C2 54
Makoua, Congo D3 54
Makrān Coast, Asia E7 42
Mākū, Iran C11 44
Makumbi, D.R.C. E4 54
Makurdi, Nig. E6 50
Makushin Volcano, vol., Ak., U.S. E6 95
Mala, Peru A2 72
Malabar, Fl., U.S. D6 102
Malabar Coast, India G2 40
Malabo, Eq. Gui. C1 54
Malacca see Melaka, Malay. C2 36
Malacca, Strait of, strt., Asia C1 36
Malad City, Id., U.S. G6 105
Maladzečna, Bela. B9 20
Málaga, Col. D5 80
Málaga, Spain I4 16
Malagarasi, Tan. E6 54
Malaimbandy, Madag. C8 56
Malaja Kuril'skaja Grjada, is., Russia B5 31
Malajaroslavec, Russia B14 20
Malaja Višera, Russia C5 22
Malakāl, Sudan I11 48
Malakoff, Tx., U.S. C4 136
Malakula, i., Vanuatu I9 62a
Malambo, Col. C5 80
Malang, Indon. E4 36
Malanje, Ang. E3 54
Malanville, Benin D5 50
Mälaren, l., Swe. G7 10
Malargüe, Arg. F4 72
Malartic, Qc., Can. k11 90
Malaspina Glacier, ice, Ak., U.S. D11 95
Malatya, Tur. C8 44
Mala Vyska, Ukr. E11 20
Malawi, ctry., Afr. A5 56
Malaŵi, Lake see Nyasa, Lake, l., Afr. F6 54
Malaya see Semenanjung Malaysia, hist. reg., Malay. C2 36
Malaybalay, Phil. E9 34
Malāyer, Iran D5 42
Malay Peninsula, pen., Asia B2 36
Malaysia, ctry., Asia C4 36
Malazgirt, Tur. C10 44
Malbaie, stm., Qc., Can. B7 90
Malbork, Pol. C5 20
Malbrán, Arg. D5 72
Malcolm, Austl. F3 60
Malden, i., Kir. E14 58
Malden, Ma., U.S. B5 114
Malden, Mo., U.S. E8 118
Malden, W.V., U.S. m12 141
Maldives, ctry., Asia I10 24
Maldonado, Ur. E7 72
Mālegaon, India E2 40
Malek Kandī, Iran D12 44
Malema, Moz. A6 56
Malha Wells, Sudan G10 48
Malheur, stm., Or., U.S. D9 130
Malheur, co., Or., U.S. D9 130
Malheur Lake, l., Or., U.S. D8 130
Mali, ctry., Afr. C4 50
Mali, Gui. D2 50
Malibu, Ca., U.S. m11 98
Malin, Or., U.S. E5 130
Malindi, Kenya D8 54
Malinga, Congo D2 54
Malka, Russia D17 26
Malkara, Tur. B2 44
Mallawi, Egypt F10 14
Malletts Bay, b., Vt., U.S. B2 138
Mallorca (Majorca), i., Spain H8 16
Malmberget, Swe. C9 10
Malmesbury, S. Afr. E2 56
Malmö, Swe. I5 10
Malmstrom Air Force Base, mil., Mt., U.S. C5 119
Maloelap, atoll, Marsh. Is. D11 58
Malolos, Phil. D8 34
Malone, N.Y., U.S. f10 125
Maloney Reservoir, res., Ne., U.S. C5 120
Malonga, D.R.C. F4 54
Malošujka, Russia B6 22
Måløy, Nor. F1 10
Malpelo, Isla de, i., Col. C3 70
Malpeque Bay, b., P.E., Can. C6 87
Malta, ctry., Eur. G5 18
Malta, Il., U.S. B5 106
Malta, Mt., U.S. B9 119
Maltahöhe, Nmb. C2 56
Maluku (Moluccas), is., Indon. D7 36
Maluku, Laut (Molucca Sea), Indon. C7 36
Malumfashi, Nig. D6 50
Mālvan, India F2 40
Malvern, Ar., U.S. C3 97
Malvern, Ia., U.S. D2 108
Malvern, Oh., U.S. B4 128
Malvern, Pa., U.S. o19 131
Malverne, N.Y., U.S. k13 125
Malyj Enisej, stm., Russia A7 28
Malyn, Ukr. D10 20
Mama, Russia D13 26
Mamala Bay, b., Hi., U.S. g10 104
Mamallapuram, hist., India G4 40
Mamaroneck, N.Y., U.S. h13 125
Mamburao, Phil. D8 34
Mamfe, Cam. B1 54
Mammoth, Az., U.S. E5 96
Mammoth Cave National Park, Ky., U.S. C4 110
Mammoth Lakes, Ca., U.S. D4 98
Mammoth Spring, Ar., U.S. A4 97
Mamoré, stm., S.A. F6 70
Mamou, Gui. D2 50
Mamou, La., U.S. D3 111
Mamoudzou, May. A8 56
Mampikony, Madag. B8 56
Mamuju, Indon. D5 36
Man, C. Iv. E3 50
Man, W.V., U.S. D3 141
Manacapuru, Braz. D7 70
Manacor, Spain H8 16
Manado, Indon. C6 36
Managua, Nic. C2 80
Managua, Lago de, l., Nic. C2 80
Manakara, Madag. C8 56
Manāli, India C3 40
Manama see Al-Manāmah, Bahr. E6 42
Manam Island, i., Pap. N. Gui. G12 32
Manana Island, i., Hi., U.S. g11 104
Mananara Avaratra, Madag. B8 56
Mananjary, Madag. C8 56
Manankoro, Mali D3 50
Manantico Creek, stm., N.J., U.S. E3 123
Mana Point, c., Hi., U.S. A2 104
Manas, China C5 28
Manas Hu, l., China B5 28
Manasquan, N.J., U.S. C4 123
Manasquan, stm., N.J., U.S. C4 123
Manassa, Co., U.S. D5 99
Manassas, Va., U.S. B5 139
Manassas National Battlefield Park, Va., U.S. g11 139
Manassas Park, Va., U.S. B5 139
Manatee, stm., Fl., U.S. E4 102
Manatee, co., Fl., U.S. E4 102
Manatuto, E. Timor E7 36
Manaus, Braz. D7 70
Manavgat, Tur. D4 44
Manawa, Wi., U.S. D5 142
Manbij, Syria D7 44
Mancelona, Mi., U.S. D5 115
Manchester, Eng., U.K. D5 12
Manchester, Ct., U.S. B5 100
Manchester, Ga., U.S. D2 103
Manchester, Ia., U.S. B6 108
Manchester, Ky., U.S. C6 110
Manchester, Ma., U.S. A6 114
Manchester, Md., U.S. A4 113
Manchester, Me., U.S. D3 112
Manchester, Mi., U.S. F6 115
Manchester, Mo., U.S. f12 118
Manchester, N.H., U.S. E4 122
Manchester, N.Y., U.S. C3 125
Manchester, Oh., U.S. D2 128
Manchester, Pa., U.S. F8 131
Manchester, Tn., U.S. B5 135
Manchester, Vt., U.S. E2 138

Name — Map Ref. — Page

Manchester Center, Vt., U.S. E2 138
Manchuria, hist. reg., China B13 28
Mancos, Co., U.S. D2 99
Mancos, stm., U.S. D2 99
Manda, Tan. F6 54
Mandabe, Madag. C7 56
Manda Island, i., Kenya D8 54
Mandal, Nor. G2 10
Mandalay, Mya. B3 34
Mandalgovĭ, Mong. B9 28
Mandali, Iraq D5 42
Mandalya, Gulf of see Güllük Körfezi, b., Tur. D2 44
Mandan, N.D., U.S. C5 127
Mandar, Teluk, b., Indon. D5 36
Mandara Mountains, mts., Afr. A2 54
Mandeb, Bab el, strt. H4 38
Mandera, Kenya C8 54
Mandeville, Jam. B4 80
Mandeville, Ar., U.S. D2 97
Mandeville, La., U.S. D5 111
Mandimba, Moz. A6 56
Mandioli, Pulau, i., Indon. D7 36
Mandla, India E4 40
Mandritsara, Madag. B8 56
Mandsaur, India E3 40
Manduria, Italy D6 18
Māndvi, India E1 40
Mandya, India G3 40
Manendragarh, India E4 40
Manfalût, Egypt E11 48
Manfredonia, Italy D5 18
Manfredonia, Golfo di, b., Italy D6 18
Manga, Braz. D3 74
Manga, reg., Niger D7 50
Mangabeiras, Chapada das, Braz. C2 74
Mangai, D.R.C. D3 54
Mangalia, Rom. H10 20
Mangalore, India G2 40
Mangchang, China F9 28
Mange, China C4 40
Manggar, Indon. D3 36
Mangkalihat, Tanjung, c., Indon. C5 36
Mangnai, China D6 28
Mangochi, Mwi. A6 56
Mangoky, stm., Madag. C7 56
Mangole, Pulau, i., Indon. D7 36
Mangum, Ok., U.S. C2 129
Manhattan, Ks., U.S. C7 109
Manhattan, Mt., U.S. E5 119
Manhattan Beach, Ca., U.S. n12 98
Manhattan Island, i., N.Y., U.S. h13 125
Manheim, Pa., U.S. F9 131
Manhuaçu, Braz. F3 74
Manica, Moz. B5 56
Manicoré, Braz. E7 70
Manicouagan, Réservoir, res., Qc., Can. h13 90
Manignan, C. Iv. D3 50
Manila, Phil. D8 34
Manila, Ar., U.S. B5 97
Manilla, Ia., U.S. C2 108
Manipur, state, India D6 40
Manisa, Tur. C2 44
Manistee, Mi., U.S. D4 115
Manistee, co., Mi., U.S. D4 115
Manistee, stm., Mi., U.S. D5 115
Manistique, Mi., U.S. C4 115
Manistique, stm., Mi., U.S. B4 115
Manistique Lake, l., Mi., U.S. B5 115
Manito, Il., U.S. C4 106
Manitoba, prov., Can. C3 86
Manitoba, Lake, l., Mb., Can. D2 86
Manitou, Mb., Can. E2 86
Manitou, Lake, l., On., Can. B3 89
Manitou Island, i., Mi., U.S. A3 115
Manitou Lake, l., Sk., Can. E1 91
Manitoulin Island, i., On., Can. B2 89
Manitou Springs, Co., U.S. C6 99
Manitowoc, Wi., U.S. D6 142
Manitowoc, co., Wi., U.S. D6 142
Manitowoc, stm., Wi., U.S. h10 142
Maniwaki, Qc., Can. C2 90
Manizales, Col. B4 70
Manja, Madag. C7 56
Manjakandriana, Madag. B8 56
Manjimup, Austl. G2 60
Mānjra, stm., India F3 40
Mankanza, D.R.C. C3 54
Mankato, Ks., U.S. C5 109
Mankato, Mn., U.S. F5 116
Manlius, N.Y., U.S. C5 125
Manly, Ia., U.S. A4 108
Manmād, India E2 40
Manna, Indon. D2 36
Mannar, Gulf of, b., Asia H3 40
Mannford, Ok., U.S. A5 129
Mannheim, Ger. F11 12
Manning, Ab., Can. A2 84
Manning, Ia., U.S. C2 108
Manning, S.C., U.S. D7 133
Mannington, W.V., U.S. B4 141
Manns Creek, stm., W.V., U.S. n14 141
Mannville, Ab., Can. C5 84
Manokin, stm., Md., U.S. D6 113
Manokotak, Ak., U.S. D8 95
Manokwari, Indon. D8 36
Manomet, Ma., U.S. C6 114
Manomet Point, c., Ma., U.S. C6 114
Manono, D.R.C. E5 54
Manor, Tx., U.S. D4 136
Manouane, Lac, l., Qc., Can. h12 90
Manresa, Spain G7 16
Mansa, Zam. A4 56
Manseau, Qc., Can. C5 90
Mansfield, Eng., U.K. D6 12
Mansfield, Ar., U.S. B1 97
Mansfield, Il., U.S. C5 106
Mansfield, La., U.S. B2 111
Mansfield, Ma., U.S. B5 114
Mansfield, Mo., U.S. D5 118
Mansfield, Oh., U.S. B3 128
Mansfield, Pa., U.S. C7 131
Mansfield, Tx., U.S. n9 136
Mansfield, Mount, mtn., Vt., U.S. B3 138
Mansfield Center, Ct., U.S. B7 100
Mansfield Hollow Lake, res., Ct., U.S. B7 100
Mansôa, Gui.-B. D1 50
Manson, Ia., U.S. B3 108
Manson, Wa., U.S. B5 140
Mansonville, Qc., Can. D5 90
Mansura, La., U.S. C3 111
Manta, Ec. D3 70
Mantachie, Ms., U.S. A5 117
Manteca, Ca., U.S. D3 98
Manteno, Il., U.S. B6 106
Manteo, N.C., U.S. B7 126
Manti, Ut., U.S. D4 137
Mantiqueira, Serra da, mts., Braz. F2 74
Manton, Mi., U.S. D5 115
Mantorville, Mn., U.S. F6 116
Mántova, Italy B3 18
Mantua, Oh., U.S. A4 128
Mantua, Ut., U.S. B4 137
Manturovo, Russia C7 22
Mäntyluoto, Fin. F9 10
Manuae, atoll, Cook Is. F14 58
Manui, Pulau, i., Indon. D6 36
Manukau, N.Z. o13 63c
Manumuskin, stm., N.J., U.S. E3 123
Manus Island, i., Pap. N. Gui. G12 32
Manvel, Tx., U.S. r14 136
Manville, N.J., U.S. B3 123
Manville, R.I., U.S. B4 132
Many, La., U.S. C2 111
Manyara, Lake, l., Tan. D7 54
Many Farms, Az., U.S. A6 96
Manyoni, Tan. E6 54
Manzanillo, Cuba A4 80
Manzanillo, Mex. D4 78
Manzanillo Bay, b., N.A. A5 80
Manzano Mountains, mts., N.M., U.S. C3 124
Manzano Peak, mtn., N.M., U.S. C3 124
Manzhouli, China B11 28
Manzini, Swaz. D5 56
Mao, Chad D8 50
Mao, Dom. Rep. B5 80
Maó, Spain H9 16
Maoke, Pegunungan, mts., Indon. G10 32
Maoming, China G10 28
Mapastepec, Mex. D6 78
Mapi, Indon. H10 32
Mapinhane, Moz. C6 56
Maple, stm., Ia., U.S. B2 108
Maple, stm., N.D., U.S. C8 127
Maple, stm., U.S. A7 134
Maple Bluff, Wi., U.S. E4 142
Maple Grove, Mn., U.S. m12 116
Maple Heights, Oh., U.S. h9 128
Maple Lake, Mn., U.S. E5 116
Maple Plain, Mn., U.S. m11 116
Maple Shade, N.J., U.S. D2 123
Maplesville, Al., U.S. C3 94
Mapleton, Ia., U.S. B2 108
Mapleton, Mn., U.S. G5 116
Mapleton, N.D., U.S. C8 127
Mapleton, Or., U.S. C3 130
Mapleton, Ut., U.S. C4 137
Maple Valley, Wa., U.S. f11 140
Mapleville, R.I., U.S. B2 132
Maplewood, Mn., U.S. n12 116
Maplewood, Mo., U.S. f13 118
Maplewood, N.J., U.S. B4 123
Maputo, Moz. D5 56
Maqteïr, reg., Maur. B2 50
Maquela do Zombo, Ang. E3 54
Maquinchao, Arg. F3 69
Maquoketa, Ia., U.S. B7 108
Maquoketa, stm., Ia., U.S. B6 108
Maquoketa, North Fork, stm., Ia., U.S. B7 108
Marabá, Braz. C2 74
Maracá, Ilha de, i., Braz. C9 70
Maracaibo, Ven. A5 70
Maracaibo, Lago de, l., Ven. B5 70
Maracaju, Braz. C6 72
Maracás, Braz. D3 74
Maracay, Ven. A6 70
Marādah, Libya E8 48
Maradi, Niger D6 50
Marāgheh, Iran C5 42
Marahuaca, Cerro, mtn., Ven. C6 70
Marais des Cygnes, stm., U.S. D8 109
Marajó, Baía de, b., Braz. B2 74
Marajó, Ilha de, i., Braz. B2 74
Maralal, Kenya C7 54
Marampa, S.L. E2 50
Marana, Az., U.S. E4 96
Marand, Iran C5 42
Maranguape, Braz. B4 74
Maranhão, stm., Braz. A8 72
Maranhão, state, Braz. B2 74
Marañón, stm., Peru D5 70
Marathon, Fl., U.S. H5 102
Marathon, Wi., U.S. D4 142
Marathon, co., Wi., U.S. D4 142
Marawi, Phil. E8 34
Marbella, Spain I4 16
Marble, Mn., U.S. C5 116
Marble, N.C., U.S. f9 126
Marble Bar, Austl. E2 60
Marble Canyon, Az., U.S. A4 96
Marble Falls, Tx., U.S. D3 136
Marble Hall, S. Afr. C4 56
Marblehead, Ma., U.S. B6 114
Marble Hill, Mo., U.S. D8 118
Marbleton, Wy., U.S. D2 143
Marburg, Ger. E11 12
Marbury, Md., U.S. C3 113
Marceline, Mo., U.S. B5 118
Marcellus, Mi., U.S. F5 115
March Air Force Base, mil., Ca., U.S. F5 98
Marche, hist. reg., Fr. D7 16
Mar Chiquita, Laguna, l., Arg. E5 72
Marco, Fl., U.S. G5 102
Marcus, Ia., U.S. B2 108
Marcus Baker, Mount, mtn., Ak., U.S. g18 95
Marcus Hook, Pa., U.S. G11 131
Marcus Island see Minami-Tori-shima, i., Japan F18 64
Marcy, Mount, mtn., N.Y., U.S. A7 125
Mardān, Pak. D10 42
Mar del Plata, Arg. F6 72
Mardin, Tur. D9 44
Maré, i., N. Cal. I9 62a
Mareeba, Austl. D4 62
Marengo, co., Al., U.S. C2 94
Marengo, Ia., U.S. C5 108
Marengo, Il., U.S. A5 106
Marengo, In., U.S. H5 107
Marfa, Tx., U.S. o12 136
Margaret, Al., U.S. B3 94
Margaret River, Austl. G1 60
Margarita, Isla de, i., Ven. A7 70
Margate, Fl., U.S. F6 102
Margate City, N.J., U.S. E3 123
Margherita Peak, mtn., Afr. C5 54
Margilan, Uzb. B10 42
Margrethe, Lake, l., Mi., U.S. D6 115
Marha, Russia C14 26
Marhanets', Ukr. F13 20
Maria, Îles, is., Fr. Poly. G14 58
María Elena, Chile B3 69
Maria Island, i., Austl. C6 60
Mariakani, Kenya D7 54
Marian, Lake, l., Fl., U.S. E5 102
Mariana Islands, is., Oc. C11 32
Mariana Ridge G17 64
Mariana Trench G17 64
Marianna, Ar., U.S. C5 97
Marianna, Fl., U.S. B1 102
Marias, stm., Mt., U.S. B4 119
Marias Pass, Mt., U.S. B3 119
Mariato, Punta, c., Pan. D3 80
Maribor, Slvn. A5 18
Marica (Évros) (Meriç), stm., Eur. C10 18
Maricopa, Az., U.S. E3 96
Maricopa, co., Az., U.S. D3 96
Maricopa, Ca., U.S. E4 98
Maricopa Mountains, mts., Az., U.S. m7 96
Marie Byrd Land, reg., Ant. D29 67
Marie-Galante, i., Guad. B7 80
Mariemont, Oh., U.S. o13 128
Mariental, Nmb. C2 56
Marienville, Pa., U.S. D3 131
Maries, co., Mo., U.S. C6 118
Mariestad, Swe. G5 10
Marietta, Ga., U.S. C2 103
Marietta, Oh., U.S. C4 128
Marietta, Ok., U.S. D4 129
Marietta, S.C., U.S. A2 133
Marieville, Qc., Can. D4 90
Marijampolė, Lith. I10 10
Marij El, state, Russia D6 26
Marília, Braz. F2 74
Marimba, Ang. E3 54
Marin, co., Ca., U.S. C2 98
Mar'ina Horka, Bela. C10 20
Marinduque, i., Phil. D8 34
Marine, Il., U.S. E4 106
Marine City, Mi., U.S. F8 115
Marine On St. Croix, Mn., U.S. E6 116
Marinette, Wi., U.S. C6 142
Marinette, co., Wi., U.S. C5 142
Maringá, Braz. F1 74
Maringouin, La., U.S. D4 111
Marion, Al., U.S. C2 94
Marion, co., Al., U.S. A2 94
Marion, Ar., U.S. B5 97
Marion, co., Ar., U.S. A3 97
Marion, co., Fl., U.S. C4 102
Marion, co., Ga., U.S. D2 103
Marion, Ia., U.S. B6 108
Marion, co., Ia., U.S. C4 108
Marion, Il., U.S. F5 106
Marion, co., Il., U.S. E4 106
Marion, In., U.S. C6 107
Marion, co., In., U.S. E5 107
Marion, Ks., U.S. D6 109
Marion, co., Ks., U.S. D6 109
Marion, Ky., U.S. e9 110
Marion, co., Ky., U.S. C4 110
Marion, La., U.S. B3 111
Marion, Mi., U.S. D5 115
Marion, co., Mo., U.S. B6 118
Marion, Ms., U.S. C5 117
Marion, co., Ms., U.S. D4 117
Marion, N.C., U.S. B1 126
Marion, Oh., U.S. B2 128
Marion, co., Oh., U.S. B2 128
Marion, co., Or., U.S. C4 130
Marion, Pa., U.S. G6 131
Marion, S.C., U.S. C9 133
Marion, co., S.C., U.S. C9 133
Marion, S.D., U.S. D8 134
Marion, co., Tn., U.S. D8 135
Marion, co., Tx., U.S. C5 136
Marion, Va., U.S. f10 139
Marion, Wi., U.S. D5 142
Marion, co., W.V., U.S. B4 141
Marion, Lake, res., S.C., U.S. E7 133
Marion Reef, rf., Austl. D5 62
Marion Station, Md., U.S. D6 113
Marionville, Mo., U.S. D4 118
Mariposa, co., Ca., U.S. D3 98
Mariscal Estigarribia, Para. C5 72
Marissa, Il., U.S. E4 106
Maritime Alps, mts., Eur. B1 18
Maritime Atlas see Atlas Tellien, mts., Alg. D4 14
Mariupol', Ukr. F14 20
Märjamaa, Est. G11 10
Marka, Som. J13 48
Mārkāpur, India F3 40
Markdale, On., Can. C4 89
Marked Tree, Ar., U.S. B5 97
Markesan, Wi., U.S. E5 142
Markham, On., Can. D5 89
Markham, Il., U.S. k9 106
Markham, Tx., U.S. E4 136
Markit, China B3 40
Markland Lock and Dam, U.S. B5 110
Markle, In., U.S. C7 107
Markovo, Russia C19 26
Marks, Russia D8 22
Marks, Ms., U.S. A3 117
Marksville, La., U.S. C3 111
Mark Twain Lake, res., Mo., U.S. B6 118
Marlboro, N.Y., U.S. D6 125
Marlboro, co., S.C., U.S. B8 133
Marlboro, Va., U.S. n17 139
Marlborough, Ct., U.S. C6 100
Marlborough, Ma., U.S. B4 114
Marlborough, N.H., U.S. E2 122
Marlette, Mi., U.S. E7 115
Marley, Md., U.S. B4 113
Marlin, Tx., U.S. D4 136
Marlinton, W.V., U.S. C4 141
Marlow, Ok., U.S. C4 129
Marlowe, W.V., U.S. B7 141
Marlton, N.J., U.S. D3 123
Marmaduke, Ar., U.S. A5 97
Marmande, Fr. E7 16
Marmara, Sea of see Marmara Denizi, Tur. B3 44
Marmara Denizi, Tur. B3 44
Marmaris, Tur. D3 44
Marmet, W.V., U.S. C3 141
Marmora, On., Can. C7 89
Marne, stm., Fr. C8 16
Maroa, Il., U.S. C5 106
Maroa, Ven. C6 70
Maroantsetra, Madag. B8 56
Maromandia, Madag. A8 56
Maromokotro, mtn., Madag. A8 56
Marondera, Zimb. B5 56
Maroni, stm., S.A. C9 70
Maros, Indon. E5 36
Maroua, Cam. A2 54
Marovoay, Madag. B8 56
Marowijne see Maroni, stm., S.A. C9 70
Marquesas Islands see Marquises, Îles, is., Fr. Poly. E16 58
Marquesas Keys, is., Fl., U.S. H4 102
Marquette, Mi., U.S. B3 115
Marquette, co., Mi., U.S. B3 115
Marquette, co., Wi., U.S. E4 142
Marquette Heights, Il., U.S. C4 106
Marquises, Îles, is., Fr. Poly. E16 58
Marrah, Jabal, Sudan H9 48
Marrakech, Mor. D3 48
Marrero, La., U.S. E5 111
Marromeu, Moz. B6 56
Mars, Pa., U.S. E1 131
Marsá al-Burayqah, Libya D8 48
Marsabit, Kenya C7 54
Marsala, Italy F4 18
Marseille, Fr. F9 16
Marseilles, Il., U.S. B5 106
Marshall, Sk., Can. D1 91
Marshall, Lib. E2 50
Marshall, co., Al., U.S. A3 94
Marshall, Ar., U.S. B3 97
Marshall, co., Ia., U.S. C4 108
Marshall, Il., U.S. D6 106
Marshall, co., Il., U.S. B4 106
Marshall, co., In., U.S. B5 107
Marshall, co., Ks., U.S. C7 109
Marshall, co., Ky., U.S. f9 110
Marshall, Mi., U.S. F6 115
Marshall, Mn., U.S. F3 116
Marshall, co., Mn., U.S. B2 116
Marshall, Mo., U.S. B4 118
Marshall, co., Ms., U.S. A4 117
Marshall, N.C., U.S. f10 126
Marshall, co., Ok., U.S. C5 129
Marshall, co., S.D., U.S. B8 134
Marshall, co., Tn., U.S. B5 135
Marshall, Tx., U.S. C5 136
Marshall, Va., U.S. B5 139
Marshall, Wi., U.S. E4 142
Marshall, co., W.V., U.S. B4 141
Marshall Islands, is., Marsh. Is. F24 4
Marshall Islands, ctry., Oc. C10 58
Marshallton, De., U.S. B3 101
Marshalltown, Ia., U.S. B5 108
Marshallville, Ga., U.S. D3 103
Marshes Siding, Ky., U.S. D5 110
Marshfield, Ma., U.S. B6 114
Marshfield, Mo., U.S. D5 118
Marshfield, Wi., U.S. D3 142
Marshfield Hills, Ma., U.S. B6 114
Marsh Fork, stm., W.V., U.S. n13 141
Mars Hill, Me., U.S. B5 112
Mars Hill, N.C., U.S. f10 126
Marsh Island, i., La., U.S. E4 111
Marsh Lake, res., Mn., U.S. E2 116
Marsh Peak, mtn., Ut., U.S. C6 137
Marshville, N.C., U.S. C2 126
Marsing, Id., U.S. F2 105
Märsta, Swe. G7 10
Marston, Mo., U.S. E8 118
Mart, Tx., U.S. D4 136
Martaban, Gulf of, b., Mya. C3 34
Martapura, Indon. D4 36
Martapura, Indon. D2 36
Marthasville, Mo., U.S. C6 118
Martha's Vineyard, i., Ma., U.S. D6 114
Martí, Cuba A4 80
Martigny, Switz. A1 18
Martigues, Fr. F9 16
Martin, Slvk. E5 20
Martin, co., Fl., U.S. E6 102
Martin, co., In., U.S. G4 107
Martin, co., Ky., U.S. C7 110
Martin, Ky., U.S. C7 110
Martin, co., Mn., U.S. G4 116
Martin, co., N.C., U.S. B5 126
Martin, S.D., U.S. D4 134
Martin, Tn., U.S. A3 135
Martin, co., Tx., U.S. C2 136
Martinez, Ca., U.S. C2 98
Martinez, Ga., U.S. C4 103
Martínez de la Torre, Mex. C5 78
Martinique, dep., N.A. F12 76
Martinique Passage, strt., N.A. B7 80
Martin Lake, res., Al., U.S. C4 94
Martin Point, c., Ak., U.S. A11 95
Martinsburg, Pa., U.S. F5 131
Martinsburg, W.V., U.S. B7 141
Martins Ferry, Oh., U.S. B5 128
Martinsville, Il., U.S. D6 106
Martinsville, In., U.S. F5 107
Martinsville, Va., U.S. D3 139
Marton, N.Z. p14 63c
Martos, Spain I5 16
Martti, Fin. C13 10
Martuni, Arm. B11 44
Marutea, atoll, Fr. Poly. F15 58
Marv Dasht, Iran D6 42
Marvell, Ar., U.S. C5 97
Marvine, Mount, mtn., Ut., U.S. E4 137
Mary, Turk. F8 26
Mary, Lake, l., Mn., U.S. E3 116
Mary, Lake, l., Ms., U.S. D2 117
Maryborough, Austl. H3 62
Maryborough, Austl. F5 62
Maryland, state, U.S. B4 113
Maryland City, Md., U.S. B4 113
Maryland Heights, Mo., U.S. f13 118
Maryland Point, c., Md., U.S. D3 113
Marys, stm., Nv., U.S. B6 121
Marys Peak, mtn., Or., U.S. C3 130
Marystown, N.L., Can. E4 88
Marysville, Ca., U.S. C3 98
Marysville, Ks., U.S. C7 109
Marysville, Mi., U.S. F8 115
Marysville, Oh., U.S. B2 128
Marysville, Pa., U.S. F8 131
Marysville, Wa., U.S. A3 140
Maryville, Mo., U.S. A3 118
Maryville, Tn., U.S. D10 135
Masai Steppe, plat., Tan. D7 54
Masaka, Ug. D6 54

Name — Map Ref. — Page

Masalembu Besar, Pulau, i., Indon. **E4** 36
Masallı, Azer. **C13** 44
Masan, S. Kor. **D13** 28
Masasi, Tan. **F7** 54
Masaya, Nic. **C2** 80
Masbate, Phil. **D8** 34
Masbate, i., Phil. **D8** 34
Mascarene Basin **J8** 64
Mascarene Islands, is., Afr. **g10** 57a
Mascarene Plateau **I8** 64
Mascasín, Arg. **E4** 72
Mascoma, stm., N.H., U.S. **C2** 122
Mascoma Lake, l., N.H., U.S. **C2** 122
Mascot, Tn., U.S. **C10** 135
Mascouche, Qc., Can. **D4** 90
Mascoutah, Il., U.S. **E4** 106
Maseru, Leso. **D4** 56
Mashapaug Pond, l., Ct., U.S. **A7** 100
Mashava, Zimb. **B5** 56
Mashhad, Iran **C7** 42
Mashra'ar Raqq, Sudan **I10** 48
Masi-Manimba, D.R.C. **D3** 54
Masindi, Ug. **C6** 54
Maşīrah, i., Oman **F7** 38
Maşīrah, Khalīj, b., Oman **G7** 38
Masjed-e Soleymān, Iran **D5** 42
Maskinongé, Qc., Can. **C4** 90
Mason, co., Il., U.S. **C4** 106
Mason, co., Ky., U.S. **B6** 110
Mason, Mi., U.S. **F6** 115
Mason, co., Mi., U.S. **D4** 115
Mason, Nv., U.S. **E2** 121
Mason, Oh., U.S. **C1** 128
Mason, Tx., U.S. **D3** 136
Mason, co., Tx., U.S. **D3** 136
Mason, co., Wa., U.S. **B2** 140
Mason, W.V., U.S. **B2** 141
Mason, co., W.V., U.S. **C3** 141
Mason City, Ia., U.S. **A4** 108
Mason City, Il., U.S. **C4** 106
Masontown, Pa., U.S. **G2** 131
Masontown, W.V., U.S. **B5** 141
Masqaţ, Oman **F7** 38
Massa, Italy **B2** 18
Massabesic Lake, l., N.H., U.S. **E4** 122
Massac, co., Il., U.S. **F5** 106
Massachusetts, state, U.S. **B4** 114
Massachusetts Bay, b., Ma., U.S. **B6** 114
Massacre Lake, l., Nv., U.S. **B2** 121
Massangena, Moz. **C5** 56
Massapoag Lake, l., Ma., U.S. **h11** 114
Massasecum, Lake, l., N.H., U.S. **D3** 122
Massawa, Erit. **G12** 48
Massena, N.Y., U.S. **f10** 125
Massenya, Chad **D8** 50
Masset, B.C., Can. **C1** 85
Massey, On., Can. **A2** 89
Massillon, Oh., U.S. **B4** 128
Massina, reg., Mali **D4** 50
Massinga, Moz. **C6** 56
Massive, Mount, mtn., Co., U.S. **B4** 99
Maştağa, Azer. **B14** 44
Masterton, N.Z. **p14** 63c
Mastic Beach, N.Y., U.S. **n16** 125
Mastung, Pak. **E9** 42
Masuda, Japan **D2** 31
Masuria see Mazury, reg., Pol. **C6** 20
Masury, Oh., U.S. **A5** 128
Masvingo, Zimb. **C5** 56
Matadi, D.R.C. **E2** 54
Matagalpa, Nic. **C2** 80
Matagorda, co., Tx., U.S. **E5** 136
Matagorda Bay, b., Tx., U.S. **E4** 136
Matagorda Island, i., Tx., U.S. **E4** 136
Matagorda Peninsula, pen., Tx., U.S. **E5** 136
Matala, Ang. **A2** 56
Matale, Sri L. **H4** 40
Matam, Sen. **C2** 50
Matamoras, Pa., U.S. **D12** 131
Matamoros, Mex. **B5** 78
Matamoros, Mex. **B4** 78
Matane, Qc., Can. **k13** 90
Matanuska, stm., Ak., U.S. **g18** 95
Matanzas, Cuba **A3** 80
Matanzas Inlet, b., Fl., U.S. **C5** 102
Matapan, Cape see Taínaron, Ákra, c., Grc. **F9** 18
Matara, Sri L. **H4** 40
Mataram, Indon. **E5** 36
Mataranka, Austl. **C5** 60
Mataró, Spain **G8** 16
Mātātīla Dam, India **D3** 40
Matawan, N.J., U.S. **C4** 123
Matehuala, Mex. **C4** 78
Matera, Italy **D6** 18
Matewan, W.V., U.S. **D2** 141
Mather, Pa., U.S. **G1** 131
Mather Peaks, mts., Wy., U.S. **B5** 143
Mathews, La., U.S. **E5** 111
Mathews, Va., U.S. **C6** 139
Mathews, co., Va., U.S. **C6** 139
Mathews, Lake, l., Ca., U.S. **n14** 98
Mathis, Tx., U.S. **E4** 136
Mathiston, Ms., U.S. **B4** 117
Mathura, India **D3** 40
Mati, Phil. **E9** 34
Matinicus Island, i., Me., U.S. **E3** 112
Mato, Cerro, mtn., Ven. **B6** 70
Matoaca, Va., U.S. **n18** 139
Mato Grosso, Braz. **E5** 68
Mato Grosso, state, Braz. **F8** 70
Mato Grosso, Planalto do, plat., Braz. **F8** 70
Mato Grosso do Sul, state, Braz. **B6** 72
Matosinhos, Port. **G2** 16
Maţraḩ, Oman **F7** 42
Matsqui, B.C., Can. **f13** 85
Matsue, Japan **D14** 28
Matsumoto, Japan **C3** 31
Matsuyama, Japan **E14** 28
Mattamiscontis Lake, l., Me., U.S. **C4** 112
Mattamuskeet, Lake, l., N.C., U.S. **B6** 126
Mattapoisett, Ma., U.S. **C6** 114
Mattaponi, stm., Va., U.S. **C5** 139
Mattawa, On., Can. **A6** 89
Mattawamkeag, Me., U.S. **C4** 112
Mattawamkeag, stm., Me., U.S. **C4** 112
Mattawamkeag Lake, l., Me., U.S. **C4** 112
Matterhorn (Cervino), mtn., Eur. **A1** 18
Matterhorn, mtn., Nv., U.S. **B6** 121
Matteson, Il., U.S. **k9** 106
Matthews, Mo., U.S. **E8** 118
Matthews, N.C., U.S. **B2** 126
Matthew Town, Bah. **A5** 80
Mattituck, N.Y., U.S. **n16** 125
Mattoon, Il., U.S. **D5** 106
Mattoon, Lake, res., Il., U.S. **D5** 106
Mattydale, N.Y., U.S. **B4** 125
Matunuck, R.I., U.S. **G3** 132
Maturín, Ven. **B7** 70
Matveev Kurgan, Russia **F15** 20
Maúa, Moz. **A6** 56
Maubeuge, Fr. **B8** 16
Maud, Ok., U.S. **B5** 129
Maués, Braz. **D8** 70
Mauganj, India **E4** 40
Maugansville, Md., U.S. **A2** 113
Maug Islands, is., N. Mar. Is. **C12** 32
Maui, i., Hi., U.S. **C6** 104
Maui, co., Hi., U.S. **B5** 104
Mauldin, S.C., U.S. **B3** 133
Maumee, Oh., U.S. **A2** 128
Maumee, stm., U.S. **A2** 128
Maumee Bay, b., U.S. **G7** 115
Maumelle, Lake, res., Ar., U.S. **C3** 97
Maumere, Indon. **E6** 36
Maun, Bots. **B3** 56
Mauna Kea, vol., Hi., U.S. **D6** 104
Maunaloa, Hi., U.S. **B4** 104
Mauna Loa, vol., Hi., U.S. **D6** 104
Maunalua Bay, b., Hi., U.S. **g10** 104
Maunawili, Hi., U.S. **g10** 104
Maupihaa, atoll, Fr. Poly. **F14** 58
Maurepas, Lake, l., La., U.S. **D5** 111
Maurice, Ia., U.S. **B1** 108
Maurice, stm., N.J., U.S. **E2** 123
Mauritania, ctry., Afr. **C2** 50
Mauritius, ctry., Afr. **f10** 57a
Mauritius, i., Mrts. **G11** 52
Maury, co., Tn., U.S. **B4** 135
Maury City, Tn., U.S. **B2** 135
Maury Island, i., Wa., U.S. **f11** 140
Mauston, Wi., U.S. **E3** 142
Maverick, co., Tx., U.S. **E2** 136
Mavinga, Ang. **B3** 56
Mawlaik, Mya. **B2** 34
Mawlamyine, Mya. **C3** 34
Maxinkuckee, Lake, l., In., U.S. **B5** 107
Maxixe, Moz. **C6** 56
Max Meadows, Va., U.S. **D2** 139
Maxton, N.C., U.S. **C3** 126
Maxville, On., Can. **B10** 89
Maxwell, Ia., U.S. **C4** 108
Maxwell Acres, W.V., U.S. **g8** 141
Maxwell Air Force Base, mil., Al., U.S. **C3** 94
Mayaguana, i., Bah. **D10** 76
Mayaguana Passage, strt., Bah. **A5** 80
Mayagüez, P.R. **B6** 80
Mayang, China **D2** 30
Mayenne, Fr. **C6** 16
Mayer, Az., U.S. **C3** 96
Mayerthorpe, Ab., Can. **C3** 84
Mayes, co., Ok., U.S. **A6** 129
Mayesville, S.C., U.S. **D7** 133
Mayfield, Ky., U.S. **f9** 110
Mayfield, Pa., U.S. **C10** 131
Mayfield Heights, Oh., U.S. **A4** 128
Mayfield Lake, res., Wa., U.S. **C3** 140
Mayflower, Ar., U.S. **C3** 97
Mayking, Ky., U.S. **C7** 110
Maymyo, Mya. **B3** 34
Maynard, Ma., U.S. **B5** 114
Maynardville, Tn., U.S. **C10** 135
Mayne, B.C., Can. **g12** 85
Mayo, stm., Mex. **B3** 78
Mayo, Md., U.S. **C4** 113
Mayo, S.C., U.S. **A4** 133
Mayodan, N.C., U.S. **A3** 126
Mayo Ndaga, Nig. **E7** 50
Mayon Volcano, vol., Phil. **D8** 34
Mayotte, dep., Afr. **A8** 56
May Park, Or., U.S. **B8** 130
Mayport Naval Station, mil., Fl., U.S. **B5** 102
Maysville, Ga., U.S. **B3** 103
Maysville, Ky., U.S. **B6** 110
Maysville, Mo., U.S. **B3** 118
Maysville, N.C., U.S. **C5** 126
Maysville, Ok., U.S. **C4** 129
Mayumba, Gabon **D2** 54
Māyūram, India **G3** 40
Mayville, Mi., U.S. **E7** 115
Mayville, N.D., U.S. **B8** 127
Mayville, N.Y., U.S. **C1** 125
Mayville, Wi., U.S. **E5** 142
Maywood, Il., U.S. **k9** 106
Maywood, N.J., U.S. **h8** 123
Mazabuka, Zam. **B4** 56
Mazamet, Fr. **F8** 16
Mazara del Vallo, Italy **F4** 18
Mazār-e Sharīf, Afg. **C9** 42
Mazaruni, stm., Guy. **D7** 80
Mazatlán, Mex. **C3** 78
Mazatzal Mountains, mts., Az., U.S. **C4** 96
Mazatzal Peak, mtn., Az., U.S. **C4** 96
Mažeikiai, Lith. **H10** 10
Mazeppa, Mn., U.S. **F6** 116
Mazomanie, Wi., U.S. **E4** 142
Mazon, Il., U.S. **B5** 106
Mazury, reg., Pol. **C6** 20
Mazyr, Bela. **C10** 20
Mbabane, Swaz. **D5** 56
M'bahiakro, C. Iv. **E4** 50
Mbaïki, C.A.R. **C3** 54
Mbaké, Sen. **D1** 50
Mbala, Zam. **E6** 54
Mbale, Ug. **C6** 54
Mbalmayo, Cam. **C2** 54
Mbamba Bay, Tan. **F6** 54
Mbandaka, D.R.C. **C3** 54
Mbanga, Cam. **C1** 54
M'banza Congo, Ang. **E2** 54
Mbanza-Ngungu (Thysville), D.R.C. **E2** 54
Mbarara, Ug. **D6** 54
Mbeya, Tan. **E6** 54
Mbigou, Gabon **D2** 54
Mbinda, Congo **D2** 54
Mbini, Eq. Gui. **C1** 54
Mboi, D.R.C. **E4** 54
Mboki, C.A.R. **B5** 54
Mbouda, Cam. **B2** 54
Mbour, Sen. **D1** 50
Mbout, Maur. **C2** 50
Mbuji-Mayi, D.R.C. **E4** 54
McAdam, N.B., Can. **D2** 87
McAdoo, Pa., U.S. **E9** 131
McAfee Peak, mtn., Nv., U.S. **B6** 121
McAlester, Ok., U.S. **C6** 129
McAlester, Lake, res., Ok., U.S. **B6** 129
McAllen, Tx., U.S. **F3** 136
McAlmont, Ar., U.S. **h10** 97
McAlpine, Md., U.S. **B4** 113
McAlpine Lock and Dam, U.S. **H6** 107
McArthur, Oh., U.S. **C3** 128
McBee, S.C., U.S. **C7** 133
McCall, Id., U.S. **E2** 105
McCalla, Al., U.S. **g6** 94
McCamey, Tx., U.S. **D1** 136
McCammon, Id., U.S. **G6** 105
McCandless, Pa., U.S. **h13** 131
McCartney Mountain, mtn., Mt., U.S. **E4** 119
McCaysville, Ga., U.S. **B2** 103
McChord Air Force Base, mil., Wa., U.S. **f11** 140
McClain, co., Ok., U.S. **C4** 129
McCleary, Wa., U.S. **B2** 140
McClintock, Mount, mtn., Ant. **D20** 67
McCloud, Ca., U.S. **B2** 98
McClure, Pa., U.S. **E7** 131
McColl, S.C., U.S. **B8** 133
McComas, W.V., U.S. **D3** 141
McComb, Ms., U.S. **D3** 117
McComb, Oh., U.S. **A2** 128
McCone, co., Mt., U.S. **C11** 119
McConnell Air Force Base, mil., Ks., U.S. **g12** 109
McConnellsburg, Pa., U.S. **G6** 131
McConnelsville, Oh., U.S. **C4** 128
McCook, Ne., U.S. **D5** 120
McCook, co., S.D., U.S. **D8** 134
McCordsville, In., U.S. **E6** 107
McCormick, S.C., U.S. **D3** 133
McCormick, co., S.C., U.S. **D3** 133
McCracken, co., Ky., U.S. **e9** 110
McCreary, Mb., Can. **D2** 86
McCreary, co., Ky., U.S. **D5** 110
McCrory, Ar., U.S. **B4** 97
McCulloch, co., Tx., U.S. **D3** 136
McCullough Mountain, mtn., Nv., U.S. **H6** 121
McCurtain, co., Ok., U.S. **C7** 129
McDermitt, Nv., U.S. **B4** 121
McDonald, co., Mo., U.S. **E3** 118
McDonough, Ga., U.S. **C2** 103
McDonough, co., Il., U.S. **C3** 106
McDougall, Mount, mtn., Wy., U.S. **D2** 143
McDowell, Ky., U.S. **C7** 110
McDowell, co., N.C., U.S. **f10** 126
McDowell, co., W.V., U.S. **D3** 141
McDowell Mountains, mts., Az., U.S. **k9** 96
McDowell Peak, mtn., Az., U.S. **k9** 96
McDuffie, co., Ga., U.S. **C4** 103
McElroy Creek, stm., W.V., U.S. **k9** 141
Mcensk, Russia **C14** 20
McEwen, Tn., U.S. **A4** 135
McFarland, Ca., U.S. **E4** 98
McFarland, Wi., U.S. **E4** 142
McGehee, Ar., U.S. **D4** 97
McGill, Nv., U.S. **D7** 121
McGrath, Ak., U.S. **C8** 95
McGregor, stm., B.C., Can. **B7** 85
McGregor, Ia., U.S. **A6** 108
McGregor, Tx., U.S. **D4** 136
McGregor Lake, l., Ab., Can. **D4** 84
McGuire, Mount, mtn., Id., U.S. **D4** 105
McGuire Air Force Base, mil., N.J., U.S. **C3** 123
McHenry, Il., U.S. **A5** 106
McHenry, co., Il., U.S. **A5** 106
McHenry, Md., U.S. **k12** 113
McHenry, co., N.D., U.S. **A5** 127
Mchinji, Mwi. **A5** 56
McIntosh, co., Ga., U.S. **E5** 103
McIntosh, Mn., U.S. **C3** 116
McIntosh, co., N.D., U.S. **C6** 127
McIntosh, co., Ok., U.S. **B6** 129
McKean, co., Pa., U.S. **C4** 131
McKee, Ky., U.S. **C6** 110
McKeesport, Pa., U.S. **F2** 131
McKees Rocks, Pa., U.S. **F1** 131
McKenzie, co., N.D., U.S. **B2** 127
McKenzie, stm., Or., U.S. **C4** 130
McKenzie, Tn., U.S. **A3** 135
McKinley, co., N.M., U.S. **B1** 124
McKinley, Mount, mtn., Ak., U.S. **C9** 95
McKinleyville, Ca., U.S. **B1** 98
McKinney, Tx., U.S. **C4** 136
McKinney, Lake, l., Ks., U.S. **E2** 109
McKittrick Summit, mtn., Ca., U.S. **E4** 98
McLaughlin, S.D., U.S. **B5** 134
McLean, co., Il., U.S. **C4** 106
McLean, Il., U.S. **C4** 106
McLean, co., Ky., U.S. **C2** 110
McLean, co., N.D., U.S. **B4** 127
McLean, Va., U.S. **g12** 139
McLeansboro, Il., U.S. **E5** 106
McLennan, Ab., Can. **B2** 84
McLennan, co., Tx., U.S. **D4** 136
McLeod, co., Mn., U.S. **F4** 116
M'Clintock Channel, strt., N.T., Can. **D19** 82
McLoud, Ok., U.S. **B4** 129
McLoughlin, Mount, mtn., Or., U.S. **D4** 130
McLouth, Ks., U.S. **C8** 109
McMechen, W.V., U.S. **B4** 141
McMillan, Lake, res., N.M., U.S. **E5** 124
McMinn, co., Tn., U.S. **D9** 135
McMinnville, Or., U.S. **B3** 130
McMinnville, Tn., U.S. **D8** 135
McMullen, co., Tx., U.S. **E3** 136
McMurdo Sound, strt., Ant. **D21** 67
McNairy, co., Tn., U.S. **B3** 135
McNary, Az., U.S. **C6** 96
McNary Dam, U.S. **B7** 130
McNeil, Ar., U.S. **D2** 97
McNeil, Mount, mtn., B.C., Can. **B2** 85
McNeil Island, i., Wa., U.S. **f10** 140
McNeill, Ms., U.S. **E4** 117
McPherson, Ks., U.S. **D6** 109
McPherson, co., Ks., U.S. **D6** 109
McPherson, co., Ne., U.S. **C4** 120
McPherson, co., S.D., U.S. **B6** 134
McQueeney, Tx., U.S. **h7** 136
McRae, Ar., U.S. **B4** 97
McRae, Ga., U.S. **D4** 103
McRoberts, Ky., U.S. **C7** 110
McSherrystown, Pa., U.S. **G7** 131
Mdandu, Tan. **E6** 54
Mead, Wa., U.S. **B8** 140
Mead, Lake, res., U.S. **A1** 96
Meade, stm., Ak., U.S. **B8** 95
Meade, Ks., U.S. **E3** 109
Meade, co., Ks., U.S. **E3** 109
Meade, co., Ky., U.S. **C3** 110
Meade, co., S.D., U.S. **C3** 134
Meaden Peak, mtn., Co., U.S. **A3** 99
Meade Peak, mtn., Id., U.S. **G7** 105
Meadow, stm., W.V., U.S. **C4** 141
Meadow Creek, stm., W.V., U.S. **n14** 141
Meadow Lands, Pa., U.S. **F1** 131
Meadow Valley Wash, val., Nv., U.S. **F7** 121
Meadowview, Va., U.S. **f10** 139
Meadville, Pa., U.S. **C1** 131
Meaford, On., Can. **C4** 89
Meagher, co., Mt., U.S. **D6** 119
Meander Creek Reservoir, res., Oh., U.S. **A5** 128
Meaux, Fr. **C8** 16
Mebane, N.C., U.S. **A3** 126
Mecca see Makkah, Sau. Ar. **F3** 38
Mecca, Ca., U.S. **F5** 98
Mechanic Falls, Me., U.S. **D2** 112
Mechanicsburg, Oh., U.S. **B2** 128
Mechanicsburg, Pa., U.S. **F7** 131
Mechanicsville, Ia., U.S. **C6** 108
Mechanicsville, Md., U.S. **D4** 113
Mechanicsville, Va., U.S. **C5** 139
Mechanicville, N.Y., U.S. **C7** 125
Mechant, Lake, l., La., U.S. **E4** 111
Mecklenburg, hist. reg., Ger. **D12** 12
Mecklenburg, co., N.C., U.S. **B2** 126
Mecklenburg, co., Va., U.S. **D4** 139
Mecklenburg Bay see Mecklenburger Bucht, b., Ger. **C12** 12
Mecklenburger Bucht, b., Ger. **C12** 12
Mecosta, co., Mi., U.S. **E5** 115
Mecúfi, Moz. **A7** 56
Medan, Indon. **C1** 36
Medanosa, Punta, c., Arg. **G3** 69
Medaryville, In., U.S. **B4** 107
Meddybumps Lake, l., Me., U.S. **C5** 112
Medellín, Col. **B4** 70
Médenine, Tun. **D7** 48
Mederdra, Maur. **C1** 50
Medfield, Ma., U.S. **h10** 114
Medford, Ma., U.S. **B5** 114
Medford, Mn., U.S. **F5** 116
Medford, Ok., U.S. **A4** 129
Medford, Or., U.S. **E4** 130
Medford, Wi., U.S. **C3** 142
Medford Lakes, N.J., U.S. **D3** 123
Medgidia, Rom. **G10** 20
Media, Pa., U.S. **G11** 131
Mediapolis, Ia., U.S. **C6** 108
Mediaş, Rom. **F8** 20
Medical Lake, Wa., U.S. **B8** 140
Medicine Bow, Wy., U.S. **E6** 143
Medicine Bow, stm., Wy., U.S. **E6** 143
Medicine Bow Mountains, mts., U.S. **E6** 143
Medicine Bow Peak, mtn., Wy., U.S. **E6** 143
Medicine Hat, Ab., Can. **D5** 84
Medicine Lodge, Ks., U.S. **E5** 109
Medicine Lodge, stm., U.S. **E4** 109
Medina see Al-Madīnah, Sau. Ar. **F3** 38
Medina, N.Y., U.S. **B2** 125
Medina, Oh., U.S. **A4** 128
Medina, co., Oh., U.S. **A4** 128
Medina, Tn., U.S. **B3** 135
Medina, stm., Tx., U.S. **k7** 136
Medina, co., Tx., U.S. **E3** 136
Medina, Wa., U.S. **e11** 140
Medina del Campo, Spain **G4** 16
Medinīpur, India **E5** 40
Mediterranean Sea **D5** 14
Mediterraneo, Mar see Mediterranean Sea **D5** 14
Mednogorsk, Russia **D10** 22
Mednyj, ostrov, i., Russia **D18** 26
Medora, In., U.S. **G5** 107
Médouneu, Gabon **C2** 54
Medvežegorsk, Russia **B5** 22
Medvežji ostrova, is., Russia **B18** 26
Medway, stm., N.S., Can. **E5** 87
Medway, Ma., U.S. **B5** 114
Medway, Me., U.S. **C4** 112
Meekatharra, Austl. **F2** 60
Meeker, Co., U.S. **A3** 99
Meeker, co., Mn., U.S. **E4** 116
Meeker, Ok., U.S. **B5** 129
Meelpaeg Lake, res., N.L., Can. **D3** 88
Meerut, India **D3** 40
Meeteetse, Wy., U.S. **B4** 143
Mēga, Eth. **C7** 54
Mégantic, Lac, l., Qc., Can. **D7** 90
Mégantic, Mont, mtn., Qc., Can. **D6** 90
Meggett, S.C., U.S. **F7** 133
Meghālaya, state, India **D6** 40
Meghri, Arm. **C12** 44
Meharry, Mount, mtn., Austl. **H20** 4
Meherrin, stm., U.S. **A4** 126
Mehlville, Mo., U.S. **f13** 118
Mehtar Lām, Afg. **D10** 42
Meia Meia, Tan. **E7** 54
Meiganga, Cam. **B2** 54
Meigs, Ga., U.S. **E2** 103
Meigs, co., Oh., U.S. **C3** 128
Meigs, co., Tn., U.S. **D9** 135
Meiktila, Mya. **B3** 34
Meiningen, Ger. **E12** 12
Meishan, China **C1** 30
Meitan, China **D2** 30
Meizhou, China **G11** 28

Name — Map Ref. — Page

Mejillones, Chile B2 69
Mékambo, Gabon C2 54
Mek'elē, Eth. H12 48
Mékhé, Sen. C1 50
Meknès, Mor. D3 48
Mekong, stm., Asia D5 34
Mékôngk see Mekong, stm., Asia D5 34
Melaka, Malay. C2 36
Melanesia, is., Oc. E10 58
Melbourne, Austl. H4 62
Melbourne, Ar., U.S. A4 97
Melbourne, Fl., U.S. D6 102
Melbourne, Ia., U.S. C4 108
Melbourne, Ky., U.S. h14 110
Melbourne Beach, Fl., U.S. D6 102
Melcher, Ia., U.S. C4 108
Melchor Múzquiz, Mex. B4 78
Melenki, Russia C7 22
Meleuz, Russia D10 22
Mélèzes, Rivière aux, stm., Qc., Can. g12 90
Melfi, Chad D8 50
Melilla, Sp. N. Afr. J5 16
Melipilla, Chile E3 72
Melita, Mb., Can. E1 86
Melitopol', Ukr. F13 20
Mellen, Wi., U.S. B3 142
Mellette, co., S.D., U.S. D5 134
Melo, Ur. E7 72
Melocheville, Qc., Can. q19 90
Melos see Mílos, i., Grc. F10 18
Melrhir, Chott, l., Alg. D6 48
Melrose, Austl. F3 60
Melrose, Fl., U.S. C4 102
Melrose, Ma., U.S. B5 114
Melrose, Mn., U.S. E4 116
Melrose, N.M., U.S. C6 124
Melton Hill Lake, res., Tn., U.S. D9 135
Meluco, Moz. A6 56
Melun, Fr. C8 16
Melvern Lake, res., Ks., U.S. D8 109
Melville, La., U.S. D4 111
Melville, Cape, c., Austl. C3 62
Melville, Lake, l., N.L., Can. B2 88
Melville Island, i., Austl. C5 60
Melville Sound, strt., N.T., Can. E18 82
Melvin, Ky., U.S. C7 110
Memboro, Indon. E5 36
Memel see Klaipėda, Lith. I9 10
Memmingen, Ger. G11 12
Mempawah, Indon. C3 36
Memphis, Fl., U.S. p10 102
Memphis, Mi., U.S. F8 115
Memphis, Mo., U.S. A5 118
Memphis, Tn., U.S. B1 135
Memphis, Tx., U.S. B2 136
Memphis Naval Air Station, mil., Tn., U.S. B2 135
Mena, Ukr. D12 20
Mena, Ar., U.S. C1 97
Menahga, Mn., U.S. D3 116
Ménaka, Mali C5 50
Menan, Id., U.S. F7 105
Menands, N.Y., U.S. C7 125
Menard, co., Il., U.S. C4 106
Menard, Tx., U.S. D3 136
Menard, co., Tx., U.S. D3 136
Menasha, Wi., U.S. D5 142
Mende, Fr. E8 16
Mendeleyev Ridge E4 144
Mendenhall, Ms., U.S. D4 117
Mendham, N.J., U.S. B3 123
Mendī, Eth. B7 54
Mendi, Pap. N. Gui. H11 32
Mendocino, co., Ca., U.S. C2 98
Mendocino Fracture Zone E23 64
Mendon, Il., U.S. C2 106
Mendon, Mi., U.S. F5 115
Mendon, Ut., U.S. B4 137
Mendota, Ca., U.S. D3 98
Mendota, Il., U.S. B4 106
Mendota, Lake, l., Wi., U.S. E4 142
Mendoza, Arg. E4 72
Mene Grande, Ven. D5 80
Menemen, Tur. C2 44
Mengcheng, China C4 30
Menggala, Indon. D3 36
Menghai, China B4 34
Mengjiawan, China B2 30
Mengzi, China G8 28
Menifee, co., Ky., U.S. C6 110
Menindee, Austl. G3 62
Menlo Park, Ca., U.S. k8 98
Menno, S.D., U.S. D8 134
Menominee, Mi., U.S. C3 115
Menominee, co., Mi., U.S. C3 115
Menominee, co., Wi., U.S. C5 142
Menominee, stm., U.S. C6 142
Menominee Indian Reservation, Wi., U.S. C5 142
Menomonee, stm., Wi., U.S. m11 142
Menomonee Falls, Wi., U.S. E5 142
Menomonie, Wi., U.S. D2 142
Menongue, Ang. A2 56
Menor, Mar, b., Spain I6 16
Menorca (Minorca), i., Spain G9 16
Mentawai, Kepulauan, is., Indon. D1 36
Mentawai, Selat, strt., Indon. D1 36
Mentone, In., U.S. B5 107
Mentor, Oh., U.S. A4 128
Mentor-on-the-Lake, Oh., U.S. A4 128
Menzel Bourguiba, Tun. F2 18
Menzies, Austl. F3 60
Meoqui, Mex. B3 78
Meppen, Ger. D10 12
Mequinenza, Embalse de, res., Spain G6 16
Mequon, Wi., U.S. E6 142
Merambéllou, Kólpos, b., Grc. G10 18
Meramec, stm., Mo., U.S. C7 118
Merano, Italy A3 18
Merasheen Island, i., N.L., Can. E4 88
Merauke, Indon. H11 32
Meraux, La., U.S. k12 111
Mercāra, India G3 40
Merced, Ca., U.S. D3 98
Merced, co., Ca., U.S. D3 98
Merced, stm., Ca., U.S. D3 98
Mercedes, Arg. D6 72
Mercedes, Ur. E6 72
Mercedes, Tx., U.S. F4 136
Mercer, co., Il., U.S. B3 106
Mercer, co., Ky., U.S. C5 110
Mercer, co., Mo., U.S. A4 118
Mercer, co., N.D., U.S. B4 127
Mercer, co., N.J., U.S. C3 123
Mercer, co., Oh., U.S. B1 128
Mercer, Pa., U.S. D1 131
Mercer, co., Pa., U.S. D1 131
Mercer, Wi., U.S. B3 142
Mercer, co., W.V., U.S. D3 141
Mercer Island, Wa., U.S. B3 140
Mercer Island, i., Wa., U.S. e11 140
Mercersburg, Pa., U.S. G6 131
Mercerville, N.J., U.S. C3 123
Mercier, Qc., Can. D4 90
Meredith, N.H., U.S. C3 122
Meredith, Lake, l., Co., U.S. C7 99
Meredith, Lake, res., Tx., U.S. B2 136
Meredosia, Il., U.S. D3 106
Meredosia Lake, l., Il., U.S. D3 106
Mereeg, Som. J14 48
Merefa, Ukr. E14 20
Merenkurkku (Norra Kvarken), strt., Eur. E9 10
Mergui, Mya. D3 34
Mergui Archipelago, is., Mya. D3 34
Meriç (Évros) (Marica), stm., Eur. D11 18
Mérida, Mex. C7 78
Mérida, Spain H3 16
Mérida, Ven. B5 70
Mérida, Cordillera de, mts., Ven. B5 70
Meriden, Ct., U.S. C4 100
Meriden, Ks., U.S. C8 109
Meridian, Id., U.S. F2 105
Meridian, Ms., U.S. C5 117
Meridian, Pa., U.S. E2 131
Meridian, Tx., U.S. D4 136
Meridian Hills, In., U.S. k10 107
Meridian Naval Air Station, mil., Ms., U.S. C5 117
Meridianville, Al., U.S. A3 94
Merikarvia, Fin. F9 10
Merín, Laguna see Mirim, Lagoa, b., S.A. E7 72
Meriwether, co., Ga., U.S. C2 103
Merkel, Tx., U.S. C2 136
Merlin, On., Can. E2 89
Mermentau, stm., La., U.S. E3 111
Mermentau, La., U.S. D3 111
Meron, Har, mtn., Isr. F6 44
Meron, Mount see Meron, Har, mtn., Isr. F6 44
Merredin, Austl. G2 60
Merriam, Ks., U.S. k16 109
Merrick, co., Ne., U.S. C7 120
Merrickville, On., Can. C9 89
Merrill, Ia., U.S. B1 108
Merrill, Mi., U.S. E6 115
Merrill, Or., U.S. E5 130
Merrill, Wi., U.S. C4 142
Merrillville, In., U.S. B3 107
Merrimac, Ma., U.S. A5 114
Merrimack, N.H., U.S. E4 122
Merrimack, co., N.H., U.S. D3 122
Merrimack, stm., U.S. A5 114
Merritt, B.C., Can. D7 85
Merritt Island, Fl., U.S. D6 102
Merritt Reservoir, res., Ne., U.S. B5 120
Merrymeeting Lake, l., N.H., U.S. D4 122
Merryville, La., U.S. D2 111
Mersa Matruh, Egypt D10 48
Mersing, Malay. C2 36
Merthyr Tydfil, Wales, U.K. E5 12
Merton, Wi., U.S. m11 142
Meru, Kenya C7 54
Merwin, Lake, res., Wa., U.S. C3 140
Merzifon, Tur. B6 44
Mesa, Az., U.S. D4 96
Mesa, co., Co., U.S. C2 99
Mesabi Range, Mn., U.S. C6 116
Mesa Mountain, mtn., Co., U.S. D4 99
Mesa Verde National Park, Co., U.S. D2 99
Mescalero, N.M., U.S. D4 124
Mescalero Indian Reservation, N.M., U.S. D4 124
Meschede, Ger. E11 12
Meshgīn Shahr, Iran C12 44
Mesilla, N.M., U.S. E3 124
Mesolóngion, Grc. E8 18
Mesopotamia, hist. reg., Asia D4 42
Mesquite, N.M., U.S. E3 124
Mesquite, Nv., U.S. G7 121
Mesquite, Tx., U.S. n10 136
Messalonskee Lake, l., Me., U.S. D3 112
Messina, Italy E5 18
Messina, S. Afr. C5 56
Messina, Stretto di, strt., Italy E5 18
Messiniakós Kólpos, b., Grc. F9 18
Mestghanem, Alg. C4 48
Mestre, Italy B4 18
Meta, stm., S.A. B5 70
Métabetchouan, Qc., Can. A6 90
Métabetchouane, stm., Qc., Can. A5 90
Metairie, La., U.S. k11 111
Metamora, Il., U.S. C4 106
Metán, Arg. D5 72
Metapán, El Sal. C2 80
Metapontum, hist., Italy D6 18
Metcalfe, On., Can. B9 89
Metcalfe, co., Ky., U.S. C4 110
Metcalfe, Ms., U.S. B2 117
Metedeconk, North Branch, stm., N.J., U.S. C4 123
Metedeconk, South Branch, stm., N.J., U.S. C3 123
Meteghan, N.S., Can. E3 87
Meteghan River, N.S., Can. E3 87
Metéora, rel., Grc. E8 18
Meteor Crater, crat., Az., U.S. C4 96
Methow, stm., Wa., U.S. A5 140
Methuen, Ma., U.S. A5 114
Metlakatla, Ak., U.S. D13 95
Metonga, Lake, l., Wi., U.S. C5 142
Metro, Indon. E3 36
Metropolis, Il., U.S. F5 106
Mettawee, stm., U.S. E2 138
Metter, Ga., U.S. D4 103
Metuchen, N.J., U.S. B4 123
Metz, Fr. C10 16
Metzger, Or., U.S. h12 130
Meulaboh, Indon. C1 36
Meuse (Maas), stm., Eur. C9 16
Mexia, Tx., U.S. D4 136
Mexia, Lake, res., Tx., U.S. D4 136
Mexiana, Ilha, i., Braz. A2 74
Mexicali, Mex. A1 78
México, state, Mex. D4 78
Mexico, ctry., N.A. C4 78
Mexico, In., U.S. C5 107
Mexico, Me., U.S. D2 112
Mexico, Mo., U.S. B6 118
Mexico, Gulf of, b., N.A. F10 92
Mexico Basin F4 66
Mexico City see Ciudad de México, Mex. D5 78
Meyersdale, Pa., U.S. G3 131
Meyīsti, i., Grc. F12 18
Meymaneh, Afg. C8 42
Mezcala, Mex. D5 78
Meždurečenskij, Russia C12 22
Mezen', Russia C6 26
Mezen', stm., Russia C6 26
Mezenskaja guba, b., Russia A7 22
Mezőtúr, Hung. F6 20
Mfangano Island, i., Kenya D6 54
Mgeta, Tan. E7 54
M'Goun, Irhil, mtn., Mor. E2 14
Mhow, India E3 40
Miahuatlán de Porfirio Díaz, Mex. D5 78
Miajadas, Spain H4 16
Miaméré, C.A.R. B3 54
Miami, Az., U.S. D5 96
Miami, Fl., U.S. G6 102
Miami, co., In., U.S. C5 107
Miami, co., Ks., U.S. D9 109
Miami, co., Oh., U.S. B1 128
Miami, Ok., U.S. A7 129
Miami Beach, Fl., U.S. G6 102
Miami Canal, Fl., U.S. F6 102
Miami International Airport, Fl., U.S. G6 102
Miamisburg, Oh., U.S. C1 128
Miami Shores, Fl., U.S. G6 102
Miami Springs, Fl., U.S. G6 102
Mianchi, China C3 30
Mīāndoāb, Iran D12 44
Miandrivazo, Madag. B8 56
Mīāneh, Iran C5 42
Mianning, China A4 34
Mianus Reservoir, res., U.S. E1 100
Miānwāli, Pak. D10 42
Mianyang, China E8 28
Mianzhu, China C1 30
Miass, Russia D8 26
Mica Mountain, mtn., Az., U.S. E5 96
Micco, Fl., U.S. E6 102
Miccosukee, Lake, res., Fl., U.S. B2 102
Michalovce, Slvk. E6 20
Michelson, Mount, mtn., Ak., U.S. B11 95
Michie, Tn., U.S. B3 135
Michigamme, Lake, l., Mi., U.S. B2 115
Michigamme Reservoir, res., Mi., U.S. B2 115
Michigan, stm., Co., U.S. A4 99
Michigan, state, U.S. E6 115
Michigan, Lake, l., U.S. C10 92
Michigan Center, Mi., U.S. F6 115
Michigan City, In., U.S. A4 107
Michigan Island, i., Wi., U.S. B3 142
Michoacán, state, Mex. D4 78
Micronesia, is., Oc. C9 58
Micronesia, Federated States of, ctry., Oc. D8 58
Mičurinsk, Russia C16 20
Mid-Atlantic Ridge F9 66
Middelburg, S. Afr. D4 56
Middelburg, S. Afr. E3 56
Middelfart, Den. I3 10
Middle, stm., Ia., U.S. C3 108
Middle, stm., Mn., U.S. B2 116
Middle America Trench G28 64
Middle Andaman, i., India G6 40
Middleboro (Middleborough Center), Ma., U.S. C6 114
Middlebourne, W.V., U.S. B4 141
Middleburg, Fl., U.S. B5 102
Middleburg, Pa., U.S. E7 131
Middleburg Heights, Oh., U.S. h9 128
Middlebury, Ct., U.S. C3 100
Middlebury, In., U.S. A6 107
Middlebury, Vt., U.S. C2 138
Middle Caicos, i., T./C. Is. A5 80
Middlefield, Ct., U.S. C5 100
Middlefield, Oh., U.S. A4 128
Middle Island Creek, stm., W.V., U.S. B3 141
Middle Nodaway, stm., Ia., U.S. C3 108
Middle Park, val., Co., U.S. A4 99
Middle Patuxent, stm., Md., U.S. B4 113
Middleport, N.Y., U.S. B2 125
Middleport, Oh., U.S. C3 128
Middle Raccoon, stm., Ia., U.S. C3 108
Middle River, Md., U.S. B5 113
Middlesboro, Ky., U.S. D6 110
Middlesbrough, Eng., U.K. C6 12
Middlesex, co., Ct., U.S. D5 100
Middlesex, co., Ma., U.S. A5 114
Middlesex, N.C., U.S. B4 126
Middlesex, N.J., U.S. B4 123
Middlesex, co., N.J., U.S. C4 123
Middlesex, co., Va., U.S. C6 139
Middlesex Fells Reservation, Ma., U.S. g11 114
Middleton, N.S., Can. E4 87
Middleton, Id., U.S. F2 105
Middleton, Ma., U.S. A5 114
Middleton, Wi., U.S. E4 142
Middletown, Ca., U.S. C2 98
Middletown, Ct., U.S. C5 100
Middletown, De., U.S. C3 101
Middletown, In., U.S. D6 107
Middletown, Ky., U.S. g11 110
Middletown, Md., U.S. B2 113
Middletown, N.J., U.S. C4 123
Middletown, N.Y., U.S. D6 125
Middletown, Oh., U.S. C1 128
Middletown, Pa., U.S. F8 131
Middletown, R.I., U.S. E5 132
Middletown, Va., U.S. A4 139
Middleville, Mi., U.S. F5 115
Midfield, Al., U.S. g7 94
Mid-Indian Basin I10 64
Mid-Indian Ridge I9 64
Midland, On., Can. C5 89
Midland, Mi., U.S. E6 115
Midland, co., Mi., U.S. E6 115
Midland, N.C., U.S. B2 126
Midland, Pa., U.S. E1 131
Midland, Tx., U.S. D1 136
Midland, co., Tx., U.S. D1 136
Midland City, Al., U.S. D4 94
Midland Park, Ks., U.S. g12 109
Midland Park, N.J., U.S. B4 123
Midland Park, S.C., U.S. k11 133
Midlothian, Il., U.S. k9 106
Midlothian, Tx., U.S. C4 136
Midongy Atsimo, Madag. C8 56
Mid-Pacific Mountains F18 64
Midvale, Ut., U.S. C4 137
Midville, Ga., U.S. D4 103
Midway, B.C., Can. E8 85
Midway, De., U.S. F5 101
Midway, Ky., U.S. B5 110
Midway, Pa., U.S. G7 131
Midway, Ut., U.S. C4 137
Midway Islands, dep., Oc. B12 58
Midwest, Wy., U.S. C6 143
Midwest City, Ok., U.S. B4 129
Midyat, Tur. D9 44
Międzyrzecz, Pol. C3 20
Miekojärvi, l., Fin. C11 10
Mielec, Pol. D6 20
Mieres, Spain F4 16
Mifflin, co., Pa., U.S. E6 131
Mifflinburg, Pa., U.S. E7 131
Mifflinville, Pa., U.S. D9 131
Miguel Alemán, Presa, res., Mex. D5 78
Miguel Auza, Mex. C4 78
Mihajlov, Russia B15 20
Mihajlovka, Russia D6 26
Mikasa, Japan C16 28
Mikínai, hist., Grc. F9 18
Mikindani, Tan. F8 54
Mikkeli, Fin. F12 10
Míkonos, i., Grc. F10 18
Mikumi, Tan. E7 54
Mikun', Russia B9 22
Milaca, Mn., U.S. E5 116
Milagro, Ec. D4 70
Milam, co., Tx., U.S. D4 136
Milan see Milano, Italy B2 18
Milan, Ga., U.S. D3 103
Milan, Il., U.S. B3 106
Milan, In., U.S. F7 107
Milan, Mi., U.S. F7 115
Milan, Mo., U.S. A4 118
Milan, N.M., U.S. B2 124
Milan, Oh., U.S. A3 128
Milan, Tn., U.S. B3 135
Milange, Moz. B6 56
Milano (Milan), Italy B2 18
Milâs, Tur. D2 44
Milazzo, Italy E5 18
Milbank, S.D., U.S. B9 134
Mildmay, On., Can. C3 89
Mildura, Austl. G3 62
Mile, China G8 28
Milesburg, Pa., U.S. E6 131
Miles City, Mt., U.S. D11 119
Milestone, Sk., Can. G3 91
Milet (Miletus), hist., Tur. D2 44
Miletus see Milet, hist., Tur. D2 44
Milford, Ct., U.S. E3 100
Milford, De., U.S. E4 101
Milford, Ia., U.S. A2 108
Milford, Il., U.S. C6 106
Milford, In., U.S. B6 107
Milford, Ma., U.S. B4 114
Milford, Me., U.S. D4 112
Milford, Mi., U.S. F7 115
Milford, Ne., U.S. D8 120
Milford, N.H., U.S. E3 122
Milford, Oh., U.S. C1 128
Milford, Pa., U.S. D12 131
Milford, Ut., U.S. E2 137
Milford Haven, Wales, U.K. E4 12
Milford Lake, res., Ks., U.S. C6 109
Milford Station, N.S., Can. D6 87
Milh, Bahr al-, res., Iraq F10 44
Mililani Town, Hi., U.S. g9 104
Milk, stm., N.A. B6 92
Mil'kovo, Russia D17 26
Milk River, Ab., Can. E4 84
Mill, stm., Ma., U.S. h9 114
Millard, co., Ut., U.S. D2 137
Millau, Fr. E8 16
Millbrae, Ca., U.S. h8 98
Millbrook, On., Can. C6 89
Millbrook, Al., U.S. C3 94
Mill Brook, stm., Vt., U.S. B5 138
Millburn, N.J., U.S. B4 123
Millbury, Ma., U.S. B4 114
Millbury, Oh., U.S. e7 128
Mill City, Or., U.S. C4 130
Mill Creek, stm., N.J., U.S. D4 123
Mill Creek, stm., Oh., U.S. B2 128
Mill Creek, stm., Tn., U.S. g10 135
Millcreek, Ut., U.S. C4 137
Mill Creek, stm., W.V., U.S. C3 141
Mill Creek, W.V., U.S. C5 141
Mill Creek, stm., W.V., U.S. m13 141
Millcreek Township, Pa., U.S. B1 131
Milledgeville, Ga., U.S. C3 103
Milledgeville, Il., U.S. B4 106
Mille Îles, Rivière des, stm., Qc., Can. p19 90
Mille Lacs, co., Mn., U.S. E5 116
Mille Lacs Indian Reservation, Mn., U.S. D5 116
Mille Lacs Lake, l., Mn., U.S. D5 116
Millen, Ga., U.S. D5 103
Miller, co., Ar., U.S. D2 97
Miller, co., Ga., U.S. E2 103
Miller, co., Mo., U.S. C5 118
Miller, S.D., U.S. C7 134
Miller, Mount, mtn., Ak., U.S. C11 95
Millerovo, Russia E7 22
Miller Peak, mtn., Az., U.S. F5 96
Miller Run, stm., Vt., U.S. B4 138
Millers, stm., Ma., U.S. A3 114
Millersburg, In., U.S. A6 107
Millersburg, Ky., U.S. B5 110
Millersburg, Oh., U.S. B4 128
Millersburg, Pa., U.S. E8 131
Millersport, Oh., U.S. C3 128
Millersville, Pa., U.S. F9 131
Millet, Ab., Can. C4 84
Mill Hall, Pa., U.S. D7 131
Millicent, Austl. H3 62
Milliken, Co., U.S. A6 99
Millington, Mi., U.S. E7 115
Millington, Tn., U.S. B2 135
Millinocket, Me., U.S. C4 112
Millinocket Lake, l., Me., U.S. B4 112
Millinocket Lake, l., Me., U.S. C4 112
Millis, Ma., U.S. B5 114
Millport, Al., U.S. B1 94
Millry, Al., U.S. D1 94
Mills, co., Ia., U.S. C2 108

Name | Map Ref. | Page

Mills, co., Tx., U.S. D3 136
Mills, Wy., U.S. D6 143
Millsboro, De., U.S. F4 101
Millsboro, Pa., U.S. G1 131
Millstadt, Il., U.S. E3 106
Millstone, stm., N.J., U.S. C4 123
Milltown, In., U.S. H5 107
Milltown, N.J., U.S. C4 123
Milltown, Wi., U.S. C1 142
Milltown [-Head of Bay d'Espoir], N.L., Can. E4 88
Millvale, Pa., U.S. k14 131
Mill Valley, Ca., U.S. D2 98
Millville, Ma., U.S. B4 114
Millville, N.J., U.S. E2 123
Millville, Pa., U.S. D9 131
Millville, Ut., U.S. B4 137
Millville Lake, N.H., U.S. E4 122
Millwood, Wa., U.S. g14 140
Millwood Lake, res., Ar., U.S. D1 97
Milner Dam, Id., U.S. G5 105
Milnor, N.D., U.S. C8 127
Milo, Ia., U.S. C4 108
Milo, Me., U.S. C4 112
Mílos, Grc. F10 18
Mílos, i., Grc. F10 18
Milparinka, Austl. F3 62
Milroy, In., U.S. F7 107
Milroy, Pa., U.S. E6 131
Milstead, Ga., U.S. C3 103
Milton, On., Can. D5 89
Milton, De., U.S. E4 101
Milton, Fl., U.S. u14 102
Milton, In., U.S. E7 107
Milton, Ma., U.S. B5 114
Milton, N.H., U.S. D5 122
Milton, Pa., U.S. D8 131
Milton, Vt., U.S. B2 138
Milton, Wa., U.S. f11 140
Milton, Wi., U.S. F5 142
Milton, W.V., U.S. C2 141
Milton, Lake, l., Oh., U.S. A4 128
Miltona, Lake, l., Mn., U.S. D3 116
Milton-Freewater, Or., U.S. B8 130
Milton Keynes, Eng., U.K. D6 12
Milton Reservoir, res., Co., U.S. A6 99
Milverton, On., Can. D4 89
Milwaukee, Wi., U.S. E6 142
Milwaukee, stm., Wi., U.S. m12 142
Milwaukee, co., Wi., U.S. E6 142
Milwaukie, Or., U.S. B4 130
Mims, Fl., U.S. D6 102
Min, stm., China F8 28
Min, stm., China D4 30
Mina, Nv., U.S. E3 121
Mīnā' al-Aḥmadī, Kuw. E5 42
Mīnāb, Iran E7 42
Minahasa, pen., Indon. C6 36
Minami-Tori-shima, i., Japan F18 64
Minas, Ur. E6 72
Minas Basin, b., N.S., Can. D5 87
Minas Channel, strt., N.S., Can. D5 87
Minas Gerais, state, Braz. E2 74
Minatare, Ne., U.S. C2 120
Minatitlán, Mex. D6 78
Minbya, Mya. B2 34
Minco, Ok., U.S. B4 129
Mindanao, i., Phil. E8 34
Mindanao Sea see Bohol Sea, Phil. E8 34
Mindelo, C.V. g10 50a
Minden, Ger. D11 12
Minden, La., U.S. B2 111
Minden, Ne., U.S. D7 120
Minden, Nv., U.S. E2 121
Minden, W.V., U.S. D3 141
Mindoro, i., Phil. D8 34
Mindoro Strait, strt., Phil. D8 34
Mine Hill, N.J., U.S. B3 123
Mineiros, Braz. B7 72
Mineola, N.Y., U.S. E7 125
Mineola, Tx., U.S. C5 136
Miner, Mo., U.S. E8 118
Miner, co., S.D., U.S. D8 134
Mineral, co., Co., U.S. D4 99
Mineral, co., Mt., U.S. C1 119
Mineral, co., Nv., U.S. E3 121
Mineral, co., W.V., U.S. B6 141
Mineral Point, Wi., U.S. F3 142
Mineral Springs, Ar., U.S. D2 97
Mineral Wells, Tx., U.S. C3 136
Minersville, Pa., U.S. E9 131
Minersville, Ut., U.S. E3 137
Minerva, Oh., U.S. B4 128
Minetto, N.Y., U.S. B4 125
Minfeng, China D4 28
Mingäçevir, Azer. B12 44
Mingäçevir su anbarı, res., Azer. B12 44
Mingechaur Reservoir see Mingäçevir su anbarı, res., Azer. B12 44
Mingenew, Austl. F2 60
Mingo, co., W.V., U.S. D2 141
Mingo Junction, Oh., U.S. B5 128
Minho (Miño), stm., Eur. G2 16
Minicoy Island, i., India H2 40
Minidoka, co., Id., U.S. G5 105
Minidoka Dam, Id., U.S. G5 105
Minier, Il., U.S. C4 106
Minisink Island, i., N.J., U.S. A3 123
Minitonas, Mb., Can. C1 86
Minle, China D8 28
Minna, Nig. E6 50
Minneapolis, Ks., U.S. C6 109
Minneapolis, Mn., U.S. F5 116
Minnedosa, Mb., Can. D2 86
Minnedosa, stm., Mb., Can. D1 86
Minnehaha, co., S.D., U.S. D9 134
Minneola, Ks., U.S. E3 109
Minneota, Mn., U.S. F3 116
Minnesota, stm., Mn., U.S. F2 116
Minnesota, state, U.S. E4 116
Minnesota Lake, Mn., U.S. G5 116
Minnetonka, Mn., U.S. n12 116
Minnetonka, Lake, l., Mn., U.S. n11 116
Minnewaska, Lake, l., Mn., U.S. E3 116
Miño (Minho), stm., Eur. F3 16
Minocqua, Wi., U.S. C4 142
Minonk, Il., U.S. C4 106
Minooka, Il., U.S. B5 106
Minot, N.D., U.S. A4 127
Minot Air Force Base, mil., N.D., U.S. A4 127
Minqin, China B1 30
Minqing, China D4 30
Minquadale, De., U.S. i7 101
Minsk, Bela. B9 20
Minster, Oh., U.S. B1 128
Mint Hill, N.C., U.S. B2 126
Minto, N.B., Can. C3 87
Minturn, Co., U.S. B4 99
Minusinsk, Russia D11 26
Minute Man National Historical Park, Ma., U.S. g10 114
Minvoul, Gabon C2 54
Minxian, China E8 28
Minya see El-Minya, Egypt E11 48
Mio, Mi., U.S. D6 115
Mīrābād, Afg. D8 42
Mirabel, Qc., Can. D3 90
Mirabella, Gulf of see Merambéllou, Kólpos, b., Grc. G10 18
Mirador, Braz. E11 70
Miraflores, Col. B5 70
Miraj, India F2 40
Miramar, Fl., U.S. s13 102
Miramar Naval Air Station, mil., Ca., U.S. F5 98
Miramichi Bay, b., N.B., Can. B5 87
Miranda, stm., Braz. B6 72
Miranda de Ebro, Spain F5 16
Mirbāṭ, Oman G6 38
Miri, Malay. C4 36
Miria, Niger D6 50
Mirim, Lagoa (Merín, Laguna), b., S.A. E7 72
Mirnyj, Russia C13 26
Mirpur, Pak. D10 42
Mīrpur Khās, Pak. E9 42
Mirror Lake, l., N.H., U.S. C4 122
Mirtóön Pélagos, Grc. F9 18
Mirzāpur, India D4 40
Miscouche, P.E., Can. C6 87
Miscou Island, i., N.B., Can. B5 87
Miscou Point, c., N.B., Can. A5 87
Misenheimer, N.C., U.S. B2 126
Mishan, China B14 28
Mishawaka, In., U.S. A5 107
Misheguk Mountain, mtn., Ak., U.S. B7 95
Mishicot, Wi., U.S. D6 142
Miskitos, Cayos, is., Nic. C3 80
Miskolc, Hung. E6 20
Misool, Pulau, i., Indon. D8 36
Mispillion, stm., De., U.S. E4 101
Miṣrātah, Libya D8 48
Missaukee, co., Mi., U.S. D5 115
Missaukee, Lake, l., Mi., U.S. D5 115
Mission, Ks., U.S. m16 109
Mission, S.D., U.S. D5 134
Mission, Tx., U.S. F3 136
Mission Range, mts., Mt., U.S. C3 119
Mission Viejo, Ca., U.S. n13 98
Missisquoi, stm., Vt., U.S. B3 138
Missisquoi Bay, b., Vt., U.S. A2 138
Mississauga, On., Can. D5 89
Mississinewa, stm., U.S. D7 107
Mississinewa Lake, res., In., U.S. C6 107
Mississippi, co., Ar., U.S. B5 97
Mississippi, co., Mo., U.S. E8 118
Mississippi, state, U.S. C4 117
Mississippi, stm., U.S. E9 92
Mississippi Delta, La., U.S. E6 111
Mississippi Sound, strt., U.S. E5 117
Mississippi State, Ms., U.S. B5 117
Missoula, Mt., U.S. D2 119
Missoula, co., Mt., U.S. D2 119
Missouri, state, U.S. C5 118
Missouri, stm., U.S. D9 92
Missouri City, Tx., U.S. r14 136
Missouri Valley, Ia., U.S. C2 108
Mistassini, Qc., Can. h12 90
Mistassini, Lac, l., Qc., Can. h12 90
Misti, Volcán, vol., Peru G5 70
Mita, Punta de, c., Mex. C3 78
Mitchell, stm., Austl. D3 62
Mitchell, Austl. F4 62
Mitchell, On., Can. D3 89
Mitchell, co., Ga., U.S. E2 103
Mitchell, co., Ia., U.S. A5 108
Mitchell, Il., U.S. E3 106
Mitchell, In., U.S. G5 107
Mitchell, co., Ks., U.S. C5 109
Mitchell, co., N.C., U.S. e10 126
Mitchell, Ne., U.S. C2 120
Mitchell, S.D., U.S. D7 134
Mitchell, co., Tx., U.S. C2 136
Mitchell, Lake, res., Al., U.S. C3 94
Mitchell, Lake, l., Mi., U.S. D5 115
Mitchell, Mount, mtn., N.C., U.S. f10 126
Mitchell Island, i., La., U.S. E6 111
Mitchellville, Ia., U.S. C4 108
Mitilíni, Grc. E11 18
Mitkof Island, i., Ak., U.S. m23 95
Mito, Japan C4 31
Mitsiwa see Massawa, Erit. G12 48
Mitú, Col. C5 70
Mitumba, Monts, mts., D.R.C. E5 54
Mitwaba, D.R.C. E5 54
Mitzic, Gabon C2 54
Miyake-jima, i., Japan E15 28
Miyako, Japan D16 28
Miyako-jima, i., Japan B9 34
Miyakonojō, Japan E14 28
Miyazaki, Japan E14 28
Miyazu, Japan D15 28
Miyoshi, Japan D2 31
Miyun, China A4 30
Mīzan Teferī, Eth. B7 54
Mizdah, Libya D7 48
Mizen Head, c., Ire. E2 12
Mizhi, China B3 30
Mizoram, state, India E6 40
Mizusawa, Japan C4 31
Mjakit, Russia C17 26
Mjölby, Swe. G6 10
Mjøsa, l., Nor. F4 10
Mkalama, Tan. D6 54
Mkokotoni, Tan. D7 54
Mladá Boleslav, Czech Rep. D3 20
Mlanje Peak see Sapitwa, mtn., Mwi. B6 56
Mława, Pol. C6 20
Mmabatho, S. Afr. D4 56
Moab, Ut., U.S. E6 137
Moala, i., Fiji m10 63b
Moamba, Moz. D5 56
Moanda, Gabon D2 54
Moapa River Indian Reservation, Nv., U.S. G7 121
Moba, D.R.C. E5 54
Mobaye, C.A.R. C4 54
Moberly, Mo., U.S. B5 118
Mobile, Al., U.S. E1 94
Mobile, stm., Al., U.S. E1 94
Mobile, co., Al., U.S. E1 94
Mobile Bay, b., Al., U.S. E1 99
Mobridge, S.D., U.S. B5 134
Mobutu Sese Seko, Lac see Albert, Lake, l., Afr. C6 54
Moca, Dom. Rep. B5 80
Mocanaqua, Pa., U.S. D9 131
Moc Chau, Viet. B4 34
Mocha see Al-Mukhā, Yemen H4 38
Mochudi, Bots. C4 56
Mocímboa da Praia, Moz. A7 56
Mocksville, N.C., U.S. B2 126
Moclips, Wa., U.S. B1 140
Môco, Morro de, mtn., Ang. F3 54
Mococa, Braz. F2 74
Moctezuma, Mex. B3 78
Mocuba, Moz. B6 56
Model Reservoir, res., Co., U.S. D6 99
Módena, Italy B3 18
Modesto, Ca., U.S. D3 98
Modoc, co., Ca., U.S. B3 98
Modowi, Indon. G9 32
Moe, Austl. H4 62
Moen-jo-Daro, hist., Pak. E9 42
Moenkopi, Az., U.S. A4 96
Moffat, co., Co., U.S. A2 99
Moffat Tunnel, Co., U.S. B5 99
Mogadishu see Muqdisho, Som. J14 48
Mogadore, Oh., U.S. A4 128
Mogaung, Mya. A3 34
Mogincual, Moz. B7 56
Mogoča, Russia D13 26
Mogogh, Sudan B6 54
Mogok, Mya. B3 34
Mogollon Mountains, mts., N.M., U.S. D1 124
Mogollon Rim, clf., Az., U.S. C5 96
Mogotón, mtn., N.A. F7 76
Mogzon, Russia A10 28
Mohall, N.D., U.S. A4 127
Mohammed, Râs, c., Egypt F10 14
Mohave, co., Az., U.S. B1 96
Mohave, Lake, res., U.S. H7 121
Mohave Mountains, mts., Az., U.S. C1 96
Mohave Valley, Az., U.S. C1 96
Mohawk, stm., N.H., U.S. g7 122
Mohawk, N.Y., U.S. C5 125
Mohawk, stm., N.Y., U.S. C6 125
Mohawk Lake, l., N.J., U.S. A3 123
Mohawk Mountains, mts., Az., U.S. E2 96
Mohe, China A12 28
Mohican, stm., Oh., U.S. B3 128
Mohns Ridge D23 144
Mohnton, Pa., U.S. F10 131
Mohnyin, Mya. B3 34
Mohyliv-Podil's'kyi, Ukr. E9 20
Mo i Rana, Nor. C6 10
Moisie, Qc., Can. h8 88
Mojave, Ca., U.S. E4 98
Mojave, stm., Ca., U.S. E5 98
Mojave Desert, des., Ca., U.S. E5 98
Mojo, Eth. B7 54
Mojynty, Kaz. E9 26
Mōkapu Peninsula, pen., Hi., U.S. g10 104
Mōkapu Point, c., Hi., U.S. g11 104
Mokelumne, stm., Ca., U.S. C3 98
Mokena, Il., U.S. k9 106
Mokhotlong, Leso. D4 56
Mokníne, Tun. G3 18
Mokolo, Cam. A2 54
Mokp'o, S. Kor. E13 28
Mokumanu, i., Hi., U.S. g11 104
Mola di Bari, Italy D6 18
Molalla, Or., U.S. B4 130
Moldavia see Moldova, ctry., Eur. F10 20
Moldavia, hist. reg., Rom. F9 20
Molde, Nor. E2 10
Moldova, ctry., Eur. F10 20
Moldoveanu, Vârful, mtn., Rom. G8 20
Molepolole, Bots. C4 56
Molfetta, Italy D6 18
Moline, Il., U.S. B3 106
Moline, Mi., U.S. F5 115
Molino, Fl., U.S. u14 102
Mollendo, Peru G5 70
Moloka'i, i., Hi., U.S. B5 104
Molokai Fracture Zone F24 64
Molokini, i., Hi., U.S. C5 104
Molopo, stm., Afr. D3 56
Molotov see Perm', Russia D7 26
Moloundou, Cam. C3 54
Molson Lake, l., Mb., Can. B3 86
Moluccas see Maluku, is., Indon. D7 36
Molucca Sea see Maluku, Laut, Indon. C7 36
Moma, Moz. B6 56
Mombasa, Kenya D7 54
Mombetsu, Japan C16 28
Momence, Il., U.S. B6 106
Mompós, Col. D5 80
Momskij hrebet, mts., Russia C16 26
Møn, i., Den. I5 10
Mona, Isla de, i., P.R. B6 80
Monaca, Pa., U.S. E1 131
Monaco, ctry., Eur. C1 18
Monadnock, Mount, mtn., N.H., U.S. E2 122
Monadnock Mountain, mtn., Vt., U.S. B5 138
Monahans, Tx., U.S. D1 136
Mona Passage, strt., N.A. B6 80
Mona Quimbundo, Ang. E3 54
Monarch Mills, S.C., U.S. B4 133
Monarch Pass, Co., U.S. C4 99
Monashee Mountains, mts., B.C., Can. D8 85
Monastir, Tun. G3 18
Monção, Braz. D10 70
Mončegorsk, Russia C15 10
Mönchengladbach, Ger. E10 12
Moncks Corner, S.C., U.S. E7 133
Monclova, Mex. B4 78
Moncton, N.B., Can. C5 87
Mondjamboli, D.R.C. C4 54
Mondovi, Wi., U.S. D2 142
Monee, Il., U.S. B6 106
Monessen, Pa., U.S. F2 131
Monett, Mo., U.S. E4 118
Monette, Ar., U.S. B5 97
Monfalcone, Italy B4 18
Monforte de Lemos, Spain F3 16
Mongalla, Sudan B6 54
Mõng Hpāyak, Mya. B3 34
Mõng Hsat, Mya. B3 34
Mongo, Chad D8 50
Mongol Altayn nuruu, mts., Asia B6 28
Mongolia, ctry., Asia B8 28
Mongonu, Nig. D7 50
Mongu, Zam. B3 56
Monhegan Island, i., Me., U.S. E3 112
Monida Pass, U.S. E6 105
Moniteau, co., Mo., U.S. C5 118
Monitor Range, mts., Nv., U.S. E5 121
Monitor Valley, val., Nv., U.S. D5 121
Monmouth, Il., U.S. C3 106
Monmouth, co., N.J., U.S. C4 123
Monmouth, Or., U.S. C3 130
Monmouth Beach, N.J., U.S. C5 123
Monmouth Mountain, mtn., B.C., Can. D6 85
Mono, co., Ca., U.S. D4 98
Monocacy, stm., Md., U.S. B3 113
Mono Lake, l., Ca., U.S. D4 98
Monomonac, Lake, l., U.S. E3 122
Monomoy Island, i., Ma., U.S. C7 114
Monomoy Point, c., Ma., U.S. C7 114
Monon, In., U.S. C4 107
Monona, Ia., U.S. A6 108
Monona, co., Ia., U.S. B1 108
Monona, Wi., U.S. E4 142
Monona, Lake, l., Wi., U.S. E4 142
Monongah, W.V., U.S. B4 141
Monongahela, Pa., U.S. F2 131
Monongahela, stm., U.S. G2 131
Monongalia, co., W.V., U.S. B4 141
Monopoli, Italy D6 18
Monor, Hung. F5 20
Monroe, co., Al., U.S. D2 94
Monroe, co., Ar., U.S. C4 97
Monroe, co., Fl., U.S. G5 102
Monroe, Ga., U.S. C3 103
Monroe, co., Ga., U.S. D3 103
Monroe, Ia., U.S. C4 108
Monroe, co., Ia., U.S. D5 108
Monroe, co., Il., U.S. E3 106
Monroe, In., U.S. C8 107
Monroe, co., In., U.S. F4 107
Monroe, co., Ky., U.S. D4 110
Monroe, La., U.S. B3 111
Monroe, Mi., U.S. G7 115
Monroe, co., Mi., U.S. G7 115
Monroe, co., Mo., U.S. B5 118
Monroe, co., Ms., U.S. B5 117
Monroe, N.C., U.S. C2 126
Monroe, N.Y., U.S. D6 125
Monroe, co., N.Y., U.S. B3 125
Monroe, Oh., U.S. C1 128
Monroe, co., Oh., U.S. C4 128
Monroe, co., Pa., U.S. D11 131
Monroe, co., Tn., U.S. D9 135
Monroe, Ut., U.S. E3 137
Monroe, Wa., U.S. B4 140
Monroe, Wi., U.S. F4 142
Monroe, co., Wi., U.S. E3 142
Monroe, co., W.V., U.S. D4 141
Monroe Center, Ct., U.S. D3 100
Monroe City, Mo., U.S. B6 118
Monroe Lake, res., In., U.S. F5 107
Monroe Park, De., U.S. h7 101
Monroeville, Al., U.S. D2 94
Monroeville, In., U.S. C8 107
Monroeville, Oh., U.S. A3 128
Monroeville, Pa., U.S. k14 131
Monrovia, Lib. E2 50
Monrovia, Ca., U.S. m13 98
Monrovia, In., U.S. E5 107
Monson, Ma., U.S. B3 114
Mönsterås, Swe. H7 10
Montague, P.E., Can. C7 87
Montague, Ca., U.S. B2 98
Montague, Mi., U.S. E4 115
Montague, co., Tx., U.S. C4 136
Montague Island, i., Ak., U.S. D10 95
Montague Peak, mtn., Ak., U.S. g18 95
Montague Strait, strt., Ak., U.S. h18 95
Mont Alto, Pa., U.S. G6 131
Montana, Blg. C9 18
Montana, state, U.S. D7 119
Montargis, Fr. C8 16
Montauban, Fr. E7 16
Montauk, N.Y., U.S. m17 125
Montbard, Fr. D9 16
Montbéliard, Fr. D10 16
Mont Belvieu, Tx., U.S. E5 136
Montblanc, Spain G7 16
Montcalm, co., Mi., U.S. E5 115
Montceau-les-Mines, Fr. D9 16
Montchanin, De., U.S. h7 101
Montclair, Ca., U.S. m13 98
Montclair, N.J., U.S. B4 123
Mont Clare, Pa., U.S. o19 131
Mont-de-Marsan, Fr. F6 16
Monteagle, Tn., U.S. D8 135
Monte Alegre, Braz. D9 70
Monte Azul, Braz. E3 74
Montebello, Qc., Can. D3 90
Montebello, Ca., U.S. m12 98
Montecarlo, Arg. D7 72
Monte Caseros, Arg. E6 72
Monte Comán, Arg. E4 72
Montecristo, Isola di, i., Italy C3 18
Montego Bay, Jam. B4 80
Montegut, La., U.S. E5 111
Montélimar, Fr. E9 16
Montello, Nv., U.S. B7 121
Montello, Wi., U.S. E4 142
Montemorelos, Mex. B5 78
Montenegro see Crna Gora, state, Serb. C7 18
Monte Patria, Chile E3 72
Montepuez, Moz. A6 56
Montepulciano, Italy C3 18
Monte Quemado, Arg. D5 72
Monterey, Ca., U.S. D3 98
Monterey, co., Ca., U.S. D3 98
Monterey, Tn., U.S. C8 135
Monterey Bay, b., Ca., U.S. D2 98
Monterey Park, Ca., U.S. m12 98
Montería, Col. B4 70

Name	Map Ref.	Page
Montero, Bol.	B5	72
Monterrey, Mex.	B4	78
Montesano, Wa., U.S.	C2	140
Montes Claros, Braz.	E3	74
Montevallo, Al., U.S.	B3	94
Montevideo, Ur.	E6	72
Montevideo, Mn., U.S.	F3	116
Monte Vista, Co., U.S.	D4	99
Montezuma, co., Co., U.S.	D2	99
Montezuma, Ga., U.S.	D2	103
Montezuma, Ia., U.S.	C5	108
Montezuma, In., U.S.	E3	107
Montezuma, Ks., U.S.	E3	109
Montezuma Castle National Monument, Az., U.S.	C4	96
Montezuma Peak, mtn., Az., U.S.	D3	96
Montgomery see Sāhīwāl, Pak.	D10	42
Montgomery, Al., U.S.	C3	94
Montgomery, co., Al., U.S.	C3	94
Montgomery, co., Ar., U.S.	C2	97
Montgomery, co., Ga., U.S.	D4	103
Montgomery, co., Ia., U.S.	C2	108
Montgomery, Il., U.S.	B5	106
Montgomery, co., Il., U.S.	D4	106
Montgomery, co., In., U.S.	D4	107
Montgomery, co., Ks., U.S.	E8	109
Montgomery, co., Ky., U.S.	B6	110
Montgomery, La., U.S.	C3	111
Montgomery, co., Md., U.S.	B3	113
Montgomery, Mn., U.S.	F5	116
Montgomery, co., Mo., U.S.	C6	118
Montgomery, co., Ms., U.S.	B4	117
Montgomery, co., N.C., U.S.	B3	126
Montgomery, N.Y., U.S.	D6	125
Montgomery, co., N.Y., U.S.	C6	125
Montgomery, co., Oh., U.S.	C1	128
Montgomery, Oh., U.S.	o13	128
Montgomery, Pa., U.S.	D8	131
Montgomery, co., Pa., U.S.	F11	131
Montgomery, co., Tn., U.S.	A4	135
Montgomery, co., Tx., U.S.	D5	136
Montgomery, co., Va., U.S.	C2	139
Montgomery, W.V., U.S.	C3	141
Montgomery City, Mo., U.S.	C6	118
Monticello, Ar., U.S.	D4	97
Monticello, Fl., U.S.	B3	102
Monticello, Ga., U.S.	C3	103
Monticello, Ia., U.S.	B6	108
Monticello, Il., U.S.	C5	106
Monticello, In., U.S.	C4	107
Monticello, Ky., U.S.	D5	110
Monticello, Mn., U.S.	E5	116
Monticello, Ms., U.S.	D3	117
Monticello, N.Y., U.S.	D6	125
Monticello, Ut., U.S.	F6	137
Monticello, Wi., U.S.	F4	142
Mont-Joli, Qc., Can.	A9	90
Mont-Laurier, Qc., Can.	C2	90
Montluçon, Fr.	D8	16
Montmagny, Qc., Can.	C7	90
Montmorenci, S.C., U.S.	D4	133
Montmorency, co., Mi., U.S.	C6	115
Monto, Austl.	E5	62
Montoro, Spain	H4	16
Montour, co., Pa., U.S.	D8	131
Montour Falls, N.Y., U.S.	C4	125
Montoursville, Pa., U.S.	D8	131
Montpelier, Id., U.S.	G7	105
Montpelier, In., U.S.	C7	107
Montpelier, Oh., U.S.	A1	128
Montpelier, Vt., U.S.	C3	138
Montpellier, Fr.	F8	16
Montréal, Qc., Can.	D4	90
Montreal, Wi., U.S.	B3	142
Montréal, Île de, i., Qc., Can.	q19	90
Montreal Lake, l., Sk., Can.	C3	91
Montréal-Nord, Qc., Can.	p19	90
Montreat, N.C., U.S.	f10	126
Montreux, Switz.	A1	18
Mont-Rolland, Qc., Can.	D3	90
Montrose, B.C., Can.	E9	85
Montrose, Scot., U.K.	B5	12
Montrose, Al., U.S.	E2	94
Montrose, Co., U.S.	C3	99
Montrose, co., Co., U.S.	C2	99
Montrose, Ia., U.S.	D6	108
Montrose, Mi., U.S.	E7	115
Montrose, Pa., U.S.	C10	131
Montrose, Va., U.S.	m18	139
Mont-Royal, Qc., Can.	p19	90
Mont-Saint-Michel, Le, rel., Fr.	C6	16
Montserrat, dep., N.A.	E12	76
Montserrat, Monasterio de, rel., Spain	G7	16
Mont-Tremblant, Parc Provincial du, Qc., Can.	C3	90
Montvale, N.J., U.S.	A4	123
Montville, Ct., U.S.	D7	100
Monument, Co., U.S.	B6	99
Monument Beach, Ma., U.S.	C6	114
Monument Peak, mtn., Co., U.S.	B3	99
Monument Peak, mtn., Id., U.S.	G4	105
Monument Valley, val., Az., U.S.	A5	96
Monywa, Mya.	B2	34
Monza, Italy	B2	18
Monze, Zam.	B4	56
Monzón, Spain	G7	16
Moodus, Ct., U.S.	D6	100
Moodus Reservoir, res., Ct., U.S.	C6	100
Moody, co., S.D., U.S.	C9	134
Moody, Tx., U.S.	D4	136
Moon Lake, l., Ms., U.S.	A3	117
Moora, Austl.	G2	60
Moorcroft, Wy., U.S.	B8	143
Moore, co., N.C., U.S.	B3	126
Moore, Ok., U.S.	B4	129
Moore, co., Tn., U.S.	B5	135
Moore, co., Tx., U.S.	B2	136
Moore, Lake, l., Austl.	F2	60
Moore Dam, U.S.	B3	122
Moorefield, W.V., U.S.	B6	141
Moore Haven, Fl., U.S.	F5	102
Mooreland, Ok., U.S.	A2	129
Moore Reservoir, res., U.S.	B3	122
Moores Creek National Military Park, N.C., U.S.	C4	126
Moores Hill, In., U.S.	F7	107
Moorestown, N.J., U.S.	D3	123
Mooresville, In., U.S.	E5	107
Mooresville, N.C., U.S.	B2	126
Moorhead, Mn., U.S.	D2	116
Moorhead, Ms., U.S.	B3	117
Mooringsport, La., U.S.	B2	111
Moorreesburg, S. Afr.	E2	56
Moose, stm., N.H., U.S.	B4	122
Moose, stm., N.Y., U.S.	B5	125
Moose, stm., Vt., U.S.	B5	138
Moosehead Lake, l., Me., U.S.	C3	112
Moose Jaw, stm., Sk., Can.	G3	91
Moose Lake, Mb., Can.	C1	86
Moose Lake, Mn., U.S.	D6	116
Moose Lake, l., Wi., U.S.	B2	142
Mooseleuk Stream, stm., Me., U.S.	B4	112
Mooselookmeguntic Lake, l., Me., U.S.	D2	112
Moose Mountain Creek, stm., Sk., Can.	H4	91
Moose Mountain Provincial Park, Sk., Can.	H4	91
Moosic, Pa., U.S.	m18	131
Moosup, Ct., U.S.	C8	100
Moosup, stm., U.S.	C1	132
Mopang Lake, l., Me., U.S.	D5	112
Mopti, Mali	D4	50
Moquegua, Peru	G5	70
Mora, Cam.	D7	50
Mora, Spain	H5	16
Mora, Swe.	F6	10
Mora, Mn., U.S.	E5	116
Mora, stm., N.M., U.S.	B5	124
Mora, co., N.M., U.S.	A5	124
Mora, N.M., U.S.	B4	124
Morādābād, India	D3	40
Morafenobe, Madag.	B7	56
Moramanga, Madag.	B8	56
Morant Cays, is., Jam.	B4	80
Moratuwa, Sri L.	H3	40
Morava, hist. reg., Czech Rep.	E4	20
Moravia, Ia., U.S.	D5	108
Morawa, Austl.	F2	60
Morawhanna, Guy.	B8	70
Moray Firth, b., Scot., U.K.	B5	12
Morbi, India	E2	40
Morden, Mb., Can.	E2	86
Mordovia see Mordovija, state, Russia	D6	26
Mordovija, state, Russia	D6	26
Mordvinia see Mordovija, state, Russia	D6	26
Moreau, stm., S.D., U.S.	B3	134
Moreauville, La., U.S.	C4	111
Morecambe Bay, b., Eng., U.K.	D5	12
Moree, Austl.	F4	62
Morehead, Ky., U.S.	B6	110
Morehead City, N.C., U.S.	C6	126
Morehouse, co., La., U.S.	B4	111
Morehouse, Mo., U.S.	E8	118
Morelia, Mex.	D4	78
Morelos, state, Mex.	D5	78
Morena, Sierra, mts., Spain	H4	16
Morenci, Az., U.S.	D6	96
Morenci, Mi., U.S.	G6	115
Moresby Island, i., B.C., Can.	C2	85
Moreton Island, i., Austl.	F5	62
Morey, Lake, l., Vt., U.S.	D4	138
Morey Peak, mtn., Nv., U.S.	E5	121
Morgan, co., Al., U.S.	A3	94
Morgan, co., Co., U.S.	A7	99
Morgan, co., Ga., U.S.	C3	103
Morgan, co., Il., U.S.	D3	106
Morgan, co., In., U.S.	F5	107
Morgan, co., Ky., U.S.	C6	110
Morgan, Mn., U.S.	F4	116
Morgan, co., Mo., U.S.	C5	118
Morgan, co., Oh., U.S.	C4	128
Morgan, co., Tn., U.S.	C9	135
Morgan, Ut., U.S.	B4	137
Morgan, co., Ut., U.S.	B4	137
Morgan, co., W.V., U.S.	B6	141
Morgan City, La., U.S.	E4	111
Morganfield, Ky., U.S.	C2	110
Morgan Hill, Ca., U.S.	D3	98
Morgan Island, i., S.C., U.S.	G6	133
Morgan Point, c., Ct., U.S.	E4	100
Morganton, N.C., U.S.	B1	126
Morgantown, In., U.S.	F5	107
Morgantown, Ky., U.S.	C3	110
Morgantown, Ms., U.S.	D2	117
Morgantown, Tn., U.S.	D8	135
Morgantown, W.V., U.S.	B5	141
Morganza, La., U.S.	D4	111
Morghāb (Murgab), stm., Asia	C8	42
Moriah, Mount, mtn., Nv., U.S.	D7	121
Moriarty, N.M., U.S.	C3	124
Moriki, Nig.	D6	50
Morinville, Ab., Can.	C4	84
Morioka, Japan	D16	28
Morlaix, Fr.	C5	16
Morley, Mo., U.S.	D8	118
Mormon Peak, mtn., Nv., U.S.	G7	121
Morning Sun, Ia., U.S.	C6	108
Mornington Island, i., Austl.	D2	62
Morobe, Pap. N. Gui.	H12	32
Morocco, ctry., Afr.	D3	48
Morocco, In., U.S.	C3	107
Morogoro, Tan.	E7	54
Moro Gulf, b., Phil.	E8	34
Morombe, Madag.	C7	56
Morón, Arg.	E6	72
Morón, Cuba	A4	80
Mörön, Mong.	B8	28
Morondava, Madag.	C7	56
Morón de la Frontera, Spain	I4	16
Moroni, Com.	A7	56
Moroni, Ut., U.S.	D4	137
Morotai, i., Indon.	C7	36
Moroto, Ug.	C6	54
Morozovsk, Russia	E7	22
Morrill, Ne., U.S.	C2	120
Morrill, co., Ne., U.S.	C2	120
Morrilton, Ar., U.S.	B3	97
Morrinhos, Braz.	E2	74
Morris, Mb., Can.	E3	86
Morris, Al., U.S.	B3	94
Morris, Il., U.S.	B5	106
Morris, co., Ks., U.S.	D7	109
Morris, Mn., U.S.	E3	116
Morris, co., N.J., U.S.	B3	123
Morris, Ok., U.S.	B6	129
Morris, co., Tx., U.S.	C5	136
Morrisburg, On., Can.	C9	89
Morris Island, i., S.C., U.S.	F8	133
Morris Jesup, Kap, c., Grnld.	B33	82
Morrison, Il., U.S.	B4	106
Morrison, co., Mn., U.S.	D4	116
Morrison, Ok., U.S.	A4	129
Morrison City, Tn., U.S.	C11	135
Morrisonville, Il., U.S.	D4	106
Morrisonville, N.Y., U.S.	f11	125
Morris Plains, N.J., U.S.	B4	123
Morristown, In., U.S.	E6	107
Morristown, Mn., U.S.	F5	116
Morristown, N.J., U.S.	B4	123
Morristown, Tn., U.S.	C10	135
Morristown National Historical Park, N.J., U.S.	B3	123
Morrisville, N.Y., U.S.	C5	125
Morrisville, Pa., U.S.	F12	131
Morrisville, Vt., U.S.	B3	138
Morro Bay, Ca., U.S.	E3	98
Morro do Chapéu, Braz.	D3	74
Morrow, Ga., U.S.	C2	103
Morrow, co., Oh., U.S.	B3	128
Morrow, Oh., U.S.	C1	128
Morrow, co., Or., U.S.	B7	130
Morrumbala, Moz.	B6	56
Morrumbene, Moz.	C6	56
Moršansk, Russia	D7	22
Morse, La., U.S.	D3	111
Morse Reservoir, res., In., U.S.	D5	107
Morses Creek, stm., N.J., U.S.	k8	123
Mortes, stm., Braz.	F9	70
Morton, Il., U.S.	C4	106
Morton, co., Ks., U.S.	E2	109
Morton, Ms., U.S.	C4	117
Morton, co., N.D., U.S.	C4	127
Morton, Tx., U.S.	C1	136
Morton, Wa., U.S.	C3	140
Morton Grove, Il., U.S.	h9	106
Morton Pass, Wy., U.S.	E7	143
Mortons Gap, Ky., U.S.	C2	110
Morwell, Austl.	H4	62
Moscow see Moskva, Russia	D5	26
Moscow, Id., U.S.	C2	105
Moscow, Pa., U.S.	m18	131
Moscow Mills, Mo., U.S.	C7	118
Mosel (Moselle), stm., Eur.	B10	16
Moselle (Mosel), stm., Eur.	C10	16
Moselle, Ms., U.S.	D4	117
Moses Coulee, val., Wa., U.S.	B6	140
Moses Lake, Wa., U.S.	B6	140
Moses Lake, l., Wa., U.S.	B6	140
Mosheim, Tn., U.S.	C11	135
Moshi, Tan.	D7	54
Mosinee, Wi., U.S.	D4	142
Mosjøen, Nor.	D5	10
Moskva (Moscow), Russia	D5	26
Mosqueiro, Braz.	B2	74
Mosquera, Col.	C4	70
Mosquito Creek Lake, res., Oh., U.S.	A5	128
Mosquito Lagoon, b., Fl., U.S.	D6	102
Mosquitos, Golfo de los, b., Pan.	D3	80
Moss, Nor.	G4	10
Mossaka, Congo	D3	54
Moss Bluff, La., U.S.	D2	111
Mosselbaai, S. Afr.	E3	56
Mossman, Austl.	D4	62
Mossoró, Braz.	C4	74
Moss Point, Ms., U.S.	E5	117
Most, Czech Rep.	D2	20
Mostar, Bos.	C6	18
Møsting, Kap, c., Grnld.	F32	82
Mosul see Al-Mawṣil, Iraq	C4	42
Møsvatnet, l., Nor.	G3	10
Moswansicut Pond, l., R.I., U.S.	C3	132
Mot'a, Eth.	A7	54
Motagua, stm., N.A.	B2	80
Motala, Swe.	G6	10
Motherwell, Scot., U.K.	C5	12
Motley, co., Tx., U.S.	B2	136
Motril, Spain	I5	16
Mott, N.D., U.S.	C3	127
Motueka, N.Z.	p13	63c
Motyklejka, Russia	D16	26
Mouaskar, Alg.	D4	14
Moudjéria, Maur.	C2	50
Mouila, Gabon	D2	54
Moulins, Fr.	D8	16
Moulouya, Oued, stm., Mor.	D4	48
Moulton, Al., U.S.	A2	94
Moulton, Ia., U.S.	D5	108
Moultrie, Ga., U.S.	E3	103
Moultrie, co., Il., U.S.	D5	106
Moultrie, Lake, res., S.C., U.S.	E7	133
Mounana, Gabon	D2	54
Mound, Mn., U.S.	n11	116
Mound Bayou, Ms., U.S.	B3	117
Mound City, Il., U.S.	F4	106
Mound City, Ks., U.S.	D9	109
Mound City, Mo., U.S.	A2	118
Mound City Group National Monument, Oh., U.S.	C2	128
Moundou, Chad	E8	50
Moundridge, Ks., U.S.	D6	109
Mounds, Il., U.S.	F4	106
Mounds, Ok., U.S.	B5	129
Mounds View, Mn., U.S.	m12	116
Moundsville, W.V., U.S.	B4	141
Moundville, Al., U.S.	C2	94
Mountainair, N.M., U.S.	C3	124
Mountainaire, Az., U.S.	B4	96
Mountain Brook, Al., U.S.	g7	94
Mountain City, Ga., U.S.	B3	103
Mountain City, Nv., U.S.	B6	121
Mountain City, Tn., U.S.	C12	135
Mountain Fork, stm., U.S.	C7	129
Mountain Grove, Mo., U.S.	D5	118
Mountain Home, Ar., U.S.	A3	97
Mountain Home, Id., U.S.	F3	105
Mountain Home Air Force Base, mil., Id., U.S.	F3	105
Mountain Iron, Mn., U.S.	C6	116
Mountain Lake, Mn., U.S.	G4	116
Mountain Lake Park, Md., U.S.	m12	113
Mountain Nile see Jabal, Baḥr al-, stm., Sudan	I11	48
Mountain Pine, Ar., U.S.	C2	97
Mountainside, N.J., U.S.	B4	123
Mountain View, Ar., U.S.	B3	97
Mountain View, Ca., U.S.	k8	98
Mountain View, Mo., U.S.	D6	118
Mountain View, N.M., U.S.	C3	124
Mountain View, Ok., U.S.	B3	129
Mountain View, Wy., U.S.	E2	143
Mountain Village, Ak., U.S.	C7	95
Mount Airy, Md., U.S.	B3	113
Mount Airy, N.C., U.S.	A2	126
Mount Albert, On., Can.	C5	89
Mount Angel, Or., U.S.	B4	130
Mount Arlington, N.J., U.S.	B3	123
Mount Augustus, Austl.	E2	60
Mount Ayr, Ia., U.S.	D3	108
Mount Barker, Austl.	G2	60
Mount Carmel, Il., U.S.	E6	106
Mount Carmel, Oh., U.S.	o13	128
Mount Carmel, Pa., U.S.	E9	131
Mount Carmel [-Mitchell's Brook-Saint Catherine's], N.L., Can.	E5	88
Mount Carroll, Il., U.S.	A4	106
Mount Clare, W.V., U.S.	B4	141
Mount Clemens, Mi., U.S.	F8	115
Mount Desert Island, i., Me., U.S.	D4	112
Mount Dora, Fl., U.S.	D5	102
Mount Forest, On., Can.	D4	89
Mount Gambier, Austl.	H3	62
Mount Gay, W.V., U.S.	D2	141
Mount Gilead, N.C., U.S.	B3	126
Mount Gilead, Oh., U.S.	B3	128
Mount Hagen, Pap. N. Gui.	H11	32
Mount Healthy, Oh., U.S.	o12	128
Mount Holly, N.C., U.S.	B1	126
Mount Holly, N.J., U.S.	D3	123
Mount Holly Springs, Pa., U.S.	F7	131
Mount Hope, stm., Ct., U.S.	B7	100
Mount Hope, Ks., U.S.	E6	109
Mount Hope, W.V., U.S.	D3	141
Mount Hope Bay, b., U.S.	D6	132
Mount Horeb, Wi., U.S.	E4	142
Mount Ida, Ar., U.S.	C2	97
Mount Isa, Austl.	E2	62
Mount Jackson, Va., U.S.	B4	139
Mount Jewett, Pa., U.S.	C4	131
Mount Joy, Pa., U.S.	F9	131
Mount Juliet, Tn., U.S.	A5	135
Mount Kisco, N.Y., U.S.	D7	125
Mount Lebanon, Pa., U.S.	F1	131
Mount Magnet, Austl.	F2	60
Mount Morris, Il., U.S.	A4	106
Mount Morris, Mi., U.S.	E7	115
Mount Morris, N.Y., U.S.	C3	125
Mount Olive, Al., U.S.	B3	94
Mount Olive, Il., U.S.	D4	106
Mount Olive, Ms., U.S.	D4	117
Mount Olive, N.C., U.S.	B4	126
Mount Olive, Tn., U.S.	n14	135
Mount Orab, Oh., U.S.	C2	128
Mount Pearl, N.L., Can.	E5	88
Mount Penn, Pa., U.S.	F10	131
Mount Pleasant, Ia., U.S.	D6	108
Mount Pleasant, Mi., U.S.	E6	115
Mount Pleasant, N.C., U.S.	B2	126
Mount Pleasant, Pa., U.S.	F2	131
Mount Pleasant, S.C., U.S.	F8	133
Mount Pleasant, Tn., U.S.	B4	135
Mount Pleasant, Tx., U.S.	C5	136
Mount Pleasant, Ut., U.S.	D4	137
Mount Pocono, Pa., U.S.	D11	131
Mount Prospect, Il., U.S.	A6	106
Mount Pulaski, Il., U.S.	C4	106
Mountrail, co., N.D., U.S.	A3	127
Mount Rainier, Md., U.S.	f9	113
Mount Rainier National Park, Wa., U.S.	C4	140
Mount Revelstoke National Park, B.C., Can.	D8	85
Mount Riddock, Austl.	E5	60
Mount Rogers National Recreation Area, Va., U.S.	D1	139
Mount Roskill, N.Z.	o13	63c
Mount Rushmore National Memorial, hist., S.D., U.S.	D2	134
Mount Savage, Md., U.S.	k13	113
Mount Shasta, Ca., U.S.	B2	98
Mount Sterling, Il., U.S.	D3	106
Mount Sterling, Ky., U.S.	B6	110
Mount Sterling, Oh., U.S.	C2	128
Mount Uniacke, N.S., Can.	E6	87
Mount Union, Pa., U.S.	F6	131
Mount Vernon, Austl.	E2	60
Mount Vernon, Al., U.S.	D1	94
Mount Vernon, Ga., U.S.	D4	103
Mount Vernon, Ia., U.S.	C6	108
Mount Vernon, Il., U.S.	E5	106
Mount Vernon, In., U.S.	I2	107
Mount Vernon, Ky., U.S.	C5	110
Mount Vernon, Mo., U.S.	D4	118
Mount Vernon, N.Y., U.S.	h13	125
Mount Vernon, Oh., U.S.	B3	128
Mount Vernon, Tx., U.S.	C5	136
Mount Vernon, Wa., U.S.	A3	140
Mount View, R.I., U.S.	D4	132
Mount Washington, Ky., U.S.	B4	110
Mount Wolf, Pa., U.S.	F8	131
Mount Zion, Il., U.S.	D5	106
Moura, Braz.	D7	70
Moussa 'Ali, mtn., Afr.	H4	38
Moussoro, Chad	D8	50
Moutong, Indon.	C6	36
Moville, Ia., U.S.	B1	108
Moweaqua, Il., U.S.	D4	106
Mower, co., Mn., U.S.	G6	116
Moxee City, Wa., U.S.	C5	140
Moyale, Kenya	C7	54
Moyamba, S.L.	E2	50
Moyen Atlas, mts., Mor.	E3	14
Moyo, Pulau, i., Indon.	E5	36
Moyobamba, Peru	E4	70
Moyock, N.C., U.S.	A6	126
Moyu, China	B3	40
Mozambique, ctry., Afr.	B5	56
Mozambique Channel, strt., Afr.	B7	56
Mozambique Plateau	L6	64
Mozdok, Russia	B4	42
Mpala, D.R.C.	E5	54
Mpanda, Tan.	E6	54
Mpika, Zam.	A5	56
Mporokoso, Zam.	E6	54
Mpulungu, Zam.	E6	54
Mpwapwa, Tan.	E7	54
Mscislaŭ, Bela.	C11	20
M'Sila, Alg.	J9	16
Mtubatuba, S. Afr.	D5	56
Mtwara, Tan.	F8	54
Muanda, D.R.C.	E2	54
Muang Hôngsa, Laos	C4	34
Muang Khammouan, Laos	C4	34
Muang Không, Laos	D5	34
Muang Khôngxédôn, Laos	C5	34
Muang Ngoy, Laos	B4	34
Muang Pak-Lay, Laos	C4	34
Muang Pakxan, Laos	C4	34
Muang Phalan, Laos	C5	34
Muang Sing, Laos	B4	34
Muang Thadua, Laos	C4	34
Muang Vangviang, Laos	C4	34
Muang Xaignabouri, Laos	C4	34
Muar, Malay.	C2	36
Muaraenim, Indon.	D2	36
Muarasiberut, Indon.	G2	32
Mubende, Ug.	C6	54

Name — Map Ref. — Page

Mubi, Nig. D7 50
Muchinga Mountains, mts., Zam. A5 56
Muckleshoot Indian Reservation, Wa., U.S. f11 140
Mucojo, Moz. A7 56
Muconda, Ang. F4 54
Mucujê, Braz. F11 70
Mud, stm., Ky., U.S. C3 110
Mud, stm., Mn., U.S. B3 116
Mud, stm., W.V., U.S. C2 141
Mudanjiang, China C13 28
Mud Creek, stm., Ok., U.S. C4 129
Muddy Boggy Creek, stm., Ok., U.S. C6 129
Muddy Creek, stm., Ut., U.S. E4 137
Muddy Creek, stm., Wy., U.S. D6 143
Muddy Creek, stm., Wy., U.S. E2 143
Muddy Creek, stm., Wy., U.S. E5 143
Muddy Creek, stm., Wy., U.S. C4 143
Muddy Mountains, mts., Nv., U.S. G7 121
Muddy Peak, mtn., Nv., U.S. G7 121
Mudgee, Austl. G4 62
Mud Lake, l., Me., U.S. A4 112
Mud Lake, l., Nv., U.S. F4 121
Mueda, Moz. A6 56
Muenster, Tx., U.S. C4 136
Mufulira, Zam. A4 56
Muğla, Tur. D3 44
Muhlenberg, co., Ky., U.S. C2 110
Mühlhausen, Ger. E12 12
Muhu, i., Est. G10 10
Muié, Ang. A3 56
Muirkirk, Md., U.S. B4 113
Muir Woods National Monument, Ca., U.S. h7 98
Muja, Russia D13 26
Mujnak, Uzb. B7 42
Mukacheve, Ukr. E7 20
Mukah, Malay. C4 36
Mukden see Shenyang, China C12 28
Mukilteo, Wa., U.S. B3 140
Mukinbudin, Austl. G2 60
Mukomuk, Indon. D2 36
Mukry, Turk. C9 42
Mukwonago, Wi., U.S. F5 142
Mula, Spain H6 16
Mulberry, Ar., U.S. B1 97
Mulberry, stm., Ar., U.S. B1 97
Mulberry, Fl., U.S. E4 102
Mulberry, In., U.S. D4 107
Mulberry, N.C., U.S. A1 126
Mulberry Fork, stm., Al., U.S. B3 94
Muldraugh, Ky., U.S. C4 110
Muldrow, Ok., U.S. B7 129
Muleshoe, Tx., U.S. B1 136
Mulgrave, N.S., Can. D8 87
Mulhacén, mtn., Spain I5 16
Mulhouse, Fr. D10 16
Mull, Island of, i., Scot., U.K. B3 12
Mullan, Id., U.S. B3 105
Mullan Pass, Mt., U.S. D4 119
Mullens, W.V., U.S. D3 141
Muller, Pegunungan, mts., Indon. C4 36
Mullet Key, i., Fl., U.S. p10 102
Mullett Lake, l., Mi., U.S. C6 115
Mullewa, Austl. F2 60
Mullica, stm., N.J., U.S. D3 123
Mullins, S.C., U.S. C9 133
Mulongo, D.R.C. E5 54
Multān, Pak. D10 42
Multnomah, co., Or., U.S. B4 130
Mulvane, Ks., U.S. E6 109
Mumbai (Bombay), India F2 40
Mumbwa, Zam. A4 56
Mummy Range, mts., Co., U.S. A5 99
Mun, stm., Thai. C4 34
Muna, Mex. C7 78
Muna, Pulau, i., Indon. D6 36
München (Munich), Ger. F12 12
Muncie, In., U.S. D7 107
Muncy, Pa., U.S. D8 131
Munday, Tx., U.S. C3 136
Mundelein, Il., U.S. A5 106
Münden, Ger. E11 12
Mundrabilla, Austl. G4 60
Munford, Al., U.S. B4 94
Munford, Tn., U.S. B2 135
Munfordville, Ky., U.S. C4 110
Mungbere, D.R.C. C5 54
Munger, India D5 40
Munhall, Pa., U.S. k14 131
Munhango, Ang. F3 54
Munich see München, Ger. F12 12
Munising, Mi., U.S. B4 115
Münster, Ger. E10 12
Munster, hist. reg., Ire. D2 12
Munster, In., U.S. A2 107
Munsungan Lake, l., Me., U.S. B3 112
Muntok, Indon. D3 36
Munuscong Lake, l., Mi., U.S. B6 115
Muojärvi, l., Fin. D13 10
Muonio, Fin. C10 10
Muqdisho, Som. J14 48
Mur (Mura), stm., Eur. F3 20
Mura (Mur), stm., Eur. F4 20
Muradiye, Tur. C10 44
Murakami, Japan C3 31
Murana, Indon. D8 36
Muraši, Russia C8 22
Murat, stm., Tur. C9 44
Murchison, stm., Austl. F1 60
Murchison Falls see Kabalega Falls, wtfl., Ug. C6 54
Murcia, Spain I6 16
Murderkill, stm., De., U.S. D4 101
Murdo, S.D., U.S. D5 134
Mureș, stm., Eur. G7 20
Muret, Fr. F7 16
Murewa, Zimb. B5 56
Murfreesboro, Ar., U.S. C2 97
Murfreesboro, N.C., U.S. A5 126
Murfreesboro, Tn., U.S. B5 135
Murgab (Morghāb), stm., Asia C8 42
Murgab, Taj. F9 26
Muriaé, Braz. F3 74
Müritz, l., Ger. D13 12
Murmansk, Russia C5 26
Murom, Russia D6 26
Muroran, Japan C16 28
Muroto, Japan D2 31
Murphy, Mo., U.S. g13 118
Murphy, N.C., U.S. f8 126
Murphy Island, i., S.C., U.S. E9 133
Murphysboro, Il., U.S. F4 106
Murray, stm., Austl. H3 62
Murray, co., Ga., U.S. B2 103
Murray, Ia., U.S. C4 108
Murray, Ky., U.S. f9 110
Murray, co., Mn., U.S. F3 116
Murray, co., Ok., U.S. C4 129
Murray, Ut., U.S. C4 137
Murray, Lake, l., Pap. N. Gui. H11 32
Murray, Lake, res., Ok., U.S. C4 129
Murray, Lake, res., S.C., U.S. C5 133
Murray Bridge, Austl. H2 62
Murray Fracture Zone E24 64
Murray Head, c., P.E., Can. C7 87
Murraysburg, S. Afr. E3 56
Murrayville, Ga., U.S. B3 103
Murree, Pak. C2 40
Murrells Inlet, S.C., U.S. D9 133
Murrells Inlet, b., S.C., U.S. D10 133
Murrumbidgee, stm., Austl. G4 62
Murrupula, Moz. B6 56
Mursala, Pulau, i., Indon. C1 36
Murua Island, i., Pap. N. Gui. H13 32
Murud, Gunong, mtn., Malay. C5 36
Murukta, Russia C12 26
Murwāra, India E4 40
Murwillumbah, Austl. F5 62
Murzuq, Libya E7 48
Murzūq, Idhān, des., Libya B7 50
Muş, Tur. C9 44
Musa Ālī Terara see Moussa 'Ali, mtn., Afr. H4 38
Musā'id, Libya E9 14
Musala, mtn., Blg. C9 18
Musan-ŭp, N. Kor. B1 31
Musay'īd, Qatar F6 42
Muscat see Masqaţ, Oman F7 38
Muscat and Oman see Oman, ctry., Asia G7 38
Muscatatuck, stm., In., U.S. G5 107
Muscatine, Ia., U.S. C6 108
Muscatine, co., Ia., U.S. C6 108
Muscle Shoals, Al., U.S. A2 94
Musclow, Mount, mtn., B.C., Can. C4 85
Muscoda, Wi., U.S. E3 142
Muscogee, co., Ga., U.S. D2 103
Musconetcong, stm., N.J., U.S. B4 123
Muse, Pa., U.S. F1 131
Musgrave Harbour, N.L., Can. D5 88
Musgravetown, N.L., Can. D5 88
Mushie, D.R.C. D3 54
Mushin, Nig. E5 50
Musi, stm., Indon. D2 36
Musicians Seamounts E22 64
Muskeg Bay, b., Mn., U.S. B3 116
Muskeget Island, i., Ma., U.S. D7 114
Muskego, Wi., U.S. F5 142
Muskego Lake, l., Wi., U.S. n11 142
Muskegon, stm., Mi., U.S. E4 115
Muskegon, Mi., U.S. E4 115
Muskegon, co., Mi., U.S. E4 115
Muskegon Heights, Mi., U.S. E4 115
Muskegon Lake, l., Mi., U.S. E4 115
Muskingum, stm., Oh., U.S. C4 128
Muskingum, co., Oh., U.S. B4 128
Muskogee, Ok., U.S. B6 129
Muskogee, co., Ok., U.S. B6 129
Musoma, Tan. D6 54
Musquacook Lakes, l., Me., U.S. B3 112
Musquodoboit Harbour, N.S., Can. E6 87
Mussau Island, i., Pap. N. Gui. G12 32
Musselshell, stm., Mt., U.S. D9 119
Musselshell, co., Mt., U.S. D8 119
Mussende, Ang. F3 54
Mussuma, Ang. A3 56
Mustafakemalpaşa, Tur. C3 44
Mustahīl, Eth. B8 54
Mustang, Ok., U.S. B4 129
Mustinka, stm., Mn., U.S. E2 116
Muswellbrook, Austl. G5 62
Mut, Tur. D5 44
Mutare, Zimb. B5 56
Mutoraj, Russia C12 26
Mutsamudu, Com. A7 56
Mutshatsha, D.R.C. F4 54
Mutsu, Japan C16 28
Mutsu-wan, b., Japan B4 31
Mutton Mountains, mts., Or., U.S. C5 130
Muxima, Ang. E2 54
Muyinga, Bdi. D6 54
Muyumba, D.R.C. E5 54
Muzaffarābād, Pak. D10 42
Muzaffargarh, Pak. D10 42
Muzaffarnagar, India D3 40
Muzaffarpur, India D5 40
Muži, Russia C8 26
Muzon, Cape, c., Ak., U.S. n23 95
Muztag, mtn., China D5 28
Mvuma, Zimb. B5 56
Mwadui, Tan. D6 54
Mwali, i., Com. A7 56
Mwanza, Tan. D6 54
Mweka, D.R.C. D4 54
Mwene-Ditu, D.R.C. E4 54
Mwenezi, Zimb. C5 56
Mweru, Lake, l., Afr. E5 54
Mwinilunga, Zam. A3 56
Myakka, stm., Fl., U.S. E4 102
Myanaung, Mya. C3 34
Myanmar (Burma), ctry., Asia B3 34
Myaungmya, Mya. C2 34
Myerstown, Pa., U.S. F9 131
Myingyan, Mya. B3 34
Myitkyinā, Mya. A3 34
Myittha, Mya. B3 34
Mykolaïv, Ukr. F11 20
Mymensingh, Bngl. E6 40
Mynaral, Kaz. A10 42
Mýrdalsjökull, ice, Ice. m19 10a
Myrhorod, Ukr. E12 20
Myrtle Beach, S.C., U.S. D10 133
Myrtle Grove, Fl., U.S. u14 102
Myrtle Point, Or., U.S. D2 130
Mysore, India G3 40
Mysore see Karnātaka, state, India G3 40
Mystic, Ct., U.S. D8 100
Mystic Lakes, l., Ma., U.S. g11 114
Mys Vhodnoj, Russia B10 26
Mys Želanija, Russia B8 26
Myszków, Pol. D5 20
My Tho, Viet. D5 34
Mzimba, Mwi. A5 56
Mzuzu, Mwi. A5 56

N

Naalehu, Hi., U.S. D6 104
Naberežnye Čelny, Russia D7 26
Nabeul, Tun. C7 48
Nabire, Indon. G10 32
Nabī Shu'ayb, Jabal an-, mtn., Yemen G4 38
Nabnasset, Ma., U.S. A5 114
Nābulus, W.B. F6 44
Nacala-a-Velha, Moz. A7 56
Naches, stm., Wa., U.S. C5 140
Nachingwea, Tan. F7 54
Náchod, Czech Rep. D4 20
Nachuge, India G6 40
Nacimiento, Lake, res., Ca., U.S. E3 98
Naco, Az., U.S. F6 96
Nacogdoches, co., Tx., U.S. D5 136
Nacogdoches, Tx., U.S. D5 136
Nacozari de García, Mex. A3 78
Nadiād, India E2 40
Nador, Mor. J5 16
Nadvirna, Ukr. E8 20
Nadym, Russia C9 26
Næstved, Den. I4 10
Nafada, Nig. D7 50
Nafī, Sau. Ar. E4 42
Naga, Phil. D8 34
Nāgāland, state, India D6 40
Nagano, Japan D15 28
Nagaoka, Japan D15 28
Nagaon, India D6 40
Nāgappattinam, India G3 40
Nagasaki, Japan E13 28
Nāgaur, India D2 40
Nagda, India E3 40
Nāgercoil, India H3 40
Nago, Japan A9 34
Nagoya, Japan D15 28
Nāgpur, India E3 40
Nagqu, China E6 28
Nags Head, N.C., U.S. B7 126
Nagykanizsa, Hung. F4 20
Naha, Japan A9 34
Nahant, Ma., U.S. g12 114
Nahāvand, Iran E13 44
Nahe, China B12 28
Nahmakanta Lake, l., Me., U.S. C3 112
Nahodka, Russia E15 26
Nahunta, Ga., U.S. E5 103
Nain, N.L., Can. g9 88
Nairobi, Kenya D7 54
Naivasha, Kenya D7 54
Najafābād, Iran D6 42
Najd, hist. reg., Sau. Ar. E4 38
Nájera, Spain F5 16
Najin, N. Kor. C14 28
Nakano-shima, i., Japan E1 31
Nakhichevan see Naxçıvan, Azer. C11 44
Nakhon Pathom, Thai. D4 34
Nakhon Phanom, Thai. C4 34
Nakhon Ratchasima, Thai. D4 34
Nakhon Sawan, Thai. C4 34
Nakhon Si Thammarat, Thai. E3 34
Nakina, On., Can. o18 89
Nakło nad Notecią, Pol. C4 20
Naknek, Ak., U.S. D8 95
Naknek Lake, l., Ak., U.S. D8 95
Nakonde, Zam. E6 54
Nakskov, Den. I4 10
Nakuru, Kenya D7 54
Nakusp, B.C., Can. D9 85
Nal'čik, Russia E6 26
Nalgonda, India F3 40
Nallihan, Tur. B4 44
Nālūt, Libya D7 48
Namak, daryācheh-ye, l., Iran D6 42
Namanga, Kenya D7 54
Namangan, Uzb. E9 26
Namanock Island, i., N.J., U.S. A3 123
Namapa, Moz. A6 56
Namarrói, Moz. B6 56
Namatanai, Pap. N. Gui. E9 58
Nambour, Austl. F5 62
Nam Co, l., China E6 28
Nam Dinh, Viet. B5 34
Namekagon, stm., Wi., U.S. B2 142
Namekagon Lake, l., Wi., U.S. B2 142
Namen see Namur, Bel. E9 12
Nametil, Moz. B6 56
Namhkam, Mya. B3 34
Namib Desert, des., Nmb. B1 56
Namibe, Ang. B1 56
Namibia, ctry., Afr. C2 56
Namīn, Iran C13 44
Namjagbarwa Feng, mtn., China F7 28
Namlea, Indon. D7 36
Nam Ngum Reservoir, res., Laos C4 34
Nampa, Id., U.S. F2 105
Nampula, Moz. B6 56
Namsang, Mya. B3 34
Namsos, Nor. D4 10
Namtu, Mya. B3 34
Namur, Bel. E9 12
Namutoni, Nmb. B2 56
Namwala, Zam. B4 56
Nan, Thai. C4 34
Nanaimo, B.C., Can. E5 85
Nanakuli, Hi., U.S. B3 104
Nanao, Japan D15 28
Nance, co., Ne., U.S. C7 120
Nancha, China A1 31
Nanchang, China F11 28
Nancheng, China D4 30
Nanchong, China E9 28
Nancy, Fr. C10 16
Nanda Devi, mtn., India C3 40
Nānded, India F3 40
Nandurbār, India E2 40
Nandyāl, India F3 40
Nanfeng, China D4 30
Nanga-Eboko, Cam. C2 54
Nanga Parbat, mtn., Pak. C10 42
Nangatayap, Indon. D4 36
Nangong, China B4 30
Nanjing, China E11 28
Nankang, China D3 30
Nanking see Nanjing, China E11 28
Nanle, China B4 30
Nannine, Austl. F2 60
Nanning, China G9 28
Nannup, Austl. G2 60
Nanping, China F11 28
Nansei-shotō (Ryukyu Islands), is., Japan A9 34
Nansemond, stm., Va., U.S. k14 139
Nansen Basin E21 144
Nansen Cordillera E22 144
Nan Shan see Qilian Shan, mts., China D7 28
Nantes, Fr. D6 16
Nanticoke, On., Can. E4 89
Nanticoke, Pa., U.S. D10 131
Nanticoke, stm., U.S. D6 113
Nanton, Ab., Can. D4 84
Nantong, China E12 28
Nantucket, Ma., U.S. D7 114
Nantucket, co., Ma., U.S. D7 114
Nantucket Island, i., Ma., U.S. D7 114
Nantucket Sound, strt., Ma., U.S. C7 114
Nantulo, Moz. A6 56
Nantuxent Point, c., N.J., U.S. E2 123
Nanty Glo, Pa., U.S. F4 131
Nanuet, N.Y., U.S. g12 125
Nanuque, Braz. E3 74
Nanusa, Kepulauan, is., Indon. C7 36
Nanxiong, China F10 28
Nanyang, China E10 28
Nanyuki, Kenya C7 54
Nanzhao, China C3 30
Naoma, W.V., U.S. n13 141
Naomi Peak, mtn., Ut., U.S. B4 137
Napa, Ca., U.S. C2 98
Napa, co., Ca., U.S. C2 98
Napanee, On., Can. C8 89
Napatree Point, c., R.I., U.S. G1 132
Napavine, Wa., U.S. C3 140
Napè, Laos C5 34
Naperville, Il., U.S. B5 106
Napier, N.Z. o14 63c
Napier Mountains, mts., Ant. C10 67
Napierville, Qc., Can. D4 90
Naples see Napoli, Italy D5 18
Naples, Fl., U.S. F5 102
Naples, Tx., U.S. C5 136
Naples, Ut., U.S. C6 137
Napo, stm., S.A. D5 70
Napoleon, N.D., U.S. C6 127
Napoleon, Oh., U.S. A1 128
Napoleonville, La., U.S. E4 111
Napoli (Naples), Italy D5 18
Napoli, Golfo di, b., Italy D5 18
Nappanee, In., U.S. B5 107
Naqadeh, Iran D11 44
Nara, Japan E15 28
Nara, Mali C3 50
Naracoorte, Austl. H3 62
Naramata, B.C., Can. E8 85
Naranja, Fl., U.S. G6 102
Narasapur, India F4 40
Narathiwat, Thai. E4 34
Nārāyanganj, Bngl. E6 40
Narberth, Pa., U.S. p20 131
Narbonne, Fr. F8 16
Nar'jan-Mar, Russia C7 26
Narmada, stm., India E2 40
Nārnaul, India D3 40
Narodnaja, gora, Russia C8 26
Naro-Fominsk, Russia B14 20
Narooma, Austl. H5 62
Narrabri, Austl. G4 62
Narragansett, R.I., U.S. F4 132
Narragansett Bay, b., R.I., U.S. E5 132
Narraguagus, stm., Me., U.S. D5 112
Narrandera, Austl. G4 62
Narrogin, Austl. G2 60
Narromine, Austl. G4 62
Narrows, Va., U.S. C2 139
Narsaq, Grnld. F30 82
Narva, Est. G13 10
Narvik, Nor. B7 10
Naryn, stm., Asia A3 40
Naryn, Kyrg. E9 26
Narynkol, Kaz. C4 28
Nāsåker, Swe. E7 10
Nasca, Peru F5 70
Naselle, Wa., U.S. C2 140
Nash, co., N.C., U.S. A4 126
Nash, Tx., U.S. C5 136
Nashawena Island, i., Ma., U.S. D6 114
Nāshik, India E2 40
Nash Stream, stm., N.H., U.S. A4 122
Nashua, Ia., U.S. B5 108
Nashua, N.H., U.S. E4 122
Nashua, stm., U.S. E3 122
Nashville, Ar., U.S. D2 97
Nashville, Ga., U.S. E3 103
Nashville, Il., U.S. E4 106
Nashville, In., U.S. F5 107
Nashville, Mi., U.S. F5 115
Nashville, N.C., U.S. B5 126
Nashville, Tn., U.S. A5 135
Nashwauk, Mn., U.S. C5 116
Nāşir, Sudan I11 48
Nasīrābād, India D2 40
Nasīrābād, Pak. E9 42
Naskaupi, stm., N.L., Can. g9 88
Nassau, Bah. D9 76
Nassau, co., Fl., U.S. B5 102
Nassau, stm., Fl., U.S. k8 102
Nassau Island, i., Cook Is. F13 58
Nassau Sound, b., Fl., U.S. B5 102
Nasser, Lake, res., Afr. F11 48
Nässjö, Swe. H6 10
Nasukoin Mountain, mtn., Mt., U.S. B2 119
Nata, Bots. C4 56
Natal, Braz. C4 74
Natalbany, La., U.S. D5 111
Natalia, Tx., U.S. E3 136
Natashquan, stm., Can. h9 88
Natchaug, stm., Ct., U.S. B7 100
Natchez, Ms., U.S. D2 117
Natchitoches, La., U.S. C2 111
Natchitoches, co., La., U.S. C2 111
Natick, Ma., U.S. B5 114
National City, Ca., U.S. F5 98
Natitingou, Benin D5 50
Natividade, Braz. F10 70
Natron, Lake, l., Afr. D7 54
Natrona, co., Wy., U.S. D5 143

Name	Map Ref.	Page
Natrona Heights, Pa., U.S.	E2	131
Natuna Besar, i., Indon.	C3	36
Natuna Besar, Kepulauan, is., Indon.	C3	36
Natuna Selatan, Kepulauan, is., Indon.	C3	36
Natural Bridge, Ut., U.S.	F3	137
Natural Bridge, Va., U.S.	C3	139
Natural Bridges National Monument, Ut., U.S.	F6	137
Naturaliste, Cape, c., Austl.	G1	60
Nau, Cap de la, c., Spain	H7	16
Naugatuck, Ct., U.S.	D3	100
Naugatuck, stm., Ct., U.S.	D3	100
Nauru, ctry., Oc.	E10	58
Naushon Island, i., Ma., U.S.	D6	114
Nautilus Park, Ct., U.S.	D7	100
Nautla, Mex.	C5	78
Nauvoo, Il., U.S.	C2	106
Navadwip, India	E5	40
Navahrudak, Bela.	C8	20
Navajo, co., Az., U.S.	B5	96
Navajo Dam, N.M., U.S.	A2	124
Navajo Indian Reservation, U.S.	A4	96
Navajo Mountain, mtn., Ut., U.S.	F5	137
Navajo National Monument, Az., U.S.	A5	96
Navajo Reservoir, res., U.S.	A2	124
Navan, On., Can.	B9	89
Navapolack, Bela.	B10	20
Navarin, mys, c., Russia	C19	26
Navarino, Isla, i., Chile	I3	69
Navarra, hist. reg., Spain	F6	16
Navarre, Oh., U.S.	B4	128
Navarro, co., Tx., U.S.	D4	136
Navasota, Tx., U.S.	D4	136
Navassa Island, i., N.A.	B4	80
Navlja, Russia	C13	20
Navoi, Uzb.	E8	26
Navojoa, Mex.	B3	78
Navsāri, India	E2	40
Nawābshāh, Pak.	E9	42
Nawiliwili Bay, b., Hi., U.S.	B2	104
Naxçıvan, Azer.	C11	44
Naxi, China	D2	30
Náxos, Grc.	F10	18
Náxos, i., Grc.	F10	18
Nayarit, state, Mex.	C4	78
Naylor, Mo., U.S.	E7	118
Nayoro, Japan	C16	28
Nazaré, Braz.	D4	74
Nazaré, Port.	H2	16
Nazareth see Nazerat, Isr.	D3	42
Nazareth, Pa., U.S.	E11	131
Nazas, stm., Mex.	B4	78
Nazas, Mex.	B4	78
Nazca Ridge	K5	66
Naze, Japan	F13	28
Naze, The see Lindesnes, c., Nor.	H2	10
Nazerat, Isr.	D3	42
Nazilli, Tur.	D3	44
Nazko, stm., B.C., Can.	C6	85
Nazran', Russia	A11	44
Nazrēt, Eth.	B7	54
Nazwá, Oman	F7	42
N'dalatando, Ang.	E2	54
Ndélé, C.A.R.	B4	54
Ndendé, Gabon	D2	54
N'Djamena, Chad	D8	50
Ndjolé, Gabon	D2	54
Ndola, Zam.	A4	56
Neagh, Lough, l., N. Ire., U.K.	C3	12
Neah Bay, Wa., U.S.	A1	140
Néa Páfos, Cyp.	E5	44
Neápolis, Grc.	F9	18
Near Islands, is., Ak., U.S.	E2	95
Nebitdag, Turk.	F7	26
Neblina, Pico da, mtn., S.A.	C6	70
Nebo, Mount, mtn., Ut., U.S.	D4	137
Nebraska, state, U.S.	C6	120
Nebraska City, Ne., U.S.	D10	120
Nechako, stm., B.C., Can.	C5	85
Neches, stm., Tx., U.S.	D5	136
Necker Island, i., Hi., U.S.	m15	104
Necochea, Arg.	F6	72
Nederland, Co., U.S.	B5	99
Nederland, Tx., U.S.	E6	136
Nêdong, China	F6	28
Nédroma, Alg.	J6	16
Nedrow, N.Y., U.S.	C4	125
Needham, Ma., U.S.	g11	114
Needle Mountain, mtn., Wy., U.S.	B3	143
Needles, Ca., U.S.	E6	98
Needville, Tx., U.S.	r14	136
Neenah, Wi., U.S.	D5	142
Neepawa, Mb., Can.	D2	86
Neffs, Oh., U.S.	B5	128
Neffsville, Pa., U.S.	F9	131
Neftçala, Azer.	C13	44
Negage, Ang.	E3	54
Negaunee, Mi., U.S.	B3	115
Negēlē, Eth.	B7	54
Negley, Oh., U.S.	B5	128
Negombo, Sri L.	H3	40
Negritos, Peru	D3	70
Negro, stm., Arg.	F4	69
Negro, stm., S.A.	D7	70
Negros, i., Phil.	E8	34
Neguac, N.B., Can.	B4	87
Nehalem, stm., Or., U.S.	A3	130
Nehbandān, Iran	D7	42
Neiges, Piton des, mtn., Reu.	g10	57a
Neijiang, China	D2	30
Neill Point, c., Wa., U.S.	f11	140
Neillsville, Wi., U.S.	D3	142
Nei Monggol Zizhiqu (Inner Mongolia), prov., China	C10	28
Neisse see Nysa, Pol.	D4	20
Neiva, Col.	C4	70
Nejd see Najd, hist. reg., Sau. Ar.	E4	38
Nek'emtē, Eth.	B7	54
Nekoosa, Wi., U.S.	D4	142
Nelidovo, Russia	C5	22
Neligh, Ne., U.S.	B7	120
Nel'kan, Russia	D15	26
Nellis Air Force Base, mil., Nv., U.S.	G6	121
Nellore, India	G4	40
Nel'ma, Russia	E15	26
Nelson, B.C., Can.	E9	85
Nelson, stm., Mb., Can.	A4	86
Nelson, N.Z.	p13	63c
Nelson, co., Ky., U.S.	C4	110
Nelson, co., N.D., U.S.	B7	127
Nelson, Ne., U.S.	D7	120
Nelson, co., Va., U.S.	C4	139
Nelson, Cape, c., Austl.	H3	62
Nelsonville, Oh., U.S.	C3	128
Nelspruit, S. Afr.	D5	56
Néma, Maur.	C3	50
Nemacolin, Pa., U.S.	G2	131
Nemadji, stm., U.S.	B1	142
Nemaha, co., Ks., U.S.	C7	109
Nemaha, co., Ne., U.S.	D10	120
Neman (Nemunas), stm., Eur.	B7	20
Nembe, Nig.	F6	50
Nemunas (Neman), stm., Eur.	B7	20
Nemuro, Japan	C17	28
Nenana, Ak., U.S.	C10	95
Nendo, i., Sol. Is.	F10	58
Neodesha, Ks., U.S.	E8	109
Neoga, Il., U.S.	D5	106
Neola, Ia., U.S.	C2	108
Neola, Ut., U.S.	C5	137
Neopit, Wi., U.S.	D5	142
Neosho, co., Ks., U.S.	E8	109
Neosho, Mo., U.S.	E3	118
Neosho, stm., Ok., U.S.	A6	129
Nepal, ctry., Asia	D4	40
Nepālganj, Nepal	D4	40
Nepaug Reservoir, res., Ct., U.S.	B3	100
Nepean, On., Can.	h12	89
Nepewassi Lake, l., On., Can.	A4	89
Nephi, Ut., U.S.	D4	137
Nepisiguit, stm., N.B., Can.	B3	87
Nepisiguit Bay, b., N.B., Can.	B4	87
Neponset, stm., Ma., U.S.	h11	114
Neptune, N.J., U.S.	C4	123
Neptune Beach, Fl., U.S.	B5	102
Neptune City, N.J., U.S.	C4	123
Nerčinsk, Russia	A11	28
Nerčinskij Zavod, Russia	D13	26
Nerehta, Russia	C7	22
Neriquinha, Ang.	B3	56
Nescopeck, Pa., U.S.	D9	131
Neshanic, stm., N.J., U.S.	C3	123
Neshoba, co., Ms., U.S.	C4	117
Neskaupstadur, Ice.	l22	10a
Nesna, Nor.	C5	10
Nesowadnehunk, l., Me., U.S.	B3	112
Nesquehoning, Pa., U.S.	E10	131
Ness, co., Ks., U.S.	D4	109
Ness, Loch, l., Scot., U.K.	B4	12
Ness City, Ks., U.S.	D4	109
Néstos, stm., Eur.	D10	18
Netanya, Isr.	D2	42
Netcong, N.J., U.S.	B3	123
Netherlands, ctry., Eur.	D9	12
Netherlands Antilles, dep., N.A.	F11	76
Netherlands Guiana see Suriname, ctry., S.A.	C8	70
Nettie, W.V., U.S.	C4	141
Nett Lake, l., Mn., U.S.	B5	116
Nett Lake Indian Reservation, Mn., U.S.	B6	116
Nettleton, Ms., U.S.	A5	117
Neubrandenburg, Ger.	D13	12
Neuchâtel, Switz.	A1	18
Neuchâtel, Lac de, l., Switz.	A1	18
Neufchâtel-en-Bray, Fr.	C7	16
Neumarkt in der Oberpfalz, Ger.	F12	12
Neumünster, Ger.	C12	12
Neuquén, Arg.	E3	69
Neuruppin, Ger.	D13	12
Neuse, stm., N.C., U.S.	B6	126
Neustrelitz, Ger.	D13	12
Neuville, Qc., Can.	C6	90
Nevada, co., Ar., U.S.	D2	97
Nevada, co., Ca., U.S.	C3	98
Nevada, Ia., U.S.	B4	108
Nevada, Mo., U.S.	D3	118
Nevada, state, U.S.	D5	121
Nevada, Sierra, mts., Ca., U.S.	D4	98
Nevada City, Ca., U.S.	C3	98
Nevado, Cerro, mtn., Arg.	F4	72
Nevado, Cerro, mtn., Col.	C5	70
Nevel', Russia	A10	20
Nevel'sk, Russia	E16	26
Never, Russia	D14	26
Nevers, Fr.	D8	16
Neversink, stm., N.Y., U.S.	D6	125
Nevinnomyssk, Russia	B4	42
Nevis, i., St. K./N.	B7	80
Nevis, Ben, mtn., Scot., U.K.	B4	12
Nevjansk, Russia	C11	22
Nevşehir, Tur.	C6	44
New, stm., Az., U.S.	k8	96
New, stm., N.C., U.S.	C5	126
New, stm., U.S.	C3	141
Newala, Tan.	F7	54
New Albany, In., U.S.	H6	107
New Albany, Ms., U.S.	A4	117
New Albany, Oh., U.S.	k11	128
New Amsterdam, Guy.	B8	70
Newark, Ar., U.S.	B4	97
Newark, Ca., U.S.	h8	98
Newark, De., U.S.	B3	101
Newark, Il., U.S.	B5	106
Newark, N.J., U.S.	B4	123
Newark, N.Y., U.S.	B3	125
Newark, Oh., U.S.	B3	128
Newark Bay, b., N.J., U.S.	k8	123
Newark Lake, l., Nv., U.S.	D6	121
New Athens, Il., U.S.	E4	106
New Augusta, Ms., U.S.	D4	117
Newaygo, Mi., U.S.	E5	115
Newaygo, co., Mi., U.S.	E5	115
New Baden, Il., U.S.	E4	106
New Baltimore, Mi., U.S.	F8	115
New Bedford, Ma., U.S.	C6	114
New Bedford, Pa., U.S.	D1	131
Newberg, Or., U.S.	B4	130
New Berlin, Il., U.S.	D4	106
New Berlin, Wi., U.S.	n11	142
New Bern, N.C., U.S.	B5	126
Newbern, Tn., U.S.	A2	135
Newberry, Fl., U.S.	C4	102
Newberry, Mi., U.S.	B5	115
Newberry, S.C., U.S.	C4	133
Newberry, co., S.C., U.S.	C4	133
New Bethlehem, Pa., U.S.	D3	131
New Bloomfield, Pa., U.S.	F7	131
New Boston, Mi., U.S.	p15	115
New Boston, Oh., U.S.	D3	128
New Boston, Tx., U.S.	C5	136
New Braunfels, Tx., U.S.	E3	136
New Bremen, Oh., U.S.	B1	128
New Brighton, Mn., U.S.	m12	116
New Brighton, Pa., U.S.	E1	131
New Britain, i., Pap. N. Gui.	H13	32
New Britain, Ct., U.S.	C4	100
New Brockton, Al., U.S.	D4	94
New Brunswick, prov., Can.	C3	87
New Brunswick, N.J., U.S.	C4	123
New Buffalo, Mi., U.S.	G4	115
Newburg, Wi., U.S.	E5	142
Newburgh, On., Can.	C8	89
Newburgh, In., U.S.	I3	107
Newburgh, N.Y., U.S.	D6	125
Newburgh Heights, Oh., U.S.	h9	128
Newburyport, Ma., U.S.	A6	114
New Caledonia, dep., Oc.	I9	62a
New Caledonia Basin	K19	64
New Canaan, Ct., U.S.	E2	100
New Carlisle, In., U.S.	A4	107
New Carlisle, Oh., U.S.	C1	128
Newcastle, Austl.	G5	62
Newcastle, N.B., Can.	C4	87
Newcastle, On., Can.	D6	89
Newcastle, S. Afr.	D4	56
New Castle, Al., U.S.	B3	94
New Castle, Co., U.S.	B3	99
New Castle, co., De., U.S.	B3	101
New Castle, De., U.S.	B3	101
New Castle, In., U.S.	E7	107
New Castle, Ky., U.S.	B4	110
Newcastle, Ok., U.S.	B4	129
New Castle, Pa., U.S.	D1	131
Newcastle, Wy., U.S.	C8	143
Newcastle upon Tyne, Eng., U.K.	C6	12
Newcastle Waters, Austl.	D5	60
New City, N.Y., U.S.	D6	125
Newcomerstown, Oh., U.S.	B4	128
New Concord, Oh., U.S.	C4	128
New Cumberland, Pa., U.S.	F8	131
New Cumberland, W.V., U.S.	A4	141
Newdegate, Austl.	G2	60
New Delhi, India	D3	40
Newell, Ia., U.S.	B2	108
Newell, S.D., U.S.	C2	134
Newell, W.V., U.S.	A4	141
New Ellenton, S.C., U.S.	E4	133
Newellton, La., U.S.	B4	111
New England, N.D., U.S.	C3	127
Newenham, Cape, c., Ak., U.S.	D7	95
New Fairfield, Ct., U.S.	D2	100
Newfane, N.Y., U.S.	B2	125
Newfields, N.H., U.S.	D5	122
New Florence, Mo., U.S.	C6	118
Newfound Gap, U.S.	f9	126
Newfound Lake, l., N.H., U.S.	C3	122
Newfoundland, i., N.L., Can.	D3	88
Newfoundland and Labrador, prov., Can.	D4	88
Newfoundland Basin	D9	66
New Franklin, Mo., U.S.	B5	118
New Freedom, Pa., U.S.	G8	131
New Georgia Sound, strt., Sol. Is.	B6	62
New Germany, N.S., Can.	E5	87
New Glarus, Wi., U.S.	F4	142
New Guinea, i.	G11	32
Newhall, Ia., U.S.	C6	108
New Hampshire, state, U.S.	C3	122
New Hampton, Ia., U.S.	A5	108
New Hanover, i., Pap. N. Gui.	G13	32
New Hanover, co., N.C., U.S.	C5	126
New Harbour, N.L., Can.	E5	88
New Harmony, In., U.S.	H2	107
New Hartford, Ct., U.S.	B4	100
New Hartford, Ia., U.S.	B5	108
New Haven, Ct., U.S.	D4	100
New Haven, co., Ct., U.S.	D4	100
New Haven, In., U.S.	B7	107
New Haven, Ky., U.S.	C4	110
New Haven, Mi., U.S.	F8	115
New Haven, Mo., U.S.	C6	118
New Haven, stm., Vt., U.S.	C2	138
New Haven, W.V., U.S.	C3	141
New Haven Harbor, b., Ct., U.S.	E4	100
New Hazelton, B.C., Can.	B4	85
New Hebrides, ctry., Oc.	F10	58
New Hebrides, is., Vanuatu	F10	58
New Hebrides Trench	K19	64
New Holland, Ga., U.S.	B3	103
New Holland, Pa., U.S.	F9	131
New Holstein, Wi., U.S.	E5	142
New Hope, Al., U.S.	A3	94
New Hope, Ky., U.S.	C4	110
New Hope, Mn., U.S.	m12	116
New Hope, Pa., U.S.	F12	131
New Hudson, Mi., U.S.	o14	115
New Iberia, La., U.S.	D4	111
Newington, Ct., U.S.	C5	100
New Inlet, b., N.C., U.S.	D5	126
New Ireland, i., Pap. N. Gui.	G13	32
New Jersey, state, U.S.	C4	123
New Johnsonville, Tn., U.S.	A4	135
New Kensington, Pa., U.S.	E2	131
New Kent, co., Va., U.S.	C5	139
Newkirk, Ok., U.S.	A4	129
New Kowloon see Xinjiulong, China	E3	30
New Laguna, N.M., U.S.	B2	124
New Lake, l., N.C., U.S.	B6	126
New Lenox, Il., U.S.	B6	106
New Lexington, Oh., U.S.	C3	128
New Lisbon, Wi., U.S.	E3	142
New Liskeard, On., Can.	p20	89
Newllano, La., U.S.	C2	111
New London, Ct., U.S.	D7	100
New London, co., Ct., U.S.	C7	100
New London, Ia., U.S.	D6	108
New London, Mn., U.S.	E4	116
New London, Mo., U.S.	B6	118
New London, N.H., U.S.	D3	122
New London, Oh., U.S.	A3	128
New London, Wi., U.S.	D5	142
New London Submarine Base, mil., Ct., U.S.	D7	100
New Madison, Oh., U.S.	C1	128
New Madrid, Mo., U.S.	E8	118
New Madrid, co., Mo., U.S.	E8	118
Newman, Austl.	E2	60
Newman, Ca., U.S.	D3	98
Newman, Il., U.S.	D6	106
New Manchester, W.V., U.S.	e8	141
Newman Grove, Ne., U.S.	C8	120
Newman Lake, l., Wa., U.S.	B8	140
Newmanstown, Pa., U.S.	F9	131
Newmarket, On., Can.	C5	89
New Market, Al., U.S.	A3	94
New Market, In., U.S.	E4	107
Newmarket, N.H., U.S.	D5	122
New Market, Tn., U.S.	C10	135
New Market, Va., U.S.	B4	139
New Martinsville, W.V., U.S.	B4	141
New Matamoras, Oh., U.S.	C4	128
New Mexico, state, U.S.	C3	124
New Miami, Oh., U.S.	C1	128
New Milford, Ct., U.S.	C2	100
New Milford, N.J., U.S.	h8	123
New Milford, Pa., U.S.	C10	131
Newnan, Ga., U.S.	C2	103
Newnans Lake, l., Fl., U.S.	C4	102
New Norfolk, Austl.	I4	62
New Orleans, La., U.S.	E5	111
New Orleans Naval Air Station, mil., La., U.S.	k11	111
New Oxford, Pa., U.S.	G7	131
New Palestine, In., U.S.	E6	107
New Paltz, N.Y., U.S.	D6	125
New Paris, In., U.S.	B6	107
New Paris, Oh., U.S.	C1	128
New Philadelphia, Oh., U.S.	B4	128
New Philadelphia, Pa., U.S.	E9	131
New Plymouth, N.Z.	o13	63c
New Plymouth, Id., U.S.	F2	105
New Point Comfort, c., Va., U.S.	C6	139
Newport, Wales, U.K.	E5	12
Newport, Ar., U.S.	B4	97
Newport, De., U.S.	B3	101
Newport, In., U.S.	E3	107
Newport, Ky., U.S.	A5	110
Newport, Me., U.S.	D3	112
Newport, Mi., U.S.	G7	115
Newport, Mn., U.S.	n13	116
Newport, N.C., U.S.	C6	126
Newport, N.H., U.S.	D2	122
Newport, Oh., U.S.	C4	128
Newport, Or., U.S.	C2	130
Newport, Pa., U.S.	F7	131
Newport, R.I., U.S.	F5	132
Newport, co., R.I., U.S.	E5	132
Newport, Tn., U.S.	D10	135
Newport, Vt., U.S.	B4	138
Newport, Wa., U.S.	A8	140
Newport Beach, Ca., U.S.	n13	98
Newport News, Va., U.S.	D6	139
New Port Richey, Fl., U.S.	D4	102
New Prague, Mn., U.S.	F5	116
New Preston, Ct., U.S.	C2	100
New Providence, i., Bah.	C9	76
New Providence, N.J., U.S.	B4	123
Newquay, Eng., U.K.	E4	12
New Richland, Mn., U.S.	G5	116
New Richmond, Qc., Can.	A4	87
New Richmond, Oh., U.S.	D1	128
New Richmond, Wi., U.S.	C1	142
New River Inlet, b., N.C., U.S.	C5	126
New Roads, La., U.S.	D4	111
New Rochelle, N.Y., U.S.	E7	125
New Rockford, N.D., U.S.	B6	127
Newry, N. Ire., U.K.	C3	12
New Salem, N.D., U.S.	C4	127
New Sarpy, La., U.S.	k11	111
New Schwabenland, reg., Ant.	D5	67
New Sharon, Ia., U.S.	C5	108
New Siberian Islands see Novosibirskie ostrova, is., Russia	B16	26
New Site, Al., U.S.	B4	94
New Smyrna Beach, Fl., U.S.	C6	102
New South Wales, state, Austl.	G4	62
New Straitsville, Oh., U.S.	C3	128
New Tazewell, Tn., U.S.	C10	135
Newton, Al., U.S.	D4	94
Newton, co., Ar., U.S.	B2	97
Newton, Ga., U.S.	E2	103
Newton, co., Ga., U.S.	C3	103
Newton, Ia., U.S.	C4	108
Newton, Il., U.S.	E5	106
Newton, co., In., U.S.	B3	107
Newton, Ks., U.S.	D6	109
Newton, Ma., U.S.	B5	114
Newton, co., Mo., U.S.	E3	118
Newton, Ms., U.S.	C4	117
Newton, co., Ms., U.S.	C4	117
Newton, N.C., U.S.	B1	126
Newton, N.J., U.S.	A3	123
Newton, Tx., U.S.	D6	136
Newton, co., Tx., U.S.	D6	136
Newton, Ut., U.S.	B4	137
Newton Falls, Oh., U.S.	A5	128
Newton Lake, res., Il., U.S.	E5	106
Newtown, Ct., U.S.	D2	100
New Town, N.D., U.S.	B3	127
Newtown, Oh., U.S.	C1	128
Newtown Square, Pa., U.S.	p20	131
New Ulm, Mn., U.S.	F4	116
New Vienna, Oh., U.S.	C2	128
Newville, Pa., U.S.	F7	131
New Washington, In., U.S.	G6	107
New Washington, Oh., U.S.	B3	128
New Waterford, Oh., U.S.	B5	128
New Westminster, B.C., Can.	E6	85
New Whiteland, In., U.S.	E5	107
New Wilmington, Pa., U.S.	D1	131
New Windsor, Il., U.S.	B3	106
New Windsor, Md., U.S.	A3	113
New Windsor, N.Y., U.S.	D6	125
New World Island, i., N.L., Can.	D4	88
New York, N.Y., U.S.	E7	125
New York, co., N.Y., U.S.	k13	125
New York, state, U.S.	C6	125
New York Mills, Mn., U.S.	D3	116
New Zealand, ctry., Oc.	H10	58
Neyrīz, Iran	E6	42
Neyshābūr, Iran	C7	42
Nezahualcóyotl, Presa, res., Mex.	D6	78
Nez Perce, co., Id., U.S.	C2	105
Nez Perce Indian Reservation, Id., U.S.	C2	105
Ngabé, Congo	D3	54
Ngangala, Sudan	C6	54
Ngangla Ringco, l., China	E4	28
Ngaoundéré, Cam.	B2	54
Ngeaur, i., Palau	E9	32
Ngidinga, D.R.C.	E3	54
Ngoring Hu, l., China	E7	28
Ngouri, Chad	D8	50
Nguigmi, Niger	D7	50
Nguru, Nig.	D7	50
Nha Trang, Viet.	D5	34
Nhill, Austl.	H3	62
Nhoma, stm., Afr.	B2	56
Niafounké, Mali	C4	50
Niagara, co., N.Y., U.S.	B2	125

Name — Map Ref. — Page

Niagara, Wi., U.S. **C6** 142
Niagara Falls, On., Can. **D5** 89
Niagara Falls, N.Y., U.S. **B1** 125
Niagara-on-the-Lake, On., Can. **D5** 89
Niah, Malay. **C4** 36
Niakaramandougou, C. Iv. **E3** 50
Niamey, Niger **D5** 50
Niangara, D.R.C. **C5** 54
Niangua, stm., Mo., U.S. **D5** 118
Nia-Nia, D.R.C. **C5** 54
Niantic, Ct., U.S. **D7** 100
Nias, Pulau, i., Indon. **C1** 36
Niatupo, Pan. **D4** 80
Nibley, Ut., U.S. **B4** 137
Nicaragua, ctry., N.A. **F7** 76
Nicaragua, Lago de, l., Nic. **C2** 80
Nicatous Lake, l., Me., U.S. **C4** 112
Nice, Fr. **F10** 16
Niceville, Fl., U.S. **u15** 102
Nichinan, Japan **E14** 28
Nicholas, co., Ky., U.S. **B6** 110
Nicholas, co., W.V., U.S. **C4** 141
Nicholas Channel, strt., N.A. **A3** 80
Nicholasville, Ky., U.S. **C5** 110
Nicholls, Ga., U.S. **E4** 103
Nichols Hills, Ok., U.S. **B4** 129
Nicholson, Ms., U.S. **E4** 117
Nickajack Lake, res., Tn., U.S. **D8** 135
Nickel Centre, On., Can. **p19** 89
Nickerson, Ks., U.S. **D5** 109
Nicobar Islands, is., India **H6** 40
Nicolet, Qc., Can. **C5** 90
Nicolet, stm., Qc., Can. **C5** 90
Nicolet, Lake, l., Mi., U.S. **B6** 115
Nicollet, co., Mn., U.S. **F4** 116
Nicollet, Mn., U.S. **F4** 116
Nicoma Park, Ok., U.S. **B4** 129
Nicosia, Cyp. **E5** 44
Nicoya, Golfo de, b., C.R. **D2** 80
Nicoya, Península de, pen., C.R. **D2** 80
Nidzica, Pol. **C6** 20
Niellé, C. Iv. **D3** 50
Nienburg, Ger. **D11** 12
Nieuw Amsterdam, Sur. **B8** 70
Nieuw Nickerie, Sur. **B8** 70
Nigadoo, N.B., Can. **B4** 87
Niğde, Tur. **D6** 44
Niger, stm., Afr. **E6** 50
Niger, ctry., Afr. **C6** 50
Nigeria, ctry., Afr. **E6** 50
Nihoa, i., Hi., U.S. **m15** 104
Niigata, Japan **D15** 28
Niihama, Japan **D2** 31
Niihau, i., Hi., U.S. **B1** 104
Nijmegen, Neth. **E10** 12
Nikel', Russia **B14** 10
Nikishka, Ak., U.S. **g16** 95
Nikkō, Japan **D15** 28
Nikol'sk, Russia **D6** 26
Nikol'sk, Russia **D8** 22
Nikopol', Ukr. **F13** 20
Niksar, Tur. **B7** 44
Nīkshahr, Iran **E8** 42
Nikšić, Serb. **C7** 18
Nila, Pulau, i., Indon. **E7** 36
Niland, Ca., U.S. **F6** 98
Nile, stm., Afr. **E11** 48
Niles, Il., U.S. **h9** 106
Niles, Mi., U.S. **G4** 115
Niles, Oh., U.S. **A5** 128
Nimach, India **E2** 40
Nimba, Mount, mtn., Afr. **E3** 50
Nîmes, Fr. **F9** 16
Nimrod Lake, res., Ar., U.S. **C2** 97
Nimule, Sudan **J11** 48
Nīnawá, hist., Iraq **C4** 42
Ninda, Ang. **A3** 56
Nine Degree Channel, strt., India **H2** 40
Nine Mile Creek, stm., Ut., U.S. **D5** 137
Ninemile Point, c., Mi., U.S. **C6** 115
Ninetyeast Ridge **J11** 64
Ninety Mile Beach, Austl. **H4** 62
Ninety Six, S.C., U.S. **C3** 133
Nineveh see Nīnawá, hist., Iraq **C4** 42
Ning'an, China **B1** 31
Ningbo, China **F12** 28
Ningcheng, China **C11** 28
Ningde, China **D4** 30
Ningdu, China **F11** 28
Ninghai, China **D5** 30
Ninghua, China **D4** 30
Ningi, Nig. **D6** 50
Ningming, China **E2** 30
Ningnan, China **A4** 34
Ningshan, China **C2** 30
Ningsia Hui Autonomous Region see Ningxia Huiza Zizhiqu, prov., China **D9** 28
Ningxia Huiza Zizhiqu, prov., China **D9** 28
Ningxiang, China **D3** 30
Ninh Binh, Viet. **B5** 34
Ninigo Group, is., Pap. N. Gui. **G11** 32
Ninigret Pond, l., R.I., U.S. **G2** 132
Ninilchik, Ak., U.S. **C9** 95
Ninnescah, stm., Ks., U.S. **E6** 109
Ninohe, Japan **B4** 31
Niobrara, co., Wy., U.S. **C8** 143
Niobrara, stm., U.S. **B7** 120
Nioki, D.R.C. **D3** 54
Niono, Mali **D3** 50
Nioro du Sahel, Mali **C3** 50
Niort, Fr. **D6** 16
Niota, Tn., U.S. **D9** 135
Nipigon, Lake, l., On., Can. **o17** 89
Nipissing, Lake, l., On., Can. **A5** 89
Nipomo, Ca., U.S. **E3** 98
Nipple Mountain, mtn., Co., U.S. **D2** 99
Niquero, Cuba **A4** 80
Nirmal, India **F3** 40
Niš, Serb. **C8** 18
Niscemi, Italy **F5** 18
Niskayuna, N.Y., U.S. **C7** 125
Nisqually, stm., Wa., U.S. **C3** 140
Nisswa, Mn., U.S. **D4** 116
Nistru (Dniester) (Dnister), stm., Eur. **F10** 20
Niterói, Braz. **F3** 74
Nitra, Slvk. **E5** 20
Nitro, W.V., U.S. **C3** 141
Niue, dep., Oc. **F13** 58
Niuke, China **C4** 40
Niulakita, i., Tuvalu **E11** 58
Niverville, Mb., Can. **E3** 86
Niwot, Co., U.S. **A5** 99
Nixa, Mo., U.S. **D4** 118
Nixon, Nv., U.S. **D2** 121
Nixon, Tx., U.S. **E4** 136
Nizāmābād, India **F3** 40
Nizhyn, Ukr. **D11** 20
Nizip, Tur. **D7** 44
Nižneangarsk, Russia **D12** 26
Nižnee Kujto, ozero, l., Russia **D14** 10
Nižnekamsk, Russia **C9** 22
Nižneudinsk, Russia **D11** 26
Nižnevartovsk, Russia **C9** 26
Nižnij Novgorod (Gor'kij), Russia **D6** 26
Nižnij Tagil, Russia **D8** 26
Nižnjaja Peša, Russia **A8** 22
Nižnjaja Tunguska, stm., Russia **C11** 26
Njandoma, Russia **C6** 26
Njazidja, i., Com. **A7** 56
Njinjo, Tan. **E7** 54
Njombe, Tan. **E6** 54
Njuhča, Russia **B8** 22
Njurba, Russia **C13** 26
Njuvčim, Russia **B9** 22
Nkambe, Cam. **B2** 54
Nkawkaw, Ghana **E4** 50
Nkhata Bay, Mwi. **A5** 56
Nkhotakota, Mwi. **A5** 56
Nkongsamba, Cam. **C1** 54
Noākhāli, Bngl. **E6** 40
Noank, Ct., U.S. **D8** 100
Noatak, Ak., U.S. **B7** 95
Noatak, stm., Ak., U.S. **B7** 95
Nobel, On., Can. **B4** 89
Nobeoka, Japan **D2** 31
Noble, co., In., U.S. **B7** 107
Noble, co., Oh., U.S. **C4** 128
Noble, Ok., U.S. **B4** 129
Noble, co., Ok., U.S. **A4** 129
Nobles, co., Mn., U.S. **G3** 116
Noblesville, In., U.S. **D6** 107
Nocatee, Fl., U.S. **E5** 102
Nocona, Tx., U.S. **C4** 136
Nodaway, co., Mo., U.S. **A3** 118
Nodaway, stm., U.S. **A2** 118
Noel, Mo., U.S. **E3** 118
Nogales, Mex. **A2** 78
Nogales, Az., U.S. **F5** 96
Nogent-le-Rotrou, Fr. **C7** 16
Noginsk, Russia **C6** 22
Nohar, India **D2** 40
Noirmoutier, Île de, i., Fr. **D5** 16
Nokaneng, Bots. **B3** 56
Nokia, Fin. **F10** 10
Nokomis, Fl., U.S. **E4** 102
Nokomis, Il., U.S. **D4** 106
Nokomis, Lake, res., Wi., U.S. **C4** 142
Nokuku, Vanuatu **j9** 62a
Nola, C.A.R. **C3** 54
Nolan, co., Tx., U.S. **C2** 136
Nolichucky, stm., Tn., U.S. **C10** 135
Nolin, stm., Ky., U.S. **C3** 110
Nolin Lake, res., Ky., U.S. **C3** 110
Nolinsk, Russia **C9** 22
Nomans Land, i., Ma., U.S. **D6** 114
Nome, Ak., U.S. **C6** 95
Nominingue, Qc., Can. **C2** 90
Nonesuch, stm., Me., U.S. **g7** 112
Nong'an, China **C13** 28
Nong Khai, Thai. **C4** 34
Nonquit Pond, l., R.I., U.S. **E6** 132
Nooksack, North Fork, stm., Wa., U.S. **A4** 140
Nooksack, South Fork, stm., Wa., U.S. **A3** 140
Noonkanbah, Austl. **D3** 60
Noorvik, Ak., U.S. **B7** 95
Nootka Sound, strt., B.C., Can. **E4** 85
No Point, Point, c., Md., U.S. **D5** 113
Noquebay, Lake, l., Wi., U.S. **C6** 142
Nóqui, Ang. **E2** 54
Noranda (part of Rouyn [-Noranda]), Qc., Can. **k11** 90
Nora Springs, Ia., U.S. **A5** 108
Norborne, Mo., U.S. **B4** 118
Norco, La., U.S. **E5** 111
Norcross, Ga., U.S. **C2** 103
Nordaustlandet, i., Nor. **A4** 26
Norden, Ger. **D10** 12
Nordenham, Ger. **D11** 12
Nordenšel'da, arhipelag, is., Russia **B11** 26
Nordfjordeid, Nor. **F2** 10
Nordhausen, Ger. **E12** 12
Nordkapp, c., Nor. **A11** 10
Nord-Ostsee-Kanal, Ger. **C11** 12
Nordre Strømfjord, b., Grnld. **E29** 82
Nordvik, Russia **B13** 26
Norfolk, Ct., U.S. **B3** 100
Norfolk, co., Ma., U.S. **B5** 114
Norfolk, Ne., U.S. **B8** 120
Norfolk, N.Y., U.S. **f9** 125
Norfolk, Va., U.S. **D6** 139
Norfolk Island, dep., Oc. **G10** 58
Norfolk Naval Base, mil., Va., U.S. **k15** 139
Norfolk Naval Shipyard, mil., Va., U.S. **k15** 139
Norfolk Ridge **K19** 64
Norfork Dam, Ar., U.S. **A3** 97
Norfork Lake, res., U.S. **A3** 97
Noril'sk, Russia **C10** 26
Norland, Fl., U.S. **s13** 102
Norlina, N.C., U.S. **A4** 126
Normal, Il., U.S. **C5** 106
Norman, co., Mn., U.S. **C2** 116
Norman, Ok., U.S. **B4** 129
Norman, Lake, res., N.C., U.S. **B2** 126
Normandie, hist. reg., Fr. **C6** 16
Normandie, Collines de, Fr. **C6** 16
Normandy see Normandie, hist. reg., Fr. **C6** 16
Normandy, Mo., U.S. **f13** 118
Normandy, Hills of see Normandie, Collines de, Fr. **C6** 16
Norman Park, Ga., U.S. **E3** 103
Normanton, Austl. **D3** 62
Norphlet, Ar., U.S. **D3** 97
Ñorquinco, Arg. **F2** 69
Norra Kvarken (Merenkurkku), strt., Eur. **E9** 10
Norrbotten, hist. reg., Swe. **C10** 10
Nørresundby, Den. **H3** 10
Norridge, Il., U.S. **k9** 106
Norridgewock, Me., U.S. **D3** 112
Norris, S.C., U.S. **B2** 133
Norris, Tn., U.S. **C9** 135
Norris Arm, N.L., Can. **D4** 88
Norris City, Il., U.S. **F5** 106
Norris Dam, Tn., U.S. **C9** 135
Norris Lake, res., Tn., U.S. **C10** 135
Norris Point, N.L., Can. **D3** 88
Norristown, Pa., U.S. **F11** 131
Norrköping, Swe. **G7** 10
Norrtälje, Swe. **G8** 10
Norseman, Austl. **G3** 60
Norsjö, Swe. **D8** 10
Norsk, Russia **D15** 26
North, stm., Al., U.S. **B2** 94
North, stm., Ia., U.S. **f8** 108
North, stm., Ma., U.S. **h12** 114
North, S.C., U.S. **D5** 133
North, stm., W.V., U.S. **B6** 141
North, Cape, c., N.S., Can. **B9** 87
North Adams, Ma., U.S. **A1** 114
North Albany, Or., U.S. **k11** 130
Northam, Austl. **G2** 60
North America, cont. **C5** 4
North American Basin **E7** 66
North Amherst, Ma., U.S. **B2** 114
Northampton, Austl. **F1** 60
Northampton, Eng., U.K. **D6** 12
Northampton, Ma., U.S. **B2** 114
Northampton, co., N.C., U.S. **A5** 126
Northampton, Pa., U.S. **E11** 131
Northampton, co., Pa., U.S. **E11** 131
Northampton, co., Va., U.S. **C7** 139
North Andaman, i., India **G6** 40
North Andover, Ma., U.S. **A5** 114
North Anna, stm., Va., U.S. **B5** 139
North Anson, Me., U.S. **D3** 112
North Apollo, Pa., U.S. **E2** 131
North Arapaho Peak, mtn., Co., U.S. **A5** 99
North Arlington, N.J., U.S. **h8** 123
North Atlanta, Ga., U.S. **h8** 103
North Attleboro, Ma., U.S. **C5** 114
North Augusta, S.C., U.S. **D4** 133
North Aurora, Il., U.S. **k8** 106
North Australian Basin **J14** 64
North Baltimore, Oh., U.S. **A2** 128
North Bay, On., Can. **A5** 89
North Beach, Md., U.S. **C4** 113
North Belmont, N.C., U.S. **B1** 126
North Bend, Ne., U.S. **C9** 120
North Bend, Or., U.S. **D2** 130
North Bend, Wa., U.S. **B4** 140
North Bennington, Vt., U.S. **F2** 138
North Bergen, N.J., U.S. **h8** 123
North Berwick, Me., U.S. **E2** 112
North Billerica, Ma., U.S. **A5** 114
Northborough, Ma., U.S. **B4** 114
North Branch, Mi., U.S. **E7** 115
North Branch, Mn., U.S. **E6** 116
North Branch, N.H., U.S. **D3** 122
North Branch, N.J., U.S. **B3** 123
North Branford, Ct., U.S. **D4** 100
Northbridge, Ma., U.S. **B4** 114
Northbrook, Il., U.S. **h9** 106
North Brookfield, Ma., U.S. **B3** 114
North Brunswick, N.J., U.S. **C4** 123
North Caicos, i., T./C. Is. **A5** 80
North Caldwell, N.J., U.S. **B4** 123
North Canadian, stm., Ok., U.S. **A5** 129
North Canton, Ga., U.S. **B2** 103
North Canton, Oh., U.S. **B4** 128
North Cape, c., P.E., Can. **B6** 87
North Cape see Nordkapp, c., Nor. **A11** 10
North Cape, c., N.Z. **n13** 63c
North Cape May, N.J., U.S. **F3** 123
North Carolina, state, U.S. **B3** 126
North Cascades National Park, Wa., U.S. **A4** 140
North Channel, strt., On., Can. **A2** 89
North Channel, strt., U.K. **C4** 12
North Charleston, S.C., U.S. **F8** 133
North Chicago, Il., U.S. **A6** 106
North Clarendon, Vt., U.S. **D3** 138
Northcliffe, Austl. **G2** 60
North College Hill, Oh., U.S. **o12** 128
North Conway, N.H., U.S. **B4** 122
North Corbin, Ky., U.S. **D5** 110
North Crossett, Ar., U.S. **D4** 97
North Cyprus, ctry., Asia **E5** 44
North Dakota, state, U.S. **B5** 127
North Dartmouth, Ma., U.S. **C6** 114
North Eagle Butte, S.D., U.S. **B4** 134
Northeast, stm., Md., U.S. **A6** 113
North East, Md., U.S. **A6** 113
North East, Pa., U.S. **B2** 131
Northeast Cape, c., Ak., U.S. **C6** 95
Northeast Cape Fear, stm., N.C., U.S. **C5** 126
Northeast Harbor, Me., U.S. **D4** 112
North Easton, Ma., U.S. **B5** 114
Northeast Pond, l., N.H., U.S. **D5** 122
North Edisto, stm., S.C., U.S. **k11** 133
North English, Ia., U.S. **C5** 108
North English, stm., Ia., U.S. **C5** 108
North Enid, Ok., U.S. **A4** 129
Northern Cheyenne Indian Reservation, Mt., U.S. **E10** 119
Northern Cook Islands, is., Cook Is. **F13** 58
Northern Donets, stm., Eur. **E15** 20
Northern Dvina see Severnaja Dvina, stm., Russia **C6** 26
Northern Indian Lake, l., Mb., Can. **A3** 86
Northern Ireland, state, N. Ire., U.K. **C3** 12
Northern Mariana Islands, dep., Oc. **C9** 58
Northern Sporades see Vórioi Sporádhes, is., Grc. **E10** 18
Northern Territory, state, Austl. **D5** 60
North Falmouth, Ma., U.S. **C6** 114
Northfield, Mn., U.S. **F5** 116
Northfield, N.H., U.S. **D3** 122
Northfield, N.J., U.S. **E3** 123
Northfield, Oh., U.S. **h9** 128
Northfield, Vt., U.S. **C3** 138
Northfield Falls, Vt., U.S. **C3** 138
North Fiji Basin **J20** 64
North Flinders Range, mts., Austl. **G2** 62
North Fond du Lac, Wi., U.S. **E5** 142
Northford, Ct., U.S. **D4** 100
North Fork Reservoir, res., Or., U.S. **B4** 130
North Fort Myers, Fl., U.S. **F5** 102
North Fox Island, i., Mi., U.S. **C5** 115
Northglenn, Co., U.S. **B6** 99
North Gower, On., Can. **B9** 89
North Grafton, Ma., U.S. **B4** 114
North Grosvenordale, Ct., U.S. **B8** 100
North Gulfport, Ms., U.S. **E4** 117
North Haledon, N.J., U.S. **B4** 123
North Hampton, N.H., U.S. **E5** 122
North Hartland Reservoir, res., Vt., U.S. **D4** 138
North Hatley, Qc., Can. **D6** 90
North Haven, Ct., U.S. **D4** 100
North Head, N.B., Can. **E3** 87
North Hero Island, i., Vt., U.S. **B2** 138
North Horn Lake, l., Tn., U.S. **e8** 135
North Industry, Oh., U.S. **B4** 128
North Inlet, b., S.C., U.S. **E9** 133
North Island, i., N.Z. **o14** 63c
North Island, i., S.C., U.S. **E9** 133
North Island Naval Air Station, mil., Ca., U.S. **o15** 98
North Islands, is., La., U.S. **E7** 111
North Judson, In., U.S. **B4** 107
North Kansas City, Mo., U.S. **h10** 118
North Kingstown, R.I., U.S. **E4** 132
North Kingsville, Oh., U.S. **A5** 128
North La Junta, Co., U.S. **C7** 99
Northlake, Il., U.S. **k9** 106
North Lakhimpur, India **D6** 40
North Laramie, stm., Wy., U.S. **D7** 143
North Las Vegas, Nv., U.S. **G6** 121
North La Veta Pass, Co., U.S. **D5** 99
North Lewisburg, Oh., U.S. **B2** 128
North Liberty, Ia., U.S. **C6** 108
North Liberty, In., U.S. **A5** 107
North Lima, Oh., U.S. **B5** 128
North Little Rock, Ar., U.S. **C3** 97
North Logan, Ut., U.S. **B4** 137
North Loon Mountain, mtn., Id., U.S. **D3** 105
North Magnetic Pole **D33** 144
North Mamm Peak, mtn., Co., U.S. **B3** 99
North Manchester, In., U.S. **C6** 107
North Manitou Island, i., Mi., U.S. **C4** 115
North Mankato, Mn., U.S. **F4** 116
North Miami, Fl., U.S. **G6** 102
North Miami Beach, Fl., U.S. **s13** 102
North Middletown, Ky., U.S. **B5** 110
North Moose Lake, l., Mb., Can. **B1** 86
North Mountain, mtn., Pa., U.S. **D9** 131
North Muskegon, Mi., U.S. **E4** 115
North Myrtle Beach, S.C., U.S. **D10** 133
North Naples, Fl., U.S. **F5** 102
North New River Canal, Fl., U.S. **F6** 102
North Ogden, Ut., U.S. **B4** 137
North Olmsted, Oh., U.S. **h9** 128
North Ossetia see Severnaja Osetija, state, Russia **E6** 26
North Palisade, mtn., Ca., U.S. **D4** 98
North Park, val., Co., U.S. **A4** 99
North Park, Il., U.S. **A4** 106
North Pass, strt., La., U.S. **E7** 111
North Pembroke, Ma., U.S. **B6** 114
North Plainfield, N.J., U.S. **B4** 123
North Plains, pl., N.M., U.S. **C1** 124
North Plains, Or., U.S. **B4** 130
North Platte, Ne., U.S. **C5** 120
North Platte, stm., U.S. **C7** 92
North Point, c., Md., U.S. **B5** 113
North Point, c., Mi., U.S. **C7** 115
North Pole **E12** 144
Northport, Al., U.S. **B2** 94
North Prairie, Wi., U.S. **F5** 142
North Providence, R.I., U.S. **C4** 132
North Raccoon, stm., Ia., U.S. **C3** 108
North Reading, Ma., U.S. **f11** 114
North Richland Hills, Tx., U.S. **n9** 136
Northridge, Oh., U.S. **C2** 128
North Ridgeville, Oh., U.S. **A3** 128
North Royalton, Oh., U.S. **h9** 128
North Rustico, P.E., Can. **C6** 87
North St. Paul, Mn., U.S. **m13** 116
North Salem, N.H., U.S. **E4** 122
North Salt Lake, Ut., U.S. **C4** 137
North Santee, stm., S.C., U.S. **E9** 133
North Saskatchewan, stm., Can. **H18** 82
North Schell Peak, mtn., Nv., U.S. **D7** 121
North Scituate, Ma., U.S. **h12** 114
North Sea, Eur. **D6** 6
North Shore City, N.Z. **o13** 63c
North Shoshone Peak, mtn., Nv., U.S. **D4** 121
North Siberian Lowland see Severo-Sibirskaja nizmennost', pl., Russia **B11** 26
North Sioux City, S.D., U.S. **E9** 134
North Skunk, stm., Ia., U.S. **C5** 108
North Springfield, Vt., U.S. **E3** 138
North Springfield Reservoir, res., Vt., U.S. **E4** 138
North Star, De., U.S. **A3** 101
North Stradbroke Island, i., Austl. **F5** 62
North Stratford, N.H., U.S. **A3** 122
North Sudbury, Ma., U.S. **g10** 114
North Swanzey, N.H., U.S. **E2** 122
North Syracuse, N.Y., U.S. **B4** 125
North Taranaki Bight, b., N.Z. **o13** 63c
North Tarrytown, N.Y., U.S. **D7** 125
North Terre Haute, In., U.S. **E3** 107
North Thompson, stm., B.C., Can. **D8** 85

Name — Map Ref. — Page

North Tonawanda, N.Y., U.S. B2 125
North Troy, Vt., U.S. B4 138
North Tunica, Ms., U.S. A3 117
North Twin Lake, l., Wi., U.S. B4 142
Northumberland, co., Pa., U.S. D8 131
Northumberland, Pa., U.S. E8 131
Northumberland, co., Va., U.S. C6 139
Northumberland Strait, strt., Can. C6 87
North Umpqua, stm., Or., U.S. D3 130
North Uxbridge, Ma., U.S. B4 114
Northvale, N.J., U.S. g9 123
North Vancouver, B.C., Can. E6 85
North Vassalboro, Me., U.S. D3 112
North Vernon, In., U.S. F6 107
Northville, Mi., U.S. p15 115
North Wales, Pa., U.S. F11 131
North Walpole, N.H., U.S. D2 122
North Warren, Pa., U.S. C3 131
North Webster, In., U.S. B6 107
North West Cape, c., Austl. E1 60
Northwest Miramichi, stm., N.B., Can. B3 87
Northwest Pacific Basin E18 64
Northwest Territories, ter., Can. E15 82
North Wildwood, N.J., U.S. E3 123
North Wilkesboro, N.C., U.S. A1 126
North Windham, Ct., U.S. C7 100
North Windham, Me., U.S. E2 112
Northwood, Ia., U.S. A4 108
Northwood, N.D., U.S. B8 127
North Woodstock, N.H., U.S. B3 122
North York, On., Can. D5 89
North York, Pa., U.S. G8 131
Norton, N.B., Can. D4 87
Norton, Ks., U.S. C4 109
Norton, co., Ks., U.S. C4 109
Norton, Ma., U.S. C5 114
Norton, Oh., U.S. A4 128
Norton, Va., U.S. f9 139
Norton Bay, b., Ak., U.S. C7 95
Norton Pond, l., Vt., U.S. B5 138
Norton Reservoir, res., Ks., U.S. C3 109
Norton Shores, Mi., U.S. E4 115
Norton Sound, strt., Ak., U.S. C6 95
Nortonville, Ks., U.S. C8 109
Nortonville, Ky., U.S. C2 110
Norvegia, Cape, c., Ant. D3 67
Norwalk, Ca., U.S. n12 98
Norwalk, Ct., U.S. E2 100
Norwalk, stm., Ct., U.S. E2 100
Norwalk, Ia., U.S. C4 108
Norwalk, Oh., U.S. A3 128
Norwalk Islands, is., Ct., U.S. E2 100
Norway, ctry., Eur. B9 8
Norway, Me., U.S. D2 112
Norway, Mi., U.S. C3 115
Norway House, Mb., Can. C3 86
Norway Lake, l., Mn., U.S. E3 116
Norwegian Basin C23 144
Norwegian Sea, Eur. I22 10a
Norwich, Eng., U.K. D7 12
Norwich, Ct., U.S. C7 100
Norwich, N.Y., U.S. C5 125
Norwich, Vt., U.S. D4 138
Norwood, On., Can. C7 89
Norwood, Ma., U.S. B5 114
Norwood, Mn., U.S. F5 116
Norwood, N.C., U.S. B2 126
Norwood, N.J., U.S. h9 123
Norwood, N.Y., U.S. f10 125
Norwood, Oh., U.S. o13 128
Norwood, Pa., U.S. p20 131
Norwoodville, Ia., U.S. e8 108
Noshiro, Japan C16 28
Nosivka, Ukr. D11 20
Nossob, stm., Afr. C2 56
Nosy-Varika, Madag. C8 56
Notasulga, Al., U.S. C4 94
Notch Peak, mtn., Ut., U.S. D2 137
Noteć, stm., Pol. C4 20
Notodden, Nor. G3 10
Noto-hantō, pen., Japan C3 31
Notre Dame, Monts, mts., Qc., Can. k13 90
Notre Dame Bay, b., N.L., Can. D4 88
Notre Dame de Lourdes, Mb., Can. E2 86
Notre-Dame-du-Lac, Qc., Can. B9 90
Nottawasaga Bay, b., On., Can. C4 89
Nottaway, stm., Qc., Can. h11 90
Nottingham, Eng., U.K. D6 12
Nottoway, stm., Va., U.S. D5 139
Nottoway, co., Va., U.S. C4 139
Nouâdhibou, Maur. B1 50
Nouâdhibou, Râs, c., Afr. B1 50
Nouakchott, Maur. C1 50
Nouâmghâr, Maur. C1 50
Nouméa, N. Cal. I9 62a
Noupoort, S. Afr. E3 56
Nouveau-Brunswick see New Brunswick, prov., Can. I26 82
Nouvelle-Calédonie, i., N. Cal. I9 62a
Nova Caipemba, Ang. E2 54
Nova Friburgo, Braz. F3 74
Nova Iguaçu, Braz. F3 74
Novaja Kazanka, Kaz. E8 22
Novaja Sibir', ostrov, i., Russia B17 26
Novaja Zemlja, is., Russia B7 26
Nova Kakhovka, Ukr. F12 20
Nova Lima, Braz. F3 74
Nova Lisboa see Huambo, Ang. F3 54
Nova Mambone, Moz. C6 56
Novara, Italy B2 18
Nova Scotia, prov., Can. D6 87
Novato, Ca., U.S. C2 98
Nova Venécia, Braz. E3 74
Novaya Zemlya see Novaja Zemlja, is., Russia B7 26
Nova Zagora, Blg. C11 18
Nové Zámky, Slvk. E5 20
Novgorod, Russia D5 26
Novhorod-Sivers'kyi, Ukr. D12 20
Novi, Mi., U.S. p15 115
Novikovo, Russia A4 31
Novi Ligure, Italy B2 18
Novi Pazar, Blg. C11 18
Novi Pazar, Serb. C8 18
Novi Sad, Serb. B7 18
Novo Aripuanã, Braz. E7 70
Novoazovs'k, Ukr. F15 20
Novočerkassk, Russia E7 22
Novodvinsk, Russia B7 22
Novo Hamburgo, Braz. D7 72
Novohrad-Volyns'kyi, Ukr. D9 20
Novokazalinsk, Kaz. E8 26
Novokujbyševsk, Russia D8 22
Novokuzneck, Russia D10 26
Novomihajlovskij, Russia G15 20
Novomoskovsk, Russia D5 26
Novomoskovs'k, Ukr. E13 20
Novomyrhorod, Ukr. E11 20
Novorossijsk, Russia E5 26
Novošahtinsk, Russia F15 20
Novosergievka, Russia D9 22
Novosibirsk, Russia D10 26
Novosibirskie ostrova, is., Russia B16 26
Novotroick, Russia D10 22
Novotroickoe, Kaz. B10 42
Novotroïts'ke, Ukr. F13 20
Novoukraïnka, Ukr. E11 20
Novouzensk, Russia D8 22
Novovjatsk, Russia C8 22
Novovolyns'k, Ukr. D8 20
Novozybkov, Russia C11 20
Novyi Buh, Ukr. F12 20
Novyj Oskol, Russia D14 20
Novyj Port, Russia C9 26
Novyj Uzen', Kaz. E7 26
Nowa Ruda, Pol. D4 20
Nowata, Ok., U.S. A6 129
Nowata, co., Ok., U.S. A6 129
Nowood, stm., Wy., U.S. B5 143
Nowra, Austl. G5 62
Nowshāk, mtn., Asia B2 40
Nowy Dwór Mazowiecki, Pol. C6 20
Nowy Sącz, Pol. E6 20
Noxon Reservoir, res., Mt., U.S. C1 119
Noxontown Lake, res., De., U.S. C3 101
Noxubee, co., Ms., U.S. B5 117
Noxubee, stm., U.S. B5 117
Noyes Island, i., Ak., U.S. n22 95
Nsanje, Mwi. B6 56
Nsawam, Ghana E4 50
Nsukka, Nig. E6 50
Nsuta, Ghana E4 50
Ntomba, Lac, l., D.R.C. D3 54
Nūbah, Jibāl an-, mts., Sudan A6 54
Nubanusit Lake, l., N.H., U.S. E2 122
Nubian Desert, des., Sudan F11 48
Nuckolls, co., Ne., U.S. D7 120
Nucla, Co., U.S. C2 99
Nueces, stm., Tx., U.S. E3 136
Nueces, co., Tx., U.S. F4 136
Nueltin Lake, l., Can. F20 82
Nueva Antioquia, Col. D6 80
Nueva Gerona, Cuba A3 80
Nueva Imperial, Chile E2 69
Nueva Italia de Ruiz, Mex. D4 78
Nueva Rosita, Mex. B4 78
Nueve de Julio, Arg. F5 72
Nuevitas, Cuba A4 80
Nuevo, Cayo, i., Mex. C6 78
Nuevo, Golfo, b., Arg. F4 69
Nuevo Casas Grandes, Mex. A3 78
Nuevo Laredo, Mex. B5 78
Nuevo León, state, Mex. B5 78
Nui, atoll, Tuvalu E11 58
Nuku'alofa, Tonga G12 58
Nukus, Uzb. E7 26
Nulato, Ak., U.S. C8 95
Nulhegan, stm., Vt., U.S. B5 138
Nullagine, Austl. E3 60
Nullarbor, Austl. G5 60
Nullarbor Plain, pl., Austl. G4 60
Numan, Nig. E7 50
Numancia, hist., Spain G5 16
Numazu, Japan D3 31
Nunavut, ter., Can. E18 82
Nunivak Island, i., Ak., U.S. D6 95
Nunjiang, China B13 28
Nuoro, Italy D2 18
Nuremberg, Pa., U.S. E9 131
Nurmes, Fin. E13 10
Nürnberg, Ger. F12 12
Nusaybin, Tur. D9 44
Nu Shan, mts., China F7 28
Nushki, Pak. E9 42
Nutley, N.J., U.S. B4 123
Nutter Fort, W.V., U.S. k10 141
Nutting Lake, Ma., U.S. f10 114
Nu'uanu Pali, c., Hi., U.S. g10 104
Nuuk see Godthåb, Grnld. F29 82
Nyabing, Austl. G2 60
Nyack, N.Y., U.S. D7 125
Nyainqêntanglha Shan, mts., China E6 28
Nyakanazi, Tan. D6 54
Nyala, Sudan H10 48
Nyamlell, Sudan B5 54
Nyanza-Lac, Bdi. D5 54
Nyasa, Lake (Malaŵi, Lake), l., Afr. F6 54
Nyasaland see Malawi, ctry., Afr. A5 56
Nyaunglebin, Mya. C3 34
Nyborg, Den. I4 10
Nybro, Swe. H6 10
Nyda, Russia C9 26
Nye, co., Nv., U.S. E5 121
Nyeri, Kenya D7 54
Nyimba, Zam. A5 56
Nyingchi, China D6 40
Nyíregyháza, Hung. F6 20
Nykøbing, Den. I4 10
Nyköping, Swe. G7 10
Nylstroom, S. Afr. C4 56
Nynäshamn, Swe. G7 10
Nyngan, Austl. G4 62
Nyš, Russia D16 26
Nysa, Pol. D4 20
Nyssa, Or., U.S. D9 130
Nyunzu, D.R.C. E5 54
Nzébéla, Gui. E3 50
Nzérékoré, Gui. E3 50
N'zeto, Ang. E2 54
Nzwani, i., Com. A7 56

O

Oahe, Lake, res., U.S. B7 92
Oahe Dam, S.D., U.S. C5 134
O'ahu, i., Hi., U.S. B4 104
Oak Bay, B.C., Can. h12 85
Oak Bluffs, Ma., U.S. D6 114
Oak Creek, Co., U.S. A4 99
Oak Creek, Wi., U.S. n12 142
Oakdale, Ca., U.S. D3 98
Oakdale, Ga., U.S. h8 103
Oakdale, La., U.S. D3 111
Oakdale, Pa., U.S. k13 131
Oakes, N.D., U.S. C7 127
Oakfield, N.Y., U.S. B2 125
Oakfield, Wi., U.S. E5 142
Oak Forest, Il., U.S. k9 106
Oak Grove, Ky., U.S. D2 110
Oak Grove, La., U.S. B4 111
Oak Grove, Or., U.S. B4 130
Oak Harbor, Oh., U.S. A2 128
Oak Harbor, Wa., U.S. A3 140
Oak Hill, mtn., Ma., U.S. f9 114
Oak Hill, Mi., U.S. D4 115
Oak Hill, Oh., U.S. D3 128
Oak Hill, W.V., U.S. D3 141
Oakhurst, Ok., U.S. A5 129
Oak Island, i., Wi., U.S. B3 142
Oak Lake, l., Mb., Can. E1 86
Oakland, Ca., U.S. D2 98
Oakland, Ia., U.S. C2 108
Oakland, Il., U.S. D5 106
Oakland, Md., U.S. m12 113
Oakland, Me., U.S. D3 112
Oakland, co., Mi., U.S. F7 115
Oakland, Ne., U.S. C9 120
Oakland, N.J., U.S. A4 123
Oakland, Ok., U.S. C5 129
Oakland, Or., U.S. D3 130
Oakland, R.I., U.S. B2 132
Oakland City, In., U.S. H3 107
Oakland Park, Fl., U.S. r13 102
Oak Lawn, Il., U.S. B6 106
Oaklawn, Ks., U.S. g12 109
Oakley, Id., U.S. G5 105
Oakley, Ks., U.S. C3 109
Oakman, Al., U.S. B2 94
Oakmont, Pa., U.S. E2 131
Oak Mountain, mtn., Ga., U.S. D2 103
Oak Orchard, De., U.S. F5 101
Oak Park, Il., U.S. B6 106
Oak Park, Mi., U.S. p15 115
Oak Ridge, N.C., U.S. A3 126
Oakridge, Or., U.S. D4 130
Oak Ridge, Tn., U.S. C9 135
Oak Ridge Reservoir, res., N.J., U.S. A3 123
Oakton, Va., U.S. g12 139
Oaktown, In., U.S. G3 107
Oak Valley, N.J., U.S. D2 123
Oakville, On., Can. D5 89
Oakville, Ct., U.S. C3 100
Oakville, Mo., U.S. g13 118
Oakwood, Ga., U.S. B3 103
Oakwood, Il., U.S. C6 106
Oakwood, Oh., U.S. C1 128
Oamaru, N.Z. q13 63c
Oaxaca, state, Mex. D5 78
Oaxaca de Juárez, Mex. D5 78
Ob', stm., Russia B9 26
Oban, Scot., U.K. B4 12
Ob Bay see Obskaja guba, b., Russia C9 26
Obed, stm., Tn., U.S. C9 135
Oberlin, Ks., U.S. C3 109
Oberlin, La., U.S. D3 111
Oberlin, Oh., U.S. A3 128
Obetz, Oh., U.S. C3 128
Obi, Kepulauan, is., Indon. D7 36
Obi, Pulau, i., Indon. D7 36
Obi, Selat, strt., Indon. D7 36
Óbidos, Braz. D8 70
Obihiro, Japan C16 28
Obion, Tn., U.S. A2 135
Obion, co., Tn., U.S. A2 135
Obion, stm., Tn., U.S. A2 135
Oblong, Il., U.S. D6 106
Obluče, Russia B14 28
Obninsk, Russia B14 20
Obo, C.A.R. B5 54
Obojan', Russia D14 20
O'Brien, co., Ia., U.S. A2 108
Obščij syrt, mts., Eur. D9 22
Observation Peak, mtn., Ca., U.S. B3 98
Obskaja guba, b., Russia C9 26
Obuasi, Ghana E4 50
Obudu, Nig. E6 50
Ocala, Fl., U.S. C4 102
Očamčira, Geor. A9 44
Ocaña, Col. B5 70
Ocaña, Spain H5 16
Occidental, Cordillera, mts., Col. E4 80
Occidental, Cordillera, mts., Peru E4 70
Ocean, co., N.J., U.S. D4 123
Oceana, co., Mi., U.S. E4 115
Oceana, W.V., U.S. D3 141
Oceana Naval Air Station, mil., Va., U.S. k15 139
Ocean Bluff, Ma., U.S. B6 114
Ocean City, Fl., U.S. u15 102
Ocean City, Md., U.S. D7 113
Ocean City, N.J., U.S. E3 123
Ocean Grove, Ma., U.S. C5 114
Ocean Island see Banaba, i., Kir. E10 58
Ocean Park, Wa., U.S. C1 140
Oceanport, N.J., U.S. C4 123
Oceanside, Ca., U.S. F5 98
Ocean Springs, Ms., U.S. E5 117
Ocean [Township], N.J., U.S. C4 123
Ocean View, De., U.S. F5 101
Ocheda Lake, l., Mn., U.S. G3 116
Ocheyedan, stm., Ia., U.S. A2 108
Ochiltree, co., Tx., U.S. A2 136
Ochlockonee, stm., Fl., U.S. B2 102
Ochoco Lake, res., Or., U.S. C6 130
Ocilla, Ga., U.S. E3 103
Ockelbo, Swe. F7 10
Ocmulgee, stm., Ga., U.S. D3 103
Ocoa, Bahía de, b., Dom. Rep. B5 80
Ocoee, Fl., U.S. D5 102
Ocoee, Lake, res., Tn., U.S. D9 135
Oconee, stm., Ga., U.S. C3 103
Oconee, co., Ga., U.S. C3 103
Oconee, co., S.C., U.S. B1 133
Oconee, Lake, res., Ga., U.S. C3 103
Oconomowoc, Wi., U.S. E5 142
Oconto, Wi., U.S. D6 142
Oconto, co., Wi., U.S. D5 142
Oconto, stm., Wi., U.S. D5 142
Oconto Falls, Wi., U.S. D5 142
Ocosingo, Mex. D6 78
Ocotal, Nic. C2 80
Ocotlán, Mex. C4 78
Ocracoke Inlet, b., N.C., U.S. B6 126
Ocracoke Island, i., N.C., U.S. B7 126
October Revolution Island see Oktjabr'skoj Revoljucii, ostrov, i., Russia B11 26
Octoraro Creek, stm., U.S. A5 113
Ocumare del Tuy, Ven. C6 80
Oda, Ghana E4 50
Oda, Jabal, mtn., Sudan F12 48
Odebolt, Ia., U.S. B2 108
Odell, Il., U.S. B5 106
Odell, Or., U.S. B5 130
Odell Lake, l., Or., U.S. E5 130
Odem, Tx., U.S. F4 136
Odemira, Port. I2 16
Ödemiş, Tur. C2 44
Odendaalsrus, S. Afr. D4 56
Odense, Den. I4 10
Odenton, Md., U.S. B4 113
Odenville, Al., U.S. B3 94
Oder, stm., Eur. C3 20
Odesa, Ukr. F11 20
Odessa, On., Can. C8 89
Odessa see Odesa, Ukr. F11 20
Odessa, De., U.S. C3 101
Odessa, Mo., U.S. C4 118
Odessa, Tx., U.S. D1 136
Odessa, Wa., U.S. B7 140
Odienné, C. Iv. E3 50
Odin, Il., U.S. E4 106
Odon, In., U.S. G4 107
O'Donnell, Tx., U.S. C2 136
Odorheiu Secuiesc, Rom. F8 20
Oeiras, Braz. C3 74
Oelwein, Ia., U.S. B6 108
Oenpelli, Austl. C5 60
Of, Tur. B9 44
O'Fallon, Il., U.S. E4 106
O'Fallon, Mo., U.S. f12 118
Ofanto, stm., Italy D5 18
Offa, Nig. E5 50
Offenburg, Ger. F10 12
Offutt Air Force Base, mil., Ne., U.S. g3 120
Ofotfjorden, b., Nor. B7 10
Ogaden, reg., Afr. I14 48
Ogallala, Ne., U.S. C4 120
Ogasawara-guntō, is., Japan F16 64
Ogbomosho, Nig. E5 50
Ogden, Ia., U.S. B3 108
Ogden, Ks., U.S. C7 109
Ogden, Ut., U.S. B4 137
Ogden, Mount, mtn., N.A. k23 95
Ogdensburg, N.J., U.S. A3 123
Ogdensburg, N.Y., U.S. f9 125
Ogeechee, stm., Ga., U.S. D5 103
Ogemaw, co., Mi., U.S. D6 115
Ogle, co., Il., U.S. A4 106
Oglesby, Il., U.S. B4 106
Oglethorpe, Ga., U.S. D2 103
Oglethorpe, co., Ga., U.S. C3 103
Oglethorpe, Mount, mtn., Ga., U.S. B2 103
Ogoja, Nig. E6 50
Ogooué, stm., Afr. D2 54
Ogre, Lat. H11 10
Ogunquit, Me., U.S. E2 112
Ogurdžaly, ostrov, i., Turk. C6 42
Oha, Russia D16 26
Ohanet, Alg. E6 48
Ohatchee, Al., U.S. B3 94
Ohio, co., In., U.S. G7 107
Ohio, co., Ky., U.S. C3 110
Ohio, co., W.V., U.S. A4 141
Ohio, state, U.S. B3 128
Ohio, stm., U.S. D10 92
Ohio Brush Creek, stm., Oh., U.S. D2 128
Ohio City, Oh., U.S. B1 128
Ohio Peak, mtn., Co., U.S. C3 99
Ohioville, Pa., U.S. E1 131
Ohoopee, stm., Ga., U.S. D4 103
Ohotsk, Russia D16 26
Ohrid, Mac. D8 18
Ohrid, Lake, l., Eur. C8 14
Oiapoque, Braz. C9 70
Oiapoque (Oyapok), stm., S.A. C9 70
Oil City, La., U.S. B2 111
Oil City, Pa., U.S. D2 131
Oil Creek, stm., Pa., U.S. C2 131
Oildale, Ca., U.S. E4 98
Oil Springs, On., Can. E2 89
Oilton, Ok., U.S. A5 129
Oise, stm., Eur. C8 16
Ōita, Japan E14 28
Ojai, Ca., U.S. E4 98
Ojinaga, Mex. B4 78
Ojmjakon, Russia C16 26
Ojocaliente, Mex. C4 78
Ojos del Salado, Cerro see Ojos del Salado, Nevado, mtn., S.A. D4 72
Ojos del Salado, Nevado, mtn., S.A. D4 72
Oka, stm., Russia D6 26
Okaba, Indon. H10 32
Okahandja, Nmb. C2 56
Okaloosa, co., Fl., U.S. u15 102
Okamanpeedan Lake, l., U.S. A3 108
Okanagan Falls, B.C., Can. E8 85
Okanagan Lake, l., B.C., Can. D8 85
Okanagan Landing, B.C., Can. D8 85
Okanogan, Wa., U.S. A6 140
Okanogan, co., Wa., U.S. A5 140
Okāra, Pak. D10 42
Okarche, Ok., U.S. B4 129
Okatibee Reservoir, res., Ms., U.S. C5 117
Okaukuejo, Nmb. B2 56
Okavango (Cubango), stm., Afr. B3 56
Okavango Delta, Bots. B3 56
Okawville, Il., U.S. E4 106
Okaya, Japan C3 31
Okayama, Japan E14 28
Okazaki, Japan D3 31
Okeechobee, co., Fl., U.S. E6 102
Okeechobee, Fl., U.S. E6 102
Okeechobee, Lake, l., Fl., U.S. F6 102
Okeene, Ok., U.S. A3 129
Okefenokee Swamp, sw., U.S. F4 103
Okemah, Ok., U.S. B5 129

Name — Map Ref. — Page

Okene, Nig. E6 50
Okfuskee, co., Ok., U.S. B5 129
Okhotsk see Ohotsk, Russia D16 26
Okhotsk, Sea of, Asia D16 26
Okhotsk Basin B7 144
Okhtyrka, Ukr. D13 20
Okinawa, Japan g6 31a
Okinawa-jima, i., Japan A9 34
Okinawa-shotō, is., Japan g6 31a
Okino-Erabu-shima, i., Japan A9 34
Okino-Tori-shima, i., Japan G15 28
Oki-shotō, is., Japan D14 28
Okitipupa, Nig. E5 50
Oklahoma, co., Ok., U.S. B4 129
Oklahoma, state, U.S. B4 129
Oklahoma City, Ok., U.S. B4 129
Oklawaha, Fl., U.S. C5 102
Oklawaha, stm., Fl., U.S. C5 102
Oklawaha, Lake, res., Fl., U.S. C5 102
Okmulgee, Ok., U.S. B6 129
Okmulgee, co., Ok., U.S. B5 129
Okoboji, Ia., U.S. A2 108
Okobojo Creek, stm., S.D., U.S. C5 134
Okolona, Ky., U.S. g11 110
Okolona, Ms., U.S. B5 117
Okondja, Gabon D2 54
Okotoks, Ab., Can. D4 84
Oktibbeha, co., Ms., U.S. B5 117
Oktjabr'sk, Kaz. E7 26
Oktjabr'skij, Russia D9 22
Oktjabr'skoe, Russia B12 22
Oktjabr'skoj Revoljucii, ostrov, i., Russia B11 26
Oktwin, Mya. C3 34
Okushiri-tō, i., Japan C15 28
Ola, Ar., U.S. B2 97
Ólafsfjörður, Ice. k19 10a
Olancha Peak, mtn., Ca., U.S. D4 98
Olanchito, Hond. B2 80
Öland, i., Swe. H7 10
Olanta, S.C., U.S. D8 133
Olathe, Co., U.S. C3 99
Olathe, Ks., U.S. D9 109
Olavarría, Arg. F5 72
Olbia, Italy D2 18
Olcott, N.Y., U.S. B2 125
Old Bahama Channel, strt., N.A. A4 80
Old Bridge, N.J., U.S. C4 123
Old Castile see Castilla la Vieja, hist. reg., Spain G5 16
Oldenburg, Ger. D11 12
Oldenburg, In., U.S. F7 107
Oldenburg in Holstein, Ger. C12 12
Old Faithful Geyser, Wy., U.S. B2 143
Old Forge, Pa., U.S. D10 131
Old Fort, N.C., U.S. f10 126
Oldham, co., Ky., U.S. B4 110
Oldham, co., Tx., U.S. B1 136
Old Harbor, Ak., U.S. D9 95
Old Hickory Lake, res., Tn., U.S. A5 135
Oldman, stm., Ab., Can. E4 84
Oldmans Creek, stm., N.J., U.S. D2 123
Old Orchard Beach, Me., U.S. E2 112
Old Perlican, N.L., Can. D5 88
Old Point Comfort, c., Va., U.S. h15 139
Old Rhodes Key, i., Fl., U.S. G6 102
Old River Lake, l., Ar., U.S. k10 97
Olds, Ab., Can. D3 84
Old Saybrook, Ct., U.S. D6 100
Oldsmar, Fl., U.S. o10 102
Old Tampa Bay, b., Fl., U.S. p10 102
Old Tappan, N.J., U.S. g9 123
Old Tate, Bots. C4 56
Old Topsail Inlet, b., N.C., U.S. C5 126
Old Town, Me., U.S. D4 112
Old Wives Lake, l., Sk., Can. G2 91
Olean, N.Y., U.S. C2 125
O'Leary, P.E., Can. C5 87
Olëkma, stm., Russia C14 26
Olekminsk, Russia C14 26
Oleksandriia, Ukr. E12 20
Olenegorsk, Russia B15 10
Olenëk, stm., Russia B13 26
Olenëk, Russia C13 26
Olenëkskij zaliv, b., Russia B14 26
Olentangy, stm., Oh., U.S. B3 128
Oléron, Île d', i., Fr. E6 16
Olevsk, Ukr. D9 20
Ol'ga, Russia E15 26
Olga, Mount, mtn., Austl. F5 60
Ölgiy, Mong. B6 28
Olhão, Port. I3 16
Olifants (Elefantes), stm., Afr. C4 56
Olifants, stm., Nmb. C2 56
Olifantshoek, S. Afr. D3 56
Ólimbos, mtn., Cyp. E5 44
Ólimbos, Óros, mtn., Grc. D9 18
Olin, Ia., U.S. B6 108
Olinda, Braz. C5 74
Olive Branch, Ms., U.S. A4 117
Olive Hill, Ky., U.S. B6 110
Olivehurst, Ca., U.S. C3 98
Oliveira, Braz. F3 74
Oliver, B.C., Can. E8 85
Oliver, co., N.D., U.S. B4 127
Oliver, Pa., U.S. G2 131
Oliver Dam, U.S. C5 94
Oliver Springs, Tn., U.S. C9 135
Olivet, Mi., U.S. F6 115
Olivia, Mn., U.S. F4 116
Oljutorskij, mys, c., Russia D19 26
Olla, La., U.S. C3 111
Ollagüe, Chile B3 69
Olmito, Tx., U.S. F4 136
Olmos, Peru E4 70
Olmos Park, Tx., U.S. k7 136
Olmsted, co., Mn., U.S. G6 116
Olmsted Falls, Oh., U.S. h9 128
Olney, Il., U.S. E5 106
Olney, Md., U.S. B3 113
Olney, Tx., U.S. C3 136
Olomouc, Czech Rep. E4 20
Olonec, Russia B5 22
Olongapo, Phil. D8 34
Oloron-Sainte-Marie, Fr. F6 16
Olot, Spain F8 16
Olovjannaja, Russia A11 28
Olsztyn, Pol. C6 20
Oltenița, Rom. G9 20
Olton, Tx., U.S. B1 136
Oltu, Tur. B10 44
Olustee, Ok., U.S. C2 129
Olympia, Wa., U.S. B3 140
Olympic Mountains, mts., Wa., U.S. B2 140
Olympic National Park, Wa., U.S. B2 140
Olympus see Ólimbos, mtn., Cyp. E5 44
Olympus, Mount see Ólimbos, Óros, mtn., Grc. D9 18
Olympus, Mount, mtn., Wa., U.S. B2 140
Olyphant, Pa., U.S. D10 131
Omagh, N. Ire., U.K. C3 12
Omaha, Ne., U.S. C10 120
Omaha Indian Reservation, Ne., U.S. B9 120
Omak, Wa., U.S. A6 140
Omak Lake, l., Wa., U.S. A6 140
Oman, ctry., Asia G7 38
Oman, Gulf of, b., Asia F7 42
Omar, W.V., U.S. D3 141
Omarama, N.Z. p12 63c
Omaruru, Nmb. C2 56
Omatako, stm., Nmb. B2 56
Ombai, Selat, strt., Asia E7 36
Omboué, Gabon D1 54
Omčak, Russia C16 26
Omdurman see Umm Durmān, Sudan G11 48
Omega, Ga., U.S. E3 103
Omemee, On., Can. C6 89
Omerville, Qc., Can. D5 90
Ometepe, Isla de, i., Nic. C2 80
Ometepec, Mex. D5 78
Omineca, stm., B.C., Can. B5 85
Omineca Mountains, mts., B.C., Can. A4 85
Ōmiya, Japan C3 31
Ommaney, Cape, c., Ak., U.S. D12 95
Omolon, stm., Russia C17 26
Ompompanoosuc, stm., Vt., U.S. D4 138
Omro, Wi., U.S. D5 142
Omsk, Russia D9 26
Omsukčan, Russia C17 26
Ōmuda (Ōmuta), Japan E14 28
Ōmura, Japan D1 31
Ōmuta (Ōmuda), Japan E14 28
Omutninsk, Russia C9 22
Onaga, Ks., U.S. C7 109
Onalaska, Wa., U.S. C3 140
Onalaska, Wi., U.S. E2 142
Onamia, Mn., U.S. D5 116
Onancock, Va., U.S. C7 139
Onarga, Il., U.S. C6 106
Onawa, Ia., U.S. B1 108
Onawa, Lake, l., Me., U.S. C3 112
Onaway, Mi., U.S. C6 115
Ondangwa, Nmb. B2 56
Ondjiva, Ang. B2 56
Ondo, Nig. E5 50
Öndörhaan, Mong. B10 28
Oneco, Fl., U.S. E4 102
Onega, stm., Russia B6 22
Onega, Russia C5 26
Onega, Lake see Onežskoe ozero, l., Russia C5 26
Onega Bay see Onežskaja guba, b., Russia B6 22
One Hundred Fifty Mile House, B.C., Can. C7 85
One Hundred Mile House, B.C., Can. D7 85
Oneida, co., Id., U.S. G6 105
Oneida, Ky., U.S. C6 110
Oneida, N.Y., U.S. B5 125
Oneida, co., N.Y., U.S. B5 125
Oneida, Oh., U.S. C1 128
Oneida, Tn., U.S. C9 135
Oneida, co., Wi., U.S. C4 142
Oneida Lake, l., N.Y., U.S. B5 125
O'Neill, Ne., U.S. B7 120
Onekotan, ostrov, i., Russia E17 26
Oneonta, Al., U.S. B3 94
Oneonta, N.Y., U.S. C5 125
Onești, Rom. F9 20
Onežskaja guba, b., Russia B6 22
Onežskoe ozero, l., Russia C5 26
Ongole, India F4 40
Onida, S.D., U.S. C5 134
Onitsha, Nig. E6 50
Onondaga, co., N.Y., U.S. C4 125
Onondaga Indian Reservation, N.Y., U.S. C4 125
Onota Lake, l., Ma., U.S. B1 114
Onoway, Ab., Can. C3 84
Onseepkans, S. Afr. D2 56
Onset, Ma., U.S. C6 114
Onslow, Austl. E1 60
Onslow, co., N.C., U.S. C5 126
Onslow Bay, b., N.C., U.S. C5 126
Onsted, Mi., U.S. F6 115
Ontario, prov., Can. C6 89
Ontario, Ca., U.S. E5 98
Ontario, co., N.Y., U.S. C3 125
Ontario, Oh., U.S. B3 128
Ontario, Or., U.S. C10 130
Ontario, Lake, l., N.A. C12 92
Ontinyent, Spain H6 16
Ontonagon, Mi., U.S. m12 115
Ontonagon, co., Mi., U.S. m12 115
Ontonagon Indian Reservation, Mi., U.S. B1 115
Oodnadatta, Austl. F2 62
Ooldea, Austl. G5 60
Oolitic, In., U.S. G4 107
Oologah, Ok., U.S. A6 129
Oologah Lake, res., Ok., U.S. A6 129
Ooltewah, Tn., U.S. D8 135
Oostburg, Wi., U.S. E6 142
Oostende, Bel. E8 12
Ootsa Lake, l., B.C., Can. C4 85
Opala, D.R.C. D4 54
Opa-Locka, Fl., U.S. s13 102
Opava, Czech Rep. E4 20
Opelika, Al., U.S. C4 94
Opelousas, La., U.S. D3 111
Opequon Creek, stm., W.V., U.S. B6 141
Opobo, Nig. F6 50
Opočka, Russia H13 10
Opole, Pol. D4 20
Opotiki, N.Z. o14 63c
Opp, Al., U.S. D3 94
Oppdal, Nor. E3 10
Oppelo, Ar., U.S. B3 97
Opportunity, Wa., U.S. B8 140
Optima Reservoir, res., Ok., U.S. e9 129
Opuwo, Nmb. B1 56
Oquawka, Il., U.S. C3 106
Oracle, Az., U.S. E5 96
Oradea, Rom. F6 20
Oradell, N.J., U.S. h8 123
Oradell Reservoir, res., N.J., U.S. h9 123
Öræfajökull, ice, Ice. l20 10a
Orai, India D3 40
Oraibi, Az., U.S. B5 96
Oran see Wahran, Alg. C4 48
Oran, Mo., U.S. D8 118
Oran, Sebkha d', l., Alg. J6 16
Orange (Oranje), stm., Afr. D2 56
Orange, Austl. G4 62
Orange, Fr. E9 16
Orange, Ca., U.S. n13 98
Orange, co., Ca., U.S. F5 98
Orange, Ct., U.S. D3 100
Orange, co., Fl., U.S. D5 102
Orange, co., In., U.S. G4 107
Orange, Ma., U.S. A3 114
Orange, co., N.C., U.S. A3 126
Orange, N.J., U.S. B4 123
Orange, co., N.Y., U.S. D6 125
Orange, Tx., U.S. D6 136
Orange, co., Tx., U.S. D6 136
Orange, Va., U.S. B4 139
Orange, co., Va., U.S. B4 139
Orange, co., Vt., U.S. D3 138
Orange, Cabo, c., Braz. C9 70
Orange Beach, Al., U.S. E2 94
Orangeburg, co., S.C., U.S. E6 133
Orangeburg, S.C., U.S. E6 133
Orange City, Fl., U.S. D5 102
Orange City, Ia., U.S. B1 108
Orange Grove, Ms., U.S. E5 117
Orange Grove, Tx., U.S. F4 136
Orange Lake, l., Fl., U.S. C4 102
Orange Park, Fl., U.S. B5 102
Orangeville, On., Can. D4 89
Orangeville, Ut., U.S. D4 137
Orange Walk, Belize B2 80
Oranienburg, Ger. D13 12
Oranje see Orange, stm., Afr. D2 56
Oranjemund, Nmb. D2 56
Oranjestad, Aruba C6 80
Orbetello, Italy C3 18
Orbost, Austl. H4 62
Orcas Island, i., Wa., U.S. A3 140
Orchard City, Co., U.S. C3 99
Orchard Homes, Mt., U.S. D2 119
Orchard Park, N.Y., U.S. C2 125
Orchards, Wa., U.S. D3 140
Orchard Valley, Wy., U.S. E8 143
Orcutt, Ca., U.S. E3 98
Ord, Ne., U.S. C7 120
Ord, Mount, mtn., Austl. D4 60
Ordu, Tur. B7 44
Ordway, Co., U.S. C7 99
Ordzhonikidze see Vladikavkaz, Russia E6 26
Ordzhonikidze, Ukr. F13 20
Ordzhonikidze see Yenakiieve, Ukr. E15 20
Ordžonikidzeabad, Taj. C9 42
Oreana, Il., U.S. D5 106
Örebro, Swe. G6 10
Oregon, Il., U.S. A4 106
Oregon, Mo., U.S. B2 118
Oregon, co., Mo., U.S. E6 118
Oregon, Oh., U.S. A2 128
Oregon, Wi., U.S. F4 142
Oregon, state, U.S. C6 130
Oregon Caves National Monument, Or., U.S. E2 130
Oregon City, Or., U.S. B4 130
Oregon Inlet, b., N.C., U.S. B7 126
Orehovo-Zuevo, Russia C6 22
Orel, Russia D5 26
Orem, Ut., U.S. C4 137
Ore Mountains see Erzgebirge, mts., Eur. E9 8
Orenburg, Russia D7 26
Orense, Arg. F6 72
Orestiás, Grc. D11 18
Orfanoú, Kólpos, b., Grc. D9 18
Orfordville, Wi., U.S. F4 142
Organ Mountains, mts., N.M., U.S. E3 124
Organ Pipe Cactus National Monument, Az., U.S. E3 96
Orgun, Afg. D9 42
Orhei, Mol. F10 20
Orhon, stm., Mong. A9 28
Oriental, N.C., U.S. B6 126
Oriental, Cordillera, mts., Col. D5 80
Oriental, Cordillera, mts., Peru F5 70
Orikhiv, Ukr. F13 20
Orillia, On., Can. C5 89
Orinoco, stm., S.A. B6 70
Oriola, Spain H6 16
Orion, Il., U.S. B3 106
Orissa, state, India E4 40
Oristano, Italy E2 18
Oristano, Golfo di, b., Italy E2 18
Orivesi, Fin. F11 10
Oriximiná, Braz. D8 70
Orizaba, Mex. D5 78
Orkney, S. Afr. D4 56
Orkney Islands, is., U.K. A5 12
Orland, Ca., U.S. C2 98
Orlando, Fl., U.S. D5 102
Orland Park, Il., U.S. k9 106
Orléanais, hist. reg., Fr. C7 16
Orléans, Fr. D7 16
Orleans, co., La., U.S. E6 111
Orleans, Ma., U.S. C7 114
Orleans, co., N.Y., U.S. B2 125
Orleans, Vt., U.S. B4 138
Orleans, co., Vt., U.S. B4 138
Orléans, Île d', i., Qc., Can. C6 90
Orlik, Russia A7 28
Orman Dam, S.D., U.S. C2 134
Ormāra, Pak. E8 42
Ormoc, Phil. D8 34
Ormond Beach, Fl., U.S. C5 102
Ormstown, Qc., Can. D3 90
Örnsköldsvik, Swe. E8 10
Orocué, Col. C5 70
Orofino, Id., U.S. C2 105
Oroluk, atoll, Micron. D9 58
Oromocto, N.B., Can. D3 87
Oromocto Lake, l., N.B., Can. D2 87
Oron, Nig. F6 50
Orono, Me., U.S. D4 112
Oronoco, Mn., U.S. F6 116
Oroquieta, Phil. E8 34
Orosei, Golfo di, b., Italy D2 18
Oroville, Ca., U.S. C3 98
Oroville, Wa., U.S. A6 140
Oroville, Lake, res., Ca., U.S. C3 98
Orrick, Mo., U.S. B3 118
Orrville, Oh., U.S. B4 128
Orša, Bela. B11 20
Orsk, Russia D7 26
Ortaca, Tur. D3 44
Ortegal, Cabo, c., Spain F3 16
Orting, Wa., U.S. B3 140
Ortiz, Mex. B2 78
Ortonville, Mi., U.S. F7 115
Ortonville, Mn., U.S. E2 116
Orto-Tokoj, Kyrg. A3 40
Orūmīyeh, Iran C5 42
Orūmīyeh, Daryācheh-ye, l., Iran C5 42
Oruro, Bol. B4 72
Orwell, Oh., U.S. A5 128
Orwigsburg, Pa., U.S. E9 131
Oš, Kyrg. E9 26
Osa, Península de, pen., C.R. D3 80
Osage, Ia., U.S. A5 108
Osage, co., Ks., U.S. D8 109
Osage, co., Mo., U.S. C6 118
Osage, stm., Mo., U.S. C3 118
Osage, co., Ok., U.S. A5 129
Osage, Wy., U.S. C8 143
Osage Beach, Mo., U.S. C5 118
Osage City, Ks., U.S. D8 109
Ōsaka, Japan E15 28
Osakis, Mn., U.S. E3 116
Osakis, Lake, l., Mn., U.S. E3 116
Osawatomie, Ks., U.S. D9 109
Osborne, Ks., U.S. C5 109
Osborne, co., Ks., U.S. C5 109
Osburn, Id., U.S. B3 105
Osceola, Ar., U.S. B6 97
Osceola, co., Fl., U.S. E5 102
Osceola, Ia., U.S. C4 108
Osceola, co., Ia., U.S. A2 108
Osceola, In., U.S. A5 107
Osceola, co., Mi., U.S. E5 115
Osceola, Mo., U.S. C4 118
Osceola, Ne., U.S. C8 120
Osceola, Wi., U.S. C1 142
Osceola Mills, Pa., U.S. E5 131
Oscoda, Mi., U.S. D7 115
Oscoda, co., Mi., U.S. D6 115
Oscura Mountains, mts., N.M., U.S. D3 124
Osgood, In., U.S. F7 107
Oshawa, On., Can. D6 89
Ō-shima, i., Japan D3 31
Oshkosh, Ne., U.S. C3 120
Oshkosh, Wi., U.S. D5 142
Oshnovīyeh, Iran D11 44
Oshogbo, Nig. E5 50
Oshtorīnān, Iran E13 44
Oshwe, D.R.C. D3 54
Osijek, Cro. B7 18
Oskaloosa, Ia., U.S. C5 108
Oskaloosa, Ks., U.S. C8 109
Oskarshamn, Swe. H7 10
Oskū, Iran D12 44
Oslo, Nor. G4 10
Oslofjorden, b., Nor. G4 10
Osmānābād, India F3 40
Osmancık, Tur. B6 44
Osmaniye, Tur. D7 44
Osmond, Ne., U.S. B8 120
Osnabrück, Ger. D11 12
Osorno, Chile F2 69
Osoyoos, B.C., Can. E8 85
Osoyoos Lake, l., Wa., U.S. A6 140
Osprey, Fl., U.S. E4 102
Ossa, Mount, mtn., Austl. I4 62
Ossabaw Island, i., Ga., U.S. E5 103
Osseo, Mn., U.S. m12 116
Osseo, Wi., U.S. D2 142
Ossian, Ia., U.S. A6 108
Ossian, In., U.S. C7 107
Ossining, N.Y., U.S. D7 125
Ossipee, stm., U.S. C5 122
Ossipee Lake, l., N.H., U.S. C4 122
Ossora, Russia D18 26
Ostaškov, Russia C5 22
Östersund, Swe. E6 10
Osterville, Ma., U.S. C7 114
Ostfriesische Inseln, is., Ger. D10 12
Ostrava, Czech Rep. E5 20
Ostróda, Pol. C5 20
Ostrogožsk, Russia D15 20
Ostroh, Ukr. D9 20
Ostrołęka, Pol. C6 20
Ostrov, Russia H13 10
Ostrowiec Świętokrzyski, Pol. D6 20
Ostrów Mazowiecka, Pol. C6 20
Ostrów Wielkopolski, Pol. D4 20
Ostuni, Italy D6 18
Ōsumi-shotō, is., Japan E14 28
Osuna, Spain I4 16
Oswegatchie, stm., N.Y., U.S. f9 125
Oswego, Il., U.S. B5 106
Oswego, Ks., U.S. E8 109
Oswego, stm., N.J., U.S. D4 123
Oswego, N.Y., U.S. B4 125
Oswego, stm., N.Y., U.S. B4 125
Oswego, co., N.Y., U.S. B4 125
Otanmäki, Fin. D12 10
Otaru, Japan C16 28
Otava, Fin. F12 10
Otavi, Nmb. B2 56
Oteen, N.C., U.S. f10 126
Otero, co., Co., U.S. D7 99
Otero, co., N.M., U.S. E3 124
Othello, Wa., U.S. C6 140
Otis Orchards, Wa., U.S. g14 140
Otis Reservoir, res., Ma., U.S. B1 114
Otisville, Mi., U.S. E7 115
Otjikondo, Nmb. B2 56
Otjiwarongo, Nmb. C2 56
Otoe, co., Ne., U.S. D9 120
Otra, stm., Nor. G2 10
Otradnyj, Russia D9 22
Ōtranto, Italy D7 18
Otranto, Strait of, strt., Eur. C7 14
Otsego, Mi., U.S. F5 115
Otsego, co., Mi., U.S. C6 115
Otsego, co., N.Y., U.S. C5 125
Otsego Lake, l., N.Y., U.S. C6 125
Ōtsu, Japan C3 31

Name — Map Ref. — Page

Ottauquechee, stm., Vt., U.S. **D4** 138
Ottawa, On., Can. **B9** 89
Ottawa, stm., Can. **I24** 82
Ottawa, Il., U.S. **B5** 106
Ottawa, Ks., U.S. **D8** 109
Ottawa, co., Ks., U.S. **C6** 109
Ottawa, co., Mi., U.S. **F4** 115
Ottawa, Oh., U.S. **A1** 128
Ottawa, stm., Oh., U.S. **e6** 128
Ottawa, co., Oh., U.S. **A2** 128
Ottawa, co., Ok., U.S. **A7** 129
Ottawa Hills, Oh., U.S. **e6** 128
Ottenby, Swe. **H7** 10
Otterbein, In., U.S. **D3** 107
Otter Brook, stm., N.H., U.S. **E2** 122
Otter Brook Lake, res., N.H., U.S. **E2** 122
Otter Creek, stm., Ut., U.S. **E4** 137
Otter Creek, stm., Vt., U.S. **C2** 138
Otter Creek Reservoir, res., Ut., U.S. **E4** 137
Otter Islands, is., S.C., U.S. **m11** 133
Otter Tail, co., Mn., U.S. **D3** 116
Otter Tail, stm., Mn., U.S. **D2** 116
Otter Tail Lake, l., Mn., U.S. **D3** 116
Otterville, On., Can. **E4** 89
Ottumwa, Ia., U.S. **C5** 108
Otway, Cape, c., Austl. **H3** 62
Otwock, Pol. **C6** 20
Ouachita, co., Ar., U.S. **D3** 97
Ouachita, co., La., U.S. **B3** 111
Ouachita, Lake, res., Ar., U.S. **C2** 97
Ouachita Mountains, mts., U.S. **E9** 92
Ouadda, C.A.R. **B4** 54
Ouagadougou, Burkina **D4** 50
Ouahigouya, Burkina **D4** 50
Ouahran see Wahran, Alg. **C4** 48
Oualâta, Maur. **C3** 50
Ouallam, Niger **D5** 50
Ouallene, Alg. **F5** 48
Ouanda Djallé, C.A.R. **B4** 54
Ouangolodougou, C. Iv. **E3** 50
Ouarâne, reg., Maur. **B2** 50
Ouarzazate, Mor. **D3** 48
Oubangui (Ubangi), stm., Afr. **D3** 54
Oudtshoorn, S. Afr. **E3** 56
Oued Rhiou, Alg. **J7** 16
Oued-Zem, Mor. **E2** 14
Ouellé, C. Iv. **E4** 50
Ouémé, stm., Benin **E5** 50
Ouessant, Île d', i., Fr. **C4** 16
Ouesso, Congo **C3** 54
Ouezzane, Mor. **D3** 48
Ouham, stm., Afr. **B3** 54
Ouidah, Benin **E5** 50
Oujda, Mor. **D4** 48
Oulu, Fin. **D11** 10
Oulujärvi, l., Fin. **D12** 10
Oulujoki, stm., Fin. **D12** 10
Oum-Chalouba, Chad **G9** 48
Oumé, C. Iv. **E3** 50
Ounianga Kébir, Chad **G9** 48
Ouray, Co., U.S. **C3** 99
Ouray, co., Co., U.S. **C3** 99
Ouray, Mount, mtn., Co., U.S. **C4** 99
Ourense, Spain **F3** 16
Ouricuri, Braz. **C3** 74
Ourinhos, Braz. **F2** 74
Ouro Preto, Braz. **F3** 74
Outagamie, co., Wi., U.S. **D5** 142
Outardes Quatre, Réservoir, res., Qc., Can. **h13** 90
Outer Hebrides, is., Scot., U.K. **B3** 12
Outer Island, i., Wi., U.S. **A3** 142
Outer Santa Barbara Passage, strt., Ca., U.S. **F4** 98
Outjo, Nmb. **C2** 56
Outpost Mountain, mtn., Ak., U.S. **B9** 95
Outremont, Qc., Can. **p19** 90
Ouvéa, i., N. Cal. **I9** 62a
Ouyen, Austl. **H3** 62
Ovalle, Chile **D2** 69
Overbrook, Ks., U.S. **D8** 109
Overgaard, Az., U.S. **C5** 96
Overland, Mo., U.S. **f13** 118
Overland Park, Ks., U.S. **m16** 109
Overlea, Md., U.S. **B4** 113
Overton, Nv., U.S. **G7** 121
Overton, co., Tn., U.S. **C8** 135
Overton, Tx., U.S. **C5** 136
Ovett, Ms., U.S. **D4** 117
Ovid, Mi., U.S. **E6** 115
Oviedo, Spain **F4** 16
Ovoot, Mong. **B10** 28
Ovruch, Ukr. **D10** 20
Owando, Congo **D3** 54
Owasco Lake, l., N.Y., U.S. **C4** 125
Owasso, Ok., U.S. **A6** 129
Owatonna, Mn., U.S. **F5** 116
Owego, N.Y., U.S. **C4** 125
Owen, co., In., U.S. **F4** 107
Owen, co., Ky., U.S. **B5** 110
Owen, Wi., U.S. **D3** 142
Owen, Lake, l., Wi., U.S. **B2** 142
Owen, Mount, mtn., Co., U.S. **C3** 99
Owendo, Gabon **C1** 54
Owens, stm., Ca., U.S. **D4** 98
Owensboro, Ky., U.S. **C2** 110
Owens Cross Roads, Al., U.S. **A3** 94
Owens Lake, l., Ca., U.S. **D5** 98
Owen Sound, On., Can. **C4** 89
Owen Sound, b., On., Can. **C4** 89
Owen Stanley Range, mts., Pap. N. Gui. **H12** 32
Owensville, In., U.S. **H2** 107
Owensville, Mo., U.S. **C6** 118
Owensville, Oh., U.S. **C1** 128
Owenton, Ky., U.S. **B5** 110
Owerri, Nig. **E6** 50
Owings Mills, Md., U.S. **B4** 113
Owingsville, Ky., U.S. **B6** 110
Owl Creek, stm., Wy., U.S. **C4** 143
Owl Creek Mountains, mts., Wy., U.S. **C4** 143
Owo, Nig. **E6** 50
Owosso, Mi., U.S. **E6** 115
Owsley, co., Ky., U.S. **C6** 110
Owyhee, co., Id., U.S. **G2** 105
Owyhee, Nv., U.S. **B5** 121
Owyhee, stm., U.S. **E9** 130
Owyhee, Lake, res., Or., U.S. **D9** 130
Owyhee Dam, Or., U.S. **D9** 130
Owyhee Mountains, mts., U.S. **G2** 105
Oxbow Dam, U.S. **E2** 105
Oxelösund, Swe. **G7** 10
Oxford, N.S., Can. **D6** 87
Oxford, Eng., U.K. **E6** 12
Oxford, Al., U.S. **B4** 94
Oxford, Ct., U.S. **D3** 100
Oxford, Ga., U.S. **C3** 103
Oxford, Ia., U.S. **C6** 108
Oxford, In., U.S. **C3** 107
Oxford, Ks., U.S. **E6** 109
Oxford, Ma., U.S. **B4** 114
Oxford, Md., U.S. **C5** 113
Oxford, Me., U.S. **D2** 112
Oxford, co., Me., U.S. **D2** 112
Oxford, Mi., U.S. **F7** 115
Oxford, Ms., U.S. **A4** 117
Oxford, N.C., U.S. **A4** 126
Oxford, Ne., U.S. **D6** 120
Oxford, N.Y., U.S. **C5** 125
Oxford, Oh., U.S. **C1** 128
Oxford, Pa., U.S. **G10** 131
Oxford Lake, l., Mb., Can. **B4** 86
Oxford Peak, mtn., Id., U.S. **G6** 105
Oxnard, Ca., U.S. **E4** 98
Oxon Hill, Md., U.S. **f9** 113
Oxus see Amu Darya, stm., Asia **B8** 42
Oyama, B.C., Can. **D8** 85
Oyapok (Oiapoque), stm., S.A. **C9** 70
Oyem, Gabon **C2** 54
Oyen, Ab., Can. **D5** 84
Oyo, Nig. **E5** 50
Oyster Bay, N.Y., U.S. **E7** 125
Oyster Keys, is., Fl., U.S. **G6** 102
Ozamis, Phil. **E8** 34
Ozark, Al., U.S. **D4** 94
Ozark, Ar., U.S. **B2** 97
Ozark, Mo., U.S. **D4** 118
Ozark, co., Mo., U.S. **E5** 118
Ozark Plateau, plat., U.S. **D9** 92
Ozark Reservoir, res., Ar., U.S. **B1** 97
Ozarks, Lake of the, res., Mo., U.S. **C5** 118
Ozaukee, co., Wi., U.S. **E6** 142
Ózd, Hung. **E6** 20
Ozernovskij, Russia **D17** 26
Ozërnyj, Russia **D11** 22
Ozette Lake, l., Wa., U.S. **A1** 140
Ozieri, Italy **D2** 18
Ozinki, Russia **D8** 22
Ozona, Fl., U.S. **o10** 102
Ozona, Tx., U.S. **D2** 136
Ozurgeti, Geor. **B10** 44

P

Paarl, S. Afr. **E2** 56
Pa'auilo, Hi., U.S. **C6** 104
Pabianice, Pol. **D5** 20
Pābna, Bngl. **E5** 40
Pacajus, Braz. **B4** 74
Pacasmayo, Peru **E4** 70
Pace, Fl., U.S. **u14** 102
Pachacamac, hist., Peru **A2** 72
Pachaug Pond, l., Ct., U.S. **C8** 100
Pachino, Italy **F5** 18
Pachuca de Soto, Mex. **C5** 78
Pacific, Mo., U.S. **C7** 118
Pacific, Wa., U.S. **f11** 140
Pacific, co., Wa., U.S. **C2** 140
Pacifica, Ca., U.S. **h8** 98
Pacific-Antarctic Ridge **O22** 64
Pacific Beach, Wa., U.S. **B1** 140
Pacific City, Or., U.S. **B3** 130
Pacific Creek, stm., Wy., U.S. **D3** 143
Pacific Grove, Ca., U.S. **D3** 98
Pacific Ocean **E20** 64
Pacific Palisades, Hi., U.S. **g10** 104
Pacific Ranges, mts., B.C., Can. **D4** 85
Pacific Rim National Park, B.C., Can. **E5** 85
Pack Monadnock Mountain, mtn., N.H., U.S. **E3** 122
Packwood, Wa., U.S. **C4** 140
Pacolet, stm., S.C., U.S. **A4** 133
Pacolet, S.C., U.S. **B4** 133
Pacolet Mills, S.C., U.S. **B4** 133
Pactola Reservoir, res., S.D., U.S. **C2** 134
Padang, Indon. **D2** 36
Padangpanjang, Indon. **D2** 36
Padangsidempuan, Indon. **C1** 36
Paddock Lake, Wi., U.S. **n11** 142
Paden City, W.V., U.S. **B4** 141
Paderborn, Ger. **E11** 12
Padma see Ganges, stm., Asia **D5** 40
Pádova, Italy **B3** 18
Padrauna, India **D4** 40
Padre Island, i., Tx., U.S. **F4** 136
Padre Island National Seashore, Tx., U.S. **F4** 136
Padua see Pádova, Italy **B3** 18
Paducah, Ky., U.S. **e9** 110
Paducah, Tx., U.S. **B2** 136
Paektu, Mount, mtn., Asia **C13** 28
Paektu-san see Paektu, Mount, mtn., Asia **C13** 28
Paestum, hist., Italy **D5** 18
Pafúri, Moz. **C5** 56
Pag, Otok, i., Cro. **B5** 18
Pagadian, Phil. **E8** 34
Pagai Selatan, Pulau, i., Indon. **D2** 36
Pagai Utara, Pulau, i., Indon. **D2** 36
Pagalu see Annobón, i., Eq. Gui. **C1** 52
Pagan, i., N. Mar. Is. **C12** 32
Pagasitikós Kólpos, b., Grc. **E9** 18
Page, Az., U.S. **A4** 96
Page, co., Ia., U.S. **D2** 108
Page, co., Va., U.S. **B4** 139
Page, W.V., U.S. **C3** 141
Pageland, S.C., U.S. **B7** 133
Pagoda Peak, mtn., Co., U.S. **A3** 99
Pago Pago, Am. Sam. **F12** 58
Pagosa Springs, Co., U.S. **D3** 99
Paguate, N.M., U.S. **B2** 124
Pāhala, Hi., U.S. **D6** 104
Pahang, stm., Malay. **C2** 36
Pāhoa, Hi., U.S. **D7** 104
Pahokee, Fl., U.S. **F6** 102
Pahrump, Nv., U.S. **G6** 121
Pahute Mesa, mtn., Nv., U.S. **F5** 121
Paia, Hi., U.S. **C5** 104
Paide, Est. **G11** 10
Päijänne, l., Fin. **F11** 10
Pailolo Channel, strt., Hi., U.S. **B5** 104
Painan, Indon. **D2** 36
Paincourtville, La., U.S. **k9** 111
Painesville, Oh., U.S. **A4** 128
Paint, stm., Mi., U.S. **B2** 115
Paint Creek, stm., Oh., U.S. **C2** 128
Paint Creek, stm., W.V., U.S. **m13** 141
Paint Creek, North Fork, stm., Oh., U.S. **C2** 128
Paint Creek Lake, res., Oh., U.S. **C2** 128
Painted Desert, des., Az., U.S. **B4** 96
Painted Post, N.Y., U.S. **C3** 125
Painted Rock Reservoir, res., Az., U.S. **D3** 96
Paintsville, Ky., U.S. **C7** 110
Paisley, On., Can. **C3** 89
Pajala, Swe. **C10** 10
Pakaraima Mountains, mts., S.A. **E7** 80
Pakistan, ctry., Asia **E9** 42
Pakistan, East see Bangladesh, ctry., Asia **B2** 34
Pakokku, Mya. **B3** 34
Pakowki Lake, l., Ab., Can. **E5** 84
Pak Phanang, Thai. **E4** 34
Paks, Hung. **F5** 20
Pakxé, Laos **C5** 34
Pala, Chad **E7** 50
Palacios, Tx., U.S. **E4** 136
Palana, Russia **D17** 26
Palangkaraya, Indon. **D4** 36
Palani, India **G3** 40
Pālanpur, India **E2** 40
Palaoa Point, c., Hi., U.S. **C4** 104
Palapye, Bots. **C4** 56
Palatine, Il., U.S. **A5** 106
Palatka, Fl., U.S. **C5** 102
Palau, ctry., Oc. **F10** 32
Palau Islands, is., Palau **E9** 32
Palaw, Mya. **D3** 34
Palawan, i., Phil. **E7** 34
Palawan Passage, strt., Phil. **E7** 34
Pālayankottai, India **H3** 40
Paldiski, Est. **G11** 10
Palembang, Indon. **D2** 36
Palencia, Spain **F4** 16
Palenque, hist., Mex. **D6** 78
Palermo, Italy **E4** 18
Palestine, hist. reg., Asia **G6** 44
Palestine, Ar., U.S. **C5** 97
Palestine, Il., U.S. **D6** 106
Palestine, Tx., U.S. **D5** 136
Palestine, Lake, res., Tx., U.S. **C5** 136
Paletwa, Mya. **B2** 34
Pālghāt, India **G3** 40
Pāli, India **D2** 40
Palikea, mtn., Hi., U.S. **g9** 104
Palikir, Micron. **D9** 58
Palisade, Co., U.S. **B2** 99
Palisades Park, N.J., U.S. **h8** 123
Palisades Reservoir, res., U.S. **F7** 105
Pālitāna, India **E2** 40
Palk Strait, strt., Asia **H3** 40
Palliser, Cape, c., N.Z. **p14** 63c
Palma, Moz. **A7** 56
Palma del Río, Spain **I4** 16
Palma de Mallorca, Spain **H8** 16
Palmares, Braz. **C4** 74
Palmas, Braz. **F10** 70
Palma Soriano, Cuba **A4** 80
Palm Bay, Fl., U.S. **D6** 102
Palm Beach, Fl., U.S. **F6** 102
Palm Beach, co., Fl., U.S. **F6** 102
Palmdale, Ca., U.S. **E4** 98
Palmeira das Missões, Braz. **D7** 72
Palmeira dos Índios, Braz. **C4** 74
Palmer, Ak., U.S. **C10** 95
Palmer, Ma., U.S. **B3** 114
Palmer, Mi., U.S. **B3** 115
Palmer, Ms., U.S. **D4** 117
Palmer, Ne., U.S. **C7** 120
Palmer, Tn., U.S. **D8** 135
Palmer, Tx., U.S. **n10** 136
Palmer Lake, Co., U.S. **B6** 99
Palmer Land, reg., Ant. **D34** 67
Palmerston, On., Can. **D4** 89
Palmerston, atoll, Cook Is. **F13** 58
Palmerston North, N.Z. **p14** 63c
Palmerton, Pa., U.S. **E10** 131
Palmetto, Fl., U.S. **E4** 102
Palmetto, Ga., U.S. **C2** 103
Palm Harbor, Fl., U.S. **o10** 102
Palmi, Italy **E5** 18
Palmira, Col. **C4** 70
Palms, Isle of, i., S.C., U.S. **F8** 133
Palm Springs, Ca., U.S. **F5** 98
Palmyra, hist., Syria **E8** 44
Palmyra see Tudmur, Syria **E8** 44
Palmyra, In., U.S. **H5** 107
Palmyra, Mo., U.S. **B6** 118
Palmyra, N.J., U.S. **C2** 123
Palmyra, N.Y., U.S. **B3** 125
Palmyra, Pa., U.S. **F8** 131
Palmyra, Wi., U.S. **F5** 142
Palo Alto, Ca., U.S. **D2** 98
Palo Alto, co., Ia., U.S. **A3** 108
Paloich, Sudan **H11** 48
Palomar Mountain, mtn., Ca., U.S. **F5** 98
Palomas Mountains, mts., Az., U.S. **D2** 96
Palo Pinto, co., Tx., U.S. **C3** 136
Palopo, Indon. **D6** 36
Palo Santo, Arg. **D6** 72
Palos Park, Il., U.S. **k9** 106
Palos Verdes Estates, Ca., U.S. **n12** 98
Palourde, Lake, l., La., U.S. **k9** 111
Palouse, Wa., U.S. **C8** 140
Palouse, stm., Wa., U.S. **C7** 140
Palu, Indon. **D5** 36
Palu, Tur. **C8** 44
Pamekasan, Indon. **E4** 36
Pamiers, Fr. **F7** 16
Pamir, mts., Asia **B2** 40
Pamlico, stm., N.C., U.S. **B6** 126
Pamlico, co., N.C., U.S. **B6** 126
Pamlico Sound, strt., N.C., U.S. **B6** 126
Pampa, reg., Arg. **F5** 72
Pampa, Tx., U.S. **B2** 136
Pampa del Infierno, Arg. **D5** 72
Pampas, Peru **A3** 72
Pamplico, S.C., U.S. **D8** 133
Pamplona, Col. **B5** 70
Pamplona, Spain **F6** 16
Pamunkey, stm., Va., U.S. **C5** 139
Pana, Il., U.S. **D4** 106
Panaca, Nv., U.S. **F7** 121
Panache, Lake, l., On., Can. **A3** 89
Panaji, India **F2** 40
Panama, ctry., N.A. **I11** 75
Panamá, Pan. **D4** 80
Panama, Ok., U.S. **B7** 129
Panamá, Bahía de, b., Pan. **D4** 80
Panamá, Canal de, Pan. **D4** 80
Panamá, Golfo de, b., Pan. **D4** 80
Panamá, Gulf of see Panamá, Golfo de, b., Pan. **D4** 80
Panamá, Istmo de, isth., Pan. **D4** 80
Panama Basin **H30** 64
Panama Canal see Panamá, Canal de, Pan. **D4** 80
Panama City see Panamá, Pan. **D4** 80
Panama City, Fl., U.S. **u16** 102
Panama City Beach, Fl., U.S. **u16** 102
Panamint Range, mts., Ca., U.S. **D5** 98
Panay, i., Phil. **D8** 34
Pancake Range, mts., Nv., U.S. **E6** 121
Pančevo, Serb. **B8** 18
Pandharpur, India **F3** 40
Pandora, Oh., U.S. **B2** 128
Panfilov, Kaz. **E9** 26
Pangala, Congo **D2** 54
Pangani, Tan. **E7** 54
Pangburn, Ar., U.S. **B4** 97
Pangi, D.R.C. **D5** 54
Pangkajene, Indon. **D5** 36
Pangkalanbuun, Indon. **D4** 36
Pangkalpinang, Indon. **D3** 36
Pango Aluquem, Ang. **E2** 54
Panguitch, Ut., U.S. **F3** 137
Pangutaran Group, is., Phil. **E7** 34
Panhandle, Tx., U.S. **B2** 136
Pāni'au, mtn., Hi., U.S. **B1** 104
Panié, Mont, mtn., N. Cal. **I8** 62a
Pānīpat, India **D3** 40
Panj see Amu Darya, stm., Asia **B8** 42
Panjang, Indon. **E3** 36
Panjgūr, Pak. **E8** 42
Pankshin, Nig. **E6** 50
Panna, India **E4** 40
Pannawonica, Austl. **E2** 60
Panola, co., Ms., U.S. **A3** 117
Panola, co., Tx., U.S. **C5** 136
Panora, Ia., U.S. **C3** 108
Pantar, Pulau, i., Indon. **E6** 36
Pantelleria, Isola di, i., Italy **F3** 18
Pánuco, stm., Mex. **C5** 78
Pánuco, Mex. **C5** 78
Panxian, China **F8** 28
Panyam, Nig. **E6** 50
Panyu, China **B6** 34
Paola, Italy **E5** 18
Paola, Ks., U.S. **D9** 109
Paoli, In., U.S. **G5** 107
Paoli, Pa., U.S. **o20** 131
Paonia, Co., U.S. **C3** 99
Pápa, Hung. **F4** 20
Pāpa'aloa, Hi., U.S. **D6** 104
Papagayo, Golfo de, b., C.R. **C2** 80
Papago Indian Reservation, Az., U.S. **E3** 96
Papantla de Olarte, Mex. **C5** 78
Papawai Point, c., Hi., U.S. **C5** 104
Papeete, Fr. Poly. **F15** 58
Papenburg, Ger. **D10** 12
Paphos see Néa Páfos, Cyp. **E5** 44
Papigochic, stm., Mex. **B3** 78
Papillion, Ne., U.S. **C9** 120
Papineauville, Qc., Can. **D2** 90
Paposo, Chile **C3** 72
Papua, Gulf of, b., Pap. N. Gui. **H11** 32
Papua New Guinea, ctry., Oc. **H11** 32
Papun, Mya. **C3** 34
Pará see Belém, Braz. **B2** 74
Pará, state, Braz. **E9** 70
Parabel', Russia **D10** 26
Paraburdoo, Austl. **E2** 60
Paracatu, Braz. **E2** 74
Paracel Islands (Xisha Qundao), is., China **C6** 34
Parachute, Co., U.S. **B2** 99
Paraćin, Serb. **C8** 18
Paracuru, Braz. **B4** 74
Paradis, La., U.S. **k11** 111
Paradise, stm., N.L., Can. **B3** 88
Paradise, Ca., U.S. **C3** 98
Paradise, Nv., U.S. **G6** 121
Paradise Hills, N.M., U.S. **B3** 124
Paradise Valley, Az., U.S. **k9** 96
Paradise Valley, Nv., U.S. **B4** 121
Pāradwīp, India **E5** 40
Paragould, Ar., U.S. **A5** 97
Paraguai (Paraguay), stm., S.A. **B6** 72
Paraguaná, Península de, pen., Ven. **C6** 80
Paraguay, ctry., S.A. **C6** 72
Paraguay (Paraguai), stm., S.A. **C6** 72
Paraíba, state, Braz. **C4** 74
Paraíba do Sul, stm., Braz. **F3** 74
Parakou, Benin **E5** 50
Paramaribo, Sur. **B8** 70
Paramirim, Braz. **F11** 70
Paramount, Md., U.S. **A2** 113
Paramus, N.J., U.S. **h8** 123
Paramušir, ostrov, i., Russia **D17** 26
Paraná, Arg. **E5** 72
Paranã, Braz. **F10** 70
Paraná, state, Braz. **C7** 72
Paranã, stm., Braz. **F5** 68
Paraná, stm., S.A. **E6** 72
Paranaguá, Braz. **D8** 72
Paranaíba, Braz. **E2** 74
Paranapanema, stm., Braz. **C7** 72
Paranavaí, Braz. **C7** 72
Parang, Phil. **E8** 34
Parangaba, Braz. **B4** 74
Paranhos, Braz. **C6** 72
Paray-le-Monial, Fr. **D9** 16
Pārbati, stm., India **D3** 40
Parbhani, India **F3** 40
Parchment, Mi., U.S. **F5** 115

Name — Map Ref. — Page

Pardeeville, Wi., U.S. **E4** 142
Pardo, stm., Braz. **F2** 74
Pardubice, Czech Rep. **E3** 20
Parecis, Braz. **A6** 72
Parecis, Chapada dos, mts., Braz. **A6** 72
Paren', Russia **C18** 26
Parepare, Indon. **D5** 36
Paria, stm., U.S. **A4** 96
Paria, Gulf of, b. **C7** 80
Pariaman, Indon. **D2** 36
Parigi, Indon. **D6** 36
Parika, Guy. **B8** 70
Paris, On., Can. **D4** 89
Paris, Fr. **C8** 16
Paris, Ar., U.S. **B2** 97
Paris, Il., U.S. **D6** 106
Paris, Ky., U.S. **B5** 110
Paris, Mo., U.S. **B5** 118
Paris, Tn., U.S. **A3** 135
Paris, Tx., U.S. **C5** 136
Paris Peak, mtn., Id., U.S. **G7** 105
Parita, Bahía de, b., Pan. **D3** 80
Park, co., Co., U.S. **B5** 99
Park, co., Mt., U.S. **E6** 119
Park, stm., N.D., U.S. **A8** 127
Park, co., Wy., U.S. **B3** 143
Park City, Ks., U.S. **g12** 109
Park City, Ut., U.S. **C4** 137
Parkdale, P.E., Can. **C6** 87
Parke, co., In., U.S. **E3** 107
Parker, Az., U.S. **C1** 96
Parker, Co., U.S. **B6** 99
Parker, Fl., U.S. **u16** 102
Parker, S.D., U.S. **D8** 134
Parker, co., Tx., U.S. **C4** 136
Parker City, In., U.S. **D7** 107
Parker Dam, U.S. **C1** 96
Parkersburg, Ia., U.S. **B5** 108
Parkersburg, W.V., U.S. **B3** 141
Parkers Prairie, Mn., U.S. **D3** 116
Parkes, Austl. **G4** 62
Parkesburg, Pa., U.S. **G10** 131
Park Falls, Wi., U.S. **C3** 142
Park Forest, Il., U.S. **B6** 106
Park Hall, Md., U.S. **D5** 113
Parkhill, On., Can. **D3** 89
Park Hills, Ky., U.S. **h13** 110
Parkin, Ar., U.S. **B5** 97
Parkland, Wa., U.S. **f11** 140
Park Layne, Oh., U.S. **C1** 128
Park Range, mts., Co., U.S. **A4** 99
Park Rapids, Mn., U.S. **D3** 116
Park Ridge, Il., U.S. **B6** 106
Park Ridge, N.J., U.S. **g8** 123
Park River, N.D., U.S. **A8** 127
Parkrose, Or., U.S. **B4** 130
Parksley, Va., U.S. **C7** 139
Parkston, S.D., U.S. **D8** 134
Parksville, B.C., Can. **E5** 85
Parkville, Md., U.S. **B4** 113
Parkville, Mo., U.S. **B3** 118
Parkwater, Wa., U.S. **g14** 140
Parkwood, N.C., U.S. **B4** 126
Parlākimidi, India **F4** 40
Parle, Lac qui, l., Mn., U.S. **E3** 116
Parlier, Ca., U.S. **D4** 98
Parma, Italy **B3** 18
Parma, Id., U.S. **F2** 105
Parma, Mi., U.S. **F6** 115
Parma, Mo., U.S. **E8** 118
Parma, Oh., U.S. **A4** 128
Parmachenee Lake, l., Me., U.S. **C2** 112
Parma Heights, Oh., U.S. **h9** 128
Parmer, co., Tx., U.S. **B1** 136
Parnaguá, Braz. **F11** 70
Parnaíba, stm., Braz. **B3** 74
Parnaíba, Braz. **B3** 74
Parnassós, mtn., Grc. **E9** 18
Pärnu, Est. **G11** 10
Paro, Bhu. **D5** 40
Paromaj, Russia **D16** 26
Parowan, Ut., U.S. **F3** 137
Par Pond, res., S.C., U.S. **D5** 133
Parral, Chile **F3** 72
Parramatta, Austl. **G5** 62
Parramore Island, i., Va., U.S. **C7** 139
Parras de la Fuente, Mex. **E9** 78
Parrish, Al., U.S. **B2** 94
Parrsboro, N.S., Can. **D5** 87
Parry, Mount, mtn., B.C., Can. **C3** 85
Parry Sound, On., Can. **B4** 89
Parshall, N.D., U.S. **B3** 127
Parsons, Ks., U.S. **E8** 109
Parsons, Tn., U.S. **B3** 135
Parsons, W.V., U.S. **B5** 141
Parsonsburg, Md., U.S. **D7** 113
Parthenay, Fr. **D6** 16
Partille, Swe. **H5** 10
Partizansk, Russia **B2** 31
Partridge Point, c., N.L., Can. **C3** 88
Paru, stm., Braz. **D9** 70
Paru de Oeste, stm., Braz. **C8** 70
Pārvatīpuram, India **F4** 40
Paryang, China **C4** 40
Parys, S. Afr. **D4** 56
Pasadena, N.L., Can. **D3** 88
Pasadena, Ca., U.S. **E4** 98
Pasadena, Md., U.S. **B4** 113
Pasadena, Tx., U.S. **r14** 136
Pascagoula, Ms., U.S. **E5** 117
Pascagoula, stm., Ms., U.S. **E5** 117
Pascagoula Bay, b., Ms., U.S. **f8** 117
Paşcani, Rom. **F9** 20
Pasco, co., Fl., U.S. **D4** 102
Pasco, Wa., U.S. **C6** 140
Pascoag, R.I., U.S. **B2** 132
Pascoag Reservoir, res., R.I., U.S. **B2** 132
Pascua, Isla de (Easter Island), i., Chile **K28** 64
Pasinler, Tur. **B9** 44
Pasir Mas, Malay. **B2** 36
Pasni, Pak. **E8** 42
Paso de los Libres, Arg. **D6** 72
Paso de los Toros, Ur. **E6** 72
Paso Robles, Ca., U.S. **E3** 98
Pasque Island, i., Ma., U.S. **D6** 114
Pasquotank, co., N.C., U.S. **A6** 126
Passaic, N.J., U.S. **B4** 123
Passaic, co., N.J., U.S. **A4** 123
Passaic, stm., N.J., U.S. **h8** 123
Passamaquoddy Bay, b., Me., U.S. **C6** 112
Passau, Ger. **F13** 12
Pass Christian, Ms., U.S. **E4** 117
Passero, Capo, c., Italy **F5** 18
Passo Fundo, Braz. **D7** 72
Passos, Braz. **F2** 74
Passumpsic, stm., Vt., U.S. **C4** 138
Pastavy, Bela. **B9** 20
Pastaza, stm., S.A. **D4** 70
Pasto, Col. **C4** 70
Pastora Peak, mtn., Az., U.S. **A6** 96
Pasuruan, Indon. **E4** 36
Pasvalys, Lith. **H11** 10
Patadkal, hist., India **F3** 40
Patagonia, reg., Arg. **F3** 69
Patagonia, Az., U.S. **F5** 96
Pātan, India **E2** 40
Patapsco, stm., Md., U.S. **B4** 113
Pataskala, Oh., U.S. **C3** 128
Patchet Brook Reservoir, res., R.I., U.S. **E6** 132
Patchogue, N.Y., U.S. **n15** 125
Pategi, Nig. **E6** 50
Pate Island, i., Kenya **D8** 54
Paterna, Spain **H6** 16
Paternò, Italy **F5** 18
Paterson, N.J., U.S. **B4** 123
Pathānkot, India **C3** 40
Pathein, Mya. **C2** 34
Pathfinder Reservoir, res., Wy., U.S. **D6** 143
Patiāla, India **C3** 40
Patience Island, i., R.I., U.S. **D5** 132
Patman, Lake, res., Tx., U.S. **C5** 136
Patna, India **D5** 40
Patnos, Tur. **C10** 44
Pato Branco, Braz. **D7** 72
Patoka, stm., In., U.S. **H2** 107
Patoka, In., U.S. **H2** 107
Patoka Lake, res., In., U.S. **H4** 107
Patos, Braz. **C4** 74
Patos, Lagoa dos, b., Braz. **E7** 72
Patos de Minas, Braz. **E2** 74
Patquía, Arg. **D4** 72
Pátrai, Grc. **E8** 18
Patraïkós Kólpos, b., Grc. **E8** 18
Patrick, co., Va., U.S. **D2** 139
Patrick Air Force Base, mil., Fl., U.S. **D6** 102
Patrocínio, Braz. **E2** 74
Pattani, Thai. **E4** 34
Patten, Me., U.S. **C4** 112
Patterson, Ga., U.S. **E4** 103
Patterson, La., U.S. **E4** 111
Patterson Creek, stm., W.V., U.S. **B5** 141
Patton, Pa., U.S. **E4** 131
Patuākhāli, Bngl. **E6** 40
Patuca, stm., Hond. **B3** 80
Patuxent, stm., Md., U.S. **D4** 113
Patuxent Naval Air Test Center, mil., Md., U.S. **D5** 113
Pátzcuaro, Mex. **D4** 78
Pau, Fr. **B3** 16
Paul, Id., U.S. **G5** 105
Paulding, co., Ga., U.S. **C2** 103
Paulding, Oh., U.S. **A1** 128
Paulding, co., Oh., U.S. **A1** 128
Paulina, La., U.S. **h10** 111
Paulina Mountains, mts., Or., U.S. **D5** 130
Paulina Peak, mtn., Or., U.S. **E5** 130
Paulins Kill, stm., N.J., U.S. **A3** 123
Paulistana, Braz. **E11** 70
Paullina, Ia., U.S. **B2** 108
Paulo Afonso, Braz. **C4** 74
Paulsboro, N.J., U.S. **D2** 123
Paul Stream, stm., Vt., U.S. **B5** 138
Pauls Valley, Ok., U.S. **C4** 129
Paungde, Mya. **C3** 34
Pāveh, Iran **E12** 44
Pavia, Italy **B2** 18
Pavilion Key, i., Fl., U.S. **G5** 102
Pāvilosta, Lat. **H9** 10
Pavlodar, Kaz. **D9** 26
Pavlof Volcano, vol., Ak., U.S. **D7** 95
Pavlohrad, Ukr. **E13** 20
Pavlovo, Russia **C7** 22
Pavo, Ga., U.S. **F3** 103
Pawcatuck, Ct., U.S. **D8** 100
Pawcatuck, stm., R.I., U.S. **G1** 132
Paw Creek, N.C., U.S. **B2** 126
Pawhuska, Ok., U.S. **A5** 129
Pawling, N.Y., U.S. **D7** 125
Pawnee, Il., U.S. **D4** 106
Pawnee, stm., Ks., U.S. **D3** 109
Pawnee, co., Ks., U.S. **D4** 109
Pawnee, co., Ne., U.S. **D9** 120
Pawnee, Ok., U.S. **A5** 129
Pawnee, co., Ok., U.S. **A5** 129
Pawnee City, Ne., U.S. **D9** 120
Pawpaw, Il., U.S. **B5** 106
Paw Paw, Mi., U.S. **F5** 115
Paw Paw, stm., Mi., U.S. **F4** 115
Pawpaw Creek, stm., W.V., U.S. **h10** 141
Pawtuckaway Pond, l., N.H., U.S. **D4** 122
Pawtucket, R.I., U.S. **C4** 132
Pawtuxet, stm., R.I., U.S. **C4** 132
Paxton, Il., U.S. **C5** 106
Paxton, Ma., U.S. **B4** 114
Payakumbuh, Indon. **D2** 36
Payeti, Indon. **E6** 36
Payette, Id., U.S. **E2** 105
Payette, co., Id., U.S. **E2** 105
Payette, North Fork, stm., Id., U.S. **E2** 105
Payette, South Fork, stm., Id., U.S. **E3** 105
Payette Lake, res., Id., U.S. **E3** 105
Payne, Oh., U.S. **A1** 128
Payne, co., Ok., U.S. **A4** 129
Payne, Lac, l., Can. **G25** 82
Paynes Find, Austl. **F2** 60
Paynesville, Mn., U.S. **E4** 116
Paysandú, Ur. **E6** 72
Payson, Az., U.S. **C4** 96
Payson, Il., U.S. **D2** 106
Payson, Ut., U.S. **C4** 137
Pazar, Tur. **B9** 44
Pazarcık, Tur. **D7** 44
Pazardžik, Blg. **C10** 18
Paz de Río, Col. **D5** 80
Pea, stm., Al., U.S. **D3** 94
Peabody, Ks., U.S. **D6** 109
Peabody, Ma., U.S. **A6** 114
Peabody, stm., N.H., U.S. **B4** 122
Peace, stm., Can. **D8** 75
Peace, stm., Fl., U.S. **E5** 102
Peace Dale, R.I., U.S. **F3** 132
Peace River, Ab., Can. **A2** 84
Peach, co., Ga., U.S. **D3** 103
Peacham Pond, res., Vt., U.S. **C4** 138
Peach Point, c., Ma., U.S. **f12** 114
Peach Springs, Az., U.S. **B2** 96
Peak Hill, Austl. **F2** 60
Peaks Island, i., Me., U.S. **g7** 112
Peale, Mount, mtn., Ut., U.S. **E6** 137
Pea Patch Island, i., De., U.S. **B3** 101
Pea Ridge, Ar., U.S. **A1** 97
Pea Ridge National Military Park, Ar., U.S. **A1** 97
Pearisburg, Va., U.S. **C2** 139
Pearl, Ms., U.S. **C3** 117
Pearl, stm., U.S. **D3** 117
Pearland, Tx., U.S. **r14** 136
Pearl and Hermes Reef, rf., Hi., U.S. **k12** 104
Pearl City, Hi., U.S. **B4** 104
Pearl Harbor, b., Hi., U.S. **B3** 104
Pearl Harbor Naval Station, mil., Hi., U.S. **g10** 104
Pearlington, Ms., U.S. **E4** 117
Pearl River, La., U.S. **D6** 111
Pearl River, co., Ms., U.S. **E4** 117
Pearl River, N.Y., U.S. **g12** 125
Pearsall, Tx., U.S. **E3** 136
Pearsoll Peak, mtn., Or., U.S. **E3** 130
Pearson, Ga., U.S. **E4** 103
Peary Land, reg., Grnld. **B32** 82
Pease, stm., Tx., U.S. **B3** 136
Pebane, Moz. **B6** 56
Peć, Serb. **C8** 18
Pecatonica, Il., U.S. **A4** 106
Pecatonica, stm., U.S. **A4** 106
Pecatonica, East Branch, stm., Wi., U.S. **F4** 142
Pečenga, Russia **C5** 26
Pechora see Pečora, Russia **C7** 26
Pechora see Pečora, stm., Russia **C7** 26
Pechora Bay see Pečorskaja guba, b., Russia **A9** 22
Peckerwood Lake, res., Ar., U.S. **C4** 97
Pečora, Russia **C7** 26
Pečora, stm., Russia **C7** 26
Pečorskaja guba, b., Russia **A9** 22
Pečorskoe more, Russia **C7** 26
Pecos, N.M., U.S. **B4** 124
Pecos, Tx., U.S. **D1** 136
Pecos, co., Tx., U.S. **D1** 136
Pecos, stm., U.S. **E7** 92
Pecos National Monument, N.M., U.S. **B4** 124
Pécs, Hung. **F5** 20
Peculiar, Mo., U.S. **C3** 118
Peddocks Island, i., Ma., U.S. **g12** 114
Pedernales, Ven. **D7** 80
Pedra Azul, Braz. **E3** 74
Pedreiras, Braz. **B3** 74
Pedro Afonso, Braz. **E10** 70
Pedro II, Braz. **B3** 74
Pedro Juan Caballero, Para. **C6** 72
Peebles, Oh., U.S. **D2** 128
Peekskill, N.Y., U.S. **D7** 125
Peel, stm., Can. **E13** 82
Pegasus Bay, b., N.Z. **p13** 63c
Pegram, Tn., U.S. **A4** 135
Pehuajó, Arg. **F5** 72
Peikang, Tai. **E5** 30
Peipus, Lake, l., Eur. **G12** 10
Peixian, China **C4** 30
Pekalongan, Indon. **E3** 36
Pekanbaru, Indon. **C2** 36
Pekin, Il., U.S. **C4** 106
Pekin, In., U.S. **G5** 107
Peking see Beijing, China **D11** 28
Pelagie, Isole, is., Italy **G4** 18
Pelahatchie, Ms., U.S. **C4** 117
Pelee Island, i., On., Can. **F2** 89
Peleng, Pulau, i., Indon. **D6** 36
Pelham, On., Can. **D5** 89
Pelham, Al., U.S. **B3** 94
Pelham, Ga., U.S. **E2** 103
Pelham, N.H., U.S. **E4** 122
Pelham Manor, N.Y., U.S. **h13** 125
Pelican Bay, b., Mb., Can. **C1** 86
Pelican Lake, l., Mb., Can. **C1** 86
Pelican Lake, l., Mn., U.S. **D3** 116
Pelican Lake, l., Mn., U.S. **B6** 116
Pelican Lake, l., Mn., U.S. **E5** 116
Pelican Lake, l., Mn., U.S. **D4** 116
Pelican Lake, l., Wi., U.S. **C4** 142
Pelican Mountain, mtn., Ab., Can. **B4** 84
Pelican Rapids, Mn., U.S. **D2** 116
Pella, Ia., U.S. **C5** 108
Pell City, Al., U.S. **B3** 94
Pell Lake, Wi., U.S. **n11** 142
Pello, Fin. **C11** 10
Peloponnesus see Pelopónnisos, pen., Grc. **F8** 18
Pelopónnisos, pen., Grc. **F8** 18
Pelotas, Braz. **E7** 72
Pelton, Lake, l., La., U.S. **E5** 111
Pemadumcook Lake, l., Me., U.S. **C3** 112
Pematangsiantar, Indon. **C1** 36
Pemba, Moz. **A7** 56
Pemba, i., Tan. **E7** 54
Pemberton, Austl. **G2** 60
Pemberville, Oh., U.S. **A2** 128
Pembina, stm., Ab., Can. **C3** 84
Pembina, N.D., U.S. **A8** 127
Pembina, co., N.D., U.S. **A8** 127
Pembroke, On., Can. **B7** 89
Pembroke, Wales, U.K. **E4** 12
Pembroke, Ga., U.S. **D5** 103
Pembroke, Ky., U.S. **D2** 110
Pembroke, Ma., U.S. **B6** 114
Pembroke, N.C., U.S. **C3** 126
Pembroke, Va., U.S. **C2** 139
Pembroke Pines, Fl., U.S. **r13** 102
Pemigewasset, stm., N.H., U.S. **C3** 122
Pemiscot, co., Mo., U.S. **E8** 118
Penang see George Town, Malay. **B2** 36
Peñaranda de Bracamonte, Spain **G4** 16
Pen Argyl, Pa., U.S. **E11** 131
Peñarroya-Pueblonuevo, Spain **H4** 16
Penas, Golfo de, b., Chile **G1** 69
Penasco, N.M., U.S. **A4** 124
Peñasco, Rio, stm., N.M., U.S. **E4** 124
Penbrook, Pa., U.S. **F8** 131
Pendembu, S.L. **E2** 50
Pendembu, S.L. **E2** 50
Pender, co., N.C., U.S. **C4** 126
Pender, Ne., U.S. **B9** 120
Pendleton, In., U.S. **E6** 107
Pendleton, co., Ky., U.S. **B5** 110
Pendleton, Or., U.S. **B8** 130
Pendleton, S.C., U.S. **B2** 133
Pendleton, co., W.V., U.S. **C5** 141
Pend Oreille, co., Wa., U.S. **A8** 140
Pend Oreille, Lake, l., Id., U.S. **A2** 105
Pend Oreille, Mount, mtn., Id., U.S. **A2** 105
Penedo, Braz. **D4** 74
Penetanguishene, On., Can. **C5** 89
Penglai, China **D12** 28
Pengshui, China **F9** 28
Pengxian, China **C1** 30
Penhold, Ab., Can. **C4** 84
Peniche, Port. **H2** 16
Penida, Nusa, i., Indon. **E5** 36
Pennant Point, c., N.S., Can. **E6** 87
Pennask Mountain, mtn., B.C., Can. **E7** 85
Pennell, Mount, mtn., Ut., U.S. **F5** 137
Penneru, stm., India **G3** 40
Penn Hills, Pa., U.S. **k14** 131
Pennington, co., Mn., U.S. **B2** 116
Pennington, co., S.D., U.S. **D2** 134
Pennington Gap, Va., U.S. **f8** 139
Pennsauken, N.J., U.S. **D2** 123
Pennsboro, W.V., U.S. **B4** 141
Pennsburg, Pa., U.S. **F11** 131
Penns Grove, N.J., U.S. **D2** 123
Pennsville, N.J., U.S. **D1** 123
Pennsylvania, state, U.S. **E7** 131
Pennville, In., U.S. **D7** 107
Penn Yan, N.Y., U.S. **C3** 125
Penobscot, stm., Me., U.S. **C4** 112
Penobscot, co., Me., U.S. **C4** 112
Penobscot Bay, b., Me., U.S. **D3** 112
Penobscot Lake, l., Me., U.S. **C2** 112
Penong, Austl. **G5** 60
Penonomé, Pan. **D3** 80
Penrhyn, atoll, Cook Is. **E14** 58
Penrith, Austl. **G5** 62
Penrith, Eng., U.K. **C5** 12
Pensacola, Fl., U.S. **u14** 102
Pensacola Bay, b., Fl., U.S. **u14** 102
Pensacola Dam, Ok., U.S. **A6** 129
Pensacola Mountains, mts., Ant. **E36** 67
Pentagon Mountain, mtn., Mt., U.S. **C3** 119
Pentecost Island see Pentecôte, i., Vanuatu **k9** 62a
Pentecôte, i., Vanuatu **k9** 62a
Penticton, B.C., Can. **E8** 85
Pentland Firth, strt., Scot., U.K. **A5** 12
Pentwater, Mi., U.S. **E4** 115
Penza, Russia **D6** 26
Penzance, Eng., U.K. **E4** 12
Penžinskaja guba, b., Russia **C18** 26
Peonan Point, c., Mb., Can. **D2** 86
Peoria, Az., U.S. **D3** 96
Peoria, Il., U.S. **C4** 106
Peoria, co., Il., U.S. **C4** 106
Peoria Heights, Il., U.S. **C4** 106
Peotone, Il., U.S. **B6** 106
Pepacton Reservoir, res., N.Y., U.S. **C6** 125
Pepeekeo, Hi., U.S. **D6** 104
Pepin, Wi., U.S. **D1** 142
Pepin, co., Wi., U.S. **D2** 142
Pepin, Lake, l., U.S. **D1** 142
Pepperell, Ma., U.S. **A4** 114
Pequannock, N.J., U.S. **B4** 123
Pequest, stm., N.J., U.S. **B2** 123
Pequop Mountains, mts., Nv., U.S. **C7** 121
Pequot Lakes, Mn., U.S. **D4** 116
Perabumulih, Indon. **D2** 36
Percival Lakes, l., Austl. **E3** 60
Percy, Il., U.S. **E4** 106
Perdido, Al., U.S. **D2** 94
Perdido, stm., U.S. **E2** 94
Perdido Bay, b., Al., U.S. **E2** 94
Pereira, Col. **C4** 70
Pereislav-Khmel'nyts'kyi, Ukr. **D11** 20
Pere Marquette, stm., Mi., U.S. **E4** 115
Pereslavl'-Zalesskij, Russia **C6** 22
Pergamino, Arg. **E5** 72
Pergamum, hist., Tur. **C2** 44
Perham, Mn., U.S. **D3** 116
Perico, Arg. **C4** 72
Pericos, Mex. **B3** 78
Peridot, Az., U.S. **D5** 96
Périgueux, Fr. **E7** 16
Perijá, Serranía de, mts., S.A. **G10** 76
Perkasie, Pa., U.S. **F11** 131
Perkins, co., Ne., U.S. **D4** 120
Perkins, Ok., U.S. **B4** 129
Perkins, co., S.D., U.S. **B3** 134
Perkinston, Ms., U.S. **E4** 117
Perlas, Archipiélago de las, is., Pan. **D4** 80
Perlas, Laguna de, b., Nic. **C3** 80
Perm', Russia **D7** 26
Pernambuco, state, Braz. **C4** 74
Pernik, Blg. **C9** 18
Perpignan, Fr. **F8** 16
Perquimans, co., N.C., U.S. **A6** 126
Perrine, Fl., U.S. **G6** 102
Perris, Ca., U.S. **F5** 98
Perro, Laguna del, l., N.M., U.S. **C4** 124
Perrot, Île, i., Qc., Can. **q19** 90
Perry, co., Al., U.S. **C2** 94
Perry, co., Ar., U.S. **C3** 97
Perry, Fl., U.S. **B3** 102
Perry, Ga., U.S. **D3** 103
Perry, Ia., U.S. **C3** 108
Perry, co., Il., U.S. **E4** 106
Perry, co., In., U.S. **H4** 107
Perry, Ks., U.S. **C8** 109
Perry, co., Ky., U.S. **C6** 110
Perry, Mi., U.S. **F6** 115
Perry, Mo., U.S. **B6** 118
Perry, co., Mo., U.S. **D8** 118
Perry, co., Ms., U.S. **D4** 117
Perry, N.Y., U.S. **C2** 125
Perry, Oh., U.S. **A4** 128
Perry, co., Oh., U.S. **C3** 128
Perry, Ok., U.S. **A4** 129
Perry, co., Pa., U.S. **F7** 131
Perry, co., Tn., U.S. **B4** 135
Perry, Ut., U.S. **B3** 137
Perry Hall, Md., U.S. **B5** 113

Name	Map Ref.	Page
Perry Lake, res., Ks., U.S.	C8	109
Perryman, Md., U.S.	B5	113
Perrysburg, Oh., U.S.	A2	128
Perry Stream, stm., N.H., U.S.	f7	122
Perry's Victory and International Peace Memorial, hist., Oh., U.S.	A2	128
Perryton, Tx., U.S.	A2	136
Perryville, Ar., U.S.	B3	97
Perryville, Ky., U.S.	C5	110
Perryville, Md., U.S.	A5	113
Perryville, Mo., U.S.	D8	118
Pershing, co., Nv., U.S.	C3	121
Persia see Iran, ctry., Asia	D6	42
Persian Gulf (The Gulf), b., Asia	E6	42
Person, co., N.C., U.S.	A3	126
Perth, Austl.	G2	60
Perth, On., Can.	C8	89
Perth, Scot., U.K.	E5	12
Perth Amboy, N.J., U.S.	B4	123
Perth-Andover, N.B., Can.	D10	87
Perth Basin	K13	64
Peru, ctry., S.A.	E4	70
Peru, Il., U.S.	B4	106
Peru, In., U.S.	C5	107
Peru, Ne., U.S.	D10	120
Peru, N.Y., U.S.	f11	125
Peru Basin	J5	66
Peru-Chile Trench	J6	66
Perugia, Italy	C4	18
Peruíbe, Braz.	C8	72
Pervari, Tur.	D10	44
Pervomais'k, Ukr.	E11	20
Pervoural'sk, Russia	D7	26
Pesaro, Italy	C4	18
Pescara, Italy	C5	18
Peshastin, Wa., U.S.	B5	140
Peshāwar, Pak.	D10	42
Peshtigo, Wi., U.S.	C6	142
Peshtigo, stm., Wi., U.S.	C5	142
Pesqueira, Braz.	C4	74
Pessac, Fr.	E6	16
Pëstraja Dresva, Russia	C17	26
Petaḥ Tiqwa, Isr.	F6	44
Petal, Ms., U.S.	D4	117
Petaluma, Ca., U.S.	C2	98
Petatlán, Mex.	D4	78
Petawawa, On., Can.	B7	89
Petawawa, stm., On., Can.	A6	89
Petenwell Lake, res., Wi., U.S.	D4	142
Peterborough, Austl.	G2	62
Peterborough, On., Can.	C6	89
Peterborough, Eng., U.K.	D6	12
Peterborough, N.H., U.S.	E3	122
Peterhead, Scot., U.K.	B6	12
Peter I Island, i., Ant.	C31	67
Peter Pond Lake, l., Sk., Can.	m7	91
Petersburg, Ak., U.S.	D13	95
Petersburg, Il., U.S.	C4	106
Petersburg, In., U.S.	H3	107
Petersburg, Mi., U.S.	G7	115
Petersburg, Oh., U.S.	B5	128
Petersburg, Tx., U.S.	C2	136
Petersburg, Va., U.S.	C5	139
Petersburg, W.V., U.S.	B5	141
Peters Creek, stm., W.V., U.S.	m14	141
Peterson, Al., U.S.	B2	94
Peterson Field, Co., U.S.	C6	99
Petersville, Al., U.S.	A2	94
Peter the Great Bay see Petra Velikogo, zaliv, b., Russia	C14	28
Pétion-Ville, Haiti	B5	80
Petit Bois Island, i., Ms., U.S.	E5	117
Petitcodiac, stm., N.B., Can.	C5	87
Petitcodiac, N.B., Can.	D4	87
Petite Amite, stm., La., U.S.	h10	111
Petite Rivière Noire, Piton de la, mtn., Mrts.	g10	57a
Petit Jean, stm., Ar., U.S.	B2	97
Petit Lac Des Allemands, l., La., U.S.	k11	111
Petit Lake, l., La., U.S.	k12	111
Petit-Rocher, N.B., Can.	B4	87
Petitsikapau Lake, l., N.L., Can.	g8	88
Peto, Mex.	C7	78
Petoskey, Mi., U.S.	C6	115
Petra see Al-Batrā', hist., Jord.	D3	42
Petra Velikogo, zaliv, b., Russia	C14	28
Petrič, Blg.	D9	18
Petrified Forest National Park, Az., U.S.	B6	96
Petrila, Rom.	G7	20
Petrodvorec, Russia	G13	10
Petrograd see Sankt-Peterburg, Russia	D5	26
Petrolândia, Braz.	C4	74
Petroleum, co., Mt., U.S.	C8	119
Petrolia, On., Can.	E2	89
Petrolina, Braz.	C3	74
Petropavlovsk, Kaz.	D8	26
Petropavlovsk-Kamčatskij, Russia	D17	26
Petrópolis, Braz.	F3	74
Petros, Tn., U.S.	C9	135
Petroşani, Rom.	G7	20
Petrovsk, Russia	D8	22
Petrozavodsk, Russia	C5	26
Pettaquamscutt Lake Shores, R.I., U.S.	F4	132
Pettingell Peak, mtn., Co., U.S.	B5	99
Pettis, co., Mo., U.S.	C4	118
Pevek, Russia	C19	26
Pevely, Mo., U.S.	g13	118
Pewaukee, Wi., U.S.	E5	142
Pewaukee Lake, l., Wi., U.S.	m11	142
Pewee Valley, Ky., U.S.	B4	110
Pha-an, Mya.	C3	34
Phalaborwa, S. Afr.	C5	56
Phalodi, India	D2	40
Phangan, Ko, i., Thai.	E4	34
Phangnga, Thai.	E3	34
Phanom Dongrak Range, mts., Asia	D4	34
Phan Rang, Viet.	D5	34
Phan Si Pan see Fan Si Pan, mtn., Viet.	B4	34
Phan Thiet, Viet.	D5	34
Pharr, Tx., U.S.	F3	136
Phatthalung, Thai.	E4	34
Phayao, Thai.	C3	34
Phelps, Ky., U.S.	C7	110
Phelps, co., Mo., U.S.	D6	118
Phelps, co., Ne., U.S.	D6	120
Phelps, N.Y., U.S.	C3	125
Phelps, Wi., U.S.	B4	142
Phelps Lake, l., N.C., U.S.	B6	126
Phenix City, Al., U.S.	C4	94
Phetchabun, Thai.	C4	34
Phetchaburi, Thai.	D3	34
Phibun Mangsahan, Thai.	C5	34
Phichit, Thai.	C4	34
Philadelphia, Ms., U.S.	C4	117
Philadelphia, Pa., U.S.	G11	131
Philadelphia, co., Pa., U.S.	G12	131
Philadelphia Naval Shipyard, mil., Pa., U.S.	P21	131
Phil Campbell, Al., U.S.	A2	94
Philip, S.D., U.S.	C4	134
Philippeville see Skikda, Alg.	C6	48
Philippi see Fílippoi, hist., Grc.	D10	18
Philippi, W.V., U.S.	B4	141
Philippine Basin	G15	64
Philippines, ctry., Asia	C8	34
Philippine Sea	H16	24
Philippine Trench	H15	64
Philippopolis see Plovdiv, Blg.	C10	18
Philipsburg, Mt., U.S.	D3	119
Philipsburg, Pa., U.S.	E5	131
Philleo Lake, l., Wa., U.S.	h14	140
Phillips, co., Ar., U.S.	C5	97
Phillips, co., Co., U.S.	A8	99
Phillips, co., Ks., U.S.	C4	109
Phillips, Me., U.S.	D2	112
Phillips, co., Mt., U.S.	B8	119
Phillips, Tx., U.S.	B2	136
Phillips, Wi., U.S.	C3	142
Phillips Brook, stm., N.H., U.S.	A4	122
Phillipsburg, Ks., U.S.	C4	109
Phillipsburg, N.J., U.S.	B2	123
Philmont, N.Y., U.S.	C7	125
Philo, Il., U.S.	C5	106
Philomath, Or., U.S.	C3	130
Philpott Reservoir, res., Va., U.S.	D2	139
Phitsanulok, Thai.	C4	34
Phnom Penh see Phnum Pénh, Camb.	D4	34
Phnum Pénh (Phnom Penh), Camb.	D4	34
Phoenix, Az., U.S.	D3	96
Phoenix, Il., U.S.	k9	106
Phoenix, N.Y., U.S.	B4	125
Phoenix, Or., U.S.	E4	130
Phoenix Islands, is., Kir.	E12	58
Phoenixville, Pa., U.S.	F10	131
Phon, Thai.	C4	34
Phôngsali, Laos	B4	34
Phrae, Thai.	C4	34
Phra Nakhon Si Ayutthaya, Thai.	D4	34
Phuket, Thai.	E3	34
Phuket, Ko, i., Thai.	E3	34
Phumĭ Chhuk, Camb.	D4	34
Phumĭ Kâmpóng Srâlau, Camb.	D5	34
Phumĭ Kaôh Kŏng, Camb.	D4	34
Phu Quoc, Dao, i., Viet.	D4	34
Piacenza, Italy	B2	18
Pianosa, Isola, i., Italy	C3	18
Piatra-Neamţ, Rom.	F9	20
Piatt, co., Il., U.S.	D5	106
Piauí, state, Braz.	C3	74
Piave, stm., Italy	A4	18
Pibor Post, Sudan	I11	48
Picacho, Az., U.S.	E4	96
Picardie, hist. reg., Fr.	C8	16
Picardy see Picardie, hist. reg., Fr.	C8	16
Picayune, Ms., U.S.	E4	117
Piccadilly, N.L., Can.	D2	88
Pichanal, Arg.	C5	72
Picher, Ok., U.S.	A7	129
Pichilemu, Chile	E3	72
Pickaway, co., Oh., U.S.	C2	128
Pickens, co., Al., U.S.	B1	94
Pickens, co., Ga., U.S.	B2	103
Pickens, Ms., U.S.	C4	117
Pickens, S.C., U.S.	B2	133
Pickens, co., S.C., U.S.	B2	133
Pickerel Lake, l., Wi., U.S.	C5	142
Pickering, On., Can.	D5	89
Pickerington, Oh., U.S.	C3	128
Pickett, co., Tn., U.S.	C8	135
Pickwick Lake, res., U.S.	A6	117
Pickworth Point, c., Ma., U.S.	f12	114
Pico de Orizaba, Volcán, vol., Mex.	D5	78
Pico Rivera, Ca., U.S.	n12	98
Picos, Braz.	C3	74
Picton, On., Can.	D7	89
Pictou Island, i., N.S., Can.	D7	87
Picture Butte, Ab., Can.	E4	84
Pictured Rocks National Lakeshore, Mi., U.S.	B4	115
Pidurutalagala, mtn., Sri L.	H4	40
Piedecuesta, Col.	D5	80
Piedmont, Al., U.S.	B4	94
Piedmont, Ca., U.S.	h8	98
Piedmont, Mo., U.S.	D7	118
Piedmont, Ok., U.S.	B4	129
Piedmont, S.C., U.S.	B3	133
Piedmont, W.V., U.S.	B5	141
Piedmont Lake, res., Oh., U.S.	B4	128
Piedra, stm., Co., U.S.	D3	99
Piedras Blancas, Point, c., Ca., U.S.	E3	98
Piedras Negras, Guat.	B1	80
Piedras Negras, Mex.	B4	78
Pieksämäki, Fin.	E12	10
Pielinen, l., Fin.	E13	10
Pierce, Co., U.S.	A6	99
Pierce, co., Ga., U.S.	E4	103
Pierce, Id., U.S.	C3	105
Pierce, co., N.D., U.S.	A5	127
Pierce, Ne., U.S.	B8	120
Pierce, co., Ne., U.S.	B8	120
Pierce, co., Wa., U.S.	C3	140
Pierce, co., Wi., U.S.	D1	142
Pierce, Lake, l., Fl., U.S.	E5	102
Pierce City, Mo., U.S.	E3	118
Pierceton, In., U.S.	B6	107
Pierre, S.D., U.S.	C5	134
Pierrefonds, Qc., Can.	q19	90
Pierre Part, La., U.S.	k9	111
Pierreville, Qc., Can.	C5	90
Pierson, Fl., U.S.	C5	102
Pierz, Mn., U.S.	E4	116
Piešt'any, Slvk.	E4	20
Pietarsaari, Fin.	E10	10
Pietermaritzburg, S. Afr.	D5	56
Pietersburg, S. Afr.	C5	56
Piet Retief, S. Afr.	D5	56
Pigeon, stm., In., U.S.	A6	107
Pigeon, Mi., U.S.	E7	115
Pigeon, stm., Mn., U.S.	h10	116
Pigeon, stm., Wi., U.S.	k10	142
Pigeon, stm., U.S.	f9	126
Pigeon Cove, Ma., U.S.	A6	114
Pigeon Forge, Tn., U.S.	D10	135
Pigeon Point, c., Mn., U.S.	h10	116
Pigg, stm., Va., U.S.	D3	139
Piggott, Ar., U.S.	A5	97
Pigüé, Arg.	F5	72
Pihlajavesi, l., Fin.	F13	10
Pihtipudas, Fin.	E11	10
Pijijiapan, Mex.	D6	78
Pike, co., Al., U.S.	D4	94
Pike, co., Ar., U.S.	C2	97
Pike, co., Ga., U.S.	C2	103
Pike, co., Il., U.S.	D2	106
Pike, co., In., U.S.	H3	107
Pike, co., Ky., U.S.	C7	110
Pike, co., Mo., U.S.	B6	118
Pike, co., Ms., U.S.	D3	117
Pike, co., Oh., U.S.	C2	128
Pike, co., Pa., U.S.	D11	131
Pike, stm., Wi., U.S.	C6	142
Pike Island Dam, U.S.	f8	141
Pike Lake, Mn., U.S.	D6	116
Pikes Peak, mtn., Co., U.S.	C5	99
Pikesville, Md., U.S.	B4	113
Piketberg, S. Afr.	E2	56
Piketon, Oh., U.S.	C2	128
Pikeville, Ky., U.S.	C7	110
Pikeville, Tn., U.S.	D8	135
Piła, Pol.	C4	20
Pilcomayo, stm., S.A.	C5	72
Pīlībhīt, India	D3	40
Pillar Point, c., Ca., U.S.	k7	98
Pílos, Grc.	F8	18
Pilot Grove, Mo., U.S.	C5	118
Pilot Knob, mtn., Id., U.S.	D3	105
Pilot Knob, Mo., U.S.	D7	118
Pilot Mound, Mb., Can.	E2	86
Pilot Mountain, N.C., U.S.	A2	126
Pilot Peak, mtn., Nv., U.S.	B7	121
Pilot Peak, mtn., Nv., U.S.	E4	121
Pilot Peak, mtn., Wy., U.S.	B3	143
Pilot Point, Tx., U.S.	C4	136
Pilot Range, mts., Nv., U.S.	B7	121
Pilot Rock, Or., U.S.	B8	130
Pilot Station, Ak., U.S.	C7	95
Pilsen see Plzeň, Czech Rep.	E2	20
Pima, Az., U.S.	E6	96
Pima, co., Az., U.S.	E3	96
Pimmit Hills, Va., U.S.	g12	139
Pinal, co., Az., U.S.	E4	96
Pinaleno Mountains, mts., Az., U.S.	E5	96
Pinal Mountains, mts., Az., U.S.	D5	96
Pinang see George Town, Malay.	B2	36
Pınarbaşı, Tur.	C7	44
Pinar del Río, Cuba	A3	80
Pinardville, N.H., U.S.	E3	122
Pincher Creek, Ab., Can.	E4	84
Pinckard, Al., U.S.	D4	94
Pinckney, Mi., U.S.	F7	115
Pinckney Island, i., S.C., U.S.	G6	133
Pinckneyville, Il., U.S.	E4	106
Pinconning, Mi., U.S.	E7	115
Pindaré-Mirim, Braz.	B2	74
Píndhos Óros, mts., Grc.	E8	18
Pindus Mountains see Píndhos Óros, mts., Grc.	E8	18
Pine, Az., U.S.	C4	96
Pine, stm., Mi., U.S.	D5	115
Pine, stm., Mi., U.S.	D7	115
Pine, co., Mn., U.S.	D6	116
Pine, stm., N.H., U.S.	C4	122
Pine, stm., Wi., U.S.	C5	142
Pine, stm., Wi., U.S.	C4	142
Pine Barrens, reg., N.J., U.S.	D3	123
Pine Bluff, Ar., U.S.	C3	97
Pinebluff, N.C., U.S.	B3	126
Pine Bluffs, Wy., U.S.	E8	143
Pine Bridge, Ct., U.S.	D3	100
Pine Castle, Fl., U.S.	D5	102
Pine City, Mn., U.S.	E6	116
Pine Creek, Austl.	C5	60
Pine Creek, stm., Nv., U.S.	C5	121
Pine Creek, stm., Pa., U.S.	C6	131
Pine Creek, stm., Wa., U.S.	B8	140
Pine Creek Lake, res., Ok., U.S.	C6	129
Pinedale, Wy., U.S.	D3	143
Pine Falls, Mb., Can.	D3	86
Pine Forest Range, mts., Nv., U.S.	B3	121
Pine Grove, Pa., U.S.	E9	131
Pine Grove Mills, Pa., U.S.	E6	131
Pine Hill, N.J., U.S.	D3	123
Pine Hills, Fl., U.S.	D5	102
Pinehouse Lake, Sk., Can.	B2	91
Pinehouse Lake, l., Sk., Can.	B2	91
Pinehurst, Ma., U.S.	f11	114
Pinehurst, N.C., U.S.	B3	126
Pine Island, i., Fl., U.S.	F4	102
Pine Island, Mn., U.S.	F6	116
Pine Island Sound, strt., Fl., U.S.	F4	102
Pine Key, i., Fl., U.S.	p10	102
Pine Knot, Ky., U.S.	D5	110
Pine Lake, Ga., U.S.	h8	103
Pine Lake, l., In., U.S.	A4	107
Pine Lake, l., Wi., U.S.	C5	142
Pine Lawn, Mo., U.S.	f13	118
Pine Level, N.C., U.S.	B4	126
Pinellas, co., Fl., U.S.	D4	102
Pinellas, Point, c., Fl., U.S.	p10	102
Pinellas Park, Fl., U.S.	E4	102
Pine Mountain, Ga., U.S.	D2	103
Pine Mountain, mtn., Or., U.S.	D6	130
Pine Mountain, mtn., Wy., U.S.	E3	143
Pine Point, Me., U.S.	E2	112
Pine Prairie, La., U.S.	D3	111
Pine Ridge, S.D., U.S.	D3	134
Pine Ridge Indian Reservation, S.D., U.S.	D3	134
Pine River, Mn., U.S.	D4	116
Pines, Isle of see Juventud, Isla de la, i., Cuba	A3	80
Pines, Lake O' the, res., Tx., U.S.	C5	136
Pinesdale, Mt., U.S.	D2	119
Pinetops, N.C., U.S.	B5	126
Pinetown, S. Afr.	D5	56
Pine Valley, val., Ut., U.S.	E2	137
Pineville, Ky., U.S.	D6	110
Pineville, La., U.S.	C3	111
Pineville, N.C., U.S.	B2	126
Pineville, W.V., U.S.	D3	141
Pinewood, S.C., U.S.	D7	133
Piney Creek, stm., W.V., U.S.	n13	141
Piney Fork, stm., W.V., U.S.	h9	141
Piney Point, Md., U.S.	D4	113
Piney View, W.V., U.S.	n13	141
Pingdu, China	B4	30
Pingelly, Austl.	G2	60
Pingjiang, China	F10	28
Pingle, China	E3	30
Pingliang, China	D9	28
Pingluo, China	B2	30
Pingquan, China	C11	28
Pingtan, China	D4	30
P'ingtung, Tai.	E5	30
Pingwu, China	E8	28
Pingxiang, China	G9	28
Pingxiang, China	F10	28
Pingyang, China	D5	30
Pingyao, China	B3	30
Pingyin, China	B4	30
Pinheiro, Braz.	B2	74
Pini, Pulau, i., Indon.	C1	36
Pinjarra, Austl.	G2	60
Pinjug, Russia	B8	22
Pinnacles National Monument, Ca., U.S.	D3	98
Pinole, Ca., U.S.	h8	98
Pinopolis Dam, S.C., U.S.	E8	133
Pinos, Mount, mtn., Ca., U.S.	E4	98
Pinrang, Indon.	D5	36
Pins, Île des, i., N. Cal.	I9	62a
Pins, Pointe aux, c., On., Can.	E3	89
Pinsk, Bela.	C9	20
Pinsk Marshes see Polesye, reg., Eur.	D8	20
Pinsk Marshes see Polesye, reg., Eur.		20
Pinson, Al., U.S.	f7	94
Pinta, Isla, i., Ec.	C1	70
Pinta, Sierra, mts., Az., U.S.	E2	96
Pintados, Chile	C4	72
Pintwater Range, mts., Nv., U.S.	G6	121
Pioche, Nv., U.S.	F7	121
Piombino, Italy	C3	18
Pioneer, Oh., U.S.	A1	128
Pioneer Mountains, mts., Id., U.S.	F5	105
Pioneer Mountains, mts., Mt., U.S.	E3	119
Pioner, ostrov, i., Russia	B10	26
Piotrków Trybunalski, Pol.	D5	20
Pīpār, India	D2	40
Pipe Spring National Monument, Az., U.S.	A3	96
Pipestem Creek, stm., N.D., U.S.	B6	127
Pipestone, Mn., U.S.	G2	116
Pipestone, co., Mn., U.S.	F2	116
Pipestone National Monument, Mn., U.S.	G2	116
Pipestone Pass, Mt., U.S.	E4	119
Pipmuacan, Réservoir, res., Qc., Can.	k12	90
Piqua, Oh., U.S.	B1	128
Piracicaba, Braz.	F2	74
Piracuruca, Braz.	B3	74
Piraeus see Piraiévs, Grc.	E9	18
Piraiévs, Grc.	E9	18
Piranhas, Braz.	E1	74
Pīrān Shahr, Iran	D11	44
Pirapora, Braz.	E3	74
Pires do Rio, Braz.	E2	74
Pírgos, Grc.	F8	18
Piripiri, Braz.	B3	74
Pirot, Serb.	C9	18
Pīr Panjāl Range, mts., Asia	E2	28
Pirtleville, Az., U.S.	F6	96
Piru, Indon.	D7	36
Pisa, Italy	C3	18
Pisagua, Chile	A2	69
Piscataqua, stm., N.H., U.S.	D5	122
Piscataquis, co., Me., U.S.	C3	112
Piscataquis, stm., Me., U.S.	C3	112
Piscataquog, stm., N.H., U.S.	D3	122
Piscataway, N.J., U.S.	B4	123
Pisco, Peru	F4	70
Piseco Lake, l., N.Y., U.S.	B6	125
Písek, Czech Rep.	E3	20
Pisgah, Al., U.S.	A4	94
Pisgah, Oh., U.S.	n13	128
Pisgah, Mount, mtn., Wy., U.S.	B8	143
Pisgah Forest, N.C., U.S.	f10	126
Pishan, China	D3	28
Pismo Beach, Ca., U.S.	E3	98
Pisticci, Italy	D6	18
Pistoia, Italy	C3	18
Pistolet Bay, b., N.L., Can.	C4	88
Pit, stm., Ca., U.S.	B3	98
Pita, Gui.	D2	50
Pitcairn, dep., Oc.	K26	64
Pitcairn, Pa., U.S.	k14	131
Piteå, Swe.	D9	10
Piteälven, stm., Swe.	C8	10
Piteşti, Rom.	G8	20
Pithara, Austl.	G2	60
Pitkin, co., Co., U.S.	B4	99
Pitkjaranta, Russia	B5	22
Pitman, N.J., U.S.	D2	123
Pitt, co., N.C., U.S.	B5	126
Pitt Island, i., B.C., Can.	C3	85
Pittsboro, In., U.S.	E5	107
Pittsboro, N.C., U.S.	B3	126
Pittsburg, Ca., U.S.	g9	98
Pittsburg, Ks., U.S.	E9	109
Pittsburg, Ky., U.S.	C5	110
Pittsburg, co., Ok., U.S.	C6	129
Pittsburg, Tx., U.S.	C5	136
Pittsburgh, Pa., U.S.	F1	131
Pittsfield, Il., U.S.	D3	106
Pittsfield, Ma., U.S.	B1	114
Pittsfield, Me., U.S.	D3	112
Pittsfield, N.H., U.S.	D4	122
Pittsford, Vt., U.S.	D2	138
Pittston, Pa., U.S.	D10	131
Pittsville, Md., U.S.	D7	113
Pittsville, Wi., U.S.	D3	142
Pittsylvania, co., Va., U.S.	D3	139
Pium, Braz.	F10	70
Piura, Peru	E3	70
Piute, co., Ut., U.S.	E3	137
Piute Peak, mtn., Ca., U.S.	E4	98
Piute Reservoir, res., Ut., U.S.	E3	137
Pivdennyi Buh, stm., Ukr.	F11	20
Pixley, Ca., U.S.	E4	98
Pjandž, stm., Asia	B1	40
Pjaozero, ozero, l., Russia	D14	10
Pjasina, stm., Russia	B10	26
Pjatigorsk, Russia	B4	42

Name | Map Ref. | Page

Placentia, N.L., Can. **E5** 88
Placentia Bay, b., N.L., Can. **E4** 88
Placer, co., Ca., U.S. **C3** 98
Placer Mountain, mtn., N.M., U.S. **k8** 124
Placerville, Ca., U.S. **C3** 98
Placetas, Cuba **A4** 80
Placid, Lake, l., Fl., U.S. **E5** 102
Placid, Lake, l., N.Y., U.S. **f11** 125
Placitas, N.M., U.S. **B3** 124
Plain City, Oh., U.S. **B2** 128
Plain City, Ut., U.S. **B3** 137
Plain Dealing, La., U.S. **B2** 111
Plainfield, Ct., U.S. **C8** 100
Plainfield, Il., U.S. **B5** 106
Plainfield, In., U.S. **E5** 107
Plainfield, N.J., U.S. **B4** 123
Plainfield, Vt., U.S. **C4** 138
Plainfield, Wi., U.S. **D4** 142
Plains, Ga., U.S. **D2** 103
Plains, Ks., U.S. **E3** 109
Plains, Mt., U.S. **C2** 119
Plains, Pa., U.S. **n17** 131
Plains, Tx., U.S. **C1** 136
Plainview, Ar., U.S. **C2** 97
Plainview, Mn., U.S. **F6** 116
Plainview, Ne., U.S. **B8** 120
Plainview, Tx., U.S. **B2** 136
Plainville, Ct., U.S. **C4** 100
Plainville, Ks., U.S. **C4** 109
Plainville, Ma., U.S. **B5** 114
Plainwell, Mi., U.S. **F5** 115
Plaistow, N.H., U.S. **E4** 122
Plampang, Indon. **E5** 36
Planeta Rica, Col. **D4** 80
Plankinton, S.D., U.S. **D7** 134
Plano, Il., U.S. **B5** 106
Plano, Tx., U.S. **C4** 136
Plantagenet, On., Can. **B9** 89
Plantation, Fl., U.S. **r13** 102
Plant City, Fl., U.S. **D4** 102
Plantersville, Al., U.S. **C3** 94
Plantersville, Ms., U.S. **A5** 117
Plantsite, Az., U.S. **D6** 96
Plantsville, Ct., U.S. **C4** 100
Plaquemine, La., U.S. **D4** 111
Plaquemines, co., La., U.S. **E6** 111
Plasencia, Spain **G3** 16
Plaster Rock, N.B., Can. **C2** 87
Plata, Río de la, est., S.A. **E6** 72
Plate, Île, i., Sey. **i13** 57b
Plato, Col. **B5** 70
Platte, stm., Mn., U.S. **E4** 116
Platte, co., Mo., U.S. **B3** 118
Platte, stm., Ne., U.S. **D6** 120
Platte, co., Ne., U.S. **C8** 120
Platte, S.D., U.S. **D7** 134
Platte, co., Wy., U.S. **D7** 143
Platte, stm., U.S. **B3** 118
Platte City, Mo., U.S. **B3** 118
Platteville, Co., U.S. **A6** 99
Platteville, Wi., U.S. **F3** 142
Plattsburg, Mo., U.S. **B3** 118
Plattsburgh, N.Y., U.S. **f11** 125
Plattsmouth, Ne., U.S. **D10** 120
Plauen, Ger. **E12** 12
Plavsk, Russia **C14** 20
Playas Lake, l., N.M., U.S. **F2** 124
Playgreen Lake, l., Mb., Can. **B2** 86
Play Ku, Viet. **D5** 34
Pleasant, stm., Me., U.S. **C3** 112
Pleasant, Lake, res., Az., U.S. **D3** 96
Pleasant Gap, Pa., U.S. **E6** 131
Pleasant Garden, N.C., U.S. **B3** 126
Pleasant Grove, Al., U.S. **g7** 94
Pleasant Grove, Ut., U.S. **C4** 137
Pleasant Hill, Ca., U.S. **h8** 98
Pleasant Hill, Ia., U.S. **e8** 108
Pleasant Hill, Il., U.S. **D3** 106
Pleasant Hill, La., U.S. **C2** 111
Pleasant Hill, Mo., U.S. **C3** 118
Pleasant Hill, Oh., U.S. **B1** 128
Pleasant Lake, In., U.S. **A7** 107
Pleasant Lake, l., Me., U.S. **C5** 112
Pleasant Lake, l., N.H., U.S. **D4** 122
Pleasanton, Ca., U.S. **h9** 98
Pleasanton, Ks., U.S. **D9** 109
Pleasanton, Tx., U.S. **E3** 136
Pleasant Prairie, Wi., U.S. **n12** 142
Pleasants, co., W.V., U.S. **B3** 141
Pleasant Valley, Ia., U.S. **g11** 108
Pleasant Valley, Mo., U.S. **h11** 118
Pleasant View, Ut., U.S. **B3** 137
Pleasantville, Ia., U.S. **C4** 108
Pleasantville, N.J., U.S. **E3** 123
Pleasantville, N.Y., U.S. **D7** 125
Pleasantville, Oh., U.S. **C3** 128
Pleasure Beach, Ct., U.S. **D7** 100
Pleasure Ridge Park, Ky., U.S. **g11** 110
Pleasureville, Ky., U.S. **B4** 110
Plenty, Bay of, b., N.Z. **o14** 63c
Plentywood, Mt., U.S. **B12** 119
Pleseck, Russia **C6** 26
Plessisville, Qc., Can. **C6** 90
Pleszew, Pol. **D4** 20
Pleven, Blg. **C10** 18
Pljussa, Russia **G13** 10
Płock, Pol. **C5** 20
Ploiești, Rom. **G9** 20
Plomosa Mountains, mts., Az., U.S. **D1** 96
Plonge, Lac la, l., Sk., Can. **B2** 91
Płońsk, Pol. **C6** 20
Plovdiv, Blg. **C10** 18
Plover, Wi., U.S. **D4** 142
Plover, stm., Wi., U.S. **D4** 142
Plum, Pa., U.S. **k14** 131
Plumas, co., Ca., U.S. **B3** 98
Plum Coulee, Mb., Can. **E3** 86
Plumerville, Ar., U.S. **B3** 97
Plum Island, i., Ma., U.S. **A6** 114
Plummer, Id., U.S. **B2** 105
Plumsteadville, Pa., U.S. **F11** 131
Plumtree, Zimb. **C4** 56
Plungė, Lith. **I9** 10
Plutarco Elías Calles, Presa, res., Mex. **B3** 78
Plymouth, Monts. **B7** 80
Plymouth, Eng., U.K. **E4** 12
Plymouth, Ct., U.S. **C3** 100
Plymouth, Fl., U.S. **D5** 102
Plymouth, co., Ia., U.S. **B1** 108
Plymouth, In., U.S. **B5** 107
Plymouth, Ma., U.S. **C6** 114
Plymouth, co., Ma., U.S. **C6** 114
Plymouth, Mi., U.S. **p15** 115
Plymouth, Mn., U.S. **m12** 116
Plymouth, N.C., U.S. **B6** 126
Plymouth, N.H., U.S. **C3** 122
Plymouth, Oh., U.S. **A3** 128
Plymouth, Pa., U.S. **D10** 131
Plymouth, Wi., U.S. **E6** 142
Plymouth Bay, b., Ma., U.S. **C6** 114
Plzeň, Czech Rep. **E2** 20
Pô, Burkina **D4** 50
Po, stm., Italy **B3** 18
Po, stm., Va., U.S. **B5** 139
Pobè, Benin **E5** 50
Pobeda, gora, mtn., Russia **C16** 26
Pobedy, Peak, mtn., Asia **B11** 42
Pocahontas, Ar., U.S. **A5** 97
Pocahontas, co., Ia., U.S. **B3** 108
Pocahontas, Ia., U.S. **B3** 108
Pocahontas, Il., U.S. **E4** 106
Pocahontas, co., W.V., U.S. **C4** 141
Pocasset, Ma., U.S. **C6** 114
Pocatalico, W.V., U.S. **C3** 141
Pocatalico, stm., W.V., U.S. **C3** 141
Pocatello, Id., U.S. **G6** 105
Počep, Russia **C12** 20
Počinok, Russia **B12** 20
Poções, Braz. **D3** 74
Pocola, Ok., U.S. **B7** 129
Pocomoke, stm., Md., U.S. **D7** 113
Pocomoke City, Md., U.S. **D6** 113
Pocomoke Sound, strt., Md., U.S. **E6** 113
Poconé, Braz. **B6** 72
Pocono Mountains, Pa., U.S. **E11** 131
Pocono Pines, Pa., U.S. **D11** 131
Poços de Caldas, Braz. **F2** 74
Pocotopaug Lake, res., Ct., U.S. **C6** 100
Podgorica, Serb. **C7** 18
Podkamennaja Tunguska, stm., Russia **C11** 26
Podkamennaja Tunguska, Russia **C10** 26
Podol'sk, Russia **C6** 22
Podor, Sen. **C2** 50
Podporože, Russia **B5** 22
Pofadder, S. Afr. **D2** 56
Poge, Cape, c., Ma., U.S. **D7** 114
Pograničnyj, Russia **C14** 28
P'ohang, S. Kor. **D13** 28
Pohénégamook, Qc., Can. **B8** 90
Pohjanmaa, reg., Fin. **D11** 10
Pohnpei, i., Micron. **D9** 58
Pohue Bay, b., Hi., U.S. **E6** 104
Pohvistnevo, Russia **D9** 22
Poinsett, co., Ar., U.S. **B5** 97
Poinsett, Cape, c., Ant. **C16** 67
Poinsett, Lake, l., Fl., U.S. **D6** 102
Poinsett, Lake, l., S.D., U.S. **C8** 134
Point Clear, Al., U.S. **E2** 94
Pointe a la Hache, La., U.S. **E6** 111
Pointe-à-Pitre, Guad. **B7** 80
Pointe-au-Pic, Qc., Can. **B7** 90
Pointe-Calumet, Qc., Can. **p19** 90
Pointe-Claire, Qc., Can. **D4** 90
Pointe Coupee, co., La., U.S. **D4** 111
Pointe-des-Cascades, Qc., Can. **q19** 90
Point Edward, On., Can. **D2** 89
Pointe-Noire, Congo **D2** 54
Pointe-Verte, N.B., Can. **B4** 87
Point Fortin, Trin. **C7** 80
Point Hope, Ak., U.S. **B6** 95
Point Imperial, mtn., Az., U.S. **A4** 96
Point Judith Pond, l., R.I., U.S. **F4** 132
Point Leamington, N.L., Can. **D4** 88
Point Marion, Pa., U.S. **G2** 131
Point Mugu Naval Air Station, mil., Ca., U.S. **E4** 98
Point of Rocks, Md., U.S. **B2** 113
Point Pelee National Park, On., Can. **F2** 89
Point Pleasant, N.J., U.S. **C4** 123
Point Pleasant, W.V., U.S. **C2** 141
Point Pleasant Beach, N.J., U.S. **C4** 123
Point Reyes National Seashore, Ca., U.S. **C2** 98
Point Roberts, Wa., U.S. **A2** 140
Poipu, Hi., U.S. **B2** 104
Poison Creek, stm., Wy., U.S. **C5** 143
Poisson Blanc, Lac du, res., Qc., Can. **C2** 90
Poitiers, Fr. **D7** 16
Poitou, hist. reg., Fr. **D6** 16
Poivre Atoll, i., Sey. **i12** 57b
Pojarkovo, Russia **B13** 28
Pokaran, India **D2** 40
Pokegama Lake, l., Mn., U.S. **C5** 116
Pokegama Lake, l., Wi., U.S. **C2** 142
Pokharā, Nepal **D4** 40
Polacca, Az., U.S. **B5** 96
Polack, Bela. **B10** 20
Pola de Lena, Spain **F4** 16
Pola de Siero, Spain **F4** 16
Poland, ctry., Eur. **C5** 20
Polar Bear Provincial Park, On., Can. **n18** 89
Polatlı, Tur. **C5** 44
Polecat Creek, stm., Ok., U.S. **B5** 129
Pol-e Khomrī, Afg. **C9** 42
Polesye, reg., Eur. **D8** 20
Polewali, Indon. **D5** 36
Policastro, Golfo di, b., Italy **E5** 18
Pólis, Cyp. **E5** 44
Poljarnyj, Russia **B15** 10
Polk, co., Ar., U.S. **C1** 97
Polk, co., Fl., U.S. **E5** 102
Polk, co., Ga., U.S. **C1** 103
Polk, co., Ia., U.S. **C4** 108
Polk, co., Mn., U.S. **C2** 116
Polk, co., Mo., U.S. **D4** 118
Polk, co., N.C., U.S. **f10** 126
Polk, co., Ne., U.S. **C8** 120
Polk, co., Or., U.S. **C3** 130
Polk, Pa., U.S. **D2** 131
Polk, co., Tn., U.S. **D9** 135
Polk, co., Tx., U.S. **D5** 136
Polk, co., Wi., U.S. **C1** 142
Polk City, Fl., U.S. **D5** 102
Polk City, Ia., U.S. **C4** 108
Pol'kino, Russia **B11** 26
Pollāchi, India **G3** 40
Pollença, Spain **H8** 16
Polo, Il., U.S. **B4** 106
Polohy, Ukr. **F14** 20
Polonnaruwa, Sri L. **H4** 40
Polonne, Ukr. **D9** 20
Polson, Mt., U.S. **C2** 119
Poltava, Ukr. **E13** 20
Põltsamaa, Est. **G12** 10
Polunočnoe, Russia **B11** 22
Polynesia, is., Oc. **I23** 64
Pombal, Braz. **C4** 74
Pomerania, hist. reg., Pol. **D14** 20
Pomeroy, Ia., U.S. **B3** 108
Pomeroy, Oh., U.S. **C3** 128
Pomeroy, Wa., U.S. **C8** 140
Pomme de Terre, stm., Mn., U.S. **E3** 116
Pomme de Terre, stm., Mo., U.S. **D4** 118
Pomme de Terre Lake, res., Mo., U.S. **D4** 118
Pomona, Ca., U.S. **E5** 98
Pomona, Ks., U.S. **D8** 109
Pomona Lake, res., Ks., U.S. **D7** 109
Pompano Beach, Fl., U.S. **F6** 102
Pompei, Italy **D5** 18
Pompéu, Braz. **E2** 74
Pompton Lakes, N.J., U.S. **A4** 123
Ponaganset, stm., R.I., U.S. **C2** 132
Ponaganset Reservoir, res., R.I., U.S. **B2** 132
Ponape see Pohnpei, i., Micron. **D9** 58
Ponca, Ne., U.S. **B9** 120
Ponca City, Ok., U.S. **A4** 129
Ponca Creek, stm., U.S. **A6** 120
Ponca Indian Reservation, Ne., U.S. **B7** 120
Ponce, P.R. **B6** 80
Ponce de Leon Bay, b., Fl., U.S. **G5** 102
Ponce de Leon Inlet, b., Fl., U.S. **C6** 102
Poncha Pass, Co., U.S. **C4** 99
Ponchatoula, La., U.S. **D5** 111
Pond, stm., Ky., U.S. **C2** 110
Pond Creek, Ok., U.S. **A3** 129
Pondera, co., Mt., U.S. **B4** 119
Pond Fork, stm., W.V., U.S. **D3** 141
Pondicherry, India **G3** 40
Pone Island, i., Md., U.S. **D5** 113
Ponferrada, Spain **F3** 16
Ponoj, Russia **C6** 26
Ponoka, Ab., Can. **C4** 84
Ponta Delgada, Port. **F7** 46
Ponta Grossa, Braz. **D8** 72
Pontalina, Braz. **E2** 74
Ponta Porã, Braz. **H8** 70
Pontarlier, Fr. **D10** 16
Pontchartrain, Lake, l., La., U.S. **D5** 111
Ponteix, Sk., Can. **H2** 91
Ponte Nova, Braz. **F3** 74
Pontevedra, Spain **F2** 16
Ponte Vedra Beach, Fl., U.S. **B5** 102
Pontiac, Il., U.S. **C5** 106
Pontiac, Mi., U.S. **F7** 115
Pontianak, Indon. **C3** 36
Pontine Islands see Ponziane, Isole, is., Italy **D4** 18
Pontoosuc Lake, l., Ma., U.S. **B1** 114
Pontotoc, Ms., U.S. **A4** 117
Pontotoc, co., Ms., U.S. **A4** 117
Pontotoc, co., Ok., U.S. **C5** 129
Pont-Rouge, Qc., Can. **C6** 90
Pontus Mountains see Doğu Karadeniz Dağları, mts., Tur. **B8** 44
Pontypool, On., Can. **C6** 89
Ponziane, Isole, is., Italy **D4** 18
Poole, Eng., U.K. **E5** 12
Pooler, Ga., U.S. **D5** 103
Pooles Island, i., Md., U.S. **B5** 113
Poolesville, Md., U.S. **B3** 113
Poopó, Bol. **B4** 72
Poopó, Lago, l., Bol. **B4** 72
Popayán, Col. **C4** 70
Pope, co., Ar., U.S. **B2** 97
Pope, co., Il., U.S. **F5** 106
Pope, co., Mn., U.S. **E3** 116
Pope Air Force Base, mil., N.C., U.S. **B3** 126
Poplar, stm., Can. **C3** 86
Poplar, stm., Mn., U.S. **C2** 116
Poplar, Mt., U.S. **B11** 119
Poplar Bluff, Mo., U.S. **E7** 118
Poplar Island, i., Md., U.S. **C5** 113
Poplarville, Ms., U.S. **E4** 117
Popocatépetl, Volcán, vol., Mex. **D5** 78
Popokabaka, D.R.C. **E3** 54
Popondetta, Pap. N. Gui. **H12** 32
Popovo, Blg. **C11** 18
Popple, stm., Wi., U.S. **C5** 142
Poprad, Slvk. **E6** 20
Poquonock, Ct., U.S. **B5** 100
Poquonock Bridge, Ct., U.S. **D7** 100
Poquoson, Va., U.S. **C6** 139
Porangatu, Braz. **D2** 74
Porbandar, India **E1** 40
Porcher Island, i., B.C., Can. **C2** 85
Porcupine, stm., N.A. **E11** 82
Porcupine Mountains, mts., Mi., U.S. **m12** 115
Pordenone, Italy **B4** 18
Pori, Fin. **F9** 10
Porirua, N.Z. **p13** 63c
Porlamar, Ven. **A7** 70
Poronajsk, Russia **E16** 26
Porpoise Bay, b., Ant. **C17** 67
Porsangen, b., Nor. **A11** 10
Porsgrunn, Nor. **G3** 10
Portachuelo, Bol. **B5** 72
Port Adelaide, Austl. **G2** 62
Portadown, N. Ire., U.K. **C3** 12
Portage, In., U.S. **A3** 107
Portage, Mi., U.S. **F5** 115
Portage, stm., Oh., U.S. **B2** 128
Portage, co., Oh., U.S. **A4** 128
Portage, Pa., U.S. **F4** 131
Portage, Wi., U.S. **E4** 142
Portage, co., Wi., U.S. **D4** 142
Portage Bay, b., Mb., Can. **D2** 86
Portage Head, c., Wa., U.S. **A1** 140
Portage Lake, l., Me., U.S. **B4** 112
Portage Lakes, Oh., U.S. **B4** 128
Portage la Prairie, Mb., Can. **E2** 86
Portageville, Mo., U.S. **E8** 118
Port Alberni, B.C., Can. **E5** 85
Portalegre, Port. **H3** 16
Portales, N.M., U.S. **C6** 124
Port Alfred, S. Afr. **E4** 56
Port Alice, B.C., Can. **D4** 85
Port Allegany, Pa., U.S. **C5** 131
Port Allen, La., U.S. **D4** 111
Port Angeles, Wa., U.S. **A2** 140
Port Antonio, Jam. **B4** 80
Port Aransas, Tx., U.S. **F4** 136
Port Arthur see Lüshun, China **D12** 28
Port Arthur, Tx., U.S. **E6** 136
Port Augusta, Austl. **G2** 62
Port au Port Bay, b., N.L., Can. **D2** 88
Port au Port [West-Aguathuna-Felix Cove], N.L., Can. **D2** 88
Port-au-Prince, Haiti **B5** 80
Port au Prince Peninsula, pen., N.L., Can. **D2** 88
Port Austin, Mi., U.S. **D7** 115
Port Barre, La., U.S. **D4** 111
Port Blair, India **G6** 40
Port Blandford, N.L., Can. **D4** 88
Port Bolivar, Tx., U.S. **E5** 136
Port Burwell, On., Can. **E4** 89
Port Byron, Il., U.S. **B3** 106
Port Carbon, Pa., U.S. **E9** 131
Port Carling, On., Can. **B5** 89
Port-Cartier-Ouest, Qc., Can. **k13** 90
Port Chalmers, N.Z. **q13** 63c
Port Charlotte, Fl., U.S. **F4** 102
Port Chester, N.Y., U.S. **E7** 125
Port Clinton, Oh., U.S. **A3** 128
Port Colborne, On., Can. **E5** 89
Port Coquitlam, B.C., Can. **E6** 85
Port Deposit, Md., U.S. **A5** 113
Port Dickinson, N.Y., U.S. **C5** 125
Port Edward, B.C., Can. **B2** 85
Port Edward, S. Afr. **E5** 56
Port Edwards, Wi., U.S. **D4** 142
Portel, Braz. **B1** 74
Port Elgin, On., Can. **C3** 89
Port Elizabeth, S. Afr. **E4** 56
Porter, In., U.S. **A3** 107
Porter, co., In., U.S. **B3** 107
Porter, Tx., U.S. **D5** 136
Porter Creek, stm., W.V., U.S. **m13** 141
Porterdale, Ga., U.S. **C3** 103
Porterville, Ca., U.S. **D4** 98
Port Ewen, N.Y., U.S. **D7** 125
Port Fairy, Austl. **H3** 62
Port Gamble Indian Reservation, Wa., U.S. **B3** 140
Port-Gentil, Gabon **D1** 54
Port Gibson, Ms., U.S. **D3** 117
Port-Harcourt, Nig. **F6** 50
Port Hedland, Austl. **E2** 60
Port Hood, N.S., Can. **C8** 87
Port Hope, On., Can. **D6** 89
Port Hope Simpson, N.L., Can. **B3** 88
Port Hueneme, Ca., U.S. **E4** 98
Port Huron, Mi., U.S. **F8** 115
Portimão, Port. **I2** 16
Port Isabel, Tx., U.S. **F4** 136
Port Jefferson, N.Y., U.S. **n15** 125
Port Jervis, N.Y., U.S. **D6** 125
Port Lairge see Waterford, Ire. **D3** 12
Portland, Austl. **H3** 62
Portland, Ct., U.S. **C5** 100
Portland, In., U.S. **D8** 107
Portland, Me., U.S. **E2** 112
Portland, Mi., U.S. **F6** 115
Portland, N.D., U.S. **B8** 127
Portland, Or., U.S. **B4** 130
Portland, Tn., U.S. **A5** 135
Portland, Tx., U.S. **F4** 136
Portland, Cape, c., Austl. **I4** 62
Portland Inlet, b., B.C., Can. **B2** 85
Port Laoise, Ire. **D3** 12
Port Lavaca, Tx., U.S. **E4** 136
Port Lincoln, Austl. **G2** 62
Port Loko, S.L. **E2** 50
Port Louis, Mrts. **f10** 57a
Port Ludlow, Wa., U.S. **B3** 140
Port Macquarie, Austl. **G5** 62
Port Madison Indian Reservation, Wa., U.S. **B3** 140
Port McNeil, B.C., Can. **D4** 85
Port McNicoll, On., Can. **C5** 89
Port Monmouth, N.J., U.S. **C4** 123
Port Moresby, Pap. N. Gui. **H12** 32
Port Morien, N.S., Can. **C10** 87
Port Neches, Tx., U.S. **E6** 136
Portneuf, Qc., Can. **C6** 90
Port Nolloth, S. Afr. **D2** 56
Porto, Port. **G2** 16
Porto Alegre, Braz. **E7** 72
Porto Amboim, Ang. **F2** 54
Portobelo, Pan. **D4** 80
Porto de Moz, Braz. **D9** 70
Porto Esperança, Braz. **G8** 70
Porto Esperidião, Braz. **G8** 70
Portoferraio, Italy **C3** 18
Port of Spain, Trin. **C7** 80
Portola, Ca., U.S. **C3** 98
Porto Murtinho, Braz. **H8** 70
Porto Nacional, Braz. **D2** 74
Porto-Novo, Benin **E5** 50
Port Orange, Fl., U.S. **C6** 102
Port Orchard, Wa., U.S. **B3** 140
Port Orford, Or., U.S. **E2** 130
Porto Santana, Braz. **B1** 74
Porto Santo, i., Port. **D1** 48
Porto Seguro, Braz. **E4** 74
Porto Torres, Italy **D2** 18
Porto-Vecchio, Fr. **D2** 18
Porto Velho, Braz. **E7** 70
Portoviejo, Ec. **D3** 70
Port Penn, De., U.S. **B3** 101
Port Phillip Bay, b., Austl. **H3** 62
Port Richey, Fl., U.S. **D4** 102
Port Rowan, On., Can. **E4** 89
Port Royal, S.C., U.S. **G6** 133
Port Royal Island, i., S.C., U.S. **G6** 133
Port Royal Sound, strt., S.C., U.S. **G6** 133
Port Said see Bûr Sa'îd, Egypt **E10** 48
Port Saint Joe, Fl., U.S. **C1** 102
Port Saint Johns, S. Afr. **E4** 56
Port Saint Lucie, Fl., U.S. **E6** 102
Port Salerno, Fl., U.S. **E6** 102
Port Saunders, N.L., Can. **C3** 88
Port Shepstone, S. Afr. **E5** 56
Portsmouth, Eng., U.K. **E6** 12
Portsmouth, N.H., U.S. **D5** 122
Portsmouth, Oh., U.S. **D3** 128
Portsmouth, R.I., U.S. **E6** 132
Portsmouth, Va., U.S. **D6** 139
Portsmouth Naval Shipyard, mil., Me., U.S. **D5** 122
Port Stanley, On., Can. **E3** 89
Port Stanley see Stanley, Falk. Is. **H5** 69
Port Sudan see Būr Sūdān, Sudan **G12** 48
Port Sulphur, La., U.S. **E6** 111
Port Talbot, Wales, U.K. **E5** 12
Porttipahdan tekojärvi, l., Fin. **B12** 10
Port Townsend, Wa., U.S. **A3** 140
Portugal, ctry., Eur. **G3** 16
Port Union, N.L., Can. **D5** 88
Port Vila, Vanuatu **k9** 62a

Name — Map Ref. — Page

Port Washington, N.Y., U.S. **h13** 125
Port Washington, Wi., U.S. **E6** 142
Port Wentworth, Ga., U.S. **D5** 103
Porum, Ok., U.S. **B6** 129
Porvenir, Chile **H2** 69
Porvoo, Fin. **F11** 10
Posadas, Arg. **D6** 72
Posen see Poznań, Pol. **C4** 20
Posen, Il., U.S. **k9** 106
Poset, Russia **E15** 26
Posey, co., In., U.S. **H2** 107
Poseyville, In., U.S. **H2** 107
Posio, Fin. **C13** 10
Poso, Indon. **D6** 36
Posse, Braz. **D2** 74
Post, Tx., U.S. **C2** 136
Post Falls, Id., U.S. **B2** 105
Postmasburg, S. Afr. **D3** 56
Postville, Ia., U.S. **A6** 108
Potawatomi Indian Reservation, Ks., U.S. **C8** 109
Potchefstroom, S. Afr. **D4** 56
Poteau, Ok., U.S. **B7** 129
Poteau, stm., U.S. **B7** 129
Poteet, Tx., U.S. **E3** 136
Potenza, Italy **D5** 18
Potgietersrus, S. Afr. **C4** 56
Poth, Tx., U.S. **E3** 136
Potholes Reservoir, res., Wa., U.S. **B6** 140
Poti, Geor. **A9** 44
Potiskum, Nig. **D7** 50
Potlatch, Id., U.S. **C2** 105
Potomac, Md., U.S. **B3** 113
Potomac, stm., U.S. **D4** 113
Potomac Heights, Md., U.S. **C3** 113
Potomac Park, Md., U.S. **k13** 113
Potosí, Bol. **B4** 72
Potosi, Mo., U.S. **D7** 118
Potsdam, Ger. **D13** 12
Potsdam, N.Y., U.S. **f10** 125
Pottawatomie, co., Ks., U.S. **C7** 109
Pottawatomie, co., Ok., U.S. **B4** 129
Pottawattamie, co., Ia., U.S. **C2** 108
Potter, co., Pa., U.S. **C6** 131
Potter, co., S.D., U.S. **B6** 134
Potter, co., Tx., U.S. **B2** 136
Potter Valley, Ca., U.S. **C2** 98
Potts Creek, stm., U.S. **C2** 139
Pottstown, Pa., U.S. **F10** 131
Pottsville, Ar., U.S. **B2** 97
Pottsville, Pa., U.S. **E9** 131
Pouce Coupe, B.C., Can. **B7** 85
Pouch Cove, N.L., Can. **E5** 88
Poughkeepsie, N.Y., U.S. **D7** 125
Poulan, Ga., U.S. **E3** 103
Poulsbo, Wa., U.S. **B3** 140
Poultney, Vt., U.S. **D2** 138
Poultney, stm., Vt., U.S. **D2** 138
Pound, Va., U.S. **e9** 139
Pound Gap, U.S. **C7** 110
Pouso Alegre, Braz. **F2** 74
Poŭthĭsăt, Camb. **D4** 34
Póvoa de Varzim, Port. **G2** 16
Povungnituk, Qc., Can. **f11** 90
Powassan, On., Can. **A5** 89
Poway, Ca., U.S. **F5** 98
Powder, stm., Or., U.S. **C9** 130
Powder, stm., U.S. **B6** 92
Powder, Middle Fork, stm., Wy., U.S. **C6** 143
Powder, North Fork, stm., Wy., U.S. **C6** 143
Powder, South Fork, stm., Wy., U.S. **C6** 143
Powder River, co., Mt., U.S. **E11** 119
Powder River Pass, Wy., U.S. **B5** 143
Powder Springs, Ga., U.S. **h8** 103
Powell, co., Ky., U.S. **C6** 110
Powell, co., Mt., U.S. **D4** 119
Powell, Oh., U.S. **B2** 128
Powell, Tn., U.S. **m13** 135
Powell, Wy., U.S. **B4** 143
Powell, stm., U.S. **C10** 135
Powell, Lake, res., U.S. **F5** 137
Powell, Lake, res., U.S. **D5** 92
Powell, Mount, mtn., Co., U.S. **B4** 99
Powell, Mount, mtn., N.M., U.S. **B1** 124
Powell Butte, Or., U.S. **C5** 130
Powell Park, reg., Co., U.S. **A2** 99
Powell River, B.C., Can. **E5** 85
Powellton, W.V., U.S. **C3** 141
Power, co., Id., U.S. **G5** 105
Powers, Or., U.S. **E2** 130
Powerview, Mb., Can. **D3** 86
Poweshiek, co., Ia., U.S. **C5** 108
Powhatan, Va., U.S. **C5** 139
Powhatan, co., Va., U.S. **C5** 139
Powhatan Point, Oh., U.S. **C5** 128
Poxoréu, Braz. **G9** 70
Poyang Hu, l., China **F11** 28
Poyang Lake see Poyang Hu, l., China **F11** 28
Poygan, Lake, l., Wi., U.S. **D5** 142
Poynette, Wi., U.S. **E4** 142
Požarevac, Serb. **B8** 18
Poza Rica, Mex. **C5** 78
Požega, Cro. **B6** 18
Poznań, Pol. **C4** 20
Pozo Redondo Mountains, mts., Az., U.S. **E3** 96
Pozuelos, Ven. **C7** 80
Prachuap Khiri Khan, Thai. **D3** 34
Prado, Braz. **G12** 70
Prague see Praha, Czech Rep. **D3** 20
Prague, Ok., U.S. **B5** 129
Praha (Prague), Czech Rep. **D3** 20
Praia, C.V. **h10** 50a
Prainha Nova, Braz. **E7** 70
Prairie, co., Ar., U.S. **C4** 97
Prairie, stm., Mn., U.S. **C5** 116
Prairie, co., Mt., U.S. **D11** 119
Prairie, stm., Wi., U.S. **C4** 142
Prairie City, Ia., U.S. **C4** 108
Prairie City, Or., U.S. **C8** 130
Prairie Creek Reservoir, res., In., U.S. **D7** 107
Prairie Dog Creek, stm., U.S. **C3** 109
Prairie du Chien, Wi., U.S. **E2** 142
Prairie du Sac, Wi., U.S. **E4** 142
Prairie Grove, Ar., U.S. **B1** 97
Prairies, Rivière des, stm., Qc., Can. **p19** 90
Prairie View, Tx., U.S. **D5** 136
Prairie Village, Ks., U.S. **m16** 109
Praslin, i., Sey. **h13** 57b
Pratāpgarh, India **E2** 40
Pratas Island see Tungsha Tao, i., Tai. **E4** 30
Prater Mountain, mtn., Wy., U.S. **C2** 143
Prato, Italy **C3** 18
Pratt, Ks., U.S. **E5** 109
Pratt, co., Ks., U.S. **E5** 109
Prattville, Al., U.S. **C3** 94
Praya, Indon. **E5** 36
Preble, co., Oh., U.S. **C1** 128
Prečistoe, Russia **B12** 20
Premont, Tx., U.S. **F3** 136
Prentiss, Ms., U.S. **D4** 117
Prentiss, co., Ms., U.S. **A5** 117
Prenzlau, Ger. **D13** 12
Preparis Island, i., Mya. **D2** 34
Preparis North Channel, strt., Mya. **C2** 34
Preparis South Channel, strt., Mya. **D2** 34
Přerov, Czech Rep. **E4** 20
Prescott, On., Can. **C9** 89
Prescott, Ar., U.S. **D2** 97
Prescott, Az., U.S. **C3** 96
Prescott, Wi., U.S. **D1** 142
Presho, S.D., U.S. **D5** 134
Presidencia Roque Sáenz Peña, Arg. **C4** 69
Presidente Dutra, Braz. **C3** 74
Presidente Epitácio, Braz. **F1** 74
Presidente Prudente, Braz. **F1** 74
Presidential Range, mts., N.H., U.S. **B4** 122
Presidio, Tx., U.S. **p12** 136
Presidio, co., Tx., U.S. **o12** 136
Prešov, Slvk. **E6** 20
Prespa, Lake, l., Eur. **D8** 18
Presque Isle, Me., U.S. **B5** 112
Presque Isle, co., Mi., U.S. **C6** 115
Prestea, Ghana **E4** 50
Preston, Eng., U.K. **D5** 12
Preston, Ia., U.S. **B7** 108
Preston, Id., U.S. **G7** 105
Preston, Mn., U.S. **G6** 116
Preston, co., W.V., U.S. **B5** 141
Preston Peak, mtn., Ca., U.S. **B2** 98
Prestonsburg, Ky., U.S. **C7** 110
Presumpscot, stm., Me., U.S. **g7** 112
Pretoria, S. Afr. **D4** 56
Prettyboy Reservoir, res., Md., U.S. **A4** 113
Pretty Prairie, Ks., U.S. **E5** 109
Préveza, Grc. **E8** 18
Prewitt Reservoir, res., Co., U.S. **A7** 99
Pribilof Islands, is., Ak., U.S. **D5** 95
Příbram, Czech Rep. **E3** 20
Price, Ut., U.S. **D5** 137
Price, stm., Ut., U.S. **D5** 137
Price, co., Wi., U.S. **C3** 142
Price Inlet, b., S.C., U.S. **k12** 133
Prichard, Al., U.S. **E1** 94
Prieska, S. Afr. **D3** 56
Priest Lake, l., Id., U.S. **A2** 105
Priest Rapids Dam, Wa., U.S. **C6** 140
Priest Rapids Lake, res., Wa., U.S. **C6** 140
Priest River, Id., U.S. **A2** 105
Prievidza, Slvk. **E5** 20
Prijedor, Bos. **B6** 18
Prilep, Mac. **D8** 18
Prim, Point, c., P.E., Can. **C6** 87
Primghar, Ia., U.S. **A2** 108
Primorsk, Russia **F13** 10
Primorsko-Ahtarsk, Russia **F15** 20
Primrose, R.I., U.S. **B3** 132
Primrose Lake, l., Can. **H18** 82
Prince, Lake, res., Va., U.S. **k14** 139
Prince Albert National Park, Sk., Can. **C2** 91
Prince Charles Mountains, mts., Ant. **D11** 67
Prince Edward, co., Va., U.S. **C4** 139
Prince Edward Island, prov., Can. **C6** 87
Prince Edward Island National Park, P.E., Can. **C6** 87
Prince Edward Islands, is., S. Afr. **N13** 46
Prince Frederick, Md., U.S. **C4** 113
Prince George, B.C., Can. **C6** 85
Prince George, co., Va., U.S. **C5** 139
Prince Georges, co., Md., U.S. **C4** 113
Prince of Wales, Cape, c., Ak., U.S. **B6** 95
Prince of Wales Island, i., Austl. **C3** 62
Prince of Wales Island, i., Ak., U.S. **n23** 95
Prince Olav Coast, is., Ant. **C9** 67
Prince Rupert, B.C., Can. **B2** 85
Princes Lakes, In., U.S. **F5** 107
Princess Anne, Md., U.S. **D6** 113
Princess Astrid Coast, Ant. **D5** 67
Princess Martha Coast, Ant. **D3** 67
Princess Ragnhild Coast, Ant. **D7** 67
Princess Royal Channel, strt., B.C., Can. **C3** 85
Princess Royal Island, i., B.C., Can. **C3** 85
Princeton, B.C., Can. **E7** 85
Princeton, Fl., U.S. **G6** 102
Princeton, Ia., U.S. **C7** 108
Princeton, Il., U.S. **B4** 106
Princeton, In., U.S. **H2** 107
Princeton, Ky., U.S. **C2** 110
Princeton, Me., U.S. **C5** 112
Princeton, Mn., U.S. **E5** 116
Princeton, Mo., U.S. **A4** 118
Princeton, N.C., U.S. **B4** 126
Princeton, N.J., U.S. **C3** 123
Princeton, Wi., U.S. **E4** 142
Princeton, W.V., U.S. **D3** 141
Princeton, Mount, mtn., Co., U.S. **C4** 99
Princeville, Qc., Can. **C6** 90
Princeville, Il., U.S. **C4** 106
Princeville, N.C., U.S. **B5** 126
Prince William, co., Va., U.S. **B5** 139
Prince William Sound, strt., Ak., U.S. **g18** 95
Príncipe, i., S. Tom./P. **C1** 54
Principe Channel, strt., B.C., Can. **C3** 85
Príncipe da Beira, Braz. **F7** 70
Prineville, Or., U.S. **C6** 130
Prineville Reservoir, res., Or., U.S. **C6** 130
Prinzapolka, Nic. **C3** 80
Prior Lake, Mn., U.S. **F5** 116
Priozersk, Russia **F14** 10
Pripet (Pryp'yat') (Pripjat'), stm., Eur. **C9** 20
Pripet Marshes, reg., Eur. **C10** 20
Pripyat see Pripet, stm., Eur. **C9** 20
Priština, Serb. **C8** 18
Pritchards Island, i., S.C., U.S. **G6** 133
Pritzwalk, Ger. **D13** 12
Privas, Fr. **E9** 16
Privolžskaja vozvyšennost', plat., Russia **D6** 26
Prizren, Serb. **C8** 18
Probolinggo, Indon. **E4** 36
Proctor, Mn., U.S. **D6** 116
Proctor, Vt., U.S. **D2** 138
Proctor Lake, res., Tx., U.S. **C3** 136
Proctorsville, Vt., U.S. **E3** 138
Proddatūr, India **G3** 40
Progreso, Mex. **C7** 78
Prohladnyj, Russia **F7** 22
Prokopevsk, Russia **D10** 26
Prokuplje, Serb. **C8** 18
Proletarskij, Russia **D13** 20
Prome, Mya. **C3** 34
Promontory Mountains, mts., Ut., U.S. **B3** 137
Prophetstown, Il., U.S. **B4** 106
Propriá, Braz. **D4** 74
Proserpine, Austl. **E4** 62
Prospect, Ct., U.S. **C4** 100
Prospect, Ky., U.S. **g11** 110
Prospect, Oh., U.S. **B2** 128
Prospect, Or., U.S. **E4** 130
Prospect, Pa., U.S. **E1** 131
Prospect Hill, mtn., Or., U.S. **k11** 130
Prospect Park, N.J., U.S. **B4** 123
Prospect Park, Pa., U.S. **p20** 131
Prosperidad, Phil. **E9** 34
Prosperity, S.C., U.S. **C4** 133
Prosperity, W.V., U.S. **n13** 141
Prosser, Wa., U.S. **C6** 140
Protection, Ks., U.S. **E4** 109
Provadija, Blg. **C11** 18
Provence, hist. reg., Fr. **F9** 16
Providence, Ky., U.S. **C2** 110
Providence, R.I., U.S. **C4** 132
Providence, co., R.I., U.S. **C2** 132
Providence, stm., R.I., U.S. **C5** 132
Providence, Ut., U.S. **B4** 137
Providence Point, c., R.I., U.S. **D5** 132
Providencia, Isla de, i., Col. **C3** 80
Providenija, Russia **C20** 26
Province Lake, l., N.H., U.S. **C5** 122
Provincetown, Ma., U.S. **B7** 114
Provins, Fr. **C8** 16
Provo, Ut., U.S. **C4** 137
Provo, stm., Ut., U.S. **C4** 137
Provost, Ab., Can. **C5** 84
Prowers, co., Co., U.S. **D8** 99
Prudence Island, i., R.I., U.S. **E5** 132
Prudentópolis, Braz. **D7** 72
Prudenville, Mi., U.S. **D6** 115
Prudhoe Bay, b., Ak., U.S. **A10** 95
Prudhoe Bay, Ak., U.S. **A10** 95
Prut, stm., Eur. **G10** 20
Pružany, Bela. **C8** 20
Pryluky, Ukr. **D12** 20
Prymors'k, Ukr. **F14** 20
Pryor, Mt., U.S. **E8** 119
Pryor, Ok., U.S. **A6** 129
Pryor Mountains, mts., Mt., U.S. **E8** 119
Pryp'yat' (Pripet) (Pripjat'), stm., Eur. **D8** 20
Przasnysz, Pol. **C6** 20
Przemyśl, Pol. **E7** 20
Psël (Ps'ol), stm., Eur. **D13** 20
Pskov, Russia **D4** 26
Pskov, Lake, l., Eur. **G13** 10
Ps'ol (Psël), stm., Eur. **D13** 20
Ptolemaïs, Grc. **D8** 18
Pucallpa, Peru **E5** 70
Pucheng, China **F11** 28
Puckaway Lake, l., Wi., U.S. **E4** 142
Pudož, Russia **B6** 22
Pudukkottai, India **G3** 40
Puebla, state, Mex. **D5** 78
Puebla de Zaragoza, Mex. **D5** 78
Pueblo, Co., U.S. **C6** 99
Pueblo, co., Co., U.S. **C6** 99
Pueblo Mountain, mtn., Or., U.S. **E8** 130
Pueblo Mountains, mts., Or., U.S. **E8** 130
Pueblo Reservoir, res., Co., U.S. **C6** 99
Puente Genil, Spain **I4** 16
Pueo Point, c., Hi., U.S. **B1** 104
Puerco, stm., U.S. **C6** 96
Puerco, Rio, stm., N.M., U.S. **B2** 124
Puerto Acosta, Bol. **B4** 72
Puerto Ángel, Mex. **D5** 78
Puerto Armuelles, Pan. **D3** 80
Puerto Asís, Col. **C4** 70
Puerto Ayacucho, Ven. **B6** 70
Puerto Baquerizo Moreno, Ec. **D2** 70
Puerto Barrios, Guat. **B2** 80
Puerto Bermúdez, Peru **F5** 70
Puerto Berrío, Col. **B5** 70
Puerto Bolívar, Col. **C5** 80
Puerto Boyacá, Col. **D5** 80
Puerto Cabello, Ven. **A6** 70
Puerto Cabezas, Nic. **C3** 80
Puerto Carreño, Col. **B6** 70
Puerto Chicama, Peru **E4** 70
Puerto Cortés, Hond. **B2** 80
Puerto Cumarebo, Ven. **A6** 70
Puerto de la Cruz, Spain **A1** 50
Puerto del Rosario, Spain **A2** 50
Puerto Deseado, Arg. **G3** 69
Puerto Esperanza, Arg. **D7** 72
Puerto Guaraní, Para. **C6** 72
Puerto Inírida, Col. **E6** 80
Puerto Juárez, Mex. **C7** 78
Puerto la Cruz, Ven. **A7** 70
Puerto Leguízamo, Col. **D5** 70
Puerto Libertad, Mex. **B2** 78
Puerto Limón, C.R. **C3** 80
Puertollano, Spain **H4** 16
Puerto Lobos, Arg. **F3** 69
Puerto Madryn, Arg. **F3** 69
Puerto Maldonado, Peru **F6** 70
Puerto Montt, Chile **F2** 69
Puerto Morazán, Nic. **C2** 80
Puerto Nariño, Col. **D6** 80
Puerto Natales, Chile **H2** 69
Puerto Padre, Cuba **A4** 80
Puerto Páez, Ven. **B6** 70
Puerto Peñasco, Mex. **A2** 78
Puerto Plata, Dom. Rep. **B5** 80
Puerto Princesa, Phil. **E7** 34
Puerto Rico, Bol. **F6** 70
Puerto Rico, dep., N.A. **B6** 80
Puerto Rico Trench **G7** 66
Puerto San José, Guat. **C1** 80
Puerto San Julián, Arg. **G3** 69
Puerto Santa Cruz, Arg. **H3** 69
Puerto Sastre, Para. **C6** 72
Puerto Suárez, Bol. **B6** 72
Puerto Vallarta, Mex. **C3** 78
Puerto Villamil, Ec. **D1** 70
Puerto Wilches, Col. **B5** 70
Puerto Ybapobó, Para. **C6** 72
Pugačov, Russia **D8** 22
Puget Sound, strt., Wa., U.S. **B3** 140
Puget Sound Naval Shipyard, mil., Wa., U.S. **e10** 140
Pugwash, N.S., Can. **D6** 87
Puhi, Hi., U.S. **B2** 104
Pukalani, Hi., U.S. **C5** 104
Pukaskwa National Park, On., Can. **o18** 89
Pukch'ŏng-ŭp, N. Kor. **C13** 28
Pukeashun Mountain, mtn., B.C., Can. **D8** 85
Pukou, China **C4** 30
Pula, Cro. **B4** 18
Pulaski, co., Ar., U.S. **C3** 97
Pulaski, co., Ga., U.S. **D3** 103
Pulaski, co., Il., U.S. **F4** 106
Pulaski, co., In., U.S. **B4** 107
Pulaski, co., Ky., U.S. **C5** 110
Pulaski, co., Mo., U.S. **D5** 118
Pulaski, N.Y., U.S. **B4** 125
Pulaski, Tn., U.S. **B4** 135
Pulaski, Va., U.S. **C2** 139
Pulaski, co., Va., U.S. **C2** 139
Pulaski, Wi., U.S. **D5** 142
Puławy, Pol. **D7** 20
Pulicat Lake, l., India **G4** 40
Pullman, Wa., U.S. **C8** 140
Pumphrey, Md., U.S. **h11** 113
Puná, Isla, i., Ec. **D3** 70
Punakha, Bhu. **D5** 40
Punata, Bol. **B4** 72
Pune, India **F2** 40
Pungo Lake, l., N.C., U.S. **B6** 126
Punia, D.R.C. **D5** 54
Punjab, state, India **C3** 40
Puno, Peru **G5** 70
Punta, Cerro de, mtn., P.R. **B6** 80
Punta Alta, Arg. **F5** 72
Punta Arenas, Chile **H2** 69
Punta de Díaz, Chile **D3** 72
Punta del Este, Ur. **F7** 72
Punta Delgada, Arg. **F4** 69
Punta Gorda, Fl., U.S. **F4** 102
Punta Gorda, Bahía de, b., Nic. **C3** 80
Puntarenas, C.R. **C2** 80
Punto Fijo, Ven. **A5** 70
Punxsutawney, Pa., U.S. **E4** 131
Puolanka, Fin. **D12** 10
Puqi, China **F10** 28
Puquio, Peru **F5** 70
Purcell, Ok., U.S. **B4** 129
Purcellville, Va., U.S. **A5** 139
Purdy, Mo., U.S. **E4** 118
Purgatoire, stm., Co., U.S. **D7** 99
Purgatoire Peak, mtn., Co., U.S. **D5** 99
Puri, India **F5** 40
Pūrnia, India **D5** 40
Purus (Purús), stm., S.A. **D7** 70
Purvis, Ms., U.S. **D4** 117
Purwakarta, Indon. **E3** 36
Purwokerto, Indon. **E3** 36
Pusan, S. Kor. **D13** 28
Pushaw Lake, l., Me., U.S. **D4** 112
Pushkar, India **D2** 40
Pushmataha, co., Ok., U.S. **C6** 129
Puškin, Russia **G15** 10
Putao, Mya. **A3** 34
Putaruru, N.Z. **o14** 63c
Putian, China **D4** 30
Puting, Tanjung, c., Indon. **D4** 36
Putnam, Ct., U.S. **B8** 100
Putnam, co., Fl., U.S. **C5** 102
Putnam, co., Ga., U.S. **C3** 103
Putnam, co., Il., U.S. **B4** 106
Putnam, co., In., U.S. **E4** 107
Putnam, co., Mo., U.S. **A4** 118
Putnam, co., N.Y., U.S. **D7** 125
Putnam, co., Oh., U.S. **B1** 128
Putnam, co., Tn., U.S. **C8** 135
Putnam, co., W.V., U.S. **C3** 141
Putney, Ga., U.S. **E2** 103
Putney, Vt., U.S. **F3** 138
Putorana, plato, plat., Russia **C11** 26
Puttalam, Sri L. **H3** 40
Puttgarden, Ger. **C12** 12
Putumayo (Içá), stm., S.A. **D5** 70
Putussibau, Indon. **C4** 36
Puukohola Heiau National Historic Site, hist., Hi., U.S. **D6** 104
Puula, l., Fin. **F12** 10
Puxico, Mo., U.S. **E7** 118
Puyallup, Wa., U.S. **B3** 140
Puyallup, stm., Wa., U.S. **C3** 140
Puyang, China **B3** 30
Pweto, D.R.C. **E5** 54
Pyandzh see Amu Darya, stm., Asia **B8** 42
Pyapon, Mya. **C3** 34
Pyhäjoki, Fin. **D11** 10
Pyhäselkä, l., Fin. **E13** 10
Pyinmana, Mya. **C3** 34
Pyles Fork, stm., W.V., U.S. **h10** 141
Pymatuning Reservoir, res., U.S. **C1** 131
P'yŏngyang, N. Kor. **D13** 28
Pyramid Lake, l., Nv., U.S. **C2** 121
Pyramid Lake Indian Reservation, Nv., U.S. **D2** 121
Pyramid Mountains, mts., N.M., U.S. **E1** 124
Pyramid Peak, mtn., N.M., U.S. **E1** 124
Pyramid Peak, mtn., Wy., U.S. **C2** 143
Pyrenees, mts., Eur. **F7** 16
Pyriatyn, Ukr. **D12** 20

Name — Map Ref. — Page

Pyu, Mya. C3 34

Q

Qaanaaq see Thule, Grnld. C26 82
Qacentina, Alg. C6 48
Qā'emshahr, Iran C6 42
Qā'en, Iran D7 42
Qaidam Pendi, bas., China D6 28
Qalāt, Afg. D9 42
Qal'at Bīshah, Sau. Ar. G4 38
Qal'at Sukkar, Iraq G12 44
Qal'eh-ye Now, Afg. D8 42
Qallābāt, Sudan H3 38
Qamar, Ghubbat al-, b., Yemen G6 38
Qamar Bay see Qamar, Ghubbat al-, b., Yemen G6 38
Qamdo, China E7 28
Qandahār see Kandahār, Afg. D9 42
Qandala, Som. H5 38
Qardho, Som. I14 48
Qareh Sū, stm., Iran C12 44
Qasr el-Boukhari, Alg. J8 16
Qasr Farâfra, Egypt E10 48
Qaṭanā, Syria F7 44
Qatar, ctry., Asia E6 42
Qattâra, Munkhafad el-, depr., Egypt E10 48
Qattara Depression see Qattâra, Munkhafad el-, depr., Egypt E10 48
Qazımämmäd, Azer. B13 44
Qazvīn, Iran C5 42
Qena, Egypt E11 48
Qeydār, Iran D13 44
Qianwei, China D1 30
Qianxi, China D2 30
Qianyang, China D3 30
Qiemo, China D5 28
Qigong, China A4 34
Qijiang, China D2 30
Qilian Shan, mts., China D7 28
Qimen, China D4 30
Qingdao, China D12 28
Qinghai, prov., China D7 28
Qinghai Hu, l., China D8 28
Qingjiang, China E11 28
Qinglong, China A4 30
Qinglong, China D2 30
Qingshen, China D1 30
Qingtang, China G10 28
Qingyang, China D9 28
Qingyuan, China E3 30
Qing Zang Gaoyuan (Tibet, Plateau of), plat., China E4 28
Qinhuangdao, China D11 28
Qin Ling, mts., China E9 28
Qinxian, China B3 30
Qinzhou, China E2 30
Qionghai, China F3 30
Qionglai, China E8 28
Qiongzhong, China H9 28
Qiongzhou Haixia, strt., China G9 28
Qiqihar, China B12 28
Qiryat Shemona, Isr. F6 44
Qishn, Yemen G6 38
Qitai, China C5 28
Qiyang, China D3 30
Qobustan, Azer. B13 44
Qogir Feng see K2, mtn., Asia B3 40
Qom, Iran D6 42
Qomolangma Feng see Everest, Mount, mtn., Asia D5 40
Qomsheh, Iran D6 42
Qorveh, Iran E12 44
Quabbin Reservoir, res., Ma., U.S. B3 114
Quaddick Reservoir, res., Ct., U.S. B8 100
Quail Oaks, Va., U.S. n18 139
Quaker Hill, Ct., U.S. D7 100
Quakertown, Pa., U.S. F11 131
Qualicum Beach, B.C., Can. E5 85
Quanah, Tx., U.S. B3 136
Quang Ngai, Viet. C5 34
Quannapowitt, Lake, l., Ma., U.S. f11 114
Quantico, Va., U.S. B5 139
Quantico Marine Corps Air Station, mil., Va., U.S. B5 139
Quanzhou, China G11 28
Quanzhou, China D3 30
Quapaw, Ok., U.S. A7 129
Qu'Appelle, Sk., Can. G4 91
Qu'Appelle, stm., Can. G4 91
Quarryville, Pa., U.S. G9 131
Quartu Sant'Elena, Italy E2 18
Quartz Mountain, mtn., Or., U.S. D4 130
Quartzsite, Az., U.S. D1 96
Quassapaug, Lake, l., Ct., U.S. C3 100
Quatsino Sound, strt., B.C., Can. D3 85
Quay, co., N.M., U.S. C6 124
Quba, Azer. B13 44
Qūchān, Iran C7 42
Queanbeyan, Austl. H4 62
Québec, Qc., Can. C6 90
Quebec, prov., Can. C5 90
Quechee, Vt., U.S. D4 138
Queen, stm., R.I., U.S. E3 132
Queen Annes, co., Md., U.S. B5 113
Queen Bess, Mount, mtn., B.C., Can. D5 85
Queen Charlotte, B.C., Can. C1 85
Queen Charlotte Islands, is., B.C., Can. C1 85
Queen Charlotte Mountains, mts., B.C., Can. C1 85
Queen Charlotte Sound, strt., B.C., Can. H14 82
Queen Charlotte Strait, strt., B.C., Can. D4 85
Queen City, Mo., U.S. A5 118
Queen City, Tx., U.S. C5 136
Queen Creek, Az., U.S. m9 96
Queen Mary Coast, Ant. C14 67
Queen Maud Land, reg., Ant. D4 67
Queen Maud Mountains, mts., Ant. E25 67
Queens, co., N.Y., U.S. E7 125
Queensland, state, Austl. E3 62
Queenstown, Austl. I4 62
Queenstown, S. Afr. E4 56
Quela, Ang. E3 54
Quelimane, Moz. B6 56
Querétaro, Mex. C4 78
Querétaro, state, Mex. C5 78
Queshan, China C3 30
Quesnel, B.C., Can. C6 85
Quesnel, stm., B.C., Can. C6 85
Quesnel Lake, l., B.C., Can. C7 85
Questa, N.M., U.S. A4 124
Quetico Provincial Park, On., Can. o17 89
Quetta, Pak. D9 42
Quevedo, Ec. D4 70
Quezon City, Phil. D8 34
Quibala, Ang. F3 54
Quibdó, Col. B4 70
Quicksand Pond, l., R.I., U.S. E6 132
Quiculungo, Ang. E3 54
Quidnessett, R.I., U.S. E4 132
Quidnick, R.I., U.S. D3 132
Quidnick Reservoir, res., R.I., U.S. D2 132
Quila, Mex. C3 78
Quilcene, Wa., U.S. B3 140
Quileute Indian Reservation, Wa., U.S. B1 140
Quillota, Chile D2 69
Quilon, India H3 40
Quimaria, Ang. E2 54
Quimilí, Arg. D5 72
Quimper, Fr. D4 16
Quimperlé, Fr. D5 16
Quinault, stm., Wa., U.S. B1 140
Quinault, Lake, l., Wa., U.S. B2 140
Quinault Indian Reservation, Wa., U.S. B1 140
Quince Mil, Peru F5 70
Quincy, Ca., U.S. C3 98
Quincy, Fl., U.S. B2 102
Quincy, Il., U.S. D2 106
Quincy, Ma., U.S. B5 114
Quincy, Mi., U.S. G6 115
Quincy, Wa., U.S. B6 140
Quincy Bay, b., Ma., U.S. g12 114
Quinebaug, Ct., U.S. A8 100
Quinebaug, stm., Ct., U.S. C8 100
Quinhagak, Ak., U.S. D7 95
Quinlan, Tx., U.S. C4 136
Quinn, stm., Nv., U.S. B3 121
Quinn Canyon Range, mts., Nv., U.S. F6 121
Quinnesec, Mi., U.S. C3 115
Quinnipiac, stm., Ct., U.S. D4 100
Quintana Roo, state, Mex. D7 78
Quinter, Ks., U.S. C3 109
Quinton, Ok., U.S. B6 129
Quirinópolis, Braz. E1 74
Quissanga, Moz. A7 56
Quiterajo, Moz. A7 56
Quitman, Ar., U.S. B3 97
Quitman, Ga., U.S. F3 103
Quitman, co., Ga., U.S. E1 103
Quitman, Ms., U.S. C5 117
Quitman, co., Ms., U.S. A3 117
Quitman, Tx., U.S. C5 136
Quito, Ec. D4 70
Quixadá, Braz. B4 74
Quixeramobim, Braz. C4 74
Qujing, China F8 28
Qumarlêb, China E7 28
Qunayyin, Sabkhat al-, l., Libya E8 14
Quonnipaug Lake, l., Ct., U.S. D5 100
Quonochontaug, R.I., U.S. G2 132
Quonochontaug Pond, l., R.I., U.S. G2 132
Quonset Point, c., R.I., U.S. E4 132
Quseir, Egypt E11 48
Qutdligssat, Grnld. D29 82
Quthing, Leso. E4 56
Qüxü, China D6 40
Quy Nhon, Viet. D5 34
Quzhou, China F11 28

R

Raab see Győr, Hung. F4 20
Raahe, Fin. D11 10
Rab, Otok, i., Cro. B5 18
Rába, stm., Eur. F4 20
Raba, Indon. E5 36
Rabat, Mor. D3 48
Rabaul, Pap. N. Gui. G13 32
Rabbit Creek, stm., S.D., U.S. B3 134
Rabbit Ears Pass, Co., U.S. A4 99
Rabi, i., Fiji m11 63b
Rābigh, Sau. Ar. F3 38
Râbniţa, Mol. F10 20
Rabun, co., Ga., U.S. B3 103
Rabun Bald, mtn., Ga., U.S. B3 103
Rabyānah, Ramlat, des., Libya F8 48
Raccoon Creek, stm., Oh., U.S. D3 128
Raccourci Island, i., La., U.S. D4 111
Race, Cape, c., N.L., Can. E5 88
Raceland, Ky., U.S. B7 110
Raceland, La., U.S. E5 111
Race Point, c., Ma., U.S. B7 114
Rach Gia, Viet. E4 34
Racine, Wi., U.S. F6 142
Racine, co., Wi., U.S. F5 142
Racine, W.V., U.S. C3 141
Racine Dam, U.S. C3 141
Rădăuţi, Rom. F8 20
Radcliff, Ky., U.S. C4 110
Radford, Va., U.S. C2 139
Radom, Pol. D6 20
Radomsko, Pol. D5 20
Radomyshl', Ukr. D10 20
Rāe Bareli, India D4 40
Raeford, N.C., U.S. C3 126
Rafaela, Arg. E5 72
Rafaḥ, Gaza G6 44
Rafḥā', Sau. Ar. E4 38
Rafsanjān, Iran D7 42
Raft, stm., Id., U.S. G5 105
Raft River Mountains, mts., Ut., U.S. B2 137
Raga, Sudan I10 48
Ragay Gulf, b., Phil. D8 34
Ragged Island, i., Me., U.S. E4 112
Ragged Island Range, is., Bah. D9 76
Ragged Lake, l., Me., U.S. C3 112
Ragged Top Mountain, mtn., Wy., U.S. E7 143
Ragland, Al., U.S. B3 94
Ragusa, Italy F5 18
Rahīmyār Khān, Pak. E10 42
Rahway, N.J., U.S. B4 123
Rahway, stm., N.J., U.S. k7 123
Rāichūr, India F3 40
Raiganj, India D5 40
Raigarh, India E4 40
Railroad Valley, val., Nv., U.S. E6 121
Rainbow Bridge National Monument, Ut., U.S. F5 137
Rainbow Falls, wtfl., Tn., U.S. D10 135
Rainbow Flowage, res., Wi., U.S. C4 142
Rainbow Lake, l., Me., U.S. C3 112
Rainelle, W.V., U.S. D4 141
Rainier, Or., U.S. A4 130
Rainier, Wa., U.S. C3 140
Rainier, Mount, mtn., Wa., U.S. C4 140
Rains, co., Tx., U.S. C5 136
Rainsville, Al., U.S. A4 94
Rainy Lake, l., Mn., U.S. B5 116
Rainy River, On., Can. o16 89
Raipur, India E4 40
Rājahmundry, India F4 40
Rajang, stm., Malay. C4 36
Rājapālaiyam, India H3 40
Rājasthān, state, India D2 40
Rajčihinsk, Russia E14 26
Rāj Gangpur, India E4 40
Rājkot, India E2 40
Rāj Nāndgaon, India E4 40
Rājshāhi, Bngl. E5 40
Rakhiv, Ukr. E8 20
Rakvere, Est. G12 10
Raleigh, Ms., U.S. C4 117
Raleigh, N.C., U.S. B4 126
Raleigh, W.V., U.S. n13 141
Raleigh, co., W.V., U.S. D3 141
Raleigh Bay, b., N.C., U.S. C6 126
Ralls, co., Mo., U.S. B6 118
Ralls, Tx., U.S. C2 136
Ralston, Ne., U.S. g12 120
Ralston Valley, val., Nv., U.S. E4 121
Ramah, N.M., U.S. B1 124
Ramah Indian Reservation, N.M., U.S. C1 124
Ramapo, stm., N.J., U.S. A4 123
Ramblewood, N.J., U.S. D3 123
Rambouillet, Fr. C7 16
Ramea, N.L., Can. E3 88
Rāmeswaram, India H3 40
Rāmhormoz, Iran D5 42
Ramm, Jabal, mtn., Jord. E3 42
Râmnicu Sărat, Rom. G9 20
Râmnicu Vâlcea, Rom. G8 20
Ramona, Ca., U.S. F5 98
Rampart Range, mts., Co., U.S. B5 99
Rāmpur, India D3 40
Ramree Island, i., Mya. C2 34
Ramsay, Mi., U.S. n12 115
Ramsele, Swe. E7 10
Ramseur, N.C., U.S. B3 126
Ramsey, Il., U.S. D4 106
Ramsey, co., Mn., U.S. E5 116
Ramsey, co., N.D., U.S. A7 127
Ramsey, N.J., U.S. A4 123
Ramsgate, Eng., U.K. E7 12
Ramshorn Peak, mtn., Mt., U.S. E5 119
Ramshorn Peak, mtn., Wy., U.S. C3 143
Ramu, Kenya C8 54
Rāna Pratāp Sāgar, res., India D2 40
Rancagua, Chile D2 69
Rancharia, Braz. F1 74
Rancheria Rock, mtn., Or., U.S. C6 130
Ranchester, Wy., U.S. B5 143
Rānchi, India E5 40
Ranchos de Taos, N.M., U.S. A4 124
Rancocas Creek, stm., N.J., U.S. C3 123
Rand, W.V., U.S. C3 141
Randall, co., Tx., U.S. B2 136
Randallstown, Md., U.S. B4 113
Randers, Den. H4 10
Randijaure, l., Swe. C8 10
Randle, Wa., U.S. C4 140
Randleman, N.C., U.S. B3 126
Randolph, co., Al., U.S. B4 94
Randolph, co., Ar., U.S. A4 97
Randolph, co., Ga., U.S. E2 103
Randolph, co., Il., U.S. E4 106
Randolph, co., In., U.S. D7 107
Randolph, Ma., U.S. B5 114
Randolph, Me., U.S. D3 112
Randolph, co., Mo., U.S. B5 118
Randolph, co., N.C., U.S. B3 126
Randolph, Ne., U.S. B8 120
Randolph, Vt., U.S. D3 138
Randolph, Wi., U.S. E5 142
Randolph, co., W.V., U.S. C5 141
Randolph Air Force Base, mil., Tx., U.S. h7 136
Randolph Hills, Md., U.S. B3 113
Random Island, i., N.L., Can. D5 88
Random Lake, Wi., U.S. E6 142
Randsfjorden, l., Nor. F4 10
Rāngāmāti, Bngl. E6 40
Rangeley, Me., U.S. D2 112
Rangeley Lake, l., Me., U.S. D2 112
Rangely, Co., U.S. A2 99
Ranger, Tx., U.S. C3 136
Ranger Lake, l., N.M., U.S. D6 124
Rangoon see Yangon, Mya. C3 34
Rangpur, Bngl. D5 40
Rānībennur, India G3 40
Rankin, co., Ms., U.S. C4 117
Rankin, Pa., U.S. k14 131
Rann of Kutch see Kutch, Rann of, reg., Asia E1 40
Ranohira, Madag. C8 56
Ranong, Thai. E3 34
Ransiki, Indon. D8 36
Ransom, co., N.D., U.S. C8 127
Ranson, W.V., U.S. B7 141
Rantauprapat, Indon. C1 36
Rantoul, Il., U.S. C5 106
Raohe, China A2 31
Raoul, Ga., U.S. B3 103
Rapallo, Italy B2 18
Rapid, stm., Mn., U.S. B4 116
Rapid City, S.D., U.S. C2 134
Rapides, co., La., U.S. C3 111
Rapid River, Mi., U.S. C4 115
Rapids City, Il., U.S. B3 106
Rappahannock, stm., Va., U.S. B5 139
Rappahannock, co., Va., U.S. B4 139
Raquette, stm., N.Y., U.S. f10 125
Raquette Lake, l., N.Y., U.S. B6 125
Raraka, atoll, Fr. Poly. F15 58
Raritan, N.J., U.S. B3 123
Raritan, stm., N.J., U.S. C4 123
Raritan Bay, b., N.J., U.S. C4 123
Rarotonga, i., Cook Is. G14 58
Ra's al-Khaymah, U.A.E. E7 42
Ras Dashen Terara, mtn., Eth. H12 48
Rashid, Egypt E10 14
Rasht, Iran C5 42
Rasšua, ostrov, i., Russia E17 26
Ratangarh, India D2 40
Rāth, India D3 40
Rathbun Lake, res., Ia., U.S. D5 108
Rathdrum, Id., U.S. B2 105
Rat Islands, is., Ak., U.S. E3 95
Ratlām, India E3 40
Ratnāgiri, India F2 40
Ratnapura, Sri L. H4 40
Raton, N.M., U.S. A5 124
Raton Pass, N.M., U.S. A5 124
Rattlesnake Creek, stm., Oh., U.S. C2 128
Rattlesnake Creek, stm., Wa., U.S. C6 140
Rättvik, Swe. F6 10
Raub, Malay. C2 36
Rauch, Arg. F6 72
Rauma, Fin. F9 10
Raurkela, India E5 40
Ravalli, co., Mt., U.S. D2 119
Raven, Va., U.S. e10 139
Ravena, N.Y., U.S. C7 125
Ravenel, S.C., U.S. k11 133
Ravenna, Italy B4 18
Ravenna, Ky., U.S. C6 110
Ravenna, Mi., U.S. E5 115
Ravenna, Ne., U.S. C7 120
Ravenna, Oh., U.S. A4 128
Raven Park, reg., Co., U.S. A2 99
Ravensburg, Ger. G11 12
Ravensthorpe, Austl. G3 60
Ravenswood, W.V., U.S. C3 141
Rāvi, stm., Asia C2 40
Ravnina, Turk. C8 42
Rawaki, atoll, Kir. E12 58
Rāwalpindi, Pak. D10 42
Rawdon, Qc., Can. C4 90
Rawhide Creek, stm., Wy., U.S. D8 143
Rawlings, Md., U.S. k13 113
Rawlinna, Austl. G4 60
Rawlins, co., Ks., U.S. C2 109
Rawlins, Wy., U.S. E5 143
Rawson, Arg. F3 69
Ray, co., Mo., U.S. B3 118
Ray, N.D., U.S. A2 127
Ray, Cape, c., N.L., Can. E2 88
Raya, Bukit, mtn., Indon. C4 36
Rāyachoti, India G3 40
Rāyadurg, India G3 40
Ray City, Ga., U.S. E3 103
Raymond, Ab., Can. E4 84
Raymond, Il., U.S. D4 106
Raymond, Mn., U.S. E3 116
Raymond, Ms., U.S. C3 117
Raymond, N.H., U.S. D4 122
Raymond, Wa., U.S. C2 140
Raymondville, Tx., U.S. F4 136
Raymore, Sk., Can. F3 91
Raymore, Mo., U.S. C3 118
Rayne, La., U.S. D3 111
Raynham, Ma., U.S. C5 114
Raynham Center, Ma., U.S. C5 114
Rayong, Thai. D4 34
Raytown, Mo., U.S. h11 118
Rayville, La., U.S. B4 111
Razdol'noe, Russia B2 31
Razgrad, Blg. C11 18
Ré, Île de, i., Fr. D6 16
Reader, W.V., U.S. B4 141
Reading, Eng., U.K. E6 12
Reading, Ma., U.S. A5 114
Reading, Mi., U.S. G6 115
Reading, Oh., U.S. C1 128
Reading, Pa., U.S. F10 131
Readlyn, Ia., U.S. B5 108
Reagan, co., Tx., U.S. D2 136
Real, co., Tx., U.S. E3 136
Real, Cordillera, mts., S.A. G6 70
Realicó, Arg. E5 72
Reamstown, Pa., U.S. F9 131
Rebiana Sand Sea see Rabyānah, Ramlat, des., Libya F8 48
Rebun-tō, i., Japan B16 28
Recherche, Archipelago of the, is., Austl. G3 60
Recife, Braz. C5 74
Reconquista, Arg. D6 72
Rector, Ar., U.S. A5 97
Rèčyca, Bela. C11 20
Red, stm., Asia B4 34
Red, stm., N.A. B8 92
Red, stm., Ky., U.S. C6 110
Red, stm., Tn., U.S. A4 135
Red, stm., U.S. E9 92
Red Bank, N.J., U.S. C4 123
Red Bank, Tn., U.S. D8 135
Red Bay, Al., U.S. A1 94
Redberry Lake, l., Sk., Can. E2 91
Red Bird, stm., Ky., U.S. C6 110
Redbird, Oh., U.S. A4 128
Red Bluff, Ca., U.S. B2 98
Red Bluff Lake, res., U.S. o12 136
Red Boiling Springs, Tn., U.S. C8 135
Red Bud, Il., U.S. E4 106
Red Butte, mtn., Ut., U.S. B2 137
Red Cedar, stm., Wi., U.S. C2 142
Red Cedar Lake, l., Wi., U.S. C2 142
Redcliff, Ab., Can. D5 84
Redcliffe, Austl. F5 62
Redcliffe, Mount, mtn., Austl. F3 60
Red Cliff Indian Reservation, Wi., U.S. B2 142
Red Cloud, Ne., U.S. D7 120
Redcloud Peak, mtn., Co., U.S. D3 99
Red Deer, Ab., Can. C4 84

Name	Map Ref.	Page
Red Deer, stm., Can.	E4	91
Red Deer, stm., Can.	D4	84
Redding, Ca., U.S.	B2	98
Redding, Ct., U.S.	D2	100
Redeye, stm., Mn., U.S.	D3	116
Redfield, Ar., U.S.	C3	97
Redfield, Ia., U.S.	C3	108
Redfield, S.D., U.S.	C7	134
Redford, Mi., U.S.	F7	115
Redgranite, Wi., U.S.	D4	142
Red Hook, N.Y., U.S.	C7	125
Red Indian Lake, l., N.L., Can.	D3	88
Red Jacket, W.V., U.S.	D2	141
Redkey, In., U.S.	D7	107
Red Lake, l., Az., U.S.	B1	96
Redlake, Mn., U.S.	C3	116
Red Lake, stm., Mn., U.S.	C2	116
Red Lake, co., Mn., U.S.	C2	116
Red Lake Falls, Mn., U.S.	C2	116
Red Lake Indian Reservation, Mn., U.S.	B3	116
Redlands, Ca., U.S.	E5	98
Red Lion, Pa., U.S.	G8	131
Red Lodge, Mt., U.S.	E7	119
Red Mill Pond, l., De., U.S.	E5	101
Redmond, Or., U.S.	C5	130
Redmond, Ut., U.S.	E4	137
Redmond, Wa., U.S.	e11	140
Red Mountain, mtn., Ca., U.S.	B2	98
Red Mountain, mtn., Mt., U.S.	C4	119
Red Mountain Pass, Co., U.S.	D3	99
Red Oak, Ga., U.S.	h7	103
Red Oak, Ia., U.S.	D2	108
Red Oak, Ok., U.S.	C6	129
Red Oak, Tx., U.S.	n10	136
Red Oaks, La., U.S.	h9	111
Redon, Fr.	D5	16
Redondo, Wa., U.S.	f11	140
Redondo Beach, Ca., U.S.	n12	98
Redoubt Volcano, vol., Ak., U.S.	g15	95
Red Peak, mtn., Co., U.S.	B4	99
Red River, co., La., U.S.	B2	111
Red River, co., Tx., U.S.	C5	136
Red Rock, stm., Mt., U.S.	F4	119
Red Rock, Lake, res., Ia., U.S.	C4	108
Redruth, Eng., U.K.	E4	12
Red Sea	F3	38
Red Springs, N.C., U.S.	C3	126
Red Table Mountain, mts., Co., U.S.	B4	99
Redwater, Ab., Can.	C4	84
Redwater, stm., Mt., U.S.	C11	119
Redwillow, stm., Can.	B7	85
Red Willow, co., Ne., U.S.	D5	120
Red Wing, Mn., U.S.	F6	116
Redwood, stm., Mn., U.S.	F3	116
Redwood, co., Mn., U.S.	F3	116
Redwood City, Ca., U.S.	D2	98
Redwood Falls, Mn., U.S.	F3	116
Redwood National Park, Ca., U.S.	B2	98
Redwood Valley, Ca., U.S.	C2	98
Ree, Lough, l., Ire.	D2	12
Reed City, Mi., U.S.	E5	115
Reedley, Ca., U.S.	D4	98
Reedsburg, Wi., U.S.	E3	142
Reeds Peak, mtn., N.M., U.S.	D2	124
Reedsport, Or., U.S.	D2	130
Reedsville, Pa., U.S.	E6	131
Reedsville, Wi., U.S.	D6	142
Reedy, stm., S.C., U.S.	C3	133
Reedy Lake, l., Fl., U.S.	E5	102
Reefton, N.Z.	p13	63c
Reelfoot Lake, l., Tn., U.S.	A2	135
Reese, Mi., U.S.	E7	115
Reese, stm., Nv., U.S.	C4	121
Reese Air Force Base, mil., Tx., U.S.	C1	136
Reeves, co., Tx., U.S.	o13	136
Reform, Al., U.S.	B1	94
Refugio, Tx., U.S.	E4	136
Refugio, co., Tx., U.S.	E4	136
Regensburg, Ger.	F12	12
Reggâne, Alg.	E4	48
Reggio di Calabria, Italy	E5	18
Reggio nell'Emilia, Italy	B3	18
Reghin, Rom.	F8	20
Regina, Sk., Can.	G3	91
Régina, Fr. Gu.	C9	70
Regina Beach, Sk., Can.	G3	91
Registro, Braz.	C8	72
Regozero, Russia	D14	10
Rehoboth, Nmb.	C2	56
Rehoboth Bay, b., De., U.S.	F5	101
Rehoboth Beach, De., U.S.	F5	101
Reid, Mount, mtn., Ak., U.S.	n24	95
Reidland, Ky., U.S.	e9	110
Reidsville, Ga., U.S.	D4	103
Reidsville, N.C., U.S.	A3	126
Reigate, Eng., U.K.	E6	12
Reims, Fr.	C9	16
Reinbeck, Ia., U.S.	B5	108
Reindeer Island, i., Mb., Can.	C3	86
Reindeer Lake, l., Can.	G19	82
Reisterstown, Md., U.S.	B4	113
Reliance, Wy., U.S.	E3	143
Remada, Tun.	D7	48
Remanso, Braz.	C3	74
Rembang, Indon.	E4	36
Remington, In., U.S.	C3	107
Remiremont, Fr.	C10	16
Remmel Dam, Ar., U.S.	g8	97
Remsen, Ia., U.S.	B2	108
Rena, Nor.	F4	10
Rend Lake, res., Il., U.S.	E5	106
Rendsburg, Ger.	C11	12
Renforth, N.B., Can.	D4	87
Renfrew, On., Can.	B8	89
Rengat, Indon.	D2	36
Rengo, Chile	E3	72
Reng Tlāng, mtn., Asia	B2	34
Rennes, Fr.	C6	16
Reno, co., Ks., U.S.	E5	109
Reno, Nv., U.S.	D2	121
Reno, Lake, l., Mn., U.S.	E3	116
Reno Hill, mtn., Wy., U.S.	D6	143
Renovo, Pa., U.S.	D6	131
Renqiu, China	B4	30
Rensselaer, In., U.S.	C3	107
Rensselaer, N.Y., U.S.	C7	125
Rensselaer, co., N.Y., U.S.	C7	125
Renton, Wa., U.S.	B3	140
Renville, Mn., U.S.	F3	116
Renville, co., Mn., U.S.	F4	116
Renville, co., N.D., U.S.	A4	127
Reo, Indon.	E6	36
Repentigny, Qc., Can.	D4	90
Repetek, Turk.	C8	42
Republic, co., Ks., U.S.	C6	109
Republic, Mi., U.S.	B3	115
Republic, Mo., U.S.	D4	118
Republic, Pa., U.S.	G2	131
Republic, Wa., U.S.	A7	140
Republican, stm., U.S.	C6	109
Republican, stm., U.S.	C8	92
Republic of Korea see Korea, South, ctry., Asia	D10	28
Reşadiye, Tur.	B7	44
Reserve, La., U.S.	h10	111
Resistencia, Arg.	D6	72
Reşiţa, Rom.	G6	20
Resolute, N.T., Can.	D20	82
Resolution Island, i., N.Z.	q12	63c
Reston, Mb., Can.	E1	86
Reston, Va., U.S.	B5	139
Réthimnon, Grc.	G10	18
Réunion, dep., Afr.	g10	57a
Reus, Spain	G7	16
Reutlingen, Ger.	F11	12
Revelo, Ky., U.S.	D5	110
Revelstoke, B.C., Can.	D8	85
Revelstoke, Lake, res., B.C., Can.	D8	85
Reventazón, Peru	E3	70
Revere, Ma., U.S.	g11	114
Revillagigedo, Islas, is., Mex.	D2	78
Revillagigedo Island, i., Ak., U.S.	n24	95
Revin, Fr.	C9	16
Rewa, India	E4	40
Rex, Ga., U.S.	h8	103
Rexburg, Id., U.S.	F7	105
Rexton, N.B., Can.	C5	87
Rey, Isla del, i., Pan.	D4	80
Reyes, Point, c., Ca., U.S.	C2	98
Reyhanlı, Tur.	D7	44
Reykjanes Ridge	B26	144
Reykjavík, Ice.	l18	10a
Reynolds, Ga., U.S.	D2	103
Reynolds, co., Mo., U.S.	D6	118
Reynoldsburg, Oh., U.S.	C3	128
Reynoldsville, Pa., U.S.	D4	131
Reynosa, Mex.	B5	78
Rezé, Fr.	D6	16
Rēzekne, Lat.	H12	10
Rhaetian Alps, mts., Eur.	A2	18
Rhea, co., Tn., U.S.	D9	135
Rheims see Reims, Fr.	C9	16
Rheine, Ger.	D10	12
Rhine (Rhein), stm., Eur.	A5	14
Rhinebeck, N.Y., U.S.	D7	125
Rhinelander, Wi., U.S.	C4	142
Rhir, Cap, c., Mor.	D2	48
Rho, Italy	B2	18
Rhode Island, i., R.I., U.S.	E5	132
Rhode Island, state, U.S.	D3	132
Rhode Island Sound, strt., U.S.	F5	132
Rhodes see Ródhos, i., Grc.	G12	18
Rhodesia see Zimbabwe, ctry., Afr.	B4	56
Rhodes Peak, mtn., Id., U.S.	C4	105
Rhodes' Tomb, hist., Zimb.	C4	56
Rhodope Mountains, mts., Eur.	D10	18
Rhône, stm., Eur.	E9	16
Riachão do Jacuípe, Braz.	D4	74
Rialto, Ca., U.S.	m14	98
Riau, Kepulauan, is., Indon.	C2	36
Riaza, Spain	G5	16
Ribáuè, Moz.	A6	56
Ribe, Den.	I3	10
Ribeira do Pombal, Braz.	D4	74
Ribeira Grande, C.V.	g9	50a
Ribeirão, Braz.	C4	74
Ribeirão Preto, Braz.	F2	74
Riberalta, Bol.	F6	70
Rib Lake, Wi., U.S.	C3	142
Riccione, Italy	B4	18
Rice, co., Ks., U.S.	D5	109
Rice, Mn., U.S.	E4	116
Rice, co., Mn., U.S.	F5	116
Riceboro, Ga., U.S.	E5	103
Rice Lake, l., On., Can.	C6	89
Rice Lake, l., Mn., U.S.	D5	116
Rice Lake, Wi., U.S.	C2	142
Riceville, Ia., U.S.	A5	108
Rich, co., Ut., U.S.	B4	137
Rich, Cape, c., On., Can.	C4	89
Richards Bay, S. Afr.	D5	56
Richardson, co., Ne., U.S.	D10	120
Richardson, Tx., U.S.	n10	136
Richardson Lakes, l., Me., U.S.	D2	112
Richard Toll, Sen.	C1	50
Richardton, N.D., U.S.	C3	127
Rich Creek, Va., U.S.	C2	139
Riche, Pointe, c., N.L., Can.	C3	88
Richfield, Mn., U.S.	F5	116
Richfield, Ut., U.S.	E3	137
Richford, Vt., U.S.	B3	138
Rich Hill, Mo., U.S.	C3	118
Richibucto, N.B., Can.	C5	87
Richland, Ga., U.S.	D2	103
Richland, co., Il., U.S.	E5	106
Richland, co., La., U.S.	B4	111
Richland, Mo., U.S.	D5	118
Richland, co., Mt., U.S.	C12	119
Richland, co., N.D., U.S.	C8	127
Richland, co., Oh., U.S.	B3	128
Richland, co., S.C., U.S.	D6	133
Richland, Wa., U.S.	C6	140
Richland, co., Wi., U.S.	E3	142
Richland Balsam, mtn., N.C., U.S.	f10	126
Richland Center, Wi., U.S.	E3	142
Richland Creek, stm., Tn., U.S.	B5	135
Richlands, N.C., U.S.	C5	126
Richlands, Va., U.S.	e10	139
Richlandtown, Pa., U.S.	F11	131
Richmond, Austl.	E3	62
Richmond, B.C., Can.	E6	85
Richmond, Qc., Can.	D5	90
Richmond, N.Z.	p13	63c
Richmond, Ca., U.S.	D2	98
Richmond, co., Ga., U.S.	C4	103
Richmond, Il., U.S.	A5	106
Richmond, In., U.S.	E8	107
Richmond, Ky., U.S.	C5	110
Richmond, Me., U.S.	D3	112
Richmond, Mi., U.S.	F8	115
Richmond, Mn., U.S.	E4	116
Richmond, Mo., U.S.	B4	118
Richmond, co., N.C., U.S.	B3	126
Richmond, co., N.Y., U.S.	E6	125
Richmond, Tx., U.S.	E5	136
Richmond, Ut., U.S.	B4	137
Richmond, Va., U.S.	C5	139
Richmond, co., Va., U.S.	C6	139
Richmond, Vt., U.S.	C3	138
Richmond Heights, Fl., U.S.	s13	102
Richmond Heights, Mo., U.S.	f13	118
Richmond Hill, On., Can.	D5	89
Richmond Hill, Ga., U.S.	E5	103
Richmond National Battlefield Park, Va., U.S.	n18	139
Rich Square, N.C., U.S.	A5	126
Richthofen, Mount, mtn., Co., U.S.	A5	99
Richton, Ms., U.S.	D5	117
Richwood, Oh., U.S.	B2	128
Richwood, W.V., U.S.	C4	141
Rickman, Tn., U.S.	C8	135
Riddle, Or., U.S.	E3	130
Riddle Mountain, mtn., Or., U.S.	D8	130
Rideau, stm., On., Can.	B9	89
Ridgecrest, Ca., U.S.	E5	98
Ridge Farm, Il., U.S.	D6	106
Ridgefield, Ct., U.S.	D2	100
Ridgefield, N.J., U.S.	h8	123
Ridgefield, Wa., U.S.	D3	140
Ridgefield Park, N.J., U.S.	B4	123
Ridgeland, Ms., U.S.	C3	117
Ridgeland, S.C., U.S.	G6	133
Ridgeley, W.V., U.S.	B6	141
Ridgely, Md., U.S.	C6	113
Ridgely, Tn., U.S.	A2	135
Ridge Spring, S.C., U.S.	D4	133
Ridgetop, Tn., U.S.	A5	135
Ridgetown, On., Can.	E3	89
Ridgeview, W.V., U.S.	C3	141
Ridgeville, In., U.S.	D7	107
Ridgeville, S.C., U.S.	E7	133
Ridgeway, Va., U.S.	D3	139
Ridgewood, N.J., U.S.	B4	123
Ridgway, Il., U.S.	F5	106
Ridgway, Pa., U.S.	D4	131
Riding Mountain National Park, Mb., Can.	D1	86
Ridley Park, Pa., U.S.	p20	131
Riesa, Ger.	E13	12
Rieti, Italy	C4	18
Rif, mts., Mor.	E3	14
Riffe Lake, res., Wa., U.S.	C3	140
Rifle, Co., U.S.	B3	99
Rifle, stm., Mi., U.S.	D6	115
Rift Valley, val., Afr.	C6	54
Rīga, Lat.	H11	10
Riga, Gulf of, b., Eur.	G10	10
Rigaud, Qc., Can.	D3	90
Rigby, Id., U.S.	F7	105
Rīgestān, reg., Afg.	D9	42
Rigo, Pap. N. Gui.	H12	32
Riihimäki, Fin.	F11	10
Riiser-Larsen Peninsula, pen., Ant.	C8	67
Rijeka, Cro.	B5	18
Riley, Ks., U.S.	C7	109
Riley, co., Ks., U.S.	C7	109
Riley, Mount, mtn., N.M., U.S.	F2	124
Rimbey, Ab., Can.	C3	84
Rimersburg, Pa., U.S.	D3	131
Rimini, Italy	B4	18
Rimouski, Qc., Can.	A9	90
Rimouski, stm., Qc., Can.	A9	90
Rimouski-Est, Qc., Can.	A9	90
Rimrock Lake, res., Wa., U.S.	C4	140
Rinca, Pulau, i., Indon.	E5	36
Rincon, Ga., U.S.	D5	103
Rincón del Bonete, Lago Artificial de, res., Ur.	E6	72
Rincón de Romos, Mex.	C4	78
Rincon Mountains, mts., Az., U.S.	E5	96
Ringdove, Vanuatu	k9	62a
Ringgold, Ga., U.S.	B1	103
Ringgold, co., Ia., U.S.	D3	108
Ringgold, La., U.S.	B2	111
Ringim, Nig.	D6	50
Ringkøbing, Den.	H3	10
Ringkøbing Fjord, b., Den.	I3	10
Ringling, Ok., U.S.	C4	129
Ringvassøya, i., Nor.	B8	10
Ringwood, N.J., U.S.	A4	123
Rinjani, Gunung, vol., Indon.	E5	36
Rio, Fl., U.S.	E6	102
Rio, Wi., U.S.	E4	142
Rio Arriba, co., N.M., U.S.	A2	124
Riobamba, Ec.	D4	70
Rio Blanco, co., Co., U.S.	B2	99
Rio Branco, Braz.	E6	70
Río Bravo, Mex.	B5	78
Rio Claro, Braz.	F2	74
Río Colorado, Arg.	E4	69
Río Cuarto, Arg.	E5	72
Rio de Janeiro, Braz.	F3	74
Rio de Janeiro, state, Braz.	F3	74
Rio Dell, Ca., U.S.	B1	98
Río Gallegos, Arg.	H3	69
Río Grande, Arg.	H3	69
Rio Grande, Braz.	E7	72
Río Grande, Mex.	C4	78
Rio Grande (Bravo), stm., N.A.	F7	92
Rio Grande, co., Co., U.S.	D4	99
Rio Grande, Oh., U.S.	D3	128
Rio Grande City, Tx., U.S.	F3	136
Rio Grande do Norte, state, Braz.	E12	70
Rio Grande do Sul, state, Braz.	D7	72
Rio Grande Reservoir, res., Co., U.S.	D3	99
Ríohacha, Col.	A5	70
Río Hato, Pan.	D3	80
Rio Hondo, Tx., U.S.	F4	136
Rio Largo, Braz.	C4	74
Riom, Fr.	E8	16
Río Mayo, Arg.	G2	69
Rionegro, Col.	D5	80
Rio Negro, Pantanal do, sw., Braz.	G8	70
Rio Rancho, N.M., U.S.	B3	124
Rio Real, Braz.	D4	74
Ríosucio, Col.	D4	80
Río Tercero, Arg.	E5	72
Rio Tinto, Braz.	C4	74
Rio Verde, Braz.	E1	74
Ríoverde, Mex.	C5	78
Rio Verde de Mato Grosso, Braz.	B7	72
Rio Vista, Ca., U.S.	C3	98
Ripley, co., In., U.S.	F7	107
Ripley, co., Mo., U.S.	E7	118
Ripley, Ms., U.S.	A5	117
Ripley, Oh., U.S.	D2	128
Ripley, Tn., U.S.	B2	135
Ripley, W.V., U.S.	C3	141
Ripon, Eng., U.K.	C6	12
Ripon, Wi., U.S.	E5	142
Rippowam, stm., Ct., U.S.	E1	100
Ririe Lake, res., Id., U.S.	F7	105
Rishiri-tō, i., Japan	B16	28
Rishon LeZiyyon, Isr.	G6	44
Rising Sun, De., U.S.	D3	101
Rising Sun, In., U.S.	G8	107
Rising Sun, Md., U.S.	A5	113
Rison, Ar., U.S.	D3	97
Ristijärvi, Fin.	D13	10
Ritchie, co., W.V., U.S.	B3	141
Ritter, Mount, mtn., Ca., U.S.	D4	98
Rittman, Oh., U.S.	B4	128
Ritzville, Wa., U.S.	B7	140
Riva del Garda, Italy	B3	18
Rivanna, stm., Va., U.S.	C4	139
Rivas, Nic.	C2	80
Rivera, Ur.	E6	72
Riverbank, Ca., U.S.	D3	98
River Bourgeois, N.S., Can.	D9	87
River Cess, Lib.	E3	50
Riverdale, Ca., U.S.	D4	98
Riverdale, Il., U.S.	k9	106
Riverdale, Md., U.S.	C4	113
River Edge, N.J., U.S.	h8	123
River Falls, Al., U.S.	D3	94
River Falls, Wi., U.S.	D1	142
River Forest, Il., U.S.	k9	106
River Grove, Il., U.S.	k9	106
Riverhead, N.Y., U.S.	n16	125
River Hebert, N.S., Can.	D5	87
River Heights, Ut., U.S.	B4	137
River Hills, Wi., U.S.	m12	142
River Pines, Ma., U.S.	f10	114
River Ridge, La., U.S.	k11	111
River Road, Or., U.S.	C3	130
River Rouge, Mi., U.S.	p15	115
Rivers, Mb., Can.	D1	86
Riversdale, S. Afr.	E3	56
Riverside, Al., U.S.	B3	94
Riverside, co., Ca., U.S.	F5	98
Riverside, Ca., U.S.	F5	98
Riverside, Ia., U.S.	C6	108
Riverside, Il., U.S.	k9	106
Riverside, N.J., U.S.	C3	123
Riverside, Pa., U.S.	E8	131
Riverside Reservoir, res., Co., U.S.	A6	99
Riverton, Mb., Can.	D3	86
Riverton, N.Z.	q12	63c
Riverton, Il., U.S.	D4	106
Riverton, Ks., U.S.	E9	109
Riverton, N.J., U.S.	C3	123
Riverton, Ut., U.S.	C4	137
Riverton, Vt., U.S.	C3	138
Riverton, Wy., U.S.	C4	143
Riverton Heights, Wa., U.S.	f11	140
River Vale, N.J., U.S.	h8	123
Riverview, Fl., U.S.	p11	102
Riverview, Mi., U.S.	p15	115
Rivesville, W.V., U.S.	B4	141
Riviera Beach, Fl., U.S.	F6	102
Riviera Beach, Md., U.S.	B4	113
Rivière-du-Loup, Qc., Can.	B8	90
Rivière-Verte, N.B., Can.	B1	87
Rivne, Ukr.	D9	20
Rivoli, Italy	B1	18
Riyadh see Ar-Riyāḍ, Sau. Ar.	F5	38
Rizhao, China	D11	28
Rjazan', Russia	D6	26
Rjažsk, Russia	C16	20
Rjukan, Nor.	G3	10
Roachdale, In., U.S.	E4	107
Road Town, Br. Vir. Is.	B7	80
Roane, co., Tn., U.S.	D9	135
Roane, co., W.V., U.S.	C3	141
Roan Mountain, Tn., U.S.	C11	135
Roanne, Fr.	D8	16
Roanoke, Al., U.S.	B4	94
Roanoke, Il., U.S.	C4	106
Roanoke, In., U.S.	C7	107
Roanoke, La., U.S.	D3	111
Roanoke, Tx., U.S.	m9	136
Roanoke, Va., U.S.	C3	139
Roanoke, co., Va., U.S.	C2	139
Roanoke, stm., U.S.	A5	126
Roanoke see Staunton, stm., U.S.	D12	92
Roanoke Island, i., N.C., U.S.	B7	126
Roanoke Rapids, N.C., U.S.	A5	126
Roanoke Rapids Lake, res., U.S.	A5	126
Roaring Fork, stm., Co., U.S.	C4	99
Roaring Spring, Pa., U.S.	F5	131
Roatán, Isla de, i., Hond.	B2	80
Robbins, Il., U.S.	k9	106
Robbins, N.C., U.S.	B3	126
Robbinsdale, Mn., U.S.	m12	116
Robbinsville, N.C., U.S.	f9	126
Robe, Austl.	H2	62
Robersonville, N.C., U.S.	B5	126
Roberta, Ga., U.S.	D2	103
Robert Lee, Tx., U.S.	D2	136
Roberts, co., S.D., U.S.	B8	134
Roberts, co., Tx., U.S.	B2	136
Roberts, Wi., U.S.	C1	142
Roberts, Point, c., Wa., U.S.	A2	140
Robert's Arm, N.L., Can.	D4	88
Roberts Creek Mountain, mtn., Nv., U.S.	D5	121
Robertsdale, Al., U.S.	E2	94
Robert S. Kerr Reservoir, res., Ok., U.S.	B6	129
Roberts Mountain, mtn., Ak., U.S.	C6	95
Roberts Mountain, mtn., Wy., U.S.	D3	143
Robertson, co., Ky., U.S.	B5	110
Robertson, co., Tn., U.S.	A5	135
Robertson, co., Tx., U.S.	D4	136
Robertsonville, Qc., Can.	C6	90
Roberts Port, Lib.	E2	50
Robertville, N.B., Can.	B4	87
Roberval, Qc., Can.	A5	90
Robeson, co., N.C., U.S.	C3	126
Robins, Ia., U.S.	B6	108
Robinson, Il., U.S.	D6	106
Róbinson Crusoe, Isla, i., Chile	E2	72
Robinson Fork, stm., W.V., U.S.	m14	141
Robinson Fork, stm., W.V., U.S.	k9	141
Robinvale, Austl.	G3	62
Roblin, Mb., Can.	D1	86

Name | Map Ref. | Page

Roboré, Bol. B6 72
Robson, Mount, mtn., B.C., Can. C8 85
Robstown, Tx., U.S. F4 136
Roca Partida, Isla, i., Mex. D2 78
Rocha, Ur. E7 72
Rochefort, Fr. E6 16
Rochelle, Ga., U.S. E3 103
Rochelle, Il., U.S. B4 106
Rochelle Park, N.J., U.S. h8 123
Rochester, Il., U.S. D4 106
Rochester, In., U.S. B5 107
Rochester, Mi., U.S. F7 115
Rochester, Mn., U.S. F6 116
Rochester, N.H., U.S. D5 122
Rochester, N.Y., U.S. B3 125
Rochester, Pa., U.S. E1 131
Rochester, Vt., U.S. D3 138
Rochester, Wa., U.S. C2 140
Rochester, Wi., U.S. n11 142
Rock, co., Mn., U.S. G2 116
Rock, co., Ne., U.S. B6 120
Rock, co., Wi., U.S. F4 142
Rock, stm., U.S. B3 106
Rock, stm., U.S. A1 108
Rockall, i., Scot., U.K. D3 6
Rockall Rise B24 144
Rockaway, N.J., U.S. B3 123
Rockaway, Or., U.S. B3 130
Rockbridge, co., Va., U.S. C3 139
Rockcastle, stm., Ky., U.S. C5 110
Rockcastle, co., Ky., U.S. C5 110
Rockcliffe Park, On., Can. h12 89
Rock Creek, Mn., U.S. E6 116
Rock Creek, stm., Nv., U.S. C5 121
Rock Creek, stm., Or., U.S. B6 130
Rock Creek, stm., Wa., U.S. B8 140
Rock Creek, stm., Wa., U.S. D5 140
Rock Creek, stm., Wy., U.S. E6 143
Rock Creek, stm., U.S. B3 113
Rock Creek, stm., U.S. h14 140
Rock Creek Butte, mtn., Or., U.S. C8 130
Rockdale, co., Ga., U.S. C3 103
Rockdale, Il., U.S. B5 106
Rockdale, Md., U.S. B4 113
Rockdale, Tx., U.S. D4 136
Rockefeller Plateau, plat., Ant. E27 67
Rockfall, Ct., U.S. C5 100
Rock Falls, Il., U.S. B4 106
Rockford, Ia., U.S. A5 108
Rockford, Il., U.S. A4 106
Rockford, Mi., U.S. E5 115
Rockford, Mn., U.S. E5 116
Rockford, Oh., U.S. B1 128
Rockford, Tn., U.S. D10 135
Rock Hall, Md., U.S. B5 113
Rockhampton, Austl. E5 62
Rockhampton Downs, Austl. D6 60
Rock Hill, S.C., U.S. B5 133
Rockingham, Austl. G2 60
Rockingham, N.C., U.S. C3 126
Rockingham, co., N.C., U.S. A3 126
Rockingham, co., N.H., U.S. D4 122
Rockingham, co., Va., U.S. B4 139
Rock Island, Qc., Can. D5 90
Rock Island, i., Fl., U.S. C3 102
Rock Island, Il., U.S. B3 106
Rock Island, co., Il., U.S. B3 106
Rock Island, i., Wi., U.S. C7 142
Rock Lake, l., Wa., U.S. B8 140
Rockland, On., Can. B9 89
Rockland, Ma., U.S. B6 114
Rockland, Me., U.S. D3 112
Rockland, co., N.Y., U.S. D6 125
Rockledge, Fl., U.S. D6 102
Rockledge, Pa., U.S. o20 131
Rocklin, Ca., U.S. C3 98
Rockmart, Ga., U.S. B1 103
Rock Mountain, mtn., Co., U.S. D3 99
Rockport, In., U.S. I3 107
Rockport, Ma., U.S. A6 114
Rockport, Me., U.S. D3 112
Rock Port, Mo., U.S. A2 118
Rockport, Tx., U.S. F4 136
Rock Rapids, Ia., U.S. A1 108
Rock River, Wy., U.S. E7 143
Rocksprings, Tx., U.S. D2 136
Rock Springs, Wy., U.S. E3 143
Rockstone, Guy. B8 70
Rockton, Il., U.S. A4 106
Rock Valley, Ia., U.S. A1 108
Rockville, In., U.S. E3 107
Rockville, Md., U.S. B3 113
Rockville Centre, N.Y., U.S. n15 125
Rockwall, Tx., U.S. C4 136
Rockwall, co., Tx., U.S. C4 136
Rockwell, Ia., U.S. B4 108
Rockwell, N.C., U.S. B2 126
Rockwell City, Ia., U.S. B3 108
Rockwell Park, N.C., U.S. B2 126
Rockwood, Mi., U.S. F7 115
Rockwood, Pa., U.S. G3 131
Rockwood, Tn., U.S. D9 135
Rocky, stm., N.C., U.S. B2 126
Rocky, stm., S.C., U.S. C2 133
Rocky, East Branch, stm., Oh., U.S. h9 128
Rocky, West Branch, stm., Oh., U.S. h9 128
Rocky Boys Indian Reservation, Mt., U.S. B7 119
Rocky Ford, Co., U.S. C7 99
Rocky Fork Lake, l., Oh., U.S. C2 128
Rocky Harbour, N.L., Can. D3 88
Rocky Hill, Ct., U.S. C5 100
Rocky Lake, l., Me., U.S. D5 112
Rocky Mount, N.C., U.S. B5 126
Rocky Mount, Va., U.S. D3 139
Rocky Mountain, mtn., Mt., U.S. C4 119
Rocky Mountain House, Ab., Can. C3 84
Rocky Mountain National Park, Co., U.S. A5 99
Rocky Mountains, mts., N.A. B5 92
Rocky Ripple, In., U.S. k10 107
Rocky River, Oh., U.S. A4 128
Rocky Top, mtn., Or., U.S. C4 130
Rodbār, Afg. D8 42
Roddickton, N.L., Can. C3 88
Rodeo, Arg. E4 72
Roderfield, W.V., U.S. D3 141
Rodez, Fr. E8 16
Ródhos, Grc. F12 18
Ródhos (Rhodes), i., Grc. G12 18
Rodney, On., Can. E3 89
Rodney, Cape, c., Ak., U.S. C6 95
Rodney Village, De., U.S. D3 101
Rodrigues, i., Mrts. F12 52
Roebourne, Austl. E2 60
Roebuck, S.C., U.S. B4 133
Roeland Park, Ks., U.S. k16 109
Roeselare, Bel. E8 12
Roff, Ok., U.S. C5 129
Roger Mills, co., Ok., U.S. B2 129
Rogers, Ar., U.S. A1 97
Rogers, Mn., U.S. E5 116
Rogers, co., Ok., U.S. A6 129
Rogers, Tx., U.S. D4 136
Rogers, Mount, mtn., Va., U.S. f10 139
Rogers City, Mi., U.S. C7 115
Rogers Lake, res., Ct., U.S. D6 100
Rogers Pass, Mt., U.S. C4 119
Rogersville, N.B., Can. C4 87
Rogersville, Al., U.S. A2 94
Rogersville, Mo., U.S. D4 118
Rogersville, Tn., U.S. C10 135
Rogue, stm., Or., U.S. E2 130
Rogue River, Or., U.S. E3 130
Rohri, Pak. E9 42
Rohtak, India D3 40
Roi Et, Thai. C4 34
Rokan, stm., Indon. C2 36
Roland, Ia., U.S. B4 108
Roland, Ok., U.S. B7 129
Roland, Lake, res., Md., U.S. g11 113
Rolette, N.D., U.S. A6 127
Rolette, co., N.D., U.S. A6 127
Rolfe, Ia., U.S. B3 108
Rolla, Mo., U.S. D6 118
Rolla, N.D., U.S. A6 127
Rollingbay, Wa., U.S. e10 140
Rolling Fork, stm., Ar., U.S. C1 97
Rolling Fork, stm., Ky., U.S. C4 110
Rolling Fork, Ms., U.S. C3 117
Rolling Meadows, Il., U.S. h8 106
Rollingstone, Mn., U.S. F7 116
Rollinsford, N.H., U.S. D5 122
Rolvsøya, i., Nor. A10 10
Roma, Austl. F4 62
Roma (Rome), Italy D4 18
Roma, Tx., U.S. F3 136
Romain, Cape, c., S.C., U.S. F9 133
Roman, Rom. F9 20
Romanche Gap I12 66
Romang, Pulau, i., Indon. E7 36
Romania, ctry., Eur. F8 20
Roman Nose Mountain, mtn., Or., U.S. D3 130
Romano, Cape, c., Fl., U.S. G5 102
Romano, Cayo, i., Cuba A4 80
Romans-sur-Isère, Fr. E9 16
Romanzof, Cape, c., Ak., U.S. C6 95
Romanzof Mountains, mts., Ak., U.S. B11 95
Rome see Roma, Italy D4 18
Rome, Ga., U.S. B1 103
Rome, Il., U.S. C4 106
Rome, N.Y., U.S. B5 125
Rome City, In., U.S. B7 107
Romeo, Mi., U.S. F7 115
Romeoville, Il., U.S. k8 106
Romney, W.V., U.S. B6 141
Romny, Ukr. D12 20
Romorantin-Lanthenay, Fr. D7 16
Romulus, Mi., U.S. p15 115
Ronan, Mt., U.S. C2 119
Roncador, Serra do, plat., Braz. D1 74
Ronceverte, W.V., U.S. D4 141
Ronda, Spain I4 16
Rondônia, state, Braz. F7 70
Rondonópolis, Braz. G9 70
Rong'an, China D2 30
Rongcheng, China B5 30
Ronge, Lac la, l., Sk., Can. B3 91
Rongelap, atoll, Marsh. Is. C10 58
Rongjiang, China D2 30
Rongxian, China E3 30
Rønne, Den. I6 10
Ronneby, Swe. H6 10
Ronne Ice Shelf, ice, Ant. D34 67
Roodhouse, Il., U.S. D3 106
Rooks, co., Ks., U.S. C4 109
Roosevelt, stm., Braz. E7 70
Roosevelt, co., Mt., U.S. B11 119
Roosevelt, co., N.M., U.S. C6 124
Roosevelt, Ut., U.S. C5 137
Roosevelt Island, i., Ant. D24 67
Roosevelt Park, Mi., U.S. E4 115
Root, stm., Mn., U.S. G7 116
Root, stm., Wi., U.S. n12 142
Roper, N.C., U.S. B6 126
Roper Valley, Austl. C5 60
Ropi, Fin. B9 10
Roraima, state, Braz. C7 70
Roraima, Mount, mtn., S.A. B7 70
Røros, Nor. E4 10
Rosamond, Ca., U.S. E4 98
Rosario, Arg. E5 72
Rosário, Braz. B3 74
Rosario, Mex. C3 78
Rosario, Para. C6 72
Rosario de la Frontera, Arg. D5 72
Rosário do Sul, Braz. E6 72
Rosário Oeste, Braz. F8 70
Roscoe, Il., U.S. A5 106
Roscoe, Tx., U.S. C2 136
Roscommon, Ire. D2 12
Roscommon, Mi., U.S. D6 115
Roscommon, co., Mi., U.S. D6 115
Rose, Mount, mtn., Nv., U.S. D2 121
Roseau, Dom. B7 80
Roseau, Mn., U.S. B3 116
Roseau, co., Mn., U.S. B3 116
Roseau, South Fork, stm., Mn., U.S. B3 116
Rose-Blanche [-Harbour le Cou], N.L., Can. E2 88
Roseboro, N.C., U.S. C4 126
Rosebud, co., Mt., U.S. D10 119
Rosebud, S.D., U.S. D5 134
Rosebud, Tx., U.S. D4 136
Rosebud Indian Reservation, S.D., U.S. D5 134
Roseburg, Or., U.S. D3 130
Rosedale, In., U.S. E3 107
Rosedale, Md., U.S. g11 113
Rosedale, Ms., U.S. B2 117
Rose Hill, Ks., U.S. E6 109
Rose Hill, N.C., U.S. C4 126
Rose Hill, Va., U.S. f8 139
Roseland, Fl., U.S. E6 102
Roseland, In., U.S. A5 107
Roseland, La., U.S. D5 111
Roseland, Oh., U.S. B3 128
Roselle, Il., U.S. k8 106
Roselle, N.J., U.S. k7 123
Roselle Park, N.J., U.S. k7 123
Rosemère, Qc., Can. p19 90
Rosemount, Mn., U.S. F5 116
Rosenberg, Tx., U.S. E5 136
Rosendale, Wi., U.S. E5 142
Rosenheim, Ger. G13 12
Rose Peak, mtn., Az., U.S. D6 96
Rosepine, La., U.S. D2 111
Rose Point, c., B.C., Can. B2 85
Roseto, Pa., U.S. E11 131
Rosetta see Rashid, Egypt E10 14
Roseville, Ca., U.S. C3 98
Roseville, Il., U.S. C3 106
Roseville, Mi., U.S. o16 115
Roseville, Mn., U.S. m12 116
Roseville, Oh., U.S. C3 128
Rosewood Heights, Il., U.S. E3 106
Rosiclare, Il., U.S. F5 106
Roşiori de Vede, Rom. G8 20
Roskilde, Den. I5 10
Roslavl', Russia C12 20
Roslyn, Wa., U.S. B4 140
Roslyn Heights, N.Y., U.S. h13 125
Ross, Oh., U.S. C1 128
Ross, co., Oh., U.S. C2 128
Rossano, Italy E6 18
Ross Barnett Reservoir, res., Ms., U.S. C3 117
Rossburn, Mb., Can. D1 86
Ross Dam, Wa., U.S. A4 140
Rossford, Oh., U.S. A2 128
Ross Ice Shelf, ice, Ant. E23 67
Rossignol, Lake, l., N.S., Can. E4 87
Ross Island, i., Ant. D22 67
Ross Island, i., Mb., Can. B3 86
Ross Lake National Recreation Area, Wa., U.S. A5 140
Rossland, B.C., Can. E9 85
Rosso, Maur. C1 50
Rossoš', Russia D15 20
Ross Sea, Ant. D24 67
Røssvatnet, l., Nor. D5 10
Rossville, Ga., U.S. B1 103
Rossville, Il., U.S. C6 106
Rossville, In., U.S. D4 107
Rossville, Ks., U.S. C8 109
Roštkala, Taj. C10 42
Rostock, Ger. D12 12
Rostov, Russia C6 22
Rostov-na-Donu, Russia E6 26
Roswell, Ga., U.S. B2 103
Roswell, N.M., U.S. D5 124
Rota, i., N. Mar. Is. D12 32
Rotan, Tx., U.S. C2 136
Rothesay, N.B., Can. D4 87
Rothschild, Wi., U.S. D4 142
Rothsville, Pa., U.S. F9 131
Roti, Pulau, i., Indon. F6 36
Rotorua, N.Z. o14 63c
Rotterdam, Neth. E9 12
Rotterdam, N.Y., U.S. C6 125
Roubaix, Fr. B8 16
Rouen, Fr. C7 16
Rouge, stm., Qc., Can. D3 90
Rough, stm., Ky., U.S. C3 110
Rough River Lake, res., Ky., U.S. C3 110
Rouiba, Alg. I8 16
Roulette, Pa., U.S. C5 131
Round Island, i., Ms., U.S. g8 117
Round Lake, Il., U.S. h8 106
Round Lake Beach, Il., U.S. h8 106
Round Mountain, Nv., U.S. E4 121
Round Rock, Tx., U.S. D4 136
Roundup, Mt., U.S. D8 119
Round Valley Indian Reservation, Ca., U.S. C2 98
Round Valley Reservoir, res., N.J., U.S. B3 123
Rouses Point, N.Y., U.S. f11 125
Routt, co., Co., U.S. A3 99
Rouyn [-Noranda], Qc., Can. k11 90
Rouzerville, Pa., U.S. G6 131
Rovaniemi, Fin. C11 10
Rovereto, Italy B3 18
Rovigo, Italy B3 18
Rovuma (Ruvuma), stm., Afr. F8 54
Rowan, co., Ky., U.S. B6 110
Rowan, co., N.C., U.S. B2 126
Rowland, N.C., U.S. C3 126
Rowlesburg, W.V., U.S. B5 141
Roxas, Phil. D8 34
Roxboro, N.C., U.S. A4 126
Roxburgh, N.Z. q12 63c
Roxton Falls, Qc., Can. D5 90
Roxton Pond, Qc., Can. D5 90
Roy, Ut., U.S. B3 137
Royal, stm., Me., U.S. g7 112
Royal Center, In., U.S. C4 107
Royale, Isle, i., Mi., U.S. h9 115
Royal Gorge, val., Co., U.S. C5 99
Royal Oak, Mi., U.S. F7 115
Royal Pines, N.C., U.S. f10 126
Royalton, Il., U.S. F4 106
Royalton, Mn., U.S. E4 116
Royan, Fr. E6 16
Royersford, Pa., U.S. F10 131
Royerton, In., U.S. D7 107
Royse City, Tx., U.S. C4 136
Royston, B.C., Can. E5 85
Royston, Ga., U.S. B3 103
Rtiščevo, Russia D7 22
Ruacana Falls, wtfl., Afr. B1 56
Ruapehu, Mount, vol., N.Z. o14 63c
Rubcovsk, Russia D10 26
Rubidoux, Ca., U.S. n14 98
Rubondo Island, i., Tan. D6 54
Ruby Dome, mtn., Nv., U.S. C6 121
Ruby Lake, l., Nv., U.S. C6 121
Ruby Mountains, mts., Nv., U.S. C6 121
Ruby Range, mts., Co., U.S. C3 99
Ruby Range, mts., Mt., U.S. E4 119
Rudnja, Russia B11 20
Rudnyj, Kaz. D8 26
Rudolf, Lake (Turkana, Lake), l., Afr. C7 54
Rudyard, Mi., U.S. B6 115
Rufiji, stm., Tan. E7 54
Rufino, Arg. E5 72
Rufisque, Sen. D1 50
Rufus Woods Lake, res., Wa., U.S. A6 140
Rugby, N.D., U.S. A6 127
Rügen, i., Ger. C13 12
Ruhengeri, Rw. D5 54
Rui'an, China F12 28
Ruidoso, N.M., U.S. D4 124
Ruidoso Downs, N.M., U.S. D4 124
Ruijin, China F11 28
Ruiz, Mex. C3 78
Ruki, stm., D.R.C. D3 54
Rukwa, Lake, l., Tan. E6 54
Ruleville, Ms., U.S. B3 117
Rum, stm., Mn., U.S. D5 116
Ruma, Serb. B7 18
Rumbek, Sudan I10 48
Rum Cay, i., Bah. D10 76
Rum Creek, stm., W.V., U.S. n12 141
Rumford, Me., U.S. D2 112
Rum Jungle, Austl. C5 60
Rumoi, Japan C16 28
Rumphi, Mwi. A5 56
Rumson, N.J., U.S. C4 123
Rumstick Point, c., R.I., U.S. D5 132
Runan, China E10 28
Rundu, Nmb. B2 56
Runge, Tx., U.S. E4 136
Rungwa, Tan. E6 54
Runnels, co., Tx., U.S. D3 136
Runnemede, N.J., U.S. D2 123
Ruoqiang, China D5 28
Rupat, Pulau, i., Indon. C2 36
Rupert, Id., U.S. G5 105
Rupert, W.V., U.S. D4 141
Rupert, Rivière de, stm., Qc., Can. h11 90
Rural Hall, N.C., U.S. A2 126
Rural Retreat, Va., U.S. D1 139
Rurrenabaque, Bol. A4 72
Rusagonis, N.B., Can. D3 87
Rusape, Zimb. B5 56
Ruse, Blg. C11 18
Rush, co., In., U.S. E6 107
Rush, co., Ks., U.S. D4 109
Rush, stm., Mn., U.S. F4 116
Rush, stm., Wi., U.S. D1 142
Rush City, Mn., U.S. E6 116
Rush Creek, stm., Oh., U.S. B2 128
Rush Creek, stm., Ok., U.S. C4 129
Rushford, Mn., U.S. G7 116
Rush Lake, l., Mn., U.S. E5 116
Rush Lake, l., Mn., U.S. D3 116
Rush Lake, l., Wi., U.S. E5 142
Rushmere, Va., U.S. h14 139
Rush Springs, Ok., U.S. C4 129
Rushville, Il., U.S. C3 106
Rushville, In., U.S. E7 107
Rushville, Ne., U.S. B3 120
Rusk, Tx., U.S. D5 136
Rusk, co., Tx., U.S. C5 136
Rusk, co., Wi., U.S. C2 142
Ruskin, Fl., U.S. E4 102
Russas, Braz. B4 74
Russell, Mb., Can. D1 86
Russell, On., Can. B9 89
Russell, co., Al., U.S. C4 94
Russell, Ks., U.S. D5 109
Russell, co., Ks., U.S. D5 109
Russell, Ky., U.S. B7 110
Russell, co., Ky., U.S. D4 110
Russell, Pa., U.S. C3 131
Russell, co., Va., U.S. f9 139
Russell, Mount, mtn., Ak., U.S. f16 95
Russell Cave National Monument, Al., U.S. A4 94
Russell Fork, stm., U.S. C7 110
Russell Springs, Ky., U.S. C4 110
Russellville, Al., U.S. A2 94
Russellville, Ar., U.S. B2 97
Russellville, Ky., U.S. D3 110
Russellville, Mo., U.S. C5 118
Russellville, Tn., U.S. C10 135
Russia, ctry., Eur. C11 26
Russian, stm., Ca., U.S. C2 98
Russiaville, In., U.S. D5 107
Russkaja Gavan', Russia B8 26
Rustavi, Geor. B11 44
Rustburg, Va., U.S. C3 139
Rustenburg, S. Afr. D4 56
Ruston, La., U.S. B3 111
Ruston, Wa., U.S. B3 140
Rutana, Bdi. D6 54
Ruteng, Indon. E6 36
Ruth, Nv., U.S. D6 121
Rutherford, co., N.C., U.S. B1 126
Rutherford, N.J., U.S. B4 123
Rutherford, Tn., U.S. A3 135
Rutherford, co., Tn., U.S. B5 135
Rutherfordton, N.C., U.S. B1 126
Ruthven, Ia., U.S. A3 108
Rutland, Ma., U.S. B4 114
Rutland, Vt., U.S. D3 138
Rutland, co., Vt., U.S. D2 138
Rutledge, Ga., U.S. C3 103
Rutledge, Tn., U.S. C10 135
Rutog, China C3 40
Rutshuru, D.R.C. D5 54
Ruvuma (Rovuma), stm., Afr. F8 54
Ruy Barbosa, Braz. D3 74
Ruzaevka, Russia D7 22
Rwanda, ctry., Afr. D5 54
Ryan, Ok., U.S. C4 129
Ryan Peak, mtn., Id., U.S. F4 105
Rybače, Kaz. E10 26
Rybačij, poluostrov, pen., Russia B15 10
Rybinsk, Russia D5 26
Rybinskoe vodohranilišče, res., Russia D5 26
Rybinsk Reservoir see Rybinskoe vodohranilišče, res., Russia D5 26
Rybnik, Pol. D5 20
Rycroft, Ab., Can. B1 84
Rye, N.H., U.S. D5 122
Rye, N.Y., U.S. h13 125
Rye Beach, N.H., U.S. E5 122
Rye Patch Dam, Nv., U.S. C3 121
Rye Patch Reservoir, res., Nv., U.S. C3 121
Ryl'sk, Russia D13 20
Ryukyu Islands see Nansei-shotō, is., Japan A9 34
Ryukyu Trench F15 64
Rzeszów, Pol. D7 20
Ržev, Russia D5 26

S

Saarbrücken, Ger. F10 12
Saaremaa, i., Est. G10 10
Saarijärvi, Fin. E11 10
Saarlouis, Ger. F10 12
Saatlı, Azer. C13 44
Saba, i., Neth. Ant. B7 80
Šabac, Serb. B7 18
Sabadell, Spain G8 16
Sabah, hist. reg., Malay. B5 36

Name	Map Ref.	Page
Sabana, Archipiélago de, is., Cuba	A3	80
Sabanalarga, Col.	C5	80
Sabattus, Me., U.S.	D2	112
Şāberī, Hāmūn-e, l., Asia	D8	42
Sabetha, Ks., U.S.	C8	109
Sabhā, Libya	E7	48
Sabi (Save), stm., Afr.	B5	56
Sabillasville, Md., U.S.	A3	113
Sabina, Oh., U.S.	C2	128
Sabinal, Tx., U.S.	E3	136
Sabinal, Cayo, i., Cuba	A4	80
Sabinas, Mex.	B4	78
Sabinas Hidalgo, Mex.	D10	78
Sabine, co., La., U.S.	C2	111
Sabine, co., Tx., U.S.	D6	136
Sabine, stm., U.S.	D6	136
Sabine, stm., U.S.	E9	92
Sabine Lake, l., U.S.	E2	111
Sabine Pass, strt., U.S.	E2	111
Sabirabad, Azer.	B13	44
Sable, Cape, c., Fl., U.S.	G5	102
Sable Island, i., N.S., Can.	F10	87
Sabrina Coast, Ant.	C16	67
Sabula, Ia., U.S.	B7	108
Şabyā, Sau. Ar.	G4	38
Sabzevār, Iran	C7	42
Sac, co., Ia., U.S.	B2	108
Sac, stm., Mo., U.S.	D4	118
Sacajawea, Lake, res., Wa., U.S.	C7	140
Sacajawea Peak, mtn., Or., U.S.	B9	130
Sacandaga Lake, l., N.Y., U.S.	B6	125
Sac and Fox Indian Reservation, Ia., U.S.	C5	108
Sacaton, Az., U.S.	D4	96
Sac City, Ia., U.S.	B2	108
Săcele, Rom.	G8	20
Sachse, Tx., U.S.	n10	136
Sachsen, hist. reg., Ger.	E13	12
Sachuest Point, c., R.I., U.S.	F6	132
Sackville, N.B., Can.	D5	87
Saco, Me., U.S.	E2	112
Saco, stm., U.S.	E2	112
Saco, East Branch, stm., N.H., U.S.	B4	122
Sacramento, Ca., U.S.	C3	98
Sacramento, stm., Ca., U.S.	C3	98
Sacramento, co., Ca., U.S.	C3	98
Sacramento, stm., N.M., U.S.	E4	124
Sacramento Mountains, mts., N.M., U.S.	E4	124
Sacramento Valley, val., Ca., U.S.	C2	98
Sacré-Coeur-Saguenay, Qc., Can.	A8	90
Sacred Heart, Mn., U.S.	F3	116
Şa'dah, Yemen	G4	38
Saddle, stm., N.J., U.S.	h8	123
Saddleback Mountain, mtn., Az., U.S.	k8	96
Saddle Brook, N.J., U.S.	h8	123
Saddlebunch Keys, is., Fl., U.S.	H5	102
Saddle Mountain, mtn., Or., U.S.	B3	130
Saddle Mountains, mts., Wa., U.S.	C5	140
Saddle River, N.J., U.S.	A4	123
Sa Dec, Viet.	D5	34
Sado, i., Japan	D15	28
Sado-kaikyō, strt., Japan	C3	31
Šadrinsk, Russia	D8	26
Saegertown, Pa., U.S.	C1	131
Safāga, Egypt	E11	48
Safety Harbor, Fl., U.S.	E4	102
Säffle, Swe.	G5	10
Safford, Az., U.S.	E6	96
Safi, Mor.	D3	48
Safonovo, Russia	A8	22
Safonovo, Russia	B12	20
Safranbolu, Tur.	B5	44
Saga, China	F5	28
Saga, Japan	D2	31
Sagadahoc, co., Me., U.S.	E3	112
Sagaing, Mya.	B3	34
Sagamore Hills, Oh., U.S.	h9	128
Saganaga Lake, l., Mn., U.S.	B7	116
Sāgar, India	E3	40
Sagarmāthā see Everest, Mount, mtn., Asia	D5	40
Sagay, Phil.	D8	34
Sag Harbor, N.Y., U.S.	m16	125
Saginaw, Mi., U.S.	E7	115
Saginaw, co., Mi., U.S.	E6	115
Saginaw, Tx., U.S.	n9	136
Saginaw Bay, b., Mi., U.S.	E7	115
Sagiz, Kaz.	E10	22
Saglek Bay, b., N.L., Can.	f9	88
Šagonar, Russia	A6	28
Saguache, co., Co., U.S.	C4	99
Sagua de Tánamo, Cuba	A4	80
Sagua la Grande, Cuba	A3	80
Saguaro Lake, res., Az., U.S.	k10	96
Saguaro National Monument (Tucson Mountain Section), Az., U.S.	E4	96
Saguaro National Monument, Az., U.S.	E5	96
Saguenay, stm., Qc., Can.	A7	90
Sagunt, Spain	H6	16
Sahagún, Col.	D4	80
Sahalin, ostrov, i., Russia	D16	26
Sahara, des., Afr.	F6	48
Sahāranpur, India	D3	40
Sahel see Sudan, reg., Afr.	H8	48
Sāhīwāl, Pak.	D10	42
Sāhīwāl, Pak.	D10	42
Şahneh, Iran	E12	44
Šahrisabz, Uzb.	F8	26
Šahty, Russia	E5	26
Sahuaripa, Mex.	B3	78
Sahuarita, Az., U.S.	F5	96
Šahunja, Russia	C8	22
Sa Huynh, Viet.	D5	34
Saibai Island, i., Austl.	B3	62
Saïda, Alg.	E4	14
Saidpur, Bngl.	D5	40
Saidu, Pak.	D10	42
Saigon see Thanh Pho Ho Chi Minh, Viet.	D5	34
Saiki, Japan	D2	31
Šaim, Russia	B11	22
Saimaa, l., Fin.	F13	10
Şā'īn Dezh, Iran	D12	44
Saint Adolphe, Mb., Can.	E3	86
Sainte-Agathe, Qc., Can.	C6	90
Sainte-Agathe-des-Monts, Qc., Can.	C3	90
Saint-Aimé (Massueville), Qc., Can.	D5	90
Saint-Alban, Qc., Can.	C5	90
Saint Alban's, N.L., Can.	E4	88
Saint Albans, Vt., U.S.	B2	138
Saint Albans, W.V., U.S.	C3	141
Saint Albans Bay, b., Vt., U.S.	B2	138
Saint Albert, Ab., Can.	C4	84
Saint-Amand-Montrond, Fr.	D8	16
Saint-Ambroise, Qc., Can.	A6	90
Saint-André-Avellin, Qc., Can.	D2	90
Saint-André-Est, Qc., Can.	D3	90
Saint Andrew Bay, b., Fl., U.S.	u16	102
Saint Andrews, N.B., Can.	D2	87
Saint Andrews, Scot., U.K.	B5	12
Saint Andrews, S.C., U.S.	F7	133
Saint Andrews, S.C., U.S.	C5	133
Saint Anne, Il., U.S.	B6	106
Sainte-Anne-de-Beaupré, Qc., Can.	B7	90
Sainte-Anne [-de-Bellevue], Qc., Can.	q19	90
Sainte Anne-de-Madawaska, N.B., Can.	B1	87
Sainte Anne-des-Chênes, Mb., Can.	E3	86
Saint-Anselme, Qc., Can.	C7	90
Saint Ansgar, Ia., U.S.	A5	108
Saint Anthony, N.L., Can.	C4	88
Saint Anthony, Id., U.S.	F7	105
Saint Antoine, N.B., Can.	C5	87
Saint-Apollinaire, Qc., Can.	C6	90
Saint Arnaud, Austl.	H3	62
Saint Arthur, N.B., Can.	B3	87
Saint-Aubert, Qc., Can.	B7	90
Saint Augustin, stm., Can.	C2	88
Saint Augustine, Fl., U.S.	C5	102
Saint Austell, Eng., U.K.	E4	12
Saint-Avold, Fr.	C10	16
Saint Basile, N.B., Can.	B1	87
Saint-Basile [-Sud], Qc., Can.	C6	90
Saint-Bernard, Qc., Can.	C6	90
Saint Bernard, Al., U.S.	A3	94
Saint Bernard, La., U.S.	E6	111
Saint Bernard, co., La., U.S.	E6	111
Saint Bernard, Oh., U.S.	o13	128
Saint Bernice, In., U.S.	E2	107
Saint Bride, Mount, mtn., Ab., Can.	D3	84
Saint Bride's, N.L., Can.	E4	88
Saint-Brieuc, Fr.	C5	16
Saint-Bruno, Qc., Can.	A6	90
Saint-Casimir, Qc., Can.	C5	90
Saint Catharines, On., Can.	D5	89
Saint Catherine, Lake, l., Vt., U.S.	E2	138
Saint Catherines Island, i., Ga., U.S.	E5	103
Saint-Célestin (Annaville), Qc., Can.	C5	90
Saint-Césaire, Qc., Can.	D4	90
Saint-Chamond, Fr.	E9	16
Saint-Charles, Qc., Can.	C7	90
Saint Charles, Il., U.S.	B5	106
Saint Charles, co., La., U.S.	E5	111
Saint Charles, Mi., U.S.	E6	115
Saint Charles, Mn., U.S.	G6	116
Saint Charles, Mo., U.S.	C7	118
Saint Charles, co., Mo., U.S.	C7	118
Saint Christopher (Saint Kitts), i., St. K./N.	B7	80
Saint Christopher and Nevis see Saint Kitts and Nevis, ctry., N.A.	E12	76
Saint-Chrysostome, Qc., Can.	D4	90
Saint Clair, co., Al., U.S.	B3	94
Saint Clair, co., Il., U.S.	E3	106
Saint Clair, Mi., U.S.	F8	115
Saint Clair, co., Mi., U.S.	F8	115
Saint Clair, Mn., U.S.	F5	116
Saint Clair, Mo., U.S.	C6	118
Saint Clair, co., Mo., U.S.	C4	118
Saint Clair, Pa., U.S.	E9	131
Saint Clair Shores, Mi., U.S.	p16	115
Saint Clairsville, Oh., U.S.	B5	128
Saint Claude, Mb., Can.	E2	86
Saint Cloud, Fl., U.S.	D5	102
Saint Cloud, Mn., U.S.	E4	116
Saint-Coeur-de-Marie, Qc., Can.	A6	90
Saint-Constant, Qc., Can.	q19	90
Sainte-Croix, Qc., Can.	C6	90
Saint Croix, co., Wi., U.S.	C1	142
Saint Croix, stm., U.S.	C1	142
Saint Croix, i., V.I.U.S.	B7	80
Saint Croix, Lake, l., U.S.	D1	142
Saint Croix Falls, Wi., U.S.	C1	142
Saint Croix Stream, stm., Me., U.S.	B4	112
Saint-Damase, Qc., Can.	D4	90
Saint David, Az., U.S.	F5	96
Saint-David-de-l'Auberivière, Qc., Can.	n17	90
Saint-Denis, Qc., Can.	D4	90
Saint-Denis, Reu.	g10	57a
Saint-Dié, Fr.	C10	16
Saint-Dizier, Fr.	C9	16
Saint-Dominique, Qc., Can.	D5	90
Saint Edward, Ne., U.S.	C8	120
Saint Eleanor's, P.E., Can.	C6	87
Saint Elias, Cape, c., Ak., U.S.	D11	95
Saint Elias, Mount, mtn., N.A.	F11	82
Saint-Élie, Fr. Gu.	C9	70
Saint Elmo, Al., U.S.	E1	94
Saint Elmo, Il., U.S.	D5	106
Saint-Éphrem [-de-Tring], Qc., Can.	C7	90
Saint-Étienne, Fr.	E9	16
Saint-Eustache, Qc., Can.	D4	90
Saint-Félicien, Qc., Can.	A5	90
Saint-Félix-de-Valois, Qc., Can.	C4	90
Saint-Ferdinand (Bernierville), Qc., Can.	C6	90
Saint-Ferréol [-les-Neiges], Qc., Can.	B7	90
Saint-Flavien, Qc., Can.	C6	90
Sainte-Foy, Qc., Can.	n17	90
Saint Francis, co., Ar., U.S.	B5	97
Saint Francis, Ks., U.S.	C2	109
Saint Francis, Mn., U.S.	E5	116
Saint Francis, S.D., U.S.	D5	134
Saint Francis, Wi., U.S.	n12	142
Saint Francis, stm., U.S.	A5	97
Saint Francis, Cape, c., N.L., Can.	E5	88
Saint Francis, Cape, c., S. Afr.	E3	56
Saint Francisville, Il., U.S.	E6	106
Saint Francisville, La., U.S.	D4	111
Saint-François, stm., Qc., Can.	D5	90
Saint Francois, co., Mo., U.S.	D7	118
Saint-François, Lac, l., Qc., Can.	D6	90
Saint Francois Mountains, Mo., U.S.	D7	118
Saint Froid Lake, l., Me., U.S.	B4	112
Saint-Fulgence, Qc., Can.	A7	90
Saint-Gabriel, Qc., Can.	C4	90
Saint-Gaudens, Fr.	F7	16
Saint-Gédéon, Qc., Can.	D7	90
Sainte Genevieve, Mo., U.S.	D7	118
Sainte Genevieve, co., Mo., U.S.	D7	118
Saint George, Austl.	F4	62
Saint George, N.B., Can.	D3	87
Saint George, On., Can.	D4	89
Saint George, S.C., U.S.	E6	133
Saint George, Ut., U.S.	F2	137
Saint George, Cape, c., N.L., Can.	D2	88
Saint George, Cape, c., Fl., U.S.	C1	102
Saint George Island, i., Ak., U.S.	D6	95
Saint George Island, i., Fl., U.S.	C2	102
Saint George's, N.L., Can.	D2	88
Saint-Georges, Qc., Can.	C5	90
Saint-Georges, Fr. Gu.	C9	70
Saint George's, Gren.	C7	80
Saint Georges, De., U.S.	B3	101
Saint George's Bay, b., N.L., Can.	D2	88
Saint Georges Bay, b., N.S., Can.	D8	87
Saint George's Channel, strt., Eur.	B3	16
Saint-Georges-Ouest (part of Ville-Saint-Georges), Qc., Can.	C7	90
Saint-Gervais, Qc., Can.	C7	90
Saint-Gilles, Qc., Can.	C6	90
Saint Gotthard Pass see San Gottardo, Passo del, Switz.	A2	18
Saint-Grégoire (Larochelle), Qc., Can.	C5	90
Saint-Guillaume-d'Upton, Qc., Can.	D5	90
Saint Helen, Lake, l., Mi., U.S.	D6	115
Saint Helena, dep., Afr.	K9	46
Saint Helena, Ca., U.S.	C2	98
Saint Helena, co., La., U.S.	D5	111
Saint Helena Island, i., S.C., U.S.	G6	133
Saint Helena Sound, strt., S.C., U.S.	G7	133
Saint Helens, Or., U.S.	B4	130
Saint Helens, Mount, vol., Wa., U.S.	C3	140
Saint Helier, Jersey	F5	12
Saint Henry, Oh., U.S.	B1	128
Saint-Honoré, Qc., Can.	D7	90
Saint-Hubert, Qc., Can.	q20	90
Saint-Hubert-de-Témiscouata, Qc., Can.	B8	90
Saint-Hyacinthe, Qc., Can.	D5	90
Saint Ignace, Mi., U.S.	C6	115
Saint Ignatius, Mt., U.S.	C2	119
Saint Isidore de Prescott, On., Can.	B10	89
Saint Jacobs, On., Can.	D4	89
Saint Jacques, N.B., Can.	B1	87
Saint-Jacques, Qc., Can.	D4	90
Saint James, co., La., U.S.	D5	111
Saint James, Mn., U.S.	G4	116
Saint James, Mo., U.S.	D6	118
Saint James, Cape, c., B.C., Can.	D2	85
Saint James City, Fl., U.S.	F4	102
Saint-Jean, stm., Qc., Can.	A7	90
Saint-Jean, Lac, l., Qc., Can.	A5	90
Saint Jean Baptiste, Mb., Can.	E3	86
Saint-Jean-Chrysostome, Qc., Can.	o17	90
Saint-Jean-d'Angély, Fr.	E6	16
Saint-Jean-sur-Richelieu, Qc., Can.	D4	90
Saint-Jérôme, Qc., Can.	D3	90
Saint Jo, Tx., U.S.	C4	136
Saint-Joachim, Qc., Can.	B7	90
Saint Joe, stm., Id., U.S.	B3	105
Saint John, N.B., Can.	D3	87
Saint John, stm., N.A.	B14	92
Saint John, In., U.S.	B3	107
Saint John, Ks., U.S.	E5	109
Saint John, i., V.I.U.S.	B7	80
Saint John, Cape, c., N.L., Can.	D4	88
Saint John Bay, b., N.L., Can.	C3	88
Saint John's, Antig.	B7	80
Saint John's, N.L., Can.	E5	88
Saint Johns, Az., U.S.	C6	96
Saint Johns, stm., Fl., U.S.	B5	102
Saint Johns, co., Fl., U.S.	C5	102
Saint Johns, Mi., U.S.	F6	115
Saint Johnsbury, Vt., U.S.	C4	138
Saint Johnsville, N.Y., U.S.	B6	125
Saint John the Baptist, co., La., U.S.	D5	111
Saint Jones, stm., De., U.S.	D4	101
Saint Joseph, N.B., Can.	D5	87
Saint Joseph, Il., U.S.	C5	106
Saint Joseph, co., In., U.S.	A5	107
Saint Joseph, La., U.S.	C4	111
Saint Joseph, Mi., U.S.	F4	115
Saint Joseph, co., Mi., U.S.	G5	115
Saint Joseph, Mn., U.S.	E4	116
Saint Joseph, Mo., U.S.	B3	118
Saint Joseph, Tn., U.S.	B4	135
Saint Joseph, stm., U.S.	F5	115
Saint-Joseph, Lac, l., Qc., Can.	n16	90
Saint Joseph, Lake, l., On., Can.	o17	89
Saint Joseph Bay, b., Fl., U.S.	C1	102
Saint-Joseph-de-Beauce, Qc., Can.	C7	90
Saint Joseph Point, c., Fl., U.S.	v16	102
Saint Joseph Sound, strt., Fl., U.S.	o10	102
Saint-Jovite, Qc., Can.	C3	90
Saint-Junien, Fr.	E7	16
Saint Kilda, i., Scot., U.K.	B2	12
Saint Kitts see Saint Christopher, i., St. K./N.	B7	80
Saint Kitts and Nevis, ctry., N.A.	E12	76
Saint-Lambert, Qc., Can.	p19	90
Saint Landry, co., La., U.S.	D3	111
Saint-Laurent, Qc., Can.	p19	90
Saint-Laurent du Maroni, Fr. Gu.	B9	70
Saint Lawrence, N.L., Can.	E4	88
Saint Lawrence, stm., N.A.	B14	92
Saint Lawrence, co., N.Y., U.S.	A5	125
Saint Lawrence, Cape, c., N.S., Can.	B9	87
Saint Lawrence, Gulf of, b., Can.	I27	82
Saint Lawrence Island, i., Ak., U.S.	C5	95
Saint Lawrence Islands National Park, On., Can.	C9	89
Saint Léonard, N.B., Can.	B2	87
Saint-Léonard [-d'Aston], Qc., Can.	C5	90
Saint-Liboire, Qc., Can.	D5	90
Saint-Lô, Fr.	C6	16
Saint-Louis, Sen.	C1	50
Saint Louis, Mi., U.S.	E6	115
Saint Louis, co., Mn., U.S.	C6	116
Saint Louis, co., Mo., U.S.	C7	118
Saint Louis, Mo., U.S.	C7	118
Saint Louis, stm., U.S.	D6	116
Saint-Louis, Lac, l., Qc., Can.	q19	90
Saint Louis Bay, b., Ms., U.S.	f7	117
Saint-Louis-de-Gonzague, Qc., Can.	D3	90
Saint Louis-de-Kent, N.B., Can.	C5	87
Saint-Louis-du-Ha! Ha!, Qc., Can.	B8	90
Saint Louis Park, Mn., U.S.	n12	116
Saint-Luc, Qc., Can.	D4	90
Saint Lucia, ctry., N.A.	F12	76
Saint Lucia, Lake, l., S. Afr.	D5	56
Saint Lucia Channel, strt., N.A.	C7	80
Saint Lucie, co., Fl., U.S.	E6	102
Saint Lucie Canal, Fl., U.S.	F6	102
Saint Lucie Inlet, b., Fl., U.S.	E6	102
Sainte-Madeleine, Qc., Can.	D4	90
Saint Magnus Bay, b., Scot., U.K.	h19	12a
Saint Malo, Mb., Can.	E3	86
Saint-Malo, Fr.	C6	16
Saint-Malo, Golfe de, b., Fr.	C5	16
Saint-Marc, Haiti	B5	80
Saint-Marc [-des-Carrières], Qc., Can.	C5	90
Saint Margaret Bay, b., N.L., Can.	C3	88
Sainte-Marguerite, stm., Qc., Can.	A7	90
Sainte-Marie, Qc., Can.	C6	90
Sainte Marie, Nosy, i., Madag.	B8	56
Saint Maries, Id., U.S.	B2	105
Sainte-Marthe, Qc., Can.	D3	90
Saint-Martin, i., N.A.	B7	80
Saint Martin, co., La., U.S.	D4	111
Saint Martin, Lake, l., Mb., Can.	D2	86
Saint Martin Island, i., Mi., U.S.	C4	115
Saint Martinville, La., U.S.	D4	111
Saint Mary, co., La., U.S.	E4	111
Saint Mary-of-the-Woods, In., U.S.	E3	107
Saint Mary Peak, mtn., Austl.	G2	62
Saint Marys, Austl.	I4	62
Saint Mary's, N.L., Can.	E5	88
Saint Marys, stm., N.S., Can.	D8	87
Saint Mary's, On., Can.	D3	89
Saint Marys, Ak., U.S.	C7	95
Saint Marys, Ga., U.S.	F5	103
Saint Marys, In., U.S.	A5	107
Saint Marys, Ks., U.S.	C7	109
Saint Marys, stm., Md., U.S.	D5	113
Saint Marys, co., Md., U.S.	D4	113
Saint Marys, Oh., U.S.	B1	128
Saint Marys, Pa., U.S.	D4	131
Saint Marys, W.V., U.S.	B3	141
Saint Marys, stm., U.S.	F5	103
Saint Marys, stm., U.S.	C8	107
Saint Mary's, Cape, c., N.L., Can.	E4	88
Saint Mary's Bay, b., N.L., Can.	E5	88
Saint Marys Bay, b., N.S., Can.	E3	87
Saint Marys City, Md., U.S.	D5	113
Saint Matthew Island, i., Ak., U.S.	C5	95
Saint Matthews, Ky., U.S.	B4	110
Saint Matthews, S.C., U.S.	D6	133
Saint-Maurice, stm., Qc., Can.	C5	90
Saint Michael, Mn., U.S.	E5	116
Saint Michaels, Md., U.S.	C5	113
Saint-Michel [-de-Bellechasse], Qc., Can.	C7	90
Saint-Nazaire, Fr.	D5	16
Saint-Nicolas, Qc., Can.	o17	90
Saint-Odilon, Qc., Can.	C7	90
Saint-Omer, Fr.	B8	16
Saint-Ours, Qc., Can.	D4	90
Saint-Pacôme, Qc., Can.	B8	90
Saint-Pamphile, Qc., Can.	C8	90
Saint Paris, Oh., U.S.	B2	128
Saint-Pascal, Qc., Can.	B8	90
Saint Paul, Ab., Can.	B5	84
Saint-Paul, Reu.	g10	57a
Saint Paul, Ak., U.S.	D5	95
Saint Paul, In., U.S.	F6	107
Saint Paul, Ks., U.S.	E8	109
Saint Paul, Mn., U.S.	F5	116
Saint Paul, Mo., U.S.	f12	118
Saint Paul, Ne., U.S.	C7	120
Saint Paul, Va., U.S.	f9	139
Saint Paul Island, i., Ak., U.S.	D5	95
Saint Paul Park, Mn., U.S.	n12	116
Saint Pauls, N.C., U.S.	C4	126
Sainte-Perpétue-de-L'Islet, Qc., Can.	B8	90
Saint Peter, Mn., U.S.	F5	116
Saint Peter Port, Guern.	F5	12
Saint Peters, N.S., Can.	D9	87

Name — Map Ref. — Page

Saint Peters, Mo., U.S. **C7** 118
Saint Petersburg see Sankt-Peterburg, Russia **D5** 26
Saint Petersburg, Fl., U.S. **E4** 102
Saint Petersburg Beach, Fl., U.S. **p10** 102
Saint Phillips Island, i., S.C., U.S. **G6** 133
Saint-Pie, Qc., Can. **D5** 90
Saint-Pierre, Reu. **g10** 57a
Saint Pierre, i., Sey. **i12** 57b
Saint-Pierre, St. P./M. **E3** 88
Saint-Pierre, Lac, l., Qc., Can. **C5** 90
Saint Pierre and Miquelon, dep., N.A. **I28** 82
Saint Pierre-Jolys, Mb., Can. **E3** 86
Saint-Prime, Qc., Can. **A5** 90
Saint Quentin, N.B., Can. **B2** 87
Saint-Quentin, Fr. **C8** 16
Saint-Raphaël, Qc., Can. **C7** 90
Saint-Raphaël, Fr. **F10** 16
Saint-Raymond, Qc., Can. **C6** 90
Saint-Rédempteur, Qc., Can. **o17** 90
Saint Regis, Mt., U.S. **C1** 119
Saint Regis, West Branch, stm., N.Y., U.S. **f10** 125
Saint-Rémi, Qc., Can. **D4** 90
Saint-Romuald, Qc., Can. **C6** 90
Saint Rose, La., U.S. **k11** 111
Sainte Rose du Lac, Mb., Can. **D2** 86
Saintes, Fr. **E6** 16
Saint Sauveur, N.B., Can. **B4** 87
Saint-Sauveur-des-Monts, Qc., Can. **D3** 90
Saint-Siméon, Qc., Can. **B8** 90
Saint Simons Island, i., Ga., U.S. **E5** 103
Saint Simons Island, Ga., U.S. **E5** 103
Saint Stephen, N.B., Can. **D2** 87
Saint Stephen, S.C., U.S. **E8** 133
Saint Tammany, co., La., U.S. **D5** 111
Sainte-Thècle, Qc., Can. **C5** 90
Sainte-Thérèse, Qc., Can. **D4** 90
Saint Thomas, On., Can. **E3** 89
Saint Thomas, i., V.I.U.S. **B6** 80
Saint Timothée, Qc., Can. **q18** 90
Saint-Tite, Qc., Can. **C5** 90
Saint-Tropez, Fr. **F10** 16
Sainte-Véronique, Qc., Can. **C3** 90
Saint-Victor, Qc., Can. **C7** 90
Saint Vincent, i., St. Vin. **C7** 80
Saint Vincent and the Grenadines, ctry., N.A. **F12** 76
Saint Vincent Island, i., Fl., U.S. **C1** 102
Saint Vincent Passage, strt., N.A. **C7** 80
Saint Vincent's [-Saint Stephens-Peter's River], N.L., Can. **E5** 88
Saint Walburg, Sk., Can. **D1** 91
Saint-Zacharie, Qc., Can. **C7** 90
Saipan, i., N. Mar. Is. **C12** 32
Sajama, Nevado, mtn., Bol. **B4** 72
Sakakawea, Lake, res., N.D., U.S. **B3** 127
Sakania, D.R.C. **F5** 54
Sakarya, Tur. **B4** 44
Sakarya, stm., Tur. **B4** 44
Sakata, Japan **D15** 28
Sakété, Benin **E5** 50
Sakha see Jakutija, state, Russia **C14** 26
Sakhalin see Sahalin, ostrov, i., Russia **D16** 26
Sakon Nakhon, Thai. **C4** 34
Sakonnet, stm., R.I., U.S. **E6** 132
Sakonnet Point, c., R.I., U.S. **F6** 132
Sakrivier, S. Afr. **E3** 56
Saky, Ukr. **G12** 20
Sal, i., C.V. **g10** 50a
Sal, Point, c., Ca., U.S. **E3** 98
Sala, Swe. **G7** 10
Salaberry-de-Valleyfield, Qc., Can. **D3** 90
Salacgrīva, Lat. **H11** 10
Sala Consilina, Italy **D5** 18
Salada, Laguna, l., Mex. **A1** 78
Saladillo, Arg. **F6** 72
Salado, stm., Arg. **F4** 72
Salado, stm., Arg. **D5** 72
Salado, stm., Arg. **F6** 72
Salado, stm., Mex. **B5** 78
Salado, Rio, stm., N.M., U.S. **C2** 124
Salaga, Ghana **E4** 50
Salal, Chad **D8** 50
Şalālah, Oman **G6** 38
Salamanca, Mex. **C4** 78
Salamanca, Spain **G4** 16
Salamanca, N.Y., U.S. **C2** 125
Salamís, i., Grc. **F9** 18
Salamis, hist., N. Cyp. **E5** 44
Salamīyah, Syria **E7** 44
Salamonie, stm., In., U.S. **C6** 107
Salamonie Lake, res., In., U.S. **C6** 107
Salavat, Russia **D7** 26
Salawati, i., Indon. **D8** 36
Sala y Gómez, Isla, i., Chile **K28** 64
Sala y Gomez Ridge **K28** 64
Saldanha, S. Afr. **E2** 56
Saldus, Lat. **H10** 10
Sale, Austl. **H4** 62
Salé, Mor. **E2** 14
Sale Creek, Tn., U.S. **D8** 135
Salehard, Russia **C8** 26
Salem, India **G3** 40
Salem, Ar., U.S. **A4** 97
Salem, Il., U.S. **E5** 106
Salem, In., U.S. **G5** 107
Salem, Ky., U.S. **e9** 110
Salem, Ma., U.S. **A6** 114
Salem, Mo., U.S. **D6** 118
Salem, N.H., U.S. **E4** 122
Salem, stm., N.J., U.S. **D2** 123
Salem, co., N.J., U.S. **D2** 123
Salem, N.J., U.S. **D2** 123
Salem, Oh., U.S. **B5** 128
Salem, Or., U.S. **C4** 130
Salem, S.D., U.S. **D8** 134
Salem, Ut., U.S. **C4** 137
Salem, Va., U.S. **C2** 139
Salem, Wi., U.S. **n11** 142
Salem, W.V., U.S. **B4** 141
Salem, Lake, l., Vt., U.S. **B4** 138
Salerno, Italy **D5** 18
Salerno, Golfo di, b., Italy **D5** 18
Salgótarján, Hung. **E5** 20
Salgueiro, Braz. **C4** 74
Salida, Co., U.S. **C5** 99
Salihli, Tur. **C3** 44
Salihorsk, Bela. **C9** 20
Salima, Mwi. **A5** 56
Salina, Ks., U.S. **D6** 109
Salina, Ok., U.S. **A6** 129
Salina, Ut., U.S. **E4** 137
Salina Cruz, Mex. **D5** 78
Salinas, Braz. **E3** 74
Salinas, Ec. **D3** 70
Salinas, stm., N.A. **B1** 80
Salinas, stm., Ca., U.S. **D3** 98
Salinas, Ca., U.S. **D3** 98
Salinas de Hidalgo, Mex. **C4** 78
Salinas Peak, mtn., N.M., U.S. **D3** 124
Salinas Pueblo Missions National Monument, N.M., U.S. **C3** 124
Saline, stm., Ar., U.S. **C1** 97
Saline, co., Ar., U.S. **C3** 97
Saline, stm., Ar., U.S. **D4** 97
Saline, co., Il., U.S. **F5** 106
Saline, stm., Ks., U.S. **C3** 109
Saline, co., Ks., U.S. **D6** 109
Saline, Mi., U.S. **F7** 115
Saline, co., Mo., U.S. **B4** 118
Saline, co., Ne., U.S. **D8** 120
Saline, North Fork, stm., Il., U.S. **F5** 106
Saline Lake, res., La., U.S. **C3** 111
Salineville, Oh., U.S. **B5** 128
Salinópolis, Braz. **B2** 74
Salisbury, Austl. **G2** 62
Salisbury, N.B., Can. **C4** 87
Salisbury, Ct., U.S. **B2** 100
Salisbury, Ma., U.S. **A6** 114
Salisbury, Md., U.S. **D6** 113
Salisbury, Mo., U.S. **B5** 118
Salisbury, N.C., U.S. **B2** 126
Salisbury see Harare, Zimb. **B5** 56
Salish Mountains, mts., Mt., U.S. **B2** 119
Salkehatchie, stm., S.C., U.S. **E5** 133
Salla, Fin. **C13** 10
Sallisaw, Ok., U.S. **B7** 129
Salluit, Qc., Can. **f11** 90
Salmās, Iran **C11** 44
Salmo, B.C., Can. **E9** 85
Salmon, stm., N.B., Can. **C4** 87
Salmon, Id., U.S. **D5** 105
Salmon, stm., Id., U.S. **D3** 105
Salmon Creek, Wa., U.S. **D3** 140
Salmon Creek Reservoir, res., Id., U.S. **G4** 105
Salmon Falls, stm., U.S. **D5** 122
Salmon Falls Creek, stm., U.S. **G4** 105
Salmon Mountains, mts., Ca., U.S. **B2** 98
Salmon Point, c., On., Can. **D7** 89
Salmon River Mountains, mts., Id., U.S. **E3** 105
Salmon River Reservoir, res., N.Y., U.S. **B5** 125
Salo, Fin. **F10** 10
Salò, Italy **B3** 18
Salome, Az., U.S. **D2** 96
Salon-de-Provence, Fr. **F9** 16
Salonika see Thessaloníki, Grc. **D9** 18
Salonika, Gulf of see Thermaïkós Kólpos, b., Grc. **D9** 18
Salonta, Rom. **F6** 20
Sal'sk, Russia **E7** 22
Salt, stm., Az., U.S. **D4** 96
Salt, stm., Ky., U.S. **C4** 110
Salt, stm., Mo., U.S. **B6** 118
Salta, Arg. **C4** 72
Salt Creek, stm., N.M., U.S. **D5** 124
Salt Creek, stm., Oh., U.S. **C3** 128
Salt Creek, stm., Wy., U.S. **C6** 143
Salter Path, N.C., U.S. **C6** 126
Salt Fork Lake, res., Oh., U.S. **B4** 128
Saltillo, Mex. **B4** 78
Saltillo, Ms., U.S. **A5** 117
Salt Lake, l., Hi., U.S. **g10** 104
Salt Lake, l., N.M., U.S. **E6** 124
Salt Lake, co., Ut., U.S. **C3** 137
Salt Lake City, Ut., U.S. **C4** 137
Salto, Ur. **E6** 72
Salton Sea, l., Ca., U.S. **F5** 98
Saltonstall, Lake, l., Ct., U.S. **D4** 100
Salt Point, c., Ca., U.S. **C2** 98
Salt River Indian Reservation, Az., U.S. **k9** 96
Salt River Range, mts., Wy., U.S. **D2** 143
Saltsburg, Pa., U.S. **F3** 131
Salt Springs, Fl., U.S. **C5** 102
Saltville, Va., U.S. **f10** 139
Salt Wells Creek, stm., Wy., U.S. **E4** 143
Saluda, S.C., U.S. **C4** 133
Saluda, stm., S.C., U.S. **C4** 133
Saluda, co., S.C., U.S. **C4** 133
Saluda Dam, S.C., U.S. **C5** 133
Salûm, Egypt **D10** 48
Sālūr, India **F4** 40
Salvador, Braz. **F12** 70
Salvador, El see El Salvador, ctry., N.A. **C2** 80
Salvador, Lake, l., La., U.S. **E5** 111
Salween, stm., Asia **G7** 28
Salyan, Azer. **C13** 44
Salyān, Nepal **D4** 40
Salyersville, Ky., U.S. **C6** 110
Salzburg, Aus. **G13** 12
Salzgitter, Ger. **D12** 12
Samah, Libya **F7** 14
Samālūṭ, Egypt **F10** 14
Samana Cay, i., Bah. **A5** 80
Samandağı, Tur. **D6** 44
Samar, i., Phil. **D9** 34
Samara (Kujbyšev), Russia **D7** 26
Samarai, Pap. N. Gui. **I13** 32
Samarinda, Indon. **D5** 36
Samarkand, Uzb. **F8** 26
Sāmarrā', Iraq **D4** 42
Samar Sea, Phil. **D8** 34
Şamaxı, Azer. **B13** 44
Samba Caju, Ang. **E3** 54
Sambalpur, India **E4** 40
Sambas, Indon. **C3** 36
Sambava, Madag. **A9** 56
Sambhal, India **D3** 40
Sāmbhar, India **D3** 40
Sambir, Ukr. **E7** 20
Samboja, Indon. **D5** 36
Samborombón, Bahía, b., Arg. **F6** 72
Samch'ŏk, S. Kor. **D13** 28
Same, Tan. **D7** 54
Samfya, Zam. **A4** 56
Şämkir, Azer. **B11** 44
Sammamish, Lake, l., Wa., U.S. **e11** 140
Samoa, ctry., Oc. **F12** 58
Samoa Islands, is., Oc. **F12** 58
Samoded, Russia **B7** 22
Sámos, i., Grc. **F11** 18
Samoset, Fl., U.S. **q10** 102
Samothrace see Samothráki, i., Grc. **D10** 18
Samothráki, i., Grc. **D10** 18
Sampit, Indon. **D4** 36
Sampit, stm., S.C., U.S. **E9** 133
Sampit, Teluk, b., Indon. **D4** 36
Sampson, co., N.C., U.S. **B4** 126
Sam Rayburn Reservoir, res., Tx., U.S. **D5** 136
Samsang, China **C4** 40
Samson, Al., U.S. **D3** 94
Sam Son, Viet. **C5** 34
Samsun, Tur. **B7** 44
Samtredia, Geor. **A10** 44
Samuels, Id., U.S. **A2** 105
Samui, Ko, i., Thai. **E4** 34
Samur, stm. **B13** 44
Samut Prakan, Thai. **D4** 34
Samut Songkhram, Thai. **D4** 34
San, Mali **D4** 50
Şan'ā', Yemen **G4** 38
Sanaba, Burkina **D4** 50
Sanaga, stm., Cam. **C2** 54
San Agustin, Cape, c., Phil. **E9** 34
San Agustin, Plains of, pl., N.M., U.S. **C2** 124
Sanak Islands, is., Ak., U.S. **E7** 95
San Ambrosio, Isla, i., Chile **H7** 2
Sanana, Pulau, i., Indon. **D7** 36
Sanandaj, Iran **C5** 42
San Andreas, Ca., U.S. **C3** 98
San Andrés, Col. **A3** 70
San Andres, Isla de, i., Col. **A3** 70
San Andres Mountains, mts., N.M., U.S. **E3** 124
San Andres Peak, mtn., N.M., U.S. **E3** 124
San Andrés Tuxtla, Mex. **D5** 78
San Angelo, Tx., U.S. **D2** 136
San Anselmo, Ca., U.S. **h7** 98
San Antonio, Chile **E3** 72
San Antonio, Tx., U.S. **E3** 136
San Antonio, Cabo, c., Arg. **F6** 72
San Antonio, Cabo de, c., Cuba **A2** 80
San Antonio Bay, b., Tx., U.S. **E4** 136
San Antonio de los Baños, Cuba **A3** 80
San Antonio Mountain, mtn., N.M., U.S. **A3** 124
San Antonio Oeste, Arg. **F4** 69
San Augustine, co., Tx., U.S. **D5** 136
San Augustine, Tx., U.S. **D5** 136
San Benedetto del Tronto, Italy **C4** 18
San Benedicto, Isla, i., Mex. **D2** 78
San Benito, Guat. **B2** 80
San Benito, co., Ca., U.S. **D3** 98
San Benito, Tx., U.S. **F4** 136
San Benito Mountain, mtn., Ca., U.S. **D3** 98
San Bernardino, Ca., U.S. **E5** 98
San Bernardino, co., Ca., U.S. **E5** 98
San Blas, Cape, c., Fl., U.S. **v16** 102
San Borja, Bol. **A4** 72
Sanborn, Ia., U.S. **A2** 108
Sanborn, co., S.D., U.S. **D7** 134
Sanbornville, N.H., U.S. **C4** 122
San Bruno, Ca., U.S. **D2** 98
San Carlos, Arg. **D4** 72
San Carlos, Chile **E2** 69
San Carlos, Phil. **C8** 34
San Carlos, Phil. **D8** 34
San Carlos, Az., U.S. **D5** 96
San Carlos, Ca., U.S. **k8** 98
San Carlos, Ven. **D6** 80
San Carlos de Bariloche, Arg. **F2** 69
San Carlos de Bolívar, Arg. **F5** 72
San Carlos del Zulia, Ven. **B5** 70
San Carlos de Río Negro, Ven. **C6** 70
San Carlos Indian Reservation, Az., U.S. **D5** 96
San Carlos Lake, res., Az., U.S. **D5** 96
Sánchez, Dom. Rep. **B6** 80
San Clemente, Ca., U.S. **F5** 98
San Clemente Island, i., Ca., U.S. **F4** 98
San Cristóbal, Arg. **E5** 72
San Cristóbal, Dom. Rep. **B5** 80
San Cristóbal, Ven. **B5** 70
San Cristóbal, Isla, i., Ec. **D2** 70
San Cristóbal de las Casas, Mex. **D6** 78
Sancti Spíritus, Cuba **A4** 80
Sancy, Puy de, mtn., Fr. **E8** 16
Sandakan, Malay. **B5** 36
Sandaré, Mali **D2** 50
Sand Creek, stm., Wy., U.S. **C7** 143
Sandefjord, Nor. **G4** 10
Sanders, Az., U.S. **B6** 96
Sanders, co., Mt., U.S. **C1** 119
Sanderson, Tx., U.S. **D1** 136
Sandersville, Ga., U.S. **D4** 103
Sandersville, Ms., U.S. **D4** 117
Sand Hill, Ma., U.S. **h13** 114
Sand Hill, stm., Mn., U.S. **C2** 116
Sandia Crest, mtn., N.M., U.S. **k8** 124
Sandia Indian Reservation, N.M., U.S. **k7** 124
Sandia Mountains, mts., N.M., U.S. **k8** 124
San Diego, Ca., U.S. **F5** 98
San Diego, stm., Ca., U.S. **o15** 98
San Diego, co., Ca., U.S. **F5** 98
San Diego, Tx., U.S. **F3** 136
San Diego, Cabo, c., Arg. **H3** 69
San Diego Naval Station, mil., Ca., U.S. **o15** 98
San Diego Naval Training Center, mil., Ca., U.S. **o15** 98
Sand Island, i., Hi., U.S. **g10** 104
Sand Island, i., Wi., U.S. **B3** 142
Sand Key, i., Fl., U.S. **E4** 102
Sandlick Creek, stm., W.V., U.S. **n13** 141
Sandnes, Nor. **G1** 10
Sandoa, D.R.C. **E4** 54
Sandoval, Il., U.S. **E4** 106
Sandoval, co., N.M., U.S. **B2** 124
Sandoway, Mya. **C2** 34
Sand Point, Ak., U.S. **D7** 95
Sandpoint, Id., U.S. **A2** 105
Sands Key, i., Fl., U.S. **s3** 102
Sand Springs, Ok., U.S. **A5** 129
Sandston, Va., U.S. **m18** 139
Sandstone, Austl. **F2** 60
Sandstone, Mn., U.S. **D6** 116
Sandusky, Mi., U.S. **E8** 115
Sandusky, stm., Oh., U.S. **B2** 128
Sandusky, co., Oh., U.S. **A2** 128
Sandusky, Oh., U.S. **A3** 128
Sandvika, Nor. **G4** 10
Sandviken, Swe. **F7** 10
Sandwich, Il., U.S. **B5** 106
Sandwich, Ma., U.S. **C7** 114
Sandwich Bay, b., N.L., Can. **B3** 88
Sandy, stm., Me., U.S. **D2** 112
Sandy, Or., U.S. **B4** 130
Sandy, Ut., U.S. **C4** 137
Sandy Cape, c., Austl. **E5** 62
Sandy Creek, stm., Oh., U.S. **B4** 128
Sandy Creek, stm., Ok., U.S. **C2** 129
Sandy Hook, Ct., U.S. **D2** 100
Sandy Hook, spit, N.J., U.S. **C5** 123
Sandy Island, i., S.C., U.S. **D9** 133
Sandykači, Turk. **F8** 26
Sandy Lake, l., N.L., Can. **D3** 88
Sandy Lake, l., On., Can. **n16** 89
Sandy Neck, pen., Ma., U.S. **C7** 114
Sandy Point, c., R.I., U.S. **h7** 132
Sandy Springs, Ga., U.S. **h8** 103
Sandy Springs, S.C., U.S. **B2** 133
Sandyville, Md., U.S. **A4** 113
San Felipe, Chile **E3** 72
San Felipe, Col. **C6** 70
San Felipe, Mex. **A2** 78
San Felipe, Ven. **A6** 70
San Felipe Indian Reservation, N.M., U.S. **k8** 124
San Felipe Pueblo, N.M., U.S. **B3** 124
San Fernando, Chile **D2** 69
San Fernando, Mex. **C5** 78
San Fernando, Phil. **C8** 34
San Fernando, Phil. **C8** 34
San Fernando, Spain **I3** 16
San Fernando, Trin. **C7** 80
San Fernando, Ca., U.S. **m12** 98
San Fernando de Apure, Ven. **B6** 70
San Fernando de Atabapo, Ven. **C6** 70
San Fernando del Valle de Catamarca, Arg. **D4** 72
Sanford, Co., U.S. **D5** 99
Sanford, Fl., U.S. **D5** 102
Sanford, Me., U.S. **E2** 112
Sanford, Mi., U.S. **E6** 115
Sanford, N.C., U.S. **B3** 126
Sanford, Mount, mtn., Ak., U.S. **C11** 95
San Francisco, Arg. **E5** 72
San Francisco, Ca., U.S. **D2** 98
San Francisco, co., Ca., U.S. **D2** 98
San Francisco, stm., U.S. **D6** 96
San Francisco Bay, b., Ca., U.S. **h8** 98
San Francisco del Oro, Mex. **B3** 78
San Francisco del Rincón, Mex. **C4** 78
San Francisco de Macorís, Dom. Rep. **B5** 80
San Gabriel Mountains, mts., Ca., U.S. **m12** 98
Sangamner, India **F2** 40
Sangamon, co., Il., U.S. **D4** 106
Sangamon, stm., Il., U.S. **C3** 106
Sangar, Russia **C14** 26
Sange, D.R.C. **E5** 54
Sanger, Ca., U.S. **D4** 98
Sanger, Tx., U.S. **C4** 136
Sanggau, Indon. **C4** 36
Sangha, stm., Afr. **D3** 54
Sangihe, Kepulauan, is., Indon. **C7** 36
Sangihe, Pulau, i., Indon. **C7** 36
San Gil, Col. **D5** 80
San Giovanni in Fiore, Italy **E6** 18
Sangiyn Dalay, Mong. **C9** 28
Sāngli, India **F2** 40
Sangmélima, Cam. **C2** 54
San Gorgonio Mountain, mtn., Ca., U.S. **E5** 98
San Gottardo, Passo del, Switz. **A2** 18
Sanibel, Fl., U.S. **F4** 102
Sanibel Island, i., Fl., U.S. **F4** 102
San Ignacio, Mex. **B2** 78
San Ignacio, Para. **D6** 72
San Ignacio de Moxo, Bol. **A4** 72
San Ignacio de Velasco, Bol. **G7** 70
Sanilac, co., Mi., U.S. **E8** 115
San Isidro, Arg. **E6** 72
San Jacinto, Col. **D4** 80
San Jacinto, Ca., U.S. **F5** 98
San Jacinto, stm., Tx., U.S. **r14** 136
San Jacinto, co., Tx., U.S. **D5** 136
San Javier, Bol. **B5** 72
San Joaquín, Bol. **F7** 70
San Joaquin, co., Ca., U.S. **D3** 98
San Joaquin, stm., Ca., U.S. **D3** 98
San Joaquin Valley, val., Ca., U.S. **D3** 98
San Jorge, Arg. **E5** 72
San Jorge, Golfo, b., Arg. **G3** 69
San José, C.R. **D3** 80
San Jose, Ca., U.S. **D3** 98
San José, Isla, i., Mex. **C2** 78
San José de Chiquitos, Bol. **B5** 72
San José de Guanipa, Ven. **D7** 80
San José de Jáchal, Arg. **E4** 72
San José de las Lajas, Cuba **A3** 80
San José del Cabo, Mex. **C3** 78
San José del Guaviare, Col. **C5** 70
San Jose Island, i., Tx., U.S. **E4** 136
San Juan, Arg. **E4** 72
San Juan, stm., N.A. **F8** 76
San Juan, P.R. **B6** 80
San Juan, co., Co., U.S. **D3** 99
San Juan, co., N.M., U.S. **A1** 124

Name — Map Ref. — Page

San Juan, Tx., U.S. F3 136
San Juan, co., Ut., U.S. F5 137
San Juan, co., Wa., U.S. A2 140
San Juan Bautista, Para. D6 72
San Juan Capistrano, Ca., U.S. F5 98
San Juan de Colón, Ven. D5 80
San Juan de la Maguana, Dom. Rep. B5 80
San Juan del Norte, Nic. C3 80
San Juan de los Morros, Ven. D6 80
San Juan del Sur, Nic. C2 80
San Juan Island, i., Wa., U.S. A2 140
San Juan Mountains, mts., Co., U.S. D3 99
San Justo, Arg. E5 72
Sankt Gallen, Switz. A2 18
Sankt-Peterburg (Saint Petersburg), Russia D5 26
Sankt Pölten, Aus. F14 12
Sankuru, stm., D.R.C. D4 54
San Lázaro, Cabo, c., Mex. C2 78
San Leandro, Ca., U.S. h8 98
Şanlıurfa, Tur. D8 44
San Lorenzo, Arg. E5 72
San Lorenzo, Bol. C5 72
San Lorenzo, Ec. C4 70
San Lorenzo, Cabo, c., Ec. D3 70
Sanlúcar de Barrameda, Spain I3 16
San Lucas, Bol. C4 72
San Lucas, Mex. C3 78
San Lucas, Cabo, c., Mex. C3 78
San Luis, Arg. E4 72
San Luis, Guat. B2 80
San Luis, Az., U.S. E1 96
San Luis, Co., U.S. D5 99
San Luis, Point, c., Ca., U.S. E3 98
San Luis Obispo, Ca., U.S. E3 98
San Luis Obispo, co., Ca., U.S. E3 98
San Luis Pass, strt., Tx., U.S. r14 136
San Luis Peak, mtn., Co., U.S. D4 99
San Luis Potosí, Mex. C4 78
San Luis Potosí, state, Mex. C4 78
San Luis Río Colorado, Mex. A2 78
San Luis Valley, val., Co., U.S. D4 99
San Manuel, Az., U.S. E5 96
San Marcos, Tx., U.S. E4 136
San Marcos, stm., Tx., U.S. h8 136
San Marino, ctry., Eur. C4 18
San Marino, Ca., U.S. m12 98
San Martín, Arg. E4 72
San Martín, Col. E5 80
San Martín, Lago, l., S.A. G2 69
San Martín de los Andes, Arg. F2 69
San Mateo, Ca., U.S. D2 98
San Mateo, co., Ca., U.S. D2 98
San Mateo Mountains, mts., N.M., U.S. D2 124
San Mateo Mountains, mts., N.M., U.S. B2 124
San Matías, Golfo, b., Arg. F4 69
Sanmenxia, China E10 28
San Miguel, El Sal. C2 80
San Miguel, stm., Co., U.S. C2 99
San Miguel, co., Co., U.S. D2 99
San Miguel, co., N.M., U.S. B5 124
San Miguel, Golfo de, b., Pan. D4 80
San Miguel de Tucumán, Arg. D4 72
San Miguel Island, i., Ca., U.S. E3 98
San Miguel Mountains, mts., Co., U.S. D2 99
Sanming, China D4 30
Sannār, Sudan H11 48
San Nicolás, Peru B2 72
San Nicolás de los Arroyos, Arg. E5 72
San Nicolás de los Garza, Mex. B4 78
San Nicolas Island, i., Ca., U.S. F4 98
Sânnicolau Mare, Rom. F6 20
Sannikova, proliv, strt., Russia B15 26
Sanok, Pol. E7 20
San Pablo, Phil. D8 34
San Pablo Bay, b., Ca., U.S. g8 98
San Patricio, co., Tx., U.S. E4 136
San Pedro, Arg. C5 72
San Pedro, Arg. E6 72
San-Pédro, C. Iv. F3 50
San Pedro, stm., N.A. A5 78
San Pedro, stm., Az., U.S. E5 96
San Pedro Bay, b., Ca., U.S. n12 98
San Pedro de las Colonias, Mex. B4 78
San Pedro de Macorís, Dom. Rep. B6 80
San Pedro de Ycuamandiyú, Para. C6 72
San Pedro Peaks, mts., N.M., U.S. A3 124
San Pedro Sula, Hond. B2 80
Sanpete, co., Ut., U.S. D4 137
San Pietro, Isola di, i., Italy E2 18
Sanpoil, stm., Wa., U.S. A7 140
San Quintín, Cabo, c., Mex. A1 78
San Rafael, Arg. E4 72
San Rafael, Ca., U.S. D2 98
San Rafael, N.M., U.S. B2 124
San Rafael, stm., Ut., U.S. D5 137
San Rafael, Ven. C5 80
San Rafael Knob, mtn., Ut., U.S. E5 137
San Rafael Mountains, mts., Ca., U.S. E4 98
San Ramon, Ca., U.S. h9 98
San Ramón de la Nueva Orán, Arg. C5 72
San Remo, Italy C1 18
San Roque, Punta, c., Mex. B2 78
San Saba, Tx., U.S. D3 136
San Saba, co., Tx., U.S. D3 136
San Salvador, i., Bah. D10 76
San Salvador, El Sal. C2 80
San Salvador de Jujuy, Arg. C4 72
Sansanné-Mango, Togo D5 50
San Sebastián see Donostia, Spain F6 16
San Severo, Italy D5 18
San Simon, stm., Az., U.S. E6 96
Santa Ana, Bol. A4 72
Santa Ana, El Sal. C1 80
Santa Ana, Mex. A2 78
Santa Ana, Ca., U.S. F5 98
Santa Ana, stm., Ca., U.S. n13 98
Santa Ana Indian Reservation, N.M., U.S. h7 124
Santa Ana Mountains, mts., Ca., U.S. n13 98
Santa Anna, Tx., U.S. D3 136
Santa Bárbara, Hond. B2 80
Santa Bárbara, Mex. B3 78
Santa Barbara, Ca., U.S. E4 98
Santa Barbara, co., Ca., U.S. E3 98
Santa Bárbara, Ven. D5 80
Santa Barbara Channel, strt., Ca., U.S. E3 98
Santa Barbara Island, i., Ca., U.S. F4 98
Santa Catalina, Gulf of, b., Ca., U.S. F5 98
Santa Catalina Island, i., Ca., U.S. F4 98
Santa Catalina Mountains, mts., Az., U.S. E5 96
Santa Catarina, state, Braz. D7 72
Santa Catarina, Ilha de, i., Braz. D8 72
Santa Clara, Cuba A3 80
Santa Clara, Ca., U.S. D2 98
Santa Clara, co., Ca., U.S. D3 98
Santa Clara, stm., Ca., U.S. E4 98
Santa Clara, Ut., U.S. F2 137
Santa Claus, In., U.S. H4 107
Santa Cruz, Phil. D8 34
Santa Cruz, co., Az., U.S. F5 96
Santa Cruz, stm., Az., U.S. E4 96
Santa Cruz, Ca., U.S. D2 98
Santa Cruz, co., Ca., U.S. D2 98
Santa Cruz, N.M., U.S. B3 124
Santa Cruz, Isla, i., Ec. D1 70
Santa Cruz de la Palma, Spain A1 50
Santa Cruz de la Sierra, Bol. B5 72
Santa Cruz del Quiché, Guat. B1 80
Santa Cruz del Sur, Cuba A4 80
Santa Cruz de Tenerife, Spain A1 50
Santa Cruz do Sul, Braz. D7 72
Santa Cruz Island, i., Ca., U.S. F4 98
Santa Cruz Islands, is., Sol. Is. F10 58
Santa Elena, Arg. E6 72
Santa Fe, Arg. E5 72
Santa Fe, N.M., U.S. B4 124
Santa Fe, stm., N.M., U.S. h8 124
Santa Fe, co., N.M., U.S. B3 124
Santa Fe, Tx., U.S. r14 136
Santa Fe Baldy, mtn., N.M., U.S. B4 124
Santa Fé do Sul, Braz. F1 74
Santa Filomena, Braz. E10 74
Santa Helena, Braz. B2 74
Santa Helena de Goiás, Braz. E1 74
Santai, China E9 28
Santa Inés, Isla, i., Chile H2 69
Santa Isabel, Arg. F4 72
Santa Isabel see Malabo, Eq. Gui. C1 54
Santa Isabel, i., Sol. Is. B6 62
Santa Lucia Range, mts., Ca., U.S. E3 98
Santa Magdalena, Isla, i., Mex. B2 78
Santa Margarita, Ca., U.S. E3 98
Santa Margarita, Isla, i., Mex. C2 78
Santa Maria, Braz. D7 72
Santa Maria, stm., Az., U.S. C2 96
Santa Maria, Ca., U.S. E3 98
Santa Maria, i., Vanuatu j9 62a
Santa Maria, Cabo de, c., Ang. A1 56
Santa María, Isla, i., Ec. D1 70
Santa Maria Mountains, mts., Az., U.S. C3 96
Santa Marta, Col. A5 70
Santa Monica, Ca., U.S. m12 98
Santana, Braz. D3 74
Santana do Livramento, Braz. E6 72
Santander, Phil. E8 34
Santander, Spain F5 16
Santanilla, Islas, is., Hond. B3 80
Sant'Antioco, Italy E2 18
Sant'Antioco, Isola di, i., Italy E2 18
Sant Antoni de Portmany, Spain H7 16
Santa Paula, Ca., U.S. E4 98
Santaquin, Ut., U.S. D4 137
Santarém, Braz. D9 70
Santarém, Port. H2 16
Santa Rita, Hond. B2 80
Santa Rita, Ven. C5 80
Santa Rosa, Arg. F5 72
Santa Rosa, Braz. D7 72
Santa Rosa, Ec. D4 70
Santa Rosa, Ca., U.S. C2 98
Santa Rosa, co., Fl., U.S. u14 102
Santa Rosa, N.M., U.S. C5 124
Santa Rosa, Ven. D6 80
Santa Rosa de Copán, Hond. C2 80
Santa Rosa Island, i., Ca., U.S. F3 98
Santa Rosa Island, i., Fl., U.S. u14 102
Santa Rosalía, Mex. B2 78
Santa Rosa Range, mts., Nv., U.S. B4 121
Šantarskie ostrova, is., Russia D15 26
Santa Sylvina, Arg. D5 72
Santa Vitória do Palmar, Braz. E7 72
Santa Ynez, Ca., U.S. E3 98
Santee, Ca., U.S. o16 98
Santee, stm., S.C., U.S. E8 133
Santee Dam, S.C., U.S. E7 133
Santee Indian Reservation, Ne., U.S. B8 120
Sant Feliu de Guíxols, Spain G8 16
Santiago, Braz. D7 72
Santiago, Chile D2 69
Santiago, i., C.V. h10 50a
Santiago, Mex. C3 78
Santiago, Pan. D3 80
Santiago, Isla, i., Ec. D1 70
Santiago de Compostela, Spain F2 16
Santiago de Cuba, Cuba B4 80
Santiago del Estero, Arg. D5 72
Santiago de los Caballeros, Dom. Rep. B5 80
Santiago Ixcuintla, Mex. C3 78
Santiago Jamiltepec, Mex. D5 78
Santiago Papasquiaro, Mex. B3 78
Santiago Peak, mtn., Ca., U.S. n13 98
Santiago Reservoir, res., Ca., U.S. n13 98
Santiam Pass, Or., U.S. C4 130
Sant Jordi, Golf de, b., Spain G7 16
Santo Amaro, Braz. D4 74
Santo André, Braz. F2 74
Santo Ângelo, Braz. D7 72
Santo Antão, i., C.V. 50a
Santo Antão, i., C.V. g9 50a
Santo António, S. Tom./P. C1 54
Santo Antônio de Jesus, Braz. D4 74
Santo Antônio do Içá, Braz. D6 70
Santo Domingo, Dom. Rep. B6 80
Santo Domingo see Hispaniola, i., N.A. A5 80
Santo Domingo Indian Reservation, N.M., U.S. h8 124
Santo Domingo Pueblo, N.M., U.S. B3 124
Santorini see Thíra, i., Grc. F10 18
Santos, Braz. F2 74
Santos Dumont, Braz. F3 74
Santo Tomé de Guayana see Ciudad Guayana, Ven. B7 70
San Valentín, Monte, mtn., Chile G2 69
San Vicente, El Sal. C2 80
San Vicente de Cañete, Peru F4 70
San Vicente del Caguán, Col. C5 70
San Vicente Reservoir, res., Ca., U.S. o16 98
San Xavier Indian Reservation, Az., U.S. E4 96
Sanya, China H9 28
Sanyuan, China E9 28
Sanza Pombo, Ang. E3 54
São Bento, Braz. B3 74
São Borja, Braz. D6 72
São Carlos, Braz. F2 74
São Domingos, Braz. A8 72
São Domingos, Gui.-B. D1 50
São Francisco, stm., Braz. C4 74
São Francisco, Braz. E3 74
São Francisco do Sul, Braz. D8 72
São Gabriel, Braz. E7 72
Sao Hill, Tan. E7 54
São João da Barra, Braz. F3 74
São João da Boa Vista, Braz. F2 74
São João da Madeira, Port. G2 16
São João Del Rei, Braz. F3 74
São João do Araguaia, Braz. E10 70
São Jorge, i., Port. F7 46
São José, Braz. D8 72
São José do Rio Preto, Braz. F2 74
São José dos Campos, Braz. F2 74
São Leopoldo, Braz. D7 72
São Lourenço, Pantanal de, sw., Braz. G8 70
São Lourenço do Sul, Braz. E7 72
São Luís, Braz. B3 74
São Luís Gonzaga, Braz. D7 72
São Manuel, stm., Braz. E8 70
São Mateus, Braz. E4 74
São Miguel, i., Port. F7 46
São Miguel do Araguaia, Braz. D1 74
Saona, Isla, i., Dom. Rep. B6 80
Saône, stm., Fr. D9 16
São Nicolau, i., C.V. g10 50a
São Paulo, Braz. C7 72
São Paulo, state, Braz. F2 74
São Paulo de Olivença, Braz. D6 70
São Raimundo Nonato, Braz. C3 74
São Roque, Cabo de, c., Braz. C4 74
São Sebastião, Braz. F2 74
São Sebastião, Ilha de, i., Braz. F2 74
São Sebastião do Paraíso, Braz. F2 74
São Simão, Represa de, res., Braz. B7 72
São Tomé, i., S. Tom./P. C1 54
São Tomé, S. Tom./P. C1 54
São Tomé, Cabo de, c., Braz. F3 74
Sao Tome and Principe, ctry., Afr. C1 54
São Vicente, Braz. F2 74
São Vicente, i., C.V. g9 50a
São Vicente, Cabo de, c., Port. I2 16
Sapé, Braz. C4 74
Sapele, Nig. E6 50
Sapelo Island, i., Ga., U.S. E5 103
Sapitwa, mtn., Mwi. B6 56
Sappa Creek, stm., U.S. E5 120
Sapphire Mountains, mts., Mt., U.S. D3 119
Sappington, Mo., U.S. f13 118
Sapporo, Japan C16 28
Sapulpa, Ok., U.S. B5 129
Sapwe, D.R.C. F5 54
Saqqez, Iran C5 42
Sarāb, Iran C5 42
Saraburi, Thai. D4 34
Saragossa see Zaragoza, Spain G6 16
Sarajevo, Bos. C7 18
Sarakhs, Iran C8 42
Saraktaš, Russia D10 22
Saraland, Al., U.S. E1 94
Saranac, Mi., U.S. F5 115
Saranac, stm., N.Y., U.S. F11 125
Saranac Lake, N.Y., U.S. f10 125
Saranac Lakes, l., N.Y., U.S. f10 125
Sarandë, Alb. E8 18
Sārangarh, India E4 40
Saranpaul', Russia B11 22
Saransk, Russia D6 26
Sarapul, Russia D7 26
Sarasota, Fl., U.S. E4 102
Sarasota, co., Fl., U.S. E4 102
Sarasota Bay, b., Fl., U.S. E4 102
Saratoga, Ca., U.S. k8 98
Saratoga, co., N.Y., U.S. B7 125
Saratoga, Tx., U.S. D5 136
Saratoga, Wy., U.S. E6 143
Saratoga Lake, l., N.Y., U.S. C7 125
Saratoga National Historical Park, N.Y., U.S. B7 125
Saratoga Springs, N.Y., U.S. B7 125
Saratov, Russia D6 26
Saratov Reservoir see Saratovskoe vodohranilišče, res., Russia D8 22
Saratovskoe vodohranilišče, res., Russia D8 22
Saravan, Laos C5 34
Sarawak, hist. reg., Malay. C4 36
Saray, Tur. B2 44
Saraya, Gui. D2 50
Sarayköy, Tur. D3 44
Sarcoxie, Mo., U.S. D3 118
Sardārshahr, India D2 40
Sar Dasht, Iran D11 44
Sardegna (Sardinia), i., Italy D2 18
Sardinia see Sardegna, i., Italy D2 18
Sardis, Ga., U.S. D5 103
Sardis, Ms., U.S. A4 117
Sardis Lake, res., Ms., U.S. A4 117
Sarek, mtn., Swe. C7 10
Sar-e Pol, Afg. C9 42
Sarepta, La., U.S. B2 111
Sargent, Ga., U.S. C2 103
Sargent, co., N.D., U.S. C8 127
Sargent, Ne., U.S. C6 120
Sargodha, Pak. D10 42
Sarh, Chad B3 54
Sārī, Iran C6 42
Sarigan, i., N. Mar. Is. C12 32
Sarıkamış, Tur. B10 44
Sarıkaya, Tur. C6 44
Sarikei, Malay. C4 36
Sarīr, Libya F8 14
Sariwŏn, N. Kor. D13 28
Sarıyar Barajı, res., Tur. C4 44
Šarja, Russia D6 26
Şarkikaraağaç, Tur. C4 44
Şarkışla, Tur. C7 44
Şarköy, Tur. B2 44
Sarmi, Indon. G10 32
Särna, Swe. F5 10
Sarnia, On., Can. E2 89
Sarny, Ukr. D9 20
Saronic Gulf see Saronikós Kólpos, b., Grc. F9 18
Saronikós Kólpos, b., Grc. F9 18
Saros Körfezi, b., Tur. B2 44
Sarpy, co., Ne., U.S. C9 120
Sarreguemines, Fr. C10 16
Sartell, Mn., U.S. E4 116
Sartène, Fr. D2 18
Šarur, Azer. C11 44
Sarus see Seyhan, stm., Tur. D6 44
Saryg-Sep, Russia D11 26
Sarykamyšskoe ozero, l., Asia B7 42
Saryozek, Kaz. E9 26
Sarysu, stm., Kaz. E8 26
Sary-Taš, Kyrg. B2 40
Sasabeneh, Eth. B8 54
Sāsarām, India E4 40
Sasebo, Japan D1 31
Saskatchewan, prov., Can. E3 91
Saskatchewan, stm., Can. H19 82
Saskylah, Russia B13 26
Sasovo, Russia B16 20
Sassafras, stm., Md., U.S. B5 113
Sassafras Mountain, mtn., U.S. A2 133
Sassandra, C. Iv. E3 50
Sassandra, stm., C. Iv. E3 50
Sassari, Italy D2 18
Sassnitz, Ger. C13 12
Satah Mountain, mtn., B.C., Can. C5 85
Sata-misaki, c., Japan D2 31
Satanta, Ks., U.S. E3 109
Sātāra, India F2 40
Säter, Swe. F6 10
Satilla, stm., Ga., U.S. E5 103
Satka, Russia D10 22
Satluj see Sutlej, stm., Asia D2 40
Satna, India E4 40
Sátoraljaújhely, Hung. E6 20
Sātpura Range, mts., India E3 40
Satsuma, Al., U.S. E1 94
Satu Mare, Rom. F7 20
Satun, Thai. E3 34
Satus Creek, stm., Wa., U.S. C5 140
Sauceda Mountains, mts., Az., U.S. E3 96
Saudárkrókur, Ice. l19 10a
Saudi Arabia, ctry., Asia F4 38
Saufley Field Naval Air Station, mil., Fl., U.S. u14 102
Saugatuck, stm., Ct., U.S. D2 100
Saugatuck, Mi., U.S. F4 115
Saugatucket, stm., R.I., U.S. F4 132
Saugatuck Reservoir, res., Ct., U.S. D2 100
Saugerties, N.Y., U.S. C7 125
Saugus, Ma., U.S. B5 114
Saugus, stm., Ma., U.S. g11 114
Sauk, stm., Mn., U.S. E4 116
Sauk, stm., Wa., U.S. A4 140
Sauk, co., Wi., U.S. E4 142
Sauk Centre, Mn., U.S. E4 116
Sauk City, Wi., U.S. E4 142
Sauk Rapids, Mn., U.S. E4 116
Saukville, Wi., U.S. E6 142
Saül, Fr. Gu. C9 70
Saulnierville, N.S., Can. E3 87
Sault-au-Mouton, Qc., Can. A8 90
Sault Sainte Marie, On., Can. p18 89
Sault Sainte Marie, Mi., U.S. B6 115
Saumarez Reef, rf., Austl. E5 62
Saumlaki, Indon. E8 36
Saumur, Fr. D6 16
Saunders, co., Ne., U.S. C9 120
Saunderstown, R.I., U.S. E4 132
Saurimo, Ang. E4 54
Sausalito, Ca., U.S. D2 98
Sava, stm., Eur. G5 20
Savage, Md., U.S. B4 113
Savage, stm., Md., U.S. k12 113
Savage River Reservoir, res., Md., U.S. k12 113
Savai'i, i., Samoa F12 58
Savalou, Benin E5 50
Savanna, Il., U.S. A3 106
Savanna, Ok., U.S. C6 129
Savannah, Ga., U.S. D5 103
Savannah, Mo., U.S. B3 118
Savannah, Tn., U.S. B3 135
Savannah, stm., U.S. E11 92
Savannah River Plant, hist., S.C., U.S. E4 133
Savannakhét, Laos C4 34
Savanna Lake, l., Md., U.S. D6 113

Name — Map Ref. — Page

Savanna-la-Mar, Jam. B4 80
Savaştepe, Tur. C2 44
Save (Sabi), stm., Afr. C5 56
Savè, Benin E5 50
Sāveh, Iran C6 42
Savelugu, Ghana E4 50
Saverne, Fr. C10 16
Saville Dam, Ct., U.S. B4 100
Savitaipale, Fin. F12 10
Savona, Italy B2 18
Savonlinna, Fin. F13 10
Savoonga, Ak., U.S. C5 95
Savoy, Il., U.S. C5 106
Savu Sea see Sawu, Laut, Indon. E6 36
Sawāi Mādhopur, India D3 40
Sawākin, Sudan G12 48
Sawankhalok, Thai. C3 34
Sawatch Range, mts., Co., U.S. B4 99
Sawdā', Jabal as-, Libya F7 14
Sawdā', Qurnat as-, mtn., Leb. E7 44
Sawnee Mountain, mtn., Ga., U.S. B2 103
Sawtooth Mountains, mts., Id., U.S. F4 105
Sawtooth National Recreation Area, Id., U.S. E3 105
Sawu, Laut (Savu Sea), Indon. E6 36
Sawu, Pulau, i., Indon. F6 36
Sawyer, co., Wi., U.S. C2 142
Sawyerville, Qc., Can. D6 90
Saxonburg, Pa., U.S. E2 131
Saxtons, stm., Vt., U.S. E3 138
Saxtons River, Vt., U.S. E3 138
Sayan Mountains, mts., Asia D11 26
Saybrook, Il., U.S. C5 106
Saybrook Manor, Ct., U.S. D6 100
Şaydā, Leb. F6 44
Saydel, Ia., U.S. e8 108
Sayhūt, Yemen G6 38
Saylac, Som. H4 38
Saylesville, R.I., U.S. B4 132
Saylorsburg, Pa., U.S. E11 131
Saylorville, Ia., U.S. e8 108
Saylorville Lake, res., Ia., U.S. C4 108
Saynshand, Mong. C10 28
Sayre, Al., U.S. B3 94
Sayre, Ok., U.S. B2 129
Sayre, Pa., U.S. C8 131
Sayreville, N.J., U.S. C4 123
Sayula, Mex. D4 78
Sayville, N.Y., U.S. n15 125
Saywūn, Yemen G5 38
Sba, Alg. F3 14
Scalp Level, Pa., U.S. F4 131
Scanlon, Mn., U.S. D6 116
Scapegoat Mountain, mtn., Mt., U.S. C3 119
Scappoose, Or., U.S. B4 130
Scarborough, On., Can. m15 89
Scarborough, Trin. C7 80
Scarborough, Eng., U.K. C6 12
Scarborough, Me., U.S. E2 112
Scarbro, W.V., U.S. n13 141
Scarsdale, N.Y., U.S. h13 125
Ščekino, Russia C14 20
Ščerbakovo, Russia C18 26
Schaefferstown, Pa., U.S. F9 131
Schaller, Ia., U.S. B2 108
Schaumburg, Il., U.S. h8 106
Schell Creek Range, mts., Nv., U.S. D7 121
Schenectady, co., N.Y., U.S. C6 125
Schenectady, N.Y., U.S. C7 125
Schererville, In., U.S. B3 107
Schertz, Tx., U.S. h7 136
Schiller Park, Il., U.S. k9 106
Schio, Italy B3 18
Schleicher, co., Tx., U.S. D2 136
Schleswig, Ger. C11 12
Schleswig, Ia., U.S. B2 108
Schley, co., Ga., U.S. D2 103
Schofield, Wi., U.S. D4 142
Schofield Barracks, mil., Hi., U.S. g9 104
Schoharie, co., N.Y., U.S. C6 125
Schoharie Creek, stm., N.Y., U.S. C6 125
Schoodic Lake, l., Me., U.S. C4 112
Schoolcraft, co., Mi., U.S. B4 115
Schoolcraft, Mi., U.S. F5 115
Schroon Lake, l., N.Y., U.S. B7 125
Schulenburg, Tx., U.S. E4 136
Schulter, Ok., U.S. B6 129
Schurz, Nv., U.S. E3 121
Schuyler, co., Il., U.S. C3 106
Schuyler, co., Mo., U.S. A5 118
Schuyler, Ne., U.S. C8 120
Schuyler, co., N.Y., U.S. C4 125
Schuylkill, co., Pa., U.S. E9 131
Schuylkill, stm., Pa., U.S. F10 131
Schuylkill Haven, Pa., U.S. E9 131
Schwaben, hist. reg., Ger. F11 12
Schwarzwald (Black Forest), mts., Ger. F11 12
Schwedt, Ger. D14 12
Schwerin, Ger. D12 12
Schwyz, Switz. A2 18
Sciacca, Italy F4 18
Science Hill, Ky., U.S. C5 110
Ščigry, Russia D14 20
Scilly, Isles of, is., Eng., U.K. F3 12
Scio, Or., U.S. C4 130
Scioto, stm., Oh., U.S. B2 128
Scioto, co., Oh., U.S. D3 128
Scituate, Ma., U.S. B6 114
Scituate Reservoir, res., R.I., U.S. C3 132
Scobey, Mt., U.S. B11 119
Scofield Reservoir, res., Ut., U.S. D4 137
Scotch Plains, N.J., U.S. B4 123
Scotia, Ca., U.S. B1 98
Scotia, N.Y., U.S. C7 125
Scotia Ridge N8 66
Scotia Sea B36 67
Scotland, On., Can. D4 89
Scotland, state, U.K. B5 12
Scotland, co., Mo., U.S. A5 118
Scotland, co., N.C., U.S. C3 126
Scotland, S.D., U.S. D8 134
Scotland Neck, N.C., U.S. A5 126
Scotlandville, La., U.S. D4 111
Scotrun, Pa., U.S. D11 131
Scotstown, Qc., Can. D6 90
Scott, co., Ar., U.S. C1 97
Scott, co., Ia., U.S. C7 108
Scott, co., Il., U.S. D3 106
Scott, co., In., U.S. G6 107
Scott, co., Ks., U.S. D3 109
Scott, co., Ky., U.S. B5 110
Scott, La., U.S. D3 111
Scott, co., Mn., U.S. F5 116
Scott, co., Mo., U.S. D8 118
Scott, co., Ms., U.S. C4 117
Scott, co., Tn., U.S. C9 135
Scott, co., Va., U.S. f9 139
Scott, Cape, c., B.C., Can. D3 85
Scott, Mount, mtn., Or., U.S. E4 130
Scott Air Force Base, mil., Il., U.S. E4 106
Scott City, Ks., U.S. D3 109
Scott City, Mo., U.S. D8 118
Scottdale, Ga., U.S. h8 103
Scottdale, Pa., U.S. F2 131
Scott Mountain, mtn., Id., U.S. E3 105
Scott Peak, mtn., Id., U.S. E6 105
Scott Reef, rf., Austl. C3 60
Scott Reservoir, res., N.C., U.S. A1 126
Scottsbluff, Ne., U.S. C2 120
Scotts Bluff, co., Ne., U.S. C2 120
Scotts Bluff National Monument, Ne., U.S. C2 120
Scottsboro, Al., U.S. A3 94
Scottsburg, In., U.S. G6 107
Scottsdale, Az., U.S. D4 96
Scottsville, Ky., U.S. D3 110
Scottsville, N.Y., U.S. B3 125
Scottville, Mi., U.S. E4 115
Scraggly Lake, l., Me., U.S. B4 112
Scranton, Ks., U.S. D8 109
Scranton, Pa., U.S. D10 131
Scranton, S.C., U.S. D8 133
Screven, Ga., U.S. E4 103
Screven, co., Ga., U.S. D5 103
Scribner, Ne., U.S. C9 120
Ščučinsk, Kaz. D8 26
Scugog, Lake, l., On., Can. C6 89
Scurry, co., Tx., U.S. C2 136
Scutari see Shkodër, Alb. C7 18
Scutari, Lake, l., Eur. C7 18
Scyros see Skíros, i., Grc. E10 18
Seaboard, N.C., U.S. A5 126
Seabreeze, De., U.S. F5 101
Seabrook, N.H., U.S. E5 122
Seabrook, Tx., U.S. r14 136
Seabrook Island, i., S.C., U.S. F7 133
Seadrift, Tx., U.S. E4 136
Seaford, De., U.S. F3 101
Seaford, Va., U.S. h15 139
Seaforth, On., Can. D3 89
Seagoville, Tx., U.S. n10 136
Seagraves, Tx., U.S. C1 136
Sea Islands, is., U.S. E11 92
Sea Isle City, N.J., U.S. E3 123
Seal Cove, N.L., Can. D3 88
Seal Point, c., P.E., Can. C5 87
Seal Rock, Or., U.S. C2 130
Sealy, Tx., U.S. E4 136
Seaman, Oh., U.S. D2 128
Seaman Range, mts., Nv., U.S. F6 121
Searchlight, Nv., U.S. H7 121
Searcy, co., Ar., U.S. B3 97
Searcy, Ar., U.S. B4 97
Searles Lake, l., Ca., U.S. E5 98
Searsport, Me., U.S. D4 112
Seaside, Or., U.S. B3 130
Seat Pleasant, Md., U.S. C4 113
Seattle, Wa., U.S. B3 140
Seattle-Tacoma International Airport, Wa., U.S. f11 140
Seaview, Wa., U.S. C1 140
Sebago Lake, Me., U.S. E2 112
Šebalino, Russia D10 26
Sebangka, Pulau, i., Indon. C2 36
Sebastian, co., Ar., U.S. B1 97
Sebastian, Fl., U.S. E6 102
Sebastian, Cape, c., Or., U.S. E2 130
Sebastian Inlet, b., Fl., U.S. E6 102
Sebastián Vizcaíno, Bahía, b., Mex. B2 78
Sebasticook Lake, l., Me., U.S. D3 112
Sebec Lake, l., Me., U.S. C3 112
Sebeka, Mn., U.S. D3 116
Šebekino, Russia D14 20
Sebeş, Rom. G7 20
Sebewaing, Mi., U.S. E7 115
Şebinkarahisar, Tur. B8 44
Seboeis, stm., Me., U.S. B4 112
Seboeis Lake, l., Me., U.S. C4 112
Seboomook Lake, l., Me., U.S. C3 112
Sebree, Ky., U.S. C2 110
Sebring, Fl., U.S. E5 102
Sebring, Oh., U.S. B4 128
Secaucus, N.J., U.S. h8 123
Sechelt, B.C., Can. E6 85
Sechura, Bahía de, b., Peru E3 70
Second Lake, l., N.H., U.S. f7 122
Second Mesa, Az., U.S. B5 96
Secret Lake, l., R.I., U.S. E4 132
Section, Al., U.S. A4 94
Security, Co., U.S. C6 99
Seda, China E8 28
Sedalia, Mo., U.S. C4 118
Sedan, Fr. C9 16
Sedan, Ks., U.S. E7 109
Sedgewick, Ab., Can. C5 84
Sedgewick, Mount, mtn., N.M., U.S. B1 124
Sedgwick, co., Co., U.S. A8 99
Sedgwick, Ks., U.S. E6 109
Sedgwick, co., Ks., U.S. E6 109
Sédhiou, Sen. D1 50
Sedley, Va., U.S. D6 139
Sedona, Az., U.S. C4 96
Sedro Woolley, Wa., U.S. A3 140
Seekonk, Ma., U.S. C5 114
Seekonk, stm., R.I., U.S. C4 132
Seeley, Ca., U.S. F6 98
Seeley Lake, Mt., U.S. C3 119
Seelyville, In., U.S. F3 107
Şefaatli, Tur. C6 44
Sefadu, S.L. E2 50
Seferihisar, Tur. C2 44
Segamat, Malay. C2 36
Segesta, hist., Italy F4 18
Segeža, Russia C5 26
Ségou, Mali D3 50
Segovia, Spain G4 16
Seguam Island, i., Ak., U.S. E5 95
Seguam Pass, strt., Ak., U.S. E5 95
Séguédine, Niger B7 50
Séguéla, C. Iv. E3 50
Seguin, Tx., U.S. E4 136
Segura, stm., Spain I6 16
Seiling, Ok., U.S. A3 129
Seinäjoki, Fin. E10 10
Seine, stm., Fr. C7 16
Seine, Baie de la, b., Fr. C6 16
Sejm, stm., Eur. D12 20
Sejmčan, Russia C17 26
Şeki, Azer. B12 44
Sekiu, Wa., U.S. A1 140
Sekondi-Takoradi, Ghana F4 50
Selah, Wa., U.S. C5 140
Selaru, Pulau, i., Indon. E8 36
Selatan, Tanjung, c., Indon. D4 36
Selawik, Ak., U.S. B7 95
Selawik Lake, l., Ak., U.S. B7 95
Selayar, Pulau, i., Indon. E6 36
Selby, S.D., U.S. B5 134
Selbyville, De., U.S. G5 101
Selçuk, Tur. D2 44
Seldovia, Ak., U.S. D9 95
Selebi-Phikwe, Bots. C4 56
Selenge, stm., Asia E12 26
Selenge, D.R.C. D3 54
Sélibabi, Maur. C2 50
Seligman, Az., U.S. B3 96
Šelihova, zaliv, b., Russia C17 26
Selinsgrove, Pa., U.S. E8 131
Seljord, Nor. G3 10
Selkirk, Mb., Can. D3 86
Sellersburg, In., U.S. H6 107
Sellersville, Pa., U.S. F11 131
Sells, Az., U.S. F4 96
Selma, Al., U.S. C2 94
Selma, Ca., U.S. D4 98
Selma, In., U.S. D7 107
Selma, N.C., U.S. B4 126
Selmer, Tn., U.S. B3 135
Selvagens, Ilhas, is., Port. D1 48
Selvas, for., Braz. E6 70
Selway, stm., Id., U.S. C3 105
Selwyn Lake, l., Can. G15 82
Selwyn Mountains, mts., Can. F13 82
Selwyn Range, mts., Austl. E3 62
Semara, W. Sah. A2 50
Semarang, Indon. E4 36
Semenanjung Malaysia, hist. reg., Malay. C2 36
Semenivka, Ukr. C12 20
Semenov, Russia C7 22
Semey see Semipalatinsk, Kaz. D10 26
Semiluki, Russia D15 20
Seminoe Mountains, mts., Wy., U.S. D6 143
Seminoe Reservoir, res., Wy., U.S. D6 143
Seminole, co., Fl., U.S. D5 102
Seminole, co., Ga., U.S. F2 103
Seminole, co., Ok., U.S. B5 129
Seminole, Ok., U.S. B5 129
Seminole, Tx., U.S. C1 136
Seminole, Lake, res., U.S. F2 103
Semipalatinsk, Kaz. D10 26
Semisopochnoi Island, i., Ak., U.S. E3 95
Semitau, Indon. C4 36
Semmes, Al., U.S. E1 94
Semnān, Iran C6 42
Senachwine Lake, l., Il., U.S. B4 106
Senador Pompeu, Braz. C4 74
Senaki, Geor. A10 44
Sena Madureira, Braz. E6 70
Senanga, Zam. B3 56
Senath, Mo., U.S. E7 118
Senatobia, Ms., U.S. A4 117
Sendai, Japan D16 28
Sendelingsdrif, Nmb. D2 56
Seneca, Il., U.S. B5 106
Seneca, Ks., U.S. C7 109
Seneca, Mo., U.S. E3 118
Seneca, co., N.Y., U.S. C4 125
Seneca, co., Oh., U.S. A2 128
Seneca, Pa., U.S. D2 131
Seneca, S.C., U.S. B2 133
Seneca Falls, N.Y., U.S. C4 125
Seneca Lake, l., N.Y., U.S. C4 125
Senecaville Lake, res., Oh., U.S. C4 128
Sénégal, stm., Afr. C2 50
Senegal, ctry., Afr. D1 50
Senekal, S. Afr. D4 56
Senftenberg, Ger. E13 12
Senhor do Bonfim, Braz. D3 74
Senica, Slvk. E4 20
Senigallia, Italy C4 18
Senja, i., Nor. B7 10
Šenkursk, Russia B7 22
Senneterre, Qc., Can. k11 90
Senoia, Ga., U.S. C2 103
Senqu see Orange, stm., Afr. D2 56
Sens, Fr. C8 16
Senta, Serb. B8 18
Sentinel, Ok., U.S. B2 129
Seoni, India E3 40
Seoul see Sŏul, S. Kor. D13 28
Sepanjang, Pulau, i., Indon. E5 36
Sepik, stm., Pap. N. Gui. G11 32
Sept-Îles (Seven Islands), Qc., Can. h13 90
Sepulga, stm., Al., U.S. D3 94
Sequatchie, stm., Tn., U.S. D8 135
Sequatchie, co., Tn., U.S. D8 135
Sequim, Wa., U.S. A2 140
Sequoia National Park, Ca., U.S. D4 98
Sequoyah, co., Ok., U.S. B7 129
Šerabad, Uzb. C9 42
Serafimovič, Russia E7 22
Seram (Ceram), i., Indon. D7 36
Seram, Laut (Ceram Sea), Indon. D7 36
Serang, Indon. E3 36
Serasan, Pulau, i., Indon. C3 36
Serasan, Selat, strt., Indon. C3 36
Serbia see Srbija, state, Serb. B8 18
Serbia and Montenegro (Yugoslavia), ctry., Eur. C8 18
Serdobsk, Russia D7 22
Sered', Slvk. E4 20
Şereflikoçhisar, Tur. C5 44
Seremban, Malay. C2 36
Serengeti Plain, pl., Tan. D6 54
Serenje, Zam. A5 56
Sergač, Russia C8 22
Sergeant Bluff, Ia., U.S. B1 108
Sergeevka, Russia B2 31
Sergeja Kirova, ostrova, is., Russia B10 26
Sergiev Posad, Russia D5 26
Serginskij, Russia C8 26
Sergipe, state, Braz. D4 74
Seria, Bru. C4 36
Serian, Malay. C4 36
Sérifos, i., Grc. F10 18
Serik, Tur. D4 44
Šerlovaja Gora, Russia A11 28
Serov, Russia D8 26
Serowe, Bots. C4 56
Serpa, Port. I3 16
Serpiente, Boca de la, strt. D7 80
Serpuhov, Russia B14 20
Serra do Navio, Braz. C9 70
Sérrai, Grc. D9 18
Serra Talhada, Braz. C4 74
Serrezuela, Arg. E4 72
Serrinha, Braz. D4 74
Sertânia, Braz. C4 74
Sêrxü, China E7 28
Sese Islands, is., Ug. D6 54
Sesfontein, Nmb. B1 56
Sesheke, Zam. B3 56
Sesser, Il., U.S. E4 106
Sestroreck, Russia F13 10
Sète, Fr. F8 16
Sete Lagoas, Braz. E3 74
Seth, W.V., U.S. C3 141
Sétif, Alg. C6 48
Seto-naikai, Japan E14 28
Setté Cama, Gabon D1 54
Setúbal, Port. H2 16
Setúbal, Baía de, b., Port. H2 16
Seul, Lac, l., On., Can. o16 89
Seul Choix Point, c., Mi., U.S. C5 115
Sevan, Arm. B11 44
Sevana Lich, l., Arm. B11 44
Sevastopol', Ukr. G12 20
Seven Devils Lake, res., Ar., U.S. D4 97
Seven Devils Mountains, mts., Id., U.S. D2 105
Seven Hills, Oh., U.S. h9 128
Seven Mile Beach, N.J., U.S. E3 123
Severn, stm., On., Can. n17 89
Severn, stm., U.K. D5 12
Severn, Md., U.S. B4 113
Severnaja Dvina, stm., Russia C6 26
Severnaja Osetija, state, Russia E6 26
Severnaja Sos'va, stm., Russia B11 22
Severnaja Zemlja, is., Russia B12 26
Severna Park, Md., U.S. B4 113
Severn River, b., Md., U.S. B4 113
Severnye uvaly, Russia D6 26
Severodvinsk, Russia C5 26
Severo-Enisejskij, Russia C11 26
Severomorsk, Russia B15 10
Severo-Sibirskaja nizmennost', pl., Russia B11 26
Severoural'sk, Russia B11 22
Sevier, co., Ar., U.S. D1 97
Sevier, co., Tn., U.S. D10 135
Sevier, stm., Ut., U.S. D3 137
Sevier, co., Ut., U.S. E4 137
Sevier Bridge Reservoir, res., Ut., U.S. D4 137
Sevier Lake, l., Ut., U.S. E2 137
Sevierville, Tn., U.S. D10 135
Sevilla, Col. E4 80
Sevilla (Seville), Spain I4 16
Seville see Sevilla, Spain I4 16
Seville, Oh., U.S. A4 128
Sewanee, Tn., U.S. D8 135
Seward, Ak., U.S. C10 95
Seward, co., Ks., U.S. E3 109
Seward, Ne., U.S. D8 120
Seward, co., Ne., U.S. D8 120
Seward Peninsula, pen., Ak., U.S. B7 95
Sewickley, Pa., U.S. E1 131
Sexsmith, Ab., Can. B1 84
Seychelles, ctry., Afr. 57b
Seychelles, ctry., Afr. h13 57b
Seychelles, is., Afr. i12 57b
Seydişehir, Tur. D4 44
Seyðisfjörður, Ice. I21 10a
Seyhan, stm., Tur. D6 44
Seyhan Barajı, res., Tur. D6 44
Seymour, Austl. H4 62
Seymour, Ct., U.S. D3 100
Seymour, Ia., U.S. D4 108
Seymour, In., U.S. G6 107
Seymour, Mo., U.S. D5 118
Seymour, Tx., U.S. C3 136
Seymour, Wi., U.S. D5 142
Seymour Inlet, b., B.C., Can. D4 85
Seymour Johnson Air Force Base, mil., N.C., U.S. B5 126
Seymour Lake, l., Vt., U.S. B4 138
Seymourville, La., U.S. h9 111
Sfântu Gheorghe, Rom. G8 20
Sfax, Tun. D7 48
's-Gravenhage (The Hague), Neth. D8 12
Shaanxi, prov., China D9 28
Shabbona, Il., U.S. B5 106
Shabeelle (Shebelē Wenz, Wabē), stm., Afr. C8 54
Shabunda, D.R.C. D5 54
Shache, China D3 28
Shackelford, co., Tx., U.S. C3 136
Shackleton Ice Shelf, ice, Ant. C14 67
Shackleton Range, mts., Ant. E2 67
Shadehill Dam, S.D., U.S. B3 134
Shadehill Reservoir, res., S.D., U.S. B3 134
Shadow Mountain National Recreation Area, Co., U.S. A4 99
Shady Cove, Or., U.S. E4 130
Shady Side, Md., U.S. C4 113
Shadyside, Oh., U.S. C5 128
Shady Spring, W.V., U.S. D3 141
Shafer, Lake, l., In., U.S. C4 107
Shafer Butte, mtn., Id., U.S. F2 105
Shafter, Ca., U.S. E4 98
Shaftsbury, Vt., U.S. E2 138
Shag Rocks, rock, S. Geor. H8 69
Shah Alam, Malay. C2 36
Shahdol, India E4 40
Shāhjahānpur, India D3 40
Shāhpura, India D2 40
Shahr-e Kord, Iran D6 42
Shahr-e Rey, Iran C6 42
Shājāpur, India E3 40
Shakawe, Bots. B3 56
Shaker Heights, Oh., U.S. A4 128
Shaki, Nig. E5 50
Shakopee, Mn., U.S. F5 116
Shala Hāyk', l., Eth. B7 54
Shallotte, N.C., U.S. D4 126

Name — Map Ref. — Page

Shallotte Inlet, b., N.C., U.S. D4 126
Shallowater, Tx., U.S. C2 136
Shām, Jabal ash-, mtn., Oman F7 38
Shambe, Sudan B6 54
Shambu, Eth. B7 54
Shamokin, Pa., U.S. E8 131
Shamokin Dam, Pa., U.S. E8 131
Shamrock, Tx., U.S. B2 136
Shamva, Zimb. B5 56
Shandī, Sudan G11 48
Shandong, prov., China D11 28
Shandong Bandao, pen., China D12 28
Shangcai, China C3 30
Shangcheng, China C4 30
Shangchuan Dao, i., China E3 30
Shangdu, China A3 30
Shanghai, China E12 28
Shanghang, China D4 30
Shangqiu, China E11 28
Shangrao, China F11 28
Shangxian, China E10 28
Shangzhi, China B13 28
Shanhaiguan, China A4 30
Shannock, R.I., U.S. F2 132
Shannon, stm., Ire. D2 12
Shannon, Ga., U.S. B1 103
Shannon, Il., U.S. A4 106
Shannon, co., Mo., U.S. D6 118
Shannon, Ms., U.S. A5 117
Shannon, co., S.D., U.S. D3 134
Shannon, Lake, l., Wa., U.S. A4 140
Shannontown, S.C., U.S. D7 133
Shantou, China G11 28
Shantung Peninsula see Shandong Bandao, pen., China D12 28
Shanxi, prov., China D10 28
Shanxian, China C4 30
Shanyin, China B3 30
Shaoguan, China G10 28
Shaowu, China F11 28
Shaoxing, China E12 28
Shaoyang, China F10 28
Shaqrā', Sau. Ar. E5 38
Shaqrā', Yemen H5 38
Šhara, gora, mtn., Asia A10 44
Shark Bay, b., Austl. F1 60
Sharkey, co., Ms., U.S. C3 117
Shark Point, c., Fl., U.S. H5 102
Sharm El Sheikh, Egypt E11 48
Sharon, Ct., U.S. B2 100
Sharon, Ma., U.S. B5 114
Sharon, Pa., U.S. D1 131
Sharon, Tn., U.S. A3 135
Sharon, Wi., U.S. F5 142
Sharon Hill, Pa., U.S. p20 131
Sharon Park, Oh., U.S. n12 128
Sharon Springs, Ks., U.S. D2 109
Sharonville, Oh., U.S. n13 128
Sharp, co., Ar., U.S. A4 97
Sharpe, Lake, res., S.D., U.S. C6 134
Sharpes, Fl., U.S. D6 102
Sharpley, De., U.S. h7 101
Sharpsburg, Md., U.S. B2 113
Sharpsburg, N.C., U.S. B5 126
Sharpsburg, Pa., U.S. k14 131
Sharpsville, In., U.S. D5 107
Sharpsville, Pa., U.S. D1 131
Sharptown, Md., U.S. C6 113
Shashe, stm., Afr. C4 56
Shashemenē, Eth. B7 54
Shashi, China E10 28
Shasta, co., Ca., U.S. B3 98
Shasta, Mount, vol., Ca., U.S. B2 98
Shasta Lake, res., Ca., U.S. B2 98
Shattuck, Ok., U.S. A2 129
Shaw, Ms., U.S. B3 117
Shaw Air Force Base, mil., S.C., U.S. D7 133
Shawano, Wi., U.S. D5 142
Shawano, co., Wi., U.S. D5 142
Shawano Lake, l., Wi., U.S. D5 142
Shawinigan, Qc., Can. C5 90
Shawinigan-Sud, Qc., Can. C5 90
Shawnee, Ks., U.S. k16 109
Shawnee, co., Ks., U.S. D8 109
Shawnee, Ok., U.S. B5 129
Shawneetown, Il., U.S. F5 106
Shawsheen, stm., Ma., U.S. f11 114
Shay Gap, Austl. E3 60
Shaykh, Jabal ash- see Hermon, Mount, mtn., Asia F6 44
Shaykh Sa'd, Iraq F12 44
Shaykh 'Uthmān, Yemen H5 38
Shebelē Wenz, Wabē (Shabeelle), stm., Afr. B8 54
Sheberghān, Afg. C9 42
Sheboygan, Wi., U.S. E6 142
Sheboygan, co., Wi., U.S. E6 142
Sheboygan, stm., Wi., U.S. k10 142
Sheboygan Falls, Wi., U.S. E6 142
Shediac, N.B., Can. C5 87
Sheenjek, stm., Ak., U.S. B11 95
Sheep Mountain, mtn., Az., U.S. E1 96
Sheep Mountain, mtn., Wy., U.S. B5 143
Sheep Mountain, mtn., Wy., U.S. C2 143
Sheep Peak, mtn., Nv., U.S. G6 121
Sheep Range, mts., Nv., U.S. G6 121
Sheet Harbour, N.S., Can. E7 87
Sheffield, Eng., U.K. D6 12
Sheffield, Al., U.S. A2 94
Sheffield, Ia., U.S. B4 108
Sheffield, Il., U.S. B4 106
Sheffield, Pa., U.S. C3 131
Sheffield Lake, Oh., U.S. A3 128
Shehong, China C2 30
Sheila, N.B., Can. B5 87
Shekhūpura, Pak. D10 42
Shelagyote Peak, mtn., B.C., Can. B4 85
Shelbiana, Ky., U.S. C7 110
Shelbina, Mo., U.S. B5 118
Shelburn, In., U.S. F3 107
Shelburne, On., Can. C4 89
Shelburne Falls, Ma., U.S. A2 114
Shelburne Pond, l., Vt., U.S. C2 138
Shelby, Al., U.S. B3 94
Shelby, co., Al., U.S. B3 94
Shelby, Ia., U.S. C2 108
Shelby, co., Ia., U.S. C2 108
Shelby, co., Il., U.S. D5 106
Shelby, In., U.S. B3 107
Shelby, co., In., U.S. E6 107
Shelby, co., Ky., U.S. B4 110
Shelby, Mi., U.S. E4 115
Shelby, co., Mo., U.S. B5 118
Shelby, Ms., U.S. B3 117
Shelby, Mt., U.S. B5 119
Shelby, N.C., U.S. B1 126
Shelby, Ne., U.S. C8 120
Shelby, Oh., U.S. B3 128
Shelby, co., Oh., U.S. B1 128
Shelby, co., Tn., U.S. B2 135
Shelby, co., Tx., U.S. D5 136
Shelbyville, Il., U.S. D5 106
Shelbyville, In., U.S. F6 107
Shelbyville, Ky., U.S. B4 110
Shelbyville, Tn., U.S. B5 135
Shelbyville, Lake, res., Il., U.S. D5 106
Sheldon, Ia., U.S. A2 108
Sheldon, Il., U.S. C6 106
Sheldon, Tx., U.S. r14 136
Shelekhov, Gulf of see Šelihova, zaliv, b., Russia C17 26
Shelikof Strait, strt., Ak., U.S. D9 95
Shell Creek, stm., Wy., U.S. B5 143
Shell Creek, stm., U.S. A2 99
Shelley, Id., U.S. F6 105
Shellharbour, Austl. G5 62
Shell Lake, l., Mn., U.S. D3 116
Shell Lake, Wi., U.S. C2 142
Shell Lake, l., Wi., U.S. C2 142
Shellman, Ga., U.S. E2 103
Shell Rock, Ia., U.S. B5 108
Shell Rock, stm., Ia., U.S. B5 108
Shellsburg, Ia., U.S. B6 108
Shelly Mountain, mtn., Id., U.S. F5 105
Shelter Island, N.Y., U.S. m16 125
Shelton, Ct., U.S. D3 100
Shelton, Ne., U.S. D7 120
Shelton, Wa., U.S. B2 140
Shemya Air Force Base, mil., Ak., U.S. E2 95
Shenandoah, Ia., U.S. D2 108
Shenandoah, Pa., U.S. E9 131
Shenandoah, Va., U.S. B4 139
Shenandoah, co., Va., U.S. B4 139
Shenandoah, stm., U.S. A5 139
Shenandoah, North Fork, stm., Va., U.S. B4 139
Shenandoah, South Fork, stm., Va., U.S. B4 139
Shenandoah Mountain, mtn., U.S. B3 139
Shenandoah National Park, Va., U.S. B4 139
Shenango River Lake, res., U.S. D1 131
Shendam, Nig. E6 50
Shenipsit Lake, l., Ct., U.S. B6 100
Shenmu, China B3 30
Shenqiu, China C4 30
Shenxian, China B4 30
Shenyang, China C12 28
Shenzhen, China E3 30
Shepaug, stm., Ct., U.S. C2 100
Shepaug Dam, Ct., U.S. D2 100
Shepaug Reservoir, res., Ct., U.S. C2 100
Shepetivka, Ukr. D9 20
Shepherd, Mi., U.S. E6 115
Shepherd, Tx., U.S. D5 136
Shepherdstown, W.V., U.S. B7 141
Shepherdsville, Ky., U.S. C4 110
Sheppard Air Force Base, mil., Tx., U.S. C3 136
Shepparton, Austl. H4 62
Sherborn, Ma., U.S. h10 114
Sherbro Island, i., S.L. E2 50
Sherbrooke, Qc., Can. D6 90
Sherburn, Mn., U.S. G4 116
Sherburne, co., Mn., U.S. E5 116
Sheridan, Ar., U.S. C3 97
Sheridan, Il., U.S. B5 106
Sheridan, In., U.S. D5 107
Sheridan, co., Ks., U.S. C3 109
Sheridan, Mi., U.S. E5 115
Sheridan, Mt., U.S. E4 119
Sheridan, co., Mt., U.S. B12 119
Sheridan, co., N.D., U.S. B5 127
Sheridan, co., Ne., U.S. B3 120
Sheridan, Or., U.S. B3 130
Sheridan, Wy., U.S. B6 143
Sheridan, co., Wy., U.S. B5 143
Sheridan, Mount, mtn., Wy., U.S. B2 143
Sherman, co., Ks., U.S. C2 109
Sherman, co., Ne., U.S. C6 120
Sherman, co., Or., U.S. B6 130
Sherman, Tx., U.S. C4 136
Sherman, co., Tx., U.S. A2 136
Sherman Reservoir, res., Ne., U.S. C7 120
Sherpur, Bngl. D6 40
Sherrill, N.Y., U.S. B5 125
Sherwood, P.E., Can. C6 87
Sherwood, Ar., U.S. C3 97
Sherwood, Or., U.S. h12 130
Sherwood, Wi., U.S. h9 142
Sherwood Manor, Ct., U.S. A5 100
Sherwood Park, De., U.S. i7 101
Shetek, Lake, l., Mn., U.S. G3 116
Shetland Islands, is., Scot., U.K. h19 12a
Shetucket, stm., Ct., U.S. C7 100
Sheyenne, stm., N.D., U.S. C8 127
Sheyenne Lake, res., N.D., U.S. B5 127
Shiawassee, co., Mi., U.S. F6 115
Shibām, Yemen G5 38
Shicheng, China A7 34
Shickshinny, Pa., U.S. D9 131
Shidao, China D12 28
Shiguaigou, China A3 30
Shijiazhuang, China D10 28
Shikārpur, Pak. E9 42
Shikoku, i., Japan E14 28
Shilabo, Eth. B8 54
Shiliguri, India D5 40
Shillington, Pa., U.S. F10 131
Shillong, India D6 40
Shiloh National Military Park, Tn., U.S. B3 135
Shimla, India C3 40
Shimoga, India G3 40
Shimonoseki, Japan E14 28
Shīndand, Afg. D8 42
Shiner, Tx., U.S. E4 136
Shinglehouse, Pa., U.S. C5 131
Shingū, Japan E15 28
Shinnston, W.V., U.S. B4 141
Shinyanga, Tan. D6 54
Shiocton, Wi., U.S. D5 142
Shiono-misaki, c., Japan D3 31
Shiping, China B4 34
Ship Island, i., Ms., U.S. E5 117
Ship Island Pass, strt., Ms., U.S. g7 117
Shippegan, N.B., Can. B5 87
Shippensburg, Pa., U.S. F6 131
Shiprock, N.M., U.S. A1 124
Ship Rock, mtn., N.M., U.S. A1 124
Shīrāz, Iran E6 42
Shiretoko-misaki, c., Japan B5 31
Shirley, In., U.S. E6 107
Shirley, Ma., U.S. A4 114
Shirley Mountains, mts., Wy., U.S. D6 143
Shīrvān, Iran C7 42
Shishaldin Volcano, vol., Ak., U.S. E7 95
Shishmaref, Ak., U.S. B6 95
Shithāthah, Iraq F10 44
Shively, Ky., U.S. B4 110
Shivpuri, India D3 40
Shizuoka, Japan C3 31
Shkodër, Alb. C7 18
Shoal Creek, stm., U.S. B4 135
Shoal Harbour, N.L., Can. D4 88
Shoal Lake, Mb., Can. D1 86
Shoals, In., U.S. G4 107
Shoals, Isles of, is., Me., U.S. E2 112
Shoalwater, Cape, c., Wa., U.S. C1 140
Shoemakersville, Pa., U.S. F10 131
Shongopovi, Az., U.S. B5 96
Shonto, Az., U.S. A5 96
Shoreham, Mi., U.S. F4 115
Shores Acres, R.I., U.S. E4 132
Shoreview, Mn., U.S. m12 116
Shorewood, Il., U.S. k8 106
Shorewood, Mn., U.S. n11 116
Shorewood, Wi., U.S. E6 142
Short Beach, Ct., U.S. D4 100
Shoshone, Id., U.S. G4 105
Shoshone, co., Id., U.S. B2 105
Shoshone, stm., Wy., U.S. B4 143
Shoshone Falls, wtfl., Id., U.S. G4 105
Shoshone Lake, l., Wy., U.S. B2 143
Shoshone Mountains, mts., Nv., U.S. E4 121
Shoshone Peak, mtn., Nv., U.S. G5 121
Shoshone Range, mts., Nv., U.S. C5 121
Shoshong, Bots. C4 56
Shoshoni, Wy., U.S. C4 143
Shostka, Ukr. D12 20
Shouchang, China D4 30
Shouguang, China B4 30
Shoup, Id., U.S. D4 105
Shouxian, China C4 30
Show Low, Az., U.S. C5 96
Shreve, Oh., U.S. B3 128
Shreveport, La., U.S. B2 111
Shrewsbury, Eng., U.K. D5 12
Shrewsbury, Ma., U.S. B4 114
Shrewsbury, N.J., U.S. C4 123
Shrewsbury, Pa., U.S. G8 131
Shuangcheng, China B13 28
Shuangjiang, China B3 34
Shuangliao, China C12 28
Shuangyashan, China B14 28
Shubenacadie, N.S., Can. D6 87
Shubrâ El-Kheima, Egypt E10 14
Shuksan, Mount, mtn., Wa., U.S. A4 140
Shule, China B3 40
Shullsburg, Wi., U.S. F3 142
Shumagin Islands, is., Ak., U.S. E7 95
Shunde, China B6 34
Shungnak, Ak., U.S. B8 95
Shurugwi, Zimb. B5 56
Shūsh, Iran F13 44
Shūshtar, Iran D5 42
Shuswap Lake, l., B.C., Can. D8 85
Shuyang, China C4 30
Shwebo, Mya. B3 34
Shwenyaung, Mya. B3 34
Shyok, stm., Asia C3 40
Siālkot, Pak. D10 42
Siam see Thailand, ctry., Asia C4 34
Siam, Gulf of see Thailand, Gulf of, b., Asia D4 34
Sian see Xi'an, China E9 28
Siargao Island, i., Phil. E9 34
Šiaškotan, ostrov, i., Russia E17 26
Siau, Pulau, i., Indon. C7 36
Sibaj, Russia D10 22
Šibenik, Cro. C5 18
Siberia see Sibir', reg., Russia C12 26
Siberut, Pulau, i., Indon. D1 36
Sibi, Pak. E9 42
Sibir' (Siberia), reg., Russia C12 26
Sibircevo, Russia B2 31
Sibirjakova, ostrov, i., Russia B9 26
Sibiti, Congo D2 54
Sibiu, Rom. G8 20
Sibley, Ia., U.S. A2 108
Sibley, La., U.S. B2 111
Sibley, co., Mn., U.S. F4 116
Sibolga, Indon. C1 36
Sibsāgar, India D6 40
Sibu, Malay. C4 36
Sibuguey Bay, b., Phil. E8 34
Sibut, C.A.R. B3 54
Sibutu Island, i., Phil. F7 34
Sibuyan Island, i., Phil. D8 34
Sibuyan Sea, Phil. D8 34
Sicamous, B.C., Can. D8 85
Sichuan, prov., China E8 28
Sicilia (Sicily), i., Italy F4 18
Sicily see Sicilia, i., Italy F4 18
Sicily, Strait of, strt. F3 18
Sico Tinto, stm., Hond. B2 80
Sicuani, Peru F5 70
Siddipet, India F3 40
Sidéradougou, Burkina D4 50
Siderno, Italy E6 18
Sidhi, India E4 40
Sīdī Barrānī, Egypt D10 48
Sidi bel Abbès, Alg. C4 48
Sidi-Ifni, Mor. E2 48
Sidley, Mount, mtn., Ant. D28 67
Sidney, B.C., Can. E6 85
Sidney, Ia., U.S. D2 108
Sidney, Il., U.S. C5 106
Sidney, Mt., U.S. C12 119
Sidney, Ne., U.S. C3 120
Sidney, N.Y., U.S. C5 125
Sidney, Oh., U.S. B1 128
Sidney Lanier, Lake, res., Ga., U.S. B2 103
Sidon see Şaydā, Leb. F6 44
Sidra, Gulf of see Surt, Khalīj, b., Libya D8 48
Sidrolândia, Braz. C6 72
Siedlce, Pol. C7 20
Siegen, Ger. E11 12
Siena, Italy C3 18
Sieradz, Pol. D5 20
Sierpc, Pol. C5 20
Sierra, co., Ca., U.S. C3 98
Sierra, co., N.M., U.S. D2 124
Sierra Blanca Peak, mtn., N.M., U.S. D4 124
Sierra Estrella, mts., Az., U.S. m8 96
Sierra Gorda, Chile C4 72
Sierra Leone, ctry., Afr. E2 50
Sierra Madre, Ca., U.S. m12 98
Sierra Nevada, mts., Ca., U.S. D4 92
Sierra Vista, Az., U.S. F5 96
Siesta Key, i., Fl., U.S. E4 102
Sieverodonets'k, Ukr. E15 20
Sífnos, i., Grc. F10 18
Sig, Alg. J6 16
Sighetu Marmaţiei, Rom. F7 20
Sighişoara, Rom. F8 20
Siglan, Russia D17 26
Siglufjörður, Ice. k19 10a
Signal Mountain, Tn., U.S. D8 135
Signal Peak, mtn., Az., U.S. D1 96
Signal Peak, mtn., Ut., U.S. F2 137
Sigourney, Ia., U.S. C5 108
Siguatepeque, Hond. C2 80
Siguiri, Gui. D3 50
Sigulda, Lat. H11 10
Siguri Falls, wtfl., Tan. E7 54
Sihanoukville see Kâmpóng Saôm, Camb. D4 34
Sihote-Alin', mts., Russia E15 26
Siirt, Tur. D9 44
Sīkar, India D3 40
Sikasso, Mali D3 50
Sikeston, Mo., U.S. E8 118
Sikiá, Grc. D9 18
Sikiang see Xi, stm., China G10 28
Sikkim, state, India D5 40
Šikotan, ostrov, i., Russia E16 26
Siktjah, Russia B14 26
Silao, Mex. C4 78
Silchar, India E6 40
Şile, Tur. B3 44
Siler City, N.C., U.S. B3 126
Silesia, hist. reg., Eur. D4 20
Siletz, Or., U.S. C3 130
Silghāt, India D6 40
Silhouette, i., Sey. h13 57b
Silifke, Tur. D5 44
Siling Co, l., China E5 28
Silistra, Blg. B11 18
Silivri, Tur. B3 44
Siljan, l., Swe. F6 10
Šilka, stm., Russia D13 26
Šilka, Russia D13 26
Silkeborg, Den. H3 10
Sillery, Qc., Can. n17 90
Sillustani, hist., Peru B3 72
Siloam Springs, Ar., U.S. A1 97
Šilovo, Russia B16 20
Silsbee, Tx., U.S. D5 136
Silt, Co., U.S. B3 99
Šilutė, Lith. I9 10
Silvan, Tur. C9 44
Silvassa, India E2 40
Silver Bay, Mn., U.S. C7 116
Silver Bow, co., Mt., U.S. E4 119
Silver City, N.M., U.S. E1 124
Silver City, Nv., U.S. D2 121
Silver Creek, Ne., U.S. C8 120
Silver Creek, N.Y., U.S. C1 125
Silver Creek, stm., Or., U.S. D7 130
Silverdale, Wa., U.S. B3 140
Silver Grove, Ky., U.S. h14 110
Silver Hill, Md., U.S. f9 113
Silver Lake, l., De., U.S. D3 101
Silver Lake, l., Ia., U.S. A3 108
Silver Lake, Ks., U.S. C8 109
Silver Lake, Ma., U.S. f11 114
Silver Lake, l., Me., U.S. C3 112
Silver Lake, Mn., U.S. F4 116
Silver Lake, l., N.H., U.S. E2 122
Silver Lake, l., N.H., U.S. C4 122
Silver Lake, l., Or., U.S. D7 130
Silver Lake, l., Wa., U.S. g13 140
Silver Lake, Wi., U.S. F5 142
Silverpeak, Nv., U.S. F4 121
Silver Peak Range, mts., Nv., U.S. F4 121
Silver Spring, Md., U.S. C3 113
Silver Springs, Nv., U.S. D2 121
Silver Star Mountain, mtn., Wa., U.S. A5 140
Silverthrone Mountain, mtn., B.C., Can. D4 85
Silvertip Mountain, mtn., Mt., U.S. C3 119
Silverton, Co., U.S. D3 99
Silverton, Id., U.S. B3 105
Silverton, N.J., U.S. C4 123
Silverton, Oh., U.S. o13 128
Silverton, Or., U.S. C4 130
Silvies, stm., Or., U.S. D7 130
Silview, De., U.S. B3 101
Silvis, Il., U.S. B3 106
Šimanovsk, Russia D14 26
Simao, China G8 28
Simav, stm., Tur. C3 44
Simba, D.R.C. C4 54
Simcoe, On., Can. E4 89
Simcoe, Lake, l., On., Can. C5 89
Simeulue, Palau, i., Indon. C1 36
Simferopol', Ukr. G13 20
Simití, Col. B5 70
Simi Valley, Ca., U.S. E4 98
Simmesport, La., U.S. D4 111
Simms Stream, stm., N.H., U.S. g7 122
Simonette, stm., Ab., Can. B1 84
Simon's Town, S. Afr. E2 56
Simpson, co., Ky., U.S. D3 110
Simpson, co., Ms., U.S. D4 117
Simpson, Pa., U.S. C11 131
Simpson Creek, stm., W.V., U.S. k10 141
Simpson Desert, des., Austl. E6 60
Simpsonville, Ky., U.S. B4 110
Simpsonville, S.C., U.S. B3 133
Simsboro, La., U.S. B3 111
Simsbury, Ct., U.S. B4 100
Simušir, ostrov, i., Russia E17 26
Sinabang, Indon. C1 36
Sinai, pen., Egypt E11 48
Sinai Peninsula see Sinai, pen., Egypt E11 48
Sinaloa, state, Mex. E3 78
Sināwin, Libya D7 48
Sincelejo, Col. B4 70

Name — Map Ref. — Page

Sinclair, Wy., U.S. E5 143
Sindangbarang, Indon. E3 36
Sindara, Gabon D2 54
Sindor, Russia B9 22
Sinfra, C. Iv. E3 50
Singalamwe, Nmb. B3 56
Singapore, ctry., Asia C2 36
Singapore, Sing. C2 36
Singaraja, Indon. H6 32
Singen, Ger. G11 12
Singida, Tan. D6 54
Singkaling Hkāmti, Mya. A3 34
Singkang, Indon. D6 36
Singkawang, Indon. C3 36
Singkep, Pulau, i., Indon. D2 36
Singleton, Austl. G5 62
Sinjai, Indon. E6 36
Sinjār, Iraq D9 44
Sinkāt, Sudan G12 48
Sinkiang see Xinjiang Uygur Zizhiqu, prov., China C5 28
Sinnemahoning Creek, stm., Pa., U.S. D5 131
Sinop, Tur. A6 44
Sinskoe, Russia C14 26
Sintang, Indon. C4 36
Sint Helenabaai, b., S. Afr. E2 56
Sinton, Tx., U.S. E4 136
Siocon, Phil. E8 34
Siófok, Hung. F5 20
Sion, Switz. A1 18
Sioux, co., Ia., U.S. A1 108
Sioux, co., N.D., U.S. C4 127
Sioux, co., Ne., U.S. B2 120
Sioux Center, Ia., U.S. A1 108
Sioux City, Ia., U.S. B1 108
Sioux Falls, S.D., U.S. D9 134
Sioux Lookout, On., Can. o17 89
Sioux Rapids, Ia., U.S. B2 108
Sipalay, Phil. E8 34
Siping, China C12 28
Sipiwesk Lake, l., Mb., Can. B3 86
Siple, Mount, mtn., Ant. D28 67
Sipsey, stm., Al., U.S. B2 94
Sipsey Fork, stm., Al., U.S. A2 94
Sipura, Pulau, i., Indon. D1 36
Siquijor Island, i., Phil. E8 34
Si Racha, Thai. D4 34
Siracusa, Italy F5 18
Sirājganj, Bngl. E5 40
Sir Douglas, Mount, mtn., Can. D3 84
Sir Edward Pellew Group, is., Austl. D6 60
Siren, Wi., U.S. C1 142
Siret, stm., Eur. G9 20
Sirjān, Iran E7 42
Şirnak, Tur. D10 44
Sirohi, India E2 40
Sironj, India E3 40
Síros, i., Grc. F10 18
Sirsa, India D3 40
Sir Sandford, Mount, mtn., B.C., Can. D9 85
Sirte, Gulf of see Surt, Khalīj, b., Libya D8 48
Sir Wilfrid Laurier, Mount, mtn., B.C., Can. C8 85
Sisaba, mtn., Tan. E5 54
Sisak, Cro. B6 18
Si Sa Ket, Thai. C4 34
Sishen, S. Afr. D3 56
Sisian, Arm. C12 44
Siskiyou, co., Ca., U.S. B2 98
Siskiyou Mountains, mts., U.S. F3 130
Siskiyou Pass, Or., U.S. E4 130
Sisŏphŏn, Camb. D4 34
Sisseton, S.D., U.S. B8 134
Sisseton Indian Reservation, U.S. B8 134
Sissiboo, stm., N.S., Can. E4 87
Sisson Branch Reservoir, res., N.B., Can. B2 87
Sissonville, W.V., U.S. C3 141
Sisters, Or., U.S. C5 130
Sistersville, W.V., U.S. B4 141
Sītāpur, India D4 40
Sitasjaure, l., Eur. C7 10
Sitka, Ak., U.S. D12 95
Sitka National Historical Park, Ak., U.S. m22 95
Sitka Sound, strt., Ak., U.S. m22 95
Sittoung, stm., Mya. C3 34
Sittwe, Mya. B2 34
Sivas, Tur. C7 44
Sivers'kyi Donets' see Northern Donets, stm., Eur. E14 20
Sivrihisar, Tur. C4 44
Siwa, Egypt E10 48
Sixian, China C4 30
Sixth Cataract, wtfl., Sudan G11 48
Siyäzän, Azer. B13 44
Siziwang Qi, China A3 30
Sjælland, i., Den. I4 10
Skadovs'k, Ukr. F12 20
Skærbæk, Den. I3 10
Skagen, Den. H4 10
Skagerrak, strt., Eur. B11 12
Skagit, co., Wa., U.S. A4 140
Skagway, Ak., U.S. D12 95
Skamania, co., Wa., U.S. D3 140
Skanderborg, Den. H3 10
Skåne, hist. reg., Swe. I5 10
Skaneateles, N.Y., U.S. C4 125
Skaneateles Lake, l., N.Y., U.S. C4 125
Skārdu, Pak. C11 42
Skarżysko-Kamienna, Pol. D6 20
Skaudvilė, Lith. I10 10
Skaw, The see Grenen, c., Den. H4 10
Skegness, Eng., U.K. D7 12
Skeleton Lake, l., On., Can. B5 89
Skellefteå, Swe. D9 10
Skellefteälven, stm., Swe. D8 10
Skidal', Bela. C8 20
Ski, Nor. G4 10
Skiatook, Ok., U.S. A5 129
Skiatook Reservoir, res., Ok., U.S. A5 129
Skien, Nor. G3 10
Skierniewice, Pol. D6 20
Skihist Mountain, mtn., B.C., Can. D7 85
Skikda, Alg. C6 48
Skillet Fork, stm., Il., U.S. E5 106
Skive, Den. H3 10
Sklad, Russia B14 26
Skokie, Il., U.S. A6 106
Skokomish Indian Reservation, Wa., U.S. B2 140
Skópelos, i., Grc. E9 18
Skopin, Russia C15 20
Skopje, Mac. C8 18
Skövde, Swe. G5 10
Skowhegan, Me., U.S. D3 112
Skull Valley, val., Ut., U.S. C3 137
Skull Valley Indian Reservation, Ut., U.S. C3 137
Skuna, stm., Ms., U.S. B4 117
Skunk, stm., Ia., U.S. D6 108
Skvyra, Ukr. E10 20
Skwentna, stm., Ak., U.S. g15 95
Skye, Island of, i., Scot., U.K. B3 12
Skykomish, stm., Wa., U.S. B4 140
Skyland, N.C., U.S. f10 126
Skyland, Nv., U.S. D2 121
Skyline, Al., U.S. A3 94
Slagnäs, Swe. D8 10
Slamet, Gunung, vol., Indon. E3 36
Slancy, Russia G13 10
Slater, Ia., U.S. C4 108
Slater, Mo., U.S. B4 118
Slater, S.C., U.S. A3 133
Slatersville, R.I., U.S. A3 132
Slatersville Reservoir, res., R.I., U.S. B3 132
Slatina, Rom. G8 20
Slatington, Pa., U.S. E10 131
Slaton, Tx., U.S. C2 136
Slaughter, La., U.S. D4 111
Slautnoe, Russia C18 26
Slave, stm., Can. F17 82
Slave Lake, Ab., Can. B3 84
Slavgorod, Russia D9 26
Slavjanka, Russia B2 31
Slavjansk-na-Kubani, Russia G15 20
Slavonia see Slavonija, hist. reg., Cro. B6 18
Slavonija, hist. reg., Cro. B6 18
Slavonski Brod, Cro. B6 18
Slavuta, Ukr. D9 20
Sławno, Pol. B4 20
Slayton, Mn., U.S. G3 116
Sleeping Bear Dunes National Lakeshore, Mi., U.S. D4 115
Sleeping Bear Point, c., Mi., U.S. D4 115
Sleepy Eye, Mn., U.S. F4 116
Slickville, Pa., U.S. F2 131
Slidell, La., U.S. D6 111
Sliderock Mountain, mtn., Mt., U.S. D3 119
Sligo, Ire. C2 12
Slinger, Wi., U.S. E5 142
Slippery Rock, Pa., U.S. D1 131
Sliven, Blg. C11 18
Sljudjanka, Russia D12 26
Sloan, Ia., U.S. B1 108
Sloan, N.Y., U.S. C2 125
Slobodskoj, Russia D7 26
Slobozia, Mol. F10 20
Slobozia, Rom. G9 20
Slocomb, Al., U.S. D4 94
Slonim, Bela. C8 20
Slope, co., N.D., U.S. C2 127
Slough, Eng., U.K. E6 12
Slovakia, ctry., Eur. E6 20
Slovenia, ctry., Eur. A5 18
Slov'ians'k, Ukr. E14 20
Sluch, stm., Ukr. D9 20
Sluck, Bela. C9 20
Słupsk, Pol. B4 20
Smackover, Ar., U.S. D3 97
Småland, hist. reg., Swe. H6 10
Small Point, c., Me., U.S. g8 112
Smallwood Reservoir, res., N.L., Can. g8 88
Smarhon', Bela. B9 20
Smederevo, Serb. B8 18
Smethport, Pa., U.S. C5 131
Smidovič, Russia B14 28
Šmidta, ostrov, i., Russia A9 26
Smila, Ukr. E11 20
Smith, co., Ks., U.S. C5 109
Smith, co., Ms., U.S. C4 117
Smith, stm., Mt., U.S. D5 119
Smith, co., Tn., U.S. A5 135
Smith, co., Tx., U.S. C5 136
Smith, stm., U.S. D3 139
Smith and Sayles Reservoir, res., R.I., U.S. B2 132
Smith Bay, b., Ak., U.S. A9 95
Smith Canyon, Co., U.S. D7 99
Smith Center, Ks., U.S. C5 109
Smithers, B.C., Can. B4 85
Smithers, W.V., U.S. C3 141
Smithfield, N.C., U.S. B4 126
Smithfield, Pa., U.S. G2 131
Smithfield, Ut., U.S. B4 137
Smithfield, Va., U.S. D6 139
Smith Island, i., Va., U.S. C7 139
Smith Island, i., U.S. D5 113
Smith Mountain Lake, res., Va., U.S. C3 139
Smith Peak, mtn., Id., U.S. A2 105
Smith Point, c., Ma., U.S. D7 114
Smith Point, c., Va., U.S. C6 139
Smiths, Al., U.S. C4 94
Smithsburg, Md., U.S. A2 113
Smiths Falls, On., Can. C8 89
Smiths Grove, Ky., U.S. C3 110
Smithton, Austl. I4 62
Smithton, Il., U.S. E4 106
Smithtown, N.Y., U.S. n15 125
Smithville, Ga., U.S. E2 103
Smithville, Mo., U.S. B3 118
Smithville, Ms., U.S. A5 117
Smithville, Oh., U.S. B4 128
Smithville, Tn., U.S. D8 135
Smithville, Tx., U.S. D4 136
Smithville Lake, res., Mo., U.S. B3 118
Smoke Creek Desert, des., Nv., U.S. C2 121
Smokey, Cape, c., N.S., Can. C9 87
Smokey Dome, mtn., Id., U.S. F4 105
Smoky, stm., Ab., Can. B1 84
Smoky Hill, stm., U.S. D5 109
Smoky Lake, Ab., Can. B4 84
Smoky Mountains, mts., Id., U.S. F4 105
Smøla, i., Nor. E3 10
Smolensk, Russia D5 26
Smoljan, Blg. D10 18
Smooth Rock Falls, On., Can. o19 89
Smoothstone Lake, l., Sk., Can. C2 91
Smyrna see İzmir, Tur. C2 44
Smyrna, stm., De., U.S. C3 101
Smyrna, De., U.S. C3 101
Smyrna, Ga., U.S. C2 103
Smyrna, Tn., U.S. B5 135
Smyth, co., Va., U.S. f10 139
Snake, stm., Mn., U.S. B1 116
Snake, stm., Ne., U.S. B4 120
Snake, stm., U.S. D5 116
Snake, stm., U.S. C4 92
Snake Range, mts., Nv., U.S. E7 121
Snake River Plain, pl., Id., U.S. F2 105
Snake River Range, mts., U.S. C2 143
Sneads, Fl., U.S. B2 102
Sneedville, Tn., U.S. C10 135
Snihurivka, Ukr. F12 20
Snipe Keys, is., Fl., U.S. H5 102
Snøhetta, mtn., Nor. E3 10
Snohomish, co., Wa., U.S. A4 140
Snohomish, Wa., U.S. B3 140
Snoqualmie, Wa., U.S. B4 140
Snoqualmie, stm., Wa., U.S. B4 140
Snoqualmie Pass, Wa., U.S. B4 140
Snøtinden, mtn., Nor. C5 10
Snowbank Lake, l., Mn., U.S. B7 116
Snowdon, mtn., Wales, U.K. D4 12
Snowdrift see Łutselk'e, N.T., Can. F17 82
Snowflake, Az., U.S. C5 96
Snow Hill, Md., U.S. D7 113
Snow Hill, N.C., U.S. B5 126
Snowking Mountain, mtn., Wa., U.S. A4 140
Snow Lake, Mb., Can. B1 86
Snowmass Mountain, mtn., Co., U.S. B3 99
Snow Peak, mtn., Wa., U.S. A7 140
Snowshoe Lake, l., Me., U.S. B4 112
Snowshoe Peak, mtn., Mt., U.S. B1 119
Snow Water Lake, l., Nv., U.S. C7 121
Snowy Mountains, mts., Austl. H4 62
Snowyside Peak, mtn., Id., U.S. F4 105
Snyder, Ok., U.S. C3 129
Snyder, co., Pa., U.S. E7 131
Snyder, Tx., U.S. C2 136
Soacha, Col. E5 80
Soalala, Madag. B8 56
Soap Lake, Wa., U.S. B6 140
Sobradinho, Represa de, res., Braz. D3 74
Sobral, Braz. B3 74
Socastee, S.C., U.S. D9 133
Soči, Russia E5 26
Social Circle, Ga., U.S. C3 103
Société, Archipel de la (Society Islands), is., Fr. Poly. F14 58
Society Hill, S.C., U.S. B8 133
Society Islands see Société, Archipel de la, is., Fr. Poly. F14 58
Socorro, Col. B5 70
Socorro, N.M., U.S. C3 124
Socorro, co., N.M., U.S. D2 124
Socorro, Isla, i., Mex. D2 78
Socotra see Suquṭrā, i., Yemen H6 38
Soc Trang, Viet. E5 34
Sodankylä, Fin. C12 10
Soda Springs, Id., U.S. G7 105
Soddy-Daisy, Tn., U.S. D8 135
Söderköping, Swe. G7 10
Södertälje, Swe. G7 10
Sodo, Eth. B7 54
Sodus, N.Y., U.S. B3 125
Soe, Indon. E6 36
Sofala, Moz. C5 56
Sofia see Sofija, Blg. C9 18
Sofija, Blg. C9 18
Sogamoso, Col. D5 80
Sognefjorden, b., Nor. F1 10
Sog Xian, China E6 28
Sointula, B.C., Can. D4 85
Soissons, Fr. C8 16
Sojat, India D2 40
Šojna, Russia A7 22
Söke, Tur. D2 44
Sokodé, Togo E5 50
Sokol, Russia C7 22
Sokol, Russia B14 26
Sokółka, Pol. C7 20
Sokolo, Mali D3 50
Sokoto, Nig. D6 50
Sokoto, stm., Nig. D5 50
Solai, Kenya C7 54
Solana, Fl., U.S. F5 102
Solano, Phil. C8 34
Solano, co., Ca., U.S. C3 98
Solāpur, India F3 40
Soldier, stm., Ia., U.S. C2 108
Soldier Key, i., Fl., U.S. s3 102
Soldotna, Ak., U.S. g16 95
Soledad, Col. A5 70
Soledad, Ca., U.S. D3 98
Soledad Díez Gutiérrez, Mex. C4 78
Solikamsk, Russia D7 26
Sol'-Ileck, Russia D10 22
Solimões see Amazon, stm., S.A. D6 70
Sollefteå, Swe. E7 10
Sóller, Spain H8 16
Šologoncy, Russia C13 26
Solomon, Ks., U.S. D6 109
Solomon, stm., Ks., U.S. C6 109
Solomon Basin I18 64
Solomon Islands, ctry., Oc. B6 62
Solomons, Md., U.S. D5 113
Solomon Sea, Oc. B5 62
Solon, China B12 28
Solon, Ia., U.S. C6 108
Solon, Oh., U.S. A4 128
Solothurn, Switz. A1 18
Solov'evsk, Russia A11 28
Solvay, N.Y., U.S. B4 125
Solway Firth, b., U.K. C5 12
Solwezi, Zam. A4 56
Soma, Tur. C2 44
Somabhula, Zimb. B4 56
Somalia, ctry., Afr. I14 46
Somali Basin H8 64
Sombor, Serb. B7 18
Sombrerete, Mex. C4 78
Sombrero Channel, strt., India H6 40
Somerdale, N.J., U.S. D2 123
Somers, Ct., U.S. B6 100
Somers, Mt., U.S. B2 119
Somerset, Mb., Can. E2 86
Somerset, Ky., U.S. C5 110
Somerset, Ma., U.S. C5 114
Somerset, co., Md., U.S. D6 113
Somerset, co., Me., U.S. C2 112
Somerset, N.J., U.S. B3 123
Somerset, co., N.J., U.S. B3 123
Somerset, Oh., U.S. C3 128
Somerset, Pa., U.S. F3 131
Somerset, co., Pa., U.S. G3 131
Somerset, Tx., U.S. k7 136
Somerset, Wi., U.S. C1 142
Somerset East, S. Afr. E4 56
Somerset Reservoir, res., Vt., U.S. E3 138
Somers Point, N.J., U.S. E3 123
Somersville, Ct., U.S. B6 100
Somersworth, N.H., U.S. D5 122
Somerton, Az., U.S. E1 96
Somervell, co., Tx., U.S. C4 136
Somerville, Ma., U.S. B5 114
Somerville, N.J., U.S. B3 123
Somerville, Tn., U.S. B2 135
Somerville, Tx., U.S. D4 136
Somerville Lake, res., Tx., U.S. D4 136
Somonauk, Il., U.S. B5 106
Son, stm., India E4 40
Sønderborg, Den. I3 10
Søndre Strømfjord, Grnld. E29 82
Søndre Strømfjord, b., Grnld. E29 82
Sondrio, Italy A2 18
Sonepur, India E4 40
Song, Nig. E7 50
Song Cau, Viet. D5 34
Songea, Tan. F7 54
Songhua, stm., China B14 28
Songhua Hu, res., China C13 28
Songkhla, Thai. E4 34
Songnim, N. Kor. D13 28
Songololo, D.R.C. E2 54
Songpan, China C1 30
Sonid Youqi, China C10 28
Sonīpat, India D3 40
Sonkël', ozero, l., Kyrg. A3 40
Son La, Viet. B4 34
Sonmiāni Bay, b., Pak. E9 42
Sonneberg, Ger. E12 12
Sonoma, co., Ca., U.S. C2 98
Sonoma, Ca., U.S. C2 98
Sonoma Peak, mtn., Nv., U.S. C4 121
Sonoma Range, mts., Nv., U.S. C4 121
Sonora, stm., Mex. B2 78
Sonora, state, Mex. B2 78
Sonora, Ca., U.S. D3 98
Sonora, Tx., U.S. D2 136
Sonoran Desert, des., N.A. E5 92
Sonoyta, Mex. A2 78
Sonqor, Iran E12 44
Sonsón, Col. D4 80
Sonsonate, El Sal. C1 80
Sonsorol Islands, is., Palau E9 32
Son Tay, Viet. B5 34
Sonthofen, Ger. G12 12
Soochow see Suzhou, China E12 28
Soperton, Ga., U.S. D4 103
Sophia, W.V., U.S. D3 141
Sopot, Pol. B5 20
Sopron, Hung. F4 20
Sopur, India C2 40
Sorel, Qc., Can. C4 90
Sorgun, Tur. C6 44
Soria, Spain G5 16
Soroca, Mol. E10 20
Sorocaba, Braz. F2 74
Soročinsk, Russia D9 22
Sorong, Indon. D8 36
Soroti, Ug. C6 54
Sørøya, i., Nor. A10 10
Sorrento, La., U.S. D5 111
Sør Rondane Mountains, mts., Ant. D7 67
Sorsele, Swe. D7 10
Sorsogon, Phil. D8 34
Sort, Spain F7 16
Sortavala, Russia F14 10
Sosnogorsk, Russia B9 22
Sosnovka, Russia A7 22
Sosnovo-Ozërskoe, Russia A10 28
Sosnowiec, Pol. D5 20
Sos'va, Russia B11 22
Sotouboua, Togo E5 50
Soubré, C. Iv. E3 50
Soucook, stm., N.H., U.S. D4 122
Soudan, Mn., U.S. C6 116
Souderton, Pa., U.S. F11 131
Souhegan, stm., N.H., U.S. E3 122
Sŏul (Seoul), S. Kor. D13 28
Souq Ahras, Alg. F1 18
Sources, Mont-aux-, mtn., Afr. D4 56
Soure, Braz. B2 74
Souris, Mb., Can. E1 86
Souris, P.E., Can. C7 87
Souris, stm., N.A. B7 92
Sousa, Braz. C4 74
Sousse, Tun. C7 48
South, stm., Ia., U.S. C4 108
South, stm., N.C., U.S. C4 126
South Acton, Ma., U.S. g10 114
South Africa, ctry., Afr. E3 56
South Amboy, N.J., U.S. C4 123
South America, cont. G9 4
South Amherst, Ma., U.S. B2 114
South Amherst, Oh., U.S. A3 128
Southampton, On., Can. C3 89
Southampton, Eng., U.K. E6 12
Southampton, N.Y., U.S. n16 125
Southampton, co., Va., U.S. D5 139
South Andaman, i., India G6 40
South Anna, stm., Va., U.S. C5 139
South Australia, state, Austl. F5 60
South Australian Basin L16 64
Southaven, Ms., U.S. A3 117
South Bald Mountain, mtn., Co., U.S. A5 99
South Baldy, mtn., N.M., U.S. D2 124
South Barre, Vt., U.S. C3 138
South Bay, Fl., U.S. F6 102
South Beloit, Il., U.S. A4 106
South Bend, In., U.S. A5 107
South Bend, Wa., U.S. C2 140
South Berwick, Me., U.S. E2 112
South Bloomfield, Oh., U.S. C3 128
South Boston, Va., U.S. D4 139
South Bound Brook, N.J., U.S. B3 123
South Branch Lake, l., Me., U.S. C4 112
Southbridge, Ma., U.S. B3 114

Name	Map Ref.	Page
South Bristol, Me., U.S.	E3	112
South Britain, Ct., U.S.	D3	100
South Broadway, Wa., U.S.	C5	140
South Burlington, Vt., U.S.	C2	138
Southbury, Ct., U.S.	D3	100
South Carolina, state, U.S.	D6	133
South Charleston, Oh., U.S.	C2	128
South Charleston, W.V., U.S.	C3	141
South Chicago Heights, Il., U.S.	m9	106
South China Basin	G14	64
South China Sea, Asia	D5	32
South Coffeyville, Ok., U.S.	A6	129
South Congaree, S.C., U.S.	D5	133
South Connellsville, Pa., U.S.	G2	131
South Dakota, state, U.S.	C5	134
South Dartmouth, Ma., U.S.	C6	114
South Daytona, Fl., U.S.	C5	102
South Deerfield, Ma., U.S.	B2	114
South Dennis, Ma., U.S.	C7	114
South Duxbury, Ma., U.S.	B6	114
South East Cape, c., Austl.	I4	62
Southeast Cape, c., Ak., U.S.	C6	95
Southeast Indian Ridge	M13	64
South Easton, Ma., U.S.	B5	114
Southeast Pacific Basin	O25	64
Southeast Pass, strt., La., U.S.	E7	111
South East Point, c., Austl.	H4	62
Southeast Point, c., R.I., U.S.	h7	132
South Elgin, Il., U.S.	B5	106
Southend-on-Sea, Eng., U.K.	E7	12
Southern Alps, mts., N.Z.	p13	63c
Southern Cook Islands, is., Cook Is.	F13	58
Southern Cross, Austl.	G2	60
Southern Indian Lake, l., Mb., Can.	f8	86
Southern Ocean	C3	67
Southern Pines, N.C., U.S.	B3	126
Southern Ute Indian Reservation, Co., U.S.	D2	99
South Euclid, Oh., U.S.	g9	128
Southey, Sk., Can.	G3	91
South Fabius, stm., Mo., U.S.	A5	118
South Fallsburg, N.Y., U.S.	D6	125
Southfield, Mi., U.S.	o15	115
South Fiji Basin	K20	64
South Fork, Pa., U.S.	F4	131
South Fox Island, i., Mi., U.S.	C5	115
South Fulton, Tn., U.S.	A3	135
South Gastonia, N.C., U.S.	B1	126
South Gate, Ca., U.S.	n12	98
Southgate, Ky., U.S.	h14	110
Southgate, Mi., U.S.	p15	115
South Georgia, i., S. Geor.	H9	69
South Glastonbury, Ct., U.S.	C5	100
South Glens Falls, N.Y., U.S.	B7	125
South Grafton, Ma., U.S.	B4	114
South Grand, stm., Mo., U.S.	C3	118
South Hadley, Ma., U.S.	B2	114
South Hadley Falls, Ma., U.S.	B2	114
South Hamilton, Ma., U.S.	A6	114
South Haven, In., U.S.	A3	107
South Haven, Mi., U.S.	F4	115
South Hero Island, i., Vt., U.S.	B2	138
South Hill, Va., U.S.	D4	139
South Hingham, Ma., U.S.	h12	114
South Holland, Il., U.S.	k9	106
South Holston Lake, res., U.S.	A9	135
South Honshu Ridge	E16	64
South Hooksett, N.H., U.S.	D4	122
South Hopkinton, R.I., U.S.	F1	132
South Houston, Tx., U.S.	r14	136
South Hutchinson, Ks., U.S.	f11	109
South Indian Basin	N12	64
South Indian Lake, Mb., Can.	A2	86
Southington, Ct., U.S.	C4	100
South International Falls, Mn., U.S.	B5	116
South Island, i., N.Z.	I10	58
South Island, i., S.C., U.S.	E9	133
South Jacksonville, Il., U.S.	D3	106
South Jordan, Ut., U.S.	C3	137
South Kenosha, Wi., U.S.	F6	142
South Korea see Korea, South, ctry., Asia	D10	28
South Lake Tahoe, Ca., U.S.	C4	98
South Lancaster, Ma., U.S.	B4	114
South Lebanon, Oh., U.S.	C1	128
South Lyon, Mi., U.S.	F7	115
South Magnetic Pole	C18	67
South Manitou Island, i., Mi., U.S.	C4	115
South Marsh Island, i., Md., U.S.	D5	113
South Miami, Fl., U.S.	G6	102
South Miami Heights, Fl., U.S.	s13	102
South Mills, N.C., U.S.	A6	126
South Milwaukee, Wi., U.S.	F6	142
Southmont, N.C., U.S.	B2	126
South Moose Lake, l., Mb., Can.	C1	86
South Mountain, mtn., Id., U.S.	G2	105
South Mountain, mtn., N.M., U.S.	k8	124
South Mountains, mts., Az., U.S.	m8	96
South Mountains, mts., N.C., U.S.	B1	126
South New River Canal, Fl., U.S.	r3	102
South Ogden, Ut., U.S.	B4	137
Southold, N.Y., U.S.	m16	125
South Orange, N.J., U.S.	B4	123
South Orkney Islands, is., Ant.	C36	67
South Paris, Me., U.S.	D2	112
South Park, val., Co., U.S.	B5	99
South Pass, strt., La., U.S.	F6	111
South Pass, Wy., U.S.	D4	143
South Patrick Shores, Fl., U.S.	D6	102
South Pekin, Il., U.S.	C4	106
South Pittsburg, Tn., U.S.	D8	135
South Plainfield, N.J., U.S.	B4	123
South Platte, stm., U.S.	C7	92
South Point, c., Mi., U.S.	D7	115
Southport (Gold Coast), Austl.	F5	62
Southport, Fl., U.S.	u16	102
Southport, In., U.S.	E5	107
Southport, N.C., U.S.	D4	126
Southport, N.Y., U.S.	C4	125
South Portland, Me., U.S.	E2	112
South Portsmouth, Ky., U.S.	B6	110
South Range, Mi., U.S.	A2	115
South River, On., Can.	B5	89
South River, b., Md., U.S.	C4	113
South River, N.J., U.S.	C4	123
South Royalton, Vt., U.S.	D3	138
South Saint Paul, Mn., U.S.	n12	116
South Sandwich Islands, is., S. Geor.	B2	67
South Sandwich Trench	N11	66
South San Francisco, Ca., U.S.	h8	98
South Shetland Islands, is., Ant.	B35	67
Southside, Al., U.S.	B3	94
Southside Place, Tx., U.S.	r14	136
South Sioux City, Ne., U.S.	B9	120
South Skunk, stm., Ia., U.S.	C4	108
South Streator, Il., U.S.	B5	106
South Taranaki Bight, b., N.Z.	o13	63c
South Tasman Rise	M17	64
South Toms River, N.J., U.S.	D4	123
South Torrington, Wy., U.S.	D8	143
South Tucson, Az., U.S.	E5	96
South Venice, Fl., U.S.	E4	102
South Ventana Cone, vol., Ca., U.S.	D3	98
South Waverly, Pa., U.S.	C8	131
South Wellfleet, Ma., U.S.	C8	114
South Wellington, B.C., Can.	f12	85
South Wenatchee, Wa., U.S.	B5	140
South West Africa see Namibia, ctry., Afr.	C2	56
South West Cape, c., N.Z.	q12	63c
Southwest Channel, strt., Fl., U.S.	E4	102
South West City, Mo., U.S.	E3	118
Southwest Harbor, Me., U.S.	D4	112
Southwest Head, c., N.B., Can.	E3	87
Southwest Indian Ridge	L8	64
Southwest Miramichi, stm., N.B., Can.	C3	87
Southwest Pacific Basin	L23	64
Southwest Pass, strt., La., U.S.	E3	111
Southwest Pass, strt., La., U.S.	F6	111
Southwest Point, c., R.I., U.S.	h7	132
South Weymouth Naval Air Station, mil., Ma., U.S.	h12	114
South Whitley, In., U.S.	B6	107
South Williamson, Ky., U.S.	C7	110
South Williamsport, Pa., U.S.	D7	131
South Windham, Ct., U.S.	C7	100
South Windham, Me., U.S.	E2	112
South Windsor, Ct., U.S.	B5	100
Southwood Acres, Ct., U.S.	A5	100
South Woodstock, Ct., U.S.	B8	100
South Yarmouth, Ma., U.S.	C7	114
South Zanesville, Oh., U.S.	C3	128
Sovetsk, Russia	C8	22
Sovetsk, Russia	I9	10
Sovetskaja Gavan', Russia	E16	26
Sovietskyi, Ukr.	G13	20
Soyo, Ang.	E2	54
Sozh, stm., Eur.	C11	20
Spain, ctry., Eur.	H5	16
Spalding, co., Ga., U.S.	C2	103
Spanaway, Wa., U.S.	B3	140
Spangler, Pa., U.S.	E4	131
Spaniard's Bay, N.L., Can.	E5	88
Spanish Fork, Ut., U.S.	C4	137
Spanish Fort, Al., U.S.	E2	94
Spanish Lake, Mo., U.S.	f13	118
Spanish Peak, mtn., Or., U.S.	C7	130
Spanish Sahara see Western Sahara, dep., Afr.	B2	50
Spanish Town, Jam.	B4	80
Sparks, Ga., U.S.	E3	103
Sparks, Nv., U.S.	D2	121
Sparta, Ga., U.S.	C4	103
Sparta, Il., U.S.	E4	106
Sparta, Mi., U.S.	E5	115
Sparta, Mo., U.S.	D4	118
Sparta, N.C., U.S.	A1	126
Sparta (Lake Mohawk), N.J., U.S.	A3	123
Sparta, Tn., U.S.	D8	135
Sparta, Wi., U.S.	E3	142
Spartanburg, S.C., U.S.	B4	133
Spartanburg, co., S.C., U.S.	B3	133
Spárti, Grc.	F9	18
Spartivento, Capo, c., Italy	E2	18
Sparwood, B.C., Can.	E10	85
Spassk-Dal'nij, Russia	E15	26
Spavinaw Creek, stm., Ok., U.S.	A7	129
Spear, Cape, c., N.L., Can.	E5	88
Spearfish, S.D., U.S.	C2	134
Spearman, Tx., U.S.	A2	136
Spearville, Ks., U.S.	E4	109
Speed, In., U.S.	H6	107
Speedway, In., U.S.	E5	107
Speke Gulf, b., Tan.	D6	54
Spence Bay see Taloyoak, N.T., Can.	E21	82
Spencer, Ia., U.S.	A2	108
Spencer, In., U.S.	F4	107
Spencer, co., In., U.S.	H4	107
Spencer, co., Ky., U.S.	B4	110
Spencer, Ma., U.S.	B4	114
Spencer, N.C., U.S.	B2	126
Spencer, Tn., U.S.	D8	135
Spencer, Wi., U.S.	D3	142
Spencer, W.V., U.S.	C3	141
Spencer, Cape, c., Austl.	H2	62
Spencer, Cape, c., Ak., U.S.	k21	95
Spencer Gulf, b., Austl.	G2	62
Spencer Lake, l., Me., U.S.	C2	112
Spencerport, N.Y., U.S.	B3	125
Spencerville, Md., U.S.	B4	113
Spencerville, Oh., U.S.	B1	128
Sperry, Ok., U.S.	A6	129
Spesutie Island, i., Md., U.S.	B5	113
Speyer, Ger.	F11	12
Spezia see La Spezia, Italy	B2	18
Spiceland, In., U.S.	E7	107
Spicer, Mn., U.S.	E4	116
Spider Lake, l., Wi., U.S.	B2	142
Spindale, N.C., U.S.	B1	126
Spink, co., S.D., U.S.	C7	134
Spirit Lake, Ia., U.S.	A2	108
Spirit Lake, l., Ia., U.S.	A2	108
Spirit Lake, Id., U.S.	B2	105
Spirit Lake, l., Wa., U.S.	C3	140
Spirit River, Ab., Can.	B1	84
Spirit River Flowage, res., Wi., U.S.	C4	142
Spiro, Ok., U.S.	B7	129
Spišská Nová Ves, Slvk.	E6	20
Spitsbergen, i., Nor.	B3	26
Spittal an der Drau, Aus.	G13	12
Split, Cro.	C6	18
Split, Cape, c., N.S., Can.	D5	87
Split Lake, l., Mb., Can.	A4	86
Split Rock Creek, stm., U.S.	G2	116
Spofford Lake, l., N.H., U.S.	E2	122
Spokane, Wa., U.S.	B8	140
Spokane, co., Wa., U.S.	B8	140
Spokane, stm., U.S.	B8	140
Spokane, Mount, mtn., Wa., U.S.	B8	140
Spokane Indian Reservation, Wa., U.S.	B8	140
Spoleto, Italy	C4	18
Spoon, stm., Il., U.S.	C3	106
Spooner, Wi., U.S.	C2	142
Spooner Lake, l., Wi., U.S.	C2	142
Spornoe, Russia	C17	26
Spotswood, N.J., U.S.	C4	123
Spotsylvania, co., Va., U.S.	B5	139
Sprague, stm., Or., U.S.	E5	130
Sprague, W.V., U.S.	n13	141
Sprague Lake, l., Wa., U.S.	B7	140
Spratly Islands, is., Asia	E6	34
Spring, stm., Ar., U.S.	A4	97
Spring Arbor, Mi., U.S.	F6	115
Spring Bay, b., Ut., U.S.	B3	137
Springbok, S. Afr.	D2	56
Springboro, Oh., U.S.	C1	128
Spring Brook, stm., Pa., U.S.	n18	131
Spring City, Pa., U.S.	F10	131
Spring City, Tn., U.S.	D9	135
Spring City, Ut., U.S.	D4	137
Spring Creek, stm., N.D., U.S.	B3	127
Spring Creek, stm., Nv., U.S.	C4	121
Spring Creek, stm., U.S.	D4	120
Springdale, N.L., Can.	D3	88
Springdale, Ar., U.S.	A1	97
Springdale, Oh., U.S.	n13	128
Springdale, Pa., U.S.	E2	131
Springdale, S.C., U.S.	D5	133
Springer, N.M., U.S.	A5	124
Springerville, Az., U.S.	C6	96
Springfield, Co., U.S.	D8	99
Springfield, Fl., U.S.	u16	102
Springfield, Ga., U.S.	D5	103
Springfield, Il., U.S.	D4	106
Springfield, Ky., U.S.	C4	110
Springfield, Ma., U.S.	B2	114
Springfield, Mn., U.S.	F4	116
Springfield, Mo., U.S.	D4	118
Springfield, Ne., U.S.	C9	120
Springfield, N.J., U.S.	B4	123
Springfield, Oh., U.S.	C2	128
Springfield, Or., U.S.	C4	130
Springfield, Pa., U.S.	p20	131
Springfield, S.D., U.S.	E8	134
Springfield, Tn., U.S.	A5	135
Springfield, Va., U.S.	g12	139
Springfield, Vt., U.S.	E4	138
Springfield, Lake, res., Il., U.S.	D4	106
Springfontein, S. Afr.	E4	56
Spring Garden, Guy.	B8	70
Spring Glen, Ut., U.S.	D5	137
Spring Green, Wi., U.S.	E3	142
Spring Grove, Il., U.S.	h8	106
Spring Grove, Mn., U.S.	G7	116
Spring Grove, Pa., U.S.	G8	131
Spring Hill, Fl., U.S.	D4	102
Spring Hill, Ks., U.S.	D9	109
Springhill, La., U.S.	A2	111
Spring Hill, Tn., U.S.	B5	135
Spring Hope, N.C., U.S.	B4	126
Spring Island, i., S.C., U.S.	G6	133
Spring Lake, l., Me., U.S.	C2	112
Spring Lake, Mi., U.S.	E4	115
Spring Lake, N.C., U.S.	B4	126
Spring Lake, N.J., U.S.	C4	123
Spring Lake, res., U.S.	B3	106
Spring Lake Heights, N.J., U.S.	C4	123
Spring Mountains, mts., Nv., U.S.	G6	121
Springport, Mi., U.S.	F6	115
Springs, S. Afr.	D4	56
Springside, Sk., Can.	F4	91
Springsure, Austl.	E4	62
Springvale, Me., U.S.	E2	112
Spring Valley, Ca., U.S.	o16	98
Spring Valley, Il., U.S.	B4	106
Spring Valley, Mn., U.S.	G6	116
Spring Valley, N.Y., U.S.	g12	125
Spring Valley, Wi., U.S.	D1	142
Springville, Al., U.S.	B3	94
Springville, Ia., U.S.	B6	108
Springville, N.Y., U.S.	C2	125
Springville, Ut., U.S.	C4	137
Spruce Fork, stm., W.V., U.S.	m12	141
Spruce Grove, Ab., Can.	C4	84
Spruce Knob, mtn., W.V., U.S.	C6	141
Spruce Knob-Seneca Rocks National Recreation Area, W.V., U.S.	C5	141
Spruce Mountain, mtn., Az., U.S.	C3	96
Spruce Mountain, mtn., Nv., U.S.	C7	121
Spruce Pine, N.C., U.S.	f10	126
Spruce Run Reservoir, res., N.J., U.S.	B3	123
Spur, Tx., U.S.	C2	136
Spurr, Mount, mtn., Ak., U.S.	g15	95
Squam Lake, l., N.H., U.S.	C4	122
Squapan Lake, l., Me., U.S.	B4	112
Square Lake, l., Me., U.S.	A4	112
Squatec, Qc., Can.	B9	90
Squaw Cap Mountain, mtn., N.B., Can.	B3	87
Squaw Hill, mtn., Wy., U.S.	E7	143
Squaw Peak, mtn., Mt., U.S.	C2	119
Squibnocket Point, c., Ma., U.S.	D6	114
Squillace, Golfo di, b., Italy	E6	18
Squire, W.V., U.S.	D3	141
Srbija (Serbia), state, Serb.	B8	18
Srbobran, Serb.	B7	18
Sredinnyj hrebet, mts., Russia	D17	26
Srednee Kujto, ozero, l., Russia	D14	10
Srednekolymsk, Russia	C17	26
Srednerusskaja vozvyšennost', plat., Russia	D5	26
Srednesibirskoe ploskogor'e, plat., Russia	C12	26
Śrem, Pol.	C4	20
Sremska Mitrovica, Serb.	B7	18
Sretensk, Russia	D13	26
Sri Jayewardenepura Kotte, Sri L.	H4	40
Srīkākulam, India	F4	40
Sri Kālahasti, India	G3	40
Sri Lanka, ctry., Asia	H4	40
Srīnagar, India	C2	40
Stack Reservoir, res., R.I., U.S.	C3	132
Stade, Ger.	D11	12
Stafford, Eng., U.K.	D5	12
Stafford, Ks., U.S.	E5	109
Stafford, co., Ks., U.S.	D5	109
Stafford, Va., U.S.	B5	139
Stafford, co., Va., U.S.	B5	139
Stafford Pond, l., R.I., U.S.	D6	132
Stafford Springs, Ct., U.S.	B6	100
Staked Plain see Estacado, Llano, pl., U.S.	E7	92
Stakhanov, Ukr.	E15	20
Stalin see Varna, Blg.	C11	18
Stalingrad see Volgograd, Russia	E6	26
Stalinogorsk see Novomoskovsk, Russia	D5	26
Stalinsk see Novokuzneck, Russia	D10	26
Stalowa Wola, Pol.	D7	20
Stambaugh, Mi., U.S.	B2	115
Stamford, Ct., U.S.	E1	100
Stamford, Tx., U.S.	C3	136
Stamford, Vt., U.S.	F2	138
Stamford, Lake, res., Tx., U.S.	C3	136
Stamping Ground, Ky., U.S.	B5	110
Stampriet, Nmb.	C2	56
Stamps, Ar., U.S.	D2	97
Stanaford, W.V., U.S.	D3	141
Stanberry, Mo., U.S.	A3	118
Standerton, S. Afr.	D4	56
Standing Rock Indian Reservation, U.S.	B4	134
Standish, Mi., U.S.	E7	115
Stanfield, Az., U.S.	E3	96
Stanfield, Or., U.S.	B7	130
Stanford, Ky., U.S.	C5	110
Stanhope, N.J., U.S.	B3	123
Stanislaus, co., Ca., U.S.	D3	98
Stanley, Falk. Is.	H5	69
Stanley, N.C., U.S.	B1	126
Stanley, N.D., U.S.	A3	127
Stanley, co., S.D., U.S.	C5	134
Stanley, Va., U.S.	B4	139
Stanley, Wi., U.S.	D3	142
Stanley Falls, wtfl., D.R.C.	C5	54
Stanley Reservoir, res., India	G3	40
Stanleytown, Va., U.S.	D3	139
Stanleyville, N.C., U.S.	A2	126
Stanly, co., N.C., U.S.	B2	126
Stanovoe nagor'e, mts., Russia	D13	26
Stanovoj hrebet, mts., Russia	D14	26
Stanovoy Mountains see Stanovoe nagor'e, mts., Russia	D13	26
Stanstead, Qc., Can.	D5	90
Stanthorpe, Austl.	F5	62
Stanton, Ia., U.S.	D2	108
Stanton, co., Ks., U.S.	E2	109
Stanton, Ky., U.S.	C6	110
Stanton, Mi., U.S.	E5	115
Stanton, Ne., U.S.	C8	120
Stanton, co., Ne., U.S.	C8	120
Stanton, Tx., U.S.	C2	136
Stantonsburg, N.C., U.S.	B5	126
Stanwood, Ia., U.S.	C6	108
Stanwood, Wa., U.S.	A3	140
Staples, Mn., U.S.	D4	116
Stapleton, Al., U.S.	E2	94
Star, Id., U.S.	F2	105
Star, N.C., U.S.	B3	126
Staraja Russa, Russia	C5	22
Stara Planina (Balkan Mountains), mts., Eur.	C9	18
Stara Zagora, Blg.	C10	18
Starbuck, i., Kir.	E14	58
Starbuck, Mn., U.S.	E3	116
Star City, Ar., U.S.	D4	97
Star City, W.V., U.S.	B5	141
Stargard Szczeciński, Pol.	C3	20
Stargo, Az., U.S.	D6	96
Stark, co., Il., U.S.	B4	106
Stark, co., N.D., U.S.	C3	127
Stark, co., Oh., U.S.	B4	128
Starke, Fl., U.S.	C4	102
Starke, co., In., U.S.	B4	107
Starks, La., U.S.	D2	111
Starkville, Ms., U.S.	B5	117
Star Lake, l., Mn., U.S.	D3	116
Starobil's'k, Ukr.	E15	20
Starodub, Russia	C12	20
Starogard Gdański, Pol.	C5	20
Star Peak, mtn., Nv., U.S.	C3	121
Starr, co., Tx., U.S.	F3	136
Startex, S.C., U.S.	B3	133
Staryj Oskol, Russia	D5	26
State Center, Ia., U.S.	B4	108
State College, Pa., U.S.	E6	131
Stateline, Nv., U.S.	E2	121
State Line, Pa., U.S.	G6	131
Staten Island see Estados, Isla de los, i., Arg.	H4	69
Staten Island, i., N.Y., U.S.	k12	125
Statenville, Ga., U.S.	F4	103
Statesboro, Ga., U.S.	D5	103
Statesville, N.C., U.S.	B2	126
Statham, Ga., U.S.	C3	103
Statue of Liberty National Monument, N.J., U.S.	k8	123
Staunton, Il., U.S.	D4	106
Staunton, Va., U.S.	B3	139
Staunton, stm., Va., U.S.	D12	92
Stavanger, Nor.	G1	10
Stavropol see Toljatti, Russia	D6	26
Stavropol', Russia	E6	26
Stawell, Austl.	H3	62
Stayner, On., Can.	C4	89
Stayton, Or., U.S.	C4	130
Steamboat, Nv., U.S.	D2	121

Name — Map Ref. — Page

Steamboat Mountain, mtn., Mt., U.S. C4 119
Steamboat Mountain, mtn., Wy., U.S. E4 143
Steamboat Springs, Co., U.S. A4 99
Stearns, Ky., U.S. D5 110
Stearns, co., Mn., U.S. E4 116
Stearns Brook, stm., N.H., U.S. A4 122
Stebbins, Ak., U.S. C7 95
Steele, Al., U.S. B3 94
Steele, co., Mn., U.S. F5 116
Steele, Mo., U.S. E8 118
Steele, N.D., U.S. C6 127
Steele, co., N.D., U.S. B8 127
Steele, Mount, mtn., Wy., U.S. E6 143
Steeleville, Il., U.S. E4 106
Steelton, Pa., U.S. F8 131
Steelville, Mo., U.S. D6 118
Steens Mountain, mts., Or., U.S. E8 130
Stefanie, Lake, l., Afr. C7 54
Steger, Il., U.S. B6 106
Steilacoom, Wa., U.S. f10 140
Steinbach, Mb., Can. E3 86
Steinhatchee, stm., Fl., U.S. C3 102
Steinkjer, Nor. E4 10
Steinkopf, S. Afr. D2 56
Stellenbosch, S. Afr. E2 56
Stendal, Ger. D12 12
Stepanakert see Xankändi, Azer. C12 44
Stephen, Mn., U.S. B2 116
Stephens, Ar., U.S. D2 97
Stephens, co., Ga., U.S. B3 103
Stephens, co., Ok., U.S. C4 129
Stephens, co., Tx., U.S. C3 136
Stephens City, Va., U.S. A4 139
Stephens Lake, res., Mb., Can. A4 86
Stephenson, co., Il., U.S. A4 106
Stephenson, Mi., U.S. C3 115
Stephens Passage, strt., Ak., U.S. m23 95
Stephenville, N.L., Can. D2 88
Stephenville, Tx., U.S. C3 136
Stephenville Crossing, N.L., Can. D2 88
Sterkstroom, S. Afr. E4 56
Sterling, Ak., U.S. g16 95
Sterling, Co., U.S. A7 99
Sterling, Il., U.S. B4 106
Sterling, Ks., U.S. D5 109
Sterling, Ok., U.S. C3 129
Sterling, co., Tx., U.S. D2 136
Sterling, Va., U.S. A5 139
Sterling City, Tx., U.S. D2 136
Sterling Heights, Mi., U.S. o15 115
Sterling Reservoir, res., Co., U.S. A7 99
Sterlington, La., U.S. B3 111
Sterlitamak, Russia D7 26
Stettler, Ab., Can. C4 84
Steuben, co., In., U.S. A7 107
Steuben, co., N.Y., U.S. C3 125
Steubenville, Oh., U.S. B5 128
Stevens, co., Ks., U.S. E2 109
Stevens, co., Mn., U.S. E3 116
Stevens, co., Wa., U.S. A7 140
Stevens Creek Dam, U.S. C4 103
Stevenson, Al., U.S. A4 94
Stevenson, Ct., U.S. D3 100
Stevenson, Wa., U.S. D4 140
Stevenson Lake, l., Mb., Can. C4 86
Stevens Pass, Wa., U.S. B4 140
Stevens Peak, mtn., Id., U.S. B3 105
Stevens Point, Wi., U.S. D4 142
Stevensville, Md., U.S. C5 113
Stevensville, Mi., U.S. F4 115
Stevensville, Mt., U.S. D2 119
Stewart, co., Ga., U.S. D2 103
Stewart, co., Tn., U.S. A4 135
Stewart Island, i., N.Z. q12 63c
Stewart Mountain, mtn., Az., U.S. k9 96
Stewartstown, Pa., U.S. G8 131
Stewartsville, Mo., U.S. B3 118
Stewartville, Mn., U.S. G6 116
Stewiacke, N.S., Can. D6 87
Steyr, Aus. F14 12
Stigler, Ok., U.S. B6 129
Stikine, stm., Ak., U.S. D13 95
Still, stm., Ct., U.S. B3 100
Stillaguamish, North Fork, stm., Wa., U.S. A4 140
Stillaguamish, South Fork, stm., Wa., U.S. A4 140
Stillhouse Hollow Lake, res., Tx., U.S. D4 136
Stillman Valley, Il., U.S. A4 106
Stillmore, Ga., U.S. D4 103
Stillwater, Mn., U.S. E6 116
Stillwater, co., Mt., U.S. E7 119
Stillwater, Ok., U.S. A4 129
Stillwater Range, mts., Nv., U.S. D3 121
Stillwater Reservoir, res., N.Y., U.S. B5 125
Stillwater Reservoir, res., R.I., U.S. B3 132
Stilwell, Ok., U.S. B7 129
Stimson, Mount, mtn., Mt., U.S. B3 119
Stine Mountain, mtn., Mt., U.S. E3 119
Stinking Lake, l., N.M., U.S. A3 124
Stinnett, Tx., U.S. B2 136
Štip, Mac. D9 18
Stirling, Austl. E5 60
Stirling, Austl. G2 60
Stirling, Ab., Can. E4 84
Stirling, On., Can. C7 89
Stockbridge, Ga., U.S. C2 103
Stockbridge, Mi., U.S. F6 115
Stockbridge-Munsee Indian Reservation, Wi., U.S. D5 142
Stockdale, Tx., U.S. E4 136
Stockholm, Swe. G8 10
Stockton, Ca., U.S. D3 98
Stockton, Il., U.S. A3 106
Stockton, Ks., U.S. C4 109
Stockton, Md., U.S. D7 113
Stockton, Mo., U.S. D4 118
Stockton Island, i., Wi., U.S. B3 142
Stockton Lake, res., Mo., U.S. D4 118
Stoddard, co., Mo., U.S. E8 118
Stoddard, Wi., U.S. E2 142
Stœng Tréng, Camb. D5 34
Stoke-on-Trent, Eng., U.K. D5 12
Stokes, co., N.C., U.S. A2 126
Stokesdale, N.C., U.S. A3 126
Stolbovoj, ostrov, i., Russia B15 26
Stolin, Bela. D9 20
Stollings, W.V., U.S. n12 141
Stone, co., Ar., U.S. B3 97
Stone, co., Mo., U.S. E4 118
Stone, co., Ms., U.S. E4 117
Stoneboro, Pa., U.S. D1 131
Stone Corral Lake, l., Or., U.S. E7 130
Stoneham, Ma., U.S. g11 114
Stonehaven, Scot., U.K. B5 12
Stonehenge, hist., Eng., U.K. E6 12
Stone Mountain, Ga., U.S. C2 103
Stone Mountain, mtn., Ga., U.S. C2 103
Stones River National Battlefield, hist., Tn., U.S. B4 135
Stoneville, N.C., U.S. A3 126
Stonewall, Mb., Can. D3 86
Stonewall, La., U.S. B2 111
Stonewall, Ms., U.S. C5 117
Stonewall, co., Tx., U.S. C2 136
Stonewood, W.V., U.S. k10 141
Stoney Creek, On., Can. D5 89
Stonington, Ct., U.S. D8 100
Stonington, Il., U.S. D4 106
Stonington, Me., U.S. D4 112
Stono, stm., S.C., U.S. k11 133
Stono Inlet, b., S.C., U.S. F8 133
Stony Brook, stm., N.J., U.S. C3 123
Stony Brook, N.Y., U.S. n15 125
Stony Creek, stm., Va., U.S. C5 139
Stony Island, i., N.Y., U.S. B4 125
Stony Plain, Ab., Can. C3 84
Stony Point, N.C., U.S. B1 126
Storavan, l., Swe. D8 10
Storebælt, strt., Den. I4 10
Storey, co., Nv., U.S. D2 121
Storlien, Swe. E5 10
Storm Bay, b., Austl. I4 62
Storm Lake, Ia., U.S. B2 108
Storm Lake, l., Ia., U.S. B2 108
Storm Mountain, mtn., Ak., U.S. h16 95
Stornoway, Scot., U.K. A3 12
Storrs, Ct., U.S. B7 100
Storsjön, l., Swe. E6 10
Storslett, Nor. B9 10
Storuman, Swe. D7 10
Storuman, l., Swe. D7 10
Story, co., Ia., U.S. B4 108
Story, Wy., U.S. B6 143
Story City, Ia., U.S. B4 108
Stoŭbcy, Bela. C9 20
Stoughton, Sk., Can. H4 91
Stoughton, Ma., U.S. B5 114
Stoughton, Wi., U.S. F4 142
Stover, Mo., U.S. C5 118
Stow, Oh., U.S. A4 128
Stow Creek, stm., N.J., U.S. E2 123
Stowe, Pa., U.S. F10 131
Stowe, Vt., U.S. C3 138
Stoyoma Mountain, mtn., B.C., Can. E7 85
Strabane, Pa., U.S. F1 131
Strafford, Mo., U.S. D4 118
Strafford, co., N.H., U.S. D4 122
Straffordville, On., Can. E4 89
Strakonice, Czech Rep. E2 20
Stralsund, Ger. C13 12
Strand, S. Afr. E2 56
Stranraer, Scot., U.K. C4 12
Strasbourg, Fr. C10 16
Strasburg, Co., U.S. B6 99
Strasburg, Oh., U.S. B4 128
Strasburg, Pa., U.S. G9 131
Strasburg, Va., U.S. B4 139
Stratford, On., Can. D3 89
Stratford, N.Z. o13 63c
Stratford, Ct., U.S. E3 100
Stratford, Ia., U.S. B4 108
Stratford, N.J., U.S. D2 123
Stratford, Ok., U.S. C5 129
Stratford, Tx., U.S. A1 136
Stratford, Wi., U.S. D3 142
Stratford Point, c., Ct., U.S. E3 100
Stratham, N.H., U.S. D5 122
Strathmore, Ab., Can. D4 84
Strathmore, Ca., U.S. D4 98
Strathroy, On., Can. E3 89
Stratton, Co., U.S. B8 99
Straubing, Ger. F13 12
Strawberry, stm., Ar., U.S. A4 97
Strawberry, stm., Ut., U.S. C5 137
Strawberry Mountain, mtn., Or., U.S. C8 130
Strawberry Point, Ia., U.S. B6 108
Strawberry Point, c., Ma., U.S. B6 114
Strawberry Range, mts., Or., U.S. C8 130
Strawberry Reservoir, res., Ut., U.S. C4 137
Streaky Bay, b., Austl. G5 60
Streator, Il., U.S. B5 106
Strelka-Čunja, Russia C12 26
Strimón (Struma), stm., Eur. D9 18
Strimon, Gulf of see Orfanoú, Kólpos, b., Grc. D9 18
Stromsburg, Ne., U.S. C8 120
Strömsund, Swe. E6 10
Strong, Ar., U.S. D3 97
Strong, Me., U.S. D2 112
Strong, stm., Ms., U.S. C4 117
Strong City, Ks., U.S. D7 109
Stronghurst, Il., U.S. C3 106
Strongsville, Oh., U.S. A4 128
Stroud, Ok., U.S. B5 129
Stroudsburg, Pa., U.S. E11 131
Stroudwater, stm., Me., U.S. g7 112
Strum, Wi., U.S. D2 142
Struma (Strimón), stm., Eur. D9 18
Strumica, Mac. D9 18
Struthers, Oh., U.S. A5 128
Strydenburg, S. Afr. D3 56
Stryi, Ukr. E7 20
Stryker, Oh., U.S. A1 128
Stuart, Fl., U.S. E6 102
Stuart, Ia., U.S. C3 108
Stuart, Ne., U.S. B6 120
Stuart, Va., U.S. D2 139
Stuart, Mount, mtn., Wa., U.S. B5 140
Stuart Lake, l., B.C., Can. B5 85
Stuarts Draft, Va., U.S. B3 139
Stull, stm., Can. B5 86
Stump Lake, l., N.D., U.S. B7 127
Stump Pond, res., R.I., U.S. D2 132
Stupino, Russia B15 20
Sturbridge, Ma., U.S. B3 114
Sturgeon, stm., Mi., U.S. B4 115
Sturgeon, Mo., U.S. B5 118
Sturgeon Bay, b., Mb., Can. C3 86
Sturgeon Bay, Wi., U.S. D6 142
Sturgeon Falls, On., Can. A5 89
Sturgeon Lake, l., On., Can. C6 89
Sturgis, Sk., Can. F4 91
Sturgis, Ky., U.S. e10 110
Sturgis, Mi., U.S. G5 115
Sturgis, S.D., U.S. C2 134
Sturtevant, Wi., U.S. F6 142
Sturt Stony Desert, des., Austl. F3 62
Stutsman, co., N.D., U.S. B6 127
Stutterheim, S. Afr. E4 56
Stuttgart, Ger. F11 12
Stuttgart, Ar., U.S. C4 97
Styr, stm., Eur. D8 20
Šu, Kaz. E9 26
Suaita, Col. D5 80
Šubarkuduk, Kaz. E10 22
Şūbāţ, stm., Sudan I11 48
Subei, China B7 40
Sublette, Ks., U.S. E3 109
Sublette, co., Wy., U.S. D2 143
Sublett Range, mts., Id., U.S. G6 105
Sublimity, Or., U.S. C4 130
Subotica, Serb. A7 18
Sucarnoochee, stm., Al., U.S. C1 94
Succasunna, N.J., U.S. B3 123
Suceava, Rom. F9 20
Sucre, Bol. B4 72
Sud, Canal du, strt., Haiti B5 80
Sudan, ctry., Afr. H10 48
Sudan, reg., Afr. H8 48
Sudbury, On., Can. A4 89
Sudbury, Ma., U.S. B5 114
Sudbury, stm., Ma., U.S. B5 114
Sudbury Center, Ma., U.S. g10 114
Sudbury Reservoir, res., Ma., U.S. g10 114
Suez see El-Suweis, Egypt E11 48
Suez, Gulf of see Suweis, Khalîg el-, b., Egypt F10 14
Suez Canal see Suweis, Qanâ el-, Egypt E10 14
Suffern, N.Y., U.S. D6 125
Suffield, Ct., U.S. B5 100
Suffolk, co., Ma., U.S. B5 114
Suffolk, co., N.Y., U.S. n15 125
Suffolk, Va., U.S. D6 139
Sugar, stm., N.H., U.S. D2 122
Sugar, stm., U.S. F4 142
Sugar City, Id., U.S. F7 105
Sugar Creek, Mo., U.S. h11 118
Sugar Creek, stm., Oh., U.S. C2 128
Sugar Creek, stm., Pa., U.S. C8 131
Sugarcreek, Pa., U.S. D2 131
Sugar Grove, Va., U.S. D1 139
Sugar Hill, Ga., U.S. B2 103
Sugar Island, i., Mi., U.S. B6 115
Sugar Land, Tx., U.S. E5 136
Sugar Loaf, Va., U.S. C3 139
Sugarloaf Mountain, mtn., Mt., U.S. C4 119
Sugar Notch, Pa., U.S. n17 131
Suggi Lake, l., Sk., Can. C4 91
Suğla Gölü, l., Tur. D5 44
Suhag, Egypt E11 48
Suhana, Russia C13 26
Şuḩār, Oman F7 38
Sühbaatar, Mong. A9 28
Suhl, Ger. E12 12
Suhona, stm., Russia C6 26
Suhumi, Geor. A9 44
Suiattle, stm., Wa., U.S. A4 140
Suichang, China D4 30
Suichuan, China D3 30
Suide, China D10 28
Suijiang, China D1 30
Suining, China C4 30
Suining, China E9 28
Suitland, Md., U.S. C4 113
Suixi, China C4 30
Suiyang, China B2 31
Suizhong, China C12 28
Suizhou, China E10 28
Sukabumi, Indon. E3 36
Sukadana, Indon. D3 36
Sukaraja, Indon. D4 36
Sukarnapura see Jayapura, Indon. G11 32
Sukhothai, Thai. C3 34
Sukkertoppen, Grnld. E29 82
Sukkozero, Russia B5 22
Sukkur, Pak. E9 42
Sukses, Nmb. C2 56
Sukumo, Japan D2 31
Sula, Kepulauan, is., Indon. D7 36
Sulaimān Range, mts., Pak. E9 42
Sulawesi (Celebes), i., Indon. D6 36
Sulawesi, Laut see Celebes Sea, Asia C6 36
Sulechów, Pol. C3 20
Sullana, Peru D3 70
Sulligent, Al., U.S. B1 94
Sullivan, Il., U.S. D5 106
Sullivan, In., U.S. F3 107
Sullivan, co., In., U.S. F3 107
Sullivan, Mo., U.S. C6 118
Sullivan, co., Mo., U.S. A4 118
Sullivan, co., N.H., U.S. D2 122
Sullivan, co., N.Y., U.S. D6 125
Sullivan, co., Pa., U.S. D9 131
Sullivan, co., Tn., U.S. C11 135
Sullivan Lake, l., Ab., Can. D5 84
Sullivans Island, S.C., U.S. k12 133
Sully, Ia., U.S. C5 108
Sully, co., S.D., U.S. C5 134
Sulmona, Italy C4 18
Sulphur, La., U.S. D2 111
Sulphur, Ok., U.S. C5 129
Sulphur, stm., U.S. D2 97
Sulphur Spring Range, mts., Nv., U.S. C5 121
Sulphur Springs, Tx., U.S. C5 136
Sultan, Wa., U.S. B4 140
Sultānpur, India D4 40
Sulu Archipelago, is., Phil. F7 34
Sulūq, Libya D9 48
Sulu Sea, Asia E7 34
Sumas, Wa., U.S. A3 140
Sumatera (Sumatra), i., Indon. C2 36
Sumatra see Sumatera, i., Indon. C2 36
Sumba, i., Indon. F5 36
Sumba, Selat, strt., Indon. E6 36
Sumbawa, i., Indon. E5 36
Sumbawa Besar, Indon. E5 36
Sumbawanga, Tan. E6 54
Sumbe, Ang. F2 54
Sumedang, Indon. E3 36
Šumen, Blg. C11 18
Sumenep, Indon. E4 36
Šumerlja, Russia C8 22
Šumiha, Russia C11 22
Sumisu-jima, i., Japan E16 28
Sumiton, Al., U.S. B2 94
Summerfield, N.C., U.S. A3 126
Summerford, N.L., Can. D4 88
Summer Island, i., Mi., U.S. C4 115
Summer Lake, l., Or., U.S. E6 130
Summerland, B.C., Can. E8 85
Summers, co., W.V., U.S. D4 141
Summerside, P.E., Can. C6 87
Summersville, W.V., U.S. C4 141
Summersville Lake, res., W.V., U.S. C4 141
Summerton, S.C., U.S. D7 133
Summertown, Tn., U.S. B4 135
Summerville, Ga., U.S. B1 103
Summerville, S.C., U.S. E7 133
Summit, co., Co., U.S. B4 99
Summit, Il., U.S. k9 106
Summit, Ms., U.S. D3 117
Summit, N.J., U.S. B4 123
Summit, co., Oh., U.S. A4 128
Summit, Tn., U.S. h11 135
Summit, co., Ut., U.S. C5 137
Summit Hill, Pa., U.S. E10 131
Summit Lake, l., Ia., U.S. C3 108
Summit Lake Indian Reservation, Nv., U.S. B2 121
Summit Mountain, mtn., Nv., U.S. D5 121
Summit Peak, mtn., Co., U.S. D4 99
Summitville, In., U.S. D6 107
Sumner, Ia., U.S. B5 108
Sumner, Il., U.S. E6 106
Sumner, co., Ks., U.S. E6 109
Sumner, co., Tn., U.S. A5 135
Sumner, Wa., U.S. B3 140
Sumner, Lake, res., N.M., U.S. C5 124
Sumner Dam, N.M., U.S. C5 124
Sumner Strait, strt., Ak., U.S. m23 95
Šumperk, Czech Rep. E4 20
Sumqayıt, Azer. B13 44
Sumrall, Ms., U.S. D4 117
Šumšu, ostrov, i., Russia D17 26
Sumter, co., Al., U.S. C1 94
Sumter, co., Fl., U.S. D4 102
Sumter, co., Ga., U.S. D2 103
Sumter, S.C., U.S. D7 133
Sumter, co., S.C., U.S. D7 133
Sumy, Ukr. D13 20
Sumzom, China D7 40
Sun, stm., Mt., U.S. C4 119
Sunapee, N.H., U.S. D2 122
Sunapee Lake, l., N.H., U.S. D2 122
Sunbright, Tn., U.S. C9 135
Sunbury, Oh., U.S. B3 128
Sunbury, Pa., U.S. E8 131
Sunchales, Arg. E5 72
Suncho Corral, Arg. D5 72
Sun City, Az., U.S. k8 96
Suncook, N.H., U.S. D4 122
Suncook, stm., N.H., U.S. D4 122
Suncook Lakes, l., N.H., U.S. D4 122
Sunda, Selat, strt., Indon. E3 36
Sundance, Wy., U.S. B8 143
Sundance Mountain, mtn., Wy., U.S. B8 143
Sundarbans, reg., Asia B1 34
Sunda Shelf H13 64
Sunda Strait see Sunda, Selat, strt., Indon. E3 36
Sunderland, On., Can. C5 89
Sunderland, Eng., U.K. C6 12
Sundown, Austl. F5 60
Sundown, Tx., U.S. C1 136
Sundre, Ab., Can. D3 84
Sundridge, On., Can. B5 89
Sundsvall, Swe. E7 10
Sunflower, Ms., U.S. B3 117
Sunflower, co., Ms., U.S. B3 117
Sunflower, Mount, mtn., Ks., U.S. C2 109
Sungaidareh, Indon. D2 36
Sungai Kolok, Thai. E4 34
Sungai Petani, Malay. B2 36
Sungari see Songhua, stm., China B14 28
Sungari Reservoir see Songhua Hu, res., China C13 28
Sungurlu, Tur. B6 44
Sunland Park, N.M., U.S. F3 124
Sunlight Creek, stm., Wy., U.S. B3 143
Sunman, In., U.S. F7 107
Sunne, Swe. G5 10
Sunnyside, N.L., Can. E5 88
Sunnyside, Wa., U.S. C5 140
Sunnyvale, Ca., U.S. k8 98
Sun Prairie, Wi., U.S. E4 142
Sunray, Tx., U.S. A2 136
Sunset, La., U.S. D3 111
Sunset, Ut., U.S. B4 137
Sunset Beach, Hi., U.S. f9 104
Sunset Crater National Monument, Az., U.S. B4 96
Sunset Lake, l., Vt., U.S. D2 138
Sunshine, Austl. H3 62
Suntar, Russia C13 26
Suntar-Hajata, hrebet, mts., Russia C16 26
Suntaug Lake, l., Ma., U.S. f11 114
Sun Valley, Id., U.S. F4 105
Sun Valley, Nv., U.S. D2 121
Sunyani, Ghana E4 50
Suojarvi, Russia B5 22
Suomussalmi, Fin. D13 10
Superior, Az., U.S. D4 96
Superior, Mt., U.S. C2 119
Superior, Ne., U.S. D7 120
Superior, Wi., U.S. B1 142
Superior, Wy., U.S. E4 143
Superior, Lake, l., N.A. B10 92
Superstition Mountains, mts., Az., U.S. m10 96
Suphan Buri, Thai. D4 34
Suquamish, Wa., U.S. B3 140
Suquṭrā, i., Yemen H6 38
Şūr, Leb. F6 44
Şūr, Oman F7 38
Sur, Point, c., Ca., U.S. D3 98
Sura, stm., Russia E15 6
Surakarta, Indon. E4 36
Sūrat, India E2 40
Sūratgarh, India D2 40

Name — Map Ref. — Page

Surat Thani, Thai. **E3** 34
Surendranagar, India **E2** 40
Surfside, Fl., U.S. **s13** 102
Surfside Beach, S.C., U.S. **D10** 133
Surgoinsville, Tn., U.S. **C11** 135
Surgut, Russia **C9** 26
Surigao, Phil. **E9** 34
Surigao Strait, strt., Phil. **E9** 34
Surin, Thai. **D4** 34
Suriname, ctry., S.A. **C8** 70
Surprise, Az., U.S. **k8** 96
Surrey, N.D., U.S. **A4** 127
Surry, co., N.C., U.S. **A2** 126
Surry, co., Va., U.S. **C6** 139
Surry Mountain Lake, res., N.H., U.S. **D2** 122
Surt, Libya **D8** 48
Surt, Khalīj, b., Libya **D8** 48
Sürüç, Tur. **D8** 44
Surulangun, Indon. **D2** 36
Šuryškary, Russia **A12** 22
Sūsangerd, Iran **G13** 44
Susanville, Ca., U.S. **B3** 98
Suşehri, Tur. **B8** 44
Susitna, stm., Ak., U.S. **C10** 95
Susquehanna, Pa., U.S. **C10** 131
Susquehanna, co., Pa., U.S. **C10** 131
Susquehanna, stm., U.S. **A5** 113
Susquehanna, West Branch, stm., Pa., U.S. **D5** 131
Sussex, N.B., Can. **D4** 87
Sussex, co., De., U.S. **F4** 101
Sussex, N.J., U.S. **A3** 123
Sussex, co., N.J., U.S. **A3** 123
Sussex, co., Va., U.S. **D5** 139
Sussex, Wi., U.S. **m11** 142
Susuman, Russia **C16** 26
Susurluk, Tur. **C3** 44
Sutherland, S. Afr. **E3** 56
Sutherland, Ia., U.S. **B2** 108
Sutherland, Ne., U.S. **C4** 120
Sutherlin, Or., U.S. **D3** 130
Sutlej (Satluj), stm., Asia **D2** 40
Sutter, co., Ca., U.S. **C3** 98
Sutter Creek, Ca., U.S. **C3** 98
Sutton, Qc., Can. **D5** 90
Sutton, Ne., U.S. **D8** 120
Sutton, co., Tx., U.S. **D2** 136
Sutton, W.V., U.S. **C4** 141
Sutton Lake, res., W.V., U.S. **C4** 141
Sutwik Island, i., Ak., U.S. **D8** 95
Süüj, Mong. **B8** 28
Suur Munamägi, Est. **H12** 10
Suva, Fiji **F11** 58
Suwałki, Pol. **B7** 20
Suwanee, Ga., U.S. **B2** 103
Suwannee, co., Fl., U.S. **B3** 102
Suwannee, stm., U.S. **C4** 102
Suwannee Sound, strt., Fl., U.S. **C3** 102
Suwanose-jima, i., Japan **F14** 28
Suwarrow, atoll, Cook Is. **F13** 58
Suweis, Khalîg el- (Suez, Gulf of), b., Egypt **F10** 14
Suweis, Qanâ el- (Suez Canal), Egypt **E10** 14
Suwŏn, S. Kor. **D13** 28
Suzak, Kaz. **B9** 42
Suzhou, China **E11** 28
Suzhou, China **E12** 28
Svalbard, dep., Nor. **D20** 144
Svaliava, Ukr. **E7** 20
Svappavaara, Swe. **C9** 10
Svatove, Ukr. **E15** 20
Svay Riĕng, Camb. **D5** 34
Sveg, Swe. **E6** 10
Švenčionėliai, Lith. **I11** 10
Svendborg, Den. **I4** 10
Svensen, Or., U.S. **A3** 130
Sverdlovsk see Ekaterinburg, Russia **D8** 26
Sverdrup, ostrov, i., Russia **B9** 26
Svetlahorsk, Bela. **C10** 20
Svetlaja, Russia **E15** 26
Svetlograd, Russia **A4** 42
Svetlyj, Russia **D13** 26
Svetlyj, Russia **D11** 22
Svetogorsk, Russia **F13** 10
Svetozarevo, Serb. **C8** 18
Svirsk, Russia **A8** 28
Svištov, Blg. **C10** 18
Svitavy, Czech Rep. **E4** 20
Svjatoj Nos, mys, c., Russia **A7** 22
Svjatoj Nos, mys, c., Russia **B15** 26
Svobodnyj, Russia **D14** 26
Svolvær, Nor. **B6** 10
Swabia see Schwaben, hist. reg., Ger. **F11** 12
Swain, co., N.C., U.S. **f9** 126
Swain Reefs, rf., Austl. **E5** 62
Swainsboro, Ga., U.S. **D4** 103
Swakopmund, Nmb. **C1** 56
Swampscott, Ma., U.S. **B6** 114
Swan, stm., Can. **C1** 86
Swan Creek, stm., Oh., U.S. **e6** 128
Swan Falls, wtfl., Id., U.S. **F2** 105
Swan Hill, Austl. **H3** 62
Swan Hills, Ab., Can. **B3** 84
Swan Islands see Santanilla, Islas, is., Hond. **B3** 80
Swan Lake, l., Mb., Can. **C1** 86
Swan Lake, l., Me., U.S. **D4** 112
Swan Lake, l., Ne., U.S. **C3** 120
Swannanoa, N.C., U.S. **f10** 126
Swan Peak, mtn., Mt., U.S. **C3** 119
Swan Range, mts., Mt., U.S. **C3** 119
Swan River, Mb., Can. **C1** 86
Swansboro, N.C., U.S. **C5** 126
Swansea, Wales, U.K. **E4** 12
Swansea, Il., U.S. **E4** 106
Swanson Lake, res., Ne., U.S. **D4** 120
Swanton, Oh., U.S. **A2** 128
Swanton, Vt., U.S. **B2** 138
Swanzey Center, N.H., U.S. **E2** 122
Swarthmore, Pa., U.S. **p20** 131
Swartswood Lake, l., N.J., U.S. **A3** 123
Swartz Creek, Mi., U.S. **F7** 115
Swayzee, In., U.S. **C6** 107
Swaziland, ctry., Afr. **D5** 56
Swea City, Ia., U.S. **A3** 108
Sweden, ctry., Eur. **E7** 10
Swedru, Ghana **E4** 50
Sweeny, Tx., U.S. **r14** 136
Sweet Grass, co., Mt., U.S. **E7** 119
Sweet Home, Or., U.S. **C4** 130
Sweetser, In., U.S. **C6** 107
Sweet Springs, Mo., U.S. **C4** 118
Sweetwater, Tn., U.S. **D9** 135
Sweetwater, Tx., U.S. **C2** 136
Sweetwater, stm., Wy., U.S. **D4** 143
Sweetwater, co., Wy., U.S. **E3** 143
Sweetwater Creek, Fl., U.S. **p10** 102
Sweetwater Creek, stm., Ok., U.S. **B1** 129
Swellendam, S. Afr. **E3** 56
Swepsonville, N.C., U.S. **A3** 126
Świdwin, Pol. **C3** 20
Świebodzin, Pol. **C3** 20
Świecie, Pol. **C5** 20
Swift, co., Mn., U.S. **E3** 116
Swift, stm., N.H., U.S. **B4** 122
Swift Creek, stm., N.C., U.S. **B5** 126
Swift Creek, stm., Va., U.S. **n17** 139
Swift Diamond, stm., N.H., U.S. **g7** 122
Swifton, Ar., U.S. **B4** 97
Swift Reservoir, res., Wa., U.S. **C3** 140
Swindon, Eng., U.K. **E6** 12
Swinomish Indian Reservation, Wa., U.S. **A3** 140
Świnoujście, Pol. **C3** 20
Swisher, Ia., U.S. **C6** 108
Swisher, co., Tx., U.S. **B2** 136
Swissvale, Pa., U.S. **k14** 131
Switzer, W.V., U.S. **D3** 141
Switzerland, ctry., Eur. **A2** 18
Switzerland, Fl., U.S. **m8** 102
Switzerland, co., In., U.S. **G7** 107
Swoyerville, Pa., U.S. **D10** 131
Syalah, Russia **C14** 26
Sycamore, Al., U.S. **B3** 94
Sycamore, Il., U.S. **B5** 106
Sycamore, Oh., U.S. **B2** 128
Sycamore Creek, stm., W.V., U.S. **m13** 141
Sydenham, On., Can. **C8** 89
Sydney, Austl. **G5** 62
Sykesville, Md., U.S. **B4** 113
Sykesville, Pa., U.S. **D4** 131
Syktyvkar, Russia **C7** 26
Sylacauga, Al., U.S. **B3** 94
Sylhet, Bngl. **E6** 40
Sylt, i., Ger. **C11** 12
Sylva, N.C., U.S. **f9** 126
Sylvania, Al., U.S. **A4** 94
Sylvania, Ga., U.S. **D5** 103
Sylvania, Oh., U.S. **A2** 128
Sylvan Lake, Ab., Can. **C3** 84
Sylvan Lake, l., In., U.S. **B7** 107
Sylvan Lake, Mi., U.S. **o15** 115
Sylvan Pass, Wy., U.S. **B2** 143
Sylvester, Ga., U.S. **E3** 103
Sym, Russia **C10** 26
Šymkent, Kaz. **E8** 26
Symmes Creek, stm., Oh., U.S. **D3** 128
Symsonia, Ky., U.S. **f9** 110
Syracuse, In., U.S. **B6** 107
Syracuse, Ks., U.S. **E2** 109
Syracuse, Ne., U.S. **D9** 120
Syracuse, N.Y., U.S. **B4** 125
Syracuse, Ut., U.S. **B3** 137
Syrdarja, Uzb. **B9** 42
Syr Darya (Syrdar'ja), stm., Asia **B9** 42
Syria, ctry., Asia **E8** 44
Syriam, Mya. **C3** 34
Syrian Desert, des., Asia **F8** 44
Syros see Ermoúpolis, Grc. **F10** 18
Sysladobsis Lake, l., Me., U.S. **C4** 112
Syvash, zatoka, strt., Ukr. **F13** 20
Syzran', Russia **D6** 26
Szamotuły, Pol. **C4** 20
Szczecin, Pol. **C3** 20
Szczecinek, Pol. **C4** 20
Szczytno, Pol. **C6** 20
Szechwan see Sichuan, state, China **E8** 28
Szeged, Hung. **F6** 20
Székesfehérvár, Hung. **F5** 20
Szekszárd, Hung. **F5** 20
Szentes, Hung. **F6** 20
Szolnok, Hung. **F6** 20
Szombathely, Hung. **F4** 20\

T

Tabar Islands, is., Pap. N. Gui. **G13** 32
Tabarka, Tun. **F2** 18
Tabasco, state, Mex. **D6** 78
Tabayin, Mya. **B3** 34
Tabbys Peak, mtn., Ut., U.S. **C3** 137
Tabelbala, Alg. **E4** 48
Taber, Ab., Can. **E4** 84
Tablas Island, i., Phil. **D8** 34
Table Head, c., N.L., Can. **B4** 88
Table Mountain, mtn., Az., U.S. **E5** 96
Table Rock Lake, res., U.S. **E4** 118
Table Top, mtn., Az., U.S. **E3** 96
Tábor, Czech Rep. **E3** 20
Tabor, Russia **B17** 26
Tabor, Ia., U.S. **D2** 108
Tabora, Tan. **D6** 54
Tabor City, N.C., U.S. **C4** 126
Tabou, C. Iv. **F3** 50
Tabrīz, Iran **C5** 42
Tabūk, Sau. Ar. **E3** 38
Tabuleiro do Norte, Braz. **C4** 74
Täby, Swe. **G8** 10
Tacloban, Phil. **D9** 34
Tacna, Peru **G5** 70
Tacoma, Wa., U.S. **B3** 140
Taconic Range, mts., U.S. **A1** 114
Tacuarembó, Ur. **E6** 72
Tacurong, Phil. **E8** 34
Tademaït, Plateau du, plat., Alg. **E5** 48
Tadjemout, Alg. **A5** 50
Tadoussac, Qc., Can. **A8** 90
T'aebaek-sanmaek, mts., Asia **D13** 28
Taegu, S. Kor. **D13** 28
Taejŏn, S. Kor. **D13** 28
Tafalla, Spain **F6** 16
Tafo, Ghana **E4** 50
Taft, Ca., U.S. **E4** 98
Taft, Tx., U.S. **F4** 136
Taganrog, Russia **F15** 20
Tagânt, reg., Maur. **C2** 50
Tagaytay, Phil. **D8** 34
Tagbilaran, Phil. **E8** 34
Taguke, China **E4** 28
Tagum, Phil. **E9** 34
Tagus, stm., Eur. **H2** 16
Tahan, Gunong, mtn., Malay. **C2** 36
Tahat, mtn., Alg. **F6** 48
Tahiataš, Uzb. **B7** 42
Tahifet, Alg. **B6** 50
Tahiti, i., Fr. Poly. **F15** 58
Tahlequah, Ok., U.S. **B7** 129
Tahoe, Lake, l., U.S. **E1** 121
Tahoe, Lake, l., U.S. **D3** 92
Tahoe City, Ca., U.S. **C3** 98
Tahoka, Tx., U.S. **C2** 136
Taholah, Wa., U.S. **B1** 140
Tahoua, Niger **D6** 50
Tahquamenon, stm., Mi., U.S. **B5** 115
Tahsis, B.C., Can. **E4** 85
Ṭahṭā, Egypt **F10** 14
Tahta-Bazar, Turk. **C8** 42
Tahtakupyr, Uzb. **B8** 42
Tahtsa Peak, mtn., B.C., Can. **C4** 85
Tahulandang, Pulau, i., Indon. **C7** 36
Tahuna, Indon. **C7** 36
Tai'an, China **D11** 28
Taibai Shan, mtn., China **C2** 30
Taibus Qi, China **A4** 30
T'aichung, Tai. **E5** 30
Taigu, China **B3** 30
Taihang Shan, mts., China **B3** 30
Taihape, N.Z. **o14** 63c
Taihe, China **D3** 30
Tai Hu, l., China **E11** 28
Taihu, China **C4** 30
Taikang, China **C4** 30
Tailai, China **B12** 28
Tai Lake see Tai Hu, l., China **E11** 28
Taimba, Russia **C11** 26
T'ainan, Tai. **E5** 30
Taínaron, Ákra, c., Grc. **F9** 18
Tainaron, Cape see Taínaron, Ákra, c., Grc. **F9** 18
T'aipei, Tai. **D5** 30
Taiping, Malay. **C2** 36
Taisha, Japan **C2** 31
Taishan, China **E3** 30
Taishun, China **F11** 28
Taitao, Península de, pen., Chile **G1** 69
T'aitung, Tai. **E5** 30
Taivalkoski, Fin. **D13** 10
Taiwan, ctry., Asia **B8** 34
Taiwan Strait, strt., Asia **E4** 30
Taiyuan, China **D10** 28
Taizhou, China **C4** 30
Ta'izz, Yemen **H4** 38
Tajikistan, ctry., Asia **B2** 40
Tāj Mahal, hist., India **D3** 40
Tajmyr, ozero, l., Russia **B12** 26
Tajmyr, poluostrov, pen., Russia **B12** 26
Tajo see Tagus, stm., Eur. **H5** 16
Tajšet, Russia **D11** 26
Tak, Thai. **C3** 34
Takāb, Iran **D12** 44
Takalar, Indon. **E5** 36
Takamatsu, Japan **E14** 28
Takaoka, Japan **C3** 31
Takasaki, Japan **C3** 31
Takatsuki, Japan **D3** 31
Takêv, Camb. **D4** 34
Takhli, Thai. **C4** 34
Takikawa, Japan **B4** 31
Takla Lake, l., B.C., Can. **B5** 85
Taklimakan Shamo, des., China **D4** 28
Takoma Park, Md., U.S. **f8** 113
Taku Glacier, ice, Ak., U.S. **k22** 95
Takum, Nig. **E7** 50
Takutea, i., Cook Is. **F14** 58
Talak, reg., Niger **C6** 50
Talara, Peru **D3** 70
Talas, Kyrg. **E9** 26
Talasea, Pap. N. Gui. **H13** 32
Talata Mafara, Nig. **D6** 50
Talaud, Kepulauan, is., Indon. **C7** 36
Talavera de la Reina, Spain **H4** 16
Talawdī, Sudan **A6** 54
Talbot, co., Ga., U.S. **D2** 103
Talbot, co., Md., U.S. **C5** 113
Talbot Island, i., Fl., U.S. **B5** 102
Talbot Lake, l., Mb., Can. **B2** 86
Talbotton, Ga., U.S. **D2** 103
Talca, Chile **E2** 69
Talcahuano, Chile **E2** 69
Taldykorgan, Kaz. **E9** 26
Talent, Or., U.S. **E4** 130
Talgar, Kaz. **B11** 42
Taliabu, Pulau, i., Indon. **D6** 36
Taliaferro, co., Ga., U.S. **C4** 103
Talihina, Ok., U.S. **C6** 129
Talish Mountains see Ṭavālesh, Kūhhā-ye, mts., Asia **D13** 44
Taliwang, Indon. **E5** 36
Talkeetna, Ak., U.S. **C10** 95
Talkeetna Mountains, mts., Ak., U.S. **f17** 95
Talladega, co., Al., U.S. **B3** 94
Talladega, Al., U.S. **B3** 94
Tall 'Afar, Iraq **D10** 44
Tallahassee, Fl., U.S. **B2** 102
Tallahatchie, stm., Ms., U.S. **B3** 117
Tallahatchie, co., Ms., U.S. **B3** 117
Tallangatta, Austl. **H4** 62
Tallapoosa, co., Al., U.S. **C4** 94
Tallapoosa, stm., Al., U.S. **C3** 94
Tallapoosa, Ga., U.S. **C1** 103
Tallassee, Al., U.S. **C4** 94
Talleyville, De., U.S. **A3** 101
Tallinn, Est. **G11** 10
Tall Kūjik, Syria **D9** 44
Tallmadge, Oh., U.S. **A4** 128
Tallulah, La., U.S. **B4** 111
Tal'ne, Ukr. **E11** 20
Talok, Indon. **C5** 36
Tāloqān, Afg. **C9** 42
Taloyoak, N.T., Can. **E21** 82
Talquin, Lake, res., Fl., U.S. **B2** 102
Talsi, Lat. **H10** 10
Taltal, Chile **C2** 69
Talu, Indon. **C1** 36
Taluk, Indon. **D2** 36
Tama, Ia., U.S. **C5** 108
Tama, co., Ia., U.S. **B5** 108
Tamale, Ghana **E4** 50
Tamalpais, Mount, mtn., Ca., U.S. **h7** 98
Tamaqua, Pa., U.S. **E10** 131
Tamaroa, Il., U.S. **E4** 106
Tamaulipas, state, Mex. **C5** 78
Tamazulapan del Progreso, Mex. **D5** 78
Tamazunchale, Mex. **C5** 78
Tambacounda, Sen. **D2** 50
Tambej, Russia **B9** 26
Tambelan, Kepulauan, is., Indon. **C3** 36
Tamberías, Arg. **E4** 72
Tambohorano, Madag. **B7** 56
Tambora, Gunung, vol., Indon. **E5** 36
Tambov, Russia **D6** 26
Tambura, Sudan **I10** 48
Tâmchekket, Maur. **C2** 50
Tame, Col. **B5** 70
Tamel Aike, Arg. **G2** 69
Tamenghest, Alg. **F6** 48
Tamiahua, Mex. **C5** 78
Tamiahua, Laguna de, l., Mex. **C5** 78
Tamiami Canal, Fl., U.S. **G6** 102
Tamil Nādu, state, India **G3** 40
Tam Ky, Viet. **C5** 34
Tampa, Fl., U.S. **E4** 102
Tampa Bay, b., Fl., U.S. **E4** 102
Tampere, Fin. **F10** 10
Tampico, Mex. **C5** 78
Tampico, Il., U.S. **B4** 106
Tam Quan, Viet. **D5** 34
Tamsagbulag, Mong. **B11** 28
Tamu, Mya. **B2** 34
Tamworth, Austl. **G5** 62
Tana (Teno), stm., Eur. **B12** 10
Tana, stm., Kenya **D7** 54
Tanabe, Japan **D3** 31
Tanafjorden, b., Nor. **A13** 10
Tanaga Island, i., Ak., U.S. **E4** 95
Tanahbala, Pulau, i., Indon. **D1** 36
Tanahjampea, Pulau, i., Indon. **E5** 36
Tanahmasa, Pulau, i., Indon. **D1** 36
Tanahmerah, Indon. **H11** 32
Tanami Desert, des., Austl. **D4** 60
Tanana, Ak., U.S. **B9** 95
Tanana, stm., Ak., U.S. **C10** 95
Tananarive see Antananarivo, Madag. **B8** 56
Tanch'ŏn-ŭp, N. Kor. **C13** 28
Tandag, Phil. **E9** 34
Ţăndărei, Rom. **G9** 20
Tandil, Arg. **F6** 72
Tanega-shima, i., Japan **E14** 28
Taney, co., Mo., U.S. **E4** 118
Taneycomo, Lake, res., Mo., U.S. **E4** 118
Taneytown, Md., U.S. **A3** 113
Tanezrouft, des., Afr. **B4** 50
Tanga, Tan. **E7** 54
Tanganyika see Tanzania, ctry., Afr. **E6** 54
Tanganyika, Lake, l., Afr. **E5** 54
Tanger, Mor. **C3** 48
Tanggula Shan, mts., China **E5** 28
Tanghe, China **C3** 30
Tangier, Va., U.S. **C7** 139
Tangier Island, i., Va., U.S. **C6** 139
Tangier Sound, strt., Md., U.S. **D6** 113
Tangipahoa, co., La., U.S. **D5** 111
Tangipahoa, stm., La., U.S. **D5** 111
Tangmai, China **C7** 40
Tangra Yumco, l., China **C5** 40
Tangshan, China **D11** 28
Tangyin, China **B3** 30
Tangyuan, China **A1** 31
Tanhoj, Russia **A9** 28
Tanimbar, Kepulauan, is., Indon. **E8** 36
Tanjungbalai, Indon. **C1** 36
Tanjungpandan, Indon. **D3** 36
Tanjungpinang, Indon. **C2** 36
Tanjungredep, Indon. **C5** 36
Tānk, Pak. **D10** 42
Tanna, i., Vanuatu **k9** 62a
Tännäs, Swe. **E5** 10
Tanner, Al., U.S. **A3** 94
Tannu-Ola Mountains, mts., Asia **A6** 28
Tanout, Niger **C6** 50
Tanta, Egypt **D11** 48
Tan-Tan, Mor. **A2** 50
Tantoyuca, Mex. **C5** 78
Tanzania, ctry., Afr. **E6** 54
Taormina, Italy **F5** 18
Taos, Mo., U.S. **C5** 118
Taos, N.M., U.S. **A4** 124
Taos, co., N.M., U.S. **A4** 124
Taos Pueblo, N.M., U.S. **A4** 124
Taoudenni, Mali **B4** 50
Taounate, Mor. **E3** 14
Taourirt, Mor. **E3** 14
Tapa, Est. **G11** 10
Tapachula, Mex. **E6** 78
Tapajós, stm., Braz. **D8** 70
Tapaktuan, Indon. **C1** 36
Taphan Hin, Thai. **C4** 34
Tāpi, stm., India **E2** 40
Tappahannock, Va., U.S. **C6** 139
Tappan, N.Y., U.S. **g13** 125
Tappan, Lake, res., N.J., U.S. **g9** 123
Tappan Lake, res., Oh., U.S. **B4** 128
Tapul Group, is., Phil. **E8** 34
Tapuruquara, Braz. **D6** 70
Taqātu' Hayyā, Sudan **G12** 48
Taquari Novo, stm., Braz. **G8** 70
Tar, stm., N.C., U.S. **B5** 126
Tara, On., Can. **C3** 89
Tara, Russia **D9** 26
Tarabuco, Bol. **B5** 72
Ţarābulus (Tripoli), Leb. **E6** 44
Ţarābulus (Tripoli), Libya **D7** 48
Ţarābulus (Tripolitania), hist. reg., Libya **E7** 14
Tarakan, Indon. **C5** 36
Taranaki, Mount (Egmont, Mount), vol., N.Z. **o13** 63c
Tarancón, Spain **G5** 16
Taranto, Italy **D6** 18
Taranto, Golfo di, b., Italy **D6** 18
Taranto, Gulf of see Taranto, Golfo di, b., Italy **D6** 18
Tarapoto, Peru **E4** 70
Taraquá, Braz. **C6** 70
Tarat, Alg. **A6** 50
Tarata, Bol. **B4** 72
Tarauacá, Braz. **E5** 70
Tarawa, atoll, Kir. **D11** 58
Tarazona, Spain **G6** 16
Tarbagatay Range, mts., Asia **B4** 28
Tarbes, Fr. **F7** 16
Tarboro, N.C., U.S. **B5** 126
Tarbū, Libya **E8** 48
Tarcoola, Austl. **G5** 60
Tardoki-Jani, gora, mtn., Russia **B15** 28

Name | Map Ref. | Page

Taree, Austl. G5 62
Tareja, Russia B11 26
Tarentum, Pa., U.S. E2 131
Tarfaya, Mor. E2 48
Targhee Pass, U.S. E7 105
Târgovište, Blg. C11 18
Târgoviște, Rom. G8 20
Târgu Jiu, Rom. G7 20
Târgu Mureș, Rom. F8 20
Târgu-Neamț, Rom. F9 20
Târgu Ocna, Rom. F9 20
Tarifa, Spain I4 16
Tariffville, Ct., U.S. B4 100
Tarija, Bol. C5 72
Tarim, stm., China C4 28
Tarim Pendi, bas., China D4 28
Tarīn Kowt, Afg. D9 42
Tarkastad, S. Afr. E4 56
Tarkio, Mo., U.S. A2 118
Tarko-Sale, Russia C9 26
Tarkwa, Ghana E4 50
Tarma, Peru F4 70
Tarn, stm., Fr. F7 16
Tärnaby, Swe. D6 10
Târnăveni, Rom. F8 20
Tarnobrzeg, Pol. D6 20
Tarnów, Pol. E6 20
Tarpey, Ca., U.S. D4 98
Tarpon, Lake, l., Fl., U.S. o10 102
Tarpon Springs, Fl., U.S. D4 102
Tarquinia, Italy C3 18
Tarragona, Spain G7 16
Tarrant, Al., U.S. B3 94
Tarrant, co., Tx., U.S. C4 136
Tarryall Mountains, mts., Co., U.S. B5 99
Tarrytown, N.Y., U.S. D7 125
Tarsus, Tur. D6 44
Tartagal, Arg. C5 72
Tärtär, Azer. B12 44
Tartu, Est. G12 10
Ṭarṭūs, Syria E6 44
Tarutung, Indon. C1 36
Tasāwah, Libya A7 50
Tasbuget, Kaz. B9 42
Taseko Mountain, mtn., B.C., Can. D6 85
Ṭashk, Daryācheh-ye, l., Iran E6 42
Tashkent see Taškent, Uzb. E8 26
Taškent, Uzb. E8 26
Taškepri, Turk. C8 42
Taşköprü, Tur. B6 44
Tasman Basin M18 64
Tasman Bay, b., N.Z. p13 63c
Tasmania, state, Austl. I4 62
Tasmania, i., Austl. I3 62
Tasman Sea, Oc. L18 64
Taşova, Tur. B7 44
Tasso, Tn., U.S. D9 135
Taštagol, Russia D10 26
Tata, Hung. F5 20
Tatarbunary, Ukr. G10 20
Tatarija, state, Russia D6 26
Tatarsk, Russia D9 26
Tatarskij proliv, strt., Russia E16 26
Tatarstan see Tatarija, state, Russia D6 26
Tatar Strait see Tatarskij proliv, strt., Russia E16 26
Tate, Ga., U.S. B2 103
Tate, co., Ms., U.S. A4 117
Tateville, Ky., U.S. D5 110
Tatnam, Cape, c., Mb., Can. f9 86
Tatta, Pak. F9 42
Tattnall, co., Ga., U.S. D4 103
Tatum, N.M., U.S. D6 124
Tatvan, Tur. C10 44
Tauá, Braz. C3 74
Taučik, Kaz. B6 42
Taujskaja guba, b., Russia D17 26
Taum Sauk Mountain, mtn., Mo., U.S. D6 118
Taunggyi, Mya. B3 34
Taungup, Mya. C2 34
Taunton, Eng., U.K. E5 12
Taunton, stm., Ma., U.S. C5 114
Taunton, Ma., U.S. C5 114
Taupo, N.Z. o14 63c
Taupo, Lake, l., N.Z. o14 63c
Tauranga, N.Z. o14 63c
Taureau, Réservoir, res., Qc., Can. C4 90
Taurus Mountains see Toros Dağları, mts., Tur. D5 44
Ṭavālesh, Kūhhā-ye, mts., Asia D13 44
Tavares, Fl., U.S. D5 102
Tavas, Tur. D3 44
Tavda, Russia D8 26
Tavda, stm., Russia D8 26
Tavernier, Fl., U.S. G6 102
Taveuni, i., Fiji m11 63b
Tavşanlı, Tur. C3 44
Tawakoni, Lake, res., Tx., U.S. C4 136
Tawas City, Mi., U.S. D7 115
Tawas Lake, l., Mi., U.S. D7 115
Tawau, Malay. C5 36
Tawitawi Group, is., Phil. E8 34
Tawkar, Sudan G12 48
Ṭāwūq, Iraq E11 44
Taxco de Alarcón, Mex. D5 78
Taxkorgan Tajik Zizhixian, China B3 40
Taylor, B.C., Can. A7 85
Taylor, Ar., U.S. D2 97
Taylor, Az., U.S. C5 96
Taylor, stm., Co., U.S. C4 99
Taylor, co., Fl., U.S. B3 102
Taylor, co., Ga., U.S. D2 103
Taylor, co., Ia., U.S. D3 108
Taylor, co., Ky., U.S. C4 110
Taylor, Mi., U.S. p15 115
Taylor, Pa., U.S. D10 131
Taylor, Tx., U.S. D4 136
Taylor, co., Tx., U.S. C3 136
Taylor, co., Wi., U.S. C3 142
Taylor, co., W.V., U.S. B4 141
Taylor, Mount, mtn., N.M., U.S. B2 124
Taylor Mill, Ky., U.S. k14 110
Taylor Mountain, mtn., Id., U.S. E4 105
Taylor Park Reservoir, res., Co., U.S. C4 99
Taylors, S.C., U.S. B3 133
Taylors Falls, Mn., U.S. E6 116
Taylors Island, i., Md., U.S. D5 113
Taylorsville, In., U.S. F6 107
Taylorsville, Ky., U.S. B4 110
Taylorsville, Ms., U.S. D4 117
Taylorsville, N.C., U.S. B1 126
Taylorville, Il., U.S. D4 106
Taymā', Sau. Ar. E3 38
Taymyr Peninsula see Tajmyr, poluostrov, pen., Russia B12 26
Tay Ninh, Viet. D5 34
Taytay, Phil. D7 34
Taz, stm., Russia D9 26
Taza, Mor. E3 14
Tazewell, co., Il., U.S. C4 106
Tazewell, Tn., U.S. C10 135
Tazewell, Va., U.S. e10 139
Tazewell, co., Va., U.S. e10 139
Tazovskij, Russia C9 26
Tbessa, Alg. C6 48
Tbilisi, Geor. B11 44
Tchaourou, Benin E5 50
Tchefuncta, stm., La., U.S. D5 111
Tchibanga, Gabon D2 54
Tchula, Ms., U.S. B3 117
Tczew, Pol. B5 20
Tea, S.D., U.S. D9 134
Teague, Tx., U.S. D4 136
Teakean Butte, mtn., Id., U.S. C2 105
Teaneck, N.J., U.S. h8 123
Teapa, Mex. D6 78
Teaticket, Ma., U.S. C6 114
Te Awamutu, N.Z. o14 63c
Tebingtinggi, Indon. C1 36
Tebingtinggi, Pulau, i., Indon. C2 36
Téboursouk, Tun. F2 18
Techlé, W. Sah. B2 50
Tecka, Arg. F2 69
Tecomán, Mex. D4 78
Tecpan de Galeana, Mex. D4 78
Tecuala, Mex. C3 78
Tecuci, Rom. G9 20
Tecumseh, On., Can. E2 89
Tecumseh, Ks., U.S. k14 109
Tecumseh, Mi., U.S. G7 115
Tecumseh, Ne., U.S. D9 120
Tecumseh, Ok., U.S. B5 129
Tedžen, Turk. F8 26
Teeli, Russia D10 26
Teeswater, On., Can. C3 89
Tefé, Braz. D7 70
Tegal, Indon. E3 36
Tégama, reg., Niger C6 50
Tegucigalpa, Hond. C2 80
Tehachapi, Ca., U.S. E4 98
Tehachapi Mountains, mts., Ca., U.S. E4 98
Tehama, co., Ca., U.S. B2 98
Tehrān, Iran C6 42
Tehuacán, Mex. D5 78
Tehuantepec, Golfo de, b., Mex. D6 78
Tehuantepec, Istmo de, isth., Mex. I13 78
Teide, Pico del, mtn., Spain A1 50
Teixeira Pinto, Gui.-B. D1 50
Tejo see Tagus, stm., Eur. H3 16
Tekamah, Ne., U.S. C9 120
Tekax, Mex. C7 78
Tekeli, Kaz. E9 26
Tekes, China A4 40
Tekirdağ, Tur. B2 44
Tekoa, Wa., U.S. B8 140
Tekonsha, Mi., U.S. F5 115
Telavi, Geor. B11 44
Tel Aviv-Yafo, Isr. D2 42
Teleckoe, ozero, l., Russia A5 28
Telêmaco Borba, Braz. C7 72
Telemark, state, Nor. G3 10
Telén, Arg. F4 72
Telescope Peak, mtn., Ca., U.S. D5 98
Telfair, co., Ga., U.S. E4 103
Telford, Eng., U.K. D5 12
Telford, Pa., U.S. F11 131
Télimélé, Gui. D2 50
Telkwa, B.C., Can. B4 85
Tell City, In., U.S. I4 107
Teller, co., Co., U.S. C5 99
Tellicherry, India G3 40
Tellico Plains, Tn., U.S. D9 135
Telluride, Co., U.S. D3 99
Telos Lake, l., Me., U.S. B3 112
Telsen, Arg. F3 69
Telukbatang, Indon. D3 36
Teluk Intan, Malay. C2 36
Tema, Ghana E5 50
Temax, Mex. C7 78
Tembilahan, Indon. D2 36
Temecula, Ca., U.S. F5 98
Teminaabuan, Indon. D8 36
Temir, Kaz. E10 22
Temirtau, Kaz. E9 26
Témiscouata, Lac, l., Qc., Can. B9 90
Te-Moak Indian Reservation, Nv., U.S. C6 121
Temora, Austl. G4 62
Temosachic, Mex. B3 78
Tempe, Az., U.S. D4 96
Temperance, Mi., U.S. G7 115
Temperance, stm., Mn., U.S. C8 116
Temple, Ga., U.S. C1 103
Temple, Ok., U.S. C3 129
Temple, Pa., U.S. F10 131
Temple, Tx., U.S. D4 136
Temple Terrace, Fl., U.S. o11 102
Temrjuk, Russia G14 20
Temuco, Chile E2 69
Tenafly, N.J., U.S. B5 123
Tenaha, Tx., U.S. D5 136
Tena Kourou, mtn., Burkina D3 50
Tenāli, India F4 40
Tenasserim, Mya. D3 34
Tendaho, Eth. H13 48
Ten Degree Channel, strt., India H6 40
Ténéré, des., Niger C6 50
Tenerife, i., Spain A1 50
Tengchong, China G7 28
Tenggara, Nusa (Lesser Sunda Islands), is., Indon. E5 36
Tengiz, ozero, l., Kaz. D8 26
Tengréla, C. Iv. D3 50
Tengxian, China E3 30
Tengxian, China B4 30
Tenino, Wa., U.S. C3 140
Tenke, D.R.C. F5 54
Tenkeli, Russia C16 26
Tenkiller Ferry Lake, res., Ok., U.S. B6 129
Tenkodogo, Burkina D4 50
Tenmile, stm., U.S. B5 132
Tenmile Creek, stm., W.V., U.S. k10 141
Tenmile Lake, l., Mn., U.S. D4 116
Tennant Creek, Austl. D5 60
Tennessee, state, U.S. B5 135
Tennessee Pass, Co., U.S. B4 99
Tennessee Ridge, Tn., U.S. A4 135
Tennille, Ga., U.S. D4 103
Teno (Tana), stm., Eur. B12 10
Tenosique, Mex. D6 78
Tensas, co., La., U.S. B4 111
Tensas, stm., La., U.S. B4 111
Tensaw, stm., Al., U.S. E2 94
Ten Sleep, Wy., U.S. B5 143
Tenterfield, Austl. F5 62
Ten Thousand Islands, is., Fl., U.S. G5 102
Teófilo Otoni, Braz. E3 74
Tepa, Indon. E7 36
Tepehuanes, Mex. B3 78
Tepic, Mex. C4 78
Téra, Niger D5 50
Teramo, Italy C4 18
Terceira, i., Port. F7 46
Terek, Russia A11 44
Terek, stm., Russia B5 42
Teresina, Braz. C3 74
Tergüün Bodg uul, mtn., Mong. C8 28
Termas de Río Hondo, Arg. D5 72
Terme, Tur. B7 44
Termez, Uzb. C9 42
Términos, Laguna de, b., Mex. D6 78
Ternej, Russia A3 31
Terneuzen, Neth. E8 12
Terni, Italy C4 18
Ternopil', Ukr. E8 20
Terpenija, mys, c., Russia E16 26
Terra Alta, W.V., U.S. B5 141
Terrace, B.C., Can. B3 85
Terracina, Italy D4 18
Terra Nova National Park, N.L., Can. D4 88
Terrassa, Spain G8 16
Terrebonne, Qc., Can. D4 90
Terrebonne, co., La., U.S. E5 111
Terrebonne, Or., U.S. C5 130
Terrebonne Bay, b., La., U.S. E5 111
Terre Haute, In., U.S. F3 107
Terre Hill, Pa., U.S. F9 131
Terrell, co., Ga., U.S. E2 103
Terrell, co., Tx., U.S. D1 136
Terrell, Tx., U.S. C4 136
Terrell Hills, Tx., U.S. k7 136
Terrenceville, N.L., Can. E4 88
Terry, Ms., U.S. C3 117
Terry, Mt., U.S. D11 119
Terry, co., Tx., U.S. C1 136
Terrytown, Ne., U.S. C2 120
Terryville, Ct., U.S. C3 100
Teruel, Spain G6 16
Teseney, Erit. G12 48
Teshekpuk Lake, l., Ak., U.S. A9 95
Teshio, Japan B4 31
Tessalit, Mali B5 50
Tessaoua, Niger D6 50
Tesuque, N.M., U.S. B4 124
Tete, Moz. B5 56
Teteriv, stm., Ukr. D10 20
Teton, co., Id., U.S. F7 105
Teton, stm., Mt., U.S. C5 119
Teton, co., Mt., U.S. C4 119
Teton, co., Wy., U.S. C2 143
Teton Pass, Wy., U.S. C2 143
Teton Range, mts., Wy., U.S. C2 143
Teton Village, Wy., U.S. C2 143
Tetouan, Mor. C3 48
Tetovo, Mac. C8 18
Teulon, Mb., Can. D3 86
Teutopolis, Il., U.S. D5 106
Tevere, stm., Italy C4 18
Teverya, Isr. D3 42
Tewksbury, Ma., U.S. A5 114
Texada Island, i., B.C., Can. E5 85
Texarkana, Ar., U.S. D1 97
Texarkana, Tx., U.S. C5 136
Texas, co., Mo., U.S. D5 118
Texas, co., Ok., U.S. e9 129
Texas, state, U.S. D3 136
Texas City, Tx., U.S. E5 136
Texel, i., Neth. D9 12
Texhoma, Ok., U.S. e9 129
Texico, N.M., U.S. C6 124
Texoma, Lake, res., U.S. D5 129
Teziutlán, Mex. D5 78
Tezpur, India D6 40
Thabana-Ntlenyana, mtn., Leso. D4 56
Thabazimbi, S. Afr. C4 56
Thai Binh, Viet. B5 34
Thailand, ctry., Asia C4 34
Thailand, Gulf of, b., Asia D4 34
Thai Nguyen, Viet. B5 34
Thames, stm., On., Can. E3 89
Thames, N.Z. o14 63c
Thames, stm., Eng., U.K. E7 12
Thames, stm., Ct., U.S. D7 100
Thamesville, On., Can. E3 89
Thāna, India F2 40
Thanh Hoa, Viet. C5 34
Thanh Pho Ho Chi Minh (Saigon), Viet. D5 34
Thanjāvūr, India G3 40
Tharād, India E2 40
Thar Desert (Great Indian Desert), des., Asia D2 40
Tharrawaddy, Mya. C3 34
Tharros, hist., Italy E2 18
Tharthār, Buḥayrat ath-, res., Iraq E10 44
Thásos, i., Grc. D10 18
Thásos, Grc. D10 18
Thatcher, Az., U.S. E6 96
Thaton, Mya. C3 34
Thayer, Mo., U.S. E6 118
Thayer, co., Ne., U.S. D8 120
Thayetmyo, Mya. C3 34
Thayne, Wy., U.S. D1 143
Thazi, Mya. B3 34
Thealka, Ky., U.S. C7 110
The Barrens, plat., Tn., U.S. B5 135
Thebes see Thívai, Grc. E9 18
The Dalles, Or., U.S. B5 130
The Dells, val., Wi., U.S. E4 142
Thedford, On., Can. D3 89
The Everglades, sw., Fl., U.S. G6 102
The Flat Tops, mts., Co., U.S. B3 99
The Flume, wtfl., N.H., U.S. B3 122
The Graves, is., Ma., U.S. g12 114
The Hague see 's-Gravenhage, Neth. D8 12
The Heads, c., Or., U.S. E2 130
The Little Minch see Little Minch, The, strt., Scot., U.K. B3 12
The Minch, strt., Scot., U.K. A4 12
The Narrows, strt., Wa., U.S. f10 140
Theodore, Al., U.S. E1 94
Theodore Roosevelt Lake, res., Az., U.S. D4 96
Theodore Roosevelt National Park (South Unit), N.D., U.S. C2 127
Theodore Roosevelt National Park (North Unit), N.D., U.S. B2 127
The Pas, Mb., Can. C1 86
The Plains, Oh., U.S. C3 128
Theresa, Wi., U.S. E5 142
Thermaïkós Kólpos, b., Grc. D9 18
Thermopílai, hist., Grc. E9 18
Thermopolis, Wy., U.S. C4 143
Thermopylae see Thermopílai, hist., Grc. E9 18
The Rockies, mts., Wa., U.S. C3 140
Thessalía, hist. reg., Grc. E9 18
Thessalon, On., Can. p19 89
Thessaloníki (Salonika), Grc. D9 18
Thessaly see Thessalía, hist. reg., Grc. E9 18
Thetford Mines, Qc., Can. C6 90
The Thimbles, is., Ct., U.S. E5 100
The Valley, Anguilla B7 80
The Village, Ok., U.S. B4 129
The Wash, b., Eng., U.K. D7 12
Thibodaux, La., U.S. E5 111
Thief, stm., Mn., U.S. B2 116
Thief Lake, l., Mn., U.S. B3 116
Thief River Falls, Mn., U.S. B2 116
Thielsen, Mount, mtn., Or., U.S. D4 130
Thiensville, Wi., U.S. E6 142
Thiès, Sen. D1 50
Thika, Kenya D7 54
Thimphu, Bhu. D5 40
Thingvellir, Ice. l18 10a
Thio, N. Cal. I9 62a
Thionville, Fr. C10 16
Thíra, i., Grc. F10 18
Third Cataract, wtfl., Sudan G11 48
Third Lake, l., N.H., U.S. f7 122
Thiruvananthapuram (Trivandrum), India H3 40
Thisted, Den. H3 10
Thistilfjörður, b., Ice. k21 10a
Thívai, Grc. E9 18
Thjórsá, stm., Ice. m18 10a
Thomas, co., Ga., U.S. F3 103
Thomas, co., Ks., U.S. C2 109
Thomas, co., Ne., U.S. C5 120
Thomas, Ok., U.S. B3 129
Thomasboro, Il., U.S. C5 106
Thomaston, Ct., U.S. C3 100
Thomaston, Ga., U.S. D2 103
Thomaston, Me., U.S. D3 112
Thomaston Reservoir, res., Ct., U.S. C3 100
Thomasville, Al., U.S. D2 94
Thomasville, Ga., U.S. F3 103
Thomasville, N.C., U.S. B2 126
Thompson, Mb., Can. B3 86
Thompson, Ct., U.S. B8 100
Thompson, N.D., U.S. B8 127
Thompson, stm., U.S. A4 118
Thompson Falls, Mt., U.S. C1 119
Thompson Island, i., Ma., U.S. g11 114
Thompson Lake, l., U.S. D2 112
Thompson Peak, mtn., Ca., U.S. B2 98
Thompson Peak, mtn., N.M., U.S. h9 124
Thompson Reservoir, res., Or., U.S. E5 130
Thomson, Ga., U.S. C4 103
Thongwa, Mya. C3 34
Thonon-les-Bains, Fr. D10 16
Thonotosassa, Fl., U.S. D4 102
Thonze, Mya. C3 34
Thorburn, N.S., Can. D7 87
Thoreau, N.M., U.S. B1 124
Thornbury, On., Can. C4 89
Thorndale, Tx., U.S. D4 136
Thornton, On., Can. C5 89
Thorntown, In., U.S. D4 107
Thorold, On., Can. D5 89
Thorp, Wi., U.S. D3 142
Thorsby, Al., U.S. C3 94
Thorshavn see Tórshavn, Far. Is. n23 10b
Thórshöfn, Ice. k21 10a
Thouars, Fr. D6 16
Thousand Islands, is., N.Y., U.S. A4 125
Thousand Lake Mountain, mtn., Ut., U.S. E4 137
Thousand Springs Creek, stm., U.S. B7 121
Thrace, hist. reg., Eur. D11 18
Thrakikón Pélagos, Grc. D10 18
Three Fingered Jack, mtn., Or., U.S. C5 130
Three Forks, Mt., U.S. E5 119
Three Hills, Ab., Can. D4 84
Three Hummock Island, i., Austl. I4 62
Three Kings Islands, is., N.Z. n13 63c
Three Lakes, Wi., U.S. C4 142
Three Mile Plains, N.S., Can. E5 87
Three Oaks, Mi., U.S. G4 115
Three Pagodas Pass, Asia C3 34
Three Points, Cape, c., Ghana F4 50
Three Rivers, Ma., U.S. B3 114
Three Rivers, Mi., U.S. G5 115
Three Rivers, Tx., U.S. E3 136
Three Sisters, mtn., Or., U.S. C5 130
Three Springs, Austl. F2 60
Throckmorton, co., Tx., U.S. C3 136
Throop, Pa., U.S. m18 131
Thule (Qaanaaq), Grnld. C26 82
Thun, Switz. A1 18
Thunder Bay, On., Can. o17 89
Thunder Bay, stm., Mi., U.S. D6 115
Thunder Bay, b., Mi., U.S. D7 115
Thunderbird, Lake, res., Ok., U.S. B4 129

Name — Map Ref. — Page

Thunderbolt, Ga., U.S. D5 103
Thunder Butte Creek, stm., S.D., U.S. B3 134
Thurmont, Md., U.S. A3 113
Thurso, Qc., Can. D2 90
Thurso, Scot., U.K. A5 12
Thurston, co., Ne., U.S. B9 120
Thurston, co., Wa., U.S. C2 140
Thy, reg., Den. H3 10
Thyolo, Mwi. B6 56
Tianchang, China C4 30
Tiandong, China E2 30
Tianguá, Braz. B3 74
Tianjin, China D11 28
Tianjun, China D7 28
Tianlin, China E2 30
Tianmen, China E10 28
Tianshui, China E9 28
Tiantai, China F12 28
Tianyang, China E2 30
Tianzhu, China D8 28
Tiassalé, C. Iv. E4 50
Tibasti, Sarīr, des., Libya B8 50
Tibati, Cam. B2 54
Tiber see Tevere, stm., Italy C4 18
Tiberias see Teverya, Isr. D3 42
Tibesti, mts., Afr. B8 50
Tibet see Xizang Zizhiqu, prov., China E5 28
Tibet, Plateau of see Qing Zang Gaoyuan, plat., China E4 28
Tiburón, Isla, i., Mex. B2 78
Tice, Fl., U.S. F5 102
Tichît, Maur. C3 50
Tickfaw, stm., La., U.S. C5 111
Ticonderoga, N.Y., U.S. B7 125
Ticul, Mex. C7 78
Tidaholm, Swe. G5 10
Tide Head, N.B., Can. B3 87
Tidjikja, Maur. C2 50
Tiébissou, C. Iv. E3 50
Tieli, China A1 31
Tieling, China C12 28
Tien Shan, mts., Asia C3 28
Tientsin see Tianjin, China D11 28
Tierp, Swe. F7 10
Tierra Amarilla, N.M., U.S. A3 124
Tierra Blanca, Mex. D5 78
Tierra de Campos, reg., Spain F4 16
Tierra del Fuego, i., S.A. H3 69
Tietê, stm., Braz. F1 74
Tieton, Wa., U.S. C5 140
Tieton, stm., Wa., U.S. C4 140
Tieton Dam, Wa., U.S. C4 140
Tiffany Mountain, mtn., Wa., U.S. A6 140
Tiffin, Oh., U.S. A2 128
Tiffin, stm., Oh., U.S. A1 128
Tift, co., Ga., U.S. E3 103
Tifton, Ga., U.S. E3 103
Tigard, Or., U.S. h12 130
Tigerton, Wi., U.S. D4 142
Tighina, Mol. F10 20
Tigil', Russia D17 26
Tignall, Ga., U.S. C4 103
Tignish, P.E., Can. C5 87
Tigris (Dicle) (Dijlah), stm., Asia D5 42
Tiguentourine, Alg. F5 14
Tihert, Alg. D4 14
Tihoreck, Russia E6 26
Tihvin, Russia C5 22
Tijuana, Mex. A1 78
Tikal, hist., Guat. B2 80
Tikamgarh, India E3 40
Tikrīt, Iraq D4 42
Tikšeozero, ozero, l., Russia C15 10
Tiksi, Russia B14 26
Tilburg, Neth. E9 12
Tilbury, On., Can. E2 89
Tilden, Il., U.S. E4 106
Tilden, Ne., U.S. B8 120
Tilghman, Md., U.S. C5 113
Tilghman Island, i., Md., U.S. C5 113
Tilimsen, Alg. D4 48
Tillabéri, Niger D5 50
Tillamook, Or., U.S. B3 130
Tillamook, co., Or., U.S. B3 130
Tillanchāng Dwīp, i., India H6 40
Tillery, Lake, res., N.C., U.S. B2 126
Tillman, co., Ok., U.S. C2 129
Tillmans Corner, Al., U.S. E1 94
Tillsonburg, On., Can. E4 89
Tílos, i., Grc. F11 18
Tilton, Il., U.S. C6 106
Tilton, N.H., U.S. D3 122
Tiltonsville, Oh., U.S. B5 128
Timanskij krjaž, Russia C7 26
Timaru, N.Z. p13 63c
Timaševsk, Russia G15 20
Timbalier Island, i., La., U.S. E5 111
Timbaúba, Braz. C4 74
Timbedgha, Maur. C3 50
Timberlake, Va., U.S. C3 139
Timberville, Va., U.S. B4 139
Timbuktu see Tombouctou, Mali C4 50
Timimoun, Alg. E5 48
Timirist, Râs, c., Maur. C1 50
Timișoara, Rom. G6 20
Timmins, On., Can. o19 89
Timmonsville, S.C., U.S. C8 133
Timms Hill, Wi., U.S. C3 142
Timon, Braz. C3 74
Timor, i., Asia E7 36
Timor Sea F6 58
Timošino, Russia B6 22
Timpanogos Cave National Monument, Ut., U.S. C4 137
Timšer, Russia B9 22
Tims Ford Lake, res., Tn., U.S. B5 135
Tinaca Point, c., Phil. E9 34
Tinaquillo, Ven. C6 80
Tindouf, Alg. E3 48
Tinghert, Ḥamādat, plat., Afr. E7 48
Tingmerkpuk Mountain, mtn., Ak., U.S. B7 95
Tingo María, Peru E4 70
Tingsryd, Swe. H6 10
Tinian, i., N. Mar. Is. D12 32
Tinker Air Force Base, mil., Ok., U.S. B4 129
Tinley Park, Il., U.S. k9 106
Tinniswood, Mount, mtn., B.C., Can. D6 85
Tinogasta, Arg. D4 72
Tínos, i., Grc. F10 18
Tinsukia, India D7 40
Tintina, Arg. D5 72
Tinton Falls, N.J., U.S. C4 123
Tioga, La., U.S. C3 111
Tioga, N.D., U.S. A3 127
Tioga, co., N.Y., U.S. C4 125
Tioga, stm., Pa., U.S. B7 131
Tioga, co., Pa., U.S. C7 131
Tiogue Lake, res., R.I., U.S. D3 132
Tioman, Pulau, i., Malay. C2 36
Tionesta Creek, stm., Pa., U.S. C3 131
Tionesta Lake, res., Pa., U.S. D3 131
Tioughnioga, stm., N.Y., U.S. C4 125
Tipitapa, Nic. C2 80
Tippah, co., Ms., U.S. A5 117
Tippah, stm., Ms., U.S. A4 117
Tipp City, Oh., U.S. C1 128
Tippecanoe, stm., In., U.S. C4 107
Tippecanoe, co., In., U.S. D4 107
Tipperary, Austl. C5 60
Tipton, Ca., U.S. D4 98
Tipton, Ia., U.S. C6 108
Tipton, In., U.S. D5 107
Tipton, co., In., U.S. D5 107
Tipton, Mo., U.S. C5 118
Tipton, Ok., U.S. C2 129
Tipton, co., Tn., U.S. B2 135
Tipton, Mount, mtn., Az., U.S. B1 96
Tiptonville, Tn., U.S. A2 135
Tirana see Tiranë, Alb. D7 18
Tiranë, Alb. D7 18
Tiraspol, Mol. F10 20
Tire, Tur. C2 44
Tirebolu, Tur. B8 44
Tiree, i., Scot., U.K. B3 12
Tírnavos, Grc. E9 18
Tiruchchirāppalli, India G3 40
Tirunelveli, India H3 40
Tirupati, India G3 40
Tiruppur, India G3 40
Tiruvannāmalai, India G3 40
Tiruvottiyūr, India G4 40
Tisa (Tisza) (Tysa), stm., Eur. G6 20
Tishomingo, co., Ms., U.S. A5 117
Tishomingo, Ok., U.S. C5 129
Tiskilwa, Il., U.S. B4 106
Tissemsilt, Alg. J7 16
Tista, stm., Asia A1 34
Tisza (Tisa) (Tysa), stm., Eur. F6 20
Titicaca, Lago, l., S.A. E4 68
Titilāgarh, India E4 40
Titograd see Podgorica, Serb. C7 18
Titonka, Ia., U.S. A3 108
Titov Veles, Mac. D8 18
Titran, Nor. E3 10
Titule, D.R.C. C5 54
Titus, co., Tx., U.S. C5 136
Titusville, Fl., U.S. D6 102
Titusville, Pa., U.S. C2 131
Tivaouane, Sen. C1 50
Tiverton, On., Can. C3 89
Tiverton, R.I., U.S. D6 132
Tizimín, Mex. C7 78
Tizi-Ouzou, Alg. C5 48
Tjeggelvas, l., Swe. C7 10
Tjukalinsk, Russia D9 26
Tjul'gan, Russia D10 22
Tjumen', Russia D8 26
Tkibuli, Geor. A10 44
Tkvarčeli, Geor. A9 44
Tlahualilo de Zaragoza, Mex. B4 78
Tlalnepantla, Mex. D5 78
Tlaquepaque, Mex. C4 78
Tlaxcala, state, Mex. D5 78
Tlaxcala de Xicohténcatl, Mex. D5 78
Tmassah, Libya A8 50
Toamasina, Madag. B8 56
Toano, Va., U.S. C6 139
Toano Range, mts., Nv., U.S. C7 121
Toast, N.C., U.S. A2 126
Toba, Danau, l., Indon. C1 36
Tobacco Root Mountains, mts., Mt., U.S. E5 119
Tobago, i., Trin. C7 80
Toba Inlet, b., B.C., Can. D5 85
Toba Kākar Range, mts., Pak. D9 42
Tobejuba, Isla, i., Ven. D7 80
Tobin, Mount, mtn., Nv., U.S. C4 121
Tobin Lake, l., Sk., Can. D4 91
Tobin Range, mts., Nv., U.S. C4 121
Tobique, stm., N.B., Can. B2 87
Tobol, stm., Asia D8 26
Tobol, Kaz. D11 22
Tobol'sk, Russia D8 26
Tobyhanna, Pa., U.S. D11 131
Tocantínia, Braz. E10 70
Tocantinópolis, Braz. C2 74
Tocantins, state, Braz. D2 74
Tocantins, stm., Braz. B2 74
Toccoa, Ga., U.S. B3 103
Toccoa, stm., Ga., U.S. B2 103
Toccoa Falls, Ga., U.S. B3 103
Tocopilla, Chile B2 69
Todd, co., Ky., U.S. D2 110
Todd, co., Mn., U.S. D4 116
Todd, co., S.D., U.S. D5 134
Tofield, Ab., Can. C4 84
Tofino, B.C., Can. E5 85
Togiak, Ak., U.S. D7 95
Togian, Kepulauan, is., Indon. D6 36
Togo, ctry., Afr. E5 50
Togtoh, China A3 30
Togwotee Pass, Wy., U.S. C2 143
Tohakum Peak, mtn., Nv., U.S. C2 121
Tohatchi, N.M., U.S. B1 124
Tohopekaliga, Lake, l., Fl., U.S. D5 102
Toiyabe Range, mts., Nv., U.S. D4 121
Tok, Ak., U.S. C11 95
Tōkamachi, Japan C3 31
Tokat, Tur. B7 44
Tokelau, dep., Oc. E12 58
Tokmak, Kyrg. A3 40
Tokmak, Ukr. F13 20
Tokoroa, N.Z. o14 63c
Toktogul, Kyrg. A2 40
Tokuno-shima, i., Japan A9 34
Tokushima, Japan D2 31
Tōkyō, Japan D16 28
Tôlañaro, Madag. D8 56
Toledo, Braz. C7 72
Toledo, Spain H4 16
Toledo, Ia., U.S. B5 108
Toledo, Il., U.S. D5 106
Toledo, Oh., U.S. A2 128
Toledo, Or., U.S. C3 130
Toledo Bend Reservoir, res., U.S. C2 111
Toledo Bend Reservoir, res., U.S. E9 92
Toler, Ky., U.S. C7 110
Toliara, Madag. C7 56
Tolima, Nevado del, vol., Col. C4 70
Tolitoli, Indon. C6 36
Toljatti, Russia D6 26
Tol'ka, Russia C10 26
Tolland, co., Ct., U.S. B6 100
Tolland, Ct., U.S. B6 100
Tollesboro, Ky., U.S. B6 110
Tolleson, Az., U.S. m8 96
Tolmezzo, Italy A4 18
Tolo, D.R.C. D3 54
Tolo, Gulf of see Tolo, Teluk, b., Indon. D6 36
Tolo, Teluk, b., Indon. D6 36
Tolono, Il., U.S. D5 106
Tolstoj, mys, c., Russia D17 26
Tolt Reservoir, res., Wa., U.S. B4 140
Tolú, Col. D4 80
Toluca, Il., U.S. C4 106
Toluca de Lerdo, Mex. D5 78
Tomah, Wi., U.S. E3 142
Tomahawk, Wi., U.S. C4 142
Tomahawk Lake, l., Wi., U.S. C4 142
Tomakomai, Japan C16 28
Tomaszów Lubelski, Pol. D7 20
Tomaszów Mazowiecki, Pol. D6 20
Tomball, Tx., U.S. D5 136
Tombe, Sudan B6 54
Tombigbee, stm., U.S. D1 94
Tombouctou, Mali C4 50
Tombstone, Az., U.S. F5 96
Tombua, Ang. B1 56
Tomé, Chile F3 72
Tomé-Açu, Braz. B2 74
Tomelloso, Spain H5 16
Tom Green, co., Tx., U.S. D2 136
Tomini, Indon. C6 36
Tomini, Gulf of see Tomini, Teluk, b., Indon. D6 36
Tomini, Teluk, b., Indon. D6 36
Tom Nevers Head, c., Ma., U.S. D8 114
Tomo, stm., Col. B6 70
Tompkins, co., N.Y., U.S. C4 125
Tompkinsville, Ky., U.S. D4 110
Tom Price, Austl. E2 60
Tomptokan, Russia D15 26
Toms, stm., N.J., U.S. C4 123
Tomsk, Russia D10 26
Toms River, N.J., U.S. D4 123
Tonalá, Mex. D6 78
Tonasket, Wa., U.S. A6 140
Tonawanda Indian Reservation, N.Y., U.S. B2 125
Tondano, Indon. C6 36
Tonekābon, Iran C6 42
Tonga, ctry., Oc. F12 58
Tonganoxie, Ks., U.S. C8 109
Tonga Ridge J21 64
Tongatapu, i., Tonga G12 58
Tonga Trench K21 64
Tongcheng, China E11 28
Tongchuan, China D9 28
Tongguan, China E10 28
Tonghai, China G8 28
Tonghua, China C13 28
Tongjiang, China A2 31
Tongjiang, China C2 30
Tongjosŏn-man, b., N. Kor. D13 28
Tongliao, China C12 28
Tongoy, Chile D2 69
Tongren, China B1 30
Tongren, China F9 28
Tongsa Dzong, Bhu. D6 40
Tongtian, stm., China E7 28
Tongue, stm., Mt., U.S. E10 119
Tongue, stm., Tx., U.S. p13 136
Tongxian, China D11 28
Tongyu, China C12 28
Tongzi, China F9 28
Tonk, India D3 40
Tonkawa, Ok., U.S. A4 129
Tonkin, Gulf of, b., Asia B5 34
Tônlé Sab, Bœng, l., Camb. D4 34
Tonle Sap see Tônlé Sab, Bœng, l., Camb. D4 34
Tonopah, Nv., U.S. E4 121
Tønsberg, Nor. G4 10
Tonstad, Nor. G2 10
Tonto National Monument, Az., U.S. D4 96
Tonto Natural Bridge, Az., U.S. C4 96
Tooele, Ut., U.S. C3 137
Tooele, co., Ut., U.S. C2 137
Toole, co., Mt., U.S. B5 119
Toombs, co., Ga., U.S. D4 103
Toomsboro, Ga., U.S. D3 103
Toora-Hem, Russia D11 26
Toowoomba, Austl. F5 62
Topeka, In., U.S. A6 107
Topeka, Ks., U.S. C8 109
Topock, Az., U.S. C1 96
Topol'čany, Slvk. E5 20
Topolobampo, Mex. B3 78
Topozero, ozero, l., Russia D14 10
Toppenish, Wa., U.S. C5 140
Topsfield, Ma., U.S. A6 114
Topsham, Me., U.S. E3 112
Top Springs, Austl. D5 60
Topton, Pa., U.S. F10 131
Toquima Range, mts., Nv., U.S. E5 121
Tor, Eth. B6 54
Torbalı, Tur. C2 44
Torbat-e Ḥeydarīyeh, Iran C7 42
Torbat-e Jām, Iran C8 42
Torbay, N.L., Can. E5 88
Torbay see Torquay, Eng., U.K. E5 12
Torbert, Mount, mtn., Ak., U.S. g15 95
Torch Lake, l., Mi., U.S. D5 115
Tordesillas, Spain G4 16
Töre, Swe. D10 10
Torez, Ukr. E15 20
Torino (Turin), Italy B1 18
Torit, Sudan J11 48
Torneälven (Tornionjoki), stm., Eur. C9 10
Torneträsk, l., Swe. B8 10
Torngat Mountains, mts., Can. f8 88
Tornio, Fin. D11 10
Tornionjoki (Torneälven), stm., Eur. C10 10
Tornquist, Arg. F5 72
Toro, Spain G4 16
Toronto, On., Can. D5 89
Toronto, Oh., U.S. B5 128
Toronto Lake, res., Ks., U.S. E7 109
Toro Peak, mtn., Ca., U.S. F5 98
Tororo, Ug. C6 54
Toros Dağları, mts., Tur. D5 44
Torquay, Eng., U.K. E5 12
Torrance, Ca., U.S. n12 98
Torrance, co., N.M., U.S. C3 124
Torrelavega, Spain F4 16
Torremolinos, Spain I4 16
Torrens, Lake, l., Austl. G2 62
Torrent, Spain H6 16
Torreón, Mex. B4 78
Torres, Îles, is., Vanuatu j9 62a
Torres Strait, strt., Oc. B3 62
Torres Vedras, Port. H2 16
Torrington, Ct., U.S. B3 100
Torrington, Wy., U.S. D8 143
Tórshavn, Far. Is. n23 10b
Tórtolas, Cerro las, mtn., S.A. D4 72
Tortosa, Spain G7 16
Tortue, Île de la, i., Haiti A5 80
Toruń, Pol. C5 20
Toržok, Russia C5 22
Tostado, Arg. D5 72
Tõstamaa, Est. G10 10
Tosya, Tur. B5 44
Totagatic, stm., Wi., U.S. B2 142
Totana, Spain I6 16
Toteng, Bots. C3 56
Tot'ma, Russia B7 22
Totowa, N.J., U.S. B4 123
Totson Mountain, mtn., Ak., U.S. C8 95
Tottenham (part of Alliston Beeton Tecumseth and Tottenham), On., Can. C5 89
Tottori, Japan C2 31
Touba, C. Iv. E3 50
Toubkal, Jebel, mtn., Mor. D3 48
Touchet, stm., Wa., U.S. C7 140
Toudao see Songhua, stm., China B14 28
Touggourt, Alg. D6 48
Touisset, Ma., U.S. C5 114
Toul, Fr. C9 16
Touliu, Tai. E5 30
Toulon, Fr. F9 16
Toulon, Il., U.S. B4 106
Toulouse, Fr. F7 16
Toumodi, C. Iv. E3 50
Toungoo, Mya. C3 34
Touraine, hist. reg., Fr. D7 16
Tournai, Bel. E8 12
Tours, Fr. D7 16
Toussaint Creek, stm., Oh., U.S. f7 128
Toussidé, Pic, vol., Chad B8 50
Toutle, North Fork, stm., Wa., U.S. C3 140
Touwsrivier, S. Afr. E3 56
Tovarkovskij, Russia C15 20
Tovuz, Azer. B11 44
Towanda, Il., U.S. C5 106
Towanda, Ks., U.S. E7 109
Towanda, Pa., U.S. C9 131
Towanda Creek, stm., Pa., U.S. C8 131
Tower City, Pa., U.S. E8 131
Town Creek, Al., U.S. A2 94
Towner, N.D., U.S. A5 127
Towner, co., N.D., U.S. A6 127
Towns, co., Ga., U.S. B3 103
Townsend, De., U.S. C3 101
Townsend, Mt., U.S. D5 119
Townshend Reservoir, res., Vt., U.S. E3 138
Townsville, Austl. D4 62
Towson, Md., U.S. B4 113
Towuti, Danau, l., Indon. D6 36
Toyama, Japan D15 28
Toyohashi, Japan D3 31
Toyota, Japan C3 31
Tozeur, Tun. D6 48
Trabzon, Tur. B8 44
Tracadie, N.B., Can. B5 87
Tracy, N.B., Can. D3 87
Tracy, Qc., Can. C4 90
Tracy, Ca., U.S. D3 98
Tracy, Mn., U.S. F3 116
Tracy City, Tn., U.S. D8 135
Tracyton, Wa., U.S. e10 140
Tradewater, stm., Ky., U.S. C2 110
Traer, Ia., U.S. B5 108
Trafford, Pa., U.S. k14 131
Trafford, Lake, l., Fl., U.S. F5 102
Trail, B.C., Can. E9 85
Trail Creek, In., U.S. A4 107
Traill, co., N.D., U.S. B8 127
Trail Ridge, mtn., U.S. F4 103
Tralee, Ire. D2 12
Tranås, Swe. G6 10
Trancas, Arg. D4 72
Trang, Thai. E3 34
Trangan, Pulau, i., Indon. E8 36
Trani, Italy D6 18
Transantarctic Mountains, mts., Ant. E32 67
Transkei, hist. reg., S. Afr. E4 56
Transylvania, hist. reg., Rom. F7 20
Transylvania, co., N.C., U.S. f10 126
Transylvanian Alps see Carpații Meridionali, mts., Rom. G7 20
Trapani, Italy E4 18
Trappe, Md., U.S. C5 113
Trapper Peak, mtn., Mt., U.S. E2 119
Traralgon, Austl. H4 62
Trârza, reg., Maur. C1 50
Trasimeno, Lago, l., Italy C3 18
Travelers Rest, S.C., U.S. B3 133
Traverse, co., Mn., U.S. E2 116
Traverse, Lake, l., U.S. B9 134
Traverse City, Mi., U.S. D5 115
Tra Vinh, Viet. E5 34
Travis, co., Tx., U.S. D4 136
Travis Air Force Base, mil., Ca., U.S. C2 98
Travnik, Bos. B6 18
Tray Mountain, mtn., Ga., U.S. B3 103
Trayning, Austl. G2 60
Treasure, co., Mt., U.S. D9 119
Treasure Island Naval Station, mil., Ca., U.S. h8 98

Name | Map Ref. | Page

Třebíč, Czech Rep. E3 20
Trebišov, Slvk. E6 20
Trego, co., Ks., U.S. D4 109
Treherne, Mb., Can. E2 86
Treinta y Tres, Ur. E7 72
Trelew, Arg. F3 69
Trelleborg, Swe. I5 10
Tremblant, Mont, mtn., Qc., Can. C3 90
Tremont, Il., U.S. C4 106
Tremont, Pa., U.S. E9 131
Tremonton, Ut., U.S. B3 137
Tremp, Spain F7 16
Trempealeau, Wi., U.S. D2 142
Trempealeau, stm., Wi., U.S. D2 142
Trempealeau, co., Wi., U.S. D2 142
Trenche, stm., Qc., Can. B5 90
Trenčín, Slvk. E5 20
Trenque Lauquen, Arg. F5 72
Trent, stm., Eng., U.K. D6 12
Trent, stm., N.C., U.S. B5 126
Trente et un Milles, Lac des, l., Qc., Can. C2 90
Trento, Italy A3 18
Trenton, On., Can. C7 89
Trenton, Fl., U.S. C4 102
Trenton, Ga., U.S. B1 103
Trenton, Il., U.S. E4 106
Trenton, Mi., U.S. F7 115
Trenton, Mo., U.S. A4 118
Trenton, Ne., U.S. D4 120
Trenton, N.J., U.S. C3 123
Trenton, Oh., U.S. C1 128
Trenton, Tn., U.S. B3 135
Trepassey, N.L., Can. E5 88
Trepassey Bay, b., N.L., Can. E5 88
Tres Arroyos, Arg. F5 72
Tresckow, Pa., U.S. E10 131
Três Corações, Braz. F2 74
Tres Esquinas, Col. C4 70
Três Lagoas, Braz. F1 74
Tres Marías, Islas, is., Mex. C3 78
Três Marias, Represa de, res., Braz. E2 74
Tres Puntas, Cabo, c., Arg. G3 69
Três Rios, Braz. F3 74
Tres Zapotes, hist., Mex. D5 78
Treutlen, co., Ga., U.S. D4 103
Treviso, Italy B4 18
Trevor, Wi., U.S. n11 142
Trevorton, Pa., U.S. E8 131
Treynor, Ia., U.S. C2 108
Trezevant, Tn., U.S. A3 135
Triadelphia, W.V., U.S. A4 141
Triadelphia Reservoir, res., Md., U.S. B3 113
Triangle, Va., U.S. B5 139
Tribune, Ks., U.S. D2 109
Tricase, Italy E7 18
Trichinopoly see Tiruchchirāppalli, India G3 40
Trichūr, India G3 40
Tri City, Or., U.S. E3 130
Trident Peak, mtn., Nv., U.S. B3 121
Trier, Ger. F10 12
Trieste, Italy B4 18
Trigg, co., Ky., U.S. D2 110
Triglav, mtn., Slvn. A4 18
Trigo Mountains, mts., Az., U.S. D1 96
Tríkala, Grc. E8 18
Trikora, Puncak, mtn., Indon. G10 32
Tri Lakes, In., U.S. B7 107
Trimble, co., Ky., U.S. B4 110
Trimble, Tn., U.S. A2 135
Trimont, Mn., U.S. G4 116
Trincomalee, Sri L. H4 40
Tring Jonction, Qc., Can. C6 90
Trinidad, Bol. A5 72
Trinidad, Col. B5 70
Trinidad, Cuba A3 80
Trinidad, i., Trin. C7 80
Trinidad, Ur. E6 72
Trinidad, Co., U.S. D6 99
Trinidad, Tx., U.S. C4 136
Trinidad and Tobago, ctry., N.A. F12 76
Trinidad Head, c., Ca., U.S. B1 98
Trinity, Al., U.S. A2 94
Trinity, stm., Ca., U.S. B2 98
Trinity, co., Ca., U.S. B2 98
Trinity, Tx., U.S. D5 136
Trinity, co., Tx., U.S. D5 136
Trinity, stm., Tx., U.S. D5 136
Trinity Bay, b., N.L., Can. D5 88
Trinity Islands, is., Ak., U.S. D9 95
Trinity Mountain, mtn., Id., U.S. F3 105
Trinity Mountains, mts., Ca., U.S. B2 98
Trinity Peak, mtn., Nv., U.S. C3 121
Trinity Range, mts., Nv., U.S. C3 121
Trion, Ga., U.S. B1 103
Tripoli see Ţarābulus, Leb. E6 44
Tripoli see Ţarābulus, Libya D7 48
Tripoli, Ia., U.S. B5 108
Tripolis, Grc. F9 18
Tripolitania see Ţarābulus, hist. reg., Libya E7 14
Tripp, S.D., U.S. D8 134
Tripp, co., S.D., U.S. D6 134
Tripura, state, India E6 40
Tristan da Cunha Group, is., St. Hel. M8 46
Triumph, La., U.S. E6 111
Trivandrum see Thiruvananthapuram, India H3 40
Trnava, Slvk. E4 20
Trochu, Ab., Can. D4 84
Troick, Russia D8 26
Troicko-Pečorsk, Russia B10 22
Trois-Pistoles, Qc., Can. A8 90
Trois-Rivières, Qc., Can. C5 90
Trois-Rivières-Ouest, Qc., Can. C5 90
Troïts'ke, Ukr. F11 20
Trollhättan, Swe. G5 10
Tromsø, Nor. B8 10
Trona, Ca., U.S. E5 98
Tronador, Monte, mtn., S.A. F2 69
Trondheim, Nor. E4 10
Trondheimsfjorden, b., Nor. E4 10
Trophy Mountain, mtn., B.C., Can. D8 85
Trotwood, Oh., U.S. C1 128
Troup, co., Ga., U.S. C1 103
Trousdale, co., Tn., U.S. A5 135
Trout, stm., Fl., U.S. m8 102
Trout, stm., Vt., U.S. B3 138
Trout Creek, On., Can. B5 89
Trout Creek Pass, Co., U.S. C5 99
Trout Lake, l., On., Can. o16 89
Trout Lake, l., Mn., U.S. B6 116
Trout Lake, Wa., U.S. D4 140
Trout Lake, l., Wi., U.S. B4 142
Troutman, N.C., U.S. B2 126
Trout Peak, mtn., Wy., U.S. B3 143
Trout River, N.L., Can. D2 88
Troy see Truva, hist., Tur. C2 44
Troy, Al., U.S. D4 94
Troy, Id., U.S. C2 105
Troy, Il., U.S. E4 106
Troy, Ks., U.S. C8 109
Troy, Mi., U.S. o15 115
Troy, Mo., U.S. C7 118
Troy, Mt., U.S. B1 119
Troy, N.C., U.S. B3 126
Troy, N.H., U.S. E2 122
Troy, N.Y., U.S. C7 125
Troy, Oh., U.S. B1 128
Troy, Pa., U.S. C8 131
Troy, Tn., U.S. A2 135
Troyes, Fr. C8 16
Troy Peak, mtn., Nv., U.S. E6 121
Trubč'evsk, Russia C12 20
Truchas Peak, mtn., N.M., U.S. B4 124
Trucial States see United Arab Emirates, ctry., Asia F6 42
Truckee, Ca., U.S. C3 98
Truckee, stm., U.S. D2 121
Trujillo, Hond. B2 80
Trujillo, Peru E4 70
Trujillo, Spain H4 16
Trujillo, Ven. B5 70
Truk Islands see Chuuk Islands, is., Micron. D9 58
Truman, Mn., U.S. G4 116
Trumann, Ar., U.S. B5 97
Trumansburg, N.Y., U.S. C4 125
Trumbull, Ct., U.S. E3 100
Trumbull, co., Oh., U.S. A5 128
Trumbull, Mount, mtn., Az., U.S. A2 96
Trussville, Al., U.S. B3 94
Trustom Pond, l., R.I., U.S. G3 132
Truth or Consequences (Hot Springs), N.M., U.S. D2 124
Truva (Troy), hist., Tur. C2 44
Tryon, N.C., U.S. f10 126
Trzcianka, Pol. C4 20
Tsaidam Basin see Qaidam Pendi, bas., China D6 28
Tsala Apopka Lake, l., Fl., U.S. D4 102
Tsaratanana, mts., Madag. A8 56
Tsaratanana, Madag. B8 56
Tsau, Bots. C3 56
Tsavo, Kenya D7 54
Tschida, Lake, res., N.D., U.S. C4 127
Tselinograd see Astana, Kaz. D9 26
Tses, Nmb. D2 56
Tsévié, Togo E5 50
Tshabong, Bots. D3 56
Tshane, Bots. C3 56
Tshela, D.R.C. E2 54
Tshikapa, D.R.C. E4 54
Tshofa, D.R.C. E5 54
Tshumbe (Chiumbe), stm., Afr. E4 54
Tsimlyansk Reservoir see Cimljanskoe vodohranilišče, res., Russia E7 22
Tsintsabis, Nmb. B2 56
Tsiombe, Madag. D8 56
Tsiroanomandidy, Madag. B8 56
Tsu, Japan D3 31
Tsugaru-kaikyō, strt., Japan C16 28
Tsumeb, Nmb. B2 56
Tsuruoka, Japan D15 28
Tsushima, is., Japan D1 31
Tsuyama, Japan C2 31
Tswaane, Bots. C3 56
Tual, Indon. E8 36
Tualatin, stm., Or., U.S. h11 130
Tuamotu, Îles, is., Fr. Poly. F15 58
Tuamotu Ridge J24 64
Tuangku, Pulau, i., Indon. C1 36
Tuapse, Russia E5 26
Tuba City, Az., U.S. A4 96
Tuban, Indon. E4 36
Tubarão, Braz. D8 72
Tübingen, Ger. F11 12
Ţubruq, Libya D9 48
Tubuai, i., Fr. Poly. G15 58
Tucacas, Ven. A6 70
Tucannon, stm., Wa., U.S. C8 140
Tucano, Braz. D4 74
Tuckahoe, stm., N.J., U.S. E3 123
Tuckahoe, N.Y., U.S. h13 125
Tuckanarra, Austl. F2 60
Tucker, Ga., U.S. h8 103
Tucker, co., W.V., U.S. B5 141
Tucker Island, i., N.J., U.S. E4 123
Tuckerman, Ar., U.S. B4 97
Tuckernuck Island, i., Ma., U.S. D7 114
Tuckerton, N.J., U.S. D4 123
Tucson, Az., U.S. E5 96
Tucumcari, N.M., U.S. B6 124
Tucumcari Mountain, mtn., N.M., U.S. B6 124
Tucupita, Ven. B7 70
Tucuruí, Braz. B2 74
Tucuruí, Represa de, res., Braz. B2 74
Tudela, Spain F6 16
Tudmur, Syria E8 44
Tugaloo Lake, res., U.S. B1 133
Tugela, stm., S. Afr. D5 56
Tug Fork, stm., U.S. C2 141
Tuguegarao City, Phil. C8 34
Tugur, Russia D15 26
Tujmazy, Russia D9 22
Tukangbesi, Kepulauan, is., Indon. E6 36
Tūkrah, Libya E8 14
Tukums, Lat. H10 10
Tukuyu, Tan. E6 54
Tukwila, Wa., U.S. f11 140
Tula, Mex. C5 78
Tula, Russia D5 26
Tulalip Indian Reservation, Wa., U.S. A3 140
Tulancingo, Mex. C5 78
Tulare, Ca., U.S. D4 98
Tulare, co., Ca., U.S. D4 98
Tulare Lake, l., Ca., U.S. D4 98
Tularosa, N.M., U.S. D3 124
Tularosa Mountains, mts., N.M., U.S. D1 124
Tularosa Valley, val., N.M., U.S. E3 124
Tulbagh, S. Afr. E2 56
Tulcán, Ec. C4 70
Tulcea, Rom. G10 20
Tul'chyn, Ukr. E10 20
Tule Lake, sw., Ca., U.S. B3 98
Tule River Indian Reservation, Ca., U.S. E4 98
Tule Valley, val., Ut., U.S. D2 137
Tuli, Zimb. C4 56
Tulia, Tx., U.S. B2 136
Tullahoma, Tn., U.S. B5 135
Tulle, Fr. E7 16
Tully, Austl. D4 62
Tulsa, Ok., U.S. A6 129
Tulsa, co., Ok., U.S. B6 129
Tuluá, Col. E4 80
Tulun, Russia D12 26
Tulungagung, Indon. E4 36
Tumacacori National Monument, Az., U.S. F4 96
Tumaco, Col. C4 70
Tuman-gang (Tumen), stm., Asia B1 31
Tumanovo, Russia B13 20
Tumbarumba, Austl. H4 62
Tumbes, Peru D3 70
Tumble Mountain, mtn., Mt., U.S. E7 119
Tumbler Ridge, B.C., Can. B7 85
Tumen (Tuman-gang), stm., Asia B1 31
Tumen, China C13 28
Tumeremo, Ven. B7 70
Tumkūr, India G3 40
Tumuc-Humac Mountains, mts., S.A. C8 70
Tumut, Austl. H4 62
Tumwater, Wa., U.S. B3 140
Tunceli, Tur. C8 44
Tunduru, Tan. F7 54
Tunga, Nig. E6 50
Tungabhadra, stm., India F3 40
Tungabhadra Reservoir, res., India F3 40
Tungkang, Tai. E5 30
Tungsha Tao (Pratas Island), i., Tai. E4 30
Tuni, India F4 40
Tunica, Ms., U.S. A3 117
Tunica, co., Ms., U.S. A3 117
Tunis, Tun. C7 48
Tunis, Golfe de, b., Tun. F3 18
Tunis, Gulf of see Tunis, Golfe de, b., Tun. F3 18
Tunisia, ctry., Afr. D7 48
Tunja, Col. B5 70
Tunkhannock, Pa., U.S. C10 131
Tunk Lake, l., Me., U.S. D4 112
Tunnel Hill, Ga., U.S. B1 103
Tunp Range, mts., Wy., U.S. D2 143
Tununak, Ak., U.S. C6 95
Tunuyán, Arg. E4 72
Tunxi, China D4 30
Tuolumne, Ca., U.S. D3 98
Tuolumne, stm., Ca., U.S. D3 98
Tuolumne, co., Ca., U.S. C4 98
Tupã, Braz. F1 74
Tupaciguara, Braz. E2 74
Tupelo, Ms., U.S. A5 117
Tupiza, Bol. C4 72
Tupper Lake, N.Y., U.S. A6 125
Tupper Lake, l., N.Y., U.S. A6 125
Tura, India D6 40
Tura, Russia C11 26
Tura, stm., Russia D18 6
Turan, Russia A6 28
Turan Lowland, pl., Asia B7 42
Turayf, Sau. Ar. G8 44
Turbat, Pak. E8 42
Turbeville, S.C., U.S. D7 133
Turbo, Col. B4 70
Turda, Rom. F7 20
Turgaj, stm., Kaz. E8 26
Turgaj, Kaz. E8 26
Turgajskaja ložbina, reg., Kaz. D8 26
Turgutlu, Tur. C2 44
Turhal, Tur. B7 44
Turia, stm., Spain H6 16
Turin see Torino, Italy B1 18
Turinsk, Russia C11 22
Turkana, Lake see Rudolf, Lake, l., Afr. C7 54
Turkestan, Kaz. E8 26
Turkey, ctry., Asia C3 38
Turkey, stm., Ia., U.S. B6 108
Turkey Creek, stm., Ok., U.S. A3 129
Turkey Point, c., Md., U.S. B5 113
Turkish Republic of Northern Cyprus see North Cyprus, ctry., Asia C2 44
Turkmenbaši, Turk. E7 26
Turkmenistan, ctry., Asia C7 42
Türkoğlu, Tur. D7 44
Turks and Caicos Islands, dep., N.A. D10 76
Turks Islands, is., T./C. Is. A5 80
Turku (Åbo), Fin. F10 10
Turley, Ok., U.S. A6 129
Turlock, Ca., U.S. D3 98
Turnbull, Mount, mtn., Az., U.S. D5 96
Turneffe Islands, is., Belize B2 80
Turner, co., Ga., U.S. E3 103
Turner, Or., U.S. C4 130
Turner, co., S.D., U.S. D8 134
Turners Falls, Ma., U.S. A2 114
Turner Valley, Ab., Can. D3 84
Turnor Lake, l., Sk., Can. m7 91
Turnu Măgurele, Rom. H8 20
Turpan, China C5 28
Turpan Pendi, depr., China C5 28
Turquino, Pico, mtn., Cuba B4 80
Turrell, Ar., U.S. B5 97
Turret Peak, mtn., Az., U.S. C4 96
Turtle Creek, Pa., U.S. k14 131
Turtle Flambeau Flowage, res., Wi., U.S. B3 142
Turtle Lake, l., Sk., Can. D1 91
Turtle Lake, N.D., U.S. B5 127
Turtle Lake, Wi., U.S. C1 142
Turtle Mountain Indian Reservation, N.D., U.S. A6 127
Turuhansk, Russia C10 26
Tuscaloosa, Al., U.S. B2 94
Tuscaloosa, co., Al., U.S. B2 94
Tuscarawas, stm., Oh., U.S. B4 128
Tuscarawas, co., Oh., U.S. B4 128
Tuscarora Indian Reservation, N.Y., U.S. B2 125
Tuscarora Mountain, mtn., Pa., U.S. F6 131
Tuscarora Mountains, mts., Nv., U.S. B5 121
Tuscola, Il., U.S. D5 106
Tuscola, co., Mi., U.S. E7 115
Tuscumbia, Al., U.S. A2 94
Tuskegee, Al., U.S. C4 94
Tusket, stm., N.S., Can. E4 87
Tustumena Lake, l., Ak., U.S. g16 95
Tutak, Tur. C10 44
Tuticorin, India H3 40
Tutrakan, Blg. B11 18
Tuttle, Ok., U.S. B4 129
Tuttle Creek Lake, res., Ks., U.S. C7 109
Tuttlingen, Ger. F11 12
Tutuila, i., Am. Sam. F12 58
Tutupaca, Volcán, vol., Peru G5 70
Tututalak Mountain, mtn., Ak., U.S. B7 95
Tutwiler, Ms., U.S. A3 117
Tuva, state, Russia D11 26
Tuvalu, ctry., Oc. E11 58
Ţuwayq, Jabal, mts., Sau. Ar. F5 38
Tuxedo, N.C., U.S. f10 126
Tuxedo Park, De., U.S. i7 101
Tuxpan, Mex. C3 78
Tuxpan de Rodríguez Cano, Mex. C5 78
Tuxtepec, Mex. D5 78
Tuxtla Gutiérrez, Mex. D6 78
Tuyen Quang, Viet. B5 34
Tuy Hoa, Viet. D5 34
Tūysarkān, Iran E13 44
Tuz, Iraq E11 44
Tuz Gölü, l., Tur. C5 44
Tuzigoot National Monument, Az., U.S. C4 96
Tuzla, Bos. B7 18
Tver', Russia D5 26
Tweed, On., Can. C7 89
Tweedsmuir Provincial Park, B.C., Can. C4 85
Tweedy Mountain, mtn., Mt., U.S. E4 119
Twelvepole Creek, stm., W.V., U.S. C2 141
Twentymile Creek, stm., W.V., U.S. C3 141
Twentynine Palms, Ca., U.S. E5 98
Twentynine Palms Marine Corps Base, mil., Ca., U.S. E5 98
Twiggs, co., Ga., U.S. D3 103
Twillingate, N.L., Can. D4 88
Twin Buttes, mtn., Or., U.S. C4 130
Twin Buttes Reservoir, res., Tx., U.S. D2 136
Twin City, Ga., U.S. D4 103
Twin Creek, stm., Oh., U.S. C1 128
Twin Falls, Id., U.S. G4 105
Twin Falls, co., Id., U.S. G4 105
Twin Knolls, Az., U.S. m9 96
Twin Lakes, l., Ct., U.S. A2 100
Twin Lakes, Ga., U.S. F3 103
Twin Lakes, l., Ia., U.S. B3 108
Twin Lakes, l., Me., U.S. C4 112
Twin Lakes, Wi., U.S. F5 142
Twin Mountains, mtn., Wy., U.S. E7 143
Twin Peaks, mts., Id., U.S. E4 105
Twin Rivers, N.J., U.S. C4 123
Twinsburg, Oh., U.S. A4 128
Twin Valley, Mn., U.S. C2 116
Twisp, Wa., U.S. A5 140
Two Harbors, Mn., U.S. C7 116
Two Hills, Ab., Can. C5 84
Two Mile Beach, N.J., U.S. F3 123
Two Rivers, Wi., U.S. D6 142
Two Rivers, North Branch, stm., Mn., U.S. B2 116
Two Rivers, South Branch, stm., Mn., U.S. B2 116
Tybee Island, Ga., U.S. D6 103
Tygart Lake, res., W.V., U.S. B5 141
Tygart River, Falls of the, wtfl., W.V., U.S. k10 141
Tygart Valley, stm., W.V., U.S. B4 141
Tyger, stm., S.C., U.S. B4 133
Tyler, Mn., U.S. F2 116
Tyler, Tx., U.S. C5 136
Tyler, co., Tx., U.S. D5 136
Tyler, co., W.V., U.S. B4 141
Tyler, Lake, res., Tx., U.S. C5 136
Tyler Branch, stm., Vt., U.S. B3 138
Tyler Heights, W.V., U.S. C3 141
Tylertown, Ms., U.S. D3 117
Tymochtee Creek, stm., Oh., U.S. B2 128
Tynda, Russia D14 26
Tyndall, S.D., U.S. E8 134
Tyndall Air Force Base, mil., Fl., U.S. u16 102
Tyne, stm., Eng., U.K. C5 12
Tyonek, Ak., U.S. C9 95
Tyre see Şūr, Leb. F6 44
Tyrifjorden, l., Nor. F3 10
Tyrma, Russia A14 28
Tyrone, N.M., U.S. E1 124
Tyrone, Ok., U.S. e9 129
Tyrone, Pa., U.S. E5 131
Tyronza, Ar., U.S. B5 97
Tyrrell, co., N.C., U.S. B6 126
Tyrrhenian Sea, Eur. D3 18
Tysa (Tisa) (Tisza), stm., Eur. E7 20
Tysnesøya, i., Nor. G1 10
Tzaneen, S. Afr. C5 56

U

Uaupés (Vaupés), stm., S.A. C6 70
Ubá, Braz. F3 74
Ubangi (Oubangui), stm., Afr. D3 54
Ubatã, Braz. D4 74
Ube, Japan E14 28
Úbeda, Spain I5 16
Uberaba, Braz. E2 74
Uberlândia, Braz. E2 74
Ubly, Mi., U.S. E8 115
Ubon Ratchathani, Thai. C4 34
Ubrique, Spain I4 16
Ubundu, D.R.C. D5 54
Učaly, Russia D10 22
Učami, Russia C11 26
Ucar, Azer. B12 44
Ucayali, stm., Peru E5 70

Name — Map Ref. — Page

Uchiura-wan, b., Japan C16 28
Uchiza, Peru E4 70
Učkuduk, Uzb. B8 42
Ucluelet, B.C., Can. E5 85
Ucon, Id., U.S. F7 105
Udagamandalam, India G3 40
Udaipur, India E2 40
Udall, Ks., U.S. E6 109
Uddevalla, Swe. G4 10
Uddjaure, l., Swe. D7 10
Udgīr, India F3 40
Udine, Italy A4 18
Udmurtia see Udmurtija, state, Russia D7 26
Udmurtija, state, Russia D7 26
Udon Thani, Thai. C4 34
Udupi, India G2 40
Ueda, Japan C3 31
Uedinenija, ostrov, i., Russia B10 26
Uele, stm., D.R.C. C4 54
Uel'kal', Russia C19 26
Uelzen, Ger. D12 12
Ufa, Russia D7 26
Uganda, ctry., Afr. C6 54
Ugarit, hist., Syria E6 44
Ugashik Lakes, l., Ak., U.S. D8 95
Uglegorsk, Russia E16 26
Uglič, Russia C6 22
Uherské Hradiště, Czech Rep. E4 20
Uhrichsville, Oh., U.S. B4 128
Uhta, Russia C7 26
Uíge, Ang. E3 54
Uil, Kaz. E9 22
Uinta, stm., Ut., U.S. C5 137
Uinta, co., Wy., U.S. E2 143
Uintah, co., Ut., U.S. D6 137
Uintah and Ouray Indian Reservation, Ut., U.S. C5 137
Uinta Mountains, mts., Ut., U.S. C5 137
Uitenhage, S. Afr. E4 56
Uivak, Cape, c., N.L., Can. f9 88
Ujar, Russia D11 26
Ujelang, atoll, Marsh. Is. D10 58
Ujiji, Tan. D5 54
Ujjain, India E3 40
Ujungpandang, Indon. E5 36
Uka, Russia D18 26
Ukara Island, i., Tan. D6 54
Ukerewe Island, i., Tan. D6 54
Ukiah, Ca., U.S. C2 98
Ukyr, Russia B9 28
Ulaanbaatar (Ulan Bator), Mong. B9 28
Ulaangom, Mong. B6 28
Ulaan-Uul, Mong. C10 28
Ulak Island, i., Ak., U.S. E4 95
Ulan Bator see Ulaanbaatar, Mong. B9 28
Ulan-Ude, Russia D12 26
Ulan Ul Hu, l., China C6 40
Ulchin, S. Kor. C1 31
Ulcinj, Serb. D7 18
Ulhāsnagar, India F2 40
Uliastay, Mong. B7 28
Ulja, Russia D16 26
Uljanovsk, Russia D6 26
Ullŭng-do, i., S. Kor. C2 31
Ulm, Ger. F11 12
Ulónguè, Moz. A5 56
Ulsan, S. Kor. C1 31
Ulster, hist. reg., Eur. C3 12
Ulster, co., N.Y., U.S. D6 125
Ulu, Indon. C7 36
Ulu, Russia C14 26
Ulúa, stm., Hond. B2 80
Ulubat Gölü, l., Tur. B3 44
Ulundi, S. Afr. D5 56
Ulungur Hu, l., China B5 28
Uluru (Ayers Rock), mtn., Austl. F5 60
Ulverstone, Austl. I4 62
Ulysses, Ks., U.S. E2 109
Umán, Mex. C7 78
Uman', Ukr. E11 20
Umanak, Grnld. D29 82
Umarkot, Pak. E9 42
Umatilla, Fl., U.S. D5 102
Umatilla, Or., U.S. B7 130
Umatilla, stm., Or., U.S. B7 130
Umatilla, co., Or., U.S. B8 130
Umatilla Indian Reservation, Or., U.S. B8 130
Umba, Russia A5 22
Umbagog Lake, l., U.S. A4 122
Umboi Island, i., Pap. N. Gui. H12 32
Umcolcus Lake, l., Me., U.S. B4 112
Umeå, Swe. E9 10
Umeälven, stm., Swe. D9 10
Umm al-'Abīd, Libya A8 50
Umm Durmān, Sudan G11 48
Umm Lajj, Sau. Ar. E3 42
Umnak Island, i., Ak., U.S. E6 95
Umpqua, stm., Or., U.S. D3 130
Umsaskis Lake, l., Me., U.S. B3 112
Umtata, S. Afr. E4 56
Umuarama, Braz. H9 70
Umzinto, S. Afr. E5 56
Unadilla, Ga., U.S. D3 103
Unadilla, stm., N.Y., U.S. C5 125
Unaí, Braz. E2 74
Unalakleet, Ak., U.S. C7 95
Unalaska Island, i., Ak., U.S. E6 95
'Unayzah, Sau. Ar. E4 38
'Unayzah, Jabal, mtn., Asia F8 44
Uncasville, Ct., U.S. D7 100
Uncompahgre, stm., Co., U.S. C3 99
Uncompahgre Mountains, mts., Co., U.S. C3 99
Uncompahgre Peak, mtn., Co., U.S. C3 99
Underwood, Al., U.S. B3 94
Underwood, N.D., U.S. B4 127
Uneča, Russia C12 20
Ungava, Péninsule d', pen., Qc., Can. g12 90
Ungava Bay, b., Can. G26 82
Ungava Peninsula see Ungava, Péninsule d', pen., Qc., Can. F25 82
União, Braz. B3 74
Uniãoda Vitória, Braz. D7 72
União dos Palmares, Braz. C4 74
Unicoi, Tn., U.S. C11 135
Unicoi, co., Tn., U.S. C11 135
Unicoi Mountains, mts., U.S. D9 135
Unimak Island, i., Ak., U.S. D7 95
Unimak Pass, strt., Ak., U.S. E6 95
Unión, Arg. F4 72
Union, co., Ar., U.S. D3 97
Union, co., Fl., U.S. B4 102
Union, co., Ga., U.S. B2 103
Union, co., Ia., U.S. C3 108
Union, co., Il., U.S. F4 106
Union, co., In., U.S. E8 107
Union, co., Ky., U.S. C2 110
Union, Ky., U.S. k13 110
Union, co., La., U.S. B3 111
Union, Mo., U.S. C6 118
Union, Ms., U.S. C4 117
Union, co., Ms., U.S. A4 117
Union, co., N.C., U.S. B2 126
Union, co., N.J., U.S. B4 123
Union, co., N.M., U.S. A6 124
Union, co., Oh., U.S. B2 128
Union, Or., U.S. B9 130
Union, co., Or., U.S. B8 130
Union, co., Pa., U.S. E7 131
Union, S.C., U.S. B4 133
Union, co., S.C., U.S. B4 133
Union, co., S.D., U.S. E9 134
Union, co., Tn., U.S. C10 135
Union, Wa., U.S. B2 140
Union, West Branch, stm., Me., U.S. D4 112
Union Beach, N.J., U.S. C4 123
Union Bridge, Md., U.S. A3 113
Union City, Ca., U.S. h8 98
Union City, Ga., U.S. C2 103
Union City, In., U.S. D8 107
Union City, Mi., U.S. F5 115
Union City, N.J., U.S. h8 123
Union City, Oh., U.S. B1 128
Union City, Ok., U.S. B4 129
Union City, Pa., U.S. C2 131
Union City, Tn., U.S. A2 135
Union Flat Creek, stm., Wa., U.S. C8 140
Union Gap, Wa., U.S. C5 140
Union Grove, Wi., U.S. F5 142
Union Lake, l., N.J., U.S. E2 123
Union Pier, Mi., U.S. G4 115
Union Point, Ga., U.S. C3 103
Union Springs, Al., U.S. C4 94
Uniontown, Al., U.S. C2 94
Uniontown, Ky., U.S. C2 110
Uniontown, Oh., U.S. B4 128
Uniontown, Pa., U.S. G2 131
Union Village, R.I., U.S. B3 132
Union Village Reservoir, res., Vt., U.S. D4 138
Unionville, Ct., U.S. B4 100
Unionville, Mo., U.S. A4 118
United Arab Emirates, ctry., Asia F6 42
United Arab Republic see Egypt, ctry., Afr. E10 48
United Kingdom, ctry., Eur. C6 12
United Nations Headquarters, N.Y., U.S. h12 125
United States, ctry., N.A. D6 92
United States Air Force Academy, Co., U.S. B6 99
United States Military Academy, mil., N.Y., U.S. C6 125
United States Naval Academy, mil., Md., U.S. C4 113
Unity Reservoir, res., Or., U.S. C8 130
University City, Mo., U.S. C7 118
University Heights, Ia., U.S. C6 108
University Heights, Oh., U.S. h9 128
University Park, Ia., U.S. C5 108
University Park, N.M., U.S. E3 124
University Park, Tx., U.S. n10 136
University Place, Wa., U.S. f10 140
Unnão, India D4 40
Unuli Horog, China B6 40
Ünye, Tur. B7 44
Unža, stm., Russia C7 22
Upata, Ven. B7 70
Upernavik, Grnld. D28 82
Upington, S. Afr. D3 56
Upland, Ca., U.S. E5 98
Upland, In., U.S. D7 107
Upolu, i., Samoa F12 58
Upolu Point, c., Hi., U.S. C6 104
Upper Ammonoosuc, stm., N.H., U.S. A4 122
Upper Arlington, Oh., U.S. B2 128
Upper Arrow Lake, res., B.C., Can. D9 85
Upperco, Md., U.S. A4 113
Upper Darby, Pa., U.S. G11 131
Upper Greenwood Lake, N.J., U.S. A4 123
Upper Humber, stm., N.L., Can. D3 88
Upper Hutt, N.Z. p14 63c
Upper Iowa, stm., Ia., U.S. A5 108
Upper Island Cove, N.L., Can. E5 88
Upper Klamath Lake, l., Or., U.S. E4 130
Upper Marlboro, Md., U.S. C4 113
Upper New York Bay, b., U.S. k8 123
Upper Red Lake, l., Mn., U.S. B4 116
Upper Saddle River, N.J., U.S. A4 123
Upper Sandusky, Oh., U.S. B2 128
Upper Sheila [Haut Sheila], N.B., Can. B5 87
Upper Volta see Burkina Faso, ctry., Afr. D4 50
Uppland, hist. reg., Swe. F7 10
Uppsala, Swe. G7 10
Upright, Cape, c., Ak., U.S. C5 95
Upshur, co., Tx., U.S. C5 136
Upshur, co., W.V., U.S. C4 141
Upson, co., Ga., U.S. D2 103
Upton, Qc., Can. D5 90
Upton, Ky., U.S. C4 110
Upton, Ma., U.S. B4 114
Upton, co., Tx., U.S. D2 136
Upton, Wy., U.S. B8 143
Uraj, Russia B12 22
Urakawa, Japan B4 31
Ural, stm. E9 22
Ural Mountains see Ural'skie gory, mts., Russia D7 26
Ural'sk, Kaz. D7 26
Ural'skie gory (Ural Mountains), mts., Russia D7 26
Urania, La., U.S. C3 111
Ura-Tjube, Taj. C9 42
Urbana, Il., U.S. C5 106
Urbana, Oh., U.S. B2 128
Urbancrest, Oh., U.S. m10 128
Urbandale, Ia., U.S. C4 108
Urbino, Italy C4 18
Ures, Mex. B2 78
Urfa see Şanlıurfa, Tur. D8 44
Urgenč, Uzb. E8 26
Ürgüp, Tur. C6 44
Uribia, Col. A5 70
Urjung-Haja, Russia B13 26
Urjupinsk, Russia D7 22
Urla, Tur. C2 44
Urmia see Orūmīyeh, Iran C5 42
Urmia, Lake see Orūmīyeh, Daryācheh-ye, l., Iran C5 42
Uromi, Nig. E6 50
Uroševac, Serb. C8 18
Urrao, Col. D4 80
Uruapan del Progreso, Mex. D4 78
Uruguai (Uruguay), stm., S.A. E6 72
Uruguaiana, Braz. D6 72
Uruguay, ctry., S.A. E6 72
Uruguay (Uruguai), stm., S.A. D6 72
Ürümqi, China C5 28
Urundi see Burundi, ctry., Afr. D5 54
Urup, ostrov, i., Russia E17 26
Urziceni, Rom. G9 20
Uržum, Russia C8 22
Usa, Japan D2 31
Uşak, Tur. C3 44
Usakos, Nmb. C2 56
Usborne, Mount, mtn., Falk. Is. H5 69
Usedom, i., Eur. B3 20
Ushuaia, Arg. H3 69
Usinsk, Russia C7 26
Usman', Russia C15 20
Usoke, Tan. E6 54
Usole-Sibirskoe, Russia D12 26
Usquepaug, R.I., U.S. F3 132
Ussuri (Wusuli), stm., Asia E15 26
Ussurijsk, Russia E15 26
Ust'-Barguzin, Russia D12 26
Ust'-Belaja, Russia C19 26
Ust'-Čaun, Russia C19 26
Ust'-Cil'ma, Russia A9 22
Ust'-Ilimsk, Russia D12 26
Ústí nad Labem, Czech Rep. D3 20
Ustinov see Iževsk, Russia D7 26
Ustka, Pol. B4 20
Ust'-Kamčatsk, Russia D18 26
Ust'-Kamenogorsk, Kaz. E10 26
Ust'-Koksa, Russia A5 28
Ust'-Kujda, Russia C15 26
Ust'-Kut, Russia D12 26
Ust'-Lyža, Russia A10 22
Ust'-Maja, Russia C15 26
Ust'-Man'ja, Russia B11 22
Ust'-Nera, Russia C16 26
Ust'-Njukža, Russia D14 26
Uštobe, Kaz. B3 28
Ust'-Tym, Russia D10 26
Ust-Urt Plateau, plat., Asia B7 42
Usu, China C4 28
Usulután, El Sal. C2 80
Usumacinta, stm., N.A. D6 78
Ušumun, Russia A13 28
Utah, co., Ut., U.S. C4 137
Utah, state, U.S. D4 137
Utah Lake, l., Ut., U.S. C4 137
Ute Creek, stm., N.M., U.S. A6 124
Ute Mountain Indian Reservation, U.S. D2 99
Utena, Lith. I11 10
Ute Reservoir, res., N.M., U.S. B6 124
Utete, Tan. E7 54
Uthai Thani, Thai. C4 34
Utiariti, Braz. F8 70
Utica, Il., U.S. B5 106
Utica, Mi., U.S. F7 115
Utica, Ms., U.S. C3 117
Utica, Ne., U.S. D8 120
Utica, N.Y., U.S. B5 125
Utica, Oh., U.S. B3 128
Utiel, Spain H6 16
Utikuma Lake, l., Ab., Can. B3 84
Utila, Isla de, i., Hond. B2 80
Utopia, Austl. E5 60
Utrecht, Neth. D9 12
Utrecht, S. Afr. D5 56
Utrera, Spain I4 16
Utsunomiya, Japan D16 28
Uttaradit, Thai. C4 34
Uttaranchal, state, India D3 40
Uttar Pradesh, state, India D3 40
Uusikaupunki, Fin. F9 10
Uvalde, Tx., U.S. E3 136
Uvalde, co., Tx., U.S. E3 136
Uvarovo, Russia D7 22
Uvinza, Tan. E6 54
Uvira, D.R.C. D5 54
Uvs Lake, l., Asia A6 28
Uwajima, Japan E14 28
Uwayl, Sudan B5 54
Uwharrie, stm., N.C., U.S. B3 126
Uxbridge, Ma., U.S. B4 114
Uyo, Nig. E6 50
Uyuni, Bol. C4 72
Uyuni, Salar de, pl., Bol. C4 72
Uzbekistan, ctry., Asia C8 42
Uzhhorod, Ukr. E7 20
Uzlovaja, Russia C15 20
Uzunköprü, Tur. B2 44
Užur, Russia D11 26

V

Vaal, stm., S. Afr. D4 56
Vaaldam, res., S. Afr. D4 56
Vaasa, Fin. E9 10
Vác, Hung. F5 20
Vaca Key, i., Fl., U.S. H5 102
Vacaria, Braz. D7 72
Vacaville, Ca., U.S. C3 98
Vache, Île à, i., Haiti B5 80
Vacherie, La., U.S. h10 111
Vadodara, India E2 40
Vadsø, Nor. A13 10
Vaduz, Liech. G11 12
Vaga, stm., Russia B7 22
Vah, stm., Russia C9 26
Váh, stm., Slvk. E4 20
Vaiden, Ms., U.S. B4 117
Vail, Co., U.S. B4 99
Vajgač, ostrov, i., Russia B7 26
Vākhān, hist. reg., Afg. C10 42
Val-Bélair, Qc., Can. n17 90
Valcourt, Qc., Can. D5 90
Valdai Hills see Valdajskaja vozvyšennost', Russia C5 22
Valdaj, Russia C5 22
Valdajskaja vozvyšennost', Russia C5 22
Val-David, Qc., Can. C3 90
Valday see Valdaj, Russia C5 22
Valdemarsvik, Swe. G7 10
Valdepeñas, Spain H5 16
Valders, Wi., U.S. D6 142
Valdés, Península, pen., Arg. F4 69
Valdese, N.C., U.S. B1 126
Valdez, Ak., U.S. C10 95
Valdivia, Chile E2 69
Val-d'Or, Qc., Can. k11 90
Valdosta, Ga., U.S. F3 103
Vale, Or., U.S. D9 130
Valemount, B.C., Can. C8 85
Valença, Braz. D4 74
Valença do Piauí, Braz. C3 74
Valence, Fr. E9 16
València, Spain H6 16
Valencia, Az., U.S. m7 96
Valencia, co., N.M., U.S. C3 124
Valencia, Ven. B6 70
València, Golf de, b., Spain H7 16
Valencia de Alcántara, Spain H3 16
Valencia Heights, S.C., U.S. D6 133
Valenciennes, Fr. B8 16
Valentine, Ne., U.S. B5 120
Valera, Ven. B5 70
Valga, Est. H12 10
Valhalla, N.Y., U.S. D7 125
Valhermoso Springs, Al., U.S. A3 94
Valjevo, Serb. B7 18
Valkeakoski, Fin. F11 10
Valladolid, Mex. C7 78
Valladolid, Spain G4 16
Vallecito Reservoir, res., Co., U.S. D3 99
Valle de la Pascua, Ven. B6 70
Valledupar, Col. A5 70
Vallée-Jonction, Qc., Can. C7 90
Vallegrande, Bol. B5 72
Valle Hermoso, Mex. B5 78
Vallejo, Ca., U.S. C2 98
Vallenar, Chile C2 69
Valletta, Malta G5 18
Valley, stm., Mb., Can. D1 86
Valley, co., Id., U.S. E3 105
Valley, co., Mt., U.S. B10 119
Valley, Ne., U.S. C9 120
Valley, co., Ne., U.S. C6 120
Valley Center, Ks., U.S. E6 109
Valley City, N.D., U.S. C8 127
Valley Cottage, N.Y., U.S. g13 125
Valley East, On., Can. p19 89
Valley Falls, Ks., U.S. C8 109
Valley Falls, R.I., U.S. B4 132
Valley Forge, Pa., U.S. o20 131
Valley Mills, Tx., U.S. D4 136
Valley Park, Mo., U.S. f12 118
Valley Springs, S.D., U.S. D9 134
Valley Station, Ky., U.S. g11 110
Valley Stream, N.Y., U.S. n15 125
Valleyview, Ab., Can. B2 84
Valley View, Pa., U.S. E8 131
Valliant, Ok., U.S. D6 129
Valls, Spain G7 16
Vallscreek, W.V., U.S. D3 141
Valmeyer, Il., U.S. E3 106
Valmiera, Lat. H11 10
Valona see Vlorë, Alb. D7 18
Vālpārai, India G3 40
Valparaíso, Chile D2 69
Valparaiso, Fl., U.S. u15 102
Valparaiso, In., U.S. B3 107
Vals, Tanjung, c., Indon. H10 32
Valsbaai, b., S. Afr. E2 56
Valtimo, Fin. E13 10
Valujki, Russia D15 20
Val Verda, Ut., U.S. C4 137
Val Verde, co., Tx., U.S. E2 136
Valverde del Camino, Spain I3 16
Van, Tur. C10 44
Van, Tx., U.S. C5 136
Van, W.V., U.S. n12 141
Vanadzor, Arm. B11 44
Van Alstyne, Tx., U.S. C4 136
Vanavara, Russia C12 26
Van Buren, Ar., U.S. B1 97
Van Buren, co., Ar., U.S. B3 97
Van Buren, co., Ia., U.S. D6 108
Van Buren, In., U.S. C6 107
Van Buren, Me., U.S. A5 112
Van Buren, co., Mi., U.S. F4 115
Van Buren, Mo., U.S. E6 118
Van Buren, co., Tn., U.S. D8 135
Vanč, Taj. C10 42
Vance, co., N.C., U.S. A4 126
Vance Air Force Base, mil., Ok., U.S. A3 129
Vanceboro, N.C., U.S. B5 126
Vanceburg, Ky., U.S. B6 110
Vancleave, Ms., U.S. E5 117
Vancouver, B.C., Can. E6 85
Vancouver, Wa., U.S. D3 140
Vancouver Island, i., B.C., Can. E4 85
Vancouver Island Ranges, mts., B.C., Can. D4 85
Vandalia, Il., U.S. E4 106
Vandalia, Mo., U.S. B6 118
Vandenberg Air Force Base, mil., Ca., U.S. E3 98
Vander, N.C., U.S. B4 126
Vanderbilt Peak, mtn., N.M., U.S. E1 124
Vanderburgh, co., In., U.S. H2 107
Vandergrift, Pa., U.S. E2 131
Vanderhoof, B.C., Can. C5 85
Vanderlin Island, i., Austl. D2 62
Van Diemen Gulf, b., Austl. C5 60
Vänern, l., Swe. G5 10
Vänersborg, Swe. G5 10
Vangaindrano, Madag. C8 56
Van Gölü, l., Tur. C10 44
Van Horn, Tx., U.S. o12 136
Van Horne, Ia., U.S. B5 108
Vanier, On., Can. h12 89
Vanimo, Pap. N. Gui. G11 32
Vanino, Russia B16 28
Vankarem, Russia C20 26
Vankleek Hill, On., Can. B10 89
Van Kull, Kill, stm., N.J., U.S. k8 123
Van Lear, Ky., U.S. C7 110
Van Meter, Ia., U.S. C4 108
Vännäs, Swe. E8 10
Vannes, Fr. D5 16
Van Rees, Pegunungan, mts., Indon. G10 32
Vanrhynsdorp, S. Afr. E2 56
Vansant, Va., U.S. e9 139
Vanua Lava, i., Vanuatu j9 62a
Vanua Levu, i., Fiji F11 58

Name Map Ref. Page

Vanuatu, ctry., Oc. F10 58
Van Vleck, Tx., U.S. r14 136
Van Wert, Oh., U.S. B1 128
Van Wert, co., Oh., U.S. B1 128
Vanwyksvlei, S. Afr. E3 56
Van Zandt, co., Tx., U.S. C5 136
Vārānasi (Benares), India D4 40
Varangerfjorden, b., Nor. A13 10
Varaždin, Cro. A6 18
Varberg, Swe. H5 10
Vardaman, Ms., U.S. B4 117
Vardar (Axiós), stm., Eur. D9 18
Varde, Den. I3 10
Vardø, Nor. A14 10
Varennes, Qc., Can. D4 90
Varese, Italy B2 18
Varginha, Braz. F2 74
Varina, Va., U.S. C5 139
Varkaus, Fin. E12 10
Värmland, hist. reg., Swe. G5 10
Varna, Blg. C11 18
Varna, Russia D11 22
Värnamo, Swe. H6 10
Varnville, S.C., U.S. F5 133
Varto, Tur. C9 44
Várzea Grande, Braz. B6 72
Vashon, Point, c., Wa., U.S. e11 140
Vashon Island, i., Wa., U.S. f11 140
Vaslui, Rom. F9 20
Vass, N.C., U.S. B3 126
Vassar, Mi., U.S. E7 115
Vastenjaure, l., Swe. C7 10
Västerås, Swe. G7 10
Västerbotten, hist. reg., Swe. D8 10
Västerdalälven, stm., Swe. F5 10
Västervik, Swe. H7 10
Vasto, Italy C5 18
Vasylivka, Ukr. F13 20
Vasyl'kiv, Ukr. D11 20
Vatican City, ctry., Eur. D4 18
Vatnajökull, ice, Ice. l20 10a
Vatomandry, Madag. B8 56
Vatra Dornei, Rom. F8 20
Vättern, l., Swe. G6 10
Vaudreuil, Qc., Can. D3 90
Vaughan, On., Can. D5 89
Vaughn, Mt., U.S. C5 119
Vaughn, N.M., U.S. C4 124
Vaukavysk, Bela. C8 20
Vaupés (Uaupés), stm., S.A. C5 70
Vauxhall, Ab., Can. D4 84
Vava'u, i., Tonga F12 58
Vavoua, C. Iv. E3 50
Vavuniya, Sri L. H4 40
Växjö, Swe. H6 10
Vaygach Island see Vajgač, ostrov, i., Russia B7 26
Važgort, Russia B8 22
Veazie, Me., U.S. D4 112
Veedersburg, In., U.S. D3 107
Veendam, Neth. D10 12
Vega, i., Nor. D4 10
Vegreville, Ab., Can. C4 84
Veinticinco de Mayo, Arg. F5 72
Vejle, Den. I3 10
Vélez-Málaga, Spain I4 16
Velika Morava, stm., Serb. B8 18
Velikie Luki, Russia D5 26
Velikij Ustjug, Russia C6 26
Vélingara, Sen. D2 50
Velletri, Italy D4 18
Vellore, India G3 40
Velma, Ok., U.S. C4 129
Vel'sk, Russia C6 26
Velva, N.D., U.S. A5 127
Venado Tuerto, Arg. E5 72
Venango, co., Pa., U.S. D2 131
Vendôme, Fr. D7 16
Veneta, Or., U.S. C3 130
Venézia (Venice), Italy B4 18
Venezuela, ctry., S.A. B6 70
Venezuela, Golfo de, b., S.A. A5 70
Venezuela, Gulf of see Venezuela, Golfo de, b., S.A. A5 70
Venezuelan Basin G7 66
Veniaminof, Mount, mtn., Ak., U.S. D8 95
Venice see Venézia, Italy B4 18
Venice, Fl., U.S. E4 102
Venice, Il., U.S. E3 106
Venice, Gulf of, b., Eur. B4 18
Venta, stm., Eur. H10 10
Ventimiglia, Italy C1 18
Ventnor City, N.J., U.S. E4 123
Ventspils, Lat. H9 10
Ventura (San Buenaventura), Ca., U.S. E4 98
Ventura, co., Ca., U.S. E4 98
Vera, Arg. D5 72
Vera, Spain I6 16
Veracruz, state, Mex. D5 78
Veracruz, Mex. D5 78
Verāval, India E2 40
Verbania, Italy B2 18
Vercelli, Italy B2 18
Verchères, Qc., Can. D4 90
Verda, Ky., U.S. D6 110
Verde, stm., Az., U.S. C4 96
Verden, Ger. D11 12
Verdi, Nv., U.S. D2 121
Verdigre, Ne., U.S. B7 120
Verdigris, Ok., U.S. A6 129
Verdigris, stm., U.S. A6 129
Verdi Peak, mtn., Nv., U.S. C6 121
Verdun, Qc., Can. q19 90
Verdun-sur-Meuse, Fr. C9 16
Vereeniging, S. Afr. D4 56
Vereščagino, Russia C10 26
Vergennes, Vt., U.S. C2 138
Verhneimbatsk, Russia C10 26
Verhnemulomskoe vodohranilišče, res., Russia B14 10
Verhnetulomskij, Russia B14 10
Verhneural'sk, Russia D10 22
Verhnij Baskunčak, Russia E8 22
Verhnij Ufalej, Russia C11 22
Verhnjaja Amga, Russia D14 26
Verhnjaja Inta, Russia A11 22
Verhnjaja Salda, Russia C11 22
Verhojansk, Russia C15 26
Verhojanskij hrebet, mts., Russia C14 26
Verhoture, Russia C11 22
Verkhoyansk see Verhojansk, Russia C15 26
Vermilion, Ab., Can. C5 84
Vermilion, stm., Ab., Can. C5 84
Vermilion, stm., Il., U.S. C5 106
Vermilion, co., Il., U.S. C6 106
Vermilion, stm., La., U.S. E3 111
Vermilion, co., La., U.S. E3 111
Vermilion, stm., Mn., U.S. B6 116
Vermilion, Oh., U.S. A3 128
Vermilion, stm., Oh., U.S. A3 128
Vermilion Bay, b., La., U.S. E3 111
Vermilion Lake, l., Mn., U.S. C6 116
Vermilion Pass, Can. D2 84
Vermillion, co., In., U.S. E2 107
Vermillion, S.D., U.S. E9 134
Vermillion, East Fork, stm., S.D., U.S. D8 134
Vermillon, stm., Qc., Can. B4 90
Vermont, Il., U.S. C3 106
Vermont, state, U.S. D3 138
Vermontville, Mi., U.S. F5 115
Vernal, Ut., U.S. C6 137
Vernon, B.C., Can. D8 85
Vernon, Al., U.S. B1 94
Vernon, co., La., U.S. C2 111
Vernon, co., Mo., U.S. D3 118
Vernon, Tx., U.S. B3 136
Vernon, co., Wi., U.S. E3 142
Vernon Hills, Il., U.S. h9 106
Vernonia, Or., U.S. B3 130
Vero Beach, Fl., U.S. E6 102
Véroia, Grc. D9 18
Verona, On., Can. C8 89
Verona, Italy B3 18
Verona, Ms., U.S. A5 117
Verona, N.J., U.S. B4 123
Verona, Pa., U.S. k14 131
Verona, Wi., U.S. E4 142
Verret, Lake, l., La., U.S. E4 111
Versailles, Fr. C8 16
Versailles, In., U.S. F7 107
Versailles, Ky., U.S. B5 110
Versailles, Mo., U.S. C5 118
Versailles, Oh., U.S. B1 128
Vert, Cap, c., Sen. D1 50
Vertientes, Cuba A4 80
Vesele, Ukr. F13 20
Vešenskaja, Russia F15 8
Vesoul, Fr. D10 16
Vestal, N.Y., U.S. C4 125
Vestavia Hills, Al., U.S. g7 94
Vesterålen, is., Nor. B6 10
Vestfjorden, b., Nor. C5 10
Vestmannaeyjar, Ice. m18 10a
Vesuvio, vol., Italy D5 18
Vesuvius see Vesuvio, vol., Italy D5 18
Veszprém, Hung. F4 20
Vetlanda, Swe. H6 10
Vetluga, stm., Russia C8 22
Vetluga, Russia C8 22
Vevay, In., U.S. G7 107
Vezirköprü, Tur. B6 44
Viacha, Bol. B4 72
Vian, Ok., U.S. B7 129
Viana, Braz. B2 74
Viana do Castelo, Port. G2 16
Viangchan (Vientiane), Laos C4 34
Viangphoukha, Laos B4 34
Viareggio, Italy C3 18
Viborg, Den. H3 10
Viborg, S.D., U.S. D8 134
Vibo Valentia, Italy E5 18
Viburnum, Mo., U.S. D6 118
Vic, Spain G8 16
Vicebsk, Bela. B11 20
Vicente, Point, c., Ca., U.S. n12 98
Vicente Guerrero, Presa, res., Mex. C5 78
Vicenza, Italy B3 18
Vichada, stm., Col. C5 70
Vichy, Fr. D8 16
Vici, Ok., U.S. A2 129
Vicksburg, Mi., U.S. F5 115
Vicksburg, Ms., U.S. C3 117
Vicksburg National Military Park, Ms., U.S. C3 117
Victor, Ia., U.S. C5 108
Victor, N.Y., U.S. C3 125
Victoria, stm., Austl. D5 60
Victoria, state, Austl. H3 62
Victoria see Limbe, Cam. C1 54
Victoria, B.C., Can. E6 85
Victoria, N.L., Can. E5 88
Victoria, Chile E2 69
Victoria see Xianggang, China E3 30
Victoria, Gui. D2 50
Victoria, Sey. h13 57b
Victoria, Ks., U.S. D4 109
Victoria, Tx., U.S. E4 136
Victoria, co., Tx., U.S. E4 136
Victoria, Lake, l., Afr. D6 54
Victoria, Mount, mtn., Pap. N. Gui. H12 32
Victoria Falls, wtfl., Afr. B4 56
Victoria Harbour, On., Can. C5 89
Victoria Island, i., Can. D18 82
Victoria Lake, res., N.L., Can. D3 88
Victoria Land, reg., Ant. D21 67
Victoria Nile, stm., Ug. C6 54
Victoria Peak, mtn., Belize B2 80
Victoria River Downs, Austl. D5 60
Victorias, Phil. D8 34
Victoriaville, Qc., Can. C6 90
Victoria West, S. Afr. E3 56
Victorville, Ca., U.S. E5 98
Vicuña Mackenna, Arg. E5 72
Vidalia, Ga., U.S. D4 103
Vidalia, La., U.S. C4 111
Vidin, Blg. C9 18
Vidisha, India E3 40
Vidor, Tx., U.S. D5 136
Viedma, Arg. F4 69
Viedma, Lago, l., Arg. G2 69
Vienna see Wien, Aus. F15 12
Vienna, Ga., U.S. D3 103
Vienna, Il., U.S. F5 106
Vienna, Mo., U.S. C6 118
Vienna, Va., U.S. B5 139
Vienna, W.V., U.S. B3 141
Vienne, Fr. E9 16
Vienne, stm., Fr. D7 16
Vientiane see Viangchan, Laos C4 34
Vieques, Isla de, i., P.R. B6 80
Vierwaldstätter See, l., Switz. A2 18
Vierzon, Fr. D8 16
Vieste, Italy D6 18
Vietnam, ctry., Asia C5 34
Viet Tri, Viet. B5 34
Vieux Desert, Lac, l., Wi., U.S. B4 142
Vigan, Phil. C8 34
Vigo, Spain F2 16
Vigo, co., In., U.S. F3 107
Vijayawāda, India F4 40
Vike, Arm. C11 44
Viking, Ab., Can. C5 84
Vikna, Nor. D4 10
Vikna, i., Nor. D4 10
Vikramasingapuram, India H3 40
Vila de Sena, Moz. B6 56
Vila do Ibo, Moz. A7 56
Vila Fontes, Moz. B6 56
Vila Gamito, Moz. A5 56
Vilagarcía de Arousa, Spain F2 16
Vilanandro, Tanjona, c., Madag. B7 56
Vilankulo, Moz. C6 56
Vilanova i la Geltrú, Spain G7 16
Vila Real, Port. G3 16
Vilas, co., Wi., U.S. B4 142
Vila Velha, Braz. F3 74
Vilejka, Bela. B9 20
Vilhelmina, Swe. D7 10
Vilhena, Braz. F7 70
Viljandi, Est. G11 10
Viljuj, stm., Russia C14 26
Viljujsk, Russia C14 26
Vil'kickogo, proliv, strt., Russia B11 26
Villa Ángela, Arg. D5 72
Villa Bella, Bol. F6 70
Villacañas, Spain H5 16
Villacarrillo, Spain H5 16
Villach, Aus. G13 12
Villa Dolores, Arg. E4 72
Villa Grove, Il., U.S. D5 106
Villaguay, Arg. E6 72
Villahermosa, Mex. D6 78
Villaldama, Mex. D4 78
Villalonga, Arg. E4 69
Villa María, Arg. E5 72
Villa Mercedes, Arg. E4 72
Villa Montes, Bol. C5 72
Villanueva de la Serena, Spain H4 16
Villa Ocampo, Arg. D6 72
Villa Ojo de Agua, Arg. D5 72
Villa Park, Il., U.S. k8 106
Villa Rica, Ga., U.S. C2 103
Villarrica, Chile E2 69
Villarrica, Para. D6 72
Villarrobledo, Spain H5 16
Villas, N.J., U.S. E3 123
Villa Unión, Mex. C3 78
Villa Valeria, Arg. E4 72
Villavicencio, Col. C5 70
Villefranche-sur-Saône, Fr. E9 16
Villena, Spain H6 16
Villeneuve-sur-Lot, Fr. E7 16
Ville Platte, La., U.S. D3 111
Ville Saint-Georges, Qc., Can. C7 90
Villeurbanne, Fr. E9 16
Villisca, Ia., U.S. D3 108
Vilnius, Lith. I11 10
Vilonia, Ar., U.S. B3 97
Vimmerby, Swe. H6 10
Viña del Mar, Chile D2 69
Vinalhaven, Me., U.S. D4 112
Vinalhaven Island, i., Me., U.S. D4 112
Vinaròs, Spain G7 16
Vincennes, In., U.S. G2 107
Vincennes Bay, b., Ant. C15 67
Vincent, Al., U.S. B3 94
Vindhya Range, mts., India E3 40
Vine Brook, stm., Ma., U.S. g11 114
Vinegar Hill, mtn., Or., U.S. C8 130
Vine Grove, Ky., U.S. C4 110
Vineland, N.J., U.S. E2 123
Vineyard Haven, Ma., U.S. D6 114
Vineyard Sound, strt., Ma., U.S. D6 114
Vinh, Viet. C5 34
Vinh Long, Viet. D5 34
Vinita, Ok., U.S. A6 129
Vinkovci, Cro. B7 18
Vinson Massif, mtn., Ant. D32 67
Vinton, Ia., U.S. B5 108
Vinton, La., U.S. D2 111
Vinton, co., Oh., U.S. C3 128
Vinton, Va., U.S. C3 139
Viola, Il., U.S. B3 106
Violet, La., U.S. k12 111
Virac, Phil. D8 34
Viramgām, India E2 40
Virandozero, Russia C14 8
Viranşehir, Tur. D8 44
Virden, Mb., Can. E1 86
Virden, Il., U.S. D4 106
Vire, Fr. C6 16
Virgin, stm., U.S. G8 121
Virgin Gorda, i., Br. Vir. Is. B7 80
Virginia, S. Afr. D4 56
Virginia, Al., U.S. g6 94
Virginia, Il., U.S. D3 106
Virginia, Mn., U.S. C6 116
Virginia, state, U.S. C4 139
Virginia Beach, Va., U.S. D7 139
Virginia City, Nv., U.S. D2 121
Virginia Peak, mtn., Nv., U.S. D2 121
Virgin Islands, dep., N.A. B7 80
Virgin Islands, is., N.A. E11 76
Viroqua, Wi., U.S. E3 142
Virovitica, Cro. B6 18
Virrat, Fin. E10 10
Virtsu, Est. G10 10
Virudunagar, India H3 40
Vis, Otok, i., Cro. C6 18
Visalia, Ca., U.S. D4 98
Visayan Sea, Phil. D8 34
Visby, Swe. H8 10
Viscount Melville Sound, strt., N.T., Can. D17 82
Viseu, Port. G3 16
Vishākhapatnam, India F4 40
Vista, Ca., U.S. F5 98
Vistula see Wisła, stm., Pol. C5 20
Vitarte, Peru F4 70
Viterbo, Italy C3 18
Viti Levu, i., Fiji F11 58
Vitim, Russia D13 26
Vitim, stm., Russia D13 26
Vitória, Braz. F3 74
Vitoria see Gasteiz, Spain F5 16
Vitória da Conquista, Braz. D3 74
Vitré, Fr. C6 16
Vitry-le-François, Fr. C9 16
Vittoria, Italy F5 18
Vittorio Veneto, Italy B4 18
Vivian, La., U.S. B2 111
Vize, ostrov, i., Russia B9 26
Vizianagaram, India F4 40
Vizinga, Russia B9 22
Vjatka, stm., Russia D7 26
Vjatskie Poljany, Russia C9 22
Vjazemskij, Russia B14 28
Vjaz'ma, Russia B13 20
Vladikavkaz, Russia E6 26
Vladikavkaz see Ordzhonikidze, Ukr. F13 20
Vladimir, Russia D6 26
Vladivostok, Russia E15 26
Vlissingen, Neth. E8 12
Vlorë, Alb. D7 18
Vogel Peak see Dimlang, mtn., Nig. E7 50
Vohimena, Tanjona, c., Madag. D8 56
Voi, Kenya D7 54
Voinjama, Lib. E3 50
Voj-Vož, Russia B9 22
Volcano, Hi., U.S. D6 104
Volcano Islands see Kazan-rettō, is., Japan F17 64
Volga, stm., Russia E6 26
Volga, S.D., U.S. C9 134
Volga-Baltic Canal see Volgo-Baltijskij kanal, Russia B6 22
Volga Plateau see Privolžskaja vozvyšennost', plat., Russia D6 26
Volgo-Baltijskij kanal, Russia B6 22
Volgodonsk, Russia E6 26
Volgograd, Russia E6 26
Volgograd Reservoir see Volgogradskoe vodohranilišče, res., Russia D8 22
Volgogradskoe vodohranilišče, res., Russia D8 22
Volhov, Russia D12 6
Volksrust, S. Afr. D4 56
Volnovakha, Ukr. F14 20
Voločanka, Russia B11 26
Volodarskoe, Kaz. D8 26
Volodymyr-Volyns'kyi, Ukr. D8 20
Vologda, Russia D6 26
Vólos, Grc. E9 18
Volos, Gulf of see Pagasitikós Kólpos, b., Grc. E9 18
Volosovo, Russia G13 10
Vol'sk, Russia D6 26
Volta, stm., Ghana E5 50
Volta Lake, res., Ghana E5 50
Volta Redonda, Braz. F3 74
Volterra, Italy C3 18
Volusia, co., Fl., U.S. C5 102
Volžsk, Russia C8 22
Volžskij, Russia E6 26
Vondrozo, Madag. C8 56
Von Frank Mountain, mtn., Ak., U.S. C9 95
Vonore, Tn., U.S. D9 135
Vordingborg, Den. I4 10
Vórioi Sporádhes, is., Grc. E10 18
Vórios Evvoïkós Kólpos, b., Grc. E9 18
Vorkuta, Russia C8 26
Vormsi, i., Est. G10 10
Voronež, Russia D5 26
Voroshilovsk see Alchevs'k, Ukr. E15 20
Vorpommern, hist. reg., Ger. D13 12
Võrtsjärv, l., Est. G12 10
Võru, Est. H12 10
Vosges, mts., Fr. C10 16
Voss, Nor. F2 10
Vostočno-Sibirskoe more, Russia B17 26
Vostočnyj Sajan, mts., Russia D11 26
Vostok, i., Kir. F14 58
Votkinsk, Russia D7 26
Votuporanga, Braz. F2 74
Voyageurs National Park, Mn., U.S. B5 116
Vožega, Russia B7 22
Voznesens'k, Ukr. F11 20
Vraca, Blg. C9 18
Vrangelja, ostrov, i., Russia B20 26
Vranje, Serb. C8 18
Vrede, S. Afr. D4 56
Vršac, Serb. B8 18
Vryburg, S. Afr. D3 56
Vryheid, S. Afr. D5 56
Vsevidof, Mount, mtn., Ak., U.S. E6 95
Vukovar, Cro. B7 18
Vulcan, Ab., Can. D4 84
Vyborg, Russia C4 26
Vyčegda, stm., Russia C6 26
Vym', stm., Russia B9 22
Vyšnij Voločok, Russia C5 22
Vytegra, Russia B6 22

W

Wa, Ghana D4 50
Waajid, Som. C8 54
Waal, stm., Eur. E9 12
Waawaa, Puu, mtn., Hi., U.S. D6 104
Wabag, Pap. N. Gui. H11 32
Wabana (Bell Island), N.L., Can. E5 88
Wabasca, Ab., Can. B4 84
Wabasca, stm., Ab., Can. f1 84
Wabash, co., Il., U.S. E6 106
Wabash, In., U.S. C6 107
Wabash, co., In., U.S. C6 107
Wabash, stm., U.S. H2 107
Wabash, stm., U.S. D10 92
Wabasha, Mn., U.S. F6 116
Wabasha, co., Mn., U.S. F6 116
Wabasso, Fl., U.S. E6 102
Wabasso, Mn., U.S. F3 116
Wabaunsee, co., Ks., U.S. D7 109
Wabeno, Wi., U.S. C5 142
Wabowden, Mb., Can. B2 86
Wabush, N.L., Can. h8 88
Waccamaw, stm., U.S. D9 133
Waccamaw, Lake, l., N.C., U.S. C4 126
Waccasassa Bay, b., Fl., U.S. C4 102
Wachusett Mountain, mtn., Ma., U.S. B4 114
Wachusett Reservoir, res., Ma., U.S. B4 114
Waco, Tx., U.S. D4 136

Name	Map Ref.	Page
Waco Lake, res., Tx., U.S.	D4	136
Waconda Lake, res., Ks., U.S.	C5	109
Waconia, Mn., U.S.	F5	116
Waddān, Libya	E8	48
Waddenzee, strt., Neth.	D9	12
Waddi Chappal, Afr.	B2	54
Waddington, Mount, mtn., B.C., Can.	D5	85
Wadena, Mn., U.S.	D3	116
Wadena, co., Mn., U.S.	D4	116
Wadesboro, N.C., U.S.	C2	126
Wādī Ḥalfā', Sudan	F11	48
Wading, stm., N.J., U.S.	D3	123
Wadley, Ga., U.S.	D4	103
Wad Madani, Sudan	H11	48
Wadmalaw Island, i., S.C., U.S.	F7	133
Wadsworth, Il., U.S.	h9	106
Wadsworth, Nv., U.S.	D2	121
Wadsworth, Oh., U.S.	A4	128
Wafangdian, China	B5	30
Wagadugu see Ouagadougou, Burkina	D4	50
Wagener, S.C., U.S.	D5	133
Wagga Wagga, Austl.	H4	62
Wagin, Austl.	G2	60
Wagner, S.D., U.S.	D7	134
Wagoner, Ok., U.S.	B6	129
Wagoner, co., Ok., U.S.	B6	129
Wagontire Mountain, mtn., Or., U.S.	D7	130
Waha, Libya	E9	48
Wahai, Indon.	D7	36
Wāh Cantonment, Pak.	D10	42
Wahiawā, Hi., U.S.	B3	104
Wahiawā Reservoir, res., Hi., U.S.	g9	104
Wahkiakum, co., Wa., U.S.	C2	140
Wahoo, Ne., U.S.	C9	120
Wahpeton, N.D., U.S.	C9	127
Wahran, Alg.	C4	48
Wahweap Creek, stm., Ut., U.S.	F4	137
Waialua, Hi., U.S.	B3	104
Waialua Bay, b., Hi., U.S.	B3	104
Wai'anae, Hi., U.S.	B3	104
Wai'anae Range, mts., Hi., U.S.	f9	104
Waidhofen an der Ybbs, Aus.	G14	12
Waigeo, Pulau, i., Indon.	C8	36
Waikabubak, Indon.	E5	36
Waikapu, Hi., U.S.	C5	104
Waikato, stm., N.Z.	o14	63c
Waikīkī Beach, cst., Hi., U.S.	g10	104
Wailua, Hi., U.S.	A2	104
Wailuku, Hi., U.S.	C5	104
Waimānalo, Hi., U.S.	B4	104
Waimānalo Bay, b., Hi., U.S.	g11	104
Waimate, N.Z.	p13	63c
Waimea, Hi., U.S.	f9	104
Waimea, Hi., U.S.	B2	104
Waimea, Hi., U.S.	C6	104
Wainganga, stm., India	E3	40
Waingapu, Indon.	E6	36
Wainwright, Ab., Can.	C5	84
Wainwright, Ak., U.S.	A8	95
Waipahu, Hi., U.S.	B3	104
Waipara, N.Z.	p13	63c
Waipi'o Acres, Hi., U.S.	g9	104
Waipi'o Peninsula, pen., Hi., U.S.	g10	104
Wairoa, N.Z.	o14	63c
Waitara, N.Z.	o13	63c
Waitemata, N.Z.	o13	63c
Waite Park, Mn., U.S.	E4	116
Waits, stm., Vt., U.S.	C4	138
Waitsburg, Wa., U.S.	C7	140
Wajir, Kenya	C8	54
Waka, D.R.C.	C4	54
Waka, Eth.	B7	54
Wakarusa, In., U.S.	A5	107
Wakarusa, stm., Ks., U.S.	D8	109
Wakasa-wan, b., Japan	C3	31
Wakatomika Creek, stm., Oh., U.S.	B3	128
Wakayama, Japan	E15	28
Wake, co., N.C., U.S.	B4	126
WaKeeney, Ks., U.S.	C4	109
Wakefield, Qc., Can.	D2	90
Wakefield, Ks., U.S.	C6	109
Wakefield, Ma., U.S.	B5	114
Wakefield, Mi., U.S.	n12	115
Wakefield, Ne., U.S.	B9	120
Wakefield, R.I., U.S.	F3	132
Wakefield, Va., U.S.	D6	139
Wake Forest, N.C., U.S.	B4	126
Wake Island, dep., Oc.	C10	58
Wakema, Mya.	C3	34
Wakeman, Oh., U.S.	A3	128
Wakkanai, Japan	B16	28
Waku Kungo, Ang.	F3	54
Wakulla, co., Fl., U.S.	B2	102
Walachia, hist. reg., Rom.	G8	20
Walbridge, Oh., U.S.	e6	128
Wałbrzych, Pol.	D4	20
Walcott, Ia., U.S.	C7	108
Walcott, Lake, res., Id., U.S.	G5	105
Wałcz, Pol.	C4	20
Walden, On., Can.	A3	89
Walden, Co., U.S.	A4	99
Walden, N.Y., U.S.	D6	125
Waldenburg see Wałbrzych, Pol.	D4	20
Walden Ridge, mtn., Tn., U.S.	D8	135
Waldheim, Sk., Can.	E2	91
Waldo, Ar., U.S.	D2	97
Waldo, co., Me., U.S.	D3	112
Waldoboro, Me., U.S.	D3	112
Waldo Lake, l., Ma., U.S.	h11	114
Waldo Lake, l., Or., U.S.	D4	130
Waldport, Or., U.S.	C2	130
Waldron, Ar., U.S.	C1	97
Waldron, In., U.S.	F6	107
Waldwick, N.J., U.S.	A4	123
Wales, state, U.K.	E4	12
Waleska, Ga., U.S.	B2	103
Walgett, Austl.	G4	62
Walgreen Coast, Ant.	D30	67
Walhalla, N.D., U.S.	A8	127
Walhalla, S.C., U.S.	B1	133
Walhonding, stm., Oh., U.S.	B3	128
Walikale, D.R.C.	D5	54
Walker, co., Al., U.S.	B2	94
Walker, co., Ga., U.S.	B1	103
Walker, Ia., U.S.	B6	108
Walker, La., U.S.	g10	111
Walker, Mi., U.S.	E5	115
Walker, Mn., U.S.	C4	116
Walker, stm., Nv., U.S.	D3	121
Walker, co., Tx., U.S.	D5	136
Walker Lake, l., Nv., U.S.	E3	121
Walker River Indian Reservation, Nv., U.S.	D3	121
Walkersville, Md., U.S.	B3	113
Walkerton, On., Can.	C3	89
Walkerton, In., U.S.	B5	107
Walkertown, N.C., U.S.	A2	126
Walkerville, Mt., U.S.	D4	119
Wall, S.D., U.S.	D3	134
Wallace, Id., U.S.	B3	105
Wallace, co., Ks., U.S.	D2	109
Wallace, N.C., U.S.	B4	126
Wallaceburg, On., Can.	E2	89
Wallace Lake, res., La., U.S.	B2	111
Walla Walla, Wa., U.S.	C7	140
Walla Walla, co., Wa., U.S.	C7	140
Walla Walla, stm., U.S.	C7	140
Walled Lake, Mi., U.S.	o15	115
Wallen, In., U.S.	B7	107
Wallenpaupack, Lake, l., Pa., U.S.	D11	131
Waller, Tx., U.S.	q14	136
Waller, co., Tx., U.S.	E4	136
Wallingford, Ct., U.S.	D4	100
Wallingford, Vt., U.S.	E3	138
Wallington, N.J., U.S.	h8	123
Wallis, Îles, is., Wal./F.	F12	58
Wallis and Futuna, dep., Oc.	F12	58
Wallkill, stm., N.Y., U.S.	D6	125
Wallkill, N.Y., U.S.	D6	125
Wall Lake, Ia., U.S.	B2	108
Wall Lake, l., Ia., U.S.	B4	108
Walloomsac, stm., U.S.	F2	138
Walloon Lake, l., Mi., U.S.	C6	115
Wallowa, Or., U.S.	B9	130
Wallowa, co., Or., U.S.	B9	130
Wallowa Mountains, mts., Or., U.S.	B9	130
Wallula, Lake, res., U.S.	C7	140
Wallum Lake, l., U.S.	A1	132
Walnut, Ia., U.S.	C2	108
Walnut, Il., U.S.	B4	106
Walnut, stm., Ks., U.S.	E6	109
Walnut Canyon National Monument, Az., U.S.	B4	96
Walnut Cove, N.C., U.S.	A2	126
Walnut Creek, Ca., U.S.	h8	98
Walnut Creek, stm., Ks., U.S.	D4	109
Walnut Grove, Al., U.S.	A3	94
Walnut Grove, Mn., U.S.	F3	116
Walnutport, Pa., U.S.	E10	131
Walnut Ridge, Ar., U.S.	A5	97
Walpole, Austl.	H2	60
Walpole, Ma., U.S.	B5	114
Walpole, N.H., U.S.	D2	122
Walsall, Eng., U.K.	D6	12
Walsenburg, Co., U.S.	D6	99
Walsh, Co., U.S.	D8	99
Walsh, co., N.D., U.S.	A8	127
Walterboro, S.C., U.S.	F6	133
Walter F. George Dam, U.S.	D4	94
Walter F. George Lake, res., U.S.	D4	94
Walters, Ok., U.S.	C3	129
Walthall, co., Ms., U.S.	D3	117
Waltham, Ma., U.S.	B5	114
Walthill, Ne., U.S.	B9	120
Walthourville, Ga., U.S.	E5	103
Walton, co., Fl., U.S.	u15	102
Walton, co., Ga., U.S.	C3	103
Walton, In., U.S.	C5	107
Walton, Ky., U.S.	B5	110
Walton, N.Y., U.S.	C5	125
Walvis Bay, Nmb.	C1	56
Walvis Bay, b., Nmb.	C1	56
Walvis Ridge	K14	66
Walworth, co., S.D., U.S.	B5	134
Walworth, Wi., U.S.	F5	142
Walworth, co., Wi., U.S.	F5	142
Wamac, Il., U.S.	E4	106
Wamba, stm., Afr.	E3	54
Wamba, D.R.C.	C5	54
Wamba, Nig.	E6	50
Wamego, Ks., U.S.	C7	109
Wamesit, Ma., U.S.	A5	114
Wamsutter, Wy., U.S.	E5	143
Wanaka, N.Z.	p12	63c
Wanamingo, Mn., U.S.	F6	116
Wanapum Dam, Wa., U.S.	C6	140
Wanapum Lake, res., Wa., U.S.	B6	140
Wanaque, N.J., U.S.	A4	123
Wanaque Reservoir, res., N.J., U.S.	A4	123
Wanatah, In., U.S.	B4	107
Wanchese, N.C., U.S.	B7	126
Wando, stm., S.C., U.S.	F8	133
Wando Woods, S.C., U.S.	k11	133
Wanfoxia, China	A7	40
Wanganui, N.Z.	p13	63c
Wangaratta, Austl.	H4	62
Wangiwangi, Pulau, i., Indon.	E6	36
Wangqing, China	B1	31
Wanigela, Pap. N. Gui.	H12	32
Wanneroo, Austl.	G2	60
Wanning, China	F3	30
Wanxian, China	E9	28
Wanyuan, China	C2	30
Wanzai, China	D3	30
Wapakoneta, Oh., U.S.	B1	128
Wapato, Wa., U.S.	C5	140
Wapawekka Lake, l., Sk., Can.	C3	91
Wapello, co., Ia., U.S.	C5	108
Wapello, Ia., U.S.	C6	108
Wapiti, stm., Can.	B1	84
Wappapello, Lake, res., Mo., U.S.	D7	118
Wappingers Falls, N.Y., U.S.	D7	125
Wapsipinicon, stm., Ia., U.S.	B6	108
War, W.V., U.S.	D3	141
Waramaug, Lake, l., Ct., U.S.	C2	100
Warangal, India	F3	40
Ward, Ar., U.S.	B4	97
Ward, co., N.D., U.S.	A4	127
Ward, co., Tx., U.S.	D1	136
Warden, Wa., U.S.	C6	140
Wardha, India	E3	40
Ward Mountain, mtn., Mt., U.S.	D2	119
Ware, co., Ga., U.S.	E4	103
Ware, Ma., U.S.	B3	114
Ware, stm., Ma., U.S.	B3	114
War Eagle Mountain, mtn., Id., U.S.	G2	105
Wareham, Ma., U.S.	C6	114
Warehouse Point, Ct., U.S.	B5	100
Waren, Indon.	G10	32
Ware Shoals, S.C., U.S.	C3	133
Warfield, B.C., Can.	E9	85
Wargla, Alg.	D6	48
Warialda, Austl.	F5	62
Warin Chamrap, Thai.	C4	34
Warmbad, Nmb.	D2	56
Warmbad, S. Afr.	C4	56
Warminster, Pa., U.S.	F11	131
Warm Springs Indian Reservation, Or., U.S.	C5	130
Warm Springs Reservoir, res., Or., U.S.	D8	130
Warner, stm., N.H., U.S.	D3	122
Warner, N.H., U.S.	D3	122
Warner, Ok., U.S.	B6	129
Warner Mountains, mts., Ca., U.S.	B3	98
Warner Peak, mtn., Or., U.S.	E7	130
Warner Robins, Ga., U.S.	D3	103
Warracknabeal, Austl.	H3	62
Warr Acres, Ok., U.S.	B4	129
Warragul, Austl.	H4	62
Warren, Ar., U.S.	D3	97
Warren, co., Ga., U.S.	C4	103
Warren, co., Ia., U.S.	C4	108
Warren, Il., U.S.	A4	106
Warren, co., Il., U.S.	C3	106
Warren, co., In., U.S.	D3	107
Warren, In., U.S.	C7	107
Warren, co., Ky., U.S.	C3	110
Warren, Ma., U.S.	B3	114
Warren, Mi., U.S.	F7	115
Warren, Mn., U.S.	B2	116
Warren, co., Mo., U.S.	C6	118
Warren, co., Ms., U.S.	C3	117
Warren, co., N.C., U.S.	A4	126
Warren, co., N.J., U.S.	B3	123
Warren, co., N.Y., U.S.	B7	125
Warren, Oh., U.S.	A5	128
Warren, co., Oh., U.S.	C1	128
Warren, Or., U.S.	B4	130
Warren, Pa., U.S.	C3	131
Warren, co., Pa., U.S.	C3	131
Warren, R.I., U.S.	D5	132
Warren, co., Tn., U.S.	D8	135
Warren, co., Va., U.S.	B4	139
Warren, Vt., U.S.	C3	138
Warren, stm., U.S.	D5	132
Warren Park, In., U.S.	k10	107
Warren Peaks, mts., Wy., U.S.	B8	143
Warrensburg, Il., U.S.	D4	106
Warrensburg, Mo., U.S.	C4	118
Warrensburg, N.Y., U.S.	B7	125
Warrensville Heights, Oh., U.S.	h9	128
Warrenton, S. Afr.	D3	56
Warrenton, Ga., U.S.	C4	103
Warrenton, Mo., U.S.	C6	118
Warrenton, N.C., U.S.	A4	126
Warrenton, Or., U.S.	A3	130
Warrenton, Va., U.S.	B5	139
Warrenville, Il., U.S.	k8	106
Warrenville, S.C., U.S.	D4	133
Warri, Nig.	E6	50
Warrick, co., In., U.S.	H3	107
Warrington, Fl., U.S.	u14	102
Warrior, Al., U.S.	B3	94
Warrior Lake, res., Al., U.S.	C2	94
Warrnambool, Austl.	H3	62
Warroad, Mn., U.S.	B3	116
Warsaw see Warszawa, Pol.	C6	20
Warsaw, Il., U.S.	C2	106
Warsaw, In., U.S.	B6	107
Warsaw, Ky., U.S.	B5	110
Warsaw, Mo., U.S.	C4	118
Warsaw, N.C., U.S.	B4	126
Warsaw, N.Y., U.S.	C2	125
Warsaw, Va., U.S.	C6	139
Warszawa (Warsaw), Pol.	C6	20
Wartburg, Tn., U.S.	C9	135
Warwick, Austl.	F5	62
Warwick, Qc., Can.	D6	90
Warwick, Md., U.S.	B6	113
Warwick, N.Y., U.S.	D6	125
Warwick, R.I., U.S.	D4	132
Wasaga Beach, On., Can.	C4	89
Wasatch, co., Ut., U.S.	C4	137
Wasco, Ca., U.S.	E4	98
Wasco, co., Or., U.S.	B5	130
Waseca, Mn., U.S.	F5	116
Waseca, co., Mn., U.S.	F5	116
Washakie, co., Wy., U.S.	C5	143
Washakie Needles, mts., Wy., U.S.	C3	143
Washburn, Ia., U.S.	B5	108
Washburn, Il., U.S.	C4	106
Washburn, Me., U.S.	B4	112
Washburn, N.D., U.S.	B5	127
Washburn, Wi., U.S.	B3	142
Washburn, co., Wi., U.S.	C2	142
Washburn, Mount, mtn., Wy., U.S.	B2	143
Wāshīm, India	E3	40
Washington, co., Al., U.S.	D1	94
Washington, co., Ar., U.S.	A1	97
Washington, co., Co., U.S.	B7	99
Washington, D.C., U.S.	C3	113
Washington, co., Fl., U.S.	u16	102
Washington, Ga., U.S.	C4	103
Washington, co., Ga., U.S.	C4	103
Washington, Ia., U.S.	C6	108
Washington, co., Ia., U.S.	C6	108
Washington, co., Id., U.S.	E2	105
Washington, Il., U.S.	C4	106
Washington, co., Il., U.S.	E4	106
Washington, In., U.S.	G3	107
Washington, co., In., U.S.	G5	107
Washington, Ks., U.S.	C6	109
Washington, co., Ks., U.S.	C6	109
Washington, Ky., U.S.	B6	110
Washington, co., Ky., U.S.	C4	110
Washington, La., U.S.	D3	111
Washington, co., La., U.S.	D5	111
Washington, co., Md., U.S.	A2	113
Washington, co., Me., U.S.	D5	112
Washington, co., Mn., U.S.	E6	116
Washington, Mo., U.S.	C6	118
Washington, co., Mo., U.S.	D7	118
Washington, Ms., U.S.	D2	117
Washington, co., Ms., U.S.	B3	117
Washington, N.C., U.S.	B5	126
Washington, co., N.C., U.S.	B6	126
Washington, co., Ne., U.S.	C9	120
Washington, N.J., U.S.	B3	123
Washington, co., N.Y., U.S.	B7	125
Washington, co., Oh., U.S.	C4	128
Washington, co., Ok., U.S.	A6	129
Washington, co., Or., U.S.	B3	130
Washington, Pa., U.S.	F1	131
Washington, co., Pa., U.S.	F1	131
Washington, co., R.I., U.S.	E2	132
Washington, co., Tn., U.S.	C11	135
Washington, co., Tx., U.S.	D4	136
Washington, Ut., U.S.	F2	137
Washington, co., Ut., U.S.	F2	137
Washington, co., Va., U.S.	f9	139
Washington, co., Vt., U.S.	C3	138
Washington, co., Wi., U.S.	E5	142
Washington, state, U.S.	B5	140
Washington, Lake, l., Fl., U.S.	D6	102
Washington, Lake, l., Mn., U.S.	E4	116
Washington, Lake, l., Ms., U.S.	B3	117
Washington, Lake, l., Wa., U.S.	e11	140
Washington, Mount, mtn., N.H., U.S.	B4	122
Washington Court House, Oh., U.S.	C2	128
Washington Island, i., Wi., U.S.	C7	142
Washington Park, Il., U.S.	E3	106
Washington Terrace, Ut., U.S.	B4	137
Washita, stm., Ok., U.S.	C4	129
Washita, co., Ok., U.S.	B2	129
Washoe, co., Nv., U.S.	C2	121
Washoe City, Nv., U.S.	D2	121
Washougal, Wa., U.S.	D3	140
Washow Bay, b., Mb., Can.	D3	86
Washtenaw, co., Mi., U.S.	F7	115
Wasilla, Ak., U.S.	C10	95
Wasior, Indon.	D8	36
Waskom, Tx., U.S.	C5	136
Waspam, Nic.	C3	80
Wasque Point, c., Ma., U.S.	D7	114
Wassookeag, Lake, l., Me., U.S.	C3	112
Wassuk Range, mts., Nv., U.S.	E3	121
Wataga, Il., U.S.	B3	106
Watampone, Indon.	D6	36
Watansopeng, Indon.	D5	36
Watauga, co., N.C., U.S.	A1	126
Watauga, stm., Tn., U.S.	C12	135
Watauga Lake, res., Tn., U.S.	C12	135
Watchaug Pond, l., R.I., U.S.	F2	132
Watch Hill Point, c., R.I., U.S.	G1	132
Watchung, N.J., U.S.	B4	123
Waterbury, Ct., U.S.	C3	100
Waterbury, Vt., U.S.	C3	138
Waterbury Center, Vt., U.S.	C3	138
Waterbury Reservoir, res., Vt., U.S.	C3	138
Wateree, stm., S.C., U.S.	D6	133
Wateree Lake, res., S.C., U.S.	C6	133
Waterford, Ire.	D3	12
Waterford, Ct., U.S.	D7	100
Waterford, N.Y., U.S.	C7	125
Waterford, Pa., U.S.	C2	131
Waterford, Wi., U.S.	F5	142
Waterhen Lake, l., Mb., Can.	C2	86
Waterloo, Bel.	E9	12
Waterloo, On., Can.	D4	89
Waterloo, Qc., Can.	D5	90
Waterloo, Ia., U.S.	B5	108
Waterloo, Il., U.S.	E3	106
Waterloo, In., U.S.	B7	107
Waterloo, N.Y., U.S.	C4	125
Waterloo, Wi., U.S.	E5	142
Waterman, Il., U.S.	B5	106
Waterman Reservoir, res., R.I., U.S.	B3	132
Waterproof, La., U.S.	C4	111
Watersmeet, Mi., U.S.	n12	115
Waterton Lakes National Park, Ab., Can.	E3	84
Watertown, Ct., U.S.	C3	100
Watertown, Ma., U.S.	g11	114
Watertown, N.Y., U.S.	B5	125
Watertown, S.D., U.S.	C8	134
Watertown, Tn., U.S.	A5	135
Watertown, Wi., U.S.	E5	142
Water Valley, Ms., U.S.	A4	117
Waterville, Ks., U.S.	C7	109
Waterville, Me., U.S.	D3	112
Waterville, Mn., U.S.	F5	116
Waterville, N.Y., U.S.	C5	125
Waterville, Oh., U.S.	A2	128
Waterville, Wa., U.S.	B5	140
Watervliet, Mi., U.S.	F4	115
Watervliet, N.Y., U.S.	C7	125
Watford, On., Can.	E3	89
Watford City, N.D., U.S.	B2	127
Wathena, Ks., U.S.	C9	109
Watheroo, Austl.	G2	60
Watkins, Mn., U.S.	E4	116
Watkins Glen, N.Y., U.S.	C4	125
Watkinsville, Ga., U.S.	C3	103
Watling Island see San Salvador, i., Bah.	D10	76
Watonga, Ok., U.S.	B3	129
Watonwan, stm., Mn., U.S.	G4	116
Watonwan, co., Mn., U.S.	F4	116
Watsa, D.R.C.	C5	54
Watseka, Il., U.S.	C6	106
Watsontown, Pa., U.S.	D8	131
Watsonville, Ca., U.S.	D3	98
Watts Bar Dam, Tn., U.S.	D9	135
Watts Bar Lake, res., Tn., U.S.	D9	135
Wattsville, S.C., U.S.	B4	133
Watubela, Kepulauan, is., Indon.	D8	36
Waubaushene, On., Can.	C5	89
Waubay, S.D., U.S.	B8	134
Waubay Lake, l., S.D., U.S.	B8	134
Wauchope, Austl.	E5	60
Wauchula, Fl., U.S.	E5	102
Wauconda, Il., U.S.	h8	106
Waugh Mountain, mtn., Id., U.S.	D4	105
Waukee, Ia., U.S.	C4	108
Waukegan, Il., U.S.	A6	106
Waukesha, Wi., U.S.	F5	142
Waukesha, co., Wi., U.S.	E5	142
Waukewan, Lake, l., N.H., U.S.	C3	122
Waukomis, Ok., U.S.	A4	129
Waukon, Ia., U.S.	A6	108
Waunakee, Wi., U.S.	E4	142
Wauneta, Ne., U.S.	D4	120
Waungumbaug Lake, l., Ct., U.S.	B6	100
Waupaca, Wi., U.S.	D4	142
Waupaca, co., Wi., U.S.	D5	142
Waupun, Wi., U.S.	E5	142
Wauregan, Ct., U.S.	C8	100
Waurika, Ok., U.S.	C4	129
Waurika Lake, res., Ok., U.S.	C3	129
Wausau, Wi., U.S.	D4	142
Wausau, Lake, res., Wi., U.S.	D4	142

Name — Map Ref. — Page

Wauseon, Oh., U.S. A1 128
Waushara, co., Wi., U.S. D4 142
Wautoma, Wi., U.S. D4 142
Wauwatosa, Wi., U.S. m12 142
Wave Hill, Austl. D5 60
Waveland, Ms., U.S. E4 117
Waverley, N.S., Can. E6 87
Waverly, Ia., U.S. B5 108
Waverly, Il., U.S. D4 106
Waverly, Ks., U.S. D8 109
Waverly, Mn., U.S. E5 116
Waverly, Mo., U.S. B4 118
Waverly, Ne., U.S. D9 120
Waverly, N.Y., U.S. C4 125
Waverly, Oh., U.S. C3 128
Waverly, Tn., U.S. A4 135
Waverly, Va., U.S. C5 139
Waverly, W.V., U.S. B3 141
Waverly Hall, Ga., U.S. D2 103
Wāw, Sudan I10 48
Wāw al-Kabīr, Libya E8 48
Wawanesa, Mb., Can. E2 86
Wawasee, Lake, l., In., U.S. B6 107
Wawayanda Lake, l., N.J., U.S. A4 123
Wawota, Sk., Can. H4 91
Waxahachie, Tx., U.S. C4 136
Waxhaw, N.C., U.S. C2 126
Waycross, Ga., U.S. E4 103
Wayland, Ia., U.S. C6 108
Wayland, Ma., U.S. g10 114
Wayland, Mi., U.S. F5 115
Wayland, N.Y., U.S. C3 125
Waylyn, S.C., U.S. k12 133
Waymart, Pa., U.S. C11 131
Wayne, co., Ga., U.S. E5 103
Wayne, co., Ia., U.S. D4 108
Wayne, co., Il., U.S. E5 106
Wayne, co., In., U.S. E7 107
Wayne, co., Ky., U.S. D5 110
Wayne, Mi., U.S. p15 115
Wayne, co., Mi., U.S. F7 115
Wayne, co., Mo., U.S. D7 118
Wayne, co., Ms., U.S. D5 117
Wayne, co., N.C., U.S. B4 126
Wayne, Ne., U.S. B8 120
Wayne, co., Ne., U.S. B8 120
Wayne, N.J., U.S. B4 123
Wayne, co., N.Y., U.S. B3 125
Wayne, co., Oh., U.S. B4 128
Wayne, co., Pa., U.S. C11 131
Wayne, co., Tn., U.S. B4 135
Wayne, co., Ut., U.S. E4 137
Wayne, W.V., U.S. C2 141
Wayne, co., W.V., U.S. C2 141
Wayne City, Il., U.S. E5 106
Waynesboro, Ga., U.S. C4 103
Waynesboro, Ms., U.S. D5 117
Waynesboro, Pa., U.S. G6 131
Waynesboro, Tn., U.S. B4 135
Waynesboro, Va., U.S. B4 139
Waynesburg, Oh., U.S. B4 128
Waynesburg, Pa., U.S. G1 131
Waynesville, Mo., U.S. D5 118
Waynesville, N.C., U.S. f10 126
Waynesville, Oh., U.S. C1 128
Waynetown, In., U.S. D3 107
Waynewood, Va., U.S. g12 139
Waynoka, Ok., U.S. A3 129
Wayzata, Mn., U.S. n11 116
Waza, Cam. D7 50
We, Pulau, i., Indon. B1 36
Weakley, co., Tn., U.S. A3 135
Weatherford, Ok., U.S. B3 129
Weatherford, Tx., U.S. C4 136
Weatherly, Pa., U.S. E10 131
Weatogue, Ct., U.S. B4 100
Weaver, Al., U.S. B4 94
Weaver Mountains, mts., Az., U.S. C3 96
Weaverville, Ca., U.S. B2 98
Weaverville, N.C., U.S. f10 126
Webb, Al., U.S. D4 94
Webb, Ms., U.S. B3 117
Webb, co., Tx., U.S. F3 136
Webb City, Mo., U.S. D3 118
Webbers Falls, Ok., U.S. B6 129
Webberville, Mi., U.S. F6 115
Webb Lake, l., Me., U.S. D2 112
Weber, co., Ut., U.S. B4 137
Weber City, Va., U.S. f9 139
Webster, co., Ga., U.S. D2 103
Webster, co., Ia., U.S. B3 108
Webster, co., Ky., U.S. C2 110
Webster, co., La., U.S. B2 111
Webster, Ma., U.S. B4 114
Webster, co., Mo., U.S. D5 118
Webster, co., Ms., U.S. B4 117
Webster, co., Ne., U.S. D7 120
Webster, N.Y., U.S. B3 125
Webster, Pa., U.S. F2 131
Webster, S.D., U.S. B8 134
Webster, co., W.V., U.S. C4 141
Webster City, Ia., U.S. B4 108
Webster Groves, Mo., U.S. f13 118
Webster Reservoir, res., Ks., U.S. C4 109
Webster Springs, W.V., U.S. C4 141
Websterville, Vt., U.S. C4 138
Weda, Indon. C7 36
Weddell Sea, Ant. C1 67
Wedgeport, N.S., Can. F4 87
Wedgewood, Mo., U.S. f13 118
Wedowee, Al., U.S. B4 94
Weed, Ca., U.S. B2 98
Weed Heights, Nv., U.S. E2 121
Weedon, Qc., Can. D6 90
Weedsport, N.Y., U.S. B4 125
Weedville, Pa., U.S. D5 131
Weehawken, N.J., U.S. h8 123
Weeksbury, Ky., U.S. C7 110
Weeping Water, Ne., U.S. D9 120
Weichang, China A4 30
Weiden in der Oberpfalz, Ger. F12 12
Weifang, China D11 28
Weihai, China D12 28
Weimar, Ger. E12 12
Weimar, Tx., U.S. E4 136
Weinan, China E9 28
Weiner, Ar., U.S. B5 97
Weippe, Id., U.S. C3 105
Weir, Ks., U.S. E9 109
Weir, Lake, l., Fl., U.S. C5 102
Weirsdale, Fl., U.S. D5 102
Weirton, W.V., U.S. A4 141
Weiser, Id., U.S. E2 105
Weiser, stm., Id., U.S. E2 105
Weishan Hu, l., China B4 30
Weissenburg in Bayern, Ger. F12 12
Weissenfels, Ger. E12 12
Weiss Lake, res., U.S. A4 94
Weixi, China A3 34
Weixian, China B4 30
Wejherowo, Pol. B5 20
Welbourn Hill, Austl. F5 60
Welch, W.V., U.S. D3 141
Welcome, Mn., U.S. G4 116
Welcome, S.C., U.S. B3 133
Weld, co., Co., U.S. A6 99
Weldon, N.C., U.S. A5 126
Weldon Spring, Mo., U.S. f12 118
Weleetka, Ok., U.S. B5 129
Welk'īt'ē, Eth. B7 54
Welkom, S. Afr. D4 56
Welland, On., Can. E5 89
Wellesley, On., Can. D4 89
Wellesley, Ma., U.S. B5 114
Wellesley Islands, is., Austl. D2 62
Wellford, S.C., U.S. B3 133
Wellington, Austl. G4 62
Wellington, On., Can. D7 89
Wellington, N.Z. I11 58
Wellington, Co., U.S. A5 99
Wellington, Ks., U.S. E6 109
Wellington, Mo., U.S. B4 118
Wellington, Nv., U.S. E2 121
Wellington, Oh., U.S. A3 128
Wellington, Tx., U.S. B2 136
Wellington, Ut., U.S. D5 137
Wellington, Isla, i., Chile G2 69
Wellman, Ia., U.S. C6 108
Wells, co., In., U.S. C7 107
Wells, Me., U.S. E2 112
Wells, Mi., U.S. C3 115
Wells, Mn., U.S. G5 116
Wells, co., N.D., U.S. B6 127
Wells, Nv., U.S. B7 121
Wells, stm., Vt., U.S. C4 138
Wellsboro, Pa., U.S. C7 131
Wellsburg, Ia., U.S. B5 108
Wellsburg, W.V., U.S. A4 141
Wellston, Oh., U.S. C3 128
Wellston, Ok., U.S. B4 129
Wellsville, Ks., U.S. D8 109
Wellsville, Mo., U.S. B6 118
Wellsville, N.Y., U.S. C3 125
Wellsville, Oh., U.S. B5 128
Wellsville, Ut., U.S. B4 137
Wellton, Az., U.S. E1 96
Wels, Aus. F13 12
Welsh, La., U.S. D3 111
Wembley, Ab., Can. B1 84
Wenatchee, Wa., U.S. B5 140
Wenatchee, stm., Wa., U.S. B5 140
Wenatchee Lake, l., Wa., U.S. B5 140
Wenatchee Mountains, mts., Wa., U.S. B5 140
Wenchang, China F3 30
Wenchi, Ghana E4 50
Wendell, Id., U.S. G4 105
Wendell, N.C., U.S. B4 126
Wendeng, China B5 30
Wendover, Ut., U.S. C1 137
Wengyuan, China E3 30
Wenham, Ma., U.S. A6 114
Wenham Lake, l., Ma., U.S. f12 114
Wenling, China D5 30
Wenona, Il., U.S. B4 106
Wenshan, China G8 28
Wenshang, China B4 30
Wensu, China A4 40
Wentworth, Austl. G3 62
Wentworth, Lake, l., N.H., U.S. C4 122
Wentzville, Mo., U.S. C7 118
Wenzhou, China F12 28
Weohyakapka, Lake, l., Fl., U.S. E5 102
Werda, Bots. D3 56
Weri, Indon. D8 36
Werribee, Austl. H3 62
Wesel, Ger. E10 12
Weser, stm., Ger. D11 12
Weslaco, Tx., U.S. F4 136
Wesleyville, N.L., Can. D5 88
Wesleyville, Pa., U.S. B2 131
Wessel, Cape, c., Austl. C6 60
Wessel Islands, is., Austl. C6 60
Wesserunsett Lake, l., Me., U.S. D3 112
Wessington Springs, S.D., U.S. C7 134
Wesson, Ms., U.S. D3 117
West, stm., Ct., U.S. D5 100
West, stm., Ma., U.S. h9 114
West, Tx., U.S. D4 136
West, stm., Vt., U.S. E3 138
West Acton, Ma., U.S. g10 114
West Alexandria, Oh., U.S. C1 128
West Allis, Wi., U.S. m11 142
West Alton, Mo., U.S. f13 118
West Andover, Ma., U.S. A5 114
West Antarctica, reg., Ant. E29 67
West Baden Springs, In., U.S. G4 107
West Baton Rouge, co., La., U.S. D4 111
West Bay, b., Fl., U.S. u16 102
West Bay, b., N.C., U.S. B6 126
West Bay, b., Tx., U.S. r15 136
West Bend, Ia., U.S. B3 108
West Bend, Wi., U.S. E5 142
West Bengal, state, India E5 40
West Berlin, N.J., U.S. D3 123
West Billerica, Ma., U.S. f10 114
West Blocton, Al., U.S. B2 94
Westborough, Ma., U.S. B4 114
West Bountiful, Ut., U.S. C4 137
West Boylston, Ma., U.S. B4 114
West Branch, Ia., U.S. C6 108
West Branch, Mi., U.S. D6 115
West Branch Reservoir, res., Ct., U.S. B3 100
West Bridgewater, Ma., U.S. B5 114
Westbrook, Ct., U.S. D6 100
Westbrook, Me., U.S. E2 112
Westbrook, Mn., U.S. F3 116
West Burlington, Ia., U.S. D6 108
West Butte, mtn., Mt., U.S. B5 119
Westby, Wi., U.S. E3 142
West Cache Creek, stm., Ok., U.S. C3 129
West Caldwell, N.J., U.S. B4 123
West Canada Creek, stm., N.Y., U.S. B6 125
West Cape Howe, c., Austl. H2 60
West Caroline Basin H16 64
West Carroll, co., La., U.S. B4 111
West Carrollton, Oh., U.S. C1 128
West Carthage, N.Y., U.S. B5 125
Westchester, Il., U.S. k9 106
Westchester, co., N.Y., U.S. D7 125
West Chester, Pa., U.S. G10 131
West Chicago, Il., U.S. k8 106
West Chop, c., Ma., U.S. D6 114
West College Corner, In., U.S. E8 107
West Columbia, S.C., U.S. D5 133
West Columbia, Tx., U.S. E5 136
West Concord, Ma., U.S. B5 114
West Concord, Mn., U.S. F6 116
West Concord, N.C., U.S. B2 126
Westconnaug Reservoir, res., R.I., U.S. C2 132
West Cote Blanche Bay, b., La., U.S. E4 111
West Covina, Ca., U.S. m13 98
West Crossett, Ar., U.S. D4 97
West Cumberland, Me., U.S. E2 112
West Dennis, Ma., U.S. C7 114
West Des Moines, Ia., U.S. C4 108
West Elk Mountains, mts., Co., U.S. C3 99
West Elk Peak, mtn., Co., U.S. C3 99
Westerly, R.I., U.S. F1 132
Western Australia, state, Austl. E2 60
Western Desert, des., Egypt F9 14
Western Dvina (Zapadnaja Dvina), stm., Eur. C4 22
Western Ghāts, mts., India F2 40
Westernport, Md., U.S. m12 113
Western Sahara, dep., Afr. B2 50
Western Samoa see Samoa, ctry., Oc. F12 58
Western Sayans see Zapadnyj Sajan, mts., Russia D11 26
Western Springs, Il., U.S. k9 106
Westerville, Oh., U.S. B3 128
West European Basin D11 66
West Falkland, i., Falk. Is. H4 69
West Falmouth, Ma., U.S. C6 114
West Fargo, N.D., U.S. C9 127
West Feliciana, co., La., U.S. D4 111
Westfield, N.B., Can. D3 87
Westfield, In., U.S. D5 107
Westfield, Ma., U.S. B2 114
Westfield, stm., Ma., U.S. B2 114
Westfield, N.J., U.S. B4 123
Westfield, N.Y., U.S. C1 125
Westfield, Pa., U.S. C6 131
Westfield, Wi., U.S. E4 142
West Fork, Ar., U.S. B1 97
West Fork, stm., W.V., U.S. B4 141
West Frankfort, Il., U.S. F5 106
West Freehold, N.J., U.S. C4 123
West Friendship, Md., U.S. B4 113
Westgate, Fl., U.S. F6 102
West Grand Lake, l., Me., U.S. C5 112
West Grove, Pa., U.S. G10 131
West Hanover, Ma., U.S. h12 114
West Hartford, Ct., U.S. B4 100
West Haven, Ct., U.S. D4 100
West Hazleton, Pa., U.S. E9 131
West Helena, Ar., U.S. C5 97
West Hill Reservoir, res., Ma., U.S. B4 114
Westhope, N.D., U.S. A4 127
West Ice Shelf, ice, Ant. C13 67
West Indies, is. D11 76
West Island, i., Ma., U.S. C6 114
West Jefferson, N.C., U.S. A1 126
West Jefferson, Oh., U.S. C2 128
West Jordan, Ut., U.S. C3 137
West Kingston, R.I., U.S. F3 132
West Lafayette, In., U.S. D4 107
West Lafayette, Oh., U.S. B4 128
Westlake, La., U.S. D2 111
West Lake, l., Me., U.S. C4 112
Westlake, Oh., U.S. h9 128
Westland, Mi., U.S. F7 115
West Laramie, Wy., U.S. E7 143
West Lawn, Pa., U.S. F10 131
West Lebanon, In., U.S. D3 107
West Liberty, Ia., U.S. C6 108
West Liberty, Ky., U.S. C6 110
West Liberty, Oh., U.S. B2 128
West Liberty, W.V., U.S. f8 141
West Linn, Or., U.S. B4 130
Westlock, Ab., Can. B4 84
West Long Branch, N.J., U.S. C4 123
West Lorne, On., Can. E3 89
West Marion, N.C., U.S. f10 126
West Medway, Ma., U.S. B5 114
West Memphis, Ar., U.S. B5 97
West Miami, Fl., U.S. s13 102
West Middlesex, Pa., U.S. D1 131
West Mifflin, Pa., U.S. F2 131
West Milton, Oh., U.S. C1 128
West Milwaukee, Wi., U.S. m12 142
Westminster, Ca., U.S. n12 98
Westminster, Co., U.S. B5 99
Westminster, Md., U.S. A4 113
Westminster, S.C., U.S. B1 133
West Monroe, La., U.S. B3 111
Westmont, Il., U.S. k9 106
Westmont, N.J., U.S. D2 123
Westmont, Pa., U.S. F4 131
Westmoreland, co., Pa., U.S. F2 131
Westmoreland, Tn., U.S. A5 135
Westmoreland, co., Va., U.S. B6 139
Westmorland, Ca., U.S. F6 98
West Musquash Lake, l., Me., U.S. C5 112
West Mystic, Ct., U.S. D8 100
West Newton, Pa., U.S. F2 131
West New York, N.J., U.S. h8 123
West Nicholson, Zimb. C4 56
West Nishnabotna, stm., Ia., U.S. C2 108
West Norriton, Pa., U.S. o20 131
Weston, Ct., U.S. E2 100
Weston, Ma., U.S. g10 114
Weston, Mo., U.S. B3 118
Weston, Oh., U.S. A2 128
Weston, Or., U.S. B8 130
Weston, W.V., U.S. B4 141
Weston, co., Wy., U.S. C8 143
Weston-super-Mare, Eng., U.K. E5 12
West Orange, N.J., U.S. B4 123
Westover, Md., U.S. D6 113
Westover, W.V., U.S. B5 141
Westover Air Force Base, mil., Ma., U.S. B2 114
West Palm Beach, Fl., U.S. F6 102
West Pawlet, Vt., U.S. E2 138
West Pearl, stm., La., U.S. D6 111
West Pelzer, S.C., U.S. B3 133
West Pensacola, Fl., U.S. u14 102
West Peoria, Il., U.S. C4 106
Westphalia, Mi., U.S. F6 115
West Pittsburg, Pa., U.S. E1 131
West Pittston, Pa., U.S. m17 131
West Plains, Mo., U.S. E6 118
West Point, mtn., Ak., U.S. C11 95
West Point, Ca., U.S. C3 98
West Point, Ga., U.S. D1 103
West Point, Ia., U.S. D6 108
West Point, Ky., U.S. C4 110
West Point, Ms., U.S. B5 117
West Point, Ne., U.S. C9 120
West Point, N.Y., U.S. D7 125
West Point, Va., U.S. C6 139
West Point Lake, res., U.S. C1 103
Westport, On., Can. C8 89
Westport, Ct., U.S. E2 100
Westport, In., U.S. F6 107
Westport, Wa., U.S. C1 140
West Portsmouth, Oh., U.S. D2 128
West Quoddy Head, c., Me., U.S. D6 112
West Reading, Pa., U.S. F10 131
West Rutland, Vt., U.S. D2 138
West Saint Paul, Mn., U.S. n12 116
West Salem, Il., U.S. E5 106
West Salem, Oh., U.S. B3 128
West Salem, Wi., U.S. E2 142
West Scarborough, Me., U.S. E2 112
West Seneca, N.Y., U.S. C2 125
West Siberian Lowland see Zapadno-Sibirskaja ravnina, pl., Russia C9 26
West Simsbury, Ct., U.S. B4 100
West Slope, Or., U.S. g12 130
West Spanish Peak, mtn., Co., U.S. D6 99
West Springfield, Ma., U.S. B2 114
West Springfield, Va., U.S. g12 139
West Swanzey, N.H., U.S. E2 122
West Terre Haute, In., U.S. F3 107
West Thompson Lake, res., Ct., U.S. B8 100
West Union, Ia., U.S. B6 108
West Union, Oh., U.S. D2 128
West Union, W.V., U.S. B4 141
West Unity, Oh., U.S. A1 128
West University Place, Tx., U.S. r14 136
West Valley City, Ut., U.S. C4 137
West Vancouver, B.C., Can. f12 85
West Van Lear, Ky., U.S. C7 110
West View, Pa., U.S. h13 131
Westville, Il., U.S. C6 106
Westville, In., U.S. A4 107
Westville, N.H., U.S. E4 122
Westville, N.J., U.S. D2 123
Westville, Ok., U.S. A7 129
Westville Lake, res., Ma., U.S. B3 114
West Virginia, state, U.S. C4 141
West Walker, stm., U.S. E2 121
West Wareham, Ma., U.S. C6 114
West Warwick, R.I., U.S. D3 132
Westwego, La., U.S. k11 111
Westwood, Ca., U.S. B3 98
Westwood, Ks., U.S. k16 109
Westwood, Ky., U.S. B7 110
Westwood, Ma., U.S. B5 114
Westwood, N.J., U.S. B4 123
Westwood Lakes, Fl., U.S. s13 102
West Wyalong, Austl. G4 62
West Wyoming, Pa., U.S. n17 131
West Yarmouth, Ma., U.S. C7 114
West Yellowstone, Mt., U.S. F5 119
West York, Pa., U.S. G8 131
Wetar, Pulau, i., Indon. E7 36
Wetar, Selat, strt., Asia E7 36
Wetaskiwin, Ab., Can. C4 84
Wete, Tan. D7 54
Wethersfield, Ct., U.S. C5 100
Wet Mountains, mts., Co., U.S. C5 99
Wetumka, Ok., U.S. B5 129
Wetumpka, Al., U.S. C3 94
Wetzel, co., W.V., U.S. B4 141
Wetzlar, Ger. E11 12
Wewahitchka, Fl., U.S. B1 102
Wewak, Pap. N. Gui. G11 32
Wewoka, Ok., U.S. B5 129
Wexford, Ire. D3 12
Wexford, co., Mi., U.S. D5 115
Weyauwega, Wi., U.S. D5 142
Weymouth, Eng., U.K. E5 12
Weymouth, Ma., U.S. B6 114
Whakatane, N.Z. o14 63c
Whaleysville, Md., U.S. D7 113
Whangarei, N.Z. o13 63c
Wharton, N.J., U.S. B3 123
Wharton, Tx., U.S. E4 136
Wharton, co., Tx., U.S. E4 136
Wharton Basin J13 64
What Cheer, Ia., U.S. C5 108
Whatcom, co., Wa., U.S. A4 140
Whatcom, Lake, l., Wa., U.S. A3 140
Wheatfield, In., U.S. B3 107
Wheatland, Ca., U.S. C3 98
Wheatland, Ia., U.S. C7 108
Wheatland, co., Mt., U.S. D7 119
Wheatland, Wy., U.S. D8 143
Wheatland Reservoir, res., Wy., U.S. E7 143
Wheatley, On., Can. E2 89
Wheaton, Il., U.S. B5 106
Wheaton, Md., U.S. B3 113
Wheaton, Mn., U.S. E2 116
Wheaton, Mo., U.S. E3 118
Wheat Ridge, Co., U.S. B5 99
Wheelbarrow Peak, mtn., Nv., U.S. F5 121
Wheeler, co., Ga., U.S. D4 103
Wheeler, Ms., U.S. A5 117
Wheeler, co., Ne., U.S. C7 120
Wheeler, co., Or., U.S. C6 130
Wheeler, Tx., U.S. B2 136
Wheeler, co., Tx., U.S. B2 136
Wheeler Air Force Base, mil., Hi., U.S. g9 104
Wheeler Lake, res., Al., U.S. A2 94
Wheeler Peak, mtn., Ca., U.S. C4 98
Wheeler Peak, mtn., N.M., U.S. A4 124
Wheeler Peak, mtn., Nv., U.S. E7 121
Wheelersburg, Oh., U.S. D3 128
Wheeling, Il., U.S. h9 106
Wheeling, W.V., U.S. A4 141
Wheeling Creek, stm., W.V., U.S. f8 141

Name — Map Ref. — Page

Wheelwright, Ky., U.S. **C7** 110
Whetstone, stm., U.S. **E2** 116
Whidbey Island, i., Wa., U.S. **A3** 140
Whidbey Island Naval Air Station, mil., Wa., U.S. **A3** 140
Whigham, Ga., U.S. **F2** 103
Whiskey Peak, mtn., Wy., U.S. **D5** 143
Whiskeytown-Shasta-Trinity National Recreation Area, Ca., U.S. **B2** 98
Whistler, B.C., Can. **D6** 85
Whitacres, Ct., U.S. **A5** 100
Whitakers, N.C., U.S. **A5** 126
Whitbourne, N.L., Can. **E5** 88
Whitby, On., Can. **D6** 89
Whitchurch-Stouffville, On., Can. **D5** 89
White, co., Ar., U.S. **B4** 97
White, stm., Az., U.S. **D5** 96
White, co., Ga., U.S. **B3** 103
White, co., Il., U.S. **E5** 106
White, stm., In., U.S. **H2** 107
White, co., In., U.S. **C4** 107
White, stm., Mi., U.S. **E4** 115
White, stm., Nv., U.S. **E6** 121
White, co., Tn., U.S. **D8** 135
White, stm., Tx., U.S. **C2** 136
White, stm., Vt., U.S. **D4** 138
White, stm., Wa., U.S. **B4** 140
White, stm., Wa., U.S. **B5** 140
White, stm., U.S. **C4** 97
White, stm., U.S. **C7** 137
White, stm., U.S. **D5** 134
White Bay, b., N.L., Can. **D3** 88
White Bear, stm., N.L., Can. **E3** 88
White Bear Lake, Mn., U.S. **E5** 116
White Bluff, Tn., U.S. **A4** 135
White Butte, mtn., N.D., U.S. **C2** 127
White Castle, La., U.S. **D4** 111
White Center, Wa., U.S. **e11** 140
White City, Or., U.S. **E4** 130
White Clay Creek, stm., U.S. **A3** 120
White Cliffs, Austl. **F3** 60
White Cliffs, Austl. **G3** 62
White Cloud, Mi., U.S. **E5** 115
Whitecourt, Ab., Can. **B3** 84
White Creek, stm., U.S. **E2** 138
Whiteday, stm., W.V., U.S. **h10** 141
White Deer, Tx., U.S. **B2** 136
White Earth Indian Reservation, Mn., U.S. **C3** 116
White Earth Lake, l., Mn., U.S. **C3** 116
Whiteface, stm., Mn., U.S. **C6** 116
Whiteface Mountain, mtn., N.Y., U.S. **f11** 125
Whitefield, N.H., U.S. **B3** 122
Whitefish, Mt., U.S. **B2** 119
Whitefish Bay, b., Mi., U.S. **B6** 115
Whitefish Bay, Wi., U.S. **m12** 142
Whitefish Lake, l., Mn., U.S. **D4** 116
Whitefish Range, mts., Mt., U.S. **B2** 119
Whiteford, Md., U.S. **A5** 113
White Hall, Al., U.S. **C3** 94
White Hall, Ar., U.S. **C3** 97
White Hall, Il., U.S. **D3** 106
Whitehall, Mi., U.S. **E4** 115
Whitehall, Mt., U.S. **E4** 119
Whitehall, N.Y., U.S. **B7** 125
Whitehall, Oh., U.S. **m11** 128
Whitehall, Wi., U.S. **D2** 142
Whitehall Reservoir, res., Ma., U.S. **h9** 114
Whitehaven, Eng., U.K. **C5** 12
White Haven, Pa., U.S. **D10** 131
Whitehorn, Point, c., Wa., U.S. **A3** 140
Whitehorse, Yk., Can. **F13** 82
White Horse, N.J., U.S. **C3** 123
Whitehouse, Oh., U.S. **A2** 128
White House, Tn., U.S. **A5** 135
White Island Shores, Ma., U.S. **C6** 114
White Knob Mountains, mts., Id., U.S. **F5** 105
White Lake, l., La., U.S. **E3** 111
Whiteman Air Force Base, mil., Mo., U.S. **C4** 118
White Mesa Natural Bridge, Az., U.S. **A4** 96
White Mountain Peak, mtn., Ca., U.S. **D4** 98
White Mountains, mts., N.H., U.S. **B3** 122
White Mountains, mts., U.S. **D4** 98
Whitemouth, stm., Mb., Can. **E4** 86
Whitemouth Lake, l., Mb., Can. **E4** 86
White Nile see Abyaḍ, Al-Baḥr al-, stm., Sudan **H11** 48
White Oak, Oh., U.S. **o12** 128
White Oak Creek, stm., Oh., U.S. **D2** 128
Whiteoak Creek, stm., Tn., U.S. **A4** 135
White Oak Lake, res., Ar., U.S. **D2** 97
White Pigeon, Mi., U.S. **G5** 115
White Pine, Mi., U.S. **m12** 115
White Pine, co., Nv., U.S. **D6** 121
White Pine, Tn., U.S. **C10** 135
White Plains, Md., U.S. **C4** 113
White Plains, N.Y., U.S. **D7** 125
Whiteriver, Az., U.S. **D6** 96
White River Junction, Vt., U.S. **D4** 138
White Rock, B.C., Can. **E6** 85
White Russia see Belarus, ctry., Eur. **C9** 20
White Salmon, Wa., U.S. **D4** 140
White Salmon, stm., Wa., U.S. **D4** 140
White Sands Missile Range, mil., N.M., U.S. **E3** 124
White Sands National Monument, N.M., U.S. **E3** 124
Whitesboro, N.Y., U.S. **B5** 125
Whitesboro, Tx., U.S. **C4** 136
Whitesburg, Ga., U.S. **C2** 103
Whitesburg, Ky., U.S. **C7** 110
Whites Creek, stm., Tn., U.S. **g10** 135
White Sea see Beloe more, Russia **C5** 26
Whiteside, co., Il., U.S. **B3** 106
White Sulphur Springs, Mt., U.S. **D6** 119
White Sulphur Springs, W.V., U.S. **D4** 141
Whitesville, Ky., U.S. **C3** 110
White Swan, Wa., U.S. **C5** 140
White Tank Mountains, mts., Az., U.S. **k7** 96
Whiteville, N.C., U.S. **C4** 126
Whiteville, Tn., U.S. **B2** 135
White Volta, stm., Afr. **E4** 50
Whitewater, Ks., U.S. **E6** 109
Whitewater, stm., Ks., U.S. **E6** 109
Whitewater, Wi., U.S. **F5** 142
Whitewater, stm., U.S. **F7** 107
Whitewater Baldy, mtn., N.M., U.S. **D1** 124
Whitewater Bay, b., Fl., U.S. **G6** 102
Whitewood, S.D., U.S. **C2** 134
Whitewright, Tx., U.S. **C4** 136
Whitfield, co., Ga., U.S. **B2** 103
Whitfield Estates, Fl., U.S. **q10** 102
Whiting, Ia., U.S. **B1** 108
Whiting, In., U.S. **A3** 107
Whiting, Wi., U.S. **D4** 142
Whiting Field Naval Air Station, mil., Fl., U.S. **u14** 102
Whitinsville, Ma., U.S. **B4** 114
Whitley, co., In., U.S. **B6** 107
Whitley, co., Ky., U.S. **D5** 110
Whitley City, Ky., U.S. **D5** 110
Whitman, Ma., U.S. **B6** 114
Whitman, co., Wa., U.S. **B8** 140
Whitman, W.V., U.S. **D2** 141
Whitman Square, N.J., U.S. **D2** 123
Whitmire, S.C., U.S. **B4** 133
Whitmore Lake, Mi., U.S. **p14** 115
Whitmore Mountains, mts., Ant. **E31** 67
Whitmore Village, Hi., U.S. **f9** 104
Whitney, S.C., U.S. **B4** 133
Whitney, Tx., U.S. **D4** 136
Whitney, Lake, res., Tx., U.S. **D4** 136
Whitney, Mount, mtn., Ca., U.S. **D4** 98
Whitney Point Lake, res., N.Y., U.S. **C5** 125
Whitsunday Island, i., Austl. **E4** 62
Whittier, Ak., U.S. **C10** 95
Whittier, Ca., U.S. **F4** 98
Whitwell, Tn., U.S. **D8** 135
Whyalla, Austl. **G2** 62
Wiarton, On., Can. **C3** 89
Wibaux, Mt., U.S. **D12** 119
Wibaux, co., Mt., U.S. **D12** 119
Wichita, co., Ks., U.S. **D2** 109
Wichita, Ks., U.S. **E6** 109
Wichita, co., Tx., U.S. **B3** 136
Wichita Falls, Tx., U.S. **C3** 136
Wichita Mountains, mts., Ok., U.S. **C3** 129
Wick, Scot., U.K. **A5** 12
Wickenburg, Az., U.S. **D3** 96
Wickham, Austl. **E2** 60
Wickham, Cape, c., Austl. **H3** 62
Wickiup Reservoir, res., Or., U.S. **E5** 130
Wickliffe, Ky., U.S. **f8** 110
Wickliffe, Oh., U.S. **A4** 128
Wicklow, Ire. **D3** 12
Wicomico, stm., Md., U.S. **D6** 113
Wicomico, co., Md., U.S. **D6** 113
Wiconisco, Pa., U.S. **E8** 131
Widefield, Co., U.S. **C6** 99
Widgiemooltha, Austl. **G3** 60
Wieluń, Pol. **D5** 20
Wien, Aus. **F15** 12
Wiener Neustadt, Aus. **G15** 12
Wieprz, stm., Pol. **D7** 20
Wiesbaden, Ger. **E11** 12
Wiggins, Ms., U.S. **E4** 117
Wiggins Peak, mtn., Wy., U.S. **C3** 143
Wight, Isle of, i., Eng., U.K. **E6** 12
Wikwemikong, On., Can. **B3** 89
Wilbarger, co., Tx., U.S. **B3** 136
Wilber, Ne., U.S. **D9** 120
Wilberforce, Oh., U.S. **C2** 128
Wilbraham, Ma., U.S. **B3** 114
Wilbur, Wa., U.S. **B7** 140
Wilburton, Ok., U.S. **C6** 129
Wilcannia, Austl. **G3** 62
Wilcox, co., Al., U.S. **D2** 94
Wilcox, co., Ga., U.S. **E3** 103
Wilcox, Pa., U.S. **C4** 131
Wild, stm., U.S. **B4** 122
Wild Ammonoosuc, stm., N.H., U.S. **B3** 122
Wild Branch, stm., Vt., U.S. **B4** 138
Wilder, Id., U.S. **F2** 105
Wilder, Vt., U.S. **D4** 138
Wilder Dam, U.S. **C2** 122
Wildhorse Creek, stm., Ok., U.S. **C4** 129
Wild Horse Reservoir, res., Nv., U.S. **B6** 121
Wildorado, Tx., U.S. **B1** 136
Wild Rice, stm., Mn., U.S. **C2** 116
Wild Rice, stm., N.D., U.S. **C8** 127
Wildwood, Fl., U.S. **D4** 102
Wildwood, N.J., U.S. **F3** 123
Wildwood Crest, N.J., U.S. **F3** 123
Wilhelm, Mount, mtn., Pap. N. Gui. **H12** 32
Wilhelmina Peak see Trikora, Puncak, mtn., Indon. **G10** 32
Wilhelmshaven, Ger. **D10** 12
Wilkes, co., Ga., U.S. **C4** 103
Wilkes, co., N.C., U.S. **A1** 126
Wilkes-Barre, Pa., U.S. **D10** 131
Wilkesboro, N.C., U.S. **A1** 126
Wilkes Land, reg., Ant. **D16** 67
Wilkin, co., Mn., U.S. **D2** 116
Wilkinsburg, Pa., U.S. **F2** 131
Wilkinson, co., Ga., U.S. **D3** 103
Wilkinson, co., Ms., U.S. **D2** 117
Wilkinson, W.V., U.S. **D3** 141
Will, co., Il., U.S. **B6** 106
Willacoochee, Ga., U.S. **E3** 103
Willacy, co., Tx., U.S. **F4** 136
Willamette, stm., Or., U.S. **C3** 130
Willamette Pass, Or., U.S. **D4** 130
Willamina, Or., U.S. **B3** 130
Willapa Bay, b., Wa., U.S. **C1** 140
Willard, Mo., U.S. **D4** 118
Willard, Oh., U.S. **A3** 128
Willard, Ut., U.S. **B3** 137
Willard Bay, b., Ut., U.S. **B3** 137
Willards, Md., U.S. **D7** 113
Willard Stream, stm., Vt., U.S. **B5** 138
Willcox, Az., U.S. **E6** 96
Willcox Playa, l., Az., U.S. **E5** 96
Willemstad, Neth. Ant. **C6** 80
William "Bill" Dannelly Reservoir, res., Al., U.S. **C2** 94
Williams, Az., U.S. **B3** 96
Williams, Ca., U.S. **C2** 98
Williams, co., N.D., U.S. **A2** 127
Williams, co., Oh., U.S. **A1** 128
Williams, stm., Vt., U.S. **E3** 138
Williams, stm., W.V., U.S. **C4** 141
Williams Bay, Wi., U.S. **F5** 142
Williamsburg, Ia., U.S. **C5** 108
Williamsburg, In., U.S. **E8** 107
Williamsburg, Ky., U.S. **D5** 110
Williamsburg, Oh., U.S. **C1** 128
Williamsburg, Pa., U.S. **F5** 131
Williamsburg, co., S.C., U.S. **D8** 133
Williamsburg, Va., U.S. **C6** 139
Williams Fork, stm., Co., U.S. **A3** 99
Williams Lake, B.C., Can. **C6** 85
Williamson, co., Il., U.S. **F4** 106
Williamson, N.Y., U.S. **B3** 125
Williamson, co., Tn., U.S. **B5** 135
Williamson, co., Tx., U.S. **D4** 136
Williamson, W.V., U.S. **D2** 141
Williamsport, In., U.S. **D3** 107
Williamsport, Md., U.S. **A2** 113
Williamsport, Pa., U.S. **D7** 131
Williamston, Mi., U.S. **F6** 115
Williamston, N.C., U.S. **B5** 126
Williamston, S.C., U.S. **B3** 133
Williamstown, Ky., U.S. **B5** 110
Williamstown, Ma., U.S. **A1** 114
Williamstown, N.J., U.S. **D3** 123
Williamstown, Pa., U.S. **E8** 131
Williamstown, Vt., U.S. **C3** 138
Williamstown, W.V., U.S. **B3** 141
Williamsville, Il., U.S. **D4** 106
Williamsville, N.Y., U.S. **C2** 125
Willimantic, Ct., U.S. **C7** 100
Willimantic, stm., Ct., U.S. **B6** 100
Willimantic Reservoir, res., Ct., U.S. **C7** 100
Willingboro, N.J., U.S. **C3** 123
Willis, Tx., U.S. **D5** 136
Willis Group, is., Austl. **D5** 62
Williston, S. Afr. **E3** 56
Williston, Fl., U.S. **C4** 102
Williston, N.D., U.S. **A2** 127
Williston, S.C., U.S. **E5** 133
Williston Lake, res., B.C., Can. **B6** 85
Willits, Ca., U.S. **C2** 98
Willmar, Mn., U.S. **E3** 116
Willoughby, Oh., U.S. **A4** 128
Willoughby, Lake, l., Vt., U.S. **B4** 138
Willoughby Hills, Oh., U.S. **A4** 128
Willow, Ak., U.S. **g17** 95
Willow Creek, stm., Nv., U.S. **E5** 121
Willow Creek, stm., Ut., U.S. **D6** 137
Willow Creek, stm., Wy., U.S. **C6** 143
Willow Grove Naval Air Station, mil., Pa., U.S. **F11** 131
Willowick, Oh., U.S. **A4** 128
Willowmore, S. Afr. **E3** 56
Willow Reservoir, res., Wi., U.S. **C3** 142
Willow Run, De., U.S. **i7** 101
Willow Run, Mi., U.S. **p14** 115
Willows, Ca., U.S. **C2** 98
Willow Springs, Il., U.S. **k9** 106
Willow Springs, Mo., U.S. **E6** 118
Wilmar, Ar., U.S. **D4** 97
Wilmerding, Pa., U.S. **k14** 131
Wilmette, Il., U.S. **A6** 106
Wilmington, De., U.S. **B3** 101
Wilmington, Il., U.S. **B5** 106
Wilmington, Ma., U.S. **A5** 114
Wilmington, N.C., U.S. **C5** 126
Wilmington, Oh., U.S. **C2** 128
Wilmington, Vt., U.S. **F3** 138
Wilmington Manor, De., U.S. **i7** 101
Wilmore, Ky., U.S. **C5** 110
Wilmot, Ar., U.S. **D4** 97
Wilson, Ar., U.S. **B5** 97
Wilson, Ks., U.S. **D5** 109
Wilson, co., Ks., U.S. **E8** 109
Wilson, La., U.S. **D4** 111
Wilson, N.C., U.S. **B5** 126
Wilson, co., N.C., U.S. **B5** 126
Wilson, Ok., U.S. **C4** 129
Wilson, Pa., U.S. **E11** 131
Wilson, co., Tn., U.S. **A5** 135
Wilson, co., Tx., U.S. **E3** 136
Wilson, Wy., U.S. **C2** 143
Wilson, Mount, mtn., Az., U.S. **B1** 96
Wilson, Mount, mtn., Ca., U.S. **m12** 98
Wilson, Mount, mtn., Co., U.S. **D2** 99
Wilson, Mount, mtn., Nv., U.S. **E7** 121
Wilson, Mount, mtn., Or., U.S. **B5** 130
Wilson Creek, stm., Wa., U.S. **B6** 140
Wilson Creek, stm., Wa., U.S. **B5** 140
Wilson Lake, res., Al., U.S. **A2** 94
Wilson Lake, res., Ks., U.S. **D4** 109
Wilsons Beach, N.B., Can. **E3** 87
Wilsons Promontory, pen., Austl. **H4** 62
Wilsonville, Al., U.S. **B3** 94
Wilsonville, Or., U.S. **h12** 130
Wilton, Al., U.S. **B3** 94
Wilton, Ct., U.S. **E2** 100
Wilton, Ia., U.S. **C6** 108
Wilton, Me., U.S. **D2** 112
Wilton, N.D., U.S. **B5** 127
Wilton, N.H., U.S. **E3** 122
Wiluna, Austl. **F3** 60
Wimauma, Fl., U.S. **E4** 102
Wimico, Lake, l., Fl., U.S. **C1** 102
Winamac, In., U.S. **B4** 107
Winburg, S. Afr. **D4** 56
Wincheck Pond, l., R.I., U.S. **E1** 132
Winchendon, Ma., U.S. **A3** 114
Winchester, On., Can. **B9** 89
Winchester, Eng., U.K. **E6** 12
Winchester, Il., U.S. **D3** 106
Winchester, In., U.S. **D8** 107
Winchester, Ks., U.S. **k15** 109
Winchester, Ky., U.S. **C5** 110
Winchester, Ma., U.S. **g11** 114
Winchester, N.H., U.S. **E2** 122
Winchester, Nv., U.S. **G6** 121
Winchester, Oh., U.S. **D2** 128
Winchester, Tn., U.S. **B5** 135
Winchester, Va., U.S. **A4** 139
Winchester Bay, Or., U.S. **D2** 130
Wind, stm., Wa., U.S. **D4** 140
Wind, stm., Wy., U.S. **C4** 143
Windber, Pa., U.S. **F4** 131
Wind Cave National Park, S.D., U.S. **D2** 134
Winder, Ga., U.S. **C3** 103
Windfall, In., U.S. **D6** 107
Windgap, Pa., U.S. **E11** 131
Windham, Ct., U.S. **C7** 100
Windham, co., Ct., U.S. **B7** 100
Windham, Oh., U.S. **A4** 128
Windham, co., Vt., U.S. **F3** 138
Windhoek, Nmb. **C2** 56
Wind Lake, Wi., U.S. **F5** 142
Wind Lake, l., Wi., U.S. **n11** 142
Windmill Point, c., Va., U.S. **C6** 139
Windom, Mn., U.S. **G3** 116
Windom Peak, mtn., Co., U.S. **D3** 99
Window Rock, Az., U.S. **B6** 96
Wind Point, Wi., U.S. **n12** 142
Wind River Indian Reservation, Wy., U.S. **C4** 143
Wind River Peak, mtn., Wy., U.S. **D3** 143
Wind River Range, mts., Wy., U.S. **C3** 143
Windsor (part of Grand Falls-Windsor), N.L., Can. **D4** 88
Windsor, On., Can. **E1** 89
Windsor, Qc., Can. **D5** 90
Windsor, Co., U.S. **A6** 99
Windsor, Ct., U.S. **B5** 100
Windsor, Il., U.S. **D5** 106
Windsor, Mo., U.S. **C4** 118
Windsor, N.C., U.S. **A6** 126
Windsor, Pa., U.S. **G8** 131
Windsor, Va., U.S. **D6** 139
Windsor, Vt., U.S. **E4** 138
Windsor, co., Vt., U.S. **D3** 138
Windsor Heights, Ia., U.S. **e8** 108
Windsor Locks, Ct., U.S. **B5** 100
Windward Islands, is., N.A. **F12** 76
Windward Passage, strt., N.A. **E10** 76
Windy Hill, S.C., U.S. **C8** 133
Windy Peak, mtn., Wa., U.S. **A6** 140
Winefred Lake, l., Ab., Can. **B5** 84
Winfield, Al., U.S. **B2** 94
Winfield, Ia., U.S. **C6** 108
Winfield, Ks., U.S. **E7** 109
Winfield, Mo., U.S. **C7** 118
Winfield, W.V., U.S. **C3** 141
Wing, stm., Mn., U.S. **D3** 116
Wingate, N.C., U.S. **C2** 126
Wingham, On., Can. **D3** 89
Winifrede, W.V., U.S. **m12** 141
Winisk, stm., On., Can. **n18** 89
Wink, Tx., U.S. **D1** 136
Winkelman, Az., U.S. **E5** 96
Winkler, Mb., Can. **E3** 86
Winkler, co., Tx., U.S. **D1** 136
Winlock, Wa., U.S. **C3** 140
Winn, co., La., U.S. **C3** 111
Winneba, Ghana **E4** 50
Winnebago, co., Ia., U.S. **A4** 108
Winnebago, stm., Ia., U.S. **A4** 108
Winnebago, Il., U.S. **A4** 106
Winnebago, co., Il., U.S. **A4** 106
Winnebago, Mn., U.S. **G4** 116
Winnebago, Ne., U.S. **B9** 120
Winnebago, co., Wi., U.S. **D5** 142
Winnebago, Wi., U.S. **h8** 142
Winnebago, Lake, l., Wi., U.S. **E5** 142
Winnebago Indian Reservation, Ne., U.S. **B9** 120
Winneconne, Wi., U.S. **D5** 142
Winnemucca, Nv., U.S. **C4** 121
Winnemucca Lake, l., Nv., U.S. **C2** 121
Winner, S.D., U.S. **D6** 134
Winneshiek, co., Ia., U.S. **A6** 108
Winnetka, Il., U.S. **A6** 106
Winnfield, La., U.S. **C3** 111
Winnibigoshish, Lake, l., Mn., U.S. **C4** 116
Winnipeg, Mb., Can. **E3** 86
Winnipeg, stm., Can. **D4** 86
Winnipeg, Lake, l., Mb., Can. **C3** 86
Winnipeg Beach, Mb., Can. **D3** 86
Winnipegosis, Mb., Can. **D2** 86
Winnipegosis, Lake, l., Mb., Can. **C2** 86
Winnipesaukee, Lake, l., N.H., U.S. **C4** 122
Winnisquam, N.H., U.S. **C3** 122
Winnisquam Lake, l., N.H., U.S. **C3** 122
Winnsboro, La., U.S. **B4** 111
Winnsboro, S.C., U.S. **C5** 133
Winnsboro, Tx., U.S. **C5** 136
Winnsboro Mills, S.C., U.S. **C5** 133
Winona, co., Mn., U.S. **F7** 116
Winona, Mn., U.S. **F7** 116
Winona, Mo., U.S. **D6** 118
Winona, Ms., U.S. **B4** 117
Winona Lake, In., U.S. **B6** 107
Winona Lake, l., Vt., U.S. **C2** 138
Winooski, Vt., U.S. **C2** 138
Winooski, stm., Vt., U.S. **C3** 138
Winslow, Az., U.S. **C5** 96
Winslow, In., U.S. **H3** 107
Winslow, Me., U.S. **D3** 112
Winsted, Ct., U.S. **B3** 100
Winsted, Mn., U.S. **F4** 116
Winston, co., Al., U.S. **A2** 94
Winston, Fl., U.S. **D4** 102
Winston, co., Ms., U.S. **B4** 117
Winston, Or., U.S. **D3** 130
Winston-Salem, N.C., U.S. **A2** 126
Winter Garden, Fl., U.S. **D5** 102
Winter Harbor, Me., U.S. **D4** 112
Winter Haven, Fl., U.S. **D5** 102
Winter Park, Fl., U.S. **D5** 102
Winter Park, N.C., U.S. **C5** 126
Winterport, Me., U.S. **D4** 112
Winter Ridge, mtn., Or., U.S. **E6** 130
Winters, Ca., U.S. **C2** 98
Winters, Tx., U.S. **D3** 136
Winterset, Ia., U.S. **C4** 108
Wintersville, Oh., U.S. **B5** 128
Winterthur, Switz. **G11** 12
Winterton, N.L., Can. **E5** 88
Winterville, Ga., U.S. **C3** 103
Winterville, N.C., U.S. **B5** 126
Winthrop, Ia., U.S. **B6** 108
Winthrop, Ma., U.S. **B6** 114
Winthrop, Me., U.S. **D3** 112
Winthrop, Mn., U.S. **F4** 116

Name — Map Ref. — Page

Winthrop, Lake, l., Ma., U.S. **h10** 114
Winthrop Harbor, Il., U.S. **A6** 106
Wintinna, Austl. **F5** 60
Winton, Austl. **E3** 62
Winton, N.Z. **q12** 63c
Winton, N.C., U.S. **A6** 126
Winton Lake, res., Oh., U.S. **o12** 129
Winyah Bay, b., S.C., U.S. **E9** 133
Wirt, co., W.V., U.S. **B3** 141
Wiscasset, Me., U.S. **D3** 112
Wisconsin, stm., Wi., U.S. **E3** 142
Wisconsin, state, U.S. **D4** 142
Wisconsin, Lake, res., Wi., U.S. **E4** 142
Wisconsin Dells, Wi., U.S. **E4** 142
Wisconsin Rapids, Wi., U.S. **D4** 142
Wise, co., Tx., U.S. **C4** 136
Wise, Va., U.S. **f9** 139
Wise, co., Va., U.S. **e9** 139
Wishek, N.D., U.S. **C6** 127
Wishram, Wa., U.S. **D4** 140
Wisła, stm., Pol. **C5** 20
Wismar, Ger. **D12** 12
Wisner, La., U.S. **C4** 111
Wisner, Ne., U.S. **C9** 120
Wissota, Lake, res., Wi., U.S. **D2** 142
Wister, Ok., U.S. **C7** 129
Wister Lake, res., Ok., U.S. **C7** 129
Witbank, S. Afr. **D4** 56
Withamsville, Oh., U.S. **C1** 128
Witherspoon, Mount, mtn., Ak., U.S. **g18** 95
Withlacoochee, stm., Fl., U.S. **C4** 102
Withlacoochee, stm., U.S. **B3** 102
Witless Bay, N.L., Can. **E5** 88
Witt, Il., U.S. **D4** 106
Wittenberg, Wi., U.S. **D4** 142
Wittenberge, Ger. **D12** 12
Wittenoom, Austl. **E2** 60
Wittlich, Ger. **E10** 12
Wittman, Md., U.S. **C5** 113
Wittmann, Az., U.S. **D3** 96
Witu Islands, is., Pap. N. Gui. **G12** 32
Wixom, Mi., U.S. **o14** 115
Wixom Lake, res., Mi., U.S. **E6** 115
Włocławek, Pol. **C5** 20
Woburn, Ma., U.S. **B5** 114
Wodonga, Austl. **H4** 62
Wokam, Pulau, i., Indon. **H9** 32
Wolcott, Ct., U.S. **C4** 100
Wolcott, In., U.S. **C3** 107
Wolcottville, In., U.S. **A7** 107
Woleai, atoll, Micron. **D8** 58
Wolf, stm., Ms., U.S. **E4** 117
Wolf, stm., Tn., U.S. **e9** 135
Wolf, stm., Wi., U.S. **C5** 142
Wolf, Volcán, vol., Ec. **C1** 70
Wolf Creek, Or., U.S. **E3** 130
Wolf Creek, stm., W.V., U.S. **m13** 141
Wolf Creek, stm., U.S. **A2** 129
Wolf Creek Pass, Co., U.S. **D3** 99
Wolfe, co., Ky., U.S. **C6** 110
Wolfeboro, N.H., U.S. **C4** 122
Wolfeboro Falls, N.H., U.S. **C4** 122
Wolfe City, Tx., U.S. **C4** 136
Wolfen, Ger. **E13** 12
Wolf Lake, l., Il., U.S. **k9** 106
Wolf Lake, Mi., U.S. **E4** 115
Wolf Mountain, mtn., Ak., U.S. **B9** 95
Wolf Point, Mt., U.S. **B11** 119
Wolfsberg, Aus. **G14** 12
Wolfsburg, Ger. **D12** 12
Wolf Swamp, sw., N.C., U.S. **C5** 126
Wollaston, Islas, is., Chile **I3** 69
Wollaston Lake, l., Sk., Can. **m8** 91
Wollongong, Austl. **G5** 62
Wolmaransstad, S. Afr. **D4** 56
Wolverhampton, Eng., U.K. **D5** 12
Woman Lake, l., Mn., U.S. **D4** 116
Womelsdorf, Pa., U.S. **F9** 131
Wonder Lake, Il., U.S. **A5** 106
Wondinong, Austl. **F2** 60
Wonewoc, Wi., U.S. **E3** 142
Wŏnsan, N. Kor. **D13** 28
Wonthaggi, Austl. **H4** 62
Wood, stm., Sk., Can. **H2** 91
Wood, co., Oh., U.S. **A2** 128
Wood, stm., R.I., U.S. **F2** 132
Wood, co., Tx., U.S. **C5** 136
Wood, co., Wi., U.S. **D3** 142
Wood, co., W.V., U.S. **B3** 141
Wood, stm., Wy., U.S. **C3** 143
Wood, Mount, mtn., Mt., U.S. **E7** 119
Woodall Mountain, mtn., Ms., U.S. **A5** 117
Woodbine, Ga., U.S. **F5** 103
Woodbine, Ia., U.S. **C2** 108
Woodbine, Ky., U.S. **D5** 110
Woodbine, N.J., U.S. **E3** 123
Woodbridge, Ct., U.S. **D3** 100
Woodbridge, Va., U.S. **B5** 139
Woodbridge [Township], N.J., U.S. **B4** 123
Woodburn, In., U.S. **B8** 107
Woodburn, Or., U.S. **B4** 130
Woodbury, Ct., U.S. **C3** 100
Woodbury, Ga., U.S. **D2** 103
Woodbury, co., Ia., U.S. **B1** 108
Woodbury, Mn., U.S. **F6** 116
Woodbury, N.J., U.S. **D2** 123
Woodbury, Tn., U.S. **B5** 135
Woodcliff Lake, N.J., U.S. **g8** 123
Woodcliff Lake, l., N.J., U.S. **g8** 123
Wood Dale, Il., U.S. **k9** 106
Wood End, spit, Ma., U.S. **B7** 114
Woodfield, S.C., U.S. **C6** 133
Woodford, co., Il., U.S. **C4** 106
Woodford, co., Ky., U.S. **B5** 110
Woodhull, Il., U.S. **B3** 106
Woodlake, Ca., U.S. **D4** 98
Woodland, Ca., U.S. **C3** 98
Woodland, Me., U.S. **C5** 112
Woodland, N.C., U.S. **A5** 126
Woodland, Wa., U.S. **D3** 140
Woodland Acres, Co., U.S. **D6** 99
Woodland Park, Co., U.S. **C5** 99
Woodlawn, Ky., U.S. **e9** 110
Woodlawn, Md., U.S. **g10** 113
Woodlawn, Oh., U.S. **n13** 128
Woodlawn, Va., U.S. **D2** 139
Woodmont, Ct., U.S. **E4** 100
Woodmoor, Md., U.S. **B4** 113
Woodridge, Il., U.S. **k8** 106
Wood-Ridge, N.J., U.S. **h8** 123
Wood River, Il., U.S. **E3** 106
Wood River, Ne., U.S. **D7** 120
Woodroffe, Mount, mtn., Austl. **F5** 60
Woodruff, co., Ar., U.S. **B4** 97
Woodruff, S.C., U.S. **B3** 133
Woodruff, Wi., U.S. **C4** 142
Woods, co., Ok., U.S. **A3** 129
Woods, Lake, res., Tn., U.S. **B5** 135
Woods, Lake of the, l., N.A. **B9** 92
Woodsboro, Tx., U.S. **E4** 136
Woods Cross, Ut., U.S. **C4** 137
Woodsfield, Oh., U.S. **C4** 128
Woods Hole, Ma., U.S. **C6** 114
Woodson, Ar., U.S. **C3** 97
Woodson, co., Ks., U.S. **E8** 109
Woodstock, N.B., Can. **C2** 87
Woodstock, On., Can. **D4** 89
Woodstock, Ga., U.S. **B2** 103
Woodstock, Il., U.S. **A5** 106
Woodstock, Md., U.S. **B4** 113
Woodstock, N.Y., U.S. **C6** 125
Woodstock, Va., U.S. **B4** 139
Woodstock, Vt., U.S. **D3** 138
Woodstown, N.J., U.S. **D2** 123
Woodsville, N.H., U.S. **B2** 122
Woodville, Fl., U.S. **B2** 102
Woodville, Ms., U.S. **D2** 117
Woodville, Oh., U.S. **A2** 128
Woodville, Tx., U.S. **D5** 136
Woodville, Wi., U.S. **D1** 142
Woodward, Ia., U.S. **C4** 108
Woodward, Ok., U.S. **A2** 129
Woodward, co., Ok., U.S. **A2** 129
Woodworth, La., U.S. **C3** 111
Woolmarket, Ms., U.S. **E5** 117
Woolrich, Pa., U.S. **D7** 131
Woolsey Peak, mtn., Az., U.S. **D3** 96
Woomera, Austl. **G2** 62
Woonsocket, R.I., U.S. **A3** 132
Woonsocket, S.D., U.S. **C7** 134
Woonsocket Reservoir Number Three, res., R.I., U.S. **B3** 132
Wooster, Oh., U.S. **B4** 128
Worcester, S. Afr. **E2** 56
Worcester, Eng., U.K. **D5** 12
Worcester, Ma., U.S. **B4** 114
Worcester, co., Ma., U.S. **A3** 114
Worcester, co., Md., U.S. **D7** 113
Worden, Il., U.S. **E4** 106
Worden Pond, l., R.I., U.S. **F3** 132
Worland, Wy., U.S. **B5** 143
Worms, Ger. **F11** 12
Worth, co., Ga., U.S. **E3** 103
Worth, co., Ia., U.S. **A4** 108
Worth, Il., U.S. **k9** 106
Worth, co., Mo., U.S. **A3** 118
Worthing, Eng., U.K. **E6** 12
Worthington, In., U.S. **F4** 107
Worthington, Ky., U.S. **B7** 110
Worthington, Mn., U.S. **G3** 116
Worthington, Oh., U.S. **B2** 128
Worthington Peak, mtn., Nv., U.S. **F6** 121
Wosu, Indon. **D6** 36
Wour, Chad **B8** 50
Wowoni, Pulau, i., Indon. **D6** 36
Woy Woy, Austl. **G5** 62
Wrangel Island see Vrangelja, ostrov, i., Russia **B20** 26
Wrangell, Ak., U.S. **D13** 95
Wrangell, Cape, c., Ak., U.S. **E2** 95
Wrangell, Mount, mtn., Ak., U.S. **f19** 95
Wrangell Island, i., Ak., U.S. **m24** 95
Wrangell Mountains, mts., Ak., U.S. **C11** 95
Wrangell-Saint Elias National Park, Ak., U.S. **C11** 95
Wrath, Cape, c., Scot., U.K. **A4** 12
Wray, Co., U.S. **A8** 99
Wrens, Ga., U.S. **C4** 103
Wrentham, Ma., U.S. **B5** 114
Wrexham, Wales, U.K. **D5** 12
Wright, co., Ia., U.S. **B4** 108
Wright, co., Mn., U.S. **E4** 116
Wright, co., Mo., U.S. **D5** 118
Wright, Mount, mtn., Mt., U.S. **C4** 119
Wright Brothers National Memorial, hist., N.C., U.S. **A7** 126
Wright City, Mo., U.S. **C8** 118
Wright City, Ok., U.S. **C6** 129
Wright Patman Lake, res., Tx., U.S. **A6** 78
Wright-Patterson Air Force Base, mil., Oh., U.S. **C1** 128
Wrightson, Mount, mtn., Az., U.S. **F5** 96
Wrightstown, N.J., U.S. **C3** 123
Wrightstown, Wi., U.S. **D5** 142
Wrightsville, Ar., U.S. **C3** 97
Wrightsville, Ga., U.S. **D4** 103
Wrightsville, Pa., U.S. **F8** 131
Wrightsville Beach, N.C., U.S. **C5** 126
Wrightsville Reservoir, res., Vt., U.S. **C3** 138
Wrocław, Pol. **D4** 20
Wu, stm., China **F9** 28
Wuchuan, China **A3** 30
Wuchuan, China **E3** 30
Wuda, China **B2** 30
Wudaoliang, China **D6** 28
Wudi, China **B4** 30
Wuding, China **A4** 34
Wudu, China **E8** 28
Wugang, China **F10** 28
Wuhai, China **D9** 28
Wuhan, China **E10** 28
Wuhe, China **C4** 30
Wuhu, China **E11** 28
Wüjang, China **E3** 28
Wukari, Nig. **E6** 50
Wuliang Shan, mts., China **G8** 28
Wuming, China **B5** 34
Wupatki National Monument, Az., U.S. **B4** 96
Wuppertal, Ger. **E10** 12
Wuqi, China **B2** 30
Wuqing, China **B4** 30
Wurno, Nig. **D6** 50
Würzburg, Ger. **F12** 12
Wushan, China **C2** 30
Wushenqi, China **D9** 28
Wusuli (Ussuri), stm., Asia **E15** 26
Wutai Shan, mtn., China **D10** 28
Wutongqiao, China **F8** 28
Wuvulu Island, i., Pap. N. Gui. **G11** 32
Wuwei, China **C4** 30
Wuwei, China **D8** 28
Wuxi, China **E12** 28
Wuyi Shan, mts., China **F11** 28
Wuyuan, China **C9** 28
Wuzhi Shan, mtn., China **H9** 28
Wuzhong, China **D9** 28
Wuzhou, China **G10** 28
Wyaconda, stm., Mo., U.S. **A6** 118
Wyandot, co., Oh., U.S. **B2** 128
Wyandotte, co., Ks., U.S. **C9** 109
Wyandotte, Mi., U.S. **F7** 115
Wyanet, Il., U.S. **B4** 106
Wye, stm., U.K. **D5** 12
Wylie, Lake, res., U.S. **A5** 133
Wyman Lake, res., Me., U.S. **C3** 112
Wymore, Ne., U.S. **D9** 120
Wyndham, Austl. **D4** 60
Wynndel, B.C., Can. **E9** 85
Wynne, Ar., U.S. **B5** 97
Wynnewood, Ok., U.S. **C4** 129
Wynoochee, stm., Wa., U.S. **B2** 140
Wyoming, On., Can. **E2** 89
Wyoming, De., U.S. **D3** 101
Wyoming, Ia., U.S. **B6** 108
Wyoming, Il., U.S. **B4** 106
Wyoming, Mi., U.S. **F5** 115
Wyoming, Mn., U.S. **E6** 116
Wyoming, co., N.Y., U.S. **C2** 125
Wyoming, Oh., U.S. **o13** 128
Wyoming, Pa., U.S. **n17** 131
Wyoming, co., Pa., U.S. **D9** 131
Wyoming, R.I., U.S. **E2** 132
Wyoming, co., W.V., U.S. **D3** 141
Wyoming, state, U.S. **C5** 143
Wyoming Peak, mtn., Wy., U.S. **D2** 143
Wyoming Range, mts., Wy., U.S. **D2** 143
Wyomissing, Pa., U.S. **F10** 131
Wyong, Austl. **G5** 62
Wysocking Bay, b., N.C., U.S. **B7** 126
Wythe, co., Va., U.S. **D1** 139
Wytheville, Va., U.S. **D1** 139

X

Xaafuun, Raas, c., Som. **H15** 48
Xaçmaz, Azer. **B13** 44
Xaidulla, China **D3** 28
Xainza, China **E5** 28
Xai-Xai, Moz. **D5** 56
Xalapa, Mex. **D5** 78
Xam Nua, Laos **B4** 34
Xá-Muteba, Ang. **E3** 54
Xangongo, Ang. **B2** 56
Xankändi, Azer. **C12** 44
Xánthi, Grc. **D10** 18
Xanxerê, Braz. **D7** 72
Xapuri, Braz. **F6** 70
Xàtiva, Spain **H6** 16
Xau, Lake, pl., Bots. **C3** 56
Xenia, Oh., U.S. **C2** 128
Xi, stm., China **G10** 28
Xiachuan Dao, i., China **E3** 30
Xiamen, China **G11** 28
Xi'an, China **E9** 28
Xianfeng, China **D2** 30
Xiang, stm., China **D3** 30
Xiangfan, China **E10** 28
Xianggang (Hong Kong), China **E3** 30
Xiangkhoang, Laos **C4** 34
Xiangride, China **D7** 28
Xiangtan, China **F10** 28
Xianju, China **D5** 30
Xianning, China **D3** 30
Xianyang, China **C2** 30
Xianyou, China **F11** 28
Xiaogan, China **E10** 28
Xiao Hinggan Ling, mts., China **A1** 31
Xiaojin, China **C1** 30
Xiapu, China **F12** 28
Xiayi, China **C4** 30
Xichang, China **F8** 28
Xigazê, China **F5** 28
Ximiao, China **C8** 28
Xin'anjiang Shuiku, res., China **D4** 30
Xinavane, Moz. **C5** 56
Xincai, China **C4** 30
Xing'an, China **F10** 28
Xingcheng, China **A5** 30
Xinghe, China **A3** 30
Xingren, China **D2** 30
Xingtai, China **D10** 28
Xingu, stm., Braz. **D9** 70
Xingxian, China **B3** 30
Xingyi, China **F8** 28
Xinhua, China **D3** 30
Xining, China **D8** 28
Xinji, China **B4** 30
Xinjiang Uygur Zizhiqu (Sinkiang), prov., China **C5** 28
Xinjin, China **C1** 30
Xinjin, China **B5** 30
Xinjiulong, China 28
Xinjiulong (New Kowloon), China **E3** 30
Xinning, China **D3** 30
Xinwen, China **B4** 30
Xinxian, China **B3** 30
Xinxiang, China **D10** 28
Xinyang, China **E10** 28
Xique-Xique, Braz. **D3** 74
Xisha Qundao (Paracel Islands), is., China **C6** 34
Xiushan, China **D2** 30
Xiushui, China **D3** 30
Xixiang, China **C2** 30
Xizang Zizhiqu (Tibet), prov., China **E5** 28
Xuancheng, China **E11** 28
Xuanhan, China **C2** 30
Xuanhua, China **A4** 30
Xuanwei, China **D1** 30
Xuchang, China **E10** 28
Xupu, China **D3** 30
Xuwen, China **G10** 28
Xuyong, China **F9** 28
Xuzhou, China **E11** 28

Y

Yaan, China **E8** 28
Yablonovy Range see Jablonovyj hrebet, mts., Russia **D13** 26
Yabrīn, Sau. Ar. **F5** 42
Yacolt, Wa., U.S. **D3** 140
Yacuiba, Bol. **C5** 72
Yādgīr, India **F3** 40
Yadkin, stm., N.C., U.S. **B2** 126
Yadkin, co., N.C., U.S. **A2** 126
Yadkinville, N.C., U.S. **A2** 126
Yadong, China **A1** 34
Yafran, Libya **E6** 14
Yagoua, Cam. **A3** 54
Yagradagzê Shan, mtn., China **D7** 28
Yahyalı, Tur. **C6** 44
Yainax Butte, mtn., Or., U.S. **E5** 130
Yakima, Wa., U.S. **C5** 140
Yakima, co., Wa., U.S. **C4** 140
Yakima, stm., Wa., U.S. **C6** 140
Yakima Indian Reservation, Wa., U.S. **C5** 140
Yako, Burkina **D4** 50
Yakobi Island, i., Ak., U.S. **m21** 95
Yakoma, D.R.C. **C4** 54
Yakumo, Japan **B3** 31
Yaku-shima, i., Japan **E14** 28
Yakutat, Ak., U.S. **D12** 95
Yakutat Bay, b., Ak., U.S. **D11** 95
Yakutia see Jakutija, state, Russia **C14** 26
Yakutsk see Jakutsk, Russia **C14** 26
Yakymivka, Ukr. **F13** 20
Yala, Thai. **E4** 34
Yale, Mi., U.S. **E8** 115
Yale, Ok., U.S. **A5** 129
Yale, Mount, mtn., Co., U.S. **C5** 99
Yale Lake, res., Wa., U.S. **D3** 140
Yalgoo, Austl. **F2** 60
Yalinga, C.A.R. **B4** 54
Yalobusha, stm., Ms., U.S. **B4** 117
Yalobusha, co., Ms., U.S. **A4** 117
Yalong, stm., China **E7** 28
Yalova, Tur. **B3** 44
Yalta, Ukr. **G13** 20
Yalu, stm., Asia **C13** 28
Yalvaç, Tur. **C4** 44
Yamachiche, Qc., Can. **C5** 90
Yamagata, Japan **D16** 28
Yamaguchi, Japan **D2** 31
Yamal Peninsula see Jamal, poluostrov, pen., Russia **B8** 26
Yambio, Sudan **J10** 48
Yamdena, Pulau, i., Indon. **E8** 36
Yamethin, Mya. **B3** 34
Yamhill, Or., U.S. **h11** 130
Yamhill, co., Or., U.S. **B3** 130
Yamoussoukro, C. Iv. **E3** 50
Yampa, stm., Co., U.S. **A2** 99
Yampil', Ukr. **E10** 20
Yamsay Mountain, mtn., Or., U.S. **E5** 130
Yamuna, stm., India **D4** 40
Yamunānagar, India **C3** 40
Yamzho Yumco, l., China **F6** 28
Yana see Jana, stm., Russia **C15** 26
Yanam, India **F4** 40
Yan'an, China **D9** 28
Yanbu'al-Baḥr, Sau. Ar. **F3** 38
Yancey, co., N.C., U.S. **f10** 126
Yanceyville, N.C., U.S. **A3** 126
Yancheng, China **E12** 28
Yanchi, China **D9** 28
Yanfolila, Mali **D3** 50
Yangambi, D.R.C. **C4** 54
Yangchun, China **E3** 30
Yanggao, China **A3** 30
Yangjiang, China **G10** 28
Yangliuqing, China **B4** 30
Yangon (Rangoon), Mya. **C3** 34
Yangquan, China **D10** 28
Yangshan, China **E3** 30
Yangshuo, China **E3** 30
Yangtze see Chang, stm., China **E9** 28
Yangxian, China **C2** 30
Yangxin, China **D4** 30
Yangzhou, China **E11** 28
Yanji, China **C13** 28
Yankton, S.D., U.S. **E8** 134
Yankton, co., S.D., U.S. **D8** 134
Yanqi, China **C5** 28
Yantai, China **D12** 28
Yantic, stm., Ct., U.S. **C7** 100
Yanting, China **C2** 30
Yanyuan, China **A4** 34
Yanzhou, China **B4** 30
Yaoundé, Cam. **C2** 54
Yap, i., Micron. **E10** 32
Yapen, Pulau, i., Indon. **G10** 32
Yaqui, stm., Mex. **B3** 78
Yardley, Pa., U.S. **F12** 131
Yardville, N.J., U.S. **C3** 123
Yarīm, Yemen **H4** 38
Yarkand see Shache, China **D3** 28
Yarkand see Yarkant, stm., China **B3** 40
Yarkant, stm., China **B3** 40
Yarloop, Austl. **G2** 60
Yarmouth, Me., U.S. **E2** 112
Yarnell, Az., U.S. **C3** 96
Yaroslavl' see Jaroslavl', Russia **D6** 26
Yarumal, Col. **B4** 70
Yass, Austl. **G4** 62
Yatağan, Tur. **D3** 44
Yaté, N. Cal. **I9** 62a
Yates, co., N.Y., U.S. **C3** 125
Yates Center, Ks., U.S. **E8** 109
Yates City, Il., U.S. **C3** 106
Yatsushiro, Japan **E14** 28
Yatta Plateau, plat., Kenya **D7** 54
Yavapai, co., Az., U.S. **C3** 96
Yavarí (Javari), stm., S.A. **D5** 70
Yavatmāl, India **E3** 40
Yaví, Cerro, mtn., Ven. **B6** 70
Yawgoog Pond, l., R.I., U.S. **E1** 132
Yazd, Iran **D6** 42
Yazoo, co., Ms., U.S. **C3** 117
Yazoo, stm., Ms., U.S. **C3** 117
Yazoo City, Ms., U.S. **C3** 117
Ye, Mya. **C3** 34
Yeadon, Pa., U.S. **p21** 131
Yeagertown, Pa., U.S. **E6** 131
Yecheng, China **D3** 28
Yecla, Spain **H6** 16
Yeeda, Austl. **D3** 60
Yei, Sudan **C6** 54
Yélimané, Mali **C2** 50
Yell, co., Ar., U.S. **B2** 97
Yellow see Huang, stm., China **D11** 28
Yellow, stm., In., U.S. **B4** 107
Yellow, stm., Wi., U.S. **C3** 142
Yellow, stm., Wi., U.S. **D3** 142
Yellow, stm., U.S. **u15** 102
Yellow Creek, stm., Tn., U.S. **A4** 135
Yellowhead Pass, Can. **C1** 84

Name	Map Ref.	Page
Yellowjacket Mountains, mts., Id., U.S.	D4	105
Yellowknife, Can.	F17	82
Yellow Lake, l., Wi., U.S.	C1	142
Yellow Medicine, co., Mn., U.S.	F2	116
Yellow Sea, Asia	D12	28
Yellow Springs, Oh., U.S.	C2	128
Yellowstone, co., Mt., U.S.	D8	119
Yellowstone, stm., U.S.	D10	119
Yellowstone Lake, l., Wy., U.S.	B2	143
Yellowstone National Park, co., Mt., U.S.	E6	119
Yellowstone National Park, U.S.	B2	143
Yellville, Ar., U.S.	A3	97
Yelm, Wa., U.S.	C3	140
Yemassee, S.C., U.S.	F6	133
Yemen, ctry., Asia	G5	38
Yenagoa, Nig.	F6	50
Yenakiieve, Ukr.	E15	20
Yenangyaung, Mya.	B2	34
Yen Bai, Viet.	B4	34
Yendéré, Burkina	D4	50
Yendi, Ghana	E4	50
Yengisar, China	D3	28
Yenice, stm., Tur.	B5	44
Yenişehir, Tur.	B3	44
Yenisey see Enisej, stm., Russia	C10	26
Yentna, stm., Ak., U.S.	f16	95
Yerevan, Arm.	B11	44
Yerington, Nv., U.S.	E2	121
Yerington Indian Reservation, Nv., U.S.	D2	121
Yerköy, Tur.	C6	44
Yermo, Ca., U.S.	E5	98
Yerupaja, Nevado, mtn., Peru	F4	70
Yerushalayim, Isr.	D3	42
Yeşilhisar, Tur.	C6	44
Yetti, reg., Afr.	A3	50
Yeu, Île d', i., Fr.	D5	16
Yevpatoriia, Ukr.	G12	20
Ygatimí, Para.	C6	72
Yi'an, China	B13	28
Yibin, China	F8	28
Yichang, China	E10	28
Yichuan, China	B3	30
Yichun, China	D3	30
Yichun, China	B13	28
Yidu, China	B4	30
Yidu, China	C3	30
Yilan, China	B13	28
Yıldızeli, Tur.	C7	44
Yiliang, China	G8	28
Yinchuan, China	D9	28
Yingde, China	E3	30
Yingkou, China	C12	28
Yingtan, China	F11	28
Yining, China	C4	28
Yinmabin, Mya.	B2	34
Yirga 'Alem, Eth.	B7	54
Yirol, Sudan	B6	54
Yishan, China	E2	30
Yitulihe, China	A12	28
Yiyang, China	F10	28
Yiyang, China	D4	30
Yizhang, China	D3	30
Yli-Kitka, l., Fin.	C13	10
Yoakum, Tx., U.S.	E4	136
Yoakum, co., Tx., U.S.	C1	136
Yockanookany, stm., Ms., U.S.	C4	117
Yocona, stm., Ms., U.S.	A4	117
Yogyakarta, Indon.	E4	36
Yoho National Park, B.C., Can.	D9	85
Yokadouma, Cam.	C2	54
Yoko, Cam.	B2	54
Yokohama, Japan	D15	28
Yokosuka, Japan	C3	31
Yokote, Japan	C4	31
Yola, Nig.	E7	50
Yolo, co., Ca., U.S.	C2	98
Yom, stm., Thai.	C3	34
Yomba Indian Reservation, Nv., U.S.	D4	121
Yonago, Japan	D14	28
Yoncalla, Or., U.S.	D3	130
Yonezawa, Japan	C3	31
Yong'an, China	F11	28
Yongchang, China	B1	30
Yongchuan, China	D2	30
Yongding, China	E4	30
Yongfeng, China	A7	34
Yongkang, China	D5	30
Yongping, China	A3	34
Yongren, China	F8	28
Yongshan, China	F8	28
Yongxiu, China	D4	30
Yongzhou, China	F10	28
Yonkers, N.Y., U.S.	E7	125
Yonne, stm., Fr.	C8	16
Yopal, Col.	D5	80
Yopurga, China	B3	40
York, Austl.	G2	60
York, stm., On., Can.	B7	89
York, On., Can.	D5	89
York, Eng., U.K.	C6	12
York, Al., U.S.	C1	94
York, Me., U.S.	E2	112
York, co., Me., U.S.	E2	112
York, Ne., U.S.	D8	120
York, co., Ne., U.S.	D8	120
York, Pa., U.S.	G8	131
York, co., Pa., U.S.	G8	131
York, S.C., U.S.	B5	133
York, co., S.C., U.S.	A5	133
York, stm., Va., U.S.	C6	139
York, co., Va., U.S.	C6	139
York, Cape, c., Austl.	C3	62
York, Kap, c., Grnld.	C26	82
York Beach, Me., U.S.	E2	112
Yorke Peninsula, pen., Austl.	G2	62
York Harbor, Me., U.S.	E2	112
Yorklyn, De., U.S.	A3	101
Yorktown, In., U.S.	D7	107
Yorktown, Tx., U.S.	E4	136
Yorktown, Va., U.S.	C6	139
Yorktown Manor, R.I., U.S.	E4	132
Yorkville, Il., U.S.	B5	106
Yorkville, N.Y., U.S.	B5	125
Yorkville, Oh., U.S.	B5	128
Yoro, Hond.	B2	80
Yoron-jima, i., Japan	g6	31a
Yosemite National Park, Ca., U.S.	D4	98
Yos Sudarso, Pulau, i., Indon.	H10	32
Yotaú, Bol.	B5	72
You, stm., China	G9	28
Youbou, B.C., Can.	g11	85
Youghiogheny, stm., U.S.	F2	131
Youghiogheny River Lake, res., U.S.	G3	131
Young, Austl.	G4	62
Young, Az., U.S.	C5	96
Young, co., Tx., U.S.	C3	136
Young Harris, Ga., U.S.	B3	103
Youngs, Lake, l., Wa., U.S.	f11	140
Youngstown, N.Y., U.S.	B1	125
Youngstown, Oh., U.S.	A5	128
Youngsville, La., U.S.	D3	111
Youngsville, Pa., U.S.	C3	131
Youngtown, Az., U.S.	k8	96
Youngwood, Pa., U.S.	F2	131
Youxian, China	D3	30
Youyang, China	F9	28
Yozgat, Tur.	C6	44
Ypacarai, Para.	D6	72
Ypsilanti, Mi., U.S.	F7	115
Yreka, Ca., U.S.	B2	98
Ystad, Swe.	I5	10
Yuanling, China	F10	28
Yuanmou, China	F8	28
Yuba, stm., Ca., U.S.	C3	98
Yuba, co., Ca., U.S.	C3	98
Yuba City, Ca., U.S.	C3	98
Yūbari, Japan	C16	28
Yucatán, state, Mex.	C7	78
Yucatan Channel, strt., N.A.	A2	80
Yucatan Peninsula, pen., N.A.	B2	80
Yucca Lake, l., Nv., U.S.	F5	121
Yucca Mountain, mtn., Nv., U.S.	G5	121
Yucheng, China	B4	30
Yudu, China	D4	30
Yueqing, China	D5	30
Yuexi, China	A4	34
Yueyang, China	F10	28
Yugoslavia see Serbia and Montenegro, ctry., Eur.	C8	18
Yukon, ter., Can.	F12	82
Yukon, stm., N.A.	F7	82
Yukon, Ok., U.S.	B4	129
Yulee, Fl., U.S.	B5	102
Yulin, China	G10	28
Yulin, China	D9	28
Yuma, Az., U.S.	E1	96
Yuma, co., Az., U.S.	E1	96
Yuma, co., Co., U.S.	A8	99
Yuma, Co., U.S.	A8	99
Yuma Marine Corps Air Station, mil., Az., U.S.	E1	96
Yumbi, D.R.C.	D3	54
Yumbo, Col.	E4	80
Yumen, China	D7	28
Yuncheng, China	D10	28
Yunnan, prov., China	G8	28
Yunxian, China	E10	28
Yunxiao, China	E4	30
Yunyang, China	C2	30
Yurimaguas, Peru	E4	70
Yuruá see Juruá, stm., S.A.	E6	70
Yushan, China	D4	30
Yü Shan, mtn., Tai.	D5	28
Yushu, China	E7	28
Yutan, Ne., U.S.	C9	120
Yutian, China	D4	28
Yuyao, China	C5	30
Yvetot, Fr.	C7	16

Z

Name	Map Ref.	Page
Žabasak, Kaz.	D11	22
Zabīd, Yemen	H4	38
Zābol, Iran	D8	42
Zacapa, Guat.	B2	80
Zacapu, Mex.	D4	78
Zacatecas, state, Mex.	C4	78
Zacatecas, Mex.	C4	78
Zachary, La., U.S.	D4	111
Zadar, Cro.	B5	18
Zadoi, China	C7	40
Zadonsk, Russia	C15	20
Zafer Burnu, c., N. Cyp.	E6	44
Zafra, Spain	H3	16
Zagazig, Egypt	E10	14
Zagora, Mor.	E2	14
Zagreb, Cro.	B5	18
Zāgros, Kūhhā-ye (Zagros Mountains), mts., Iran	D6	42
Zagros Mountains see Zāgros, Kūhhā-ye, mts., Iran	D6	42
Zāhedān, Iran	D8	42
Zahīrābād, India	F3	40
Zaḥlah, Leb.	F6	44
Zaire see Congo, Democratic Republic of the, ctry., Afr.	D4	54
Zaïre see Congo, stm., Afr.	D2	54
Zaječar, Serb.	C9	18
Zajsan, Kaz.	E10	26
Zajsan, ozero, l., Kaz.	E10	26
Zakamensk, Russia	D12	26
Zākho, Iraq	D10	44
Zákinthos, i., Grc.	F8	18
Zákinthos, Grc.	F8	18
Zakopane, Pol.	E6	20
Zakouma, Chad	A3	54
Zalaegerszeg, Hung.	F4	20
Zalău, Rom.	F7	20
Zalishchyky, Ukr.	E8	20
Zamantı, stm., Tur.	D6	44
Zambeze (Zambezi), stm., Afr.	A3	56
Zambezi (Zambeze), stm., Afr.	B5	56
Zambezi, Zam.	A3	56
Zambia, ctry., Afr.	E5	52
Zamboanga, Phil.	E8	34
Zamboanga Peninsula, pen., Phil.	E8	34
Zambrów, Pol.	C7	20
Zâmbuè, Moz.	B5	56
Žambyl, Kaz.	E9	26
Zamora, Spain	G4	16
Zamora de Hidalgo, Mex.	D4	78
Zamość, Pol.	D7	20
Zanaga, Congo	D2	54
Žanatas, Kaz.	B9	42
Zanesville, Oh., U.S.	C4	128
Zanjān, Iran	C5	42
Zante see Zákinthos, i., Grc.	F8	18
Zanthus, Austl.	G3	60
Zanzibar, Tan.	E7	54
Zanzibar, i., Tan.	E7	54
Zanzibar Channel, strt., Tan.	E7	54
Zaozhuang, China	C4	30
Zapadno-Sibirskaja ravnina, pl., Russia	C9	26
Zapadnyj Sajan, mts., Russia	D11	26
Zapala, Arg.	E2	69
Zapata, co., Tx., U.S.	F3	136
Zapata, Tx., U.S.	F3	136
Zapopan, Mex.	C4	78
Zaporizhzhia, Ukr.	F13	20
Zaqatala, Azer.	B12	44
Zara, Tur.	C7	44
Zaragoza, Spain	G6	16
Zarajsk, Russia	B15	20
Zaranj, Afg.	D8	42
Zarasai, Lith.	I12	10
Zárate, Arg.	E6	72
Zarembo Island, i., Ak., U.S.	m23	95
Zarghon Shahr, Afg.	D9	42
Zaria, Nig.	D6	50
Žarkamys, Kaz.	E10	22
Žarma, Kaz.	B4	28
Žary, Pol.	D3	20
Zāskār Mountains, mts., Asia	C3	40
Zavala, co., Tx., U.S.	E3	136
Zave, Zimb.	B5	56
Zavitinsk, Russia	A13	28
Zawiercie, Pol.	D5	20
Zāwiyat Masūs, Libya	E8	14
Zaysan, Lake see Zajsan, ozero, l., Kaz.	E10	26
Zdolbuniv, Ukr.	D9	20
Zduńska Wola, Pol.	D5	20
Zearing, Ia., U.S.	B4	108
Zebulon, Ga., U.S.	C2	103
Zebulon, N.C., U.S.	B4	126
Zeehan, Austl.	I4	62
Zeeland, Mi., U.S.	F5	115
Zeerust, S. Afr.	D4	56
Zeigler, Il., U.S.	F4	106
Zeja, Russia	D14	26
Zeja, stm., Russia	D14	26
Zejskoe vodohranilišče, res., Russia	D14	26
Zelenogorsk, Russia	F13	10
Zelenokumsk, Russia	B4	42
Železnodorožnyj, Russia	B9	22
Železnogorsk, Russia	C13	20
Železnogorsk-Ilimskij, Russia	D12	26
Zelienople, Pa., U.S.	E1	131
Zell am See, Aus.	G13	12
Zémio, C.A.R.	B5	54
Zenica, Bos.	B6	18
Zenith, Wa., U.S.	f11	140
Zenobia Peak, mtn., Co., U.S.	A2	99
Zenza do Itombe, Ang.	E2	54
Zephyr Cove, Nv., U.S.	E2	121
Zephyrhills, Fl., U.S.	D4	102
Žerdevka, Russia	D7	22
Zestafoni, Geor.	A10	44
Zeya see Zeja, stm., Russia	D14	26
Zeya Reservoir see Zejskoe vodohranilišče, res., Russia	D14	26
Žezkazgan, Kaz.	E8	26
Zgierz, Pol.	D5	20
Zhalun, China	C4	40
Zhangjiakou, China	C10	28
Zhangping, China	F11	28
Zhangpu, China	E4	30
Zhangye, China	D8	28
Zhangzhou, China	G11	28
Zhanhua, China	B4	30
Zhanjiang, China	G10	28
Zhao'an, China	G11	28
Zhaojue, China	D1	30
Zhaoqing, China	G10	28
Zhaotong, China	F8	28
Zhashkiv, Ukr.	E11	20
Zhaxigang, China	E3	28
Zhdanov see Mariupol', Ukr.	F14	20
Zhejiang, prov., China	F11	28
Zhenghe, China	D4	30
Zhenglan Qi, China	A4	30
Zhengzhou, China	D10	28
Zhenjiang, China	C4	30
Zhenning, China	D2	30
Zhenping, China	E10	28
Zhenxiong, China	D1	30
Zhenyuan, China	F9	28
Zhidoi, China	C6	40
Zhijiang, China	D2	30
Zhmerynka, Ukr.	E10	20
Zhob, stm., Pak.	D9	42
Zhob, Pak.	D9	42
Zhongba, China	E4	28
Zhongdian, China	F7	28
Zhongning, China	D9	28
Zhongshan, China	B6	34
Zhongwei, China	B2	30
Zhongxian, China	C2	30
Zhongxiang, China	E10	28
Zhoushan Qundao, is., China	E12	28
Zhovtneve, Ukr.	F12	20
Zhuanghe, China	B5	30
Zhucheng, China	B4	30
Zhumadian, China	C3	30
Zhuolu, China	A4	30
Zhuozhou, China	D11	28
Zhushan, China	E10	28
Zhuzhou, China	F10	28
Zhytomyr, Ukr.	D10	20
Zia Indian Reservation, N.M., U.S.	h7	124
Zibo, China	D11	28
Ziebach, co., S.D., U.S.	C4	134
Zielona Góra, Pol.	D3	20
Žigalovo, Russia	D12	26
Žigansk, Russia	C14	26
Zigong, China	F8	28
Ziguinchor, Sen.	D1	50
Zihuatanejo, Mex.	D4	78
Zile, Tur.	B6	44
Žilina, Slvk.	E5	20
Zillah, Libya	E8	48
Zillah, Wa., U.S.	C5	140
Zilwaukee, Mi., U.S.	E7	115
Zima, Russia	D12	26
Zimbabwe, ctry., Afr.	B4	56
Zimi, S.L.	E2	50
Zimmerman, Mn., U.S.	E5	116
Zinder, Niger	D6	50
Zion, Il., U.S.	A6	106
Zion National Park, Ut., U.S.	F3	137
Zion Reservoir, res., Az., U.S.	C6	96
Zionsville, In., U.S.	E5	107
Zipaquirá, Col.	D5	80
Zirkel, Mount, mtn., Co., U.S.	A4	99
Zitong, China	C2	30
Zittau, Ger.	E14	12
Zitundo, Moz.	D5	56
Ziway Hāyk', l., Eth.	B7	54
Ziyun, China	D2	30
Zlatoust, Russia	D7	26
Zlītan, Libya	D7	48
Žlobin, Bela.	C11	20
Złotów, Pol.	C4	20
Zmeinogorsk, Russia	A4	28
Znam'ianka, Ukr.	E12	20
Znojmo, Czech Rep.	E4	20
Žodzina, Bela.	B10	20
Zolfo Springs, Fl., U.S.	E5	102
Zomba, Mwi.	B6	56
Zonguldak, Tur.	B4	44
Zouar, Chad	B8	50
Zouérat, Maur.	B2	50
Zrenjanin, Serb.	B8	18
Žuantobe, Kaz.	B9	42
Zug, Switz.	A2	18
Zugdidi, Geor.	A9	44
Zugspitze, mtn., Eur.	G12	12
Žukovka, Russia	C12	20
Zumbo, Moz.	B5	56
Zumbro, stm., Mn., U.S.	F6	116
Zumbrota, Mn., U.S.	F6	116
Zuni (Zuni Pueblo), N.M., U.S.	B1	124
Zuni, stm., U.S.	C6	96
Zuni Indian Reservation, N.M., U.S.	B1	124
Zuni Mountains, mts., N.M., U.S.	B1	124
Zunyi, China	F9	28
Zūrābād, Iran	C11	44
Zurich, On., Can.	D3	89
Zürich, Switz.	A2	18
Zurich, Lake see Zürichsee, l., Switz.	A2	18
Zürichsee, l., Switz.	A2	18
Zuru, Nig.	D6	50
Zuwārah, Libya	E6	14
Zvishavane, Zimb.	C4	56
Zvolen, Slvk.	E5	20
Zwedru, Lib.	E3	50
Zwickau, Ger.	E13	12
Zwolle, Neth.	D10	12
Zwolle, La., U.S.	C2	111
Żyrardów, Pol.	C6	20
Zyrjanka, Russia	C17	26
Zyrjanovsk, Kaz.	E10	26
Żywiec, Pol.	E5	20